PUBLICATIONS OF
THE ISRAEL ACADEMY OF SCIENCES
AND HUMANITIES

SECTION OF HUMANITIES

———

FONTES AD RES JUDAICAS SPECTANTES

Greek and Latin Authors
on Jews and Judaism

Volume One

FROM HERODOTUS TO PLUTARCH

GREEK AND LATIN AUTHORS
ON JEWS AND JUDAISM

Edited with Introductions, Translations

and Commentary

by

MENAHEM STERN

Volume One

FROM HERODOTUS TO PLUTARCH

Jerusalem 1974

The Israel Academy of Sciences and Humanities

Preparation and publication of this volume
was made possible by a grant from the
Memorial Foundation for Jewish Culture

Memoriae Johannis Lewy

Sacrum

PREFACE

SINCE THE EARLY NINETEENTH CENTURY scholars have recognized the need to assemble a collection of Greek and Latin literature relating to Jews and Judaism in ancient times. Attempts at such an undertaking were made in both Germany[1] and England,[2] beginning in 1832. These first efforts were eclipsed by the remarkable achievement of the Jewish-French scholar Théodore Reinach, who published his *Textes d'auteurs grecs et latins relatifs au Juifs et Judaïsme* in 1895. An outstanding historian of ancient times and profoundly interested in the Jewish past, Reinach's work comprised most of the important texts, French translations made by two assistants under his supervision, and brief notes.

This work marked an immense advance over that of his predecessors; it also gave great impetus to the study of Jewish history in Hellenistic times and under the Roman Empire. However, Reinach's work was not without omissions. Among these are the main passages of the Autobiography of Nicolaus of Damascus, bearing on the history of Judaea; a famous chapter of Tacitus (*Annales*, XII, 54), dealing with the Roman procuratorial régime in that country; the discussion of Moses in Galenus; and many texts from later Antiquity. Critics pointed out some of the omissions,[3] and, in his great work, Jean Juster emphasized the need for a more comprehensive collection.[4] In spite of Reinach's great achievement, it became apparent that his work was no longer adequate for the modern student; subsequent editions of the ancient writers and the general progress of historical and philological scholarship demanded a new collection and a more complete commentary.

It was Hans (Johanan) Lewy (1901–1945) who embarked on a new edition of the texts. A student of Ed. Norden in Germany, and later a lecturer in Latin literature at the Hebrew University of Jerusalem,

1. See F. C. Meier, *Judaica seu veterum scriptorum profanorum de rebus Judaicis fragmenta*, Jena 1832.
2. See J. Gill, *Notices of the Jews and their Country by the Classic Writers of Antiquity*, London 1872; Schürer, III, p. 150, n.1.
3. See H. Willrich, *Berliner philologische Wochenschrift*, 1895, pp. 987 ff.
4. See Juster, I, pp. 31 f.

Lewy was deeply imbued with knowledge of ancient literature, thought and religion. His main fields of research were Jewish-Hellenistic literature and the religious syncretism of the Roman Empire. As a kind of preliminary work, he published articles in German (on Hecataeus), in English (on Clearchus) and in Hebrew (on Cicero, Tacitus and Julian).

Lewy's untimely death prevented him from going on with the project. He left notes in his private copy of Reinach, as well as a collection of material and German translations of some of the texts. These were all put at my disposal in 1959 by Professor Gershom Scholem, Lewy's friend and now President of the Israel Academy of Sciences and Humanities.

I have worked on the principle that the present corpus of Graeco-Latin fragments on Jews and Judaism should include all references to these subjects in ancient pagan literature, as well as all passages relating to the country of Judaea. This, of course, raises the question which area of Palestine may be defined as Judaea, because boundaries changed over the course of time. I have generally elected passages which refer to or were written at a time when a specific part of the country was ruled or inhabited mainly by Jews. I have also included texts referring to Jewish individuals active in a non-Jewish environment and fragments relating to Samaritans.

I have excluded some texts incorporated by Reinach, when the connection with Jews and Judaism seemed to me highly improbable (e.g. Choirilus, Thrasyllus). I also differ from Reinach in that I have not separated Latin and Greek authors, but have followed a chronological order.

At the beginning of each fragment I have given the name of the editor of one of the main critical editions, where the reader may find information on the manuscript tradition together with the key to the *sigla*.

In this first volume, which covers authors from Herodotus to Plutarch, I have endeavoured to take into consideration scholarly work published by 1971, and only some of the work which appeared in 1972, as the book went to press in that year.[5] The second volume will contain writings from Tacitus to later Antiquity.

5. A new papyrus (P. Oxy., XLI, No. 2944) constitutes a tale of a judgement (quoted by Philiscus of Miletus, a pupil of Isocrates) which is identical with that of Solomon (I Kings iii : 16 ff.). It should be noted, however, that neither Solomon nor the Jews are mentioned in this papyrus.

Preface

My thanks are due to Professors G. Scholem and Ch. Wirszubski, who suggested that I undertake the work; to my friends Professor A. Fuks, who offered me continual encouragement during all stages of its preparation, and Dr D. Rokeah, who helped me read the proofs.

I also wish to acknowledge my debt to the indefatigable staff of the Israel Academy of Sciences and Humanities.

I am grateful to Harvard University Press for permission to reprint many translations published by them in their edition of the Loeb Classical Library, and to Cambridge University Press for allowing me to use their translations of two fragments.

Finally, I would like to thank the National and University Library in Jerusalem for their assistance to me during the preparation of the work.

Menahem Stern

The Hebrew University of Jerusalem, 1974

TABLE OF CONTENTS

Table of Contents

Table of Contents

LIST OF ABBREVIATIONS

AASOR	*Annual of the American Schools of Oriental Research*
Abel	F. M. Abel, *Géographie de la Palestine*, I–II, Paris 1933–1938
AJA	*American Journal of Archeology*
AJP	*American Journal of Philology*
Alt	A. Alt, *Kleine Schriften zur Geschichte des Volkes Israel*, I–III, Munich 1953–1959
BASOR	*Bulletin of the American Schools of Oriental Research*
Bengtson	H. Bengtson, *Die Strategie in der hellenistischen Zeit*, I–III, Munich 1937–1952
Bernays	J. Bernays, *Gesammelte Abhandlungen*, I–II, Berlin 1885
BGU	*Aegyptische Urkunden aus den Königlichen Museen zu Berlin*, Berlin 1895 →
Bidez & Cumont	J. Bidez & F. Cumont, *Les mages hellénisés*, I–II, Paris 1938
BIFAO	*Bulletin de l'institut français d'archéologie orientale*
Böhl	F. M. T. de Liagre Böhl, *Opera Minora*, Groningen–Djakarta 1953
CAH	*The Cambridge Ancient History*, I–XII, Cambridge 1923–1939
Cichorius	C. Cichorius, *Römische Studien*, Leipzig–Berlin 1922
CII	J. B. Frey, *Corpus Inscriptionum Iudaicarum*, I–II, Rome–Paris 1936–1952
CIL	*Corpus Inscriptionum Latinarum*
CPJ	V. A. Tcherikover, A. Fuks & M. Stern, *Corpus Papyrorum Judaicarum*, I–III, Cambridge (Mass.) 1957–1964
CQ	*The Classical Quarterly*
Derenbourg	J. Derenbourg, *Essai sur l'histoire et la géographie de la Palestine*, Paris 1867
F. Gr. Hist.	F. Jacoby, *Die Fragmente der griechischen Historiker*, Berlin–Leiden 1923 →
FHG	C. & T. Müller, *Fragmenta Historicorum Graecorum*, I–V
Fraser	P. M. Fraser, *Ptolemaic Alexandria*, I–III, Oxford 1972
Freudenthal	J. Freudenthal, *Hellenistische Studien*, I–II, *Alexander Polyhistor und die von ihm erhaltenen Reste jüdischer und samaritanischer Geschichtswerke*, Breslau 1874–1875
Friedländer	L. Friedländer, *Darstellungen aus der Sittengeschichte Roms in der Zeit von Augustus bis zum Ausgang der Antonine*, Leipzig, I–II, 1922; III, 1923; IV, 1921
Gabba	E. Gabba, *Iscrizioni greche e latine per lo studio della Bibbia*, Turin 1958

xv

List of Abbreviations

Gager	J. G. Gager, *Moses in Greco-Roman Paganism*, Nashville, 1972
Geyer	P. Geyer, *Itinera Hierosolymitana Saeculi, IIII–VIII*, Prague–Vienna–Leipzig 1898
Ginzberg	L. Ginzberg, *The Legends of the Jews*, I–VII, Philadelphia 1925–1938
Goodenough	E. R. Goodenough, *Jewish Symbols in the Greco-Roman Period*, I–XII, New York 1953–1965
Gutschmid	A. v. Gutschmid, *Kleine Schriften*, I-V, Leipzig 1889–1894
Hengel	M. Hengel, *Judentum und Hellenismus — Studien zu ihrer Begegnung unter besonderer Berücksichtung Palästinas bis zur Mitte des 2 Jh. v. Chr.*, Tübingen 1969
HTR	*The Harvard Theological Review*
HUCA	*Hebrew Union College Annual*
IEJ	*Israel Exploration Journal*
IG	*Inscriptiones Graecae*
ILS	H. Dessau, *Inscriptiones Latinae Selectae*, I–III, Berlin 1892–1916
JAOS	*Journal of the American Oriental Society*
JBL	*Journal of Biblical Literature*
JEA	*The Journal of Egyptian Archeology*
Jeremias	J. Jeremias, *Jerusalem zur Zeit Jesu*[3], Göttingen 1962
JHS	*The Journal of Hellenic Studies*
JNES	*Journal of Near Eastern Studies*
JQR	*The Jewish Quarterly Review*
JR	*Journal of Religion*
JRS	*The Journal of Roman Studies*
JTS	*The Journal of Theological Studies*
Juster	J. Juster, *Les Juifs dans l'empire Romain*, I–II, Paris 1914
Kahrstedt	U. Kahrstedt, *Syrische Territorien in hellenistischer Zeit*, Berlin 1926
Theol. Wörterbuch	G. Kittel (ed.), *Theologisches Wörterbuch zum Neuen Testament*, Stuttgart 1933 →
LCL	The Loeb Classical Library, Cambridge (Mass.)–London
Leon	H. J. Leon, *The Jews of Ancient Rome*, Philadelphia 1960
Ed. Meyer	E. Meyer, *Ursprung und Anfänge des Christentums*, I–III, Stuttgart–Berlin 1921–1923
MGWJ	*Monatsschrift für Geschichte und Wissenschaft des Judentums*
Momigliano	A. Momigliano, *Ricerche sull' organizzazione della Giudea sotto il dominio romano (Annali della R. Scuola Normale Superiore de Pisa)*, Series II, Vol. III (1934)
Müller	J. G. Müller, *Des Flavius Josephus Schrift gegen den Apion*, Basel 1877
Niese	B. Niese, *Geschichte der griechischen und makedonischen Staaten seit der Schlacht bei Chaeronea*, I–III, Gotha 1893–1903

NNM	Numismatic Notes and Monographs
Norden	E. Norden, *Kleine Schriften zum klassischen Altertum*, Berlin 1966
OGIS	W. Dittenberger, *Orientis Graeci Inscriptiones Selectae*, I–II, Leipzig 1903–1905
Otto	W. Otto, *Herodes — Beiträge zur Geschichte des letzten jüdischen Königshauses*, Stuttgart 1913
PAAJR	*Proceedings of the American Academy for Jewish Research*
P. Columbia Zenon	W. L. Westermann et al., *Zenon papyri — Business Papers in the Third Century B. C. dealing with Palestine and Egypt* (*Columbia Papyri, Greek Series*, Nos. 3–4), I–II, New York 1934–1940
PCZ	C. C. Edgar, *Zenon Papyri*, I–IV, Cairo 1925–1931
PG	*Patrologia Graeca*
PIR²	*Prosopographia Imperii Romani Saeculi I. II. III*, editio altera, Berlin–Leipzig 1933 →
PL	*Patrologia Latina* →
P. Lond	*Greek Papyri in the British Museum*, London 1893→
P. Oxy.	*The Oxyrhynchus Papyri*, London 1898 →
PSI	Papiri greci e latini — *Pubblicazioni della Società italiana per la ricerca dei Papiri greci e latini in Egitto*, Florence 1912→
P. Tebtunis	*The Tebtunis Paypri*, I–III, London – New York– California 1902–1938
PW	Pauly-Wissowa, *Real-encyclopädie der classischen Altertumswissenschaft*, Stuttgart 1893 →
R	T. Reinach, *Textes d'auteurs grecs et romains relatifs au Judaïsme*, Paris 1895
Radin	M. Radin, *The Jews among the Greeks and Romans*, Philadelphia 1915
RB	*Revue biblique*
REA	*Revue des études anciennes*
REG	*Revue des études grecques*
Reinach (Budé)	Flavius Josèphe, Contre Apion, texte établi et annoté par T. Reinach, Collection de l'Association Guillaume Budé, Paris 1930
REJ	*Revue des études juives*
Rhein. Museum	Rheinisches Museum für Philologie
RHR	*Revue de l'histoire des religions*
RIDA	*Revue internationale des droits de l'antiquité*
SEHHW	M. Rostovtzeff, *Social and Economic History of the Hellenistic World*, I–III, Oxford 1953
Schanz & Hosius	M. Schanz & C. Hosius, *Geschichte der römischen Literatur*, I–II⁴, Munich 1927-1935
Schmid & Stählin, II	*Wilhelm von Christs Geschichte der griechischen Litteratur*, sechste Auflage unter Mitwirkung von O. Stählin bearbeitet von Wilhelm Schmid, Part II, Munich 1920–1924

List of Abbreviations

Schürer	E. Schürer, *Geschichte des jüdischen Volkes im Zeitalter Jesu Christi*, I–III, Leipzig 1901–1909
SEG	*Supplementum Epigraphicum Graecum*, Leiden 1923 →
Stähelin	F. Stähelin, *Der Antisemitismus des Altertums*, Basel 1905
Strack & Billerbeck	H. L. Strack, P. Billerbeck & J. Jeremias, *Kommentar zum Neuen Testament aus Talmud und Midrasch*, I–VI, Munich 1922–1961
Susemihl	F. Susemihl, *Geschichte der griechischen Litteratur in der Alexandrinerzeit*, I–II, Leipzig 1891–1892
SVF	J. [H.] de Arnim, *Stoicorum Veterum Fragmenta*, I–IV, Leipzig 1903–1924
Sylloge	W. Dittenberger, *Sylloge Inscriptionum Graecarum*, I–IV, Leipzig 1915–1924
TAPA	*Transactions and Proceedings of the American Philological Association*
Tcherikover	V. Tcherikover, *Hellenistic Civilization and the Jews*, Philadelphia 1959
YCS	*Yale Classical Studies*
ZAW	*Zeitschrift für die alttestamentliche Wissenschaft*
ZDMG	*Zeitschrift der Deutschen morgenländischen Gesellschaft*
ZDPV	*Zeitschrift des Deutschen Palästinavereins*
ZNTW	*Zeitschrift für die neutestamentliche Wissenschaft*

xviii

I. HERODOTUS

Fifth century B.C.E.

"The Father of History" does not expressly refer either to the Jews or to Judaea. However, it seems that in his statement about the Syrians in Palestine who practise circumcision (No. 1) the Jews are implied. Presumably he also alludes to one of the events of the political history of Judah, namely, the Battle of Megiddo (No. 2). The significance of the first passage was realized by Josephus, who ignored the second. On the other hand, there is no plausibility in the suggestion put forward by Josephus (Antiquitates, VIII, 253) identifying Sesostris (Herodotus, II, 102 ff.) with Shishak, the Pharaoh who led a military expedition against Rehoboam, King of Judah (I Kings xiv : 25).[1]

Nos. 1–2 are taken from the second book of the Historiae, *a book which centres on Egypt and in which the Egyptian viewpoint is discernible. It is certain that the historian visited Palestine, but his visit was probably confined to the coast. From II, 44 we learn about his stay at Tyre. It seems that he also saw Gaza (= Cadytis), the size of which he compares with the size of Sardis. It stands to reason that we should connect this visit with his Egyptian journey, which is generally dated to the forties of the fifth century B.C.E.[2] In any case, in view of his rather short sojourn in Egypt itself,[3] Herodotus could not have stayed long in Palestine.*

---

1 Aly has pointed out that Herodotus (II, 172) appears to allude to Isaiah xliv : 12 ff. and to Jeremiah x : 3; see W. Aly, *Volksmärchen, Sage und Novelle bei Herodot und seinen Zeitgenossen*, Göttingen 1921, p.71. The parallels are not too close, and one should by no means suggest that the historian depended on Hebrew prophecy. Herodotus was not the first Greek writer to mention places in Palestine. He was preceded by Alcaeus, who refers to Ascalon; cf. E. Lobel & D. Page, *Poetarum Lesbiorum Fragmenta*, Oxford 1955, F 48, l.11, p. 134; J. D. Quinn, *BASOR*, 164 (1961), pp. 19 f.

2 Cf. F. Jacoby, PW, Suppl. II, p. 266 = *Griechische Historiker*, Stuttgart 1956, p. 37; P. E. Legrand, *Hérodote — Introduction*, Paris 1932, p. 25; E. Lüddeckens, *ZDMG*, CIV (1954), p. 332. Powell distinguishes between a journey made before 461 B. C. E. and one made after 455 or 448 B. C. E. ; see J. E. Powell, *The History of Herodotus*, Cambridge 1939, p. 26. However, this suggestion seems rather superfluous; cf. C. W. Fornara, *Herodotus*, Oxford 1971, p. 24.

3 Cf. T. S. Brown, *AJP*, LXXXVI (1965), p. 60.

1

Historiae, II, 104:1–3 — Legrand = F1R

*(1) Φαίνονται μὲν γὰρ ἐόντες οἱ Κόλχοι Αἰγύπτιοι. νοήσας δὲ πρότερον
αὐτὸς ἢ ἀκούσας ἄλλων λέγω· ὡς δέ μοι ἐν φροντίδι ἐγένετο, εἰρόμην
ἀμφοτέρους, καὶ μᾶλλον οἱ Κόλχοι ἐμεμνέατο τῶν Αἰγυπτίων ἢ οἱ Αἰγύπτιοι τῶν Κόλχων· (2) νομίζειν δ' ἔφασαν οἱ Αἰγύπτιοι τῆς Σεσώστριος*
5 *στρατιῆς εἶναι τοὺς Κόλχους. αὐτὸς δὲ εἴκασα τῇδε· καὶ ὅτι μελάγχροές
εἰσι καὶ οὐλότριχες (καὶ τοῦτο μὲν ἐς οὐδὲν ἀνήκει· εἰσὶ γὰρ καὶ ἕτεροι
τοιοῦτοι), ἀλλὰ τοισίδε καὶ μᾶλλον ὅτι μοῦνοι πάντων ἀνθρώπων
Κόλχοι καὶ Αἰγύπτιοι καὶ Αἰθίοπες περιτάμνονται ἀπ' ἀρχῆς τὰ αἰδοῖα.
(3) Φοίνικες δὲ καὶ Σύριοι οἱ ἐν τῇ Παλαιστίνῃ καὶ αὐτοὶ ὁμολογέουσι*
10 *παρ' Αἰγυπτίων μεμαθηκέναι, Σύριοι δὲ οἱ περὶ Θερμώδοντα ποταμὸν
καὶ Παρθένιον καὶ Μάκρωνες οἱ τούτοισι ἀστυγείτονες ἐόντες ἀπὸ Κόλχων
φασὶ νεωστὶ μεμαθηκέναι.*

| 1 οἱ om. DRSV | 2 ἠρόμην ABCP | 4 οἱ om. PDRSV |
| 7 τοῖσδε C | καὶ om. PDRSV | 9 σύριοι ABC / οἱ om. DR |

(1) For it is plain to see that the Colchians are Egyptians; and this
that I say I myself noted before I heard it from others. When I began
to think on this matter, I inquired of both peoples; and the Colchians
remembered the Egyptians better than the Egyptians remembered
the Colchians; (2) the Egyptians said that they held the Colchians to
be part of Sesostris' army. I myself guessed it to be so, partly because
they are dark-skinned and wooly-haired; though that indeed goes for
nothing, seeing that other peoples, too, are such; but my better
proof was that the Colchians and Egyptians and Ethiopians are the
only nations that have from the first practised circumcision. (3) The
Phoenicians and the Syrians of Palestine acknowledge of themselves
that they learnt the custom from the Egyptians, and the Syrians of
the valleys of the Thermodon and the Parthenius, as well as their
neighbours the Macrones, say that they learnt it lately from the
Colchians.   (trans. A. D. Godley, *LCL*)

2   τῆς Σεσώστριος στρατιῆς: Sesostris was a name borne by Pharaohs of the
twelfth dynasty. The name also refers to a legendary national hero of Egypt,
who is credited with having performed striking military exploits at different
periods; see Kees, PW, Ser. 2, II, pp. 1861 ff.; M. Malaise, *Chronique d'Égypte*,
XLI (1966), pp. 244 ff.; M. Braun, *History and Romance in Graeco-Oriental
Literature*, Oxford 1938, pp. 13 ff. Josephus accuses Herodotus of attributing to
Sesostris the exploits of the Libyan Pharaoh Shishak, who led a military expedition into Palestine after the death of Solomon (I Kings xiv:25 f.; II Chron.

xii:2 ff.). On this, see B. Mazar, *Suppl. to Vetus Testamentum*, IV (1957), pp. 57 ff.
μοῦνοι πάντων ἀνθρώπων Κόλχοι καὶ Αἰγύπτιοι ... περιτάμνονται: In II, 36 Herodotus also mentions the practice of circumcision by the Egyptians; cf. Diodorus, I, 28 : 3; 55 : 5 (Nos. 55, 57); Agatharchides, *De Mari Erythraeo*, 61 in: *Geographi Graeci Minores*, I, p. 154; Strabo, *Geographica*, XVI, 4 : 17, p. 776; XVII, 2 : 5, p. 824; Philo, *De Specialibus Legibus*, I, 2; Celsus, apud: Origenes, *Contra Celsum*, V, 41; *Epistula Barnabae*, IX:6; Hieronymus, *Commentarius in Ieremiam*, IX:25 f.; *PL*, XXIV, Col. 746; Suda, s.v. ψωλός. That circumcision was practised by the Egyptians is also implied by Josh. v : 9, see Ed. Meyer, *Geschichte des Altertums*, II, 1, Stuttgart–Berlin 1928, p. 559, n.1). It is confirmed by Egyptian documents; see G. Foucart, "Circumcision (Egyptian)", in: J. Hastings, *Encyclopaedia of Religion and Ethics*, III, pp. 670 ff. At least the priests in Egypt were obliged to practise circumcision; cf. *Contra Apionem*, II, 141; Origenes, *Homiliae ad Ieremiam*, v : 14 (ed. Klostermann, 1901, p. 43); idem, *Commentarius in Epistulam ad Romanos*, II : 13 (*PG*, XIV, Col. 911); Epiphanius, *Panarion*, XXX, 33 : 3. Cf. also the papyrological evidence in L. Mitteis & U. Wilcken, *Grundzüge und Chrestomathie der Papyruskunde*, Vol. I, Part 2, Leipzig 1912, Nos. 74–77 (second century C. E.).

3 Φοίνικες δὲ καὶ Σύριοι οἱ ἐν τῇ Παλαιστίνῃ: The Σύριοι οἱ ἐν τῇ Παλαιστίνῃ are also mentioned in VII, 89 : 1; together with the Phoenicians they furnish ships for the Persian navy. The name Παλαιστίνη is used again in the same chapter. In other places Herodotus refers to Παλαιστίνη Συρία (I,105; II,106) or to Συρίη ἡ Παλαιστίνη (III, 91; IV, 39). The Greek name Παλαιστίνη derives from the name of the southern part of the coast, which was inhabited by the Philistines and which was thus named not later than the eighth century B. C. E., as attested, e.g., by Isa. xIV: 29, 31 and by Assyrian documents relating to the same period; cf. M. Noth, *ZDPV*, LXII (1939), p. 134. Hence, it is commonly assumed that Herodotus also denotes the coastal strip in the south of Phoenicia by Παλαιστίνη or Συρία ἡ Παλαιστίνη. Still, perhaps we should not completely exclude the possibility that already in Herodotus some parts of the interior were somewhat vaguely included in this term. See also the discussion of O. Leuze, *Die Satrapieneinteilung in Syrien und im Zweistromlande von 520–320*, Halle 1935, p. 261 (p. 105) ff.; the introduction to Aristotle, *Meteorologica*, II, p. 359a (No. 3).

On circumcision among the Phoenicians, see F. C. Movers, *Die Phönizier*, I, Bonn 1841, pp. 60 f. Herodotus himself states that circumcision was by no means usual among the Phoenicians, and Ezek. xxxii : 30 seems to imply that the Sidonians were uncircumcised. On the other hand, cf. Aristophanes, *Aves*, 505 ff.

Who are the Σύριοι οἱ ἐν τῇ Παλαιστίνῃ, who, according to Herodotus, adopted the practice of circumcision from the Egyptians? Josephus (*Ant.*, VIII, 262; *Contra Apionem*, I, 168 ff.) had no doubt whatever that those Syrians could only be Jews, since among all the inhabitants of Syria the Jews alone practised circumcision. This interpretation may be traced back, perhaps, to Hecataeus, through Diodorus, I, 28 (No. 55). The Philistines themselves were the uncircumcised (ערלים) par excellence; see, e.g., Jud. xiv : 3; xv : 18; I Sam. xiv : 6; xvii : 26, 36; xviii : 27; xxxi : 4; II Sam. i : 20; iii : 14; I Chron. x : 4. However, we also hear about other people in these regions, apart from the Jews, who were circumcised; see, e. g., Hieronymus, *loc. cit.*: "multarum ex quadam parte gentium, et maxime quae Iudaeae Palaestinaeque confines sunt, usque hodie populi circumciduntur, et praecipue Aegyptii et Idumaei, Ammonitae et Moabitae et omnis regio Saracenorum quae habitat in solitudine." Cf. also *Epistula Barnabae*, IX : 6: Καὶ μὴν περιτέτμηται ὁ λαὸς εἰς σφραγῖδα. ἀλλὰ καὶ πᾶς Σύρος καὶ Ἄραψ καὶ πάντες οἱ ἱερεῖς τῶν εἰδώλων. Above all, there is ample evidence that circumcision was practised among at least some of the Arabs; see also Origenes, *Commentarius in Epistulam ad Romanos*, II : 13 (*PG*, XIV, Col. 911); Eusebius, *Praeparatio Evangelica*, VI, 11 : 69; Epiphanius, *Panarion*, XXX, 33 : 3; Philostorgius, *Historia Ecclesiastica*, III, 4; Sozomenus, *Historia Ecclesiastica*, VI, 38 : 11.

In view of the strong Arab infiltration into the southern part of Palestine during the Persian age, it might be suggested that Herodotus meant Arabs when he spoke of the Syrians who practised circumcision. However, considering the fact that Herodotus knew the Arabs as a people distinct from the Syrians and that the Phoenicians are mentioned by him separately, there seems to be sufficient ground for the interpretation that Josephus (or, for that matter, Hecataeus and Diodorus) put on the passage. In any case, Wiedemann goes too far in his condemnation of Josephus; see A. Wiedemann, *Herodots zweites Buch mit sachlichen Erläuterungen*, Leipzig 1890, p. 412; cf. also Radin, pp. 80 f. We may endorse with little hesitation the view that Herodotus obtained his version of the origins of circumcision in Egypt itself. For a suggestion that he received it from the Phoenicians, see J. G. Müller, *Theologische Studien und Kritiken*, 1843, p. 900.

2

Historiae, II, 159:2 — Legrand = F2R

Καὶ ταύτῃσί τε ἐχρᾶτο ἐν τῷ δέοντι καὶ Συρίοισι πεζῇ ὁ Νεκῶς συμβαλὼν ἐν Μαγδώλῳ ἐνίκησε, μετὰ δὲ τὴν μάχην Κάδυτιν πόλιν τῆς Συρίης ἐοῦσαν μεγάλην εἷλε.

1 σύροισι ABCP   2 μαγδόλω D²SV   μαγδάλω R, Lex Vind., p. 165

Nechos used these ships at need, and with his land army met and defeated the Syrians at Magdolus, taking the great Syrian city of Cadytis after the battle.   (trans. A. D. Godley, *LCL*)

ὁ Νεκῶς συμβαλὼν ἐν Μαγδώλῳ: Most scholars identify Magdolus here with Megiddo and suppose that Herodotus alludes to the victory of the Pharaoh Necho over Josiah, King of Judah (II Kings xxiii : 29 f.; II Chron. xxxv : 20 ff.); see Ed. Meyer, *Geschichte des Altertums*, III, Stuttgart 1937, p. 162; W. W. Cannon, *ZAW*, XLIV (1926), pp. 63 f.; A. Malamat, *JNES*, IX (1950), p. 221. However, some scholars think that Herodotus confuses this city with the Egyptian border-fortress, the Biblical Migdal (Exod. xiv : 2); see T. Nöldeke, *Hermes*, V, 1871, p. 451. On the other hand, Böhl (p. 114) denies the existence of any confusion of this kind and maintains that the historian does refer to some military operations at Migdal at the beginning of Necho's campaign. However, there is nothing to support this view, which implies aggressive action from the direction of Syria against the Egyptian border. Schwartz quite plausibly suggests that the historian really wrote ΜΑΓΙΔΔΩ,

Herodotus

and that the reading Μαγδωλω is due only to the errors of copyists; see E. Schwartz, *Philologus*, LXXXVI (1931), p. 387, n. 15 = *Gesammelte Schriften*, II, Berlin 1956 p. 255, n.1.

Κάδυτιν πόλιν: Cadytis is also mentioned by Herodotus in III, 5, as follows: ...πόλιος ἐούσης, ὡς ἐμοὶ δοκέει, Σαρδίων οὐ πολλῷ ἐλάσσονος, where it is implied that Cadytis was a city situated near the coast and that the historian knew it by autopsy. It should be identified with Gaza; see K. B. Stark, *Gaza und die philistäische Küste*, Jena 1852, pp. 218 ff.; H. Matzat, *Hermes*, VI (1872), pp. 424 ff.; Wiedemann, *op. cit.* (supra, p. 4), pp. 566 f.; Leuze, *op. cit.* (supra, p. 3), p. 262 (p. 106); H. Tadmor, *Biblical Archaeologist*, XXIX (1966), p. 102, n. 60; cf. also the discussion by H. de Meulenaere, *Herodotos over de 26ste Dynastie*, Louvain 1951, p. 58. It is difficult to accept the view that distinguishes between the Cadytis in Herodotus, III, 5 (= Gaza) and the Cadytis here, which is identified with Kadesh on the Orontes; cf. H. R. Hall, *CAH*, III, 1925, p. 297, n.1. It seems rather that the capture of Gaza by Necho accords with the steps he took after his victory at Megiddo in 609 B. C. E. (cf., for the chronology, H. Tadmor, *JNES*, XV, 1956, p. 228). The capture of Gaza is also referred to in Jer. xlvii : 1; cf. Matzat, *op. cit.*, p. 427; A. Malamat, *IEJ*, I (1950–51), pp. 154 ff.

II. ARISTOTLE

384–322 B.C.E.

There is no mention of Jews or of the Jewish religion in the existing works of Aristotle, and there is no hint whatsoever that he referred to either of them in his lost dialogues.[1] In his Meteorologica, *however, we find a reference to a lake in Palestine, which, though not specified, should certainly be identified with the Dead Sea.*

Aristotle states there that if one binds a man (or a beast) and throws him in this lake, he will not sink. He also says that the lake is so bitter and salty that no fish live in it, and that when clothes are soaked in it and are then shaken, they are cleansed. For this last statement we have no parallels in Greek and Latin literature apart from those of Alexander of Aphrodisias (No. 400) and the pseudo-Aristotelian Problemata, *III, 49 (No. 401). It is noteworthy that Aristotle does not locate the lake in Judaea, as do the majority of later writers, or in Coele-Syria, or, for that matter, in the Nabataean country, as is done by Hieronymus (No. 10), but in Palestine. It may thus be argued that Aristotle already uses the name Palestine in the same broad sense as it seems to have been used, somewhat vaguely, by Herodotus; cf. the commentary to No. 1. However, one may assert that Aristotle had a rather unclear idea about the exact location of the lake (εἰ δ᾽ ἔστιν ὥσπερ μυθολογοῦσί τινες ἐν Παλαιστίνῃ τοιαύτη λίμνη), and this impression gains some support from the fact that even later writers, ranging from Xenophilus (No. 22), as quoted from Callimachus by Antigonus of Carystus, to Vitruvius,* De Architectura, *VIII, 3:8 (No. 140), imply a connection of the Dead Sea with Jaffa.*

---

1 Jaeger maintains that if there had been any mention of the Jews in the lost dialogues, later Jewish writers would have discovered and utilized this testimony; see W. Jaeger, *JR*, XVIII (1938), p. 130. That in itself is perhaps not wholly cogent, as only a part of Jewish-Hellenistic literature has reached us. One should also note that it was left to Porphyry to resuscitate for us the description of Jews by Theophrastus (No. 4), which seemingly made no impression on Jewish authors.

6

Aristotle

3

Meteorologica, II, p. 359a — Fobes = F4R

Εἰ δ' ἔστιν ὥσπερ μυθολογοῦσί τινες ἐν Παλαιστίνῃ τοιαύτη λίμνη,
εἰς ἣν ἐάν τις ἐμβάλῃ συνδήσας ἄνθρωπον ἢ ὑποζύγιον ἐπιπλεῖν καὶ
οὐ καταδύεσθαι κατὰ τοῦ ὕδατος, μαρτύριον ἂν εἴη τι τοῖς εἰρημένοις·
λέγουσι γὰρ πικρὰν οὕτως εἶναι τὴν λίμνην καὶ ἁλμυρὰν ὥστε μηδένα
5 ἰχθὺν ἐγγίγνεσθαι, τὰ δὲ ἱμάτια ῥύπτειν, ἐάν τις διασείσῃ βρέξας.

1 παλαιστίνοις J₁   2 ἐμβαλεῖ J₁   ἐμβάλλῃ H   ἐμβάλει N₁
3 κατὰ om. F   4 γὰρ] δὲ F   5 ῥύπτειν ex ῥίπτειν corr. N₁ /
διασείσει N

If there were any truth in the stories they tell about the lake in Palestine it would further bear out what I say. For they say if you bind a
man or beast and throw him into it he floats and does not sink beneath
the surface; and that the lake is so bitter and salty that there are no
fish in it, and that if you wet clothes in it and shake them out it
cleans them.

(trans. H. D. P. Lee, LCL)

ὥσπερ μυθολογοῦσί τινες: It is difficult to suggest a probable source for the
passage that follows. It is still debatable whether the *Meteorologica* should be
dated before or after Alexander's expedition to the East; see W. Jaeger, *Aristotle*,
Oxford 1948, p. 307, n. 1. However, the first possibility is to be preferred; cf.
I. Düring, PW, Suppl. XI, pp. 247 f.
ἐν Παλαιστίνῃ: For the use of the term "Palestine" in the Hellenistic period, see
Agatharchides of Cnidus, *Geographi Graeci Minores*, I, p. 176 = Diodorus, III,
42 : 5; Strabo, *Geographica*, XVI, 4 : 18, p. 776, which derives from Artemidorus.
These passages certainly refer to the southern coast of the country; cf. M. Noth,
ZDPV, LXII (1939), p. 140. See also the introduction to Polybius, the commentary
to Polemo, apud: Eusebius, *Praeparatio Evangelica*, X, 10 : 15 (No. 29); Ovidius,
Ars Amatoria, I, 416 (No. 142). See also *Inscriptions de Délos*, (edited by P. Roussel
& M. Launey, Paris 1937, No. 2549 (a poem), ll. 2, 21.
ἐάν τις ἐμβάλῃ συνδήσας ἄνθρωπον ἢ ὑποζύγιον ... οὐ καταδύεσθαι: The fact
that living creatures do not sink in the Dead Sea is stressed by the later sources,
and the same holds true for the statement that fish cannot live in it; see the commentary to Diodorus, XIX, 98 (No. 62).

III. THEOPHRASTUS
372–288/7 B.C.E.

Theophrastus, the disciple of Aristotle, describes the Jews in a fragment of his work De Pietate. *He traces the development of sacrifice and expresses his disapproval of animal sacrifice, which, according to him, only slowly won its way into divine worship. The Jewish cult is a case in point. The Jews practise animal sacrifice, but the way they do it contrasts glaringly with that of the Greeks. They do not eat the meat, and they sacrifice only holocausts; even these they sacrifice only in haste and in the darkness of the night, and they pour out much honey and wine. Although they are, as a matter of fact, the people who started to sacrifice living creatures, they did so reluctantly.*

This emphasis on the Jewish reluctance to initiate such a custom is in keeping with the tone of the whole passage, which is favourable to the Jews and which declares them to be philosophers (ἄτε φιλόσοφοι), who converse about God during the sacrifice, and observe the stars. The last feature is a rather important constituent of a philosophical religion, according to the schools of Plato and Aristotle. The esteem in which the Jews are held by Theophrastus is also in accordance with his admiration for the Egyptians.[1]

It seems that the view of Bernays, followed by Reinach, that Theophrastus was the first Greek writer to deal expressly with the Jews, still holds true, notwithstanding Jaeger's arguments to the contrary. Jaeger maintains that, since Theophrastus — as attested in his work De Lapidibus — *presumably knew of Hecataeus' work on Egypt, his description of the Jews in* De Pietate *depends on Hecataeus' references to them, and that, accordingly, we should attribute* De Pietate *to Theophrastus' later years. Hecataeus would then emerge as the first Greek writer on the Jews.*

Jaeger's proofs are hardly convincing: (a) Even if we were absolutely certain that De Lapidibus *is dependent upon the above-mentioned work of Hecataeus, we should not automatically infer that* De Pietate

---

1 W. Pötscher, *Theophrastos, Περὶ Εὐσεβείας*, Leiden 1964, F 2: τό γε πάντων λογιώτατον γένος καὶ τὴν ἱερωτάτην ὑπὸ τοῦ Νείλου κτισθεῖσαν χώραν κατοικοῦν; see also F 13, the passage which immediately follows that on the Jews: μάθοι δ' ἄν τις ἐπιβλέψας τοὺς λογιωτάτους πάντων Αἰγυπτίους.

8

also draws on that writer.[2] *The more so, as Jaeger's dating of* De Lapidibus *after 300 B.C.E. and the resultant inference regarding the dependence of* De Lapidibus *on Hecataeus seem untenable.*[3] (*b*) *The descriptions of the Jews by Hecataeus and Theophrastus have nothing specific in common, as far as they are known to us.* (*c*) *The general consensus as to the date of* De Pietate *tends to place it among the earlier works of Theophrastus,*[4] *which would preclude any dependence on Hecataeus.* (*d*) *Theophrastus could have obtained his rather vague knowledge of Jewish customs from many sources other than Hecataeus, since his information about the countries of the East, as attested by his botanical works, is considerable. He might even have met Jews, e.g., in Egypt, a country which he presumably knew by autopsy.*[5]

Theophrastus nowhere mentions the country of Judaea, the city of Jerusalem, or, for that matter, Palestine. He does, however, refer to the onions of Ascalon.[6] *He also presents us with a most detailed description of the balsam of Judaea, but locates it vaguely "in the valley of Syria" (No. 9). He is no more explicit about the palm tree (No. 6).*

Bibliography

J. Bernays, *Theophrastos' Schrift über Frömmigkeit*, Berlin 1866, pp. 108 ff.; Radin, pp. 81 ff.; A. Büchler, *ZAW*, XXII (1902), pp. 202 ff.; W. Jaeger, *Diokles von Karystos*, Berlin 1938, pp. 134 ff.; idem, *JR*, XVIII (1938), pp. 131 ff.; A. D. Nock, *HTR*, XXXVII (1944), p. 174; Y. Gutman, *The Beginnings of Jewish-Hellenistic Literature*, Jerusalem 1958, pp. 74 ff. (in Hebrew); Hengel, pp. 466 f.; M. Stern, *Zion*, XXXIV (1969), pp. 121 ff.

2 Pötscher, *op. cit.*, p. 123.

3 Theophrastus, *De Lapidibus*, edited by D. E. Eichholz, Oxford 1965, pp. 8 ff.

4 Pötscher, *op. cit.*, p. 125. Pötscher suggests 315 or 314 B. C. E. as a probable date for the work. As a matter of fact, Regenbogen also thought that *De Pietate* belonged to an early stage of Theophrastus' writing, and that it is not dependent on Hecataeus. He probably wavered only when he was influenced by the specific arguments of Jaeger. Cf. O. Regenbogen, PW, Suppl. VII, pp. 1515 f.

5 For Theophrastus' personal knowledge of Egypt, see W. Capelle, *Wiener Studien* LXIX (1956) = *Festschrift Albin Lesky*, pp. 173 ff.

6 See Theophrastus, *Historia Plantarum*, VII, 4 : 8–9.

4

De Pietate, apud: Porphyrius, *De Abstinentia*, II, 26 — Nauck = W. Pötscher, *Theophrastos*,
Περὶ Εὐσεβείας, Leiden 1964, F13 = F5R

Καίτοι Σύρων, ὧν μὲν Ἰουδαῖοι, διὰ τὴν ἐξ ἀρχῆς θυσίαν ἔτι καὶ νῦν,
φησὶν ὁ Θεόφραστος, ζῳοθυτούντων εἰ τὸν αὐτὸν ἡμᾶς τρόπον τις κελεύοι θύειν, ἀποσταίημεν ἂν τῆς πράξεως. οὐ γὰρ ἐστιώμενοι τῶν τυθέντων, ὁλοκαυτοῦντες δὲ ταῦτα νυκτὸς καὶ κατ' αὐτῶν πολὺ μέλι καὶ οἶνον
5 λείβοντες ἀναλίσκουσι τὴν θυσίαν θᾶττον, ἵνα τοῦ δεινοῦ μηδ' ὁ πανόπτης
γένοιτο θεατής. καὶ τοῦτο δρῶσιν νηστεύοντες τὰς ἀνὰ μέσον τούτων
ἡμέρας· κατὰ δὲ πάντα τοῦτον τὸν χρόνον, ἅτε φιλόσοφοι τὸ γένος ὄντες,
περὶ τοῦ θείου μὲν ἀλλήλοις λαλοῦσι, τῆς δὲ νυκτὸς τῶν ἄστρων ποιοῦνται
τὴν θεωρίαν, βλέποντες εἰς αὐτὰ καὶ διὰ τῶν εὐχῶν θεοκλυτοῦντες.
10 κατήρξαντο γὰρ οὗτοι πρῶτοι τῶν τε λοιπῶν ζῴων καὶ σφῶν αὐτῶν,
ἀνάγκῃ καὶ οὐκ ἐπιθυμίᾳ τοῦτο πράξαντες.

1 Σύρων, ὧν Mras   Σύρων μὲν codd.   καθότι Σύρων μὲν Ἰουδαῖοι... ζῳοθυτοῦσιν
Bernays / διὰ] κατὰ Nauck / θυσίαν] συνήθειαν Nauck   2 ζῳοθυτούντων Eus. ζῳοθυτοῦντες codd. / εἰ Eus. εἰς codd. / τρόπον τις ex Eus.
2-3 κελεύοι Eus.   κελεύοιεν codd.   5 ἀναλίσκουσι Bernays   ἀνήλισκον
codd. / μηδ' ὁ πανόπτης Eus.   μὴ ὁ πανόπτης codd.   μὴ Ἥλιος ὁ πανόπτης
Bernays   6 τούτων Eus.   τούτου codd.   7 κατὰ δὲ πάντα Eus.
καὶ κατὰ πάντα codd.   9 εὐχῶν] νυκτῶν Bernays ex Eus.

And indeed, says Theophrastus, the Syrians, of whom the Jews
constitute a part, also now sacrifice live victims according to their
old mode of sacrifice; if one ordered us to sacrifice in the same way
we would have recoiled from the entire business. For they are not
feasted on the sacrifices, but burning them whole at night and pouring
on them honey and wine, they quickly destroy the offering, in order
that the all-seeing sun should not look on the terrible thing. And
they do it fasting on the intervening days.

During this whole time, being philosophers by race, they converse with
each other about the deity, and at night-time they make observations
of the stars, gazing at them and calling on God by prayer. They were
the first to institute sacrifices both of other living beings and of
themselves; yet they did it by compulsion and not from eagerness for it.

Σύρων, ὧν μὲν Ἰουδαῖοι: For the Jews as a part of the Syrian nation, see Clearchus,
apud: Josephus, *Contra Apionem*, I, 179 (No. 15); Megasthenes, apud: Clemens
Alexandrinus, *Stromata*, I, 15 : 72 : 5 (No. 14). In spite of the objections raised
by Jaeger, one still feels that Bernays may have been right here in interpreting
Theophrastus as meaning that the Jews were a type of philosophical caste among
the Syrians; see W. Jaeger, *Diokles von Karystos*, Berlin 1938, p. 139; idem, *JR*,
XVIII (1938), p. 132, n. 14; Bernays, *op. cit.* (supra, p. 9), p. 111. Cf. also the

Theophrastus

following statement of Theophrastus: ἄτε φιλόσοφοι τὸ γένος ὄντες.
ἔτι καὶ νῦν, φησὶν ὁ Θεόφραστος: Cf. Bernays, *op. cit.* (supra, p. 9), pp. 108 f.;
Pötscher, *op. cit.* (supra, p. 8, n. 1), p. 82. By repeating the name of Theophrastus,
Porphyrius wants to make it clear to the reader that he is referring to the time of
Theophrastus and not to his own time.
οὐ γὰρ ἑστιώμενοι τῶν τυθέντων: Cf. *Contra Apionem*, II, 195: θύομεν τὰς
θυσίας οὐκ εἰς μέθην ἑαυτοῖς ... ἀλλ' εἰς σωφροσύνην. Though holocausts were
not the only sacrifices known to Jews, they were the most characteristic; see, e.g.,
Oracula Sibyllina, III, 579: βωμῷ ἐπὶ μεγάλῳ ἁγίως ὁλοκαρπεύοντες.
The daily holocaust constituted the chief part of the Jewish public cult; cf. Schürer,
II, pp. 345 ff. The Greeks, on the other hand, knew holocausts mainly in connection
with chthonic cults; see P. Stengel, *Die griechischen Kultusaltertümer*, Munich
1920, p. 241. On the contrast between Greeks and Jews in the matter of holocausts,
see Philo, *Legatio ad Gaium*, 356: οὐ τὸ μὲν αἷμα τῷ βωμῷ περισπείσαντες τὰ δὲ
κρέα εἰς θοίνην καὶ εὐωχίαν οἴκαδε κομίσαντες; cf. also E. J. Bickerman, *Classical
Philology*, LX (1965), pp. 64 f.
πολὺ μέλι ... λείβοντες: Here Theophrastus is notoriously mistaken; see Lev.
ii : 11; Plutarchus, *Quaestiones Convivales*, IV, 6 : 2, p. 672 B (No. 258): μέλι μὲν οὐ
προσφέρουσι ταῖς ἱερουργίαις, ὅτι δοκεῖ φθείρειν τὸν οἶνον κεραννύμενον.
ἵνα τοῦ δεινοῦ μηδ' ὁ πανόπτης γένοιτο θεατής: πανόπτης usually means the sun,
though for a Jew it might instead signify God; cf. the *Letter of Aristeas*, 16: τὸν γὰρ
πάντων ἐπόπτην καὶ κτίστην θεὸν οὗτοι σέβονται, and the commentary of
R. Tramontano, *La Lettera di Aristea a Filocrate*, Naples 1931, p. 30.
καὶ τοῦτο δρῶσιν νηστεύοντες: Bernays suggested that there is some connection
here with the fasting of the members of the various *ma'amadot* in the townships of
Judaea, which was based on the division of the Jewish population into twenty-four
priestly courses and twenty-four lay *ma'amadot*; see Bernays, *op. cit.* (supra, p. 9),
p. 114. We may, however, doubt whether Theophrastus had any real knowledge of
this custom and even whether the custom was already established at the beginning
of the Hellenistic age; cf. Büchler, *op. cit.* (supra, p. 9), pp. 212 f.
περὶ τοῦ θείου μὲν ἀλλήλοις λαλοῦσι: Jaeger assumes that though Theophrastus
does not explicitly mention the Jewish belief in one God, he must have known
this fact, and that it may have been the main reason why he thought of the Jewish
religion as a philosophical one; see Jaeger, *JR*, XVIII, p. 133. He suggests that the
monistic character of the Jewish belief is implied by the conversation of the Jews on
"the Divine" (τὸ θεῖον), since in the pre-Socratic systems τὸ θεῖον had always
denoted the philosophical concept of the "One Highest Being" that governs
the world, in contrast to the popular belief in a plurality of mythical deities.
τῆς δὲ νυκτὸς τῶν ἄστρων ποιοῦνται τὴν θεωρίαν: We must remember that in
the eyes of the Greek philosophers the orderly motion of the heavenly bodies constituted one of the chief demonstrations of the existence of God; cf. W. Jaeger,
loc. cit.; cf. also Aristotle, *Dialogue on Philosophy* (*Aristotelis Fragmenta*, ed.
Rose, Leipzig 1886, Nos. 10–11); R. Walzer, *Aristotelis Dialogorum Fragmenta*,
Florence 1934, pp. 75 f. On the occupation of the Egyptian priests as described
by Chaeremon, see Chaeremon, apud: Porphyrius, *De Abstinentia*, IV, 8 = *F. Gr.
Hist.*, III C, 618 F 6: διῄρουν δὲ νύκτα μὲν εἰς ἐπιτήρησιν οὐρανίων. For the
Druids of Gaul, cf. *Bellum Gallicum*, VI, 14 : 6: "multa praeterea de sideribus
atque eorum motu... disputant."
κατήρξαντο γὰρ οὗτοι ... καὶ σφῶν αὐτῶν: How did Theophrastus arrive at this

11

startling statement? It may be that he did so under the influence of the well-known and widely-spread Phoenician custom; or perhaps we may assume with Jaeger that Theophrastus had some vague knowledge of the attempted sacrifice of Isaac, as related in Genesis; see Jaeger, *Diokles von Karystos*, p. 143, n. 1.

5

De Legibus, apud: Josephus, *Contra Apionem*, I, 166–167 — Niese = F6R = Reinach (Budé), p. 32

(166) ῞Ην δὲ καὶ κατὰ πόλεις οὐκ ἄγνωστον ἡμῶν πάλαι τὸ ἔθνος, καὶ πολλὰ τῶν ἐθῶν εἴς τινας ἤδη διαπεφοιτήκει καὶ ζήλου παρ᾽ ἐνίοις ἠξιοῦτο. δηλοῖ δὲ ὁ Θεόφραστος ἐν τοῖς περὶ νόμων· *(167)* λέγει γάρ, ὅτι κωλύουσιν οἱ Τυρίων νόμοι ξενικοὺς ὅρκους ὀμνύειν, ἐν οἷς
5 μετά τινων ἄλλων καὶ τὸν καλούμενον ὅρκον κορβὰν καταριθμεῖ. παρ᾽ οὐδενὶ δ᾽ ἂν οὗτος εὑρεθείη πλὴν μόνοις ᾽Ιουδαίοις, δηλοῖ δ᾽ ὡς ἂν εἴποι τις ἐκ τῆς ῾Εβραίων μεθερμηνευόμενος διαλέκτου δῶρον θεοῦ.

6 οὐδέσι Niese

(166) In ancient times various cities were acquainted with the existence of our nation, and to some of these many of our customs have now found their way, and here and there been thought worthy of imitation. This is apparent from a passage in the work of Theophrastus on Laws, (167) where he says that the laws of the Tyrians prohibit the use of foreign oaths, in enumerating which he includes among others the oath called "Corban". Now this oath will be found in no other nation except the Jews, and, translated from the Hebrew, one may interpret it as meaning "God's gift".

(trans. H. St. J. Thackeray, *LCL*)

This passage derives from the work *De Legibus*; cf. Regenbogen, *op. cit.* (supra, p. 9, n. 4), pp. 1519 ff.

167 λέγει γάρ, ὅτι κωλύουσιν οἱ Τυρίων νόμοι ξενικοὺς ὅρκους ὀμνύειν, ἐν οἷς μετά τινων ἄλλων καὶ τὸν καλούμενον ὅρκον κορβὰν καταριθμεῖ: Theophrastus expressly lists the κορβάν among the foreign oaths whose use is forbidden by the laws of the Tyrians, which in itself seems to refute the view that Josephus misinterpreted this passage and that, in fact, κορβάν implies a native Phoenician oath, since there is practically no difference between the Hebrew and the Phoenician languages; see, e.g., Müller, p. 164; cf. also the conclusion of Gutschmid, IV, p. 561: "Die Combination des Josephos scheint eine berechtigte zu sein." ὅρκος should probably be understood to denote a vow, a connotation illustrated by the New Testament; cf. Mark vii : 11; Matt. xxvii : 6. See also *Ant.*, IV, 73: καὶ οἱ κορβᾶν αὐτοὺς ὀνομάσαντες τῷ θεῷ; cf. J. H. A. Hart, *JQR*, XIX (1907), pp. 615 ff.; Rengstorf, apud: G. Kittel, *Theologisches Wörterbuch*, III, 1938, pp. 860 ff.; S. Zeitlin,

JQR, LIII (1962–1963), pp. 160 ff; see also H. Grégoire, *La Nouvelle Clio*, V (1953) = *Mélanges Carnoy*, pp. 450 f.; J. D. M. Derrett, *New Testament Studies*, XVI (1969–1970), pp. 364 ff.

6

Historia Plantarum, II, 6:2, 5, 8 — Hort

(2) Πανταχοῦ γὰρ ὅπου πλῆθος φοινίκων ἁλμώδεις αἱ χῶραι· καὶ γὰρ ἐν Βαβυλῶνί φασιν, ὅπου οἱ φοίνικες πεφύκασι, καὶ ἐν Λιβύῃ δὲ καὶ ἐν Αἰγύπτῳ καὶ Φοινίκῃ καὶ τῆς Συρίας δὲ τῆς κοίλης, ἐν ᾗ γ᾽ οἱ πλεῖστοι τυγχάνουσιν, ἐν τρισὶ μόνοις τόποις ἁλμώδεσιν εἶναι τοὺς δυναμένους
5 *θησαυρίζεσθαι...*
(5) Ἄλλοι δέ τινες λέγουσιν ὡς οἵ γε κατὰ Συρίαν οὐδεμίαν προσάγουσιν ἐργασίαν ἀλλ᾽ ἢ διακαθαίρουσι καὶ ἐπιβρέχουσιν, ἐπιζητεῖν δὲ μᾶλλον τὸ ναματιαῖον ὕδωρ ἢ τὸ ἐκ τοῦ Διός· εἶναι δὲ πολὺ τοιοῦτον ἐν τῷ αὐλῶνι ἐν ᾧ καὶ τὰ φοινικόφυτα τυγχάνει, τὸν
10 *αὐλῶνα δὲ τοῦτον λέγειν τοὺς Σύρους ὅτι διατείνει διὰ τῆς Ἀραβίας μέχρι τῆς ἐρυθρᾶς θαλάσσης καὶ πολλοὺς φάσκειν ἐληλυθέναι· τούτου δὲ ἐν τῷ κοιλοτάτῳ πεφυκέναι τοὺς φοίνικας...*
(8) ...Θησαυρίζεσθαι δὲ μόνους δύνασθαί φασι τῶν ἐν Συρίᾳ τοὺς ἐν τῷ αὐλῶνι, τοὺς δ᾽ ἐν Αἰγύπτῳ καὶ Κύπρῳ καὶ παρὰ τοῖς ἄλλοις χλω-
15 *ροὺς ἀναλίσκεσθαι.*

11 διεληλυθέναι Wimmer

(2) Wherever date-palms grow abundantly, the soil is salt, both in Babylon, they say, where the tree is indigenous, in Libya, in Egypt and in Phoenicia; while in Coele-Syria, where are most palms, only in three districts, they say, where the soil is salt, are dates produced which can be stored... (5) However some say that the people of Syria use no cultivation, except cutting out wood and watering, also that the date-palm requires spring water rather than water from the skies; and that such water is abundant in the valley in which are the palm-groves. And they add that the Syrians say that this valley extends through Arabia to the Red Sea, and that many profess to have visited it, and that it is in the lowest part of it that the date-palms grow... (8) The only dates that will keep, they say, are those which grow in the Valley of Syria, while those that grow in Egypt, Cyprus and elsewhere are used when fresh. (trans. A. Hort, *LCL*)

This passage is a part of Theophrastus' discussion of palms and their propagation. Theophrastus maintains that wherever date palms grow abundantly, the soil is salty.

2 *καὶ τῆς Συρίας δὲ τῆς κοίλης*: The meaning of Coele-Syria underwent many changes throughout the ages. On the origin of the name and its various connotations, which gave rise to many discussions, see W. Otto, *Beiträge zur Seleukidengeschichte des 3. Jahrhunderts v. Chr.*, Munich 1928, pp. 30 ff.; E. Schwartz, *Philologus*, LXXXVI (1931), pp. 373 ff. (= *Gesammelte Schriften*, II, Berlin 1956, pp. 240 ff.,); *ibid.*, LXXXVII (1932), pp. 261 ff. (= *Gesammelte Schriften*, II, p. 270 ff.); K. Galling, *ZDPV*, LXI (1938), pp. 85 ff.; E. Bikerman, *RB*, LIV (1947), pp. 256 ff.; A. Shalit, *Scripta Hierosolymitana*, I, 1954, pp. 64 ff.; W. Brandenstein, *Anzeiger für die Altertumswissenschaft*, VIII (1955), pp. 62 ff. It seems that we must look for a Semitic origin for the term, something like the Hebrew כל סוריה (the whole of Syria, in *status constructus*); cf. Otto, *op. cit.*, p. 34, n.1; Schwartz, Shalit. Owing to the similarity of sound, this became *Κοίλη Συρία* (the hollow Syria), a combination well adapted to the Greek ear. The Semitic name seems still to be echoed by Diodorus, XIX, 57 : 1: *Συρίαν δὲ πᾶσαν Πτολεμαίῳ*; cf. XIX, 94 : 1. Originally Coele-Syria was identical with the whole Persian province of עבר נהרא, that is,with Syria. This is the meaning of Coele-Syria that emerges from our two oldest sources, both from the fourth century B. C. E., in which the name occurs, namely, Ctesias, (apud: Diodorus, II, 2 : 3): *κατεστρέψατο μὲν γὰρ ... τήν τε Αἴγυπτον καὶ Φοινίκην, ἔτι δὲ Κοίλην Συρίαν καὶ Κιλικίαν...*; Pseudo-Scylax; cf. *ZDPV*, LXI (1938), p. 90.

However, already at the beginning of the Hellenistic period the upper — i.e. the northern — parts of Syria were no longer included in Coele-Syria; whether the Orontes at first constituted the border between *ἡ ἄνω Συρία* and *Κοίλη Συρία* we cannot be sure; cf. Diodorus, XVIII, 6 : 3 (a list of the satrapies of Alexander's empire at the time of his death in 323 B.C.E., presumably deriving from Hieronymus of Cardia), where *Συρία ἡ ἄνω* is contrasted with *Κοίλη Συρία*. The same holds true for Diodorus, XIX, 93 : 1, and for Eratosthenes, apud: Strabo, *Geographica*, II, 5 : 38. This somewhat limited meaning of Coele-Syria, which excludes northern Syria, will suit both Theophrastus and Clearchus, apud: Josephus, *Contra Apionem*, I, 179 (No. 15). It seemingly continued to prevail through the third century B. C. E., though it was not in official use under the Ptolemies, who ruled the territories and called them Syria and Phoenicia; cf. Bengtson, III, pp. 166 ff. After Antiochus III conquered the Syrian possessions of the Ptolemies in 200–198 B. C. E., Coele-Syria became the official name; see *OGIS*, No. 230: *Πτολεμαῖος Θρασέα, στραταγὸς καὶ ἀρχιερεὺς Συρίας Κοίλας καὶ Φοινίκας* (on the correct dating of the inscription, after 197 B.C.E., see M. Holleaux, *Études d'épigraphie et d'histoire grecques*, III, Paris 1942, p. 161, n. 6; Gabba, No. II, pp. 18 f.); see also II Macc., iii : 5; iv : 4; viii : 8; x : 11; I Macc, x : 69; Polybius V, 80 : 3. On the later use of the name, see the exhaustive treatment of Bikerman.

Till the middle of the second century B. C. E, — i.e. till the establishment of the free Hasmonaean state — Judaea was undoubtedly included in Coele-Syria. Thus, one may assume that Theophrastus, when speaking here of the palms in Coele-Syria, has in mind the world-famous palms of Judaea, those growing in the Jordan Valley in the vicinity of Jericho. This assumption is reinforced by the account that follows of the Valley of Syria (clearly a reference to the Jordan Valley), in the lowest part of which date-palms grow, and which extends through Arabia.

Theophrastus

7

Historia Plantarum, IV, 4:14 — Hort

(4:14) Περιττότερα δὲ τῶν φυομένων καὶ πλεῖστον ἐξηλλαγμένα πρὸς τὰ ἄλλα τὰ εὔοσμα τὰ περὶ Ἀραβίαν καὶ Συρίαν καὶ Ἰνδούς, οἷον ὅ τε λιβανωτὸς καὶ ἡ σμύρνα καὶ ἡ κασία καὶ τὸ ὀποβάλσαμον καὶ τὸ κινάμωμον καὶ ὅσα ἄλλα τοιαῦτα...

Among the plants that grow in Arabia, Syria and India the aromatic plants are somewhat exceptional and distinct from the plants of other lands; for instance, frankincense, myrrh, cassia, opobalsam, cinnamon and all other such plants.   (trans. A. Hort, *LCL*)

8

Historia Plantarum, IX, 1:6 — Hort

Τὸν δὲ λιβανωτὸν καὶ τὴν σμύρναν ὑπὸ Κύνα φασὶ καὶ ταῖς θερμοτάταις ἡμέραις ἐντέμνειν· ὡσαύτως δὲ καὶ τὸ ἐν Συρίᾳ βάλσαμον.

The frankincense and myrrh trees they say should be cut at the rising of the Dogstar and on the hottest days, and so also the "Syrian balsam".   (trans. A. Hort, *LCL*)

9

Historia Plantarum, IX, 6:1–4 — Hort

(1) Τὸ δὲ βάλσαμον γίνεται μὲν ἐν τῷ αὐλῶνι τῷ περὶ Συρίαν. παραδείσους δ᾽ εἶναί φασι δύο μόνους, τὸν μὲν ὅσον εἴκοσι πλέθρων τὸν δ᾽ ἕτερον πολλῷ ἐλάττονα. τὸ δὲ δένδρον μέγεθος μὲν ἡλίκον ῥόα μεγάλη πολύκλαδον δὲ σφόδρα· φύλλον δὲ ἔχειν ὅμοιον πηγάνῳ, πλὴν ἔκλευκον,
5 ἀείφυλλον δὲ εἶναι· καρπὸν δὲ παρόμοιον τῇ τερμίνθῳ καὶ μεγέθει καὶ σχήματι καὶ χρώματι· εὐῶδες σφόδρα καὶ τοῦτο καὶ μᾶλλον τοῦ δακρύου.
(2) Τὸ δὲ δάκρυον ἀπὸ ἐντομῆς συλλέγειν, ἐντέμνειν δὲ ὄνυξι σιδηροῖς ὑπὸ τὸ ἄστρον, ὅταν μάλιστα πνίγη ὦσι, καὶ τὰ στελέχη καὶ τὰ ἄνω.
10 τὴν δὲ συλλογὴν ὅλον τὸ θέρος ποιεῖσθαι· οὐκ εἶναι δὲ πολὺ τὸ ῥέον, ἀλλ᾽ ἐν ἡμέρᾳ τὸν ἄνδρα συλλέγειν ὅσον κόγχην· τὴν δ᾽ ὀσμὴν διαφέρουσαν καὶ πολλήν, ὥστε ἀπὸ μικροῦ πολὺν ἐφικνεῖσθαι τόπον. ἀλλ᾽ οὐ φοιτᾶν

6 εὐώδη σφόδρα καὶ τοῦτον Wimmer

15

ἐνταῦθα ἄκρατον, ἀλλὰ τὸ συνηγμένον κεκραμένον· πολλὴν γὰρ δέχεσθαι
κρᾶσιν· καὶ τὸ ἐν τῇ Ἑλλάδι πολλάκις εἶναι κεκραμένον· εὔοσμα δὲ σφόδρα
15 καὶ τὰ ῥαβδία· (3) καθαίρειν γὰρ καὶ τῶνδε ἔνεκα καὶ του διαφόρου· πωλεῖσθαι ⟨γὰρ⟩ τίμια. καὶ τὴν ἐργασίαν τὴν περὶ τὰ δένδρα σχεδὸν ἐν ταὐτῇ
αἰτίᾳ εἶναι καὶ τὴν βροχήν· βρέχεσθαι γὰρ συνεχῶς. συναιτίαν δὲ δοκεῖν
εἶναι τοῦ μὴ μεγάλα γίνεσθαι τὰ δένδρα καὶ τὴν τῶν ῥαβδίων τομήν. διὰ
γὰρ τὸ πολλάκις ἐπικείρεσθαι ῥάβδους ἀφιέναι καὶ οὐκ εἰς ἓν ἐκτείνειν
20 τὴν ὁρμήν.
(4) Ἄγριον δὲ οὐδὲν εἶναι βάλσαμον οὐδαμοῦ· γίνεσθαι δὲ ἐκ μὲν
τοῦ μείζονος παραδείσου ἀγγείδια δώδεκα ὅσον ἡμιχοαῖα, ἐκ δὲ τοῦ
ἑτέρου δύο μόνον· πωλεῖσθαι δὲ τὸ μὲν ἄκρατον δὶς πρὸς ἀργύριον τὸ
δ' ἄλλο κατὰ λόγον τῆς μίξεως· καὶ τοῦτο μὲν διαφέρον τι φαίνεται
κατὰ τὴν εὐοσμίαν.

15 του Hort in ed. Loeb τοῦ codd.　　16 ⟨γὰρ⟩ Schneider ／ ἐν ταὐτῇ αἰτίᾳ
Hort in ed. Loeb　　ταύτην αἰτίαν codd.　　ἐν ταύτῃ αἰτίᾳ Wimmer

(1) Balsam grows in the valley of Syria. They say that there are only
two parks in which it grows, one of about four acres, the other much
smaller. The tree is as tall as a good-sized pomegranate and is much
branched; it has a leaf like that of rue, but is pale; and it is evergreen;
the fruit is like that of the terebinth in size, shape and colour, and
this too is very fragrant, indeed more so than the gum.
(2) The gum, they say, is collected by making incisions, which is done
with bent pieces of iron at the time of the Dog-star, when there is
scorching heat; and the incisions are made both in the trunks and in
the upper parts of the tree. The collecting goes on throughout the
summer; but the quantity which flows is not large; in a day a single
man can collect a shell-full; the fragrance is exceeding great and
rich, so that which comes from a small amount is perceived for a wide
distance. However it does not reach us in a pure state; what is collected
is mixed with other things; for it mixes freely with other things; and
what is known in Hellas is generally mixed with something else. The
boughs are also very fragrant. (3) In fact it is on account of these
boughs, they say, that the tree is pruned (as well for a different reason),
since the boughs cut off can be sold for a good price. In fact the culture
of the trees has the same motive as the irrigation (for they are con-
stantly irrigated). And the cutting of the boughs seems likewise to be
partly the reason why the trees do not grow tall; for, since they are
often cut about, they send out branches instead of putting out all
their energy in one direction.
(4) Balsam is said not to grow wild anywhere. From the larger park

16

are obtained twelve vessels containing each about three pints, from the other only two such vessels; the pure gum sells for twice its weight in silver, the mixed sort at a price proportionate to its purity. Balsam then appears to be of exceptional fragrance.

(trans. A. Hort, *LCL*)

1 Τὸ δὲ βάλσαμον γίνεται μὲν ἐν τῷ αὐλῶνι τῷ περὶ Συρίαν: This refers to the Jordan Valley, since that is the only place in Syria where the balsam grows. Cf. Diodorus, II, 48 : 9 (No. 59): γίνεται δὲ περὶ τοὺς τόπους ἐν αὐλῶνί τινι καὶ τὸ καλούμενον βάλσαμον ... οὐδαμοῦ μὲν τῆς ἄλλης οἰκουμένης εὑρισκομένου τοῦ φυτοῦ τούτου; cf. also Dioscorides, *De Materia Medica*, I, 19 : 1 (No. 179): κατά τινα αὐλῶνα; Strabo, *Geographica*, XVI, 2 : 41, p. 763 (No. 115): ἐνταῦθα μόνον γεννᾶται; Plinius, *Naturalis Historia*, XII, 111 (No. 213): "Sed omnibus odoribus praefertur balsamum, uni terrarum Iudaeae concessum..."
παραδείσους δ'εἶναί φασι δύο μόνους: Cf. Strabo, *Geographica*, XVI, 2:41, p. 763: ἔστι δ'αὐτοῦ καὶ βασίλειον καὶ ὁ τοῦ βαλσάμου παράδεισος. In Theophrastus we find the first and also the most detailed description of the balsam of Judaea to appear in Greek literature.
φύλλον δὲ ἔχειν ὅμοιον πηγάνῳ: Cf. Dioscorides, *De Materia Medica*, I, 19 : 1 (No. 179) φύλλα ἔχον ὅμοια πηγάνῳ, λευκότερα δὲ πολλῷ καὶ ἀειθαλέστερα, γεννώμενον ἐν μόνῃ Ἰουδαίᾳ.
καρπὸν δὲ παρόμοιον τῇ τερμίνθῳ: Cf. Strabo, *Geographica*, XVI, 2 : 41, p. 763: κυτίσῳ ἐοικὸς καὶ τερμίνθῳ.
4 πωλεῖσθαι δὲ τὸ μὲν ἄκρατον δὶς πρὸς ἀργύριον: Cf. Plinius, *Naturalis Historia*, XII, 117 (No. 213): "cum et duplo rependebatur argento."

V. HIERONYMUS OF CARDIA

Second half of the fourth century to first half of the third century B.C.E.

Hieronymus, the foremost historian of the early Hellenistic age and the ultimate authority for what we know of the political history of the years 323-272 B.C.E., stayed in Palestine for some time and took an active part in the political and military events that took place in that country c. 312 B.C.E. It was on Hieronymus that Antigonus Monophthalmus imposed the task of supervising the Dead Sea and collecting the asphalt; cf. Diodorus, XIX, 100: 1-2: ἐπὶ μὲν ταύτης ἐπιμελητὴν ἔταξεν Ἱερώνυμον τὸν τὰς Ἱστορίας συγγράψαντα, τούτῳ δὲ συνετέτακτο πλοῖα παρασκευάσασθαι καὶ πᾶσαν τὴν ἄσφαλτον ἀναλαβόντα συνάγειν εἴς τινα τόπον. *Nevertheless, Hieronymus never refers either to Judaea or to the Jews. In describing the Dead Sea, he refers only to the Nabataeans (*ἐν τῇ Ναβαταίων χώρᾳ τῶν Ἀράβων εἶναι λίμνην πικράν), *and Josephus already expressed his disappointment with Hieronymus' omission of any mention of Jews, contrasting him with his contemporary, Hecataeus; see* Contra Apionem, *I, 214:* ἀλλ᾽ ὅμως Ἑκαταῖος μὲν καὶ βιβλίον ἔγραψεν περὶ ἡμῶν, Ἱερώνυμος δ᾽ οὐδαμοῦ κατὰ τὴν ἱστορίαν ἐμνημόνευσε καίτοι σχεδὸν ἐν τοῖς τόποις διατετριφώς.

Hieronymus is the first Greek writer known to us to speak of the Nabataeans. Our passage, which expressly testifies to Hieronymus' statement that the Dead Sea is situated in "the Land of the Nabataeans", derives from a work, De Aquis Mirabilibus. *This is a collection of* paradoxa *by an anonymous writer who lived in the Roman Empire and who is known as the Florentine Paradoxographer.*[1]

Our knowledge of Hieronymus' description of the Dead Sea is not, however, confined to the Paradoxographer's brief remark. As a matter of fact, we find it also in the chapters dedicated to the Dead Sea by Diodorus (Nos. 59 and 62). For Diodorus' dependence on Hieronymus,

---

1 For the Florentine Paradoxographer, cf. H. Öhler, "Paradoxographi Florentini Anonymi Opusculum de Aquis Mirabilibus", Ph. D. Thesis, Tübingen 1913; K. Ziegler, PW, XVIII, pp. 1161 f. On our passage, cf. especially Öhler, *op. cit.*, pp. 108 f.

see the introduction to Diodorus. Here it will suffice to point out the close similarity of content between our passage and that of Diodorus.

Bibliography

R. Schubert, *Die Quellen zur Geschichte der Diadochenzeit*, Leipzig 1914, pp. 6 ff., especially p. 16; F. Jacoby, PW, VIII, pp. 1540 ff. = *Griechische Historiker*, Stuttgart 1956, pp. 245 ff.; T. S. Brown, *American Historical Review*, LII (1946–1947), pp. 684 ff.; M. J. Fontana, "Le lotte per la successione di Alessandro Magno", *Atti della Accademia di Scienze, Lettere e Arti di Palermo*, Ser. 4, Vol. XVIII, Part 2, 1957–1958 (1960) pp. 257 f.

10

Historia Diadochorum, apud: Paradoxographus Florentinus, *De Aquis Mirabilibus*, 33 — Öhler = *F. Gr. Hist.*, II, B, 154 F5 = *Paradoxographorum Graecorum Reliquiae*, ed. A. Giannini, Milano 1965, p. 324

Ἱερώνυμος ἱστόρησεν ἐν τῇ Ναβαταίων χώρᾳ τῶν Ἀράβων εἶναι λίμνην πικράν, ἐν ᾗ οὔτε ἰχθῦς οὔτε ἄλλο τι τῶν ἐνύδρων ζῴων γίνεσθαι· ἀσφάλτου δὲ πλίνθους ἐξ αὐτῆς αἴρεσθαι ὑπὸ τῶν ἐπιχωρίων.

1 Ναβαταίων] βαταναίων U

Hieronymus recorded that there was in the country of the Nabataeans a bitter lake in which neither fish nor any other kind of animals living in water are born; bricks of asphalt are drawn out from it by the people of the country.

V. HECATAEUS OF ABDERA

c. 300 B.C.E.

Hecataeus lived in the time of Alexander the Great and Ptolemy I.[1] Under the last-mentioned ruler he visited Egypt, venturing as far as Thebes.[2] He was a prolific writer,[3] and according to Diogenes Laertius (IX, 69), he was counted a pupil of Pyrron the Sceptic. While we cannot assign him to any particular philosophical school, he is conspicuous as spokesman for the trends and ideas prevalent in the great age of transition in which he lived.[4] His most famous book was the Aegyptiaca,[5] a panegyrical exposition of the culture, history, political organization and religion of the ancient Egyptians. This book served as the main source for the description of Egypt in the first book of Diodorus. From the same book of Diodorus one might reasonably infer that in his Aegyptiaca Hecataeus refers to Jews in connection with his survey of the emigration of Egyptians to foreign countries (I, 28 = No. 55). However, a much more detailed description of Jews, and one that expressly derives from Hecataeus, has come down to us in the fortieth book of Diodorus, through the Bibliotheca of Photius. In it we find the oldest account of Jewish origins in Greek literature, though not necessarily the first reference to Jews; cf. the introduction to Theophrastus. Diodorus uses this account in connection with Pompey's capture of Jerusalem, but he does not specify which of Hecataeus' works he used or in what context he found the material concerning the Jews.[6]

---

1 See *Contra Apionem*, I, 183: Ἀλεξάνδρῳ τῷ βασιλεῖ συνακμάσας καὶ Πτολεμαίῳ τῷ Λάγου συγγενόμενος. Cf. Suda s.v. Ἑκαταῖος Ἀβδηρίτης... γέγονε δὲ ἐπὶ τῶν διαδόχων.

2 See Diodorus, I, 46 : 8.

3 The list of his works in Suda, *loc. cit.*, has been lost. Here we only find the name of one of them: Περὶ τῆς ποιήσεως Ὁμήρου καὶ Ἡσιόδου. From other sources we learn about a work by him that deals with the Hyperboreans; cf. Plinius, *Naturalis Historia*, VI, 55; *Scholia to Apollonius Rhodius*, II, 675.

4 E. Schwartz, *Rhein. Mus.*, XL (1885), pp. 223 ff.; F. Jacoby, PW, VII, pp. 2753 ff. = *Griechische Historiker*, Stuttgart 1956, pp. 229 ff.

5 As a matter of fact, we do not know the exact name of the work; see Jacoby, PW, VII, p. 2752 = *Griechische Historiker*, p. 228.

6 It is noteworthy that there is a conspicuous difference between the "Jewish

20

Hecataeus of Abdera

The following are some of the main features of the picture of the Jews that emerges from Hecataeus:

a. Hecataeus' starting point is Egypt. The Jews are a people who were expelled from Egypt, and this event has had an effect on their customs and constitution. Moreover, some of their institutions closely resemble those of the Egyptians, as described by Hecataeus.

b. Hecataeus uses also a Jewish source, and it seems that it was an oral one. This is evidenced by the high esteem in which he holds Moses and by his usage of an almost direct reference to the Bible: προσγέγραπται δὲ καὶ τοῖς νόμοις ἐπὶ τελευτῆς ὅτι Μωσῆς ἀκούσας τοῦ θεοῦ τάδε λέγει τοῖς Ἰουδαίοις.

c. The Jewish community is one that is ruled by priests. In this statement, as in some others, Hecataeus is influenced by the actual contemporary situation in Judaea.

d. Hecataeus is devoid of anti-Semitic feelings, and his attitude to Jews is, if anything, sympathetic. In their expulsion from Egypt, the Jews are coupled with the emigrants to Greece, led by Cadmus and Danaus.

e. Hecataeus knows about Jewish monotheism and its opposition to anthropomorphism. He even alludes to the division of the Jewish people into twelve tribes, but he is ignorant of the whole period of Jewish history that preceded the Persian rule.

f. He notes that the ancestral customs of the Jews changed as a result of Persian and Macedonian rule. But, as far as we may judge from the extant text, he does not criticize the change.

g. In his history of Jewish settlement, he conforms more to the common schemata of Greek colonization than to the traditional Hebrew version. Thus, according to Hecataeus, Moses came to Judaea, founded Jerusalem and drew up the Jewish constitution there.

Diodorus does not use all the material found in the relevant chapter of Hecataeus, and, as a matter of fact, we sometimes feel that he refers only briefly to subjects that Hecataeus deals with at some length.[7] We must also bear in mind that Diodorus, while summarizing and condensing his source, might have introduced stylistic changes. Thus, we cannot be sure of the ipsissima verba *of Hecataeus.*

Apart from the Jewish chapter in Diodorus, Josephus, in Contra Apionem, *I, 183, expressly refers to a work of Hecataeus that was wholly*

chapter" in the fortieth book of Diodorus, where the Jews appear as foreigners expelled from Egypt, and the first book of Diodorus, where a voluntary emigration of the Jews, who were originally Egyptians, is implied. Cf. also *F. Gr. Hist.* IIIa, p. 50.

7 W. Jaeger, *Diokles von Karystos*, Berlin 1938, pp. 150 f.

dedicated to Jews (οὐ παρέργως, ἀλλὰ περὶ αὐτῶν Ἰουδαίων συγγέγραφε βιβλίον). The same work is attested by Origenes, Contra Celsum, I, 15, where it is stated that its authenticity was suspected by Herennius Philo:
καὶ Ἑκαταίου δὲ τοῦ ἱστορικοῦ φέρεται περὶ Ἰουδαίων βιβλίον, ἐν ᾧ προστίθεται μᾶλλόν πως ὡς σοφῷ τῷ ἔθνει ἐπὶ τοσοῦτον, ὡς καὶ Ἑρέννιον Φίλωνα ἐν τῷ περὶ Ἰουδαίων συγγράμματι πρῶτον μὲν ἀμφιβάλλειν, εἰ τοῦ ἱστορικοῦ ἐστι τὸ σύγγραμμα, δεύτερον δὲ λέγειν ὅτι, εἴπερ ἐστὶν αὐτοῦ, εἰκὸς αὐτὸν συνηρπάσθαι ἀπὸ τῆς παρὰ Ἰουδαίοις πιθανότητος καὶ συγκατατεθεῖσθαι αὐτῶν τῷ λόγῳ.

Another book by Hecataeus, one that deals with Abraham, is referred to in Antiquitates, *I, 159. The same work appears under the name of* Abraham and the Egyptians *in* Clemens Alexandrinus, Stromata, *V, 113 =* Eusebius, Praeparatio Evangelica, *XIII, 13:40:* Ἑκαταῖος ὁ τὰς ἱστορίας συνταξάμενος ἐν τῷ κατ' Ἄβραμον καὶ τοὺς Αἰγυπτίους.

The admiration Hecataeus displays for the Jewish religion is also stressed in the Letter of Aristeas, *the pseudoepigraphical work composed, as it seems, c. 100 B. C. E.,*[8] *where (§31) we read:*
Διὸ πόρρω γεγόνασιν οἵ τε συγγραφεῖς καὶ ποιηταὶ καὶ τὸ τῶν ἱστορικῶν πλῆθος τῆς ἐπιμνήσεως τῶν προειρημένων βιβλίων...διὰ τὸ ἁγνήν τινα καὶ σεμνὴν εἶναι τὴν ἐν αὐτοῖς θεωρίαν, ὥς φησιν Ἑκαταῖος ὁ Ἀβδηρίτης·

The book about Abraham may be assumed, with almost absolute certainty, to be a product of Jewish religious propaganda, since it includes, according to the evidence of Clemens of Alexandria, spurious verses of Sophocles that have a militant monotheistic ring.

The main problem arises in connection with the somewhat extensive chapter found in Contra Apionem, *I, 183 ff., where Josephus states that he excerpted from Hecataeus' work about Jews. It is given in the form of Hecataeus' memories, or, at least, this is the impression given in the first passage, which concerns the chief priest Ezekias, and by the last one, namely, the story of the Jewish mounted archer Mosollamus. It is expressly stated that the latter story comes from the personal experience of the writer. The intermediate passages stress the loyalty of Jews to their laws — a loyalty that did not shrink from martyrdom*

8 Cf. A. Momigliano, *Aegyptus*, XII (1932), pp. 161 ff.; W.W. Tarn, *The Greeks in Bactria and India*[2], Cambridge 1951, pp. 424 f.; O. Murray, *JTS*, XVIII (1967), pp. 338 f. A somewhat earlier date in the second century B.C.E. is maintained with strong arguments by E. Van't Dack; see *Antidorum W. Peremans Sexagenario ab Alumnis Oblatum*, Louvain 1968, pp. 263 ff. Again, an early date is postulated by U. Rappaport, *Studies in the History of the Jewish People and the Land of Israel in Memory of Zvi Avneri*, Haifa 1970, pp. 37 ff. (in Hebrew).

under either the Persians or Alexander. These passages also refer to the vast population of Judaea and to the size of the country, and they give a description of Jerusalem and the Temple.

The authenticity of the passages from Hecataeus in Contra Apionem has often been questioned, e.g., by Willrich, Schürer, Jacoby, Stein, Dalbert, Schaller and Fraser. Others defend it, e.g., Schlatter, Wendland, Engers, Lewy, Gutman and Gager. Tcherikover uses it for his survey of Hellenistic Judaea, and Jaeger seems to suspend judgment.[9]

The chief arguments adduced against the authenticity of the chapter may be summarized as follows:

a. We know for certain that Jewish apologetic writers attached the name of Hecataeus to at least one book fabricated by them—that about Abraham. They may have used the same device on more than one occasion. It has even been suggested by Schürer that the work on the Jews should be considered identical with the one on Abraham.

b. The passages in question include anachronistic details that reflect conditions subsequent to the Hasmonaean revolt (cf. recently, Schaller). Moreover, the emphasis put on the Jewish spirit of martyrdom would be more consonant with the atmosphere prevailing after the persecution launched by Antiochus Epiphanes.

c. The fact that Herennius Philo already had grave doubts about the authenticity of the excerpt carries some weight with modern scholars.

d. It is maintained that the general tenor of the passages in Contra Apionem differs considerably from that characterizing the Jewish chapter in Diodorus. While the tone of the latter is a detached one, that of the former is in the nature of a panegyric.

Most of these arguments may be rebutted:

a. The existence of a Jewish pseudo-Hecataeus renders it indeed possible that he might also be the author of Περὶ Ἰουδαίων, but it does not prove that he was; the assumption that Περὶ Ἰουδαίων is identical with the work on Abraham is wholly unwarranted.

b. None of the details in the fragments of Περὶ Ἰουδαίων have really been shown to be anachronisms. This also holds true for the question of the tithes, discussed recently by Schaller; cf. the commentary.

c. The doubts of Herennius Philo express no more than his personal feelings. As a contemporary of Hadrian he could not understand the sympathetic attitude shown to the Jews by the older writer.[10]

d. It is true that Hecataeus' general tone concerning the Jews in

9 Jaeger, *loc. cit.* (supra, n. 7).
10 Cf. also J. G. Gager, *ZNTW*, LX (1969), p. 132.

Contra Apionem *is more laudatory than the tone in Diodorus. Yet, we must also remember that the passages in Diodorus reveal Hecataeus' high esteem for Moses and for the Jewish constitution. We must also take into account the fact that the description in Diodorus presumably derives from Hecataeus'* Aegyptiaca, *with its Egyptian point of view, while the Περὶ Ἰουδαίων may be supposed to have been a wholly independent work. Hecataeus may have been more dependent on Jewish oral sources in the latter work than he was in his treatment of Jews in his* Aegyptiaca.

It should be added that Hecataeus lived in an age that thought rather highly of Jews, as is attested by the attitude of Theophrastus, apud: Porphyrius, De Abstinentia, *II, 26 (No. 4); Megasthenes, apud: Clemens Alexandrinus,* Stromata, *I, 15:72:5 (No. 14); and Clearchus, apud: Josephus,* Contra Apionem, *I, 176–183 (No. 15). Moreover, some of the main champions of the view that the fragments are not authentic (Schürer and Jacoby) do admit that they excel the common pseudo-epigraphic compositions in sobriety. Still, there are some expressions and nuances that are perhaps difficult to attribute to the real Hecataeus, especially his approval of the Jews' destruction of pagan temples and altars erected in their country (καὶ προσεπιτίθησιν, ὅτι δίκαιον ἐπὶ τούτοις αὐτούς ἐστι θαυμάζειν)·*

Therefore, it seems that Josephus had before him a Jewish revision, however slight, of the book of Hecataeus. In this revised version the Greek writer's tone toward the Jews became more laudatory.[11]

---

11 Even Schürer admits that authentic passages of Hecataeus lie at the bottom of the presumably spurious work Περὶ Ἰουδαίων and that "schon bei den Exzerpten des Josephus hat man zum Teil den Eindruck der Echtheit"; cf. Schürer, III, p. 606.

Hecataeus of Abdera

Bibliography

Susemihl, II, pp. 644 f.; A. Schlatter, *Zur Topographie und Geschichte Palästinas*, Stuttgart 1893, pp. 333 ff.; H. Willrich, *Juden und Griechen vor der makkabäischen Erhebung*, Göttingen 1895, pp. 20 ff., 48 ff.; idem, *Judaica*, Göttingen 1900, pp. 86 ff.; P. Wendland, *Philologische Wochenschrift*, XX, (1900), pp. 1199 ff.; J. Geffcken, *Neue Jahrbücher für das klassische Altertum*, XV (1905), pp. 627 f.; idem, *Zwei griechische Apologeten*, Leipzig-Berlin 1907, pp. XI ff.; Schürer, III, pp. 603 ff.; Radin, pp. 92 ff.; Ed. Meyer, II, p. 24, n. 2; pp. 28 ff.; M. Engers, *Mnemosyne*, NS LI (1923), pp. 229 ff.; W. Bousset & H. Gressmann, *Die Religion des Judentums im späthellenistischen Zeitalter*, Tübingen 1926, pp. 26 f.; K. Reinhardt, *Poseidonios über Ursprung und Entartung*, Heidelberg 1928, pp. 9 f., 19 ff.; T. Reinach, in the Budé edition of *Contra Apionem*, Paris 1930, pp. XXXI f.; H. Lewy, *ZNTW*, XXXI (1932), pp. 117 ff.; M. Stein, *Zion*, OS VI (1934), pp. 1 ff.; J. Jeremias, *ZAW*, LII (1934), pp. 109 f.; H. Diels & W. Kranz, *Die Fragmente der Vorsokratiker*, II [5], Berlin 1935, p. 245; A. T. Olmstead, *JAOS*, LVI (1936), pp. 243 f.; W. Jaeger, *Diokles von Karystos*, Berlin 1938, pp. 135 ff.; idem, *JR*, XVIII (1938), pp. 127 ff.; F. Dornseiff, *ZAW*, LVI (1938), p. 76, n. 1; idem, *Echtheitsfragen antik-griechischer Literatur*, Berlin 1939, pp. 52 ff.; Bidez & Cumont, I, pp. 240 ff.; *F. Gr. Hist.*, IIIa, 1943, pp. 46 ff., 61 ff.; P. Dalbert, *Die Theologie der hellenistisch-jüdischen Missions-Literatur*, Hamburg 1954, pp. 65 ff.; W. Aly, *Strabon von Amaseia*, Bonn 1957, pp. 197 ff.; Y. Gutman, *The Beginnings of Jewish-Hellenistic Literature*, Jerusalem 1958, pp. 39 ff. (in Hebrew); Tcherikover, pp. 58 f., 119 f., 122 f.; B. Schaller, *ZNTW*, LIV (1963), pp. 15 ff.; N. Walter, *Der Thoraausleger Aristobulos*, Berlin 1964, pp. 172 ff.; O. Murray, *JTS*, XVIII (1967), p. 342, n. 4; J. G. Gager, *ZNTW*, LX (1969), pp. 130 ff.; Hengel, pp. 465 ff.; O. Murray, *JEA*, LVI (1970), pp. 144 f., p. 158; W. Speyer, *Die literarische Fälschung im heidnischen und christlichen Altertum*, Munich 1971, pp. 160 f.; Fraser, I, p. 496; Gager, pp. 26 ff.

11

Aegyptiaca, apud: Diodorus Siculus, *Bibliotheca Historica*, XL, 3 — Dindorf = Photius, Cod. 244 —
Bekker = ed. Henry, Vol• VI, pp. 134 ff = F9R = *F. Gr. Hist.*, III, A264, F6

*(1) Κατὰ τὴν Αἴγυπτον τὸ παλαιὸν λοιμικῆς περιστάσεως γενομένης,
ἀνέπεμπον οἱ πολλοὶ τὴν αἰτίαν τῶν κακῶν ἐπὶ τὸ δαιμόνιον· πολλῶν
γὰρ καὶ παντοδαπῶν κατοικούντων ξένων καὶ διηλλαγμένοις ἔθεσι χρωμέ-
νων περὶ τὸ ἱερὸν καὶ τὰς θυσίας, καταλελύσθαι συνέβαινε παρ' αὐ-*
5 *τοῖς τὰς πατρίους τῶν θεῶν τιμάς· (2) ὅπερ οἱ τῆς χώρας ἐγγενεῖς
ὑπέλαβον, ἐὰν μὴ τοὺς ἀλλοφύλους μεταστήσωνται, κρίσιν οὐκ ἔσεσθαι
τῶν κακῶν. εὐθὺς οὖν ξενηλατουμένων τῶν ἀλλοεθνῶν, οἱ μὲν ἐπιφανέστατοι καὶ δραστικώτατοι συστραφέντες ἐξερρίφησαν, ὥς τινές φασιν,
εἰς τὴν Ἑλλάδα καί τινας ἑτέρους τόπους, ἔχοντες ἀξιολόγους ἡγεμόνας,*
10 *ὧν ἡγοῦντο Δαναὸς καὶ Κάδμος τῶν ἄλλων ἐπιφανέστατοι· ὁ δὲ πολὺς
λεὼς ἐξέπεσεν εἰς τὴν νῦν καλουμένην Ἰουδαίαν, οὐ πόρρω μὲν κειμένην
τῆς Αἰγύπτου, παντελῶς δὲ ἔρημον οὖσαν κατ' ἐκείνους τοὺς χρόνους.
(3) ἡγεῖτο δὲ τῆς ἀποικίας ὁ προσαγορευόμενος Μωσῆς, φρονήσει τε
καὶ ἀνδρείᾳ πολὺ διαφέρων. οὗτος δὲ καταλαβόμενος τὴν χώραν ἄλλας*
15 *τε πόλεις ἔκτισε καὶ τὴν νῦν οὖσαν ἐπιφανεστάτην, ὀνομαζομένην
Ἱεροσόλυμα. ἱδρύσατο δὲ καὶ τὸ μάλιστα παρ' αὐτοῖς τιμώμενον ἱερόν,
καὶ τὰς τιμὰς καὶ ἁγιστείας τοῦ θείου κατέδειξε, καὶ τὰ κατὰ τὴν
πολιτείαν ἐνομοθέτησέ τε καὶ διέταξε. διεῖλε δὲ τὸ πλῆθος εἰς δώδεκα
φυλὰς διὰ τὸ τὸν ἀριθμὸν τοῦτον τελεότατον νομίζεσθαι καὶ σύμφωνον*
20 *εἶναι τῷ πλήθει τῶν μηνῶν τῶν τὸν ἐνιαυτὸν συμπληρούντων. (4) ἄ-
γαλμα δὲ θεῶν τὸ σύνολον οὐ κατεσκεύασε διὰ τὸ μὴ νομίζειν ἀνθρω-
πόμορφον εἶναι τὸν θεόν, ἀλλὰ τὸν περιέχοντα τὴν γῆν οὐρανὸν
μόνον εἶναι θεὸν καὶ τῶν ὅλων κύριον. τὰς δὲ θυσίας ἐξηλλαγμένας
συνεστήσατο τῶν παρὰ τοῖς ἄλλοις ἔθνεσι, καὶ τὰς κατὰ τὸν βίον ἀγωγάς·*
25 *διὰ γὰρ τὴν ἰδίαν ξενηλασίαν ἀπάνθρωπόν τινα καὶ μισόξενον βίον
εἰσηγήσατο. ἐπιλέξας δὲ τῶν ἀνδρῶν τοὺς χαριεστάτους καὶ μάλιστα
δυνησομένους τοῦ σύμπαντος ἔθνους προΐστασθαι, τούτους ἱερεῖς
ἀπέδειξε· τὴν δὲ διατριβὴν ἔταξεν αὐτῶν γίνεσθαι περὶ τὸ ἱερὸν καὶ
τὰς τοῦ θεοῦ τιμάς τε καὶ θυσίας. (5) τοὺς αὐτοὺς δὲ καὶ δικαστὰς*
30 *ἀπέδειξε τῶν μεγίστων κρίσεων, καὶ τὴν τῶν νόμων καὶ τῶν ἐθῶν
φυλακὴν τούτοις ἐπέτρεψε· διὸ καὶ βασιλέα μὲν μηδέποτε τῶν Ἰουδαίων,
τὴν δὲ τοῦ πλήθους προστασίαν δίδοσθαι διὰ παντὸς τῷ δοκοῦντι τῶν
ἱερέων φρονήσει καὶ ἀρετῇ προέχειν. τοῦτον δὲ προσαγορεύουσιν*

5 διόπερ Herwerden / εὐγενεῖς A   6 κρίσιν] λύσιν Nock ap. Walton in ed.
Loeb   ἔκλυσιν vel ἔκβασιν Herwerden   9 ἡγεμόνας] δυνάμεις? Jacoby
13–14 τε καὶ A^mg   δὲ καὶ A   δὲ πολλῇ καὶ ς   14 πολὺ] πλεῖστον ς
19 τελεώτατον ς   27 σύμπαντος] συμπαρόντος ς

ἀρχιερέα, καὶ νομίζουσιν αὐτοῖς ἄγγελον γίνεσθαι τῶν τοῦ θεοῦ
35 προσταγμάτων. (6) τοῦτον δὲ κατὰ τὰς ἐκκλησίας καὶ τὰς ἄλλας
συνόδους φησὶν ἐκφέρειν τὰ παραγγελλόμενα, καὶ πρὸς τοῦτο τὸ μέρος
οὕτως εὐπιθεῖς γίνεσθαι τοὺς Ἰουδαίους ὥστε παραχρῆμα πίπτοντας
ἐπὶ τὴν γῆν προσκυνεῖν τὸν τούτοις ἑρμηνεύοντα ἀρχιερέα. προσγέγραπται δὲ καὶ τοῖς νόμοις ἐπὶ τελευτῆς ὅτι Μωσῆς ἀκούσας τοῦ
40 θεοῦ τάδε λέγει τοῖς Ἰουδαίοις. ἐποιήσατο δ' ὁ νομοθέτης τῶν τε πολεμικῶν ἔργων πολλὴν πρόνοιαν καὶ τοὺς νέους ἠνάγκαζεν ἀσκεῖν ἀν-
δρείαν τε καὶ καρτερίαν καὶ τὸ σύνολον ὑπομονὴν πάσης κακοπαθείας.
(7) ἐποιεῖτο δὲ καὶ στρατείας εἰς τὰ πλησιόχωρα τῶν ἐθνῶν, καὶ
πολλὴν κατακτησάμενος χώραν κατεκληρούχησε, τοῖς μὲν ἰδιώταις
45 ἴσους ποιήσας κλήρους, τοῖς δ' ἱερεῦσι μείζονας, ἵνα λαμβάνοντες
ἀξιολογωτέρας προσόδους ἀπερίσπαστοι συνεχῶς προσεδρεύωσι ταῖς
τοῦ θεοῦ τιμαῖς. οὐκ ἐξῆν δὲ τοῖς ἰδιώταις τοὺς ἰδίους κλήρους
πωλεῖν, ὅπως μή τινες διὰ πλεονεξίαν ἀγοράζοντες τοὺς κλήρους
ἐκθλίβωσι τοὺς ἀπορωτέρους καὶ κατασκευάζωσιν ὀλιγανδρίαν. (8) τεκ-
50 νοτροφεῖν τε ἠνάγκαζε τοὺς ἐπὶ τῆς χώρας· καὶ δι' ὀλίγης δαπάνης
ἐκτρεφομένων τῶν βρεφῶν ἀεὶ τὸ γένος τῶν Ἰουδαίων ὑπῆρχε πολυάνθρωπον. καὶ τὰ περὶ τοὺς γάμους δὲ καὶ τὰς τῶν τελευτώντων ταφὰς
πολὺ τὸ παρηλλαγμένον ἔχειν ἐποίησε νόμιμα πρὸς τὰ τῶν ἄλλων ἀνθρώπων. κατὰ δὲ τὰς ὕστερον γενομένας ἐπικρατείας ἐκ τῆς τῶν ἀλλο-
55 φύλων ἐπιμιξίας ἐπί τε τῆς τῶν Περσῶν ἡγεμονίας καὶ τῶν ταύτην κατα-
λυσάντων Μακεδόνων πολλὰ τῶν πατρίων τοῖς Ἰουδαίοις νομίμων ἐκι-
νήθη... περὶ μὲν τῶν Ἰουδαίων Ἑκαταῖος ὁ Ἀβδηρίτης ταῦτα ἱστόρηκεν.

37 εὐπειθεῖς ς   46 προσεδρεύσωσι ς   54 γενομένας] ἐγνωσμένας B
55 ἐπί τε τῆς Bekker   ἐπὶ τετάρτης codd.   56 Ἰουδαίοις om. A^{ac}
57 Ἀβδηρίτης Wesseling   Μιλήσιος codd.

(1) When in ancient times a pestilence arose in Egypt, the common
people ascribed their troubles to the workings of a divine agency; for
indeed with many strangers of all sorts dwelling in their midst and
practising different rites of religion and sacrifice, their own traditional
observances in honour of the gods had fallen into disuse. (2) Hence
the natives of the land surmised that unless they removed the foreigners, their troubles would never be resolved. At once, therefore,
the aliens were driven from the country, and the most outstanding
and active among them banded together and, as some say, were
cast ashore in Greece and certain other regions; their leaders were
notable men, chief among them being Danaus and Cadmus. But
the greater number were driven into what is now called Judaea,
which is not far distant from Egypt and was at that time utterly

27

uninhabited. (3) The colony was headed by a man called Moses, outstanding both for his wisdom and for his courage. On taking possession of the land he founded, besides other cities, one that is now the most renowned of all, called Jerusalem. In addition he established the temple that they hold in chief veneration, instituted their forms of worship and ritual, drew up their laws and ordered their political institutions. He also divided them into twelve tribes, since this is regarded as the most perfect number and corresponds to the number of months that make up a year. (4) But he had no images whatsoever of the gods made for them, being of the opinion that God is not in human form; rather the Heaven that surrounds the earth is alone divine, and rules the universe. The sacrifices that he established differ from those of other nations, as does their way of living, for as a result of their own expulsion from Egypt he introduced an unsocial and intolerant mode of life. He picked out the men of most refinement and with the greatest ability to head the entire nation, and appointed them priests; and he ordained that they should occupy themselves with the temple and the honours and sacrifices offered to their God. (5) These same men he appointed to be judges in all major disputes, and entrusted to them the guardianship of the laws and customs. For this reason the Jews never have a king, and authority over the people is regularly vested in whichever priest is regarded as superior to his colleagues in wisdom and virtue. They call this man the high priest, and believe that he acts as a messenger to them of God's commandments. (6) It is he, we are told, who in their assemblies and other gatherings announces what is ordained, and the Jews are so docile in such matters that straightway they fall to the ground and do reverence to the high priest when he expounds the commandments to them. And at the end of their laws there is even appended the statement: "These are the words that Moses heard from God and declares unto the Jews." Their lawgiver was careful also to make provision for warfare, and required the young men to cultivate manliness, steadfastness, and, generally, the endurance of every hardship. (7) He led out military expeditions against the neighbouring tribes, and after annexing much land apportioned it out, assigning equal allotments to private citizens and greater ones to the priests, in order that they, by virtue of receiving more ample revenues, might be undistracted and apply themselves continually to the worship of God. The common citizens were forbidden to sell their individual plots, lest there be some who for their own advantage should buy them up, and by oppressing the poorer classes bring on a scarcity of manpower.

(8) He required those who dwelt in the land to rear their children, and since offspring could be cared for at little cost, the Jews were from the start a populous nation. As to marriage and the burial of the dead, he saw to it that their customs should differ widely from those of other men. But later, when they became subject to foreign rule, as a result of their mingling with men of other nations (both under Persian rule and under that of the Macedonians who overthrew the Persians), many of their traditional practices were disturbed. Such is the account of Hecataeus of Abdera in regard to the Jews.

(trans. F. R. Walton, *LCL*)

1 τὸ παλαιὸν λοιμικῆς περιστάσεως γενομένης: In contrast to the later Graeco-Egyptian writers, Hecataeus does not supply us with a clear chronological framework for the events he describes. From the expression τὸ παλαιὸν and the references to Cadmus and Danaus we can only infer that, according to his view, the expulsion of the foreigners from Egypt took place in the mythical past. Manetho (apud: Josephus, *Contra Apionem*, I, 228 ff., below, No. 21) and Chaeremon (*ibid.*, I, 288; below, No. 178) dated the event to the time of Amenophis and Ramses. Ptolemy of Mendes (No. 157) dated it to the reign of Amosis, while Lysimachus (apud: Josephus, *Contra Apionem*, I, 305 ff.; below, No. 158) and Tacitus (*Historiae*, V, 3; below, No. 281) connected it with the reign of Bocchoris. Pestilences were generally regarded as punishments inflicted by the gods for sins. On the expression λοιμικὴ περίστασις, see, e.g., Polybius, VI, 5 : 5. This punishment was quite often accompanied by λιμός, ἀκαρπία and ἀφορία.
ἀνέπεμπον ... ἐπὶ τὸ δαιμόνιον: For people asking an oracle the cause of a pestilence, cf., e.g., Phylarchus, apud: Jacoby, *F. Gr. Hist.*, II, A 81 F 69; Diodorus, III, 59 : 7.
καταλελύσθαι ... τὰς πατρίους τῶν θεῶν τιμάς: Cf. Herodotus, I, 172.
2 ὅπερ οἱ τῆς χώρας ἐγγενεῖς ὑπέλαβον κτλ: Here Hecataeus draws on Egyptian tradition, as Egyptian prophecies often included a description of foreigners' campaigns in Egypt, causing the abolishment of the cults, the desolation of the temples and the spreading of pestilence and hunger over the country — till a saviour king appeared who brought about the expulsion of the foreigners and restored the former order of things. In Hecataeus' version the pestilence is an expression of the wrath of the gods, similar to the dream in Chaeremon's *Aegyptiaca Historia*, apud: Josephus, *Contra Apionem*, I, 288–292 (No. 178), and the drought described by Lysimachus, apud: Josephus, *Contra Apionem*, I, 304–311 (No. 158).
Κάδμος: Cadmus, the son of Agenor, is usually considered a Phoenician and the founder of Thebes. However, as we see already in Diodorus, I, 23 : 4 (Κάδμον ἐκ Θηβῶν ὄντα τῶν Αἰγυπτίων γεννῆσαι σὺν ἄλλοις τέκνοις καὶ Σεμέλην), a tradition existed that connected Cadmus with Egypt. This tradition probably derives from the fact that there was a city called Thebes both in Egypt and in Boeotia; cf. F. Vian, *Les origines de Thèbes*, Paris 1963, pp. 32 ff.
παντελῶς δὲ ἔρημον οὖσαν: This statement contradicts the Biblical tradition, though it incidentally accords well with the conclusion reached by the great modern scholar Alt and his followers, who maintain that the settlement of the tribes of

29

Israel encompassed mainly the hilly and yet unsettled parts of the country; see Alt, I, pp. 89 ff.; cf. also Judith V : 19: *καὶ κατῳκίσθησαν ἐν τῇ ὀρεινῇ, ὅτι ἦν ἔρημος.* Hecataeus, of course, knew nothing about the ancient history of Canaan, and his statement is to be explained by parallel examples from ethnographical literature. Here he uses a well-known and typical motive of ancient ethnography, one employed in descriptions of the settlement of new countries in the mythical age; cf., e.g., Herodotus' narrative on the settlement of Scythians in a desolate country (IV, 11:4), the story of the settlement of Italy by the Oenotrians in Dionysius Halicarnassensis (I, 12 : 1, 13 : 3) and the settlement of Sicily in an account by the same author (I, 22 : 2). Cf. also Strabo, *Geographica*, XVI, 2 : 36, p. 761 (No. 115), on the immigration of the Jews into Judaea. Strabo explains that this was possible because the country had been poor and uninhabited.

3 *Μωσῆς, φρονήσει τε καὶ ἀνδρείᾳ πολὺ διαφέρων*: Hecataeus' attitude to Moses is one of admiration; cf. Diodorus, V, 71 : 1: *Διενέγκαι δὲ τὸν θεὸν τοῦτον ἁπάντων ἀνδρείᾳ καὶ συνέσει καὶ δικαιοσύνῃ καὶ ταῖς ἄλλαις ἁπάσαις ἀρεταῖς.* Bidez and Cumont miss *εὐσέβεια* among the attributes of Moses.

καὶ τὴν νῦν ... ὀνομαζομένην Ἱεροσόλυμα: This, of course, does not agree with the main Hebrew tradition, which accepts that Jerusalem was a Jebusite town captured by King David.

διεῖλε δὲ τὸ πλῆθος εἰς δώδεκα φυλὰς διὰ τὸν ἀριθμὸν τοῦτον τελειότατον νομίζεσθαι...: Cf. Philo, *De Fuga*, 184 f.: *τέλειος δ'ἀριθμὸς ὁ δώδεκα. μάρτυς δ'ὁ ζῳδιακὸς ἐν οὐρανῷ κύκλος ... Μωυσῆς δ'οὐκ ἐν ὀλίγοις ὑμνεῖ τὸν ἀριθμόν, δώδεκα φυλὰς τοῦ ἔθνους ἀναγράφων.* See also Aristotle, F 385 (Rose): *ὅπως γένηται τὰ πάντα δώδεκα μέρη, καθάπερ οἱ μῆνες εἰς τὸν ἐνιαυτόν*; cf. also Herodotus, I, 145, 149; Plato, *Leges*, V, 745 B–C.

4 *ἄγαλμα δὲ θεῶν τὸ σύνολον οὐ κατεσκεύασε*: The first nation known to the Greeks to have spurned idolatry were the Persians; see Herodotus, I, 131. Herodotus, who had some difficulty in defining an abstract deity, thought that the Persians worshipped the sky. Hecataeus explains Jewish worship in the same way; cf. Strabo, *Geographica*, XVI, 2 : 35, p. 761 (No. 115).

καὶ τῶν ὅλων κύριον: Cf. Diodorus, III, 61 : 4.

τὰς δὲ θυσίας ἐξηλλαγμένας...: Hecataeus seems to have said more about Jewish sacrifices, but this material was omitted in Diodorus' abridgement. Also Theophrastus stresses the difference between Jewish sacrificial customs and those of other peoples; apud: Porphyrius, *De Abstinentia*, II, 26 (No. 4). Perhaps Hecataeus was also aware of this difference. The *τόπος τῶν θυσιῶν* was a fixed component of ethnographical literature. In the Persian *λόγος* of Herodotus (I, 132) the discussion of sacrifices follows one on the deity worshipped by the Persians. We should not see an expression of anti-Semitic feeling in Hecataeus' description of the peculiarities of the Jewish system of religion, but rather the traces of ethnographical literature.

διὰ γὰρ τὴν ἰδίαν ξενηλασίαν ἀπάνθρωπόν τινα καὶ μισόξενον βίον εἰσηγήσατο: Here we have a good example of the aetiological way of thinking that was characteristic of ancient ethnography. In their descriptions of various nations, Greek writers dwelt on their relations with foreigners; see, e.g., Aristotle, F 611 : 15 (Rose); Diodorus, III, 56 : 2; V, 34; Eratosthenes, apud: Strabo, XVII, 1 : 19, p. 802. *Ξενηλασία* was thought to have been a custom common to all barbarians; see Eratosthenes, *loc. cit.*: *φησὶ δ' Ἐρατοσθένης κοινὸν μὲν εἶναι τοῖς βαρβάροις πᾶσιν ἔθος τὴν ξενηλασίαν.*

ἐπιλέξας ... τούτους ἱερεῖς ἀπέδειξε: In the narrative of Dionysius of Halicarnassus (II, 21) concerning Romulus we have a parallel to the appointment of the priests by Moses. Hecataeus does not enter into the question of the transmission of the priesthood here, although he may have done so in a passage that Diodorus did not summarize.

τὴν δὲ διατριβὴν ἔταξεν...: On the tasks imposed on the priesthood by the Torah, see Deut. xix : 17; xxi : 5.

5 τοὺς αὐτοὺς δὲ καὶ δικαστάς...: With the leadership of the priests in the Jewish society, as depicted by Hecataeus, cf. the description of the utopian state of Panachaia (Diodorus, V, 45 : 4): οἱ μὲν οὖν ἱερεῖς τῶν ἁπάντων ἦσαν ἡγεμόνες, τάς τε τῶν ἀμφισβητήσεων κρίσεις ποιούμενοι καὶ τῶν ἄλλων τῶν δημοσίᾳ πραττομένων κύριοι.

See also Aelianus, *Varia Historia*, XIV, 34: δικασταὶ δὲ τὸ ἀρχαῖον παρ᾽ Αἰγυπτίοις οἱ ἱερεῖς ἦσαν; Caesar, *Bellum Gallicum*, VI, 13 : 5: "nam fere de omnibus controversiis publicis privatisque constituunt et, si quod est admissum facinus... idem decernunt, praemia poenasque constituunt." On the concentration of judicial powers in the hands of the priests, according to Mosaic Law, see Deut. xvii : 8 ff.

διὸ καὶ βασιλέα μὲν μηδέποτε τῶν Ἰουδαίων...: Hecataeus is wholly ignorant of the dynastic period of Israel and Judah; instead he reflects the actual situation in Hellenistic Judaea, which, in the absence of royal power, did conform to the original Mosaic constitution. We must remember that, apart from Nicolaus, who refers to David (No. 84), Pompeius Trogus, who speaks of ancient Jewish kings (No. 137) and some writers who refer to Solomon (Nos. 35–37), there is no mention of Biblical Jewish kings in Greek and Roman literature of the Hellenistic and early Roman periods. In fact, Philo and Josephus also tend to ignore the monarchy in their general surveys of the Jewish constitution. It was the hierocracy that was considered to be the specific Jewish form of government, the πάτριος πολιτεία of the Jews, as it was expressed, e.g., in *Ant.*, XIV, 41, and in Diodorus, XL, 2 (No. 64).

τῷ δοκοῦντι τῶν ἱερέων φρονήσει καὶ ἀρετῇ προέχειν: Hecataeus seems not to have known that in the period of the Second Temple the high priesthood usually passed from father to oldest son in direct succession, and that all high priests from the Exile to the time of Hecataeus himself belonged to the Zadokite house and were descendants of Yehoshua ben Yehozadak. However, with respect to this family, there were some exceptions to the rule of direct succession; it was felt that members of the house, other than the eldest son of the late high priest, also had claim to the high priesthood. Thus, e. g., according to *Ant.*, XII 44, after the death of the High Priest Simon the First, his office passed into the hands of his brother Eleazar. Josephus explains that this happened because Simon's son Onias was a minor. It is noteworthy, however, that Eleazar was succeeded by his uncle Manasseh, and that only at the death of the latter did Onias become high priest; cf. G. Alon, *Studies in Jewish History*, I, Tel Aviv 1957, p. 72 (in Hebrew). Alon maintains that the succession of the high priests was not wholly fixed in the Hellenistic age. Cf. the *Letter of Aristeas*, 98: ὁ κριθεὶς ἄξιος τούτων ἐν ταῖς λειτουργίαις.

ἄγγελον γίνεσθαι τῶν τοῦ θεοῦ προσταγμάτων: Cf. Diodorus, V, 75 : 2; cf. also F.R. Walton, *HTR*, XLVIII (1955), pp. 255 ff. The ceremony of the Day of Atonement, when the high priest enters into the Holy of Holies, may have had some influence on this characterization of the high priest as the authoritative

31

interpreter of the ordinances of God. On the spirit of prophecy possessed, e.g., by John Hyrcan, see *TP Soṭa* ix, 24b; *TB Soṭa* 33a; see also Derenbourg, pp. 73 f.

6 οὕτως εὐπιθεῖς γίνεσθαι: The credulity of the Jews became a recurrent theme in ancient literature, from Hecataeus onwards. In the eyes of the Greeks it was a characteristic of barbarians in general; see Herodotus, I, 60 : 3.

ὥστε... πίπτοντας ἐπὶ τὴν γῆν...: On the splendour of the high priest's appearance when seen by the congregation, see especially Siracides, L; see also *Contra Apionem*, II, 193 f.

προσγέγραπται δὲ καὶ τοῖς νόμοις ἐπὶ τελευτῆς: Cf. Lev. xxvi : 46; xxvii : 34; Num. xxxvi : 13. Among the Greeks there was much discussion regarding the origin of the laws, i.e. whether they were divinely inspired or only products of the human mind; see, e.g., Plato, *Leges*, 624 A; see also Bidez & Cumont, I, p. 241.

ἐποιήσατο δ'ὁ νομοθέτης τῶν τε πολεμικῶν ἔργων πολλὴν πρόνοιαν: We may compare this with the description of the Spartan constitution given by Polybius, VI, 48 : 3 f.: ἡ δὲ πρὸς τοὺς πόνους καὶ πρὸς τὰ δεινὰ τῶν ἔργων ἄσκησις ἀλκίμους καὶ γενναίους ἀποτελέσειν ἄνδρας. ἑκατέρων δὲ τούτων ὁμοῦ συνδραμόντων εἰς μίαν ψυχὴν ἢ πόλιν, ἀνδρείας καὶ σωφροσύνης, οὔτ' ἐξ αὐτῶν φῦναι κακίαν εὐμαρές... On a possible visit by Hecataeus to Sparta, see F. Jacoby, PW, VII, p. 2752. Jaeger thinks that Hecataeus' description of Jewish education was influenced by Plato's *Republic*, especially by the features attributed to the military caste of the φύλακες.

7 ἐποιεῖτο δὲ καὶ στρατείας: According to the Biblical account, the conquests of Moses were confined to Trans-Jordan and preceded the occupation of the country west of the Jordan by the tribes of Israel. The conquered territories were allotted to the tribes of Reuben, Gad and half the tribe of Manasseh. Hecataeus, however, speaks of Moses' capture of enemy territory as being subsequent to the foundation of Jerusalem. He even differentiates, it seems, between the Israelite settlement of the area of Jerusalem, which had been an uninhabited country, and the later conquests of inhabited lands. Hecataeus' version of Moses' activities is that of a leader and legislator, who was active in Judaea. Hecataeus' knowledge of Jewish tradition was rather vague, and he used it in a way natural to a Greek. Since Hecataeus knew that Moses was the Jewish legislator, he quite naturally supposed that Moses led his people to their country; therefore, he dated Moses' legislation to the period after the foundation of the capital and the conquest of the land.

τοῖς δ' ἱερεῦσι μείζονας: According to Num. xxxv : i ff. and Josh. xxi, the Levites and priests were allotted certain cities, but were not, it is emphasized in other passages of the Torah, given a share in the land; cf. Deut. x : 9; xii : 12; xviii : 1; Num. xviii : 24. This is also stressed by Philo, *De Specialibus Legibus*, I, 131: τοῖς ἱερεῦσιν οὐκ ἀπένειμε χώρας ἀποτομὴν ὁ νόμος. See also *Siracides*, xlv : 22. Hecataeus' statement concerning the priests of Judaea has parallels in both Egyptian conditions and Greek Utopias. On the priests of Egypt, see Diodorus, I, 73 : 2; see also Artapanus, in: *F. Gr. Hist.*, III, C 726 F 3, p. 682. The remarks of Euhemerus, in whose Utopia the priests get a double share (Diodorus, V, 45 : 5), are very illuminating. Still, it is quite possible that in this respect Hecataeus' account reflects the actual economic conditions prevailing in Judaea in the Hellenistic age, when the priests constituted the ruling class and enjoyed material advantages. In fact, we find concrete examples of priests who were land owners already in the period of the First Temple, e.g. Ebiathar, the high priest in the time of David, who owned land at 'Anatot (I Kings ii : 26), and the priest Amaziah of

Hecataeus of Abdera

Bethel (Amos vii : 17); see also Alt, III, pp. 359 f. The same holds true for the Roman period, as attested, e.g., by Josephus, *Vita*, 422 (τοὺς ἀγροὺς οὓς εἶχον ἐν τοῖς Ἱεροσολύμοις), and the talmudic sources; see, e.g., the tradition concerning the legendary wealth of the priest Eleazar, the son of Ḥarsom (*TP Ta'anit* iv, 69a; *TB Yoma* 35b).

οὐκ ἐξῆν... κλήρους πωλεῖν: According to the Torah, the sale of any land was temporary, and the land was to be returned to its former owner in the year of the Jubilee (Lev. xxv: 13). Did Hecataeus know of this law? There is no proof of the continued existence of the Jubilee in the period of the Second Temple, but there is some basis for Tcherikover's suggestion (p. 122), that a law was promulgated in Judaea that aimed at preventing the land from being concentrated in the hands of great land owners. From Neh. v we learn of a regulation requiring the return of mortgaged land to the debtors. Hecataeus took a lively interest in this problem, which was acute in the Greek world and caused heated debates among statesmen and thinkers.The ἀνισότης in connection with landownership was thought of as one of the chief sources of social trouble and as the cause of ὀλιγανδρία, many citizens being deprived of the minimum conditions necessary for raising children. See Aristotle, *Politica*, II, 1266 A, about Phaleas of Chalcedon, who wanted the citizens' estates to be equal; and 1266 B 19 f., concerning the law of Locri, which prevented the sale of land; cf. D. Asheri, *Distribuzioni di terre nell' antica Grecia*, 1966, pp. 16 ff. (*Memoria dell' accademia delle scienze di Torino, classe di Scienze Morali, Storiche e Filologiche*, Ser. 4ª, n. 10).

8 τεκνοτροφεῖν τε ἠνάγκαζε: The Jews' religious duty to rear all their children and their view that the exposure of new-born children is tantamount to murder offer a striking contrast to the Greek habit of killing, or ἔκθεσις, of infants, a constant feature of Greek life, as exemplified in Greek literature (especially the comedy) and evidenced by documents; see Rostovtzeff, *SEHHW*, II, p. 623. Polybius' complaint about the dwindling of the population of Greece is well known; Polybius, XXXVI, 17 : 5 ff.; cf. W.W. Tarn, *Hellenistic Civilisation*[3], London 1952, pp. 100 ff. On the other hand, we can follow a trend wholly opposed to that; see M.P. Nilsson, *Geschichte der griechischen Religion*, II[2], Munich 1961, p. 291; cf. also F. Sokolowski, *Lois sacrées de l'Asie mineure*, Paris 1955, No. 20, l. 20 f. [from Philadelphia in Asia Minor: μὴ φθορεῖν, μὴ (ἀτ)οκεῖον μ(ὴ ἄλλο τι παιδο) φόνον μήτε αὐτοὺς ἐπιτελεῖν, μήτε (ἑτέρῳ συμβου) λεύειν μηδὲ συνιστορεῖν]; No. 84, l. 2 ff.; p. 188, n.1. However, as these last-mentioned views were not of cardinal importance in the development of Greek society, both Greek and Roman writers were struck by the contrast afforded by the Jews; cf., in general, R. Tolles, "Untersuchungen zur Kindesaussetzung bei den Griechen", Ph.D. Thesis, Breslau 1941; and the commentary to Tacitus, *Historiae*, V, 5 (No. 281). The Jewish view has been well-expressed by Josephus, *Contra Apionem*, II, 202: τέκνα τρέφειν ἅπαντα προσέταξεν [scil. Moses], καὶ γυναιξὶν ἀπεῖπεν μήτ'ἀμβλοῦν τὸ σπαρὲν μήτε διαφθείρειν ἀλλὰ ἢν φανείη τεκνοκτόνος ἂν εἴη ψυχὴν ἀφανίζουσα καὶ τὸ γένος ἐλαττοῦσα. See also Philo, *De Specialibus Legibus*, III, 110: ἕτερόν τι μεῖζον ἀπηγόρευνται, βρεφῶν ἔκθεσις; *De Virtutibus*, 131 f. (cf. I. Heinemann, *Philons griechische und jüdische Bildung*, Breslau 1932, pp. 392 ff.); *Oracula Sibyllina*, III, 765; *Didache*, II : 2: οὐ φονεύσεις τέκνον ἐν φθορᾷ οὐδὲ γεννηθὲν ἀποκτενεῖς; G. Alon, *Studies in Jewish History*, I, Tel Aviv 1957, pp. 279 f. (in Hebrew); cf. also Bernays, I, pp. 242 f., S. Belkin, *JQR*, XXVII (1936–1937), pp. 7 ff. F. Geiger, *Philon von Alexandreia als sozialer Denker*, Stuttgart 1932, pp. 46 ff.

33

According to Dionysius of Halicarnassus, II, 15 : 2, Romulus also restricted the practice of killing new-born infants, but the exception allowed by the Roman legislator (ἀποκτιννύναι δὲ μηδὲν τῶν γεννωμένων νεώτερον τριετοῦς, πλὴν εἴ τι γένοιτο παιδίον ἀνάπηρον) reveals a world of difference between the Jewish law in the matter of infanticide and that promulgated by the founder of Rome. Cf. Diodorus, I, 77 : 7, who mentions that Egyptian parents who had slain their children were, to some degree, punished.

δι' ὀλίγης κτλ.: The same reason is adduced by Hecataeus for the Egyptian πολυανθρωπία; cf. Diodorus, I, 80 : 3; see also I, 73 : 8.

τὸ γένος τῶν Ἰουδαίων ὑπῆρχε πολυάνθρωπον: The populousness of Judaea in the Hellenistic age is corroborated by other sources. The number of Jews who had returned from the Babylonian Exile amounted to no more than 42,360, excluding more than seven thousand slaves (Ezra ii : 64–65). To these should be added the remnant of the population of Judaea, who remained there throughout the Exile. During the Persian rule the Judaean population seems to have increased to the point where the country had difficulty in supporting all its inhabitants. Many residents of Judaea resettled in the other parts of Palestine or emigrated to other countries. We have practically no reliable details on the number of Jews at the beginning of the Hellenistic period. The *Letter of Aristeas* (12 f) maintains that at the end of the fourth century B. C. E. some one hundred thousand Jews were deported from Judaea to Egypt by Ptolemy Soter, and that thirty thousand were garrisoned in that country. We also have figures on the manpower of Judaea at the time of the Hasmonaean revolt, some of which are quite high. If these are reliable, they would prove that Judaea and the adjoining districts, which were inhabited by Jews, had a very considerable population at that time. In I Macc. v : 20, we read that in 164 B. C. E. Judas took a force of eight thousand fighters with him on his expedition to Galaaditis and also allotted three thousand men to his brother Simon for the fighting in Western Galilee, leaving still another force in Judaea itself (I Macc. v: 18). Forty thousand is the highest figure mentioned in connection with the armed forces of Judaea in the second century B. C. E. This is the number of soldiers led by Jonathan against Tryphon (I Macc. xii : 41); cf. the commentary to Strabo, *Geographica*, XVI, 2 : 28, p. 759 (No. 114), and to Tacitus, *Historiae*, V, 13 (No. 281).

καὶ τὰς τῶν τελευτώντων ταφάς: The reference to burial customs (περὶ ταφῶν) follows at the end of the general account of the Jews. The same is true in some other ethnographical descriptions, as already exemplified by Herodotus; cf. K. Trüdinger, *Studien zur Geschichte der griechisch-römischen Ethnographie*, Basel 1918, p. 26. For the τόπος περὶ ταφῶν, cf. also A. Schroeder, "De Ethnographiae Antiquae Locis Quibusdam Communibus Observationes", Ph.D. Thesis, Halle 1921, pp. 25 ff. It is very likely that in his unabridged work Hecataeus dwelt on the adoption by the Jews of some burial customs of the Egyptians, though perhaps he emphasized the differences between the usages of the two nations; cf. Tacitus, *Historiae*, V, 5 (No. 281). The Egyptian burial practices are described by Herodotus (II, 85 ff.) and by Diodorus (I, 91 f.).

Ἑκαταῖος ὁ Ἀβδηρίτης ταῦτα ἱστόρηκεν: In the Mss. of Photius we read Μιλήσιος. However, from the time of Wesseling onwards there has been an almost unanimous consensus of scholarly opinion to the effect that Μιλήσιος should be emended to Ἀβδηρίτης. One notable exception is Dornseiff, *op. cit.* (supra, p. 25), but his arguments are hardly convincing; cf. F. Jacoby, PW, VII,

Hecataeus of Abdera

p. 2752; *F. Gr. Hist.*, IIIa. pp. 46 ff; W. Jaeger, *JR*, XVIII (1938), p. 139, n. 37. It is by no means probable that the old Milesian Hecataeus would have described the Jews as is done here; on the other hand, the text accords well with the writing of Hecataeus of Abdera, as illustrated by the first book of Diodorus.

12

De Iudaeis, apud: Josephus, *Contra Apionem*, I, 183–204 — Niese = Append. II A R = *F. Gr. Hist.*, *III*, A264, F21 = Reinach (Budé), pp. 35 ff.

(183) ῾Εκαταῖος δὲ ὁ ᾽Αβδηρίτης, ἀνὴρ φιλόσοφος ἅμα καὶ περὶ τὰς πράξεις ἱκανώτατος, ᾽Αλεξάνδρῳ τῷ βασιλεῖ συνακμάσας καὶ Πτολεμαίῳ τῷ Λάγου συγγενόμενος, οὐ παρέργως, ἀλλὰ περὶ αὐτῶν ᾽Ιουδαίων συγγέγραφε βιβλίον, ἐξ οὗ βούλομαι κεφαλαιωδῶς ἐπιδραμεῖν ἔνια
5 τῶν εἰρημένων. *(184)* καὶ πρῶτον ἐπιδείξω τὸν χρόνον· μνημονεύει γὰρ τῆς Πτολεμαίου περὶ Γάζαν πρὸς Δημήτριον μάχης· αὕτη δὲ γέγονεν ἑνδεκάτῳ μὲν ἔτει τῆς ᾽Αλεξάνδρου τελευτῆς, ἐπὶ δὲ ὀλυμπιάδος ἑβδόμης καὶ δεκάτης καὶ ἑκατοστῆς, ὡς ἱστορεῖ Κάστωρ. *(185)* προσθεὶς γὰρ ταύτην τὴν ὀλυμπιάδα φησίν·
10 «᾽Επὶ ταύτης Πτολεμαῖος ὁ Λάγου ἐνίκα ⟨τῇ⟩ κατὰ Γάζαν μάχῃ Δημήτριον τὸν ᾽Αντιγόνου τὸν ἐπικληθέντα Πολιορκητήν.» ᾽Αλέξανδρον δὲ τεθνάναι πάντες ὁμολογοῦσιν ἐπὶ τῆς ἑκατοστῆς τεσσαρεσκαιδεκάτης ὀλυμπιάδος. δῆλον οὖν, ὅτι καὶ κατ᾽ ἐκεῖνον καὶ κατὰ ᾽Αλέξανδρον ἤκμαζεν ἡμῶν τὸ ἔθνος. *(186)* λέγει τοίνυν ὁ ῾Εκαταῖος πάλιν τάδε,
15 ὅτι μετὰ τὴν ἐν Γάζῃ μάχην ὁ Πτολεμαῖος ἐγένετο τῶν περὶ Συρίαν τόπων ἐγκρατής, καὶ πολλοὶ τῶν ἀνθρώπων πυνθανόμενοι τὴν ἠπιότητα καὶ φιλανθρωπίαν τοῦ Πτολεμαίου συναπαίρειν εἰς Αἴγυπτον αὐτῷ καὶ κοινωνεῖν τῶν πραγμάτων ἠβουλήθησαν. *(187)* ὧν εἷς ἦν, φησίν, ᾽Εζεκίας ἀρχιερεὺς τῶν ᾽Ιουδαίων, ἄνθρωπος τὴν μὲν ἡλικίαν ὡς ἑξη-
20 κονταὲξ ἐτῶν, τῷ δ᾽ ἀξιώματι τῷ παρὰ τοῖς ὁμοέθνοις μέγας καὶ τὴν ψυχὴν οὐκ ἀνόητος, ἔτι δὲ καὶ λέγειν δυνατὸς καὶ τοῖς περὶ τῶν πραγμάτων, εἴπερ τις ἄλλος, ἔμπειρος. *(188)* καίτοι, φησίν, οἱ πάντες ἱερεῖς τῶν ᾽Ιουδαίων οἱ τὴν δεκάτην τῶν γινομένων λαμβάνοντες καὶ τὰ κοινὰ διοικοῦντες περὶ χιλίους μάλιστα καὶ πεντακοσίους εἰσίν.» *(189)* πάλιν δὲ
25 τοῦ προειρημένου μνημονεύων ἀνδρός «οὗτος, φησίν, ὁ ἄνθρωπος τετευχὼς τῆς τιμῆς ταύτης καὶ συνήθης ἡμῖν γενόμενος, παραλαβών τινας τῶν μεθ᾽ ἑαυτοῦ τήν τε διφθέραν ἀνέγνω πᾶσαν αὐτοῖς· εἶχεν γὰρ τὴν κατοίκησιν αὐτῶν καὶ τὴν πολιτείαν γεγραμμένην.» *(190)* εἶτα ῾Εκαταῖος δηλοῖ πάλιν, πῶς ἔχομεν πρὸς τοὺς νόμους, ὅτι πάντα πάσχειν ὑπὲρ

3 ⟨ἴδιον⟩ περὶ Reinach   10 ⟨τῇ⟩ κατὰ Niese   21 τοῖς περὶ damnavit Hudson   23 τὴν δεκάτην] decatas Lat.   27 διφθέραν Lewy   διαφορὰν L

30 τοῦ μὴ παραβῆναι τούτους προαιρούμεθα καὶ καλὸν εἶναι νομίζομεν.
_(191)_ «τοιγαροῦν, φησί, καὶ κακῶς ἀκούοντες ὑπὸ τῶν ἀστυγειτόνων
καὶ τῶν εἰσαφικνουμένων πάντες καὶ προπηλακιζόμενοι πολλάκις ὑπὸ τῶν
Περσικῶν βασιλέων καὶ σατραπῶν οὐ δύνανται μεταπεισθῆναι τῇ
διανοίᾳ, ἀλλὰ γεγυμνωμένως περὶ τούτων καὶ αἰκίαις καὶ θανάτοις
35 δεινοτάτοις μάλιστα πάντων ἀπαντῶσι μὴ ἀρνούμενοι τὰ πάτρια.»
_(192)_ παρέχεται δὲ καὶ τεκμήρια τῆς ἰσχυρογνωμοσύνης τῆς περὶ
τῶν νόμων οὐκ ὀλίγα· φησὶ γάρ, Ἀλεξάνδρου ποτὲ ἐν Βαβυλῶνι γενομένου
καὶ προελομένου τὸ τοῦ Βήλου πεπτωκὸς ἱερὸν ἀνακαθᾶραι καὶ πᾶσιν
αὐτοῦ τοῖς στρατιώταις ὁμοίως φέρειν τὸν χοῦν προστάξαντος,
40 μόνους τοὺς Ἰουδαίους οὐ προσσχεῖν, ἀλλὰ καὶ πολλὰς ὑπομεῖναι
πληγὰς καὶ ζημίας ἀποτῖσαι μεγάλας, ἕως αὐτοῖς συγγνόντα τὸν
βασιλέα δοῦναι τὴν ἄδειαν. _(193)_ ἔτι γε μὴν τῶν εἰς τὴν χώραν, φησίν,
πρὸς αὐτοὺς ἀφικνουμένων νεὼς καὶ βωμοὺς κατασκευασάντων ἅπαντα
ταῦτα κατέσκαπτον, καὶ τῶν μὲν ζημίαν τοῖς σατράπαις ἐξέτινον,
45 περί τινων δὲ καὶ συγγνώμης μετελάμβανον. καὶ προσεπιτίθησιν,
ὅτι δίκαιον ἐπὶ τούτοις αὐτούς ἐστι θαυμάζειν. _(194)_ λέγει δὲ καὶ περὶ
τοῦ πολυανθρωπότατον γεγονέναι ἡμῶν τὸ ἔθνος· «πολλὰς μὲν γὰρ ἡμῶν,
φησίν, ἀνασπάστους εἰς Βαβυλῶνα Πέρσαι πρότερον αὐτῶν ἐποίησαν
μυριάδας, οὐκ ὀλίγαι δὲ καὶ μετὰ τὸν Ἀλεξάνδρου θάνατον εἰς Αἴγυπτον
50 καὶ Φοινίκην μετέστησαν διὰ τὴν ἐν Συρίᾳ στάσιν.» _(195)_ ὁ δὲ αὐτὸς
οὗτος ἀνὴρ καὶ τὸ μέγεθος τῆς χώρας ἣν κατοικοῦμεν καὶ τὸ κάλλος
ἱστόρηκεν· «τριακοσίας γὰρ μυριάδας ἀρουρῶν σχεδὸν τῆς ἀρίστης
καὶ παμφορωτάτης χώρας νέμονται, φησίν· ἡ γὰρ Ἰουδαία τοσαύτη
πλῆθός ἐστιν.» _(196)_ ἀλλὰ μὴν ὅτι καὶ τὴν πόλιν αὐτὴν τὰ Ἱεροσόλυμα
55 καλλίστην τε καὶ μεγίστην ἐκ παλαιοτάτου κατοικοῦμεν καὶ περὶ
πλήθους ἀνδρῶν καὶ περὶ τῆς τοῦ νεὼ κατασκευῆς οὕτως αὐτὸς διηγεῖται.
_(197)_ «ἔστι γὰρ τῶν Ἰουδαίων τὰ μὲν πολλὰ ὀχυρώματα κατὰ τὴν
χώραν καὶ κῶμαι, μία δὲ πόλις ὀχυρὰ πεντήκοντα μάλιστα σταδίων
τὴν περίμετρον, ἣν οἰκοῦσι μὲν ἀνθρώπων περὶ δώδεκα μυριάδες,
60 καλοῦσι δ᾽ αὐτὴν Ἱεροσόλυμα. _(198)_ ἐνταῦθα δ᾽ ἐστὶ κατὰ μέσον μάλιστα
τῆς πόλεως περίβολος λίθινος μῆκος ὡς πεντάπλεθρος, εὖρος δὲ πηχῶν
ρ᾽, ἔχων διπλᾶς πύλας, ἐν ᾧ βωμός ἐστι τετράγωνος ἀτμήτων συλλέκτων
ἀργῶν λίθων οὕτως συγκείμενος, πλευρὰν μὲν ἑκάστην εἴκοσι πηχῶν,

30 τούτους ed. pr.   τοῦτο L   34 γεγυμνασμένως intellexit Lat.
35 πάτρια Niese   πατρῷα L   40 προσσχεῖν Bekker   προσχεῖν L
42 ἔτι Niese   ἐπεῖ L   44 ἐξέτινον Dindorf   ἐξέτεινον L   46 τούτοις
ed. pr.   τούτους L   47 ἡμῶν]² αὐτῶν Bekker   48 αὐτῶν secl. Bekker
54 πλάτος Hudson   55 κατοικοῦμεν ed pr.   _inhabitamus_ Lat.   κατοικου-
μένην L   56 αὐτὸς] _idem ipse_ Lat.   αὖ vel ὁ αὐτὸς Bekker   59 δώδεκα
μυριάδες] _CL milia_ Lat.   62 οὐκ ἐκ τμητῶν ἀλλ᾽ ἐκ συλλέκτων Naber

ὕψος δὲ δεκάπηχυ. καὶ παρ' αὐτὸν οἴκημα μέγα, οὗ βωμός ἐστι καὶ
65 λυχνίον ἀμφότερα χρυσᾶ δύο τάλαντα τὴν ὁλκήν. (199) ἐπὶ τούτων φῶς
ἐστιν ἀναπόσβεστον καὶ τὰς νύκτας καὶ τὰς ἡμέρας. ἄγαλμα δὲ οὐκ
ἔστιν οὐδὲ ἀνάθημα τὸ παράπαν οὐδὲ φύτευμα παντελῶς οὐδὲν οἷον
ἀλσῶδες ἤ τι τοιοῦτον. διατρίβουσι δ' ἐν αὐτῷ καὶ τὰς νύκτας καὶ τὰς
ἡμέρας ἱερεῖς ἁγνείας τινὰς ἁγνεύοντες καὶ τὸ παράπαν οἶνον οὐ πίνοντες
70 ἐν τῷ ἱερῷ.» (200) ἔτι γε μὴν ὅτι καὶ ᾿Αλεξάνδρῳ τῷ βασιλεῖ
συνεστρατεύσαντο καὶ μετὰ ταῦτα τοῖς διαδόχοις αὐτοῦ μεμαρτύρηκεν.
οἷς δ' αὐτὸς παρατυχεῖν φησιν ὑπ' ἀνδρὸς ᾿Ιουδαίου κατὰ τὴν στρατείαν
γενομένοις, τοῦτο παραθήσομαι. (201) λέγει δ' οὕτως· «ἐμοῦ γοῦν ἐπὶ
τὴν ᾿Ερυθρὰν θάλασσαν βαδίζοντος συνηκολούθει τις μετὰ τῶν ἄλλων
75 τῶν παραπεμπόντων ἡμᾶς ἱππέων ᾿Ιουδαίων ὄνομα Μοσόλλαμος,
ἄνθρωπος ἱκανῶς κατὰ ψυχὴν εὔρωστος καὶ τοξότης δὴ πάντων ὁμολογου-
μένως καὶ τῶν ῾Ελλήνων καὶ τῶν βαρβάρων ἄριστος· (202) οὗτος οὖν
ὁ ἄνθρωπος διαβαδιζόντων πολλῶν κατὰ τὴν ὁδὸν καὶ μάντεώς
τινος ὀρνιθευομένου καὶ πάντας ἐπισχεῖν ἀξιοῦντος ἠρώτησε, διὰ τί
80 προσμένουσι. (203) δείξαντος δὲ τοῦ μάντεως αὐτῷ τὸν ὄρνιθα καὶ
φήσαντος, ἐὰν μὲν αὐτοῦ μένῃ προσμένειν συμφέρειν πᾶσιν, ἂν δ' ἀναστὰς
εἰς τοὔμπροσθεν πέτηται προάγειν, ἐὰν δὲ εἰς τοὔπισθεν ἀναχωρεῖν
αὖθις, σιωπήσας καὶ παρελκύσας τὸ τόξον ἔβαλε καὶ τὸν ὄρνιθα πατάξας
ἀπέκτεινεν. (204) ἀγανακτούντων δὲ τοῦ μάντεως καί τινων ἄλλων καὶ
85 καταρωμένων αὐτῷ, «τί μαίνεσθε, ἔφη, κακοδαίμονες;» εἶτα τὸν ὄρνιθα
λαβὼν εἰς τὰς χεῖρας, «πῶς γάρ, ἔφη, οὗτος τὴν αὐτοῦ σωτηρίαν οὐ
προϊδὼν περὶ τῆς ἡμετέρας πορείας ἡμῖν ἄν τι ὑγιὲς ἀπήγγελλεν; εἰ
γὰρ ἠδύνατο προγιγνώσκειν τὸ μέλλον, εἰς τὸν τόπον τοῦτον οὐκ ἂν ἦλθε
φοβούμενος, μὴ τοξεύσας αὐτὸν ἀποκτείνῃ Μοσόλλαμος ὁ ᾿Ιουδαῖος.»

64 δεκάπηχυς Bekker   73 τοῦτο] ταῦτα Holwerda   75 ᾿Ιουδαῖος Niese
76 ἱκανῶς Eus., cod. J   ἱκανὸς L, Lat., Eus., cod. G   76-77 ὁμολογου-
μένως Niese   ὁμολογούμενος L, Eus.   indubitanter Lat.   80 τὸν Eus.
τὴν L   81 συμφέρειν Eus., cod. G   συμφέρῃ L   συμφέρει Eus., cod. J
83 τὸν Eus.   τὴν L   85 κακοδαίμονες· εἶτα τὸν Eus.   κακοδαιμονέστατον
L, Lat.   86 λαβὼν Eus.   λαβόντες L, Lat. / ἔφη Eus. om. L, Lat.
89 Μοσόμαμος Eus.   a mosollamo Lat.

(183) Of a different nature is the evidence of Hecataeus of Abdera,
at once a philosopher and a highly competent man of affairs, who
rose to fame under King Alexander, and was afterwards associated
with Ptolemy, son of Lagus. He makes no mere passing allusion to
us, but wrote a book entirely about the Jews, from which I propose
briefly to touch on some passages. (184) I will begin with fixing his
date. He mentions the battle near Gaza between Ptolemy and Demetrius, which, as Castor narrates, was fought eleven years after the

death of Alexander, in the 117th Olympiad. (185) For under the head of this Olympiad he says:

"In this period Ptolemy, son of Lagus, defeated in a battle at Gaza Demetrius, son of Antigonus, surnamed Poliorcetes." And all agree that Alexander died in the 114th Olympiad. It is evident, therefore, that our race was flourishing both under Ptolemy and under Alexander. (186) Hecataeus goes on to say that after the battle of Gaza Ptolemy became master of Syria, and that many of the inhabitants, hearing of his kindliness and humanity, desired to accompany him to Egypt and to associate themselves with his realm. (187) "Among these (he says) was Ezechias, a chief priest of the Jews, a man of about sixty-six years of age, highly esteemed by his countrymen, intellectual, and moreover an able speaker and unsurpassed as a man of business. (188) Yet (he adds) the total number of Jewish priests who receive a tithe of the revenue and administer public affairs is about fifteen hundred." (189) Reverting to Ezechias, he says: "This man, after obtaining this honour and having been closely in touch with us, assembled some of his friends and read to them his whole scroll, in which was written the story of their settlement and the constitution of the state".[1] (190) In another passage Hecataeus mentions our regard for our laws, and how we deliberately choose and hold it a point of honour to endure anything rather than transgress them. (191) "And so (he says), neither the slander of their neighbours and of foreign visitors, to which as a nation they are exposed, nor the frequent outrages of Persian kings and satraps can shake their determination; for these laws, naked and defenceless, they face tortures and death in its most terrible form, rather than repudiate the faith of their forefathers." (192) Of this obstinacy in defence of their laws he furnishes several instances. He tells how on one occasion Alexander, when he was at Babylon and had undertaken to restore the ruined temple of Bel, gave orders to all his soldiers, without distinction, to bring materials for the earthworks; and how the Jews alone refused to obey, and even submitted to severe chastisement and heavy fines, until the king pardoned them and exempted them from this task. (193) Again, when temples and altars were erected in the country by its invaders, the Jews razed them all to the ground, paying in some cases a fine to the satraps, and in others obtaining pardon. For such conduct, he adds, they deserve admiration. (194) Then he goes on to

---

[1] The translation, based as it is on the emendation διφθέραν, differs from that of Thackeray.

speak of our vast population, stating that, though many myriads of our race had already been deported to Babylon by the Persians, yet after Alexander's death myriads more migrated to Egypt and Phoenicia in consequence of the disturbed condition of Syria. (195) The same writer has referred to the extent and beauty of the country which we inhabit in the following words: "They occupy almost three million *arourae* of the most excellent and fertile soil, productive of every variety of fruits. Such is the extent of Judaea." (196) Again, here is his description of Jerusalem itself, the city which we have inhabited from remote ages, of its great beauty and extent, its numerous population, and the temple buildings: (197) "The Jews have many fortresses and villages in different parts of the country, but only one fortified city, which has a circumference of about fifty *stades* and some hundred and twenty thousand inhabitants; they call it Jerusalem. (198) Nearly in the centre of the city stands a stone wall, enclosing an area about five *plethra* long and a hundred cubits broad, approached by a pair of gates. Within this enclosure is a square altar, built of heaped up stones, unhewn and unwrought; each side is twenty cubits long and the height ten cubits. Beside it stands a great edifice, containing an altar and a lampstand, both made of gold, and weighing two talents; (199) upon these is a light which is never extinguished by night or day. There is not a single statue or votive offering, no trace of a plant, in the form of a sacred grove or the like. Here priests pass their nights and days performing certain rites of purification, and abstaining altogether from wine while in the temple." (200) The author further attests the share which the Jews took in the campaigns both of King Alexander and of his successors. One incident on the march, in which a Jewish soldier was concerned, he states that he witnessed himself. I will give the story in his own words: (201) "When I was on the march towards the Red Sea, among the escort of Jewish cavalry which accompanied us was one named Mosollamus, a very intelligent man, robust, and, by common consent, the very best of bowmen, whether Greek or barbarian. (202) This man, observing that a number of men were going to and fro on the route and that the whole force was being held up by a seer who was taking the auspices, inquired why they were halting. (203) The seer pointed out to him the bird he was observing, and told him that if it stayed in that spot it was expedient for them all to halt; if it stirred and flew forward, to advance; if backward, then to retire. The Jew, without saying a word, drew his bow, shot and struck the bird, and killed it. (204) The seer and some others were indignant, and heaped curses upon him. 'Why so mad,

39

you poor wretches?' he retorted; and then, taking the bird in his hands, continued, 'Pray, how could any sound information about our march be given by this creature, which could not provide for its own safety? Had it been gifted with divination, it would not have come to this spot, for fear of being killed by an arrow of Mosollamus the Jew.' "

(trans. H. St. J. Thackeray, LCL)

186 Μετὰ τὴν ἐν Γάξῃ μάχην ὁ Πτολεμαῖος ... πυνθανόμενοι τὴν ἠπιότητα καὶ φιλανθρωπίαν τοῦ Πτολεμαίου: The Battle of Gaza is dated to 312 B. C. E. Ptolemy Soter invaded the country four times, presumably in 320, 312, 302 and 301; see Tcherikover, pp. 56 f. During one of these invasions Jerusalem suffered much at the hands of Ptolemy; see Agatharchides, apud: Josephus, *Contra Apionem*, I, 205–211 (No. 30); Appianus, *Syriaca*, 50 : 252 (No. 343). The ἠπιότης and the φιλανθρωπία of the king, mentioned in the present passage, are not discredited by that episode, since the events related in our text did not necessarily occur in the same year that was implied for capture of Jerusalem by Agatharchides and Appian. On the benevolent character of Ptolemy, see Diodorus, XVIII, 14 : 1; XIX, 86 : 3.

187 Ἐζεκίας ἀρχιερεὺς τῶν Ἰουδαίων: The lists of high priests in Josephus do not include a high priest of that name in this or any other period, though the name does occur among priests and high-priestly houses during the period of the Second Temple; see Josephus, *BJ*, II, 429. In the opinion of some scholars, therefore, the high priest Ezekias was a later Jewish fabrication and constituted one of the chief arguments against the authenticity of the passage. Willrich (*Juden und Griechen*, p. 32) sees in the emigration of Ezekias to Egypt a reflection of events that occurred in the reign of Antiochus Epiphanes, when Onias escaped to Egypt. We should not, however, take ἀρχιερεύς here as a reference to the high priest par excellence. We know that, at least in the last generations of the Second Temple, the terms ἀρχιερεύς and ἀρχιερεῖς were used loosely to denote different members of the high-priestly oligarchy and the chief dignitaries of the Temple of Jerusalem. In any case, these titles were not confined to actual high priests or ex-high priests. For a discussion of the meaning of this term, see E. Schürer, *Theologische Studien und Kritiken*, 1872, pp. 593 ff.; Jeremias, pp. 197 ff.; E. Haenchen, *Die Apostelgeschichte*[13], Göttingen 1961, p.174, n.5. It seems very likely that this loose meaning of the term originated in the Hellenistic age; cf. Schlatter, *op. cit.* (supra, p. 25), p. 340. We may, therefore, suggest that Ezekias was one of the chief priestly dignitaries in Judaea, though not the high priest. This view gains strong support from a coin found in the excavations of Bet-Ẓur, which bears two legends in archaic Hebrew script and has the well-known figure of the Athenian owl. Behind the owl is written יהוד (Yehud), and in front of it we recognize the personal name יחזקיה (Ezekias), which may well be that of the person mentioned by Hecataeus. This has been the view of Sellers and Avigad, though, as Lapp points out, the frequency of paponymy makes the identification somewhat less certain, and the Ezekias of the Bet-Ẓur coin may have been the grandfather of that referred to by Hecataeus; cf. O. R. Sellers, *The Citadel of Beth-Zur*, Philadelphia 1933, p. 73; N. Avigad, *IEJ*, VII (1957), p. 149; P. W. Lapp, *BASOR*, 172 (1963), p. 34, n. 59. It is perhaps reasonable to assume that Ezekias acted as the treasurer of the Temple and of the autonomous State of Judaea. The appearance of his name on a coin of Yehud may be similar to that of Uriah probably from the priestly family of Haqoṣ, on seals; cf. Avigad, *op. cit.* pp. 146 ff.; W. F. Albright, *BASOR*, 148 (1957), pp. 28 ff.; cf. also Gager. *ZNTW*, LX (1969), pp. 138 f.

188 πάντες ἱερεῖς τῶν Ἰουδαίων οἱ τὴν δεκάτην τῶν γινομένων λαμβάνοντες: This statement about the priests' receiving the tithes is Schaller's chief argument against attributing the passage to Hecataeus, as mentioned in the introduction. However, Schaller's argument is by no means convincing. He bases his contention on the contradiction between our passage, which maintains as an established fact that the tithes belong to the priests, and the regulations of the Torah, which prescribe that they should be given to the Levites (Num. xviii : 21, 24). These regulations still remained in force in the time of Nehemiah (x : 38–39) in the fifth century B. C. E. On the other hand, in the period following the Hasmonaean Revolt the situation wholly changed, and it was mainly the priests who benefited from the tithes; see, e.g., *Ant.*, XX, 206 (τὰς τῶν ἱερέων δεκάτας ἐλάμβανον βι-αζόμενοι); XX, 181; *Vita*, 80 (ἀλλ᾽ οὐδὲ τὰς ὀφειλομένας μοι [scil. Josephus] ὡς ἱερεῖ δεκάτας ἀπελάμβανον); see also *Vita*, 63; *Ant.* IV, 68, 205 (the tithes pertain both to the priests and the Levites). The author of *The Letter to the Hebrews* (vii : 5) also holds the view that the tithes belong to the priests, and the same is attested by Philo, *De Virtutibus*, 95: κελεύουσιν οἱ νόμοι δεκάτας μὲν ἀπό τε σίτου καὶ οἴνου καὶ ἐλαίου καὶ θρεμμάτων ἡμέρων καὶ ἐρίων ἀπάρχεσθαι τοῖς ἱερωμένοις, though, in his *De Specialibus Legibus*, I, 156, Philo states that the tithes were to be given to the Levites. This situation is also echoed in various passages of the talmudic literature, where both views are expressed; cf. *TP Ma'aser Sheni* V, 56b; *TB Ketubbot* 26a. The change is implied by the Talmud to have existed already in the time of John Hyrcan (134–104 B. C. E.); see *TB Soṭa* 47b–48a; in fact, books like Jubilees (xxxii : 15) and Judith (xi : 13) already testify to the change. Schaller dates this change to the Maccabaean period, giving as decisive proof the divergence between the books of Nehemiah and Tobit (cf. I : 7, according to the Sinaiticus: καὶ ἐδίδουν αὐτὰ τοῖς ἱερεῦσιν τοῖς υἱοῖς Ἀαρὼν πρὸς τὸ θυσιαστήριον καὶ τὴν δεκάτην τοῦ σίτου καὶ τοῦ οἴνου καὶ ἐλαίου κτλ. τοῖς υἱοῖς Λευΐ τοῖς θεραπεύουσιν ἐν Ἱερουσαλήμ), on the one hand, both of which know that the tithes belong to the Levites, and the books of Jubilees and Judith, on the other, which assign the tithes to the priests. Since Schaller dates the Book of Tobit to the fourth (or third) century, and the books of Judith and Jubilees to the period following the Maccabaean revolt, he asserts that the change occurred in the Hasmonaean epoch. This conclusion, however, is hardly called for, even on Schaller's chronological assumptions. If the Book of Tobit had been composed, e.g., in the fourth century — i.e. perhaps still under Persian rule — it could have preceded the change, which might have occurred at some date later in the same century, but before the time in which Hecataeus wrote. We should add that certain scholars have adduced arguments, which are by no means negligible, in favour of dating Judith to the Persian period; see, e.g., the elaborate discussion by Y. M. Grintz, *The Book of Judith*, Jerusalem 1957 (in Hebrew). Moreover, to date the change in the late Persian period would accord well with the increased influence of the priesthood and the assumption by it of the leadership of the Jewish society at that period, a process favoured by the Persian government. This change also had its justification in the large number of priests who returned from the Babylonian Exile, in comparison with the rather meagre number of Levites who returned. It is noteworthy that already in the Talmud we find the

41

transfer of the tithes to the priests explained as a punishment inflicted by Ezra on the Levites for not returning from Babylon; cf. Grintz, *op. cit.*, p. 192. As for Hecataeus, it may also be that he distinguished hardly at all between priests and Levites, and this possibility considerably weakens Schaller's argumentation; cf. Gager, *op. cit.* (supra, p. 41), pp. 137 f.

καὶ τὰ κοινὰ διοικοῦντες περὶ χιλίους μάλιστα καὶ πεντακοσίους εἰσίν: The figure of 1,500 is too small for the number of priests to be found in the whole country. Already in Ezra ii : 36 ff. we find 4,289 given as the number of priests, and, according to Neh. xi : 10 ff., the priesthood of Jerusalem alone totalled 1,192, a figure that approximates the one mentioned by Hecataeus; cf. I Chron. ix : 13, which refers to 1,760 priests. It lends support to Büchler's suggestion that in our passage of Hecataeus only the priests of Jerusalem are taken into account; see A. Büchler, *Die Priester und der Cultus*, Vienna 1895, p. 49. For other explanations, see S. Lieberman, *Tarbiz*, III, p. 211; S. Klein, *The Land of Judaea*, Tel Aviv 1939, pp. 37 f. (in Hebrew); Jeremias, pp. 225 ff. The *Letter of Aristeas* (95), refers to seven hundred priests who were occupied with the Temple service; possibly he was referring only to the members of one of the twenty-four priestly courses (*mishmarot*). *Contra Apionem* (II, 108) puts the number of the Jewish priests at twenty thousand.

189 διφθέραν: This is a brilliant emendation by Lewy for διαφοράν of the manuscript tradition, which caused so much difficulty to the interpreters; see H. Lewy, *ZNTW*, XXXI (1932), p. 123; cf., e.g., Willrich, *Judaica*, p. 91; Engers, *op. cit.* (supra, p. 25), p. 236. As Lewy has put it: "διαφορά ist korrupt und in διφθέρα ("Buch") zu verbessern." διφθέρα would mean a scroll, and in our case it denotes the Torah written on a scroll. Zuntz also approves of Lewy's emendation; see G. Zuntz, *Journal of Semitic Studies*, III (1958), p. 311, n. 3. The same emendation has been suggested, without a reference to Lewy, by Q. Cataudella, *Rivista di Filologia Classica*, LXI (1933), pp. 75 f.

εἶχεν ... κατοίκησιν αὐτῶν καὶ τὴν πολιτείαν γεγραμμένην: Hecataeus probably refers to the reading of the Torah on the Sabbath or on one of the Jewish festivals, according to the well-known custom that goes back to the period of the Second Temple.

191 καὶ προπηλακιζόμενοι πολλάκις ὑπὸ τῶν Περσικῶν βασιλέων ...: Some scholars have seen in this passage a reflection of the time of persecution under Antiochus Epiphanes. But we know very little about the relations between the Persian state and the Jews during the latter part of the fifth century and the fourth century. A deterioration in those relations is, perhaps, echoed in *Ant.*, XI, 297 ff.; one must also remember the Book of Esther. It is likewise possible that some version of the story of Daniel and his companions at the Babylonian Court was disseminated in the time of Hecataeus, and that the difference between the Persian and Babylonian kings became somewhat blurred at that time. On this possibility, see P. Wendland, *Philologische Wochenschrift*, 1900, p. 1200; see also the commentary to Solinus, *Collectanea*, 35 : 4 (No. 449).

192 καὶ προελομένου τὸ τοῦ Βήλου πεπτωκὸς ἱερὸν ἀνακαθᾶραι...: On the rebuilding of the temple of Bel by Alexander the Great, see Arrianus, *Anabasis*, VII, 17 : 1 ff.; Strabo, *Geographica*, XVI, 1 : 5, p. 738 (where a tomb of Bel is referred to); see also H. Berve, *Das Alexanderreich auf prosopographischer Grundlage*, I, Munich 1926, p. 88, n. 4; p. 98.

ἕως αὐτοῖς συγγνόντα τὸν βασιλέα δοῦναι τὴν ἄδειαν: On Alexander's consideration for the religious feelings of the conquered people, see, e.g., Strabo, *Geographica*, XV, 1 : 63, p. 715; Curtius Rufus, IV, 7 : 5. Cf. also the attitude of Antiochus Sidetes to the Jews, according to Nicolaus of Damascus, apud: Josephus, *Ant.*, XIII, 250 f. (No. 88).

194 περὶ τοῦ πολυανθρωπότατον γεγονέναι ἡμῶν τὸ ἔθνος: Cf. the passage from Diodorus, above (No. 11).

πολλὰς... ἀνασπάστους εἰς Βαβυλῶνα Πέρσαι... ἐποίησαν: We also know of the banishment of the Jews from the territory of Jericho under Artaxerxes III Ochus from other sources; see Solinus, *loc. cit.* (supra, p. 42); Eusebius, *Chronicle* (ed. Schöne), II, p. 112; Orosius, III, 7 : 6; Syncellus (ed. Dindorf) I, p. 486. The three last-mentioned sources refer to a banishment of Jews to Hyrcania on the Caspian Sea. Only Syncellus adds Babylon.

εἰς Αἴγυπτον καὶ Φοινίκην μετέστησαν: Jewish emigration to Egypt is abundantly proved by the relatively large number of papyri dating from the third century B. C. E. We have no definite knowledge of the Jewish settlements in Phoenicia, but that is purely fortuitous. There were presumably quite a few such settlements.

197 πόλις ὀχυρά: On the strength of Jerusalem, see Agatharchides, (No. 30a); Strabo, *Geographica*, XVI, 2 : 36, p. 761 (No. 115).

πεντήκοντα μάλιστα σταδίων τὴν περίμετρον: The *Schoinometresis* of Syria gives it only twenty-seven stadia (No. 42). The *Letter of Aristeas* (105) mentions forty stadia, and the same figure is referred to by Timochares, apud: Eusebius, *Praeparatio Evangelica*, ix : 35, 1 (No. 41). Josephus (*BJ*, V, 159) states that the circumference of Jerusalem at the beginning of the siege was 33 stadia. On the basis of archaeological finds, Avi-Yonah estimates the circumference of the First Wall of Jerusalem as *c.* 3,800 m, while he fixes the circumference of the city after the building of the Third Wall as 5,550 m; see M. Avi-Yonah, *Book of Jerusalem*, I, Jerusalem 1956, p. 319 (in Hebrew). This compares with the circumference, e.g., of the city of Antigoneia, built by Antigonus Monophthalmus, which, according to Diodorus (XX, 47 : 5), was 70 stadia. The size of Sebaste, which "did not fall short of that of the most renowned cities", was 20 stadia; see *Ant.*, XV, 297.

198 κατὰ μέσον μάλιστα τῆς πόλεως: Lewy aptly remarks that locating the temple of Jerusalem in the middle of the city, which is contrary to the facts, would accord with the Greek way of building; see H. Lewy, *op. cit.* (supra, p. 42), p. 128; cf., e.g., Hellanicus, apud: Athenaeus, *Deipnosophistae*, XV, 679 F=*F. Gr. Hist.*, I, A 4 F 54.

ἀτμήτων... λίθων: Cf. Exod. xx : 22; Deut. xxvii : 5 f.; I Macc. iv : 47; Philo, *De Specialibus Legibus*, I, 274; *Ant.*, IV, 200; *M. Middot*, III, 4.

199 οἶνον οὐ πίνοντες ἐν τῷ ἱερῷ: Cf. Lev. x : 9; Ezek. xliv : 21; Philo, *De Specialibus Legibus*, I, 98; *Ant.*, III, 279; *BJ*, V, 229.

200 ὅτι καὶ Ἀλεξάνδρῳ τῷ βασιλεῖ συνεστρατεύσαντο: On Jewish soldiers in the Ptolemaic army, see the *Letter of Aristeas*, 13, 36; and the documents in *CPJ*, Nos. 18–32. On Jewish soldiers in the Seleucid empire, see *Ant.*, XII, 149 (cf. also A. Schalit, *JQR*, L, 1959–1960, pp. 289 ff.); II Macc. viii : 20 (cf. also I. Lévy, *Mélanges Grégoire*, II, Brussels 1950, pp. 681 ff.); I Macc. x : 36 f. Thus, the statement of Hecataeus here accords well with other sources. See, in general, Hengel, pp. 21 ff.

201 τῶν... ἱππέων Ἰουδαίων: On Jewish cavalry-men, see II Macc. xii : 35; I Macc. xvi : 4.

Μοσόλλαμος: It is the well-known Biblical name משולם; see, e.g., II Kings, xxii : 3; II Chron. xxxiv : 12; Ezra x : 29; Neh. iii : 4; see also *Ant.*, XIII, 75 (Μεσσάλαμος).

203 καὶ τὸν ὄρνιθα... ἀπέκτεινεν: Cf. H.D. Jocelyn, *The Tragedies of Ennius*, Cambridge 1967, l. 267, p. 128 F CXXXIV: "qui sibi semitam non sapiunt alteri monstrant viam."

13

De Iudaeis, apud: Josephus, *Contra Apionem*, II, 43 — Niese = Append. 2B R = *F. Gr. Hist.*, III, A264, F22 = Reinach (Budé), p. 66

Ἐτίμα γὰρ ⟨scil. Ἀλέξανδρος⟩ ἡμῶν τὸ ἔθνος, ὡς καί φησιν Ἑκαταῖος περὶ ἡμῶν, ὅτι διὰ τὴν ἐπιείκειαν καὶ πίστιν, ἣν αὐτῷ παρέσχον Ἰουδαῖοι, τὴν Σαμαρεῖτιν χώραν προσέθηκεν ἔχειν αὐτοῖς ἀφορολόγητον.

The honour in which he [scil. Alexander] held our nation may be illustrated by the statement of Hecataeus that, in recognition of the consideration and loyalty shown to him by the Jews, he added to their territory the district of Samaria free of tribute.

(trans. H. St. J. Thackeray, *LCL*)

τὴν Σαμαρεῖτιν χώραν προσέθηκεν: Here Josephus seems to have given the content of the relevant passage of Hecataeus rather inaccurately. Indeed, we know from other sources that the relations between Alexander and the Samaritans became strained; see Curtius Rufus, IV, 8 : 9–11 (No. 197). Nevertheless, it is very unlikely that the whole Samaritan territory was annexed to Judaea at any time. We cannot seek refuge in our ignorance of the period in view of all the subsequent political and territorial history. It may be suggested, however, that in the time of Alexander some territorial changes, which preceded the incorporation of southern Samaria into Judaea in the forties of the second century B. C. E., were made in favour of Judaea; see I Macc. x : 38; xi : 34; cf. also G. Beyer, *ZDPV*, LVI (1933), pp. 233 f.; Alt, II, p. 348. These changes, which may have been referred to by Hecataeus, are magnified, through Josephus' loose paraphrasing, into the annexation of the whole of Samaria to Judaea.

VI. MEGASTHENES

c. 300 B.C.E.

Megasthenes, a contemporary of Seleucus Nicator, visited India and spent there some years (between 302 and 288 B.C.E.).[1] His work on that country, Indica, *from which the reference to Jews derives, became authoritative. His appraisal of the Jews as a philosophical group among the Syrians reminds one of Theophrastus and Clearchus, and his comparison of the Syrian Jews and the Indian Brahmans[2] is similar to Clearchus' comparison of the Jews and the Indian Calani. Jaeger suggests the direct dependence of Clearchus on Megasthenes,[3] but as the former refers to Calani instead of to Brahmans, one may feel rather sceptical about this view, especially as the presence of Clearchus in Bactria is attested by inscriptional evidence so that we may even suppose that he had the opportunity of directly observing the religion of India.[4] Josephus mentions Megasthenes twice,[5] but it is certain that he did not have the whole* Indica *before him, for in that case he would undoubtedly have quoted the present passage in his* Contra Apionem.

1 See A. Dahlquist, *Megasthenes and Indian Religion*, Stockholm–Göteborg–Uppsala 1962, p. 9. Stein also dates Megasthenes' sojourn in India between 303 and 292 B.C.E.; see O. Stein, PW, XV, p. 232.
2 On the Brahmans in Megasthenes, see I. Dziech, *Eos*, XLIV (1950), pp. 9 ff.
3 W. Jaeger, *Diokles von Karystos*, Berlin 1938, pp. 140 ff.; idem, *JR*, XVIII (1938), p. 132, n. 14.
4 Cf. L. Robert, *Comptes rendus de l'Académie des Inscriptions et Belles Lettres*. 1968, pp. 451 ff.
5 See *Antiquitates* X, 227; *Contra Apionem*, I, 144.

14

Indica, apud: Clemens Alexandrinus, *Stromata*, I, 15:72:5 — Stählin & Früchtel = F8R = *Megasthenes*, ed. E.A. Schwanbeck, Bonn 1846, F42 = *F. Gr. Hist.*, III, C715, F3

Μεγασθένης ὁ συγγραφεὺς ὁ Σελεύκῳ τῷ Νικάτορι συμβεβιωκὼς
ἐν τῇ τρίτῃ τῶν Ἰνδικῶν ὧδε γράφει· «ἅπαντα μέντοι τὰ περὶ φύσεως
εἰρημένα παρὰ τοῖς ἀρχαίοις λέγεται καὶ παρὰ τοῖς ἔξω τῆς Ἑλλάδος
φιλοσοφοῦσι, τὰ μὲν παρ᾽ Ἰνδοῖς ὑπὸ τῶν Βραχμάνων, τὰ δὲ ἐν τῇ
5 Συρίᾳ ὑπὸ τῶν καλουμένων Ἰουδαίων.»

4 παρὰ τοῖς Eus. | τῇ om. Eus.

Megasthenes, the writer who was a contemporary of Seleucus Nicator,
writes in the third book of his *Indica*: "All the opinions expressed by
the ancients about nature are found also among the philosophers
outside Greece, some among the Indian Brahmans and others in
Syria among those called Jews."

VII. CLEARCHUS OF SOLI

c. 300 B.C.E.

Clearchus of the Cyprian city Soli is commonly designated a pupil of Aristotle, although his view of the soul is closer to Plato's than to that of the Peripatos. Among his works there is a dialogue, De Somno, *in which Aristotle appears as one of the main interlocutors. The reference to the Jews, which Clearchus has Aristotle aver in* De Somno, *derives from the discussion of the separate existence of the soul.*

The authenticity of the meeting between Aristotle and the Jew in the afore-mentioned work can hardly be maintained. It is true that we are well informed about the philosopher's sojourn in Asia Minor in the forties of the fourth century B.C.E.[1] and that later he was at the head of a school at Mytilene, but there is no more reason to consider the above-mentioned meeting as historical fact than other supposed encounters between famous Greek thinkers and representatives of Eastern wisdom. Cf., e.g., what Aristoxenus, another Peripatetic writer, has to say about the meeting between Socrates and an Indian sage; Eusebius, Praeparatio Evangelica, *XI, 3:8=F. Wehrli*, Die Schule des Aristoteles, *II,[2] Basel–Stuttgart 1967, F53:* φησὶ δ' 'Αριστόξενος ὁ μουσικὸς 'Ινδῶν εἶναι τὸν λόγον τοῦτον. 'Αθήνησι γὰρ ἐντυχεῖν Σωκράτει τῶν ἀνδρῶν ἐκείνων ἕνα κτλ.

Clearchus may have met Jews in his native Cyprus or elsewhere. From his description of the Jew who spoke Greek and who had the soul of a Greek, one gets the impression that Clearchus had in mind, however vaguely, one of those Hellenistic Jews so typical of the Jewish Diaspora. But apart from this, his reference to the Jews hardly necessitates the supposition that he had very much concrete knowledge of them. Rather, it represents the views of the time on Eastern wisdom and especially on that of well-defined priestly groups in the East. Clearchus' assertion that Jewish origins can be traced back to the Indian philosophers is similar in style to his assertion in De Educatione *that the Indian gymnosophists are descended from the Magi; see Diogenes Laertius I,9. Clearchus' passage on the Jews has been preserved by Josephus in*

---

1 W. Jaeger, *Aristotle*, Oxford 1948, pp. 105 ff.; A. H. Chroust, *Historia*, XXI (1972), pp. 170 ff.

From Herodotus to Plutarch

Contra Apionem. *Eusebius, in turn, derives it from Josephus. Clemens of Alexanderia refers only to the meeting between Aristotle and the Jew, without quoting the whole passage; cf.* Stromata, *I, 15:70:2:* Κλέαρχος δὲ ὁ Περιπατητικὸς εἰδέναι φησί τινα᾿Ιουδαῖον, ὃς ᾿Αριστοτέλει συνεγένετο.

It is almost certain that Josephus did not have access to the complete dialogue De Somno, and that he cited it only from some florilegium.

Bibliography

J. Bernays, *Theophrastos' Schrift über Frömmigkeit*, Berlin 1866, pp. 110, 187; Gutschmid, IV, pp. 578 ff.; H. Willrich, *Juden und Griechen vor der makkabäischen Erhebung*, Göttingen 1895, pp. 45 ff.; O. Stein, *Philologus*, LXXXVI, pp. 258 f.; U. v. Wilamowitz-Moellendorff, *Der Glaube der Hellenen*, II, Berlin 1932, p. 255, n. 2; E. Silberschlag, *JBL*, LII (1933), pp. 66 ff.; F. M. Abel, *RB*, XLIII (1934), pp. 535 f.; W. Jaeger, *Diokles von Karystos*, Berlin 1938, pp. 140 ff.; idem, *JR*, XVIII (1938), pp. 130 f.; H. Lewy, *HTR*, XXXI (1938), pp. 205 ff.; A. J. Festugière, *RHR*, CXXX (1945), pp. 29 ff.; F. Wehrli, *Die Schule des Aristoteles*, III [2], Basel–Stuttgart 1969, pp. 47 f.; Y. Gutman, *The Beginnings of Jewish-Hellenistic Literature*, Jerusalem 1958, pp. 91 ff. (in Hebrew); Hengel, pp. 467 ff. For new epigraphic evidence for Clearchus and his sojourn in Bactria cf. L. Robert, *Comptes rendus de l'Académie des Inscriptions et Belles Lettres*, 1968, pp. 422, 441 ff.

Clearchus of Soli

15

De Somno, apud: Josephus, *Contra Apionem*, I, 176–183 — Niese = F7R = F. Wehrli, *Die Schule des Aristoteles*, III, Basel–Stuttgart 1969, F6 = Reinach (Budé), pp. 34 f.

(176) Κλέαρχος γάρ, ὁ Ἀριστοτέλους ὢν μαθητὴς καὶ τῶν ἐκ τοῦ
Περιπάτου φιλοσόφων οὐδενὸς δεύτερος, ἐν τῷ πρώτῳ περὶ ὕπνου
βιβλίῳ φησὶν Ἀριστοτέλην τὸν διδάσκαλον αὐτοῦ περί τινος ἀνδρὸς
Ἰουδαίου ταῦτα ἱστορεῖν, αὐτῷ τε τὸν λόγον Ἀριστοτέλει ἀνατίθησι·
5 *(177)* ἔστι δὲ οὕτω γεγραμμένον· «ἀλλὰ τὰ μὲν πολλὰ μακρὸν ἂν εἴη
λέγειν, ὅσα δ᾽ ἔχει τῶν ἐκείνου θαυμασιότητά τινα καὶ φιλοσοφίαν
ὁμοίως διελθεῖν οὐ χεῖρον. σαφῶς δ᾽ ἴσθι, εἶπεν, Ὑπεροχίδη, θαυμαστὸν
ὀνείροις ἴσα σοι δόξω λέγειν. καὶ ὁ Ὑπεροχίδης εὐλαβούμενος, δι᾽ αὐτὸ
γάρ, ἔφη, τοῦτο καὶ ζητοῦμεν ἀκοῦσαι πάντες· *(178)* οὐκοῦν, εἶπεν ὁ
10 Ἀριστοτέλης, κατὰ τὸ τῶν ῥητορικῶν παράγγελμα τὸ γένος αὐτοῦ
πρῶτον διέλθωμεν, ἵνα μὴ ἀπειθῶμεν τοῖς τῶν ἀπαγγελιῶν διδασκάλοις.
λέγε, εἶπεν ὁ Ὑπεροχίδης, εἴ τί σοι δοκεῖ. *(179)* κἀκεῖνος τοίνυν τὸ
μὲν γένος ἦν Ἰουδαῖος ἐκ τῆς Κοίλης Συρίας. οὗτοι δέ εἰσιν ἀπόγονοι
τῶν ἐν Ἰνδοῖς φιλοσόφων, καλοῦνται δέ, ὥς φασιν, οἱ φιλόσοφοι παρὰ
15 μὲν Ἰνδοῖς Καλανοί, παρὰ δὲ Σύροις Ἰουδαῖοι, τοὔνομα λαβόντες ἀπὸ
τοῦ τόπου· προσαγορεύεται γὰρ ὃν κατοικοῦσι τόπον Ἰουδαία. τὸ δὲ τῆς
πόλεως αὐτῶν ὄνομα πάνυ σκολιόν ἐστιν· Ἱερουσαλήμην γὰρ αὐτὴν
καλοῦσιν. *(180)* οὗτος οὖν ὁ ἄνθρωπος ἐπιξενούμενός τε πολλοῖς κἀκ
τῶν ἄνω τόπων εἰς τοὺς ἐπιθαλαττίους ὑποκαταβαίνων Ἑλληνικὸς ἦν οὐ
20 τῇ διαλέκτῳ μόνον, ἀλλὰ καὶ τῇ ψυχῇ. *(181)* καὶ τότε διατριβόντων
ἡμῶν περὶ τὴν Ἀσίαν παραβαλὼν εἰς τοὺς αὐτοὺς τόπους ἄνθρωπος
ἐντυγχάνει ἡμῖν τε καί τισιν ἑτέροις τῶν σχολαστικῶν πειρώμενος αὐτῶν
τῆς σοφίας. ὡς δὲ πολλοῖς τῶν ἐν παιδείᾳ συνῳκείωτο, παρεδίδου τι
μᾶλλον ὧν εἶχεν.» *(182)* ταῦτ᾽ εἴρηκεν ὁ Ἀριστοτέλης παρὰ τῷ Κλεάρχῳ
25 καὶ προσέτι πολλὴν καὶ θαυμάσιον καρτερίαν τοῦ Ἰουδαίου ἀνδρὸς ἐν τῇ
διαίτῃ καὶ σωφροσύνην διεξιών. ἔνεστι δὲ τοῖς βουλομένοις ἐξ αὐτοῦ
τὸ πλέον γνῶναι τοῦ βιβλίου· φυλάττομαι γὰρ ἐγὼ [τὰ] πλείω τῶν
ἱκανῶν παρατίθεσθαι.*(183)* Κλέαρχος μὲν οὖν ἐν παρεκβάσει ταῦτ᾽

3 βιβλίῳ Eus.   βίβλῳ L   4 ἀνατίθησι Eus.   παρατιθείς L   ascribit
Lat.   περιτίθησι Gutschmid   5 ἂν εἴη Eus.   εἴη L   6 τῶν Eus.
τὴν L   7 οὐ χεῖρον Eus.   οὐ χεῦρον L   operae pretium est Lat. / δ᾽ ἴσθι
εἶπεν Eus.   δέ σοι εἰπεῖν L   11 ἀπαγγελιῶν Eus.   ἐπαγγελιῶν L
praeceptorum Lat.   12 εἴ τί σοι] οὕτως εἰ Eus.   ὅτι ed. pr.   13 γένος
<ἔφη> vel <εἶπεν> Niese   17 Ἱερουσαλὴμ Eus.   hierosolyma Lat.
19 ἐπιθαλαττίους Eus.   θαλαττίους L   21 ἄνθρωπος (vel ὁ ἄνθρωπος)
Niese   ἄνθρωπον L   ἄνθρωπος Eus.   23 πολλοῖς Eus.   πολλοὶ L, Lat.
27 τὰ secl. Niese   28 παραθέσθαι Niese

εἴρηκεν, τὸ γὰρ προκείμενον ἦν αὐτῷ καθ᾽ ἕτερον, οὕτως ἡμῶν
30 μνημονεύσας.

30 μνημονεύσας Hudson   μνημονεῦσαι L   ἐμνημόνευσεν vir doctus ap.
Hudsonum, Niese

(176) Clearchus, a disciple of Aristotle, and in the very first rank of
peripatetic philosophers, relates, in his first book on Sleep, the following anecdote told of a certain Jew by his master. He puts the words into
the mouth of Aristotle himself. (177) I quote the text "It would take
too long to repeat the whole story, but there were features in that
man's character, at once strangely marvellous and philosophical,
which merit description. 'I warn you, Hyperochides', he said, 'that
what I am about to say will seem to you as wonderful as a dream.'
Hyperochides respectfully replied, 'That is the very reason why we
are all anxious to hear it.' (178) 'Well', said Aristotle, 'in accordance
with the precepts of rhetoric, let us begin by describing his race, in
order to keep to the rules of our masters in the art of narration.' 'Tell
the story as you please', said Hyperochides. (179) 'Well,' he replied, 'the man was a Jew of Coele-Syria. These people are descended from the Indian philosophers. The philosophers, they say, are
in India called Calani, in Syria by the territorial name of Jews; for
the district which they inhabit is known as Judaea. Their city has a
remarkably odd name: they call it Hierusaleme. (180) Now this man,
who was entertained by a large circle of friends and was on his way
from the interior to the coast, not only spoke Greek, but had the soul
of a Greek. (181) During my stay in Asia, he visited the same places
as I did, and came to converse with me and some other scholars, to
test our learning. But as one who had been intimate with many
cultivated persons, it was rather he who imparted to us something of
his own.'" (182) These are the words of Aristotle as reported by Clearchus, and he went on to speak of the great and astonishing endurance
and sobriety displayed by this Jew in his manner of life. Further
information can be obtained, if desired, from the book itself; I forbear
to quote more than is necessary. (183) This allusion of Aristotle to
us is mentioned parenthetically by Clearchus, who was dealing with
another subject.   (trans. H. St. J. Thackeray, *LCL*)

176 Κλέαρχος γάρ, ὁ Ἀριστοτέλους ὢν μαθητής: On Clearchus as a pupil of
Aristotle, see Wehrli, *op. cit.* (supra, p. 48), Nos. 8, 37, 64, 91, 108.
αὐτῷ τε τὸν λόγον Ἀριστοτέλει ἀνατίθησι: Already in his own dialogues Aristotle
appears as chief debater in the discussion; cf. R. Hirzel, *Der Dialog*, I, Leipzig
1895, pp. 292 f.

177 οὖ χεῖρον: A common expression both in Plato and in Aristotle; see, e.g., *Phaedo*, 105a; *Ethica Nicomachea*, IV, 1127a; *Politica*, VII, 1316b.

179 ἐκ τῆς Κοίλης Συρίας: On the meaning of Coele-Syria in the early Hellenistic age, see the commentary to Theophrastus, *Historia Plantarum*, II, 6 : 2 (No. 6). ἀπόγονοι τῶν ἐν Ἰνδοῖς φιλοσόφων: Cf. Megasthenes, apud: Clemens Alexandrinus, *Stromata*, I, 15 : 72 : 5 (No. 14). Megasthenes, however, only draws a comparison between the Indian philosophers and the Syrian philosophers, i.e. the Jews. It seems to have been the habit of Clearchus to account for kindred spiritual phenomena by a hypothesis of physical kinship; cf. Diogenes Laertius, I, 9 = Wehrli F 13: Κλέαρχος δὲ ὁ Σολεὺς ἐν τῷ περὶ παιδείας καὶ τοὺς γυμνοσοφιστὰς ἀπογόνους εἶναι τῶν μάγων φησίν. Cf. Wehrli, *op. cit.* (supra, p. 48), p. 50.

Καλανοί: Clearchus does not refer to the Indian philosophers by the name of Brahmans. Calanus is the name of an Indian sage in the time of Alexander the Great, who burnt himself before the Macedonian army, thereby leaving a lasting impression on the Greeks; see Kroll, PW, X, pp. 1544 ff.; Berve, *op. cit.* (supra, p. 42), pp. 187 f.; L. Wallach, *PAAJR*, XI (1941), p. 60. In a passage from Nearchus, apud: Strabo, *Geographica*, XV, 1 : 66, p. 716, we read: Νέαρχος δὲ περὶ τῶν σοφιστῶν οὕτω λέγει τοὺς μὲν Βραχμᾶνας πολιτεύεσθαι καὶ παρακολουθεῖν τοῖς βασιλεῦσι συμβούλους, τοὺς δ'ἄλλους σκοπεῖν τὰ περὶ τὴν φύσιν . τούτων δ'εἶναι καὶ Κάλανον. See also Suda, s.v. "Kalanos" (certainly the grafting of the name to a tradition that did not have it): Κάλανος, Ἰνδός, ἐκ τῶν Βραχμάνων. οὕτω δὲ πάντα σοφὸν οἱ Ἰνδοὶ προσαγορεύουσιν.

179 Ἰουδαία: This name also occurs in Hecataeus. It was already the official name of the land at the beginning of the Hellenistic period; *pace* G. Hölscher, *Palästina in der persischen und hellenistischen Zeit*, Berlin 1903, pp. 76 ff.

Ἱερουσαλήμην: This form for Jerusalem is unique to Greek literature, whose authors consistently use the plural form Ἱεροσόλυμα.

180 οὗτος οὖν ὁ ἄνθρωπος... ὑποκαταβαίνων: This piece of information alone, even if authentic, does not prove that Jewish settlements existed in western Asia Minor in the second half of the fourth century. We can only imply from it the sojourn of an individual Jew to those parts. The first express statement about Jewish settlements in the area is found in *Ant.*, XII, 125, which refers to the reign of Antiochus II Theos. More circumstantial information is given regarding the settlement of two thousand Jewish families from Babylonia in Lydia and Phrygia in the reign of Antiochus III (223–187 B. C. E.); see *Ant.*, XII, 147 ff. Nevertheless, there is no reason to preclude the supposition that considerable numbers of Jews came in contact with western Asia Minor before the middle of the third century, and new findings may confirm this conjecture. It is noteworthy that a new inscription shows that a Jew lived in Greece in the third century B. C. E.; see *SEG*, XV, No. 293; cf. D.M. Lewis, *Journal of Semitic Studies*, II, 1957, p. 264. Also, there is much to be said for the view that Jews lived at Sardis in the Persian period; see W. Kornfeld, *Mélanges bibliques rédigés en l'honneur de André Robert*, Paris [1957] pp. 180 ff.

181 τῶν σχολαστικῶν πειρώμενος: On σχολαστικοί, see Festugière, *op. cit.* (supra, p. 48), p. 30, n. 3.

182 καρτερίαν τοῦ Ἰουδαίου ἀνδρός: Cf. Athenaeus, *Deipnosophistae*, XIII, 93, p. 611 B = Wehrli, F 16: συνελόντι δὲ εἰπεῖν κατὰ τὸν Σολέα Κλέαρχον οὐ καρτερικὸν βίον ἀσκεῖτε. On the motive of καρτερία in meetings of this kind, see Festugière, p. 31.

From Herodotus to Plutarch

φυλάττομαι γὰϱ ἐγὼ πλείω τῶν ἱκανῶν παϱατίθεσθαι: Undoubtedly there is a gap between the promise of Aristotle ὀνείϱοις ἴσα σοι δόξω λέγειν and the actual facts related here. The question arises why Josephus was content to refer to the original work of Clearchus but did not think it worthwhile to quote at length the story of Aristotle and the Jew if this story really did redound to the glory of Judaism. One might reply that the reason is a purely technical one. Josephus did not have the original work of Clearchus before him and took recourse in some sort of *florilegium*. If the compiler of this latter work was another Jewish apologetic writer, the problem would only be transferred to an earlier period. If, however, it was an anthology on the Jews by a pagan Greek writer, such as Alexander Polyhistor, the above-mentioned technical reason would sufficiently account for Josephus' omission of further details, since a pagan writer would not have felt it necessary to cite everything that was implicitly in favour of Judaism. Some, however, may feel — with Gutschmid and Lewy — that another explanation is needed for Josephus' procedure here, namely, that the continuation of the story was not, in the opinion of the Jewish historian, wholly to the credit of the Jewish religion. Following Gutschmid, *op. cit.* (supra, p. 48), pp. 587 f., Lewy has adduced at length arguments for the identification of the Jew with the magician who was able to draw out the soul from the body of a sleeping boy with the help of a magic wand, a story known to us from Proclus; cf. Lewy, *op. cit.* (supra, p. 48); cf. also Proclus, *In Platonis Rem Publicam*, II, p.122, ll. 22 ff. ed. Kroll (=Wehrli F7), who refers to Clearchus' Πεϱὶ ὕπνου: ὅτι δὲ καὶ ἐξιέναι τὴν ψυχὴν καὶ εἰσιέναι δυνατὸν εἰς τὸ σῶμα, δηλοῖ καὶ ὁ παϱὰ τῷ Κλεάϱχῳ τῇ ψυχουλκῷ ῥάβδῳ χϱησάμενος ἐπὶ τοῦ μειϱακίου τοῦ καθεύδοντος καὶ πείσας τὸν δαιμόνιον 'Αϱιστοτέλη, καθάπεϱ ὁ Κλέαϱχος ἐν τοῖς πεϱὶ ὕπνου φησίν, πεϱὶ τῆς ψυχῆς, ὡς ἄϱα χωϱίζεται τοῦ σώματος καὶ ὡς εἴσεισιν εἰς τὸ σῶμα καὶ ὡς χϱῆται αὐτῷ οἷον καταγωγίῳ. τῇ γὰϱ ῥάβδῳ πλήξας τὸν παῖδα τὴν ψυχὴν ἐξείλκυσεν καὶ οἷον ἄγων δι'αὐτῆς πόϱϱω τοῦ σώματος ἀκίνητον ἐνέδειξε τὸ σῶμα καὶ ἀβλαβὲς σῳζόμενον ἀναισθητεῖν.... Proclus, however, nowhere alludes to the magician as a Jew. This is explained away by Lewy as the result of the Neoplatonic writer's desire to omit everything connected with either Judaism or Christianity. Though one may doubt whether Lewy wholly proves his case, namely, that this magician should be identified with the Jewish sage, it is, nevertheless, quite reasonable to assume that a similar story, connected with magic, was also told about the Jew.

VIII. EUHEMERUS

First half of the third century B.C.E.

Euhemerus is included by Josephus in a group of eight writers who "have made more than a passing allusion to us". None of the writers can be identified with absolute certainty and, thus, dated; but even if some of them could be, it would not help us much to fix the date of our Euhemerus, since a similar list in Contra Apionem *(II, 84)) does not give the names of the writers in sequence, and it is doubtful whether Josephus knew the correct chronological order.*

Consequently, we can only conjecture that the Euhemerus in our passage is the famous Euhemerus, the author of ʿΙεϱὰ ᾿Αναγϱαφή. It has been suggested with some plausibility that he lived in Egypt and that his work appeared c. 280 B.C.E.[1] Thus, Euhemerus takes his place with Theophrastus, Hecataeus, Megasthenes and Clearchus as one of the earliest Hellenistic writers to refer to the Jews.[2] We do not know, of course, in what regard Euhemerus made mention of the Jews and their religion.[3] It should only be noted that certain features ascribed by Euhemerus to the community of Panchaia are also mentioned by Hecataeus in his description of the Jewish community.[4]

1 Cf. F. Jacoby, PW, VI, p. 953 = *Griechische Historiker*, Stuttgart 1956, p. 176. Vallauri suggests a date *c.* 270 B.C.E.; cf. G. Vallauri, *Evemero di Messene*, Turin 1956, p. 5. Cf. on him also Fraser, I, pp. 289 ff.

2 Cf. also H.F. van der Meer, "Euhemerus van Messene", Ph. D. Thesis, Amsterdam 1949, p. 73.

3 We read in Lactantius that Zeus used to assume the names of his hosts and, thus welcome the erection of sanctuaries in his honour under the names of Zeus Kasios, Zeus Atabyrios, etc. It has been surmised that the Jewish God was also included among the hosts of Zeus; cf. Lactantius, *Institutiones Divinae*, I, 22 : 22 = Vallauri, *op. cit.*, F 23, p. 41. Cf. also R. de Block, *Evhémère*, Mons 1876, p. 15. In any case, I see no ground whatever for Willrich's suggestion that it was Euhemerus who invented the combination Jupiter-Sabazius that we meet in Valerius Maximus, I, 3 : 3 (No. 147); see H. Willrich, *Juden und Griechen vor der makkabäischen Erhebung*, Göttingen 1895, p. 52.

4 Cf. Hecataeus, apud: Diodorus, XL, 3 : 5 (No. 11): τοὺς αὐτοὺς δὲ καὶ δικαστὰς ἀπέδειξε τῶν μεγίστων κρίσεων with Diodorus, V, 42 : 5: καὶ αὐτοὶ δὲ οὗτοι τὰ μέγιστα ἐπὶ τοὺς ἱερεῖς ἀναφέρουσιν; cf. also XL, 3 : 7 with V, 45 : 5.

16

apud: Josephus, *Contra Apionem*, I, 215–216 — Niese = G. Vallauri,

Evemero di Messene, Turin 1956, F 11

(215) Ἀρκοῦσι δὲ ὅμως εἰς τὴν ἀπόδειξιν τῆς ἀρχαιότητος αἵ τε
Αἰγυπτίων καὶ Χαλδαίων καὶ Φοινίκων ἀναγραφαὶ πρὸς ἐκείναις τε τοσοῦτοι τῶν Ἑλλήνων συγγραφεῖς· *(216)* ἔτι δὲ πρὸς τοῖς εἰρημένοις Θεόφιλος ⟨No. 38⟩ καὶ Θεόδοτος καὶ Μνασέας ⟨No. 27⟩ καὶ Ἀριστοφάνης
5 ⟨No. 24⟩ καὶ Ἑρμογένης ⟨No. 199⟩ Εὐήμερός τε καὶ Κόνων ⟨No. 144⟩
καὶ Ζωπυρίων ⟨No. 198⟩ καὶ πολλοί τινες ἄλλοι τάχα, οὐ γὰρ ἔγωγε
πᾶσιν ἐντετύχηκα τοῖς βιβλίοις, οὐ παρέργως ἡμῶν ἐμνημονεύκασιν.

3 ἔτι δὲ Eus.   ἔτι δὲ καὶ L

(215) However, our antiquity is sufficiently established by the Egyptian,
Chaldaean, and Phoenician records, not to mention the numerous
Greek historians. (216) In addition to those already cited, Theophilus,
Theodotus, Mnaseas, Aristophanes, Hermogenes, Euhemerus, Conon,
Zopyrion, and, maybe, many more — for my reading has not been
exhaustive — have made more than a passing allusion to us.

(trans. H. St. J. Thackeray, *LCL*)

IX. BEROSSUS

Third century B.C.E.

Berossus was a Babylonian priest of Bel, who lived in the time of Antiochus I (281/80–262/61 B.C.E.). To this king he also dedicated his work, written in Greek, on Babylonian history. The work begins with the story of Creation and ends with the writer's own time. Just as Manetho strove to supersede Herodotus as the chief authority on Egyptian history for the Greeks, so Berossus wanted to render the great past of Babylonia accessible to Greeks by publishing a historical work, based on local tradition, that would replace the fantastic romances related after the manner of Ctesias. History, however, seems to have disappointed these hopes. Greek writers rarely referred to the work of the Babylonian priest, and it was used only by Graeco-Jewish apologetic writers searching for an independent testimony on the antiquity of the Jews.

The main passage of Berossus that has any bearing on Jewish history is found in Contra Apionem, *I, 130 ff. (No. 17).*

It is doubtful that the righteous man experienced in celestial affairs, who, according to Berossus, lived ten generations after the Flood, can be identified with Abraham (Ant., I, 158). It seems that Josephus drew this equation from Jewish-Hellenistic circles. Probability was lent to this interpretation by the fact that, according to Genesis, ten generations spanned the interval from Noah to Abraham. Consequently, I do not consider it necessary to include this passage in the present collection.

Babyloniaca, apud: Josephus, *Contra Apionem*, I, 130–141 — Niese (135–141 repet. in: Josephus, *Antiquitates Judaicae*, X, 220–226) = F13R = P. Schnabel, *Berossos und die babylonisch-hellenistische Literatur*, Leipzig 1923, F49 = Reinach (Budé), pp. 25 ff. = *F. Gr. Hist.*, III, C680, F8

   (130) Οὗτος τοίνυν ὁ Βηρῶσος ταῖς ἀρχαιοτάταις ἐπακολουθῶν ἀναγραφαῖς περί τε τοῦ γενομένου κατακλυσμοῦ καὶ τῆς ἐν αὐτῷ φθορᾶς τῶν ἀνθρώπων καθάπερ Μωσῆς οὕτως ἱστόρηκεν καὶ περὶ τῆς λάρνακος, ἐν ᾗ Νῶχος ὁ τοῦ γένους ἡμῶν ἀρχηγὸς διεσώθη
5 *προσενεχθείσης αὐτῆς ταῖς ἀκρωρείαις τῶν Ἀρμενίων ὀρῶν. (131) εἶτα τοὺς ἀπὸ Νώχου καταλέγων καὶ τοὺς χρόνους αὐτοῖς προστιθεὶς ἐπὶ Ναβοπαλάσσαρον παραγίνεται τὸν Βαβυλῶνος καὶ Χαλδαίων βασιλέα (132) καὶ τὰς τούτου πράξεις ἀφηγούμενος λέγει, τίνα τρόπον πέμψας ἐπὶ τὴν Αἴγυπτον καὶ ἐπὶ τὴν ἡμετέραν γῆν τὸν υἱὸν τὸν ἑαυτοῦ*
10 *Ναβοκοδρόσορον μετὰ πολλῆς δυνάμεως, ἐπειδήπερ ἀφεστῶτας αὐτοὺς ἐπύθετο, πάντων ἐκράτησεν καὶ τὸν ναὸν ἐνέπρησε τὸν ἐν Ἱεροσολύμοις ὅλως τε πάντα τὸν παρ᾽ ἡμῶν λαὸν ἀναστήσας εἰς Βαβυλῶνα μετῴκισεν, συνέβη δὲ καὶ τὴν πόλιν ἐρημωθῆναι χρόνον ἐτῶν ἑβδομήκοντα μέχρι Κύρου τοῦ Περσῶν βασιλέως. (133) κρατῆσαι δέ φησι τὸν Βαβυλώνιον*
15 *Αἰγύπτου Συρίας Φοινίκης Ἀραβίας πάντας δὲ ὑπερβαλόμενον ταῖς πράξεσι τοὺς πρὸ αὐτοῦ Χαλδαίων καὶ Βαβυλωνίων βεβασιλευκότας. (134) [εἶθ᾽ ἑξῆς ὑποκαταβὰς ὀλίγον ὁ Βηρῶσος πάλιν παρατίθεται ἐν τῇ τῆς ἀρχαιότητος ἱστοριογραφίᾳ]. αὐτὰ δὲ παραθήσομαι τὰ τοῦ Βηρώσου τοῦτον ἔχοντα τὸν τρόπον (135) «ἀκούσας δ᾽ ὁ πατὴρ αὐτοῦ*
20 *Ναβοπαλάσαρος, ὅτι ὁ τεταγμένος σατράπης ἔν τε Αἰγύπτῳ καὶ τοῖς περὶ τὴν Συρίαν τὴν Κοίλην καὶ τὴν Φοινίκην τόποις ἀποστάτης γέγονεν, οὐ δυνάμενος αὐτὸς ἔτι κακοπαθεῖν συστήσας τῷ υἱῷ Ναβοκοδροσόρῳ ὄντι ἔτι ἐν ἡλικίᾳ μέρη τινὰ τῆς δυνάμεως ἐξέπεμψεν ἐπ᾽ αὐτόν. (136) συμμίξας δὲ Ναβοκοδρόσορος τῷ ἀποστάτῃ καὶ παραταξάμενος αὐτοῦ τ᾽*
25 *ἐκράτει καὶ τὴν χώραν ἐξ ἀρχῆς ὑπὸ τὴν αὐτῶν βασιλείαν ἐποιήσατο. τῷ τε πατρὶ αὐτοῦ συνέβη Ναβοπαλασάρῳ κατὰ τοῦτον τὸν καιρὸν ἀρρωστήσαντι ἐν τῇ Βαβυλωνίων πόλει μεταλλάξαι τὸν βίον ἔτη βεβασιλευκότι κα´. (137) αἰσθόμενος δὲ μετ᾽ οὐ πολὺ τὴν τοῦ πατρὸς τελευτὴν Ναβουκοδρόσορος, καταστήσας τὰ κατὰ τὴν Αἴγυπτον*

   3 Μωυσῆς ed. pr.   6 αὐτοῖς] αὐτῶν Reinach (*eorum* Lat.)
7 Ναβοπαλάσσαρον Niese   ναβολάσσαρον L / Βαβυλωνίων Reinach
10 Ναβοκοδρόσορον Niese   ναβουχοδονοσὸρ L   11 ἐπύθετο Lambertus
ὑπέθετο L   12 μετῴκισεν ed. pr.   μετῴκησεν L   14 ⟨πρώτου⟩
Περσῶν Reinach   15 δὲ om. Niese   δὴ Gutschmid   16 αὐτοῦ
ed. pr.   αὐτῶν L   17–18 εἶθ᾽... ἱστοριογραφίᾳ secl. Niese (om. Lat.)
25 ἐκράτει Niese   κρατεῖ Syncellus   ἐκράτησε Ant.   ἐκυρίευσε L, Eus.
ἐποιήσατο Niese   ἐποίησεν L   28 κα´] εἰκοσιέν Ant.   εἰκοσιεννέα L

30 πράγματα καὶ τὴν λοιπὴν χώραν καὶ τοὺς αἰχμαλώτους Ἰουδαίων τε
καὶ Φοινίκων καὶ Σύρων καὶ τῶν κατὰ τὴν Αἴγυπτον ἐθνῶν συντάξας
τισὶ τῶν φίλων μετὰ τῆς βαρυτάτης δυνάμεως καὶ τῆς λοιπῆς ὠφελείας
ἀνακομίζειν εἰς τὴν Βαβυλωνίαν, αὐτὸς ὁρμήσας ὀλιγοστὸς παρεγένετο
διὰ τῆς ἐρήμου εἰς Βαβυλῶνα. (138) καταλαβὼν δὲ τὰ πράγματα
35 διοικούμενα ὑπὸ Χαλδαίων καὶ διατηρουμένην τὴν βασιλείαν ὑπὸ τοῦ
βελτίστου αὐτῶν, κυριεύσας ὁλοκλήρου τῆς πατρικῆς ἀρχῆς τοῖς μὲν
αἰχμαλώτοις παραγενομένοις συνέταξεν [αὐτοῖς] κατοικίας ἐν τοῖς
ἐπιτηδειοτάτοις τῆς Βαβυλωνίας τόποις ἀποδεῖξαι, (139) αὐτὸς δὲ
ἀπὸ τῶν ἐκ τοῦ πολέμου λαφύρων τό τε Βήλου ἱερὸν καὶ τὰ λοιπὰ
40 κοσμήσας φιλοτίμως τήν τε ὑπάρχουσαν ἐξ ἀρχῆς πόλιν ‹ἀνακαινίσας›
καὶ ἑτέραν ἔξωθεν προσχαρισάμενος καὶ ἀναγκάσας * πρὸς τὸ μηκέτι
δύνασθαι τοὺς πολιορκοῦντας τὸν ποταμὸν ἀναστρέφοντας ἐπὶ τὴν πόλιν
κατασκευάζειν, περιεβάλετο τρεῖς μὲν τῆς ἔνδον πόλεως περιβόλους,
τρεῖς δὲ τῆς ἔξω, τούτων δὲ τοὺς μὲν ἐξ ὀπτῆς πλίνθου καὶ ἀσφάλτου,
45 τοὺς δὲ ἐξ αὐτῆς τῆς πλίνθου. (140) καὶ τειχίσας ἀξιολόγως τὴν πόλιν
καὶ τοὺς πυλῶνας κοσμήσας ἱεροπρεπῶς προσκατεσκεύασεν τοῖς
πατρικοῖς βασιλείοις ἕτερα βασίλεια ἐχόμενα ἐκείνων, ὑπὲρ ὧν
τἀνάστημα καὶ τὴν λοιπὴν πολυτέλειαν μακρὸν ἴσως ἔσται, ἐάν τις
ἐξηγῆται, πλὴν ὡς ὄντα γε ὑπερβολὴν [ὡς] μεγάλα καὶ ὑπερήφανα
50 συνετελέσθη ἡμέραις δεκαπέντε. (141) ἐν δὲ τοῖς βασιλείοις τούτοις
ἀναλήμματα λίθινα ὑψηλὰ ἀνοικοδομήσας καὶ τὴν ὄψιν ἀποδοὺς
ὁμοιοτάτην τοῖς ὄρεσι, καταφυτεύσας δένδρεσι παντοδαποῖς ἐξ-
ειργάσατο καὶ κατεσκεύασε τὸν καλούμενον κρεμαστὸν παράδεισον διὰ
τὸ τὴν γυναῖκα αὐτοῦ ἐπιθυμεῖν τῆς ὀρείας διαθέσεως τεθραμμένην ἐν
55 τοῖς κατὰ τὴν Μηδίαν τόποις.»

30 τε Eus., ed. pr., *Ant.* δὲ L 31 καὶ τῶν *Ant.* τῶν L 35–36 τῶν
βελτίστων? Reinach 36 ὁλοκλήρου Syncellus ἐξ ὁλοκλήρου L 37 παραγενομένοις *Ant.* παραγενόμενος L / αὐτοῖς om. Lat., *Ant.* αὐτόθι Gutschmid / κατοικίας Syncellus ἀποικίας L, *Ant.* 40 ‹ἀνακαινίσας›
Naber 41 καταχαρισάμενος *Ant.* προκαθιδρυσάμενος Gutschmid προσο-
χυρισάμενος Herwerden / καὶ ἀναγκάσας secl. Reinach 42 ἀποστρέ-
φοντας Ernesti 43 περιεβάλετο ed. pr. *Antiquitatum* ὑπερεβάλετο L *Ant.*
40–43 τήν τε ὑπάρχουσαν ἐξ ἀρχῆς πόλιν καὶ ἑτέραν ἔξωθεν προσχωρησομένην
κατανοήσας, πρὸς τὸ μηκέτι δύνασθαι τοὺς πολιορκοῦντας τὸν ποταμὸν ἀναστρέφοντας ἐπὶ τὴν πόλιν κατασπιλάζειν, ὑπερεβάλετο G. Giangrande, *CQ*, LVI
(1962), pp. 109 ff. 44 τούτων δὲ τοὺς μὲν Niese τούτων τότε μὲν L
46 προσκατεσκεύασεν Syncellus προσκατεσκεύακεν L 47 ὑπὲρ ὧν Syncellus ὧν *Ant.* ἐπαίρων L 48 τἀνάστημα Gutschmid ἀνάστημα L
τὸ μὲν ἀνάστημα *Ant.*, Syncellus / λοιπὴν *Ant.*, Syncellus πολλὴν L /
μακρὸν Niese μακρὰ δ᾽ L 49 πλὴν ὡς *Ant.* πλὴν L / ὡς secl.
Reinach 51 ἀνοικοδομήσας Syncellus ἀνῳκοδομήσας L ἀνῳκοδόμησε
Ant. 52 καταφυτεύσας ‹δὲ› Gutschmid

57

(130) This Berosus, following the most ancient records, has, like Moses, described the flood and the destruction of mankind thereby, and told of the ark in which Noah, the founder of our race, was saved when it landed on the heights of the mountains of Armenia. (131) Then he enumerates Noah's descendants, appending dates, and so comes down to Nabopalassar, king of Babylon and Chaldaea. (132) In his narrative of the actions of this monarch he relates how he sent his son Nabuchodorosor with a large army to Egypt and to our country, on hearing that these people had revolted, and how he defeated them all, burnt the temple at Jerusalem, dislodged and trans-ported our entire population to Babylon, with the result that the city lay desolate for seventy years until the time of Cyrus, king of Persia. (133) He adds that the Babylonian monarch conquered Egypt, Syria, Phoenicia, and Arabia, his exploits surpassing those of all previous kings of Chaldaea and Babylon. (134) [Then again a passage a little lower down in Berosus is cited in his history of antiquity.] But I will quote Berosus's own words, which are as follows: (135) "His father Nabopalassar, hearing of the defection of the satrap in charge of Egypt, Coele-Syria, and Phoenicia, and being himself unequal to the fatigues of a campaign, committed part of his army to his son Nabuchodorosor, still in the prime of life, and sent him against the rebel. (136) Nabuchodorosor engaged and defeated the latter in a pitched battle and replaced the district under Babylonian rule. Meanwhile, as it happened, his father Nabopalassar sickened and died in the city of Babylon, after a reign of twenty-one years. (137) Being informed ere long of his father's death, Nabuchodorosor settled the affairs of Egypt and the other countries. The prisoners — Jews, Phoenicians, Syrians, and those of Egyptian nationality — were consigned to some of his friends, with orders to conduct them to Babylonia, along with the heavy troops and the rest of the spoils; while he himself, with a small escort, pushed across the desert to Babylon. (138) There he found the administration in the hands of the Chaldaeans and the throne reserved for him by their chief nobleman. Being now master of his father's entire realm, he gave orders to allot to the captives, on their arrival, settlements in the most suitable dis-tricts of Babylonia. (139) He then magnificently decorated the temple of Bel and the other temples with the spoils of war, *restored* the old city, and added a new one outside the walls, and, in order to prevent the possibility in any future siege of *access being gained* to the city by a diversion of the course of the river, he enclosed both the inner and the outer city with three lines of ramparts, those of the

inner city being of baked brick and bitumen, those of the outer city of rough brick. (140) After fortifying the city on this grand scale and adorning the gateways in a manner worthy of their sanctity, he constructed a second palace adjoining that of his father. It would perhaps be tedious to describe the towering height and general magnificence of this building; it need only be remarked that, notwithstanding its immense and imposing proportions, it was completed in fifteen days. (141) Within this palace he erected lofty stone terraces, in which he closely reproduced mountain scenery, completing the resemblance by planting them with all manner of trees and constructing the so-called hanging garden; because his wife, having been brought up in Media, had a passion for mountain surroundings."

(trans. H. St. J. Thackeray, *LCL*)

135 ἀκούσας…: On this passage in general, see Gutschmid's commentary to *Contra Apionem*. There is much to be said for the view that Josephus did not use Berossus directly, but only through Alexander Polyhistor. However, as it was Polyhistor's habit to give his excerpts in indirect speech, we may assume that Josephus changed them into direct speech. We can detect a similar procedure by Josephus in *Ant.*, I, 118 — a quotation of the Sibyl by Josephus. On the use of Berossus by Josephus, see P. Schnabel, *Berossos und die babylonisch-hellenistische Literatur*, Leipzig–Berlin 1923, pp. 166 f. On the relation between Berossus and Alexander Polyhistor, see Schnabel, *op. cit.*, pp. 134 ff.

ὁ πατὴρ αὐτοῦ Ναβοπαλάσαρος: It was Nabopalasaros who, in alliance with the Medes, put an end to the Assyrian empire.

ὁ τεταγμένος σατράπης ἔν τε Αἰγύπτῳ: This can only imply Pharaoh Necho. From the point of view of those who regarded the neo-Babylonian empire as a continuation of the Assyrian, the conquest of Coele-Syria and Phoenicia by the Egyptian ruler might be interpreted as the rape of Babylonian territory. Still, the labelling of Necho as a rebellious satrap calls for some explanation. Should we look here for some notion of a universal empire centred around Babylon, or have we perhaps some reference to the subjugation of Egypt by the Assyrians in the seventh century B. C. E.?

περὶ τὴν Συρίαν τὴν Κοίλην: On Coele-Syria, see the commentary to Theophrastus, *Historia Plantarum*, II, 6 : 2 (No. 6). On Necho's conquests in these parts, see II Kings, xxiii : 29; Herodotus (II, 159; No. 2) refers to the conquest of Gaza by the Egyptian king.

συστήσας τῷ υἱῷ Ναβοκοδροσόρῳ…: Cf. D.J. Wiseman, *Chronicles of Chaldaean Kings (626–556 B.C.) in the British Museum*, London 1956, pp. 20 f.

136 συμμίξας δὲ Ναβοκοδρόσορος…: The decisive battle, in which the Egyptian army was crushed, was fought at Carchemish in 605 B. C. E.; see the description of these events as they emerge from the *Babylonian Chronicle* (British Museum, No. 21946) in Wiseman, *op. cit.* pp. 67 ff. :"(1.1) In the twenty-first year the king of Akkad stayed in his own land, Nebuchadrezzar his eldest son, the crown prince, (1.2) mustered [the Babylonian army] and took command of his troops; he marched to Carchemish, which is on the bank of the Euphrates, (1.3) and crossed the river

[to go] against the Egyptian army which lay in Carchemish (1.4)... fought with each other, and the Egyptian army withdrew before him. (1.5) He accomplished their defeat and to non-existence [beat?] them. As for the rest of the Egyptian army (1.6) which had escaped from the defeat [so quickly that] no weapon had reached them, in the district of Hamath (1.7) the Babylonian troops overtook and defeated them so that not a single man [escaped] to his own country."

On the battle of Carchemish, see Jer. xlvi : 2; II Chron. xxxv : 20; *Ant.*, X, 84 ff. As a result of this victory and the extinction of the retreating Egyptian army at Hamath, Nebuchadrezzar became the master of all of Syria; see Wiseman, *op. cit.*, p. 69, 1.8 of the *Chronicle*: "At that time Nebuchadrezzar conquered the whole area of the Hati country"; cf. also for these events, R. Campbell Thompson, *CAH*, III, 1925, pp. 210 ff.; A. Gardiner, *Egypt of the Pharaohs*, Oxford 1961, pp. 358 f.

συνέβη Ναβοπαλασάρῳ ... μεταλλάξαι τὸν βίον ἔτη βεβασιλευκότι κα': Cf. the above-mentioned *Chronicle*, 1.9 ff.: "for twenty-one years Nabopolassar had been king of Babylon. On the eighth of the month of Ab he died. In the month of Elul Nebuchadrezzar returned to Babylon and on the first day of the month of Elul he sat on the royal throne in Babylon."

137 καὶ τοὺς αἰχμαλώτους Ἰουδαίων: Perhaps these Jewish prisoners were auxiliaries in Pharaoh's army, sent there by the King of Judah, who was a vassal of Pharaoh as a result of the changes that occurred after the Battle of Megiddo; or it may be that Nebuchadrezzar, after Jehoyakim had submitted to him voluntarily, took some Jews as hostages, as reflected in Dan. 1:3 f.; cf.Wiseman, *op. cit.*(supra, p. 59), p. 26. In any case, Berossus does not refer here to the later deportations of the Jews in the time of Jehoyakim (598 B. C. E.) and Zedekiah (587 B. C. E.). The passage that Tatian derives from Berossus (No. 18) may suggest that Berossus referred to these later events elsewhere.

18

Babyloniaca, apud: Tatianus, *Oratio ad Graecos*, 36 — Schwartz = Schnabel, *op. cit.*, F51 = F. *Gr. Hist.*, III, C680, T2 + F8b

Βηρωσὸς ἀνὴρ Βαβυλώνιος, ἱερεὺς τοῦ παρ' αὐτοῖς Βήλου, κατ' Ἀλέξανδρον γεγονώς, Ἀντιόχῳ τῷ μετ' αὐτὸν τρίτῳ τὴν Χαλδαίων ἱστορίαν ἐν τρισὶ βιβλίοις κατατάξας καὶ τὰ περὶ τῶν βασιλέων ἐκθέμενος, ἀφηγεῖταί τινος αὐτῶν ὄνομα Ναβουχοδονόσορ, τοῦ στρατεύσαντος ἐπὶ
5 Φοίνικας καὶ Ἰουδαίους.

1 βηρωσσὸς V, Eus. / τοῦ om. P / κατὰ V, Eus., JOGD   2 γενόμενος Eus.   3 ἐκτιθέμενος Eus.   4 ναβουχοδονόσωρ MV in ναβουχοδονόσορ corr. P / συστρατεύσαντος Eus., JOGDN

Berosus, a Babylonian, a priest of their god Belus, born in the time of Alexander, composed for Antiochus, the third after him, the history of the Chaldaeans in three books; and, narrating the acts of the kings, he mentions one of them Nabuchodonosor by name, who made war against the Phoenicians and Jews.   (trans. B. P. Pratten, Edinburgh 1867)

Ναβουχοδονόσορ, τοῦ στρατεύσαντος ἐπὶ Φοίνικας καὶ 'Ιουδαίους: Here it seems that the reference is to the events that led up to the fall of Jerusalem in 587 B. C. E. At that time the Phoenician cities of Tyre and Sidon took common action with the Kingdom of Judah against Nebuchadrezzar. The representatives of the kings of Tyre, Moab and Ammon met in Jerusalem and planned a revolt; see Jer. xxvii : 2 ff.; cf. W.B. Fleming, *The History of Tyre*, New York 1915, p. 43; Eissfeldt, PW, Ser. 2, VII, pp. 1889 f. The Babylonians first attacked Jerusalem and captured it, then they subdued Phoenicia, and they also attacked Tyre, which was besieged for thirteen years. Tatian may have derived the reference to Berossus, independently of Josephus, from some Jewish-Hellenistic source. Still, the possibility remains that the words στρατεύσαντος ἐπὶ Φοίνικας καὶ 'Ιουδαίους are an addition by Tatian, who thus described the Babylonian conqueror more explicitly.

X. MANETHO

Third century B.C.E.

Manetho, born at Sebennytus and a priest in Heliopolis, is the Egyptian parallel to the Babylonian Berossus. He was well versed in Egyptian national tradition and was associated with the religious policy of the Ptolemies, namely, the introduction of the cult of Sarapis. He was also the first Egyptian writer to give an account of his country's past in Greek. Some fragments of his Aegyptiaca, *which are actually the only substantial narrative passages left from Manetho's work, have been preserved by Josephus in his* Contra Apionem. *It seems, however, that Josephus did not use Manetho directly,[1] but was acquainted only with abridgements made by his predecessors among Hellenistic Jewry who sought support in Manetho and, at the same time, attempted to refute him in their polemic against Graeco-Egyptian anti-Semites.*

The historical importance of Manetho assumes greater dimensions if we regard him as the first literary exponent of the anti-Jewish trend in Graeco-Roman Egypt and as the man who was instrumental in creating, or at least in popularizing, some of the oft-recurring anti-Semitic motifs. This has been denied by many scholars, who distinguish Manethonian from pseudo-Manethonian elements in the fragments quoted or summarized by Josephus. According to their view it is only pseudo-Manetho who may be labelled an anti-Semite, while the authentic Manetho made no mention of the Jews.

The fragments of Manetho in Contra Apionem *fall into two main divisions. The first (No. 19) relates the history of the Hyksos rule in Egypt. The Hyksos are stated to have been a people of ignoble origin, who burnt the cities of Egypt, destroyed the temples of the gods and dealt very cruelly with the native population. This characterization of the Hyksos is in line with the later Egyptian tradition (cf. the commentary). After their expulsion from Egypt the Hyksos crossed the desert to Syria. Once there, terrified by the might of Assyria, they built a city in "the country now called Judaea" and gave it the name of Jerusalem. Though Manetho does not expressly refer to Jews in connection with*

---

1 Cf., e.g., Ed. Meyer, *Aegyptische Chronologie*, Berlin 1904, p. 71; R. Weill, *La fin du Moyen Empire Égyptien*, Paris, p. 70.

the Hyksos, he seems to do so by implication. The fact that he makes the Hyksos emigrate to Judaea, which in Manetho's time was not identical with the whole of Palestine, and ascribes to them the founding of Jerusalem, can be explained only on the assumption of an identification of the Hyksos with the ancestors of the Jewish nation.[2] And there was nothing significant in the history of Jerusalem, apart from its being the capital of the Jews,[3] to make it the centre of the Hyksos' settlement after their withdrawal from Egypt. On the other hand, one should point out that in existing later Greek and Latin literature there is no parallel to the connection between the Hyksos and the Jews suggested by Manetho.

The second Manethonian version of the origin of the Jewish nation (No. 21) was destined to have greater currency, though it must be emphasized, that we can by no means discern its direct influence on later literature, but can only trace parallel stories and traditions.

Josephus stated that Manetho himself distinguishes between his first version and the second one, where he uses fables and current reports (μυθευόμενα καὶ λεγόμενα). The main theme of his story runs as follows: King Amenophis wished to be granted a vision of the gods. In order to achieve his desire, he acted upon the counsel of his namesake Amenophis, son of Paapis, and made an attempt to purge the country of lepers and other polluted persons. He collected about eighty thousand of them and assigned them to toil in the stone quarries of the Nile. Subsequently he agreed to their request to allot them the old Hyksos capital, Avaris. There, an ex-priest of Heliopolis, named Osarsiph, became their leader. He ordained that they should neither worship the gods nor abstain from the flesh of animals revered in Egypt, and he enjoined that they should foster relations only with the members of their own community. Moreover, he sent a delegation to the inhabitants of Jerusalem, who had once been expelled from Egypt. In a common effort, the Solymites and the polluted Egyptians subdued the country and maltreated the population even more brutally than the Hyksos. At the end comes the most interesting passage — that in which Osarsiph is identified with Moses (§250).

Many scholars argued against Manetho's authorship of the whole

2 This has rightly been pointed out in Bousset, *Berliner Philologische Wochenschrift*, XXVII (1907), p. 1166.
3 Jerusalem is already mentioned in connection with Egypt in the Tel el-Amarna correspondence, but nothing is stated there to give it pre-eminence among the other cities of the land; see J.B. Pritchard, *Ancient Near Eastern Texts Relating to the Old Testament*[2], Princeton 1955, p. 488.

Osarsiph version. Others found it enough to attribute only the equation Osarsiph = Moses to pseudo-Manetho, thereby removing from that version the main passage that buttresses the contention that Manetho must have been an anti-Semite,[4] though the role ascribed to the Solymites may be enough for the purpose even without that equation. Yet, no valid reason seems to exist for denying to Manetho either the whole story, or even the crucial paragraph. On the whole, the story shows many traits also found in the Prophecy of the Lamb *or the* Oracle of the Potter,[5] *and it could easily be combined with anti-Jewish elements. The Jewish story of the Exodus made an Egyptian reply urgent even before the Bible was translated into Greek, because the Jewish presentation of the clash between the Egyptians and the ancestors of the Jewish people had presumably won some adherents in non-Jewish circles. Moreover, an anti-Jewish atmosphere in Egypt should not be considered typical of only the later Ptolemaic or early Roman age; we have clear evidence that there was religious tension between the Egyptians and Jewish settlers in Egypt in the Persian period (end of the fifth century).[6] From Hecataeus, apud: Diodorus, XL (No. 11), we learn that the account of the Jewish Exodus had, in his time, already been merged with a story concerning the expulsion of foreigners at the behest of the gods, due to misfortunes that befell the land. Hence it can hardly be supposed that it was Manetho who first combined the story of the defiled people with that of Moses and the Jews. He may have merely included in his* Aegyptiaca *a version already current.*

4 See *FHG*, II, p. 514; Bousset, *loc. cit.* (supra, n. 2); see also Ed. Meyer, *op. cit.* (supra, n. 1), p. 77 (with some hesitation, p. 79, n. 2); Laqueur, PW XIV, p. 1071; Weill, *op. cit.*, p. 101. This view is also shared by Heinemann.

5 The *Oracle of the Potter* undoubtedly originated in Pharaonic Egypt, but its Greek form is Hellenistic. The versions of the *Oracle of the Potter* do not show anti-Semitic traits. An anti-Jewish tendency is, however, found in a Graeco-Egyptian prophecy found on a papyrus; cf. *PSI*, No. 982 = *CPJ*, No. 520. For the *Oracle of the Potter*, see C. Wessely, *Denkschriften der Kaiserlichen Akademie der Wissenschaften, Wien*, XLII, 1893, 2, pp. 3 ff.; U. Wilcken, *Hermes*, XL (1905), pp. 544 ff.; R. Reitzenstein & H. H. Schaeder, *Studien zum antiken Synkretismus*, Leipzig-Berlin 1926, pp. 39 f.; G. Manteuffel, *De Opusculis Graecis Aegypti e Papyris, Ostracis Lapidibusque Collectis*, Warsaw 1930, pp. 99 ff.; *P. Oxy.*, XXII, 2332 (Roberts); L. Koenen, *Zeitschrift für Papyrologie und Epigraphik*, II (1968), pp. 178 ff.

6 See A. Cowley, *Aramaic Papyri of the Fifth Century B. C.*, Oxford 1923, Nos. 30–31. That Manetho is also the author of the second version is maintained by Gutschmid and by Willrich (though the argumentation of the latter scholar is much vitiated by some fallacious preconceptions that he clings to obstinately, e.g., his denial of the existence of a Jewish diaspora in third-century Egypt), as well as by Reinach, Schürer and Tcherikover. See also Fraser, II, p. 733, no. 116.

From Manetho onwards, we frequently meet with this combination of narratives, although nowhere else is it exactly the same as in Manetho's version. While in Manetho the expulsion is motivated by a royal wish to see the gods, in Chaeremon and in a Graeco-Egyptian prophecy on papyrus[7] the wrath of Isis is the cause. In the same connection, Lysimachus, apud: Josephus, Contra Apionem, I, 304–311. (No. 158) stresses the disease of the defiled people as the reason for their expulsion, while Pompeius Trogus, apud: Iustinus, XXXVI, 2 : 12 (No. 137) speaks of the physical misfortunes of the Egyptians themselves. Cf. also Tacitus, Historiae, V, 3 (No. 281), and the commentary to that passage. They differ also in regard to the dating of the events. Among the later writers, Chaeremon alone concurs with Manetho in dating them to the reign of Amenophis, but even he contradicts Manetho in many of his details.[8]

Bibliography

Müller, pp. 120 ff., 185 ff., 214 ff.; J. Krall, "Die Composition und die Schicksale des Manethonischen Geschichtswerkes", *Sitzungsberichte der Wiener Akademie* (philosophisch-historische Classe), XCV, 1879 (1880), pp. 152 ff.; Gutschmid, I, p. 350; IV, pp. 419 ff.; H. Willrich, *Juden und Griechen vor der makkabäischen Erhebung*, Göttingen 1895, pp. 53 ff.; Ed. Meyer, *Aegyptische Chronologie*, Berlin 1904, pp. 71 ff.; Stähelin, pp. 9 ff.; Schürer, III, pp. 529 ff.; Radin, pp. 99 ff.; R. Weill, *La fin du Moyen Empire Égyptien*, Paris 1918, pp. 68 ff.; Laqueur, PW, XIV, pp. 1060 ff.; Ed. Meyer, *Geschichte des Altertums*, III ², Stuttgart–Berlin 1928, pp. 420 ff.; I. Heinemann, PW, Suppl. V, pp. 26 f.; A. Momigliano, *Rivista di Filologia*, LIX (1931), pp. 490 ff.; W. G. Waddell, *Manetho*, 1940, *LCL*, VII ff.; A.M.A. Hospers-Jansen, *Tacitus over de Joden*, Groningen 1949, p. 119; J. Schwartz, *BIFAO*, XLIX (1950), pp. 73 ff.; W. Helck, *Untersuchungen zu Manetho und den ägyptischen Königslisten*, Berlin 1956, pp. 38 ff.; Tcherikover, pp. 361 ff.; J. Yoyotte, *RHR*, CLXIII (1963), pp. 133 ff.; J. van Seters, *The Hyksos*, New Haven 1966, pp. 121 ff.; Gager, pp. 113 ff.; Fraser, I, pp. 505 ff.

7 Cf. for the emergence of anti-Semitic feelings in Egyptian priestly circles, J. Yoyotte, *RHR*, CLXIII (1963), pp. 133 ff.
8 For a useful table of motifs, cf. Weill, *op. cit.* (supra, n. 1), p. 109. For interesting remarks concerning the localization of the events and the differences relating to them in literary tradition, cf. J. Schwartz, *BIFAO*, XLIX (1950), pp. 77 f.

Aegyptiaca, apud: Josephus, *Contra Apionem*, I, 73–91 — Niese =F10R = *F. Gr. Hist.*, III, C609,
F1,8 = Reinach (Budé), pp. 15 ff. = W.G. Waddell, *Manetho*, Cambridge Mass. 1940, F42

(73) Ἄρξομαι δὲ πρῶτον ἀπὸ τῶν παρ᾽ Αἰγυπτίοις γραμμάτων. αὐτὰ
μὲν οὖν οὐχ οἷόν τε παρατίθεσθαι τἀκείνων, Μάνεθως δ᾽ ἦν τὸ γένος
Αἰγύπτιος, ἀνὴρ τῆς Ἑλληνικῆς μετεσχηκὼς παιδείας, ὡς δῆλός
ἐστιν· γέγραφεν γὰρ Ἑλλάδι φωνῇ τὴν πάτριον ἱστορίαν ἔκ τε τῶν ἱερῶν,
5 ὥς φησιν αὐτός, μεταφράσας καὶ πολλὰ τὸν Ἡρόδοτον ἐλέγχει τῶν
Αἰγυπτιακῶν ὑπ᾽ ἀγνοίας ἐψευσμένον. *(74)* οὗτος δὴ τοίνυν ὁ Μάνεθως
ἐν τῇ δευτέρᾳ τῶν Αἰγυπτιακῶν ταῦτα περὶ ἡμῶν γράφει. παραθήσομαι δὲ τὴν λέξιν αὐτοῦ καθάπερ αὐτὸν ἐκεῖνον παραγαγὼν μάρτυρα.
«*(75)* ✳ τοῦ τίμαιος ὄνομα· ἐπὶ τούτου οὐκ οἶδ᾽ ὅπως θεὸς
10 ἀντέπνευσεν καὶ παραδόξως ἐκ τῶν πρὸς ἀνατολὴν μερῶν ἄνθρωποι
τὸ γένος ἄσημοι καταθαρρήσαντες ἐπὶ τὴν χώραν ἐστράτευσαν καὶ
ῥᾳδίως ἀμαχητὶ ταύτην κατὰ κράτος εἷλον, *(76)* καὶ τοὺς ἡγεμονεύσαντας
ἐν αὐτῇ χειρωσάμενοι τὸ λοιπὸν τάς τε πόλεις ὠμῶς ἐνέπρησαν καὶ τὰ
τῶν θεῶν ἱερὰ κατέσκαψαν, πᾶσι δὲ τοῖς ἐπιχωρίοις ἐχθρότατά πως
15 ἐχρήσαντο, τοὺς μὲν σφάζοντες, τῶν δὲ καὶ τὰ τέκνα καὶ γυναῖκας εἰς
δουλείαν ἄγοντες. *(77)* πέρας δὲ καὶ βασιλέα ἕνα ἐξ αὐτῶν ἐποίησαν,
ᾧ ὄνομα ἦν Σάλιτις. καὶ οὗτος ἐν τῇ Μέμφιδι κατεγίνετο τήν τε ἄνω
καὶ κάτω χώραν δασμολογῶν καὶ φρουρὰν ἐν τοῖς ἐπιτηδειοτάτοις
καταλιπὼν τόποις. μάλιστα δὲ καὶ τὰ πρὸς ἀνατολὴν ἠσφαλίσατο μέρη
20 προορώμενος Ἀσσυρίων ποτὲ μεῖζον ἰσχυόντων ἐσομένην ἐπιθυμίᾳ
τῆς αὐτοῦ βασιλείας ἔφοδον· *(78)* εὑρὼν δὲ ἐν νομῷ τῷ Σαΐτῃ πόλιν
ἐπικαιροτάτην, κειμένην μὲν πρὸς ἀνατολὴν τοῦ Βουβαστίτου ποταμοῦ,
καλουμένην δ᾽ ἀπό τινος ἀρχαίας θεολογίας Αὔαριν, ταύτην ἔκτισέν τε
καὶ τοῖς τείχεσιν ὀχυρωτάτην ἐποίησεν, ἐνοικίσας αὐτῇ καὶ πλῆθος
25 ὁπλιτῶν εἰς εἴκοσι καὶ τέσσαρας μυριάδας ἀνδρῶν προφυλακήν.
(79) ἔνθα δὲ κατὰ θέρειαν ἤρχετο, τὰ μὲν σιτομετρῶν καὶ μισθοφορίαν
παρεχόμενος, τὰ δὲ καὶ ταῖς ἐξοπλισίαις πρὸς φόβον τῶν ἔξωθεν γυμνάζων.
ἄρξας δ᾽ ἐννεακαίδεκα ἔτη τὸν βίον ἐτελεύτησε. *(80)* μετὰ τοῦτον δὲ
ἕτερος ἐβασίλευσεν τέσσαρα καὶ τεσσαράκοντα ἔτη καλούμενος Βηών·

1 δὲ Eus.   δὴ L   2 *Μάνεθως* Eus.   μανεθὼν ex μανέθων L
3 *Αἰγύπτιος ἀνὴρ* Niese   ἀνὴρ αἰγύπτιος L, Eus., cod. G   4 τε τῶν]
δέλτων Gutschmid   5 *καὶ*] ὃς καὶ Eus.   6 οὗτος Eus.   αὐτὸς L
ipse Lat.   9 *Τουτίμαιος* Gutschmid   *honorabile nomen* Lat.   ἐγένετο
βασιλεὺς ἡμῖν *Τίμαιος* ὄνομα ed. pr.   /   ὁ θεὸς Eus.   19 *καταλείπων* ed.
pr.   20 ἐπιθυμίᾳ Bekker   ἐπιθυμίαν L   21 αὐτοῦ Niese   αὐτῆς
L   /   *Σαΐτῃ*] *Σεθροΐτῃ* Bernard ex Africano et *Schol. Plat.*   24 ἐνοικίσας
ed. pr.   ἐνοικήσας L   *collocans* Lat.   26 ἔνθα δὲ Niese   ἐνθάδε L
hic autem Lat.   29 *Βνών* Gutschmid ex *Schol. Plat.* et Africano

Manetho

30 μεθ' ὃν ἄλλος 'Απαχνὰς ἓξ καὶ τριάκοντα ἔτη καὶ μῆνας ἑπτά. ἔπειτα
δὲ καὶ "Απωφις ἓν καὶ ἑξήκοντα καὶ 'Ιαννὰς πεντήκοντα καὶ μῆνα ἕνα.
(81) ἐπὶ πᾶσι δὲ καὶ "Ασσις ἐννέα καὶ τεσσαράκοντα καὶ μῆνας δύο.
καὶ οὗτοι μὲν ἓξ ἐν αὐτοῖς ἐγενήθησαν πρῶτοι ἄρχοντες, ποθοῦντες
ἀεὶ καὶ μᾶλλον τῆς Αἰγύπτου ἐξᾶραι τὴν ῥίζαν. (82) ἐκαλεῖτο δὲ τὸ
35 σύμπαν αὐτῶν ἔθνος Ὑκσώς, τοῦτο δέ ἐστιν βασιλεῖς ποιμένες· τὸ γὰρ
ὓκ καθ' ἱερὰν γλῶσσαν βασιλέα σημαίνει, τὸ δὲ σὼς ποιμήν ἐστι καὶ
ποιμένες κατὰ τὴν κοινὴν διάλεκτον, καὶ οὕτως συντιθέμενον γίνεται
Ὑκσώς. τινὲς δὲ λέγουσιν αὐτοὺς "Αραβας εἶναι. (83) ἐν δ' ἄλλῳ ἀντιγράφῳ οὐ βασιλεῖς σημαίνεσθαι διὰ τῆς ὓκ προσηγορίας, ἀλλὰ τοὐναντίον
40 αἰχμαλώτους δηλοῦσθαι ποιμένας· τὸ γὰρ ὓκ πάλιν Αἰγυπτιστὶ καὶ
τὸ ἃκ δασυνόμενον αἰχμαλώτους ῥητῶς μηνύει. καὶ τοῦτο μᾶλλον
πιθανώτερόν μοι φαίνεται καὶ παλαιᾶς ἱστορίας ἐχόμενον. (84) τούτους
τοὺς προκατωνομασμένους βασιλέας [καὶ] τοὺς τῶν ποιμένων καλουμένων καὶ τοὺς ἐξ αὐτῶν γενομένους κρατῆσαι τῆς Αἰγύπτου
45 φησὶν ἔτη πρὸς τοῖς πεντακοσίοις ἕνδεκα. (85) μετὰ ταῦτα δὲ τῶν ἐκ
τῆς Θηβαΐδος καὶ τῆς ἄλλης Αἰγύπτου βασιλέων γενέσθαι φησὶν ἐπὶ
τοὺς ποιμένας ἐπανάστασιν καὶ πόλεμον αὐτοῖς συρραγῆναι μέγαν καὶ
πολυχρόνιον. (86) ἐπὶ δὲ βασιλέως, ᾧ ὄνομα εἶναι Μισφραγμούθωσις
ἡττωμένους φησὶ τοὺς ποιμένας ἐκ μὲν τῆς ἄλλης Αἰγύπτου πάσης
50 ἐκπεσεῖν, κατακλεισθῆναι δ' εἰς τόπον ἀρουρῶν ἔχοντα μυρίων τὴν
περίμετρον· Αὔαριν ὄνομα τῷ τόπῳ. (87) τοῦτόν φησιν ὁ Μάνεθως
ἅπαντα τείχει τε μεγάλῳ καὶ ἰσχυρῷ περιβαλεῖν τοὺς ποιμένας, ὅπως
τήν τε κτῆσιν ἅπασαν ἔχωσιν ἐν ὀχυρῷ καὶ τὴν λείαν τὴν ἑαυτῶν.
(88) τὸν δὲ Μισφραγμουθώσεως υἱὸν Θούμμωσιν ἐπιχειρῆσαι μὲν αὐτοὺς
55 διὰ πολιορκίας ἑλεῖν κατὰ κράτος, ὀκτὼ καὶ τεσσαράκοντα μυριάσι
στρατοῦ προσεδρεύσαντα τοῖς τείχεσιν· ἐπεὶ δὲ τῆς πολιορκίας ἀπέγνω,
ποιήσασθαι συμβάσεις, ἵνα τὴν Αἴγυπτον ἐκλιπόντες, ὅποι βούλονται,
πάντες ἀβλαβεῖς ἀπέλθωσι. (89) τοὺς δὲ ἐπὶ ταῖς ὁμολογίαις πανοικησίᾳ
μετὰ τῶν κτήσεων οὐκ ἐλάττους μυριάδων ὄντας εἴκοσι καὶ τεσσάρων
60 ἀπὸ τῆς Αἰγύπτου τὴν ἔρημον εἰς Συρίαν διοδοιπορῆσαι· (90) φοβουμένους
δὲ τὴν Ἀσσυρίων δυναστείαν, τότε γὰρ ἐκείνους τῆς Ἀσίας κρατεῖν,

---

31 'Αννὰς vel "Ανναν Gutschmid   Samnas Lat.   Ιανίας ed. pr.
33 ποθοῦντες ed. pr.   πορθοῦντες L   35 σύμπαν αὐτῶν Eus., Lat.   om. L /
'Υκουσσὼς Eus.   Sesos Lat.   36 οὐσσὼς Eus.   40 αἰχμαλώτους
Eus.   βασιλεῖς αἰχμαλώτους L /   ποιμένας Eus.   οὐ ποιμένας L   neque
pastores Lat.   43 καὶ secl. Reinach   47 αὐτοῖς om. Eus.
48 ἐπὶ Eus.   ἐπεὶ L /   Μισφραγμούθωσις Eus.   ἀλισφραγμούθωσις L
alisfragmuthos Lat.   49 ἡττημένους Cobet /   post ποιμένας add. ἐξ αὐτοῦ
L (ὑπ'αὐτοῦ ed. pr.)   om. Eus.   54 Θμούθωσιν Eus.   56 τὴν
πολιορκίαν Eus.   60 διοδοιπορῆσαι Eus.   ὁδοιπορῆσαι L

67

ἐν τῇ νῦν Ἰουδαίᾳ καλουμένῃ πόλιν οἰκοδομησαμένους τοσαύταις μυριάσιν ἀνθρώπων ἀρκέσουσαν Ἱεροσόλυμα ταύτην ὀνομάσαι. *(91)* ἐν
ἄλλῃ δέ τινι βίβλῳ τῶν Αἰγυπτιακῶν Μάνεθως τοῦτό φησιν τὸ ἔθνος
65 τοὺς καλουμένους ποιμένας αἰχμαλώτους ἐν ταῖς ἱεραῖς αὐτῶν βίβλοις
γεγράφθαι, λέγων ὀρθῶς· καὶ γὰρ τοῖς ἀνωτάτω προγόνοις ἡμῶν τὸ
ποιμαίνειν πάτριον ἦν καὶ νομαδικὸν ἔχοντες τὸν βίον οὕτως ἐκαλοῦντο
ποιμένες.

63 ὀνομάσαι Eus.   ὠνόμασαν L   64 τοῦτό] τὸ αὐτὸ Gutschmid

(73) I will begin with Egyptian documents. These I cannot indeed
set before you in their ancient form; but in Manetho we have a native
Egyptian who was manifestly imbued with Greek culture. He wrote
in Greek the history of his nation, translated, as he himself tells us,
from sacred tablets; and on many points of Egyptian history he
convicts Herodotus of having erred through ignorance. (74) In the
second book of his *History of Egypt*, this writer Manetho speaks
of us as follows. I shall quote his own words, just as if I had brought
forward the man himself as a witness: (75) "Tutimaeus. (?) In his
reign, for what cause I know not, a blast of God smote us; and
unexpectedly, from the regions of the East, invaders of obscure race
marched in confidence of victory against our land. By main force they
easily seized it without striking a blow; (76) and having overpowered
the rulers of the land, they then burned our cities ruthlessly, razed to
the ground the temples of the gods, and treated all the natives with a
cruel hostility, massacring some and leading into slavery the wives and
children of others. (77) Finally, they appointed as king one of their
number whose name was Salitis. He had his seat at Memphis, levying
tribute from Upper and Lower Egypt, and always leaving garrisons
behind in the most advantageous positions. Above all, he fortified the
district to the east, foreseeing that the Assyrians, as they grew stronger,
would one day covet and attack his kingdom. (78) In the Saïte nome
he found a city very favourably situated on the east of the Bubastite
branch of the Nile, and called Auaris after an ancient religious tradition. This place he rebuilt and fortified with massive walls, planting
there a garrison of as many as 240,000 heavy-armed men to guard his
frontier. (79) Here he would come in summer-time, partly to serve out
rations and pay his troops, partly to train them carefully in manoeuvres
and so strike terror into foreign tribes. After reigning for 19 years,
Salitis died; (80) and a second king, named Beon, succeeded and reigned
for 44 years. Next to him came Apachnas, who ruled for 36 years and
7 months; then Apophis for 61, and Iannas for 50 years and 1 month;

(81) then finally Assis for 49 years and 2 months. These six kings, their first rulers, were ever more and more eager to extirpate the Egyptian stock. (82) Their race as a whole was called Hyksos, that is 'king-shepherds': for *hyk* in the sacred language means 'king,' and *sos* in common speech is 'shepherd' or 'shepherds': hence the compound word 'Hyksos'. Some say that they were Arabs." (83) In another copy the expression *hyk*, it is said, does not mean "kings": on the contrary, the compound refers to "captive-shepherds". In Egyptian *hyk*, in fact, and *hak* when aspirated expressly denote "captives". This explanation seems to me the more convincing and more in keeping with ancient history. (84) These kings whom I have enumerated above, and their descendants, ruling over the so-called Shepherds, dominated Egypt, according to Manetho, for 511 years. (85) Thereafter, he says, there came a revolt of the kings of the Thebaïd and the rest of Egypt against the Shepherds, and a fierce and prolonged war broke out between them. (86) By a king whose name was Misphragmuthosis, the Shepherds, he says, were defeated, driven out of all the rest of Egypt, and confined in a region measuring within its circumference 10,000 *arourae*, by name Auaris. (87) According to Manetho, the Shepherds enclosed this whole area with a high, strong wall, in order to safeguard all their possessions and spoils. (88) Thummosis, the son of Misphragmuthosis (he continues), attempted by siege to force them to surrender, blockading the fortress with an army of 480,000 men. Finally, giving up the siege in despair, he concluded a treaty by which they should all depart from Egypt and go unmolested where they pleased. (89) On these terms the Shepherds, with their possessions and households complete, no fewer than 240,000 persons, left Egypt and journeyed over the desert into Syria. (90) There, dreading the power of the Assyrians who were at that time masters of Asia, they built in the land now called Judaea a city large enough to hold all those thousands of people, and gave it the name of Jerusalem. (91) In another book of his *History of Egypt* Manetho says that this race of so-called Shepherds is in the sacred books of Egypt described as "captives"; and his statement is correct. With our remotest ancestors, indeed, it was a hereditary custom to feed sheep; and as they lived a nomadic life, they were called Shepherds.   (trans. W. G. Waddell, *LCL*)

---

75 τοῦ τίμαιος ὄνομα: This reading of the Laurentianus, which also occurs in Eusebius (*Praeparatio Evangelica*), is clearly corrupt. Basing himself on the emendation (*Τον*) τίμαιος, Säve-Söderbergh has suggested that this king be identified with Dedumose, an Upper-Egyptian king of the thirteenth dynasty; see. T. Säve-

Söderbergh, *JEA*, XXXVII (1951), p. 62. This identification, however, seems to raise some phonetic difficulties; see A. Gardiner, *Egypt of the Pharaohs*, Oxford 1961, p. 157.

ἐκ τῶν πρὸς ἀνατολὴν μερῶν ἄνθρωποι... ἐπὶ τὴν χώραν ἐστράτευσαν καὶ... κατὰ κράτος εἷλον: On this conquest of Egypt by foreigners from the East known as the Hyksos and, in general, on their rule over the country, see P.C. Labib, *Die Herrschaft der Hyksos in Ägypten und ihr Sturz*, Ph. D. Thesis, Berlin 1936; Alt III, pp. 72 ff.; Säve-Söderbergh, *op. cit.*, pp. 53 ff.; Gardiner, *op. cit.*, pp. 155 ff.; W.C. Hayes, *Egypt from the Death of Ammenemes III to Seqenenre II*, *CAH*, 1962 (rev. ed.), Vol. II, Part 2, pp. 15 ff.; W. Helck, *Die Beziehungen Aegyptens zu Vorderasien im 3. und 2. Jahrtausend v. Chr.*, Wiesbaden 1962, pp. 92 ff. The majority of scholars who have dealt with the question hold the view that the Hyksos rule over Egypt was the result of a gradual process of infiltration and not of a short act of conquest, thereby invalidating the evidence of Manetho. According to the prevalent view, the Hyksos first occupied the Delta and only later extended their rule to the other parts of the country, including even Upper Egypt. Also basing themselves on the so-called Stele of 400 Years, many scholars are of the opinion that the Hyksos rule in the Delta goes back to 1730–1720 B. C. E., the beginning of this rule having been marked by the introduction of the cult of Seth-Sutekh, the chief deity of the Hyksos, into Tanis; cf. Säve-Söderbergh, *op. cit.*, pp. 64; Van Seters, *op. cit.*, pp. 97 ff. It is often assumed, too, that the Hyksos were mostly Semites; for a formulation of this view, see Labib, *op. cit.*, p. 16. This whole concept of the Hyksos and their rule over Egypt has recently been challenged by Helck. Helck does not see any connection between the Stele of Tanis and the Hyksos, and he revives the theory of the Hurrian origin of the Hyksos. Moreover, Helck defends Manetho and his description of the conquest of Egypt by the Hyksos against the modern theory of infiltration. See, however, the contrary arguments of Van Seters, *op. cit.*, pp. 121 ff.

76 καὶ τοὺς ἡγεμονεύσαντας ἐν αὐτῇ χειρωσάμενοι... καὶ τὰ τῶν θεῶν ἱερὰ κατέσκαψαν...: The cruel treatment of the Egyptians by the Hyksos became a fixed motif in later Egyptian sources; cf. Säve-Söderbergh, *op. cit.*, p. 55. Modern scholars, on the other hand, emphasize the integration of the Hyksos rulers into the Egyptian cultural and religious tradition. This was expressed by some Hyksos rulers taking names that incorporated that of the god Re, or in their making copies of Egyptian works of literature. Nevertheless, one should not exclude the possibility that there were different phases in Hyksos–Egyptian relations. Allowance must also be made for changes of attitude towards the Egyptian population and its traditions.

77 ᾧ ὄνομα ἦν Σάλιτις: Modern scholars — other than Helck — distinguish between the first settlement of the Hyksos in the Delta and the time when the Hyksos dynasty (the fifteenth in Manetho's list) began to rule the whole country. The rise of the fifteenth dynasty is dated to the first half of the seventeenth century, presumably 1674 B. C. E.; see Hayes, *op. cit.*, p. 19. For parallels containing the list of the fifteenth dynasty (Africanus, Eusebius), see *F. Gr. Hist.*, III C, p. 72. The identity of Salitis is not clear, though Hayes suggests that Salitis stands for King Sharek, or Shalek, who is found in a genealogical table of Memphite priests; see Hayes, p. 20. For a discussion of the Hyksos royal lists, see Ed. Meyer, *Chronologie*, pp. 80 ff.

προορώμενος Ἀσσυρίων ποτὲ μεῖζον ἰσχυόντων ἐσομένην ἐπιθυμίᾳ τῆς αὐτοῦ βασιλείας ἔφοδον: It is enough to say that the reference to the Assyrians is anachronistic.

Manetho

Manetho's statement presupposes the Greek view on the great Assyrian world-empire founded by Ninus and Semiramis.

78 *ἐν νομῷ τῷ Σαΐτῃ*: Since the Saite *nomos* did not seem to suit the context, most editors discarded the reading of the Laurentianus for that of Eusebius and Syncellus, reading instead *Σεθροΐτῃ*. However, as Avaris is now commonly identified with Tanis (cf. the following note), which was the capital of the Tanite *nomos*, and not of the Sethroite, the reading *Σεθροΐτῃ* does not carry conviction either. Accordingly, Collomp, basing himself on Montet, proposes to retain the reading of the Laurentianus on the supposition that one of the two forms under which the region of Tanis could appear in Greek was *Σαΐτικος*, thus implying a *nomos* that is distinguished from that west of the Delta; cf. P. Collomp, *REA*, XLII (1940), pp. 74 ff. = *Mélanges Radet*: "Il serait donc très normal que des copistes ou des érudits postérieurs à Manéthon, qui ne savaient plus qu'Avaris était Tanis, pour qui le nome Saïte était celui des Saïs, presque à l'Ouest du Delta, qui apprenaient de Manéthon qu'Avaris était à l'Est de la branche Bubastite, bien loin donc de Saïs,... aient mis à sa place le nom du plus oriental de tous les nomes" (p. 84).

καλουμένην ... Αὔαριν: The location of Avaris (Hatwaret, Haware) has given rise to much discussion. Many scholars believe that it should be identified with the subsequently famous city of Tanis (Zoʿan), which was the same as Pi-Ramesses; see, e.g., J. Leibovitch, *IEJ*, III (1953), p. 102. For dissenting voices, see R. Weill, *JEA*, XXI (1935), pp. 10 ff.; B. Couroyer, *RB*, LIII (1946), pp. 75 ff. Weill argues against the identification of Tanis with Avaris, and Couroyer disputes its being the same as Pi-Ramesses. Van Seters agrees with those scholars who locate Avaris (= Pi-Ramesses) in the district of Khatane Qantîr; see Van Seters, *op. cit.* (supra, p. 70), pp. 127 ff.; cf. Gardiner, *op. cit.*, p. 164.

79 *ἔνθα δὲ κατὰ θέρειαν ἤρχετο*: This must mean that the royal residence was generally at Memphis, but that in summer the king stayed at Avaris.

80 *καὶ Ἄπωφις*: The first king of the fifteenth dynasty whose name has an Egyptian sound. In Egyptian sources it appears as Awessere. On the monuments of the reign of Awessere, see Labib, *op. cit.* (supra, p. 70), p. 27.

Ἰαννὰς: He is assumed to be Chian of the Egyptian monuments; see Labib, *ibid.*, pp. 31 ff.

81 *Ἄσσις*: Hayes thinks that Assis is probably the King Asehre mentioned on a small obelisk from San el-Hagar, in the vicinity of ancient Avaris; cf. Hayes, *op. cit.* (supra, p. 70), p. 24.

ἐννέα καὶ τεσσαράκοντα καὶ μῆνας δύο: The six Hyksos kings reigned for a total of two hundred and fifty-nine years. However, such a long period for the fifteenth dynasty is incompatible with our more exact information about Egyptian chronology; see G. Farina, *Il papiro dei re* (= *The Turin Papyrus*), Rome 1938, p. 56; see also W.F. Albright, *BASOR*, 99 (1945), p. 17.

ποθοῦντες ἀεὶ καὶ μᾶλλον τῆς Αἰγύπτου ἐξᾶραι τὴν ῥίζαν: Again the hostility of the Hyksos is emphasized, in even stronger terms than before. On the Egyptian tradition on the Persian rule and its atrocities, see J. Schwartz, *BIFAO*, XLVIII (1949), pp. 65 ff.

82 *Ὑκσώς, τοῦτο δέ ἐστιν βασιλεῖς ποιμένες*: Cf. Gardiner, *op. cit.* (supra, p. 70), p. 156, according to whom "the word Hyksos undoubtedly derives from the expression hikkhase 'chieftain of a foreign hill-country' ", which from the Middle Kingdom onwards was used to designate Bedouin sheikhs. Gardiner adds that the term refers to the rulers only and not to the entire race. Hayes (*op. cit.*, pp. 15 f.)

explains Hikau-khoswet as princes of the desert uplands or rulers of foreign countries. The term had already been applied before to both Nubian chieftains and the Bedouin princes of Syria and Palestine.

καθ'ἱεϱὰν γλῶσσαν... κατὰ τὴν κοινὴν διάλεκτον: This explanation, which implies that the one word is composed of both a hieratic and a demotic component, is, in itself, open to suspicion.

τινὲς δὲ λέγουσιν αὐτοὺς Ἄϱαβας εἶναι: This statement does not seem to derive from Manetho, but constitutes an addition by Josephus, as evinced by the fact that ἐν δ'ἄλλῳ ἀντιγϱάφῳ οὐ βασιλεῖς σημαίνεσθαι..., which undoubtedly is not by Manetho, is dependent on τινὲς δὲ λέγουσιν; see Gutschmid, IV, p. 431. Gutschmid also points out that Africanus and Eusebius, as well as the "Scholia Platonica" to Timaeus, give as a heading for the Hyksos dynasty: Φοίνικες ξένοι βασιλεῖς. He suggests, therefore, that Manetho held them to be Canaanites. Gutschmid's argument, however, loses force if we presume that Φοίνικες is only an addition to the text of Manetho; cf. Collomp, *op. cit.* (supra, p. 71), p. 79.

Perhaps the theory that identifies the Hyksos with the Arabs is echoed in a papyrus dating from the Roman period, where ἄμμος Ὑκσιωτική is found listed among Arab exports; see U. Wilcken, *Archiv für Papyrusforschung*, III, pp. 188 ff.

83 ἐν δ'ἄλλῳ ἀντιγϱάφῳ: If we take this sentence at face value, it means that Josephus, or his source, consulted another copy of Manetho, one which included the alternative explanation of Hyksos. Although there is no reason why Josephus should not have done this, a suspicion arises in view of the subsequent reference (§91) to the same explanation's occurrence: ἐν ἄλλῃ δέ τινι βίβλῳ τῶν Αἰγυπτιακῶν. As ἀντίγϱαφον can by no means be equated with βίβλος, and in view of the proximity of two other marginal notes (in § 92 and § 98), both Niese and Thackeray athetized the passage. Reinach, on the other hand, maintains that it should not be considered a marginal annotation of the archetype of the Laurentianus, since it appears in Eusebius; see Reinach: (Budé), p. 17, n. 2. Ed. Meyer has suggested that Josephus, who did not use Manetho directly but only through some intermediary source, misunderstood that source, presumably confusing ἀντίγϱαφον with βίβλος; see Ed. Meyer, *Chronologie*, p. 72. Cf. the discussion by Laqueur, *op. cit.* (supra, p. 65), pp. 1067 ff.

84 τούτους τοὺς προκατωνομασμένους βασιλέας... κρατῆσαι τῆς Αἰγύπτου φησὶν ἔτη πϱὸς τοῖς πεντακοσίοις ἕνδεκα: The following passage constitutes a free summary from Manetho, and not a verbal quotation. This summary, which begins with φησὶν, continues in indirect speech until § 90. It includes the story of the Egyptian uprising against the Hyksos; the capture of their last stronghold in the country, Avaris; their arrival at Syria; and the building of a large city named Jerusalem in Judaea.

85 τῶν ἐκ τῆς Θηβαΐδος καὶ τῆς ἄλλης Αἰγύπτου βασιλέων γενέσθαι φησὶν ἐπὶ τοὺς ποιμένας ἐπανάστασιν...: The initial phases of the Egyptian uprising against the Hyksos are illustrated by *P. Sallier*, I, in a tale dating from the Ramesside age, which describes a clash between Sekenenrè, the Egyptian ruler of Thebes, and one of the Hyksos rulers; see the Egyptian text in: A.H. Gardiner, *Late Egyptian Stories*, Brussels 1932, pp. 85 ff.; for an English translation, see B. Gunn & A. H. Gardiner, *JEA*, V (1918), pp. 40 ff. The struggle was continued by Sekenenre's brother and successor, Kamose, whose military operations against the Hyksos king Aweserre

Manetho

Apopi are mentioned on a stela unearthed at Karnak in 1954; see *Annales du Service*, LIII (1956), pp. 195 ff.

86 Μισφραγμούθωσις: Misphragmuthosis plays a part here that is roughly comparable with that played by Kamose in the Egyptian sources. It seems, however, that the name Μισφραγμούθωσις makes its appearance here as a result of some confusion. The same name reappears later in Manetho's list as that of the fifth king in the line of successors to the king who expelled the Hyksos (§ 95). There he is succeeded by King Thmosis, as here he is succeeded by Thumosis.

Αὔαριν ὄνομα τῷ τόπῳ: Avaris is referred to here as if it had not been mentioned before (cf. § 78). Also, the statement about its walls is repeated, though the reason given here for enclosing the place with a strong wall, namely, that it was to serve as a place of security for safeguarding possessions and spoils, differs slightly from that suggested before, to wit, that it could also serve as a bulwark against the Assyrians.

88 υἱὸν Θούμμωσιν ἐπιχειρῆσαι μὲν αὐτοὺς διὰ πολιορκίας ἑλεῖν... : The real conqueror of the Hyksos was not Tuthmosis, but the founder of the eighteenth dynasty, Ahmose I, in Greek Amosis, under which name he appears in Manetho's list cited in Africanus; see Ptolemy of Mendes (No. 157); *Apion* (No. 163). In the list in *Contra Apionem*, I, 94, the name was changed, as it seems, under the influence of our passage. We learn about the fall of Avaris in the time of Ahmose from an inscription engraved on the wall of a tomb at el-Kab, which belonged to an Egyptian officer, Ahmose son of Abana; cf. *JEA*, V (1918), pp. 48 ff. For the chronology of the Pharaonic Eighteenth Dynasty, see D.B. Redford, *JNES*, XXV (1966), pp. 113 ff.

ὀκτὼ καὶ τεσσαράκοντα μυριάσι στρατοῦ προσεδρεύσαντα τοῖς τείχεσιν: This is double the number of the besieged; cf. above § 78.

89 ἀπὸ τῆς Αἰγύπτου τὴν ἔρημον εἰς Συρίαν διοδοιπορῆσαι; We know from the above-mentioned inscription that the capture of Avaris did not put an end to the Hyksos–Egyptian struggle. The struggle went on in Palestine, where the Egyptian army besieged the Hyksos at Sharuhen for three years (Sharuhen is sometimes identified with Tell el-Farah).

90 φοβουμένους δὲ τὴν Ἀσσυρίων δυναστείαν: The reason given here for the building of Jerusalem is the same as that given above for the building of Avaris.

ἐν τῇ νῦν Ἰουδαίᾳ καλουμένῃ πόλιν οἰκοδομησαμένους... Ἱεροσόλυμα: Manetho speaks only of the founding of Jerusalem by the Hyksos, though he does not expressly identify them with the Jews. That, however, is probably implied by his narrative, if we are to judge by Hecataeus (apud: Diodorus, XL; No. 11), who thinks of Moses and his Hebrew contemporaries as the founders of Jerusalem and wholly ignores the pre-Judaean existence of the town; cf. the introduction. Whether the alleged connection between the Hyksos and the ancestors of the Jews has any historical foundation is another question, and a long-debated one. Though only few will now be inclined to assert that the Hyksos should be identified with the Hebrews, there still remains the plausible hypothesis that the descent of the ancestors of Israel to Egypt was somehow connected with the Hyksos' movement. This theory has chronological probability and is somewhat supported by the occurrence of names formed with the element Jacob — e.g. Yaqob-har — among the Hyksos chiefs; cf. J.H. Breasted, *A History of Egypt*, London 1945, p. 220 ('the Hebrews in Egypt will have been but a part of the Beduin allies of the Hyksos'); R. de Vaux, *RB*, LV (1948), p. 336; W.F. Albright, *From the Stone Age to Christi-*

From Herodotus to Plutarch

anity, Baltimore 1940, p. 184; Leibovitch, *op. cit.* (supra, p. 71), p. 111.

τοσαύταις μυριάσιν ἀνθρώπων ἀρκέσουσαν: Again it is worthwhile comparing Manetho with Hecataeus (apud: Josephus, *Contra Apionem*, I, 197; No. 12), who gives the number of inhabitants in Jerusalem during his time as one hundred and twenty thousand.

91 ἐν ἄλλῃ δέ τινι βίβλῳ: From the fact that Josephus does not state the number of the book of the *Aegyptiaca* referred to by him we may infer either that he did not have the original work of Manetho before him and, therefore, used it only through intermediary sources, or that this particular piece of information, giving the etymology of the name Hyksos,was not found in the copy of Manetho that Josephus generally used.

λέγων ὀρθῶς: Cf. *Ant.*, VII, 103: οὐ διήμαρτε τῆς ἀληθείας (scil. Νικόλαος).

20

Aegyptiaca, apud: Josephus, *Contra Apionem*, I, 93–105 — Niese = F10R = *F. Gr. Hist.*, III, C609, F9 = Reinach (Budé), pp. 19 ff. = Waddell, *op. cit.*, F50

(93) Πάλιν οὖν τὰ τοῦ Μανέθω πῶς ἔχει πρὸς τὴν τῶν χρόνων τάξιν ὑπογράψω. *(94)* φησὶ δὲ οὕτως· «μετὰ τὸ ἐξελθεῖν ἐξ Αἰγύπτου τὸν λαὸν τῶν ποιμένων εἰς Ἱεροσόλυμα ὁ ἐκβαλὼν αὐτοὺς ἐξ Αἰγύπτου βασιλεὺς Τέθμωσις ἐβασίλευσεν μετὰ ταῦτα ἔτη εἰκοσιπέντε καὶ μῆνας
5 τέσσαρας καὶ ἐτελεύτησεν, καὶ παρέλαβεν τὴν ἀρχὴν ὁ αὐτοῦ υἱὸς Χέβρων ἔτη δεκατρία. *(95)* μεθ᾽ ὃν Ἀμένωφις εἴκοσι καὶ μῆνας ἑπτά. τοῦ δὲ ἀδελφὴ Ἀμεσσὴς εἰκοσιὲν καὶ μῆνας ἐννέα. τῆς δὲ Μήφρης δώδεκα καὶ μῆνας ἐννέα. τοῦ δὲ Μηφραμούθωσις εἰκοσιπέντε καὶ μῆνας δέκα. *(96)* τοῦ δὲ Θμῶσις ἐννέα καὶ μῆνας ὀκτώ. τοῦ δ᾽ Ἀμένωφις
10 τριάκοντα καὶ μῆνας δέκα. τοῦ δὲ Ὧρος τριακονταὲξ καὶ μῆνας πέντε. τοῦ δὲ θυγάτηρ Ἀκεγχερὴς δώδεκα καὶ μῆνα ἕνα. τῆς δὲ Ῥάθωτις ἀδελφὸς ἐννέα. *(97)* τοῦ δὲ Ἀκεγχήρης δώδεκα καὶ μῆνας πέντε. τοῦ δὲ Ἀκεγχήρης ἕτερος δώδεκα καὶ μῆνας τρεῖς. τοῦ δὲ Ἅρμαῖς τέσσαρα καὶ μῆνα ἕνα. τοῦ δὲ Ῥαμέσσης ἓν καὶ μῆνας τέσσαρας. τοῦ δὲ Ἁρμέσσης
15 Μιαμοῦν ἑξηκονταὲξ καὶ μῆνας δύο. τοῦ δὲ Ἀμένωφις δεκαεννέα καὶ μῆνας ἕξ. *(98)* τοῦ δὲ Σέθως ὁ καὶ Ῥαμέσσης ἱππικὴν καὶ ναυτικὴν ἔχων δύναμιν τὸν μὲν ἀδελφὸν Ἅρμαῖν ἐπίτροπον τῆς Αἰγύπτου κατέστησεν καὶ πᾶσαν μὲν αὐτῷ τὴν ἄλλην βασιλικὴν περιέθηκεν ἐξουσίαν, μόνον δὲ ἐνετείλατο διάδημα μὴ φορεῖν μηδὲ τὴν βασιλί-

1 Μανέθω Niese μανεθῶνος L   7 Ἀμέσση Theophilus   Amenses Eus. Ἀμενσὶς Africanus ap. Syncellum   16 Σέθως ὁ καὶ Ῥαμέσσης Böckh ex Eus. Arm.   σέθωσις καὶ ῥαμέσσης L   18 κατέστησεν] εὑρέθη ἐν ἑτέρῳ ἀντιγράφῳ οὕτως. μεθ᾽ ὃν σέθωσις καὶ ῥαμέσσης δύο ἀδελφοί· ὁ μὲν ναυτικὴν ἔχων δύναμιν τοὺς κατὰ θάλατταν ἀπαντῶντας καὶ διαχειρωμένους (διαπειρωμένους Naber) ἐπολιόρκει· μετ᾽ οὐ πολὺ δὲ καὶ τὸν ῥαμέσσην ἀνελὼν ἅρμαῖν ἄλλον αὐτοῦ ἀδελφὸν ἐπίτροπον τῆς αἰγύπτου καταστῆσαι in marg. L m. 1

74

20 δα μητέρα τε τῶν τέκνων ἀδικεῖν, ἀπέχεσθαι δὲ καὶ τῶν ἄλλων βασιλικῶν παλλακίδων. *(99)* αὐτὸς δὲ ἐπὶ Κύπρον καὶ Φοινίκην καὶ πάλιν Ἀσσυρίους τε καὶ Μήδους στρατεύσας ἅπαντας τοὺς μὲν δόρατι, τοὺς δὲ ἀμαχητὶ φόβῳ δὲ τῆς πολλῆς δυνάμεως ὑποχειρίους ἔλαβε καὶ μέγα φρονήσας ἐπὶ ταῖς εὐπραγίαις ἔτι καὶ θαρσαλεώτερον ἐπεπορεύετο τὰς
25 πρὸς ἀνατολὰς πόλεις τε καὶ χώρας καταστρεφόμενος. *(100)* χρόνου τε ἱκανοῦ γεγονότος Ἀρμαῒς ὁ καταλειφθεὶς ἐν Αἰγύπτῳ πάντα τἄμπαλιν οἷς ἀδελφὸς παρῄνει μὴ ποιεῖν ἀδεῶς ἔπραττεν· καὶ γὰρ τὴν βασιλίδα βιαίως ἔσχεν καὶ ταῖς ἄλλαις παλλακίσιν ἀφειδῶς διετέλει χρώμενος, πειθόμενός τε ὑπὸ τῶν φίλων διάδημα ἐφόρει καὶ ἀντῆρε τῷ ἀδελφῷ.
30 *(101)* ὁ δὲ τεταγμένος ἐπὶ τῶν ἱερέων τῆς Αἰγύπτου γράψας βιβλίον ἔπεμψε τῷ Σεθώσει δηλῶν αὐτῷ πάντα καὶ ὅτι ἀντῆρεν ὁ ἀδελφὸς αὐτῷ Ἀρμαῒς. παραχρῆμα οὖν ὑπέστρεψεν εἰς Πηλούσιον καὶ ἐκράτησεν τῆς ἰδίας βασιλείας. *(102)* ἡ δὲ χώρα ἐκλήθη ἀπὸ τοῦ αὐτοῦ ὀνόματος Αἴγυπτος· λέγει γάρ, ὅτι μὲν Σέθως ἐκαλεῖτο Αἴγυπτος, Ἀρμαῒς δὲ
35 ὁ ἀδελφὸς αὐτοῦ Δαναός.
(103) Ταῦτα μὲν ὁ Μάνεθως. δῆλον δέ ἐστιν ἐκ τῶν εἰρημένων ἐτῶν τοῦ χρόνου συλλογισθέντος, ὅτι οἱ καλούμενοι ποιμένες ἡμέτεροι δὲ πρόγονοι τρισὶ καὶ ἐνενήκοντα καὶ τριακοσίοις πρόσθεν ἔτεσιν ἐκ τῆς Αἰγύπτου ἀπαλλαγέντες τὴν χώραν ταύτην ἐπῴκησαν ἢ Δαναὸν εἰς
40 Ἄργος ἀφικέσθαι· καίτοι τοῦτον ἀρχαιότατον Ἀργεῖοι νομίζουσι. *(104)* δύο τοίνυν ὁ Μάνεθως ἡμῖν τὰ μέγιστα μεμαρτύρηκεν ἐκ τῶν παρ' Αἰγυπτίοις γραμμάτων, πρῶτον μὲν τὴν ἑτέρωθεν ἄφιξιν εἰς Αἴγυπτον, ἔπειτα δὲ τὴν ἐκεῖθεν ἀπαλλαγὴν οὕτως ἀρχαίαν τοῖς χρόνοις, ὡς ἐγγύς που προτερεῖν αὐτὴν τῶν Ἰλιακῶν ἔτεσι χιλίοις.
45 *(105)* ὑπὲρ ὧν δ' ὁ Μάνεθως οὐκ ἐκ τῶν παρ' Αἰγυπτίοις γραμμάτων, ἀλλ' ὡς αὐτὸς ὡμολόγηκεν ἐκ τῶν ἀδεσπότως μυθολογουμένων προστέθεικεν, ὕστερον ἐξελέγξω κατὰ μέρος ἀποδεικνὺς τὴν ἀπίθανον αὐτοῦ ψευδολογίαν.

25 καταστρεφόμενος Cobet   26 τοὔμπαλιν ed. pr.   27 ἀδελφὸς Gutschmid   ἀδελφὸς L   29 τε Niese   δὲ L   30 ἱερῶν Hudson   31 Σέθῳ Niese / αὐτῷ Niese   αὐτοῦ L   34 λέγει] λόγος vel λέγεται Gutschmid   37 δὲ Eus.   om. L   43 ἀρχαίαν Eus.   ἀρχαῖον L   44 που προτερεῖν Eus.   τοῦ πρότερον L   45 γραμμάτων ed. pr.   litteris Lat.   πραγμάτων L

(93) I shall therefore resume my quotations from Manetho's works in their reference to chronology. (94) His account is as follows: "After the departure of the tribe of Shepherds from Egypt to Jerusalem, Tethmosis, the king who drove them out of Egypt, reigned for 25 years 4 months until his death, when he was succeeded by his son Chebron,

who ruled for 13 years. (95) After him Amenophis reigned for 20 years 7 months; then his sister Amessis for 21 years 9 months; then her son Mephres for 12 years 9 months; then his son Mephramuthosis for 25 years 10 months; (96) then his son Thmosis for 9 years 8 months; then his son Amenophis for 30 years 10 months; then his son Orus for 36 years 5 months; then his daughter Acencheres for 12 years 1 month; then her brother Rathotis for 9 years; (97) then his son Acencheres for 12 years 5 months, his son Acencheres II for 12 years 3 months, his son Harmaïs for 4 years 1 month, his son Ramesses for 1 year 4 months, his son Harmesses Miamun for 66 years 2 months, his son Amenophis for 19 years 6 months, (98) and his son Sethos, also called Ramesses, whose power lay in his cavalry and his fleet. This king appointed his brother Harmaïs viceroy of Egypt, and invested him with all the royal prerogatives, except that he charged him not to wear a diadem, not to wrong the queen, the mother of his children, and to refrain likewise from the royal concubines. (99) He then set out on an expedition against Cyprus and Phoenicia and later against the Assyrians and the Medes; and he subjugated them all, some by the sword, others without a blow and merely by the menace of his mighty host. In the pride of his conquests, he continued his advance with still greater boldness, and subdued the cities and lands of the East. (100) When a considerable time had elapsed, Harmaïs who had been left behind in Egypt, recklessly contravened all his brother's injunctions. He outraged the queen and proceeded to make free with the concubines; then, following the advice of his friends, he began to wear a diadem and rose in revolt against his brother. (101) The warden of the priests of Egypt then wrote a letter which he sent to Sethosis, revealing all the details, including the revolt of his brother Harmaïs. Sethosis forthwith returned to Pelusium and took possession of his kingdom; (102) and the land was named Aegyptus after him. It is said that Sethos was called Aegyptus and his brother Harmaïs, Danaus."

(103) Such is Manetho's account; and, if the time is reckoned according to the years mentioned, it is clear that the so-called Shepherds, our ancestors, quitted Egypt and settled in our land 393 years before the coming of Danaus to Argos. Yet the Argives regard Danaus as belonging to a remote antiquity. (104) Thus Manetho has given us evidence from Egyptian records upon two very important points: first, upon our coming to Egypt from elsewhere; and secondly, upon our departure from Egypt at a date so remote that it preceded the Trojan war by wellnigh a thousand years. (105) As for the additions which Manetho has made, not from the Egyptian records, but, as he has him-

Manetho

self admitted, from anonymous legendary tales, I shall later refute
them in detail, and show the improbability of his lying stories.

(trans. W. G. Waddell, LCL)

93 πάλιν οὖν τὰ τοῦ Μανέθω πῶς ἔχει πρὸς τὴν τῶν χρόνων τάξιν ὑπογράψω:
The list that follows, which includes names of kings of the eighteenth and nineteenth dynasties, is inaccurate; see Ed. Meyer, *Chronologie*, pp. 88 ff.; Gardiner, *op.
cit.* (supra, p. 70), pp. 241 f.

94 Τέθμωσις: Tethmosis stands for Amosis (Ahmose), the founder of the
eighteenth dynasty.

καὶ παρέλαβεν τὴν ἀρχὴν ὁ αὐτοῦ υἱὸς Χέβρων: a son of Ahmose and presumably
his successor, is unknown from other sources, which record that Ahmose was
succeeded by Amenophis I (died *c.* 1528 B. C. E.).

95 τοῦ δὲ ἀδελφὴ Ἀμεσσῆς εἰκοσιὲν καὶ μῆνας ἐννέα: It is noteworthy that the
real successor of Amenophis, namely, Tuthmosis I, is not mentioned in the list.
Amesses may stand for Princess Ahmose, the wife of Tuthmosis; this marriage constituted Tuthmosis' chief title to the throne.

τῆς δὲ Μήφρης δώδεκα καὶ μῆνας ἐννέα: Tuthmosis II is not mentioned at all.
Mephramutosis may be identical with Tuthmosis III. Mephres is probably the
same as the Mespheres referred to by Plinius, *Naturalis Historia*, XXXVI, 64, 69.
Ed. Meyer (*Chronologie*, p. 89) thinks that both Mephres and Mephramutosis are
identical with Tuthmosis III, who will thus be allotted thirty-eight years and seven
months; Tuthmosis III actually reigned for fifty-three years and ten months.

96 τοῦ δὲ Θμῶσις... τοῦ δ᾽Ἀμένωφις... τοῦ δὲ Ὧρος: This part of the list is, in
any case, confused. Ed. Meyer (*loc. cit.*) proposes that the places of Thmosis
(= Tuthmosis IV) and Amenophis II (1436 – 1413 B. C. E.) should be interchanged on the list and that Oros should be identified with Amenophis III (*c.*
1405–1367 B. C. E.). Gardiner, on the other hand, holds the view that Oros is the
same as Haremhab, since the Abydos and Sakkara king-lists, "ignoring Akhenaten
and his three successors as tainted with Atheism, place Haremhab immediately
after Amenophis III, thus agreeing with the Oros of Manetho"; see Gardiner,
op. cit. (supra, p. 70). Gardiner, however, thinks that Haremhab appears a second
time under the name of Harmais (§ 97).

97 τοῦ δὲ Ῥαμέσσης ἓν καὶ μῆνας τέσσαρας: This is Ramesses I (1308 B. C. E.),
the first pharaoh of the nineteenth dynasty. The length of his reign may be accurate
as given here; cf. Gardiner, *op. cit.* (supra, p. 70), p. 248.

Ἁρμέσσης Μιαμοῦν ἑξηκονταὲξ καὶ μῆνας δύο: Here, too, the list that deals with
the nineteenth dynasty is very confused. The span given to the reign of Harmesses
Miamoun is entirely consonant with that of Ramesses II; the reign of Sethos I,
which preceded that of Ramesses II (1290–1224 B. C. E.), is not mentioned at all.
τοῦ δὲ Ἀμένωφις δεκαεννέα καὶ μῆνας ἕξ: It seems that Amenophis stands here
for Merneptah (1224–1214 B. C. E.).

98 τοῦ δὲ Σέθως ὁ καὶ Ῥαμέσσης: Here, again, Ramesses II appears to have
been confused with his father Sethos.

ἱππικὴν καὶ ναυτικὴν ἔχων δύναμιν τὸν μὲν ἀδελφὸν Ἁρμαῖν ἐπίτροπον τῆς
Αἰγύπτου κατέστησεν: On King Sesostris, see Herodotus, II, 107; Diodorus,
I, 57 : 6 f.

102 λέγει γάρ, ὅτι μὲν Σέθως ἐκαλεῖτο Αἴγυπτος, Ἁρμαῖς δὲ ὁ ἀδελφὸς αὐτοῦ

Δαναός: Ed. Meyer plausibly argues that the whole of Manetho's list of kings was adduced by Josephus in order to establish, by synchronism with Greek history, the greater antiquity of the Jews, who were identified with the Hyksos; cf. Ed. Meyer, *Chronologie*, p. 75.

21

Aegyptiaca, apud: Josephus, *Contra Apionem*, I, 228–252 — Niese = F11R = *F. Gr. Hist.*, III, C609, F10 = Reinach (Budé), pp. 43 ff. = Waddell, *op. cit.*, F54

(228) Ὁ γὰρ Μανεθὼς οὗτος ὁ τὴν Αἰγυπτιακὴν ἱστορίαν ἐκ τῶν ἱερῶν γραμμάτων μεθερμηνεύειν ὑπεσχημένος, προειπὼν τοὺς ἡμετέρους προγόνους πολλαῖς μυριάσιν ἐπὶ τὴν Αἴγυπτον ἐλθόντας κρατῆσαι τῶν ἐνοικούντων, εἶτ᾽ αὐτὸς ὁμολογῶν χρόνῳ πάλιν ὕστερον ἐκπεσόντας 5 τὴν νῦν Ἰουδαίαν κατασχεῖν καὶ κτίσαντας Ἱεροσόλυμα τὸν νεὼ κατασκευάσασθαι, μέχρι μὲν τούτων ἠκολούθησε ταῖς ἀναγραφαῖς. *(229)* ἔπειτα δὲ δοὺς ἐξουσίαν αὑτῷ διὰ τοῦ φάναι γράψειν τὰ μυθευόμενα καὶ λεγόμενα περὶ τῶν Ἰουδαίων λόγους ἀπιθάνους παρενέβαλεν, ἀναμῖξαι βουλόμενος ἡμῖν πλῆθος Αἰγυπτίων λεπρῶν καὶ ἐπὶ ἄλλοις ἀρρωστήμασιν, 10 ὥς φησι, φυγεῖν ἐκ τῆς Αἰγύπτου καταγνωσθέντων. *(230)* Ἀμένωφιν γὰρ βασιλέα προσθεὶς ψευδὲς ὄνομα καὶ διὰ τοῦτο χρόνον αὐτοῦ τῆς βασιλείας ὁρίσαι μὴ τολμήσας, καίτοι γε ἐπὶ τῶν ἄλλων βασιλέων ἀκριβῶς τὰ ἔτη προστιθείς, τούτῳ προσάπτει τινὰς μυθολογίας ἐπιλαθόμενος σχεδόν, ὅτι πεντακοσίοις ἔτεσι καὶ δεκαοκτὼ πρότερον ἱστόρηκε γενέσθαι 15 τὴν τῶν ποιμένων ἔξοδον εἰς Ἱεροσόλυμα. *(231)* Τέθμωσις γὰρ ἦν βασιλεὺς ὅτε ἐξῄεσαν, ἀπὸ δὲ τούτου τῶν μεταξὺ βασιλέων κατ᾽ αὐτόν ἐστι τριακόσια ἐνενηκοντατρία ἔτη μέχρι τῶν δύο ἀδελφῶν Σέθω καὶ Ἑρμαίου, ὧν τὸν μὲν Σέθων Αἴγυπτον, τὸν δὲ Ἕρμαιον Δαναὸν μετονομασθῆναί φησιν, ὃν ἐκβαλὼν ὁ Σέθως ἐβασίλευσεν ἔτη νθ᾽ καὶ μετ᾽ αὐτὸν 20 ὁ πρεσβύτερος τῶν υἱῶν αὐτοῦ Ῥάμψης ξς᾽. *(232)* τοσούτοις οὖν πρότερον ἔτεσιν ἀπελθεῖν ἐξ Αἰγύπτου τοὺς πατέρας ἡμῶν ὡμολογηκὼς εἶτα τὸν Ἀμένωφιν εἰσποιήσας ἐμβόλιμον βασιλέα φησὶν τοῦτον ἐπιθυμῆσαι θεῶν γενέσθαι θεατήν, ὥσπερ Ὧρ εἷς τῶν πρὸ αὐτοῦ βεβασιλευκότων, ἀνενεγκεῖν δὲ τὴν ἐπιθυμίαν ὁμωνύμῳ μὲν αὐτῷ 25 Ἀμενώφει πατρὸς δὲ Παάπιος ὄντι, θείας δὲ δοκοῦντι μετεσχηκέναι φύσεως κατά τε σοφίαν καὶ πρόγνωσιν τῶν ἐσομένων. *(233)* εἰπεῖν οὖν αὐτῷ τοῦτον τὸν ὁμώνυμον, ὅτι δυνήσεται θεοὺς ἰδεῖν, εἰ καθαρὰν ἀπό τε λεπρῶν καὶ τῶν ἄλλων μιαρῶν ἀνθρώπων τὴν χώραν ἅπασαν

5 νεῶν Dindorf   11 προθείς Cobet   16 τούτου
τῶν μεταξὺ Niese τούτων μεταξὺ τῶν L   18 Ἕρμαιον ed. pr.   ἑρμᾶν L
20 πρεσβύτατος Niese   23 Ὧρος Hudson   24 αὐτοῦ Naber
25 Παάπιος ed. pr.   πάπιος L

ποιήσειεν. *(234)* ἠσθέντα δὲ τὸν βασιλέα πάντας τοὺς τὰ σώματα
30 λελωβημένους ἐκ τῆς Αἰγύπτου συναγαγεῖν· γενέσθαι δὲ τὸ πλῆθος
μυριάδας ὀκτώ· *(235)* καὶ τούτους εἰς τὰς λιθοτομίας τὰς ἐν τῷ πρὸς
ἀνατολὴν μέρει τοῦ Νείλου ἐμβαλεῖν αὐτόν, ὅπως εἰργάζοιντο καὶ τῶν
ἄλλων Αἰγυπτίων οἱ ἐγκεχωρισμένοι. εἶναι δέ τινας ἐν αὐτοῖς καὶ τῶν
λογίων ἱερέων φησὶ λέπρᾳ συγκεχυμένους. *(236)* τὸν δὲ ᾿Αμένωφιν
35 ἐκεῖνον, τὸν σοφὸν καὶ μαντικὸν ἄνδρα, ὑποδεῖσαι πρὸς αὐτόν τε καὶ
τὸν βασιλέα χόλον τῶν θεῶν, εἰ βιασθέντες ὀφθήσονται. καὶ προσθέμε-
νον εἰπεῖν, ὅτι συμμαχήσουσί τινες τοῖς μιαροῖς καὶ τῆς Αἰγύπτου
κρατήσουσιν ἐπ᾿ ἔτη δεκατρία, μὴ τολμῆσαι μὲν αὐτὸν εἰπεῖν ταῦτα τῷ
βασιλεῖ, γραφὴν δὲ καταλιπόντα περὶ πάντων ἑαυτὸν ἀνελεῖν, ἐν
40 ἀθυμίᾳ δὲ εἶναι τὸν βασιλέα. *(237)* κἄπειτα κατὰ λέξιν οὕτως γέγραφεν·
«τῶν δ᾿ ἐν ταῖς λατομίαις ὡς χρόνος ἱκανὸς διῆλθεν ταλαιπωρούντων,
ἀξιωθεὶς ὁ βασιλεύς, ἵνα [πρὸς] κατάλυσιν αὐτοῖς καὶ σκέπην ἀπομερίσῃ,
τὴν τότε τῶν ποιμένων ἐρημωθεῖσαν πόλιν Αὔαριν συνεχώρησεν· ἔστι
δ᾿ ἡ πόλις κατὰ τὴν θεολογίαν ἄνωθεν Τυφώνιος. *(238)* οἱ δὲ εἰς ταύτην
45 εἰσελθόντες καὶ τὸν τόπον τοῦτον εἰς ἀπόστασιν ἔχοντες ἡγεμόνα
αὐτῶν λεγόμενόν τινα τῶν ῾Ηλιοπολιτῶν ἱερέων ᾿Οσάρσηφον ἐστήσαντο
καὶ τούτῳ πειθαρχήσοντες ἐν πᾶσιν ὡρκωμότησαν. *(239)* ὁ δὲ πρῶτον
μὲν αὐτοῖς νόμον ἔθετο μήτε προσκυνεῖν θεοὺς μήτε τῶν μάλιστα ἐν
Αἰγύπτῳ θεμιστευομένων ἱερῶν ζῴων ἀπέχεσθαι μηδενός, πάντα δὲ
50 θύειν καὶ ἀναλοῦν, συνάπτεσθαι δὲ μηδενὶ πλὴν τῶν συνομωμοσμένων.
(240) τοιαῦτα δὲ νομοθετήσας καὶ πλεῖστα ἄλλα μάλιστα τοῖς Αἰγυπτίοις
ἐθισμοῖς ἐναντιούμενα ἐκέλευσεν πολυχειρίᾳ τὰ τῆς πόλεως ἐπισκευάζειν
τείχη καὶ πρὸς πόλεμον ἑτοίμους γίνεσθαι τὸν πρὸς ᾿Αμένωφιν τὸν
βασιλέα. *(241)* αὐτὸς δὲ προσλαβόμενος μεθ᾿ ἑαυτοῦ καὶ τῶν ἄλλων
55 ἱερέων καὶ συμμεμιαμμένων ἔπεμψε πρέσβεις πρὸς τοὺς ὑπὸ Τεθμώσεως
ἀπελαθέντας ποιμένας εἰς πόλιν τὴν καλουμένην ῾Ιεροσόλυμα, καὶ τὰ
καθ᾿ ἑαυτὸν καὶ τοὺς ἄλλους τοὺς συνατιμασθέντας δηλώσας ἠξίου
συνεπιστρατεύειν ὁμοθυμαδὸν ἐπ᾿ Αἴγυπτον. *(242)* ἐπάξειν μὲν οὖν
αὐτοὺς ἐπηγγείλατο πρῶτον μὲν εἰς Αὔαριν τὴν προγονικὴν αὐτῶν

30 τὸ πλῆθος Niese   τοῦ πλήθους L   33 οἱ ἐγκεχειρισμένοι Hudson   οἱ
ἐκκεχωρισμένοι Bekker   εἶεν κεχωρισμένοι Holwerda   34 συνεσχημένους
(vel συνεισχημένους) Niese   perfusos Lat.   35 ὑποδεῖσαι Dindorf   ὑπο-
δεῖσθαι L   36–37 προθέμενον ed. pr.   προσθεμένων G. Giangrande,
CQ, LVI (1962), p. 114   προορώμενον Reinach   37 εἰπεῖν secl. Reinach
41 δ᾿ ἐν Bekker   δὲ L   42 πρὸς secl. Niese   45 εἰς secl. Niese
ὁρμητήριον εἰς Holwerda   46 ᾿Οσάρσιφον Hudson   47 πειθαρχήσοντες ed.
pr. πειθαρχήσαντες L | ὡρκωμότησαν Bekker   ὁρκωμότησαν L   50 συν-
ομωμσμένων Niese   συνωμοσμένων L   55 συμμεμιασμένων ed. pr.
56 ἀπελαθέντας Dindorf   ἀπελασθέντας L   58 ἀπάξειν Lowth
ἐπανάξειν Cobet

79

60 πατρίδα καὶ τὰ ἐπιτήδεια τοῖς ὄχλοις παρέξειν ἀφθόνως, ὑπερμαχήσεσ-
θαι δὲ ὅτε δέοι καὶ ῥαδίως ὑποχείριον αὐτοῖς τὴν χώραν ποιήσειν.
(243) οἱ δὲ ὑπερχαρεῖς γενόμενοι πάντες προθύμως εἰς κ΄ μυριάδας ἀνδρῶν
συνεξώρμησαν καὶ μετ᾽ οὐ πολὺ ἧκον εἰς Αὔαριν. Ἀμένωφις δ᾽ ὁ τῶν
Αἰγυπτίων βασιλεὺς ὡς ἐπύθετο τὰ κατὰ τὴν ἐκείνων ἔφοδον, οὐ
65 μετρίως συνεχύθη τῆς παρὰ Ἀμενώφεως τοῦ Παάπιος μνησθεὶς
προδηλώσεως. (244) καὶ πρῶτον συναγαγὼν πλῆθος Αἰγυπτίων καὶ
βουλευσάμενος μετὰ τῶν ἐν τούτοις ἡγεμόνων τά τε ἱερὰ ζῷα τὰ
[πρῶτα] μάλιστα ἐν τοῖς ἱεροῖς τιμώμενα ὡς ἑαυτὸν μετεπέμψατο καὶ
τοῖς κατὰ μέρος ἱερεῦσι παρήγγελλεν ὡς ἀσφαλέστατα τῶν θεῶν
70 συγκρύψαι τὰ ξόανα. (245) τὸν δὲ υἱὸν Σέθω τὸν καὶ Ῥαμεσσῆ ἀπὸ
Ῥαψηοῦς τοῦ πατρὸς ὠνομασμένον πενταέτη ὄντα ἐξέθετο πρὸς τὸν
ἑαυτοῦ φίλον. αὐτὸς δὲ διαβὰς ⟨σὺν⟩ τοῖς ἄλλοις Αἰγυπτίοις οὖσιν εἰς
τριάκοντα μυριάδας ἀνδρῶν μαχιμωτάτων καὶ τοῖς πολεμίοις ἀπαντήσας
οὐ συνέβαλεν, (246) ἀλλὰ μέλλειν θεομαχεῖν νομίσας παλινδρομήσας
75 ἧκεν εἰς Μέμφιν ἀναλαβών τε τόν τε Ἆπιν καὶ τὰ ἄλλα τὰ ἐκεῖσε
μεταπεμφθέντα ἱερὰ ζῷα εὐθὺς εἰς Αἰθιοπίαν σὺν ἅπαντι τῷ στόλῳ καὶ
πλήθει τῶν Αἰγυπτίων ἀνήχθη· χάριτι γὰρ ἦν αὐτῷ ὑποχείριος ὁ τῶν
Αἰθιόπων βασιλεύς. (247) ὃς ὑποδεξάμενος καὶ τοὺς ὄχλους πάντας
ὑπολαβὼν οἷς ἔσχεν ἡ χώρα τῶν πρὸς ἀνθρωπίνην τροφὴν ἐπιτηδείων,
80 καὶ πόλεις καὶ κώμας ⟨παρασχὼν⟩ πρὸς τὴν τῶν πεπρωμένων
τρισκαίδεκα ἐτῶν ἀπὸ τῆς ἀρχῆς αὐτοῦ εἰς τὴν ἔκπτωσιν αὐτάρκεις,
οὐχ ἧττον δὲ καὶ στρατόπεδον Αἰθιοπικὸν πρὸς φυλακὴν ἐπέταξε τοῖς
παρ᾽ Ἀμενώφεως τοῦ βασιλέως ἐπὶ τῶν ὁρίων τῆς Αἰγύπτου. (248) καὶ
τὰ μὲν κατὰ τὴν Αἰθιοπίαν τοιαῦτα. οἱ δὲ Σολυμῖται κατελθόντες
85 σὺν τοῖς μιαροῖς τῶν Αἰγυπτίων οὕτως ἀνοσίως καὶ τοῖς ἀνθρώποις
προσηνέχθησαν, ὥστε τὴν τῶν προειρημένων κράτησιν χρυσὸν φαίνεσθαι τοῖς τότε τὰ τούτων ἀσεβήματα θεωμένοις· (249) καὶ γὰρ οὐ
μόνον πόλεις καὶ κώμας ἐνέπρησαν οὐδὲ ἱεροσυλοῦντες οὐδὲ λυμαινόμενοι
ξόανα θεῶν ἠρκοῦντο, ἀλλὰ καὶ τοῖς αὐτοῖς ὀπτανίοις τῶν σεβα-
90 στευομένων ἱερῶν ζῴων χρώμενοι διετέλουν καὶ θύτας καὶ σφαγεῖς
τούτων ἱερεῖς καὶ προφήτας ἠνάγκαζον γίνεσθαι καὶ γυμνοὺς ἐξέβαλλον.
(250) λέγεται δέ, ὅτι τὴν πολιτείαν καὶ τοὺς νόμους αὐτοῖς καταβαλόμενος
ἱερεὺς τὸ γένος Ἡλιοπολίτης ὄνομα Ὀσαρσὶφ ἀπὸ τοῦ ἐν Ἡλιουπόλει

66 πρῶτον Niese   πρότερον L   68 πρῶτα secl. Bekker / ἑαυτὸν Cobet
γε αὐτὸν L   69 παρήγγειλεν ed. pr.   70 Σέθων ... Ῥαμέσσην ed. pr.
71 Ῥάμψεως Hudson   72 ⟨σὺν⟩ Niese   73 καὶ] καίτοι Holwerda /
ἀπαντήσας Cobet   ἀπαντήσασιν L   77 ⟨τῷ⟩ πλήθει Niese   78 ὃς
Niese   ὅθεν L / ὑποδεξάμενος ⟨αὐτὸν⟩ Reinach   80 ⟨παρασχὼν⟩ Hudson   ⟨παρέσχε⟩ Reinach   81 εἰς τὴν om. ed. pr.   89 αὐτοῖς]
ἀδύτοις Bekker   92 ⟨ὁ⟩ τὴν πολιτείαν Cobet   93 ὄνομα ⟨δὲ⟩ Reinach

Manetho

θεοῦ Ὀσίρεως, ὡς μετέβη εἰς τοῦτο τὸ γένος, μετετέθη τοὔνομα καὶ
95 προσηγορεύθη Μωυσῆς.»
(251) ῞Α μὲν οὖν Αἰγύπτιοι φέρουσι περὶ τῶν Ἰουδαίων ταῦτ' ἐστὶ καὶ
ἕτερα πλείονα, ἃ παρίημι συντομίας ἕνεκα. λέγει δὲ ὁ Μανεθὼς πάλιν,
ὅτι μετὰ ταῦτα ἐπῆλθεν ὁ Ἀμένωφις ἀπὸ Αἰθιοπίας μετὰ μεγάλης
δυνάμεως καὶ ὁ υἱὸς αὐτοῦ ῾Ράμψης καὶ αὐτὸς ἔχων δύναμιν, καὶ
100 συμβαλόντες οἱ δύο τοῖς ποιμέσι καὶ τοῖς μιαροῖς ἐνίκησαν αὐτοὺς
καὶ πολλοὺς ἀποκτείναντες ἐδίωξαν αὐτοὺς ἄχρι τῶν ὁρίων τῆς Συρίας.
(252) ταῦτα μὲν καὶ τὰ τοιαῦτα Μανεθὼς συνέγραψεν.

97 ἃ παρίημι ed. pr.   παρ' ἡμῖν L

(228) I refer to Manetho. This writer, who had undertaken to translate
the history of Egypt from the sacred books, began by stating that our
ancestors came against Egypt with many tens of thousands and gained
the mastery over the inhabitants; and then he himself admitted that
at a later date again they were driven out of the country, occupied
what is now Judaea, founded Jerusalem, and built the temple.
Up to this point he followed the chronicles: (229) thereafter, by
offering to record the legends and current talk about the Jews,
he took the liberty of interpolating improbable tales in his desire to
confuse with us a crowd of Egyptians, who for leprosy and other maladies had been condemned, he says, to banishment from Egypt.
(230) After citing a king Amenophis, a fictitious person—for which
reason he did not venture to define the length of his reign, although
in the case of the other kings he adds their years precisely—Manetho
attaches to him certain legends, having doubtless forgotten that according to his own chronicle the exodus of the Shepherds to Jerusalem
took place 518 years earlier. (231) For Tethmosis was king when they
set out; and, according to Manetho, the intervening reigns thereafter
occupied 393 years down to the two brothers Sethos and Hermaeus,
the former of whom, he says, took the new name of Aegyptus, the
latter that of Danaus. Sethos drove out Hermaeus and reigned for
59 years; then Rampses, the elder of his sons, for 66 years. (232)
Thus, after admitting that so many years had elapsed since our
forefathers left Egypt, Manetho now interpolates this intruding Amenophis. This king, he states, conceived a desire to behold the gods, as
Or, one of his predecessors on the throne, had done; and he communi-
cated his desire to his namesake Amenophis, Paapis' son, who, in
virtue of his wisdom and knowledge of the future, was reputed to be
a partaker in the divine nature. (233) This namesake, then, replied that
he would be able to see the gods if he cleansed the whole land of

81

lepers and other polluted persons. (234) The king was delighted, and assembled all those in Egypt whose bodies were wasted by disease: they numbered 80,000 persons. (235) These he cast into the stone-quarries to the east of the Nile, there to work segregated from the rest of the Egyptians. Among them, Manetho adds, there were some of the learned priests, who had been attacked by leprosy. (236) Then this wise seer Amenophis was filled with dread of divine wrath against himself and the king if the outrage done to these persons should be discovered; and he added a prediction that certain allies would join the polluted people and would take possession of Egypt for 13 years. Not venturing to make this prophecy himself to the king, he left a full account of it in writing, and then took his own life. The king was filled with despondency. (237) Then Manetho continues as follows (I quote his account *verbatim*): "When the men in the stone-quarries had suffered hardships for a considerable time, they begged the king to assign to them as a dwelling-place and a refuge the deserted city of the Shepherds, Auaris, and he consented. According to religious tradition this city was from earliest times dedicated to Typhon. (238) Occupying this city and using the region as a base for revolt, they appointed as their leader one of the priests of Heliopolis called Osarseph, and took an oath of obedience to him in everything. (239) First of all, he made it a law that they should neither worship the gods nor refrain from any of the animals prescribed as especially sacred in Egypt, but should sacrifice and consume all alike, and that they should have intercourse with none save those of their own confederacy. (240) After framing a great number of laws like these, completely opposed to Egyptian custom, he ordered them with their multitude of hands, to repair the walls of the city and make ready for war against King Amenophis. (241) Then, acting in concert with certain other priests and polluted persons like himself, he sent an embassy to the Shepherds who had been expelled by Tethmosis, in the city called Jerusalem; and, setting forth the circumstances of himself and his companions in distress, he begged them to unite wholeheartedly in an attack upon Egypt. (242) He offered to conduct them first to their ancestral home at Auaris, to provide their hosts with lavish supplies, to fight on their behalf whenever need arose, and to bring Egypt without difficulty under their sway. (243) Overjoyed at the proposal, all the Shepherds, to the number of 200,000, eagerly set out, and before long arrived at Auaris. When Amenophis, king of Egypt, learned of their invasion, he was sorely troubled, for he recalled the prediction of Amenophis, son of Paapis. (244) First, he gathered a multitude of

Egyptians; and having taken counsel with the leading men among them, he summoned to his presence the sacred animals, which were held in greatest reverence in the temples, and gave instructions to each group of priests to conceal the images of the gods as securely as possible. (245) As for his five-year-old son Sethos, also called Ramesses after his grandfather Rapses, he sent him safely away to his friend. He then crossed the Nile with as many as 300,000 of the bravest warriors of Egypt, and met the enemy. But, instead of joining battle, (246) he decided that he must not fight against the gods, and made a hasty retreat to Memphis. There he took into his charge Apis and the other sacred animals which he had summoned to that place; and forthwith he set off for Ethiopia with his whole army and the host of Egyptians. The Ethiopian king, who was under obligation to him and at his service (247) welcomed him, maintained the whole multitude with such products of the country as were fit for human consumption, assigned to them cities and villages sufficient for the destined period of 13 years' banishment from his realm, and especially stationed an Ethiopian army on the frontiers of Egypt to guard King Amenophis and his followers. (248) Such was the situation in Ethiopia. Meanwhile, the Solymites made a descent along with the polluted Egyptians, and treated the people so impiously and savagely that the domination of the Shepherds seemed like a golden age to those who witnessed the present enormities. (249) For not only did they set towns and villages on fire, pillaging the temples and mutilating images of the gods without restraint, but they also made a practice of using the sanctuaries as kitchens to roast the sacred animals which the people worshipped; and they would compel the priests and prophets to sacrifice and butcher the beasts, afterwards casting the men forth naked. (250) It is said that the priest who framed their constitution and their laws was a native of Heliopolis, named Osarseph after the god Osiris, worshipped at Heliopolis; but when he joined this people, he changed his name and was called Moses."

(251) Such, then, are the Egyptian stories about the Jews, together with many other tales which I pass by for brevity's sake. Manetho adds, however, that, at a later date, Amenophis advanced from Ethiopia with a large army, his son Rampses also leading a force, and that the two together joined battle with the Shepherds and their polluted allies, and defeated them, killing many and pursuing the others to the frontiers of Syria. (252) This then, with other tales of a like nature, is Manetho's account.

(trans. W.G. Waddell, *LCL*)

From Herodotus to Plutarch

228 καὶ κτίσαντας Ἱεροσόλυμα τὸν νεὼ κατασκευάσασθαι: There is no allusion to the building of the Temple in Manetho's narrative of the expulsion of the Hyksos, as related by Josephus. It does appear, however, in the tale of Moses' achievement by Hecataeus, apud: Diodorus, XL (No. 11).

μέχρι μὲν τούτων ἠκολούθησε ταῖς ἀναγραφαῖς...: As Ed. Meyer remarks, this assertion of Josephus is true only if we take the ἱεραὶ ἀναγραφαί, to mean "schriftliche ägyptische Vorlagen", but not in the authentic meaning, ἀναγραφαί, which may stand in marked contrast to the following narrative concerning Osarsiph; see Ed. Meyer, Chronologie, p. 79. According to Ed. Meyer, this narrative contains a historic account that is no less true than those about the Hyksos, about Sethos and Harmais, or, for that matter, than the story about King Bocchoris and the Prophecy of the Lamb, known from a demotic papyrus; cf. H. Gressmann, Altorientalische Texte zum Alten Testament, Berlin–Leipzig 1926, pp. 48 f.

230 Ἀμένωφιν γὰρ βασιλέα προσθεὶς ψευδὲς ὄνομα: Manetho obtained this name from his Egyptian source. It also occurs as the name of the Pharaoh of the Time of Troubles in the Oracle of the Potter; see U. Wilcken, Hermes, XL (1905), p. 549, Col. II, ll. 17, 22. The Amenophis mentioned here by Manetho, as well as the Amenophis of the Oracle of the Potter, remains a problem. Schwartz rightly notes that the occurrence in this context of a pharaoh named Amenophis is not of much historical importance, since both he and Bocchoris serve as figures of legendary kings "parfaitement interchangeables"; see J. Schwartz, BIFAO, XLIX (1950), p. 80. Manetho had already mentioned two kings named Amenophis (§ 95 ff.). Meyer identifies the present — i.e. the third — Amenophis with Merneptah, the son of Ramesses II, during whose reign Egypt underwent a Syrian invasion; his personality, however, was confused with that of Amenophis IV (Akhenaten); see Ed. Meyer, Geschichte des Altertums, Vol. II, Part 1², Stuttgart–Berlin 1928, p. 421; cf. also Helck, op. cit. (supra, p. 65), pp. 42 f.

Chaeremon, apud: Josephus, Contra Apionem, I, 288 ff. (No. 178), also places the expulsion of the defiled people in the reign of Amenophis; cf. the introduction.

ἐπιλαθόμενος σχεδόν, ὅτι πεντακοσίοις ἔτεσι καὶ δεκαοκτὼ πρότερον ἱστόρηκε γενέσθαι τὴν τῶν ποιμένων ἔξοδον εἰς Ἱεροσόλυμα: As it stands, the argumentation of Josephus is hardly convincing, since it is clear that Manetho distinguished between the departure of the Hyksos, which culminated in the foundation of Jerusalem, and the much later events, in which the lepers and Osarsiph took part. Perhaps what Josephus really meant was something like the following: since Manetho's former narrative implies that the Hebrews founded Jerusalem, it cannot be true that the Jewish legislator (Osarsiph = Moses), the formative years of the Jewish constitution and the emergence of the religious laws should have occurred at a much later time.

232 τοῦτον ἐπιθυμῆσαι θεῶν γενέσθαι θεατήν: Cf. Herodotus, II 42 : 3.

ὥσπερ Ὧρ εἷς τῶν πρὸ αὐτοῦ βεβασιλευκότων: On this pharaoh, see Contra Apionem, I, 96 (No. 20), and the commentary ad loc.

Ἀμενώφει, πατρὸς δὲ Παάπιος ὄντι: This is Amenhotpe, the son of Hapu, one of the important persons in the reign of Amenophis III; he was even deified; see Waddell, op. cit. (supra, p. 65), p. 122, n. 1; Gardiner, op. cit. (supra, p. 70), pp. 209 ff.; J. Schwartz, BIFAO, XLIX (1950), p. 80 n. 2. In Chaeremon (No. 178) a similar part is played by Phritibautes, the hiero-grammateus.

233 ὅτι δυνήσεται θεοὺς ἰδεῖν, εἰ καθαρὰν ἀπό τε λεπρῶν καὶ τῶν ἄλλων μιαρῶν ἀνθρώπων τὴν χώραν ἅπασαν ποιήσειεν: For a comparative table of motifs occurring

in the narrative of Manetho and in other Graeco-Latin writers, cf. Weill, *op. cit.* (supra, p. 65), p. 109. For interesting remarks bearing upon the localities of the events and upon their identification in literary tradition, cf. Schwartz, *BIFAO*, XLIX, pp. 77 f. Hecataeus (No. 11) does not connect the purgation of Egypt from elements unwelcome to the gods with the wish of the king to see the gods. He stresses only the pestilence that overwhelmed the country. According to Hecataeus, the persons concerned were not lepers, but foreigners, whose presence caused the neglect of the national cults. The motif of the expulsion of the lepers occurs, however, in Diodorus, XXXIV–XXXV, 1 : 2 (No. 63), where it is καθαρμοῦ χάριν, and in Pompeius Trogus, apud: Iustinus, XXXVI, 2 : 12 (No. 137). Neither one, however, refers to the desire of the king for a vision of the gods; nor does Chaeremon, according to whom the actions of Amenophis were instigated by the appearance of Isis in a dream. Isis reproached the king for the destruction of her temple (No. 178). The version of Lysimachus (apud: Josephus, *Contra Apionem*, I, 304–311; No. 158), who, contrary to Manetho and Chaeremon, dates the events to the time of Bocchoris, connects the leprosy of the Jews with a dearth that ensued throughout Egypt. Tacitus (*Historiae*, V, 3; No. 281) is mainly dependent on Lysimachus' version; cf. commentary *ad loc*. In both of them the oracle of Ammon is consulted by King Bocchoris.

234 γενέσθαι δὲ τὸ πλῆθος μυριάδας ὀκτώ: Lysimachus (No. 160) and Apion (No 165) give the number of those expelled from Egypt as one hundred and ten thousand; Chaeremon (No. 178) states that the king collected and banished two hundred and fifty thousand afflicted persons.

235 καὶ τούτους εἰς τὰς λιθοτομίας... ἐμβαλεῖν...: This story on maimed people who were sent to work in the stone-quarries is not found outside Manetho. Hecataeus, Diodorus, Pompeius Trogus, Chaeremon and Tacitus speak plainly of an expulsion from Egypt, and Lysimachus of sending them to desert places.

εἶναι δέ... καὶ τῶν λογίων ἱερέων: Cf. the *New Phrynichus*, ed. W.G. Rutherford, London 1881, p. 284: λόγιος... ἐπὶ τοῦ τὰ ἐν ἑκάστῳ ἔθνει ἐπιχώρια ἐξηγουμένου ἐμπείρως. See also Plutarchus, *Sulla*, 7: οἱ λογιώτατοι Τυρρηνῶν; Arrianus, *Anabasis*, VII, 16 : 5; Herodotus, II, 3 : 1: οἱ γὰρ Ἡλιοπολῖται λέγονται Αἰγυπτίων εἶναι λογιώτατοι; cf. E. Orth, *Logios*, Leipzig 1926.

238 ἡγεμόνα αὐτῶν λεγόμενόν τινα τῶν Ἡλιοπολιτῶν ἱερέων Ὀσάρσηφον ἐστήσαντο: This is the only place in ancient literature where the Jewish legislator is called by this name. In Strabo, *Geographica*, XVI, 2 : 35, p. 760 (No. 115), Moses is also stated to have been an Egyptian priest, and in Chaeremon, apud: Josephus, *Contra Apionem*, I, 290 (No. 178), both he and Joseph are designated ἱερογραμματεῖς. The Heliopolitan origin of Moses is also emphasized in Apion, apud: Josephus, *Contra Apionem*, II, 10 (No. 164). It has been suggested that the name Osarseph is in fact an Egyptian form of Joseph, in which the letters Io were taken for the name of the Jewish God and superseded by Osiris; see, e.g., Reinach (Budé), p. 45, n. 1. In Chaeremon (No. 178) the name Tisithen stands for Moses; cf. Gager, p. 115 n. 5.

239 μήτε τῶν μάλιστα ἐν Αἰγύπτῳ θεμιστευομένων ἱερῶν ζῴων ἀπέχεσθαι μηδενός: Cf. Tacitus, *Historiae*, V, 4 (No. 281).

συνάπτεσθαι δὲ μηδενὶ πλὴν τῶν συνομωμοσμένων: For the motif of *coniuratio* in ancient literature, in which the formula συνάπτεσθαι... μηδενὶ πλὴν τῶν συνομωμοσμένων constitutes a standing τόπος, and for the history of the Jewish *coniuratio*, see E. Bickermann, *MGWJ*, LXXI (1927) pp. 173 ff.; the commentary to Apion (No. 171).

243 οἱ δὲ ὑπερχαρεῖς γενόμενοι πάντες προθύμως... συνεξώρμησαν: The fertile land of Egypt always had a strong attraction for invaders; cf. Gen. xiii : 10, where the Garden of God is equated with the Land of Egypt.

246 ἀλλὰ μέλλειν θεομαχεῖν νομίσας: On the concept of θεομαχεῖν, see Euripides, *Bacchae*, 45, 325, 1255 (cf. the second edition of the commentary by E.R. Dodds, Oxford 1960, p. 68); Diodorus, XIV, 69 : 2; II Macc. vii : 19; Acts v : 39; Epictetus, III, 24 : 24. See, in general, J.C. Kamerbeek, *Mnemosyne*, Ser. 4, Vol. I, 1948, pp. 271 ff.

248 χρυσὸν φαίνεσθαι: Cf. Euripides, *Troiades*, 432; Conon, 13, apud: Photius, 186, p. 133a; Plutarchus, *Sertorius*, 5.

250 λέγεται δέ, ὅτι... Ὀσαρσίφ... μετετέθη τοὔνομα καὶ προσηγορεύθη Μωυσῆς: The way in which Manetho adduces the identification of Osarsiph with Moses (by λέγεται) implies that it was an addition to the main narrative, after it had already been traditionally fixed. This additional material, however, seems to have coloured the main narrative by Manetho, since the identification of Osarsiph with Moses implies the identification of the defiled people with the Jews.

XI. XENOPHILUS

Third century B.C.E.

Xenophilus (this emendation for Zenophilus seems plausible) remains almost unknown to us. He seems to be identical with Xenophilus, the historian of Lydia,[1] about whose personality and time we know next to nothing.
In any case, the following passage cannot be dated after c. 240 B. C. E., since it reached Antigonus of Carystus through Callimachus, who died c. 240 B. C. E.[2] Xenophilus is by no means the first Greek writer to mention the Dead Sea; cf. Aristotle, Meteorologica, II, p. 359a (No. 3) and Hieronymus (No. 10).

---

1 See *FHG*, IV, p. 530; Susemihl, I, p. 617. Cf. *F. Gr. Hist.*, III, C 767, F 1: Ξενό-
φιλος ὁ τὰς Λυδικὰς ἱστορίας γράψας. See also H. Herter, PW, Ser. 2, IX,
pp. 1566 f.
2 For Antigonus the paradoxographer, cf. U. v. Wilamowitz-Moellendorff,
Antigonos von Karystos, Berlin 1881, pp. 16 ff.

22

apud: Antigonus Carystius, *Historiarum Mirabilium Collectio*, 151, ed. A. Giannini, *Paradoxographorum Graecorum Reliquiae*, Milano 1965, p. 96 = *Callimachus*, ed. R. Pfeiffer, I, Oxford 1949, F407 (XXIII), p. 334

Ξενόφιλον δὲ ἐν μὲν τῇ πλησίον Ἰόππης οὐ μόνον ἐπινήχεσθαι πᾶν βάρος, ἀλλὰ καὶ παρὰ τρίτον ἔτος φέρειν ὑγρὰν ἄσφαλτον· ὅταν δὲ γίγνηται τοῦτο, παρὰ τοῖς ἐντὸς τριάκοντα σταδίων οἰκοῦσιν κατιοῦσθαι χαλκώματα.

1 Ξενόφιλον edd.   ζηνόφιλον P   Ζηνόθεμιν Oehler / Ἰόππης edd.
ἰόππῃ P   Ἰόππης <λίμνη> Keller / ἐπινήχεσθαι Meursius   ἐπιδέχεσθαι P
3 κατιοῦσθαι Casaubonus   μειοῦσθαι P   ἰοῦσθαι Meursius Keller

Xenophilus says that in the lake near Joppe not only every weight floats, but every third year it brings forth wet asphalt; when this happens, vessels of copper among the people living in a circumference of thirty stades become tarnished.

Ξενόφιλον δὲ...: From the 129th chapter onward, Antigonus uses Callimachus (Πεποίηται δέ τινα καὶ Κυρηναῖος Καλλίμαχος ἐκλογὴν τῶν παραδόξων ἧς ἀναγράφομεν ὅσα ποτὲ ἡμῖν ἐφαίνετο εἶναι ἀκοῆς ἄξια). On the paradoxographical work of Callimachus, which was geographically arranged, see Herter, PW, Suppl. V (1931), p. 403. On the use of Callimachus by Antigonus of Carystus, see Wilamowitz, *op. cit.* (supra, p. 87, n. 2), pp. 20 f.

ἐν μὲν τῇ πλησίον Ἰόππης...: Xenophilus, like Aristotle, *Meteorologica* (No. 3), does not call the lake by its name. The vicinity of the lake to Jaffa reappears in Vitruvius, VIII, 3 : 8 (No. 140). Antigonus began his discussion of the lakes in the previous paragraph.

οὐ μόνον ἐπινήχεσθαι πᾶν βάρος: Cf. Aristotle, *loc. cit.*

παρὰ τρίτον ἔτος...: In Diodorus, II, 48 (No. 59), we read that it happens annually, while Strabo, *Geographica*, XVI, 2 : 42, p. 763 (No. 115), says: αὕτη δὲ ἀναφυσᾶται κατὰ καιροὺς ἀτάκτους ἐκ μέσου τοῦ βάθους.

κατιοῦσθαι χαλκώματα: Cf. Diodorus (No. 59): καὶ πᾶς ὁ περὶ τὸν τόπον ἄργυρός τε καὶ χρυσὸς καὶ χαλκὸς ἀποβάλλει τὴν ἰδιότητα τοῦ χρώματος. See also Strabo, *Geographica* (No. 115): συναναφέρεται δὲ καὶ ἄσβολος πολλή, καπνώδης μέν... ὑφ᾽ ἧς κατιοῦται καὶ χαλκὸς καὶ ἄργυρος καὶ πᾶν τὸ στιλπνὸν μέχρι καὶ χρυσοῦ.

XII. ERATOSTHENES

275–194 B.C.E.

We learn about Eratosthenes' view of the formation of the country around the Dead Sea through Strabo, who made great use of Eratosthenes' geographical work in his own Geographica.[1] Strabo tells us of the repeated assertion of the local people that thirteen cities, the chief of which was Sodoma, were destroyed as a result of earthquakes and fires that caused the lake to burst its bounds and the rocks to catch fire. Eratosthenes, on the contrary, stated that the country was originally a lake, the greater part of which was uncovered by these outbreaks.[2]

1 On Strabo's frequent use of Eratosthenes in his sixteenth book of the *Geography*, cf. 1:12, p. 741; 1:21, p. 746; 1:22, p. 746; 3:2, p. 765; 4:2, p. 767; 4:19, p. 778. In XVI, 4:2, p. 767, the words ἥτις ἐστὶ μεταξὺ τῆς τε εὐδαίμονος Ἀραβίας καὶ τῆς Κοιλοσύρων καὶ τῶν Ἰουδαίων, which describe the situation of the desert part of Arabia mentioned by Eratosthenes, seem to be an explanation by Strabo himself.
2 In this connection, Reinhardt defines Eratosthenes as a neptunist, in contrast to Posidonius the vulcanist; cf. K. Reinhardt, *Poseidonios über Ursprung und Entartung*, Heidelberg 1928, p. 69.

23

apud: Strabo, *Geographica*, XVI, 2:44, p. 764 — Kramer = *F. Gr. Hist.*, II, A87, F70, p. 267

Ἐρατοσθένης δέ φησι τἀναντία, λιμναζούσης τῆς χώρας, ἐκρήγμασιν
ἀνακαλυφθῆναι τὴν πλείστην, καθάπερ τὴν * θάλατταν.

2 θάλατταν] Θετταλίαν Corais   τὴν θάλατταν <ταπεινωθῆναι> Letronne
καθάπερ τὴν πλείστην <τὴν περὶ> τὴν θάλατταν K. Reinhardt, *Poseidonios über
Ursprung und Entartung*, Heidelberg 1928, p. 69

But Eratosthenes says, on the contrary, that the country was a lake,
and that most of it was uncovered by outbreaks, as was the case with
the sea.   (trans. H. L. Jones, *LCL*)

XIII. ARISTOPHANES

c. 200 B.C.E.

Josephus lists Aristophanes between Mnaseas and Hermogenes — among those writers who dealt extensively with Jews.
We have no clue as to the identity of this Aristophanes. It has been suggested that he is the same as the great Alexandrian philologist Aristophanes of Byzantium.[1]

---

1 See Müller, p. 181; cf. R. Pfeiffer, *History of Classical Scholarship, from the Beginnings to the End of the Hellenistic Age*, Oxford 1968, pp. 171 ff; Fraser, I, pp. 459 ff.

24

apud: Josephus, *Contra Apionem*, I, 215–216 — Niese = Reinach (Budé), p. 41

(215) ’Αρκοῦσι δὲ ὅμως εἰς τὴν ἀπόδειξιν τῆς ἀρχαιότητος αἵ τε
Αἰγυπτίων καὶ Χαλδαίων καὶ Φοινίκων ἀναγραφαὶ πρὸς ἐκείναις τε τοσοῦτοι τῶν Ἑλλήνων συγγραφεῖς· *(216)* ἔτι δὲ πρὸς τοῖς εἰρημένοις Θεόφιλος
〈No. 38〉 καὶ Θεόδοτος καὶ Μνασέας 〈No. 27〉 καὶ ’Αριστοφάνης
5 καὶ Ἑρμογένης 〈No. 199〉 Εὐήμερός 〈No. 16〉 τε καὶ Κόνων 〈No. 144〉
καὶ Ζωπυρίων 〈No. 198〉 καὶ πολλοί τινες ἄλλοι τάχα, οὐ γὰρ ἔγωγε
πᾶσιν ἐντετύχηκα τοῖς βιβλίοις, οὐ παρέργως ἡμῶν ἐμνημονεύκασιν.

3 ἔτι δὲ Eus.   ἔτι δὲ καὶ L

(215) However, our antiquity is sufficiently established by the
Egyptian, Chaldaean, and Phoenician records, not to mention the
numerous Greek historians. (216) In addition to those already cited,
Theophilus, Theodotus, Mnaseas, Aristophanes, Hermogenes, Euhemerus, Conon, Zopyrion, and, may be, many more — for my reading has not been exhaustive — have made more than a passing allusion
to us.   (trans. H. St. J. Thackeray, *LCL*)

XIV. HERMIPPUS OF SMYRNA

c. 200 B.C.E.

Both Josephus and Origenes quote statements of Hermippus concerning
Pythagoras' debt to Judaism. Josephus presents us with a story taken
from the first book of Hermippus' De Pythagora, according to which the
soul of one of Pythagoras' pupils warned the philosopher not to pass a
certain spot on which an ass had collapsed, to abstain from thirst-
producing water and to avoid all calumny.[1] Then, Josephus seems to
quote directly from a passage in Hermippus that emphasizes Pythagoras' dependence on the doctrines of the Jews and the Thracians. Finally,
Josephus adds that Pythagoras is said to have introduced many Jewish
concepts into his philosophy. This does not represent a citation from
Hermippus, but it does give us the current view of Hellenistic Jewry.[2]

Origenes does not quote Hermippus directly, but derives his statement
about the influence of Judaism on Pythagoras only from "what is said"
(ὡς λέγεται). However, Origenes' source bases itself on Hermippus'
work On Legislators and not, like Josephus, on the first book of De
Pythagora. This consideration lends support to the opinion of Gutschmid
(IV, pp. 557 f.), who maintains that Origenes does not depend on Josephus, a view that seems preferable to that of Schürer (III, p. 626),
who claims that there was a direct connection between Josephus and
Origenes.

Nobody should contest the authenticity of the contents of the passage
from Hermippus, which is to be found in Contra Apionem. As there is
nothing specifically Jewish in it, there is no reason to suppose that a
Jewish writer invented it. It hardly enhances the glory of the Jewish
people, for the Jews are put on the same level as the Thracians. There is
also nothing to preclude the possibility that, in another of his works,
Hermippus also refers to the Jewish inspiration behind some of the Pythagorean tenets, though the generalizing tone found in Origenes may
perhaps be attributed to some Jewish intermediary.

1 For the nature of the Pythagorean symbols, with which the above-mentioned
   are in line, see W. K. C. Guthrie, A History of Greek Philosophy, I, Cambridge
   1962, pp. 183 ff.
2 Cf. the Jewish philosopher Aristobulus of the second century B.C.E., apud:
   Eusebius, Praeparatio Evangelica, XIII, 12 : 4; cf. also N. Walter, Der Thoraausleger Aristobulos, Berlin 1964.

*One should also remember that there is nothing surprising in the fact
that Hermippus traces some of the Pythagorean customs to Jews, since
even in the fourth century B.C.E. we encounter the opinion that the
philosopher learned much Eastern lore; cf. Isocrates, Busiris, 28:
Πυθαγόρας ὁ Σάμιος...ἀφικόμενος εἰς Αἴγυπτον καὶ μαθητὴς ἐκείνων
γενόμενος.³ For the Eastern connections of Pythagoras, see also
Porphyrius, Vita Pythagorae, 6; Iamblichus, De Vita Pythagorica;⁴
Clemens Alexandrinus, Stromata, I, 15:66:2; VI, 2:27:2; Suda, s.v.
δογματίζει: ᾿Αναξαγόρας δὲ καὶ Πυθαγόρας εἰς Αἴγυπτον ἀφικόμενοι
καὶ τοῖς Αἰγυπτίων καὶ ῾Εβραίων αὐτόθι σοφοῖς ὁμιλήσαντες κτλ.
Cf. also Antonius Diogenes, apud: Porphyrius, Vita Pythagorae, 11
(No. 250). Moreover, at the beginning of the Hellenistic age the Jews
were regarded as a philosophical people, and Hermippus "the Peripatetic"
might likewise have been sympathetic to them.⁵*

---

3 For a repertory of traditions about Pythagoras' sojourn in the East, cf.
   T. Hopfner, *Orient und griechische Philosophie*, Leipzig 1925, pp. 3 ff.
4 Cf. I. Lévy, *La légende de Pythagore de Grèce en Palestine*, Paris 1927, pp. 20 ff.
5 Hermippus seems to have accepted a suggestion from an earlier authority;
   cf. A. Momigliano, *The Development of Greek Biography*, Cambridge, Mass.
   1971, pp. 79 f.

25

De Pythagora, apud: Josephus, *Contra Apionem*, I, 162–165 — Niese =
F 14 R = Reinach (Budé) pp. 31 f.

(162) Πυθαγόρας τοίνυν ὁ Σάμιος ἀρχαῖος ὤν, σοφίᾳ δὲ καὶ τῇ περὶ
τὸ θεῖον εὐσεβείᾳ πάντων ὑπειλημμένος διενεγκεῖν τῶν φιλοσοφησάν-
των, οὐ μόνον ἐγνωκὼς τὰ παρ᾽ ἡμῖν δῆλός ἐστιν, ἀλλὰ καὶ ζηλωτὴς
αὐτῶν ἐκ πλείστου γεγενημένος. *(163)* αὐτοῦ μὲν οὖν οὐδὲν ὁμολογεῖ-
5 ται σύγγραμμα, πολλοὶ δὲ τὰ περὶ αὐτὸν ἱστορήκασι, καὶ τούτων
ἐπισημότατός ἐστιν Ἕρμιππος ἀνὴρ περὶ πᾶσαν ἱστορίαν ἐπιμελής.
(164) λέγει τοίνυν ἐν τῷ πρώτῳ τῶν περὶ Πυθαγόρου βιβλίων, ὅτι
Πυθαγόρας ἑνὸς αὐτοῦ τῶν συνουσιαστῶν τελευτήσαντος, τοὔνομα
Καλλιφῶντος τὸ γένος Κροτωνιάτου, τὴν ἐκείνου ψυχὴν ἔλεγε συν-
10 διατρίβειν αὐτῷ καὶ νύκτωρ καὶ μεθ᾽ ἡμέραν· καὶ ὅτι παρεκελεύετο
μὴ διέρχεσθαι τόπον, ἐφ᾽ ὃν ὄνος ὀκλάσῃ, καὶ τῶν διψίων ὑδάτων
ἀπέχεσθαι καὶ πάσης [ἀπέχειν] βλασφημίας. *(165)* εἶτα προστίθησι
μετὰ ταῦτα καὶ τάδε· «ταῦτα δὲ ἔπραττεν καὶ ἔλεγε τὰς Ἰουδαίων καὶ
Θρακῶν δόξας μιμούμενος καὶ μεταφέρων εἰς ἑαυτόν. λέγεται γὰρ ὡς
15 ἀληθῶς ὁ ἀνὴρ ἐκεῖνος πολλὰ τῶν παρὰ Ἰουδαίοις νομίμων εἰς τὴν
αὐτοῦ μετενεγκεῖν φιλοσοφίαν.»

4 ἐκ πλείστου] *ex multis apparet* Lat.   10 μεθ᾽ ed. pr.   καθ᾽ L
11 ὃν ἂν ed. pr.   οὗ ἂν Niese   12 ἀπέχειν secl. Herwerden.
ἀποστῆναι Reinach   16 αὐτοῦ Naber: αὐτοῦ L

(162) Now, Pythagoras, that ancient sage of Samos, who for wisdom
and piety is ranked above all the philosophers, evidently not only
knew of our institutions, but was to a very great degree an admirer of
them. (163) Of the master himself we possess no authentic work, but
his history has been told by many writers. The most distinguished of
these is Hermippus, always a careful historian. (164) Now, in the first
book of his work on Pythagoras, this author states that the philosopher, on the death of one of his disciples, named Calliphon, a native of
Cortona, remarked that his pupil's soul was with him night and day,
and admonished him not to pass a certain spot, on which an ass had
collapsed, to abstain from thirst-producing water, and to avoid all
calumny. (165) Then he proceeds as follows: "In practising and repeating these precepts he was imitating and appropriating the doctrines
of Jews and Thracians. In fact, it is actually said that that great man
introduced many points of Jewish law into his philosophy."

(trans. H. St. J. Thackeray, *LCL*)

164 ἐν τῷ πρώτῳ τῶν περὶ Πυθαγόρου βιβλίων: Cf. Diogenes Laertius, VIII, 10: ὥς φησιν ῞Ερμιππος ἐν δευτέρῳ περὶ Πυθαγόρου.

Καλλιφῶντος: Calliphon should probably be identified with Calliphon, the father of Democedes; cf. Herodotus, III, 125; cf. also Gossen, PW, X, p. 1656.

ἐφ᾽ὃν ὄνος ὀκλάσῃ: It is difficult to determine whether Hermippus intended to connect all the prohibitions with both the Jews and the Thracians. Gutschmid refers to the story of Balaam and the she-ass (Num. xxii : 21 ff.), and it is noteworthy that in the version in *Ant.*, IV, 109 we read: ἡ ὄνος τυπτομένη ὤκλασε κατὰ βούλησιν θεοῦ ... But we may doubt the dependence of Hermippus on the story of Balaam.

διψίων ὑδάτων: Probably salty water. This is taken to mean uncovered water by S. Liebermann, *Ha-Yerushalmi Kiphshuto*, I, 1, Jerusalem 1934, p. 49.

καὶ πάσης ἀπέχειν βλασφημίας: Cf. Exod. xxii : 27.

165 Θρακῶν δόξας μιμούμενος: Willrich thinks that the Jews and the Thracians are coupled together here because the latter worshipped the god Sabazius, who was identified with the Jewish God; see H. Willrich, *Juden und Griechen vor der makkabäischen Erhebung*, Göttingen 1895, pp. 59 f.; cf. also the commentary to Valerius Maximus, I, 3 : 3 (No. 147).

26

De Legislatoribus, apud: Origenes, *Contra Celsum*, I, 15:334 — Koetschau = F14b R

Λέγεται δὲ καὶ ῞Ερμιππον ἐν τῷ πρώτῳ περὶ νομοθετῶν ἱστορηκέναι Πυθαγόραν τὴν ἑαυτοῦ φιλοσοφίαν ἀπὸ ᾿Ιουδαίων εἰς ῞Ελληνας ἀγαγεῖν.

It is said that also Hermippus, in his first book on legislators, related that Pythagoras brought his own philosophy from the Jews to the Greeks.

περὶ νομοθετῶν: Cf., e.g., Athenaeus, *Deipnosophistae*, IV, 41, p. 154 D: ῞Ερμιππος δ᾽ ἐν πρώτῳ περὶ νομοθετῶν; XIII, 2, p. 555 C; XIV, 10, p. 619 B; Porphyrius, *De Abstinentia*, IV, 22.

XV. MNASEAS OF PATARA

c. 200 B.C.E.

Mnaseas was a writer from Lycian Patara,[1] who was stated by Suda
(s.v. Ἐρατοσθένης) to have been a pupil of Eratosthenes.[2] Among his
compositions there was a collection of mythological tales and θαυμάσ α,
arranged in geographical order.

Josephus mentions a writer named Mnaseas three times: (a) among
writers referring to the Flood (Ant., I, 94); (b) in a list of writers
who wrote about the Jews (No. 27); (c) as one of Apion's sources on the
Jews (No. 28), where the emendation to Mnaseas seems almost certainly correct.

It is reasonable to assume that Josephus had the same author in mind in
all three references.

Since Eratosthenes died in the nineties of the second century B.C.E.,
it is quite possible that the book by his pupil Mnaseas, which included
the story about the relations between the Idumaeans and the Jews, was
written before the time of Antiochus Epiphanes' persecution. Mnaseas
is the first known writer to mention the ass-worship of the Jews. He
states that the Jews adore a golden asinine head, and in that he is followed
by Apion (No. 170) and Damocritus (No. 247), though we should not
postulate a direct derivation. Diodorus, XXXIV–XXXV, 1 : 3 (No. 63)
tells us about a statue, discovered by Antiochus Epiphanes in the Temple
of Jerusalem, of a man — identified with Moses — mounted on an ass.
Tacitus mentions the part played by a herd of wild asses in conducting
the Jewish exiles from Egypt to a place with water; see Historiae, V, 4
(No. 281). Cf. Plutarchus, Quaestiones Convivales, IV, 5 : 2, p. 670 E
(No. 258). Moreover, the fable of ass-worship became attached to the
Christians in due time; cf. Tertullianus, Apologeticus, XVI, 1–3;
Ad Nationes, I, 14; Minucius Felix, Octavius, IX, 3: "Audio eos
turpissimae pecudis caput asini consecratum inepta nescio qua persua-
sione venerari: digna et nata religio talibus moribus."[3]

It seems that the fable, to which Mnaseas is the first to testify, was

---

1 See P. Oxy., XIII, No. 1611, F 2, Col. I, ll. 128 f.
2 For Mnaseas, see FHG, III, pp. 149 ff., Susemihl, I, pp. 679 f.; Laqueur, PW,
  XV, pp. 2250 ff.; Fraser, II, p. 755, n. 41.
3 Cf. L. Vischer, RHR, LXX (1951), pp. 14 ff.

born in Hellenistic Egypt in an atmosphere hostile to the Jews. It is a well-established fact that the ass was an animal connected with Typhon-Seth, the enemy of Osiris.[4] *Moreover, it is clear from Plutarchus, De Iside et Osiride, 31, p. 363 C–D (No. 259), that Jewish origins were sometimes associated with Typhon-Seth. In addition, the fact that the name Iao, known also to pagan circles as the name of the God of the Jews,*[5] *is similar in sound to the Egyptian word for ass probably contributed something to the emergence of the fable.*[6]

The fable of Jewish ass-worship was combined early with the story of the Jewish-Idumaean struggle, which presumably continued on Egyptian soil. We have some evidence of Idumaeans living in Egypt already in the third century B.C.E. (P. Tebtunis, No. 815, F5, l. 29), and that evidence becomes more extensive in the second century B.C.E.[7]

It seems that both the Jewish and Idumaean immigrants to Egypt carried on their long-standing mutual hostility. It is hardly to be supposed that Mnaseas invented either the original fable or its association with Palestinian conditions. He must have taken it over from his sources, in accordance with his usual procedure.[8] *Thus, we need not assume that later sources connecting Jews with ass-worship should be traced back to Mnaseas.*

Bibliography (On Mnaseas and Jewish ass-worship)

H. Willrich, *Juden und Griechen vor der makkabäischen Erhebung*, Göttingen 1895, pp. 52 f.; A. Büchler, *ZAW*, XXII (1902), pp. 224 ff.; Stähelin, pp. 14 ff.; Schürer, III, pp. 531 f.; J. Halévy, *Revue sémitique*, XVIII (1910), pp. 218 ff.; Radin, pp. 168 ff.; Ed. Meyer, II, p. 33; W. Bousset & H. Gressmann, *Die Religion des Judentums im späthellenistischen Zeitalter*, Tübingen 1926, p. 76, n. 1; E. Bickermann, *MGWJ*, LXXI (1927), pp. 255 ff.; I. Heinemann, PW, Suppl. V, pp. 28 f.; Y. Gutman, *Ziyunim — Simḥoni Memorial Book* (in Hebrew), Berlin 1929, pp, 181 ff.; T. Hopfner, *Die Judenfrage bei Griechen und Römern*, Prague 1943, pp. 58 f.; A. H. Krappe, *Classical Philology*, XLII (1947), p. 232; A. M. A. Hospers-Jansen, *Tacitus over de Joden*, Groningen 1949, pp. 122 ff.; Böhl, pp. 123 ff.; Tcherikover, pp. 365 f.; R. Neher-Bernheim, *Zion*, XXVIII (1963), pp. 106 ff. (in Hebrew).

4 Cf. Plutarchus, *De Iside et Osiride*, 30, p. 362 F: ὄνον δὲ καὶ κατακρημνίζοντες [scil. Αἰγύπτιοι], ὡς Κοπτῖται, διὰ τὸ πυρρὸν γεγονέναι τὸν Τυφῶνα καὶ ὀνώδη τὴν χρόαν. The ass, also in the opinion of the Egyptians, excelled in folly; cf. Plutarchus, *op. cit.*, 50, p. 371 C: Διὸ καὶ τῶν μὲν ἡμέρων ζῴων ἀπονέμουσιν αὐτῷ [scil. Τυφῶνι] τὸ ἀμαθέστατον. The enemy of the Egyptians, Artaxerxes Ochus, deified the ass; cf. Aelianus, *Historia Animalium*, X, 28. See also G. Michailides, *Aegyptus*, XXXII (1952), pp. 45 ff.

5 See the commentary to No. 58.

6 Cf. A. Jacoby, *Archiv für Religionswissenschaft*, XXV (1927), pp. 265 ff.

7 Cf. M. Launey, *Recherches sur les armées hellénistiques*, I, Paris 1949, pp. 556 ff.; E. Kiessling, *Archiv für Papyrusforschung*, XV (1953), p. 42; U. Rapaport, *Revue de Philologie*, XLIII (1969), pp. 73 ff.

8 Cf. Laqueur, PW, XV, p. 2251.

Mnaseas of Patara

27

apud: Josephus, *Contra Apionem*, I, 215–216 — Niese = Reinach (Budé), p. 41

(215) Ἀρκοῦσι δὲ ὅμως εἰς τὴν ἀπόδειξιν τῆς ἀρχαιότητος αἵ τε
Αἰγυπτίων καὶ Χαλδαίων καὶ Φοινίκων ἀναγραφαὶ πρὸς ἐκείναις τε
τοσοῦτοι τῶν ῾Ελλήνων συγγραφεῖς· (216) ἔτι δὲ πρὸς τοῖς εἰρημένοις
Θεόφιλος ⟨No. 38⟩ *καὶ Θεόδοτος καὶ Μνασέας καὶ Ἀριστοφάνης*
5 ⟨No. 24⟩ *καὶ ῾Ερμογένης* ⟨No. 199⟩ *Εὐήμερός* ⟨No. 16⟩ *τε καὶ Κόνων*
⟨No. 144⟩ *καὶ Ζωπυρίων* ⟨No. 198⟩ *καὶ πολλοί τινες ἄλλοι τάχα, οὐ*
γὰρ ἔγωγε πᾶσιν ἐντετύχηκα τοῖς βιβλίοις, οὐ παρέργως ἡμῶν
ἐμνημονεύκασιν.

3 ἔτι δὲ Eus.   ἔτι δὲ καὶ L

(215) However, our antiquity is sufficiently established by the
Egyptian, Chaldaean, and Phoenician records, not to mention the
numerous Greek historians. (216) In addition to those already cited,
Theophilus, Theodotus, Mnaseas, Aristophanes, Hermogenes, Euhemerus, Conon, Zopyrion, and, may be, many more — for my reading
has not been exhaustive — have made more than a passing allusion
to us.   (trans. H. St. J. Thackeray, *LCL*)

216 *καὶ Μνασέας*: Mnaseas is mentioned in a list of writers who, according to
Josephus, testify to the antiquity of the Jews. We have, however, no means of
ascertaining whether Mnaseas made other references to Jews apart from the story
related in No. 28. This story, however, could have been Josephus' justification for
including Mnaseas among the writers who dealt with Jewish antiquities. The
events described in No. 28, which refer to the hostile relations between Jews and
Idumaeans, might well be regarded as having taken place in the remote past.

28

apud: Josephus, *Contra Apionem*, II, 112–114 — Niese = F19 R = Reinach (Budé) p. 77

(112) Rursumque tamquam piissimus deridet adiciens fabulae suae Mnaseam. Ait enim illum retulisse, dum bellum Iudaei contra Idumaeos
haberent longo quodam tempore in aliqua civitate Idumaeorum, qui
Dorii nominantur, quendam eorum qui in ea Apollinem colebat venisse
5 ad Iudaeos, cuius hominis nomen dicit Zabidon, deinde qui eis promisisset traditurum se eis Apollinem deum Doriensium venturumque illum

1 *piissimos* Niese ap. Boysen   1-2 Mnaseam Niese   *mnafeam* Lat.
2 *Idumaeos* Gelenius   *iudaeos* Lat.   3 *Idumaeorum* Gelenius   *iudaeorum*
                                Lat.   5 *quia* Boysen

ad nostrum templum, si omnes abscederent. (113) Et credidisse omnem
multitudinem Iudaeorum; Zabidon vero fecisse quoddam machinamentum ligneum et circumposuisse sibi et in eo tres ordines infixisse lucerna-
10 rum et ita ambulasse, ut procul stantibus appareret, quasi stellae per terram *(114)* τὴν πορείαν ποιουμένων, τοὺς μὲν Ἰουδαίους ὑπὸ τοῦ παραδόξου τῆς θέας καταπεπληγμένους πόρρω μένοντας ἡσυχίαν ἄγειν, τὸν δὲ
Ζάβιδον ἐπὶ πολλῆς ἡσυχίας εἰς τὸν ναὸν παρελθεῖν καὶ τὴν χρυσῆν
ἀποσῦραι τοῦ κάνθωνος κεφαλήν, οὕτω γὰρ ἀστεϊζόμενος γέγραφεν,
15 καὶ πάλιν εἰς Δῶρα τὸ τάχος ἀπελθεῖν.

12 μένοντας Bekker   μὲν ὄντας L   *constitutos* Lat.   14 κάνθωνος Hudson
ἀκανθῶνος L   *asini* Lat.   15 εἰς Δῶρα Niese   *ad dora* Lat.   εἰς
δῶριν L   εἰς δώραν ed. pr. / τὸ τάχος] κατὰ τάχος ed. pr.

(112) This model of piety derides us again in a story which he attributes to Mnaseas. The latter, according to Apion, relates that in
the course of a long war between the Jews and the Idumaeans, an
inhabitant of an Idumaean city, called Dorii, who worshipped
Apollo and bore (so we are told) the name of Zabidus, came out to
the Jews and promised to deliver into their hands Apollo, the god of
his city, who would visit our temple if they all took departure.
(113) The Jews all believed him; whereupon Zabidus constructed an
apparatus of wood, inserted in it three rows of lamps, and put it over
his person. Thus arrayed he walked about, presenting the appearance
to distant onlookers of stars (114) perambulating the earth. Astounded
at this amazing spectacle, the Jews kept their distance, in perfect
silence. Meanwhile, Zabidus stealthily passed into the sanctuary,
snatched up the golden head of the pack-ass (as he facetiously calls
it), and made off post-haste to Dora.   (trans. H. St. J. Thackeray, *LCL*)

112 *Dum bellum Iudaei contra Idumaeos haberent*: Since the main work of
Mnaseas followed a geographical arrangement, we must assume that he spoke of
this incident in connection with the θαυμάσια of the country. We know that
Mnaseas dealt with Ascalon in the second of his books concerning Asia; cf.
FHG, III, p. 155. The wars between the Jews and the Idumaeans in the time of Judas
the Maccabaean and John Hyrcan are well known; but these conflicts occurred too
late to serve as a background for events related by Mnaseas. We know, however,
that the relations between the Jews and the Idumaeans were also very strained in
the period preceding the Hasmonaean Revolt, and, in fact, from the time of the
Babylonian Exile; cf., e.g., Siracides, L : 25 f. This friction presumably caused
quite a few incidents between the neighbouring peoples, and the prevailing hostile
atmosphere may have caused the Idumaeans living in their native country or those
who had emigrated to Egypt to produce a story of this kind. The historical setting
of this narrative could be placed either in the recent, or, better still, in the remote

past. Such considerations seem to somewhat weaken Jacoby's supposition that the story reflects the struggles of the Maccabaean period; cf. A. Jacoby, *op. cit.* (supra, p. 98, n. 6), p. 281.

Idumaeorum, qui Dorii nominantur: Since the Dorii are designated Idumaeans by Mnaseas, they cannot be regarded as inhabitants of Dora (Dor) on the seacoast south of Mt. Carmel. The Dorii of Mnaseas must be identical with the Adorii, i.e. the inhabitants of Adora, the ancient Judaean township that, during the period of the Second Temple, constituted one of the main centres of Idumaea (in *PCZ*, No. 59006, Col. 3, it appears as 'Ἀδώρεον); see I Macc. xiii : 20 (″Ἀδωρα). Adora was captured by the Jews in the time of John Hyrcan, in the twenties of the second century B. C. E,; see *Ant.*, XIII, 257; *BJ*, I, 63; the Book of Jubilees xxxviii : 8 f. It is noteworthy that in the MSS *FLAMVW* of *Ant.*, XIV, 88, the place is also called Δῶρα (here it appears alongside Idumaean Marissa; in the parallel narrative of *BJ*, I, 166, it is called 'Ἀδώρεος) and *Ant.*, XIII, 207, has Dora, a city of Idumaea, instead of Adora. Also, in modern Arabic the place is known as Dura (a village southwest of Hebron); cf. G. Beyer, *ZDPV*, LIV (1931), p. 251; Abel, II, p. 239. From Josephus we see that the text of Apion used by him had the reading Dorii, which may even go back to Mnaseas himself.

Apollinem: Apollo stands for Cos, the national god of the Idumaeans; see *OGIS*, No. 737, a decree of the Idumaeans in the temple of Apollo in Memphis, and the Idumaean persons bearing names derived from Apollo; cf. M. Launey, *Recherches sur les armées hellénistiques*, II, Paris 1950, pp. 1236 ff.

113 *Et credidisse omnem multitudinem Iudaeorum*: On the motif of Jewish credulousness, see Horatius, *Sermones*, I, 5 : 100 (No. 128).

Zabidon vero fecisse quoddam machinamentum . . .: For this motif, cf. Herodotus, I, 60 : 4 f.

XVI. POLEMO OF ILIUM?

First half of the second century B.C.E.

Polemo lived in the time of Ptolemy V Epiphanes.[1] *The passage included here was taken by Eusebius, through Julius Africanus, from the* Historia Graeca *by Polemo. The work is also mentioned elsewhere as that of Polemo (cf. the commentary). It has, however, been argued that the fact that the passage tolerates the hiatus is contrary to Polemonian usage.*[2]

There is no express allusion to Jews here, but only a reference to the settlement of a part of the Egyptian army in Palestine under the leadership of Apis, the son of Phoroneus. Yet, it seems that we are justified in relating this statement to the traditions, which found their way into Greek literature at an early date, of the emigration from Egypt that laid the foundation of Judaea.

---

1 Polemo appears among the proxeni of Delphi (Πολέμων Μιλησίου Ἰλιεύς) in *Sylloge*[3], No. 585, p. 99.
2 Cf. K. Deichgräber, PW, XXI, p. 1303.

Polemo of Ilium

29

Historia Graeca, apud: Eusebius, *Praeparatio Evangelica*, X, 10:15 — Mras = F15R = L. Preller, *Polemonis Periegetae Fragmenta*, Leipzig 1838, F 13

Πολέμων μὲν ἐν τῇ πρώτῃ τῶν Ἑλληνικῶν ἱστοριῶν λέγων· «Ἐπὶ Ἄπιδος τοῦ Φορωνέως μοῖρα τοῦ Αἰγυπτίων στρατοῦ ἐξέπεσεν Αἰγύπτου, οἳ ἐν τῇ Παλαιστίνῃ καλουμένῃ Συρίᾳ οὐ πόρρω Ἀραβίας ᾤκησαν.»

2 τοῦ²] τῶν I   3 Ἀραβίας] συρίας B

Polemo, in the first book of the *Greek Histories*, states: "In the reign of Apis the son of Phoroneus, a part of the Egyptian army was expelled from Egypt and established itself in the country called Syria-Palaestina not far from Arabia."

ἐν τῇ πρώτῃ τῶν Ἑλληνικῶν ἱστοριῶν: This work is also referred to in the scholia to Aelius Aristides, *Panathenaicus* (ed. Dindorf, Vol. III, p. 322 = *FHG*, III, p. 119, F 11) as "Hellenic History" (ἐν τῇ Ἑλληνικῇ ἱστορίᾳ); cf. also Schmid & Stählin, II, 1, p. 244, n. 1.

ἐπὶ Ἄπιδος τοῦ Φορωνέως: On this Apis, King of Argos and grandson of Inachus, see W.H. Roscher, *Ausführliches Lexikon der griechischen und römischen Mythologie*, Vol. I, Part, 1, Leipzig 1884–1886, pp. 421 f. Cf. also the list of the Argive kings, according to Africanus, in: H. Gelzer, *Sextus Julius Africanus*, I, Leipzig 1880, p. 143.

οἳ ἐν τῇ Παλαιστίνῃ καλουμένῃ Συρίᾳ: On the use of Palestine in the Hellenistic age, see the commentaries to Herodotus *Historiae*, II, 104:3 (No. 1), Aristotle, *Meteorologica*, II, p. 359a (No. 3), and the introduction to Polybius.

XVII. AGATHARCHIDES OF CNIDUS

Second century B.C.E.

A historian and scholar of the Middle Hellenistic age, Agatharchides was a native of Cnidus, who stayed in Alexandria for some time during the reigns of Ptolemy VI Philometor and Ptolemy Physcon. His chief historical works, for which he is famous, are his History of Asia, in ten books, and his History of Europe, in forty-nine books. The following passage referring to Jews derives from one of these works.

During his sojourn in Egypt Agatharchides undoubtedly had an opportunity to meet many Jews, as they played a conspicuous part in the life and politics of second-century Egypt.[1]

Like Theophrastus and Clearchus, Agatharchides was counted among the followers of the Peripatos.[2] It is by no means certain whether he referred to the Jews anywhere in his works, apart from this short passage quoted by Josephus. The view that Agatharchides became an authority on Jewish history and that his writings were valued as a source of information by later writers [3] can hardly be substantiated.

---

1 Agatharchides was closely associated with Heracleides Lembus. Some scholars are of the opinion that Suda, s. v. ʿΗρακλείδης ʾΟξυρυγχίτης (...γεγονὼς ἐπὶ Πτολεμαίου τοῦ ἕκτου, ὃς τὰς πρὸς ʾΑντίοχον ἔθετο συνθήκας) implies diplomatic activity on the part of Heracleides that has a bearing upon the relations between Ptolemy Philometor and Antiochus Epiphanes. Cf. *F. Gr. Hist.*, II C, p. 151; E. R. Bevan, *The House of Seleucus*, II, London 1902, p. 141, n. 1; and, as it seems, E. van't Dack, *Antidorum W. Peremans sexagenario ab alumnis oblatum*, Louvain 1968, pp. 274 f. Thus, we could postulate that Agatharchides gained specific information concerning the disturbed situation in Judaea. However, the whole interpretation of the passage seems mistaken, and the ὃς τὰς πρὸς ʾAντίοχον ἔθετο συνθήκας seems to be Ptolemy himself; cf. Niese, III, p. 172, n. 4.

2 See Strabo, *Geographica*, XIV, 2 : 15, p. 656. On his philosophical views, cf. H. Leopoldi, "De Agatharchide Cnidio", Ph. D. Thesis, Rostock 1892, pp. 53 ff.

3 See E. A. Wagner, "Agatharchides und der mittlere Peripatos", Suppl. *Jahresbericht des königlichen Realgymnasiums zu Annaberg*, Leipzig 1901, pp. 5 f.; Fraser I, p. 517; II, p. 783, n. 204 finds in Agatharchides' work on the Red Sea signs of knowledge of the Septuagint and compares Diodorus III, 40 : 7 (τὸ πνεῦμα τῇ δούσῃ φύσει πάλιν ἀπέδωκάν) with LXX, Eccl. xii : 7 (καὶ τὸ πνεῦμα ἐπιστρέψῃ πρὸς τὸν θεόν). However, I doubt whether we should see here a direct dependence of Agatharchides on the Septuagint.

In any case, the passage adduced by Josephus derives from one of the chief works of Agatharchides, and not from a chapter dealing mainly with Jews. It is quoted by Josephus twice, once in Antiquitates *and again in* Contra Apionem. *The latter version is the fuller one.*

Agatharchides' knowledge of Judaism seems to rest on firmer ground than that of his early Hellenistic predecessors. He is the first to mention the Seventh Day as a day of rest, and this statement is not marred by the mistake, common to many later writers, that it was a fast day.

We should hardly be justified in regarding Agatharchides' statement as an expression of nascent anti-Semitism. He refers to the superstition of the Jews in the same spirit as to that of Stratonice.[4]

---

4 One may also point to the general interest taken by Agatharchides in irrational human behaviour; see A. Dihle, in: *Grecs et barbares — Entretiens sur l'antiquité classique*, 1961, VIII (1962), p. 223. On the mentality of Agatharchides, cf. also the summary of O. Immisch, *Agatharchidea*, Heidelberg 1919, pp. 108 f.

From Herodotus to Plutarch

30a

apud: Josephus, *Contra Apionem*, I, 205–211 — Niese = F16R = *F. Gr. Hist.*, II, A86, F20a = Reinach (Budé), pp. 39 f.

(205) Οὐκ ὀκνήσω δὲ καὶ τὸν ἐπ' εὐηθείας διασυρμῷ, ... μνήμην πεποιημένον ἡμῶν Ἀγαθαρχίδην ὀνομάσαι· (206) διηγούμενος γὰρ τὰ περὶ Στρατονίκην, ὃν τρόπον ἦλθεν μὲν εἰς Συρίαν ἐκ Μακεδονίας καταλιποῦσα τὸν ἑαυτῆς ἄνδρα Δημήτριον, Σελεύκου δὲ γαμεῖν αὐτὴν
5 *οὐ θελήσαντος, ὅπερ ἐκείνη προσεδόκησεν, ποιουμένου [δὲ] τὴν ἀπὸ Βαβυλῶνος στρατείαν αὐτοῦ τὰ περὶ τὴν Ἀντιόχειαν ἐνεωτέρισεν. (207) εἶθ' ὡς ἀνέστρεψεν ὁ βασιλεύς, ἁλισκομένης τῆς Ἀντιοχείας εἰς Σελεύκειαν φυγοῦσα, παρὸν αὐτῇ ταχέως ἀποπλεῖν ἐνυπνίῳ κωλύοντι πεισθεῖσα ἐλήφθη καὶ ἀπέθανεν. (208) ταῦτα προειπὼν ὁ Ἀγαθαρχίδης*
10 *καὶ ἐπισκώπτων τῇ Στρατονίκῃ τὴν δεισιδαιμονίαν παραδείγματι χρῆται τῷ περὶ ἡμῶν λόγῳ καὶ γέγραφεν οὕτως· (209) «οἱ καλούμενοι Ἰουδαῖοι πόλιν οἰκοῦντες ὀχυρωτάτην πασῶν, ἣν καλεῖν Ἱεροσόλυμα συμβαίνει τοὺς ἐγχωρίους, ἀργεῖν εἰθισμένοι δι' ἑβδόμης ἡμέρας καὶ μήτε τὰ ὅπλα βαστάζειν ἐν τοῖς εἰρημένοις χρόνοις μήτε γεωργίας*
15 *ἅπτεσθαι μήτε ἄλλης ἐπιμελεῖσθαι λειτουργίας μηδεμιᾶς, ἀλλ' ἐν τοῖς ἱεροῖς ἐκτετακότες τὰς χεῖρας εὔχεσθαι μέχρι τῆς ἑσπέρας, (210) εἰσιόντος εἰς τὴν πόλιν Πτολεμαίου τοῦ Λάγου μετὰ τῆς δυνάμεως καὶ τῶν ἀνθρώπων ἀντὶ τοῦ φυλάττειν τὴν πόλιν διατηρούντων τὴν ἄνοιαν, ἡ μὲν πατρὶς εἰλήφει δεσπότην πικρόν, ὁ δὲ νόμος ἐξηλέγχθη*
20 *φαῦλον ἔχων ἐθισμόν. (211) τὸ δὲ συμβὰν πλὴν ἐκείνων τοὺς ἄλλους πάντας δεδίδαχε τηνικαῦτα φυγεῖν εἰς ἐνύπνια καὶ τὴν περὶ τοῦ νόμου παραδεδομένην ὑπόνοιαν, ἡνίκα ἂν τοῖς ἀνθρωπίνοις λογισμοῖς περὶ τῶν διαπορουμένων ἐξασθενήσωσιν.»*

5 δὲ secl. Niese   6 στρατείαν Bekker   στρατιὰν L, Lat.   14 μήτε
Bekker   μήδε L   17 πόλιν] χώραν Reinach   21 νόμου] θείου
Herwerden   23 ἐξασθενήσωσιν Bekker   ἐξασθενήσουσιν L

(205) There is another writer whom I shall name without hesitation, although he mentions us only to ridicule our folly—I mean Agatharchides. (206) He is telling the story of Stratonice, how she deserted her husband Demetrius and came from Macedonia to Syria, and how, when Seleucus disappointed her by refusing to marry her, she created a revolution at Antioch while he was starting on a campaign from Babylon; (207) and then how, after the king's return and the capture of Antioch, she fled to Seleucia, and instead of taking sail immediately, as she might have done, let herself be stopped by a dream, was captured and put to death. (208) After telling this story and deriding

106

Agatharchides of Cnidus

the superstition of Stratonice, Agatharchides quotes in illustration a tale told about us. The following are his words: (209) "The people known as Jews, who inhabit the most strongly fortified of cities, called by the natives Jerusalem, have a custom of abstaining from work every seventh day; on those occasions they neither bear arms nor take any agricultural operations in hand, nor engage in any other form of public service, but pray with outstretched hands in the temples until the evening. (210) Consequently, because the inhabitants, instead of protecting their city, persevered in their folly, Ptolemy, son of Lagus, was allowed to enter with his army; the country was thus given over to a cruel master, and the defect of a practice enjoined by law was exposed. (211) That experience has taught the whole world, except that nation, the lesson not to resort to dreams and traditional fancies about the law, until the difficulties are such as to baffle human reason."   (trans. H. St. J. Thackeray, *LCL*)

206 διηγούμενος γὰρ τὰ περὶ Στρατονίκην: Stratonice was a Seleucid princess, the daugher of Antiochus I of Syria and wife of Demetrius II of Macedon. After running away from Macedon and returning to Syria, she provoked a revolt against her nephew Seleucus II, and, in consequence, lost her life; see Niese, II, pp. 166 f; K. J. Beloch, *Griechische Geschichte*, Vol. IV, Part I, Berlin–Leipzig 1925, pp. 684 f.; IV, 2, 1927, p. 330, n. 1.; E. Will, *Histoire politique du monde hellénistique*, I, Nancy 1966, pp. 269 f.

208 ταῦτα προειπὼν ὁ ᾽Αγαθαρχίδης: It is by no means simple to decide whether Agatharchides referred to the capture of Jerusalem in his European or in his Asiatic History. Müller (*FHG*, III, p. 196) chooses the latter possibility, while Jacoby (*F. Gr. Hist.*, II C, p. 154) prefers the former, since it was the fate of Stratonice, the wife of a Macedonian prince, that was the starting point of Agatharchides. But, considering the fact that she was originally a Seleucid princess and that she ultimately lost her life in Syria, there is still something to be said for Müller's view.

209 πόλιν οἰκοῦντες ὀχυρωτάτην πασῶν: The strength of Jerusalem is also emphasized in other Hellenistic writings; see, e.g., Timochares, apud: Eusebius, *Praeparatio Evangelica*, IX, 35 : 1 (No. 41): εἶναι δ᾽αὐτὴν δυσάλωτον.

ἀργεῖν εἰθισμένοι δι᾽ ἑβδόμης ἡμέρας: On the loyalty of the Jews of that period to their religion, see Hecataeus, in *Contra Apionem*, I, 192 (No. 12). Agatharchides' remarks on the strict observance of the Sabbath by the Jews are corroborated by I Macc. ii : 32 ff., where we read that a multitude of Hasidim, who refrained from defending themselves on the Sabbath, were slaughtered by the soldiers of Antiochus on the holy day; cf. A. Büchler, *REJ*, XXXIV (1897), pp. 72 f.; K. D. Schunck, "Die Quellen des I. and II. Makkabäerbuches", Ph.D. Thesis, Greifswald (Halle) 1954, p. 61. The Jews began to defend themselves on the Sabbath only at the instigation of Mattathias the Hasmonaean; cf. the commentary to Frontinus, *Strategemata*, II, 1 : 17 (No. 229). Agatharchides uses the expression "the seventh day" and not a transcription of the Hebrew word for Sabbath, as in the phrase ἡμέρα τῶν σαββάτων.

210 ἡ μὲν πατρὶς εἰλήφει δεσπότην πικρόν: We also learn of the fate of Jerusalem in the time of Ptolemy I Soter from Appianus, S*yriaca*, 50 : 252 (No. 343). The *Letter of Aristeas*, 12, tells us of the great number of prisoners taken in Judaea in the time of the above-mentioned king: ἐκεῖνος γὰρ ἐπελθὼν τὰ κατὰ Κοίλην Συρίαν καὶ Φοινίκην ἅπαντα... τοὺς μὲν μετῴκιζεν, οὓς δὲ ἠχμαλώτιζε. Ptolemy conquered Palestine four times (a) In 320 B. C. E. he took the country from Laomedon, and he ruled over it for five years, till it was overrun by the army of Antigonus Monophthalmus; (b) in 312, the year of his victory over Demetrius Poliorcetes in the Battle of Gaza, a short time after which the country was regained by Antigonus; (c) in 302, at the time of the grand alliance formed against Antigonus; (d) in 301, the year of the final annexation of Palestine to the Ptolemaic Empire. Some scholars date the events in Judaea alluded to by Agatharchides to 320 B. C. E.; see, e.g., J. G. Droysen, *Geschichte des Hellenismus*, II, Gotha 1878, pp. 167 f. Others prefer the year 312; e.g. H. Willrich, *Juden und Griechen vor der makkabäischen Erhebung*, Göttingen 1895, p. 23; Ed. Meyer, II, p. 24; F.M. Abel, *RB*, XLIV (1935), p. 576. Tcherikover (pp. 57 f.) has adduced strong arguments for 302. The evidence of Agatharchides concerning the capture of Jerusalem by Ptolemy Soter is by no means invalidated by the argumentation of E.L. Abel, *REJ*, CXXVII (1968), pp. 253 ff.

30 b

apud: Josephus, *Antiquitates Judaicae*, XII, 5–6 — Niese = *F. Gr. Hist.*, II, A86, F20b

(5) Μαρτυρεῖ δὲ τῷ λόγῳ τούτῳ καὶ ᾿Αγαθαρχίδης ὁ Κνίδιος ὁ τὰς τῶν διαδόχων πράξεις συγγραψάμενος, ὀνειδίζων ἡμῖν δεισιδαιμονίαν ὡς δι᾿ αὐτὴν ἀποβαλοῦσι τὴν ἐλευθερίαν, λέγων οὕτως· (6) «ἔστιν ἔθνος ᾿Ιουδαίων λεγόμενον, οἳ πόλιν ὀχυρὰν καὶ μεγάλην ἔχοντες ῾Ιεροσόλυμα
5 *ταύτην περιεῖδον ὑπὸ Πτολεμαίῳ γενομένην ὅπλα λαβεῖν οὐ θελήσαντες, ἀλλὰ διὰ τὴν ἄκαιρον δεισιδαιμονίαν χαλεπὸν ὑπέμειναν ἔχειν δεσπότην.»*

5 περιεῖδον Niese   ὑπερῖδον P   ὑπὲρ ἰδων L¹   ὑπερεῖδον cett.

(5) This account is attested by Agatharchides of Cnidus, the historian of the Diadochi, who reproaches us for our superstition, on account of which we lost our liberty, in these words: "(6) There is a nation called Jews, who have a strong and great city called Jerusalem, which they allowed to fall into the hands of Ptolemy by refusing to take up arms and, instead, through their untimely superstition submitted to having a hard master."   (trans. R. Marcus, *LCL*)

5 ὁ τὰς τῶν διαδόχων πράξεις συγγραψάμενος: It seems that this was not the true name of the historical work of Agatharchides. The History of the Diadochi constituted only a part of his great historical work; cf. Jacoby, *op. cit.* (supra, p. 107 n. 1), p. 150.

Agatharchides of Cnidus

6 ἔστιν ἔθνος 'Ιουδαίων...: The entry of Agatharchides is given here in a shorter version. Josephus does not reproduce the context in which the mention of the Jewish δεισιδαιμονία occurred in the work of Agatharchides (the story of Stratonice's death), and there are also some differences in the wording: Ptolemy is designated πικρός in Contra Apionem and χαλεπός in Ant., where Jerusalem is described as a big city as well as a strong one. In Ant., the word δεισιδαιμονία in relation to the Jews forms part of the excerpt from Agatharchides, while in Contra Apionem it occurs only in Josephus' introductory sentence and in relation to Stratonice. Koets rightly emphasizes the fact that δεισιδαιμονία is used here in an unfavourable sense, which is perhaps less characteristic of Josephus himself; see P.J. Koets,"Δεισιδαιμονία — A Contribution to the Knowledge of the Religious Terminology in Greek", Ph.D. Thesis, Utrecht, 1929, pp. 65 f.

XVIII. POLYBIUS

End of the third century to *c*. 120 B.C.E.

In the course of narrating the struggle between the Ptolemaic and Seleucid empires in his Historiae, *Polybius often dwells on events connected with Palestine. This country looms especially large in the history of the Fourth Syrian War, which culminated in the battle of Raphia (the fifth book). Although there is no allusion in this part of his work to the plight of Judaea during the eventful years preceding the decisive battle or in the period after the battle, Polybius relates at length the military operations in other parts of Palestine, including Samaria. The omission of any reference to the Jews in the time of the Fourth Syrian War testifies to the insignificant part they played in that war and reminds one of the similar omission of any mention of the Jews by Hieronymus of Cardia; cf. the introduction to Hieronymus.*

On the other hand, we may see from the fragments of the sixteenth book that Polybius included a description of the political and military situation in Judaea in his treatment of the Fifth Syrian War. He also refers to the Jews in connection with the activities of Antiochus Epiphanes in Jerusalem. In that context he presumably gives a sort of general survey of the Jews, allotting a central place to their temple and religion.

As a young statesman of the Achaean League, Polybius already showed much interest in the fate of the Hellenistic monarchies of the East. In 181 or 180 B.C.E. he was designated as one of the Achaean ambassadors to the court of Ptolemy V Epiphanes, but the mission was cancelled on the death of the King (XXIV, 6:5 ff.). He was conspicuous in his efforts to bring about Achaean military intervention on behalf of Ptolemaic Egypt at the time of the invasion by the armies of Antiochus Epiphanes (XXIX, 23:3), and later it was Polybius who inspired Demetrius I to make an attempt to regain his ancestral throne (XXXI, 11–15).[1]

Some time after 145 B.C.E., in the reign of Ptolemy Physcon, Polybius visited Alexandria,[2] *but whether he also knew some parts of the Syrian,*

1 Cf. R. Laqueur, *Hermes*, LXV (1930) pp. 129 ff.
2 See E. Mioni, *Polibio*, Padua 1949, p. 15; F. W. Walbank, *A Historical Commentary on Polybius*, I, Oxford 1957, p. 5; P. Pédech, *La méthode historique de Polybe*, Paris 1964, pp. 561 f.

110

Polybius

or even the Palestinian coast by autopsy cannot be stated with any degree of certainty.[3]

The scantiness of the Polybian fragments dealing with the Jews prevents us from forming an opinion about Polybius' view of them. Still, some points emerge clearly: (a) Polybius has, perhaps, some feeling of respect for the Jewish Temple, which in his eyes constituted the centre and main institution of the Jewish people. (b) He does not view the policy of Antiochus Epiphanes in Judaea sympathetically.[4] The anti-Jewish measures of Antiochus are not interpreted by the historian as the expression of a general policy of a militant Hellenism, but are explained as the outcome of the financial straits in which the King found himself.

There is no doubt that Polybius' description of Jerusalem can be said to have left its mark on later writers, e.g., Livius, Periochae, 102 (No. 131); less certainty attaches to the presumable dependence of Strabo on Polybius.[5]

3 Autopsy is suggested by Pédech, op. cit.
4 For the personality of Antiochus as it emerges in the Polybian tradition, cf. F. Reuter, "Beiträge zur Beurteilung des Königs Antiochos Epiphanes", Ph. D. Thesis, Münster 1938, pp. 17 ff.
5 Such a dependence has been postulated by E. Norden, Festgabe Harnack, Tübingen 1921, p. 296 = Kleine Schriften, p. 280. I have not found it necessary to include in the present collection of texts the reference to Γίττα πόλις Παλαιστίνης in Stephanus Byzantius (= Polybius, XVI, 40), which presumably derives from the narrative of the fifth Syrian War. Whatever the identification of Γίττα, it is obvious that neither then, nor when Polybius wrote the sixteenth book, did it belong to Judaea; and the historian located it in Palestine, not in Judaea.
The main cities eligible for identification with the Gitta mentioned by Polybius are the Gitta situated, according to Eusebius, between Antipatris and Jamnia (Onomasticon, ed. Klostermann, p. 72; cf. Abel, II, p. 338) and the more northern city, mentioned also in Plinius, Naturalis Historia, V, 75; cf. A. Alt, Palästinajahrbuch, XXI (1925), p. 48, n. 3; see also M. Noth, ZDPV, LXII (1939), p. 139; Walbank, op. cit. (supra, n. 2), II, 1967, p. 547.

111

From Herodotus to Plutarch

31

Historiae, V, 71:11–12 — Büttner-Wobst

*(11) Οὗ γενομένου κυριεύσας τῶν ῾Ραββαταμάνων ἐπὶ μὲν τούτων
ἀπέλιπε Νίκαρχον μετὰ φυλακῆς τῆς ἁρμοζούσης· ῾Ιππόλοχον δὲ καὶ
Κεραίαν τοὺς ἀποστάντας μετὰ πεζῶν πεντακισχιλίων ἐξαποστείλας
ἐπὶ τοὺς κατὰ Σαμάρειαν τόπους, καὶ συντάξας προκαθῆσθαι καὶ
πᾶσι τὴν ἀσφάλειαν προκατασκευάζειν τοῖς ὑπ᾽ αὐτὸν ταττομένοις,
(12) ἀνέζευξε μετὰ τῆς δυνάμεως ὡς ἐπὶ Πτολεμαΐδος, ἐκεῖ ποιεῖσθαι
διεγνωκὼς τὴν παραχειμασίαν.*

(11) After this had happened, Antiochus got possession of Rab-
batamana and left Nicarchus in it with an adequate garrison, and now
sending the revolted leaders Hippolochus and Ceraeas with a force of
five thousand foot to the district of Samaria, with orders to protect
the conquered territory and assure the safety of all the troops he left
in it, (12) he returned with his army to Ptolemais, where he had decided
to pass the winter. (trans. W. R. Paton, *LCL*)

This passage is taken from the account of the conquests of Antiochus III, who
captured northern Palestine and a part of Transjordan from the Ptolemaic forces in
218 B. C. E. On the so-called Fourth Syrian War, see E.R. Bevan, *The House of
Seleucus*, I, London 1902, pp. 311 ff.; K.J. Beloch, *Griechische Geschichte²*, Vol.
IV, Part 1, Berlin–Leipzig 1925, pp. 689 ff.; W.W. Tarn, *CAH*, VII, 1928, pp.
726 ff.; F.W. Walbank, *op. cit.* (supra, p. 110, n. 2), pp. 585 ff.; Pédech, *op. cit.*
(supra, p. 110, n. 2), pp. 140 ff.; H.J. Thissen, *Studien zum Raphiadekret*, Meisenheim am Glan 1966; E. Will, *Histoire politique du monde hellénistique*, II, Nancy
1967, pp. 21 ff.

11 *τῶν ῾Ραββαταμάνων*: Though Rabbat-Ammon had become a Greek city
called Philadelphia, Polybius continues to call it by the traditional Semitic name;
see Tcherikover, pp. 100 f. The same may be said of Greek documentary evidence
from the third century B. C. E.; see *PSI*, No. 616, 1.27.

῾Ιππόλοχον δὲ καὶ Κεραίαν: Both of them were Ptolemaic commanders who
deserted to the Seleucid side; see Polybius, V, 70 : 10–11; cf. also Walbank, *op. cit.*
(supra, p. 110, n. 2), p. 596.

κατὰ Σαμάρειαν τόπους: This implies the whole district of Samaria, which constituted one of the divisions of Ptolemaic Syria and Seleucid Coele-Syria, and the capital
of which was the city of Samaria; cf. Bengtson, II, p. 170. Polybius makes no
reference to Jerusalem or to any military operations in Judaea (consequently
Graetz maintains that Judaea remained under Ptolemaic sway all this time; see
H. Graetz, *Geschichte der Juden*, Vol. II, Part 2, p. 250, n. 1). However, we cannot
be certain, from the silence of Polybius, that Judaea was not conquered by the
Seleucid army. He also fails to relate the capture of the coastal line between Dora
and Gaza, although this is implied by Antiochus' subsequent retreat to Gaza after
the Battle of Raphia; see Beloch, *op. cit.*, p. 693, n. 4. On the other hand, Büchler's

112

Polybius

view that Judaea is included here in Samaria cannot be proved; see, A. Büchler, *Die Tobiaden und Oniaden*, Vienna 1899, pp. 65 f. Bengtson concurs with the general view that Judaea was administratively dependent on Samaria; see Bengtson, *loc. cit.* (supra, p. 112). However, this view cannot be proved either.

32

Historiae, apud: Josephus, *Antiquitates Judaicae*, XII, 135–136 — Niese = Polybius, *Historiae*, XVI, 39:1, 3, 4 — Büttner-Wobst = F21R

(135) Μαρτυρεῖ τούτοις ἡμῶν τοῖς λόγοις Πολύβιος ὁ Μεγαλοπολίτης· ἐν γὰρ τῇ ἑξκαιδεκάτῃ τῶν ἱστοριῶν αὐτοῦ φησιν οὕτως. «ὁ δὲ τοῦ Πτολεμαίου στρατηγὸς Σκόπας ὁρμήσας εἰς τοὺς ἄνω τόπους κατεστρέψατο ἐν τῷ χειμῶνι τὸ Ἰουδαίων ἔθνος.» (136) λέγει δὲ ἐν τῇ
5 *αὐτῇ βίβλῳ, ὡς τοῦ Σκόπα νικηθέντος ὑπ᾽ Ἀντιόχου τὴν μὲν Βατανέαν καὶ Σαμάρειαν καὶ Ἄβιλα καὶ Γάδαρα παρέλαβεν Ἀντίοχος, μετ᾽ ὀλίγον δὲ προσεχώρησαν αὐτῷ καὶ τῶν Ἰουδαίων οἱ περὶ τὸ ἱερὸν τὸ προσαγορευόμενον Ἱεροσόλυμα κατοικοῦντες, ὑπὲρ οὗ καὶ πλείω λέγειν ἔχοντες καὶ μάλιστα περὶ τῆς γενομένης περὶ τὸ ἱερὸν ἐπιφανείας,*
10 *εἰς ἕτερον καιρὸν ὑπερθησόμεθα τὴν διήγησιν.»*

2 ἑκκαιδεκάτη AW ις V XII Lat. 4 τὸ τῶν FLAVW
5-6 Βατανέαν Niese βαταναίαν codd. *bataniam* Lat. 6 γάδειρα W
gadera Lat. 9 περὶ τῆς γενομένης] διὰ τὴν FLV / ἐπιφάνειαν FLV

(135) Polybius of Megalopolis attests these statements of mine; for in the sixteenth book of his History he says the following: "Scopas, the general of Ptolemy, set out for the upper country and during the winter subdued the Jewish nation." (136) And in the same book he says that, after Scopas was defeated by Antiochus, "Antiochus took Batanaia, Samaria, Abila and Gadara, and after a short time there also came over to him those Jews, who live near the temple of Jerusalem, as it is called, concerning which we have more to say, especially concerning the renown of the temple, but we shall defer the account to another occasion." (trans. R. Marcus, *LCL*)

Josephus had already related accounts of the war waged by Antiochus III against Scopas and the way in which the Jews assisted Antiochus in the Fifth Syrian War. He also quotes Polybius in *Ant.*, XII, 358, in connection with the death of Antiochus Epiphanes. It seems that either direct or, more probably, indirect use of Polybius coloured the account of non-Jewish history included in the latter part of the twelfth book and the first part of the thirteenth book of *Antiquitates*, cf. M. Nussbaum, "Observationes in Flavii Josephi Antiquitates.", Ph. D. Thesis, Göttingen 1875, p. 27; J. v. Destinon, *Die Quellen des Flavius Josephus*, Kiel 1882, pp. 46 ff.

From Herodotus to Plutarch

135 ἐν γὰρ τῇ ἑξκαιδεκάτῃ τῶν ἱστοριῶν: Josephus expressly quotes the sixteenth book of Polybius, which comprised the events of 201 and 200 B. C. E. Thus, we must date the Battle of Panium and the subsequent subjugation of Judaea not later than 200 B. C. E., since Josephus found them narrated in the same book of Polybius; cf. ἐν τῇ αὐτῇ βίβλῳ. Some scholars cling to the view that these events should be dated to 198 B. C. E. and even propose to emend the text of Josephus to make it fit the latter date; see, e.g., G. de Sanctis, *Storia dei Romani*, Vol. IV, Part 1², Florence 1969, p. 115, n. 8. However, the arguments for 200 B. C. E. as the year of the Battle of Panium are convincing enough; see the main discussion in M. Holleaux, *Études d'épigraphie et d'histoire grecques*, III, Paris 1942, pp. 317 ff. The correct date is also given by others, e.g. by Niese, II, p. 578, n. 6; O. Leuze, *Hermes*, LVIII (1923), p. 192; E. Täubler, *JQR*, NS XXXVII, (1946–1947), p. 10. Yet, the last remnants of the Ptolemaic dominion fell into the hands of Antiochus only in 198; see Livius, XXXIII, 19 : 8. Cf. for all these events, Walbank, *op. cit.* (supra, p. 110, n. 2), II, 1967, pp. 523 f.; 546 f. See also the inscription found at Ḥefzibah, seven kilometres northwest of Bet She'an, and published by Y. H. Landau, *IEJ*, XVI (1966), pp. 54 ff.; Jeanne Robert & L. Robert, *REG*, LXXXIII (1970), pp. 469 ff.

Σκόπας: On him, see H. Benecke, "Die Seepolitik der Aitoler", Ph.D. Thesis, Hamburg 1934, pp. 38 ff; Dumrese, PW, Suppl. VII, pp. 1211 ff.

κατεστρέψατο ἐν τῷ χειμῶνι: Holleaux suggested the following chronological scheme: (a) 201 B. C. E. — the capture of Gaza by the Seleucid army; (b) winter 201–200 — the counter-offensive of the Ptolemaic forces under the command of Scopas; (c) 200 — the Battle of Panium, the conquest of Batanaia, etc. Thus, the winter during which Scopas subdued the Jews would be that of 201–200 B. C. E.; cf. H. H. Schmitt, *Untersuchungen zur Geschichte Antiochos' des Grossen und seiner Zeit*, Wiesbaden 1964, pp. 236 f.

τὸ 'Ιουδαίων ἔθνος: On the concept of ἔθνος in the Seleucid administration, see E. Bikerman, *Institutions des Séleucides*, Paris 1938, pp. 164 f. On the conquest of Jerusalem during the counter-offensive of Scopas, see Hieronymus (presumably from Porphyry), on Dan. xi : 13 f. = *F. Gr. Hist.*, II, B 260, F 45 "cepitque Iudaeam [scil. Scopas] et optimates Ptolemaei partium secum abducens."

136 Σκόπα νικηθέντος ὑπ' 'Αντιόχου: The Battle of Panium is implied here. For an attempt to describe it, see De Sanctis, *op. cit.*, pp. 115 ff.

οἱ περὶ τὸ ἱερὸν τὸ προσαγορευόμενον 'Ιεροσόλυμα κατοικοῦντες: Cf. *Oracula Sibyllina*, III, 702 f.: υἱοὶ δ᾽ αὖ μεγάλοιο θεοῦ περὶ ναὸν ἅπαντες ἡσυχίως ζήσοντ᾽ εὐφραινόμενοι ἐπὶ τούτοις.

Polybius calls the Temple itself by the name of Hierosolyma. Yet, we should not infer from this passage that Judaea was envisaged at that period as a temple-state, after the fashion of the temple-states of Asia Minor and Syria. Contrary to these temples, the one in Jerusalem was not in possession of landed estates, and the territory of Judaea was by no means regarded as its property. However, since the Temple eclipsed all the other institutions of Judaea with its splendour and importance and since it constituted the indisputable centre of the Jews, Polybius used that expression; cf. Livius, *Periochae*, CII (No. 131).

γενομένης περὶ τὸ ἱερὸν ἐπιφανείας: ἐπιφάνεια in the sense of renown; cf., e.g., Polybius, VI, 43 : 7: τῆς τότε γενομένης περὶ τὴν Θηβαίων πόλιν ἐπιφανείας; Diodorus, XL, 3 : 3 (No. 65), where Jerusalem is described as καὶ τὴν νῦν οὖσαν ἐπιφανεστάτην. Cf. also E. Pax, 'Επιφάνεια, Munich 1955, p. 13. The alternative

Polybius

interpretation of ἐπιφάνεια as a divine manifestation should be discarded; cf. R. Marcus, *Josephus (LCL)* VII, p. 69, n.g.

εἰς ἕτερον καιρὸν ὑπερθησόμεθα τὴν διήγησιν: It seems that the more detailed discussion of the Jewish Temple was reserved for the account of the activities of Antiochus Epiphanes; cf. the following passage (No. 33); H. Willrich, *Juden und Griechen vor der makkabäischen Erhebung*, Göttingen 1895, pp. 60 f.; E. Norden, *Festgabe Harnack*, p. 295 = *Kleine Schriften*, p. 279; Pédech, *op. cit.* (supra, p. 110, n.2), p. 562, n. 276.

33

Historiae, apud: Josephus, *Contra Apionem*, II, 83–84 — Niese = Reinach (Budé), pp. 72 f.

(83) Quia vero Antiochus neque iustam fecit templi depraedationem, sed egestate pecuniarum ad hoc accessit, cum non esset hostis, et super nos auxiliatores suos et amicos adgressus est nec aliquid dignum derisione illic invenit, (84) multi et digni conscriptores super
5 hoc quoque testantur, Polybius Megalopolita, Strabon Cappadox ⟨No. 98⟩, Nicolaus Damascenus ⟨No. 87⟩, Timagenes ⟨No. 80⟩ et Castor ⟨No. 77⟩ temporum conscriptor et Apollodorus ⟨No. 34⟩, ⟨qui⟩ omnes dicunt pecuniis indigentem Antiochum transgressum foedera Iudaeorum expoliasse templum auro argentoque plenum.

6 *Timagenes* Boysen   *Timagenis* Lat.   8 *⟨qui⟩* Hudson
9 *expoliasse* Niese   *et spoliasse* Lat.

(83) That the raid of Antiochus on the temple was iniquitous, that it was impecuniosity which drove him to invade it, when he was not an open enemy, that he attacked us, his allies and friends, and that he found there nothing to deserve ridicule; (84) these facts are attested by many sober historians: Polybius of Megalopolis, Strabo the Cappadocian, Nicolaus of Damascus, Timagenes, Castor the chronicler, and Apollodorus, who all assert that it was impecuniosity which induced Antiochus, in violation of his treaties with the Jews, to plunder the temple with its stores of gold and silver.

(trans. H. St. J. Thackeray, *LCL*)

Josephus did not directly consult all the writers enumerated here. It appears that he knew Polybius only through Nicolaus or Strabo. Yet, we may assume that most of the other five writers, if not all of them, are also dependent on Polybius as their ultimate source for the history of the relations between Antiochus and the Jews.
83 *Fecit templi depraedationem*: On the pillage of the Temple by Antiochus Epiphanes, see I Macc. i : 20 ff.; II Macc. v : 15 f.; v : 21; *Ant.*, XII, 249 ff.

115

Polybius' comments on the event corroborate the version of I Macc., according to which Antiochus committed the sacrilegious robbery with no provocation from the Jews, while II Macc. sets the event after the revolt of Jason and the capture of rebellious Jerusalem; cf. E. Bickermann, *Der Gott der Makkabäer*, Berlin 1937, pp. 160 ff. According to I Macc., the pillage took place in the year 143 of the Seleucid Era. From the fragment of Polybius that follows it would seem impossible to date Jason's revolt to 169 B. C. E. instead of to 168 B. C. E., as suggested by Kolbe and Otto; see W. Kolbe, *Beiträge zur syrischen und jüdischen Geschichte*, Stuttgart 1926, p. 152; W. Otto, *Zur Geschichte der Zeit des 6. Ptolemäers*, Munich 1934, pp. 65 f. The passage testifies to the fact that the pillage of the Temple, for which the only possible date is 169 B. C. E., was not caused by a hostile act on the part of the Jews. On those events, see now O. Mørkholm, *Antiochus IV of Syria*, Copenhagen 1966, pp. 142 f.

XIX. APOLLODORUS OF ATHENS

Second century B.C.E.

Apollodorus, the famous compiler of a chronicle in metre, was active both in Alexandria and in Pergamum. He was a younger contemporary of Polybius, but we cannot say whether he derived his information about Antiochus Epiphanes from that historian.

It is unlikely that Josephus used Apollodorus' work directly. He presumably got his reference to Apollodorus from one of the other writers cited by him as witnesses to the policy of Antiochus. It was either Nicolaus or Strabo who mentioned Apollodorus in this connection. Although Apollodorus should have come after Polybius chronologically, he is quoted the last in the series of authors.

34

apud: Josephus, *Contra Apionem*, II, 83–84 — Niese = *F. Gr. Hist.*, II, B244, F79 = Reinach (Budé), pp. 72 f.

(83) Quia vero Antiochus neque iustam fecit templi depraedationem, sed egestate pecuniarum ad hoc accessit, cum non esset hostis, et super nos auxiliatores suos et amicos adgressus est nec aliquid dignum derisione illic invenit, (84) multi et digni conscriptores super
5 hoc quoque testantur, Polybius Megalopolita ⟨No. 33⟩, Strabon Cappadox ⟨No. 98⟩, Nicolaus Damascenus ⟨No. 87⟩, Timagenes ⟨No. 80⟩ et Castor ⟨No. 77⟩ temporum conscriptor et Apollodorus, ⟨qui⟩ omnes dicunt pecuniis indigentem Antiochum transgressum foedera Iudaeorum expoliasse templum auro argentoque plenum.

6 *Timagenes* Boysen, *Timagenis* Lat.   7 *⟨qui⟩* Hudson
9 *expoliasse* Niese *et spoliasse* Lat.

(83) That the raid of Antiochus on the temple was iniquitous, that it was impecuniosity which drove him to invade it, when he was not an open enemy, that he attacked us, his allies and friends, and that he found there nothing to deserve ridicule; (84) these facts are attested by many sober historians: Polybius of Megalopolis, Strabo the Cappadocian, Nicolaus of Damascus, Timagenes, Castor the chronicler, and Apollodorus, who all assert that it was impecuniosity which induced Antiochus, in violation of his treaties with the Jews, to plunder the temple with its stores of gold and silver.

(trans. H. St. J. Thackeray, *LCL*)

Quia vero Antiochus neque iustam fecit templi depraedationem . . .: Cf. the commentary to Polybius (No. 33).

118

XX. MENANDER OF EPHESUS

Second century B.C.E.

*Menander was a Greek writer, who composed a work "on the achieve-
ments of the kings among the Greeks and barbarians"; cf.* Contra
Apionem, *I, 116:* γέγραφεν δὲ οὗτος τὰς ἐφ᾽ ἑκάστου τῶν βασιλέων
πράξεις τὰς παρὰ τοῖς Ἕλλησι καὶ βαρβάροις γενομένας. *If we accept
the identification of Menander of Ephesus with Aristarchus' pupil mentioned in Suda, s.v.* Eratosthenes = F. Gr. Hist., *III, C783, T1, he lived
in the second century B.C.E.*[1]
*Josephus asserts that Menander derived his material from the native
sources of the people, whose past he related in Greek. A part of the
work was allotted to the Tyrian kings.*[2]
*The preservation of the Menandrian fragments is due entirely to
Josephus. The most important fragment, found in* Contra Apionem, *I,
117 ff., includes the history of Hiram and a list of subsequent kings.
The end of the passage, which comprises two chronological remarks,
the last of which is connected with the date of the foundation of the
Temple at Jerusalem, does not constitute a direct quotation from
Menander. It is nevertheless probable that its contents derive from that
writer.*
*The portion of the fragment that deals with Hiram and his relations with
Solomon — the only one bearing upon the Jews — resembles the fragment
of Dius, apud:* Contra Apionem, *I, 112–115 (No. 36), and is also found
in* Ant., *VIII, 144 ff.*
Other fragments of Menander are preserved in Ant., *VIII, 324 (the
drought of the time of Ithobalus) and IX, 284 ff. (the war of the
Assyrians against Tyre). It also seems that Josephus' account of Tyrian
history from Nebuchadrezzar to Cyrus, in* Contra Apionem, *I, 156 ff.,
derives from Menander.*

---

1 See also Laqueur, PW, XV, p. 762.
2 For Gutschmid's view that the whole work dealt only with Phoenician history,
see Gutschmid, IV, p. 471.

apud: Josephus, *Contra Apionem*, I, 116–120, 126 — Niese (repet. *Antiquitates Judaicae*, VIII.
144–146) = F17R = *F. Gr. Hist.*, III, C783, F1 = Reinach (Budé), pp. 23 ff.

(116) Ἀλλὰ πρὸς τούτῳ ⟨scil. *Δίῳ*⟩ *παραθήσομαι καὶ Μένανδρον τὸν
Ἐφέσιον. γέγραφεν δὲ οὗτος τὰς ἐφ᾽ ἑκάστου τῶν βασιλέων πράξεις τὰς
παρὰ τοῖς Ἕλλησι καὶ βαρβάροις γενομένας ἐκ τῶν παρ᾽ ἑκάστοις ἐπιχωρίων γραμμάτων σπουδάσας τὴν ἱστορίαν μαθεῖν. (117) γράφων τοίνυν*
5 *περὶ τῶν ἐν Τύρῳ βεβασιλευκότων ἔπειτα γενόμενος κατὰ τὸν Εἴρωμον
ταῦτά φησι· «τελευτήσαντος δὲ Ἀβιβάλου διεδέξατο τὴν βασιλείαν
αὐτοῦ ὁ υἱὸς Εἴρωμος, ὃς βιώσας ἔτη νγ᾽ ἐβασίλευσεν ἔτη λδ᾽. (118) οὗτος
ἔχωσε τὸν Εὐρύχωρον τόν τε χρυσοῦν κίονα τὸν ἐν τοῖς τοῦ Διὸς
ἀνέθηκεν, ἐπί τε ὕλην ξύλων ἀπελθὼν ἔκοψεν ἀπὸ τοῦ λεγομένου Λιβάνου*
10 *ὄρους κέδρινα ξύλα εἰς τὰς τῶν ἱερῶν στέγας, καθελών τε τὰ ἀρχαῖα
ἱερὰ καινὰ ᾠκοδόμησεν τό τε τοῦ Ἡρακλέους καὶ τῆς Ἀστάρτης,
(119) πρῶτόν τε τοῦ Ἡρακλέους ἔγερσιν ἐποιήσατο ἐν τῷ Περιτίῳ
μηνί, τοῖς τε Κιτίοις ἐπεστρατεύσατο μὴ ἀποδιδοῦσι τοὺς φόρους· οὓς
καὶ ὑποτάξας ἑαυτῷ πάλιν ἀνέστρεψεν. (120) ἐπὶ τούτου ἦν Ἀβδήμουνος*
15 *παῖς νεώτερος, ὃς ἀεὶ ἐνίκα τὰ προβλήματα, ἃ ἐπέταττε Σολομὼν ὁ
Ἱεροσολύμων βασιλεύς»... (126) συνάγεται πᾶς ὁ χρόνος ἀπὸ τῆς
Εἰρώμου βασιλείας μέχρι Καρχηδόνος κτίσεως ἔτη ρνε᾽ μῆνες η᾽. ἐπεὶ
δὲ δωδεκάτῳ ἔτει τῆς αὐτοῦ βασιλείας ὁ ἐν Ἱεροσολύμοις ᾠκοδομήθη
ναός, γέγονεν ἀπὸ τῆς οἰκοδομήσεως τοῦ ναοῦ μέχρι Καρχηδόνος*
20 *κτίσεως ἔτη ρμγ᾽ μῆνες η᾽.*

1 καὶ Lat, Eus.   om. L   2 τὰς² Eus.   om. L.   3 ἑκάστοις Eus.,
Lat.   ἐκείνοις L   4 τοίνυν Eus.   δὴ L   enim Lat.   5 ἐν Τύρῳ
βεβασιλευκότων Eus.   βεβασιλευκότων ἐν τύρῳ L   7 ὃς Ant. om. L /
νγ᾽... ἔτη Ant.   om. L, Lat.   8 τὸ Εὐρύχωρον Ant.   9 ἐπί τε Eus.
ἔπειτα L   ἔτι τε Ant.   9–10 ἀπὸ τοῦ ὄρους τοῦ λεγομένου Λιβάνου Ant.
11 καινὰ Niese   καὶ ναοὺς L   ναὸν Eus.   καὶ ναὸν Ant. /   Ἀστάρτης Eus.,
Ant.   ἀστάρτης τέμενος ἀνιέρευσεν L   12 πρῶτόν (πρῶτός Ant.) τε
τοῦ Ἡρακλέους ἔγερσιν Eus., Ant.   καὶ τὸ μὲν τοῦ ἡρακλέους πρῶτον L
13 εἶτα τὸ τῆς Ἀστάρτης post μηνί add. L /   τοῖς τε Κιτίοις Albright   ὁπότε
τιτνοῖς L   τοῖς τε Τιτναίοις Eus.   τοῖς τε Ἰυκέοις Ant.   τοῖς τε Ἰτυκαίοις
Gutschmid   ὁπότε Τυρίοις Lowth /   ἐπεστρατεύσατο Ant.   ἐπεστράτευσεν
L /   τὸν φόρον Eus. /   οὓς om. Ant.   14 ἑαυτῷ πάλιν Ant.   πάλιν
ἑαυτῷ L /   Ἀβδήμονος Ant.   Ἀβδούμηνος Eus.   abdemonus Lat.   Ἀβδή-
μων Reinach   15 ἀεὶ Ant.   om. L /   τὰ] λύων τὰ Eus. /   Σολομὼν
Ant.   σαλομὼν L   16 συνάγεται δὲ Eus.   συνάγεται οὖν Theophilus
συνάγεται δὴ ed. pr.   17 μέχρι Eus.   ἄχρι L   18 αὐτοῦ Eus.
εἰρώμου L   Ἱερώμου Theophilus   19 ναός Eus.   ὁ ναός L /
μέχρι Eus.   ἄχρι L

Menander of Ephesus

(116) I will, however, cite yet a further witness, Menander of Ephesus. This author has recorded the events of each reign, in Hellenic and non-Hellenic countries alike, and has taken the trouble to obtain his information in each case from the national records. (117) Writing on the kings of Tyre, when he comes to Hirom he expresses himself thus: "On the death of Abibalus the kingdom passed to his son Hirom, who lived fifty-three years and reigned thirty-four. (118) He laid the embankment of the Broad Place, dedicated the golden pillar in the temple of Zeus, went and cut down cedar wood on the mount called Libanus for timber for the roofs of temples, demolished the ancient temples, and built new shrines dedicated to Heracles and Astarte. (119) He was the first to celebrate the Awaking of Heracles,[1] in the month Peritius. He undertook a campaign against the people of Citium,[2] and did not return home till he had reduced them to submission. (120) Under his reign lived Abdemun, a young lad, who always succeeded in mastering the problems set by Solomon, king of Jerusalem...." (126) The whole period from the accession of Hirom to the foundation of Carthage thus amounts to 155 years and eight months; and since the temple at Jerusalem was built in the twelfth year of King Hirom's reign, 143 years and eight months elapsed between the erection of the temple and the foundation of Carthage.

(trans. H. St. J. Thackeray, LCL)

116 παραθήσομαι καὶ Μένανδρον τὸν Ἐφέσιον: The Phoenician writers Dius and Menander are referred to in a different order in *Ant.*, VIII than in *Contra Apionem*.
117 περὶ τῶν ἐν Τύρῳ βεβασιλευκότων: Menander preserves the character of the Tyrian annals in his work.
ἐβασίλευσεν ἔτη λδ΄: According to the prevalent chronological system, Hiram reigned at Tyre in the years 969–936 B. C. E.
118 τὸν Εὐρύχωρον: On the "Broad Space", see F.C. Movers, *Die Phönizier*, Vol. II, Part 1, Bonn 1849, pp. 190 ff. Menander has in mind Hiram's achievement, which is also referred to by Dius (No. 36), namely, the bridging of the two islands that made up Tyre.
119 τοῦ Ἡρακλέους ἔγερσιν: The Tyrian Heracles stands for Melkart. The celebration alluded to here is connected with the ritual of the god who dies and comes back to life. This tradition about the death and resurrection of Heracles is preserved by Athenaeus, *Deipnosophistae*, IX, 47, p. 392 D–E; cf. J. Frazer, *Adonis, Attis, Osiris*, I, London 1927, pp. 110 ff.; see also J. Morgenstern, *Vetus Testamentum*, X (1960), pp. 163 ff. Thackeray translated the passage as implying the erection of a temple to Heracles. His interpretation has been recently approved by H. J. Katzenstein, *JNES*, XXIV (1965), pp. 116 f.

1 I have changed the translation of Thackeray here.
2 According to the emendation of Albright.

From Herodotus to Plutarch

τοῖς Κιτίοις: This is an emendation proposed by Albright, implying a campaign by Hiram against the people of Citium on the island of Cyprus; see G. E. Wright (ed.) *The Bible and the Ancient Near East — Essays in Honor of W.F. Albright*, New York 1961, p. 361, n. 101; Movers, *op. cit.* (supra, p. 121), pp. 330 f. This seems more plausible than Gutschmid's emendation Ἰτυκαίοις; see also B. Mazar, "The Philistines and the Rise of Israel and Tyre", *Proceedings of the Israel Academy of Sciences and Humanities*, I, Jerusalem 1964, No. 7, p. 15.

120 Ἀβδήμουνος παῖς νεώτερος: The passage from Dius (No. 36) does not describe him as a boy, but calls him a man of Tyre: Ἀβδήμουνόν τινα Τύριον ἄνδρα. ὁ Ἱεροσολύμων βασιλεύς: The same designation is also found in Dius.

126 μέχρι Καρχηδόνος κτίσεως ἔτη ρνέ: The main tradition, as represented by the Graeco-Sicilian historian Timaeus, dates the foundation of Carthage to 814 B. C. E., thirty-eight years before the First Olympiad; see Timaeus, apud: Dionysius Halicarnassensis, I, 74 : 1 = *F. Gr. Hist.*, III, B 566, F 60. Cf. also O. Meltzer, *Geschichte der Kartager*, I, Berlin 1879, pp. 100 ff.; *F. Gr. Hist. op. cit.* III b, pp. 331 f., notes; T. S. Brown, *Timaeus of Tauromenium*, Berkeley–Los Angeles 1958, pp. 35 f. Taking this date as a basis, scholars can fix the various Tyrian reigns. Since, according to Menander, Hiram began to reign one hundred and fifty-five years before the foundation of Carthage, it follows that he became king in 969 B. C. E. and died in 936, after a reign of thirty-four years; cf. Ed. Meyer, *Geschichte des Altertums*, Vol. II, Part 2, Stuttgart–Berlin 1931, p. 125, n. 2; W. F. Albright, *Annuaire de l'institut de philologie et d'histoire orientales et slaves*, XIII, 1953 (1955), pp. 6 ff.; J. M. Peñuela, *Sefarad*, XIII (1953), p. 231. Liver, on the other hand, argues for a somewhat earlier date for the accession of Hiram, namely 979–978 B. C. E.; see J. Liver, *IEJ*, III (1953), pp. 113 ff.

ἐπεὶ δὲ δωδεκάτῳ ἔτει τῆς αὐτοῦ βασιλείας...: Most scholars doubt whether this synchronism really derives from Menander. Gutschmid (IV, p. 488) suggests that it stems from Alexander Polyhistor. Ed. Meyer thinks that Josephus used a version of Menander's work already reworked by Jews; *op. cit.*, p. 79, n. 2. Still, it is possible that Menander did mention the building of the Temple of Jerusalem. Since that event shed lustre on Tyre, it is by no means improbable that it had its place in the historical tradition of that city. It may even be that this tradition related the event in a way that did not wholly accord with Jewish feelings and that, therefore, either Josephus himself, or his presumed Jewish source, did not directly quote Menander on the building of the Temple, though he did so on the synchronism; cf. M. B. Rowton, *BASOR*, 119 (1950), p. 21, n. 1.

XXI. DIUS

Second century B.C.E.

We know of the Greek writer Dius through Contra Apionem *and through* Ant., *VIII, 147 ff. In the first-mentioned work Josephus asserts that Dius composed a history of Phoenicia, and that he was thought to be an authority on that subject. We do not know when he lived. For the most part, the information attributed to Dius agrees with that of Menander of Ephesus. In* Contra Apionem, *Dius' work is mentioned before Menander's as the oldest evidence for the antiquity of the Jewish nation found in Phoenician sources. In the* Antiquitates, *Dius' name follows that of Menander. The fragment of Dius that is quoted by Josephus deals with the activities of King Hiram and his relations with Solomon.*

apud: Josephus, *Contra Apionem*, I, 112–115 — Niese (repet. *Antiquitates Judaicae*, VIII, 147–149)

= F18R = *F. Gr. Hist.*, III, C785, T1 + F1 = Reinach (Budé), pp. 22 f.

(112) "Ότι δ' οὐ λόγος ἐστὶν ὑπ' ἐμοῦ συγκείμενος ὁ περὶ τῶν παρὰ τοῖς Τυρίοις γραμμάτων, παραθήσομαι μάρτυρα Δῖον ἄνδρα περὶ τὴν Φοινικικὴν ἱστορίαν ἀκριβῆ γεγονέναι πεπιστευμένον. οὗτος τοίνυν ἐν ταῖς περὶ Φοινίκων ἱστορίαις γράφει τὸν τρόπον τοῦτον· *(113)* «Ἀβι-
5 βάλου τελευτήσαντος ὁ υἱὸς αὐτοῦ Εἴρωμος ἐβασίλευσεν. οὗτος τὰ πρὸς ἀνατολὰς μέρη τῆς πόλεως προσέχωσεν καὶ μεῖζον τὸ ἄστυ ἐποίησεν καὶ τοῦ Ὀλυμπίου Διὸς τὸ ἱερὸν καθ' ἑαυτὸ ὂν ἐν νήσῳ, χώσας τὸν μεταξὺ τόπον, συνῆψε τῇ πόλει καὶ χρυσοῖς ἀναθήμασιν ἐκόσμησεν, ἀναβὰς δὲ εἰς τὸν Λίβανον ὑλοτόμησεν πρὸς τὴν τῶν ἱερῶν
10 κατασκευήν. *(114)* τὸν δὲ τυραννοῦντα Ἱεροσολύμων Σολομῶνα πέμψαι φασὶ πρὸς τὸν Εἴρωμον αἰνίγματα καὶ παρ' αὐτοῦ λαβεῖν ἀξιοῦν, τὸν δὲ μὴ δυνηθέντα διακρῖναι τῷ λύσαντι χρήματα ἀποτίνειν. *(115)* ὁμο-λογήσαντα δὲ τὸν Εἴρωμον καὶ μὴ δυνηθέντα λῦσαι τὰ αἰνίγματα πολλὰ τῶν χρημάτων εἰς τὸ ἐπιζήμιον ἀναλῶσαι. εἶτα δὲ Ἀβδήμουνόν
15 τινα Τύριον ἄνδρα τά τε προτεθέντα λῦσαι καὶ αὐτὸν ἄλλα προβαλεῖν, ἃ μὴ λύσαντα τὸν Σολομῶνα πολλὰ τῷ Εἰρώμῳ προσαποτῖσαι χρήματα.»

3 Φοινικικὴν Syncellus   φοινικὴν L, Eus.   7 ἐποίησε Eus., *Ant.*   πεποίηκεν L   9 ἱερῶν Eus., *Ant.*   ναῶν L   11 εἴρωμον L¹ Ἴρωμον
Eus.   Εἴρωμον Syncellus / λύσιν post ἀξιοῦν add. Eus.   14 δὲ Eus.,
Ant.   δὴ L   δι' Syncellus / Ἀβδάμονον Eus.   Ἀβδήμονα *Ant.*
abdemonum Lat.

(112) To prove that these assertions about the Tyrian archives are not of my own invention, I will call upon Dius, who is regarded as an accurate historian of Phoenicia, for my witness. In his history of the Phoenicians he writes as follows: (113) "On the death of Abibalus, his son Hirom came to the throne. He levelled up the eastern part of the city with embankments, enlarged the town, united to it by a causeway the temple of Olympian Zeus, which was isolated on an island, and adorned it with offerings of gold; he also went up to Libanus and had timber cut down for the construction of temples. (114) It is said that Solomon, the sovereign of Jerusalem, sent riddles to Hirom and asked for others from him, on the understanding that the one who failed to solve them should pay a sum of money to him who succeeded. (115) Hirom agreed, and being unable to guess the riddles, spent a large part of his wealth on the fine. Afterwards they were solved by a certain Abdemun of Tyre, who propounded others.

Dius

Solomon, failing to solve these, paid back to Hirom more than he had received."　　　　　　　　　　　　　　　　(transl. H. St. J. Thackeray, *LCL*)

112 *"Ότι δ'οὐ λόγος ἐστὶν...*: Josephus had written previously about the Tyrian archives, stating that they testify to the building of the Temple at Jerusalem by Solomon, one hundred and forty-three years and eight months before Carthage was founded by the Tyrians, and that the correspondence between Solomon and Hiram is still kept at Tyre.

113 *'Αβιβάλου τελευτήσαντος*: This Abibal is also known from Menander, apud: Josephus, *Contra Apionem*, I, 117 (No. 35).

Εἴρωμος ἐβασίλευσεν: According to the generally accepted chronology, Hiram I, a contemporary of Solomon, reigned between 969 and 936 B. C. E.; see the commentary to Menander of Ephesus. For the relations between Hiram and David and Solomon, see II Sam. v : 11; I Kings v : 16 ff.; ix : 10 ff.; x : 11, 22; I Chron. xiv : 1; II Chron. ii : 2 ff.; ix : 21; see also the correspondence between Hiram and Solomon in *Ant.*, VIII, 50 ff.; the fragments from the work of the Jewish-Hellenistic historian Eupolemus (*F. Gr. Hist.*, III, C 723, F 2); and the material referred to by Ginzberg (VI p. 288, n. 36). On Hiram, see W.B. Fleming, *The History of Tyre*, New York 1915, pp. 16 ff.; Ed. Meyer, *Geschichte des Altertums*, II, 2², Stuttgart-Berlin 1931, pp. 123 f.; Eissfeldt, PW, Ser. 2, VII, p. 1884; Alt, II, pp. 144 f.; J. Liver, *Encyclopaedia Biblica*, III, 1958, pp. 122 ff. (in Hebrew).

τοῦ 'Ολυμπίου Διὸς τὸ ἱερόν: Zeus Olympius represents Baalshamin, the chief deity of the Phoenician pantheon; see Gutschmid, IV, p. 468; see also O. Eissfeldt, PW, XX, p. 361; E. Bickermann, *Der Gott der Makkabäer*, Berlin 1937, p. 112.

χώσας τὸν μεταξὺ τόπον: The ancient city of Tyre consisted of two islands: the larger one, to the north, which included the main part of the city, and the smaller one, to the south, where the temple was situated. The latter was joined to the northern island by Hiram; see Eissfeldt, *loc. cit.*, pp. 1877 ff. Menander speaks of the same accomplishment as the covering of the "Broad Space".

καὶ χρυσοῖς ἀναθήμασιν ἐκόσμησεν: Menander writes that Hiram dedicated a golden pillar in the temple of Zeus.

ἀναβὰς δὲ εἰς τὸν Λίβανον...: Cf. Menander (No. 35); see also I Kings v : 20.

114 *τὸν δὲ τυραννοῦντα τῶν 'Ιεροσολύμων Σολομῶνα*: It is true that in later times a distinction was made between king and tyrannos; see, e.g., *P. Oxy.*, No. 33 = H. Musurillo, *Acts of the Pagan Martyrs*, Oxford 1954, No. XI, Col. II, ll. 5 f. In this case, however, we should not expect Dius to characterize Solomon as a tyrant; the expression is only an example of the older Greek usage.

πέμψαι... αἰνίγματα: Cf. I Kings x : 1.

115 *ὁμολογήσαντα δὲ τὸν Εἴρωμον καὶ μὴ δυνηθέντα λῦσαι κτλ.*: In Menander we miss Solomon's victory in the solution of the riddles. Reinach surmises that Dius represents an amalgam of Jewish and Phoenician traditions.

εἶτα δὲ 'Αβδήμουννόν τινα Τύριον ἄνδρα: For this name, 'Αβδήμων, a Phoenician king who ruled Cyprus in the first century B. C. E., see Diodorus, XIV, 98 : 1. He appears in Theopompus as 'Αβδύμων; see *F. Gr. Hist.*, II, B 115, F 103.

XXII. THEOPHILUS

Second century B.C.E.

Alexander Polyhistor cites Theophilus[1] *as a witness to corroborate the statement of the Jewish Hellenistic historian Eupolemus, who reports that Solomon sent a golden pillar to be exhibited in the temple of Zeus; cf. Eusebius,* Praeparatio Evangelica *IX, 34:18* = F. Gr. Hist., *III, 723 F 2,* ad fin.: τῷ δὲ Σούρωνι εἰς Τύρον πέμψαι τὸν χρυσοῦν κίονα τὸν ἐν Τύρῳ ἀνακείμενον ἐν τῷ ἱερῷ τοῦ Διός.[2]

Theophilus may be the same as the Theophilus listed by Josephus in Contra Apionem, *I, 216 (No. 38), among writers testifying to the antiquity of the Jews.*

1 Cf. R. Laqueur, PW, Ser. 2, V, pp. 2137 f.
2 Cf. Freudenthal, pp. 117 f.

Theophilus

37

apud: Eusebius, *Praeparatio Evangelica*, IX, 34:19 — Mras = F20R = *F. Gr. Hist.*, III, C733, F1

Θεόφιλος δέ φησι τὸν περισσεύσαντα χρυσὸν τὸν Σολομῶνα τῷ Τυρίων βασιλεῖ πέμψαι· τὸν δὲ εἰκόνα τῆς θυγατρὸς ζῷον ὁλοσώματον κατασκευάσαι, καὶ ἔλυτρον τῷ ἀνδριάντι τὸν χρυσοῦν κίονα περιθεῖναι.

1 περιττεύσαντα Β | τὸν σολομῶντα Β
τω σολομῶντι ΟΝ   2 ζῷον om. Β

Theophilus says that Solomon sent to the king of the Tyrians the gold which had been left. The last-mentioned king made a full-length statue of his daughter and used the golden column to cover it.

τὸν περισσεύσαντα χρυσόν: I.e. the gold left from that which Hiram sent to Solomon (I Kings ix : 11 ff.).

τὸν δὲ εἰκόνα τῆς θυγατρός: The daughter given in marriage to Solomon is meant here; see the commentary to Laetus, apud: Tatianus, *Oratio ad Graecos*, 37 (No. 39). It seems that Theophilus mentioned this marriage before.

τὸν χρυσοῦν κίονα: This is the pillar referred to by Eupolemus; see the introduction.

38

apud: Josephus, *Contra Apionem*, I, 215–216 = Reinach (Budé), p. 41

(215) ᾿Αρκοῦσι δὲ ὅμως εἰς τὴν ἀπόδειξιν τῆς ἀρχαιότητος αἵ τε Αἰγυπτίων καὶ Χαλδαίων καὶ Φοινίκων ἀναγραφαὶ πρὸς ἐκείναις τε τοσοῦτοι τῶν ῾Ελλήνων συγγραφεῖς· *(216)* ἔτι δὲ πρὸς τοῖς εἰρημένοις Θεόφιλος καὶ Θεόδοτος καὶ Μνασέας ⟨No. 27⟩ καὶ ᾿Αριστοφάνης
5 ⟨No. 24⟩ καὶ ῾Ερμογένης ⟨No. 199⟩ Εὐήμερός ⟨No. 16⟩ τε καὶ Κόνων ⟨No. 144⟩ καὶ Ζωπυρίων ⟨No. 198⟩ καὶ πολλοί τινες ἄλλοι τάχα, οὐ γὰρ ἔγωγε πᾶσιν ἐντετύχηκα τοῖς βιβλίοις, οὐ παρέργως ἡμῶν ἐμνημονεύκασιν.

3 ἔτι δὲ] Eus.   ἔτι δὲ καὶ L

(215) However, our antiquity is sufficiently established by the Egyptian, Chaldaean, and Phoenician records, not to mention the numerous Greek historians. (216) In addition to those already cited, Theophilus, Theodotus, Mnaseas, Aristophanes, Hermogenes, Euhemerus, Conon, Zopyrion and, may be, many more — for my reading has not been exhaustive — have made more than a passing allusion to us.

(trans. H. St. J. Thackeray, *LCL*)

XXIII. LAETUS

Second century B.C.E.

Laetus was a historian who wrote, in Greek, about Phoenician history. He was thought of as one of those who translated the works of Phoenician writers into Greek, like Berossus, who claimed to have translated Babylonian documents; Manetho, who translated the Egyptian records; and Philo of Byblus, who rendered the work of Sanchuniaton.

The following passage is quoted by both Tatianus and Eusebius, Praeparatio Evangelica *X, 11:10 f. Clemens of Alexandria has an abridged version in which Laetus is closely coupled with Menander; see* Stromata, *I, 21:114:2.*

apud: Tatianus, *Oratio ad Graecos*, 37 — Schwartz = F 123 R = *F. Gr. Hist.*, III, C784, T1 + F1a

Μετὰ δὲ τοὺς Χαλδαίους τὰ Φοινίκων οὕτως ἔχει. γεγόνασι παρ᾿ αὐτοῖς
ἄνδρες τρεῖς, Θεόδοτος, Ὑψικράτης, Μῶχος· τούτων τὰς βίβλους εἰς
Ἑλληνίδα κατέταξεν φωνὴν Λαῖτος ὁ καὶ τοὺς βίους τῶν φιλοσόφων
ἐπ᾿ ἀκριβὲς πραγματευσάμενος. ἐν δὴ ταῖς τῶν προειρημένων ἱστορίαις
5 δηλοῦται κατὰ τίνα τῶν βασιλέων Εὐρώπης ἁρπαγὴ γέγονεν Μενελάου
τε εἰς τὴν Φοινίκην ἄφιξις καὶ τὰ περὶ Χείραμον, ὅστις Σολομῶνι
τῷ Ἰουδαίων βασιλεῖ πρὸς γάμον δοὺς τὴν ἑαυτοῦ θυγατέρα καὶ ξύλων
παντοδαπῶν ὕλην εἰς τὴν τοῦ ναοῦ κατασκευὴν ἐδωρήσατο.

3 κατέταξε V, Eus.   κατέταξαν P | Λαῖτος Clemens   χαῖτος MPV   ἄδιτος
Eus., JOGN   ἄσιτος D   4 δὴ Eus.   δὲ MPV   4–5 ἱστορίαις
δηλοῦται Eus.   δηλοῦται ἱστορίαις MPV   5 ἁρπαγὴ Eus.   ἁρπαγὴν
MPV | γέγονεν Wilamowitz   γεγονέναι MPV, Eus.   6 Εἴραμον Eus.
7 ἑαυτοῦ Eus.   om. MPV   8 νεὼ Eus.

After the Chaldaeans, the testimony of the Phoenicians is as follows:
There were among them three men, Theodotus, Hypsicrates and
Mochus. Laetus, who also composed with exactness the lives of the
philosophers, translated their books into Greek. Now, in the histories
of the aforesaid writers it is shown under which of the kings occurred the abduction of Europa; the arrival of Menelaus to Phoenicia;
and the events relating to Hiram, who gave his daughter to Solomon
the king of the Jews and supplied wood from all kinds of trees for
the building of the Temple.

Θεόδοτος: We know of no author of this name who dealt with Phoenician history;
however, we do know of a Jewish or Samaritan poet who wrote an epic on Shechem
from Eusebius, *Praeparatio Evangelica*, IX, 22; cf. R.J. Bull, *HTR*, LX (1967),
pp. 221 ff. The Theodotus referred to by Tatianus may be identical with the
Theodotus that Josephus mentions in *Contra Apionem*, I, 216, among the non-
Jewish authors who wrote about Jews.
Ὑψικράτης: Hypsicrates is also unknown to us as a historian of Phoenicia. For
the Greek historian Hypsicrates, see No. 79.
Μῶχος: Mochus is known from other sources, the oldest among them being Strabo,
Geographica, XVI, 2 : 24, p. 757, which refers to Posidonius: Εἰ δὲ δεῖ Ποσειδωνίῳ
πιστεῦσαι καὶ τὸ περὶ τῶν ἀτόμων δόγμα παλαιόν ἐστιν ἀνδρὸς Σιδονίου Μώχου
πρὸ τῶν Τρωϊκῶν χρόνων γεγονότος. If, indeed, Posidonius knew Mochus only
through Laetus, it would give us a *terminus ante quem* for the time of Laetus of
no later than the second century B. C. E. Against Reinach, who dates Laetus in the
second century C. E., see Laqueur, PW, XII, p. 518. Mochus is also mentioned by
Josephus, (*Ant.*, I, 107), Athenaeus, Diogenes Laertius, Iamblichus and Damascius;
see these texts in *F. Gr. Hist.* 784 F 2–6.

From Herodotus to Plutarch

Λαῖτος: In the MSS of Tatianus and Eusebius the name is χαῖτος or ἄδιτος(ἄσιτος); however, it is found in the correct form in Clemens of Alexandria and twice in Plutarchus, *Aetia Physica*, 2, p. 912 A; *ibid.* 6, p. 913 E.

ὁ καὶ τοὺς βίους τῶν φιλοσόφων... πραγματευσάμενος: We know nothing about this work of Laetus.

περὶ Χείραμον, ὅστις Σολομῶνι... δοὺς τὴν ἑαυτοῦ θυγατέρα: In I Kings xi : 1 we are only told that Solomon married Sidonian women, but not that he married Hiram's daughter.

ὕλην... ἐδωρήσατο: Cf. I Kings v : 22, 24; ix : 11; x : 11; II Chron. ii : 7.

XXIV. OCELLUS LUCANUS

Second century B.C.E.

The Pythagorean work De Universi Natura, *which is attributed to Ocellus Lucanus, may be dated as early as the second century B.C.E.; in any case, it precedes Varro.*[1]
By accepting the reading of M (the Marcianus 263 from the fifteenth century), which has πληροῦσθαι *in § 46, p. 22, l. 18 (ed. Harder),*[2] *we probably get an allusion to the Septuagint translation of Genesis i: 28:* Αὐξάνεσθε καὶ πληθύνεσθε καὶ πληρώσατε τὴν γῆν. *This should by no means cause much surprise in a Pythagorean work of the Hellenistic age and much coloured, moreover, by Peripatetic influence. One must recall the sympathetic attitude shown to Judaism by some of the Peripatetic philosophers; cf. Theophrastus, apud:* Porphyrius, De Abstinentia, *II, 26 = No. 4, and Clearchus, apud:* Contra Apionem, *I, 176 – 183 = No. 15, as well as the tradition of Pythagoras' dependence on the Jews, as it emerges from Hermippus (Nos. 25–26).*[3]
*The context of this probable allusion to the Septuagint is as follows: Ocellus argues that the organs and impulses of sexual intercourse were supplied by God not for the sake of pleasure, but in order to perpetuate the human race. Therefore, a man should not desert the hearth of his family, his city or God Himself, but he must fulfil his prescribed duty. However, he should not accomplish this in the manner of unintelligent animals, but should regard as necessary and good that which is thought to be so by good men, namely, not only that the families should abound in men (*πολυανδρεῖσθαι*) and that most of the earth should be filled (here*

---

1 See the summary by R. Harder, *Ocellus Lucanus — Text und Kommentar,* Berlin 1926, pp. 149 ff.; cf. H. Thesleff, *Eranos,* LX (1962), pp. 10 f.; H. Dörrie, PW, XXIV, p. 272.
2 There are some other passages in the book where M alone preserves the correct reading. Cf. Harder, *op. cit.,* p. IV. In his commentary (pp. 128 ff.) Harder seems to have made a good case for πληροῦσθαι on the grounds of style and content. For W. Theiler's reservations, cf. *Gnomon,* II (1926), pp. 589 f.
3 Harder's opinion that this passage of Ocellus Lucanus refers to Genesis has been accepted by others, e. g., by R. Walzer, *Galen on Jews and Christians,* Oxford 1949, p. 22.

πληροῦσθαι) *by them, but — and this is the most important thing — that there should be an abundance of good men* (εὐανδρεῖσθαι).

Naturally, the first chapter of Genesis suggested itself to the minds of both Ocellus Lucanus and the author of De Sublimitate, *IX:9 (No. 148).*

Ocellus Lucanus

40

De Universi Natura, 45–46 — *The Pythagorean Texts of the Hellenistic Period*, ed. H. Thesleff, Åbo 1965, pp. 135 f. = R. Harder, *Ocellus Lucanus, Text und Kommentar*, Berlin 1926, p. 22

(45) "Εν οὖν τοῦτο πρῶτον δεῖ θεωρεῖν ὅτι οὐχ ἡδονῆς ἕνεκα ἡ μῖξις· ἔπειτα δὲ καὶ αὐτὴν τὴν τοῦ ἀνθρώπου σύνταξιν πρὸς τὸ ὅλον, ὅτι μέρος ὑπάρχων οἴκου τε καὶ πόλεως καί, τὸ μέγιστον, κόσμου συμπληροῦν ὀφείλει τὸ ἀπογινόμενον τούτων ἕκαστον, ἐὰν μέλλῃ μήτε
5 συγγενικῆς ἑστίας λειποτάκτης γίνεσθαι μήτε πολιτικῆς μήτε μὴν τῆς θείας. οἱ γὰρ καθάπαξ μὴ διὰ παιδοποιίαν συναπτόμενοι ἀδικήσουσι τὰ τιμιώτατα τῆς κοινωνίας συστήματα· εἰ δὲ καὶ γεννήσουσιν οἱ τοιοῦτοι μεθ᾽ ὕβρεως καὶ ἀκρασίας, μοχθηροὶ οἱ γενόμενοι καὶ κακοδαίμονες ἔσονται καὶ βδελυροὶ ὑπό τε θεῶν καὶ δαιμόνων καὶ ἀνθρώπων
10 καὶ οἴκων καὶ πόλεων. *(46)* ταῦτα οὖν προδιανοουμένους οὐ δεῖ ὁμοίως τοῖς ἀλόγοις ζῴοις προσέρχεσθαι τοῖς ἀφροδισίοις, ἀλλ᾽ ὡς ἀναγκαῖον ‹καὶ› καλὸν ἡγουμένους ὅπερ ἀναγκαῖον καὶ καλὸν εἶναι νομίζουσιν οἱ ἀγαθοὶ τῶν ἀνθρώπων, τὸ μὴ μόνον πολυανδρεῖσθαι τοὺς οἴκους καὶ τὸν πλείονα τῆς γῆς τόπον πληροῦσθαι (ἡμερώτατον γὰρ πάντων καὶ
15 βέλτιστον ζῷον ὁ ἄνθρωπος), ἀλλὰ καί, τὸ μέγιστον, εὐανδρεῖσθαι.

2 αὐτὴν τὴν τοῦ ἀνθρώπου Jaeger   τὴν αὐτὴν τῷ ἀνθρώπῳ AMBR
4 μέλῃ AM   5 γενέσθαι M / πολίτης AB   6 ἁπτόμενοι R
8 ἐκρασίας M / γεννώμενοι A   10 οὐ δεῖ] δεῖ (μὴ superscr.) A
12 ‹καὶ› Rudolph / ὅπερ] ἅπερ MB   εἴπερ Nogarola   14 πληροῦσθαι
om. ABR   14–15 πάντων post βέλτιστον posuerunt ABR   15 ζῷον
Nogarola   ζῴων AMBR / τοῦ μεγίστου BR

(45) First of all it should be perceived that sexual intercourse does not exist for pleasure's sake. Secondly we have to consider man's relative position in the universe, that since he constitutes a part of his family and of his city, and above all of the world, he has to fill up the losses of each of them if he is not to become a deserter of his family hearth, neither of that of the city nor of the divine one. For those who once and for all renounce intercourse in order to beget children will injure the most honourable bodies of association; and if indeed such people will beget with lust and incontinence, the progeny will be wretched, unhappy and abhorred by gods, semi-divine beings, men, households and cities. (46) People have to think over these matters beforehand and thus not come to sexual intercourse like irrational animals, but to consider as necessary and good that which good men think necessary and good, namely, that households not only will abound in men and the greater part of the earth will be filled (man is indeed the gentlest and best of all creatures), but, which is the most important thing, that they will also have an abundance of good men.

133

XXV. TIMOCHARES

Second half of the second century B.C.E.

The following fragment, quoted by Eusebius from Alexander Polyhistor, is the only one of Timochares that has come down to us. We know that Timochares wrote a Historia Antiochi, *but we cannot tell which of the Seleucid kings with that name is referred to here. It is certain that at least three of the Syrian Antiochi were engaged in military operations against Jerusalem:*

a. Antiochus III (c. 200 B.C.E.), who fought against the Ptolemaic garrison in the Citadel; cf. Ant., XII, 133; Hieronymus (Porphyry) in his commentary to Dan. xi:13–14 = F. Gr. Hist., II, B260, F46 (No. 463).

b. Antiochus IV Epiphanes; cf. II Macc. v:11. Antiochus Epiphanes' capture of Jerusalem was related by many Greek historians, including Polybius (cf. Contra Apionem, *II, 83–84 = No. 33). Laqueur[1] is inclined to identify Antiochus Epiphanes with the Antiochus of Timochares, and the same view is held by Pédech.[2]*

c. Antiochus VII Sidetes, who besieged Jerusalem for a long time; see Ant., XIII, 236 ff.; Diodorus, XXXIV–XXXV, 1:1–5 (No. 63); pseudo-Plutarchus, Regum et Imperatorum Apophthegmata, *p. 184 E–F (No. 260).[3] To judge from Diodorus and pseudo-Plutarchus, this event was also well known to Greek historiography.*

The last possibility seems to be most plausible, as the siege at that time happened to be a lengthy one and needed some explanation. Timochares explained that it was so long because of the strength of the city, the abundance of water found there and the barrenness of its vicinity.

---

1 PW, Ser. 2, VI, p. 1258.
2 P. Pédech, *La méthode historique de Polybe*, Paris 1964, p. 562, n. 276.
3 Cf. Schürer, I, p. 259, n. 5.

Timochares

41

Historia Antiochi, apud: Eusebius, *Praeparatio Evangelica*, IX, 35:1 — Mras = F22R = F. Gr. *Hist.*,II, B165, F1

Τιμοχάρης δέ φησιν ἐν τοῖς Περὶ ᾿Αντιόχου τὰ ῾Ιεροσόλυμα τὴν μὲν περίμετρον ἔχειν σταδίους μ'· εἶναι δ᾿ αὐτὴν δυσάλωτον, πάντοθεν ἀπορρῶξι περικλειομένην φάραγξιν. ὅλην δὲ τὴν πόλιν ὕδασι καταρρεῖσθαι, ὥστε καὶ τοὺς κήπους ἐκ τῶν ἀπορρεόντων ὑδάτων ἐκ τῆς πόλεως
5 ἄρδεσθαι· τὴν δὲ μεταξὺ ἀπὸ τῆς πόλεως ἄχρι τεσσαράκοντα σταδίων ἄνυδρον εἶναι, ἀπὸ δὲ τῶν μ' σταδίων πάλιν κάθυδρον ὑπάρχειν.

1 αἱμοχάρης B   5 ἀπὸ om. ON   6 δὲ τῶν om. B

Timochares says in the *History of Antiochus* that Jerusalem has a circumference of 40 stades. It is hard to capture her, as she is enclosed on all sides by abrupt ravines. The whole city has a plenitude of running waters, so that the gardens are also irrigated by the waters streaming from the city. An area extending to a distance of 40 stades from the city is waterless; beyond the 40 stades the land becomes moist again.

ἔχειν σταδίους μ': The *Letter of Aristeas* (105) gives the same circumference for Jerusalem: οἷον τεσσαράκοντα σταδίων ὄντος τοῦ περιβόλου καθόσον εἰκάσαι δυνατόν. In the anonymous Schoinometresis of Syria (apud: Eusebius, *Praeparatio Evangelica*, IX, 36 : 1 = No. 42) the circumference is twenty-seven stadia, while Hecataeus (apud: Josephus, *Contra Apionem*, I, 197 = No. 12) speaks of *c*. fifty stadia; see also *BJ*, V, 159: τῆς πόλεως δ᾿ ὁ πᾶς κύκλος σταδίων ἦν τριακοντατριῶν. εἶναι δ᾿ αὐτὴν δυσάλωτον... φάραγξιν: This is somewhat of an overstatement of the natural strength of Jerusalem. The town was open to attack on the northern side, and it was on this side that the enemies of the Jews, among them Antiochus Sidetes, concentrated their main efforts; see *Ant.*, XIII, 238: κατὰ δὲ τὸ βόρειον μέρος τοῦ τείχους, καθ᾿ ὃ συνέβαινεν αὐτὸ καὶ ἐπίπεδον εἶναι, πύργους ἀναστήσας ἑκατὸν τριωρόφους ἀνεβίβασεν ἐπ᾿ αὐτοὺς στρατιωτικὰ τάγματα.

ὕδασι καταρρεῖσθαι: On the abundance of water in Jerusalem, see the *Letter of Aristeas*, 89: ὕδατος δὲ ἀνέκλειπτός ἐστι σύστασις... See also R. Tramontano, *La lettera di Aristea a Filocrate*, Naples 1931, pp. 95 f.; the Jewish-Hellenistic epic poet, Philo the Elder, apud: Eusebius, *Praeparatio Evangelica*, IX, 37 = F. Gr. *Hist.*, III, C 729, F 2; and the above-mentioned Schoinometresis. On the water installations of Jerusalem, see M. Hecker, *The Book of Jerusalem*, I (ed. M. Avi-Yonah), Jerusalem 1956, pp. 191 ff. (in Hebrew), which deals mainly with the biblical period; Schürer, I, p. 490, n. 146.

κήπους... ἄρδεσθαι: Cf. Jeremias, pp. 47 ff.

τὴν δὲ μεταξὺ... ἄνυδρον εἶναι: The shortage of water constituted a serious drawback for Antiochus during the siege of Jerusalem, *Ant.*, XIII, 237. A similar description, from the standpoint of the besiegers, may be found in Strabo, *Geographica*, XVI, 2 : 40 (No. 115): ἐντὸς μὲν εὔυδρον, ἐκτὸς δὲ παντελῶς διψηρόν.

From Herodotus to Plutarch

See also the description of Petra in Strabo, *Geographica*, XVI, 4 : 21, p. 779, which reminds us in some ways of Timochares' description of Jerusalem: κεῖται γὰρ ἐπὶ χωρίου τἆλλα ὁμαλοῦ καὶ ἐπιπέδου, κύκλῳ δὲ πέτρᾳ φρουρουμένου, τὰ μὲν ἐκτὸς ἀποκρήμνου καὶ ἀποτόμου, τὰ δ' ἐντὸς πηγὰς ἀφθόνους ἔχοντος εἴς τε ὑδρείαν καὶ κηπείαν.

XXVI. SCHOINOMETRESIS SYRIAE
(XENOPHON OF LAMPSACUS?)

c. 100 B.C.E.

The following quotation, which Eusebius owes to Alexander Polyhistor, derives from an anonymous Schoinometresis Syriae, *a work which may be supposed to be in the tradition of the bematists of the time of Alexander.*[1] *We know from Stephanus Byzantius s.v.* 'Ωρωπός (F. Gr. Hist., IIIA, 273, F72), *who draws on Alexander Polyhistor's* 'Περὶ Συρίας', *that there was a writer called Xenophon who wrote* 'Αἱ ἀναμετρήσεις τῶν ὁρῶν'. *It is usually assumed that this Xenophon is to be identified with Xenophon of Lampsacus, who was one of the sources of the* Naturalis Historia, *and who is well attested as the author of a Periplus; see Valerius Maximus, VIII, 13:7; Plinius,* Naturalis Historia, *VII, 155.*[2] *There is also much plausibility in the identification of Xenophon—the author of the* Αἱ ἀναμετρήσεις τῶν ὁρῶν *as quoted from Polyhistor's* Περὶ Συρίας *—with the anonymous author of the* Schoinometresis Syriae. *If all these identifications hold, then the work should be dated c. 100 B.C.E.,*[3] *and thus may perhaps be considered roughly contemporary with Timochares (No. 41). What the fragment contains regarding the circumference of Jerusalem and its water supply has its parallels in other sources; in addition, it contains some specific remarks about the nature of the wall of Jerusalem, certain parts of which consist of hewn stone, but most of which is gravel.*

---

1 See H. Berve, *Das Alexanderreich auf prosopographischer Grundlage*, I, Munich 1926, pp. 51 f.

2 Cf. Susemihl, I, p. 692; F. Gisinger, PW, Ser. 2, IX, pp. 2051 f.

3 For the date of Xenophon of Lampsacus, see Gisinger, *loc. cit.*

42

apud: Eusebius, *Praeparatio Evangelica*, IX, 36:1 — Mras = F23R = *F. Gr. Hist.*, III, C849, F1

ʿΟ δὲ τῆς Συρίας [σχοινομέτρης] σχοινομέτρησιν γράψας ἐν τῇ πρώτῃ
φησὶ κεῖσθαι ʿΙεροσόλυμα ἐπὶ μετεώρου τε καὶ τραχέος τόπου· ᾠκο-
δομῆσθαι δέ τινα μὲν μέρη τοῦ τείχους ἀπὸ λίθου ξεστοῦ, τὰ δὲ πλείονα
ἀπὸ χάλικος· καὶ ἔχειν τὴν περίμετρον τὴν πόλιν σταδίων κζ', ὑπάρχειν
5 δὲ καὶ πηγὴν ἐν τῷ χωρίῳ ὕδωρ δαψιλὲς ἀναβλύζουσαν.

1 σχοινομέτρης secl. Gaisford / σχοινομέτρησιν om. I

The author of *The Land-Survey of Syria* states in his first book that
Jerusalem is situated on a high and rough terrain; some parts of the
wall are built of hewn stone, but most of it consists of gravel. The city
has a circumference of 27 stades, and in that place there is a
fount from which water spouts out in abundance.

κεῖσθαι ʿΙεροσόλυμα ἐπὶ μετεώρου τε καὶ τραχέος τόπου: Cf. Strabo, *Geographica*,
XVI, 2 : 40, p. 762 (No. 115): ἦν γὰρ πετρῶδες καὶ εὐερκὲς ἔρυμα.

ἔχειν τὴν περίμετρον τὴν πόλιν σταδίων κζ: This circumference is smaller
than that found in Timochares, apud: Eusebius, *Praeparatio Evangelica*, IX,
35 : 1 (No. 41), where it is estimated at forty stadia. In Hecataeus, apud: Josephus,
Contra Apionem, I, 197 (No. 12) it is given as fifty stadia. Josephus, *BJ*, V, 159,
states that the circumference of the city in 70 C. E. — when it was certainly larger
than in the Hellenistic period — was thirty-three stadia.

ὑπάρχειν δὲ καὶ πηγήν: Cf. Timochares (No. 41) and Tacitus, *Historiae*, V, 12
(No. 281), and the commentaries *ad loc.*

XXVII. MELEAGER

End of the second century B.C.E. to beginning
of the first century B.C.E. ?

*Although a quite impressive number of Greek writers came from the
Hellenistic cities of Palestine (Gadara, Ascalon, Gaza, Gerasa), the
only remaining reference to Jews in their works is the one given here
from Meleager. Despite the statement in Diogenes Laertius, VI, 99,
that Meleager is a contemporary of Menippus, who lived in the third
century B.C.E.,[1] it is now commonly assumed, on the basis of a note
of the lemmatist (ἤκμασεν ἐπὶ Σελεύκου τοῦ ἐσχάτου, i.e. Seleucus
VI),[2] that Meleager lived at the end of the second century and the
beginning of the first.[3]*
*On the evidence of Meleager himself, he was born at Gadara, grew up at
Tyre and spent his old age in Cos; cf.* Anthologia Graeca, *VII, 418:*
Πρῶτα μοι Γαδάρων κλεινὰ πόλις ἔπλετο πάτρα, ἤνδρωσεν δ' ἱερὰ
δεξαμένα με Τύρος· εἰς γῆρας δ' ὅτ' ἔβην, ‹ἁ› καὶ Δία θρεψαμένα
Κῶς κἀμὲ θετὸν Μερόπων ἀστὸν ἐγηροτρόφει; *see also ibid., 417, 419.*
*The view that Meleager left Gadara for Tyre because of political events,
namely, the capture of the first-named city by the Hasmonaeans,[4] cannot
be substantiated.[5]*

---

1 Gow and Page suggest that Diogenes may have drawn a false inference from
  Meleager's profession that he was a follower of Menippus; see A. S. F. Gow &
  D. L. Page, *The Greek Anthology — Hellenistic Epigrams* I, Cambridge
  1965, p. XVI, n. 2. However, there are some scholars who argue strongly for
  a third-century date for Meleager, e. g., L. A. Stella, *Cinque poeti dell' antologia
  palatina*, Bologna 1949, pp. 232 ff.
2 When Seleucus VI captured Antioch in 95 B. C. E., he issued two series of
  coins, whose different monograms show them to belong to different Seleucid
  years. Cf. E. T. Newell, *The Seleucid Mint of Antioch*, New York 1918, pp.
  111 ff.; A. R. Bellinger, "The End of the Seleucids", *The Connecticut Academy
  of Arts and Sciences*, XXXVIII (1949), p. 73.
3 Cf., e. g., H. Ouvré, *Méléagre de Gadara*, Paris 1894, pp. 19 ff.; C. Radinger,
  Meleagros von Gadara, Innsbruck 1895, pp. 73 ff.; Gow & Page, *op. cit.*
  (supra, n. 1), pp. XIV ff.
4 *Ant.*, XIII, 356; *B. J.*, I, 86; cf. Radinger, *op. cit.*, p. 5.
5 For Meleager and the Jews, see also N. Bentwich. *JQR*, XXIII (1932–1933),
  pp. 183 f.

From Herodotus to Plutarch

43

Anthologia Graeca, V, 160 — Waltz = XXVI, Page — in: A.S.F. Gow & D. L. Page, *The Greek Anthology* — *Hellenistic Epigrams*, I, Cambridge 1965, p. 223 = F24R

Δημὼ λευκοπάρειε, σὲ μέν τις ἔχων ὑπόχρωτα
τέρπεται, ἃ δ᾽ ἐν ἐμοὶ νῦν στενάχει κραδία.
εἰ δέ σε σαββατικὸς κατέχει πόθος, οὐ μέγα θαῦμα·
ἐστὶ καὶ ἐν ψυχροῖς σάββασι θερμὸς Ἔρως.

White-cheeked Demo, some one hath thee named next him and is taking his delight, but my own heart groans within me. If thy lover is some Sabbath-keeper no great wonder! Love burns hot even on cold Sabbaths.   (trans. W. R. Paton, *LCL*)

1 Δημὼ λευκοπάρειε: Demo also appears elsewhere in the poems of Meleager; see *Anthologia Graeca*, V, 172, 173, 197. For this name in a Jewish inscription from Larisa in Thessaly, see *IG*, IX, 2, No. 988b = *CII*, No. 700,
3 σαββατικὸς πόθος: Meleager is one of the first pagan writers to refer to the Sabbath. If we accept the dating of Stella, he would be the very first, even preceding Agatharchides.
4 ἐν ψυχροῖς σάββασι: The Sabbath is designated cold because Jews were forbidden to light fires on that day. This has become a motif in pagan literature; see Rutilius Namatianus, *De Reditu Suo*, I, 389 (No. 542): "cui frigida sabbata cordi." For the dative σάββασι, see now A. Pelletier, *Vetus Testamentum*, XXII (1972), p. 441.

XXVIII. POSIDONIUS

c. 135–51 B.C.E.?

There is a paucity of references to Jews or to Judaea that may, with any
degree of certainty, be attributed to Posidonius. What they amount to,
in fact, is one statement by Josephus[1] that Posidonius' influence was
paramount, alongside that of Apollonius Molon, in the anti-Semitic work
of Apion, and a single passage in Strabo's Geographica, in which
Posidonius describes the people engaged in cutting asphalt — presumably extracted from the Dead Sea — as sorcerers using incantations.
The plain meaning of Josephus' statement about Posidonius' attitude
to the Jews is that the philosopher was by no means sympathetic toward
them, and that, like Apollonius Molon, he charged the Jews with abstention from worshipping the gods worshipped by others; moreover, he told
lies about the Temple in Jerusalem. Thus, both writers supplied Apion
with material against the Jews. After the statement referred to, Josephus
cites specimens of Apion's calumnies regarding Jewish worship at the
Temple, namely, the reference to the cult of an asinine head in Jerusalem
and the story of the annual murder of a Greek in the Temple. It is
clear that Josephus implies that Apion derived his calumnies about the
Jewish Temple from Posidonius and Apollonius Molon, and that there
seems to be no reason to differentiate between the two sources, or
between the two slanders. Yet, it may be assumed that Apollonius Molon
is dependent on Posidonius and not vice versa.[2]
A question that arises is: Where did Josephus obtain his information
about the views of Posidonius? The way he expresses himself about the
relationship of the two writers with Apion does not necessarily imply that
he compared the allegations of Posidonius and Apollonius with Apion's
libels and thus reached the conclusion that it was they who supplied the
pernicious material to Apion. It seems rather that Apion, who wanted to
lend more authority to his calumnies, traced them to the works of such
illustrious predecessors as Posidonius and Apollonius. It is also note-

1 Contra Apionem, II, 79 ff. (No. 44).
2 See Müller, p. 259.

worthy that nowhere in his works does Josephus show any direct acquaintance with the works of Posidonius.[3]

Since Posidonius was a prolific writer with a wide range of interests and knowledge, one can hardly be sure where he placed his description of the Jewish Temple. However, his History is the most likely work.[4] *As we are certain that this work begins where Polybius leaves off, namely, in the forties of the second century B.C.E.,*[5] *the calumnies that Josephus alluded to do not accord with the date of the relations between Antiochus Epiphanes and the Jews, notwithstanding the fact that this king played a part in the stories told by Apion. We should, therefore, assume that Posidonius discusses the nature of the Jewish worship and the Temple service in another section of his History.*

This recalls the passage of Diodorus the Sicilian in a fragment of his thirty-fourth book, 1, 1–5 (No. 63), which deals with the struggle between Antiochus VII Sidetes and the Jews (134–132 B.C.E.). There the anti-Semitic advisers of the victorious Seleucid king suggest that he should storm Jerusalem and destroy Judaism, adducing as a precedent the attempt made in his time by Antiochus Epiphanes. Among other things, the advisers state that Antiochus Epiphanes found the statue of a bearded man sitting on an ass in the Jewish Temple, and that he identified the statue with Moses, the founder of Jerusalem. The entire argumentation of Sidetes' friends shows a marked anti-Semitic tendency; however, it must be noted that this is not the view of the historian himself, who praises the king for not listening to his friends: ὁ δὲ βασιλεὺς μεγαλό-ψυχος ὢν καὶ τὸ ἦθος ἥμερος, λαβὼν ὁμήρους ἀπέλυσε τῶν ἐγκλημάτων τοὺς Ἰουδαίους.

The common view that this passage derives from Posidonius is based mainly on the prevalent opinion that Diodorus' narrative from the thirty-third book on derives from Posidonius.[6] *The case seems particularly strong for the account of the First Sicilian Revolt (XXXIV–XXXV, 2 : 34 ff.), and a fortiori it may be suggested that the Syrian Posidonius*

3 See R. Scheppig, "De Posidonio Apamensi Rerum Gentium Terrarum Scriptore", Ph. D. Thesis, Halle 1869, pp. 33 f.
4 The existence of a special monograph by Posidonius on Pompey, as maintained by Reinhardt, is problematic; see K. Reinhardt, PW, XXII, pp. 638 f.
5 For the History, see Reinhardt, *op. cit.*, pp. 630 ff.; M. Laffranque, *Poseidonios d'Apamée*, Paris 1964, pp. 109 ff.
6 See E. Schwartz, PW, V, p. 690. = *Griechische Geschichtsschreiber*, Leipzig 1959, pp. 76 f. See also P. Toepelmann, *De Posidonio Rhodio Rerum Scriptore*, Bonn 1867, p. 44; Scheppig, *op. cit.*, (supra n. 3), p. 37.

was used by Diodorus for his history of Syria. This sounds plausible, though positive proof is missing.

This supposition involves, however, no small difficulties. The passage in Diodorus undoubtedly does not show any sympathy for the anti-Semites. Furthermore, the anti-Semites allude to a man sitting on an ass, but not to an asinine head worshipped by the Jews. The first difficulty can only be resolved by suggesting that Apion purposely blurred the fact that it was the opinion of Sidetes' friends, and not that of Posidonius, which was obviously inspired by anti-Semitism, and that Josephus, who had no direct knowledge of Posidonius, supposed the Apamean himself to have been biased against the Jews. Also, one may distinguish between Posidonius' objection to a policy of pitiless extermination of the Jews, as proposed by the King's friends, and his general criticism of Jewish exclusiveness which might even have caused him to transmit calumnious reports about the Jewish worship and the Temple. As to the contradiction between the asinine head of Contra Apionem *and the man sitting on the ass described by Diodorus, it may possibly be explained by the supposition that the two statements derive from different passages of Posidonius, or that Posidonius incorporated, even in the same passage, different versions of the same charge. Yet, all these explanations are, of course, no more than pure conjecture.[7] Even more problematic is the attribution to Posidonius of the account of the development of the Jewish religion in Strabo's* Geographica. *Thus, we must pronounce a* non liquet *on the question of Posidonius' real views on the Jews and their religion.*

It is also worth mentioning that in later times Apamea, Posidonius' birthplace, had quite a good record of relations with the Jews, and that it produced Numenius, who showed much respect and sympathy for Judaism; cf. the introduction to Numenius. This, of course, is not conclusive, and in view of the fact that it is doubtful whether the passages bearing upon Jews in Diodorus and Strabo actually derive from Posidonius, we are left with the slight and somewhat imprecise allusion of Josephus.

It may indeed be that Josephus' historical narrative in Antiquitates *was indirectly, though considerably, influenced by Posidonius, through, let us say, Nicolaus. Some resemblance between Josephus* (Ant., XIII, 245)

---

7 Against the derivation of the Diodorian passage from Posidonius, see Böhl, p. 124; see also W. Aly, *Strabon von Amaseia*, Bonn 1957, pp. 199 f. Yet this is assumed without question by other scholars; cf. recently, e. g., M. Adriani, *Studi e materiali di storia delle religioni*, XXXVI (1965), p. 88.

and the above-mentioned passage of Diodorus lends support to such considerations.[8] Yet, no certain conclusions can be arrived at on the basis of existing material.

There is no close parallel in other writers to Posidonius' statement about the extraction of asphalt (No. 45).

---

8 Nussbaum even envisages the possibility of a direct use of Posidonius, which is improbable; see M. Nussbaum,"Observationes in Flavii Josephi Antiquitates", Ph. D. Thesis, Göttingen 1875, p. 8; see also J. v. Destinon, *Die Quellen des Flavius Josephus*, Kiel 1882, pp. 46 ff.

44

apud: Josephus, *Contra Apionem*, II, 79–80, 89, 91–96 — Niese = *F. Gr. Hist.*, II, A 87, F 69 =
Reinach (Budé), pp. 72 ff. = L. Edelstein & I. G. Kidd, *Posidonius*, I, *The Fragments*, Cambridge
1972, F 278.

(79) Ammiror autem etiam eos, qui ei ⟨scil. Apioni⟩ huiusmodi fomitem praebuerunt id est Posidonium et Apollonium Molonem ⟨No. 48⟩,
quoniam accusant quidem nos, quare nos eosdem deos cum aliis non
colimus, mentientes autem pariter et de nostro templo blasphemias
5 componentes incongruas non se putant impie agere, dum sit valde
turpissimum liberis qualibet ratione mentiri multo magis de templo
apud cunctos homines nominato ⟨et⟩ tanta sanctitate pollente. (80) In
hoc enim sacrario Apion praesumpsit edicere asini caput collocasse
Iudaeos et eum colere ac dignum facere tanta religione, et hoc affirmat
10 fuisse depalatum, dum Antiochus Epiphanes expoliasset templum et
illud caput inventum ex auro compositum multis pecuniis dignum...
(89) Alteram vero fabulam derogatione nostra plenam de Graecis
apposuit...
(91) Dixit Antiochum in templo invenisse lectum et hominem in
15 eo iacentem et propositam ei mensam maritimis terrenisque et
volatilium dapibus plenam, et obstipuisset his homo. (92) Illum
vero mox adorasse regis ingressum tamquam maximum ei solacium praebiturum ac procidentem ad eius genua extensa dextra
poposcisse libertatem; et iubente rege, ut confideret et diceret,
20 quis esset vel cur ibidem habitaret vel quae esset causa ciborum
eius, tunc hominem cum gemitu et lacrimis lamentabiliter suam
narrasse necessitatem. (93) Ait, inquit, esse quidem se Graecum,
et dum peragraret provinciam propter vitae causam direptum se
subito ab alienigenis hominibus atque deductum ad templum et
25 inclusum illic, et a nullo conspici sed cuncta dapium praeparatione
saginari. (94) Et primum quidem haec sibi inopinabilia beneficia
prodidisse et detulisse laetitiam deinde suspicionem postea stuporem,
ac postremum consulentem a ministris ad se accedentibus audisse
legem ineffabilem Iudaeorum, pro qua nutriebatur, et hoc illos facere
30 singulis annis quodam tempore constituto. (95) Et compraehendere
quidem Graecum peregrinum eumque annali tempore saginare et
deductum ad quandam silvam occidere quidem eum hominem eiusque
corpus sacrificare secundum suas sollemnitates et gustare ex eius
visceribus et iusiurandum facere in immolatione Graeci, ut inimicitias
35 contra Graecos haberent, et tunc in quandam foveam reliqua hominis

2 *Molonem* Reinach   *molonis* Lat.   23 *direptum* ed. pr.   *directum* Lat.

145

pereuntis abicere. (96) Deinde refert eum dixisse paucos iam dies de vita sibimet superesse atque rogasse, ut erubescens Graecorum deos et superantes in suo sanguine insidias Iudaeorum de malis eum circumastantibus liberaret.

36-37 *de vita* Boysen   *debita* Lat.

(79) I am no less amazed at the proceedings of the authors who supplied him with his materials, I mean Posidonius and Apollonius Molon. On the one hand they charge us with not worshipping the same gods as other people; on the other, they tell lies and invent absurd calumnies about our temple, without showing any consciousness of impiety. Yet to high-minded men nothing is more disgraceful than a lie, of any description, but above all on the subject of a temple of world-wide fame and commanding sanctity. (80) Within this sanctuary Apion has the effrontery to assert that the Jews kept an ass's head, worshipping that animal and deeming it worthy of the deepest reverence; the fact was disclosed, he maintains, on the occasion of the spoliation of the temple by Antiochus Epiphanes, when the head, made of gold and worth a high price, was discovered...

(89) He adds a second story, about Greeks, which is a malicious slander upon us from beginning to end...

(91) and asserts that Antiochus found in the temple a couch, on which a man was reclining, with a table before him laden with a banquet of fish of the sea, beasts of the earth, and birds of the air, at which the poor fellow was gazing in stupefaction. (92) The king's entry was instantly hailed by him with adoration, as about to procure him profound relief; falling at the king's knees, he stretched out his right hand and implored him to set him free. The king reassured him and bade him tell him who he was, why he was living there, what was the meaning of his abundant fare. Thereupon, with sighs and tears, the man, in a pitiful tone, told the tale of his distress. (93) He said, Apion continues, that he was a Greek and that, while travelling about the province for his livelihood, he was suddenly kidnapped by men of a foreign race and conveyed to the temple; there he was shut up and seen by nobody, but was fattened on feasts of the most lavish description. (94) At first these unlooked for attentions deceived him and caused him pleasure; suspicion followed, then consternation. Finally, on consulting the attendants who waited upon him, he heard of the unutterable law of the Jews, for the sake of which he was being fed. The practice was repeated by them annually at a fixed season. (95) They would kidnap a Greek foreigner, fatten him up for a year, and then

146

Posidonius

convey him to a wood, where they slew him, sacrificed his body
with their customary ritual, partook of his flesh, and, while immolating the Greek, swore an oath of hostility to the Greeks. The
remains of their victim were then thrown into a pit. (96) The man
(Apion continues) stated that he had now but a few days left to live, and
implored the king, out of respect for the gods of Greece, to defeat
this Jewish plot upon his life-blood and to deliver him from his
miserable predicament.　　　　　　　　　　(trans. H. St. J. Thackeray, *LCL*)

45

apud: Strabo, *Geographica*, XVI, 2:43, p. 764 = *F. Gr. Hist.*, II, A87, F70, p. 266
= Edelstein & Kidd, *Posidonius*, I, *The Fragments*, Cambridge 1972, F 279.

Γόητας δὲ ὄντας σκήπτεσθαί φησιν ἐπῳδὰς ὁ Ποσειδώνιος τοὺς ἀνθρώ-
πους καὶ οὖρα καὶ ἄλλα δυσώδη ὑγρά, ἃ περικαταχέαντας καὶ ἐκπιά-
σαντας πήττειν τὴν ἄσφαλτον, εἶτα τέμνειν.

2 ἃ secl. Corais / περικαταχέαντας Kramer　περικαταχέοντας codd.

But according to Posidonius the people are sorcerers and pretend
to use incantations, as also urine and other malodorous liquids which
they pour over the solidified substance, and squeeze out the asphalt
and harden it, and then cut it into pieces.　　　　(trans. H. L. Jones, *LCL*)

σκήπτεσθαί φησιν ἐπῳδὰς ὁ Ποσειδώνιος: Strabo found it necessary to state
explicitly his authority for the rather singular procedure used in the extraction of
asphalt; cf. Aly, *op. cit.* (supra, p. 143, n. 7), pp. 208 f.
οὖρα καὶ ἄλλα δυσώδη ὑγρά: Posidonius does not expressly mention, as do some
other writers, the use of the blood of menstruation; see Plinius, *Naturalis Historia*,
VII, 65 (No. 207); *BJ*, IV, 480; see also Tacitus, *Historiae*, V, 6 (No. 281);
K. Reinhardt, *Poseidonios über Ursprung und Entartung*, Heidelberg 1928, pp. 65 f.

XXIX. APOLLONIUS MOLON

First century B.C.E.

Apollonius Molon, a renowned rhetor, was born at Alabanda in Caria. Later the island of Rhodes became the main centre of his activity. He was chosen by the Rhodians to represent their city before the Romans in the time of Sulla. Some of the most prominent Romans, including Cicero and Caesar, were among his pupils at Rhodes.[1]

Apollonius Molon seems to have been the first Greek writer after Hecataeus who is reported to have written a special book about the Jews. The most important fragment of his work has been transmitted through the work of his contemporary Alexander Polyhistor and preserved by Eusebius in his Praeparatio Evangelica.

Josephus considers Apollonius a fanatic anti-Semite, a source of inspiration for the acrimonious Apion and his equal in hatred of the Jews. He tries also to disparage Apollonius' intellectual power and his character (No. 50), in contrast to Plutarch (Caesar, 3), who covers him with praise. From the fragments quoted by Josephus we learn that Apollonius charges the Jews with xenophobia and exclusiveness, that he maintains that Moses was a cheat and that the Jewish law taught nothing good. Apollonius attributes to the Jews both cowardice and the courage of despair. According to him the Jews were the least able among the barbarians and were the only nation that added absolutely nothing to the civilization of mankind.

However, Josephus says that Apollonius did not write a continuous indictment of the Jews, but that such charges are scattered throughout his work. The fragment found in Eusebius does not show any marked anti-Semitic features.[2] What Apollonius relates here about the Jewish past depends indirectly on the biblical narratives. The interpretation he suggests for the name of the second of the Patriarchs might have reached him, either directly or indirectly, from Jewish-Hellenistic circles. On the other hand, there is no trace in the quotation of the Graeco-Egyptian account of Jewish origins, and it seems to be more related to

---

1 See Cicero, *Brutus*, 316; Plutarchus, *Cicero*, 4; *Caesar*, 3.
2 See Radin, pp. 198 f.

Apollonius Molon

the tradition, represented by Pompeius Trogus (*No. 137*), that connected the Jews with Syria.

Apollonius did not lack the opportunity to obtain first-hand knowledge of Jews in his native Caria, where we find Jewish settlements already in the second and first centuries B.C.E.[3] His personality gains interest from the fact that he was a teacher of some of the most influential Romans of the last generation of the Republic.[4]

---

3 See Juster, I, p. 191.

4 For his influence on Cicero, see F. Portalupi, *Sulla corrente rodiese*, Università di Torino, Pubblicazioni della Facoltà di Magistero, 7, 1957, pp. 16 f.; J. C. Davies, *CQ*, NS XVIII (1968), pp. 303 ff.

46

De Iudaeis, apud: Eusebius, *Praeparatio Evangelica*, IX, 19:1–3 — Mras = F26R =
F. Gr. Hist.,III, C728, F1

*(1) Ὁ δὲ τὴν συσκευὴν τὴν κατὰ Ἰουδαίων γράψας Μόλων μετὰ τὸν
κατακλυσμόν φησιν ἀπὸ τῆς Ἀρμενίας ἀπελθεῖν τὸν περιλειφθέντα
ἄνθρωπον μετὰ τῶν υἱῶν, ἐκ τῶν ἰδίων ἐξελαυνόμενον ὑπὸ τῶν
ἐγχωρίων· διανύσαντα δὲ τὴν μεταξὺ χώραν ἐλθεῖν εἰς τὴν ὀρεινὴν*
5 *τῆς Συρίας οὖσαν ἔρημον. (2) μετὰ δὲ τρεῖς γενεὰς Ἀβραὰμ γενέσθαι,
ὃν δὴ μεθερμηνεύεσθαι πατρὸς φίλον, ὃν δὴ σοφὸν γενόμενον τὴν
ἐρημίαν μεταδιώκειν· λαβόντα δὲ δύο γυναῖκας, τὴν μὲν ἐντοπίαν,
συγγενῆ, τὴν δὲ Αἰγυπτίαν, θεράπαιναν, ἐκ μὲν τῆς Αἰγυπτίας γεννῆσαι
δώδεκα υἱούς, οὓς δὴ εἰς Ἀραβίαν ἀπαλλαγέντας διελέσθαι τὴν χώραν*
10 *καὶ πρώτους βασιλεῦσαι τῶν ἐγχωρίων· ὅθεν ἕως καθ᾽ ἡμᾶς δώδεκα
εἶναι βασιλεῖς Ἀράβων ὁμωνύμους ἐκείνοις. (3) ἐκ δὲ τῆς γαμετῆς
υἱὸν αὐτῷ γενέσθαι ἕνα, ὃν Ἑλληνιστὶ Γέλωτα ὀνομασθῆναι. καὶ τὸν
μὲν Ἀβραὰμ γήρᾳ τελευτῆσαι, Γέλωτος δὲ καὶ γυναικὸς ἐγχωρίου
υἱοὺς ἕνδεκα γενέσθαι καὶ δωδέκατον Ἰωσὴφ καὶ ἀπὸ τοῦδε τρίτον Μωσῆν.*

1 τὴν κατὰ ἰουδαίων συσκευὴν B / μήλων I   6–7 ὃν...μεταδιώκειν om. B

(1) Molon, who composed the invective against the Jews, relates that
the man who survived the flood left Armenia with his sons, having
been expelled from his native place by the inhabitants of the land.
Having traversed the intermediate country, he came to the mountainous part of Syria, which was desolate. (2) After three generations
Abraam was born, whose name signifies the friend of the father. This
man was wise and eagerly went to the desert. He took two wives, one
a local one and a relative of his, and the other an Egyptian handmaid.
The Egyptian woman bore him twelve sons, who emigrated to Arabia
and divided the country between themselves; they were the first to
be kings over the inhabitants of that country. Consequently, till our
times there are twelve kings among the Arabs who are namesakes
of the sons of Abraam. (3) Of his lawful wife one son was born to him,
whose name translated into Greek signifies *Gelos* [laughter]. Abraam
died of old age, while to Gelos and a native woman there were born
eleven sons, and a twelfth one Joseph. His grandson was Moses.

1 τὴν συσκευὴν τὴν κατὰ Ἰουδαίων: The words τὴν συσκευὴν do not belong
to the name of the book. Eusebius uses the same words in relation to the work of
Porphyry.
τὸν περιλειφθέντα ἄνθρωπον: Noah is not mentioned by name by Apollonius;
however, we cannot tell whether or not this omission is due to the transmission by
Alexander Polyhistor.

Apollonius Molon

ἐξελαυνόμενον ὑπὸ τῶν ἐγχωρίων: According to the biblical story only Noah, his wife, his sons and his daughters-in-law were saved from the Flood, but the Babylonian tradition, which was contaminated with the Jewish account in the Hellenistic period, records that many people were saved on Mount Ararat.

ἐλθεῖν εἰς τὴν ὀρεινὴν τῆς Συρίας: The Bible does not state that Noah emigrated to Palestine.

2 μετὰ δὲ τρεῖς γενεὰς ᾽Αβραὰμ γενέσθαι: According to Gen. xi, Abraham lived ten generations after Noah.

πατρὸς φίλον: This etymology contradicts Gen. xvii : 5 (אב המון גויים = אברהם); see, however, Isa. xli : 8 (זרע אברהם אהבי) and II Chron. xx : 7; cf. Ginzberg, V, p. 207, n. 4. Israel Levi (apud: Reinach) remarks that Apollonius' etymology probably derives from the Aramaic root רחם (= to love) and was suggested to him or to his source by the similarity of sound between this Aramaic verb and Abraham.

σοφὸν γενόμενον: Here we have a parallel to the later Jewish tradition, which tells how Abraham realized the folly of the Chaldaean astral cult and decided to emigrate to Canaan; cf. Ginzberg, p. 210, n. 16. Since Molon had already recounted the emigration of Noah to Syria, he now passes over the emigration of Abraham to Canaan, and refers instead to Abraham the Wise, who retired to the desert due to the ignorance of his fellow men. For the motif, in later Judaism, of retirement into the desert, see M. Hengel, Die Zeloten, Leiden–Cologne 1961, pp. 255 ff.

συγγενῆ: On the relationship of Sarah to Abraham, see Gen. xx : 12; Jubilees xii : 9.

Αἰγυπτίαν, θεράπαιναν: Hagar is meant here; see Gen. xvi : 1.

δώδεκα υἱούς: According to Gen. xxv : 13 ff., Ishmael, the son of Abraham by Hagar, was the father of twelve sons, not Abraham; cf. Ant., I, 220 f.

3 Γέλωτα: For the name Γέλως for Isaac, see Philo, De Mutatione Nominum, 261; De Abrahamo, 201; De Praemiis et Poenis, 31. For Γέλως as a Greek proper name, see, e.g., L. Robert, Hellenica, II, Paris 1946, p. 6, l. 28.

γήρᾳ τελευτῆσαι: Cf. Gen. xxv : 8.

καὶ δωδέκατον ᾽Ιωσήφ: Apollonius confuses Isaac with his son Jacob, whose name he seems not to have known.

ἀπὸ τοῦδε τρίτον Μωσῆν: Apollonius makes Moses a grandson of Joseph. A similar tradition is found in Pompeius Trogus (apud: Iustinus, XXXVI, 2 : 11 = No. 137), which describes Moses as the son of Joseph. Chaeremon (apud: Josephus Contra Apionem, I, 290 = No. 178) only makes them contemporaries, without asserting any relationship between them. According to Exod. vi : 16 ff., Moses is a descendant of Levi, the brother of Joseph, in the fourth generation.

47

De Iudaeis, apud: Josephus, Contra Apionem, II, 16 — Niese = 27aR = F. Gr. Hist., III, C 728, F2 = Reinach (Budé), p. 61

Μανεθὼς μὲν γὰρ κατὰ τὴν Τεθμώσιος βασιλείαν ἀπαλλαγῆναί φησιν ἐξ Αἰγύπτου τοὺς ᾽Ιουδαίους πρὸ ἐτῶν τριακοσίων ἐνενηκοντατριῶν

1 pathmosii Lat.

τῆς εἰς ῎Αργος Δαναοῦ φυγῆς, Λυσίμαχος ⟨No. 159⟩ δὲ κατὰ Βόκχοριν
τὸν βασιλέα, τουτέστι πρὸ ἐτῶν χιλίων ἑπτακοσίων, Μόλων δὲ καὶ
5 ἄλλοι τινὲς ὡς αὐτοῖς ἔδοξεν.

3 bochore Lat.

Well, Manetho states that the departure of the Jews from Egypt occurred in the reign of Tethmosis, 393 years before the flight of Danaus
to Argos; Lysimachus says, under King Bocchoris, that is to say,
1700 years ago; Molon and others fix a date to suit themselves.

(trans. H. St. J. Thackeray, *LCL*)

Apollonius Molon does touch upon the subject of the Exodus elsewhere in his
writings.

48

De Iudaeis, apud: Josephus, *Contra Apionem*, II, 79–80, 89, 91–96 — Niese = F27bR = Reinach
(Budé), pp. 72 ff.

(79) Ammiror autem etiam eos, qui ei ⟨scil. Apioni⟩ huiusmodi
fomitem praebuerunt id est Posidonium ⟨No. 44⟩ et Apollonium Molonem, quoniam accusant quidem nos, quare nos eosdem deos cum aliis
non colimus, mentientes autem pariter et de nostro templo blasphemias
5 componentes incongruas non se putant impie agere, dum sit valde turpissimum liberis qualibet ratione mentiri multo magis de templo apud
cunctos homines nominato ⟨et⟩ tanta sanctitate pollente. (80) In hoc
enim sacrario Apion ⟨170⟩ praesumpsit edicere asini caput collocasse
Iudaeos et eum colere ac dignum facere tanta religione, et hoc affirmat
10 fuisse depalatum, dum Antiochus Epiphanes expoliasset templum et
illud caput inventum ex auro compositum multis pecuniis dignum...
(89) Alteram vero fabulam derogatione nostra plenam de Graecis
apposuit...
(91) Dixit Antiochum in templo invenisse lectum et hominem
15 in eo iacentem et propositam ei mensam maritimis terrenisque et
volatilium dapibus plenam, et obstipuisset his homo. (92) Illum vero
mox adorasse regis ingressum tamquam maximum ei solacium
praebiturum ac procidentem ad eius genua extensa dextra poposcisse
libertatem; et iubente rege, ut confideret et diceret, quis esset vel cur
20 ibidem habitaret vel quae esset causa ciborum eius, tunc hominem
cum gemitu et lacrimis lamentabiliter suam narrasse necessitatem.

2–3 Molonem Reinach   molonis Lat.

152

Apollonius Molon

(93) Ait, inquit, esse quidem se Graecum, et dum peragraret provinciam propter vitae causam direptum se subito ab alienigenis hominibus atque deductum ad templum et inclusum illic, et a nullo conspici sed cuncta dapium praeparatione saginari. (94) Et primum quidem haec sibi inopinabilia beneficia prodidisse et detulisse laetitiam deinde suspicionem postea stuporem, ac postremum consulentem a ministris ad se accedentibus audisse legem ineffabilem Iudaeorum, pro qua nutriebatur, et hoc illos facere singulis annis quodam tempore constituto. (95) Et compraehendere quidem Graecum peregrinum eumque annali tempore saginare et deductum ad quandam silvam occidere quidem eum hominem eiusque corpus sacrificare secundum suas sollemnitates et gustare ex eius visceribus et iusiurandum facere in immolatione Graeci, ut inimicitias contra Graecos haberent, et tunc in quandam foveam reliqua hominis pereuntis abicere. (96) Deinde refert eum dixisse paucos iam dies de vita sibimet superesse atque rogasse, ut erubescens Graecorum deos et superantes in suo sanguine insidias Iudaeorum de malis eum circumastantibus liberaret.

23 *direptum* ed. pr.   *directum* Lat.   36 *de vita* Boysen   *debita* Lat.

(79) I am no less amazed at the proceedings of the authors who supplied him with his materials, I mean Posidonius and Apollonius Molon. On the one hand they charge us with not worshipping the same gods as other people; on the other, they tell lies and invent absurd calumnies about our temple, without showing any consciousness of impiety. Yet to high-minded men nothing is more disgraceful than a lie, of any description, but above all on the subject of a temple of world-wide fame and commanding sanctity. (80) Within this sanctuary Apion has the effrontery to assert that the Jews kept an ass's head, worshipping that animal and deeming it worthy of the deepest reverence; the fact was disclosed, he maintains, on the occasion of the spoliation of the temple by Antiochus Epiphanes, when the head, made of gold and worth a high price, was discovered. . .

(89) He adds a second story, about Greeks, which is a malicious slander upon us from beginning to end. . .

(91) He asserts that Antiochus found in the temple a couch, on which a man was reclining, with a table before him laden with a banquet of fish of the sea, beasts of the earth, and birds of the air, at which the poor fellow was gazing in stupefaction. (92) The king's entry was instantly hailed by him with adoration, as about to procure him profound relief; falling at the king's knees, he stretched out his right hand and implored him to set him free. The king reassured him and

153

bade him tell who he was, why he was living there, what was the meaning of his abundant fare. Thereupon, with sighs and tears, the man, in a pitiful tone, told the tale of his distress. (93) He said, Apion continues, that he was a Greek and that, while travelling about the province for a livelihood, he was suddenly kidnapped by men of a foreign race and conveyed to the temple; there he was shut up and seen by nobody, but was fattened on feasts of the most lavish description. (94) At first these unlooked for attentions deceived him and caused him pleasure; suspicion followed, then consternation. Finally, on consulting the attendants who waited upon him, he heard of the unutterable law of the Jews, for the sake of which he was being fed. The practice was repeated annually at a fixed season. (95) They would kidnap a Greek foreigner, fatten him for a year, and then convey him to a wood, where they slew him, sacrificed his body with their customary ritual, partook of his flesh, and, while immolating the Greek, swore an oath of hostility to the Greeks. The remains of their victim were then thrown into a pit. (96) The man (Apion continues) stated that he had now but a few days left to live, and implored the king, out of respect for the gods of Greece, to defeat this Jewish plot upon his life-blood and to deliver him from his miserable predicament.

(trans. H. St. J. Thackeray, *LCL*)

See the introduction to Posidonius.

49

De Iudaeis, apud: Josephus, *Contra Apionem*, II, 145, 148 — Niese = F27c + dR = *F. Gr. Hist.* III, C728, T3a + F3a = Reinach (Budé), pp. 82 f.

(145) Ἐπεὶ δὲ καὶ Ἀπολλώνιος ὁ Μόλων καὶ Λυσίμαχος ⟨No. 161⟩ καί τινες ἄλλοι τὰ μὲν ὑπ᾽ ἀγνοίας, τὸ πλεῖστον δὲ κατὰ δυσμένειαν περί τε τοῦ νομοθετήσαντος ἡμῖν Μωσέως καὶ περὶ τῶν νόμων πεποίηνται λόγους οὔτε δικαίους οὔτε ἀληθεῖς, τὸν μὲν ὡς γόητα καὶ ἀπατεῶνα διαβάλλοντες, τοὺς νόμους δὲ κακίας ἡμῖν καὶ οὐδεμιᾶς ἀρετῆς φάσκοντες εἶναι διδασκάλους, βούλομαι συντόμως καὶ περὶ τῆς ὅλης ἡμῶν καταστάσεως τοῦ πολιτεύματος καὶ περὶ τῶν κατὰ μέρος ὡς ἂν ὦ δυνατὸς εἰπεῖν...

(148) Ἄλλως τε καὶ τὴν κατηγορίαν ὁ Ἀπολλώνιος οὐκ ἀθρόαν ὥσπερ ὁ

1 Ἐπεὶ δὲ Dindorf   ἐπειδὴ L   quoniam vero Lat
3 *moyse* Lat. Μωϋσέως Reinach

Apollonius Molon

10 'Απίων ⟨No. 177⟩ ἔταξεν, ἀλλὰ σποράδην, καὶ δὴ εἶπας ποτὲ μὲν ὡς
ἀθέους καὶ μισανθρώπους λοιδορεῖ, ποτὲ δ' αὖ δειλίαν ἡμῖν ὀνειδίζει καὶ
τοὔμπαλιν ἔστιν ὅπου τόλμαν κατηγορεῖ καὶ ἀπόνοιαν. λέγει δὲ καὶ
ἀφυεστάτους εἶναι τῶν βαρβάρων καὶ διὰ τοῦτο μηδὲν εἰς τὸν βίον
εὕρημα συμβεβλῆσθαι μόνους.

10 δὴ εἶπας] δὴ ἡμᾶς Reinach   καὶ δὴ εἶπας ποτὲ μὲν ⟨δεισιδαιμονεστάτους
πάντων ἄλλοτε⟩ ὡς ἀθέους Niese

(145) Seeing, however, that Apollonius Molon, Lysimachus, and
others, partly from ignorance, mainly from ill will, have made reflections, which are neither just nor true, upon our lawgiver Moses
and his code, maligning the one as charlatan and impostor, and
asserting that from the other we receive lessons in vice and none in
virtue, I desire to give, to the best of my ability, a brief account of
our constitution as a whole and of its details. . .
(148) I adopt this line the more readily because Apollonius, unlike
Apion, has not grouped his accusations together, but scattered them
here and there all over his work, reviling us in one place as atheists
and misanthropes, in another reproaching us as cowards, whereas
elsewhere, on the contrary, he accuses us of temerity and reckless
madness. He adds that we are the most witless of all barbarians,
and are consequently the only people who have contributed no
useful invention to civilization.   (trans. H. St. J. Thackeray, LCL)

145 ὡς γόητα καὶ ἀπατεῶνα: Cf. Plinius, Naturalis Historia, XXX, 11 (No. 221).
See also Ant., II, 284: ἐξ ἀπάτης αὐτοῦ τὴν ἄφιξιν πεποιημένον καὶ τερατουργίαις
καὶ μαγείαις καταπλήξειν ἐπικεχειρηκότα.
148 ποτὲ μὲν ὡς ἀθέους: For the accusation of ἀθεότης, see E. Fascher, Festschrift
für Otto Michel, Leiden–Cologne 1963, pp. 78 ff.
καὶ ἀπόνοιαν: This implies a contrast (καὶ τοὔμπαλιν) to δειλία = cowardice, and
means courage deriving from despair. Cf. Tacitus, Historiae, V, 5 (No. 281):
moriendi contemptus
μηδὲν εἰς τὸν βίον εὕρημα: This argument was repeated by Apion (Contra Apionem,
II, 135 = No. 175) and by Celsus (Contra Celsum, IV, 31 = No. 375).
For a list of inventions and inventors, see Plinius, Naturalis Historia, VII, 191 ff.;
see also M. P. Nilsson, Geschichte der griechischen Religion, II ², Munich 1961,
p. 284; K. Thraede, Rhein. Mus., CV (1962), pp. 158 ff.

50

De Iudaeis, apud: Josephus, Contra Apionem, II, 236, 255, 258, 295 — Niese = 27e + 27fR =
F. Gr. Hist., III, C728, T3b + 3c + 3d; F3b = Reinach (Budé), pp. 100 f., 104, 110

(236) Εἶτα Λυσίμαχοι ⟨No. 162⟩ καὶ Μόλωνες καὶ τοιοῦτοί τινες ἄλλοι
1 Μόλωνες ed. pr. ex Lat.   σόλωνες L

From Herodotus to Plutarch

συγγραφεῖς, ἀδόκιμοι σοφισταί, μειρακίων ἀπατεῶνες, ὡς πάνυ ἡμᾶς
φαυλοτάτους ἀνθρώπων λοιδοροῦσιν...

(255) Ἀπολλώνιος μὲν οὖν ὁ Μόλων τῶν ἀνοήτων εἷς ἦν καὶ τετυ-
5 φωμένων, τοὺς μέντοι κατ' ἀλήθειαν ἐν τοῖς Ἑλληνικοῖς φιλοσοφήσαν-
τας οὔτε τῶν προειρημένων οὐδὲν διέλαθεν οὔτε τὰς ψυχρὰς προφάσεις
τῶν ἀλληγοριῶν ἠγνόησαν, διόπερ τῶν μὲν εἰκότως κατεφρόνησαν, εἰς
δὲ τὴν ἀληθῆ καὶ πρέπουσαν περὶ τοῦ θεοῦ δόξαν ἡμῖν συνεφώνησαν...

(258) Ὧν οὐδὲν λογισάμενος ὁ Μόλων Ἀπολλώνιος κατηγόρησεν, ὅτι
10 μὴ παραδεχόμεθα τοὺς ἄλλαις προκατειλημμένους δόξαις περὶ θεοῦ μηδὲ
κοινωνεῖν ἐθέλομεν τοῖς καθ' ἑτέραν συνήθειαν βίου ζῆν προαιρουμένοις...

(295) Εἰ δὲ καὶ χρώμενοι μάλιστα πάντων βλεπόμεθα καὶ τὴν πρώτην
εὕρεσιν αὐτῶν ἡμετέραν οὖσαν ἐπεδείξαμεν, Ἀπίωνες ⟨No. 177⟩ μὲν καὶ
Μόλωνες καὶ πάντες ὅσοι τῷ ψεύδεσθαι καὶ λοιδορεῖν χαίρουσιν ἐξελη-
15 λέγχθωσαν.

5 τοῖς ἕλλησι Niese   6 ψυχρὰς ed. pr.   ψυχὰς L

(236) For all that, the Lysimachuses and Molons and other writers
of that class, reprobate sophists and deceivers of youth, rail at us as
the very vilest of mankind...

(255) Apollonius Molon was but one of the crazy fools. The genuine
exponents of Greek philosophy were well aware of all that I have
said, nor were they ignorant of the worthless shifts to which the
allegorists have resort. That was why they rightly despised them
and agreed with us in forming a true and befitting conception of
God...

(258) Of these facts Apollonius Molon took no account when he condemned us for refusing admission to persons with other preconceived
ideas about God, and for declining to associate with those who
have chosen to adopt a different mode of life...

(295) If, however, it is seen that no one observes them better than
ourselves, and if we have shown that we were the first to discover
them, then the Apions and Molons and all who delight in lies and
abuse may be left to their own confusion.

(trans. H. St. J. Thackeray, *LCL*)

258 ὅτι μὴ παραδεχόμεθα...: For this argument, cf. Iuvenalis, XIV, 103 f. (No.
301); Tacitus, *Historiae*, V, 5 (No. 281).

XXX. ALEXANDER POLYHISTOR

First century B.C.E.

Alexander Polyhistor was a Greek writer from Miletus. He was brought to Rome as a slave and was among those who were manumitted by Sulla. Among his many compilations there was a Περὶ Ἰουδαίων, which well illustrates the great interest in Jews that was current in the generation of the capture of Jerusalem by Pompey, and which is also reflected in the works of some of Alexander's Asian contemporaries, e.g., Teucer of Cyzicus and Apollonius Molon. It is also in line with the way in which Pythagoreanism and the abstruse lore of the East took hold in Roman society.

The surviving fragments of Alexander Polyhistor's Περὶ Ἰουδαίων have been preserved in Eusebius' Praeparatio Evangelica (IX, 17–39). From them we learn that Alexander derived his knowledge about Jews from a large number of Jewish-Hellenistic authors and from some non-Jewish writers, and he quotes them according to the chronology of their contents. He does not seem to change their style to any extent, but only renders them into indirect speech and supplies the connecting sentences. Among the Jewish writers who furnished him with material were Demetrius, Eupolemus, Artapanus, Malchus-Cleodemus, Aristeas, the epic poet Philo and Ezekiel the dramatist. Among the pagan writers consulted by him were Timochares and Apollonius Molon.

Josephus, too, quotes Alexander Polyhistor, deriving from him a notice by Cleodemus; whether the excerpt is from the Περὶ Ἰουδαίων or from the Libyca *is not certain.[1] However, apart from the above-mentioned quotation, it is hard to assess to what extent Josephus is indebted to Alexander Polyhistor.[2]*

---

1 The first view is Jacoby's. The second is propounded by Gutschmid and endorsed, as it seems, by Schwartz.

2 The extensive dependence of Josephus on Alexander Polyhistor is maintained, e. g., by Hölscher and by Norden, but the evidence is far from clear; see G. Hölscher, *Die Quellen des Josephus*, Leipzig 1904, pp. 43 ff.; E. Norden, *Neue Jahrbücher für das klassische Altertum*, XXXI 1913, p. 661 = *Kleine Schriften*, p. 269; B. Motzo, *Saggi di storia e letteratura Giudeo-Ellenistica*, Florence 1924, p. 193.

In the connecting sentences of Alexander there are some references to the "Holy Book" (ἱερὰ βίβλος) or the "Holy Books".[3] These should be explained by Alexander's verbal dependence on his Jewish sources. Two passages from Alexander relating to the Jews are quoted in Suda (No. 52) and in Stephanus Byzantius (No. 53). The first passage derives from his Περὶ ʿΡώμης, and neither, as is clearly implied by their contents, depends on Jewish sources.

Bibliography

Freudenthal; Gutschmid, II, pp. 180 ff.; Susemihl, II, pp. 356 ff.; Schwartz, PW, I, pp. 1449 ff. = *Griechische Geschichtsschreiber*, Leipzig 1959, pp. 240 ff.; Schürer, III, pp. 469 ff.; *F. Gr. Hist.*, IIIa, pp. 248 ff.

3 Cf. Eusebius, *Praeparatio Evangelica*, IX, 24 : 1 = *F. Gr. Hist.*, III, C 729, F 3; Eusebius, *Praeparatio Evangelica*, IX, 29 : 1 = *F. Gr. Hist.*, III, C 722, F 2; Eusebius, *Praeparatio Evangelica*, IX, 29 : 15 = *F. Gr. Hist.*, III, C 722, F 4.

51a

De Iudaeis, apud: Eusebius, *Praeparatio Evangelica*, IX, 17–39 — Mras = F. Gr. Hist.,
III, A 273, F19a

(17) Ταῦτα ὁ Ἰώσηπος. συνᾴδει δὲ τούτοις καὶ ὁ Πολυΐστωρ Ἀλέξανδρος... ὃς ἐν τῇ περὶ Ἰουδαίων συντάξει τὰ κατὰ τὸν Ἀβραὰμ τοῦτον ἱστορεῖ κατὰ λέξιν τὸν τρόπον· «Εὐπόλεμος δὲ ἐν τῷ Περὶ Ἰουδαίων... *(18)* Ἀρτάπανος δέ φησιν ἐν τοῖς Ἰουδαϊκοῖς... *(19)* ὁ δὲ τὴν συσκευὴν
5 τὴν κατὰ Ἰουδαίων γράψας Μόλων ⟨cf. No. 46⟩»... τοσαῦτα ὁ Πολυΐστωρ, οἷς μεθ᾿ ἕτερα ἐπιφέρει λέγων· «μετ᾿ οὐ πολὺν δὲ χρόνον τὸν θεὸν τῷ Ἀβραὰμ προστάξαι Ἰσαὰκ τὸν υἱὸν ὁλοκαρπῶσαι αὐτῷ. τὸν δὲ ἀναγαγόντα τὸν παῖδα ἐπὶ τὸ ὄρος πυρὰν νῆσαι καὶ ἐπιθεῖναι τὸν Ἰσαάκ· σφάζειν δὲ μέλλοντα κωλυθῆναι ὑπὸ ἀγγέλου, κριὸν αὐτῷ πρὸς τὴν
10 κάρπωσιν παραστήσαντος· τὸν δὲ Ἀβραὰμ τὸν μὲν παῖδα καθελεῖν ἀπὸ τῆς πυρᾶς, τὸν δὲ κριὸν καρπῶσαι.»
(20) φησὶ δὲ περὶ τούτου καὶ Φίλων ἐν τῷ πρώτῳ τῶν Περὶ Ἱεροσόλυμα... ταῦτα μὲν δὴ ἀπὸ τῆς προειρημένης τοῦ Πολυΐστορος γραφῆς.
Καὶ ὁ Ἰώσηπος δὲ ἐν τῇ πρώτῃ τῆς Ἀρχαιολογίας τοῦ αὐτοῦ μνημονεύει...
15 «μαρτυρεῖ δέ μου τῷ λόγῳ Ἀλέξανδρος ὁ Πολυΐστωρ λέγων οὕτως...»
Τὰ μὲν οὖν περὶ τοῦ Ἀβραὰμ ὡς ἐν ὀλίγοις τοσαῦτα παρακείσθω.
(21) ἀπίωμεν δὲ πάλιν ἐπὶ τὸν Πολυΐστορα «Δημήτριός φησι...»
ταῦτά μοι κείσθω ἀπὸ τῆς Ἀλεξάνδρου τοῦ Πολυΐστορος γραφῆς,
ἑξῆς δ᾿ ἐπισυνήφθω καὶ τάδε· *(22)* «τὰ δὲ Σίκιμά φησι Θεόδοτος ἐν τῷ
20 Περὶ Ἰουδαίων...» τούτοις καὶ τὰ ἑξῆς περὶ τοῦ Ἰωσὴφ ἐκ τῆς αὐτῆς τοῦ Πολυΐστορος γραφῆς ἐπισυνήφθω· *(23)* «Ἀρτάπανος δέ φησιν ἐν τῷ Περὶ Ἰουδαίων τῷ Ἀβραὰμ Ἰωσὴφ ἀπόγονον γενέσθαι...» *(24)* «μαρτυρεῖ δὲ ταῖς ἱεραῖς βίβλοις καὶ Φίλων ἐν τῇ ιδ´ τῶν Περὶ Ἱεροσόλυμα...»
Ταῦτα καὶ περὶ τοῦ Ἰωσήφ. ἄκουε δὲ οἷα καὶ περὶ τοῦ Ἰὼβ ὁ αὐτὸς
25 ἱστορεῖ·
(25) «Ἀριστέας δέ φησιν ἐν τῷ Περὶ Ἰουδαίων...» *(28)* «περὶ δὲ τοῦ τὸν Μώϋσον ἐκτεθῆναι ὑπὸ τῆς μητρὸς εἰς τὸ ἕλος καὶ ὑπὸ τῆς τοῦ βασιλέως θυγατρὸς ἀναιρεθῆναι καὶ τραφῆναι ἱστορεῖ καὶ Ἐζεκίηλος ὁ τῶν τραγῳδιῶν ποιητής... *(29)* Δημήτριος δὲ περὶ τῆς ἀναιρέσεως τοῦ
30 Αἰγυπτίου καὶ τῆς διαφορᾶς τῆς πρὸς τὸν μηνύσαντα τὸν τελευτήσαντα ὁμοίως τῷ τὴν ἱερὰν βίβλον γράψαντι ἱστόρησε... λέγει δὲ περὶ τούτων καὶ Ἐζεκίηλος ἐν τῇ Ἐξαγωγῇ...» πάλιν μεθ᾿ ἕτερα ἐπιλέγει· «φησὶ δὲ καὶ Ἐζεκίηλος... παρεισάγων ἄγγελον λέγοντα τήν τε τῶν Ἑβραίων διάθεσιν καὶ τὴν τῶν Αἰγυπτίων φθορὰν οὕτως...» καὶ πάλιν μετ᾿ ὀλίγα·
35 «ἐκεῖθεν ἦλθον ἡμέρας τρεῖς, ὡς αὐτός τε ὁ Δημήτριος λέγει καὶ συμφώνως τούτῳ ἡ ἱερὰ βίβλος, μὴ ἔχοντα δὲ ὕδωρ ἐκεῖ γλυκύ, ἀλλὰ πικρόν, τοῦ θεοῦ εἰπόντος ξύλον τι ἐμβαλεῖν εἰς τὴν πηγήν, καὶ γενέσθαι

159

γλυκὺ τὸ ὕδωρ. ἐκεῖθεν δὲ εἰς Ἐλεὶμ ἐλθεῖν, καὶ εὑρεῖν ἐκεῖ δώδεκα μὲν πηγὰς ὑδάτων, ἑβδομήκοντα δὲ στελέχη φοινίκων. περὶ τούτων καὶ
40 τοῦ φανέντος ὀρνέου Ἐζεκιῆλος ἐν τῇ Ἐξαγωγῇ παρεισάγει τινὰ λέγοντα τῷ Μωσεῖ...» καὶ μετὰ βραχέα· «ἐπιζητεῖν δέ τινα πῶς οἱ Ἰσραηλῖται ὅπλα ἔσχον, ἄνοπλοι ἐξελθόντες. ἔφασαν γὰρ τριῶν ἡμερῶν ὁδὸν ἐξελθόντες καὶ θυσιάσαντες πάλιν ἀνακάμψειν. φαίνεται οὖν τοὺς μὴ κατακλυσθέντας τοῖς ἐκείνων ὅπλοις χρήσασθαι.»
45 (30) «Εὐπόλεμος δέ φησιν ἔν τινι περὶ τῆς Ἠλίου προφητείας Μωσῆν προφητεῦσαι ἔτη μ'... (34:19) Θεόφιλος ⟨No. 37⟩ δέ φησι τὸν περισσεύσαντα χρυσὸν τὸν Σολομῶνα τῷ Τυρίων βασιλεῖ πέμψαι... ποιῆσαι δέ φησιν ὁ Εὐπόλεμος τὸν Σολομῶνα καὶ ἀσπίδας χρυσᾶς χιλίας... βιῶσαι δὲ αὐτὸν ἔτη πεντήκοντα δύο, ὧν ἐν εἰρήνῃ βασιλεῦσαι ἔτη μ'.»
50 (35) «Τιμοχάρης ⟨No. 41⟩ δέ φησιν ἐν τοῖς Περὶ Ἀντιόχου τὰ Ἱεροσόλυμα τὴν μὲν περίμετρον ἔχειν σταδίους μ'... (36) ὁ δὲ τῆς Συρίας σχοινομέτρησιν γράψας ⟨No. 42⟩ ἐν τῇ πρώτῃ φησὶ κεῖσθαι Ἱεροσόλυμα ἐπὶ μετεώρου τε καὶ τραχέος τόπου... (37) φησὶ δὲ ὁ Φίλων ἐν τοῖς Περὶ Ἱεροσολύμων κρήνην εἶναι...» τοσαῦτα μὲν δὴ τὰ
55 ἀπὸ τῶν Ἀλεξάνδρου τοῦ Πολυΐστορος...
(39) Ἐπὶ τούτοις καὶ τῆς Ἱερεμίου προφητείας τοῦ Πολυΐστορος μνήμην πεποιημένου (ex Eupolemo), ἡμᾶς ἀποσιωπῆσαι ταύτην πάντων ἂν εἴη παραλογώτατον. κείσθω τοίνυν καὶ αὕτη. «εἶτα Ἰωναχείμ· ἐπὶ τούτου προφητεῦσαι Ἱερεμίαν τὸν προφήτην. τοῦτον ὑπὸ τοῦ θεοῦ
60 ἀποσταλέντα καταλαβεῖν τοὺς Ἰουδαίους θυσιάζοντας εἰδώλῳ χρυσῷ, ᾧ εἶναι ὄνομα Βάαλ. τοῦτον δὲ αὐτοῖς τὴν μέλλουσαν ἀτυχίαν δηλῶσαι. τὸν δὲ Ἰωναχεὶμ ζῶντα αὐτὸν ἐπιβαλέσθαι κατακαῦσαι· τὸν δὲ φάναι τοῖς ξύλοις τούτοις Βαβυλωνίοις ὀψοποιήσειν, καὶ σκάψειν τὰς τοῦ Τίγριδος καὶ Εὐφράτου διώρυγας αἰχμαλωτισθέντας. τὸν δὲ τῶν Βαβυλωνίων
65 βασιλέα ἀκούσαντα Ναβουχοδονόσορ τὰ ὑπὸ τοῦ Ἱερεμίου προμαντευθέντα παρακαλέσαι Ἀστιβάρην τὸν Μήδων βασιλέα συστρατεύειν αὐτῷ. παραλαβόντα δὲ Βαβυλωνίους καὶ Μήδους καὶ συναγαγόντα πεζῶν μὲν ὀκτὼ καὶ δέκα, ἱππέων δὲ μυριάδας δώδεκα καὶ [πεζῶν] ἅρματα μυρία, πρῶτον μὲν τὴν Σαμαρεῖτιν καταστρέψασθαι καὶ Γαλιλαίαν καὶ Σκυθό-
70 πολιν καὶ τοὺς ἐν Γαλααδίτιδι οἰκοῦντας Ἰουδαίους, αὖθις δὲ τὰ Ἱεροσόλυμα παραλαβεῖν καὶ τὸν Ἰουδαίων βασιλέα Ἰωναχεὶμ ζωγρῆσαι· τὸν δὲ χρυσὸν τὸν ἐν τῷ ἱερῷ καὶ ἄργυρον καὶ χαλκὸν ἐκλέξαντα εἰς Βαβυλῶνα ἀποστεῖλαι, χωρὶς τῆς κιβωτοῦ καὶ τῶν ἐν αὐτῇ πλακῶν·
75 ταύτην δὲ τὸν Ἱερεμίαν κατασχεῖν.»

43 ἐξελθόντες καὶ θυσιάσαντες Stephanus   ἐξελθόντας καὶ θυσιάσαντας codd.
58 ἰωνεχείμ B   68 πεζῶν secl. Vigerus   70 γαλαδίτιδι I   γαλατίδι
    ON   Γαλαατίδι Stephanus   72 ἐκλέξαντα Freudenthal
    ἐκλέξαντας codd.

(17) So far Josephus. Alexander Polyhistor is in accord with him. . . who in his work about the Jews speaks about Abraam verbatim as follows: "Eupolemus in his work on Jews. . . (18) Artapanus in his Jewish History says. . . (19) Molon the writer of the invective against Jews." So far Polyhistor, to which *inter alia*, he adds: "Shortly afterwards God commanded Abraam to bring him Isaac as a holocaust. Abraam led the child up the mountain, piled up a funeral pyre and placed Isaac upon it; however, when he was on the point of slaying him, he was prevented from doing so by an angel, who provided him with a ram for the offering. Abraam, then, removed the child from the pyre, and he sacrificed the ram."

(20) Philo, too, speaks of this in the first book of his work on Jerusalem. . . these quotations are taken from the aforementioned writing of Polyhistor.

'Also Josephus in the first book of his *Antiquities* refers to him. . . : "Alexander Polyhistor testifies to what I say, stating as follows:'. . . This will be enough about Abraam, as befits the shortness of our exposition.' (21) Let us return to Polyhistor. "Demetrius says. . ." This I quote from the writing of Alexander Polyhistor; thereto I subjoin also the following: (22) "Theodotus in his *On Jews* says that Shechem. . ." To this must be added also from the same book of Polyhistor the next excerpt about Joseph: (23) "Artapanus states in his work on Jews that Joseph was a descendant of Abraam. . ." (24) "Also Philo in his fourteenth book *On Jerusalem* bears witness to the sacred books."

So far about Joseph. Listen now to what the same writer [i.e. Polyhistor] narrates of Job:

(25) "Aristeas says in his *On Jews* . . ." (28) "The story of the exposure of Moysos by his mother at the marsh and of his being taken and reared by the king's daughter also Ezekiel the tragic poet relates. . . (29)Demetrius states the same as the writer of the Holy Book concerning the killing of the Egyptian and the quarrel with the person who announced his death. . . also Ezekiel in *The Exodus* speaks about these matters". . . again after other subjects he adds: "also Ezekiel says. . . introducing a messenger who describes the condition of the Hebrews and the destruction of the Egyptians in the following manner. . .", and again after a brief interval he adds: "Thence they went three days, as Demetrius himself says, his statement being in agreement with the Holy Book; and not having there sweet water but only bitter, he threw at the behest of God a piece of wood into the fountain, and the water became sweet. Thence they went to

161

Eleim and found there twelve fountains of water and seventy trunks
of date-palms. In regard to these and the bird that appeared, Ezekiel
in *The Exodus* introduces some person who tells Moses. . .", and
shortly afterwards he declares: "One may inquire how it happened
that the Israelites got arms, since they went out unarmed, for they
said that they went forth for a three days' journey and that after
sacrificing they would return. It seems indeed that they, who were
not drowned, used the arms of the Egyptians, who were."

(30) "Eupolemus says in a passage on the Prophecy of Elias that
Moses acted as prophet during forty years. . . [34:19] And Theophilus [No. 37] says that Solomon sent to the king of the Tyrians
the gold which had been left. . . and Eupolemus says that Solomon
also made a thousand golden shields. . . and that he [scil. the king
of the Tyrians] lived fifty-two years, of which he reigned in peace forty
years."

(35)"Timochares says in the *History of Antiochus* that Jerusalem
has a circumference of 40 stades. . . (36) The author of the *Land-
Survey of Syria* states in his first book that Jerusalem is situated on
a high and rough terrain. . . (37) Philo in his work on Jerusalem says
that there is a well. . ." (38) These passages derive from Alexander
Polyhistor.

(39) Since in addition to these Polyhistor refers also to the prophecy
of Jeremiah, it would be an extremely illogical proceeding on our
part to pass that over in silence. Let us therefore subjoin this reference:
"Then Jonacheim. In his reign Jeremiah the prophet delivered his
prophecies. He was sent by God, found the Jews sacrificing to a golden
idol, named Baal, and he foretold them their future misfortune.
Jonacheim intended to burn him alive, while Jeremiah asserted that
this wood would serve him for making food for the Babylonians,
and that the Jews taken prisoners would dig the conduits of the
Tigris and the Euphrates. When Nabuchodonosor the king of the
Babylonians heard of the prophecies of Jeremiah, he exhorted As-
tibares the king of Medians to join him in the expedition. And he
took with him the Babylonians and the Medians, bringing together
an army of one hundred and eighty thousand infantry and one
hundred and twenty thousand cavalry and ten thousand war-chariots
and subdued at first Samaritis and Galilaea and Scythopolis and the
Jews inhabiting Galaaditis. Later he took also Jerusalem and took
captive Jonacheim the king of the Jews. The gold found in the temple,
the silver and the copper he picked out and sent to Babylon, apart
from the Ark and the Tables found in it, which were kept by Jeremiah."

51 b

De Iudaeis, apud: Clemens Alexandrinus, Stromata, I, 21:130:3 — Stählin & Früchtel =
F. Gr. Hist., III, A273, F19b

'Αλέξανδρος δὲ ὁ Πολυΐστωρ ἐπικληθεὶς ἐν τῷ Περὶ 'Ιουδαίων συγγράμματι ἀνέγραψέν τινας ἐπιστολὰς Σολομῶνος μὲν πρός τε Οὐ-
άφρην τὸν Αἰγύπτου βασιλέα πρός τε τὸν Φοινίκης Τυρίων τάς τε αὐτῶν πρὸς Σολομῶντα, καθ' ἃς δείκνυται ὁ μὲν Οὐάφρης ὀκτὼ μυριάδας
5 ἀνδρῶν Αἰγυπτίων ἀπεσταλκέναι αὐτῷ εἰς οἰκοδομὴν τοῦ νεώ, ἄτερος
δὲ τὰς ἴσας σὺν ἀρχιτέκτονι Τυρίῳ ἐκ μητρὸς 'Ιουδαίας ἐκ τῆς φυλῆς
Δαβίδ, ὡς ἐκεῖ γέγραπται, 'Υπέρων τοὔνομα.

Alexander surnamed Polyhistor in the treatise *On Jews* recorded
some letters of Solomon both to Uaphres king of Egypt and to the
king of the Tyrians of Phoenicia, and also those written by them to
Solomon. From them it emerges that Uaphres sent him eighty thousand Egyptian men for the building of the temple, and that the other
king sent the same number and in addition the Tyrian architect
born of a Judaean mother of the tribe of David, as it is written there,
named Hyperon.

52

De Roma, apud: Suda s.v. 'Αλέξανδρος ὁ Μιλήσιος — Adler = F28R =
F. Gr. Hist., III, A273, F70

Καὶ Περὶ 'Ρώμης βιβλία ε'. ἐν τούτοις λέγει, ὡς γυνὴ γέγονεν 'Εβραία
Μωσώ, ἧς ἐστι σύγγραμμα ὁ παρ' 'Εβραίοις νόμος.

And about Rome five books, in which he states that there lived a
Hebrew woman Moso, who composed the Law of the Hebrews.

Περὶ 'Ρώμης βιβλία ε: There is nothing left of this work by Alexander Polyhistor,
which may, however, be identical with his 'Ιταλικά. Rauch suggested that some
words, namely, περὶ 'Ιουδαίων, were dropped after περὶ 'Ρώμης, and that Alexander Polyhistor wrote five books about the Jews. It seems more likely that Alexander
Polyhistor recounted the tradition of the female Jewish lawgiver in connection
with King Numa and the Nymph Egeria.
Μωσώ stands for Moses, as the lawgiver of the Jews. Though Alexander was well
aware of the Jewish tradition about Moses, he saw nothing wrong in relating a
version that contradicted it and which may even have mocked the Jewish people;
see Heinemann, PW, XVI, p. 360. Müller, followed by Freudenthal, suggests that

163

the notion of the female Jewish lawgiver originated with the history of the Sibyls; see Freudenthal, p. 29; Reinach, *ad loc.*

ὁ παρ᾽Ἑβραίοις νόμος: "Moso" is designated here as the Hebrew, and the Jews are called "Hebrews". Thus, Alexander Polyhistor is the first pagan writer to substitute the term *"Hebrew"* for *"Jew"*; see the commentary to Charax of Pergamon (No. 335). The alternative view that the use of this name derives from Hesychius of Milet, the source of Suda, has little basis, as Alexander Polyhistor also uses the term "Hebrews" in his connecting sentences, found in Eusebius, *Praeparatio Evangelica*, IX, 29 : 14; IX, 22 : 2. It seems that he became accustomed to the term from the Jewish sources that he used, e.g. the poet-playwright Ezekiel, apud: Eusebius, *Praeparatio Evangelica*, IX, 28 : 2–3; 29 : 8.

53

apud: Stephanus Byzantius, s.v. Ἰουδαία — Meineke = F29R = *F. Gr. Hist.*, III, A273, F121

Ἰουδαία. Ἀλέξανδρος ὁ Πολυΐστωρ, ἀπὸ τῶν παίδων Σεμιράμιδος Ἰούδα καὶ Ἰδουμαίας.

2 Ἰδουμαίας? Meineke   ἰδουμαία codd.

Judaea.—Alexander Polyhistor says that the name derives from that of the children of Semiramis Juda and Idumaea [?].

For the use of Alexander Polyhistor by Stephanus Byzantius, see Honigmann, PW, Ser. 2, III, p. 2384.

Ἰουδαία: This passage may derive from Alexander's special work on the Jews or from some part of his Chaldaic history.

ἀπὸ τῶν παίδων Σεμιράμιδος: This fantastic etymology assumes the truth of Ctesias' story about Semiramis' rule over the East and her founding many cities in Asia; see Diodorus, II, 14 : 1; Plinius, *Naturalis Historia*, VI, 8, 92, 145. Semiramis is said to have laid the foundations of Judaea and Idumaea in the same way as Osiris founded Macedonia, through his son Macedon; see Diodorus, I, 20 : 3. The reference to Semiramis may have some connection with the tradition concerning the Babylonian-Assyrian origin of the Jews, which is reflected in Greek and Latin literature; see Pompeius Trogus, apud: Iustinus, XXXVI, 2 : 1 (No. 137); Tacitus, *Historiae*, V, 2 (No. 281); see also Nicolaus of Damascus, apud: Josephus, *Ant.*, I, 159–160 (No. 83). On this tradition, see also T. Labhardt, *Quae de Iudaeorum Origine Iudicaverint Veteres*, Augsburg 1881, pp. 42 ff.

Ἰούδα καὶ Ἰδουμαίας: Ἰούδα appears before Ἰδουμαία as a consequence of the political ascendancy of Judaea over Idumaea in the Hellenistic period, especially from the time of the conquest of Idumaea by John Hyrcan in the twenties of the second century B. C. E; however, this is contrary to Biblical tradition, according to which Esau, the ancestor of the Idumaeans, was the first-born of the twins; see Gen. xxv : 25.

The genealogical affinity between Judaea and Idumaea is based not only on geography and Biblical tradition, but also on the religious and ethnic intermingling of the two people. The eponymic explanation conforms to the common usage of antiquity; see Plutarchus *De Iside et Osiride*, 31, p. 363 D (No. 259).

XXXI. TEUCER OF CYZICUS

First century B.C.E.?

Teucer was a very prolific author, who, according to Suda, wrote many books. Among them was a Historia Judaica *in six parts. Since one of his works deals with Mithridates (Μιθριδατικῶν πράξεων), we have at least a* terminus post quem, *and some scholars suppose that he did not live later than the first century B.C.E. Yet, it is difficult to substantiate the view of Gutschmid and Laqueur that the victories of Pompey constituted the focal point of Teucer's literary work, and that his purpose was to describe the various peoples with whom Pompey came in contact. It is even more difficult to corroborate Jacoby's view that Teucer was anti-Roman and sided with Mithridates. A priori, it seems strange that a citizen of Cyzicus, a city that heroically withstood the Pontic king and was saved from destruction by Roman intervention, would become a writer of marked anti-Roman tendencies. In any event, there is no trace whatsoever of Teucer's having been an anti-Roman partisan of Pontus after the manner, for example, of Metrodorus of Scepsis.*

Teucer is the third writer from Asia Minor, along with Apollonius Molon and Alexander Polyhistor, to dedicate a special monograph to the Jews, and it seems probable that he, too, lived in the first century B.C.E. This may be partly explained by the collision between Rome and Judaea in the time of Pompey, which may have acted as a stimulus to the writing of works on Jews. The role that writers from Asia Minor played in this respect is a natural outcome of both the prominence of Asia Minor in Greek literature and the large numbers of Jews in the cities of Asia Minor at that period.

Bibliography

Gutschmid, I, p. 15; II, pp. 708 ff.; Schürer, I, pp. 70 f.; Juster, I, p. 32; R. Laqueur, PW, Ser. 2, V, pp. 1131 f.; *F. Gr. Hist.*, IIIa, pp. 314 f.

54

Historia Iudaica, apud: Suda s.v. *Τεῦκρος ὁ Κυζικηνός* — Adler = F122R = *F. Gr. Hist.*, III, A 274 T1

Τεῦκρος ὁ Κυζικηνός, ὁ γράψας Περὶ χρυσοφόρου γῆς, Περὶ τοῦ
Βυζαντίου, Μιθριδατικῶν πράξεων βιβλία ε´, Περὶ Τύρου ε´, Ἀραβικῶν
ε´, Ἰουδαϊκὴν ἱστορίαν ἐν βιβλίοις ς´, Ἐφήβων τῶν ἐν Κυζίκῳ ἄσκησιν
γ´, καὶ λοιπά.

2 μιθριδατινῶν V   2–3 Ἀραβικῶν ε´ om. G
3 Ἰουδαϊκὴν] Χαλδαϊκὴν Müller

Teucer of Cyzicus, who wrote about gold-producing land, about
Byzantium, five books about the achievements of Mithridates, five
about Tyre, five of Arabian history, a Jewish History in six books,
three books on the training of ephebes at Cyzicus, and more works.

Ἰουδαϊκὴν ἱστορίαν: Contrary to the now-prevalent view concerning the date of
Teucer, Wilamowitz-Moellendorff held the view that the work dealt with the
history of the Great Revolt, see U. v. Wilamowitz-Moellendorff, *Isyllos von Epi-
dauros*, Berlin 1886, p. 122, n. 12. Müller's emendation into Χαλδαϊκὴν is arbitrary and unnecessary.
ἐν βιβλίοις ς: The relatively large number of books that constituted the *Historia
Iudaica* of Teucer is not so extraordinary if we compare it with the five books of his
History of Tyre and the five books of his *Arabian History*.

XXXII. DIODORUS

First century B.C.E.

The Bibliotheca Historica *of Diodorus the Sicilian, who was the least original of all known ancient historians, is of value mainly because it is a compilation that slavishly transmits the contents and views of earlier writers which would otherwise have been lost to us.[1] With regard to the passages bearing upon the Jews, unfortunately we cannot always state Diodorus' source with any degree of certainty. His main account of the Jews, their history and their religion is included in his narrative on the first capture of Jerusalem by the Romans (63 B.C.E.). This was a natural procedure on the part of an ancient historian; Diodorus himself states his authority for Jewish origins, namely, Hecataeus (No. 65). Yet, the source whence he obtained his description of the tribulations of the Jewish state and the story of the appearance of the Jewish delegates at Damascus can only be conjectured; cf. the commentary to No. 64.*

Nos. 55 and 57, which express the view that the Jews should be included among the original colonists sent out from Egypt, and which substantiates this view with a reference to the custom of circumcision prevalent among them, also derive from Hecataeus. Not so No. 58, which speaks of Moyses and mentions the name of Iao. Moyses is the last in the list of legislators, which also includes Minos, Lycurgus, Zathraustes and Zalmoxis, all of whom claimed to receive their laws from deities. The description of the Dead Sea, which first occurs in No. 59, is repeated within the framework of the Wars of the Diadochi.[2]

The history of the Age of the Diadochi in Diodorus stems, at least ultima-

---

1 Diodorus' method of composition may best be seen by comparing the excerpt from Agatharchides included in Photius (cod. 250) with the relevant chapters of Diodorus (III), and also parts of Diodorus' work with the corresponding sections of Polybius' *Historiae.* Diodorus' originality was confined, for the most part, to changes in style and language and to some occasional comments; cf. J. Palm, *Über Sprache und Stil des Diodoros von Sizilien,* Lund 1955, pp. 15 ff. At times he also inserted into the main narrative a passage taken from another source.

2 Cf. P. Krumbholz, *Rhein. Mus.,* XLIV (1889), pp. 286 ff.

167

tely, from Hieronymus of Cardia.[3] *This is fully confirmed by the fact that although Diodorus describes the Dead Sea and refers to both Jaffa and Samaria, he ignores Jerusalem and Judaea in that context; cf. also the introduction to Hieronymus.*

The source for the history of the clash between Antiochus Sidetes and the Jews (No. 63) may be Posidonius, as is maintained by many scholars, but there can be no certainty in the matter (cf. the introduction to Posidonius).

---

3 Not a few scholars postulate an intermediate source. See, e. g., E. Schwartz, PW, V, 685 = *Griechische Historiker*, Leipzig 1959, p. 68; C. Bottin, *Revue belge de philologie et d'histoire*, VII (1928), p. 1316; R. H. Simpson, *AJP*, LXXX (1959), p. 370.

55

Bibliotheca Historica, I, 28 : 1–3 — Vogel = F 33 R

(1) Οἱ δ'οὖν Αἰγύπτιοί φασι καὶ μετὰ ταῦτα ἀποικίας πλείστας ἐξ
Αἰγύπτου κατὰ πᾶσαν διασπαρῆναι τὴν οἰκουμένην. εἰς Βαβυλῶνα
μὲν γὰρ ἀγαγεῖν ἀποίκους Βῆλον τὸν νομιζόμενον Ποσειδῶνος εἶναι
καὶ Λιβύης... *(2)* λέγουσι δὲ καὶ τοὺς περὶ τὸν Δαναὸν ὁρμηθέντας
5 ὁμοίως ἐκεῖθεν συνοικίσαι τὴν ἀρχαιοτάτην σχεδὸν τῶν παρ᾽ Ἕλλησι
πόλεων Ἄργος, τό τε τῶν Κόλχων ἔθνος ἐν τῷ Πόντῳ καὶ τὸ τῶν
Ἰουδαίων ἀνὰ μέσον Ἀραβίας καὶ Συρίας οἰκίσαι τινὰς ὁρμηθέντας
παρ᾽ ἑαυτῶν· *(3)* διὸ καὶ παρὰ τοῖς γένεσι τούτοις ἐκ παλαιοῦ
παραδεδόσθαι τὸ περιτέμνειν τοὺς γεννωμένους παῖδας, ἐξ Αἰγύπτου
10 μετενηνεγμένου τοῦ νομίμου.

7 Ἰουδαίων] ἰσορρεπῶν C   ἰσορραιων F / ὄντας ἀνὰ D

(1) Now the Egyptians say that also after these events a great number
of colonies were spread from Egypt over all the inhabited world.
To Babylon, for instance, colonists were led by Belus, who was held
to be the son of Poseidon and Libya;... (2) They say also that those
who set forth with Danaus, likewise from Egypt, settled what is
practically the oldest city of Greece, Argos, and that the nation of
the Colchi in Pontus and that of the Jews, which lies between Arabia
and Syria, were founded as colonies by certain emigrants from their
country; (3) and this is the reason why it is a long-established institution among these two peoples to circumcise their male children,
the custom having been brought over from Egypt.

(trans. C. H. Oldfather, *LCL*)

56

Bibliotheca Historica, I, 31 : 2 — Vogel

Ἡ τετάρτη τοίνυν πλευρὰ πᾶσα σχεδὸν ἀλιμένῳ θαλάττῃ προσκλυζομένη
προβέβληται τὸ Αἰγύπτιον πέλαγος, ὃ τὸν μὲν παράπλουν ἔχει μακρότατον,
τὴν δ᾽ ἀπόβασιν τὴν ἐπὶ τὴν χώραν δυσπροσόρμιστον· ἀπὸ γὰρ Παραιτονίου τῆς Λιβύης ἕως Ἰόππης τῆς ἐν τῇ Κοίλῃ Συρίᾳ, ὄντος τοῦ
5 παράπλου σταδίων σχεδὸν πεντακισχιλίων, οὐκ ἔστιν εὑρεῖν ἀσφαλῆ
λιμένα πλὴν τοῦ Φάρου.

4 Ἰόπης Vogel

The fourth side, which is washed over its whole extent by waters
which are practically harbourless, has for a defence before it the

Egyptian Sea. The voyage along the coast of this sea is exceedingly
long, and any landing is especially difficult; for from Paraetonium
in Libya as far as Jope in Coele-Syria, a voyage along the coast of
some five thousand stades, there is not to be found a safe harbour
except Pharos. (trans. C. H. Oldfather, *LCL*)

ἀπὸ γὰρ Παραιτονίου τῆς Λιβύης ἕως Ἰόππης... οὐκ ἔστιν εὑρεῖν ἀσφαλῆ λιμένα
πλὴν τοῦ Φάρου: This passage reflects the paramount importance of the port of
Jaffa in the Hellenistic period. In fact, Jaffa was the main port of Judaea at the
period in which Diodorus wrote, but the statement is no less suited to the situation
at the beginning of the Hellenistic age. In the Persian period Jaffa came under the
rule of Eshmunezer, the King of Sidon; see *Corpus Inscriptionum Semiticarum* Vol. II,
Paris 1881, p. 14, l. 19 = G. A. Cooke, *A Text-Book of North-Semitic Inscriptions*,
Oxford 1903, No. 5. The city is not mentioned in connection with the overrun-
ning of the Palestinian coast by Alexander the Great, but it played some part in the
Wars of the Diadochi; see Diodorus, XIX, 59 : 2 (No. 60); XIX, 93 : 7 (No. 61).
One of the Ptolemaic mints was situated at Jaffa in the third century B. C. E.,
a fact attested by coins from the time of Ptolemy II Philadelphus and Ptolemy III
Euergetes. For a summary of the history of Jaffa in the Hellenistic age, see S. Tol-
kowsky, *The Gateway of Palestine—A History of Jaffa*, London 1924, pp. 44 ff.
There is also a very interesting inscription bearing upon the Hellenistic ruler cult;
see B. Lifshitz, *ZDPV*, LXXVIII (1962), pp. 82 ff. Jaffa appears also in some
of the Zeno papyri; see *PSI*, No. 406; *PCZ*, Nos. 59011, 59093. Jews lived in
Jaffa even before the establishment of the Hasmonaean state (II Macc. XII: 3),
but only with its final capture by Simon the Hasmonaean did it become a Jewish
city; see I Macc. XIII : 11. It was at all times regarded as Judaea's chief outlet to
the sea; see the *Letter of Aristeas*, 115; Strabo, *Geographica*, XVI, 2 : 28, p. 759
(No. 114).

τῆς ἐν τῇ Κοίλῃ Συρίᾳ: For Coele-Syria, see the commentary to Theophrastus,
Historia Plantarum, II, 6 : 2 (No. 6).

57

Bibliotheca Historica, I, 55:5 — Vogel = F 33b R

Ὅτι δὲ τοῦτο τὸ γένος ⟨scil. τὸ Κόλχων⟩ Αἰγυπτιακόν ἐστι σημεῖον
εἶναι τὸ περιτέμνεσθαι τοὺς ἀνθρώπους παραπλησίως τοῖς κατ' Αἴγυπτον,
διαμένοντος τοῦ νομίμου παρὰ τοῖς ἀποίκοις, καθάπερ καὶ παρὰ τοῖς
Ἰουδαίοις.

And the proof which they offer of the Egyptian origin of this nation
is the fact that the Colchi practise circumcision even as the Egyptians
do, the custom continuing among the colonists sent out from Egypt
as it also did in the case of the Jews. (trans. C. H. Oldfather, *LCL*)

58

Bibliotheca Historica, I, 94:1–2 — Vogel = F34R = Bidez & Cumont, II, B19

(1) Μετὰ γὰρ τὴν παλαιὰν τοῦ κατ᾽ Αἴγυπτον βίου κατάστασιν, τὴν μυθολογουμένην γεγονέναι ἐπί τε τῶν θεῶν καὶ τῶν ἡρώων, πεῖσαί φασι πρῶτον ἐγγράπτοις νόμοις χρήσασθαι τὰ πλήθη τὸν Μνεύην, ἄνδρα καὶ τῇ ψυχῇ μέγαν καὶ τῷ βίῳ κοινότατον τῶν μνημονευομένων.
5 *προσποιηθῆναι δ᾽ αὐτῷ τὸν Ἑρμῆν δεδωκέναι τούτους, ὡς μεγάλων ἀγαθῶν αἰτίους ἐσομένους, καθάπερ παρ᾽ Ἕλλησι ποιῆσαί φασιν ἐν μὲν τῇ Κρήτῃ Μίνωα, παρὰ δὲ Λακεδαιμονίοις Λυκοῦργον, τὸν μὲν παρὰ Διός, τὸν δὲ παρ᾽ Ἀπόλλωνος φήσαντα τούτους παρειληφέναι.*
(2) καὶ παρ᾽ ἑτέροις δὲ πλείοσιν ἔθνεσι παραδέδοται τοῦτο τὸ γένος
10 *τῆς ἐπινοίας ὑπάρξαι καὶ πολλῶν ἀγαθῶν αἴτιον γενέσθαι τοῖς πεισθεῖσι· παρὰ μὲν γὰρ τοῖς Ἀριανοῖς Ζαθραύστην ἱστοροῦσι τὸν ἀγαθὸν δαίμονα προσποιήσασθαι τοὺς νόμους αὐτῷ διδόναι, παρὰ δὲ τοῖς ὀνομαζομένοις Γέταις τοῖς ἀπαθανατίζουσι Ζάλμοξιν ὡσαύτως τὴν κοινὴν Ἑστίαν, παρὰ δὲ τοῖς Ἰουδαίοις Μωυσῆν τὸν Ἰαὼ ἐπικαλούμενον θεόν, εἴτε*
15 *θαυμαστὴν καὶ θείαν ὅλως ἔννοιαν εἶναι κρίναντας τὴν μέλλουσαν ὠφελήσειν ἀνθρώπων πλῆθος, εἴτε καὶ πρὸς τὴν ὑπεροχὴν καὶ δύναμιν τῶν εὑρεῖν λεγομένων τοὺς νόμους ἀποβλέψαντα τὸν ὄχλον μᾶλλον ὑπακούσεσθαι διαλαβόντας.*

3–4 τὸν Μνεύην ἄνδρα] βιοῦν τὸν ἄνδρα D   καὶ βιοῦν τὸν ἄνδρα C   καὶ βιοῦν τὸν Μωσῆν ἄνδρα F   11 ἀρειανοῖς F   ἀριμασποῖς C   13 τοῖς ἀπαθανατίζουσι om. CF   14 ἰάω D

(1) After the establishment of settled life in Egypt in early times, which took place, according to the mythical account, in the period of the gods and heroes, the first, they say, to persuade the multitudes to use written laws was Mneves, a man not only great of soul but also in his life the most public-spirited of all lawgivers whose names are recorded. According to the tradition he claimed that Hermes had given the laws to him with the assurance that they would be the cause of great blessings, just as among the Greeks, they say, Minos did in Crete and Lycurgus among the Lacedaemonians, the former saying that he received his laws from Zeus and the latter his from Apollo. (2) Also among several other peoples tradition says that this kind of a device was used and was the cause of much good to such as believed it. Thus it is recorded that among the Arians Zathraustes claimed that the Good Spirit gave him his laws, among the people known as the Getae who represent themselves to be immortal. Zalmoxis asserted the same of their common goddess Hestia, and

among the Jews Moyses referred his laws to the god who is invoked as Iao. They all did it either because they believed that a conception which would help humanity was marvellous and wholly divine, or because they held that the common crowd would be more likely to obey the laws if their gaze was directed towards the majesty and power of those to whom their laws were ascribed.   (trans. C. H. Oldfather, *LCL*)

2   Ζαθραύστην: For this form see Bidez & Cumont, II B 19, p. 31, n. 3; K. Ziegler, PW, Ser. 2, IX, p. 2331.

τὸν Ἰαὼ ἐπικαλούμενον θεόν: Here, for the first time in Greek literature, the name Ἰάω designates the Jewish God. It does not occur in the Septuagint, having become a *vocabulum ineffabile* for the Jews. We find it used by Egyptian Jews under Persian rule, as attested by the papyri from Elephantine; see A. Cowley, *Aramaic Papyri of the Fifth Century*, Oxford 1923; E. G. Kraeling, *The Brooklyn Museum Aramaic Papyri*, New Haven 1953. Thus, for example, we find oaths there ביהו אלהא; see also the Mishna, *Succa*, iv : 5. The two other pagan literary sources that mention Iao are Varro, apud: Lydus, *De Mensibus*, IV, 53 (No. 75); and Labeo, apud: Macrobius, I, 18 : 18–21 (No. 445). However, this name is very common in magical papyri and amulets; see Ganschinietz, PW, IX, pp. 698 ff.; Goodenough, II, pp. 192 ff.; O. Eissfeldt, *Kleine Schriften*, I, Tübingen 1962, pp. 157 ff.

εἴτε καὶ πρὸς τὴν ὑπεροχὴν καὶ δύναμιν τῶν εὑρεῖν λεγομένων... τὸν ὄχλον μᾶλλον ὑπακούσεσθαι διαλαβόντας: For the same idea, see Strabo, *Geographica*, XVI, 2 : 38–39, pp. 761 f. (No. 115). Because of the general similarity between Diodorus and Strabo, scholars such as Heinemann and Pfligersdorffer have maintained that the present passage derives from Posidonius; see I. Heinemann, *MGWJ*, LXIII, (1919), pp. 117 f.; G. Pfligersdorffer, *Studien zu Poseidonios*, Vienna 1959, p. 145. Other scholars take into account the possibility that Hecataeus, the main source of Diodorus' first book, also constitutes his source for the name Ἰάω. This is the view held by Bidez & Cumont (I, pp. 20 f.; II, B 19, p. 31, n. 3). Jacoby, who sees no reason to doubt the Hecataean origin of Chaps. 94–95 of Diodorus, did not find it necessary to include them in the appendix to *F. Gr. Hist.*, III, A 264 = Hecataeus; cf. F. Jacoby, PW, VII, p. 2760. On the other hand, Schwartz expresses himself categorically against this view; see Schwartz, PW, V, p. 670: "der mit der Königsgeschichte nicht übereinstimmende Excurs über die ägyptischen Gesetzgeber (I, 94, 95) hat sich bis jetzt auf keinen bestimmten Gewährsmann mit Sicherheit zurückführen lassen." Aly, also, objects to the view that the name Iao derives from Hecataeus and thinks that pagan writers learnt of it at a much later date; see W. Aly, *Strabon von Amaseia*, Bonn 1957, pp. 200 f.; see also the commentary to Varro (No. 75). Most probably the name Iao derives from a source later than Hecataeus. However, in view of the insufficient data at our disposal, we cannot reach reliable conclusions as to the ultimate, or even secondary, origin of the catalogue of legislators in Diodorus.

59

Bibliotheca Historica, II, 48:6–9 — Vogel = F35R

(6) "Εστι δ' ἐν τῇ χώρᾳ τῶν Ναβαταίων καὶ πέτρα καθ' ὑπερβολὴν

172

Diodorus

ὀχυρά, μίαν ἀνάβασιν ἔχουσα, δι᾽ ἧς κατ᾽ ὀλίγους ἀναβαίνοντες ἀποτίθενται τὰς ἀποσκευάς· λίμνη τε μεγάλη φέρουσα πολλὴν ἄσφαλτον, ἐξ ἧς λαμβάνουσιν οὐκ ὀλίγας προσόδους. (7) αὕτη δ᾽ ἔχει τὸ μὲν
5 μῆκος σταδίων ὡς πεντακοσίων, τὸ δὲ πλάτος ὡς ἑξήκοντα, τὸ δ᾽ ὕδωρ δυσῶδες καὶ διάπικρον, ὥστε μὴ δύνασθαι μήτ᾽ ἰχθὺν τρέφειν μήτ᾽ ἄλλο τῶν καθ᾽ ὕδατος εἰωθότων ζῴων εἶναι. ἐμβαλλόντων δ᾽ εἰς αὐτὴν ποταμῶν μεγάλων τῇ γλυκύτητι διαφόρων, τούτων μὲν περιγίνεται κατὰ τὴν δυσωδίαν, ἐξ αὑτῆς δὲ μέσης κατ᾽ ἐνιαυτὸν ἐκφυσᾷ ἀσφάλτου
10 μέγεθος ποτὲ μὲν μεῖζον ἢ τρίπλεθρον, ἔστι δ᾽ ὅτε δυοῖν πλέθρων· ἐφ᾽ ᾧ δὴ συνήθως οἱ περιοικοῦντες βάρβαροι τὸ μὲν μεῖζον καλοῦσι ταῦρον τὸ δ᾽ ἔλαττον μόσχον ἐπονομάζουσιν. (8) ἐπιπλεούσης δὲ τῆς ἀσφάλτου πελαγίας ὁ τύπος φαίνεται τοῖς [μὲν] ἐξ ἀποστήματος θεωροῦσιν οἱονεὶ νῆσος. τὴν δ᾽ ἔκπτωσιν τῆς ἀσφάλτου συμβαίνει
15 φανερὰν γίνεσθαι τοῖς ἀνθρώποις πρὸ ἡμερῶν εἴκοσι [δύο]· κύκλῳ γὰρ τῆς λίμνης ἐπὶ πολλοὺς σταδίους ὀσμὴ προσπίπτει μετὰ πνεύματος, καὶ πᾶς ὁ περὶ τὸν τόπον ἄργυρός τε καὶ χρυσὸς καὶ χαλκὸς ἀποβάλλει τὴν ἰδιότητα τοῦ χρώματος. ἀλλ᾽ αὕτη μὲν ἀποκαθίσταται πάλιν, ἐπειδὰν ἀναφυσηθῆναι συμβῇ πᾶσαν τὴν ἄσφαλτον· ὁ δὲ πλησίον τόπος
20 ἔμπυρος ὢν καὶ δυσώδης ποιεῖ τὰ σώματα τῶν ἀνθρώπων ἐπίνοσα καὶ παντελῶς ὀλιγοχρόνια. (9) ἀγαθὴ δ᾽ ἐστὶ φοινικόφυτος ὅσην αὐτῆς συμβαίνει ποταμοῖς διειλῆφθαι χρησίμοις ἢ πηγαῖς δυναμέναις ἀρδεύειν. γίνεται δὲ περὶ τοὺς τόπους τούτους ἐν αὐλῶνί τινι καὶ τὸ καλούμενον βάλσαμον, ἐξ οὗ πρόσοδον ἁδρὰν λαμβάνουσιν, οὐδαμοῦ μὲν τῆς ἄλλης
25 οἰκουμένης εὑρισκομένου τοῦ φυτοῦ τούτου, τῆς δ᾽ ἐξ αὐτοῦ χρείας εἰς φάρμακα τοῖς ἰατροῖς καθ᾽ ὑπερβολὴν εὐθετούσης.

9 ἐκφύουσα DF   11 ᾧ Vogel   ὧν codd.   13 τύπος Schaefer
τόπος codd. / μὲν secl. Vogel   15 δύο secl. Vogel   19 ἀναφυσηθῆναι Vogel   ἀναφυσῆσαι codd.   23 τούτους om. CDF

(6) There is also in the land of the Nabataeans a rock, which is exceedingly strong since it has but one approach, and using this ascent they mount it a few at a time and thus store their possessions in safety. And a large lake is also there which produces asphalt in abundance, and from it they derive not a little revenue. (7) It has a length of about five hundred stades and a width of about sixty, and its water is so ill-smelling and so very bitter that it cannot support fish or any of the other animals which commonly live in water. And although great rivers of remarkable sweetness empty into it, the lake gets the better of them by reason of its evil smell, and from its centre it spouts forth once a year a great mass of asphalt, which sometimes extends for more than three plethra, and sometimes for only two; and when

173

this occurs the barbarians who live about the lake usually call the larger flow a "bull" and to the smaller one they give the name "calf". (8) Since the asphalt floats on the surface of the lake, to those who view it from a distance it takes the appearance of an island. And the fact is that the emission of the asphalt is made known to the natives twenty days before it takes place; for to a distance of many stades around the lake the odour, borne on the wind, assails them, and every piece of silver and gold and brass in the locality loses its characteristic lustre. But this returns again as soon as all the asphalt has been spouted forth; and the region round about, by reason of its being exposed to fire and to the evil odours, renders the bodies of the inhabitants susceptible to disease and makes the people very short-lived. (9) Yet the land is good for the growing of palms, wherever it happens to be traversed by rivers with usable water or to be supplied with springs which can irrigate it. And there is also found in these regions in a certain valley the balsam tree, as it is called, from which they receive a substantial revenue, since this tree is found nowhere else in the inhabited world and the use of it for medicinal purposes is most highly valued by physicians.

(trans. C. H. Oldfather, *LCL*)

The entire description of the Dead Sea in this chapter is repeated almost verbatim in Diodorus, XIX, 98, (No. 62), with the exception of one insignificant detail concerning the size of the flow of asphalt. Here it comes in the middle of the survey of Arabia; in No. 62 it is found in the framework of the campaign of Demetrius Poliorcetes against the Nabataeans. The circumstantial description of the asphalt collection given in Diodorus, XIX, 99, is not found here; nor is there any reference to the fact that it was used for embalming the dead and that it was exported to Egypt. Though there are parallels in other Greek or Latin writers for some of the features of the Dead Sea and the collection of the asphalt as Diodorus describes them, the description on the whole does not have a close counterpart in existing literature; see the commentary to Diodorus, XIX, 98–99 (No. 62). Diodorus probably goes back to Hieronymus, but we cannot ascertain whether or not he owes anything to an intermediate source; see the introduction. It should be pointed out that the fragment of Hieronymus (No. 10) is the only one of our sources to state, as does Diodorus (II, 48), that the lake in question is situated in the country of the Nabataeans.

60

Bibliotheca Historica, XIX, 59:1–2 — Fischer

(1) Ὄντος δ' αὐτοῦ περὶ ταῦτα παρῆν Ἀγησίλαος ὁ πεμφθεὶς εἰς Κύπρον πρεσβευτής, ἀπαγγέλλων ὅτι Νικοκρέων μὲν καὶ τῶν ἄλλων

Diodorus

οἱ κράτιστοι βασιλεῖς πρὸς Πτολεμαῖον πεποίηνται συμμαχίαν, ὁ δὲ
Κιτιεὺς καὶ Λαπίθιος, ἔτι δὲ Μαριεὺς καὶ Κερυνίτης τὴν πρὸς αὐτὸν
φιλίαν συντέθεινται. (2) ἀκούσας δὲ ταῦτα τρισχιλίους μὲν στρατιώτας
καὶ στρατηγὸν Ἀνδρόνικον κατέλιπεν ἐπὶ τῆς πολιορκίας, αὐτὸς δὲ
μετὰ τῆς δυνάμεως ἀναζεύξας τήν τ' Ἰόππην καὶ Γάζαν ἀπειθούσας
κατὰ κράτος εἷλε καὶ τοὺς μὲν καταληφθέντας Πτολεμαίου στρατιώτας
ἐπιδιεῖλεν εἰς τὰς ἰδίας τάξεις, εἰς δὲ τὰς πόλεις παρεισήγαγε φρουρὰν
10 τὴν ἀναγκάσουσαν πειθαρχεῖν τοὺς ἐνοικοῦντας.

4 Μαριεὺς Gronovius μάριος codd.   7 Ἰόππην Dindorf
10 ἀναγκάζουσαν RX

(1) While Antigonus was thus engaged, Agesilaus, the envoy whom
he sent to Cyprus, arrived with the information that Nicocreon and
the most powerful of the other kings had made an alliance with Ptolemy, but that the kings of Cition, Lapithus, Marion, Ceryneia had
concluded a treaty of friendship with himself. (2) On learning this,
Antigonus left three thousand soldiers under Andronicus to carry
on the siege, but he himself set out with the army and took by storm
Joppa and Gaza, cities that had refused obedience. The soldiers of
Ptolemy whom he captured he distributed among his own ranks,
but he placed in each city a garrison to force the inhabitants to obey
him.   (trans. R. M. Geer, LCL)

From the narrative of the campaign of Antigonus Monophthalmus against Ptolemy
I in 315 B. C. E. Cf. Niese, I, pp. 275 f.; K. J. Beloch, Griechische Geschichte, IV, 1,
Berlin–Leipzig 1925, p. 118.
2 τήν τ' Ἰόππην καὶ Γάζαν ἀπειθούσας κατὰ κράτος εἷλε: Ptolemy had presumably ruled over Palestine for some five years, i.e. since its conquest by his
forces in 320 B. C. E.; cf. Tcherikover, pp. 50 f.

61
Bibliotheca Historica, XIX, 93:7 — Fischer

Διὸ καὶ κρίνας ⟨scil. Πτολεμαῖος⟩ ἐκλιπεῖν τὴν Συρίαν κατέσκαψε τὰς
ἀξιολογωτάτας τῶν κεκρατημένων πόλεων, Ἄκην μὲν τῆς Φοινίκης
Συρίας, Ἰόππην δὲ καὶ Σαμάρειαν καὶ Γάζαν τῆς Συρίας, αὐτὸς δὲ
τὴν δύναμιν ἀναλαβὼν καὶ τῶν χρημάτων ὅσα δυνατὸν ἦν ἄγειν ἢ φέρειν
ἐπανῆλθεν εἰς Αἴγυπτον·

3 ἰόπην F

Deciding, therefore, to leave Syria, he razed the most noteworthy
of the cities that he had captured: Ake in Phoenician Syria, and Joppe,

175

Samaria, and Gaza in Syria; then he himself, taking the army and what of the booty it was possible to drive or carry, returned into Egypt. (trans. R. M. Geer, *LCL*)

62

Bibliotheca Historica, XIX, 98–99 — Fischer = F 35b R

(98) Ὁ μὲν οὖν Δημήτριος λαβὼν ὁμήρους καὶ τὰς ὁμολογηθείσας δωρεὰς ἀνέζευξεν ἀπὸ τῆς πέτρας· διατείνας δὲ σταδίους τριακοσίους κατεστρατοπέδευσε πλησίον τῆς Ἀσφαλτίτιδος λίμνης, ἧς τὴν φύσιν οὐκ ἄξιον παραδραμεῖν ἀνεπισήμαντον. κεῖται γὰρ κατὰ μέσην τὴν
5 σατραπείαν τῆς Ἰδουμαίας, τῷ μὲν μήκει παρεκτείνουσα σταδίους μάλιστά που πεντακοσίους, τῷ δὲ πλάτει περὶ ἑξήκοντα· τὸ δ' ὕδωρ ἔχει διάπικρον καὶ καθ' ὑπερβολὴν δυσῶδες, ὥστε μήτ' ἰχθὺν δύνασθαι τρέφειν μήτ' ἄλλο τῶν καθ' ὕδατος εἰωθότων ζῴων ‹εἶναι›. ἐμβαλλόντων δ' εἰς αὐτὴν ποταμῶν μεγάλων τῇ γλυκύτητι διαφόρων τούτων μὲν
10 περιγίνεται κατὰ τὴν δυσωδίαν, ἐξ αὐτῆς δὲ μέσης ἐκφυσᾷ κατ' ἐνιαυτὸν ἀσφάλτου στερεᾶς μέγεθος ποτὲ μὲν μεῖζον ἢ τρίπλεθρον, ἔστι δ' ὅτ' οὐ πολὺ λειπόμενον πλέθρου· ἐφ' ᾧ δὴ συνήθως οἱ περιοικοῦντες βάρβαροι τὸ μὲν μεῖζον καλοῦσι ταῦρον, τὸ δὲ ἔλασσον μόσχον. ἐπιπλεούσης δὲ τῆς ἀσφάλτου πελαγίας ὁ τόπος φαίνεται τοῖς ἐξ
15 ἀποστήματος θεωροῦσιν οἱονεί τις νῆσος. τὴν δ' ἔκπτωσιν φανερὰν συμβαίνει γίνεσθαι πρὸ ἡμερῶν εἴκοσι· κύκλῳ γὰρ τῆς λίμνης ἐπὶ πολλοὺς σταδίους ὀσμὴ τῆς ἀσφάλτου προσπίπτει ‹μετὰ› πνεύματος μοχθηροῦ καὶ πᾶς ὁ περὶ τὸν τόπον ἄργυρος κα[ὶ] χρυσὸς καὶ χαλκὸς ἀποβάλλει τὴν ἰδιότητα τοῦ χρώματος. ἀλλ' αὕτη μὲν ἀποκαθίσταται
20 πάλιν, ἐπειδὰν ἀναφυσηθῆναι συμβῇ πᾶσαν τὴν ἄσφαλτον· ὁ δὲ πλησίον τόπος ἔμπυρος ὢν καὶ δυσώδης ποιεῖ τὰ σώματα τῶν περιοικούντων ἐπίνοσα καὶ παντελῶς ὀλιγοχρόνια. ἀγαθὴ δ' ἐστὶ φοινικόφυτος ὅσην αὐτῆς συμβαίνει διειλῆφθαι ποταμοῖς χρησίμοις ἢ πηγαῖς δυναμέναις ἀρδεύειν· γίνεται δὲ περὶ τοὺς τόπους τούτους ἐν αὐλῶνί τινι καὶ τὸ
25 καλούμενον βάλσαμον, ἐξ οὗ πρόσοδον ἁδρὰν εἶναι συμβαίνει, οὐδαμοῦ μὲν τῆς ἄλλης οἰκουμένης εὑρισκομένου τοῦ φυτοῦ, τῆς δ' ἐξ αὐτοῦ χρείας εἰς φάρμακα τοῖς ἰατροῖς καθ' ὑπερβολὴν εὐθετούσης.

5 τῆς Ἰδουμαίας om. RX   6 που] ὡς F   8 ‹εἶναι› Stephanus / ἐμβαλόντων F   10 κατὰ τὴν δυσωδίαν] κατὰ τὴν ἄλμην Reiske 12 ἐφ' ᾧ Fischer   ἐφ' ὧν codd.   14 τόπος] τύπος Schaefer   14–15 ἐκ διαστήματος F   16 συμβαίνει γινέσθαι φανερὰν F   17 ‹ἀπὸ› τῆς ἀσφάλτου Reiske / ‹μετὰ› Wesseling   18 μοχθηροῦ om. RX   23 αὐτὴν RX

Diodorus

(99:1) τὴν δ' ἐκπίπτουσαν ἄσφαλτον οἱ περιοικοῦντες ἐξ ἀμφοτέρων τῶν μερῶν τὴν λίμνην διαρπάζουσι πολεμικῶς διακείμενοι πρὸς ἀλλήλους,
30 *ἄνευ πλοίων ἰδιαζόντως τὴν κομιδὴν ποιούμενοι. παρασκευασάμενοι γὰρ δέσμας καλάμων εὐμεγέθεις ἐμβάλλουσιν εἰς τὴν λίμνην· ἐπὶ δὲ τούτων ἐπικάθηνται οὐ πλείω τριῶν, <ὧν> δύο μὲν ἔχοντες προσδεδεμένας πλάτας κωπηλατοῦσιν, εἷς δὲ φορῶν τόξα τοὺς προσπλέοντας ἐκ τοῦ πέραν ἢ βιάζεσθαι τολμῶντας ἀμύνεται, (2) ὅταν δὲ πλησίον*
35 *γένωνται τῆς ἀσφάλτου, πελέκεις ἔχοντες ἐπιπεδῶσι καὶ καθάπερ μαλακῆς πέτρας ἀποκόπτοντες γεμίζουσι τὴν δέσμην, εἶτα ἀποπλέουσιν εἰς τοὐπίσω. ἂν δέ τις αὐτῶν ἀποπέσῃ τῆς δέσμης διαλυθείσης μὴ δυνάμενος νεῖν, οὐ καταδύεται καθάπερ ἐν τοῖς ἄλλοις ὕδασιν, ἀλλὰ ἐπινήχεται τοῖς ἐπισταμένοις ὁμοίως. (3) φύσει γὰρ τοῦτο τὸ ὑγρὸν*
40 *παραδέχεται βάρος ὃ συμβαίνει μετέχειν αὐξήσεως ἢ πνεύματος, ἔξω τῶν στερεῶν, ἃ τὴν πυκνότητα δοκεῖ παραπλησίαν ἔχειν ἀργύρῳ καὶ χρυσῷ καὶ μολύβδῳ καὶ τοῖς ὁμοίοις· καὶ ταῦτα μὲν πολὺ βραδύτερον καταφέρεται τῶν ἐν ταῖς ἄλλαις λίμναις ῥιπτουμένων. ταύτην δ' ἔχοντες οἱ βάρβαροι πρόσοδον ἀπάγουσι τὴν ἄσφαλτον εἰς τὴν Αἴγυπτον*
45 *καὶ πωλοῦσιν εἰς τὰς ταριχείας τῶν νεκρῶν· μὴ μιγνυμένης γὰρ ταύτης τοῖς λοιποῖς ἀρώμασιν οὐ δυνατὸν γενέσθαι τὴν τῶν σωμάτων φυλακὴν πολυχρόνιον.*

32 <ὧν> Schaefer   32–33 δεδεμένας F   40 ᾧ συμβαίνει Reiske
42 μὲν] μέντοι Dindorf   46 τὴν τῶν om. F

(98) Demetrius received hostages and the gifts that had been agreed upon and departed from the rock. After marching for three hundred stades, he camped near the Dead Sea, the nature of which ought not to be passed over without remark. It lies along the middle of the satrapy of Idumaea, extending in length about five hundred stades and in width about sixty. Its water is very bitter and of exceedingly foul odour, so that it can support neither fish nor any of the other creatures usually found in water. Although great rivers whose waters are of exceptional sweetness flow into it, it prevails over these by reason of its foulness; and from its centre each year it sends forth a mass of solid asphalt, sometimes more than three plethra in area, sometimes a little less than one plethrum. When this happens the barbarians who live near habitually call the larger mass a bull and the smaller one a calf. When the asphalt is floating on the sea, its surface seems to those who see it from a distance just like an island. It appears that the ejection of the asphalt is indicated twenty days in advance, for on every side about the sea for a distance of many stades the odour of the asphalt spreads with a noisome exhalation,

177

and all the silver, gold, and bronze in the region lose their proper
colours. These, however, are restored as soon as all the asphalt has
been ejected; but the neighbouring region is very torrid and ill smell-
ing, which makes the inhabitants sickly in body and exceedingly
short-lived. Yet the land is good for raising palm trees in whatever
part it is crossed by serviceable rivers or is supplied with springs that
can irrigate it. In a certain valley in this region there grows what is
called balsam, from which there is a great income since nowhere
else in the inhabited world is this plant found, and its use as a drug
is very important to physicians.

(99: 1) When the asphalt has been ejected, the people who live about
the sea on both sides carry it off like plunder of war since they are
hostile to each other, making the collection without boats in a peculiar
fashion. They make ready large bundles of reeds and cast them into
the sea. On these not more than three men take their places, two of
whom row with oars, which are lashed on, but one carries a bow
and repels any who sail against them from the other shore or who
venture to interfere with them. (2) When they have come near the
asphalt they jump upon it with axes and, just as if it were soft stone,
they cut out pieces and load them on the raft, after which they sail
back. If the raft comes to pieces and one of them who does not know
how to swim falls off, he does not sink as he would in other waters,
but stays afloat as well as do those who do know. (3) For this liquid
by its nature supports heavy bodies that have the power of growth
or of breathing, except for solid ones that seem to have a density
like that of silver, gold, lead, and the like; and even these sink much
more slowly than do these same bodies if they are cast into other
lakes. The barbarians who enjoy this source of income take the asphalt
to Egypt and sell it for the embalming of the dead; for unless this
is mixed with the other aromatic ingredients, the preservation of the
bodies cannot be permanent.   (trans. R. M. Geer, *LCL*)

---

98 Ὁ μὲν οὖν Δημήτριος λαβὼν ὁμήρους...: For the expedition of Demetrius
against the Nabataeans, see F.M. Abel, *RB*, XLVI (1937), pp. 373 ff.; G. Elkeles,
"Demetrios der Städtebelagerer", Ph.D. Thesis, Breslau 1941, pp. 10 f.; J. Starcky,
Biblical Archaeologist, XVIII (1955), pp. 84 f.
Ἀσφαλτίτιδος λίμνης: The Dead Sea is also referred to under this name by Plinius
in *Naturalis Historia*, II, 226; V, 71 ff. (Nos. 203–204); by Galenus in *De Simplicium
Medicamentorum Temperamentis ac Facultatibus*, IV, 20 (No. 381); and, very
often, by Josephus in *Ant.*, I, 174; IV, 85; IX, 7; XV, 168; *BJ*, I, 657; III, 515;
IV, 437 f., 453, 455 f., 474, 476; VII, 281; *Contra Apionem*, I, 174.
κεῖται γὰρ κατὰ μέσην τὴν σατραπείαν τῆς Ἰδουμαίας: The designation of Idumaea as a satrapy contradicts Diodorus, XIX, 95 : 2, where the same country is

Diodorus

designated as an eparchy. The term *eparchia* does not occur elsewhere in connection with any part of Hellenistic Palestine. According to a theory propounded by Tarn, the eparchy in the Seleucid empire constituted a subdivision of the satrapy; see W. W. Tarn, *Proceedings of the British Academy*, XVI, 1930, pp. 129 ff.; idem, *The Greeks in Bactria and India²*, Cambridge 1951, p. 2. The use of the term "satrapy" is better attested in the Hellenistic period, though hardly in connection with the administrative divisions of Palestine, although the Septuagint does refer to the five Philistine districts as satrapies in Jos. xiii : 3 and Judges iii : 3; cf., e.g., Polybius, V, 54 : 9; C.B. Welles, *Royal Correspondence in the Hellenistic Period*, New Haven 1934, Nos. 11, 37,70. Strabo, however, deriving expressly from Posidonius, XVI, 2 : 4, p. 750, asserts that Coele-Syria, which included the whole of Palestine in the Seleucid period, was divided into four satrapies; see the commentary to Theophrastus, *Historia Plantarum*, II, 6 : 2 (No. 6). This piece of information undoubtedly relates to the administrative division of the second century B. C. E., but not to the latter part of the century, when Hasmonaean Judaea obtained full independence and initiated the Jewish expansion over most parts of the country. In any event, in the sixties of the second century Idumaea constituted a separate administrative unit (II Macc. xii : 32), and it would not be too far-fetched to suppose that Idumaea was among the four satrapies alluded to by Posidonius. But how are we to account for the fact that Diodorus, after having called Idumaea an eparchy, calls it a satrapy? It may be that the explanation lies in Diodorus' indifference to exact administrative nomenclature. Still, much is to be said for Tarn's view that the term in 95 : 2 derives directly from Hieronymus, while here we have Diodorus' own remark; see Tarn, *Proceedings*, p. 134, n. 2; Jacoby, PW, VIII, p. 1555. In that case, Diodorus would reflect later Seleucid terminology.

Some difficulty is still attached to the statement that the Dead Sea was situated in the middle of the satrapy of Idumaea. We may explain it as an inaccuracy on the part of Diodorus, but it is equally possible that, according to the Seleucid division, the satrapy of Hellenistic Idumaea included the eastern shore of the Dead Sea, though we have no information to that effect from other sources. Thus, the satrapy of Idumaea was a much larger unit than the *meris* of Idumaea proper. This conjecture obviates the necessity for Bengtson's suggestion that we omit the words τῆς Ἰδουμαίας after κατὰ μέσην τὴν σατραπείαν, in accordance with MSS R and X, where it is implied that the satrapy included the entire province of Συρία καὶ Φοινίκη, mentioned before in 94 : 1; see Bengtson, II, pp. 35 f. In Hieronymus' reference to the Dead Sea, as cited by the Florentine Paradoxographer (No. 10), he states only that it is situated in the Land of the Nabataeans; the same holds true for Diodorus, II, 48 (No. 59).

τῷ μὲν μήκει παρεκτείνουσα σταδίους μάλιστά που πεντακοσίους, τῷ δὲ πλάτει περὶ ἑξήκοντα: Strabo (*Geographica*, XVI, 2 : 42, p. 763= No. 115) asserts that some reckon the circumference of the Lake at one thousand stadia, but this probably refers to Lake Sirbonis; see C. Burchard, *RB*, LXIX (1962), p. 546 n. 57. In *BJ*, IV, 482, Josephus estimates the length at five hundred and eighty stadia and the width at one hundred and fifty stadia. Plinius, *Naturalis Historia*, V, 72 (No. 204) says: "longitudine excedit C p., latitudine maxima LXXV implet, minima VI." Tacitus states that it is huge; *Historiae*, V, 6 (No. 281). The magnitude of the Dead Sea is also stressed by Pompeius Trogus, apud: Iustinus, XXXVI, 3 : 6 (No. 137); Strabo *loc. cit.* πολλὴ μέν ἐστι, In September 1966 the Dead Sea was found to be *c.* 76 km long and 17.5 km at its maximal width.

179

From Herodotus to Plutarch

τὸ δ'ὕδωρ ἔχει διάπικρον καὶ... δυσῶδες, ὥστε μήτ'ἰχθὺν δύνασθαι τρέφειν: Cf. Aristotle (No. 3); Hieronymus (No. 10); *BJ*, IV, 476; Tacitus (No. 281); Pausanias, V, 7:5 (No. 356); Galenus, *De Simplicium Medicamentorum Temperamentis ac Facultatibus*, IV, 20 (No. 381).

ἐμβαλλόντων δ'εἰς αὐτὴν ποταμῶν μεγάλων...: The most important rivers that flow into the Dead Sea are the Jordan from the north and the Arnon from the east; see Abel, I, pp. 176 ff.; see also Galenus, *loc. cit.*

ἐξ αὐτῆς δὲ μέσης ἐκφυσᾷ κατ' ἐνιαυτόν: Cf. Strabo, XVI, 2:42 (No. 115): ἐκ μέσου τοῦ βάθους, but Strabo states (scil. ἡ ἄσφαλτος)ἀναφυσᾶται κατὰ καιροὺς ἀτάκτους. Tacitus, *loc. cit.* (No. 281) says: "certo anni tempore", while Xenophilus (No. 22) has παρὰ τρίτον ἔτος φέρειν ὑγρὰν ἄσφαλτον.

ἀσφάλτου στερεᾶς: Cf. Strabo, *Geographica*, XVI, 2 : 42, p. 764: ἔστι δ'ἡ ἄσφαλτος γῆς βῶλος, ὑγραινομένη μὲν ὑπὸ θερμοῦ καὶ ἀναφυσωμένη καὶ διαχεομένη, πάλιν δὲ μεταβάλλουσα εἰς πάγον ἰσχυρὸν... ὥστε τομῆς καὶ κοπῆς δεῖσθαι. See also Tacitus, *loc. cit.* (No. 281): "manuque trahi ad litus... securibus cuneisque... discindi"; *BJ*, IV, 479: τῆς μέντοι ἀσφάλτου κατὰ πολλὰ μέρη βώλους μελαίνας ἀναδίδωσιν.

ποτὲ μὲν μεῖζον ἢ τρίπλεθρον...: Among classical sources only Diodorus gives the size of the floating asphalt masses.

τὸ μὲν μεῖζον καλοῦσι ταῦρον: Cf. *BJ*, IV, 479: αἱ δ' [scil. βῶλοι μέλαιναι) τό τε σχῆμα καὶ τὸ μέγεθος ταύροις ἀκεφάλοις παραπλήσιαι. It seems that the statement of Plinius in *Naturalis Historia* (V, 72 = No. 204), "tauri camelique fluitant", derives from a misunderstanding of his source. See also *Mandeville's Travels*, London 1953, texts and translations by M. Letts, I, p. 71: "And men may find ilk a day on ilk side of this sea great lumps thereof, yea as great als a horse."

οἱονεί τις νῆσος: Cf. Strabo, *Geographica*, XVI, 2 : 42, p. 763 (No. 115): κυρτουμένη δ'ἡ ἐπιφάνεια λόφου φαντασίαν παρέχει.

καὶ πᾶς ὁ περὶ τὸν τόπον ἄργυρος καὶ χρυσὸς καὶ χαλκὸς ἀποβάλλει τὴν ἰδιότητα τοῦ χρώματος: Strabo, *loc. cit.* (No. 115) refers to the tarnishing of the metals (copper, silver, gold) under the influence of the soot that comes from the asphalt. Cf. also Xenophilus (No. 22): παρὰ τοῖς ἐντὸς τριάκοντα σταδίων οἰκοῦσιν κατιοῦσθαι χαλκώματα.

ποιεῖ τὰ σώματα τῶν περιοικούντων ἐπίνοσα καὶ παντελῶς ὀλιγοχρόνια: The statement about the sickness and the short life-span of the inhabitants of the vicinity has a parallel in Tacitus, *loc. cit.* (No. 281): "lacus ... gravitate odoris accolis pestifer."

ἀγαθὴ δ' ἐστὶ φοινικόφυτος: The renowned dates grown in Jericho are meant here. Diodorus does not mention the name of any place in the region of the Dead Sea.

γίνεται δὲ... ἐν αὐλῶνί τινι καὶ τὸ καλούμενον βάλσαμον: For the balsam of these regions, see Theophrastus, *Historia Plantarum*, IX 6 : 1–4 (No. 9); Strabo, *Geographica*, XVI, 2 : 41, p. 763 (No. 115); Pompeius Trogus, apud: Iustinus, XXXVI, 3 : 3–4 (No. 137); Plinius, *Naturalis Historia*, XII, 111–123 (No. 213); Tacitus, *loc. cit.* (No. 281); and the commentaries *ad loc.* Strabo states that "Hiericus is a plain surrounded by a mountainous country ... where the palm grove is to be found".

οὐδαμοῦ μὲν τῆς ἄλλης οἰκουμένης εὑρισκομένου τοῦ φυτοῦ: The same is maintained by Strabo and Plinius; see Strabo, *loc. cit.* (No. 115): τίμιος οὖν ἐστι, καὶ διότι ἐνταῦθα μόνον γεννᾶται; Plinius, *Naturalis Historia*, XII, 111 (No. 213): "uni terrarum Iudaeae concessum."

180

Diodorus

τῆς δ'ἐξ αὐτοῦ χρείας εἰς φάρμακα... εὐθετούσης: For the use of the balsam for medical purposes, see Strabo, loc. cit. (No. 115), who says that the juice of the balsam cures headaches, incipient cataracts and dimness of sight.

99 : 1 τὴν δ'ἐκπίπτουσαν ἄσφαλτον οἱ περιοικοῦντες ἐξ ἀμφοτέρων τῶν μερῶν τὴν λίμνην διαρπάζουσι...: On collecting the asphalt, see Strabo, Geographica, XVI, 2 : 42, p. 764 (No. 115); BJ, IV, 480; Tacitus, loc. cit. (No. 281). The description in Diodorus is more circumstantial than in any of the other sources.

πολεμικῶς διακείμενοι πρὸς ἀλλήλους: Perhaps this implies hostility between the old Idumaean inhabitants and the Nabataean invaders or, what seems to me more likely, a rivalry between different Arab tribes; see Kahrstedt, p. 36.

παρασκευασάμενοι γὰρ δέσμας καλάμων...: Cf. Strabo, loc. cit. (No. 115): προσπλεύσαντες δὲ ταῖς σχεδίαις.

99 : 2-3 οὐ καταδύεται καθάπερ ἐν τοῖς ἄλλοις ὕδασιν, ἄλλα ἐπινήχεται... φύσει γὰρ τοῦτο τὸ ὑγρὸν παραδέχεται βάρος ὃ συμβαίνει μετέχειν αὐξήσεως ἢ πνεύματος: Cf. Aristotle, Meteorologica, II, p. 359a (No. 3): εἰς ἣν ἐάν τις ἐμβάλῃ συνδήσας ἄνθρωπον ἢ ὑποζύγιον ἐπιπλεῖν καὶ οὐ καταδύεσθαι κατὰ τοῦ ὕδατος; Strabo, Geographica, XVI, 2 : 42, p.763 (No. 115): ὥστε μὴ δεῖν κολύμβου, ἀλλὰ τὸν ἐμβάντα καὶ μέχρις ὀμφαλοῦ προβάντα εὐθὺς ἐξαίρεσθαι; BJ, IV, 477; Tacitus, loc. cit. (No.281): "periti imperitique nandi perinde attolluntur". All these passages constitute a parallel to the first part of Diodorus' statement, namely, that living bodies do not sink in the Dead Sea. Pompeius Trogus (apud: Iustinus, XXXVI, 3:7=No.137) only emphasizes that "omnia vita carentia in profundum merguntur; nec materiam ullam sustinet, nisi quae alumine incrustatur"; however, Iustinus does not give us Pompeius Trogus' views on the fate of living bodies. In Pausanias, loc. cit. (No. 356), we find a description, which like the account of Diodorus, takes into consideration the whole question of sinking in the Dead Sea. Cf. also Xenophilus (No. 22): ἐπινήχεσθαι πᾶν βάρος; Plinius, Naturalis Historia, V, 72 (No. 204): "Nullum corpus animalium recipit, tauri camelique fluitant; inde fama nihil in eo mergi" (cf. idem, II, 226 = No. 203: "nihil in Asphaltite Iudaeae lacu, qui bitumen gignit, mergi potest"); Galenus, loc. cit. (No. 381).

ἀπάγουσι τὴν ἄσφαλτον εἰς τὴν Αἴγυπτον καὶ πωλοῦσιν εἰς τὰς ταριχείας τῶν νεκρῶν: Cf. Strabo (Geographica, XVI, 2 : 45, p. 764=No. 115),who says the same thing. It is, therefore, useless to deny that, at least in the Graeco-Roman period, the asphalt of the Dead Sea was used in embalming; cf. R. J. Forbes, Bitumen and Petroleum in Antiquity, Leiden 1936, pp. 93 f.; P. C. Hammond, Biblical Archaeologist, XXII (1959), pp. 44 ff. For the various uses of asphalt in antiquity, see Abel, I, pp. 193 ff.; Forbes, op. cit., pp. 42 ff.; Hammond, op. cit., pp. 40 ff.; N. Davey, A History of Building Materials, London 1961, pp. 128 ff. Josephus (BJ, IV, 481) stresses its use for both caulking ships and as an ingredient in medicine. For the medical use of the asphalt, see also Galenus, De Simplicium Medicamentorum Temperamentis ac Facultatibus, XI, 2 : 10 (No. 386).

63

Bibliotheca Historica, XXXIV–XXXV, 1:1–5 — Dindorf = Photius, cod. 244, p. 379 — Bekker = ed. Henry, Vol. VI, pp. 132 ff. = F25R = F. Gr. Hist., II, A 87 F 109

(1:1) Ὡς Ἀντίοχος ὁ βασιλεύς, φησίν, ἐπολιόρκει τὰ Ἱεροσόλυμα, οἱ δὲ

Ἰουδαῖοι μέχρι μέν τινος ἀντέσχον, ἐξαναλωθέντων δὲ τῶν ἐπιτηδείων
ἁπάντων ἠναγκάσθησαν περὶ διαλύσεως διαπρεσβεύσασθαι. οἱ δὲ πλείους
αὐτῷ τῶν φίλων συνεβούλευον κατὰ κράτος αἱρήσειν τὴν πόλιν καὶ τὸ
5 γένος ἄρδην ἀνελεῖν τῶν Ἰουδαίων· μόνους γὰρ ἁπάντων ἐθνῶν ἀκοινωνήτους εἶναι τῆς πρὸς ἄλλο ἔθνος ἐπιμιξίας καὶ πολεμίους ὑπολαμβάνειν
πάντας. ἀπεδείκνυον δὲ καὶ τοὺς προγόνους αὐτῶν ὡς ἀσεβεῖς καὶ
μισουμένους ὑπὸ τῶν θεῶν ἐξ ἁπάσης τῆς Αἰγύπτου πεφυγαδευμένους.
(2) τοὺς γὰρ ἀλφοὺς ἢ λέπρας ἔχοντας ἐν τοῖς σώμασι, καθαρμοῦ χάριν
10 ὡς ἐναγεῖς συναθροισθέντας ὑπερορίους ἐκβεβλῆσθαι· τοὺς δὲ ἐξορισθέν-
τας καταλαβέσθαι μὲν τοὺς περὶ τὰ Ἱεροσόλυμα τόπους, συστησαμέ-
νους δὲ τὸ τῶν Ἰουδαίων ἔθνος παραδόσιμον ποιῆσαι τὸ μῖσος τὸ πρὸς
τοὺς ἀνθρώπους· διὰ τοῦτο δὲ καὶ νόμιμα παντελῶς ἐξηλλαγμένα
καταδεῖξαι, τὸ μηδενὶ ἄλλῳ ἔθνει τραπέζης κοινωνεῖν μηδ᾽ εὐνοεῖν τὸ
15 παράπαν. *(3)* ὑπέμνησαν δὲ αὐτὸν καὶ περὶ τοῦ προγενομένου μίσους
τοῖς προγόνοις πρὸς τοῦτο τὸ ἔθνος. Ἀντίοχος γὰρ ὁ προσαγορευθεὶς
Ἐπιφανὴς καταπολεμήσας τοὺς Ἰουδαίους εἰσῆλθεν εἰς τὸν ἄδυτον τοῦ
θεοῦ σηκόν, οἷ νόμιμον εἰσιέναι μόνον τὸν ἱερέα· εὑρὼν δὲ ἐν αὐτῷ
λίθινον ἄγαλμα ἀνδρὸς βαθυπώγωνος καθήμενον ἐπ᾽ ὄνου, μετὰ χεῖρας
20 ἔχον βιβλίον, τοῦτο μὲν ὑπέλαβε Μωσέως εἶναι τοῦ κτίσαντος τὰ
Ἱεροσόλυμα καὶ συστησαμένου τὸ ἔθνος, πρὸς δὲ τούτοις νομοθετήσαντος
τὰ μισάνθρωπα καὶ παράνομα ἔθη τοῖς Ἰουδαίοις· αὐτὸς δὲ στυγήσας
τὴν μισανθρωπίαν πάντων ἐθνῶν ἐφιλοτιμήθη καταλῦσαι τὰ νόμιμα.
(4) διὸ τῷ ἀγάλματι τοῦ κτίστου καὶ τῷ ὑπαίθρῳ βωμῷ τοῦ θεοῦ
25 μεγάλην ὗν θύσας τό τε αἷμα προσέχεεν αὐτοῖς καὶ τὰ κρέα σκευάσας
προσέταξε τῷ μὲν ἀπὸ τούτων ζωμῷ τὰς ἱερὰς αὐτῶν βίβλους καὶ
περιεχούσας τὰ μισόξενα νόμιμα καταρρᾶναι, τὸν δὲ ἀθάνατον λεγόμενον
παρ᾽ αὐτοῖς λύχνον καὶ καόμενον ἀδιαλείπτως ἐν τῷ ναῷ κατασβέσαι,
τῶν τε κρεῶν ἀναγκάσαι προσενέγκασθαι τὸν ἀρχιερέα καὶ τοὺς ἄλλους
30 Ἰουδαίους. *(5)* Ταῦτα δὴ διεξιόντες οἱ φίλοι τὸν Ἀντίοχον παρεκάλουν
μάλιστα μὲν ἄρδην ἀνελεῖν τὸ ἔθνος, εἰ δὲ μή, καταλῦσαι τὰ νόμιμα
καὶ συναναγκάσαι τὰς ἀγωγὰς μεταθέσθαι. ὁ δὲ βασιλεὺς μεγαλόψυχος
ὢν καὶ τὸ ἦθος ἥμερος, λαβὼν ὁμήρους ἀπέλυσε τῶν ἐγκλημάτων
τοὺς Ἰουδαίους, φόρους τε τοὺς ὀφειλομένους πραξάμενος καὶ τὰ τείχη
35 περιελὼν τῶν Ἱεροσολύμων.

14–15 τὸ παράπαν μηδ᾽ εὐνοεῖν ς   15 γενομένου ς   18 οἱ Bekker
ἢ A   οὖ ς   22 στυγήσας Bekker   συστῆσαι codd.   συννοήσας Reiske
26 αὐτοῦ A   28 καιόμενον A   29 ἀναγκάσας A   ἀναγκάσαι A²
ἠνάγκασε Reiske

(1:1) When King Antiochus, says Diodorus, was laying siege to Jerusalem, the Jews held out for a time, but when all their supplies were

182

Diodorus

exhausted they found themselves compelled to make overtures for a cessation of hostilities. Now the majority of his friends advised the king to take the city by storm and to wipe out completely the race of Jews, since they alone of all nations avoided dealings with any other people and looked upon all men as their enemies. They pointed out, too, that the ancestors of the Jews had been driven out of all Egypt as men who were impious and detested by the gods. (2) For by way of purging the country all persons who had white or leprous marks on their bodies had been assembled and driven across the border, as being under a curse; the refugees had occupied the territory round about Jerusalem, and having organized the nation of the Jews had made their hatred of mankind into a tradition, and on this account had introduced utterly outlandish laws: not to break bread with any other race, nor to show them any good will at all. (3) His friends reminded Antiochus also of the enmity that in times past his ancestors had felt for this people. Antiochus, called Epiphanes, on defeating the Jews had entered the innermost sanctuary of the god's temple, where it was lawful for the priest alone to enter. Finding there a marble statue of a heavily bearded man seated on an ass, with a book in his hands, he supposed it to be an image of Moses, the founder of Jerusalem and organizer of the nation, the man, moreover, who had ordained for the Jews their misanthropic and lawless customs. And since Epiphanes was shocked by such hatred directed against all mankind, he had set himself to break down their traditional practices. (4) Accordingly, he sacrificed before the image of the founder and the open-air altar of the god a great sow, and poured its blood over them. Then, having prepared its flesh, he ordered that their holy books, containing the xenophobic laws, should be sprinkled with the broth of the meat; that the lamp, which they call undying and which burns continually in the temple, should be extinguished; and that the high priest and the rest of the Jews should be compelled to partake of the meat. (5) Rehearsing all these events, his friends strongly urged Antiochus to make an end of the race completely, or, failing that, to abolish their laws and force them to change their ways. But the king, being a magnanimous and mild-mannered person, took hostages but dismissed the charges against the Jews, once he had exacted the tribute that was due and had dismantled the walls of Jerusalem. (trans. F. R. Walton, *LCL*)

1 ὡς ᾿Αντίοχος ὁ βασιλεύς... ἐπολιόρκει τὰ ῾Ιεροσόλυμα: After failing in his military attempts against Judaea in the time of Simon (I Macc. xv–xvi), Antiochus

From Herodotus to Plutarch

Sidetes made new moves at the beginning of the rule of John Hyrcan; see *Ant.*, XIII, 236. Diodorus' narrative here is very similar to that of Josephus in both content and language, and even in many details. Thus, we may be justified in assuming that both historians had recourse to a common source, though Josephus used it only through the medium of an intermediate source. Most scholars suggest that Posidonius was Diodorus' source; see J. G. Müller, *Theologische Studien und Kritiken*, 1843, pp. 908 f.; T. Reinach, I. Heinemann, *MGWJ*, LXIII (1919), pp. 119 f.; K. Reinhardt, *Poseidonios über Ursprung und Entartung*, Heidelberg 1928, pp. 28 f.; E. Norden, *Festgabe Harnack*, p. 297 = *Kleine Schriften*, pp. 281 f.; Ed. Meyer, II, p. 268, n.3; E. Bickermann, *MGWJ*, LXXI (1927), p. 260. This sounds plausible enough, although it is not strictly proven; cf. the introduction to Posidonius. In any case, Josephus does not seem to use Posidonius directly; it was probably Nicolaus of Damascus who served as his intermediate source. It is noteworthy that the ultimate source, as expressed not only in Josephus but also in Diodorus, does not agree with the arguments of the anti-Semites, but instead praises Antiochus Sidetes for not having been won over by them: cf. ὁ δὲ βασιλεὺς μεγαλόψυχος ὢν καὶ τὸ ἦθος ἥμερος... ἀπέλυσε τῶν ἐγκλημάτων τοὺς Ἰουδαίους. On deliberations by the victors after the defeat of a city, see, e.g., Iustinus, XI, 3 : 8 ff. (after the defeat of Thebes by Alexander). The arguments of the anti-Semites in the entourage of Antiochus Sidetes reflect the well-known Graeco-Egyptian version of historical events; cf. M. Friedländer, *Geschichte der jüdischen Apologetik*, Zürich 1903, pp. 123 ff.

οἱ δὲ Ἰουδαῖοι μέχρι μέν τινος ἀντέσχον: The siege of Jerusalem lasted at least a year; see Schürer, I, p. 259, n. 5; Ed. Meyer, II, p. 268, n. 1.

ἐξαναλωθέντων δὲ τῶν ἐπιτηδείων ἁπάντων: Cf. ἀναλισκομένων τε τῶν ἐπιτηδείων in *Ant.*, XIII, 240.

καὶ τὸ γένος ἄρδην ἀνελεῖν τῶν Ἰουδαίων: Cf. ὁ δὲ ἀπωσάμενος τὴν ἐπιβουλὴν τῶν μὲν παραινούντων ἐξελεῖν τὸ ἔθνος (*op. cit.*, 245).

ἀκοινωνήτους εἶναι τῆς πρὸς ἄλλο ἔθνος ἐπιμιξίας: Cf. διὰ τὴν πρὸς ἄλλους αὐτῶν τῆς διαίτης ἀμιξίαν (*loc. cit*).

3 οἱ νόμιμον εἰσιέναι μόνον τὸν ἱερέα: By ἱερεύς, the high priest is meant. In fact, even he was allowed to enter there only once a year, on the Day of Atonement.

εὑρὼν δὲ ἐν αὐτῷ λίθινον ἄγαλμα: On the alleged Jewish ass-worship, see Mnaseas, apud: Josephus, *Contra Apionem*, II, 112–114 (No. 28); Apion, apud: *Contra Apionem*, II, 80 (No. 170). In Diodorus, however, we do not actually have a statement concerning ass-worship, but only a description of a statue of the Jewish law-giver riding on an ass. This difference between Diodorus and Apion (who refers to Apollonius Molon and Posidonius as his sources) led Böhl to suggest that Diodorus is independent of Posidonius here; see Böhl, p. 124. Bickermann, on the other hand, maintains that Posidonius is Diodorus' source, and that it was Posidonius who blunted the anti-Semitic edge of the story; see Bickermann, *op. cit.* Cf. now the reservations made by Gager, pp. 124 ff.

πρὸς δὲ τούτοις νομοθετήσαντος τὰ μισάνθρωπα καὶ παράνομα ἔθη τοῖς Ἰουδαίοις: This is still part of the representations of the anti-Semites in the camp of Antiochus Sidetes and not an expression of the views of the source itself.

αὐτὸς δὲ στυγήσας τὴν μισανθρωπίαν: Cf. H. Fuchs, *Vigiliae Christianae*, IV (1950), pp. 86 f.; E. Bickermann, *Der Gott der Makkabäer*, Berlin 1937, pp. 21 ff.

4 μεγάλην ὗν θύσας...: Cf. *Ant.*, XIII, 243: πλεῖστον Ἀντιόχου τοῦ Ἐπιφανοῦς

184

Diodorus

διενέγκας, ὃς τὴν πόλιν ἑλὼν οὓς μὲν κατέθυσεν ἐπὶ τὸν βωμόν, τὸν νεὼν δὲ τῷ ζωμῷ τούτων περιέρρανε...

τῶν τε κρεῶν ἀναγκάσαι προσενέγκασθαι τὸν ἀρχιερέα καὶ τοὺς ἄλλους Ἰουδαίους: At the time of the persecution (167 B. C. E.) it was the notorious Menelaus who acted as high priest. He needed little encouragement to desecrate his faith, even if he was not the chief instigator of the persecution as Bickermann maintains. For another view, see I. Heinemann, *MGWJ*, LXXXII (1938), pp. 145 ff.

5 ὁ δὲ βασιλεὺς μεγαλόψυχος ὢν καὶ τὸ ἦθος ἥμερος: Cf. *Ant.*, XIII, 244 f. λαβὼν ὁμήρους: Cf. *Ant.*, XIII 247.

64

Bibliotheca Historica, XL, 2 — Dindorf = Constantinus Porphyrogenitus, *Excerpta de Sententiis* — Boissevain, pp. 404 f. = F 36 R

Ὅτι περὶ Δαμασκὸν τῆς Συρίας διατρίβοντος Πομπηίου ἧκε πρὸς αὐτὸν Ἀριστόβουλος ὁ τῶν Ἰουδαίων βασιλεὺς καὶ Ὑρκανὸς ὁ ἀδελφὸς ἀμφισβητοῦντες περὶ τῆς βασιλείας. οἱ δὲ ἐπιφανέστατοι, πλείους ὄντες τῶν διακοσίων, κατήντησαν πρὸς τὸν αὐτοκράτορα, καὶ ἀπεφήναντο
5 τοὺς προγόνους ἑαυτῶν ἀφεστηκότας τοῦ ἱεροῦ πεπρεσβευκέναι πρὸς τὴν σύγκλητον, καὶ παρειληφέναι τὴν προστασίαν τῶν Ἰουδαίων ἐλευθέρων καὶ αὐτονόμων, οὐ βασιλέως χρηματίζοντος ἀλλ᾽ ἀρχιερέως ⟨τοῦ⟩ προεστηκότος τοῦ ἔθνους. ⟨p. 405⟩ τούτους δὲ νῦν δυναστεύειν καταλελυκότας τοὺς πατρίους νόμους καὶ καταδεδουλῶσθαι τοὺς πολίτας ἀδίκως· μισθο-
10 φόρων γὰρ πλήθει καὶ αἰκίαις καὶ πολλοῖς φόνοις ἀσεβέσι περιπεποιῆσθαι τὴν βασιλείαν. ὁ δὲ περὶ μὲν τῶν ἀμφισβητήσεων εἰς ὕστερον ὑπερεβάλετο καιρόν, περὶ δὲ τῆς παρανομίας τῶν Ἰουδαίων καὶ τῶν εἰς Ῥωμαίους ἀδικημάτων πικρῶς ἐπιτιμήσας τοῖς περὶ τὸν Ὑρκανὸν ἀξίους μὲν αὐτοὺς ἔφησεν εἶναι καὶ μείζονος καὶ πικροτέρας ἐπιστροφῆς,
15 ὅμως δὲ διὰ τὴν πάτριον ἐπιείκειαν τῶν Ῥωμαίων, εἰ ἀπὸ τῆς νῦν πείθωνται, συγγνώμης αὐτοὺς ἀξιώσειν.

3 ἐπιφανέστατοι ⟨τῶν Ἰουδαίων⟩ Herwerden   5 ἑαυτῶν] αὐτῶν Dindorf / προεστηκότας τοῦ ἱεροῦ Dindorf   ἀφεστηκότας τοῦ Συρίου (τοῦ Σύρου Boissevain) Herwerden   ἀφεστηκότας τοῦ Δημητρίου Walton   7–8 ⟨τοῦ⟩ προεστηκότος Nock   12 παρανομίας ⟨τῆς κατὰ⟩ Herwerden   15 εἰ] ἐὰν Walton / τῆς] τοῦ Dindorf

During Pompey's stay in Damascus of Syria, Aristobulus, the king of the Jews, and Hyrcanus his brother came to him with their dispute over the kingship. Likewise the leading men, more than two hundred in number, gathered to address the general and explain that their forefathers, having revolted from Demetrius,[1] had sent an embassy to the senate, and received from them the leadership of the Jews,

185

who were, moreover, to be free and autonomous, their ruler being called High Priest, not King. Now, however, these men were lording it over them, having overthrown the ancient laws and enslaved the citizens in defiance of all justice; for it was by means of a horde of mercenaries, and by outrages and countless impious murders that they had established themselves as kings. Pompey put off till a later occasion the settlement of their rival claims, but as to the lawless behaviour of the Jews and the wrongs committed against the Romans he bitterly upbraided the party of Hyrcanus. They deserved, he said, some graver and harsher visitation; nevertheless, in the spirit of Rome's traditional clemency, he could, if they were obedient henceforward, grant them pardon. (trans. F. R. Walton, *LCL*)

1 According to the emendation of Walton.

Diodorus' narrative closely resembles that of Josephus in *Ant.*, XIV, 41 ff. Presumably they drew on a common source, which has been tentatively identified with the history of Theophanes of Mytilene, the friend and freedman of Pompey; see *F. Gr. Hist.*, II, B 188; cf. R. Laqueur, *Der jüdische Historiker Flavius Josephus*, Giessen 1920, pp. 149 ff. However, other possibilities should not be excluded; see, e.g., Ed. Meyer, II, p. 314, n. 1. On Theophanes as one of the main sources on the conquest of Syria by Pompey, see F. P. Rizzo, *Le fonti per la storia della conquista pompeiana della Siria*, Palermo 1963, pp. 35 ff.

ἀμφισβητοῦντες περὶ τῆς βασιλείας: Upon the appearance of Scaurus in Syria, Hyrcan and his Nabataean allies were compelled to escalate the effort to besiege Jerusalem. Their forces were defeated near Papyron by the army of Aristobulus; see *Ant.*, XIV, 29 ff.; *BJ*, I, 128 ff. After the arrival of Pompey at Damascus each brother implored the Roman general to recognize him as king of Judaea; for the course of events, see Schürer, I, p. 296; J. van Ooteghem, *Pompée le Grand*, Brussels 1954, pp. 230 f.

ἀφεστηκότας τοῦ ἱεροῦ: It is clear that this makes no sense. Dindorf suggested προεστηκότας. Other scholars have sought the source of corruption in ἱεροῦ. Herwerden read ἀφεστηκότας τοῦ Συρίου (which was improved into τοῦ Σύρου by Boissevain). The same line of thought has been set forth by Walton, who has emended ἱεροῦ into Δημητρίου, having in mind Demetrius I, during whose reign (161 B. C. E.) the Jews concluded their first alliance with Rome (I Macc. viii); cf. F. R. Walton, *AJP*, LXXVII (1956), pp. 413 f; Pompeius Trogus, apud: Iustinus, XXXVI, 3 : 9 (No. 137): "a Demetrio cum descivissent."

οὐ βασιλέως χρηματίζοντος: On χρηματίζειν, see E. Bickerman, *HTR*, XLII (1949), pp. 109 ff. (*Ant.*, XIII, 318: χρηματίσας μὲν Φιλέλλην).

προεστηκότος: Nock's proposal to add τοῦ before προεστηκότος seems excellent; see Walton, *op. cit.*, p. 414.

The argument used here is identical with that put forth by the representatives of the Jewish nation in *Antiquitates*, namely, the opposition to the constitutional change and the enslavement of the people; cf. Strabo, *Geographica*, XVI, 2 : 40, p. 762 (No. 115): ἤδη δ'οὖν φανερῶς τυραννουμένης τῆς Ἰουδαίας. On the other hand, in the passage of *Antiquitates* there is no mention of the embassy sent to Rome.

Diodorus

τοὺς πατρίους νόμους: Cf. the πάτριον γὰρ εἶναι in Josephus.

μισθοφόρων γὰρ πλήθει... περιπεποιῆσθαι τὴν βασιλείαν: The first of the Hasmonaeans to employ mercenaries was John Hyrcan; see *Ant.*, XIII, 249. This policy was continued by Alexander Jannaeus, who had recourse to soldiers from Pisidia and Cilicia; see *Ant.*, XIII, 374; *BJ*, 88. He seems to have been given the nickname Thracidas as a protest against his employment of foreign mercenaries and against his cruelty in using them; see *Ant.*, XIII, 383; Syncellus, I, p. 558, ed. Dindorf; cf. M. Stern, *Tarbiz*, XXIX (1960), pp. 207 ff. His antagonists held to their conviction that a mercenary army constitutes the mainstay of royal absolutism and makes it possible for the ruler to do away with the representative institutions of the country. On the connection between absolutism and mercenary armies, see V. G. Kiernan, *Past and Present*, XI (1957), pp. 66 ff. Even Jannaeus' widow, though pious and inclined towards Pharisaism, continued the recruitment of mercenaries; see *Ant.*, XIII, 409.

καὶ πολλοῖς φόνοις: Above all, Jannaeus was known for his cruelty; see, e.g., *Ant.*, XIII, 380 ff.

τῶν εἰς Ῥωμαίους ἀδικημάτων: This allusion is rather obscure, and the other sources are silent about this point. Some scholars think that what is meant here are piratical raids in which the Jews took part; see, e.g., Laqueur *op. cit.* (supra, p. 186), pp. 149, 153; cf. Dobiáš, *Archiv Orientální*, III (1931), pp. 247 f.; U. Rappaport, *REJ*, CXXVII (1968), pp. 340 ff. Piratical raids under the rule of Hyrcan could only have taken place in 67 B. C. E., that is, during the short time after his mother's death, when Hyrcan was king of Judaea. However, it may be that Pompey hinted at some hostilities by the partisans of Hyrcan, against the Romans under Scaurus, who saved Aristobulus from the siege by Hyrcan and his Nabataean allies.

Other scholars think that the names of Hyrcan and Aristobulus were mistakenly interchanged here; see, e.g., J. Wellhausen, *Israelitische und jüdische Geschichte*[8], Berlin–Leipzig 1921, p. 273; Ooteghem, *loc. cit.* (supra, p. 186). This view is corroborated by *Ant.*, XIV, 43: τάς τε καταδρομὰς τὰς ἐπὶ τοὺς ὁμόρους καὶ τὰ πειρατήρια τὰ ἐν τῇ θαλάττῃ τοῦτον (scil. Ἀριστόβουλον) εἶναι τὸν συστήσαντα διέβαλεν (scil. Ὑρκανός).

65

Bibliotheca Historica, XL, 3 — Dindorf = Photius, cod. 244, pp. 380a, 381a — Bekker = ed. Henry, Vol. VI, pp. 134, 137

Ἡμεῖς δὲ μέλλοντες ἀναγράφειν τὸν πρὸς Ἰουδαίους πόλεμον, οἰκεῖον εἶναι διαλαμβάνομεν προδιελθεῖν ἐν κεφαλαίοις τήν τε τοῦ ἔθνους τούτου ἐξ ἀρχῆς κτίσιν, καὶ τὰ παρ' αὐτοῖς νόμιμα. κατὰ τὴν Αἴγυπτον τὸ παλαιὸν λοιμικῆς περιστάσεως γενομένης ἀνέπεμπον οἱ πολλοὶ τὴν αἰτίαν
5 τῶν κακῶν ἐπὶ τὸ δαιμόνιον... ⟨cf. No. 11⟩ ... περὶ μὲν τῶν Ἰουδαίων Ἑκαταῖος ὁ Ἀβδηρίτης ταῦτα ἱστόρηκεν.

6 Ἀβδηρίτης Wesseling   Μιλήσιος codd.

Now that we are about to record the war against the Jews, we con-

sider it appropiate to give first a summary account of the establishment
of the nation, from its origins, and of the practices observed among
them. When in ancient times a pestilence arose in Egypt, the common
people ascribed their troubles to the working of a divine agency...
Such is the account of Hecataeus of Abdera in regard to the Jews.

(trans. F. R. Walton, *LCL*)

66

Bibliotheca Historica, XL, 4 — Dindorf = Constantinus Porphyrogenitus, *Excerpta de Sententiis* —
Boissevain, pp. 405 f.

῞Οτι ὁ Πομπήιος τὰς ἰδίας πράξεις ἃς συνετέλεσεν ἐπὶ τῆς ᾽Ασίας
ἀναγράψας ἀνέθηκεν, ὧν ἐστιν ἀντίγραφον τόδε· Πομπήιος Γναίου υἱὸς
Μέγας αὐτοκράτωρ τὴν παράλιον τῆς οἰκουμένης καὶ πάσας τὰς ἐντὸς
᾽Ωκεανοῦ νήσους ἐλευθερώσας τοῦ πειρατικοῦ πολέμου, ὁ ῥυσάμενός ποτε
5 πολιορκουμένην τὴν ᾽Αριοβαρζάνου βασιλείαν, Γαλατίαν τε καὶ τὰς
ὑπερκειμένας χώρας καὶ ἐπαρχίας, ᾽Ασίαν, Βιθυνίαν, ὑπερασπίσας
δὲ Παφλαγονίαν τε καὶ τὸν Πόντον, ᾽Αρμενίαν τε καὶ ᾽Αχαῖαν, ἔτι
δὲ ᾽Ιβηρίαν, Κολχίδα, Μεσοποταμίαν, Σωφηνήν, Γορδυηνήν, ὑποτάξας
δὲ βασιλέα Μήδων Δαρεῖον, βασιλέα ᾽Αρτώλην ᾽Ιβήρων, βασιλέα
10 ᾽Αριστόβουλον ᾽Ιουδαίων, βασιλέα ᾽Αρέταν Ναβαταίων [βασιλέα] ᾽Αρά-
βων, καὶ τὴν κατὰ Κιλικίαν Συρίαν, ᾽Ιουδαίαν, ᾽Αραβίαν, Κυρηναϊκὴν
ἐπαρχίαν, ᾽Αχαιούς, ᾽Ιοζυγούς, Σοανούς, ῾Ηνιόχους καὶ τὰ λοιπὰ φῦλα
⟨τὰ⟩ μεταξὺ Κολχίδος καὶ Μαιώτιδος λίμνης τὴν παράλιον διακατέχον-
τα καὶ τοὺς τούτων βασιλεῖς ἐννέα τὸν ἀριθμὸν καὶ πάντα τὰ ἔθνη
15 τὰ ἐντὸς τῆς Ποντικῆς καὶ τῆς ᾽Ερυθρᾶς θαλάσσης κατοικοῦντα, καὶ τὰ
ὅρια τῆς ἡγεμονίας τοῖς ὅροις τῆς γῆς προσβιβάσας, καὶ τὰς προσόδους
῾Ρωμαίων φυλάξας, ἃς δὲ προσαυξήσας, τούς τε ἀνδριάντας καὶ τὰ λοιπὰ
ἀφιδρύματα τῶν θεῶν καὶ τὸν λοιπὸν κόσμον τῶν πολεμίων ἀφελόμενος,
ἀνέθηκε τῇ θεῷ χρυσοῦς μυρίους καὶ δισχιλίους ἑξήκοντα, ἀργυρίου
20 τάλαντα τριακόσια ἑπτά.

9 Δαρεῖον Μήδων? Boissevain / ᾽Αρτώκην Dindorf   10 βασιλέα² secl.
Dindorf   12 Σοανούς Dindorf   Σολνούς Vat.   13 ⟨τὰ⟩ μεταξὺ
Dindorf   17 ⟨ἃς μὲν διὰ⟩φυλάξας Herwerden

4. Pompey had inscribed on a tablet, which he set up as a dedication,
the record of his achievements in Asia. Here is a copy of the inscription: "Pompey the Great, son of Gnaeus, Imperator, having liberated
the seacoast of the inhabited world and all islands this side Ocean
from the war with the pirates—being likewise the man who delivered

Diodorus

from siege the kingdom of Ariobarzanes, Galatia and the lands and provinces lying beyond it, Asia, and Bithynia; who gave protection to Paphlagonia and Pontus, Armenia and Achaia, as well as Iberia, Colchis, Mesopotamia, Sophene, and Gordyene; brought into subjection Darius king of the Medes, Artoles king of the Iberians, Aristobulus king of the Jews, Aretas king of the Nabataean Arabs, Syria bordering on Cilicia, Judaea, Arabia, the province of Cyrene, the Achaeans, the Iozygi, the Soani, the Heniochi and the other tribes along the seacoast between Colchis and the Maeotic Sea, with their kings, nine in number, and all the nations that dwell between the Pontic and the Red Seas; extended the frontiers of the Empire to the limits of the earth; and secured and in some cases increased the revenues of the Roman people—he, by confiscation of the statues and the images set up to the gods, as well as other valuables taken from the enemy, has dedicated to the goddess twelve thousand and sixty pieces of gold and three hundred and seven talents of silver."

(trans. F. R. Walton, *LCL*)

Cf. the *praefatio* of the triumph of Pompey in Plinius, *Naturalis Historia*, VII, 98 (No. 208); Appianus, *Mithridatica*, 114 : 556; 117 : 571–573 (Nos. 345–346).

XXXIII. LUCRETIUS

c. 99–55 B.C.E.

In the sixth book of his De Rerum Natura Lucretius describes some mirabilia, to which he altogether denies supernatural explanations. The description of the Avernian Lake in the vicinity of Cumae, whose sulphur springs are fatal to birds in their flight, is followed by a reference to the well-known story that the temple of Athena on the Acropolis is shunned by crows because of the wrath of Athena. This paradoxon precedes one connected with a place in Syria where not only birds but quadrupeds (quadrupedes quoque) fall dead as soon as they enter.

Bailey[1] cannot find any data definitely identifying the place in Syria mentioned by Lucretius. Yet there is much to be said for identifying "the place in Syria" with the vicinity of the Dead Sea, whose exhalations were thought to be pestilential,[2] although an alternative locality may be suggested.

In a similar way Seneca presumably alludes to the Dead Sea as "in Syria stagnum, in quo natant lateres et mergi proiecta non possunt"; Quaestiones Naturales, III, 25 : 5 (No. 187). Lucretius uses "Syria" in an extended sense, to include both Palestine and Phoenicia; cf. De Rerum Natura, VI, 585: "in Syria Sidone quod accidit"; see also the commentary to Seneca, (No. 187).

Lucretius probably got his knowledge of "the place in Syria" from a work that dealt with mirabilia. It is noteworthy that Antigonus of Carystus, the paradoxographer, related the above-mentioned paradoxon

---

1 In his Commentary, III, Oxford 1947, p. 1667.
2 See J. Gill, *Notices of the Jews and their Country by the Classic Writers of Antiquity*, London 1872, pp. 111 f; cf. Tacitus, *Historiae*,V, 7 (No. 281). Some scholars refer instead to the description of the Plutonium in Hierapolis found in Strabo, *Geographica*, XIII, 4 : 14, pp. 629 f.; cf., e.g.,*T. Lucreti Cari De Rerum Natura*, edited by W. E. Leonard & S. B. Smith, Madison 1942, p. 828. However, the Hierapolis alluded to in Strabo is not the Syrian one.

190

of the Avernian Lake[3] *and also referred to the strange qualities of the Lake near Jaffa (No. 22).*

3 Cf. Antigonus Carystius, *Historiarum Mirabilium Collectio*, 152b, edited by A. Giannini, *Paradoxographorum Graecorum Reliquiae*, Milan 1965, p. 98: ὃ δὴ καὶ περὶ τὴν Ἄορνίν τι δοκεῖ γίγνεσθαι καὶ κατίσχυκεν ἡ φήμη παρὰ τοῖς πλείστοις. According to Antigonus, the reported events at the Avernian Lake are the same as those he relates immediately before this passage (152a, p. 96), on the authority of Heracleides, that occurred at the lake in the Sarmatian country: Τὴν δὲ ἐν τοῖς Σαρμάταις λίμνην Ἡρακλείδην γράφειν, ὅτι οὐδὲν τῶν ὀρνέων ὑπεραίρειν, τὸ δὲ προσελθὸν ὑπὸ τῆς ὀσμῆς τελευτᾶν.

67

De Rerum Natura, VI, 756–759 — Bailey

In Syria quoque fertur item locus esse videri,
quadrupedes quoque quo simul ac vestigia primum
intulerint, graviter vis cogat concidere ipsa,
manibus ut si sint divis mactata repente.

In Syria also, as it is said, another such place is to be seen; whither so soon as ever four-footed beasts direct their steps, its natural power forces them of themselves heavily to fall, as if they were suddenly slain in sacrifices to the infernal gods.   (trans. W. H. D. Rouse, LCL)

XXXIV. CICERO

106–43 B.C.E.

The attitude towards the Jews of Cicero, the greatest orator of Rome and a writer whose influence subsequently dominated European humanism, is, of course, of the greatest interest. From the outset one should stress the fact that the Jews and their religion are conspicuously absent from the whole range of Cicero's philosophical works, though one might have expected some reference to Judaism, if Cicero had taken even the slightest interest in it, in a treatise like De Natura Deorum. *In this respect Cicero differs from his contemporary Varro, who much appreciated the incorporeal character of the Jewish Deity, and from his successors in Latin literature, Seneca and Tacitus, who adopted a clearly hostile stand towards Judaism. As Cicero does not allude to Jews, even in his voluminous correspondence, apart from nicknaming Pompey "Hierosolymarius" (No. 69), we must conclude that the Jews were not much within the orbit of his immediate interests.*

Jews appear only in the speeches Pro Flacco *and* De Provinciis Consularibus, *delivered in 59 B.C.E. and 56 B.C.E., respectively. In both cases it was the nature of the situation that imposed the speaker's disparaging remarks about Jews. On the first occasion the Jews were instrumental in the prosecution of Flaccus, who was defended by Cicero. In the second speech his brief reference to Jews and Syrians served his purpose — to impugn Gabinius, the enemy of the Roman Publicani — since he was so closely connected with them. As propraetor, Flaccus ruled the province of Asia and was sued for* repetundae *by Laelius, who acted on behalf of the cities of the province. Among the charges of the prosecution was that he confiscated Jewish money during his stay in Asia.*

Cicero, who with Hortensius acted as defending counsel for Flaccus, also dwells, as might be expected, on the charge relating to the Jewish money. He does this in a twofold manner: by trying to show that there was nothing illegal in Flaccus' proceedings, and by casting aspersions on the Jews. First, he defines the religion of the Jews as "barbara superstitio". *Then, he points to the "raging" of the Roman Jews in the* contiones. *He also explains to the judges that Pompey's abstention from pillaging the Temple at Jerusalem did not derive from respect*

193

towards Jews, who were enemies, but from his own feeling of honour and from considerations of political expediency. Cicero finishes his outburst against the Jews by showing the contrast between the Jewish religion and Roman ancestral institutions, and by emphasizing the recent war waged by the Jews against Rome.

In assessing the contents of this passage we must bear in mind its judicial context and Cicero's common practice, wherever such a procedure suited the nature of the case, of denigrating opposing witnesses by incriminating their national character. Thus, little is left of Cicero's supposed anti-Semitism. One need only recall the way he treated the Gauls in Pro Fonteio, *or the Sardinians in* Pro Scauro, *to see that the Jews fare no worse than other nations in his speeches. In* Pro Flacco *itself, the Graeco-Asianic witnesses, labelled by the speaker as Phrygians, Mysians, Carians and Lydians, are made to appear in no better light than the Jews. Indeed, Cicero himself stresses the difference between his personal views and those expressed by him as a pleader.[1] One is sometimes surprised to find radically contrasting opinions concerning the same persons in Cicero's speeches. When the circumstances warrant it, even the arch-enemy Catilina receives some words of posthumous tribute from the lips of Cicero.[2]*

It is noteworthy that in spite of his sojourn at Rhodes and his connections with Apollonius Molon, Cicero did not take recourse to any of the specific arguments of Hellenistic anti-Semitism and did not charge the Jews with misanthropy, with being the least able among the barbarians, or with contributing nothing to the advancement of civilization.

In view of the fact that the Optimates consistently opposed the intrusion of foreign cults into the city of Rome, while the Populares favoured them, and also considering the prohibition of the collegia in 64 B.C.E.[3] — though we are not sure how far the Jewish religious associations were affected by it — we may concur with Lewy that the Jewish multitudes

---

1 See *Pro Cluentio*, 139: "Sed errat vehementer, si quis in orationibus nostris quas in iudiciis habuimus auctoritates nostras consignatas se habere arbitratur. Omnes enim illae causarum ac temporum sunt, non hominum ipsorum aut patronorum."

2 *Pro Caelio*, 12.

3 See Asconius, edited by A. C. Clark, p. 7. They were restored by P. Clodius.

194

in the contiones *were enlisted on the side of the Populares, i.e. Cicero's enemies, in 59 B.C.E.*[4]

4 We owe the most detailed study of Cicero's attitude to the Jews to J. Lewy, *Zion*, VII (1941–1942), pp. 109 ff. (in Hebrew) = *Studies in Jewish Hellenism*, Jerusalem 1960, pp. 79 ff. See also J. A. Hild, *REJ*, VIII (1884), pp. 19 ff.; H.Vogelstein & P. Rieger, *Geschichte der Juden in Rom*, Berlin 1896, I, pp. 7 ff.; Radin, p. 221; E. Bickermann, *Berliner Philologische Wochenschrift*, XLVI (1926), pp. 907 ff.; D. Magie, *Roman Rule in Asia Minor*, I, Princeton 1950, p. 381; Leon, pp. 5 ff.; L. Herrmann, *Atti del Congresso internazionale di Studi Ciceroniani*, I, 1961, pp. 113 ff. On the general circumstances of the speech *Pro Flacco*, see W. Drumann & P. Groebe, *Geschichte Roms in seinem Übergange von der republikanischen zur monarchischen Verfassung*, V, Leipzig 1919, pp. 613 ff.; E. Ciaceri, *Cicerone e i suoi tempi*, II, Milan–Genoa–Rome–Naples 1930, pp. 42 ff.

(28 : 66) Sequitur auri illa invidia Iudaici. Hoc nimirum est illud quod non longe a gradibus Aureliis haec causa dicitur. Ob hoc crimen hic locus abs te, Laeli, atque illa turba quaesita est; scis quanta sit manus, quanta concordia, quantum valeat in contionibus. Sic submissa voce
5 agam tantum ut iudices audiant; neque enim desunt qui istos in me atque in optimum quemque incitent; quos ego, quo id facilius faciant, non adiuvabo. (67) Cum aurum Iudaeorum nomine quotannis ex Italia et ex omnibus nostris provinciis Hierosolymam exportari soleret, Flaccus sanxit edicto ne ex Asia exportari liceret. Quis est, iudices,
10 qui hoc non vere laudare possit? Exportari aurum non oportere cum saepe antea senatus tum me consule gravissime iudicavit. Huic autem barbarae superstitioni resistere severitatis, multitudinem Iudaeorum flagrantem non numquam in contionibus pro re publica contemnere gravitatis summae fuit. At Cn. Pompeius captis
15 Hierosolymis victor ex illo fano nihil attigit. (68) In primis hoc, ut multa alia, sapienter; in tam suspiciosa ac maledica civitate locum sermoni obtrectatorum non reliquit. Non enim credo religionem et Iudaeorum et hostium impedimento praestantissimo imperatori, sed pudorem fuisse. Ubi igitur crimen est, quoniam quidem furtum
20 nusquam reprehendis, edictum probas, iudicatum fateris, quaesitum et prolatum palam non negas, actum esse per viros primarios res ipsa declarat? Apameae manifesto comprehensum ante pedes praetoris in foro expensum est auri pondo c paulo minus per Sex. Caesium, equitem Romanum, castissimum hominem atque integerrimum,
25 Laodiceae XX pondo paulo amplius per hunc L. Peducaeum, iudicem nostrum, Adramytii ⟨c⟩ per Cn. Domitium legatum, Pergami non multum. (69) Auri ratio constat, aurum in aerario est; furtum non reprehenditur, invidia quaeritur; a iudicibus oratio avertitur, vox in coronam turbamque effunditur. Sua cuique civitati religio, Laeli, est,
30 nostra nobis. Stantibus Hierosolymis pacatisque Iudaeis tamen istorum religio sacrorum a splendore huius imperi, gravitate nominis nostri, maiorum institutis abhorrebat; nunc vero hoc magis, quod illa gens quid de nostro imperio sentiret ostendit armis; quam cara dis immor-

1 *illud est* c   4 *valet* Σbχ   7 *Iudaeorum nomine aurum* c
8 *nostris* Σb¹k   om. cett.   *vestris* Faernus   *Hierosolyma* Ernesti
19 *quoniam*] *quando* ς   20 *indicatum* Pantagathus   22 *manifesto* Σ b¹
manifeste cett.   23 *est*] *esse* Σ / *cesiuium* Σ   26 *Adramytii*
Sylvius   *adrimeti* Σbχ   *adrumeti* ς / ⟨c⟩ Clark   28 *convertitur* Σb¹

talibus esset docuit, quod est victa, quod elocata, quod serva facta.

34 *victa*] *unita* Σk | *elocata* Σb¹   *est locata* cett. | *serva facta* Sylvius   *servata* codd.

(28:66) There follows the odium that is attached to Jewish gold. This is no doubt the reason why this case is being tried not far from the Aurelian Steps. You procured this place and that crowd, Laelius, for this trial. You know what a big crowd it is, how they stick together, how influential they are in informal assemblies. So I will speak in a low voice so that only the jurors may hear; for those are not wanting who would incite them against me and against every respectable man. I shall not help them to do this more easily. (67) When every year it was customary to send gold to Jerusalem on the order of the Jews from Italy and from all our provinces, Flaccus forbade by an edict its exportation from Asia. Who is there, gentlemen, who could not honestly praise this action? The senate often earlier and also in my consulship most urgently forbade the export of gold. But to resist this barbaric superstition was an act of firmness, to defy the crowd of Jews when sometimes in our assemblies they were hot with passion, for the welfare of the state was an act of the greatest seriousness. "But Gnaeus Pompey when Jerusalem was captured laid his victorious hands on nothing in that shrine." (68) In that he was especially wise — as in many other matters. In a state so given to suspicion and calumny he left his critics no opportunity for gossip. But I do not think that illustrious general was hindered by the religious feelings of the Jews and his enemies, but by his sense of honour. Where, then, is the ground for an accusation against Flaccus, since, indeed, you never make any charge of theft, you approve his edict, you confess that there was judgement, you do not deny that the business was openly proposed and published, and that the facts show that it was administered by excellent men? At Apamea a little less than a hundred pounds of gold was openly seized and weighed before the seat of the praetor in the forum through the agency of Sextius Caesius, a Roman knight, an upright and honourable man; at Laodicea a little more than twenty pounds by Lucius Peducaeus, our juror. At Adramyttium hundred pounds by Gnaeus Domitius, the commissioner, at Pergamum a small amount. (69) The accounting for the gold is correct. The gold is in the treasury, no embezzlement is charged, it is just an attempt to fix odium on him. The plea is not addressed to the jury; the voice of the advocate is directed to the attendant crowd and the mob. Each state, Laelius, has its own religious scruples, we have ours. Even while Jerusalem was stand-

From Herodotus to Plutarch

ing and the Jews were at peace with us, the practice of their sacred rites was at variance with the glory of our empire, the dignity of our name, the customs of our ancestors. But now it is even more so, when that nation by its armed resistance has shown what it thinks of our rule; how dear it was to the immortal gods is shown by the fact that it has been conquered, let out for taxes, made a slave.

(trans. L. E. Lord, *LCL*)

66 *auri* ... *Iudaici*: We read below that this gold was exported to Jerusalem from Italy and from all the provinces. There is little doubt that it was the annual half-shekel payment for the Temple in Jerusalem, which was also known as the *didrachmon*; see Cassius Dio, LXVI, 7 : 2 (No. 430). The tax was levied on all Jews over the age of twenty, including freedmen and proselytes. On this tax, see the *Mishna* and the *Tosefta Sheqalim*, which constitute our main sources of information on the subject. The amount of the levy was fluid and changed throughout the ages (*M. Sheqalim* ii : 4). Though, in later times, the origin of the tax was thought to go back to Exod. xxx : 11 ff., there was no real connection between the Biblical regulation and the contribution that became customary during the period of the Second Temple, which, strictly speaking, was of a different character; cf. J. Liver, *HTR*, LVI (1963), pp. 173 ff. The main purpose of the tax in the later period was the maintenance of the public cult, that is, of the sacrifices in the Temple (*M. Sheqalim* iv : 1; *Tosefta Sheqalim* i : 6). However, the surplus was used freely for other purposes, including the municipal needs of Jerusalem.
In the period of the First Temple the expenses of the cult were defrayed by the King. Ezekiel (xlv : 17), in his utopian picture of the future, also thinks of the prince as responsible for public sacrifices. It seems, however, that the Persian sovereigns took over the obligations of the kings of Judaea with regard to the maintenance of the Jewish cult. Thus, Darius I in his edict (Ezra vi : 8 ff.) expressly asserts these obligations. The same probably holds true for the edict of Artaxerxes (Ezra vii:17), though in the latter case it is not wholly clear whether the King's grant to Ezra was meant to constitute a perpetual grant. At any rate, we see that the grants of the Persian government were not sufficiently regular to defray the expenses and that Nehemiah found it necessary to obligate all members of the Jewish community to pay an annual tax of a third of a shekel (Neh. x : 33 f.). On the incidence of the tax, see J. N. Epstein, *Introduction to Tannaitic Literature*, Jerusalem 1957, p. 337 (in Hebrew). Nehemiah expressly states that this tax has been levied to defray the cost of the various sacrifices and כל מלאכת בית אלהינו, whatever it means. Thus, a new tax, generally identical with that known during the whole period of the Second Temple, was instituted by Nehemiah. However, we do not know to what extent this obligation applied to the Jews of the Diaspora; nor do we know whether this tax was intended to be permanent or whether it was only a temporary expedient in view of the Persian government's negligence in fulfilling its obligations towards the Jewish cult. At any rate, in Seleucid Judaea the expenses of the Jewish cult were believed to be regularly paid by the central government: συνέβαινε καὶ αὐτοὺς τοὺς βασιλεῖς τιμᾶν τὸν τόπον καὶ τὸ ἱερὸν ἀποστολαῖς ταῖς κρατίσταις δοξάζειν, ὥστε καὶ Σέλευκον τὸν τῆς Ἀσίας βασιλέα χορηγεῖν ἐκ τῶν ἰδίων προσόδων πάντα τὰ πρὸς τὰς λειτουργίας τῶν θυσιῶν ἐπιβάλλοντα δαπανήματα

198

Cicero

(II Macc. iii: 2–3); cf. *Ant.*, XII, 140. On the other hand, there is no allusion in the Jewish literature of that period to the payment of a third of a shekel, or of a half-shekel, as it was called later; see also E. Bikerman, *Annuaire de l'institut de philologie et d'histoire orientales et slaves*,VII, (1939–1944), p. 14. It seems that it was not until the Hasmonaean period that the half-shekel contribution became the sole financial support of the cult at the Temple in Jerusalem. Some trace of the beginnings of this may perhaps be found in the Hebrew scholion to *Ta'anit* (*HUCA*, VIII–IX, 1931–1932, p. 323); cf. Lichtenstein's comments, *ibid.*, pp. 290 ff. See also the different view concerning the exact chronology held by A. Schwarz, *MGWJ*, LXIII (1919), pp. 230 ff. Strabo (apud: Josephus, *Ant.*, XIV, 111–113 = No. 102) testifies that the Jews of Asia Minor contributed to the tax in the time of Mithridates (88 B. C. E.), that is, some decades before the propraetorship of Flaccus. Of course, the *aurum Iudaicum* mentioned here may have included contributions to the Temple other than the *didrachmon*; see, e.g., *Ant.*, XVIII, 312: τό τε δίδραχμον... καὶ ὁπόσα δὲ ἄλλα ἀναθήματα.

a gradibus Aureliis: the *gradus Aurelii* are also referred to in *Pro Cluentio*, 93, and were probably erected by M. Aurelius Cotta, the consul of 74 B. C. E. More often Cicero refers to the *tribunal Aurelii*; see S. B. Platner & T. Ashby, *A Topographical Dictionary of Ancient Rome*, Oxford 1929, pp. 539 f. We should not, however, suppose that the *gradus Aurelii* were situated near a special concentration of Jews. It seems instead that the turbulent *contiones*, in which the Jews also participated, took place in the neighbourhood of the *gradus Aurelii*; see below: "multitudinem Iudaeorum flagrantem in contionibus"; cf. *Pro Cluentio*, 93: "Accusabat tribunus plebis idem in contionibus, idem ad subsellia; ad iudicium non modo de contione sed etiam cum ipsa contione veniebat. Gradus illi Aurelii tum novi quasi pro theatro illi iudicio aedificati videbantur; quos ubi accusator concitatis hominibus complerat, non modo dicendi ab reo sed ne surgendi quidem potestas erat."

quanta concordia: On the Jewish *concordia*, see Tacitus, *Historiae*, V, 5 (No. 281).

quantum valeat in contionibus: The Jewish influence in the *contiones*, even if much exaggerated by Cicero, can only be explained if we suppose that the Jewish population of Rome was already quite considerable before Pompey captured Jerusalem; see L. Geiger, *Quid de Judaeorum Moribus atque Institutis Scriptoribus Romanis Persuasum Fuerit*, Berlin 1872, pp. 7 f.; Radin, pp. 227 ff.; Leon, pp. 4 f. However, there is nothing in our sources to justify Haskell's statement that there were a considerable number of Jewish businessmen in Rome and that Cicero recognized their political power; see H. J. Haskell, *This was Cicero*, New York 1942, p. 229. For the view that the supposed anti-Semitism of Cicero drew its inspiration from the rivalry of Jewish businessmen with Roman equites, see Herrmann, *loc. cit.* (supra, p. 195, n. 4).

in optimum quemque: *optimus* is used here in the usual sense it had in the political phraseology of the age of Cicero; see J. Hellegouarc'h, *Le vocabulaire latin des relations et des partis politiques sous la république*, Paris 1963, pp. 495 ff.

67 *tum me consule gravissime iudicavit*: Cf. *In Vatinium*, 12: "missusne sis a me consule Puteolos, ut inde aurum exportari argentumque prohiberes."

barbarae superstitioni: On *superstitio* as opposed to *religio*, see W. F. Otto, *Archiv für Religionswissenschaft*, XII (1909), pp. 533 ff.; XIV, (1911), pp. 406 ff.; R. Freudenberger, *Das Verhalten der römischen Behörden gegen die Christen im 2. Jahrhundert*, Munich 1967, pp. 189 ff.

At Cn. Pompeius. . . : Here we may infer from Cicero's words that Laelius emphasized the quite unusual behaviour of Pompey,who had spared the gold found in the Jewish Temple. Cicero disputes the claim that Pompey did this out of respect for the Jewish religion. This explanation was probably advanced by Laelius and is also found in *Ant.*, XIV, 72 (= *BJ*, I, 153): ὄντων δὲ τραπέζης... χωρὶς δὲ τούτων ἐν τοῖς θησαυροῖς ἱερῶν χρημάτων εἰς δύο χιλιάδας ταλάντων, οὐδενὸς ἥψατο δι᾽ εὐσέβειαν, ἀλλὰ κἂν τούτῳ ἀξίως ἔπραξεν τῆς περὶ αὐτὸν ἀρετῆς.

68 *iudicatum fateris*: The word *iudicatum* has caused much trouble to commentators; see A. du Mesnil, *Ciceros Rede für L. Flaccus*, Leipzig 1883, p. 164. In view of the previous use of *iudicavit* in connection with the decision of the senate ("cum saepe antea senatus, tum me consule gravissime iudicavit"), Webster has suggested that *iudicatum fateris* should be translated: "you admit the previous decision of the senate"; see T. B. L. Webster, *Pro. L. Flacco Oratio*, edited with introduction and notes, Oxford 1931, p. 91. However, this interpretation is rather artificial. It seems that Flaccus, after promulgating his edict prohibiting the export of gold, went before a tribunal to accuse the Jews of disregarding the order. After the tribunal passed judgment on the Jews and their illegal export of the gold became *res iudicata*, Flaccus confiscated it; cf. J. Lewy, *Zion.* VII (1941–1942), p. 113, n. 35.

Apameae: On the Jewish connections with Apamea in Phrygia, see Schürer, III, pp. 18 ff.; Juster, I, p. 191, n. 19; *CII*, II, Nos. 773–774.

Laodiceae: Cf. Juster, I, p. 191, n. 17; *Ant.*, XIV, 241 f.

Adramytii: We know almost nothing about the Jews and their connection with this city of the Troad.

Pergami: On the connection between Pergamum and the Jews as early as the end of the second century B. C. E., see *Ant.*, XIV, 247 ff. On the date of the document, see M. Stern, *Zion*, XXVI (1961), pp. 12 ff. We know of other important cities in Asia Minor (Ephesus, Sardis, Miletus) where Jews lived in considerable numbers in the first century B. C. E. Still, these do not occur as names of places in which Flaccus confiscated Jewish money. Alon has explained this omission by suggesting that only in these four expressly-mentioned cities did the confiscation bear a legal character, which it lacked in other places, and that it was for this reason that Cicero found it convenient to refer only to them; see G. Alon, apud: J. Lewy, *Zion*, VII, p. 124, n. 117. We know also from Josephus that the Jews stored the sacred funds that were to be sent to Jerusalem in some of the great cities; see *Ant.*, XVIII, 311 f., where he tells us that in Babylonia, Nearda and Nisibis served as depots for the didrachmon.

69 *furtum non reprehenditur, invidia quaeritur*: From the comparison drawn by Laelius between the behaviour of Pompey and that of Flaccus we learn that the Jews' main complaint against Flaccus was that he confiscated this money. They could plead that even on the basis of Flaccus' edict there was no justification for accusing them before a tribunal and for confiscating the funds, since they had not been found smuggling the money out of the province, but merely storing it in some of the chief cities until they could obtain permission from the propraetor to export the gold. Cicero defended Flaccus by claiming that the latter's action was a *res iudicata* — and not, therefore, an arbitrary act — and that therefore he did not commit a *furtum*. Juster thinks that the Jews accused Flaccus of depriving them of the privilege of exporting money, a privilege recognized by former Roman authorities; see Juster, I, p. 379, n.7; cf. Radin, pp. 225 f.

invidia: On *invidia*, see Lewy, *Zion*, VII. Lewy refers here to *Ad Herennium*, I, 5 : 8,

Cicero

where the author suggests *invidia* as a weapon against adversaries. The optimates were also accustomed to viewing the vehement attacks on them by their adversaries as an expression of *popularis invidia*.

pacatisque Iudaeis: *pacatis* in the frequently used sense of "being at peace", not "having been subdued"; see Webster, *op. cit.* (supra, p. 200), p. 92.

quam cara dis immortalibus esset . . . : For the same logic, see *Contra Apionem*, II, 125 (No. 174); Celsus, apud: Origenes, *Contra Celsum* (No. 375); Minucius Felix, *Octavius*, 10 : 4: "Iudaeorum sola et misera gentilitas unum et ipsi deum, sed palam, sed templis, aris, victimis caerimoniisque coluerunt, cuius adeo nulla vis nec potestas est, ut sit Romanis hominibus cum sua sibi natione captivus." On the other hand, we meet with the idea that an empire of the entire world was bestowed upon the Romans because of their piety; cf. Cicero, *De Haruspicum Responso*, 19; Tertullianus, *Apologeticus*, 25, 2: ". . . praesumptio dicentium Romanos pro merito religiositatis diligentissimae in tantum sublimitatis elatos, ut orbem occuparint."

quod elocata: There is no justification for Bernays' doubts regarding the reading *elocata*; see Bernays, II, p. 309. Judaea had to pay its first tribute not after the deposition of Archelaus in 6 C. E., but already as a result of the conquest by Pompey; see *Ant.*, XIV, 74: καὶ τὰ μὲν Ἱεροσόλυμα ὑποτελῆ φόρου Ῥωμαίοις ἐποίησεν; *BJ*, I, 154: τῇ τε χώρᾳ καὶ τοῖς Ἱεροσολύμοις ἐπιτάσσει φόρον. See also the commentary to *De Provinciis Consularibus* (No. 70).

69

Ad Atticum, II, 9:1 — Watt

Si vero, quae de me pacta sunt, ea non servantur, in caelo sum; tum sciat hic noster Hierosolymarius traductor ad plebem quam bonam meis praestantissimis orationibus gratiam rettulerit; quarum exspecta divinam παλινῳδίαν.

1 *tum* Watt *ut* codd. ⟨*et faciam*⟩ *ut* Koch   3 *praestantissimis* Watt *putissimis* ΣM   *potissimis* Hδ   *politissimis* Boot

If the compact about me is not kept, I am in the seventh heaven at thinking how that Jerusalemite plebeian-monger will learn what a pretty return he has made for all my choicest panegyrics; and you may expect recantation of eclipsing brilliancy.   (trans. E.O. Winstedt, *LCL*)

This letter, dated to April 59 B.C.E., reflects the mood of Cicero at the time of the First Triumvirate. His enemy Clodius joined forces with Julius Caesar and, with the consent of Pompey, was transferred from the patricians to the plebeians in order to be elected tribune. In this passage Cicero refers to Clodius' promise to Pompey that he would not act against Cicero. For this letter, see Tyrrell & Purser, *The Correspondence of Cicero* [3], I, Dublin 1904, pp. 293 ff.; J. van Ooteghem, *Pompée le Grand, bâtisseur d'empire*, Brussels 1954, pp. 311 f.; D. R. Shackleton Bailey, *Cicero's Letters to Atticus*, I, Cambridge 1965, pp. 369 f.

From Herodotus to Plutarch

Hierosolymarius: An allusion to the capture of Jerusalem by Pompey in 63 B. C. E. In other letters Pompey is nicknamed Sampsiceramus, after the ruler of Emesa; see *Ad Atticum*, II, 14, 16, 17, 23. All four letters are dated to 59 B. C. E. In *Ad Atticum*, II, 17 : 3, Pompey is referred to as Arabarches.

70

De Provinciis Consularibus, 5:10–12 — Peterson = F127R

(10) Iam vero publicanos miseros — me etiam miserum illorum ita de me meritorum miseriis ac dolore! — tradidit in servitutem Iudaeis et Syris, nationibus natis servituti. Statuit ab initio, et in eo perseveravit, ius publicano non dicere; pactiones sine ulla iniuria factas rescidit;
5 custodias sustulit; vectigalis multos ac stipendiarios liberavit; quo in oppido ipse esset aut quo veniret, ibi publicanum aut publicani servum esse vetuit. Quid multa? crudelis haberetur si in hostis animo fuisset eo quo fuit in civis Romanos, eius ordinis praesertim qui est semper ⟨pro⟩ dignitate sua benignitate magistratuum sustentatus. (11) Itaque,
10 patres conscripti, videtis non temeritate redemptionis aut negoti gerendi inscitia, sed avaritia, superbia, crudelitate Gabini paene adflictos iam atque eversos publicanos: quibus quidem vos in his angustiis aerari tamen subveniatis necesse est, etsi iam multis non potestis, qui propter illum hostem senatus, inimicissimum ordinis
15 equestris bonorumque omnium, non solum bona sed etiam honestatem miseri deperdiderunt, quos non parsimonia, non continentia, non virtus, non labor, non splendor tueri potuit contra illius helluonis et praedonis audaciam. (12) Quid? qui se etiam nunc subsidiis patrimoni aut amicorum liberalitate sustentant, hos perire patiemur? An si qui
20 frui publico non potuit per hostem, hic tegitur ipsa lege censoria: quem is frui non sinit qui est, etiam si non appellatur, hostis, huic ferri auxilium non oportet? Retinete igitur in provincia diutius eum qui de sociis cum hostibus, de civibus cum sociis faciat pactiones, qui hoc etiam se pluris esse quam conlegam putet, quod ille vos tristitia
25 vultuque deceperit, ipse numquam se minus quam erat nequam esse simularit. Piso autem alio quodam modo gloriatur se brevi tempore perfecisse ne Gabinius unus omnium nequissimus existimaretur.

9 ⟨*pro*⟩ Pluygers | *magistratuum* Kayser *magistratus* codd.

(10) Then, too, there are those unhappy revenue-farmers—and what misery to me were the miseries and troubles of those to whom I owed so much! — he handed them over as slaves to Jews and Syrians, them-

202

selves peoples born to be slaves. From the beginning he made it a rule, in which he persisted, not to hear any suits brought by revenue-farmers; he revoked agreements which had been made in which there was no unfairness; removed guards; released many imposts or tribute, forbade a revenue-farmer or any of his slaves to remain in any town where he himself was on the point of going. In a word, he would be considered cruel, if he had shown the same feelings towards our enemies as he showed towards Roman citizens, and they too, members of an Order which has always been supported in a way befitting its position by the good-will of our magistrates. (11) And so, Conscript Fathers, you see that the revenue-farmers have already been almost crushed and ruined, not by any rashness in making their contracts, nor ignorance in conducting their business, but by the avarice, the arrogance, the cruelty of Gabinius; yet, in spite of the present exhaustion of the Treasury it is your bounden duty to come to their assistance; although there are many past your aid, who, owing to that enemy of the Senate, the bitter foe of the Equestrian Order and of all good citizens, have not only lost their goods but also their honoured name in society — unfortunates whom neither economy nor self-restraint, neither integrity nor toil nor the highest personal character, has been able to defend against the effrontery of that glutton and robber. (12) Again, are we to suffer those to perish who even now support themselves on their partrimony or the generosity of their friends? If a man has been unable "by the action of an enemy" to enjoy a public right, his contract with the censors itself protects him; but when a man is prevented from such enjoyment by one who, though not called an enemy, is one, ought not such a man to receive assistance? Very well, retain still longer in his province a man who makes compacts with enemies against allies, with allies against citizens, who even counts himself of more value than his colleague, just because his colleague has deceived you by his grim and gloomy looks, whereas he himself has never pretended to be less wicked than he was. Piso, on the other hand, parades a somewhat different claim to distinction, seeing that in a brief space he has deprived Gabinius of his reputation as the most villainous of men. (trans. R. Gardner, *LCL*)

Cicero's speech *De Provinciis Consularibus* was delivered in 56 B. C. E. The question to be decided here was which provinces should be allotted to the consuls of 55 B. C. E. Some people sought to hurt Caesar by depriving him of the Gallic provinces, or at least of one of them. Cicero, on the other hand, suggested that Syria should be taken away from Gabinius and Macedonia from Piso; both had been consuls in 58 B. C. E., the year in which Cicero was banished from Rome, and he regarded them as his personal enemies. Cicero's main argument against the prolongation of Gabinius' governorship in Syria was that he had shown an improper attitude to the publicani and had caused their financial ruin by surrendering them to the Syrians and the Jews, "nations born to slavery".

We know more details about the activities of Aulus Gabinius in Judaea from Josephus (*Ant.*, XIV, 82 ff.; *BJ*, I, 160 ff.) and from Cassius Dio, XXXIX, 56 : 5–6 (No. 408). Gabinius acted as governor of Syria in 57–55 B. C. E. On his governorship, see Schürer, I, pp. 305 f., 339 ff., V. Mühll, PW, VII, pp. 427 ff.; Kahrstedt, p. 99; Momigliano, pp. 188 ff.; E. M. Sanford, *TAPA*, LXX (1939), pp. 80 ff.; S. J. de Laet, *Portorium*, Brugge 1949, pp. 86 f.; Rostovtzeff, SEHHW, II, 980 ff.; E. M. Smallwood, *Journal of Jewish Studies*, XVIII (1967), pp. 89 ff. On his early career, see E. Badian, *Philologus*, CIII (1959), pp. 87 ff. It seems that the policy of Gabinius, which, according to Cicero, involved the ruin of the publicani, tended to abolish the direct taxes by the Roman societies of publicani and to replace them with taxes levied by the local authorities. This is also probably implied by the words of Cassius Dio, *loc. cit.* (No. 408): καὶ φόρον τοῖς ᾿Ιουδαίοις ἐπέταξε. It is very likely that the five synhedria,which represented Gabinius' five divisions of what was still left of the Hasmonaean state (*Ant.*, XIV, 91; *BJ*, I, 170), were made responsible for the regular collection of taxes. Though in his speech Cicero asserts that Gabinius surrendered the publicani to the Syrians and the Jews, we must remember that the essential feature of Gabinius' activities in Judaea and of his administrative reforms tended to weaken the political power of the Jewish population of the country and to destroy its unity. On the other hand, Gabinius, together with Pompey, was the chief restorer of Hellenistic city life in Palestine. Nevertheless, his financial reforms were also of some benefit to the Jews in view of the well-known rapacity of the Roman publicani, which constituted a real calamity for the inhabitants of the provinces. This is attested by sources on the Roman province of Asia; see T. R. S. Broughton, apud: T. Frank, *An Economic Survey of Ancient Rome*, IV, Baltimore 1938, pp. 535 ff. In this connection, we should also pay attention to the humane behaviour of Gabinius after he quelled the frequent Jewish revolts during his governorship. Though the revolts were fierce, Gabinius never executed any of the Jewish leaders who fell into his hands. For the relations between Gabinius and the publicani, see also Cicero, *Ad Quintum Fratrem*, III, 2 : 2.

10 *natis servituti*: This emphasis on the Jews' being born to slavery may have suggested itself to Cicero due to the large number of Jewish slaves who were brought to Rome after the capture of Jerusalem by Pompey; see Philo, *Legatio ad Gaium*, 155; see also Appianus, *Bella Civilia*, II, 74 : 308: ἀνδράποδα ταῦτ᾿ ἐστὶ Σύρια καὶ Φρύγια καὶ Λύδια, φεύγειν αἰεὶ καὶ δουλεύειν ἕτοιμα; Livius, XXXVI, 17 : 5 "vilissima genera hominum et servituti nata". On the nationality of slaves in Rome, see M. L. Gordon, *JRS*, XIV (1924), pp. 93 ff.

custodias sustulit: Cf. De Laet, *op. cit.*, p. 106.

71

Ad Familiares, XII, 11 — Purser

Scr. in castris Taricheis Non. Mart. a 711 (43)

C. Cassius procos. S. D. M. Ciceroni

S. v. b. e. e. q. v. In Syriam me profectum esse scito ad. L. Murcum

et Q. Crispum imp. Viri fortes optimique cives, postea quam audierunt
5 quae Romae gererentur, exercitus mihi tradiderunt ipsique mecum una
fortissimo animo rem p. administrant. Item legionem quam Q. Caecilius Bassus habuit ad me venisse scito, quattuorque legiones quas
A. Allienus ex Aegypto eduxit traditas ab eo mihi esse scito. (2) Nunc
te cohortatione non puto indigere ut nos absentis remque p. quantum
10 est in te, defendas. Scire te volo firma praesidia vobis senatuique non
deesse, ut optima spe et maximo animo rem p. defendas. Reliqua
tecum aget L. Carteius, familiaris meus. Vale. D. Nonis Martiis ex
castris Taricheis.

10 *in te* om. M

Camp at Taricheae, March 7th, 43 B.C.E.
Cassius procunsul to Cicero

(1) If you are well, all is right; I too am well. You must know that I
have started for Syria to join L. Murcus and Q. Crispus, commanders-
in-chief. When those gallant men and admirable citizens heard what
was going on in Rome, they handed their armies over to me, and are
themselves administering the affairs of the State side by side with me,
and with the utmost resolution. I beg to inform you also that the legion
which Q. Caecilius Bassus had, has come over to me, and I beg to
inform you that the four legions A. Allienus brought out of Egypt
have been handed over by him to me. (2) For the present I do not suppose that there is any need of my exhorting you to defend us while we
are away, and the Republic too, as far as in you lies. I should like you
to be assured that neither all of you, nor the Senate are without strong
safeguards, so that you may defend the Republic in the best of hopes
and with the highest spirit. What business remains will be transacted
with you by L. Carteius, an intimate friend of mine. Dated the 7th of
March, from camp at Taricheae.   (trans. W. Glynn Williams, *LCL*)

This letter was written to Cicero by C. Cassius in March 43 B. C. E. Cassius informs
Cicero of the events in Syria, where the local Roman commanders joined forces
with him. The letter was written in the camp of Taricheae, which seems to be
identical with the Galilaean township of that name. We do know that Cassius
took punitive measures against the Jewish inhabitants of Taricheae on an earlier
occasion, after the death of Crassus in 53 B. C. E., when he attacked the town
and enslaved thousands of its inhabitants (*Ant.*, XIV, 120; *BJ*, I, 180). On the
contents of the present letter, see *Ad Familiares*, XII, 12; *Ad Brutum*, II, 3; *Philippicae*, XI, 12:30; Velleius Paterculus, II, 69:2; Appianus, *Bella Civilia*, III, 78:319:
καὶ αὐτὸν (scil. ᾽Αλλιηνὸν) ὁ Κάσσιος οὐδὲν προπεπυσμένον ἐν τῇ Παλαιστίνῃ

From Herodotus to Plutarch

περιέλαβέ τε καὶ ἠνάγκασεν ἑαυτῷ προσθέσθαι; IV, 59 : 255 f.; Cassius Dio, XLVII, 28 (No. 410); J. Dobiáš, *Dějiny řísmké provincie syrské*, I, Prague 1924, p. 182. In *Ant.*, XIV, 274, Josephus describes the situation in Galilee, where Herod promptly raised the sum imposed by Cassius.

XXXV. VARRO

116–27 B.C.E.

In the few passages that illustrate Varro's views on the Jewish religion, the greatest scholar of republican Rome and the forerunner of the Augustan religious restoration[1] is most sympathetic. These passages put him in the company of such writers as Strabo, rather than with some of the later celebrities of the literature of imperial Rome.
The two main passages (No. 72 a–b) derive from Varro's great work, Res Divinae, which constitutes the later part of the Antiquitates Rerum Humanarum et Divinarum, compiled between 63 and 47 B.C.E.[2] They belong to the first book, and have been transmitted by Augustine.[3] We learn from one of them (No. 72b) that Varro identifies the Jewish God with Jupiter. In the second (No. 72a) he adduces that the Jewish form of divine worship, because of its opposition to cultic images, is an example of a pure and useful worship and one that resembles the original cult of old Rome in this respect.
In his censure of the cult of images Varro follows a long tradition of Greek philosophical thought.[4] This cult had already been disparaged by Stoic philosophers from Zeno onwards,[5] and the same opinion was later expressed by Seneca in his De Superstitione, apud: Augustinus, De Civitate Dei, VI, 10. Lucilius, in his time (vv. 486 ff., ed. Marx) also poured ridicule on images. But the specific argument against images, namely, that image worship detracts from the fear of the gods, has no parallel in these writers.

---

1 For Varro's theology, see P. Boyancé, REA, LVII (1955), pp. 57 ff.; see also the succinct summary by K. Latte, Römische Religionsgeschichte, Munich 1960, pp. 291 ff.

2 H. Dahlmann, PW, Suppl. VI, p. 1234. It was dedicated to Caesar in 47 B. C. E. Cf. F. Della Corte, Varrone, Genoa 1954, p. 133, n. 19.

3 It may be taken for granted that both passages derive from Antiquitates; cf. B. Cardauns, Varros Logistoricus über die Götterverehrung, Würzburg 1960, p. 50.

4 Cf. J. Geffcken, Neue Jahrbücher für das klassische Altertum, XV, 1905, pp. 630 f. Cf., in general, B. de Borries, "Quid Veteres Philosophi de Idolatria Senserint", Ph. D. Thesis, Göttingen 1918.

5 See SVF, I, F 264.

From Herodotus to Plutarch

We cannot suggest any known philosophical authority — Posidonius or Antiochus of Ascalon — as the source of Varro's views on the Jewish religion.[6] It is quite probable that Varro did have some direct knowledge of Judaism, since by his time the Jews had spread to most Mediterranean countries, and he could have met them both at Rome and in the provinces.[7]

Bibliography

E. Norden, *Festgabe Harnack*, Tübingen 1921, pp. 298 ff. = *Kleine Schriften*, pp. 282 ff.; W. Fink, *Der Einfluss der jüdischen Religion auf die griechisch-römische*, Bonn 1932, pp. 51 ff.; Cardauns, *op. cit.* (supra n. 3), p. 58, n. 17; B. Wacholder, *HTR*, LXI (1968), pp. 469 f.; Hengel, pp. 472 f.

6 On Varro and Antiochus of Ascalon, see G. Langenberg, "M. Terenti Varronis Liber de Philosophia", Ph. D. Thesis, Köln 1959, pp. 29 f.
7 Varro had some personal knowledge of Asia Minor, but he seems not to have visited Syria. Cf. Cichorius, pp. 203 f.; cf. pp. 195 f.

Varro

72 a

apud: Augustinus, *De Civitate Dei*, IV, 31 — Dombart & Kalb = F128R = F703, Burkhart
Cardauns, apud: H. Hagendahl, *Augustine and the Latin Classics*, I, Göteborg 1967

Dicit ⟨scil. Varro⟩ etiam antiquos Romanos plus annos centum et
septuaginta deos sine simulacro coluisse. "Quod si adhuc, inquit, man-
sisset, castius dii observarentur." Cui sententiae suae testem adhibet
inter cetera etiam gentem Iudaeam; nec dubitat eum locum ita con-
cludere, ut dicat, qui primi simulacra deorum populis posuerunt, eos
civitatibus suis et metum dempsisse et errorem addidise, prudenter
existimans deos facile posse in simulacrorum stoliditate contemni.

4 *etiam* om. L¹

He [scil. Varro] also says that for more than one hundred and
seventy years the ancient Romans worshipped the gods without an
image. "If this usage had continued to our own day", he says, "our
worship of the gods would be more devout." And in support of his
opinion he adduces, among other things, the testimony of the Jewish
race. And he ends with the forthright statement that those who first set
up images of the gods for the people diminished reverence in their
cities as they added to error, for he wisely judged that gods in the
shape of senseless images might easily inspire contempt.

(trans. W. M. Green, *LCL*)

*antiquos Romanos ... deos sine simulacro coluisse ... cui sententiae suae testem
adhibet inter cetera etiam gentem Iudaeam*: Cf. Strabo, *Geographica*, XVI, 2 : 35,
pp. 760 f. (No. 115) and the commentary *ad loc*. The sympathy shown by Varro for
the Jewish religion stands in marked contrast to his attitude towards the idolatrous
oriental cults; see Servius, *In Aeneidem* VIII, 698: "Varro indignatur Alexandrinos
deos Romae coli." In other places Varro expresses his opposition to divine statues
and even his contempt for it, and he contrasts them with real gods; see Varro,
apud: Arnobius, *Adversus Nationes*, VII, 1: "Dii veri neque desiderant ea [scil.
sacrificia] neque deposcunt, ex aere autem facti, testa, gypso vel marmore multo
minus haec curant. Carent enim sensu ..." On the imageless cult of the ancient
Romans, see Plutarchus, *Numa*, 8.

72 b

apud: Augustinus, *De Consensu Evangelistarum*, I, 22:30 — Weihrich = F672, Burkhart Cardauns,
apud: Hagendahl, *op. cit.*, = A. G. Condemi, *M. Terenti Varronis Antiquitates Rerum
Divinarum*, I–II: *Fragmenta*, Bologna 1964, F48

Varro autem ipsorum, quo doctiorem aput se neminem inveniunt,
deum Iudaeorum Iovem putavit nihil interesse censens, quo nomine

209

nuncupetur, dum eadem res intellegatur, credo illius summitate deter-
ritus. Nam quia nihil superius solent colere Romani quam Iovem,
5 quod Capitolium eorum satis aperteque testatur, eumque regem omnium deorum arbitrantur, cum animadverteret Iudaeos summum
deum colere, nihil aliud potuit suspicari quam Iovem.

4 *nam* om. p   6 *animadverteret et* B

Yet Varro, one of themselves — to a more learned man they cannot
point — thought the God of the Jews to be the same as Jupiter,
thinking that it makes no difference by which name he is called, so
long as the same thing is understood. I believe that he did it being
terrified by his sublimity. Since the Romans habitually worship nothing
superior to Jupiter, a fact attested well and openly by their Capitol,
and they consider him the king of all the gods, and as he perceived
that the Jews worship the highest God, he could not but identify
him with Jupiter.

*Deum Iudaeorum Iovem putavit nihil interess censens, quo nomine nuncupetur, dum
eadem res intellegatur*: Cf. the words of Varro, as quoted by Augustinus in *De
Civitate Dei*, IV, 9: "Hunc Varro credit etiam ab his coli, qui unum deum solum
sine simulacro colunt, sed alio nomine nuncupari." Cf. also the *Letter of Aristeas*, 16; Labeo, apud: Macrobius, *Saturnalia*, I, 18 : 18–21 (No. 445).

72c

apud: Augustinus, *De Consensu Evangelistarum*, I, 23:31 — Weihrich = F673, Burkhart Cardauns,
apud: Hagendahl, *op. cit.*

Merito ergo et Varro Iovem opinatus est coli a Iudaeis.

Justly therefore also Varro thinks that it is Jupiter who is worshipped by the Jews.

72d

apud: Augustinus, *De Consensu Evangelistarum*, I, 27:42 — Weihrich = F676, Burkhart Cardauns
apud: Hagendahl, *op. cit.*

Si deum Israhel Iovem putant, sicut Varro scripsit, interim ut secundum
eorum opinionem loquar, cur ergo Iovi non credunt idola esse delenda?

2 *credant* CPV

If they think Jupiter to be the God of Israel, as Varro wrote, let me

Varro

speak meanwhile according to their opinion, why therefore don't they believe Jupiter that idols ought to be destroyed.

73

Res Rusticae, II, 1:27 — Goetz

Neque enim hirundines et ciconiae, quae in Italia pariunt, in omnibus terris pariunt. Non scitis palmulas careotas Syrias parere in Iudaea, in Italia non posse?

2 *Syrias* Keil   *syriam* codd. | *Iudaea* Victorius   *iurea* codd.

Swallows and storks, for instance, which bear in Italy, do not bear in all lands. Surely you are aware that the date-palms of Syria bear fruit in Judaea but cannot in Italy.   (trans. W. D. Hooper, *LCL*)

palmulas careotas Syrias parere in Iudaea: Cf. Strabo, *Geographica*, XVI, 2 : 41, p. 763 (No. 115), which states that the palm grove in the vicinity of Jericho is the only place where the caryotic palm grows. The name of the palm is derived from its nut-like fruit; see Steier, PW, XX, pp. 387 f.

74

apud: Plinius, *Naturalis Historia*, XXXIII, 136 — Mayhoff = F224R

Congerant excedentes numerum opes, quota tamen portio erunt Ptolemaei, quem Varro tradit Pompeio res gerente circa Iudaeam octona milia equitum sua pecunia toleravisse, mille convivas totidem aureis potoriis, mutantem ea vasa cum ferculis, saginasse!

But let them amass uncountable riches, yet what fraction will they be of the riches of the Ptolemy who is recorded by Varro, at the time when Pompey was campaigning in the regions adjoining to Judaea, to have maintained 8000 horses at his own charge, to have given a lavish feast to a thousand guests, with 1000 gold goblets, which were changed at every course.   (trans. H. Rackham, *LCL*)

75

apud: Lydus, *De Mensibus*, IV, 53, pp. 110 f. — Wünsch

Ὁ δὲ Ῥωμαῖος Βάρρων περὶ αὐτοῦ διαλαβών φησι παρὰ Χαλδαίοις ἐν τοῖς μυστικοῖς αὐτὸν λέγεσθαι Ἰάω.

211

The Roman Varro defining him [scil. the Jewish God] says that
he is called Iao in the Chaldaean mysteries.

Βάρρων περὶ αὐτοῦ διαλαβών... λέγεσθαι 'Ιάω: On the name 'Ιάω in Graeco-
Roman literature, see the commentary to Diodorus, I, 94 (No. 58). We cannot say
where Varro got the name. Norden suggests that he derived it from *De Diis* by
Nigidius Figulus, the neo-Pythagoraean. On his religious views, see Latte, *op. cit.*
(supra, p. 207, n. 1), pp. 289 ff. Aly also suggests neo-Pythagoraean circles as the
source; see W. Aly, *Strabon von Amaseia*, Bonn 1957, pp. 200 f.

XXXVI. ASINIUS POLLIO

First century B.C.E.

*A famous statesman, orator, poet and historian, Pollio seems to have
been on friendly terms with Herod of Judaea. He was one of the consuls
of 40 B.C.E., the year that Herod, at the instigation of Mark Antony
and with the approval of Octavian, was proclaimed king* (Ant., *XIV,
389*). *This and their common friendship with Antony may have drawn
Pollio and Herod together, for we learn later that Alexander and
Aristobulus, the sons of the King of Judaea, lived at Pollio's house
during their stay at Rome; see* Ant., *XV, 343:* τούτοις ἀνελθοῦσιν
καταγωγὴ μὲν ἦν Πολλίωνος οἶκος ἀνδρὸς τῶν μάλιστα σπουδασάντων
περὶ τὴν 'Ηρώδου φιλίαν.[1]
*Pollio is known to have written a history of the Roman Civil Wars that
covered the period from the year of the First Triumvirate to the Battle of
Actium.*[2] *It is this work that Josephus had in mind when he quoted
Pollio about the part Hyrcan played in the rescue of Caesar in Egypt
(47 B.C.E.).*
Since Josephus cites Pollio only on the authority of Strabo,[3] *it is certain
that he did not consult his work directly.*[4]

1 This house of Pollio is commonly assumed to have been that of Asinius Pollio;
  cf. Schürer, I, p. 407; Otto, p. 71; L. H. Feldman, *TAPA*, LXXXIV (1953),
  p. 79. Niese and Willrich denied this, maintaining that a Jew named Pollio is
  meant here; see B. Niese in his index to Josephus; H. Willrich, *Das Haus des
  Herodes*, Heidelberg 1929, pp. 184 f. Stein also expressed his doubts over the
  identification of the host of Herod's sons with Asinius Pollio; see A. Stein,
  PIR, I², 1933, p. 253. Syme has even suggested that we should identify this host
  with the notorious Vedius Pollio, who had a distinguished career in Asia Minor,
  but there is a strong case for the older view; see R. Syme, *JRS*, LI (1961), p.
  30, addendum; M. Grant, *Herod the Great*, London 1971, p. 145.
2 See J. André, *La vie et l'œuvre d'Asinius Pollion*, Paris 1949, pp. 41 ff.
3 Aly maintains that the Asinius cited by Strabo was not the Roman statesman,
  but his freedman, Asinius Pollio of Tralles, who, according to Suda (s. v.
  Πωλίων, ὁ 'Ασίνιος χρηματίσας F. Gr. Hist., II, B 193, T 1), wrote a work about
  the war between Caesar and Pompey. This statement, however, is probably
  due to confusion between the two; see W. Aly, *Strabon von Amaseia*, Bonn
  1957, p. 90.
4 Against the view that a Greek version of Asinius' History exists, see R. Häus-
  sler, *Rhein. Mus.*, CIX (1966), pp. 339 ff.; cf. P. Treves, *Il mito di Alessandro
  e la Roma d'Augusto*, Milan–Naples 1953, p. 67.

76

apud: Josephus, *Antiquitates Judaicae*, XIV, 138 — Niese = F129R

Λέγεται δ᾽ ὑπὸ πολλῶν ʿΥρκανὸν ταύτης κοινωνῆσαι τῆς στρατείας καὶ
ἐλθεῖν εἰς Αἴγυπτον, μαρτυρεῖ δέ μου τῷ λόγῳ καὶ Στράβων ὁ Καππάδοξ
λέγων ἐξ ᾽Ασινίου ὀνόματος οὕτως· «μετὰ τὸν Μιθριδάτην εἰσβαλεῖν
εἰς τὴν Αἴγυπτον καὶ ʿΥρκανὸν τὸν τῶν ᾽Ιουδαίων ἀρχιερέα.»

1 στρατείας Dindorf   στρατιᾶς codd.   2 καὶ om. FLAMW
3 μετὰ δὲ FLAMW / τὸν] τὸ M et ex corr. A / εἰσβάλλειν FL

It is said by many writers that Hyrcanus took part in this campaign
and came to Egypt. And this statement of mine is attested by Strabo
of Cappadocia, who writes as follows, on the authority of Asinius:
"After Mithridates, Hyrcanus, the high priest of the Jews, also invaded Egypt."   (trans. R. Marcus, *LCL*)

Στράβων... ἐξ ᾽Ασινίου ὀνόματος: For the use of Asinius Pollio by Strabo, see
Geographica, IV, 3 : 3, p. 193.

μετὰ τὸν Μιθριδάτην εἰσβαλεῖν εἰς τὴν Αἴγυπτον: On these events, see W. Judeich,
Caesar im Orient, Leipzig 1885, pp. 92 ff.; T. Rice Holmes, *The Roman Republic
and the Founder of the Empire*, III, Oxford 1923, pp. 198 ff.; P. J. Sijpesteijn,
Latomus, XXIV (1965), pp. 122 ff.; H. Heinen, "Rom und Ägypten von 51 bis
47 v. Chr.", Ph.D.Thesis, Tübingen 1966, pp. 69 ff. Julius Caesar was besieged in
Alexandria in 47 B. C. E. The army that came to his help, under the command of
Mithridates of Pergamon, included a Jewish force.

καὶ ʿΥρκανὸν τὸν τῶν ᾽Ιουδαίων ἀρχιερέα: The quotation from Asinius Pollio
implies the direct participation of Hyrcan II, the Jewish High Priest and Ethnarch in
the expedition to Egypt. This also emerges from Hypsicrates (No. 79) and is
supported by an edict of Julius Caesar referred to in *Ant.*, XIV, 192 f.: ἐπεὶ ʿΥρκανὸς
᾽Αλεξάνδρου ᾽Ιουδαῖος... καὶ ἐν τῷ ἔγγιστα ἐν ᾽Αλεξανδρείᾳ πολέμῳ μετὰ χιλίων
πεντακοσίων στρατιωτῶν ἧκεν σύμμαχος καὶ...πάντας ἀνδρείᾳ τοὺς ἐν τάξει ὑπερ-
έβαλεν. On the other hand, in his narrative of these events, Josephus, contrary to
Pollio's statement, ignores the personal intervention of Hyrcan in the war in Egypt
and emphasizes only the role of his minister Antipater.This may be explained by the
historian's dependence on his principal source, Nicolaus of Damascus, the friend of
Antipater's son, Herod; see B. R. Motzo, *Studi Cagliaritani di Storia e Filologia*,
I (1927), pp. 1 ff.; see also P. Graindor, *La guerre d'Alexandrie*, Cairo 1931, p. 17.
Though Destinon defends Nicolaus' version, the document quoted above, which
expressly refers to the personal valour of Hyrcan in the Egyptian campaign, is in
itself enough to refute Nicolaus; see J. v. Destinon, *Die Quellen des Flavius
Josephus*, Kiel 1882, p. 104; B. Niese, *Hermes*, XI (1876), p. 471. It seems that the
personal appearance of the High Priest was needed to influence the Jews on the
Egyptian border. So, there is no doubt that preference should be given to Asinius
Pollio's version.

XXXVII. CASTOR OF RHODES

First century B.C.E.

There are two fragments from the Chronicle of Castor of Rhodes that have bearing on the history of Palestine. One is connected with the Battle of Gaza; the second is presented here. It is possible that Castor used the work of his predecessor Apollodorus (No. 34).

77

apud: Josephus, *Contra Apionem*, II 83–84— Niese = *F. Gr. Hist.*, II, B250, F13 = Reinach (Budé) = pp. 72 f.

(83) Quia vero Antiochus neque iustam fecit templi depraedationem, sed egestate pecuniarum ad hoc accessit, cum non esset hostis, et super nos auxiliatores suos et amicos adgressus est nec aliquid dignum derisione illic invenit, (84) multi et digni conscriptores super hoc

5 quoque testantur, Polybius Megalopolita ⟨No. 33⟩, Strabon Cappadox ⟨No. 98⟩, Nicolaus Damascenus ⟨No. 87⟩, Timagenes ⟨No. 80⟩ et Castor temporum conscriptor et Apollodorus ⟨No. 34⟩, ⟨qui⟩ omnes dicunt pecuniis indigentem Antiochum transgressum foedera Iudaeorum expoliasse templum auro argentoque plenum.

6 *Timagenes* Boysen   *Timagenis* Lat.   7 *⟨qui⟩* Hudson   9 *expoliasse*
Niese   *et spoliasse* Lat.

(83) That the raid of Antiochus on the temple was iniquitous, that it was impecuniosity which drove him to invade it, when he was not an open enemy, that he attacked us, his allies and friends, and that he found there nothing to deserve ridicule; (84) these facts are attested by many sober historians: Polybius of Megalopolis, Strabo the Cappadocian, Nicolaus of Damascus, Timagenes, Castor the chronicler, and Apollodorus who all assert that it was impecuniosity which induced Antiochus, in violation of his treaties with the Jews, to plunder the temple with its stores of gold and silver.

(trans. H. St. J. Thackeray, *LCL*)

quia vero Antiochus neque iustam fecit templi depraedationem . . .: Cf. the commentary to Polybius (No. 33).

XXXVIII. CRINAGORAS OF MYTILENE

Second half of the first century B.C.E.

Crinagoras was a Lesbian poet of the age of Augustus, some of whose epigrams are preserved in the Anthologia Graeca. *One of these deals with the fate of a man called Philostratus, who lost favour and was presumably banished to the sandy Ostracine. The "Judaean boundaries" are mentioned in connection with the downfall of this man. Yet, the exact significance of the part those boundaries play in the epigram is obscure and, in fact, depends on the interpretation we adopt of ll. 3–4. The usual interpretation, based on the reading* ἦ *in l. 3 and* κεῖσαι *in l. 4, implies that Philostratus, in his low estate, will be seen or looked upon with disdain from the Judaean borders. On the other hand, Cichorius*[1] *suggests other readings (see the commentary) and thinks that what Crinagoras wants to convey is that Judaea, like Egypt, was witness to the past splendour of Philostratus.*[2]

---

1 Cichorius, pp. 314 ff.
2 Cichorius (p. 317) also suggests that *Ant.*, X, 228, where Philostratus appears as a writer on Indian and Phoenician history, be emended to read: ἐν ταῖς Ἰουδαικαῖς καὶ Φοινικικαῖς ἱστορίαις instead of ἐν ταῖς Ἰνδικαῖς καὶ Φοινικικαῖς ἱστορίαις. This emendation, though undoubtedly brilliant, is still far from certain, and consequently I have not included Philostratus as one of the writers on Jewry in the present collection.

From Herodotus to Plutarch

78

Anthologia Graeca, VII, 645 — Waltz = XX, Page, in: A.S.F. Gow & D.L. Page, *The Greek Anthology* — *The Garland of Philip*, I, Cambridge 1968, p. 210 = F30R = M. Rubensohn, *Crinagorae Mytilenaei Epigrammata*, Berlin 1888, No. 23

ᵂΩ δύστην' ὄλβοιο Φιλόστρατε, ποῦ σοι ἐκεῖνα
σκῆπτρα καὶ αἱ βασιλέων ἄφθονοι εὐτυχίαι,
αἷσιν ἐπηώρησας ἀεὶ βίον; ἦ ἐπὶ Νείλῳ
‹κεῖσαι 'Ιου›δαίοις ὢν περίοπτος ὅροις;
5 ὀθνεῖοι καμάτους τοὺς σοὺς διεμοιρήσαντο,
σὸς δὲ νέκυς ψαφαρῇ κείσετ' ἐν 'Οστρακίνῃ

3 βίον; ἦ] βίον ἦ Cichorius   4 κεῖσαι 'Ιουδαίοις man. rec. in P sane ex
Aldi Manutii coniectura   ...δαίοις P¹ Planudes   ἦ παρ' (?) 'Ιου› δαίοις
Cichorius / ὅροις Planudes   ὅρρις P   6 ἐν Οστρακίνη Boissonade
ἐνοστρακίνη P   ἐν ὀστρακίνη Planudes

Ill-starred in your prosperity, Philostratus, where are those sceptres
and abundant princely blessings on which you ever made your life
depend, a man of eminence whether on the Nile or within the boundaries of Judaea?[1] Strangers have shared out the fruits of your labour,
and your corpse shall lie in sandy Ostracina.

(trans. D. L. Page)

[1] The translation here is based on the emendation of Cichorius; cf. the *apparatus criticus*.

1 Φιλόστρατε: This Philostratus is commonly identified with the Academic
philosopher who belonged to the intimate circle of Antony and Cleopatra and
whose life was spared by Octavian after the conquest of Egypt (30 B. C. E.); see
Plutarchus, *Antonius*, 80, p. 953 A; M. Rubensohn, *Crinagorae Mytilenaei Vita et
Epigrammata*, Berlin 1887, pp. 10f.; see also K. v. Fritz, PW, XX, pp. 123 f.; Solmsen,
ibid., p. 124
4 ('Ιου)δαίοις: This restoration is generally accepted, although opinions differ
regarding the word preceding it. Cichorius argues against the reading κεῖσαι,
since in that case the word κείσετ' of 1.6 would be a superfluous repetition; see
Cichorius, pp. 316 f. He also reads ἦ and not ἦ in 1.3. Thus, Judaea is implied as
"ein zweiter Schauplatz von Philostratos' Auftreten". Cichorius also supposes
that the βασιλέων εὐτυχίαι of 1.2 may allude to Philostratus' sojourn at the
Herodian court, as well as at Alexandria. It is true that the examples adduced by
Cichorius of the bright intellects who passed from the service of Cleopatra to that of
Herod do not carry the same weight, since they (e.g. Nicolaus) made the change
only after Cleopatra's collapse, but the disgraced Philostratus could hardly have
been welcomed by Herod. Still, there is nothing to preclude the possibility that
Philostratus stayed in Jerusalem for some time in the years preceding Actium. In
any case, περίοπτος should be understood as meaning conspicuous; see Page, *op.
cit.*, II, p. 228; Fraser, II, p. 710, n. 112.

Crinagoras of Mytilene

6 ἐν Ὀστρακίνῃ: In north-eastern Egypt, east of Pelusium; see H. Kees, PW, XVIII, pp. 1673 f. From the contents of the epigram it seems that at that time Philostratus, though he had lost his standing and property, had not yet died; Crinagoras merely foretells his burial in miserable Ostracine; see *BJ*, IV, 661: κατὰ τὴν Ὀστρακίνην· οὗτος ὁ σταθμὸς ἦν ἄνυδρος, ἐπεισάκτοις δ᾽ ὕδασιν οἱ ἐπιχώριοι χρῶνται.

XXXIX. HYPSICRATES

First century B.C.E.

A historian and grammarian, referred to several times by Strabo in his Geographica, *Josephus owes his knowledge of Hypsicrates to the* Histories *of Strabo. The fragment of Hypsicrates, like that of Asinius Pollio, emphasizes the prominent part played by Hyrcan II in the campaign launched for the rescue of Caesar in Alexandria (47 B.C.E.), an aspect that is ignored by the main narrative of Josephus, since it is based on Nicolaus (cf. also the commentary to No. 76).*

Hypsicrates

79

apud: Josephus, *Antiquitates Judaicae*, XIV, 139 — Niese = F37 R = *F. Gr. Hist.*, II, B190, F1

Ὁ δ'αὐτὸς οὗτος Στράβων καὶ ἐν ἑτέροις πάλιν ἐξ Ὑψικράτους
ὀνόματος λέγει οὕτως· «τὸν δὲ Μιθριδάτην ἐξελθεῖν μόνον, κληθέντα δ' εἰς
Ἀσκάλωνα Ἀντίπατρον ὑπ' αὐτοῦ τὸν τῆς Ἰουδαίας ἐπιμελητὴν τρισχιλίους αὐτῷ στρατιώτας συμπαρασκευάσαι καὶ τοὺς ἄλλους δυνάστας
5 προτρέψαι, κοινωνῆσαι δὲ τῆς στρατείας καὶ Ὑρκανὸν τὸν ἀρχιερέα.»

5 στρατείας Dindorf   στρατιᾶς codd.

And again this same Strabo in another passage writes as follows,
on the authority of Hypsicrates. "Mithridates went out alone, but
Antipater, the procurator of Judaea, was called to Ascalon by him and
provided him with an additional three thousand soldiers, and won over
the other princes; and the high priest Hyrcanus also took part in the
campaign."   (trans. R. Marcus, *LCL*)

Ἀντίπατρον... τῆς Ἰουδαίας ἐπιμελητήν: Antipater is also designated ἐπιμελητής
in *Ant.*, XIV, 127. Schürer regards this as proof that Antipater was appointed
general supervisor of taxes as a result of the administrative reforms of Gabinius;
see Schürer, I, p. 343, n. 14; cf. Momigliano, p. 207.

τρισχιλίους αὐτῷ στρατιώτας συμπαρασκευάσαι: The edict of Caesar (*Ant.*,
XIV, 193) refers to only one thousand five hundred Jewish soldiers participating in
the war under Hyrcan; cf. *Ant.*, XVI, 52 — a speech of Nicolaus — where two
thousand soldiers are mentioned.

κοινωνῆσαι δὲ τῆς στρατείας καὶ Ὑρκανὸν τὸν ἀρχιερέα: In this Hypsicrates
agrees with Asinius Pollio. On the other hand, he does not ignore Antipater and
ascribes to him important military and political activities. On the designation of
Hyrcan as βασιλεύς, see the commentary to Cassius Dio, XXXVII, 16 : 4 (No.
406).

XL. TIMAGENES

First century B.C.E.

Timagenes was born in Alexandria and was transported to Rome by Gabinius. In Rome, where he was set free, he taught rhetoric and entered the highest circles of Roman society of the Augustan age. His sharp tongue caused his relations with Augustus to be severed, but he found a protector in the person of Asinius Pollio.

Timagenes wrote many works; see Suda, s.v. = F. Gr. Hist., II, A 88, T 1. However, the name, or a part of it, of only one of them has come down to us. This is referred to as βασιλεῖς *by Stephanus Byzantius, s.v.* Μιλύαι *= F. Gr. Hist., II, A 88, F1. Otherwise, Timagenes is designated in a general way as a "writer of history"; see Seneca, De Ira, III, 23:4: "Timagenes historiarum scriptor." There is reason to suppose that the work on the kings was a comprehensive history built upon a royal and dynastic principle. Thus, it follows that the references to the Jews also derive from this work. Yet, we do not know whether Timagenes dedicated a special part of his History to the Jews. The first reference (No. 80) may be a brief remark in the narrative relating to the deeds of Antiochus Epiphanes, and the third (No. 82) derives from the history of the campaigns of Ptolemy Lathyrus. The second fragment (No. 81), bearing upon the Hasmonaean ruler Aristobulus I, may also have come from some chapter of Seleucid history. Still, it is not unlikely that Timagenes devoted special chapters to the Jewish monarchy and included there a detailed account of the country, religion and history of the Jews. This would be a certainty if we were sure that Pompeius Trogus' Historiae Philippicae does, as is widely maintained, depend on Timagenes.[1]*

Timagenes was a writer well known to later authors, both Greek (Plutarch) and, even more, Latin; see Curtius Rufus, IX, 5:21:21; Plinius, Naturalis Historia, *III, 132;* Quintilianus, Institutio Oratoria,

---

1 This view has been held, e.g., by Gutschmid, Stähelin and Jacoby; cf. Schanz & Hosius II, pp. 322 f. Objections have been raised by Momigliano and Seel; see A. Momigliano, *Athenaeum*, NS XII (1934), p. 56; O. Seel, *Die Preafatio des Pompeius Trogus*, Erlangen 1955, pp. 18 ff. Of course, we should not assume that Timagenes was the sole or even the main source of Trogus' work. Still, in some parts of it Trogus is likely to have used him. The excursus on the Jews may be one of those parts.

Timagenes

I, 10:10; Ammianus Marcellinus, XV, 9:2. However, it is difficult to assess to what extent, apart from the presumed influence on Pompeius Trogus, he moulded later traditions about Jews and Judaism.[2] *It is noteworthy that Timagenes is the only Graeco-Alexandrian writer whose attitude to the Jews was not hostile. This emerges clearly from his sympathetic characterization of Aristobulus I, which contrasts conspicuously with the main narrative of Josephus, derived from the pro-Herodian Nicolaus.*

Bibliography

Susemihl, II, pp. 377 ff.; C. Wachsmuth, *Rhein. Mus.* XLVI (1891), pp. 465 ff.; idem, *Einleitung in das Studium der alten Geschichte*, Leipzig 1895, pp. 114 f., 450; J. Kaerst, *Philologus*, LVI (1897), pp. 621 ff.; Gutschmid, V, pp. 218 ff.; Schürer, I, pp. 43 f.; Stähelin, pp. 26 f.; *F. Gr. Hist.*, II C, pp. 220 f.; R. Laqueur, PW, Ser. 2, VI, pp. 1063 ff.; P. Treves, *Il mito di Alessandro e la Roma d'Augusto*, Milan–Naples 1953, pp. 58 ff. et passim; R. Syme, *Harvard Studies in Classical Philology*, LXIV (1959), p. 65; G. W. Bowersock, *Augustus and the Greek World*, Oxford 1965, pp. 125 f.; H. R. Breitenbach, *Museum Helveticum*, XXVI (1969), pp. 156 f; Fraser, I, p. 518 f.

2 As Laqueur aptly puts it: "Es mag sehr wohl sein, dass T. eine grössere Rolle in der antiken Überlieferung gespielt hat, als wir beweisen können; aber wirklich greifbar is sie nicht;" see R. Laqueur, PW, Ser. 2, VI, p. 1071.

223

80

apud: Josephus, *Contra Apionem*, II,83–84 — Niese = *F. Gr. Hist.*,II, A88, F4 = Reinach
(Budé), pp. 72 f.

(83) Quia vero Antiochus neque iustam fecit templi depraedationem, sed egestate pecuniarum ad hoc accessit, cum non esset hostis, et super nos auxiliatores suos et amicos adgressus est nec aliquid dignum derisione illic invenit, (84) multi et digni conscriptores super hoc quoque tes-
5 tantur, Polybius Megalopolita ⟨No. 33⟩, Strabon Cappadox ⟨No. 98⟩, Nicolaus Damascenus ⟨No. 87⟩, Timagenes et Castor ⟨No. 77⟩ temporum conscriptor et Apollodorus ⟨No. 34⟩, ⟨qui⟩ omnes dicunt pecuniis indigentem Antiochum transgressum foedera Iudaeorum expoliasse templum auro argentoque plenum.

6 *Timagenes* Boysen   *Timagenis* Lat.   7 ⟨qui⟩ Hudson   8 *expoliasse*
Niese   *et spoliasse* Lat.

(83) That the raid of Antiochus on the temple was iniquitous, that it was impecuniosity which drove him to invade it, when he was not an open enemy, that he attacked us, his allies and friends, and that he found there nothing to deserve ridicule; (84) these facts are attested by many sober historians. Polybius of Megalopolis, Strabo the Cappadocian, Nicolaus of Damascus, Timagenes, Castor the chronicler and Apollodorus all assert that it was impecuniosity which induced Antiochus, in violation of his treaties with the Jews, to plunder the temple with its stores of gold and silver.

(trans. H. St. J. Thackeray, *LCL*)

On the whole passage, see the commentary to Polybius (No. 33). It is almost certain that Josephus did not use primary sources for all the writers to whom he alludes here. In view of No. 81, where Josephus owes his knowledge of Timagenes to Strabo, it seems safe to assume that he also here derives the name of Timagenes from Strabo's *Historica Hypomnemata*.

81

apud: Josephus, *Antiquitates Judaicae*, XIII, 319 — Niese = F31R =*F. Gr. Hist.*, II, A88, F5

Φύσει δ' ἐπιεικεῖ κέχρητο καὶ σφόδρα ἦν αἰδοῦς ἥττων, ὡς μαρτυρεῖ τούτῳ καὶ Στράβων ἐκ τοῦ Τιμαγένους ὀνόματος λέγων οὕτως· «ἐπιεικὴς τε ἐγένετο οὗτος ὁ ἀνὴρ ⟨scil. Ἀριστόβουλος⟩ καὶ πολλὰ τοῖς Ἰουδαίοις χρήσιμος· χώραν τε γὰρ αὐτοῖς προσεκτήσατο καὶ τὸ μέρος τοῦ τῶν
5 Ἰτουραίων ἔθνους ᾠκειώσατο, δεσμῷ συνάψας τῇ τῶν αἰδοίων περιτομῇ.»
5 Ἰτουραίων] Ἰδουμαίων? Ed. Meyer

224

Timagenes

He had a kindly nature, and was wholly given to modesty, as Strabo also testifies on the authority of Timagenes, writing as follows: "This man was a kindly person and very serviceable to the Jews, for he acquired additional territory for them, and brought over to them a portion of the Ituraean nation, whom he joined to them by the bond of circumcision." (trans. R. Marcus, *LCL*)

ἐπιεικής τε ἐγένετο οὗτος ὁ ἀνήρ: For the contrast between the characterization of Aristobulus I, the Hasmonaean king (104–103 B. C. E.), as it emerges from the main narrative of Josephus, and that drawn by Timagenes, see the commentary to Strabo, *Historica Hypomnemata* (No. 100).

καὶ τὸ μέρος τοῦ τῶν Ἰτουραίων ἔθνους ᾠκειώσατο: The Ituraeans are mentioned in the Bible (Gen. xxv : 15; I Chron. i : 31; v : 19), and they appear in the historical work of the Jewish-Hellenistic writer Eupolemus (apud: Eusebius, *Praeparatio Evangelica*, IX, 30 : 3 = F. Gr. Hist. III, C 723, F 2b) among the enemies of David. They mainly inhabited the area of the Libanus and the Antilibanus, but not much is known about their expansion before the first century B. C. E.; see Schürer, I, pp. 707 ff.; R. Dussaud, *La pénétration des Arabes en Syrie avant l'Islam*, Paris 1955, pp. 176 ff. Timagenes does not specify the territories captured from the Ituraeans by Aristobulus. Many scholars hold the opinion that Timagenes' statement about the judaization of the Ituraeans implies the forceful judaization of the whole Galilee and that it was Aristobulus who both started and accomplished the process; see, e.g., Schürer, I, pp. 275 f.; II, pp. 10 ff.; G. Bertram, *Archiv für Religionswissenschaft*, XXXII (1935), p. 269. This view, at least in its extreme formulation, cannot be accepted, due to the following considerations:

a. The continuity of the occupation of parts of Galilee, either by the successors of the ancient Israelite population or by Jews, has never been wholly interrupted. The evacuation of Galilaean Jews, as related in I Macc. v : 14 ff., was evidently confined to a part of Western Galilee. It emerges from I Macc. ix : 2 that some years later (160 B. C. E.) the Jewish inhabitants of Arbel in Eastern Galilee made an attempt to stop the advance of the Seleucid general, Bacchides; see F. M. Abel, *Les livres des Maccabées*, Paris 1949, p. 159.

b. According to Josephus (*Ant.*, XIII, 322), Alexander Jannaeus, the brother of Aristobulus, was educated in Galilee during their father's lifetime. Thus, we may infer that parts of Galilee were Jewish, and were probably even included in the Jewish state under John Hyrcan.

c. Josephus (*Ant.*, XIII, 337) relates that Ptolemy Lathyrus deliberately attacked the Galilaean township of Asochis on Saturday (*c.* 102 B. C. E.). From this we may conclude that a year or so after the death of Aristobulus the inhabitants of Asochis were devoted Jews, a fact hardly compatible with the suggestion that they had been compelled to become Jews only recently. See also Alt, II, pp. 407 ff.; K. Galling, *Palästinajahrbuch*, XXXVI (1940), pp. 62 ff. These scholars cogently argue that there was continuity from the old Israelite population of Galilee to the Galilaean Jews at the period of the Second Temple. Still, we may assume that the Ituraeans penetrated into parts of Northern and North-Eastern Galilee and occupied them at an unknown time. These Ituraean settlers seem to be implied by Timagenes. The suggestion of Ed. Meyer, that we take Ἰτουραῖοι as a mistake for Ἰδουμαῖοι,

From Herodotus to Plutarc

already found by Josephus in his source, has not much to commend itself; therefore, the question-mark put by Jacoby after 'Ιτουραίων is superfluous; see Ed. Meyer, II, p. 274, n. 4. The Idumaeans were already part of the Jewish nation in the time of John Hyrcan, in the twenties of the second century B. C. E.; see *Ant.*, XIII, 257 f.

δεσμῷ συνάψας τῇ τῶν αἰδοίων περιτομῇ: It is noteworthy that Timagenes views Aristobulus' effort to enforce circumcision as a political measure and consequently does not blame him for it.

82

apud: Josephus, *Antiquitates Judaicae*, XIII, 344 — Niese = F32R = *F. Gr. Hist.*, II, A88, F6

Τρισμυρίους γοῦν ἔφασαν αὐτῶν ἀποθανεῖν, Τιμαγένης δὲ πεντακισμυρίους εἴρηκεν, τῶν δὲ ἄλλων τοὺς μὲν αἰχμαλώτους ληφθῆναι, τοὺς δ' εἰς τὰ οἰκεῖα διαφυγεῖν χωρία.

3 διαφυγεῖν Niese   διαφεύγειν PFL   φεύγειν AMWE

It was said in fact, that thirty thousand of them perished — Timagenes says that there were fifty thousand — while as for the rest, some were taken captive, and others escaped to their native places.

(trans. R. Marcus, *LCL*)

Τιμαγένης δὲ πεντακισμυρίους εἴρηκεν: Here Josephus describes the victory of Lathyrus in the Battle of Asophon. It stands to reason that here, too, he quotes Timagenes from Strabo, who is mentioned expressly by him in § 347; see Schürer, I, p. 44; G. Hölscher, *Die Quellen des Josephus für die Zeit vom Exil bis zum jüdischen Kriege*, Leipzig 1904, p. 15. Even the number of thirty thousand casualties suffered by the Jews in one battle seems too high. Timagenes' figure of fifty thousand deaths derives from his well-known inclination to exaggeration and sensational narrative; see, e.g., Strabo, *Geographica*, IV, 1 : 13, p. 188 = *F. Gr. Hist.* II, A 88, F 11; see also Strabo, *Geographica*, XV, 1 : 57, p. 711 = *F. Gr. Hist.*, II, A 88, F 12.

XLI. NICOLAUS OF DAMASCUS

c. 64 B.C.E. to the beginning of the first century C.E.

A historian, scholar and prolific writer, born at Damascus c. *64 B.C.E., Nicolaus came from a prominent family in his native city. His father, Antipater, fulfilled various tasks on behalf of the community; he served on foreign missions and was also elected to the municipal ἀρχαί of Damascus. Nicolaus' descendants were still conspicuous in that city after many generations.*[1]
The part played by his father in the municipal life of Damascus implies that Nicolaus was not of a Jewish family, and this becomes undisputable with the statement in Suda, s.v. 'Αντίπατρος, *that before his death Antipater ordered his two sons, Nicolaus and Ptolemy, to fulfil his vow to Zeus.*[2] *His Hellenic consciousness and sympathies are well illustrated by the counsel he gave to Archelaus, the heir of Herod, not to object to the bestowal of autonomy on Greek cities formerly included in his father's kingdom, and by his refusal to represent the same Archelaus on the question of that autonomy before Augustus.*
Nicolaus was included among the Peripatetics. He had the wide scholarly and literary range of interests commonly attributed to the members of that school, also excelling as a rhetor and a diplomat. Owing to his varied talents, he early established connections with some of the leading personalities of his time. He acted as a teacher of the children of Antony and Cleopatra, and some time after their fall he passed over to the court of Herod, to whom he may have been known from his years of association with Antony.
Nicolaus entered the service of Herod by 14 B.C.E. at the latest. He supervised the King's education and was one of his chief counsellors, representing him on various occasions. In 14 B.C.E. he accompanied Herod on his journey to Asia Minor. There he defended the interests of the Jewish communities against the claims of the Greek cities (Ant., XVI, 27 ff.) before Agrippa. Nevertheless, he took care to ingratiate

---

1 Sophronius of Damascus, *PG*, LXXXVII, 3, Col. 3621 = *F. Gr. Hist.*, II, A 90, T 2; A. Brinkmann, *Rhein. Mus.*, LX (1905), pp. 634 f.
2 See Gutschmid, V, p. 539; K. Patsch, *Wiener Studien*, XII (1890), pp. 231 ff.

227

*himself and his royal master with the Greeks of Asia Minor, e.g.
by effecting a reconciliation between the people of Ilium and the same
Agrippa. In 12 B.C.E. he went to Italy with Herod on the so-called
"second journey of Herod". After the relations between Herod
and the Princeps had deteriorated as a result of the military reprisals
of Herod in Arabia, it was Nicolaus who undertook and succeeded
in effecting a reconciliation with the Princeps. At the end of Herod's
reign Nicolaus played a prominent part in the judicial proceedings
against Antipater, the King's eldest son. After the death of the King
Nicolaus represented the interests of Archelaus against the claims of
his opponents. Once more his influence and his rhetorical talent prevailed, and Augustus confirmed, in the main, the testament of Herod.
This was Nicolaus' last act relating to Jewish affairs. He seems to have
spent his last years at Rome.*

Nicolaus' greatest literary achievement is his Historiae, *which
consists of 144 books, beginning with the ancient history of eastern
monarchies. It becomes more detailed as it approaches the author's
own time. It was Herod who urged Nicolaus to launch upon this* magnum
opus, *and it may be surmised that at least a part of it was published
in the King's lifetime. As a courtier of Herod and a man who played a
not undistinguished part in the events of Herod's reign, it is not surprising
that he recounts them in great detail. One only need mention the fact
that he dealt with the question of Jewish rights in Asia Minor in both
the 123rd and the 124th books of his work!*

*Also important for the study of Jewish history is his autobiography,
published after the death of Herod, fragments of which were preserved
in the* Excerpta de Virtutibus *and* Excerpta de Insidiis *of Constantinus
Porphyrogenitus. There we find some details concerning Herod's reign
and its aftermath that are missing in Josephus'* Antiquitates. *Moreover,
much interest attaches to a comparison between these fragments and
the narrative of Josephus, itself based on the* Historiae *of Nicolaus.
Important parts of the first seven books of the* Historiae *have also been
transmitted in the tenth-century excerpts of Constantinus Porphyrogenitus, but these do not include any reference to Jews. Only small fragments
of the later books have come down to us, transmitted by Athenaeus and,
above all, by Josephus. All the fragments of the* Historiae *bearing upon
Jews are from the* Antiquitates.

*From these fragments we learn that Nicolaus refers to Jews, on various
occasions, in connection with: the history of the Aramaic monarchy
(No. 84); the reign of Antiochus Epiphanes (No. 87); the Parthian
expedition of Antiochus Sidetes (No. 88); and the wars of Ptolemy*

Lathyrus (No. 89). We also note that he describes the expeditions of Pompey and Gabinius against the Jews (Nos. 91 and 92).
Nicolaus finds it proper to mention famous Jewish personalities — e.g., Abraham and Moses — in contexts that do not, in the main, relate to Jews. In one of these fragments (No. 83) we find the statement that he will deal with the offspring of Abraham on another occasion. This promised account of the Jews has not come down to us. Nevertheless, we are much more indebted to Nicolaus for our knowledge of Jewish history in the Hellenistic and early Roman period than would seem possible from the few fragments of his work, because the historical works of Josephus depend so heavily on the Historiae *of Nicolaus.*
It is the consensus of scholars, e.g. Schürer, Hölscher and Thackeray, that Nicolaus' writings constitute the main source of the Bellum Judaicum *for the whole period between Antiochus Epiphanes and the accession of Archelaus. The same holds true for books fourteen to seventeen of the* Antiquitates, *which comprise the history of Herod's time. When Josephus ceases to use Nicolaus as a source, as is the case in both his works from the time of Archelaus onward, the Jewish historian becomes much less circumstantial and his narrative is no longer comparable to that in his history of Herod.*
Apart from supplying Josephus with the material, Nicolaus left his imprint on the passionate and dramatic description of the domestic tragedy of Herod and his house as given by Josephus, and this seems to be typical of the literary technique of Nicolaus.[3] The encomiastic treatment of Herod and his father in Bellum Judaicum, *and, on the other hand, the account full of hatred displayed towards the younger Antipater, are also to be explained as deriving from Nicolaus.*
In his Antiquitates *Josephus becomes more restrained in his attitude to Herod. He even strongly criticizes the laudatory approach of Nicolaus in his account of the reign of his royal benefactor (No. 93). Despite this criticism, Josephus continues to draw upon the* Historiae *of Nicolaus. Moreover, it should be stated that this change of tone in Josephus' work should not be attributed to any additional sources of material, but rather to the altered circumstances in which he lived when writing his later works.[4]*
Some scholars, e.g. Otto, Jacoby and Hölscher, maintain that in the books of Antiquitates *relating to the reign of Herod, Josephus uses*

3 Cf. Jakob, "De Nicolai Damasceni Sermone", pp. 62 ff.
4 See R. Laqueur, *Der jüdische Historiker Flavius Josephus*, Giessen 1920, pp. 128 ff. This is an analysis of the fourteenth book of Josephus' *Antiquitates*, in which the defence of the main thesis seems to be overdone.

Nicolaus only through an intermediate source, namely, a Jewish anonymous writer unsympathetic to Herod; but this view has nothing to commend it.

With regard to method, it should be emphasized that not everything found in Antiquitates *and missing in* Bellum Judaicum *is necessarily explained by postulating sources other than Nicolaus, since it is clear that in his* Antiquitates *Josephus drew to an even greater extent on the material provided by Nicolaus'* Historiae. *On the other hand, not everything common to both of Josephus' works necessarily derives from Nicolaus. A case in point is the fantastic story related by Josephus about Herod's order to imprison the Jewish notables and to slaughter them indiscriminately upon his death, thus preventing an outburst of joy on the part of the population of his kingdom (Ant., XVII, 174 ff.; BJ, I, 659 f.). Such a tale, whatever its historical worth, is so derogatory to the memory of Herod that it can hardly be attributed to Nicolaus.*

Another set of problems arises with respect to Josephus' dependence on Nicolaus in those chapters that relate the story of the greatness of the Hasmonaean state, i.e. from the murder of Simon the Hasmonaean to the death of Salome-Alexandra (BJ, I, 54 ff.; the major part of the thirteenth book of Antiquitates). *It seems that Nicolaus also constituted the chief source of the Jewish historian's narrative on this subject, though in his* Antiquitates *he added some other sources, especially Strabo. This explains the rather strange fact that Josephus, notwithstanding his patriotism and the pride he took in his kinship with the Hasmonaeans, presents us with a rather cold picture of the three main figures of the Hasmonaean monarchy, namely, Aristobulus I, Alexander Jannaeus and Salome-Alexandra. Moreover, the account shows some sympathy with Hellenisitc Gaza, which succumbed to the onslaught of the Jews; see especially Ant., XIII, 359 ff. It even looks as if the victories of Alexander Jannaeus are deliberately somewhat played down; cf., e.g., Ant., XIII, 389 ff., with Syncellus (edited by Dindorf, I, p. 559), which is presumably independent of Josephus and where we read of Alexander's victory over Antiochus Dionysus.[5] The prosopographical material relating to the Greek side is also somewhat richer than that relating to the Jewish side. This would be fully consonant with the point of view of Nicolaus, the Syrian Greek and friend of Herod, who had very little reason to sympathize with the Hasmonaean destroyers of the Hellenistic cities and with*

5 On the information supplied by Syncellus, cf. H. Gelzer, *Sextus Julius Africanus*, I, Leipzig 1880, pp. 256 ff.

the members of a house that had, in fact, been replaced and even exterminated by Herod.[6] *The account of the reign of Aristobulus I may also be considered as deriving from Nicolaus, against the view of Destinon and Schürer.*[7] *The story of the relations between Aristobulus and Antigonus and of their death is pathetically told* (BJ, I, 70–84; *and* Ant., XIII, 301–317); *it concentrates on the domestic tragedy, almost wholly omitting any reference to the main political and military events of the reign of Aristobulus. Nicolaus' version stands in marked contrast to the shorter one of Timagenes, transmitted to Josephus by Strabo* (Nos. 81 and 100).

Nicolaus was indeed a Damascene, though a Hellenized one. In contrast to many famous writers and philosophers, he never deemed it necessary to abandon his own city[8] *and to obtain citizenship in a famous Greek city. It may be seen from the fragments of his* Historiae *that Nicolaus took pride in the past of Aramaic Damascus. However, it would be unjustified, it seems, to put Nicolaus in the same category with such exponents of ancient Eastern culture as Berossus, Manetho, or, for that matter, the Jewish-Hellenistic writers, who, basing themselves on original national traditions, made an attempt to give some account of the ancient history of their nation in Greek. We do not know whether Nicolaus knew Aramaic, or whether he considered himself a descendant of the Greeks or of native Syrians.*

As we should naturally expect from a historian who was a personal friend and servant of a Jewish king and who defended Jewish rights before Agrippa, Nicolaus showed more respect for the Jewish past and traditions than most of the Graeco-Roman writers, and the historical information supplied by the Bible ranked high with him. On the other hand, as we have seen, his treatment of the Hasmonaean royal house was coloured by his connection with Herod and by his natural sympathy with the cause of Syrian Greeks. Apart from the works of Josephus, we cannot trace any direct influence of Nicolaus' Historiae *on later references to Jews in Graeco-Roman literature.*

I have abstained from including here the speeches attributed by Josephus to Nicolaus (e.g. Ant., XVI, 31 ff.) *not only because they do not constitute the* ipsissima verba *of Nicolaus, but also because we*

---

6 See M. Stern, *Tarbiz*, XXXIII (1964), pp. 335 f. (in Hebrew).
7 See J. v. Destinon, *Die Quellen des Flavius Josephus*, Kiel 1882, p. 41; Schürer, I, p. 83.
8 *F. Gr. Hist.*, II, A 90, F 137, pp. 425 f.; cf. Wacholder, *Nicolaus of Damascus*, pp. 15 f.

cannot even be sure how far they are true to the general ideas expressed by Nicolaus on these occasions. It was in the speeches that Josephus was sometimes able to show his originality and rhetorical power, and his Bellum Judaicum *supplies abundant evidence of his ability as speech composer. In any case, it seems to me that the mere fact that Josephus attributes these orations to Nicolaus does not signify that they are any more characteristic of Nicolaus than the general narrative of Josephus, although in this Josephus does not expressly assert his dependence on his predecessor.*

Additional Note

In the Corpus Aristotelicum *the work* De Plantis *is usually included. In fact, the Greek printed edition is a translation from the Latin, which is itself translated from the Arabic. The work is not by Aristotle but, as it seems, by Nicolaus of Damascus. The Greek original has been lost, and we can only go back to the Arabic translation.*

I give here the Greek translation of De Plantis, *II, p. 824a (edited by Apelt, 1888), which bears on the Dead Sea:* Οὕτω φυσικῶς ἐν τῇ νεκρᾷ θαλάσσῃ οὔτε καταδύεται ζῷον, οὔτε γεννᾶται· κυριεύει γὰρ ἡ ξηρότης ἐν αὐτῷ, καὶ ἐν παντὶ ὅπερ ἐστὶ πλησίον τοῦ σχήματος τῆς γῆς.[9]

Bibliography

FHG, III, pp. 343 ff.; Susemihl, II, pp. 309 ff.; Gutschmid, V, pp. 536 ff.; F. Münzer, *Deutsche Litteraturzeitung*, XXI (1900) pp. 2983 f.; Schürer, I, pp. 50 ff.; G. Misch, *Geschichte der Autobiographie*, I, Leipzig–Berlin 1907, pp. 183 ff.; P. Jakob, "De Nicolai Damasceni Sermone et Arte Historica Quaestiones Selectae", Ph. D. Thesis, Göttingen 1911; Schmid & Stählin, II, 1, pp. 374 ff.; E. Täubler, *Byzantinische Zeitschrift*, XXV (1925), pp. 33 ff.; *F. Gr. Hist.*, II C, pp. 229 ff.; H. Willrich, *Das Haus des Herodes*, Heidelberg 1929, pp. 112 ff.; R. Laqueur, PW, XVII, pp. 362 ff.; B. Wacholder, *Nicolaus of Damascus*, Berkeley–Los Angeles 1962; G. W. Bowersock, *Augustus and the Greek World*, Oxford 1965, pp. 134 ff.; D. A. W. Biltcliffe, *Rhein. Mus.*, CXII (1969), pp. 85 ff.
For the use of Nicolaus by Josephus, see H. Bloch, *Die Quellen des Flavius Josephus*, Leipzig 1879, pp. 106 ff.; J. v. Destinon, *Die Quellen des Flavius Josephus*, Kiel 1882, pp. 91 ff.; P. Otto, *Leipziger Studien zur classischen Philologie*, XI, Suppl., 1889, pp. 225 ff.; A. Büchler, *JQR*, IX (1897), pp. 325 ff.; Schürer, I, pp. 82 ff.; K. Albert, "Strabo als Quelle des Flavius Josephus", Ph.D. Thesis, Würzburg 1902, pp. 10 ff.; G. Hölscher, *Die Quellen des Josephus für die Zeit vom Exil bis zum jüdischen Kriege*, Leipzig 1904, pp. 17 ff.; idem, PW, IX, pp. 1944 ff.; idem, *Die Hohenpriesterliste bei Josephus und die evangelische Chronologie*, Heidelberg

9 On the pseudo-Aristotelian *De Plantis*, cf. H. J. Drossaart-Lulofs, *JHS*, LXXVII (1957), pp. 75 ff.; B. Hemmerdinger, *Philologus*, CXI (1967), pp. 56 ff.

Nicolaus of Damascus

1940, pp. 3 f.; Otto, pp. 4 f.; R. Laqueur, *Der jüdische Historiker Flavius Josephus*, Giessen 1920, pp. 128 ff.; idem, PW, XVII, pp. 392 ff.; Ed. Meyer, II, pp. 164, 328, n. 5; A. Schlatter, *Geschichte Israels von Alexander dem Grossen bis Hadrian*[3], Stuttgart 1925, pp. 241 ff.; H. St. J. Thackeray, *Josephus the Man and the Historian*, New York 1929, pp. 40 f.; 59, 65 ff.; R. J. H. Shutt, *Studies in Josephus*, London 1961, pp. 79 ff.; Gager, p. 21; M. Stern, *Studies in Bible and Jewish History Dedicated to the Memory of Jacob Liver*, Tel Aviv 1971, pp. 375 ff. (in Hebrew).

83

Historiae, apud: Josephus, *Antiquitates Judaicae*, I, 159–160 — Niese = Eusebius, *Praeparatio Evangelica*, IX, 16 = F38R = *F. Gr. Hist.*, II, A90, F19

(159) Νικόλαος δὲ ὁ Δαμασκηνὸς ἐν τῇ τετάρτῃ τῶν ἱστοριῶν λέγει οὕτως· «Ἀβράμης ἐβασίλευσεν Δαμασκοῦ ἔπηλυς σὺν στρατῷ ἀφιγμένος ἐκ τῆς γῆς τῆς ὑπὲρ Βαβυλῶνος Χαλδαίων λεγομένης. (160) μετ' οὐ πολὺν δὲ χρόνον μεταναστὰς καὶ ἀπὸ ταύτης τῆς χώρας σὺν τῷ
5 *σφετέρῳ λαῷ εἰς τὴν τότε μὲν Χαναναίαν λεγομένην, νῦν δὲ Ἰουδαίαν μετῴκησε καὶ οἱ ἀπ' ἐκείνου πληθύσαντες, περὶ ὧν ἐν ἑτέρῳ λόγῳ διέξειμι τὰ ἱστορούμενα. τοῦ δὲ Ἀβράμου ἔτι καὶ νῦν ἐν τῇ Δαμασκηνῇ τὸ ὄνομα δοξάζεται καὶ κώμη δείκνυται ἀπ' αὐτοῦ Ἀβράμου οἴκησις λεγομένη.»*

2 ἄβραμος L   ἀβράμης Exc.   Ἀβραάμης Eus. | ἐβασίλευε Eus. |
Δαμασκοῦ om. RO   3 χαλδαιας SP Exc.   4 πολὺ δὲ L   δὲ πολὺν RO |
μεταστὰς P   ἐξαναστὰς Eus. | ἀπ' αὐτῆς RO   6 πλήθους ὄντες R
πλήθους ὄντες O   πληθύναντες SL

(159) Nicolaus of Damascus in the fourth book of his Histories makes the following statement: "Abrames reigned in Damascus, a foreigner who had come with an army from the country beyond Babylon called the land of the Chaldees. (160) But, not long after, he left this country also with his people for the land then called Canaan but now Judaea, where he settled, he and his numerous descendants, whose history I shall recount in another book. The name of Abram is still celebrated in the region of Damascus, and a village is shown that is called after him 'Abram's abode.'"   (trans. H. St. J. Thackeray, *LCL*)

159 *Νικόλαος δὲ ὁ Δαμασκηνὸς ... λέγει οὕτως*: It is not clear in what connection Nicolaus came to speak of Abraham; perhaps he did it in connection with the Lydian expeditions to Syria; see *FHG*, III, p. 373, n. 30.
Ἀβράμης ἐβασίλευσεν Δαμασκοῦ: Abraham is designated Prince of God (נשיא אלהים) in Gen. xxiii : 6. For various midrashic traditions about Abraham as king, see Ginzberg, V, p. 216, n. 46; see also Philo, *De Virtutibus*, 216: *ὡς παρὰ τοῖς*

ὑποδεξαμένοις νομίζεσθαι βασιλεύς, οὐχὶ ταῖς παρασκευαῖς — ἰδιώτης γὰρ ἦν —, ἀλλὰ τῷ περὶ τὴν ψυχὴν μεγέθει, φρονήματος ὢν βασιλικοῦ.

τῆς ὑπὲρ Βαβυλῶνος Χαλδαίων λεγομένης: Nicolaus follows the biblical tradition with respect to the Chaldaic origin of Abraham. Ur of the Chaldeans, Abraham's place of origin according to the Bible, is translated in the Septuagint as χώρα τῶν Χαλδαίων (Gen. xi : 28, 31). The Bible does not refer to Abraham's sojourn at Damascus. Only his servant Eliezer came from that city (Gen. xv : 2). There is also a reference to Damascus in connection with Abraham's pursuit of Chedorlaomer, King of Elam, and his allies (Gen. xiv : 15). However, the tradition of Abraham's sojourn at Damascus derives from the fact that the road from Haran, where Abraham had been staying after leaving Ur, to the land of Canaan, led through Damascus. It seems that a tradition on Abraham and Damascus had arisen in Jewish circles in Syria and that Nicolaus included it in his history, both to enhance the past glory of Damascus and to flatter Herod. For this last factor see Wacholder, *op. cit.* (supra, p. 232), p. 55. On Abraham's connection with Damascus, see Pompeius Trogus, apud: Iustinus, XXXVI, 2 : 1 ff. (No. 137). While Nicolaus does not conceal the Chaldaic origin of Abraham, in the Epitome of Justin, Abraham emerges as a Damascene; see I. Heinemann, PW, Suppl. V, p. 23.

160 Χαναναίαν λεγομένην: Χαναναία is the usual form in *Antiquitates*.

νῦν δὲ 'Ιουδαίαν: In Nicolaus 'Ιουδαία is identical with the whole Χαναναία; here it has the broad meaning it assumed as a result of the Hasmonaean conquests.

περὶ ὧν ἐν ἑτέρῳ λόγῳ διέξειμι τὰ ἱστορούμενα: Probably in connection with the activities of Antiochus Epiphanes against Jerusalem.

'Αβράμου οἴκησις λεγομένη: There is also a Muslim tradition that honours Masdjid Ibrahim in Berze, north of Damascus, as the birthplace of Abraham; see R. Hartmann, *The Encyclopaedia of Islam*, Vol. I, Part 2, 1911, p. 903. We may also point to several traditions which originated in Jewish-Hellenistic circles on Abraham's connection with various countries. Thus, Eupolemus (apud: Eusebius, *Praeparatio Evangelica*, IX, 17 : 4) tells us that Abraham, coming from the Chaldaean country, settled in Phoenicia, while Cleodemus-Malchus (*Ant.*, I, 241) informs us that Abraham's sons went with Heracles to Lybia. Artapanus (apud: Eusebius, *Praeparatio Evangelica*, IX, 18 : 1) tells of Abraham's emigration to Egypt, where he instructed the king in astrology. Cf. the traditions on Pergamon and the Jews in the time of Abraham (*Ant.*, XIV, 255) and on Abraham and Sparta (I Macc. xii : 21; *Ant.*, XII, 226; F. Dornseiff, *Würzburger Jahrbücher für die Altertumswissenschaft*, I, 1946, pp. 128 ff.). Cf. also the commentary to Claudius Iolaus (No. 249) and the bibliography listed there on the relations between Sparta and the Jews. One should also note that there is some doubt as to whether the last sentence should be included in the quotation from Nicolaus. It may be that, in spite of Niese and Jacoby, it should end with διέξειμι τὰ ἱστορούμενα. See already E. Nestle, *ZAW*, XXVI (1906) p. 282; XXIX, (1909), p. 60; see also the notes of Lommatzsch & Denk in *Biblische Zeitschrift*, VI (1908), p. 265. On Abraham in Damascus, see also R. Fruin, *Nieuw Theologisch Tijdschrift*, XV (1926), pp. 3 ff.

84

Historiae, apud: Josephus, *Antiquitates Judaicae*, VII, 101–103 — Niese = F 39 R = *F. Gr. Hist.*, II, A 90, F 20

(101) Μέμνηται δὲ τούτου τοῦ βασιλέως καὶ Νικόλαος ἐν τῇ τετάρτῃ

Nicolaus of Damascus

τῶν ἱστοριῶν αὐτοῦ λέγων οὕτως· «μετὰ δὲ ταῦτα πολλῷ χρόνῳ ὕστερον τῶν ἐγχωρίων τις "Αδαδος ὄνομα πλεῖον ἰσχύσας Δαμασκοῦ τε καὶ τῆς ἄλλης Συρίας ἔξω Φοινίκης ἐβασίλευσε. πόλεμον δ᾽ ἐξενέγκας πρὸς
5 Δαυίδην τὸν βασιλέα τῆς Ἰουδαίας καὶ πολλαῖς μάχαις κριθείς, ὑστάτῃ δὲ παρὰ τὸν Εὐφράτην, ἐν ᾗ ἡττᾶτο, ἄριστος ἔδοξεν εἶναι βασιλέων ῥώμῃ καὶ ἀνδρείᾳ.» (102) πρὸς τούτοις δὲ καὶ περὶ τῶν ἀπογόνων αὐτοῦ φησιν, ὡς μετὰ τὴν ἐκείνου τελευτὴν ἐξεδέχοντο παρ᾽ ἀλλήλων καὶ τὴν βασιλείαν καὶ τὸ ὄνομα, λέγων οὕτως· «τελευτήσαντος δὲ
10 ἐκείνου ἀπόγονοι ἐπὶ δέκα γενεὰς ἐβασίλευον, ἑκάστου παρὰ τοῦ πατρὸς ἅμα καὶ τὴν ἀρχὴν καὶ τοὔνομα τούτου ἐκδεχομένου, ὥσπερ οἱ Πτολεμαῖοι ἐν Αἰγύπτῳ. (103) μέγιστον δὲ ἁπάντων δυνηθεὶς ὁ τρίτος ἀναμαχέσασθαι βουλόμενος τὴν τοῦ προπάτορος ἧτταν στρατεύσας ἐπὶ τοὺς Ἰουδαίους ἐπόρθησε τὴν νῦν Σαμαρεῖτιν καλουμένην γῆν.»

2 αὐτοῦ om. MSP, Lat.   6 ἥττητο RO   10 οἱ ἀπόγονοι SP
12 δὲ πάντων MSP   13 προπάτορος] avi Lat.   πατρὸς RO   14 τοὺς
om. MSP / γῆν om. MSP

(101) This king is also mentioned by Nicolaus in the fourth book of his History, who writes as follows: "A long while after this, one of the natives, Adados by name, attained to great power and became ruler of Damascus and the rest of Syria excepting Phoenicia. He waged war against David, king of Judaea, and, after trial of many battles, the last of which was fought beside the Euphrates, where he was defeated, he gained the reputation of being the most vigorous and courageous of kings." (102) In addition, he speaks also of his descendants and tells how, after his death, they succeeded one another in his kingdom and his name. This is what he says: "Upon his death, his posterity reigned for ten generations, each receiving from his father both his authority and his name, as did the Ptolemies in Egypt. (103) The most powerful of all these kings was the third, who, in his desire to make good his grandfather's defeat, marched against the Jews and sacked the country now called Samaritis."   (trans. R. Marcus, *LCL*)

101 "Αδαδος... Δαμασκοῦ τε καὶ τῆς ἄλλης Συρίας ἔξω Φοινίκης ἐβασίλευσε: The most important Aramaean king among the contemporaries of David was Hadadezer, King of Aram-Ẓobah, not of Damascus, though the latter city was presumably included in the federation of Aramaean and non-Aramaean political units led by Aram-Ẓobah. The centre of this Kingdom was, it seems, in the northern part of the Lebanon valley. In order to stress the importance of Damascus, Nicolaus describes David's chief enemy as the King of Damascus. For Hadadezer, King of Ẓobah, see A. Malamat, *Encyclopaedia Biblica*, II, pp. 791 f. (in Hebrew). The dominion of Hadadezer extended from the Euphrates in the north-east to the Batanitis in the south. His conquests are attested in Assyrian documents. The

names Hadadezer and (H)Adados both derive from the name of the god Hadad. For the interchange between the names Ben-Hadad and Hadadezer, see J. B. Pritchard, *Ancient Near Eastern Texts Relating to the Old Testament*[2], Princeton 1955, p. 278. Here Adad-idri — i.e. Hadadezer — of Damascus stands for Ben-Hadad.

πόλεμον δ'ἐξενέγκας πρὸς Δαυίδην: This is the only passage from a pagan writer before the spread of Christianity in which there is a reference to King David. πολλαῖς μάχαις κριθείς: Cf. II Sam. x : 7 ff.; I Chron. xix : 6 ff. (the victories in the vicinity of Rabbah of the Ammonites and Helam); II Sam. viii : 3 ff.; I Chron. xviii : 3 ff. (the victories in the heart of Syria); cf. also Alt, II, pp. 71 f. On the whole question of the relations between Aram and Israel, see M. F. Unger, *Israel and the Aramaeans of Damascus*, London 1957, pp. 48 ff.; B. Mazar, *Biblical Archaeologist*, XXV (1962), pp. 98 ff.

102 τελευτήσαντος δὲ ἐκείνου ἀπόγονοι ἐπὶ δέκα γενεὰς ἐβασίλευον ...: The kings of Damascus referred to by Nicolaus are not known from the Bible to have been descendants of Hadadezer of Zobah. The man who liberated Damascus from Judaean rule was Rezon, the son of Eliada (I Kings xi : 23), while the first Damascene king to interfere in the affairs of Israel after the partition of the Kingdom is designated as Ben-Hadad, the son of Tabrimmon, who was the son of Hezion (I Kings xv : 18).

καὶ τὴν ἀρχὴν καὶ τοὔνομα τούτου ἐκδεχομένου, ὥσπερ οἱ Πτολεμαῖοι: We know of three Aramaic kings called Ben-Hadad. Mazar suggests that Ben-Hadad is not a personal name, but a title common to kings of Aram-Damascus, as Nicolaus expressly states; see Mazar, p. 106; cf. *Ant.*, VIII, 156, where Josephus explains the name Pharaoh in the same way.

103 ὁ τρίτος ἀναμαχέσασθαι βουλόμενος ... ἐπόρθησε τὴν νῦν Σαμαρεῖτιν καλουμένην γῆν: Josephus identifies him with the Adados (Ben-Hadad) who waged war against Samaria in the time of Ahab. This king is generally understood to have been Ben-Hadad II, though some scholars now identify him with the above mentioned Ben-Hadad I, the son of Tabrimmon, who defeated Baasha, the King of Israel; see S. Loewenstamm, *Encyclopaedia Biblica*, II, p. 155 ff. (in Hebrew); cf. also W. F. Albright, *BASOR*, 87 (1942), p. 26; Unger, *op. cit.*, pp. 59 ff. On the wars between Ben-Hadad II and Ahab, see I Kings xx : 22. These wars lasted a long time. At one stage Ben-Hadad besieged Samaria but was severely repulsed. A second time he was defeated by Ahab in the Battle of Aphek. He avenged these defeats in his last battle with Ahab, fought at Ramot-Gilead, which ended in the death of Ahab and in an Aramaean victory.

85

Historiae, apud: Josephus, *Antiquitates Judaicae*, I, 93–95 — Niese = F41R = *F. Gr. Hist.*, II, A90, F72

(93) Τοῦ δὲ κατακλυσμοῦ τούτου καὶ τῆς λάρνακος μέμνηνται πάντες οἱ τὰς βαρβαρικὰς ἱστορίας ἀναγεγραφότες, ὧν ἐστι Βηρωσσὸς ὁ Χαλδαῖος... (94) μέμνηται δὲ τούτων καὶ Ἱερώνυμος ὁ Αἰγύπτιος... καὶ Νικόλαος δὲ ὁ Δαμασκηνὸς ἐν τῇ ἐνενηκοστῇ καὶ ἕκτῃ βίβλῳ ἱστορεῖ περὶ αὐτῶν

Nicolaus of Damascus

5 λέγων οὕτως· (95) «ἔστιν ὑπὲρ τὴν Μιννάδα μέγα ὄρος κατὰ τὴν
'Αρμενίαν Βάρις λεγόμενον, εἰς ὃ πολλοὺς συμφυγόντας ἐπὶ τοῦ
κατακλυσμοῦ λόγος ἔχει περισωθῆναι καί τινα ἐπὶ λάρνακος ὀχούμενον
ἐπὶ τὴν ἀκρώρειαν ὀκεῖλαι καὶ τὰ λείψανα τῶν ξύλων ἐπὶ πολὺ σωθῆναι.
γένοιτο δ' ἂν οὗτος, ὅντινα καὶ Μωυσῆς ἀνέγραψεν ὁ 'Ιουδαίων
10 νομοθέτης.»

5 μηννάδα ROL   Μιλνάδα I. Vossius   6 βάρεις R
  beris Hieronymus   7 λάρνακα RO

(93) The flood and the ark are mentioned by all who have written
histories of the barbarians. Among these is Berossus the Chaldaean...
(94) These matters are also mentioned by Hieronymus the Egyptian...
and Nicolaus of Damascus in his ninety-sixth book relates the story
as follows: (95) "There is above the country of Minyas in Armenia
a great mountain called Baris, where, as the story goes, many refugees found safety at the time of the flood, and one man, transported
upon an ark, grounded upon the summit, and relics of the timber were
for long preserved; this might well be the same man of whom Moses,
the Jewish legislator, wrote."   (trans. H. St. J. Thackeray, *LCL*)

95 ὑπὲρ τὴν Μιννάδα: There is much to be said for the identification of Minyas
with the kingdom of Minni, mentioned in Jer. li : 27, with that of Ararat; cf.
Schachermeyr, PW, XV, p. 2017. Thus, there is no need for the emendation Μιλνάδα
for Μιννάδα; see Müller, *FHG*, III, p. 415, n. 76. The Greeks seem to have connected
the name with the Thessalian Minyans, Armenia having been founded, according
to the Greek tradition, by one of the companions of Jason; see Iustinus, XLII,
2 : 7 ff.; Strabo, *Geographica*, XI, 14 : 12, p. 530. Jacoby thinks it probable that
Nicolaus wrote about Minyas in connection with Parthian history, since Justin,
too, related the *Armeniae origo* in that connection; see Jacoby, *F. Gr. Hist.*, II C,
p. 254. The reading Μιννάδα, however, is discarded by Huxley, who prefers the
reading Μηννάδα of ROL, connecting the name with Menua, the old Urartian
conqueror (800 B. C. E.); see G. Huxley, *Greek, Roman and Byzantine Studies*,
IX, (1968), pp. 319 f.

Βάρις: Strabo (*Geographica*, XI, 14 : 14, p. 531) mentions a temple of Baris in
Armenia: μέρη δ' ἐστὶ τοῦ Ταύρου ταῦτα, ὧν ὁ "Αβος ἐγγύς ἐστι τῆς ὁδοῦ τῆς εἰς
'Εκβάτανα φερούσης παρὰ τὸν τῆς Βάριδος νεών. It stands to reason that this temple
is related to the Armenian mountain Baris. It may even be that the Jews who had
been living in Armenia already in pre-Christian times identified Βάρις with the
mountain of Noah's Ark, because the Bible identifies the place where the Ark
touched land as Mt. Ararat, i.e. in Armenia; cf. J. Neusner, *JAOS*, LXXXIV (1964),
pp. 230 ff.

εἰς ὃ πολλοὺς συμφυγόντας ἐπὶ τοῦ κατακλυσμοῦ λόγος ἔχει περισωθῆναι:
Compare this with the Babylonian tradition, as expressed in the fragments of
Berossus in *Ant.*, I, 93; Syncellus, I, ed. Dindorf, p. 55; cf. *F. Gr. Hist.*, III, C 680,
F 4c; see also P. Schnabel, *Berossos*, Leipzig 1923, pp. 180 ff. Berossus, too, locates

the remnants of the Ark in Armenia πρὸς τῷ ὄρει τῶν Κορδναίων; cf. E. G. Kraeling, *JAOS*, LXVII (1947), p. 181. However, he, as well as other historians Josephus quotes in this connection (Hieronymus, Mnaseas), in contrast to Nicolaus, do not refer to Noah.

86

Historiae, apud: Josephus, *Antiquitates Judaicae*, XII, 125–127 — Niese = F43R = *F. Gr. Hist.*, II, A90, F81

(125) "Ομοιον δέ τι τούτῳ καὶ Μᾶρκον 'Αγρίππαν φρονήσαντα περὶ τῶν 'Ιουδαίων οἴδαμεν· τῶν γὰρ 'Ιώνων κινηθέντων ἐπ' αὐτοὺς καὶ δεομένων τοῦ 'Αγρίππου, ἵνα τῆς πολιτείας, ἣν αὐτοῖς ἔδωκεν 'Αντίοχος ὁ Σελεύκου υἱωνὸς ὁ παρὰ τοῖς "Ελλησιν Θεὸς λεγόμενος, μόνοι μετ-
5 έχωσιν, (126) ἀξιούντων δ' εἰ συγγενεῖς εἰσιν αὐτοῖς 'Ιουδαῖοι, σέβεσθαι τοὺς αὐτῶν θεούς, καὶ δίκης περὶ τούτων συστάσης ἐνίκησαν οἱ 'Ιουδαῖοι τοῖς αὐτῶν ἔθεσι χρῆσθαι συνηγορήσαντος αὐτοῖς Νικολάου τοῦ Δαμασκηνοῦ· ὁ γὰρ 'Αγρίππας ἀπεφήνατο μηδὲν αὐτῷ καινίζειν ἐξεῖναι. (127) τὸ δ' ἀκριβὲς εἴ τις βούλεται καταμαθεῖν, ἀναγνώτω
10 τοῦ Νικολάου τὴν ἑκατοστὴν καὶ εἰκοστὴν καὶ τρίτην καὶ τετάρτην.

1 τούτων PVWE   τούτοις Niese   4 υἱὸς W   4–5 μετέχωσιν E
μετέλθωσιν codd.   *possiderent* Lat.   6 αὐτῶν] ἰδίους αὐτῶν FLV
ἰουδαίους αὐτῶν E   *proprios eorum* Lat.   / καὶ om. Lat.   7 αὐτῶν]
αὐτοῖς FLV   10 τῶν νικολάου ἱστοριῶν FLAVW, Lat.

(125) And we know that Marcus Agrippa had a similar view concerning the Jews, for when the Ionians agitated against them and petitioned Agrippa that they alone might enjoy the citizenship which Antiochus, the grandson of Seleucus, called Theos by the Greeks, had given them, (126) and claimed that, if the Jews were to be their fellows, they should worship the Ionians' gods, the matter was brought to trial and the Jews won the right to use their own customs, their advocate being Nicolaus of Damascus; for Agrippa gave his opinion that it was not lawful for him to make a new rule. (127) But if anyone wishes to learn the details, let him read the hundred and twenty-third and hundred and twenty-fourth books of Nicolaus' History.

(trans. R. Marcus, *LCL*)

126 καὶ δίκης περὶ τούτων συστάσης ἐνίκησαν: Cf. *Ant.*, XVI, 27 ff.; G. Hölscher, PW, IX, p. 1979, n. 1; Laqueur, PW, XVII, pp. 394 f.
127 τὴν ἑκατοστὴν καὶ εἰκοστὴν καὶ τρίτην καὶ τετάρτην: In his *Historiae* Nicolaus seems to deal at great length with the question of Jewish rights in Ionia, since he took an active part in their establishment. It should be noted that the

number of the books in his *Historiae* as given here by Josephus lends support to Athenaeus (*Deipnosophistae*, VI, 54, p. 249 A), who states that the *Historiae* consisted of 144 books and not of 80, as found in Suda, s.v. Νικόλαος Δαμασκηνός.

87

Historiae, apud: Josephus, *Contra Apionem*, II, 83–84 — Niese = *F. Gr. Hist.*, II, A90, F91 = Reinach (Budé), pp. 72 f.

(83) Quia vero Antiochus neque iustam fecit templi depraedationem, sed egestate pecuniarum ad hoc accessit, cum non esset hostis, et super nos auxiliatores suos et amicos adgressus est nec aliquid dignum derisione illic invenit, (84) multi et digni conscriptores super hoc quoque testan-
5 tur, Polybius Megalopolita 〈No. 33〉, Strabon Cappadox 〈No. 98〉, Nicolaus Damascenus, Timagenes 〈No. 80〉 et Castor 〈No. 77〉 tempo-rum conscriptor et Apollodorus 〈No. 34〉, 〈qui〉 omnes dicunt pecuniis indigentem Antiochum transgressum foedera Iudaeorum expoliasse templum auro argentoque plenum.

6 *Timagenes* Boysen *Timagenis* Lat. 7 〈*qui*〉 Hudson 8 *expoliasse*
Niese *et spoliasse* Lat.

(83) That the raid of Antiochus on the temple was iniquitous, that it was impecuniosity which drove him to invade it, when he was not an open enemy, that he attacked us, his allies and friends, and that he found there nothing to deserve ridicule; (84) these facts are at-tested by many sober historians: Polybius of Megalopolis, Strabo the Cappadocian, Nicolaus of Damascus, Timagenes, Castor the chroni-cler, and Apollodorus who all assert that it was impecuniosity which induced Antiochus, in violation of his treaties with the Jews, to plunder the temple with its stores of gold and silver.

(trans. H. St. J. Thackeray, *LCL*)

See the commentary to Polybius (No. 33). It seems plausible that most of the authors referred to here by Josephus were known to him only through Nicolaus.

88

Historiae, apud: Josephus, *Antiquitates Judaicae*, XIII, 250–251 — Niese = F40R = *F. Gr. Hist.*, II, A90, F92

(250) Γίνεται δ' αὐτῷ 〈scil. Ὑρκανῷ〉 καὶ πρὸς Ἀντίοχον φιλία καὶ συμμαχία, καὶ δεξάμενος αὐτὸν εἰς τὴν πόλιν ἀφθόνως πάντα τῇ

239

From Herodotus to Plutarch

στρατιᾷ καὶ φιλοτίμως παρέσχεν. καὶ ποιουμένῳ τὴν ἐπὶ Πάρθους
αὐτῷ στρατείαν συνεξώρμησεν Ὑρκανός. μάρτυς δὲ τούτων ἡμῖν
5 ἐστιν καὶ Νικόλαος ὁ Δαμασκηνὸς οὕτως ἱστορῶν· (251) «τρόπαιον
δὲ στήσας Ἀντίοχος ἐπὶ τῷ Λύκῳ ποταμῷ νικήσας Ἰνδάτην τὸν
Πάρθων στρατηγὸν αὐτόθι ἔμεινεν ἡμέρας δύο δεηθέντος Ὑρκανοῦ
τοῦ Ἰουδαίου διά τινα ἑορτὴν πάτριον, ἐν ᾗ τοῖς Ἰουδαίοις οὐκ ἦν
νόμιμον ἐξοδεύειν.»

6 σινδάτην PFV   indatim Lat.   Σίνδαν τινὰ Syncellus

(250) And he [scil. Hyrcanus] made a friendly alliance with Antiochus, and admitting him into the city, lavishly and generously supplied his army with all they needed. And when Antiochus undertook
an expedition against the Parthians, Hyrcanus set out with him. On
this we have the testimony of Nicolaus of Damascus, who writes as
follows. "After defeating Indates, the Parthian general, and setting
up a trophy at the Lycus river, Antiochus remained there two days at
the request of the Jew Hyrcanus because of a festival of his nation on
which it was not customary for the Jews to march out."

(trans. R. Marcus, LCL)

250 συνεξώρμησεν Ὑρκανός: John Hyrcan joined Antiochus VII Sidetes in his
campaign against the Parthians as a result of the victory of the Seleucid king over
the Jews. The war between Antiochus and the Jews went on till 132 B. C. E.; see
Schürer, I, p. 259, n. 5. On the war of Antiochus with the Parthians, see Niese, III,
pp. 297 f.; N. C. Debevoise, A Political History of Parthia, Chicago 1938, pp.
31 ff.; T. Fischer, "Untersuchungen zum Partherkrieg Antiochos' VII im Rahmen
der Seleukidengeschichte", Ph.D. Thesis, Tübingen 1970.
251 ἐπὶ τῷ Λύκῳ ποταμῷ: The river Lycus is the Great Zab.
νικήσας Ἰνδάτην: The event should be dated to 130 B. C. E. In 129 B. C. E., the
year of Antiochus' death, Hyrcan does not appear to have been with him any
longer; see Ant., XIII, 254.
Ὑρκανοῦ τοῦ Ἰουδαίου: From the fact that Hyrcan is designated here as a Jew one
may surmise that the quotation from Nicolaus does not derive from a consecutive
narrative of the history of Judaea, but from a chapter of Seleucid history instead;
cf. A. Büchler, JQR, IX (1897), pp. 313 ff.; Wacholder, op. cit. (supra, p. 232),
p. 59.

89

Historiae, apud: Josephus, Antiquitates Judaicae, XIII, 345–347 — Niese = F. Gr. Hist.,
II, A90, F93

(345) Πτολεμαῖος δὲ μετὰ τὴν νίκην προσκαταδραμὼν τὴν χώραν

1 προσκαταλαβὼν PF   peragrans Lat.

240

Nicolaus of Damascus

ὀψίας ἐπιγενομένης ἔν τισι κώμαις τῆς Ἰουδαίας κατέμεινεν, ἃς γυναικῶν
εὑρὼν μεστὰς καὶ νηπίων ἐκέλευσεν τοὺς στρατιώτας ἀποσφάττοντας
αὐτοὺς καὶ κρεουργοῦντας, ἔπειτα εἰς λέβητας ζέοντας ἐνιέντας τὰ μέλη
5 ἀπάρχεσθαι. (346) τοῦτο δὲ προσέταξεν, ἵν᾽ οἱ διαφυγόντες ἐκ τῆς μάχης
καὶ πρὸς αὑτοὺς ἐλθόντες σαρκοφάγους ὑπολάβωσιν εἶναι τοὺς πολεμίους,
καὶ διὰ τοῦτο ἔτι μᾶλλον αὐτοὺς καταπλαγῶσι ταῦτ᾽ ἰδόντες. (347) λέγει
δὲ καὶ Στράβων ⟨No. 101⟩ καὶ Νικόλαος, ὅτι τοῦτον αὐτοῖς ἐχρήσαντο
τὸν τρόπον, καθὼς κἀγὼ προείρηκα.

2 κώμαις] χώραις AMWE   5 ἀπέρχεσθαι Naber   6 καὶ om. AMWE
8 ἐχρήσατο Gutschmid

(345) After this victory Ptolemy overran other territory, and when
evening fell, halted in some villages of Judaea, which he found full of
women and infants; he thereupon commanded his soldiers to cut their
throats and chop them up, and then to fling the pieces into boiling
cauldrons and to taste of them. (346) This order he gave that those who
had escaped from the battle and had returned to their homes might get
the notion that the enemy were eaters of human flesh, and so might
be terrified by this sight. (347) And both Strabo and Nicolaus say
they treated the Jews in the manner which I have just mentioned.

(trans. R. Marcus, *LCL*)

See the commentary to Strabo, *Historica Hypomnemata* (No. 101); see also
Wacholder, *op. cit.* (supra, p. 232), p. 61.

90

Historiae, apud: Josephus, *Antiquitates Judaicae*, XIV, 8–9 — Niese = F42R = *F. Gr. Hist.*, II,
A90, F96

(8) Φίλος δέ τις Ὑρκανοῦ Ἰδουμαῖος, Ἀντίπατρος λεγόμενος, πολλῶν
μὲν εὐπόρει χρημάτων, δραστήριος δὲ ὢν τὴν φύσιν καὶ στασιαστὴς
ἀλλοτρίως εἶχεν πρὸς τὸν Ἀριστόβουλον καὶ διαφόρως διὰ τὴν πρὸς
τὸν Ὑρκανὸν εὔνοιαν. (9) Νικόλαος μέντοι φησὶν ὁ Δαμασκηνὸς
5 τοῦτον εἶναι γένος ἐκ τῶν πρώτων Ἰουδαίων τῶν ἐκ Βαβυλῶνος
εἰς τὴν Ἰουδαίαν ἀφικομένων. ταῦτα δὲ λέγει χαριζόμενος Ἡρώδῃ
τῷ παιδὶ αὐτοῦ βασιλεῖ τῶν Ἰουδαίων ἐκ τύχης τινὸς γενομένῳ.

(8) But there was a certain friend of Hyrcanus, an Idumaean called
Antipater, who, having a large fortune and being by nature a man of
action and a trouble-maker, was unfriendly to Aristobulus and quar-

241

relled with him because of his friendliness toward Hyrcanus. (9) Nicolaus of Damascus, to be sure, says that his family belonged to the leading Jews who came to Judaea from Babylon. But he says this in order to please Antipater's son Herod, who became king of the Jews by a certain turn of fortune. (trans. R. Marcus, *LCL*)

9 τοῦτον εἶναι γένος ἐκ τῶν πρώτων Ἰουδαίων: On the other hand, Josephus consistently maintains that Antipater was an Idumaean. In the parallel narrative (*BJ*, I, 123) Josephus does not mention Nicolaus' version of the Jewish origin of Antipater. He simply states Antipater's Idumaean ancestry, though he emphasizes the nobility of this ancestry. In *Antiquitates*, Josephus criticizes Nicolaus for embellishing Herod's family. Antipater no doubt belonged to one of the noble Idumaean families that had become proselytes in the time of John Hyrcan. His father and namesake (Antipas = Antipater) had already served as strategos of Idumaea under Alexander Jannaeus and his wife, Queen Alexandra; see *Ant.*, XIV, 10. In the eyes of many Jews this Idumaean ancestry constituted a serious obstacle to Herod's becoming King of Judaea; see, e.g., the contention of his rival Antigonus before the Roman commander Silo and his army (*Ant.*, XIV, 403): ὡς παρὰ τὴν αὐτῶν δικαιοσύνην Ἡρώδῃ δώσουσιν τὴν βασιλείαν ἰδιώτῃ τε ὄντι καὶ Ἰδουμαίῳ, τουτέστιν ἡμιουδαίῳ. The non-Jewish origin of the house was remembered as late as the time of King Agrippa, who, loyal to Judaism, shed tears when he came to the passage of Deuteronomy (xvii : 14 ff.) where it is written that only Israelites may be appointed king. The people present then had to assure him that he was their brother, i.e. a Jew; see *M. Sota* vii : 8; Derenbourg, pp. 216 f. It is, therefore, not surprising that pro-Herodian propaganda attempted to legitimatize Herod's royalty by asserting that his ancestors were Jews who had returned from the Babylonian Exile. On the other hand, a hostile tradition grudged him even his Idumaean ancestry and stated that Herod's grandfather, also called Herod, had been a hierodule in the temple of Apollo at Ascalon, and that Antipater had been carried away to Idumaea by brigands; cf. Justinus Martyr, *Dialogus cum Tryphone*, 52; Eusebius, *Historia Ecclesiastica*, I, 6 : 2; 7 : 11. Cf. also the derivative traditions referred to by Schürer, I, p. 292, n. 3; H. Gelzer, *Sextus Julius Africanus*, I, Leipzig 1880, pp. 258 ff.; Otto, pp. 1 f. Schalit argues that this hostile tradition arose in anti-Herodian Jewish circles, and that the Christians only took it over; see A. Schalit, *Annual of the Swedish Theological Institute*, I (1962), pp. 109 ff.

91

Historiae, apud: Josephus, *Antiquitates Judaicae*, XIV, 66–68 — Niese = *F. Gr Hist.*, II, A90, F98

(66) Καὶ γὰρ ἁλούσης τῆς πόλεως περὶ τρίτον μῆνα τῇ τῆς νηστείας ἡμέρᾳ κατὰ ἐνάτην καὶ ἑβδομηκοστὴν καὶ ἑκατοστὴν ὀλυμπιάδα ὑπατευόντων Γαΐου Ἀντωνίου καὶ Μάρκου Τυλλίου Κικέρωνος οἱ

1 τρίτον] τέταρτον Scaliger / τῇ om. FLAMVW, Lat. (?)   2 τὴν ἐνάτην
   FLAMVW   3 Τυλλίου Niese   τυλαίου P   τουλίου FLAMW

Nicolaus of Damascus

πολέμιοι μὲν εἰσπεσόντες ἔσφαττον τοὺς ἐν τῷ ἱερῷ, (67) οἱ δὲ πρὸς
5 ταῖς θυσίαις οὐδὲν ἧττον ἱερουργοῦντες διετέλουν, οὔτε ὑπὸ τοῦ φόβου
τοῦ περὶ τῆς ψυχῆς οὔθ᾽ ὑπὸ τοῦ πλήθους τῶν ἤδη πεφονευμένων
ἀναγκασθέντες ἀποδρᾶναι πᾶν θ᾽ ὅ τι δέοι παθεῖν τοῦτο παρ᾽ αὐτοῖς
ὑπομεῖναι τοῖς βωμοῖς κρεῖττον εἶναι νομίζοντες ἢ παρελθεῖν τι τῶν
νομίμων. (68) ὅτι δὲ οὐ λόγος ταῦτα μόνον ἐστὶν ἐγκώμιον ψευδοῦς
10 εὐσεβείας ἐμφανίζων, ἀλλ᾽ ἀλήθεια, μαρτυροῦσι πάντες οἱ τὰς κατὰ
Πομπήιον πράξεις ἀναγράψαντες, ἐν οἷς καὶ Στράβων ⟨No. 104⟩ καὶ
Νικόλαος καὶ πρὸς αὐτοῖς Τίτος Λίβιος ⟨No. 132⟩ ὁ τῆς Ῥωμαϊκῆς
ἱστορίας συγγραφεύς.

4 ἐπιπεσόντες E / ἔσφαζον FLAMW   6 πλήθους] dolore Lat. /
πεφονευμένων Niese   φονευμένων P   φονευομένων FLAMVW

(66) And indeed when the city was taken, in the third month, on
the Fast Day, in the hundred and seventy-ninth Olympiad, in the consulship of Gaius Antonius and Marcus Tullius Cicero, and the enemy
rushed in and were slaughtering the Jews in the temple, (67) those who
were busied with the sacrifices none the less continued to perform the
sacred ceremonies; nor were they compelled, either by fear for their
lives or by the great number of those already slain, to run away, but
thought it better to endure whatever they might have to suffer there
beside the altars than to neglect any of the ordinances. (68) And that
this is not merely a story to set forth the praises of a fictitious piety,
but the truth, is attested by all those who have narrated the exploits
of Pompey, among them Strabo and Nicolaus and, in addition, Titus
Livius, the author of a History of Rome.   (trans. R. Marcus, *LCL*)

66 καὶ γὰρ ἁλούσης τῆς πόλεως: See the commentary to Strabo, *Historica
Hypomnemata* (No. 104).

92

Historiae, apud: Josephus, *Antiquitates Judaicae* XIV, 104 — Niese = *F. Gr. Hist.*, II, A90, F97

Περὶ δὲ τῆς Πομπηίου καὶ Γαβινίου στρατείας ἐπὶ Ἰουδαίους γράφει
Νικόλαος ὁ Δαμασκηνὸς καὶ Στράβων ὁ Καππάδοξ ⟨No. 106⟩ οὐδὲν
ἕτερος ἑτέρου καινότερον λέγων.

1 στρατιᾶς FL

Now the expeditions of Pompey and Gabinius against the Jews have

243

From Herodotus to Plutarch

been written about by Nicolaus of Damascus and Strabo of Cappadocia, neither of whom differs in any respect from the other.

(trans. R. Marcus, *LCL*)

Περὶ δὲ τῆς Πομπηίου: See the commentary to Strabo, *Historica Hypomnemata* (No. 106).

93

Historiae, apud: Josephus, *Antiquitates Judaicae* XVI, 179–185 — Niese = F44R = *F. Gr. Hist.*, II, A90, F101–102

(179) ʿΟ γὰρ ʿΗρώδης πολλοῖς τοῖς ἀναλώμασιν εἴς τε τὰς ἔξω ‹χρείας› καὶ τὰς ἐν τῇ βασιλείᾳ χρώμενος, ἀκηκοὼς ἔτι τάχιον ὡς ʿΥρκανὸς... ἀνοίξας τὸν Δαυίδου τάφον ἀργυρίου λάβοι τρισχίλια τάλαντα... *(180)* ἀνοίξας τὸν τάφον εἰσέρχεται... *(181)* ἀποθέσιμα μὲν οὖν χρήματα
5 καθάπερ ʿΥρκανὸς οὐχ εὗρεν, κόσμον δὲ χρυσοῦν καὶ κειμηλίων πολύν, ὃν ἀνείλετο πάντα. σπουδὴν δ᾽ εἶχεν ἐπιμελεστέραν ποιούμενος τὴν ἔρευναν ἐνδοτέρω τε χωρεῖν καὶ κατὰ τὰς θήκας, ἐν αἷς ἦν Δαυίδου καὶ τοῦ Σολομῶνος τὰ σώματα· *(182)* καὶ δύο μὲν αὐτῷ τῶν δορυφόρων διεφθάρησαν φλογὸς ἔνδοθεν εἰσιοῦσιν ἀπαντώσης, ὡς ἐλέγετο, περίφοβος
10 δ᾽ αὐτὸς ἐξῄει, καὶ τοῦ δέους ἱλαστήριον μνῆμα λευκῆς πέτρας ἐπὶ τῷ στομίῳ κατεσκευάσατο πολυτελὲς τῇ δαπάνῃ. *(183)* τούτου καὶ Νικόλαος ὁ κατ᾽ αὐτὸν ἱστοριογράφος μέμνηται τοῦ κατασκευάσματος, οὐ μὴν ὅτι καὶ κατῆλθεν, οὐκ εὐπρεπῆ τὴν πρᾶξιν ἐπιστάμενος. διατελεῖ δὲ καὶ τἆλλα τοῦτον τὸν τρόπον χρώμενος τῇ γραφῇ· *(184)* ζῶντι
15 γὰρ ἐν τῇ βασιλείᾳ καὶ σὺν αὐτῷ κεχαρισμένως ἐκείνῳ καὶ καθ᾽ ὑπηρεσίαν ἀνέγραφεν, μόνων ἁπτόμενος τῶν εὔκλειαν αὐτῷ φερόντων, πολλὰ δὲ καὶ τῶν ἐμφανῶς ἀδίκων ἀντικατασκευάζων καὶ μετὰ πάσης σπουδῆς ἐπικρυπτόμενος, *(185)* ὅς γε καὶ τὸν Μαριάμμης θάνατον καὶ τῶν παίδων αὐτῆς οὕτως ὠμῶς τῷ βασιλεῖ πεπραγμένον εἰς εὐπρέπειαν
20 ἀνάγειν βουλόμενος ἐκείνης τε ἀσέλγειαν καὶ τῶν νεανίσκων ἐπιβουλὰς καταψεύδεται, καὶ διατετέλεκεν τῇ γραφῇ τὰ μὲν πεπραγμένα δικαίως τῷ βασιλεῖ περιττότερον ἐγκωμιάζων, ὑπὲρ δὲ τῶν παρανομηθέντων ἐσπουδασμένως ἀπολογούμενος.

1 ἔξω ‹χρείας› Bekker   6 ἀνείλετο E   ἀνείλατο codd.   7 κατὰ] καταγνύναι Marcus in ed. Loeb   10 δέους] θεοῦ Marcus   11 τῶν στομίων E / πολυτελεστάτῃ ΑΜΕ   *magnificentissimis* Lat.   14 ζῶν τε Cocceji   συζῶν γε Gutschmid   16 γέγραφεν Naber   ἔγραφεν Niese / πρὸς εὔκλειαν ΑΜW   19 πεπραγμένον ed. pr.   πεπραγμένων codd.

(179) Now Herod, who had spent large sums of money both on external needs and on those of the realm and had heard even earlier

244

Nicolaus of Damascus

that Hyrcanus... had opened David's tomb and taken three thousand talents of silver... (180) opened the tomb and entered it...(181) Unlike Hyrcanus, however, he did not find money stored there but he did find many ornaments of gold and other valuable deposits, all of which he took away. He was intent upon making a more careful search, penetrating farther and breaking open[1] the coffins in which the bodies of David and Solomon lay. (182) But as two of his bodyguards were destroyed, it is said, by a flame that met them as they entered, the king himself became frightened, and as propitiation of the terror he built at the entrance a memorial of white marble, which was a huge expense. (183) This structure is also mentioned by his contemporary, the historian Nicolaus, but he does not say that the king also went down [into the tomb], for he considered this action improper. Indeed Nicolaus continues to write in this manner about other things. (184) For since he lived in Herod's realm and was one of his associates, he wrote to please him and to be of service to him, dwelling only on those things that redounded to his glory, and transforming his obviously unjust acts into the opposite or concealing them with the greatest care. (185) For example, in his desire to give a colour of respectability to the putting to death of Mariamme and her sons, which had been so cruelly ordered by the king, Nicolaus makes false charges of licentiousness against her and of treachery against the youths. And throughout his work he has been consistent in excessively praising the king for his just acts, and zealously apologizing for his unlawful ones.

(trans. R. Marcus, *LCL*)

1 According to the emendation of Marcus.

183 διατελεῖ δὲ καὶ τἆλλα τοῦτον τὸν τρόπον...: Josephus' attack on Nicolaus is not the result of his use of a new anti-Herodian source; see, e.g., Otto, p. 11 ff.; G. Hölscher, *Die Hohenpriesterliste bei Josephus und die evangelische Chronologie,* Heidelberg 1940, pp. 3 f. It is either an expression of Josephus' change of mind or of the altered circumstances in which he lived; see the introduction.

185 ἐκείνης τε ἀσέλγειαν καὶ τῶν νεανίσκων ἐπιβουλὰς καταψεύδεται: No clue is found in *De Vita Sua* as to whether Mariamme was guilty. However, from No. 97 we see that Nicolaus clearly states that her sons were not guilty, but only victims of the machinations of Antipater. He expresses another view in *Historiae;* cf. Otto, p. 4, note, against the view of J. v. Destinon, *Die Quellen des Flavius Josephus,* pp. 114 ff. There are even some vestiges in *Antiquitates* of Nicolaus' views on the guilt of Alexander and Aristobulus, as expressed in *Historiae;* see especially the speech of Nicolaus in *Ant.,* XVII, 108: νεωτέρους γὰρ καὶ κακίᾳ συμβούλων διεφθαρμένους ἀπαλεῖψαι τὰ τῆς φύσεως δικαιώματα ἀρχῆς θᾶσσον ἢ χρῆν μεταποιεῖσθαι σπουδάσαντας... Even in this speech, however, we find allusions to Antipater's false accusations of the brothers (*ibid.,* 114). For the expression ἐκείνης

τε ἀσέλγειαν, cf. *BJ*, I, 439: δὶ ὑπερβολὴν ἀσελγείας ἀποῦσαν δείξειεν ἑαυτὴν ἀνθρώπῳ γυναικομανοῦντι (scil. Mariamme to Marc Antony).

94

De Vita Sua, apud: Constantinus Porphyrogenitus, *Excerpta de Virtutibus et Vitiis*, I — Büttner-Wobst, p. 326 = *F. Gr. Hist.*, II, A90, F133

⟨p. 326⟩ *** καὶ παρακαλέσας οἷα δὴ φιλόσοφον καὶ ἀμνησίκακον ἐν πολὺ πλείονι ἦγε τιμῇ καὶ εὐνοίᾳ.

And Herod, exhorting Nicolaus as befits a philosopher and a man who forgives, treated him with much more respect and goodwill.

Καὶ παρακαλέσας οἷα δὴ φιλόσοφον καὶ ἀμνησίκακον: The φιλόσοφος καὶ ἀμνησίκακος is Nicolaus, Herod being the subject of the sentence. We do not know what is implied here by ἀμνησίκακος, namely, what wrong he had to forgive.

95

De Vita Sua, apud: Constantinus Porphyrogenitus, *Excerpta de Virtutibus et Vitiis*, I — Büttner-Wobst, pp. 326f. = *F. Gr. Hist.*, II, A90, F134

⟨p. 326⟩ Ὅτι ἐπράχθη τι φιλανθρωπίας πολλῆς ἐχόμενον Νικολάῳ. Ἰλιεῖς γάρ, ἀφικνουμένης νύκτωρ ὡς αὐτοὺς Ἰουλίας τῆς Καίσαρος μὲν θυγατρός, γυναικὸς δὲ Ἀγρίππα, καὶ τοῦ Σκαμάνδρου μεγάλου ῥυέντος ὑπὸ χειμάρρων πολλῶν, κινδυνευούσης περὶ τὴν διάβασιν
5 ἀπολέσθαι σὺν τοῖς κομίζουσιν αὐτὴν οἰκέταις οὐκ ᾔσθοντο. ἐφ᾽ οἷς ἀγανακτήσας ὁ Ἀγρίππας, ὅτι οὐ παρεβοήθησαν οἱ Ἰλιεῖς, δέκα μυριάσιν αὐτοὺς ἐζημίωσεν ἀργύριον. οἱ δὲ ἀπόρως ἔχοντες, καὶ ἅμα οὐ προϋπιδόμενοι τὸν χειμῶνα οὐδὲ ὅτι ἐξίοι ἡ παῖς, Ἀγρίππᾳ μὲν οὐδ᾽ ὁτιοῦν εἰπεῖν ἐτόλμησαν, ἥκοντα δὲ τὸν Νικόλαον δεόμενοι παρα-
10 σχεῖν αὐτοῖς Ἡρώδην βοηθὸν καὶ προστάτην. καὶ ὃς μάλα προθύμως ὑπέστη διὰ τὴν τῆς πόλεως δόξαν καὶ ἐδεήθη τοῦ βασιλέως διηγήσατό τε αὐτῷ τὸ πρᾶγμα, ὡς οὐ δικαίως αὐτοῖς ὀργίζεται, οὔτε προειπὼν ὅτι πέμποι τὴν γυναῖκα ὡς αὐτοὺς οὔθ᾽ ὅλως ἐκείνων προῃσθημένων διὰ τὸ νυκτὸς ἰέναι. τέλος δ᾽ οὖν ἀναδεξάμενος ὁ ἀνὴρ τὴν προστασίαν
15 εὑρίσκεται αὐτοῖς τὴν ἄφεσιν τῆς ζημίας καὶ τὴν ὑπὲρ ταύτης ἐπιστολήν, ἅτε δὴ ἀπεληλυθότων ἤδη διὰ τὸ ἀπογνῶναι τὴν ἀπόλυσιν, Νικολάῳ δίδωσι πλέοντι ἐπὶ Χίου καὶ Ῥόδου, ἔνθα ἦσαν αὐτῷ οἱ υἱεῖς· αὐτὸς

8 προϋπιδόμενοι Dindorf   προυπειδόμενοι P   9 Νικόλαον ⟨ἐπεκαλοῦντο⟩ Müller   10 αὐτοῖς Valesius   αὐτοῖς Büttner-Wobst   αὐτοὺς P

Nicolaus of Damascus

γὰρ ἐπὶ Παφλαγονίας ᾔει σὺν Ἀγρίππᾳ. Νικόλαος δὲ ἐκ τῆς Ἀμισοῦ πλεύσας ἐπὶ Βυζάντιον κἀκεῖθεν εἰς τὴν Τρῳάδα γῆν ἀνέβη εἰς 20 Ἴλιον καὶ τὴν τῆς ἀπολύσεως τοῦ ⟨p. 327⟩ χρέους ἐπιστολὴν ἀποδοὺς σφόδρα ὑπὸ τῶν Ἰλιέων αὐτός τε καὶ ἔτι μᾶλλον ὁ βασιλεὺς ἐτιμήθη.

A great act of humanity was done by Nicolaus. The people of Ilium did not know that Julia, the daughter of Caesar and wife of Agrippa, came to them at night-time and was in danger of being drowned with the servants carrying her when crossing the Scamander which was overflowing because of the many torrents. Agrippa, therefore, became vexed with the people of Ilium because they had not come to his wife's succour and imposed on them a fine of hundred thousand silver drachmas. The people of Ilium were at a loss to know what to do. They did not dare to tell Agrippa that they had not foreseen the storm and had not even known that the girl had gone out, and so they approached Nicolaus, who had come there, with the request to let them have Herod as a helper and protector. Nicolaus undertook this eagerly because of the city's fame. He approached the king with the request and told him about the matter, namely, that there was no just reason for Agrippa's anger with the people of Ilium, as he had not told them beforehand that he had sent his wife to them, nor had they by any means perceived it since she went at night. At last Herod undertook their protection and succeeded in freeing them from the fine. The Ilian representatives had already left, since they despaired of obtaining annulment of the fine, and so Herod gave the letter concerning it to Nicolaus, who was then on the point of sailing to Chios and Rhodes where his sons were staying. Herod himself went to Paphlagonia with Agrippa. Nicolaus, having sailed from Amisus to Byzantium and thence to the land of Troy, went up to Ilium, and delivering to its people the letter concerning the cancellation of the debt he, and even more so the king, were very much honoured by the people of Ilium.

γυναικὸς δὲ Ἀγρίππα: Agrippa acted as regent of the eastern part of the Roman Empire between 16 and 13 B. C. E. The presence in Asia of his wife Julia, the daughter of Augustus, though not mentioned in other literary sources, is well attested by inscriptional evidence; see M. Reinhold, *Marcus Agrippa*, Geneva – New York 1933, p. 117. The incident in the vicinity of Ilium occurred at the time that Agrippa was dealing with the situation in the Bosporus (14 B. C. E.). For Agrippa's sojourn in the East, see Reinhold, *op. cit.*, pp. 106 ff.; D. Magie, *Roman Rule in Asia Minor*, I, Princeton 1950, pp. 476 ff.

παρασχεῖν αὐτοῖς Ἡρώδην βοηθὸν καὶ προστάτην: The intervention of Herod on behalf of Ilium is only briefly referred to by Josephus; see *Ant.*, XVI, 26: Ἰλιεῦσι μέν γε αὐτὸν διήλλαξεν ὀργιζόμενον. Josephus does not state the reasons for this

247

From Herodotus to Plutarch

anger, and he wholly ignores Nicolaus' part in the affair. Herod came to Asia
to aid Agrippa in his expedition to the Bosporus. He followed after Agrippa with
his ships and caught up with him at Sinope. According to Josephus (*Ant.*, XVI,
22), who is obviously dependent on Nicolaus, Herod proved himself extremely
useful to the Roman statesmen: πᾶν γοῦν ἦν αὐτῷ κατὰ τὴν στρατείαν Ἡρώδης
ἔν τε τοῖς πραγματικοῖς συναγωνιστής, κἂν τοῖς κατὰ μέρος σύμβουλος, ἡδὺς δὲ
κἂν ταῖς ἀνέσεσι, καὶ μόνος ἀπάντων κοινωνός.
They did not return by sea, but made their way via Paphlagonia, Cappadocia and
Great Phrygia to Ephesus; from Ephesus they crossed the sea to Samos. See also
Sylloge, No. 776: Agrippa is honoured in an inscription by the people of Ilium.
εὑρίσκεται αὐτοῖς τὴν ἄφεσιν τῆς ζημίας: The friendship between Agrippa and
Herod was of old standing. It dates from as early as 23–22 B. C. E. (or 22–21
B. C. E.), that is, during Agrippa's first stay in the East; see Schürer, I, p. 369,
n. 11; Reinhold, *op. cit.* (supra, p. 247), p. 84, n. 47. In 15 B. C. E. Agrippa paid a
visit to Herod in Judaea, made a sacrifice in the Temple of Jerusalem and even
feasted the population of Jerusalem; see *Ant.*, XVI, 13 ff.; Philo, *Legatio ad Gaium*,
294 ff. When some of the citizens of the Greek city of Gadara accused Herod
before Agrippa, he did not give them a hearing, but sent them in chains to the King;
see *Ant.*, XV, 351; cf. Otto, p.74. See also the exaggerated evaluation of the relations
between Agrippa and Herod in *Ant.*, XV, 361, presumably stemming from Nicolaus:
Ἀγρίππας δὲ μετὰ Καίσαρα πρῶτον ἀπεδίδου φιλίας τόπον Ἡρώδῃ. On Agrippa's
attitude to the Jews of the Diaspora, see Leon, pp. 140 f. On the relations between
Herod and Agrippa, see V. Gardthausen, *Augustus und seine Zeit*, Vol. I, Part 2,
Leipzig 1896, pp. 836 ff.; R. Daniel, "M. Vipsanius Agrippa", Ph. D. Thesis,
Breslau 1933, pp. 31 ff.; R. Hanslik, PW, Ser. 2, IX, pp. 1262 ff.
Herod's intercession for the inhabitants of Ilium was not the only benefaction he
bestowed on the Greek inhabitants of Asia at the time of his sojourn with Agrippa —
he paid also the money owed by the people of Chios to Caesar's procurators; see
Ant., XVI, 26; cf. F. Millar, *JRS*, LIII (1963), p. 32.

96

De Vita Sua, apud: Constantinus Porphyrogenitus, *Excerpta de Virtutibus et Vitiis*, I — Büttner-
Wobst, p. 327 = *F. Gr. Hist.*, II, A90, F135

⟨p. 327⟩ Ὅτι Ἡρώδης πάλιν διαμεθεὶς τὸν φιλοσοφίας ἔρωτα, ὃ φιλεῖ
τοῖς ἐν ὑπεροχῇ οὖσι συμβαίνειν διὰ τὸ πλῆθος τῶν ἐξαλλαττόντων
αὐτοὺς ἀγαθῶν, ἐπεθύμησε πάλιν ῥητορικῆς καὶ Νικόλαον ἠνάγκαζε
συρρητορεύειν αὐτῷ, καὶ κοινῇ ἐρρητόρευον. αὖθις δ' ἱστορίας αὐτὸν
5 ἔλαβεν ⟨ἔρως⟩, ἐπαινέσαντος Νικολάου τὸ πρᾶγμα καὶ πολιτικώτατον
εἶναι λέγοντος, χρήσιμον δὲ καὶ βασιλεῖ, ὡς τὰ τῶν προτέρων ἔργα
καὶ πράξεις ἱστοροίη. καὶ ἐπὶ τοῦτο ὁρμήσας προύτρεψε καὶ Νικόλαον
πραγματευθῆναι τὰ περὶ ἱστορίαν. ὁ δὲ μειζόνως ἔτι ὥρμησεν ἐπὶ τὸ
πρᾶγμα, πᾶσαν ἀθροίσας τὴν ἱστορίαν μέγαν τε πόνον ὑποστὰς καὶ

1 ὃ φιλεῖ Valesius   â ὀφείλη P   5 ἔλαβεν ⟨ἔρως⟩ Büttner-Wobst   ⟨ἔρως⟩
  ἔλαβεν Valesius   6 πρότερον Büttner-Wobst

248

Nicolaus of Damascus

10 οἷον οὐκ ἄλλος· ἐν πολλῷ δὲ χρόνῳ φιλοπονήσας ἐξετέλεσεν αὐτὴν
ἔλεγέ τε ὡς τοῦτον τὸν ἄθλον Εὐρυσθεὺς εἰ προύτεινεν Ἡρακλεῖ,
σφόδρα ἂν αὐτὸν ἀπέτρυσεν. ἐκ τούτου πλέων εἰς Ῥώμην ὡς Καίσαρα
Ἡρώδης ἐπῆγε<το> τὸν Νικόλαον ὁμοῦ ἐπὶ τῆς αὐτῆς νηός, καὶ κοινῇ
ἐφιλοσόφουν.

11-12 τοῦτον... ἀπέτρυσεν Suda s.   ἀπετρύετο   13 ἐπήγετο Corais
ἐπῆγε P / ὁμοῦ Valesius   ὁμοίως P

Herod again having given up his enthusiasm for philosophy, as it
commonly happens with people in authority because of the abundance
of goods that distract them, was eager again for rhetoric and pressed
Nicolaus to practise rhetoric together with him, and they practised
rhetoric together. Again, he was seized by love of history, Nicolaus
praising the subject and saying that it was proper for a statesman, and
useful also for a king, to know the works and achievements of the
former generations. And Herod, becoming eager to study this subject, also influenced Nicolaus to busy himself with history. He applied
himself vigorously to that undertaking, collecting material for the
whole of history, and working incomparably harder than other people,
completed the project after a long toil. He used to say that if Eurys-
theus had suggested this task to Heracles, he would have very much
worn him out. Then Herod, when sailing to Rome to meet Caesar,
took Nicolaus with him on the same ship, and they discussed philosophy together.

Ἡρώδης πάλιν διαμεθεὶς τὸν φιλοσοφίας ἔρωτα... ἐπεθύμησε πάλιν ῥητορικῆς:
The intellectual pursuits of Herod are not mentioned in the historical works of
Josephus. *Ant.*, XV, 373, refers only incidentally to Herod's attending a school
when he was a child. However, Josephus has more to say about the education of
the royal sons, all of whom presumably received what was then considered a good
education; see *Ant.*, XVI, 242, where there is a reference to Andromachus and
Gemellus as men who helped to educate the royal sons; cf. also Otto, p. 90. *Ant.*,
XVI 203, alludes to the good education received by the sons of Herod: τὸ νῦν
ἐπιμελὲς αὐτῶν καὶ πρὸς παιδείαν ἐσπουδασμένον. Herod's interest in the
various aspects of contemporary culture conforms with the general trend of the
Augustan age to foster culture. It is noteworthy that some of the vassal kings of
Rome became well-known writers in Greek, e.g. Archelaus of Cappadocia; see
Berger, PW, II, pp. 451 f. Another, somewhat later, was Juba of Mauretania.
καὶ κοινῇ ἐρρητόρευον: Wacholder suggests, in view of the apologetic nature of
the Autobiography, that Nicolaus attempts to defend his association with a man
notorious for inhumanity by stressing Herod's intellectual activity; see Wacholder,
op. cit. (supra, p. 232), p. 30. On Nicolaus as teacher of the children of Antony
and Cleopatra, see the introduction.
ἐν πολλῷ δὲ χρόνῳ φιλοπονήσας ἐξετέλεσεν αὐτήν: Since the historical work of

249

Nicolaus also includes events subsequent to the death of Herod, the whole work could not have been published during the lifetime of the King. Large parts of it, however, could have appeared, especially as Nicolaus was interested in gratifying his benefactor; cf. Gutschmid, V, p. 537.

ἔλεγέ τε ὡς τοῦτον τὸν ἆθλον...: The *Historiae* of Nicolaus, which consisted of 144 books, was indeed one of the most voluminous works of the historical literature of Antiquity. The histories of Polybius and Diodorus consisted of only forty books each, but Livy's *Ab Urbe Condita* approaches it in length, and it was surpassed by Valerius Antias' work.

ἐκ τούτου: This sounds out of place here, and it is likely that the excerptor omitted some passage that would have accounted for these words; cf. R. Laqueur, PW, XVII, p. 368.

πλέων εἰς ῾Ρώμην ὡς Καίσαρα ῾Ηρώδης: Josephus refers to Herod's three voyages to Rome during the principate of Augustus.

a. The first voyage is recounted in *Ant.*, XVI, 6. It was undertaken, according to Josephus, for the purpose of meeting Augustus and seeing his sons Alexander and Aristobulus, who were residing at Rome. Herod was given a friendly reception by Augustus, and he took his sons home. This voyage should be dated between 19 and 16 B. C. E.; see Schürer I, p. 370. Korach suggests the years 18 or 17; see L. Korach, *MGWJ*, XXXVIII (1894), pp. 529 f. Corbishley dates it to 17–16 B. C. E.; see T. Corbishley, *JTS*, XXXVI (1935), pp. 27 ff.

b. The second voyage is connected with the quarrel between Herod and his sons. Herod accused his sons before Augustus in order to avoid a careless or rash mistake; see *Ant.*, XVI, 90 ff.; *BJ*, I, 452 ff. According to *Ant.*, XVI, 91, the meeting took place at Aquileia. An important piece of evidence for dating this event is afforded by *Ant.*, XVI, 128: ἐν δὲ ταῖς ὑστέραις ἡμέραις ῾Ηρώδης μὲν ἐδωρεῖτο Καίσαρα τριακοσίοις ταλάντοις, θέας τε καὶ διανομὰς ποιούμενον τῷ ῾Ρωμαίων δήμῳ. This is usually taken to imply the *congiaria* of 12 B. C. E. referred to in the *Monumentum Ancyranum*, 15; see Korach, *op. cit.*, pp. 530 ff.; Schürer, I, p. 371; Corbishley, *op. cit.*, pp. 30 ff.

c. Herod's third journey to Rome is alluded to in *Ant.*, XVI, 271; see Schürer, I, p. 373, n. 17. However, some scholars think this journey a fiction, originating in a duplication of the second journey by Josephus; see Korach, *op. cit.*, pp. 533 ff.; T. Corbishley, *JRS*, XXIV (1934), pp. 43 ff. In view of the fact that the reference to the journey occurs in the *Excerpta de Virtutibus*, where it follows the incident between Agrippa and the city of Ilium in 14 B. C. E., the journey mentioned here must be the second.

ἐπῆγετο τὸν Νικόλαον: In the works of Josephus there is no reference to Nicolaus accompanying Herod on any of his journeys to Rome.

97

De Vita Sua, apud: Constantinus Porphyrogenitus, *Excerpta de Insidiis* — de Boor, pp. 1 f. = F. Gr. Hist., II, A90, F136

⟨p. 1⟩ ῞Οτι ἐστράτευσεν ἐπὶ τὴν ᾿Αραβίαν ῾Ηρώδης, οὐ συνδοκοῦν Καίσαρι, ἐφ᾿ οἷς ἐκεῖνος ἠφίει φωνάς, καὶ ὀργὴν εἶχε χαλεπὴν εἰς τὸν ῾Ηρώδην ἐπέστειλέ τε αὐτῷ πικρότατα, καὶ τοὺς ἥκοντας παρ᾿ αὐτοῦ

πρέσβεις οὐ κατὰ κόσμον ἀπέλυσεν· ἀφικόμενος δ' ὡς Καίσαρα Νικόλαος
5 οὐ μόνον τῶν ἐγκλημάτων ἐρρύσατο ῾Ηρώδην, ἀλλὰ καὶ τὴν ὀργὴν
ἀπέστρεψεν ἐπὶ τοὺς κατηγόρους. ὁ μὲν οὖν ῎Αραψ ἤδη ἐτεθνήκει, τοῦ
δὲ διοικητοῦ ἤδη κατέγνω πεισθεὶς τῇ Νικολάου κατηγορίᾳ, καὶ
ὕστερον εὑρὼν κάκιστον ἀπέκτεινεν.

᾿Εν τούτῳ δὲ ῾Ηρώδου ὁ οἶκος ἐταράχθη, τοῦ πρεσβυτάτου τῶν υἱέων
10 τοὺς μετ' αὐτὸν δύω διαβάλλοντος ⟨ὡς⟩ ἐπιβουλεύοντας τῷ πατρί,
οἳ τῇ μὲν ἡλικίᾳ μετ' αὐτὸν ἦσαν, ἀξιώματι δὲ πρότεροι διὰ τὸ ἐκ
βασιλίδος γεγονέναι, τὸν δὲ ἐξ ἰδιώτιδος γυναικός. πρὶν δὲ ἐλθεῖν ἐκ
῾Ρώμης Νικόλαον ἐν συνεδρίῳ κατεδικάσθησαν οἱ νεανίσκοι, ⟨καὶ⟩
παρωξυσμένος εὖ μάλα ὁ πατὴρ ἔμελλεν αὐτοὺς ἀναιρήσειν· καταπλεύ-
15 σαντι δὲ Νικολάῳ περὶ τῶν γεγονότων ἀπήγγελλε καὶ σύμβουλον ἐποιεῖτο. ὁ δὲ αὐτῷ παρῄνεσεν ἀποθέσθαι αὐτοὺς ἔν τινι τῶν ἐρυμάτων, ἄχρις
ἂν ἐν τῷ πλέονι χρόνῳ βουλεύσαιτο περὶ αὐτῶν ἄμεινον, μὴ δοκοίη ὑπ'
ὀργῆς προαχθεὶς ἀνήκεστόν τι γνῶναι περὶ τῶν ἀναγκαίων. αἰσθόμενος
δὲ τοῦτο ᾿Αντίπατρος τόν τε Νικόλαον ὑπέβλεπε καὶ ἄλλους ἐπ' ἄλλοις
20 αὐτὸς καθιεὶς τὸν πατέρα ἐφόβει, ὡς αὐτίκα μάλα ἀναιρεθησόμενον
ὑπὸ τῶν νεανίσκων διεφθαρκότων καὶ τὸ στρατιωτικὸν ἅπαν, ὡς
ἔφη, καὶ τοὺς ἀπὸ τῆς θεραπείας, εἰ μὴ διὰ ταχέων ἐκποδῶν αὐτοὺς
ποιήσαιτο. καὶ ὃς δείσας περὶ αὐτοῦ θᾶττον ἢ κάλλιον ἐβουλεύσατο,
⟨p. 2⟩ οὐδὲν ἔτι μεταδοὺς Νικολάῳ, ἀλλὰ νύκτωρ τοὺς ἀναιρήσοντας
25 ὑποπέμψας. καὶ οἱ μὲν ἀπέθανον, ῾Ηρώδῃ δὲ τῶν συμπάντων ἤδη
γίνεται κακῶν ἀρχή, τὰ πρὸ τούτων εὖ ἐστώτων αὐτῷ τῶν πραγμάτων.
ἐχθρὸν δ' ἡγεῖτο ᾿Αντίπατρος Νικόλαον ἀνελὼν τοὺς ἀδελφούς, ἐμισεῖτό
γε μὴν δεινόν τι μῖσος οὐχ ὑπὸ τῆς βασιλείας μόνον, ἀλλὰ καὶ τῆς Συρίας
καὶ τῶν πέραν οἰκούντων. ἐχώρει δὲ ὁ λόγος καὶ εἰς ῾Ρώμην, καὶ οὐδεὶς
30 ἦν οὔτε μέγας οὔτε μικρός, ὃς οὐκ ἐμίσει τὸν ἄνθρωπον δι' ἀμφότερα,
καὶ ὅτι πολὺ κρείττους αὐτοῦ ἀδελφοὺς ἀπέκτεινε καὶ ὅτι τὸν πατέρα
ἔπεισε τοιούτου προσάψασθαι μύσους καὶ τὴν προϋποῦσαν εὔνοιαν αἰσχῦ-
ναι. ἐπεὶ δ' οὖν τὰ ἀκόλουθα δρῶν τοῖς προτέροις ἀνὴρ καὶ ἐπὶ τὸν πατέρα
ὥρμησε, θᾶττον ἐπειγόμενος τὴν βασιλείαν λαβεῖν, καὶ τὸ φάρμακον
35 ἐώνητο ἐξ Αἰγύπτου, ὅπερ ἐμήνυσεν εἷς τῶν κοινωνούντων τῆς πράξεως,
ἐβασάνιζέ τε τοὺς οἰκέτας αὐτοῦ ὁ πατήρ, οἳ δὴ τὸ σύμπαν φανερὸν
ἐποίησαν, ὡς καὶ τὴν τηθίδα ἔμελλεν ἀναιρήσειν καὶ τοὺς ἄλλους
ἀδελφοὺς ὄντας τούς τε τῶν ἀνῃρημένων παῖδας, ὡς μηδείς λείποιτο
κληρονόμος, ἐτύρευσε δέ τι μιαρὸν καὶ εἰς τὸν οἶκον Καίσαρος πολὺ
40 μεῖζον τῶν εἰς τὸ γένος παρανομημάτων, ἧκε μὲν ὁ τῆς Συρίας

7 πεισθεὶς edd.   τεισθεὶς S   10 διαβαλόντος Müller / ⟨ὡς⟩ edd.
13 ⟨καὶ⟩ edd.   16 ἄχρις] ς add. m²   23 αὐτοῦ edd.   αὑτοῦ S
24 ἔτι μεταδοὺς edd.   ἔτι μετὰ δὲ S   32 προϋποῦσαν]
προυπάρχουσαν? Müller

στρατηγὸς Οὖαρος καὶ οἱ ἄλλοι ἐπιμεληταί, καθίζει δὲ συνέδριον ὁ
πατὴρ αὐτοῦ, παρηνέχθη δὲ εἰς μέσον τὸ φάρμακον καὶ αἱ τῶν οἰκετῶν
βάσανοι τά τε ἐκ ʿΡώμης γράμματα, Νικολάῳ δὲ τὸν ἀγῶνα ἐπέτρεψεν
ὁ βασιλεύς. κατηγόρει μὲν οὗτος, ἀπελογεῖτο δὲ Ἀντίπατρος, ἔκρινεν
45 δὲ Οὖαρος μετὰ τῶν φίλων. καταδικάζεται δ᾽ οὖν Ἀντίπατρος, καὶ
τὴν ἐπὶ θανάτῳ παραδίδοται. Νικόλαος δὲ καὶ τότε παρῄνει πέμπειν
αὐτὸν ἐπὶ Καίσαρα, ἐπεὶ καὶ εἰς αὐτὸν ἠδίκησεν, καὶ ὅ τι ἂν ἐκεῖνος
γνῷ, τοῦτο πράττειν. ἔφθη δὲ τὰ παρὰ Καίσαρος γράμματα ἥκοντα
καὶ τῷ πατρὶ κολάζειν αὐτὸν ἐπιτρέποντα. καὶ ὁ μὲν ἐκολάσθη, ἀπέκτεινεν
50 δὲ καὶ ὁ Καῖσαρ τὴν συγκακουργήσασαν αὐτῷ ἀπελευθέραν. οὐδεὶς δὲ ἦν
ὃς οὐχὶ Νικόλαον * κάλλιστα κατηγορήσαντα τοῦ πατραλοίου τε καὶ
ἀδελφοκτόνου.
Μετὰ δὲ ταῦτα ὀλίγου χρόνου διελθόντος τελευτᾷ καὶ ὁ βασιλεύς, καὶ
τὸ ἔθνος ἐπανίσταται τοῖς τέκνοις αὐτοῦ καὶ τοῖς Ἕλλησιν. ἦσαν δὲ
55 πλείους μυρίων. γενομένης δὲ μάχης νικᾷ τὸ Ἑλληνικόν. ⟨p. 3⟩ καὶ ὁ
διάδοχος Ἀρχέλαος εἰς ʿΡώμην πλέων ἕνεκα τῆς ὅλης ἀρχῆς μετὰ τῶν
ἄλλων ἀδελφῶν παρακαλεῖ συμπλεῦσαι Νικόλαον, ἀναχωρεῖν ἤδη ὡς
ἑαυτὸν ἐγνωκότα· καὶ γὰρ ἦν περὶ ξ᾽ ἔτη· συνέπλευσε δ᾽ οὖν, καὶ εὗρεν
πάντα κατηγόρων πλέα ἐπὶ τὸν Ἀρχέλαον. χωρὶς μὲν γὰρ ὁ νεώτερος
60 ἀδελφὸς τῆς βασιλείας ἀντεποιεῖτο, χωρὶς δ᾽ οἱ συγγενεῖς ἅπαντες κατηγόρουν αὐτοῦ, οὐ τῷ νεωτέρῳ συναγωνιζόμενοι. ἐπρεσβεύσαντο δὲ καὶ αἱ
ὑφ᾽ Ἡρώδῃ Ἑλληνίδες πόλεις αἰτούμεναι τὴν ἐλευθερίαν παρὰ Καίσαρος,
καὶ ὅλον δὲ τὸ Ἰουδαίων ἔθνος ἐπικαλοῦν φόνον τρισχιλίων ἀνδρῶν τῶν
ἐν τῇ μάχῃ πεσόντων, καὶ ἀξιοῦν μάλιστα μὲν ὑπὸ Καίσαρι εἶναι, εἰ δὲ
65 μή, ὑπό γε οὖν τῷ νεωτέρῳ ἀδελφῷ. τοσούτων δὲ δικῶν ἐπηγγελμένων,
ἀγωνισάμενος ὑπὲρ Ἀρχελάου Νικόλαος τὸν πρὸς συγγενεῖς ἀγῶνα
πρῶτον κατώρθωσεν, ἔπειτα δὲ τὸν πρὸς τοὺς ὑπηκόους Ἰουδαίους·
τὸν μέντοι πρὸς τὰς Ἑλληνίδας πόλεις οὐκ ἠξίου, ἀλλὰ καὶ Ἀρχελάῳ
παρῄνει μὴ ἐναντιοῦσθαι αὐταῖς ἐλευθερίας γλιχομέναις· ἀρκεῖν γὰρ
70 αὐτῷ τὴν ἄλλην δυναστείαν. ὁμοίως δ᾽ οὐδὲ πρὸς τὸν ἀδελφὸν αὐτοῦ
ἠξίου ἀγωνίζεσθαι διὰ τὴν πρὸς τὸν κοινὸν αὐτῶν πατέρα φιλίαν.
διῄτησε δὲ Καῖσαρ καὶ τὸ ὅλον, ἑκάστῳ τῶν παίδων μέρος ἀποδοὺς
τῆς ἀρχῆς, τὴν δ᾽ ἡμίσειαν μοῖραν Ἀρχελάῳ· καὶ Νικόλαον μὲν ἐτί-
μησεν ὁ Καῖσαρ, Ἀρχέλαον δὲ ἐθνάρχην κατέστησεν· ὑπέσχετο δέ, εἰ
75 αὐτὸν ἄξιον παρασκευάσειεν, καὶ βασιλέα ταχὺ ποιήσειν· τοὺς δὲ μετ᾽
αὐτὸν ἀδελφοὺς Φίλιππον καὶ Ἀντίπαν τετράρχας ἀπέδειξεν.

44 κατηγόρει edd.   κατηγορεῖ S   49 ἐπιτρέποντα Feder   ἐπίτροπον
ὄντα S   ἐπιτροπεύοντα Müller   61 αὐτοῦ Müller   αὐτῳ S   63 ἐπικαλοῦν Feder   ἐπεκάλουν S   67 πρῶτον Feder   πρῶτος S   69 ἐλευθερίας edd.   ἐλευθέραις S   72 καὶ secl. Müller

(p. 1) Herod went on an expedition against Arabia without the approval of Caesar. In view of this the latter expressed his displeasure and was very angry with Herod, writing to him very harshly and dismissing his ambassadors with disrespect. Appearing before Caesar, Nicolaus not only exonerated Herod from the charges, but also turned Caesar's anger against the accusers. The Arab king had already died, and Caesar, being convinced by the accusation lodged by Nicolaus, condemned the Arabian minister, and later, finding him a very evil man, had him executed.

At the same time the court of Herod was thrown into confusion, since the eldest of his sons falsely accused the two next born of plotting against their father. These were indeed younger than he, but were his superiors in rank, because they were children of a queen, whereas his mother was a commoner. Before Nicolaus had returned from Rome, the young men were convicted by the council, and the father, having been much exasperated, was on the point of having them executed. After Nicolaus had sailed home, Herod informed him of what happened and asked his advice. Nicolaus suggested that they should be removed to one of the fortresses, in order to gain time for better consultation, and thus not appear to make a fatal decision concerning his nearest while actuated by anger. Antipater perceiving this, looked on Nicolaus with suspicion, and, suborning various persons, frightened his father into the belief that he was in danger of being immediately killed by his sons who had corrupted the whole army, as he maintained, and his service, and that his only safety lay in their quick execution. And Herod, being afraid for his life, took a quick but not a good decision. (p. 2) No more did he communicate about the matter with Nicolaus, but at night he secretly sent the executioners. Thus the sons died, and this constituted the beginning of all evil for Herod, while everything had gone well with him before. After Antipater had caused the death of his brothers, he thought Nicolaus to be his enemy, while he himself, in turn, was bitterly hated not only by the inhabitants of the realm, but also, by those of Syria and those living beyond. The tale of the events reached Rome as well, and none was to be found either great or small who did not hate the man both for the reason that he had caused the death of his brothers who were much his betters and because he had persuaded his father to be involved in such defilement and to dishonour his former goodwill. And since the later activities of Antipater were in line with his former misdeeds, and he formed a plot against his father, being eager to become king sooner, and bought poison from Egypt about which one of his accomplices

253

confessed, Herod put his slaves to torture. Those divulged everything, namely that he intended to kill his aunt and his other brothers as well as the children of his formerly executed brothers, in order that no heir would be left. He contrived also a plot against the house of Caesar that was much more dreadful than the transgressions he committed against his own house. When also Varus, the governor of Syria, and the other officials arrived, his father convened a tribunal; the poison as well as the confessions of the slaves under torture and the letters from Rome were publicly brought forth, and the king entrusted the delivery of the speech to Nicolaus. Thus, Nicolaus lodged the accusation, Antipater spoke in his defence, while Varus and his friends acted as judges. Antipater was convicted and handed over for execution. Even then Nicolaus proposed to send him to Caesar, since he had also committed an offence against him, and to do whatever Caesar would decide. But a letter coming from Caesar, who allowed the father to punish Antipater, reached them first; and he was executed, while Caesar also killed the freedwoman, who had been his accomplice. There was none who did not praise * Nicolaus for his excellent arraignment of the parricide and murderer of his brothers.

After these events, when a short time passed, the king also died, and the nation rose against his children and against the Greeks. The last-mentioned numbered more than ten thousand. In the battle which ensued (p. 3) the Greeks had the upper hand. And Archelaus, the heir, sailed away to Rome to deal with the whole question of his rule together with his brothers, and he exhorted Nicolaus, who had already been bent on retiring from public affairs since he was about 60 years old, to sail in his company. Thus he sailed in his company [to Rome] and he found that everywhere Archelaus' accusers were active. On the one hand, the younger brother lay claim to the crown, and, on the other hand, all the relatives levelled charges against him, though not working in the interest of the younger brother. Also the Greek cities subject to Herod sent emissaries petitioning Caesar to grant them freedom. The representatives of the whole Jewish nation accused Archelaus of the murder of three thousand men who fell in the battle, and above all asked to be subject to the rule of Caesar, and, if not, to that of the younger brother. So many trials having been announced, Nicolaus first fought for Archelaus in the contest against the relatives and then against his Jewish subjects, and won. But the contest against the Greek cities he did not think fit for him to undertake, and he also exhorted Archelaus not to oppose their striving for freedom, as the remaining dominion would be enough for him. For the same reason

Nicolaus of Damascus

he did not choose to contend against his brother, because of his friendship with their common father. Caesar settled the question of the whole inheritance, allotting to each of Herod's children a part of the realm, Archelaus' share amounting to a half of the whole. And Caesar honoured Nicolaus and appointed Archelaus ethnarch. He promised that if he proved himself worthy, he would soon appoint him king. His younger brothers Philip and Antipas he appointed tetrarchs.

(p. 1) ἐστράτευσεν ἐπὶ τὴν Ἀραβίαν Ἡρώδης οὐ συνδοκοῦν Καίσαρι: The relations between Herod and the Nabataean kingdom were somewhat strained from the beginning. Although his father Antipater was on very friendly terms with the Nabataeans and his mother was of Arab origin, Herod's policy was a continuation of that of the later Hasmonaeans, the military rivals of the Nabataeans. Already at the time of Actium, Herod and Malchus, King of the Nabataeans, had an encounter that ended in a victory for Herod; see *Ant.*, XV, 147 ff.; *BJ*, I, 364 ff. Furthermore, old Hyrcan was accused of treacherous connections with Malchus; see *Ant.*, XV, 165 ff. The relations between the two vassal-states of Rome, Judaea and the Nabataean kingdom, do not seem to have improved much under the rule of the new Arab king, Obodas; for a chronological table of the Nabataean rulers, see R. Dussaud, *La pénétration des Arabes en Syrie avant l'Islam*, Paris 1955, p. 54; A. Grohmann, PW, XVI, p.1459. Obodas mostly left the reins of government to his minister Syllaeus, who had already played a prominent part in the Arab expedition of Aelius Gallus. Syllaeus was also a lover of Salome, Herod's sister, and wanted to marry her. This, however, did not come to pass, as Herod would allow it only if Syllaeus would become a proselyte; see *Ant.*, XVI, 225: ἐγγραφῆναι τοῖς τῶν Ἰουδαίων ἔθεσι καὶ τότε γαμεῖν. After his disappointment, Syllaeus became embittered against Herod. On Syllaeus and his influence in the Nabataean kingdom, see C. Clermont-Ganneau, *Recueil d'archéologie orientale*, VII, Paris 1906, pp. 305 ff.; A. Kammerer, *Pétra et la Nabatène*, I, Paris 1929, pp. 190 ff.; Stein, PW, Ser. 2, IV, pp. 1041 ff.
Herod's campaign against Arabia, referred to by Nicolaus in *De Vita Sua*, is described with much more detail in *Ant.*, XVI, 271 ff., which draws on the *Historiae* of Nicolaus. Trouble arose among the inhabitants of Trachonitis during Herod's absence on a voyage to Rome. After a report was spread about the king's death, the population revolted and began to attack their neighbours. Herod's generals crushed the revolt, but forty of the chief brigands escaped to Arabia, where they were well received by Syllaeus, who gave them a fortified place to live in, Rhaepta, and thus provided them with a base of operation.When Herod was informed of the revolt upon his return from Rome, he retaliated by slaughtering the relatives whom the brigands had left in Trachonitis. The brigands, angered by this action, continued to raid Herod's territory. Herod discussed the matter with Saturninus, governor of Syria, and with Volumnius, presumably a procurator, and demanded that the brigands be handed over to him for punishment. The brigands, however, multiplied their efforts to destroy Herod's kingdom, plundering towns and villages and slaughtering the people. Incensed at these actions, Herod again demanded that the culprits be handed over to him and also that the Nabataean king repay a debt of sixty talents lent through the agency of Syllaeus. But Syllaeus, who was then the

255

actual ruler of the Nabataean state, denied that the brigands were in Arabia and also delayed payment of the debt. At last, at the instigation of Saturninus and Volumnius, the Arabs undertook to pay Herod the money within thirty days, and both sides agreed to return refugees from the other's realm, but the Arabs did not fulfil their obligation. After Saturninus and Volumnius gave Herod permission to act, he led his forces into Arabia and demolished Rhaepta. When the Arab chief Nakeb came to the brigands' assistance, a battle ensued in which Nakeb and twenty-five of his men fell. Herod informed the Roman chiefs — i.e. Saturninus and Volumnius — of his action, averring that he had done no more than necessary against the obstinate Arabs. Upon investigating the matter, the Romans found that he had told them the truth. On these events, see Otto, pp. 126 ff.; H. Willrich, *Das Haus des Herodes*, Heidelberg 1929, pp. 73 ff.; A. H. M. Jones, *The Herods of Judaea*, Oxford 1938, pp. 123 ff.; A. Schalit, *König Herodes*, Berlin 1969, pp. 613 ff.; see also O. Bohn, *Qua Condicione Iuris Reges Socii Populi Romani Fuerint*, Berlin 1877, p. 41, n. 87.

ἐπέστειλέ τε αὐτῷ πικρότατα: Josephus (*Ant.*, XVI, 286 ff.) proceeds to narrate the repercussions of Herod's action at Rome. Syllaeus, then sojourning at Rome, complained to Augustus, asserting that 2,500 leading Arabs had perished and that he would never have left his country had he not been convinced that it was of importance to Augustus that the two countries should be at peace with each other. Since the friends of Herod could not deny that he led an army out of Judaea, the angered Augustus wrote a letter to Herod, the main argument of which was ὅτι πάλαι χρώμενος αὐτῷ φίλῳ, νῦν ὑπηκόῳ χρήσεται (*ibid.*, 290).

καὶ τοὺς ἥκοντας παρ' αὐτοῦ πρέσβεις, οὐ κατὰ κόσμον ἀπέλυσεν: Since the situation in Trachonitis had deteriorated to the point where its inhabitants rose against Herod's Idumaean settlers, pillaging their lands with the help of the Arabs, Herod sent envoys to Rome to plead his case. Augustus, however, refused to receive them and sent them back to Judaea (*ibid.*, 293). Josephus' narrative here, to which there is no parallel in *Bellum Judaicum*, is wholly dependent on Nicolaus' *Historiae*. It describes Herod's action as completely innocent and undertaken with the knowledge of the Roman governor of Syria, making Augustus' anger incomprehensible.

Ὁ... Ἄραψ ἤδη ἐτεθνήκει: I.e. King Obodas (9 B. C. E.), who was succeeded by Aretas IV (9 B. C. E. to 40 C. E.).

τοῦ δὲ διοικητοῦ: I.e. Syllaeus.

ἤδη κατέγνω πεισθεὶς τῇ Νικολάου κατηγορίᾳ: According to *Ant.*, XVI, 295, Syllaeus strove to unseat the new Arab king. To this end he distributed much money to the members of the imperial court. Augustus was angry with Aretas for assuming the royal title before obtaining permission. Aretas then sent a letter and gifts to Augustus, accusing Syllaeus of having poisoned Obodas. Augustus ignored these charges, and the relations between Judaea and Arabia further deteriorated. Since Herod could not anticipate an end to the frictions, he sent Nicolaus to Rome in a new attempt at reconciliation. The story of this embassy is narrated in *Ant.*, XVI, 335 ff. — undoubtedly derived from Nicolaus' *Historiae*. From this account we learn that Nicolaus decided not only to defend Herod, but also to attain a general indictment against Syllaeus. After receiving information about Syllaeus' crimes from some Arabs, Nicolaus accused him before Augustus of causing the death of Obodas, of borrowing money for unlawful purposes, of being guilty of adultery with women both in Arabia and in Rome and of telling Augustus

Nicolaus of Damascus

lies about Herod. The intervention of Nicolaus so affected Augustus that he decided to condemn Syllaeus.

καὶ ὕστερον εὑρὼν κάκιστον ἀπέκτεινεν: We see here that Syllaeus' execution did not immediately follow Nicolaus' persuasions at Rome. From *Ant.*, XVI, 352 f., we learn that Syllaeus was condemned to death as a result of these persuasions, but only after he was sent back to pay his debts. The subsequent history of Syllaeus is related in *Ant.*, XVII, 54 ff., 81; cf. *BJ*, I, 574 ff. From this passage it emerges that Syllaeus did not carry out Augustus' orders, and that upon his return to Rome he was charged with the attempted murder of Herod by Antipater, Herod's son. He was also accused by Aretas of the murder of many of the leading men of Petra, and of Fabatus, one of the imperial slaves. Syllaeus' death is not expressly mentioned in the relevant passage of *Antiquitates* or *Bellum Judaicum*, but it is referred to by Strabo, *Geographica*, XVI, 4 : 24, p. 782: ὁ δ'αἴτιος τούτων [scil. of the failure of the expedition of Aelius Gallus] ὁ Συλλαῖος ἔτισε δίκας ἐν ʽΡώμῃ, προσποιούμενος μὲν φιλίαν, ἐλεγχθεὶς δὲ πρὸς ταύτῃ τῇ πονηρίᾳ καὶ ἄλλα κακουργῶν καὶ ἀποτμηθεὶς τὴν κεφαλήν.
Strabo gives no clue as to the time of his death. Obviously we must distinguish between two main phases in Augustus' procedure against Syllaeus; cf. Stein, *op. cit.* (supra, p. 255), p. 1043. One of them occurred at the time of Nicolaus' sojourn at Rome; the second ended in the execution of Syllaeus following the accusations of Antipater and Aretas (4 B. C. E.); cf. also Otto, p. 129, note; Wacholder, *op. cit.* (supra, p. 232), pp. 62 f.

τοῦ πρεσβυτάτου τῶν υἱέων τοὺς μετ'αὐτὸν δύω διαβάλλοντος: The eldest son of Herod was Antipater; next came Alexander, and then Aristobulus.

⟨ὡς⟩ ἐπιβουλεύοντας τῷ πατρί: It is clear that, at least in *De Vita Sua*, Nicolaus maintained the view that the guilt of Alexander and Aristobulus had not been proved; see also the commentary to No. 93.

ἀξιώματι δὲ πρότεροι διὰ τὸ ἐκ βασιλίδος γεγονέναι: The mother of Alexander and Aristobulus was Mariamme the Hasmonaean; Antipater's mother, Doris, married Herod (*Ant.*, XIV, 300; *BJ*, I, 241) and bore Antipater before Herod became king (*Ant.*, XVI, 78; *BJ*, I, 432 f.). The contrast between Doris and Mariamme is stressed by Josephus (*BJ*, I, 517), who puts the words into the mouth of Eurycles the Spartan, when he talks to Alexander: εἰ γεγενημένος ἐκ βασιλίδος ... ἐάσει διαδέχεσθαι τὴν ἀρχὴν τὸν ἐξ ἰδιώτιδος.

ἐν συνεδρίῳ κατεδικάσθησαν οἱ νεανίσκοι: On the last chapter of the life of Alexander and Aristobulus, see *Ant.*, XVI, 300 ff.; *BJ*, I, 513 ff.; cf. Schürer, p. 373, n. 18; Otto, pp. 137 ff.; Willrich, *op. cit.* (supra, p. 256), pp. 123 ff.; Jones, *op. cit.* (supra, p. 256), pp. 128 ff.; Schalit, *op. cit.* (supra, p. 256), pp. 588 ff. They were executed in 7 B. C. E. After Herod became convinced of his sons' intention to murder him, he sent a letter to Augustus on this matter. Augustus suggested that he convene a συνέδριον at the Roman colony of Berytus, to which he would invite the leading Romans of Syria, and also Archelaus of Cappadocia; see *Ant.*, XVI, 356 ff.; *BJ*, I, 536 ff. Herod, acting accordingly, convened the principal Romans of Syria, including the governor Saturninus, but not Archelaus. The majority of the one hundred fifty members of the synedrion concurred with Herod's view and condemned his sons to death.

καταπλεύσαντι δὲ Νικολάῳ... μὴ δοκοίη ὑπ' ὀργῆς προαχθεὶς ἀνήκεστόν τι γνῶναι: Cf. *Ant.*, XVI, 370 ff. Herod left Berytus for Tyre, and meeting Nicolaus there on his way back from Rome, asked him what his friends in Rome thought about his

257

sons. Nicolaus replied that they strongly disapproved of the intentions of Herod's sons, but their opinion was also that χρῆναι μέντοι αὐτοὺς καθείρξαντα δεσμώτας φυλάττειν καὶ εἰ μὲν ἑτέρως σοι δοκοίη κολάζειν αὐτούς, μὴ φαίνοιο ὀργῇ τὸ πλέον ἢ γνώμῃ κεχρῆσθαι, εἰ δὲ τἀναντία ἀπολύειν, μὴ ἀνεπανόρθωτον εἴη σοι τὸ ἀτύχημα. What in *De Vita Sua* is given as the view of Nicolaus himself, is represented in *Antiquitates* as that of Herod's friends in Rome; compare ὑπ'ὀργῆς προαχθεὶς of *De Vita Sua* with μὴ φαίνοιο ὀργῇ... κέχρησθαι of *Antiquitates* and ἀνήκεστόν τι γνῶναι of Nicolaus with ἀνεπανόρθωτον εἴη of Josephus.

αἰσθόμενος δὲ τοῦτο 'Αντίπατρος: In this connection Josephus does not emphasize the part played by Antipater.

ὑπὸ τῶν νεανίσκων διεφθαρκότων καὶ τὸ στρατιωτικὸν ἅπαν: For the sympathy shown by the military to Alexander and Aristobulus, see *Ant.*, XVI, 375 ff.; *BJ*, I, 544 ff. The spokesman for the soldiers was a man named Tiron, whose son was a friend of Alexander; see especially *Ant.*, XVI, 383, where Tiron states that the army and its chiefs pity the youths; cf. *BJ*, I, 546; *Ant.*, XVI, 386; 393, where it is related that Herod brought three hundred of the officers before an assembly, where they were killed by the crowd.

καὶ τοὺς ἀπὸ τῆς θεραπείας: In both *Ant.*, (XVI, 387) and *BJ*, (I, 547) Josephus tells of a Court barber named Tryphon as connected with a plot against the king's life. On the expression θεραπεία, see Otto, p. 87, n. 3.

(p. 2) ἀλλὰ νύκτωρ τοὺς ἀναιρήσοντας ὑποπέμψας: Cf. *Ant.*, XVI, 394; *BJ*, I, 551. We learn from Josephus that both sons were led to Sebaste and strangled there. In *Ant.*, *loc. cit.*, we read that their bodies were brought at night (νύκτωρ) to Alexandrion.

ἐμισεῖτό γε μὴν...: On the fall of Antipater, see *Ant.*, XVII; *BJ*, I, 552 ff.; cf. also Schürer, I, pp. 412 ff.; Otto, pp. 141 ff.; Willrich, *op. cit.* (supra, p. 256), pp. 127 ff.; Jones, *op. cit.* (supra, p. 256), pp. 137 ff.; Schalit, *op. cit.* (supra, p. 256), pp. 628 ff. On the hatred felt for Antipater, see *BJ*, I, 552: μῖσος μὲν ἀφόρητον ἐκ τοῦ ἔθνους ἐπεγείρεται; see also *Ant.*, XVII, 82: μῖσος τῶν ἀνθρώπων τὸ πρὸς 'Αντίπατρον. Antipater was particularly affected by the hatred of the military; see *Ant.*, XVII, 2.

καὶ τὸ φάρμακον ἐώνητο ἐξ Αἰγύπτου: On the poison imported from Egypt, see *Ant.*, XVII, 70; *BJ*, I, 592: (μετεπέμψατο μὲν 'Αντίπατρος ἐξ Αἰγύπτου δηλητήριον φάρμακον.) The drug was brought by Antiphilus, a friend of Antipater. The poison had been sent by Theudion, the maternal uncle of Antipater, to Pheroras, the brother of Herod. Pheroras gave it to his wife to keep. After the death of Pheroras all this was divulged to Herod.

εἷς τῶν κοινωνούντων τῆς πράξεως: It was a Samaritan, also named Antipater, ἐπιτροπεύων τὸν υἱὸν τοῦ βασιλέως (scil. Antipater), who revealed the matter under torture; see *Ant.*, XVII, 69 ff.; *BJ*, *loc. cit.* The widow of Pheroras made a similar confession.

ἐβασάνιζέ τε τοὺς οἰκέτας αὐτοῦ ὁ πατήρ: Herod tortured one of the brothers of Antiphilus and his mother; see *Ant.*, XVII, 77; *BJ*, I, 598. In connection with the trial of Antipater, see also *Ant.*, XVII, 93: εἰσεκλήθησαν δὲ καὶ οἱ ἀμφοῖν φίλοι καὶ οἱ συγγενεῖς ... εἴτ' εἴ τινες μηνύσειν ἔμελλον καὶ ὧν βάσανοι γεγόνασιν. The last-mentioned need not necessarily be identical with Antiphilus' brother and mother.

καὶ τὴν τηθίδα ἔμελλεν ἀναιρήσειν: Salome, the sister of Herod, had always been suspicious of the machinations of Antipater, and the relations between the two

Nicolaus of Damascus

continued to be strained; see *Ant.*, XVII, 38 ff.; *BJ*, I, 573. Antipater's attempt to kill Salome, mentioned by Nicolaus, should be connected with the intrigues of Antipater, to which Acme was a party; see *Ant.*, XVII, 137: καὶ ἀντίγραφον ποιήσασα τῇ πρὸς τὴν ἐμὴν κυρίαν ὡς παρὰ Σαλώμης ἔγραψα, ἣν ἀναγνοὺς οἶδ᾽ ὅτι τιμωρήσεται Σαλώμην ὡς ἐπίβουλον; cf. *BJ*, I, 643. καὶ τοὺς ἄλλους ἀδελφοὺς ὄντας...: Cf. *Ant.*, XVII, 80; *BJ*, I, 602 f., 637: ἐπιβουλεύειν δὲ αὐτὸν ἔλεγεν καὶ τοῖς περιοῦσιν ὡς ἐφέδροις τῆς διαδοχῆς (Nicolaus in his speech); cf. also Otto, p. 145.

ἐτύρευσε δέ τι μιαρὸν καὶ εἰς τὸν οἶκον Καίσαρος: The only event described by Josephus that might be the same as the one alluded to by Nicolaus concerns the relationship between Antipater and Acme, a Jewish slave (or freedwoman) of the Empress Livia; cf. the words of Nicolaus: ἀπέκτεινεν δὲ καὶ ὁ Καῖσαρ τὴν συγκακουργήσασαν αὐτῷ ἀπελευθέραν. On the affair of Acme, see *Ant.*, XVII, 134, 137 ff.; *BJ*, I, 641. Acme helped Antipater plot against Salome. She forged a letter from Salome to Livia, which incriminated Herod. Nicolaus' attitude toward Antipater's transgression is accounted for by his feelings for Augustus and his house.

ἧκε μὲν ὁ τῆς Συρίας στρατηγὸς Οὔαρος: Cf. *Ant.*, XVII, 89 ff.; *BJ*, I, 617 ff. Nicolaus' speech against Antipater is related at length in *Antiquitates*, and, in a shorter form, in *Bellum Judaicum*. On the style of this passage of *De Vita Sua*, see Laqueur, PW, XVII, p. 423.

Νικόλαος δὲ καὶ τότε παρῄνει πέμπειν αὐτὸν ἐπὶ Καίσαρα: In spite of his hatred of Antipater, Nicolaus advised that execution of his sentence be postponed for political reasons. As we learn from *Ant.*, XVI, 355, the internal struggle in Herod's Court had already done much harm to the prestige of Herod. On the reaction of Augustus to the behaviour of Herod towards his sons, see Macrobius, *Saturnalia*, II, 4 : 11 (No. 543); see also *Ant.*, XVII, 144 f., where it is stated that Herod intended to send his son to Augustus to stand trial at Rome, but, fearing that Antipater might escape with the help of friends, decided to keep him imprisoned and again sent letters to Augustus indicting him. On the difficulties inherent in this passage when compared with the parallel passages in Josephus, see E. Täubler, *Byzantinische Zeitschrift*, XXV (1925), pp. 33 ff.

ἔφθη δὲ τὰ παρὰ Καίσαρος γράμματα: Cf. *Ant.*, XVII, 182, *BJ*, I, 661. The letter, in fact, came from Herod's envoys at Rome. The substance of the letter was that Augustus left it to the discretion of Herod whether to banish Antipater or execute him.

καὶ ὁ μὲν ἐκολάσθη: Cf. *Ant.*, XVII, 187; *BJ*, I, 664.

ἀπέκτεινεν δὲ καὶ ὁ Καῖσαρ τὴν συγκακουργήσασαν αὐτῷ: Cf. *Ant.*, XVII, 182 f.; *BJ*, I, 661. From Josephus we learn that the execution of Acme preceded that of Antipater.

καὶ τὸ ἔθνος ἐπανίσταται τοῖς τέκνοις: On the events in Judaea after the death of Herod, see *Ant.*, XVII, 200 ff.; *BJ*, II, 1 ff.; see also Tacitus, *Historiae*, V, 9 (No. 281). The revolt of the Jews spread over most parts of Herod's former kingdom, i.e. Judaea proper, Peraea and Galilaea; see Schürer, I, p. 418 ff.; Graetz, *Geschichte der Juden*, III 1⁵, Leipzig 1905, pp. 247 ff.; Otto, pp. 166 f.; M. Brann, *De Herodis, qui Dicitur, Magni Filiis Patrem in Imperio Secutis*, I, Breslau 1873, pp. 16 ff.

καὶ τοῖς Ἕλλησιν: The description of the revolt, as directed against the Greek element in the state, is not emphasized by Josephus, though in his account of the reign of Herod, the Jewish historian does sometimes dwell on Herod's preference of foreigners to Jews.

259

From Herodotus to Plutarch

ἦσαν δὲ πλείους μυρίων: Wacholder, *op. cit.* (supra, p. 232), p. 63, assumes that the subject of this sentence is the rebels (τὸ ἔθνος), but we prefer to interpret it as referring to the ῞Ελληνες. It seems that the relatively high number of "Greeks" includes the armed forces which were mainly recruited from the "Greek" population, especially from the Hellenistic cities of Sebaste and Caesarea. On the prevalence of the Greek element in the Herodian monarchy, see Otto, pp. 88 ff.; pp. 107 ff.; Jeremias, pp. 103 f.

νικᾷ τὸ ῾Ελληνικόν: Nicolaus probably refers to the slaughter of three thousand Jews on Passover of 4. B.C.E., in which, it seems, the soldiers from Sebaste and Caesarea took a leading part. The massacre preceded Archelaus' sailing to Rome; see *Ant.*, XVII, 215 ff.; *BJ*, II, 11 ff.

᾿Αρχέλαος εἰς ῾Ρώμην πλέων... παρακαλεῖ συμπλεῦσαι Νικόλαον: Cf. *Ant.*, XVII, 219; *BJ*, II, 14.

ὁ νεώτερος ἀδελφὸς τῆς βασιλείας ἀντεποιεῖτο: Herod Antipas, the younger brother of Archelaus, sailed to Rome to claim the throne for himself. He did this at the instigation of Salome, basing himself on an earlier will of Herod, which he claimed was more valid than the later one; see *Ant.*, XVII, 224; *BJ*, II, 20 ff. Among the supporters of Antipas was Ptolemy, the brother of Nicolaus.

οἱ συγγενεῖς ἅπαντες κατηγόρουν αὐτοῦ, οὐ τῷ νεωτέρῳ συναγωνιζόμενοι: Cf. *Ant.*, XVII, 227: ἐπεὶ δ᾿εἰς τὴν ῾Ρώμην ἀφίκετο [scil. Antipas] καὶ πάντων τῶν συγγενῶν ἀπόστασις ἦν πρὸς αὐτόν, οὐκ εὐνοίᾳ τῇ ἐκείνου, μίσει δὲ τῷ πρὸς ᾿Αρχέλαον; cf. *BJ*, II, 22. The most hostile relative of Archelaus was Antipater, Salome's son and Archelaus' cousin, who delivered a speech against him before Augustus; see *Ant.*, XVII, 230 ff.; *BJ*, II, 26 ff. For an analysis of this passage, see Täubler, *op. cit.* (supra, p. 259), pp. 36 ff.; see also J. Crook, *Consilium Principis*, Cambridge 1955, pp. 32 f. H. W. Hoehner, *Herod Antipas*, Cambridge 1972, pp. 18 ff.

῾Ελληνίδες πόλεις αἰτούμεναι τὴν ἐλευθερίαν παρὰ Καίσαρος: It seems that the Greek cities implied here are Gaza, Hippos and Gadara, which were subsequently set free by Augustus; see *Ant.*, XVII, 320; *BJ*, II, 97.

τὸ ᾿Ιουδαίων ἔθνος ἐπικαλοῦν φόνον τρισχιλίων ἀνδρῶν: For the speech of the Jewish envoys recalling the misdeeds of the late Herod and accusing Archelaus, see *Ant.*, XVII, 304 ff., especially 313: τρισχιλίων ὁμοφύλων ἀνδρῶν σφαγὴν ἐν τῷ τεμένει ποιησάμενον; see also *BJ*, II, 89.

καὶ ἀξιοῦν μάλιστα μὲν ὑπὸ Καίσαρι εἶναι: Josephus, too, relates that the Jewish delegates asked for Judaea's incorporation into Syria; see *Ant.*, XVII, 314; *BJ*, II, 91. Josephus, however, does not refer to the alternative mentioned by Nicolaus. For a similar request on the part of a population of a vassal kingdom, see Tacitus, *Annales*, II, 42: "per idem tempus Antiocho Commagenorum, Philopatore Cilicum regibus defunctis turbabantur nationes; plerisque Romanum, aliisque regium imperium cupientibus."

ἀγωνισάμενος ὑπὲρ ᾿Αρχελάου Νικόλαος τὸν πρὸς συγγενεῖς ἀγῶνα: Cf. *Ant.*, XVII, 240 ff.; *BJ*, II, 34 ff.

ἔπειτα δὲ τὸν πρὸς ὑπηκόους ᾿Ιουδαίους: Cf. *Ant.*, XVII, 315 f.; *BJ*, II, 92.

διῄτησε δὲ Καῖσαρ: Cf. *Ant.*, XVII, 317 ff., *BJ*, II, 93 ff. Archelaus received Judaea, Idumaea and Samaria as his portion. Antipas received Galilaea and Peraea, while Batanaea, Trachonitis and Auranitis were allotted to Philip.

τὴν δ᾿ἡμίσειαν: Cf. *Ant.*, XVII, 317; *BJ.*, II, 93.

ὑπέσχετο... καὶ βασιλέα ταχὺ ποιήσειν: Cf. *Ant.*, XVII, 317; *BJ*, II, 93.

260

XLII. STRABO OF AMASEIA

c. 64 B.C.E. to the twenties of the first century C.E.

*Chance ordained that one of the most circumstantial surveys of the
country and religion of the Jews that has come down to us in Greek
and Latin literature is contained in the* Geographica *of Strabo. Strabo
was equally distinguished as a historian and as a geographer. A native
of Pontus and of illustrious ancestry, Strabo travelled widely, knew
at least some parts of Asia Minor well, stayed for a time in Egypt and
visited Rome. According to his own assertion, he travelled from the
Euxine to Ethiopia and from Armenia to Etruria* (Geographica, *II, 5:11,
p. 117). However, it seems that neither Syria nor Judaea were included
within the range of his autopsy.*[1]

*The historical work of Strabo covered mainly the period from the time
at which Polybius stopped to the capture of Alexandria by Octavian.*[2] *It
consisted of forty-three books and had four introductory volumes, which
dealt summarily with the preceding period. Most of the fragments left
to us from Strabo's lost historical work have been transmitted by
Josephus'* Antiquitates *and, thus, naturally refer to events connected
with Jews. The first event bearing upon Jews that is mentioned in these
fragments is the sack of the Temple of Jerusalem by Antiochus Epiphanes (No. 98). The last reference by Josephus to Strabo's* Historica
Hypomnemata *relates to the execution of Antigonus the Hasmonaean
by Antony in 37 B.C.E. (No. 108).*

*Already from the few fragments quoted by Josephus one can see that
Strabo used many written sources in his* History, *and he expressly
refers to three of them: Timagenes, Asinius Pollio and Hypsicrates.
Once (No. 103) Strabo even quotes a document that he himself saw,
namely, the inscription written on a gift sent by a Hasmonaean king
(either Aristobulus II or his father Alexander; cf. the commentary to
that place). What is certain is that Strabo could not have had recourse in*

---

1 W. Aly, *Strabon von Amaseia*, Bonn 1957, p. 48.
2 R. Syme, *Harvard Studies in Classical Philology*, LXIV (1959), p. 65. For a
   somewhat later date (27–25 B. C. E.), see E. Honigmann, PW, Ser. 2, IV, p.
   90; C. Wachsmuth, *Einleitung in das Studium der alten Geschichte*, Leipzig
   1895, p. 654.

his historical work to Nicolaus' Historiae, *which was published at a later date.*[3] *Consequently, whenever Josephus testifies to the consonance between Strabo and Nicolaus in their accounts of Jewish history, it should be explained by (a) intrinsic correctness of the facts independently related by the two writers; (b) their independent derivation from common sources; or (c) a not impossible, though not very probable, use of Strabo by Nicolaus.*

There is much more in books thirteen and fourteen of the Antiquitates *that depends on Strabo's* Historica Hypomnemata *than Josephus' express references to Strabo. Nevertheless, one should not go to the length of attributing all the material on Syrian and Egyptian history to Strabo — as was done, for example, by Hölscher.*

Strabo was able to make a more detached evaluation of the Hasmonaean dynasty than Nicolaus, who had personal ties with Herod and who was, as a native of Damascus, more sympathetic to the fate of the Hellenistic population of Syria. Thus, Strabo stresses the high esteem in which Herod's arch-enemy, King Antigonus, was held by the Jews, and he does not, in contrast to Nicolaus (cf. the commentary to No. 107), suppress Hyrcan's role in bringing succour to Julius Caesar when he found himself in trouble in Egypt. In addition, without any qualms he quotes Timagenes, who praises Aristobulus I, thus allowing the latter to emerge here as quite a different ruler and man (No. 100) than the one pictured by Nicolaus, whose opinion has been preserved in the main narrative of Josephus.

However, because the bulk of Strabo's Historica Hypomnemata *has been lost, it is mainly in the* Geographica *that we find his views about the Jews, their religion, their state and their history. Strabo's* Geographica, *like his* Historica Hypomnemata, *was destined chiefly for men of affairs and statesmen. It bears the imprint of the Principates of Augustus and Tiberius, at which time it received its final form.*[4] *It was an elaborate composition, and many sources, belonging to different periods, contributed to its contents.*

Naturally, the description of Judaea and the Jews finds its place within the framework of the geography of Syria. Already in the introductory chapter (No. 111) Strabo refers to the opinion of those who divide the whole population of Syria into Coele-Syrians, Syrians proper and Phoenicians, and adds that four other ἔθνη are mixed in with these: the Jews, the Idumaeans, the Gazaeans and the Azotians. The authorities used

---

3 For the relation between Strabo and Nicolaus, see also F. Münzer, *Deutsche Litteraturzeitung,* XXI (1900), p. 2983.

4 E. Pais, *Ancient Italy,* Chicago–London 1908, pp. 379 ff.

here by Strabo reflect conditions that hardly prevailed after the second century B. C. E., since the Idumaeans lost their identity in the twenties of the second century B. C. E., the Azotians approximately at the same time, while Gaza was captured c. 96 B. C. E.

On the other hand, when, in a later chapter, Strabo comes to the definition of Coele-Syria in both its broader and narrower senses, and to that of Phoenicia, he states that the territory extending into the interior beyond Phoenicia, as far as the area occupied by the Arabians, between Gaza and the Anti-Lebanon, is called Judaea (No. 113). This, of course, implies that the results of the Hasmonaean conquests were already taken into consideration, and that Strabo uses the name Judaea in the meaning attached to it from the Hasmonaean age to the time of Hadrian.

In his description of the Palestinian coast, Strabo uses older sources, but he is, to some extent, conscious of the change that had occurred in more recent times. Thus, when he mentions the old townships of Sycaminopolis, Bucolopolis or Crocodilopolis, he adds that only their names remain. Not always, however, does he succeed in noting the changes so as to reflect contemporary conditions. When he speaks of Gaza, he still considers it uninhabited, thereby ignoring its restoration by the Romans after the downfall of the Hasmonaean state. Nor does he take notice of the fact that the Tower of Strato has become Caesarea.

In his description of the interior, he shows full knowledge of the judaization of the Idumaeans, but he confuses Lake Sirbonis with the Dead Sea. He emphasizes the mixed character of the population inhabiting Galilaea, Hiericus, Philadelphia and Samaria, and, in respect of the last-mentioned, he notes that Herod surnamed it Sebaste. He concludes, however, basing himself on the most prevalent reports concerning the Temple of Jerusalem, that the ancestors of the present Jews were Egyptians, a view he had already propounded in his History *(No. 105). This theory provided the background for his account of the origins of the Jewish religion and for his famous chapters on Moses, the main outline of which is: the Egyptian origin of Moses; his renunciation of any representation of the Divine Being by images; his establishment of a cult without images; his concept of God as that which encompasses mankind, land and sea and is identical with heaven, the universe and the nature of existence; his arrival, along with that of many of his thoughtful followers, at the rocky and unenviable site where Jerusalem was founded; his organization of a remarkable kind of government; the attraction his teaching and ethical standards had for the neighbouring peoples; the maintenance of the same way of life by immediate successors, who continued to act righteously; the deterioration that set in when credulous priests*

263

arose who introduced superstitious customs; the tyrannies, robberies and the subjugation of much of Syria and Phoenicia that followed.

In connection with the personality and the achievement of Moses, Strabo enters into a digression on other famous legislators and the nature of their work. Moses belongs to the category of people that includes Minos, Lycurgus, Tiresias and many others, all of whom also claimed to have divine inspiration.

The evaluation of Moses in these chapters of Strabo is outstanding in its sympathy, and recalls that of Hecataeus (No. 11). Strabo's praise of abstract worship reminds one of Varro's remarks (No. 72). In contrast to Hecataeus, Strabo does not attribute the change in the character of Judaism to external causes, such as the assimilation of foreign manners, but considers this a result of an internal process.

The question of where Strabo derived his views of Moses and the history of the Jewish religion has given rise to much discussion. The prevalent opinion is that he owes it to Posidonius. Heinemann and Reinhardt were the chief champions of this view, which has been already stated by Reitzenstein. It also won the approval of many others, e.g. Jacoby, Morr, Honigmann, Saliternik, Strasburger and Pohlenz, although Aly remained one of its chief opponents. One must admit that there is much to be said for the Posidonian derivation. First,we are certain that Strabo used Posidonius a great deal in the sixteenth book of his Geographica, *and according to him Posidonius was ἀνὴρ τῶν καθ'ἡμᾶς φιλοσόφων πολυμαθέστατος (XVI, 2 : 10. p. 753). Strabo also expressly mentions his view concerning the habits of the people living in the neighbourhood of the Dead Sea. Further, the passage on revelation through* incubatio, *attributed by Strabo to the Jewish religion, may have something in common with Posidonius' view, since we learn from Cicero* (De Divinatione, *I, 64) that Posidonius was much occupied with that problem.[5] Moreover, there is hardly any difference between the sympathetic account of the origins of the Jewish religion found in Strabo and the view emerging from the chapter in Diodorus (No. 63) that summarizes the opinion of the anti-Semitic advisers of Antiochus Sidetes — a chapter also generally thought to derive from Posidonius. It is obvious that the anti-Semitic opinions expressed there are not shared by the author, who bestows praise on the King for his refusal to comply with the anti-Semitic suggestions. Also, the fact that in* Contra Apionem *Josephus couples Posidonius, with Apollonius Molon, as a foremost representative of anti-Semitism (No. 44), can be explained as*

5 Nock, *JRS,* XLIX (1959), p. 9.

the mistaken conception of a writer who had no direct acquaintance with Posidonius (cf. the introduction to Posidonius).

The scholars who believe in the Posidonian origin of the chapters on Moses are somewhat uneasy about the exact location of the excursus on the Jews in the lost History of Posidonius. As it is commonly accepted that his History did not go beyond the eighties of the first century B. C. E., the most natural context for the inclusion of the chapters on Moses would be the description of the clash between Antiochus Sidetes and Hasmonaean Judaea, c. 134 B. C. E. If one assumes that Strabo derived his account from Posidonius, one must suppose that Posidonius also proleptically reviewed the subsequent history of the Hasmonaean state from the stages of its gradual moral deterioration to the reign of Alexander Jannaeus, including most of the reign of that ruler and, of course, that of his immediate predecessors — who were all distinguished by their conquest of neighbouring territory and most of whom were noted for their destruction of Hellenistic municipal life.

Yet, Reinhardt has maintained, though not with sufficiently convincing arguments, that the excursus on the Jews could have been written only in the context of the Roman conquest. He has suggested, and Pohlenz agrees with him, that Strabo is indebted not to Posidonius' History, but to his monograph on Pompey, the existence of which is rather doubtful.[6] Jacoby, on the other hand, prefers the view that Strabo derived the excursus from an intermediate source, namely, the History of Timagenes, and that it was Timagenes who connected it with the events of 63 B. C. E. Though the work of Timagenes was well known to Strabo and we are certain that he drew on it in his own History, *Jacoby's assumption does not seem necessary, and what he attributes to Timagenes may as easily be attributed to Strabo himself.*

However, a striking fact emerges: while there is perhaps no absolutely cogent argument to refute the view that the chapters on Moses in Strabo's Geographica *depend on Posidonius, neither is there any positive proof of that dependence. At most, one may feel that these chapters owe something to Posidonius' views on religion, without being sure that it was Posidonius himself who applied them to the Jewish*

---

6 In order to meet the difficulty, Strasburger is even prepared to go to the length of invalidating the somewhat obscure evidence of Suda and of postulating a later date for the termination of the History of Posidonius; see H. Strasburger, *JRS*, LV (1965), p. 44. In his time Dubois supposed Strabo to be dependent on Posidonius in his account of the campaigns of Pompey in Judaea. He did not, however, enter into details; see M. Dubois, *Examen de la géographie de Strabon*, Paris 1891, p. 327.

religion. Some scholars — e.g., Schürer, Stähelin, Nock and Gager — thought that Strabo depends here on a Jewish source. Nock has considered the possibility that the excursus reproduces "the creation of a Jew familiar with the ideas of Posidonius, a Jew whose Hellenization was not, like Philo's, controlled by an overpowering loyalty to Scripture. Such a Jew might have resented legalism on the one hand and Hasmonaean militancy on the other". Adherents of this view encounter not only the obvious difficulty that the story of Exodus, as related in the Scripture, wholly contradicts the contents of the chapters on Moses in Strabo, but also that this view assumes nothing less than that a Jew attributed the founding of Judaism to the Egyptians. At most, we know that Jews such as the historian Artapanus, in order to emphasize the Jewish contribution to civilization, went to the length of ascribing the origins of Egyptian polytheism to Moses, but we have no ground for assuming the opposite. Thus, it seems best to look for a pagan philosophical source, whatever it may be, for the chapters on Moses. It seems also that one should not, after all, exclude the possibility that Strabo is not merely derivative. Owing to his wide reading and travels, including his long stay in Egypt, and the relatively strong concern in his History *with events relating to the Jews, he probably acquired no inconsiderable knowledge of the various theories regarding the origin of the Jewish religion, as well as a general outline of the history of the Hasmonaean state. He may have combined this information with prevailing philosophical ideas on the emergence and development of religions. The contrast between the august character of the original Mosaic religion and its contemporary stage, which was marked by "superstitious" dietary laws and a militant spirit aimed at the destruction of the city centres of Hellenistic civilization, might have been well accounted for by current philosophical views regarding the process of deterioration in religion. Such views were also maintained by thinkers prior to Posidonius, e.g. Theophrastus, by whom Strabo could, of course, have been influenced through Posidonius.*

Strabo, like the Greek and Latin writers from Hecataeus to Tacitus, with very few exceptions, skips the whole period of the Hebrew kingdoms as related in the Scripture. In contrast, however, to the above-mentioned writers, he also omits in his Geographica *the period of foreign rule, Persian as well as Greek. After Moses, the first personality in Jewish history that Strabo names in his* Geographica *is Alexander Jannaeus, who he claims substituted monarchical rule for a priestly one. Strabo dwells at some length on the conquest of Judaea by Pompey and gives a description of the strength of Jerusalem. Again, as on two former occasions — the description of Jaffa and the process of deterioration under-*

Strabo of Amaseia

gone by the Jewish religion—he defines the Jewish fortresses as haunts of robbers.

As Strabo referred to the Jordan and the Lake of Gennesareth in an earlier passage, he does not return to them, but dwells on the valley of Jericho and its remarkable products: the balsam and its medical qualities, and the palms. Reinhardt [7] has suggested that Artemidorus was the source for Strabo's description of the balsam and the palm groves of Jericho, but no proof can be adduced for this view. Nor can we be certain as to the source of Strabo's information concerning the conquest of Judaea in 63 B. C. E., or of his brief account of the reign of Herod and the fate of his family after his death. It is only reasonable to presume that Theophanes of Mytilene, the friend and historian of Pompey, supplied him with the information bearing upon the events of 64-63 B. C. E. Since Strabo was a contemporary of Herod and his successors, there is no need to assume his dependence on the Historiae of Nicolaus for information on this period, though such a possibility cannot, of course, be excluded.

Bibliography:
J. G. Müller, Theologische Studien und Kritiken, (1843), pp. 912 ff.; R. Kunze, "Symbolae Strabonianae", Ph. D. Thesis, Leipzig 1892, pp. 1 ff.; R. Reitzenstein, Zwei religionsgeschichtliche Fragen, Strasbourg 1901, p. 77, n. 2; K. Albert, "Strabo als Quelle des Flavius Josephus", Ph. D. Thesis, Würzburg 1902; G. Hölscher, Die Quellen des Josephus, Leipzig 1904, pp. 36 ff.; Stähelin, pp. 27 f.; J. Geffcken, Zwei griechische Apologeten, Leipzig–Berlin 1907, p. XI, n. 5; I. Heinemann, MGWJ, LXIII (1919), pp. 113 ff.; E. Norden, Festgabe Harnack, Tübingen 1921, pp. 292 ff. = Kleine Schriften, pp. 276 ff.; F. Gr. Hist., II C, pp. 196 ff.; J. Morr, Philologus, LXXXI, pp. 256 ff.; I. Heinemann, Poseidonios' metaphysische Schriften, II, Breslau 1928, pp. 72 ff.; K. Reinhardt, Poseidonios über Ursprung und Entartung, Heidelberg 1928, pp. 6 ff., 56 ff.; D. Saliternik, Journal of Jewish Palestine Exploration Society, 1934–1935, pp. 227 ff. (in Hebrew); K. Reinhardt, PW, XXII, pp. 638 ff.; M. Pohlenz, Die Stoa 2, II, Göttingen 1955, p. 105; W. Aly, Strabon von Amaseia, Bonn 1957, pp. 191 ff.; A. D. Nock, JRS, XLIX (1959), pp. 5 ff.; Hengel, pp. 469 ff.; M. Stern, Essays in Jewish History and Philology in Memory of Gedaliahu Alon, Tel Aviv 1970, pp. 169 ff. (in Hebrew); Gager, pp. 38 ff.

7 Reinhardt, Poseidonios über Ursprung und Entartung, p. 75.

98

Historica Hypomnemata, apud: Josephus, *Contra Apionem*, II, 83–84 — Niese = *F. Gr. Hist.*, II,
A91, F10 = Reinach (Budé), pp. 72 f.

(83) Quia vero Antiochus neque iustam fecit templi depraedationem,
sed egestate pecuniarum ad hoc accessit, cum non esset hostis, et super
nos auxiliatores suos et amicos adgressus est nec aliquid dignum derisione illic invenit, (84) multi et digni conscriptores super hoc quoque
5 testantur, Polybius Megalopolita ⟨No. 33⟩, Strabon Cappadox, Nicolaus
Damascenus ⟨No. 87⟩, Timagenes ⟨No. 80⟩ et Castor ⟨No. 77⟩ temporum conscriptor et Apollodorus ⟨No. 34⟩, ⟨qui⟩ omnes dicunt pecuniis
indigentem Antiochum transgressum foedera Iudaeorum expoliasse
templum auro argentoque plenum.

6 *Timagenes* Boysen   *Timagenis* Lat.   7 *⟨qui⟩* Hudson
8 *expoliasse* Niese   *et spoliasse* Lat.

(83) That the raid of Antiochus on the temple was iniquitous, that it
was impecuniosity which drove him to invade it, when he was not
an open enemy, that he attacked us, his allies and friends, and that he
found there nothing to deserve ridicule; (84) these facts are attested
by many sober historians: Polybius of Megalopolis, Strabo the Cappadocian, Nicolaus of Damascus, Timagenes, Castor the chronicler,
and Apollodorus who all assert that it was impecuniosity which induced Antiochus, in violation of his treaties with the Jews, to plunder
the temple with its stores of gold and silver.

(trans. H. St. J. Thackeray, *LCL*)

84 *Strabo Cappadox*: Cf. the commentary to No. 33.

99

Historica Hypomnemata, apud: Josephus, *Antiquitates Judaicae*, XIII, 284–287 — Niese = F48R =
F.Gr.Hist., II, A91, F4

*(284) Κατὰ δὲ τοῦτον ἔτυχε τὸν καιρὸν μὴ μόνον τοὺς ἐν Ἱεροσολύμοις
καὶ τῇ χώρᾳ Ἰουδαίους εὐπραγεῖν, ἀλλὰ καὶ τοὺς ἐν Ἀλεξανδρείᾳ
κατοικοῦντας καὶ ἐν Αἰγύπτῳ καὶ Κύπρῳ· (285) Κλεοπάτρα γὰρ ἡ
βασίλισσα πρὸς τὸν υἱὸν στασιάζουσα Πτολεμαῖον τὸν Λάθουρον ἐπιλε-
5 γόμενον κατέστησεν ἡγεμόνας Χελκίαν καὶ Ἀνανίαν υἱοὺς ὄντας Ὀνίου
τοῦ οἰκοδομήσαντος τὸν ναὸν ἐν τῷ Ἡλιοπολίτῃ νομῷ... (286) παρα-
δοῦσα δὲ τούτοις ἡ Κλεοπάτρα τὴν στρατιὰν οὐδὲν δίχα τῆς τούτων γνώ-
μης ἔπραττεν, ὡς μαρτυρεῖ καὶ Στράβων ἡμῖν ὁ Καππάδοξ λέγων οὕτως·*

(287) «οἱ γὰρ πλείους, οἵ τε συγκατελθόντες καὶ οἱ ὕστερον ἐπι-
10 πεμπόμενοι παρὰ τῆς Κλεοπάτρας εἰς Κύπρον, μετεβάλοντο παραχρῆμα
πρὸς τὸν Πτολεμαῖον· μόνοι δὲ οἱ ἐκ τῆς Ὀνίου γενόμενοι Ἰουδαῖοι
συνέμενον διὰ τὸ τοὺς πολίτας αὐτῶν εὐδοκιμεῖν μάλιστα παρὰ τῇ
βασιλίσσῃ Χελκίαν τε καὶ Ἀνανίαν.» ταῦτα μὲν οὖν ὁ Στράβων φησίν.

9 συνελθόντες PFVE   qui cum eo descenderunt Lat.

11 γενόμενοι] λεγόμενοι FLAMVWE

(284) At this time not only were the Jews in Jerusalem and in the
country in a flourishing condition, but also those who lived in Alexandria and in Egypt and Cyprus. (285) For Queen Cleopatra, who was
at war with her son Ptolemy, surnamed Lathyrus, appointed as her
generals Chelkias and Ananias, sons of the Onias, who had built the
temple in the nome of Heliopolis... (286) And having entrusted her
army to them, Cleopatra did nothing without their approval, as
Strabo of Cappadocia also testifies, when he writes as follows.
(287) "For the majority, both those who came back from exile and
those, who were later sent to Cyprus by Cleopatra, immediately went
over to Ptolemy. And only the Jews of the district named 'the Land of
Onias' remained faithful to her, because their fellow-citizens Chelkias
and Ananias were held in special favour by the queen." This, then, is
what Strabo says.   (trans. R. Marcus, *LCL*)

284 κατὰ δὲ τοῦτον ἔτυχε τὸν καιρόν...: The starting point for Josephus'
quotation from Strabo's *Historica Hypomnemata* is John Hyrcan's successful
military operations against Samaria. In *Ant.*, XIII, 278, Josephus relates the
help sent by Ptolemy Lathyrus in a belated, unsuccessful attempt to save the town
from capture by the Jews. The military activity against Ptolemy Lathyrus by the Jews
both of Judaea and of Egypt links the events in Palestine with those in Cyprus.
285 Ὀνίου τοῦ οἰκοδομήσαντος τὸν ναὸν ἐν τῷ Ἡλιοπολίτῃ νομῷ: On Onias
IV, the founder of the temple at Leontopolis, and the part he played in the politics
of Ptolemaic Egypt, see the commentary to No. 167.
286 Lathyrus' mother expelled him from Egypt for the last time in 107 B.C.E.; see
T.C. Skeat, *The Reigns of the Ptolemies*, Munich 1954, p. 35, n. 15; A.E. Samuel,
Ptolemaic Chronology, Munich 1962, pp. 150 f. We do not know the exact date of
the events Strabo alludes to, but Cleopatra III's last document is dated 14 October
101 B.C.E.; see Samuel, *op. cit.*, p. 152. Since Chelkias had already died in the
reign of this Cleopatra (*Ant.*, XIII, 351), the *terminus ante quem* for the operations
related by Strabo is 101 B.C.E., while the *terminus post quem* is *c.* 107 B.C.E. We
may also assume that all these events occurred before 104 B.C.E., i.e. before the
death of John Hyrcan. After his expulsion from Egypt, Ptolemy Lathyrus established
himself in Cyprus. Apart from Strabo, Pompeius Trogus is the only ancient writer
to mention this stage of Cleopatra III's struggle against her son; cf. Iustinus,
XXXIX, 4 : 2: "Nec filium regno expulisse contenta, bello Cypri exulantem perse-

quitur. Unde pulso, interficit ducem exercitus sui, quod vivum eum e manibus emisisset, quamquam Ptolemaeus verecundia materni belli, non viribus minor ab insula recessisset." Lathyrus left Cyprus for Syria; see Pompeius Trogus, *Prologus Libri*, XXXIX: "expulsus est a matre Cyprum et in Syria bello petitus ab eadem." Lathyrus' sojourn at Seleucia is implied by Diodorus, XXXIV–XXXV, 39a; cf. also A. Bouché-Leclercq, *Histoire des Lagides*, II, Paris 1904, p. 97; H. Volkmann, PW, XXIII, p. 1741. However, it seems that Cleopatra made a new attempt to dislodge him from Cyprus after he regained it. This time the attempt failed, since only the Jewish soldiers from the "Land of Onias" remained loyal to the queen. These events are referred to here by Strabo; cf. W. Otto & H. Bengtson, *Zur Geschichte des Niederganges des Ptolemäerreiches*, Munich 1938, pp. 184 ff.

287 οἱ ἐκ τῆς ᾿Ονίου γενόμενοι ᾿Ιουδαῖοι: The "Land of Onias" was named so after Onias IV. For this expression, cf. *Ant.*, XIV, 131; *BJ*, I, 190 (οἱ τὴν ᾿Ονίου προσαγορευομένην χώραν κατέχοντες—); VII, 421; *CII*, No. 1530, l. 4: ᾿Ονίου γᾶ τροφὸς ἀμετέρα. The Land of Onias was situated around the Temple of Onias at Leontopolis, a place identified with Tell el-Yehoudieh in the Heliopolite nome in the eastern part of the Delta. For the Graeco-Jewish inscriptions of Tell el-Yehoudieh, see *CII*, Nos. 1450–1530; see also E. Naville, *The Mound of the Jew and the City of Onias*, London 1890; Schürer, III, p. 145, n. 34; Le Comte du Mesnil du Buisson, *BIFAO*, XXIX (1929), pp. 155 ff.; XXXV (1935), pp. 59 ff.; H. Kees, PW, XVIII, pp. 477 ff.

διὰ τὸ τοὺς πολίτας αὐτῶν εὐδοκιμεῖν... Χελκίαν τε καὶ ᾿Ανανίαν: Cf. *Contra Apionem*, II, 49 (No. 167): ῾Ο δὲ Φιλομήτωρ Πτολεμαῖος καὶ ἡ γυνὴ αὐτοῦ Κλεοπάτρα τὴν βασιλείαν ὅλην τὴν ἑαυτῶν ᾿Ιουδαίοις ἐπίστευσαν καὶ στρατηγοὶ πάσης τῆς δυνάμεως ἦσαν ᾿Ονίας καὶ Δοσίθεος ᾿Ιουδαῖοι. As Josephus states earlier (*Ant.*, XIII, 285), both Chelkias and Ananias were sons of Onias IV. They were heirs to his positions as the leader of the Jews in the Land of Onias and as the mainstay of the royal power in Egypt. As we learn from the following narrative of Josephus (*ibid.*, 349 ff.), they continued to play a prominent part in the struggle between Cleopatra and Lathyrus. After Lathyrus defeated Alexander Jannaeus in battle and subjugated Gaza, Cleopatra sent an expeditionary force against him under the command of Chelkias and Ananias. Chelkias died during the operations that ensued (*ibid.*, 351), but Ananias was of much service to the Jews of Judaea in defending their independence and by being instrumental in forming an alliance between Cleopatra III and the Jewish king (*ibid.*, 355).

An inscription found in the Heliopolite nome apparently has some connection with Chelkias; see *CII*, No. 1450 = Gabba, No. XI. In l. 2. of the inscription we read Χελκίου, while in l.7 we find στρατηγὸν. On this inscription, see T. Reinach, *REJ*, XL (1900), pp. 50 ff.; H. Willrich, *Archiv für Papyrusforschung*, I, pp. 48 ff.; M.L. Strack, *Archiv für Papyrusforschung*, II, p. 554; L. Fuchs, *Die Juden Aegyptens in ptolemäischer und römischer Zeit*, Vienna 1924, p. 16; J. Cohen, *Judaica et Aegyptiaca*, Groningen 1941, p. 58. The mutilated condition of the inscription prevents us from positively determining its contents. While Willrich and Cohen think that it refers to Chelkias, it is regarded as a reference to his son by Strack, Fuchs and Gabba.

Strabo of Amaseia

100

Historica Hypomnemata, apud: Josephus, *Antiquitates Judaicae*, XIII, 319 — Niese = *F. Gr. Hist.*, II, A91, F11

Φύσει δ' ἐπιεικεῖ κέχρητο καὶ σφόδρα ἦν αἰδοῦς ἥττων, ὡς μαρτυρεῖ τούτῳ καὶ Στράβων ἐκ τοῦ Τιμαγένους ὀνόματος λέγων οὕτως· «ἐπιεικής τε ἐγένετο οὗτος ὁ ἀνὴρ ⟨scil. Ἀριστόβουλος⟩ καὶ πολλὰ τοῖς Ἰουδαίοις χρήσιμος· χώραν τε γὰρ αὐτοῖς προσεκτήσατο καὶ
5 τὸ μέρος τοῦ τῶν Ἰτουραίων ἔθνους ᾠκειώσατο, δεσμῷ συνάψας τῇ τῶν αἰδοίων περιτομῇ.»

5 Ἰτουραίων] Ἰδουμαίων? Ed. Meyer

He [scil. Aristobulus I] had a kindly nature and was wholly given to modesty, as Strabo also testifies on the authority of Timagenes, writing as follows. "This man was a kindly person and very serviceable to the Jews, for he acquired additional territory for them, and brought over to them a portion of the Ituraean nation, whom he joined to them by the bond of circumcision." (trans. R. Marcus, *LCL*)

Στράβων ἐκ τοῦ Τιμαγένους ὀνόματος: Cf. the commentary to Timagenes (No. 81). This passage may show how one can use Strabo's tradition to correct the picture that emerges from Nicolaus.

101

Historica Hypomnemata, apud: Josephus, *Antiquitates Judaicae*, XIII, 345-347 — Niese = F49R = *F. Gr. Hist.*, II, A91, F12

(345) Πτολεμαῖος δὲ μετὰ τὴν νίκην προσκαταδραμὼν τὴν χώραν ὀψίας ἐπιγενομένης ἔν τισι κώμαις τῆς Ἰουδαίας κατέμεινεν, ἃς γυναικῶν εὑρὼν μεστὰς καὶ νηπίων ἐκέλευσεν τοὺς στρατιώτας ἀποσφάττοντας αὐτοὺς καὶ κρεουργοῦντας ἔπειτα εἰς λέβητας ζέοντας
5 ἐνιέντας τὰ μέλη ἀπάρχεσθαι. (346) τοῦτο δὲ προσέταξεν, ἵν' οἱ διαφυγόντες ἐκ τῆς μάχης καὶ πρὸς αὐτοὺς ἐλθόντες σαρκοφάγους ὑπολάβωσιν εἶναι τοὺς πολεμίους, καὶ διὰ τοῦτο ἔτι μᾶλλον αὐτοὺς καταπλαγῶσι ταῦτ' ἰδόντες. (347) λέγει δὲ καὶ Στράβων καὶ Νικόλαος, ὅτι τοῦτον αὐτοῖς ἐχρήσαντο τὸν τρόπον, καθὼς κἀγὼ προείρηκα.

5 ἀπέρχεσθαι Naber   9 ἐχρήσατο Gutschmid

(345) After this victory Ptolemy overran other territory, and when evening fell, halted in some villages of Judaea, which he found full of women and infants; he thereupon commanded his soldiers to

cut their throats and chop them up and then to fling the pieces into boiling cauldrons and to taste of them. (346) This order he gave that those who had escaped from the battle and had returned to their homes might get the notion that the enemy were eaters of human flesh, and so might be the more terrified by this sight. (347) And both Strabo and Nicolaus say that they treated the Jews in the manner which I have just mentioned. (trans. R. Marcus, *LCL*)

345 Πτολεμαῖος δὲ μετὰ τὴν νίκην...: Cf. the commentary to Nicolaus (No. 89). Josephus continues the narrative of the war between Lathyrus and Alexander Jannaeus.

ἀποσφάττοντας αὐτοὺς καὶ κρεουργοῦντας: On this act of deliberate cruelty, cf. Frontinus, *Strategemata*, III, 5 : 1: "Aliquem ex captivis in conspectu iussit occidi [scil. Clearchus Lacedaemonius] et membratim tamquam alimenti causa in contubernia distribui: Thraces nihil non facturum perseverantiae causa eum credentes, qui tam detestabiles epulas sustinuisset experiri." According to Nonius Marcellus, the Carthaginian commander tortured the Roman prisoners in order to crush the spirit of the Romans ("quo metu debilitaret nostros"); cf. Nonius Marcellus, *De Conpendiosa Doctrina*, p. 163 M, 24 ff., from Varro, *De Vita Populi Romani*, III. The best parallel to Lathyrus' deed that I know is perhaps to be found in the chronicles of the First Crusade relating to Bohemond the Norman and the events of 1098 C.E.; see William of Tyre, *Historia Rerum in Partibus Transmarinis Gestarum*, IV, 23 (*Recueil des Historiens des Croisades: Historiens occidentaux*, Vol. I, Part 1, Paris 1844, p. 190): "Boamundus vero, promissi memor, circa primum noctis crepusculum cum alii per castra pro coenae apparatu, more solito, essent solliciti, educi praecipit Turcos aliquot, quos habebat in vinculis et tradens eos carnificibus iugulari mandat; et igne copioso supposito, quasi ad opus coenae, diligenter assari praecipit et studiosius praeparari; praecipiens suis, quod si ab aliquibus interrogati essent, quidnam sibi coena talis vellet, responderent, quod inter principes convenerat, ut quotquot deinceps de hostibus aut eorum exploratoribus caperentur omnes prandiis et principum et populi ex seipsis escas, via simili, cogerentur persolvere."

102

Historica Hypomnemata, apud: Josephus, *Antiquitates Judaicae*, XIV, 111–113 — Niese = F50R = F. *Gr. Hist.*, II, A91, F6

(111) Οὐκ ἔστι δὲ ἀμάρτυρον τὸ μέγεθος τῶν προειρημένων χρημάτων, οὐδ᾽ ὑπὸ ἀλαζονείας ἡμετέρας καὶ περιττολογίας ἐπὶ τοσοῦτον ἐξαίρεται πλῆθος, ἀλλὰ πολλοί τε ἄλλοι τῶν συγγραφέων ἡμῖν μαρτυροῦσιν καὶ Στράβων ὁ Καππάδοξ λέγων οὕτως· (112) «πέμψας δὲ Μιθριδάτης εἰς Κῶ ἔλαβε τὰ χρήματα, ἃ παρέθετο ἐκεῖ Κλεοπάτρα ἡ βασίλισσα, καὶ τὰ τῶν Ἰουδαίων ὀκτακόσια τάλαντα.» (113) ἡμῖν δὲ δημόσια

5 εἰς Κῶ om. P / ἡ om. P

Strabo of Amaseia

χρήματα οὐκ ἔστιν ἢ μόνα τὰ τοῦ θεοῦ, καὶ δῆλον, ὅτι ταῦτα μετήνεγκαν
εἰς Κῶ τὰ χρήματα οἱ ἐν τῇ ᾿Ασίᾳ ᾿Ιουδαῖοι διὰ τὸν ἐκ Μιθριδάτου
φόβον· οὐ γὰρ εἰκὸς τοὺς ἐν τῇ ᾿Ιουδαίᾳ πόλιν τε ὀχυρὰν ἔχοντας καὶ
10 τὸν ναὸν πέμπειν χρήματα εἰς Κῶ, ἀλλ᾽ οὐδὲ τοὺς ἐν ᾿Αλεξανδρείᾳ
κατοικοῦντας ᾿Ιουδαίους πιθανὸν τοῦτ᾽ ἐστὶ ποιῆσαι μηδὲν Μιθριδάτην
δεδιότας.

8 ἐκ om. P

(111) And there is no lack of witnesses to the great amount of
the sums mentioned, nor have they been raised to so great a figure
through boastfulness or exaggeration on our part, but there are many
historians who bear us out, in particular Strabo of Cappadocia, who
writes as follows. (112) "Mithridates sent to Cos and took the money
which Queen Cleopatra had deposited there, and eight hundred talents
of the Jews." (113) Now there is no public money among us except
that which is God's and it is therefore evident that this money was
transferred to Cos by the Jews of Asia because of their fear of Mithridates. For it is not likely that those in Judaea, who possessed a
fortified city and the temple, would have sent money to Cos, nor is
it probable that the Jews living in Alexandria would have done this
either, since they had no fear of Mithridates.   (trans. R. Marcus, *LCL*)

On this passage, see T. Reinach, *REJ*, XVI (1888), pp. 204 ff.; Albert, *op.
cit.* (supra, p. 267), pp. 35 ff.; A. Bouché-Leclercq, *Histoire des Lagides*, II,
Paris 1904, pp. 117 f.; H. Willrich, *Hermes*, XXXIX (1904), p. 250; idem,
Urkundenfälschung in der hellenistisch-jüdischen Literatur, Göttingen 1924, p. 74;
Otto & Bengtson, *op. cit.* (supra, p. 270), pp. 16, 190; Cohen, *op. cit.* (supra,
p. 270), pp. 59 ff.

112 Κλεοπάτρα ἡ βασίλισσα: This Cleopatra seems to be Cleopatra III; see *Ant.*,
XIII, 349: τὰ δὲ πολλὰ τοῦ πλούτου αὐτῆς καὶ τοὺς υἱωνοὺς καὶ διαθήκας
πέμψασα [scil. Cleopatra] Κῴοις παρέθετο. Josephus' statement is confirmed by
Appianus, *Mithridatica*, 23 : 92 f.: Μιθριδάτης δὲ ἐς μὲν Κῶ κατέπλευσε, Κῴων
αὐτὸν ἀσμένως δεχομένων, καὶ τὸν ᾿Αλεξάνδρου παῖδα τοῦ βασιλεύοντος Αἰγύπτου
σὺν χρήμασι πολλοῖς ὑπὸ τῆς μάμμης Κλεοπάτρας ἐν Κῶ καταλελειμμένον παραλα-
βὼν ἔτρεφε βασιλικῶς ἐκ τε τῶν Κλεοπάτρας θησαυρῶν γάζαν πολλὴν καὶ τέχνην
καὶ λίθους καὶ κόσμους γυναικείους καὶ χρήματα πολλὰ εἰς τὸν Πόντον ἔπεμψεν.
This fact as related by Appian refutes the arguments of Willrich. According to
Appian, Cleopatra was the grandmother of the young prince. Willrich maintains
that it was Cleopatra Berenice, the wife of Ptolemy Alexander I, who sent her son,
the future Alexander II, together with her treasures to Cos (Willrich, *loc. cit.*).
We must admit, however, that some difficulty is attached to the long interval that
elapsed between the sending of Cleopatra III's grandson (before 101 B.C.E.) and
his capture by Mithridates (88 B.C.E.). For an attempt to explain this, see Cohen,
op. cit., p. 60.

καὶ τὰ τῶν Ἰουδαίων ὀκτακόσια τάλαντα: Jacoby, following Otto, is of the opinion that the money belonged to the Jews of Alexandria, who in this instance imitated their queen. The same view is held by Willrich. It contradicts, however, the interpretation given to the passage by Josephus, who states that the Jewish money deposited at Cos belonged to the Jews of Asia. Josephus bases his interpretation on the argument that the Jews, both of Judaea and of Alexandria, would not have sent their money to Cos, since they had no fear of Mithridates. To validate this argument, we must presume that Josephus assumes that the depositing of the Jewish money at Cos took place at the time of Mithridates' invasion of Asia. However, this invasion was not, contemporary with Cleopatra's deposit of her treasures, since she died in 101 B.C.E. Nonetheless, the language of the passage from Strabo does not necessitate a direct temporal or logical connection between the two deposits of money and there is nothing in the passage to contradict Josephus' interpretation.

We know almost nothing about Jews living at Cos itself. We have some documents that point to Jewish connections with Cos, but they do not prove that Jews permanently lived on the island. For the letter referring to the Jewish ambassadors returning from Rome to their country, written by the consul C. Fannius Strabo and sent to Cos in 161 B.C.E., see *Ant.*, XIV, 233, as interpreted and dated by B. Niese, *Orientalische Studien Theodor Nöldeke gewidmet*, II, Giessen 1906, pp. 817 ff.; see also F. Münzer, *Hermes*, LV (1920), p. 437, n. 1. For the letter of Lucius, presumably L. Caecilius Metellus, consul in 142 B. C. E., cf. I Macc. xv : 23. On the gifts of Herod to Cos, see *BJ*, I, 423. For the visit of Euaratus the Coan to Herod's court in Jerusalem, see *BJ*, I, 532; *Ant.*, XVI, 312. However, there is insufficient evidence to assume with Ruppel that there is a connection between *OGIS*, No. 192, and the Jewish community of Cos; cf. W. Ruppel, *Philologus*, LXXXII, pp. 437 ff. Whatever the number of the Jewish population of Cos, it would not account for the vast treasure alluded to by Strabo.

In Josephus' opinion the vast amount of money mentioned by Strabo was money collected by the Jews for the Temple in Jerusalem. However, Reinach, *op. cit.* (supra, p. 273), aptly remarks that the sum of eight hundred talents is too large to represent only the annual collection for the Temple. It does not compare with the treasure of the Temple, which consisted of only 2,000 talents when it was robbed by Crassus (*Ant.*, XIV, 105). We should conclude that the money also included much of the private fortunes of the Asian Jews.

103

Historica Hypomnemata, apud: Josephus, *Antiquitates Judaicae*, XIV, 34–36 — Niese = F52R = *F. Gr. Hist.*, II, A91, F14

(34) Μετ᾽ οὐ πολὺ δὲ Πομπηίου εἰς Δαμασκὸν ἀφικομένου καὶ Κοίλην Συρίαν ἐπιόντος ἧκον παρ᾽ αὐτὸν πρέσβεις ἐξ ὅλης Συρίας καὶ Αἰγύπτου καὶ ἐκ τῆς Ἰουδαίας· ἔπεμψε γὰρ αὐτῷ μέγα δῶρον Ἀριστόβουλος ἄμπελον χρυσῆν ἐκ πεντακοσίων ταλάντων. (35) μέμνηται δὲ τοῦ
5 δώρου καὶ Στράβων ὁ Καππάδοξ λέγων οὕτως· «ἦλθεν δὲ καὶ ἐξ

Strabo of Amaseia

Αἰγύπτου πρεσβεία καὶ στέφανος ἀπὸ χρυσῶν τετρακισχιλίων καὶ ἐκ τῆς Ἰουδαίας εἴτε ἄμπελος εἴτε κῆπος· τερπωλὴν ὠνόμαζον τὸ δημιούργημα. (36) τοῦτο μέντοι τὸ δῶρον ἱστορήκαμεν καὶ ἡμεῖς ἀνακείμενον ἐν Ῥώμῃ ἐν τῷ ἱερῷ τοῦ Διὸς τοῦ Καπετωλίου ἐπιγραφὴν 10 ἔχον Ἀλεξάνδρου τοῦ τῶν Ἰουδαίων βασιλέως. ἐτιμήθη δὲ εἶναι πεντακοσίων ταλάντων.» Ἀριστόβουλον μὲν οὖν τοῦτο λέγεται πέμψαι τὸν Ἰουδαίων δυνάστην.

10 Ἀλεξάνδρου] ἀριστοβούλου E   aristoboli filii alexandri Lat.
‹Ἀριστοβούλου τοῦ› Ἀλεξάνδρου G. C. Richards & R. J. H. Shutt, CQ, XXXI
(1937), p. 173

(34) When Pompey not long afterward came to Damascus and was advancing into Coele-Syria, there came to him envoys from all of Syria and Egypt and Judaea. Aristobulus for example, sent him a fine gift, which was a golden vine worth five hundred talents. (35) This gift is also mentioned by Strabo of Cappadocia in the following words: "There also came from Egypt an embassy and a crown worth four thousand pieces of gold, and from Judaea either a vine or garden; terpole (delight) is what they called this work of art. (36) Moreover we ourselves have examined this gift, which has been set up in the temple of Jupiter Capitolinus at Rome, and has an inscription reading, 'From Alexander, the king of the Jews.' It was valued at five hundred talents." And it is said to have been sent by Aristobulus, the ruler of the Jews.

(trans. R. Marcus, LCL)

34 μετ᾽οὐ πολὺ δὲ Πομπηίου εἰς Δαμασκὸν ἀφικομένου: Josephus did not succeed in integrating Strabo with his main source, presumably Nicolaus. The result is that Pompey's arrival at Damascus is told twice, here and in Ant., XIV, 40: διελθὼν δὲ τὰς πόλεις... εἰς Δαμασκὸν ἦκεν—; cf. B. Niese, Hermes, XI (1876), p. 471; L. Korach, "Über den Wert des Josephus als Quelle für die römische Geschichte", Ph.D. Thesis, Leipzig 1895, pp. 22 f.; Albert, op. cit. (supra, p. 267), pp. 32 ff.
35 τερπωλὴν ὠνόμαζον τὸ δημιούργημα: Cf. W. Wreszinski, Orientalistische Literaturzeitung, XXVII (1924), pp. 570 ff.; K. Galling, ZAW, Suppl., LXXVII (1958), pp. 49 ff.
36 Ἀλεξάνδρου: That is, Alexander Jannaeus, the father of Aristobulus. Only the Epitome reads Ἀριστοβούλου, while the Latin translation has "aristoboli filii alexandri". The reading of the Greek MSS may, after all, be the true one, because the exquisite τερπωλή had been made in the time of Alexander. It had his name inscribed on it, though it was presented to the Romans by Aristobulus. However, it could be that the τερπωλή Strabo saw at Rome was, in fact, a present sent to Rome by Alexander Jannaeus, who presumably followed his father, John Hyrcan in renewing the treaty of alliance between Judaea and Rome; cf. T. Reinach, REJ, XXXVIII (1899), p. 170. Another example of Strabo's sojourn in Rome is given in Geographica, VI, 2 : 6, p. 273.

104

Historica Hypomnemata, apud: Josephus, *Antiquitates Judaicae*, XIV, 66–68 — Niese =
F. Gr. Hist., II, A91, F15

(66) Καὶ γὰρ ἁλούσης τῆς πόλεως περὶ τρίτον μῆνα τῇ τῆς νηστείας
ἡμέρᾳ κατὰ ἐνάτην καὶ ἑβδομηκοστὴν καὶ ἑκατοστὴν ὀλυμπιάδα
ὑπατευόντων Γαΐου Ἀντωνίου καὶ Μάρκου Τυλλίου Κικέρωνος οἱ
πολέμιοι μὲν εἰσπεσόντες ἔσφαττον τοὺς ἐν τῷ ἱερῷ, (67) οἱ δὲ πρὸς
5 *ταῖς θυσίαις οὐδὲν ἧττον ἱερουργοῦντες διετέλουν, οὔτε ὑπὸ τοῦ φόβου*
τοῦ περὶ τῆς ψυχῆς οὔθ᾿ ὑπὸ τοῦ πλήθους τῶν ἤδη πεφονευμένων
ἀναγκασθέντες ἀποδρᾶναι πᾶν θ᾿ ὅ τι δέοι παθεῖν τοῦτο παρ᾿ αὐτοῖς
ὑπομεῖναι τοῖς βωμοῖς κρεῖττον εἶναι νομίζοντες ἢ παρελθεῖν τι τῶν
νομίμων. (68) ὅτι δὲ οὐ λόγος ταῦτα μόνον ἐστὶν ἐγκώμιον ψευδοῦς
10 *εὐσεβείας ἐμφανίζων, ἀλλ᾿ ἀλήθεια, μαρτυροῦσι πάντες οἱ τὰς κατὰ*
Πομπήιον πράξεις ἀναγράψαντες, ἐν οἷς καὶ Στράβων καὶ Νικόλαος
⟨No. 91⟩ *καὶ πρὸς αὐτοῖς Τίτος Λίβιος* ⟨No. 132⟩ *ὁ τῆς Ῥωμαϊκῆς*
ἱστορίας συγγραφεύς.

3 Τυλλίου Niese   τυλαιου P   τουλίου FLAMW   6 πεφονευμένων Niese
         φονευμένων P   φονευομένων FLAMW

(66) And indeed when the city was taken, in the third month, on the
Fast Day, in the hundred and seventy-ninth Olympiad, in the consulship of Gaius Antonius and Marcus Tullius Cicero, and the enemy rushed in and were slaughtering the Jews in the temple, (67) those who
were busied with the sacrifices none the less continued to perform the
sacred ceremonies; nor were they compelled, either by fear for their
lives or by the great number of those already slain, to run away, but
thought it better to endure whatever they might have to suffer there
beside the altars than to neglect any of the ordinances. (68) And that
this is not merely a story to set forth the praises of a fictitious piety, but
the truth, is attested by all those who have narrated the exploits
of Pompey, among them Strabo and Nicolaus and, in addition, Titus
Livius, the author of a History of Rome.   (trans. R. Marcus, *LCL*)

66 καὶ γὰρ ἁλούσης τῆς πόλεως περὶ τρίτον μῆνα τῇ τῆς νηστείας ἡμέρᾳ:
The statement about Jerusalem's capture on the Day of Atonement cannot be
accepted, though some scholars take it at its face value and have even attempted to
support it with a misinterpreted allusion in the Commentary to Habakkuk found in
the Dead Sea Scrolls; see, e.g., J. van Ooteghem, *Pompée le Grand*, Brussels 1954,
p. 233, n. 6. By περὶ τρίτον μῆνα the third month of the siege is meant, and not
the third month of the Jewish year. This is proved by a comparison with *BJ*, I,
149 (τρίτῳ γὰρ μηνὶ τῆς πολιορκίας ... εἰσέπιπτον εἰς τὸ ἱερόν); V, 397; cf.
Orosius, *Adversus Paganos*, VI, 6 : 3; Eutropius, VI, 14 (No. 489).

Strabo of Amaseia

The mention of the Day of Atonement contradicts the statement that Jerusalem fell in the third month of the siege, since the siege had already begun in the spring; see M. B. Dagut, *Biblica*, XXXII (1951), pp. 542 ff. As Magie remarks, the Day of Atonement was observed in October, and it is hard to see how Pompey could have remained so long in Judaea and still have reached Amisus before winter began, since it was necessary for him to cross the Taurus before the Cilician Gates were blocked by snow; see D. Magie, *Roman Rule in Asia Minor*, II, Princeton 1950, p. 1229. The mention of the Day of Atonement also is suspicious in view of Josephus' statement that in 37 B. C. E. Jerusalem, too, was captured on the Day of the Fast; see *Ant.*, XIV, 487: ὥσπερ ἐκ περιτροπῆς τῆς γενομένης ἐπὶ Πομπηίου τοῖς Ἰουδαίοις συμφορᾶς.

Cassius Dio asserts that the capture of Jerusalem by Pompey occurred on a Sabbath, and not on the Day of Atonement; see Cassius Dio, XXXVII, 16 : 4 (No. 406). Therefore, we should follow the suggestion expressed by Herzfeld and followed by many scholars that the mention of the Day of Atonement derives from the mistake prevalent in pagan literature that the Sabbath was a fast day; see the commentary to Suetonius (No. 303); cf. L. Herzfeld, *MGWJ*, IV (1855), pp. 109 ff.; J. Kromayer, *Hermes*, XXIX (1894), pp. 563 ff.; Korach, *op. cit.* (supra, p. 270), p. 29; Schürer, I, p. 298, n. 23; Dagut, *op. cit.* We may be sure that Josephus' mistake derives from Strabo, and not from Nicolaus, for the following reasons: (a) It is very unlikely that Nicolaus, who lived at the Court of Herod and had a first-hand knowledge of the Jews, would have been guilty of such confusion; (b) it does not occur in *Bellum Judaicum*, where Josephus used Nicolaus, but not Strabo; (c) the supposition is corroborated by the parallel narrative in Strabo's *Geographica* XVI, 2 : 40, p. 763 (No. 115): κατελάβετο δ', ὥς φασι, τηρήσας τὴν τῆς νηστείας ἡμέραν. Cf. also D. L. Drew, *Bulletin of the Faculty of Arts, Fouad University*, XIII, Part I (1951), pp. 83 ff. The arguments of Morr that Jerusalem fell on the Day of Atonement do not carry conviction; see J. Morr, *Philologus*, LXXXI, pp. 266 ff.; see also the commentary to Strabo, *loc. cit.* (No. 115). The year of the siege, 63 B.C.E., is upheld by the mention of the consulates of Cicero and Antonius.

105

Historica Hypomnemata, apud: Josephus, *Antiquitates Judaicae*, XIV, 114–118 — Niese = F51R = F. Gr. Hist., II, A91, F7

(114) Μαρτυρεῖ δὲ καὶ ἐν ἑτέρῳ τόπῳ ὁ αὐτὸς Στράβων, ὅτι καθ' ὃν καιρὸν διέβη Σύλλας εἰς τὴν Ἑλλάδα πολεμήσων Μιθριδάτῃ καὶ Λεύκολλον πέμψας ἐπὶ τὴν ἐν Κυρήνῃ στάσιν ★ τοῦ ἔθνους ἡμῶν ἡ οἰκουμένη πεπλήρωτο, λέγων οὕτως· *(115)* «τέτταρες δ' ἦσαν ἐν τῇ
5 πόλει τῶν Κυρηναίων, ἥ τε τῶν πολιτῶν καὶ ἡ τῶν γεωργῶν, τρίτη δ' ἡ τῶν μετοίκων, τετάρτη δ' ἡ τῶν Ἰουδαίων. αὕτη δ' εἰς πᾶσαν πόλιν

3 πέμψαι FLAMVW   ἔπεμψεν Gutschmid / post στάσιν lacunam indicavit Niese   4 ἦσαν ‹στάσεις›? Jacoby   5 Κυρηναίων ‹μερίδες›

Richards & Shutt, supra, p. 275

277

ἤδη καὶ παρελήλυθεν καὶ τόπον οὐκ ἔστι ῥᾳδίως εὑρεῖν τῆς οἰκουμένης,
ὃς οὐ παραδέδεκται τοῦτο τὸ φῦλον μηδ᾽ ἐπικρατεῖται ὑπ᾽ αὐτοῦ.
(116) τῆς τε Αἰγύπτου τὴν Κυρηναίων ἅτε τῶν αὐτῶν ἡγεμόνων
10 τυχοῦσαν τῶν τε ἄλλων συχνὰ ζηλῶσαι συνέβη καὶ δὴ τὰ συντάγματα
τῶν Ἰουδαίων θρέψαι διαφερόντως καὶ συναυξῆσαι χρώμενα τοῖς
πατρίοις τῶν Ἰουδαίων νόμοις. *(117)* ἐν γοῦν Αἰγύπτῳ κατοικία τῶν
Ἰουδαίων ἐστὶν ἀποδεδειγμένη χωρίς, καὶ τῆς Ἀλεξανδρέων πόλεως
ἀφώρισται μέγα μέρος τῷ ἔθνει τούτῳ. καθίσταται δὲ καὶ ἐθνάρχης
15 αὐτῶν, ὃς διοικεῖ τε τὸ ἔθνος καὶ διαιτᾷ κρίσεις καὶ συμβολαίων
ἐπιμελεῖται καὶ προσταγμάτων, ὡς ἂν πολιτείας ἄρχων αὐτοτελοῦς.
(118) ἐν Αἰγύπτῳ μὲν οὖν ἴσχυσε τὸ ἔθνος διὰ τὸ Αἰγυπτίους εἶναι
τὸ ἐξ ἀρχῆς τοὺς Ἰουδαίους, καὶ διὰ τὸ πλησίον θέσθαι τὴν κατοικίαν
τοὺς ἀπελθόντας ἐκεῖθεν, εἰς δὲ τὴν Κυρηναίαν μετέβη διὰ τὸ καὶ
20 ταύτην ὅμορον εἶναι τῇ τῶν Αἰγυπτίων ἀρχῇ, καθάπερ τὴν Ἰουδαίαν ⋆
μᾶλλον δὲ τῆς ἀρχῆς ἐκείνης πρότερον.» Στράβων μὲν δὴ ταῦτα λέγει.

9 τῆς τε Αἰγύπτου τὴν Κυρηναίων Niese   τήν τε αἴγυπτον καὶ τὴν κυρηναίων
PF κυρηναίαν LAMVW   12 κατοικία Gutschmid   13 χώρα Gutschmid
18 θέσθαι Bekker   ἔσεσθαι codd.   20 ἀρχῇ secl. Niese

(114) And this same Strabo in another passage testifies that at the time
when Sulla crossed over to Greece to make war on Mithridates, and
sent Lucullus to put down the revolt in Cyrene⋆ the habitable world was
filled with our nation, for he writes as follows: (115) "There were four
classes in the state of Cyrene; the first consisted of citizens, the second
of farmers, the third of resident aliens (metics), and the fourth of Jews.
This people has already made its way into every city, and it is not easy
to find any place in the habitable world which has not received this
nation and in which it has not made its power felt. (116) And it has
come about that Cyrene, which had the same rulers as Egypt, has imitated it in many respects, particularly in notably encouraging and
aiding the expansion of the organized groups of Jews, which observe
the national Jewish laws. (117) In Egypt for example, territory has been
set apart for a Jewish settlement, and in Alexandria a great part of the
city has been allocated to this nation. And an ethnarch of their own has
been installed, who governs the people and adjudicates suits and
supervises contracts and ordinances, just as if he were the head of a
sovereign state. (118) And so this nation has flourished in Egypt
because the Jews were originally Egyptians and because those who left
that country made their homes near by; and they migrated to Cyrene
because this country bordered on the kingdom of Egypt, as did
Judaea — or rather, it formerly belonged (?) to that kingdom." These
are Strabo's own words.   (trans. R. Marcus, *LCL*)

Strabo of Amaseia

114 καὶ Λεύκολλον πέμψας ἐπὶ τήν ἐν Κυρήνῃ στάσιν: The mission of Lucullus to Cyrene is referred to also by Plutarch (*Lucullus*, 2 : 3 ff.). Appianus (*Mithridatica*, 33 : 131) mentions only his being sent by Sulla to Alexandria and to Syria in 86 B.C.E. Plutarch, in this connection, does not refer to the Jews, but in general he agrees with Josephus, saying: ἐξέπεμψεν ἐπ' Αἰγύπτου καὶ Λιβύης τὸν Λεύκολλον ἄξοντα ναῦς ἐκεῖθεν... καὶ Κυρηναίους καταλαβὼν ἐκ τυραννίδων συνεχῶν καὶ πολέμων ταραττομένους ἀνέλαβε... δ καὶ τότε Κυρηναίους νομοθετοῦντι Λευκόλλῳ πρῴους παρέσχεν. On the events in Cyrene, see Gelzer, PW, XIII, p. 378; P. Romanelli, *La Cirenaica Romana*, Verbania 1943, pp. 43 f.; E. J. Bickerman, *PAAJR*, XX (1951), p. 131; S. I. Oost, *Classical Philology*, LVIII (1963), pp. 18 f.

115 τετάρτη δ'ἡ τῶν 'Ιουδαίων: The origins of the Jewish population of Cyrenaica go back at least to the early Hellenistic age, as we learn from *Contra Apionem*, II, 44: καὶ Κυρήνης ἐγκρατῶς ἀρχεῖν βουλόμενος [scil. Πτολεμαῖος ὁ Λάγου] καὶ τῶν ἄλλων τῶν ἐν τῇ Λιβύῃ πόλεων εἰς αὐτὰς μέρος 'Ιουδαίων ἔπεμψε κατοικῆσον. The inscriptional evidence tends to confirm the Egyptian origin of a part of Cyrenaican Jewry; see S. Applebaum, *Journal of Jewish Studies*, XIII (1962), p. 34. There were considerable Jewish communities in most of the cities of Cyrenaica, namely, in Cyrene, in Teucheira and in Berenice; see S. Applebaum, *Scripta Hierosolymitana*, VII, 1961, pp. 30 f. Several inscriptions teach us something about the organization of the Jewish community of Berenice. An inscription from this city dates from the time of Augustus; see J. & G. Roux, *REG*, LXII (1949), pp. 281 ff. It includes a decree of the Jewish *politeuma*; cf. Ruppel, *op. cit.*, (supra, p. 274), pp. 439 ff. It honours a member of the *politeuma*, Decimus Valerius Dionysius. Another decree emanating from that *politeuma*, dating from 24–25 C.E., honours a Roman official; cf. Roux, *loc. cit.* We learn from both inscriptions that a body of archontes headed the Jewish *politeuma* of Berenice. The organization of the Jewish community there emerges also from a third inscription, from the second year of Nero (56 C.E.) published by G. Caputo, *La Parola del Passato*, XII (1957), pp. 132 ff.=*SEG*, XVII, No. 823; cf. J. & L. Robert, *REG*, LXXII (1959), pp. 275 f. This inscription honours some members of the Jewish community, first of them the archontes, for repairing the local synagogue. We may assume that the Jews of Cyrene were similarly organized in a regular *politeuma*, the members of which enjoyed well-defined privileges in the city, being neither citizens of Cyrene nor *metoikoi*. New inscriptions from Cyrene seem to suggest that individual Jews played their part in the municipal life of the city in the first century C.E. We learn from an inscription dating from 60–61 C.E. that one of the *nomophylakes* was a Jew; see *Quaderni di Archaeologia della Libia*, IV (1961), p. 16. Jewish names ('Ιησοῦς, 'Ιούδας, 'Ελάζαρ) surprisingly make their appearance in a list of ephebes that dates from 3–28 C.E.; see J. & L. Robert, *REG*, LXXV (1962), p. 218. The high cultural level already attained by the Jews of Cyrene in the Hellenistic age is well illustrated by the historian Jason, who wrote a five-book history of the Hasmonaean revolt, in which he combined Hellenistic historical style with Jewish orthodoxy.

We do not know the exact nature of the *stasis* Lucullus had to settle in Cyrene. From Josephus (*Ant.*, XVI, 160) we learn about a struggle between the Jews and the Greeks of Cyrene in the time of Augustus. Josephus maintains that, although the kings had formerly granted the Jews *isonomia*, their rights were not respected by the Greeks. On an intercession of Marcus Agrippa on behalf of the Jews of Cyrene, see *Ant.*, XVI, 169 f.

279

καὶ τόπον οὐκ ἔστι ῥᾳδίως εὑρεῖν τῆς οἰκουμένης...: For the nature of the diffusion of the Jews throughout the world, see also Philo, *Legatio ad Gaium*, 281 f.: αὕτη... μητρόπολις δὲ οὐ μιᾶς χώρας Ἰουδαίας, ἀλλὰ καὶ τῶν πλείστων, διὰ τὰς ἀποικίας ἃς ἐξέπεμψεν... καὶ οὐ μόνον αἱ ἤπειροι μεσταὶ τῶν Ἰουδαϊκῶν ἀποικιῶν εἰσιν, ἀλλὰ καὶ νήσων αἱ δοκιμώταται.

ἐπικρατεῖται ὑπ' αὐτοῦ: Heinemann translates: "wo nicht Juden Aufnahme gefunden und sich behauptet hätten"; see I. Heinemann, PW, Suppl. V (1931), p. 16. Roos interprets ἐπικρατεῖν in the sense it has in private law, as attested in the papyri: "das Besitzrecht über etwas ausüben, den Besitz von etwas ergreifen"; see A.G. Roos, *Mnemosyne*, Ser. 3, II (1935), pp. 236 f. Nevertheless, we may assume that ἐπικρατεῖν in our passage has its common meaning of ruling, and that Strabo exaggerates in order to emphasize the pervasiveness of Jewish influence.

117 καὶ τῆς Ἀλεξανδρέων πόλεως ἀφώρισται μέγα μέρος τῷ ἔθνει τούτῳ: Strabo does not state which part of Alexandria had been allotted to the Jews, but in view of *BJ*, II, 495, we may surmise that it was identical with the Delta (... δέλτα, συνῴκιστο γὰρ ἐκεῖ τὸ Ἰουδαϊκόν) or, perhaps, the Delta with the addition of some other quarter, since Philo (*In Flaccum*, 55) states that two of the five quarters denoted by the first letters of the alphabet were Jewish. For their enumeration, see pseudo-Callisthenes, I, 32; see also P.M. Fraser, *JEA*, XXXVII (1951), p. 104, referring to a Syriac source; J. Seyfarth, *Aegyptus*, XXXV (1955), p. 15. On the location of the original Jewish centre at Alexandria, see the commentary to No. 166.

ἐθνάρχης αὐτῶν: Strabo testifies here in the clearest terms to the "monarchical" organization of Egyptian — or at least Alexandrian — Jewry in the time of Augustus. His statement is supported by Philo (*In Flaccum*, 74), though Philo does not speak of an ethnarch, but of a genarch; see also *Ant.*, XIX, 283. Our sources are silent about the ethnarch in the Ptolemaic period. In fact, the only source that refers to the organization of the Jewish community in Alexandria at that period is the *Letter of Aristeas*, 310, which implies the existence of a Jewish politeuma: ... καὶ τῶν ἀπὸ τοῦ πολιτεύματος οἵ τε ἡγούμενοι τοῦ πλήθους. For an interpretation of this passage, see A. Pelletier, *Flavius Josèphe adaptateur de la lettre d'Aristée*, Paris 1962, pp. 187 f. However, there is no mention of an ethnarch. Yet, the passage is too short to make any inference from its silence on the date of the ethnarchy's emergence. According to Philo (*In Flaccum*, 74); a genarch, who is presumably identical with the ethnarch, died when Magius Maximus was to become prefect of Egypt for the second time in 11–12 C. E.; see A. Stein, *Die Präfekten von Ägypten in der römischen Kaiserzeit*, Bern 1950, pp. 22 f. After the death of the genarch Augustus created a gerusia, which assumed the leadership of Alexandrian Jewry; see Schürer, III, pp. 77 ff.; Tcherikover, p. 302. After this we hear no more of a single ethnarch or genarch at the head of the Jewish community of Alexandria. Nevertheless, from the edict of Claudius preserved in *Ant.*, XIX, 283, we learn that Augustus did not prevent the appointment of ethnarchs (μὴ κεκωλυκέναι ἐθνάρχας γίγνεσθαι) after the death of the Jewish ethnarch in 10–11 C.E., when Aquila served as prefect; see Stein, *op. cit.*, pp. 21 f. However, from Philo's statement we must assume that some radical reform was introduced *c.* 11 C.E., of which the chief importance was the strengthening of the Jewish gerusia, which subsequently weakened the power of the ethnarchs. The ethnarchs, however, continued to play a role in the life of the Jewish community. The πρωτεύοντες τῆς γερουσίας (*BJ*, VII, 412) can hardly be identified with ethnarchs. On the ethnarch and the Jewish gerusia of Alexandria, see also P. Jouguet, *La vie municipale dans l'Égypte romaine*, Paris 1911, pp. 38 f.; M. Engers, *Klio*, XVIII, 1923, p. 79; L. Fuchs, *Die Juden Aegyptens in ptolemäischer und römischer Zeit*, Vienna 1924, pp. 90 ff.

We have no information as to the territorial extent of the ethnarch's jurisdiction. Was he the leader only of the Jewish *politeuma* of Alexandria or of all Egyptian Jewry? Some scholars prefer the second possibility. For a view that wavers between the two possibilities see A. Bludau, *Juden und Judenverfolgungen im alten Alexandria*, Münster 1906, p. 14; cf. Y. Gutman, *JQR*, L (1959–1960), p. 282. Both in Philo and in the edict of Claudius the death of an ethnarch or genarch at the end of the principate of Augustus assumed great importance. We may conclude from this that the office was neither annual nor short-term, but probably life-long, as the death of a magistrate chosen only for a short time would not have suggested to Augustus a special opportunity for reform. One may even surmise that the death of this unknown ethnarch was significant because he was the last of a dynasty, possibly a descendant of Onias IV.

καὶ διαιτᾷ κρίσεις καὶ συμβολαίων ἐπιμελεῖται: The autonomous jurisdiction of Jewish courts in Egypt is well-attested by talmudic sources; see *Tosefta Pe'ah* 4 : 6; *Ketubbot* 3 : 1; cf. S. Lieberman, *Tosefta ki-Fshuṭah*, I, New York 1955, p. 182. Also, a Jewish archive is mentioned in *CPJ*, No. 143, ll. 7 f.: καθ᾽ἣν ἔθετο διαθήκ<ην> διὰ τοῦ τῶν ᾽Ιουδαίων ἀρχείου. From this papyrus we learn that a certain Theodorus deposited his will in the Jewish archive (13 B.C.E.). However, unfortunately this is the only clear reference in the papyri to autonomous legal institutions of Egyptian Jewry in the Hellenistic and Roman age. Especially disappointing in this respect are the legal documents drawn up in the typical form of συγχώρησις, deriving from the excavations conducted at Abusir el-Meleq in the Heracleopolite nome and bearing on the conditions of Alexandria in the time of Augustus. Jews appear, at least, in eight of the papyri (*CPJ*, Nos. 142–149), but, though they are of a legal character, they do not contain any allusion that may shed some light on the actual operation of the Jewish judiciary in Alexandria referred to by Strabo, except for the above-mentioned reference to the Jewish archive. Yet, one should remember that these documents were drawn up in the form of a *synchoresis* in a non-Jewish office, according to the requirements of the general law prevalent in Alexandria. The problem is why the Jews, although having autonomous courts, resorted to non-Jewish tribunals. This implies, no doubt, that the jurisdiction of the Jewish courts of Alexandria was not compulsory; see H. J. Wolff, *Das Justizwesen der Ptolemäer*, Munich 1962, p. 21; see also J. Modrzejewski, *Zeitschrift der Savigny-Stiftung für Rechtsgeschichte*, LXXX (1963), pp. 50 f. There is also a strong presumption that in some of the afore-mentioned documents, if not in all of them, only one party in the contract was Jewish.

The legal documents from the χώρα bearing on Jews show that they freely used the Hellenistic law of Ptolemaic Egypt; see *CPJ*, Sect. III. However, we should remember that these documents derive from an environment of Jewish soldiers and military settlers in the Fayum in the third and second centuries B.C.E., when specific Jewish organization and law were not yet established in the diaspora communities. Zucker suggested that ἐν τοῖς πολιτικοῖς νόμοις (*Flinders Petrie Papyri*, III, Dublin 1905, No. 21g, l.47 = *CPJ*, No. 19) refers to Jewish law; see F. Zucker, *Beiträge zur Kenntnis der Gerichtsorganisation im ptolemäischen und römischen Aegypten*, Leipzig 1911, pp. 52 f. The question is still controversial; cf. Tcherikover *ad loc.*

From Herodotus to Plutarch

On the problem of Jewish and Hellenistic law among the Jews of Egypt, see V. Tcherikover, *The Jews of Egypt in the Hellenistic-Roman Age in the Light of the Papyri*[2], Jerusalem 1963, pp. 95 ff. (in Hebrew).

118 διὰ τὸ Αἰγυπτίους εἶναι τὸ ἐξ ἀρχῆς τοὺς Ἰουδαίους: On the Egyptian origin of the Jews, see also Strabo, *Geographica*, XVI, 2 : 35, p. 760 (No. 115).

106

Historica Hypomnemata, apud: Josephus, *Antiquitates Judaicae*, XIV, 104 — Niese = *F. Gr. Hist.*, II, A91, F13

Περὶ δὲ τῆς Πομπηίου καὶ Γαβινίου στρατείας ἐπὶ Ἰουδαίους γράφει Νικόλαος ὁ Δαμασκηνός ⟨No. 92⟩ καὶ Στράβων ὁ Καππάδοξ οὐδὲν ἕτερος ἑτέρου καινότερον λέγων·

Now the expeditions of Pompey and Gabinius against the Jews have been written about by Nicolaus of Damascus and Strabo of Cappadocia, neither of whom differs in any respect from the other.

(trans. R. Marcus, *LCL*)

... οὐδὲν ἕτερος ἑτέρου καινότερον λέγων: Cf. Albert, *op. cit.* (supra, p. 267), pp. 21 f. For the whole passage, see the commentary to Nicolaus' *Historiae*, apud: Josephus, *Ant.*, XIV, 104 (No. 92). The similarity between Nicolaus and Strabo, as testified by Josephus, should be explained by their common source. The fact that Josephus stresses the consonance of both reports should not exclude the possibility that they contained details specific to each of them.

107

Historica Hypomnemata, apud: Josephus, *Antiquitates Judaicae*, XIV, 138–139 — Niese = *F. Gr. Hist.*, II, A91, F16 + 17; cf. Asinius Pollio (No. 76); Hypsicrates (No. 79)

(138) Λέγεται δ' ὑπὸ πολλῶν Ὑρκανὸν ταύτης κοινωνῆσαι τῆς στρατείας καὶ ἐλθεῖν εἰς Αἴγυπτον, μαρτυρεῖ δέ μου τῷ λόγῳ καὶ Στράβων ὁ Καππάδοξ λέγων ἐξ Ἀσινίου ὀνόματος οὕτως· «μετὰ τὸν Μιθριδάτην εἰσβαλεῖν εἰς τὴν Αἴγυπτον καὶ Ὑρκανὸν τὸν τῶν Ἰουδαίων ἀρχιερέα.» *(139)* ὁ δ' αὐτὸς οὗτος Στράβων καὶ ἐν ἑτέροις πάλιν ἐξ Ὑψικράτους ὀνόματος λέγει οὕτως· «τὸν δὲ Μιθριδάτην ἐξελθεῖν μόνον, κληθέντα δ' εἰς Ἀσκάλωνα Ἀντίπατρον ὑπ' αὐτοῦ τὸν τῆς Ἰουδαίας ἐπιμελητὴν τρισχιλίους αὐτῷ στρατιώτας συμπαρασκευάσαι καὶ τοὺς ἄλλους δυνάστας προτρέψαι, κοινωνῆσαι δὲ τῆς στρατείας καὶ Ὑρκανὸν τὸν ἀρχιερέα.» ταῦτα μὲν Στράβων φησίν.

1–2 στρατείας Dindorf στρατιᾶς codd.   2 καὶ² om. FLAMW   4 εἰσβάλλειν FL   6 δὲ] μὲν FLAMW   9 στρατείας Dindorf στρατιᾶς codd.

282

Strabo of Amaseia

(138) It is said by many writers that Hyrcanus took part in this campaign and came to Egypt. And this statement of mine is attested by Strabo of Cappadocia, who writes as follows, on the authority of Asinius. "After Mithridates, Hyrcanus, the high priest of the Jews, also invaded Egypt." (139) And again this same Strabo in another passage writes as follows, on the authority of Hypsicrates. "Mithridates went out alone, but Antipater, the procurator of Judaea, was called to Ascalon by him and provided him with an additional three thousand soliders, and won over the other princes; and the high priest Hyrcanus also took part in the campaign." These are Strabo's own words. (trans. R. Marcus, *LCL*)

138 Μαρτυρεῖ δέ μου τῷ λόγῳ καὶ Στράβων: Cf. Albert, *op. cit.* (supra, p. 267), pp. 39 ff. Again, we have an example of a discrepancy in Josephus between Strabo's tradition and that of Nicolaus; cf. the commentaries to Asinius Pollio, apud: Josephus, *Ant.*, XIV, 138 (No. 76) and Hypsicrates, apud: Josephus, *Ant.*, XIV, 139 (No. 79). While Nicolaus does not mention Hyrcan's participation in the Egyptian campaign, the sources used by Strabo expressly refer to it.

108

Historica Hypomnemata, apud: Josephus, *Antiquitates Judaicae*, XV, 8-10 — Niese = F53R = F. Gr. Hist., II, A91, F18

(8) Ἀντώνιος δὲ λαβὼν αἰχμάλωτον τὸν Ἀντίγονον δέσμιον ἔγνω μέχρι τοῦ θριάμβου φυλάττειν, ἐπεὶ δ᾽ ἤκουσεν νεωτερίζειν τὸ ἔθνος κἀκ τοῦ πρὸς Ἡρώδην μίσους εὔνουν Ἀντιγόνῳ διαμένον, ἔγνω τοῦτον ἐν Ἀντιοχείᾳ πελεκίσαι· σχεδὸν γὰρ οὐδ᾽ ἄλλως ἠρεμεῖν ἠδύναντο οἱ
5 Ἰουδαῖοι. (9) μαρτυρεῖ δέ μου τῷ λόγῳ Στράβων ὁ Καππάδοξ λέγων οὕτως· «Ἀντώνιος δὲ Ἀντίγονον τὸν Ἰουδαῖον ἀχθέντα εἰς Ἀντιόχειαν πελεκίζει. καὶ ἔδοξε μὲν οὗτος πρῶτος Ῥωμαίων βασιλέα πελεκίσαι, οὐκ οἰηθεὶς ἕτερον τρόπον μεταθεῖναι ἂν τὰς γνώμας τῶν Ἰουδαίων, ὥστε δέξασθαι τὸν ἀντ᾽ ἐκείνου καθεσταμένον Ἡρώδην· οὐδὲ γὰρ βασανιζόμενοι
10 βασιλέα ἀναγορεύειν αὐτὸν ὑπέμειναν· (10) οὕτως μέγα τι ἐφρόνουν περὶ τοῦ πρώτου βασιλέως. τὴν οὖν ἀτιμίαν ἐνόμισε μειώσειν ⋆ τῆς πρὸς αὐτὸν μνήμης, μειώσειν δὲ καὶ τὸ πρὸς Ἡρώδην μῖσος.» ταῦτα μὲν ὁ Στράβων.

4 οὐδ᾽ ἄλλως Niese   οὐδαμῶς codd.   οὐδαμοῦ Gutschmid   11 πρώτου] πρὸ τοῦ Gutschmid   12 μειώσειν <μέν τι> Richards & Shutt, supra, p. 275

(8) Now Antony, on taking Antigonus captive, decided to keep him until his triumph, but when he heard that the nation was rebel-

lious and had remained loyal to Antigonus out of hatred for Herod, he decided to behead him in Antioch, for the Jews could hardly be kept quiet in any other way. (9) And my words are borne out by the testimony of Strabo of Cappadocia, who writes as follows: "When Antigonus was brought to Antioch, Antony beheaded him. He was the first Roman who decided to behead a king, since he believed that in no other way could he change the attitude of the Jews so that they would accept Herod, who had been appointed in his place. For not even under torture would they submit to proclaiming him king (10), so highly did they regard their former king. And so he thought that the disgrace would somewhat dim their memory of him and would also lessen their hatred of Herod." That is Strabo's account.

(trans. R. Marcus, *LCL*)

8 Ἀντώνιος δὲ λαβὼν αἰχμάλωτον...: As usual in Josephus, the quotation from Strabo is preceded by a paraphrase of that quotation. One detail found in this paraphrase that is lacking in the quotation is Antony's primary intention to keep Antigonus until his triumph.

9 Ἀντίγονον τὸν Ἰουδαῖον: The life of Antigonus, the last ruler of the Hasmonaean house, was spent mainly in a struggle against the power of Rome and the House of Antipater. As the younger son of Aristobulus II, he was carried off to Rome by Pompey, together with his father and his sisters; see *Ant.*, XIV, 79; *BJ*, I, 158. Subsequently, he fled with his father, who led a rebellion against the Romans in 55 B.C.E. He was taken prisoner at the capture of Machaerus (*Ant.*, XIV, 96; *BJ*, I, 173). However, he was released by the Senate. Later, he found refuge with Ptolemy of Chalcis (*Ant.*, XIV, 126; *BJ*, I, 186). After the victory of Julius Caesar, his father's supporter, Antigonus accused Antipater before Caesar, but without much success (*Ant.*, XIV, 140 ff.; *BJ*, I, 195 ff.). Nor had he better luck in his attempt to invade Judaea during the civil wars after the death of Caesar (*Ant.*, XIV, 297 ff.; *BJ*, I, 239 f.). The Parthian invasion of Syria presented him with a great opportunity. Antigonus was restored to the throne of Judaea by the Parthians (*Ant.*, XIV, 330 ff.; *BJ*, I, 248 ff.), which he maintained for three years (40–37 B.C.E.). Rome countered the restoration of the Hasmonaean prince by declaring Herod King of Judaea in 40 B.C.E. (*Ant.*, XIV, 382). The struggle between the rival kings was finally decided by the victory of the Romans over the Parthians. For some time Antigonus tried bribery to gain the favour of the local Roman commanders in charge of the forces operating in Judaea (*Ant.*, XIV, 392 f.; *BJ*, I, 288 f.); in the end a strong Roman legionary force under the command of Sosius arrived to sustain Herod in his struggle, and Jerusalem was overcome after a valiant defence (37 B.C.E.). For the chronology, see the commentary to Cassius Dio, XLIX, 23 : 1 (No. 414).

ἀχθέντα... πελεκίζει: The reference to the death of Antigonus in Plutarchus, *Vita Antonii*, 36 : 4 (No. 266) recalls Strabo's statement: ὃν καὶ προαγαγὼν ἐπελέκισεν οὐδενὸς πρότερον ἑτέρου βασιλέως οὕτω κολασθέντος. Cassius Dio relates that Antigonus had been flogged and then crucified, adding in connection with this that no other king received such treatment from the Romans, and only then says:

Strabo of Amaseia

καὶ μετὰ τοῦτο καὶ ἀπέσφαξεν. The marked pro-Herodian narrative, which is dependent on Nicolaus of Damascus and echoes the official propaganda of Herod, attempts to throw an unfavourable light on the last moments of Antigonus; cf. *BJ*, I, 357: τοῦτον μὲν οὖν φιλοψυχήσαντα μέχρις ἐσχάτου διὰ ψυχρᾶς ἐλπίδος ἄξιος τῆς ἀγεννείας πέλεκυς ἐκδέχεται; see also *Ant.*, XIV, 481 (= *BJ*, I, 353): ἔνθα καὶ Ἀντίγονος μήτε τῆς πάλαι μήτε τῆς τότε τύχης ἔννοιαν λαβὼν κάτεισι μὲν ἀπὸ τῆς βάρεως, προσπίπτει δὲ τοῖς Σοσσίου ποσίν, κἀκεῖνος μηδὲν αὐτὸν οἰκτείρας πρὸς τὴν μεταβολὴν ἐπεκρότησεν μὲν ἀκρατῶς καὶ Ἀντιγόνην ἐκάλεσεν. On the other hand, the passage according to which Herod bribed Antony and persuaded him to put Antigonus to death (*Ant.*, XIV, 490) is not likely to derive from Herod's adherent Nicolaus. Jacoby, who suggests Nicolaus as the source, adds question marks to his suggestion. Whatever its ultimate origin, the passage in *Antiquitates* should be explained by the emergence of an anti-Herodian bias in the later writings of Josephus.

10 οὕτως μέγα τι ἐφρόνουν...: Strabo gives as the most obvious reason for Antigonus' ignominious death Sosius' wish to disgrace him. Sosius felt this was necessary to undermine the Jews' deep respect for Antigonus as the last great representative of the Hasmonaean House, which caused them to regard Herod as an intruder and to stubbornly refuse to acknowledge him as their king. Sosius further wished to disgrace Antigonus before the Romans, who might find the feelings of the Jews justifiable; see *Ant.*, XIV, 489: δείσας δὲ Ἡρώδης μὴ φυλαχθεὶς Ἀντίγονος ὑπ᾽ Ἀντωνίου καὶ κομισθεὶς εἰς Ῥώμην ὑπ᾽ αὐτοῦ δικαιολογήσηται πρὸς τὴν σύγκλητον ἐπιδεικνὺς αὐτὸν μὲν ἐκ βασιλέων, Ἡρώδην δὲ ἰδιώτην, καὶ ὅτι προσῆκεν αὐτοῦ βασιλεύειν τοὺς παῖδας διὰ τὸ γένος, εἰ καὶ αὐτὸς εἰς Ῥωμαίους ἐπεξήμαρτεν. For a similar sentiment, cf. also *Ant.*, XIV, 386, 403. It is noteworthy that from the brief statement of Strabo, Antigonus emerges as one whom the nation esteemed highly. The respect of the nation for him was probably due not only to his Hasmonaean origin, but also to his qualities as a leader. It should be remembered that he only succumbed under tremendous odds; see *Ant.*, XIV, 469. He also showed great dexterity in dealing with the Roman and Parthian commanders. The vast majority of the people supported him from the start, and without substantial Roman assistance Herod would have had no chance to overcome his opponents in Judaea. After Antigonus' death his memory continued to be cherished. Even Antipater, Herod's eldest son, found it convenient to marry the daughter of the dead Hasmonaean king (*Ant.*, XVII, 92).

ταῦτα μὲν ὁ Στράβων: On this passage and the death of Antigonus, see Albert, *op. cit.* (supra, p. 267), pp. 41 ff.; Otto, pp. 34 ff.; see also the commentaries to Seneca the Rhetor, *Suasoriae*, II, 21 (No. 149); Plutarchus, *Vita Antonii*, 36 : 4 (No. 266); Cassius Dio, XLIX, 22 : 6 (No. 414). For the suggestion, that Strabo's source for the execution of Antigonus was Timagenes, see G. W. Bowersock, *Augustus and the Greek World*, Oxford 1965, p. 125 n. 5.

109

Geographica, I, 2:35, pp. 42 f. — Sbordone

Εἰσὶ δὲ οἳ καὶ τὴν Αἰθιοπίαν εἰς τὴν καθ᾽ ἡμᾶς Φοινίκην μετάγουσι

1 οἳ om. WBv

καὶ τὰ περὶ τὴν Ἀνδρομέδαν ἐν Ἰόπῃ συμβῆναί φασιν· οὐ δήπου κατ᾽ ἄγνοιαν τοπικὴν καὶ τούτων λεγομένων, ἀλλ᾽ ἐν μύθου μᾶλλον σχήματι.

2 Ἰόππῃ Xylander

And there are some who transfer Ethiopia also to our Phoenicia, and who say that the adventure of Andromeda took place in Joppa, though the story is surely not told in ignorance of its local setting but rather in the guise of myth. (trans. H. L. Jones, *LCL*)

Εἰσὶ δ᾽οἳ καὶ τὴν Αἰθιοπίαν εἰς τὴν καθ᾽ ἡμᾶς Φοινίκην μετάγουσι: Cf. H. Lewy, *MGWJ*, LXXXI (1937), pp. 65 ff., and the commentary to Tacitus, *Historiae*, V, 2 (No. 281).

καὶ τὰ περὶ τὴν Ἀνδρομέδαν: Cf. the commentary to Pausanias, *Graeciae Descriptio*, IV, 35:9 (No. 354) and to Conon, *Narrationes*, apud: Photius, Cod. 186 (No. 145).

110

Geographica, XVI, 1:1, pp. 736 f. — Kramer

Τῇ δὲ Περσίδι καὶ τῇ Σουσιανῇ συνάπτουσιν οἱ Ἀσσύριοι· καλοῦσι δ᾽ οὕτω τὴν Βαβυλωνίαν καὶ πολλὴν τῆς κύκλῳ γῆς, ἧς ἐν μέρει καὶ ἡ Ἀτουρία ἐστίν, ἐν ᾗπερ ἡ Νίνος καὶ ἡ Ἀπολλωνιᾶτις καὶ Ἑλυμαῖοι καὶ Παραιτάκαι καὶ ἡ περὶ τὸ Ζάγρον ὄρος Χαλωνῖτις καὶ τὰ περὶ
5 τὴν Νίνον πεδία, Δολομηνή τε καὶ Καλαχηνὴ καὶ Χαζηνὴ καὶ Ἀδιαβηνή, καὶ τὰ τῆς Μεσοποταμίας ἔθνη τὰ περὶ Γορδυαίους καὶ τοὺς περὶ Νίσιβιν Μυγδόνας μέχρι τοῦ Ζεύγματος τοῦ κατὰ τὸν Εὐφράτην καὶ τῆς πέραν τοῦ Εὐφράτου πολλή, ἣν Ἄραβες κατέχουσι, καὶ οἱ ἰδίως ὑπὸ τῶν νῦν λεγόμενοι Σύροι μέχρι Κιλίκων καὶ Φοινίκων καὶ Ἰουδαίων
10 καὶ τῆς θαλάττης τῆς κατὰ τὸ Αἰγύπτιον πέλαγος καὶ τὸν Ἰσσικὸν κόλπον.

3 Νίνος Corais νῖνος codd. 4 ζάδρον E ζάγριον Dhix / Χαλωνῖτις Casaubonus χαλωνίτης D χαωνῖτις cett. 8 πολλή Kramer πολλῆς codd. 9 ιουδαίων post νῦν add. sw. / Ἰουδαίων] λιβύων codd., sed in marg. Fz pr. m. add. καὶ ιουδαίων, in marg. C. add. ιουδαίων καὶ ιουδαίων καὶ λιβύων x

The country of the Assyrians borders on Persis and Susiana. This name is given to Babylonia and to much of the country all around, which latter in part is also called Aturia, in which are Ninus, Apolloniatis, the Elymaei, the Paraetacae, the Chalonitis in the neighbourhood of Mt. Zagrus, the plains in the neighbourhood of Ninus, and also Dolomene and Calachene and Chazene and Adiabene, and the

Strabo of Amaseia

tribes of Mesopotamia, in the neighbourhood of the Gordyaeans, and the Mygdonians in the neighbourhood of Nisibis, as far as the Zeugma of the Euphrates, as also much of the country on the far side of the Euphrates, which is occupied by Arabians, and those people which in a special sense of the term are called by the men of to-day Syrians, who extend as far as the Cilicians and the Phoenicians and the Judaeans and the sea that is opposite the Egyptian Sea and the Gulf of Issus.

(trans. H. L. Jones, *LCL*)

111

Geographica, XVI, 2:2, p. 749 — Kramer = F54R

Μέρη δ' αὐτῆς ⟨scil. Συρίας⟩ τίθεμεν ἀπὸ τῆς Κιλικίας ἀρξάμενοι καὶ τοῦ Ἀμανοῦ τήν τε Κομμαγηνὴν καὶ τὴν Σελευκίδα καλουμένην τῆς Συρίας, ἔπειτα τὴν Κοίλην Συρίαν, τελευταίαν δ' ἐν μὲν τῇ παραλίᾳ τὴν Φοινίκην, ἐν δὲ τῇ μεσογαίᾳ τὴν Ἰουδαίαν. ἔνιοι δὲ τὴν Συρίαν
5 ὅλην εἴς τε Κοιλοσύρους καὶ Σύρους καὶ Φοίνικας διελόντες τούτοις ἀναμεμῖχθαί φασι τέτταρα ἔθνη, Ἰουδαίους, Ἰδουμαίους, Γαζαίους, Ἀζωτίους, γεωργικοὺς μέν, ὡς τοὺς Σύρους καὶ Κοιλοσύρους, ἐμπο-ρικοὺς δέ, ὡς τοὺς Φοίνικας.

1 αὐτοῖς Dh / τίθενται F τίθεται s   5 καὶ Σύρους om. codd. exc. E

We set down as parts of Syria, beginning at Cilicia and Mt. Amanus, both Commagene and the Seleucis of Syria, as the latter is called; and then Coele-Syria, and last, on the seaboard, Phoenicia, and, in the interior, Judaea. Some writers divide Syria as a whole into Coele-Syrians and Syrians and Phoenicians, and say that four other tribes are mixed up with these, namely, Judaeans, Idumaeans, Gazaeans, and Azotians, and that they are partly farmers, as the Syrians and Coele-Syrians, and partly merchants as the Phoenicians.

(trans. H. L. Jones, *LCL*)

ἔνιοι δὲ τὴν Συρίαν ὅλην... διελόντες τούτοις ἀναμεμῖχθαί φασι τέτταρα ἔθνη, Ἰουδαίους, Ἰδουμαίους, Γαζαίους, Ἀζωτίους...: This view of ἔνιοι reflects a situation that existed before the twenties of the second century B.C.E., since afterwards the Idumaeans merged into the Jewish nation. As to Azotus, it constituted an important administrative centre in the Assyrian, Persian and Hellenistic periods. It was also one of the bases for military operations against Judaea in the time of the Hasmonaean revolt. It cannot be stated positively when it was annexed by the Hasmonaeans to Judaea, but it seems that it happened under John Hyrcan. On the history of Azotus, see Alt, II, pp. 234 ff. Gaza was captured by Alexander Jannaeus c. 96 B.C.E.

287

Δύο δὲ ταῦτ᾽ ἐστὶν ὄρη τὰ ποιοῦντα τὴν Κοίλην καλουμένην Συρίαν,
ὡς ἂν παράλληλα, ὅ τε Λίβανος καὶ ὁ Ἀντιλίβανος, μικρὸν ὕπερθεν
τῆς θαλάττης ἀρχόμενα ἄμφω· ὁ μὲν Λίβανος τῆς κατὰ Τρίπολιν,
κατὰ τὸ τοῦ Θεοῦ μάλιστα πρόσωπον, ὁ δ᾽ Ἀντιλίβανος τῆς κατὰ
5 Σιδόνα· τελευτῶσι δ᾽ ἐγγύς πως τῶν Ἀραβίων ὀρῶν τῶν ὑπὲρ τῆς
Δαμασκηνῆς καὶ τῶν Τραχώνων ἐκεῖ λεγομένων εἰς ἄλλα ὄρη γεώ-
λοφα καὶ καλλίκαρπα. ἀπολείπουσι δὲ μεταξὺ πεδίον κοῖλον. πλάτος
μὲν τὸ ἐπὶ τῇ θαλάττῃ διακοσίων σταδίων, μῆκος δὲ τὸ ἀπὸ τῆς
θαλάττης ἐς τὴν μεσόγαιαν ὁμοῦ τι διπλάσιον. διαρρεῖται δὲ ποταμοῖς
10 ἄρδουσι χώραν εὐδαίμονα καὶ πάμφορον, μεγίστῳ δὲ τῷ Ἰορδάνῃ.
ἔχει δὲ καὶ λίμνην ἣ φέρει τὴν ἀρωματῖτιν σχοῖνον καὶ κάλαμον, ὡς δ᾽
αὕτως καὶ ἕλη· καλεῖται δ᾽ ἡ λίμνη Γεννησαρῖτις· φέρει δὲ καὶ βάλσαμον.
τῶν δὲ ποταμῶν ὁ μὲν Χρυσορρόας, ἀρξάμενος ἀπὸ τῆς Δαμασκηνῶν
πόλεως καὶ χώρας, εἰς τὰς ὀχετείας ἀναλίσκεται σχεδόν τι· πολλὴν γὰρ
15 ἐπάρδει καὶ βαθεῖαν σφόδρα· τὸν δὲ Λύκον καὶ τὸν Ἰορδάνην ἀναπλέουσι
φορτίοις, Ἀράδιοι δὲ μάλιστα.

1 Συρίαν] γωνίαν CDhmsxz   γονίαν F in marg.   6 Τραχώνων Tzschucke
τραχανῶν codd.   9 ὁμοῦ] σχεδὸν E   11 σχῖνον Tzschucke, Corais

Here are two mountains, Libanus and Antilibanus, which form
Coele-Syria, as it is called, and are approximately parallel to each
other. They both begin slightly above the sea-Libanus above the sea
near Tripolis and nearest to Theuprosopon, and Antilibanus above
the sea near Sidon: and somewhere in the neighbourhood of the
Arabian mountains above Damascene and the Trachones, as they are
called, the two mountains terminate in other mountains that are hilly
and fruitful. They leave a hollow plain between them, the breadth of
which, near the sea, is two hundred stadia, and the length, from the
sea into the interior, is about twice that number. It is intersected by
rivers, the Jordan being the largest, which water a country that is
fertile and all-productive. It also contains a lake which produces the
aromatic rush and reed; and likewise marshes. The lake is called
Gennesaritis. The plain also produces balsam. Among the rivers is
the Chrysorrhoas, which begins at the city and country of the Damasceni and is almost wholly used up in the conduits, for it irrigates a large
territory that has a very deep soil; but the Lycus and the Jordan are
navigated inland with vessels of burden, mostly by the Aradians.

(trans. H. L. Jones, *LCL*)

Strabo of Amaseia

Δύο δὲ ταῦτ' ἐστὶν ὄρη τὰ ποιοῦντα τὴν Κοίλην καλουμένην Συρίαν, ὡς ἂν παράλληλα, ὅ τε Λίβανος καὶ ὁ 'Αντιλίβανος: Here we meet with the limited meaning of Κοίλη Συρία, referring to the valley between the Libanus and the Anti-Libanus. However, this valley comprises, according to Strabo, the whole country intersected by the Jordan, including the Lake of Gennesareth and the plain that produces balsam, i.e. the Valley of Jericho. On the varied uses of Coele-Syria by Strabo, see E. Bikerman, RB, LIV (1947), pp. 265 f.

καὶ τῶν Τραχώνων: Cf. below, XVI, 2 : 20. Trachonitis or Trachon was the name of a territory in North-Eastern Transjordan. On the division of Trachonitis into two, see Hölscher, PW, Ser. 2, VI, pp. 1865 f.; R. Dussaud, Topographie historique de la Syrie antique et médiévale, Paris 1927, pp. 371 ff. This territory comprised the two lava stretches, the Lega and the Safa, to the south-east of Damascus.

μεγίστῳ δὲ τῷ 'Ιορδάνῃ: For other, specific references to the Jordan by Graeco-Roman writers, see Plinius, Naturalis Historia, V, 71 (No. 204); Tacitus, Historiae, V, 6 (No. 281); Pausanias, Graeciae Descriptio, V, 7 : 4 (No. 356).

βάλσαμον: Reinach (ad loc.) suggests that the lake implied by Strabo is the more northern one, Lake Merom, and that the words καλεῖται δ'ἡ λίμνη... βάλσαμον should be considered as an interpolation "provenant de deux gloses marginales primitivement indépendantes". He argues that, according to Strabo, the Lake of Gennesareth is situated in Galilaea and not in Coele-Syria, and that the balsam was cultivated only at Jericho; cf. Abel, I, 478, 491. However, Strabo actually seems to have included the whole Jordan Valley in Coele-Syria. Still, it is possible that Strabo confused the two lakes, since the description suits the Lake Merom (Semechonitis) more than the Lake of Gennesareth; cf., however, J.P. Rey-Coquais, Mélanges de l'Université Saint Joseph, XL (1964), pp. 306 ff.

'Αράδιοι δὲ μάλιστα: Of the part played by the Aradians in the navigation of the Jordan we learn only here. On Aradus' importance in the Hellenistic period, see Strabo, Geographica, XVI, 2 : 13 f. p. 754; Ant., XIV, 323; cf. H. Seyrig, NNM, CXIX (1950), pp. 17 ff. Rey-Coquais argues that the statement concerning the navigation of the Jordan by the Aradians arose from a palaeographical confusion between the Orontes and the Jordan (ὀρόντην, ἰορδάνην); cf. Rey-Coquais, op. cit., pp. 308 ff.; ibid., XLI (1965), pp. 226 ff.

113

Geographica, XVI, 2:21, p. 756 — Kramer = F54R

῍Απασα μὲν οὖν ἡ ὑπὲρ τῆς Σελευκίδος ὡς ἐπὶ τὴν Αἴγυπτον καὶ τὴν 'Αραβίαν ἀνίσχουσα χώρα Κοίλη Συρία καλεῖται, ἰδίως δ' ἡ τῷ Λιβάνῳ καὶ τῷ 'Αντιλιβάνῳ ἀφωρισμένη. τῆς δὲ λοιπῆς ἡ μὲν ἀπὸ 'Ορθωσίας μέχρι Πηλουσίου παραλία Φοινίκη καλεῖται, στενή τις καὶ ἁλιτενής· ἡ δ' ὑπὲρ ταύτης μεσόγαια μέχρι τῶν 'Αράβων ἡ μεταξὺ Γάζης καὶ 'Αντιλιβάνου 'Ιουδαία λέγεται.

2 ἐν post ἡ add. E

Now the whole of the country above the territory of Seleucis, extending approximately to Egypt and Arabia, is called Coele-Syria; but the country marked off by the Libanus and the Antilibanus is called by that name in a special sense. Of the remainder the seaboard from Orthosia to Pelusium is called Phoenicia, which is a narrow country and lies flat along the sea, whereas the interior above Phoenicia, as far as the Arabians, between Gaza and Antilibanus, is called Judaea.

(trans. H. L. Jones, *LCL*)

῎Απασα μὲν... χώρα Κοίλη Συρία καλεῖται: Κοίλη Συρία is used here in its broader sense; cf. the commentary to Theophrastus, *Historia Plantarum*, II, 6 : 2 (No. 6).

ἡ μὲν ἀπὸ ᾿Ορθωσίας μέχρι Πηλουσίου παραλία Φοινίκη καλεῖται: We must go back to the Persian period for the inclusion of the Palestinian coast in Phoenicia. It seems that under the Seleucid rule the whole seaboard constituted one of the main subdivisions of the province of Coele-Syria and Phoenicia. Whenever later writers — e.g. Pliny or Herennius Philo (No. 327) — use the term Phoenicia in relation to the Palestinian coast, they either continue the Hellenistic use or go back to an even older source. On the development of the term Phoenicia from the Persian period onwards, see Kahrstedt, pp. 37 ff., 97, 116 f.

114

Geographica, XVI, 2:27–30, pp. 758 f. — Kramer = F 54 R

(27) Μετὰ δὲ τὴν ῎Ακην Στράτωνος πύργος, πρόσορμον ἔχων. μεταξὺ δὲ ὅ τε Κάρμηλος τὸ ὄρος καὶ πολιχνίων ὀνόματα, πλέον δ᾿ οὐδέν, Συκαμίνων πόλις, Βουκόλων καὶ Κροκοδείλων πόλις καὶ ἄλλα τοιαῦτα· εἶτα δρυμὸς μέγας τις.

5 *(28)* Εἶτα ᾿Ιόπη, καθ᾿ ἣν ἡ ἀπὸ τῆς Αἰγύπτου παραλία σημειωδῶς ἐπὶ τὴν ἄρκτον κάμπτεται, πρότερον ἐπὶ τὴν ἕω τεταμένη. ἐνταῦθα δὲ μυθεύουσί τινες τὴν ᾿Ανδρομέδαν ἐκτεθῆναι τῷ κήτει· ἐν ὕψει γάρ ἐστιν ἱκανῶς τὸ χωρίον, ὥστ᾿ ἀφορᾶσθαί φασιν ἀπ᾿ αὐτοῦ τὰ ῾Ιεροσόλυμα, τὴν τῶν ᾿Ιουδαίων μητρόπολιν· καὶ δὴ καὶ ἐπινείῳ τούτῳ κέχρηνται
10 καταβάντες μέχρι θαλάττης οἱ ᾿Ιουδαῖοι· τὰ δ᾿ ἐπίνεια τῶν ληστῶν ληστήρια δηλονότι ἐστί. τούτων δὲ καὶ ὁ Κάρμηλος ὑπῆρξε καὶ ὁ δρυμός· καὶ δὴ καὶ εὐάνδρησεν οὗτος ὁ τόπος, ὥστ᾿ ἐκ τῆς πλησίον κώμης ᾿Ιαμνείας καὶ τῶν κατοικιῶν τῶν κύκλῳ τέτταρας μυριάδας ὁπλίζεσθαι. εἰσὶ δ᾿ ἐντεῦθεν εἰς τὸ Κάσιον τὸ πρὸς Πηλουσίῳ μικρῷ
15 πλείους ἢ χίλιοι στάδιοι, τριακόσιοι δ᾿ ἄλλοι πρὸς αὐτὸ τὸ Πηλούσιον. *(29)* ᾿Εν δὲ τῷ μεταξὺ καὶ ἡ Γαδαρίς ἐστιν, ἣν καὶ αὐτὴν ἐξιδιάσαντο

5 Ἰόππη codd. exc. Emoz   7 γάρ] δέ? Kramer
14 τῷ ante Πηλουσίῳ add. moz

Strabo of Amaseia

οἱ Ἰουδαῖοι· εἶτ' Ἄζωτὸς καὶ Ἀσκάλων. ἀπὸ δὲ Ἰαμνείας εἰς Ἄζωτὸν
καὶ Ἀσκάλωνά εἰσιν ὅσον διακόσιοι στάδιοι. κρομμύῳ τ' ἀγαθός
ἐστιν ἡ χώρα τῶν Ἀσκαλωνιτῶν, πόλισμα δὲ μικρόν. ἐντεῦθεν ἦν
20 Ἀντίοχος ὁ φιλόσοφος, μικρὸν πρὸ ἡμῶν γεγονώς. ἐκ δὲ τῶν Γαδάρων
Φιλόδημός τε ὁ Ἐπικούρειος [γεγονὼς] καὶ Μελέαγρος καὶ Μένιππος
ὁ σπουδογέλοιος καὶ Θεόδωρος ὁ καθ' ἡμᾶς ῥήτωρ.
(30) Εἶθ' ὁ τῶν Γαζαίων λιμὴν πλησίον· ὑπέρκειται δὲ καὶ ἡ πόλις
ἐν ἑπτὰ σταδίοις, ἔνδοξός ποτε γενομένη, κατεσπασμένη δ' ὑπὸ Ἀλεξ-
25 άνδρου καὶ μένουσα ἔρημος.

18 κρομμύῳ Kramer   κρομμύων X   κρομμύοις moz   21 γεγονὼς secl. edd.

(27) After Acre one comes to the Tower of Strato, which has a
landing-place for vessels. Between the two places is Mt. Carmel, as
also towns of which nothing more than the names remain—I mean
Sycaminopolis, Bucolopolis, Crocodeilopolis, and others like them.
And then one comes to a large forest.

(28) Then one comes to Jope, where the seaboard from Egypt,
though at first stretching towards the east, makes a significant bend
towards the north. Here it was, according to certain writers of myths,
that Andromeda was exposed to the sea-monster; for the place is
situated at a rather high elevation—so high, it is said, that Jerusalem,
the metropolis of the Judaeans, is visible from it; and indeed the
Judaeans have used this place as a seaport when they have gone down
as far as the sea; but the seaports of robbers are obviously only robbers' dens. To these people belonged not only Carmel, but also the
forest; and indeed this place was so well supplied with men that it
could muster forty thousand men from the neighbouring village Iamnia and the settlements all round. Thence to Mt. Casius near Pelusium
the distance is a little more than one thousand stadia; and, three
hundred stadia farther, one comes to Pelusium itself.

(29) But in the interval one comes to Gadaris, which the Judaeans
appropriated to themselves; and then to Azotus and Ascalon. The
distance from Iamnia to Azotus and Ascalon is about two hundred
stadia. The country of the Ascalonitae excels in onion, but the town
is small. Antiochus the philosopher, who was born a little before
my time, was a native of this place. Philodemus the Epicurean, and
Meleager and Menippus, the satirist, and Theodorus, the rhetorician
of my own time, were natives of Gadaris.

(30) Then, near Ascalon, one comes to the harbour of the Gazaeans.
The city of the Gazaeans is situated inland at a distance of seven

stadia; it became famous at one time, but was rased to the ground by Alexander and remains uninhabited. (trans. H. L. Jones, *LCL*)

27 Στράτωνος πύργος: Alexander Jannaeus captured the Tower of Strato; see *Ant.* XIII, 395. In its vicinity Herod founded the large city of Caesarea with its famous port. Since Strabo does not refer to the place under its new name, it may be assumed that he reflects a pre-Herodian source, prior to the foundation of Caesarea.

Κάρμηλος τὸ ὄρος: Cf. Tacitus, *Historiae*, II, 78 (No. 278) and the commentary *ad loc.*

Συκαμίνων πόλις: For the same name, cf. Pseudo-Scylax, *ZDPV*, LXI (1938), p. 90; *Ant.*, XIII, 332; cf. also Plinius, *Naturalis Historia*, V, 75 (No. 204; Sycaminum); Antoninus of Placentia, in: Geyer, p. 160; *Itinerarium Burdigalense*, *ibid.*, p. 19. The statement of Eusebius that Sycaminus is called Haifa contradicts all other evidence; see *Onomasticon*, ed. Klostermann, p. 108, l. 30 f. We know about a place called Shikmona from talmudic literature; see *M. Demai* i : 1; *TB Baba Batra* 119a. The place is to be identified with Tell es-Semak, on the coast southwest of Haifa; see S. Klein, *The Land of Galilee*, Jerusalem 1945, p. 63 (in Hebrew); Abel, II, p. 472.

Βουκόλων καὶ Κροκοδείλων πόλις: Galling has suggested that מגדל־עדר is the Semitic equivalent of Βουκόλων πόλις; see K. Galling, *ZDPV*, LXI (1938), p. 80. He identifies מגדל־עדר with Atlit. For Κροκοδείλων πόλις, cf. Pseudo-Scylax, *op. cit.*, p. 90; Plinius, *Naturalis Historia*, V, 75. The nearby river with the same name is better known; cf. Abel, I, pp. 470 f.

εἶτα δρυμὸς μέγας τις: Cf. *BJ*, I, 250: ὁ δὲ αὐτοὺς [scil. Ἀντίγονος] ἐπὶ τὸν καλούμενον Δρυμὸν προέπεμψεν τὸ χωρίον καταλαβεῖν where the δρυμός is referred to after the mention of the Carmel; cf. *Ant.*, XIV, 334: ἐκ δὲ τῶν περὶ Κάρμηλον τὸ ὄρος Ἰουδαίων πρὸς Ἀντίγονον ἐλθόντων καὶ συνεισβαλεῖν ἑτοίμως ἐχόντων, προσεδόκα δὲ τῆς χώρας μέρος τι λαβεῖν ὁ Ἀντίγονος, δρυμοὶ δὲ τὸ χωρίον καλεῖται... The Septuagint, Isa. lxv : 10, translates the Sharon as δρυμός. The Carmel is also mentioned together with the Sharon in the Masoretic text of Isa. xxxv : 2. In both Strabo and Josephus it is hard to determine whether by δρυμός the whole Plain of Sharon is implied or only a part of it.

28 εἶτα Ἰόππη: Jaffa became a Jewish town in 143 B.C.E.; see I Macc. xiii : 11. It was detached from Judaea by Pompey and restored to it by Caesar.

ὥστ᾽ ἀφορᾶσθαί φασιν ἀπ᾽ αὐτοῦ τὰ Ἱεροσόλυμα: This, of course, is not true. Josephus (*Ant.*, XI, 329) refers in similar terms to Σαφεῖν... τά τε γὰρ Ἱεροσόλυμα καὶ τὸν ναὸν συνέβαινεν ἐκεῖθεν ἀφορᾶσθαι.

τὰ δ᾽ ἐπίνεια τῶν λῃστῶν λῃστήρια δηλονότι ἐστί: Cf. *Ant.*, XIV, 43: τάς τε καταδρομὰς τὰς ἐπὶ τοὺς ὁμόρους καὶ τὰ πειρατήρια τὰ ἐν τῇ θαλάττῃ τοῦτον εἶναι τὸν συστήσαντα; see also Diodorus, XL, 2 (No. 64); cf. λῃστήρια, below (§ 40); J. Dobiáš, *Archiv Orientální*, III (1931), p. 248.

τούτων δὲ καὶ ὁ Κάρμηλος ὑπῆρξε καὶ ὁ δρυμός. καὶ δὴ καὶ εὐάνδρησεν οὗτος ὁ τόπος...: Strabo uses here the aorist to indicate that the Carmel, the Drymos and Jamnia belonged to the Jews. All these places were incorporated in the Jewish state under the Hasmonaeans. They were lost to it as a result of the dismemberment of the Hasmonaean kingdom by Pompey, but were included again in Judaea under the reign of Herod. Therefore, one might say that Strabo's point of view is post-Pompeian, but pre-Herodian.

292

Strabo of Amaseia

ὥστ᾽ἐκ τῆς πλησίον κώμης Ἰαμνείας καὶ τῶν κατοικιῶν τῶν κύκλῳ τέτταρας μυριάδας ὁπλίζεσθαι: Jamnia had been a non-Jewish town in the Hellenistic age and constituted one of the Seleucid bases against the Jews; see I Macc. iv : 15; v : 58; x : 69; xv : 40; II Macc. xii : 8, 9. The assertion of *Ant.*, XIII, 215, is hardly accurate; cf. *BJ*, I, 50. Jamnia seems to have become Jewish only under John Hyrcan; see Avi-Yonah, *Historical Geography of Palestine*, Jerusalem 1962 (in Hebrew), p. 43. In any case, it is listed among the towns found under the rule of Alexander Jannaeus (*Ant.*, XIII, 395) and mentioned among the towns detached from Judaea by Pompey (*Ant.*, XIV, 75; *BJ*, I, 156). It was resettled by Gabinius (*BJ*, I, 166). On the territory of Jamnia, see G. Beyer, *ZDPV*, LVI (1933), pp. 246 f. It is noteworthy that Strabo designates Jamnia as a village. In fact, we have no reference in our sources to Jamnia as a *polis* in the period of the Second Temple.
The figure of forty thousand armed men is very high and represents the highest number of soldiers ever mustered by one of the Hasmonaean brothers in their struggle against the Seleucids; cf. I Macc. xii : 41 (Jonathan against Tryphon). We do not know exactly which area is implied by Strabo — he may include also the Sharon and the toparchy of Lydda. Hieronymus, in his commentary to Isa. xxxiii : 9, states that "Saron autem omnis iuxta Joppen Liddamque appellatur regio in qua latissimi campi fertilesque tenduntur"; see *PL*, XXIV, Col. 365.
The information supplied by Strabo — although its exact meaning is not clear — well illustrates the populousness of the Hasmonaean state and the denseness of the Jewish settlement west of Judaea proper as a result of the Hasmonaean expansion. The other figures at our disposal regarding the manpower of Judaea at the zenith of the Hasmonaean monarchy are mainly derived from Josephus' not very reliable account of the fighting forces taking part in some of the battles, the casualties and the prisoners; see, e.g., *Ant.*, XIII, 344, 376 f.; XIV, 120. The populousness of Judaea had already made a great impression on Hecataeus; see Diodorus, *Bibliotheca Historica* XL, 3 : 8 (No. 11); cf. Tacitus, *Historiae*, V, 5 (No. 281).

29 Ἐν δὲ τῷ μεταξὺ καὶ ἡ Γαδαρίς ἐστιν: Since Strabo refers to this place after having mentioned Jamnia and before mentioning Azotus and Ascalon, it is clear that it cannot be identical with the famous Gadara in Transjordan. He probably confused it with that city, as may be deduced from the way he later refers to the real Gadara (Ἐκ δὲ τῶν Γαδάρων...). This Gadaris in western Palestine, which was situated not far from Jamnia and Azotus, should be identified with Gazara, the pronounciation of which was confused with that of Gadara; see H. Ouvré, *Méléagre de Gadara*, Paris 1894, p. 36, n.1.; Schürer, I, p. 245, n. 12; p. 339, n. 5; R. Marcus, note to Josephus, *Ant.*, XIV, 91 (*LCL*, Vol. VII, p. 494, note d).
ἣν καὶ αὐτὴν ἐξιδιάσαντο οἱ Ἰουδαῖοι: Gazara was captured by the Jews in the time of Simon the Hasmonaean; see Schürer, I, p. 245, n. 12. Gadara was captured by Alexander Jannaeus; see *Ant.*, XIII, 356, 396; *BJ*, I, 86.

30 ὑπέρκειται δὲ καὶ ἡ πόλις... κατεσπασμένη δ᾽ ὑπὸ Ἀλεξάνδρου καὶ μένουσα ἔρημος: Taken at its face value, this statement would mean that Gaza was razed to the ground by Alexander the Great and remained so till Strabo's days. This cannot be true, since we know much about the part played continuously by Gaza in the history of the country from the time of the Diadochi to the time of Alexander Jannaeus. The Alexander referred to by Strabo should be identified with Alexander Jannaeus, who captured Gaza c. 96 B.C.E. and destroyed it; see *Ant.*, XIII, 364: καὶ τὴν πόλιν... ἐπικατασκάψας. After its liberation by Pompey Gaza's municipal life was restored. The information supplied by Strabo, therefore, seems

293

to derive from a source reflecting the conditions prevailing in the first half of the first century B.C.E.; Schürer, II, p. 114, n. 79; Benzinger, PW, VII, p. 883; Tcherikover, p. 96.

ἐν ἑπτὰ σταδίοις: This is inaccurate. The distance was about twenty stadia, as Arrianus attested for old Gaza; see *Anabasis*, II, 26.

115

Geographica, XVI, 2:34–46, pp. 760–765 — Kramer = F54R = *F. Gr. Hist.*, II, A87, F70

(34) Τῆς δ' Ἰουδαίας τὰ μὲν ἑσπέρια ἄκρα τὰ πρὸς τῷ Κασίῳ κατέχουσιν Ἰδουμαῖοί τε καὶ ἡ λίμνη. Ναβαταῖοι δ' εἰσὶν οἱ Ἰδουμαῖοι· κατὰ στάσιν δ' ἐκπεσόντες ἐκεῖθεν προσεχώρησαν τοῖς Ἰουδαίοις καὶ τῶν νομίμων τῶν αὐτῶν ἐκείνοις ἐκοινώνησαν· πρὸς θαλάττῃ δὲ ἡ
5 Σιρβωνὶς τὰ πολλὰ κατέχει καὶ ἡ συνεχὴς μέχρι Ἱεροσολύμων· καὶ γὰρ ταῦτα πρὸς θαλάττῃ ἐστίν· ἀπὸ γὰρ τοῦ ἐπινείου τῆς Ἰόπης εἴρηται ὅτι ἐστὶν ἐν ὄψει. ταῦτα μὲν προσάρκτια· τὰ πολλὰ δ' ὡς ἕκαστά εἰσιν ὑπὸ φύλων οἰκούμενα μικτῶν ἔκ τε Αἰγυπτίων ἐθνῶν καὶ Ἀραβίων καὶ Φοινίκων· τοιοῦτοι γὰρ οἱ τὴν Γαλιλαίαν ἔχοντες καὶ
10 τὸν Ἱερικοῦντα καὶ τὴν Φιλαδέλφειαν καὶ Σαμάρειαν, ἣν Ἡρώδης Σεβαστὴν ἐπωνόμασεν. οὕτω δ' ὄντων μιγάδων, ἡ κρατοῦσα μάλιστα φήμη τῶν περὶ τὸ ἱερὸν τὸ ἐν τοῖς Ἱεροσολύμοις πιστευομένων Αἰγυπτίους ἀποφαίνει τοὺς προγόνους τῶν νῦν Ἰουδαίων λεγομένων.

(35) Μωσῆς γάρ τις τῶν Αἰγυπτίων ἱερέων, ἔχων τι μέρος τῆς ⟨κάτω⟩
15 καλουμένης χώρας, ἀπῆρεν ἐκεῖσε ἐνθένδε, δυσχεράνας τὰ καθεστῶτα, καὶ συνεξῆραν αὐτῷ πολλοὶ τιμῶντες τὸ θεῖον. ἔφη γὰρ ἐκεῖνος καὶ ἐδίδασκεν, ὡς οὐκ ὀρθῶς φρονοῖεν οἱ Αἰγύπτιοι θηρίοις εἰκάζοντες καὶ βοσκήμασι τὸ θεῖον οὐδ' οἱ Λίβυες· οὐκ εὖ δὲ οὐδ' οἱ Ἕλληνες, ἀνθρωπομόρφους τυποῦντες· ⟨p. 761⟩ εἴη γὰρ ἓν τοῦτο μόνον θεὸς
20 τὸ περιέχον ἡμᾶς ἅπαντας καὶ γῆν καὶ θάλατταν, ὃ καλοῦμεν οὐρανὸν καὶ κόσμον καὶ τὴν τῶν ὄντων φύσιν. τούτου δὴ τίς ἂν εἰκόνα πλάττειν θαρρήσειε νοῦν ἔχων ὁμοίαν τινὶ τῶν παρ' ἡμῖν; ἀλλ' ἐᾶν δεῖν πᾶσαν ξοανοποιίαν, τέμενος ⟨δ'⟩ ἀφορίσαντας καὶ σηκὸν ἀξιόλογον τιμᾶν ἕδους χωρίς. ἐγκοιμᾶσθαι δὲ καὶ αὐτοὺς ὑπὲρ ἑαυτῶν καὶ ὑπὲρ τῶν
25 ἄλλων ἄλλους τοὺς εὐονείρους· καὶ προσδοκᾶν δεῖν ἀγαθὸν παρὰ τοῦ

2 τε om. E   5 σερβωνὶς E, Aldina / κατέχει Corais   κατεῖχε codd. /
καὶ Ἱεροσολύμων F   6 ἰόππης CF   10 ἱεριχοῦντα E, Aldina
ἐρικοῦντα cett. / Φιλαδέλφειαν edd.   φιλαδελφίαν codd.   14 ⟨κάτω⟩
Corais   15 ἐκεῖθεν F   17 οἱ om. Corais   18 οὐδ' οἱ Λίβυες
secl. Jacoby   22 τινὶ Casaubonus   τινά codd. / δεῖν Corais δεῖ codd.
23 ⟨δ'⟩ Corais   24 ἕδους h   αἰδοῦς FD   εἴδους cett.   24–25 ἐγκοιμᾶσθαι . . . εὐονείρους secl. Jacoby

294

θεοῦ καὶ δῶρον ἀεί τι καὶ σημεῖον τοὺς σωφρόνως ζῶντας καὶ μετὰ
δικαιοσύνης, τοὺς δ᾽ ἄλλους μὴ προσδοκᾶν.

(36) Ἐκεῖνος μὲν οὖν τοιαῦτα λέγων ἔπεισεν εὐγνώμονας ἄνδρας οὐκ
ὀλίγους καὶ ἀπήγαγεν ἐπὶ τὸν τόπον τοῦτον, ὅπου νῦν ἐστι τὸ ἐν τοῖς
30 Ἱεροσολύμοις κτίσμα. κατέσχε δὲ ῥᾳδίως, οὐκ ἐπίφθονον ὃν τὸ χωρίον,
οὐδ᾽ ὑπὲρ οὗ ἄν τις ἐσπουδασμένως μαχέσαιτο· ἔστι γὰρ πετρῶδες,
αὐτὸ μὲν εὔυδρον, τὴν δὲ κύκλῳ χώραν ἔχον λυπρὰν καὶ ἄνυδρον, τὴν
δ᾽ ἐντὸς ἑξήκοντα σταδίων καὶ ὑπόπετρον. ἅμα δ᾽ ἀντὶ τῶν ὅπλων τὰ
ἱερὰ προὐβάλλετο καὶ τὸ θεῖον, ἵδρυσιν τούτου ζητεῖν ἀξιῶν, καὶ
35 παραδώσειν ὑπισχνούμενος τοιοῦτον σεβασμὸν καὶ τοιαύτην ἱεροποιίαν,
ἥτις οὔτε δαπάναις ὀχλήσει τοὺς χρωμένους οὔτε θεοφορίαις οὔτε ἄλλαις
πραγματείαις ἀτόποις. οὗτος μὲν οὖν εὐδοκιμήσας τούτοις συνεστήσατο
ἀρχὴν οὐ τὴν τυχοῦσαν, ἁπάντων προσχωρησάντων ῥᾳδίως τῶν κύκλῳ
διὰ τὴν ὁμιλίαν καὶ τὰ προτεινόμενα.

40 (37) Οἱ δὲ διαδεξάμενοι χρόνους μέν τινας ἐν τοῖς αὐτοῖς διέμενον
δικαιοπραγοῦντες καὶ θεοσεβεῖς ὡς ἀληθῶς ὄντες· ἔπειτ᾽ ἐφισταμένων
ἐπὶ τὴν ἱερωσύνην τὸ μὲν πρῶτον δεισιδαιμόνων, ἔπειτα τυραννικῶν
ἀνθρώπων, ἐκ μὲν τῆς δεισιδαιμονίας αἱ τῶν βρωμάτων ἀποσχέσεις,
ὧνπερ καὶ νῦν ἔθος ἐστὶν αὐτοῖς ἀπέχεσθαι καὶ ⟨αἱ⟩ περιτομαὶ καὶ αἱ
45 ἐκτομαὶ καὶ εἴ τινα τοιαῦτα ἐνομίσθη, ἐκ δὲ τῶν τυραννίδων τὰ
λῃστήρια· οἱ μὲν γὰρ ἀφιστάμενοι τὴν χώραν ἐκάκουν καὶ αὐτὴν
καὶ τὴν γειτνιῶσαν, οἱ δὲ συμπράττοντες τοῖς ἄρχουσι καθήρπαζον
τὰ ἀλλότρια καὶ τῆς Συρίας κατεστρέφοντο καὶ τῆς Φοινίκης πολλήν.
ἦν δ᾽ ὅμως εὐπρέπειά τις περὶ τὴν ἀκρόπολιν αὐτῶν, οὐχ ὡς τυραννεῖον
50 βδελυττομένων, ἀλλ᾽ ὡς ἱερὸν σεμνυνόντων καὶ σεβομένων.

(38) Πέφυκε γὰρ οὕτω, καὶ κοινόν ἐστι τοῦτο καὶ τοῖς Ἕλλησι καὶ
τοῖς βαρβάροις. πολιτικοὶ γὰρ ὄντες ἀπὸ προστάγματος κοινοῦ ζῶσιν·
ἄλλως γὰρ οὐχ οἷόν τε τοὺς πολλοὺς ἕν τι καὶ ταὐτὸ ποιεῖν ἡρμοσμένως
ἀλλήλοις, ὅπερ ἦν τὸ πολιτεύεσθαι, καὶ ἄλλως πως νέμειν βίον κοινόν.
55 τὸ δὲ πρόσταγμα διττόν· ⟨p. 762⟩ ἢ γὰρ παρὰ θεῶν ἢ παρὰ ἀνθρώπων·
καὶ οἵ γε ἀρχαῖοι τὸ παρὰ τῶν θεῶν ἐπρέσβευον μᾶλλον καὶ ἐσέμνυνον,
καὶ διὰ τοῦτο καὶ ὁ χρηστηριαζόμενος ἦν τότε πολὺς καὶ τρέχων εἰς
μὲν Δωδώνην, ὅπως

ἐκ δρυὸς ὑψικόμοιο Διὸς βουλὴν ἐπακούσῃ

60 συμβούλῳ τῷ Διὶ χρώμενος, εἰς δὲ Δελφούς,

36 οὔτε¹ Corais   οὐδὲ codd.   38 προχωρησάντων F   44 ⟨αἱ⟩ Kramer   49 τύραννον CDF hi (in marg. D et F pr. m. add. τυραννοίον)
53 καὶ ταὐτὸ Corais   κατ᾽ αὐτὸ CDF hir   κατὰ ταὐτὸ moxz, Aldina
54 ἄλλως πως] ἀμωσγέπως Corais   57 ὁ om. C   59 ἐπακούσῃ Corais
ὑπακούσῃ codd.

τὸν ἐκτεθέντα παῖδα μαστεύων μαθεῖν
εἰ μηκέτ᾽ εἴη·

αὐτὸς δ᾽ ὁ παῖς

ἔστειχε τοὺς τεκόντας ἐκμαθεῖν θέλων
65 πρὸς δῶμα Φοίβου

καὶ ὁ Μίνως παρὰ τοῖς Κρησὶν

ἐννέωρος βασίλευε Διὸς μεγάλου ὀαριστής·

δι᾽ ἐννέα ἐτῶν, ὥς φησι Πλάτων, ἀναβαίνων ἐπὶ τὸ ἄντρον τοῦ Διὸς
καὶ παρ᾽ ἐκείνου τὰ προστάγματα λαμβάνων καὶ παρακομίζων εἰς
70 τοὺς ἀνθρώπους. τὰ δ᾽ ὅμοια ἐποίει καὶ Λυκοῦργος ὁ ζηλωτὴς αὐτοῦ·
πυκνὰ γάρ, ὡς ἔοικεν, ἀποδημῶν ἐπυνθάνετο παρὰ τῆς Πυθίας, ἃ
προσήκει παραγγέλλειν τοῖς Λακεδαιμονίοις·
(39) Ταῦτα γὰρ ὅπως ποτὲ ἀληθείας ἔχει, παρά γε τοῖς ἀνθρώποις
ἐπεπίστευτο καὶ ἐνενόμιστο, καὶ διὰ τοῦτο καὶ οἱ μάντεις ἐτιμῶντο,
75 ὥστε καὶ βασιλείας ἀξιοῦσθαι, ὡς τὰ παρὰ τῶν θεῶν ἡμῖν ἐκφέροντες
παραγγέλματα καὶ ἐπανορθώματα καὶ ζῶντες καὶ ἀποθανόντες·
καθάπερ καὶ ὁ Τειρεσίας·

τῷ καὶ τεθνηῶτι νόον πόρε Περσεφόνεια
οἴῳ πεπνῦσθαι· τοὶ δὲ σκιαὶ ἀΐσσουσι.

80 τοιοῦτος δὲ ὁ Ἀμφιάρεως καὶ ὁ Τροφώνιος καὶ <ὁ> Ὀρφεὺς καὶ ὁ
Μουσαῖος καὶ ὁ παρὰ τοῖς Γέταις θεός, τὸ μὲν παλαιὸν Ζάμολξις,
Πυθαγόρειός τις, καθ᾽ ἡμᾶς δὲ ὁ τῷ Βυρεβίστᾳ θεσπίζων, Δεκαίνεος·
παρὰ δὲ τοῖς Βοσπορηνοῖς Ἀχαΐκαρος, παρὰ δὲ τοῖς Ἰνδοῖς οἱ γυμνο-
σοφισταί, παρὰ δὲ τοῖς Πέρσαις οἱ Μάγοι καὶ νεκυομάντεις καὶ ἔτι οἱ
85 λεγόμενοι λεκανομάντεις καὶ ὑδρομάντεις, παρὰ δὲ τοῖς Ἀσσυρίοις οἱ
Χαλδαῖοι, παρὰ δὲ τοῖς Ῥωμαίοις οἱ Τυρρηνικοὶ ⋆ ὡροσκόποι. τοιοῦτος
δέ τις ἦν καὶ ὁ Μωσῆς καὶ οἱ διαδεξάμενοι ἐκεῖνον, τὰς μὲν ἀρχὰς
λαβόντες οὐ φαύλας, ἐκτραπόμενοι δ᾽ ἐπὶ τὸ χεῖρον.
(40) Ἤδη δ᾽ οὖν φανερῶς τυραννουμένης τῆς Ἰουδαίας, πρῶτος ἀνθ᾽ ἱε-
90 ρέως ἀνέδειξεν ἑαυτὸν βασιλέα Ἀλέξανδρος· τούτου δ᾽ ἦσαν υἱοὶ Ὑρκανός
τε καὶ Ἀριστόβουλος· διαφερομένων δὲ περὶ τῆς ἀρχῆς, ἐπῆλθε Πομπήιος
καὶ κατέλυσεν αὐτοὺς καὶ τὰ ἐρύματα αὐτῶν κατέσπασε καὶ αὐτὰ ἐν
πρώτοις τὰ Ἱεροσόλυμα βίᾳ καταλαβών· ἦν γὰρ πετρῶδες καὶ εὐερκὲς

69 διακομίζων moz   72 προσῆκε sive προσήκοι Corais   προσῆκεν
Meineke   80 δὲ <καὶ> Corais / <ὁ> Kramer   82 πυθαγόριος
CDFxz / Βυρεβίστᾳ] βυρεβισθα CDFh   βυβεβίθα i   Βοιρεβίστα Corais
83 βοσπορινοῖς mowxz, Aldina   Βοσπορανοῖς Xylander   86 ἱεροσκόποι
Letronne   οἰωνοσκόποι Corais   89 δ᾽ om. moxz   93 καταλαβών
Casaubonus   καταβαλὼν codd.

ἔρυμα, ⟨p. 763⟩ ἐντὸς μὲν εὔυδρον, ἐκτὸς δὲ παντελῶς διψηρόν, τάφρον
95 λατομητὴν ἔχον βάθος μὲν ἑξήκοντα ποδῶν, πλάτος δὲ πεντήκοντα
καὶ διακοσίων· ἐκ δὲ τοῦ λίθου τοῦ λατομηθέντος ἐπεπύργωτο τὸ
τεῖχος τοῦ ἱεροῦ. κατελάβετο δ᾽, ὥς φασι, τηρήσας τὴν τῆς νηστείας
ἡμέραν, ἡνίκα ἀπείχοντο οἱ Ἰουδαῖοι παντὸς ἔργου, πληρώσας τὴν
τάφρον καὶ ἐπιβαλὼν τὰς διαβάθρας· κατασπάσαι δ᾽ οὖν ἐκέλευσε τὰ
100 τείχη πάντα καὶ ἀνεῖλεν εἰς δύναμιν τὰ ληστήρια καὶ τὰ γαζοφυλάκια
τῶν τυράννων· ἦν δὲ δύο μὲν τὰ ταῖς εἰσβολαῖς ἐπικείμενα τοῦ Ἱερι-
κοῦντος Θρήξ τε καὶ Ταῦρος, ἄλλα δὲ Ἀλεξάνδριόν τε καὶ Ὑρκάνιον
καὶ Μαχαιροῦς καὶ Λυσιὰς καὶ τὰ περὶ τὴν Φιλαδέλφειαν καὶ ἡ περὶ
Γαλιλαίαν Σκυθόπολις.
105 (41) Ἱερικοῦς δ᾽ ἐστὶ πεδίον κύκλῳ περιεχόμενον ὀρεινῇ τινι καί που
καὶ θεατροειδῶς πρὸς αὐτὸ κεκλιμένῃ· ἐνταῦθα δ᾽ ἐστὶν ὁ φοινικών,
μεμιγμένην ἔχων καὶ ἄλλην ὕλην ἥμερον καὶ εὔκαρπον, πλεονάζων δὲ
τῷ φοίνικι, ἐπὶ μῆκος σταδίων ἑκατόν, διάρρυτος ἅπας καὶ μεστὸς
κατοικιῶν· ἔστι δ᾽ αὐτοῦ καὶ βασίλειον καὶ ὁ τοῦ βαλσάμου παράδεισος.
110 ἔστι δὲ τὸ φυτὸν θαμνῶδες, κυτίσῳ ἐοικὸς καὶ τερμίνθῳ, ἀρωματίζον·
οὗ τὸν φλοιὸν ἐπισχίσαντες ὑπολαμβάνουσιν ἀγγείοις τὸν ὀπόν,
γλίσχρῳ γάλακτι παραπλήσιον· ἀναληφθεὶς δ᾽ εἰς κογχάρια λαμβάνει
πῆξιν· λύει δὲ κεφαλαλγίας θαυμαστῶς καὶ ὑποχύσεις ἀρχομένας καὶ
ἀμβλυωπίας· τίμιος οὖν ἐστι, καὶ διότι ἐνταῦθα μόνον γεννᾶται· καὶ
115 ὁ φοινικὼν δὲ τοιοῦτος, ἔχων τὸν καρυωτὸν φοίνικα ἐνταῦθα μόνον,
πλὴν τοῦ Βαβυλωνίου καὶ τοῦ ἐπέκεινα, πρὸς τὴν ἕω· μεγάλη οὖν ἀπ᾽
αὐτῶν ἡ πρόσοδος. καὶ τῷ ξυλοβαλσάμῳ δὲ ὡς ἀρώματι χρῶνται.
(42) Ἡ δὲ Σιρβωνὶς λίμνη πολλὴ μέν ἐστι· καὶ γὰρ χιλίων σταδίων
εἰρήκασί τινες τὸν κύκλον· τῇ μέντοι παραλίᾳ παρεκτέταται μικρῷ τι
120 πλέον τῶν διακοσίων σταδίων μῆκος ἐπιλαμβάνουσα, ἀγχιβαθής,
βαρύτατον ἔχουσα ὕδωρ, ὥστε μὴ δεῖν κολύμβου, ἀλλὰ τὸν ἐμβάντα
καὶ μέχρις ὀμφαλοῦ προβάντα εὐθὺς ἐξαίρεσθαι· μεστὴ δ᾽ ἐστὶν ἀσφάλ-
του· αὕτη [τοῦτο] δὲ ἀναφυσᾶται κατὰ καιροὺς ἀτάκτους ἐκ μέσου τοῦ
βάθους μετὰ πομφολύγων, ὡς ἂν ζέοντος ὕδατος· κυρτουμένη δ᾽ ἡ
125 ἐπιφάνεια λόφου φαντασίαν παρέχει· συναναφέρεται δὲ καὶ ἄσβολος
πολλή, καπνώδης μέν, πρὸς δὲ τὴν ὄψιν ἄδηλος, ὑφ᾽ ἧς κατιοῦται καὶ
χαλκὸς καὶ ἄργυρος καὶ πᾶν τὸ στιλπνὸν μέχρι καὶ χρυσοῦ· ἀπὸ δὲ

---

102 ἀλεξάνδρειον Dh / ὑρκάνειον Dh   103 λύδας post Μαχαιροῦς add.
w / λύδας post Λυσιὰς add. F / Φιλαδέλφειαν Corais   φιλαδελφίαν codd.
105 Ἱερικοῦς Tzschucke   ἱεριχοὺς E   ἱερικοὺς cett.   111 ἀπολαμβάνουσιν
moz / ἀγγείῳ E   114 ἐστὶ ⟨καὶ διὰ τοῦτο⟩ Corais   118 σερβωνὶς E
119 μικρὸν moz   121 βαθύτατον xz   122 προεμβάντα CDFhi   προ-
ελθόντα x   om. epitome   123 τοῦτο del. Groskurd

297

τοῦ κατιοῦσθαι τὰ σκεύη γνωρίζουσιν οἱ περιοικοῦντες ἀρχομένην τὴν
ἀναβολὴν τοῦ ἀσφάλτου, καὶ παρασκευάζονται πρὸς τὴν μεταλλείαν
130 αὐτοῦ, ποιησάμενοι σχεδίας καλαμίνας. ⟨p. 764⟩ ἔστι δ᾽ ἡ ἄσφαλτος
γῆς βῶλος, ὑγραινομένη μὲν ὑπὸ θερμοῦ καὶ ἀναφυσωμένη καὶ
διαχεομένη, πάλιν δὲ μεταβάλλουσα εἰς πάγον ἰσχυρὸν ὑπὸ τοῦ ψυχροῦ
ὕδατος, οἷόν ἐστι τὸ τῆς λίμνης ὕδωρ, ὥστε τομῆς καὶ κοπῆς δεῖσθαι·
εἶτ᾽ ἐπιπολάζουσα διὰ τὴν φύσιν τοῦ ὕδατος, καθ᾽ ἣν ἔφαμεν μηδὲ
135 κολύμβου δεῖσθαι, μηδὲ βαπτίζεσθαι τὸν ἐμβάντα, ἀλλ᾽ ἐξαίρεσθαι·
προσπλεύσαντες δὲ ταῖς σχεδίαις κόπτουσι καὶ φέρονται τῆς ἀσφάλτου
ὅσον ἕκαστος δύναται.

(43) Τὸ μὲν οὖν συμβαῖνον τοιοῦτον· γόητας δὲ ὄντας σκήπτεσθαί
φησιν ἐπῳδὰς ὁ Ποσειδώνιος ⟨No. 45⟩ τοὺς ἀνθρώπους καὶ οὖρα καὶ
140 ἄλλα δυσώδη ὑγρά, ἃ περικαταχέαντας καὶ ἐκπιάσαντας πήττειν τὴν
ἄσφαλτον, εἶτα τέμνειν· εἰ μή τίς ἐστιν ἐπιτηδειότης τῶν οὔρων τοιαύτη,
καθάπερ καὶ ἐν ταῖς κύστεσι τῶν λιθιώντων, καὶ ἐκ τῶν παιδικῶν οὔρων
ἡ χρυσόκολλα συνίσταται· ἐν μέσῃ δὲ τῇ λίμνῃ τὸ πάθος συμβαίνειν
εὔλογον, ὅτι καὶ ἡ πηγὴ τοῦ πυρὸς καὶ τῆς ἀσφάλτου κατὰ μέσον ἐστὶ
145 καὶ τὸ πλῆθος· ἄτακτος δὲ ἡ ἀναφύσησις, ὅτι καὶ ἡ τοῦ πυρὸς κίνησις
οὐκ ἔχει τάξιν ἡμῖν φανεράν, ὥσπερ καὶ ἄλλων πνευμάτων πολλῶν.
τοιαῦτα δὲ καὶ τὰ ἐν Ἀπολλωνίᾳ τῇ Ἠπειρώτιδι.

(44) Τοῦ δ᾽ ἔμπυρον τὴν χώραν εἶναι καὶ ἄλλα τεκμήρια φέρουσι
πολλά· καὶ γὰρ πέτρας τινὰς ἐπικεκαυμένας δεικνύουσι τραχείας περὶ
150 Μοασάδα καὶ σήραγγας πολλαχοῦ καὶ γῆν τεφρώδη, σταγόνας τε
πίσσης ἐκ λισσάδων λειβομένας καὶ δυσώδεις πόρρωθεν ποταμοὺς
ζέοντας, κατοικίας τε ἀνατετραμμένας σποράδην· ὥστε πιστεύειν
τοῖς θρυλουμένοις ὑπὸ τῶν ἐγχωρίων, ὡς ἄρα ᾠκοῦντό ποτε τρισκαίδεκα
πόλεις ἐνταῦθα, ὧν τῆς μητροπόλεως Σοδόμων σῴζοιτο κύκλος ἑξή-
155 κοντά που σταδίων· ὑπὸ δὲ σεισμῶν καὶ ἀναφυσημάτων πυρὸς καὶ
θερμῶν ὑδάτων ἀσφαλτωδῶν τε καὶ θειωδῶν ἡ λίμνη προπέσοι καὶ
πέτραι πυρίληπτοι γένοιντο, αἵ τε πόλεις αἱ μὲν καταποθεῖεν, ἃς δ᾽ ἐκ-
λίποιεν οἱ δυνάμενοι φυγεῖν. Ἐρατοσθένης δέ ⟨No. 23⟩ φησι τἀναντία,
λιμναζούσης τῆς χώρας, ἐκρήγμασιν ἀνακαλυφθῆναι τὴν πλείστην,
160 καθάπερ τὴν ✶ θάλατταν.

(45) Ἔστι δὲ καὶ ἐν τῇ Γαδαρίδι ὕδωρ μοχθηρὸν λιμναῖον, οὗ τὰ
γευσάμενα κτήνη τρίχας καὶ ὁπλὰς καὶ κέρατα ἀποβάλλει. ἐν δὲ ταῖς

140 περικαταχέαντας Kramer   περικαταχέοντας codd. | ἐκπιέσαντας i
ἐκπιάζοντας x   148 καὶ] τὰ Casaubonus   150 βοασάδα Dh
151 πίττης Meineke   153 θρυλουμένοις] λεγομένοις D | ᾤκουν πώποτε
D   157 ⟨αἱ⟩ πέτραι Corais   160 θάλατταν] Θετταλίαν Corais   τὴν
θάλατταν ⟨ταπεινωθῆναι⟩ Letronne   καθάπερ τὴν πλείστην ⟨τὴν περὶ⟩ τὴν
θάλατταν Reinhardt   161 γαρίτιδι Dhi

Strabo of Amaseia

καλουμέναις Ταριχέαις ἡ λίμνη μὲν ταριχείας ἰχθύων ἀστείας παρέχει,
φύει δὲ δένδρα καρποφόρα, μηλέαις ἐμφερῆ· χρῶνται δ' Αἰγύπτιοι τῇ
165 ἀσφάλτῳ πρὸς τὰς ταριχείας τῶν νεκρῶν.

(46) Πομπήιος μὲν οὖν περικόψας τινὰ τῶν ἐξιδιασθέντων ⟨p. 765⟩
ὑπὸ τῶν Ἰουδαίων κατὰ βίαν ἀπέδειξεν Ἡρώδῃ τὴν ἱερωσύνην·
τῶν δ' ἀπὸ γένους τις ὕστερον Ἡρώδης, ἀνὴρ ἐπιχώριος, παραδὺς
εἰς τὴν ἱερωσύνην, τοσοῦτον διήνεγκε τῶν πρὸ αὐτοῦ, καὶ μάλιστα
170 τῇ πρὸς Ῥωμαίους ὁμιλίᾳ καὶ πολιτείᾳ, ὥστε καὶ βασιλεὺς ἐχρημάτισε,
δόντος τὸ μὲν πρῶτον Ἀντωνίου τὴν ἐξουσίαν, ὕστερον δὲ καὶ Καίσαρος
τοῦ Σεβαστοῦ· τῶν δ' υἱῶν τοὺς μὲν αὐτὸς ἀνεῖλεν, ὡς ἐπιβουλεύσαντας
αὐτῷ, τοὺς δὲ τελευτῶν διαδόχους ἀπέλιπε, μερίδας αὐτοῖς ἀποδούς.
Καῖσαρ δὲ καὶ τοὺς υἱοὺς ἐτίμησε τοῦ Ἡρώδου καὶ τὴν ἀδελφὴν
175 Σαλώμην καὶ τὴν ταύτης θυγατέρα Βερενίκην· οὐ μέντοι εὐτύχησαν
οἱ παῖδες, ἀλλ' ἐν αἰτίαις ἐγένοντο, καὶ ὁ μὲν ἐν φυγῇ διετέλει, παρὰ
τοῖς Ἀλλόβριξι Γαλάταις λαβὼν οἴκησιν, οἱ δὲ θεραπείᾳ πολλῇ μόλις
εὕροντο κάθοδον, τετραρχίας ἀποδειχθείσης ἑκατέρῳ.

163 Ταριχέαις Salmasius   ταριχίαις F   ταριχείαις cett.   167 Ἡρώδῃ]
Ὑρκανῷ Corais   171 καὶ om. Dhw   175 θυγατέρα Βερενίκην edd.
βερενίκην θυγατέρα codd.   177 τὴν οἴκησιν Dh, Aldina   178 ἀπο-
δοθείσης Aldina

---

(34) As for Judaea, its western extremities towards Casius are occupied by the Idumaeans and by the lake. The Idumaeans are Nabataeans, but owing to a sedition they were banished from there, joined
the Judaeans, and shared in the same customs with them. The greater
part of the region near the sea is occupied by Lake Sirbonis and by
the country continuous with the lake as far as Jerusalem; for this city
is also near the sea; for, as I have already said, it is visible from the
seaport of Iope. This region lies towards the north; and it is inhabited
in general, as is each place in particular, by mixed stocks of people
from Egyptian and Arabian and Phoenician tribes; for such are
those who occupy Galilee and Hiericus and Philadelphia and Samaria,
which last Herod surnamed Sebaste. But though the inhabitants are
mixed up thus, the most prevalent of the accredited reports in regard
to the temple at Jerusalem represents the ancestors of the present
Judaeans, as they are called, as Egyptians.
(35) Moses, namely, was one of the Egyptian priests, and held
a part of Lower Egypt, as it is called, but he went away from there
to Judaea, since he was displeased with the state of affairs there, and
was accompanied by many people who worshipped the Divine
Being. For he said, and taught, that the Egyptians were mistaken in

299

representing the Divine Being by the images of beasts and cattle, as were also the Libyans; and that the Greeks were also wrong in modelling gods in human form; for, according to him, God is the one thing alone that encompasses us all and encompasses land and sea — the thing which we call heaven, or universe, or the nature of all that exists. What man, then, if he has sense, could be bold enough to fabricate an image of God resembling any creature amongst us? Nay, people should leave off all image-carving, and, setting apart a sacred precinct and a worthy sanctuary, should worship God without an image; and people who have good dreams should sleep in the sanctuary, not only themselves on their own behalf, but also others for the rest of the people; and those who live self-restrained and righteous lives should always expect some blessing or gift or sign from God, but no other should expect them.

(36) Now Moses, saying things of this kind, persuaded not a few thoughtful men and led them away to this place where the settlement of Jerusalem now is; and he easily took possession of the place, since it was not a place that would be looked on with envy, nor yet one for which anyone would make a serious fight; for it is rocky, and, although it itself is well supplied with water, its surrounding territory is barren and waterless, and the part of the territory within a radius of sixty stadia is also rocky beneath the surface. At the same time Moses, instead of using arms, put forward as defence his sacrifices and his Divine Being, being resolved to seek a seat of worship for Him and promising to deliver to the people a kind of worship and a kind of ritual which would not oppress those who adopted them either with expenses or with divine obsessions or with other absurd troubles. Now Moses enjoyed fair repute with these people, and organised no ordinary kind of government, since the people all round, one and all, came over to him, because of his dealings with them and of the prospects he held out to them.

(37) His successors for some time abided by the same course, acting righteously and being truly pious toward God; but afterwards, in the first place, superstitious men were appointed to the priesthood, and then tyrannical people; and from superstition arose abstinence from flesh, from which it is their custom to abstain even to-day, and circumcisions and excisions (i.e. of the females) and other observances of the kind. And from the tyrannies arose the bands of robbers; for some revolted and harassed the country, both their own country and that of their neighbours, whereas others, co-operating with the rulers, seized the property of others and subdued much of Syria and Phoenicia.

But still they had respect for their acropolis, since they did not loathe it as the seat of tyranny, but honoured and revered it as a holy place. (38) For this is natural; and it is common to the Greeks and the barbarians; for, being members of states, they live under common mandates; for otherwise it would be impossible for the mass of people in any country to do one and the same thing in harmony with one another, which is precisely what life in a free state means, or in any other way to live a common life. And the mandates are twofold; for they come either from gods or from men; and the ancients, at least, held those from the gods in greater honour and veneration; and on this account men who consulted oracles were much in evidence at that time—men who ran to Dodona "to hear the will of Zeus from the high-tressed oak," thus using Zeus as their counsellor, and also to Delphi, "seeking to learn whether the child which had been exposed to die was no longer alive;" but the child himself "was on his way to the home of Phoebus, wishing to discover his parents." And among the Cretans Minos "reigned as king, who held converse with great Zeus every ninth year," every nine years, as Plato says, when he would go up to the cave of Zeus and receive decrees from him and carry them to the people. And Lycurgus, his emulator, did likewise; for oftentimes, as it appears, he would go abroad to inquire of the Pythian priestess what ordinances it was proper for him to report to the Lacedaemonians.

(39) For these things, whatever truth there may be in them, have at least been believed and sanctioned among men; and for this reason the prophets too were held in so much honour that they were deemed worthy to be kings, on the ground that they promulgated to us ordinances and amendments from the gods, not only when they were alive, but also when they were dead, as, for example, Teiresias, 'to whom even in death Persephone granted reason, that he alone should have understanding, whereas the others flit about as shadows.' Such, also, were Amphiaraus, Trophonius, Orpheus, Musaeus, and the god among the Getae, who in ancient times was Zamolxis, a Pythagoreian, and in my time was Decaeneus, the diviner of Byrebistas; and, among the Bosporeni, Acheacarus; and, among the Indians, the Gymnosophists; and, among the Persians, the Magi and the necromancers, as also the dish-diviners and water-diviners, as they were called; and, among the Assyrians, the Chaldaeans; and, among the Romans, the Tyrrhenian nativity-casters. Moses was such a person as these, as also his successors, who, with no bad beginning, turned out for the worse.

(40) At any rate, when now Judaea was under the rule of tyrants,

Alexander was first to declare himself king instead of priest; and both Hyrcanus and Aristobulus were sons of his; and when they were at variance about the empire, Pompey went over and overthrew them and rased their fortifications, and in particular took Jerusalem itself by force; for it was a rocky and well-walled fortress; and though well supplied with water inside, its outside territory was wholly without water; and it had a trench cut in rock, sixty feet in depth and two hundred and fifty feet in breadth; and, from the stone that had been hewn out, the wall of the temple was fenced with towers. Pompey seized the city, it is said, after watching for the day of fasting, when the Judaeans were abstaining from all work; he filled up the trench and threw ladders across it; moreover, he gave orders to rase all the walls and, so far as he could, destroyed the haunts of robbers and the treasure-holds of the tyrants. Two of these were situated on the passes leading to Hiericus, I mean Threx and Taurus, and others were Alexandrium and Hyrcanium and Machaerus and Lysias and those in the neighbourhood of Philadelphia and Scythopolis in the neighbourhood of Galilaea.

(41) Hiericus is a plain surrounded by a kind of mountainous country which, in a way, slopes towards it like a theatre. Here is the Phoenicon, which is mixed also with other kinds of cultivated and fruitful trees, though it consists mostly of palm trees; it is one hundred stadia in length, and is everywhere watered with streams and full of dwellings. Here are also the palace and the balsam park. The balsam is of the shrub kind, resembling cytisus and terminthus, and has a spicy flavour. The people make incisions in the bark and catch the juice in vessels. This juice is a glutinous, milk-white substance; and when it is put up in small quantities it solidifies; and it is remarkable for its cure of headache and of incipient cataracts and of dimness of sight. Accordingly, it is costly; and also for the reason that it is produced nowhere else. Such is also the case with the Phoenicon, which alone has the caryotic palm, excepting the Babylonian and that beyond Babylonia towards the east. Accordingly, the revenue derived from it is great. And they use the xylo-balsam as spice.

(42) Lake Sirbonis is large; in fact some state that it is one thousand stadia in circuit; however, it extends parallel to the coast to a length of slightly more than two hundred stadia, is deep to the very shore, and has water so very heavy that there is no use for divers, and any person who walks into it and proceeds no farther than up to his navel is immediately raised afloat. It is full of asphalt. The asphalt is blown to the surface at irregular intervals from the midst of the deep, and with

it rise bubbles, as though the water were boiling; and the surface of the lake, being convex, presents the appearance of a hill. With the asphalt there arises also much soot, which though smoky, is imperceptible to the eye; and it tarnishes copper and silver and anything that glistens, even gold; and when their vessels are becoming tarnished the people who live round the lake know that the asphalt is beginning to rise; and they prepare to collect it by means of rafts made of reed. The asphalt is a clod of earth, which at first is liquefied by heat, and is blown up to the surface and spreads out; and then again, by reason of the cold water, the kind of water the lake in question has, it changes to a firm, solidified substance, and therefore requires cutting and chopping; and then it floats, because of the nature of the water, owing to which, as I was saying, there is no use for divers; and no person who walks into it can immerse himself either, but is raised afloat. They reach the asphalt on rafts and chop it and carry off as much as they each can.

(43) Such, then, is the fact in the case; but according to Poseidonius the people are sorcerers and pretend to use incantations, as also urine and other malodorous liquids, which they first pour all over the solidified substance, and squeeze out the asphalt and harden it, and then cut it into pieces; unless there is some suitable element of this kind in urine, such, for example, as chrysocolla, which forms in the bladder of people who have bladder-stones and is derived from the urine of children. It is reasonable that this behaviour should occur in the middle of the lake, because the source of the fire and also the greater part of the asphalt is at the middle of it; but the bubbling up is irregular, because the movement of the fire, like that of many other subterranean blasts, follows no order known to us. Such, also, are the phenomena at Apollonia in Epirus.

(44) Many other evidences are produced to show that the country is fiery; for near Moasada are to be seen rugged rocks that have been scorched, as also, in many places, fissures and ashy soil, and drops of pitch dripping from smooth cliffs, and boiling rivers that emit foul odours to a great distance, and ruined settlements here and there; and therefore people believe the oft-repeated assertions of the local inhabitants, that there were once thirteen inhabited cities in that region of which Sodom was the metropolis, but that a circuit of about sixty stadia of that city escaped unharmed; and that by reason of earthquakes and of eruptions of fire and of hot waters containing asphalt and sulphur, the lake burst its bounds, and rocks were enveloped with fire; and as for the cities, some were swallowed

303

up and others were abandoned by such as were able to escape. But Eratosthenes says, on the contrary, that the country was a lake, and that most of it was uncovered by outbreaks, as was the case with the sea.

(45) In Gadaris, also, there is noxious lake water; and when animals taste it they lose hair and hoofs and horns. At the place called Taricheae the lake supplies excellent fish for pickling; and on its banks grow fruit-bearing trees resembling apple trees. The Egyptians use the asphalt for embalming the bodies of the dead.

(46) Now Pompey clipped off some of the territory that had been forcibly appropriated by the Judaeans, and appointed Herod to the priesthood; but later a certain Herod, a descendant of his and a native of the country, who slinked into the priesthood, was so superior to his predecessors, particularly in his intercourse with the Romans and in his administration of affairs of state, that he received the title of king, being given that authority first by Antony and later by Augustus Caesar. As for his sons, he himself put some of them to death, on the ground that they had plotted against him; and at his death left others as his successors, having assigned to them portions of his kingdom. Caesar also honoured the sons of Herod and his sister Salome and her daughter Berenice. However, his sons were not successful, but became involved in accusations; and one of them spent the rest of his life in exile, having taken up his abode among the Allobrogian Gauls, whereas the others, by much obsequiousness, but with difficulty, found leave to return home, with a tetrarchy assigned to each. (trans. H. L. Jones, *LCL*)

---

34 Ναβαταῖοι δ'εἰσὶν οἱ 'Ιδουμαῖοι· κατὰ στάσιν δ' ἐκπεσόντες: The Idumaeans certainly were not originally Nabataeans. The truth is that they were driven northwards by the Nabataean invasion. Their old capital, Petra, became the capital of the new Nabataean kingdom, while the Idumaeans occupied the southern territories of old Judah, including Hebron, Adora and Marissa.

προσεχώρησαν τοῖς 'Ιουδαίοις καὶ τῶν νομίμων τῶν αὐτῶν ἐκείνοις ἐκοινώνησαν: Strabo does not stress the compulsory character of the Judaization of the Idumaeans, but rather describes it as a voluntary act. On the other hand, cf. *Ant.*, XIII, 257: 'Υρκανὸς... ἐπέτρεψεν αὐτοῖς μένειν ἐν τῇ χώρᾳ, εἰ περιτέμνοιντο τὰ αἰδοῖα καὶ τοῖς 'Ιουδαίων νόμοις χρῆσθαι θέλοιεν; cf. also Ptolemy (No. 146), who designates the Idumaeans not as former Nabataeans, but as Phoenicians and Syrians whom the Jews compelled to undergo circumcision. Churgin prefers Strabo's version; see P. Churgin, *Studies in the Times of the Second Temple*, New York 1949, p. 79 (in Hebrew).

τοιοῦτοι γὰρ οἱ τὴν Γαλιλαίαν ἔχοντες: Strabo is the first pagan writer to use the form Γαλιλαία, already known from the Septuagint. A papyrus from the third

Strabo of Amaseia

century B.C.E. (*P. Columbia Zenon*, No. 2, l.22) has the form Γαλιλα. On the population problems and the ethnic character of Hellenistic Galilaea, see Alt, II, pp. 384 ff.

'Ιεϱικοῦντα: The Septuagint usually has the transcription Ιεϱιχω. Josephus has either 'Ιεϱιχώ or 'Ιεϱιχοῦς; cf. *PCZ*, No. 59004, Col. 1, l.4: ἐν 'Εϱιχο(ῖ). Jericho was already included in Judaea proper in the Persian period. It seems, however, to have had a mixture of non-Jewish inhabitants.

καὶ τὴν Φιλαδέλφειαν: On Philadelphia, the ancient Rabbat-Ammon, see Schürer, II, pp. 189 ff.; Tcherikover, pp. 100 f. Its territory bordered on that of Jewish Peraea; see *Ant.*, XX, 2. On the Pompeian Era at Philadelphia, see A. Alt, *ZDPV*, LV (1932), pp. 132 ff.

Σαμάϱειαν, ἣν 'Ηϱώδης Σεβαστὴν ἐπωνόμασεν: In 27 B.C.E.

φήμη... Αἰγυπτίους ἀποφαίνει τοὺς πϱογόνους τῶν νῦν 'Ιουδαίων λεγομένων: Strabo declares that the ancestors of the Jews were Egyptians, in contrast to Hecataeus, who considered them foreigners in Egypt. Strabo's view, however, is paralleled by that of Celsus. Moreover, it is implied in the hostile account of Jewish origins given by the enemies of the Jews in the time of Antiochus Sidetes; see Diodorus, *Bibliotheca Historica*, XXXIV–XXXV, 1 (No. 63); Chaeremon, apud: Josephus, *Contra Apionem*, I, 288–292 (No. 178).

35 Μωσῆς: For the different forms of the name in Greek, see Heinemann, PW, XVI, p. 360. Also in Hecataeus we find the form Μωσῆς; see Diodorus, XL, 3 : 3 (No.11). The same form occurs in Apollonius Molon (No.46), but not in Diodorus, XXXIV–XXXV, 1 : 3 (No. 63); I, 94 (No. 58); cf. Aly, *op. cit.* (supra, p. 267), p. 199.

τις τῶν Αἰγυπτίων ἱεϱέων: On Moses as an Egyptian priest, see Manetho, apud: Josephus, *Contra Apionem*, I, 250 (No. 21) and Chaeremon, apud: Josephus, *Contra Apionem*, I, 290 (No. 178). It is noteworthy that Strabo refers to the sojourn of both Plato and Eudoxus in the priestly centre of Heliopolis; *Geographica*, XVII, 1 : 29, p. 806. For the respect which Strabo had for Egyptian civilization in general, see *ibid.*, 1 : 3, p. 787.

εἴη γὰϱ ἓν τοῦτο μόνον θεὸς τὸ πεϱιέχον ἡμᾶς ἅπαντας καὶ γῆν καὶ θάλατταν, ὃ καλοῦμεν οὐϱανὸν καὶ κόσμον: Cf. Hecataeus, apud: Diodorus, XL, 3 : 4 (No.11):"Ἄγαλμα δὲ θεῶν τὸ σύνολον οὐ κατεσκεύασε διὰ τὸ μὴ νομίζειν ἀνθϱωπομόϱφον εἶναι τὸν θεόν, ἀλλὰ τὸν πεϱιέχοντα τὴν γῆν οὐϱανὸν μόνον εἶναι θεὸν καὶ τῶν ὅλων κύϱιον. Both Hecataeus and Strabo regard heaven as the God of the Jews, but Strabo also equates it with the universe and with the nature of all existence. Both writers declare that this god — namely, heaven — encompasses the earth. But here, again, Strabo goes beyond Hecataeus in coupling the sea and ἡμᾶς ἅπαντας with the earth. Both writers depict the God of Moses in marked contrast to the anthropomorphic deities worshipped by the Greeks, and both emphasize the Jews' belief in the oneness of God. Thus, we may even assume that the concept of the Jewish God as it emerges in Strabo is an elaboration of that represented by Hecataeus. Whether this elaboration is due to Strabo or to some intermediate source cannot be determined. Reinhardt, who attributes the whole passage to Posidonius, holds the view that the differences between Hecataeus and Strabo are very significant and that the latter expresses the philosophy of Posidonius: " ... die Formel selbst verwandelt ihren Sinn: indem das 'Uns-Umfangende' neben das, was die 'Erde und das Meer umfängt', sich stellt, sogar davor sich stellt, bleibt das Umfangende nicht mehr im Räumlichen, es wird zum Tragenden, Umfangenden in einem

305

From Herodotus to Plutarch

anderen Sinn ..."; cf. K. Reinhardt, *Poseidonios über Ursprung und Entartung*, Heidelberg 1928, pp. 10 f. Whether this was the philosophy of Posidonius is still to be disputed. According to the Scholia to Lucan (*Pharsalia*, IX, 578), the view of Posidonius was that θεός ἐστι πνεῦμα νοερὸν διῆκον δι'ἁπάσης οὐσίας, which has a pantheistic ring and does not accord with Strabo's view that the deity encompasses the world; cf. Aly, *op. cit.* (supra, p. 267), pp. 196 f. On the other hand, I cannot agree with Aly that there is a similarity between Strabo's statement and Gen. i : 2: καὶ πνεῦμα θεοῦ ἐπεφέρετο ἐπάνω τοῦ ὕδατος.

τούτου δὴ τίς ἂν εἰκόνα πλάττειν θαρρήσειε νοῦν ἔχων...: On the philosophical — especially Stoic — opposition to the cult of images, see the introduction to Varro.

ἀλλ' ἐᾶν δεῖν πᾶσαν ξοανοποιίαν: On the discarding of image-making by Jews, see also Hecataeus (No. 11), Varro (No. 72), Livy (No. 133),Tacitus (No. 281, § 5), Cassius Dio (No. 406). On the Stoic views, see the commentary to Varro.

τέμενος δ' ἀφορίσαντας καὶ σηκὸν ἀξιόλογον: Σηκός means here the inner part of the Temple. It is also used by Diodorus XXXIV–XXXV, 1 : 3 (No. 63) with reference to the Temple of Jerusalem; see also II Macc. xiv : 33.

ἐγκοιμᾶσθαι δὲ καὶ αὐτοὺς ὑπὲρ ἑαυτῶν: For *incubatio* in Strabo's *Geographica* see also XIV, 1 : 44, p. 649; XVII, 1 : 17, p. 801: ἐγκοιμᾶσθαι αὐτοὺς ὑπὲρ ἑαυτῶν ἢ ἑτέρους.

36 κατέσχε δὲ ῥαδίως οὐκ ἐπίφθονον ὃν τὸ χωρίον...: Cf. Hecataeus, apud: Diodorus, XL, 3:2 (No. 11). Hecataeus refers to Judaea as having been uninhabited at the time of the Jews' arrival.

αὐτὸ μὲν εὔυδρον...: Cf. Timochares, apud: Eusebius, *Praeparatio Evangelica*, IX, 35 : 1 (No. 41): Τὴν δὲ μεταξὺ ἀπὸ τῆς πόλεως ἄχρι τεσσαράκοντα σταδίων ἄνυδρον εἶναι.

ἥτις οὔτε δαπάναις ὀχλήσει τοὺς χρωμένους: Cf. the various passages referred to by A. Wilhelm, *Rhein. Mus.*, LXX (1915), p. 219; I. Heinemann, *MGWJ*, (1919), p. 114, n. 3; see also Theophrastus, apud: Porphyrius, *De Abstinentia*, II, 15: τὸ εὐδάπανον φίλον θεοῖς.

ἁπάντων προσχωρησάντων ῥαδίως τῶν κύκλῳ...: Here again Strabo stresses the peaceful conversion of the neighbouring people to Judaism.

37 ἐκ μὲν τῆς δεισιδαιμονίας: On Strabo's negative attitude to δεισιδαιμονία, see P. J. Koets, "Δεισιδαιμονία — A Contribution to the Knowledge of the Religious Terminology in Greek", Ph. D. Thesis, Utrecht 1929, pp. 63 ff.

αἱ τῶν βρωμάτων ἀποσχέσεις: Cf. Tacitus, *Historiae*, V, 5 (No. 281): "separati epulis".

καὶ αἱ ἐκτομαί: On excisions of females, see Strabo, *Geographica*, XVI, 4 : 9, p. 771 (No. 118): αἱ γυναῖκες Ἰουδαϊκῶς ἐκτετμημέναι; XVII, 2 : 5, p. 824. In fact, nothing like this exists in the Jewish religion, but this custom is well known elsewhere; cf. L. H. Gray, in: *Encyclopaedia of Religion and Ethics*, III, London 1910, p. 659.

ἐκ δὲ τῶν τυραννίδων τὰ ληστήρια: Cf. Strabo, *Geographica*, XVI, 2 : 28; Pompeius Trogus, *Historiae Philippicae*, Prologus, XXXIX (No. 138): "Iudaei et Arabes terrestribus latrociniis."

καὶ τῆς Συρίας κατεστρέφοντο καὶ τῆς Φοινίκης πολλήν: The Hasmonaean conquests are implied.

ἦν δ' ὅμως εὐπρέπειά τις...: Cf. Hecataeus, apud: Diodorus, *Bibliotheca Historica*, XL, 3 : 3 (No. 11): Ἱδρύσατο δὲ καὶ τὸ μάλιστα παρ' αὐτοῖς τιμώμενον ἱερόν.

306

Strabo of Amaseia

38 καὶ ὁ Μίνως... καὶ Λυκοῦργος...: For a similar list of names, cf. Diodorus, *Bibliotheca Historica*, I, 94 (No. 58). In Diodorus we find Minos, Lycurgus, Zathraustes, Zalmoxis and Moyses, all of whom, with the exception of Zathraustes, are also listed by Strabo. Strabo, however, refers to the magi in general. On the other hand, Strabo does not mention the name of Iao as that of the Jewish God.

39 Δεκαίνεος: On this contemporary of Julius Caesar and of Burebistas, King of the Getae, see Strabo, *Geographica*, VII, 3 : 5, p. 298; cf. *ibid.*, 3 : 11, p. 304: πρὸς δὲ τὴν εὐπείθειαν τοῦ ἔθνους συναγωνιστὴν ἔσχε [scil. Βοιρεβίστας], Δεκαίνεον ἄνδρα γόητα.

40 πρῶτος ἀνθ' ἱερέως ἀνέδειξεν ἑαυτὸν βασιλέα 'Αλέξανδρος: Strabo's statement that Alexander — (i.e. Alexander Jannaeus, 103–76 B.C.E.) — was the first to declare himself king contradicts Josephus (*Ant.*, XIII, 301; *BJ*, I, 70). Josephus expressly says that it was Aristobulus (104–103 B.C.E.) who became the first king of Hasmonaean Judaea. It seems to me that the Jewish historian's version which gives a much more circumstantial account of the Hasmonaean history should be preferred to that of Strabo, especially as we cannot see any cogent reason for Josephus' attribution of this step to Aristobulus if it was not historically true. It may be suggested that there should be a distinction between Aristobulus' title in his relations with foreign states and the one he continued to use among his Jewish subjects. It may be that for his subjects he remained simply high priest, while he called himself king only in his foreign contacts. Subsequently, Alexander Jannaeus completely transformed the government of Judaea into a monarchy; cf. E.R. Bevan, *Jerusalem under the High Priests*, London 1904, p. 115; Tcherikover, p. 490, n. 25. That Aristobulus bears the traditional title of high priest on the coins is inconclusive. Too much importance is ascribed to this fact by scholars, e.g., H. Box, *JRS*, XXIX (1939), p. 250. However, we are by no means sure that the coins in question belong to Aristobulus I, and not to his nephew, Aristobulus II. On ἀνάδειξις, see E. Bikerman, *Annuaire de l'institut de philologie et d'histoire orientales et slaves*, V (1937), pp. 117 ff.

ἐντὸς μὲν εὔυδρον, ἐκτὸς δὲ παντελῶς διψηρόν...: Cf. again Timochares, apud: Eusebius, *Praeparatio Evangelica*, IX, 35 : 1. (No. 41): "Ολην δὲ τὴν πόλιν ὕδασι καταρρεῖσθαι, ὥστε καὶ τοὺς κήπους ἐκ τῶν ἀπορρεόντων ὑδάτων ἐκ τῆς πόλεως ἄρδεσθαι. τὴν δὲ μεταξὺ... ἄνυδρον εἶναι.

κατελάβετο... τηρήσας τὴν τῆς νηστείας ἡμέραν: This does not mean the Day of Atonement, which seems to be excluded by chronology; cf. the commentary to Strabo, *Historica Hypomnemata*, apud: Josephus, *Ant.*, XIV : 66 (No. 104). Strabo, like other ancient writers, thought the Sabbath was a fast day. As we learn from Josephus (*Ant.*, XIV, 63 f.), the soldiers of Pompey abstained from attacking the Jews on the Sabbath and instead raised earthworks and brought up their siege-engines, because, although the Jews were allowed to defend themselves against a direct attack on the Sabbath, they were not allowed to fight against enemies engaged in preparatory activities. Thus, it was more advantageous to refrain from attacking the Jews on the Day of Atonement or on any Sabbath and to carry out the preliminary work instead. However, there is nothing to refute the additional supposition that on one of these Sabbaths the Romans, after filling the trenches undisturbed, also started a general attack and captured the Temple on the same day. Nevertheless, it seems more plausible that Strabo condensed the events and created the impression that the Temple fell on a Sabbath, which, to him, was a fast day.

From Herodotus to Plutarch

Θρήξ τε καὶ Ταῦρος: The name of the first of the fortresses is to be connected with Thracian mercenaries who served in the armies of the Jewish kings. We know that Thracian soldiers served under Herod (*Ant.*, XVII, 198; *BJ*, I, 672), and it stands to reason that Alexander Jannaeus already had recourse to Thracian mercenaries; cf. his nickname Thracidas in *Ant.*, XIII, 383. On these fortresses, see also J.L. Kelso, *Biblical Archaeologist*, XIV (1951), p. 38.

Ἀλεξάνδριον (Ἀλεξάνδρειον): Alexandrion is identified with Karn Sartaba, north of Jericho; see Abel, II, pp. 241 f.; O. Plöger, *ZDPV*, LXXI (1955), pp. 142 ff.; N. Schmidt, *JBL*, XXIX (1910), pp. 77 ff. The fortress was presumably built by Alexander Jannaeus.

Ὑρκάνιον (Ὑρκανία): Hyrcania is identified with Khirbet-Mird, to the south-east of Jerusalem, a fortress built by John Hyrcan; see Abel, II, p. 350; Plöger, *op. cit.*, pp. 148 ff.

Μαχαιροῦς: A strong fortress to the east of the Dead Sea; see the commentary to Plinius' *Naturalis Historia*, V, 72 (No. 204).

Λυσιάς: This name is probably corrupt; one may suggest some connection with Lysias, a fortress in the region of Lebanon ruled by the Jew Silas and destroyed by Pompey.

41 Ἱερικοῦς δ᾽ἐστὶ πεδίον...: Pompeius Trogus (apud: Iustinus, *Epitoma*, XXXVI, 3 : 2 = No. 137) refers to Ericus as a valley "quae continuis montibus...clauditur".

ἔστι δ᾽αὐτοῦ καὶ βασίλειον: A palace built by Herod.

ἔστι δὲ τὸ φυτὸν θαμνῶδες: For the other main descriptions of the balsam, see Theophrastus, *Historia Plantarum*, IX, 6:1–4 (No. 9). For the most detailed description, cf. Plinius, *Naturalis Historia*, XII, 111–123 (No. 213); see also Dioscorides, *De Materia Medica*, I, 19 : 1 (No. 179).

κυτίσῳ ἐοικὸς καὶ τερμίνθῳ: Cf. Theophrastus, *Historia Plantarum*, IX, 6:1 (No. 9): καρπὸν δὲ παρόμοιον τῇ τερμίνθῳ καὶ μεγέθει καὶ σχήματι καὶ χρώματι.

οὗ τὸν φλοιὸν ἐπισχίσαντες...: On the mode of the incision, see Plinius, *loc. cit.* (No. 213); Tacitus, *Historiae*, V, 6 (No. 281).

λύει δὲ κεφαλαλγίας: On the medical qualities of the balsam, see Diodorus, II, 48 : 9 (No. 59); Plinius, *Naturalis Historia*, XII, 118 (No. 213); Dioscorides, *De Materia Medica*, I, 19; Nicander, *Theriaca*, 947; Celsus, *De Medicina*, V, 3–6, 18 : 3, 23 : 1; Galenus, XI (Kühn), p. 846; XII, p. 554; XIII, pp. 567 f.

τίμιος οὖν ἐστι: Cf. Plinius, *Naturalis Historia*, XII, 117 f. (No. 213).

καὶ διότι ἐνταῦθα μόνον γεννᾶται: For a similar statement, see Diodorus, *loc. cit.* (No. 59); Pompeius Trogus, apud: Iustinus, XXXVI, 3 : 1 (No. 137): "opes genti ex vectigalibus opobalsami crevere quod in his tantum regionibus gignitur." See also Plinius, *Naturalis Historia*, XII, 111 (No. 213): "uni terrarum Iudaeae concessum"; Dioscorides, *De Materia Medica*, I, 19 : 1 (No. 179). Dioscorides adds Egypt to Judaea as a country where balsam grows. On the balsam, see also the commentary to Plinius, *Naturalis Historia*, XII, 111 ff. (No. 213).

ἔχων τὸν καρυωτὸν φοίνικα ἐνταῦθα μόνον: Cf. Varro, *Res Rusticae*, II, 1 : 27 (No. 73); Galenus, *De Alimentorum Facultatibus*, II, 26 (No. 379): ὥσπερ οἱ καλούμενοι καρυωτοί, κάλλιστοι δ᾽οὗτοι γεννῶνται κατὰ τὴν Παλαιστίνην Συρίαν and the commentary *ad loc*. On the use of *palmae caryotae* for medical purposes, see Scribonius Largus, 74, 148; cf. also Dioscorides, *De Materia Medica*, I, 109.

καὶ τῷ ξυλοβαλσάμῳ δὲ ὡς ἀρώματι χρῶνται: Cf. Plinius, *Naturalis Historia*, XII, 118 (No. 213): "et sarmenta quoque in merce sunt . . . xylobalsamum vocatur et coquitur in unguentis."

308

Strabo of Amaseia

42 'Η δὲ Σιρβωνὶς λίμνη: Strabo confuses Lake Sirbonis with the Dead Sea. Though he gives the lake the name of the Egyptian Sirbonis, all the features he attributes to it are those peculiar to the Dead Sea, with the exception, perhaps, of its circumference. On the measurements of the Dead Sea given by various writers, see the commentary to Diodorus (No. 62).

βαρύτατον ἔχουσα ὕδωρ, ὥστε μὴ δεῖν κολύμβου: Cf. Aristoteles, Meteorologica, II, p. 359a (No. 3); Plinius, Naturalis Historia, V, 72 (No. 204); BJ, IV, 476 f.; Tacitus, Historiae, V, 6 (No. 281); Pausanias, V, 7 : 5 (No. 356).

ἀναφυσᾶται κατὰ καιροὺς ἀτάκτους: On the contrary we read in Diodorus, Bibliotheca Historica, II, 48 : 7 (No. 59): ἐξ αὐτῆς δὲ μέσης κατ' ἐνιαυτὸν ἐκφυσᾷ ἀσφάλτου μέγεθος; Tacitus, Historiae, V, 6 (No. 281): "certo anni tempore"; cf. also Reinhardt, op. cit. (supra, p. 306), pp. 62 ff.

συναναφέρεται δὲ καὶ ἄσβολος ... ὑφ' ἧς κατιοῦται καὶ χαλκὸς καὶ ἄργυρος: On the tarnishing of metals due to the asphalt, see Diodorus (Nos. 59, 62). The statement that it is caused by the smoky soot is unique to Strabo.

ποιησάμενοι σχεδίας καλαμίνας: Cf. Diodorus, Bibliotheca Historica, XIX, 99 : 1 (No. 62): παρασκευασάμενοι γὰρ δέσμας καλάμων εὐμεγέθεις...

43 γόητας δὲ ὄντας σκήπτεσθαί φησιν ἐπῳδὰς ὁ Ποσειδώνιος: Cf. the commentary to Posidonius (No. 45). It constitutes the only express reference to Posidonius in Strabo's description of Judaea.

τοιαῦτα δὲ καὶ τὰ ἐν 'Απολλωνίᾳ τῇ 'Ηπειρώτιδι: Cf. Strabo, Geographica, VII, 5 : 8, p. 316.

44 περὶ Μοασάδα: Cf. the commentary to Plinius, Naturalis Historia, V, 73 (No. 204).

45 ἔστι δὲ καὶ ἐν τῇ Γαδαρίδι ὕδωρ...: Which town is meant by Strabo — Gadaris (= Gazara) or Gadara? It seems that the second possibility is preferable. ἐν δὲ ταῖς καλουμέναις Ταριχέαις: On Taricheae, see also the commentary to Plinius, Naturalis Historia, V, 71 (No. 204). By using Pliny's location of the town to the south of the Sea of Gennesareth as a basis, many scholars identified the town with Khirbet Kerak. For this view, see G. Hölscher, PW, Ser. 2, IV, p. 2317. This identification, however, seems to be precluded by other evidence, which suggests that Taricheae is identical with Mejdel, the talmudic Migdal Nounaya, north of Tiberias; cf. S. Klein, Beiträge zur Geographie und Geschichte Galiläas, Leipzig 1909, pp. 76 ff.; W.F. Albright, AASOR, II–III, 1921–1922 (1923), pp. 29 ff.; Abel, II, pp. 476 f.; Avi-Yonah, op. cit. (supra, p. 293), p. 140; see also A. H. M. Jones, The Cities of the Eastern Roman Provinces, Oxford 1971, p. 274 f.; Alt, II, pp. 449 f. Strabo is the first writer to give us information concerning this town. It already had a large Jewish population in the middle of the first century B.C.E.; see Ant., XIV, 120; BJ, I, 180; see also Cicero, Ad Familiares, XII, 11 (No. 71).

χρῶνται δ'Αἰγύπτιοι τῇ ἀσφάλτῳ πρὸς τὰς ταριχείας τῶν νεκρῶν: Similar information is supplied by Diodorus, Bibliotheca Historica, XIX, 99 : 3 (No. 62).

46 Πομπήιος... περικόψας τινὰ τῶν ἐξιδιασθέντων ὑπὸ τῶν 'Ιουδαίων κατὰ βίαν: It is obvious that ἐξιδιασθέντα ὑπὸ τῶν 'Ιουδαίων implies the territorial aggrandizement of Judaea. Reinhardt's interpretation has no foundation; see Reinhardt, op. cit. (supra, p. 306), p. 26: "Pompeius, indem er gewisse Auswüchse in ihren Sitten abstellt, setzt die alte Priesterherrschaft wieder ein." Cf. also Reinhardt, PW, (supra, p, 267), p. 639. For Pompey's conquest of Judaea, see Ant., XIV, 74: ἃς δὲ πρότερον οἱ ἔνοικοι πόλεις ἐχειρώσαντο τῆς κοίλης Συρίας

From Herodotus to Plutarch

ἀφελόμενος ὑπὸ τῷ σφετέρῳ στρατηγῷ ἔταξεν καὶ τὸ σύμπαν ἔθνος ἐπὶ μέγα πρότερον αἱρόμενον ἐντὸς τῶν ἰδίων ὅρων συνέστειλεν; see also *BJ*, I, 155.

ἀπέδειξεν ῾Ηρώδῃ τὴν ἱερωσύνην: This statement, as it stands, sounds strange. In fact, Pompey confirmed Hyrcan as high priest, and not Herod. Herod was at that time about ten years old. His first official appointment was under Julius Caesar, when he was made governor of Galilee; see *Ant.*, XIV, 158 = *BJ*, I, 203. Strabo distinguishes between Herod and the high priest appointed by Pompey: τῶν δ'ἀπὸ γένους τις ὕστερον ῾Ηρώδης: Thus, there is much to be said for the emendation of Corais, who substitutes Hyrcan for Herod.

ἀνὴρ ἐπιχώριος: On Herod's origins, see the commentary to Nicolaus, apud: Josephus, *Ant.*, *XIV*, 9 (No. 90).

παραδὺς εἰς τὴν ἱερωσύνην: Otto (p. 18), thinks that at the bottom of this statement lies an attempt by Herod to gain access into the priestly order. This, however, is unlikely. Strabo uses ἱερωσύνη in the sense of ἀρχιερωσύνη. In the Hasmonaean period the rulers of Judaea usually fulfilled the function of high priest, which was considered by their subjects to be their main function; cf. also Tacitus, *Historiae*,V, 8 (No. 281). Strabo also mistakenly refers to Herod as a high priest since he did not know the details of Jewish law, which restricted the priesthood only to those of priestly origin. It also seems that Strabo confuses ἱερωσύνη with "kingdom"; cf. Cassius Dio, XXXVII, 15 : 2 (No. 406): ὑπὲρ τῆς . . . ἱερωσύνης· οὕτω γὰρ τὴν βασιλείαν σφῶν ὠνόμαζον; see also Iustinus, Epitoma, XXXVI, 2 : 16 (No. 137).

δόντος τὸ μὲν πρῶτον ᾿Αντώνιον τὴν ἐξουσίαν: Cf. *Ant.*, XIV, 381 ff.; *BJ*, I, 282 ff.

ὕστερον δὲ καὶ Καίσαρος τοῦ Σεβαστοῦ: Cf. *Ant.*, XV, 195; *BJ*, I, 391 f.

τῶν δ' υἱῶν τοὺς μὲν αὐτὸς ἀνεῖλεν, ὡς ἐπιβουλεύσαντας αὐτῷ: Herod sentenced to death Alexander and Aristobulus, his sons from Mariamme, and his eldest son Antipater, who was executed a few days before his own death; cf. Nicolaus, *De Vita Sua* (No. 97).

μερίδας αὐτοῖς ἀποδούς: Archelaus received Judaea, Idumaea and Samaria as his portion; Herod Antipas was given Galilaea and Peraea; and Philip received the north-eastern parts of the Herodian Kingdom; see *Ant.*, XVII, 188 f.

καὶ τὴν ἀδελφὴν Σαλώμην: Salome, Herod's sister, maintained close relations with the Empress Livia. She also received a portion in her brother's testament, consisting of Jamnia, Azotus and Phasaelis, to which Augustus added the royal palace of Ascalon; see *Ant.*, XVII, 321; *BJ*, II, 98. Salome's influence at the imperial court is reflected in the Acts of the Pagan Martyrs; see H. Musurillo, *The Acts of the Pagan Martyrs*, Oxford 1954, Acta Isidori, Recension A, Col. III, l. 11 f., p. 19: σὺ δὲ ἐκ Σαλώμη (ς) (τ)ῆς ᾿Ιουδα(ίας ν)ἱὸς (ἀπό)βλητος = *CPJ* Vol. II. No. 156d.

Βερενίκην: Berenice was the daughter of Salome and her Idumaean husband Costobar. One of her sons was the famous Agrippa I. While Strabo refers to Berenice's being honoured by Augustus, we know from Josephus about her friendship with Antonia, the wife of Augustus' step-son Drusus and the mother of Claudius; see *Ant.*, XVIII, 143; cf. also A. H. M. Jones, *The Herods of Judaea*, Oxford 1938, pp. 184, 222.

οὐ μέντοι εὐτύχησαν οἱ παῖδες...: On the end of Archelaus, see *Ant.*, XVII, 342 ff.; *BJ*, II, 111. According to Josephus, the complaint of the Jews and the Samaritans concerning Archelaus' cruelty constituted the immediate cause of his exile. Archelaus was banished in 6 C.E. to Vienna in Gaul, the capital of the Allobrogi; cf. the commentary to Cassius Dio, LV, 27 : 6 (No. 418).

310

Strabo of Amaseia

οἱ δὲ θεραπείᾳ πολλῇ μόλις εὗροντο κάθοδον: According to Strabo, it seems
that at the same time the positions of Antipas and Philip were endangered, and
they were called to Rome to answer before the Emperor for their conduct. However,
this is not stated by Josephus; cf. Otto, pp.178 ff. For a different view, see H.Willrich,
Das Haus des Herodes zwischen Jerusalem und Rom, Heidelberg 1929, p. 188.
Otto's view has also been accepted by H. Dessau, *Geschichte der römischen Kaiserzeit*, Vol. II, Part 2, Berlin 1930, p. 776. See also H. W. Hoehner, *Herod Antipas*,
Cambridge 1972, p. 103.

τετραρχίας ἀποδειχθείσης ἑκατέρῳ: If we accept Otto's interpretation, we
should understand that Strabo refers to a reconfirmation of the rule of Antipas and
Philip over their respective territories. After Herod's death (4 B.C.E.) Archelaus
became ethnarch, while his two brothers had to content themselves with the title of
tetrarch; cf. W. Schwahn, PW, Ser. 2, V, pp. 1094 f.

116

Geographica, XVI, 3 : 1, p. 765 — Kramer

Ὑπέρκειται δὲ τῆς Ἰουδαίας καὶ τῆς Κοίλης Συρίας μέχρι Βαβυλωνίας
καὶ τῆς τοῦ Εὐφράτου ποταμίας πρὸς νότον Ἀραβία πᾶσα χωρὶς τῶν
ἐν τῇ Μεσοποταμίᾳ Σκηνιτῶν.

2 νότου E

Above Judaea and Coele-Syria, as far as Babylonia and the river-
country of the Euphrates towards the south, lies the whole of Arabia,
with the exception of the Scenitae in Mesopotamia.

(trans. H.L. Jones, *LCL*)

117

Geographica, XVI, 4:2, p. 767 — Kramer

Ἐπάνειμι δὲ ἐπὶ τὰς Ἐρατοσθένους ἀποφάσεις, ἃς ἑξῆς περὶ τῆς
Ἀραβίας ἐκτίθεται. φησὶ δὲ περὶ τῆς προσαρκτίου καὶ ἐρήμης, ἥτις
ἐστὶ μεταξὺ τῆς τε εὐδαίμονος Ἀραβίας καὶ τῆς Κοιλοσύρων καὶ
τῶν Ἰουδαίων, μέχρι τοῦ μυχοῦ τοῦ Ἀραβίου κόλπου, διότι ἀπὸ
5 Ἡρώων πόλεως, ἥτις ἐστὶ πρὸς τῷ Νείλῳ μυχὸς τοῦ Ἀραβίου κόλπου,
πρὸς μὲν τὴν Ναβαταίων Πέτραν εἰς Βαβυλῶνα πεντακισχίλιοι ἑξα-
κόσιοι... ὑπὲρ δὲ τούτων ἡ Εὐδαίμων ἐστίν... ἔχουσι δ' αὐτὴν οἱ μὲν
πρῶτοι μετὰ τοὺς Σύρους καὶ τοὺς Ἰουδαίους ἄνθρωποι γεωργοί.

5 ἥτις ἐστὶν ἐν τῷ πρὸς τὸν Νεῖλον μυχῷ Corais

But I return to Eratosthenes, who next sets forth his opinions concerning Arabia. He says concerning the northerly, or desert, part of

311

From Herodotus to Plutarch

Arabia, which lies between Arabia Felix and Coele-Syria and Judaea, extending as far as the recess of the Arabian Gulf that from the City of Heroes, which forms a recess of the Arabian Gulf near the Nile, the distance in the direction of the Petra of the Nabataeans to Babylon is five thousand six hundred stadia. . . Above these lies Arabia Felix. . . The first people who occupy Arabia Felix, after the Syrians and Judaeans, are farmers.   (trans. H. L. Jones, *LCL*)

118

Geographica, XVI, 4:9, p. 771 — Kramer

Εἶτα ὁ ᾿Αντιφίλου λιμὴν καὶ οἱ ὑπὲρ τούτου Κρεοφάγοι, κολοβοὶ τὰς βαλάνους καὶ αἱ γυναῖκες ᾿Ιουδαϊκῶς ἐκτετμημέναι.

1 οἱ om. Casaubonus

And then to the Harbour of Antiphilus, and, above this, to the Creophagi, of whom the males have their sexual glands mutilated and the women are excised in the Jewish fashion.   (trans. H. L. Jones, *LCL*)

119

Geographica, XVI, 4:21, p. 779 — Kramer

῎Εξω δὲ τοῦ περιβόλου χώρα ἔρημος ἡ πλείστη ⟨scil. ἡ τῶν Ναβαταίων⟩, καὶ μάλιστα ἡ πρὸς ᾿Ιουδαίᾳ· ταύτῃ δὲ καὶ ἐγγυτάτω ἐστὶ τριῶν ἢ τεττάρων ὁδὸς ἡμερῶν εἰς ῾Ιερικοῦντα, εἰς δὲ τὸν φοινικῶνα πέντε.

3 ἐρικοῦντα CDF hw   ἱεριχοῦντα moxz

Outside the circuit of the rock most of the territory is desert, in particular that towards Judaea. Here, too, is the shortest road to Hiericus, a journey of three or four days, as also to the grove of palm trees, a journey of five days.   (trans. H. L. Jones, *LCL*)

ταύτῃ δὲ καὶ ἐγγυτάτω ἐστὶ τριῶν ἢ τεττάρων ὁδὸς ἡμερῶν εἰς ῾Ιερικοῦντα... εἰς δὲ τὸν φοινικῶνα πέντε: On Jericho and the Phoinikon; see *Geographica*, XVI, 2 : 41 (No. 115), where we read that the Phoinikon was situated in the Plain of Jericho, while here we meet with a statement that implies a distance of two days' journey, presumably between the city of Jericho and the Phoinikon.

312

Strabo of Amaseia

120

Geographica, XVI, 4:23, p. 780 — Kramer = F55R

Γνοὺς δὲ διεψευσμένος ⟨scil. Αἴλιος Γάλλος⟩ ἐναυπηγήσατο σκευαγωγὰ
ἑκατὸν καὶ τριάκοντα, οἷς ἔπλευσεν ἔχων περὶ μυρίους πεζοὺς τῶν
ἐκ τῆς Αἰγύπτου 'Ρωμαίων καὶ τῶν συμμάχων, ὧν ἦσαν 'Ιουδαῖοι
μὲν πεντακόσιοι, Ναβαταῖοι δὲ χίλιοι μετὰ τοῦ Συλλαίου.

1 διεψευσμένους F

But when he [scil. Aelius Gallus] realised that he had been thoroughly
deceived, he built one hundred and thirty vessels of burden, on which
he set sail with about ten thousand infantry, consisting of Romans in
Egypt, as also of Roman allies, among whom were five hundred Jews
and one thousand Nabataeans under Syllaeus.

(trans. H. L. Jones, *LCL*)

On the expedition of Aelius Gallus, commonly dated to 25–24 B.C.E., see
Cassius Dio, LIII, 29; *Ant.*, XV, 317; Plinius, *Naturalis Historia*, VI, 160 f.; cf.
V. Gardthausen, *Augustus und seine Zeit*, Vol. I, Part 2, Leipzig 1896, pp. 788 ff.;
Schürer, I, p. 367, n. 9; Otto, p. 70; A. Kammerer, *Pétra et la Nabatène*, Paris 1929,
pp. 196 ff.; T. Rice-Holmes, *The Architect of the Roman Empire*, II, Oxford
1931, pp. 19 f.; W. Aly, *Strabon von Amaseia*, Bonn 1957, pp. 165 ff. For the
dating of the expedition to 26–25 B.C.E., see Shelagh Jameson, *JRS*, LVIII
(1968), pp. 76 ff.

ὧν ἦσαν 'Ιουδαῖοι μὲν πεντακόσιοι: Cf. *Ant.*, XV, 317: Περὶ δὲ τὸν χρόνον ἐκεῖνον
καὶ συμμαχικὸν ἔπεμψε [scil. Herod] Καίσαρι πεντακοσίους ἐπιλέκτους τῶν σω-
ματοφυλάκων, οὓς Γάλλος Αἴλιος ἐπὶ τὴν 'Ερυθρὰν θάλασσαν ἦγεν.
Ναβαταῖοι δὲ χίλιοι μετὰ τοῦ Συλλαίου: On Syllacus, see the commentary to
Nicolaus (No. 97).

121

Geographica, XVII, 1:15, p. 800 — Kramer

'Η δὲ βύβλος ἐνταῦθα μὲν οὐ πολλὴ φύεται (οὐ γὰρ ἀσκεῖται), ἐν δὲ
τοῖς κάτω μέρεσι τοῦ Δέλτα πολλή, ἡ μὲν χείρων, ἡ δὲ βελτίων, ἡ
ἱερατική· κἀνταῦθα δέ τινες τῶν τὰς προσόδους ἐπεκτείνειν βουλομένων
μετήνεγκαν τὴν 'Ιουδαϊκὴν ἐντρέχειαν, ἣν ἐκεῖνοι παρεῦρον ἐπὶ τοῦ
5 φοίνικος, καὶ μάλιστα τοῦ καρυωτοῦ, καὶ τοῦ βαλσάμου· οὐ γὰρ
ἐῶσι πολλαχοῦ φύεσθαι, τῇ δὲ σπάνει τιμὴν ἐπιτιθέντες τὴν πρόσοδον
οὕτως αὔξουσι, τὴν δὲ κοινὴν χρείαν διαλυμαίνονται.

1 βίβλος C moxz   3 τὴν πρόσοδον Ε   6 ἐπιθέντες CDEh
7 ὄντως CDFhswx   αὐτοῖς Corais

313

As for the byblus, it does not grow in large quantities here (for it is not cultivated) but it grows in large quantities in the lower parts of the Delta, one kind being inferior, and the other superior, that is, the Hieratica. And here, too, certain of those who wished to enhance the revenues adopted the shrewd practice of the Judaeans, which the latter had invented in the case of the palm tree (particularly the caryotic palm) and the balsam tree; for they do not allow the byblus to grow in many places, and because of the scarcity they set a higher price on it and thus increase the revenues, though they injure the common use of the plant. (trans. H. L. Jones, *LCL*)

122

Geographica, XVII, 1: 21 p. 803 — Kramer

Ταύτη δὲ καὶ δυσείσβολός ἐστιν ἡ Αἴγυπτος ἐκ τῶν ἑωθινῶν τόπων τῶν κατὰ Φοινίκην καὶ τὴν Ἰουδαίαν.

2 τὴν om. E

Here, too, Egypt is difficult to enter, I mean from the eastern regions about Phoenicia and Judaea. (trans. H. L. Jones, *LCL*)

123

Geographica, XVII, 1:51, p. 818 — Kramer

Καθ᾽ ὅλην δὲ τὴν Αἴγυπτον τοῦ φοίνικος ἀγεννοῦς ὄντος καὶ ἐκφέροντος καρπὸν οὐκ εὔβρωτον ἐν τοῖς περὶ τὸ Δέλτα τόποις καὶ περὶ τὴν Ἀλεξάνδρειαν, ὁ ἐν τῇ Θηβαΐδι φοῖνιξ ἄριστος τῶν ἄλλων φύεται. θαυμάζειν οὖν ἄξιον, πῶς ταὐτὸ κλίμα οἰκοῦντες τῇ Ἰουδαίᾳ καὶ
5 ὅμοροι οἱ περὶ τὸ Δέλτα καὶ τὴν Ἀλεξάνδρειαν, τοσοῦτον διαλλάττουσιν, ἐκείνης πρὸς ἄλλῳ φοίνικι καὶ τὸν καρυωτὸν γεννώσης, οὐ πολὺ κρείττονα τοῦ Βαβυλωνίου. διττὸς δ᾽ ἐστὶν ὅ τε ἐν τῇ Θηβαΐδι καὶ ὁ ἐν τῇ Ἰουδαίᾳ, ὅ τε ἄλλος καὶ ὁ καρυωτός· σκληρότερος δ᾽ ὁ Θηβαϊκός, ἀλλὰ τῇ γεύσει εὐστομώτερος.

2-3 τὴν περὶ ἀλεξάνδρειαν CDFh   τοῖς περὶ ἀλεξάνδρειαν E
5 τοσοῦτο CD   τοσούτῳ Ehi   6 οὐ del. Corais   7 κρείττονα]
χείρονα Salmasius

Throughout the whole of Egypt the palm tree is not of a good species; and in the region of the Delta and Alexandria it produces fruit that is not good to eat; but the palm tree in the Thebais is better than any of the rest. Now it is a thing worth marvelling at, that the country which is in the same latitude as Judaea and borders on it, I mean the country round the Delta and Alexandria, differs so much, since Judaea, in addition to another palm, produces also the caryotic, which is somewhat better than the Babylonian. There are two kinds in the Thebais as well as in Judaea, both the caryotic and the other; and the Thebaic date is harder, but more agreeable to the taste.

(trans. H. L. Jones, LCL)

124

Geographica, XVII, 2, 5, p. 824 — Kramer

Καὶ τοῦτο δὲ τῶν μάλιστα ζηλουμένων παρ' αὐτοῖς τὸ πάντα τρέφειν τὰ γεννώμενα παιδία καὶ τὸ περιτέμνειν καὶ τὰ θήλεα ἐκτέμνειν, ὅπερ καὶ τοῖς Ἰουδαίοις νόμιμον· καὶ οὗτοι δ' εἰσὶν Αἰγύπτιοι τὸ ἀνέκαθεν, καθάπερ εἰρήκαμεν ἐν τῷ περὶ ἐκείνων λόγῳ.

One of the customs most zealously observed among the Egyptians is this, that they rear every child that is born, and circumcise the males, and excise the females, as is also customary among the Jews, who are also Egyptians in origin, as I have already stated in my account of them.

(trans. H. L. Jones, LCL)

XLIII. VIRGIL

70–19 B.C.E.

The world-famous palms of Judaea are called by Virgil "Idumaean".
This is the first example in Latin poetry of the interchange between
Judaea and Idumaea, of which we find more instances in later times,[1] and
the only reference to Judaea in the works of Virgil. Concerning the
presumable Jewish influence on the fourth Eclogue, it may be said that
the arguments for it now seem rather weak.[2]

1 Cf. Lucanus, *Pharsalia*, III, 216 (No. 192): "Arbusto palmarum dives Idume";
Silius Italicus, *Punica*, III, 600 (No. 227): "palmiferamque ... domitabit
Idymen"; Valerius Flaccus, *Argonautica*, I, 12 (No. 226): "versam proles tua
pandet Idumen"; Martialis, II, 2 : 5 (No. 238): "frater Idumaeos meruit cum
patre triumphos"; Statius, *Silvae*, I, 6 : 13 (No. 232); III, 2 : 138 (No. 234); V,
2 : 139 (No. 237); Iuvenalis, VIII, 160 (No. 300).

2 Jewish Messianic influence has been suggested by, e. g., F. Marx, *Neue Jahrbücher für das klassische Altertum*, I, (1898), pp. 105 ff.; H. W. Garrod, *Classical Review*, XIX (1905) pp. 37 f.; J. B. Mayor, *Sources of the Fourth Eclogue*
in: J. B. Mayor, W. Warde Fowler & R. S. Conway, *Virgil's Messianic Eclogue*,
London 1907, pp. 87 ff.; A. Kurfess, *Historisches Jahrbuch*, LXXIII (1954),
pp. 120 ff. See also T. F. Royds, *Virgil and Isaiah*, Oxford 1918. Against this view,
cf., e.g., E. Norden, *Die Geburt des Kindes*, Leipzig 1924, pp. 52 f.; H. J. Rose,
The Eclogues of Vergil, Berkeley 1942, p. 194; L. Herrmann, *L'antiquité classique*,
XIV (1945), pp. 85 ff. Against the Messianic character of the *fourth Eclogue*,
even in Norden's sense, see J. Carcopino, *Virgile et le mystère de la IVe églogue*,
Paris 1930, pp. 29 f.

125

Georgica, III, 12–15 — Sabbadini

Primus Idumaeas referam tibi, Mantua, palmas
et viridi in campo templum de marmore ponam
propter aquam, tardis ingens ubi flexibus errat
15 Mincius et tenera praetexit harundine ripas.

1 *idumeas* P   *idymeas* FM   *idymaeas* M¹V

I will be the first to bring back to thee, my Mantua, the palms of
Idumea, and on the broad green sward I will build a temple of marble
by the water's side, where Mincius trails his great breadth along in
lazy windings, and fringes his banks with soft rushes as he goes.

(trans. J. Conington, London 1893)

XLIV. TIBULLUS

Second half of the first century B.C.E.

The "Day of Saturn" in the first book of the Elegiae, *published before Tibullus' death in 19 B.C.E., takes its place alongside other references to the Jewish Sabbath in Augustan literature, namely, those in Horatius,* Sermones, *I, 9:69 (No. 129) and Ovidius,* Ars Amatoria, *I, 76, 416 (Nos. 141 and 142). They all demonstrate the impression that the diffusion of Jewish customs made on Roman society.*

Besides the allusion to the Sabbath, the first book of Tibullus includes not a few references to Oriental cults. Delia herself is an adherent of the cult of Isis (I, III:23: "quid tua nunc Isis mihi"), and Osiris is also mentioned twice (I, VII:27, 43). Also noteworthy is the appearance of the "alba Palaestino sancta columba Syro", the sacred dove revered at Ascalon (I, VII:18).

126

Carmina, I, 3:15–18 — Lenz = F133R

15 Ipse ego solator, cum iam mandata dedissem,
quaerebam tardas anxius usque moras.
Aut ego sum causatus aves aut omina dira,
Saturni sacram me tenuisse diem.

17 *aut* Itali Scaliger   *dant* ωΥ   18 *Saturni aut* ed. Regiensis
Saturnive exemplar codicis Q? / *sacram*] *sanctam* Vat. 2794   *sacrum* E. Fraenkel,
Glotta, VIII, p. 62

Yea, even I her comforter, after I had given my parting charge, sought
still in my disquiet for reasons to linger and delay. Either birds or
words of evil omen were my pretexts, or there was the accursed day
of Saturn to detain me.   (trans. J. P. Postgate, *LCL*)

ipse ego solator ...: Tibullus leaves for the East with Messalla (31 B.C.E.). There
he becomes ill and blames himself for leaving his beloved Delia. Surely he could
have found an excuse for staying in Rome, such as portents against the journey,
bodeful birds or the day of Saturn.
aut omina dira: The reading *dant* is rejected by most editors, from Scaliger to
Levy (Teubner edition, 1927) and Lenz (second edition, 1964), who prefer the
reading *aut*, though some, like Calonghi in his edition of 1928, print *dant*; see the
discussion by M. Schuster, *Tibull-Studien*, Vienna 1930, pp. 125 ff.
Saturni sacram me tenuisse diem: In the use of *dies Saturni* for the Sabbath the
parallel diffusions of the Jewish week and the planetary week tended to merge
them into one. For inscriptional evidence on the spread of the planetary week in
the time of Augustus, see Boll, PW, VII, p. 2573. See also E.J. Bickerman, *Chronology of the Ancient World*, London 1968, pp. 59 ff. Gradually, the Jews began to
refer to the astrological week, which is apparent from Jewish literature; see
S. Gandz, *PAAJR*, XVIII (1948–1949), pp. 213 ff. For the identification of Saturn
with the Jewish divinity, see Tacitus, *Historiae*, V, 4 (No. 281) and the commentary
ad loc.
Saturni sacram ... This constitutes an asyndeton, whereas the first and second
parts of the sentence are connected by *aut*. The *editio Regiensis* of 1481 tried
to solve this difficulty by adding a third *aut*. Goldbacher has suggested the reading: "aut ego sum causatus aves aut — omina dira! — Saturn isacram me tenuisse diem"; see Goldbacher, *Wiener Studien*, VII '1885', pp. 163 f. Levy disagrees
with this interpretation; see F. Levy, *Philologische Wochenschrift*, XLVII (1927),
p. 893. Levy prefers the usual punctuation, though he admits that he cannot
find an exact parallel in the literature of the Augustan age (p. 894). He tries to
resolve the difficulty by the conjecture that Tibullus, "um der Gewichtigkeit und
Fülle der sich ihm aufdrängenden Entschuldigungsgründe stärkeren Ausdruck zu
geben ... das letzte Glied als das stärkste Argument enthaltend, asyndetisch
angefügt hat." Still, something is to be said for the reading *Saturnive*, which is
accepted by some scholars as the best solution; see Schuster, *op. cit.* Schuster

also thinks it unjustified to emend *sacram* into *sacrum*, as proposed by E. Fraenkel, *Glotta*, VIII (1917), p. 62. It is almost needless to remark that Tibullus' reference to Saturday implies no more real understanding of the Jewish Sabbath than that shown by Fuscus Aristius; cf. No. 129.

XLV. HORACE

65–8 B.C.E.

There are four certain references to Jews in the poetry of Horace. This in itself well attests to the impact made by the Jews on the Roman society of the Augustan age, and is paralleled by some passages in the poetry of Tibullus (No. 126) and Ovid (Nos. 141–143).

Once Horace alludes to the missionary zeal of the Jews (No. 127); a second time he laughs at their credulousness, which became proverbial (No. 128). He also shows knowledge of Jewish circumcision and of the Sabbath (No. 129). All this occurs in his Sermones. *In his* Epistulae *(No. 130) he mentions Herod and also refers to the world-famous palm groves.*[1]

Since Horace was a freedman from Apulian Venusia, there is much room for conjecture as to his ultimate ethnic origin. Some suppose it to have been Oriental,[2] *without assigning him to a particular Oriental people. Others have suggested that he was of Jewish stock.*[3] *One scholar has even attempted to account for the poet's silence about his mother by claiming that she was Jewish.*[4] *Yet, I must state that no positive proof,*

1 Scholars like Dornseiff accept the view that the passage in *Sermones*, II, 3: 288 ff. ("Iuppiter ingentis qui das adimisque dolores, mater ait pueri mensis iam quinque cubantis, frigida si puerum quartana reliquerit, illo mane die, quo tu indicis ieiunia, nudus in Tiberi stabit") implies an allusion to Jewish customs; see F. Dornseiff, "Verschmähtes zu Vergil, Horaz und Properz", *Berichte über die Verhandlungen der Sächsischen Akademie der Wissenschaften zu Leipzig*, Philologisch-historische Klasse, XCVII, 6, 1951, pp. 67 ff. However, mention of a cold bath in the river need not be a specific reference to a Jewish custom. Dornseiff (*op. cit.*, pp. 64 ff.) also finds biblical motifs in some other passages of Horace's *Sermones*, but he has not proved his case; cf. M. Hadas, *Hellenistic Culture*, New York 1959, p. 244. Nor is there much to be learned from the table of comparisons between the Bible and Horace drawn by I. Handel, *Eos*, XXXI (1928), pp. 501 ff.

2 K. Mras, *Wiener Studien*, LIV (1936), pp. 70 ff.

3 E. g., O. Seeck, *Kaiser Augustus*, Bielefeld–Leipzig 1902, p. 134. Seeck admits the possibility that Horace was a "Stammesgenosse" of Heine and Börne.

4 W. H. Alexander, *Classical Philology*, XXXVII (1942), pp. 385 ff. Dornseiff (*op. cit.*, p. 65) suggests that Horace's father was a proselyte.

however slight, has been adduced to buttress these speculations, and the Jewish ancestry of Horace should probably be relegated to the realm of pure conjecture.[5]

5 See R. Hanslik, *Das Altertum*, I (1955), p. 231: "Was freilich Horaz selbst von seinem Vater in *Sat*. I. 4 und 6 berichtet... das erweckt nicht den Anschein, als habe sich dieser als Jude, Grieche oder Levantiner gefühlt."

127

Sermones, I, 4:139–143 — Bo = F131aR

... Hoc est mediocribus illis
140 ex vitiis unum; cui si concedere nolis,
multa poetarum veniat manus, auxilio quae
sit mihi: nam multo plures sumus, ac veluti te
Iudaei cogemus in hanc concedere turbam.

140 *noles* Bentley   141 *venit* E   *veniet* ς sch. ΓVvc

This is one of those lesser frailties I spoke of, and if you should make
no allowance for it, then would a big band of poets come to my
aid — for we are the big majority — and we, like the Jews, will compel
you to make one of our throng.   (trans. H. Rushton Fairclough, *LCL*)

142–143 *ac veluti te Iudaei cogemus in hanc concedere turbam*: The comparison
implies strong Jewish missionary activity in Rome. On such activity already in the
second century B. C. E., see Valerius Maximus, *Facta et Dicta Memorabilia*,
III, 3 : 3 (No. 147). Proselytization also helped to cause the expulsion of the
Roman Jews in the times of Tiberius; see the commentary to Tacitus, *Annales*,
II, 85 (No. 284). See also the well-known passage in Matt. xxiii : 15 concerning the
enthusiasm of the Pharisees for winning proselytes; cf. Strack & Billerbeck, I, pp.
924 ff.; B. J. Bamberger, *Proselytism in the Talmudic Period*, Cincinnati 1939, pp.
267 ff.; K. G. Kuhn & H. Stegemann, PW, Suppl., IX (1962), pp. 1248 ff. Zielinski's
comments seem somewhat far-fetched; see T. Zielinski *Eos*, XXX (1927), p. 58.
For this sort of threat, Lejay aptly refers to passages from Plato; see F. Plessis &
P. Lejay, *Oeuvres d'Horace — Satires*, Paris 1911, p. 133.

128

Sermones, I, 5:96–104 — Bo = F131bR

Postera tempestas melior, via peior ad usque
Bari moenia piscosi; dein Gnatia Lymphis
iratis extructa dedit risusque iocosque,
dum flamma sine tura liquescere limine sacro
100 persuadere cupit. Credat Iudaeus Apella,
non ego: namque deos didici securum agere aevom
nec, siquid miri faciat natura, deos id
tristis ex alto caeli demittere tecto.
Brundisium longae finis chartaeque viaeque est.

97 *dehinc* g φψϱ   *deinc* R^2 in rasura   *hinc* Peerlkamp   99 *lumine* E
flumine Cg   100 *credet* Cg / *appella* UR^{1}ϱ ante rasuram, ed. Med. 1486,
        Aldus, alii   *apellam* M

Next day's weather was better, but the road worse, right up to the walls of Barium, a fishing town. Then Gnatia, built under the wrath of the water-nymphs brought us laughter and mirth in its effort to convince us that frankincense melts without fire at the temple's threshold. Apella, the Jew may believe it, not I; for I "have learned that the gods lead a care-free life", and if Nature works any marvel, the gods do not send it down from their heavenly home aloft when in surly mood! Brundisium is the end of a long story and a long journey.

(trans. H. Rushton Fairclough, LCL)

97 *Dein Gnatia*: On his voyage to Brundisium the poet arrives at Gnatia. There he is told about the miracle of the frankincense melting without fire; cf. Plinius, *Naturalis Historia*, II, 240.

100 *credat Iudaeus Apella*: "urbanissimum nomen Iudaeo imposuit 'Apella' dicens, quasi quod pellem in parte genitali Iudaei non habeant" (Pomponius Porphyrio *ad loc.*). Bentley explained the occurrence of this name as a common name for libertini, the class of the majority of Roman Jews; see R. Bentley, *Epistola ad Joannem Millium*, Toronto 1962, pp. 345 f. (131 f.); cf. also N. Rudd, *CQ*, NS (1960), p. 170. However, in the inscriptions from the Jewish catacombs we do not find this name; cf. Leon, p. 12. n. 1. The name occurs, however, on a Jewish ostracon from Edfu from the end of the first century C.E. (*CPJ*, II, No. 188), according to which Nicon, the son of Apellas, paid the Jewish tax. For 'Aπ(ελ)λᾱ in an inscription from Eumeneia in Phrygia, see *CII*, No. 761. In spite of the silence of the inscriptions, the name could have been common among the Jews of ancient Rome, and the poet might have been thinking about a certain Jew by this name. Jewish credulity had become proverbial. For a similar allusion to Gallic credulity, see Martialis, V, 1 : 10.

101 *namque deos didici securum agere aevom*: For this Epicurean tenet, see Lucretius, V, 82.

<h1 align="center">129</h1>

Sermones, I, 9:60–78 — Bo = F131cR

60 ... ... Haec dum agit, ecce
   Fuscus Aristius occurrit, mihi carus et illum
   qui pulchre nosset. Consistimus. "Unde venis" et
   "quo tendis?" rogat et respondet. Vellere coepi
   et prensare manu lentissima bracchia, nutans,
65 distorquens oculos, ut me eriperet. Male salsus
   ridens dissimulare; mecum iecur urere bilis.
   "Certe nescio quid secreto velle loqui te

62 *venisset* D pr. gR ante rasuram φ ante corr. ψϱ ante rasuram   63 *tendit*
   φψϱ¹   64 *pressare* Da² gR φψϱ   66 bellis R¹φψ¹

aiebas mecum." "Memini bene, sed meliore
tempore dicam; hodie tricensima, sabbata: vin tu
70 curtis Iudaeis oppedere?" "Nulla mihi" inquam
"religio est." "At mi: sum paulo infirmior, unus
multorum. Ignosces; alias loquar." Huncine solem
tam nigrum surrexe mihi! fugit inprobus ac me
sub cultro linquit. Casu venit obvius illi
75 adversarius et "quo tu, turpissime?" magna
inclamat voce, et "licet antestari?" Ego vero
oppono auriculam. Rapit in ius; clamor utrimque,
undique concursus. Sic me servavit Apollo.

69 *tricensima* R¹   *trigensima* ϱ ante rasuram   *trigesima* ϱ post
rasuram *tricesima* cett.   *tristissima* Linkerus   post *tricensima* interpungunt
Stowasser, Bo, alii

While he is thus running on, lo! there comes up Aristius Fuscus,
a dear friend of mine, who knew the fellow right well. We halt.
"Whence come you? Whither go you?" he asks and answers. I begin
to twitch his cloak and squeeze his arms—they were quite unfeeling—
nodding and winking hard for him to save me. The cruel joker laughed,
pretending not to understand. I grew hot with anger. "Surely you
said that there was something you wanted to tell me in private."
"I mind it well, but I'll tell you at a better time. To day is the thirtieth
day, a Sabbath. Would you affront the circumcised Jews?"
"I have no scruples", say I.
"But I have. I am a somewhat weaker brother, one of the many. You
will pardon me; I'll talk another day."
To think so black a sun as this has shone for me! The rascal runs
away and leaves me under the knife.
It now chanced that the plaintiff came face to face with his opponent.
"Where go you, you scoundrel?" he loudly shouts, and to me "May
I call you as witness?" I offer my ear to touch. He hurries the man
to court. There is shouting here and there, and on all sides a running
to and fro. Thus was I saved by Apollo.

(trans. H. Rushton Fairclough, *LCL*)

60–61 *haec dum agit, ecce Fuscus Aristius*: While the bore was tiring him, Horace
met the poet Fuscus Aristius; cf. *Carmina*, I, 22 : 4; *Sermones*, I, 10 : 83; *Epistulae*,
I, 10 : 1. He hoped to find a saviour in this poet and pretended to have something
to discuss with him privately. Fuscus, however, did not show any readiness to
help Horace, declaring that, as the day was Sabbath he could not offend the Jews
by talking business.

69 *tricensima, sabbata*: The form in the plural is the common one among Greek-speaking Jews, as attested by the Septuagint. But why the thirtieth? The most prevalent explanation is that this is an allusion to the celebration of the new moon by the Jews; cf., e.g., B. Dombart, *Archiv für lateinische Lexikographie und Grammatik*, VI (1889), p. 272; Schürer, III, p. 142, n. 27; Juster, I, p. 363, n. 1; Friedländer, III, p. 217, n. 10; see also S. Sabbadini, *Athenaeum*, VIII (1920), pp. 160 ff.; Dornseiff, *op. cit.* (supra, p. 321, n. 1), p. 67, n. 1; E. Lohse, in: *Theologisches Wörterbuch zum Neuen Testament*, VII, 1964, p. 17, n. 136. Lohse accepts the following punctuation: "hodie tricesima, sabbata" ("heute ist Neumond, also Sabbatruhe"), which has also been adopted by some of the editors, among them Bo.

The identification of *tricensima* with the new moon goes back to the scholiasts; cf. Pomponius Porphyrio, *ad loc.* "sabbata lunaria significat, quae vulgares homines ferias sibi adsumunt"; Pseudacro: "Tricesima sabbata quae Iudei Neomenias dicunt, quoniam per sabbata Iudei numeros appellant lunares. ...Item: tricesima sabbata dicuntur, quando veniunt Kalendae in prima luna per sabbata, qui dies maxime a Iudeis observatur, aut quia tricesima sabbata religiosius colebantur"; cf. also Commodianus, *Instructiones*, I, 40 : 3; idem, *Carmen Apologeticum*, 688.

Some modern scholars think that we have to count the thirtieth Sabbath from the beginning of the Jewish year, starting from April (i.e. Nissan), so that it would fall in the Feast of Tabernacles. Others maintain that there was no such Jewish festival, and Fuscus only invented it for the occasion. Recently Baumgarten has suggested that the poet's reference was simply to the weekly Sabbath, as he knew that the Jews designated their Sabbaths numerically, and *tricensima* looked prosodically suitable to him; see J. M. Baumgarten, *Vetus Testamentum*, XVI (1966), p. 285 f. In any case, "Aristius n'est pas un 'sabbatisant'; autrement la plaisanterie manquerait de sel. Tout ce que dit Aristius de lui-même est parfaitement ironique"; Lejay, *op. cit.* (supra, p. 323), p. 246. The incident seems to have taken place beyond the Sacra Via, near the Temple of Vesta; cf. Leon, p. 12.

130

Epistulae, II, 2:183–189 — Bo = F132R

Cur alter fratrum cessare et ludere et ungui
praeferat Herodis palmetis pinguibus, alter
185 dives et inportunus ad umbram lucis ab ortu
silvestrem flammis et ferro mitiget agrum,
scit Genius, natale comes qui temperat astrum,
naturae deus humanae, mortalis in unum
quodque caput, voltu mutabilis, albus et ater.

184 *heroidis* L[1]   *heredis* R pr.   / *polmetis* C pr.   *palmentis* M[1]

Of two brothers one prefers, above Herod's rich palm-groves, idling and playing and the anointing of himself; the other, wealthy and untiring, from dawn to shady eve subdues his woodland farm with flames and iron plough. Why so, the Genius alone knows—that companion who rules our star of birth, the god of human nature, though mortal for each single life, and changing in countenance, white or black.   (trans. H. Rushton Fairclough, *LCL*)

This passage discusses the various forms of wealth; some care nothing for what others value highly.

184 *Herodis palmetis*: Cf. Otto, pp. 45, 92.

XLVI. LIVY

59 B.C.E. to 17 C.E.[1]

Livy mentions the Jews at least twice in his History. The first time he does so in his account of Pompey's conquest of Syria, and the second time, when he relates the capture of Jerusalem by Antony's commanders (37 B.C.E.). In connection with the first event he seems to give a description of the Jewish religion that stresses the anonymity of the Jewish God and the absence in the Temple at Jerusalem of any statue to represent the Deity; cf. Cassius Dio, XXXVII, 17:2 (No. 406). Whether Livy took an interest in the Jews and their relations with Rome in the period prior to Pompey is a matter open to conjecture (cf. the introduction to Valerius Maximus).

---

1 For slightly different dates (64 B. C. E.–12 C. E.), see R. Syme, *Harvard Studies in Classical Philology*, LXIV (1959), pp. 40 ff.

131

Periochae, CII — Rossbach = F136aR

Cn. Pompeius Iudaeos subegit, fanum eorum Hierosolyma, inviolatum ante id tempus, cepit.

1 *ierusolyma* P   *Hierosolymam* Lovelianus 2   *in hierosolyma* Leidensis
2 *ad id* Leidensis

Cn. Pompeius conquered the Jews and captured their temple Jerusalem, never invaded before.

Cn. Pompeius Iudaeos subegit: The 102nd book of Livy's History starts with the transformation of Pontus into a Roman province. This was followed by the capture of Jerusalem, and, later, the conspiracy of Catilina, another event of 63 B.C.E. For Livy and the Livian tradition as a source for Pompey's conquest of Syria, see F.P. Rizzo, *Le fonti per la storia della conquista pompeiana della Siria*, Palermo 1963, pp. 39 ff.

fanum eorum Hierosolyma: The designation of Jerusalem as a temple goes back to Polybius though he, of course, applied it in the quite different context of Jerusalem's capture by Antiochus III; see Polybius, *Historiae*, apud: Josephus, *Ant.*, XII, 135–136 (No. 32). It is, however, noteworthy, that the emphasis Livy puts on the Temple, and not on the city, had some justification in what really happened in Pompey's time: the city of Jerusalem surrendered without resistance to the Roman legions, and only the Temple put up an obstinate defence. Thus, the capture of the Temple constituted Pompey's main military achievement in Judaea.

inviolatum ante id tempus: This is a quite misleading assertion. It is enough to mention the City's capture and the violation of the Temple's sanctity by Antiochus Epiphanes. Livy certainly bases his statement on a source that wished to magnify Pompey's feat as much as possible. It is interesting that Josephus speaks of this almost in the same vein; see *Ant.*, XIV, 71: παρηνομήθη δὲ οὐ σμικρὰ περὶ τὸν ναὸν ἄβατόν τε ὄντα ἐν τῷ πρὶν χρόνῳ καὶ ἀόρατον. It seems that both Livy and Josephus ultimately drew upon the same source, who, we surmise, was Theophanes of Mytilene, though one should remember that our knowledge is extremely scanty concerning the sources for Livy's later books; see Klotz, PW, XIII, p. 846.

Extensive exaggeration of this sort is well illustrated by an inscription in honour of Titus, dated 80 C.E.; see *CIL*, VI, No. 944 = *ILS*, No. 264 = Gabba, No. XXVII: "gentem Iudeorum domuit et urbem Hierusolymam, omnibus ante se ducibus regibus gentibus aut frustra petitam aut omnino intemptatam delevit." For an attempt to tone down the exaggeration, see H. U. Instinsky, *Philologus*, XCVII (1948), pp. 370 f.

132

apud: Josephus, *Antiquitates Judaicae*, XIV, 68 — Niese = 136bR

῞Οτι δὲ οὐ λόγος ταῦτα μόνον ἐστὶν ἐγκώμιον ψευδοῦς εὐσεβείας
1 λόγοις W / μόνων W / ἐστὶν om. W

ἐμφανίζων, ἀλλ' ἀλήθεια, μαρτυροῦσι πάντες οἱ τὰς κατὰ Πομπήιον πράξεις ἀναγράψαντες, ἐν οἷς καὶ Στράβων ⟨No. 104⟩ καὶ Νικόλαος ⟨No. 92⟩ καὶ πρὸς αὐτοῖς Τίτος Λίβιος ὁ τῆς Ῥωμαϊκῆς ἱστορίας
5 συγγραφεύς.

3 καί¹ om. P   4 τούτοις V

And that this is not merely a story to set forth the praises of a fictitious piety, but the truth, is attested by all those who have narrated the exploits of Pompey, among them Strabo and Nicolaus and, in addition, Titus Livius, the author of a History of Rome.

(trans. R. Marcus, *LCL*)

As we may infer from the former passage (No. 131), Livy dealt with these events in the 102nd book of his History. It cannot be determined whether Josephus used Livy independently.

133
Scholia in Lucanum, II, 593 — Usener

Incerti Iudea dei. Livius de Iudaeis "Hierosolimis fanum cuius deorum sit non nominant, neque ullum ibi simulacrum est, neque enim esse dei figuram putant."

And Judaea given over to the worship of an unknown God. Livy on Jews: "They do not state to which deity pertains the temple at Jerusalem, nor is any image found there, since they do not think the God partakes of any figure."

Livius de Iudaeis: This, too, is taken from the 102nd book of Livy's History. Livy, according to the habit of ancient historians when about to tell the story of Jerusalem's capture, found it appropriate to describe at this place the nation with which the Romans clashed for the first time.
neque ullum ibi simulacrum est: Cf. Varro, apud: Augustinus, *De Civitate Dei*, IV, 31 (No. 72).

134
apud: Lydus, *De Mensibus*, IV, 53 — Wünsch, p. 109

Λίβιος δὲ ἐν τῇ καθόλου Ῥωμαϊκῇ ἱστορίᾳ ἄγνωστον τὸν ἐκεῖ τιμώμενόν φησι.

1 Λίβιος Wünsch   λίλαιος S

Livy in his general Roman History says that the God worshipped there
is unknown.

ἄγνωστον τὸν ἐκεῖ τιμώμενόν φησι: Lydus probably got his reference to Livy
from the scholia to Lucan, which often served as his source; cf. E. Norden, *Agnostos
Theos*, Leipzig–Berlin 1913, p. 59. The expression *ignotus* itself is not found in
Livy, who only states that the Jewish God has no name. It seems that Lydus
adapted a Neoplatonic term to designate the Jewish deity. On the unknown God
in Neoplatonism, see Proclus, *The Elements of Theology*[2], revised edition by
E. R. Dodds, Oxford 1963, pp. 310 ff.

135

Periochae, CXXVIII — Rossbach = F137R

P. Ventidius, legatus M. Antoni, Parthos in Syria proelio vicit regem-
que eorum occidit. Iudaei quoque a legatis Antoni subacti sunt.

2 *occidit*] *interemit* ed. pr.

P. Ventidius, one of the lieutenants of M. Antonius, defeated the
Parthians in a battle in Syria and killed their king. The Jews were
also conquered by the lieutenants of Antonius.

Iudaei quoque a legatis Antoni subacti sunt: An allusion to the capture of Jerusalem
by C. Sosius in 37 B.C.E.; see also Cassius Dio, XLIX, 22 : 3 ff. (No. 414).

XLVII. POMPEIUS TROGUS

End of the first century B.C.E. to beginning of the first century C.E.

The Historiae Philippicae *of Pompeius Trogus centre on the history of the Macedonian-Hellenistic states. The work has not been preserved, and only the Epitome* of Justin, *composed in the third or fourth century C. E., and the* Prologues, *which are independent of this Epitome, have come down to us. Pompeius Trogus touches upon the Jewish past in connection with the history of the Seleucid monarchy, the events in the reign of Antiochus Sidetes serving as a proper background* (*book thirty-six*). *From the prologue of the thirty-ninth book* (*No. 138*) *we may infer that he also dwelt on the later Hasmonaean activities, which, at least in part, were censured by him.*

Pompeius Trogus' main survey of the Jews in the thirty-sixth book is divided into three parts: (*a*) *Jewish antiquity;* (*b*) *a geographical description of Judaea;* (*c*) *a history of the Jews from the Persian period onwards.*

The account of Jewish antiquity, to judge from its remnants in the Epitome, is fairly circumstantial. It constitutes a combination of different versions: a biblical version, a Damascene version and the hostile Graeco-Egyptian version. All three have left their imprint on the narration of the events and also, implicitly, on the evaluation of the Jewish past. Thus, on the one hand, we get the well-known statement that the ancestors of the Jews were lepers, while on the other hand, the account of antiquity, as it stands in the Epitome, ends with the appreciative remark on the effectiveness of the Jewish body-politic: "quorum iustitia religione permixta incredibile quantum coaluere." *The emphasis placed by Pompeius Trogus on the link between the priesthood and the monarchy is a natural reflection of the conditions prevailing in the Hasmonaean kingdom.*

The geographical description in the Epitome is brief — in consonance with Justin's habit of omitting or heavily abridging such descriptions.[1] As a matter of fact, the geographical survey of Judaea is confined to a portrayal of the Valley of Jericho and the Dead Sea (*Mare Mortuum*).

---

1 See A. Klotz, PW, XXI, p. 2304.

Pompeius Trogus

The historical survey yields only one substantial piece of information, namely, the account of the alliance between Rome and the Jews in the reign of Demetrius I. This constitutes an independent confirmation of what is related about the same event in I Macc. viii.

Nobody will question the dependence of Pompeius Trogus on Greek sources. It may be that he used Timagenes, a plausible view that is widely current; cf. the introduction to Timagenes. Much more problematical is Trogus' use of Posidonius.

The division of the material by Pompeius Trogus greatly resembles that of the survey of the Jews and Judaea in the Historiae of Tacitus (No. 281), but they differ in content. This amounts to saying no more than that both historians followed a common ethnographic method.

Bibliography

T. Labhardt, *Quae de Iudaeorum Origine Iudicaverint Veteres*, Augsburg 1881, pp. 39 ff.; C. Wachsmuth, *Einleitung in das Studium der alten Geschichte*, Leipzig 1895, pp. 108 ff.; Schürer, I, p. 111; III, p. 544, n. 86; Stähelin, pp. 26 f.; J. Morr, *Philologus*, LXXXI, pp. 278 f.; I. Heinemann, *Poseidonios' metaphysische Schriften*, II, Breslau 1928, pp. 80 f.; P. Treves, *Il mito di Alessandro e la Roma d'Augusto*, Milan–Naples 1953, pp. 43 f.; O. Seel, *Die Praefatio des Pompeius Trogus*, Erlangen 1955; L. Ferrero, *Struttura e metodo dell' Epitome di Giustino*, Turin 1957, pp. 120 ff.; E. Cavaignac, *Mélanges bibliques rédigés en l'honneur de André Robert*, Paris [1957], p. 350; G. Forni, *Valore storico e fonti di Pompeo Trogo*, Urbino 1958, pp. 80 f.; Gager, pp. 48 ff.

333

136

Historiae Philippicae, Prologus Libri XXXVI — Seel = F138aR

Sexto et tricensimo volumine continentur haec. Ut Trypho pulso Syria Demetrio captoque a Parthis bellum gessit cum fratre eius Antiocho cognomine Sidete. Ut Antiochus interfecto Hyrcano Iudaeos subegit. Repetita inde in excessu origo Iudaeorum.

1-3 *Trypho pulso ... captoque ... Sidete. Ut* Bongars   *cypro pulsus ... captaque ... sed ut* codd.

Contents of the XXXVIth book: How, when Demetrius was expelled from Syria and captured by the Parthians, Trypho waged a war against his brother Antiochus, surnamed Sidetes. How Antiochus, Hyrcanus having been killed, subdued the Jews. Then a digression in which one follows the origins of the Jews.

Ut Antiochus interfecto Hyrcano Iudaeos subegit: On the war between Antiochus Sidetes and John Hyrcan, see *Ant.*, XIII, 236 ff.; see also Diodorus, *Bibliotheca Historica*, XXXIV-XXXV, 1 (No. 63); Plutarchus, *Regum et Imperatorum Apophthegmata*, p. 184 F (No. 260). The Jewish ruler, however, was not killed in that war. He died in 104 B.C.E., almost twenty-five years after the death of Antiochus Sidetes. It cannot be determined whether the mistake was made by Pompeius Trogus himself or by the writer of the prologue. Since Justin does not relate this event, I prefer the second possibility.

in excessu: This expression is very common in the prologues of Pompeius Trogus; see, e.g., the prologues to books seven ("in excessu Illyrorum et Maeonum origines"), eleven, thirteen, fifteen and eighteen. It is a translation of the Greek ἐν παρεκβάσει; cf. Ferrero, *op. cit.* (supra, p. 333), p. 16.

137

apud: Iustinus, *Historiae Philippicae*, Libri XXXVI Epitoma, 1:9-3:9 — Seel = F138 bR

(1:9) Igitur Antiochus, memor quod et pater propter superbiam invisus et frater propter segnitiam contemptus fuisset, ne in eadem vitia incideret, recepta in matrimonium Cleopatra, uxore fratris, civitates, quae initio fraterni imperii defecerant, summa industria persequitur,
₅ domitasque rursus regni terminis adicit; (10) Iudaeos quoque, qui in Macedonico imperio sub Demetrio patre armis se in libertatem vindicaverant, subegit. Quorum vires tantae fuere, ut post haec

3 *accepta* C   5-6 *qui a* C   *qui* ι   7 *post hunc* ιC

nullum Macedonum regem tulerint domesticisque imperiis usi Syriam
magnis bellis infestaverint.

10 (2:1) Namque Iudaeis origo Damascena, Syriae nobilissima civitas,
unde et Assyriis regibus genus ex regina Samirami fuit. (2) Nomen
urbi a Damasco rege inditum, in cuius honorem Syri sepulcrum Arathis, uxoris eius, pro templo coluere, deamque exinde sanctissimae
religionis habent. (3) Post Damascum Azelus, mox Adores et Abra-
15 hames et Israhel reges fuere. (4) Sed Israhelem felix decem filiorum
proventus maioribus suis clariorem fecit. (5) Itaque populum in
decem regna divisum filiis tradidit, omnesque ex nomine Iudae,
qui post divisionem decesserat, Iudaeos appellavit colique memoriam
eius ab omnibus iussit, cuius portio omnibus accesserat. (6) Minimus
20 aetate inter fratres Ioseph fuit, cuius excellens ingenium fratres
veriti clam interceptum peregrinis mercatoribus vendiderunt. (7) A
quibus deportatus in Aegyptum, cum magicas ibi artes sollerti
ingenio percepisset, brevi ipsi regi percarus fuit. (8) Nam et
prodigiorum sagacissimus erat et somniorum primus intellegentiam
25 condidit, nihilque divini iuris humanique ei incognitum videbatur,
(9) adeo ut etiam sterilitatem agrorum ante multos annos providerit;
perissetque omnis Aegyptus fame, nisi monitu eius rex edicto servari
per multos annos fruges iussisset; (10) tantaque experimenta eius
fuerunt, ut non ab homine, sed a deo responsa dari viderentur. (11) Fi-
30 lius eius Moyses fuit, quem praeter paternae scientiae hereditatem
etiam formae pulchritudo commendabat. (12) Sed Aegyptii, cum
scabiem et vitiliginem paterentur, responso moniti eum cum aegris,
ne pestis ad plures serperet, terminis Aegypti pellunt. (13) Dux
igitur exulum factus sacra Aegyptiorum furto abstulit, quae repetentes
35 armis Aegyptii domum redire tempestatibus conpulsi sunt. (14) Itaque Moyses Damascena, antiqua patria, repetita montem Sinam
occupat, in quo septem dierum ieiunio per deserta Arabiae cum
populo suo fatigatus cum tandem venisset, septimum diem more
gentis Sabbata appellatum in omne aevum ieiunio sacravit, quoniam
40 illa dies famem illis erroremque finierat. (15) Et quoniam metu
contagionis pulsos se ab Aegypto meminerant, ne eadem causa
invisi apud incolas forent, caverunt, ne cum peregrinis converent;

---

8 *ut siriam et* C   11 *ex regina Samirami* Seel   *ex regina semirami (seminarum*
Q) τ   *et reginae samirami (-mis* LE) ι   *et reginae samiramidis* C   *et reginae*
Samiramidi Ruehl   12–13 *arates* ι   *ariarathes* C   *Atarathes* Gutschmid
14 *zelus* C   14–15 *et abramas* C   26 *agrorum ante* om. C
29 *dari* om. C   30 *eius Moyses*] *autem iosepho moses* C   36 *syneum* C
       sinay ς   *Sinaeum* Nöldeke   41 *ab* del. Ruehl

quod ex causa factum paulatim in disciplinam religionemque
convertit. (16) Post Moysen etiam filius eius Arruas sacerdos sacris
45 Aegyptiis, mox rex creatur; semperque exinde hic mos apud Iudaeos
fuit, ut eosdem reges et sacerdotes haberent, quorum iustitia religione
permixta incredibile quantum coaluere.
(3:1) Opes genti ex vectigalibus opobalsami crevere, quod in his tantum
regionibus gignitur. (2) Est namque vallis, quae continuis montibus
50 velut muro quodam ad instar castrorum clauditur (spatium loci
ducenta iugera; nomine Aricus dicitur); (3) in ea silva est et ubertate
et amoenitate insignis, siquidem palmeto et opobalsameto distin-
guitur. (4) Et arbores opobalsami similem formam piceis arboribus
habent, nisi quod sunt humiles magis et in vinearum morem exco-
55 luntur. Hae certo anni tempore balsamum sudant. (5) Sed non minor
loci eius apricitatis quam ubertatis admiratio est; quippe cum toto
orbe regionis eius ardentissimus sol sit, ibi tepidi aëris ⟨flatu⟩ naturalis
quaedam ac perpetua opacitas inest. (6) In ea regione latus lacus est,
qui propter magnitudinem aquae et inmobilitatem Mortuum Mare
60 dicitur. (7) Nam neque ventis movetur, resistente turbinibus bitumine,
quo aqua omnis stagnatur, neque navigationis patiens est, quoniam
omnia vita carentia in profundum merguntur; nec materiam ullam
sustinet, nisi quae alumine incrustatur.
(8) Primum Xerxes, rex Persarum, Iudaeos domuit; postea cum
65 ipsis Persis in dicionem Alexandri Magni venere diuque in potestate
Macedonici imperii subiecti Syriae regno fuere. (9) A Demetrio cum
descivissent, amicitia Romanorum petita primi omnium ex Orientali-
bus libertatem acceperunt, facile tunc Romanis de alieno largientibus.

46 *religioni* C   50 *castrorum*] *ortorum* C   *hortorum* Ruehl   51 *nomen*
C / *arcus* τ   *ricis* EF   *ricus* L   om. S   *eruchis* C   *Jericho* ς *Ericus*
Gutschmid   53 *picies* AG¹   *species* R   *specie* VQ   57 ⟨*flatu*⟩ Walter
lacunam ind. Ruehl   59 *et aquae* C   *atque* Ieep   63 *lumine* πιC
bitumine Ruehl ex ς / *incrustatur* Ieep   *illustratur* codd.   65 *venere*] *fuere* C

(1:9) Then Antiochus, remembering that his father had been hated
for his pride and his brother despised for his indolence, was anxious
not to fall into the same vices, and having married Cleopatra, his
brother's wife, proceeded to make war, with the utmost vigour on
the cities that had revolted at the beginning of his brother's government, and after subduing them, reunited them to his kingdom.
(10) He also reduced the Jews, who during the Macedonian rule
under his father Demetrius had recovered their liberty by force of

arms and whose strength was such that they would submit to no
Macedonian king afterwards, but commanded by rulers of their
own nation harassed Syria with fierce wars.

(2:1) The origin of the Jews was from Damascus, the most illustrious city
of Syria, whence also the stock of the Assyrian kings through queen
Samiramis had sprung. (2) The name of the city was given by King
Damascus, in honour of whom the Syrians consecrated the sepulchre
of his wife Arathis as a temple, and regard her since then as a goddess
worthy of the most sacred worship. (3) After Damascus, Azelus,
and then Adores, Abraham, and Israhel were their kings. (4) But a
felicitous progeny of ten sons made Israhel more famous than any of
his ancestors. (5) Having divided his people, in consequence, into
ten kingdoms, he committed them to his sons, and called them all
Jews from Judas, who died soon after this division, and ordered his
memory, whose portion was added to theirs, to be held in veneration
by them all. (6) The youngest of the brothers was Joseph, whom the
others, fearing his extraordinary abilities, secretly made prisoner and
sold to some foreign merchants. (7) Being carried by them into Egypt,
and having there, by his shrewd nature, made himself master of the
arts of magic, he found in a short time great favour with the king;
(8) for he was eminently skilled in prodigies, and was the first to establish the science of interpreting dreams; and nothing indeed of
divine or human law seemed to have been unknown to him, (9) so that
he foretold a dearth in the land some years before it happened, and
all Egypt would have perished by famine had not the king, by his
advice, ordered the corn to be laid up for several years; (10) such
being the proofs of his knowledge that his admonitions seemed to
proceed, not from a mortal, but a god. (11) His son was Moyses,
whom, besides the inheritance of his father's knowledge, the comeli-
ness of his person also recommended. (12) But the Egyptians, being
troubled with scabies and leprosy and warned by an oracle, expelled
him, with those who had the disease, out of Egypt, that the distemper
might not spread among a greater number. (13) Becoming leader,
accordingly, of the exiles, he carried off by stealth the sacred utensils
of the Egyptians, who, trying to recover them by force of arms, were
compelled by tempests to return home. (14) Thus Moyses, having
reached Damascus, his ancestral home, took possession of mount
Sinai, on his arrival at which, after having suffered together with
his followers, from a seven days' fast in the deserts of Arabia, he,
for all time, consecrated the seventh day, which used to be called
Sabbath by the custom of the nation, for a fast-day, because that

337

day had ended at once their hunger and their wanderings. (15) And as they remembered that they had been driven from Egypt for fear of spreading infection, they took care, in order that they might not become odious, from the same cause, to their neighbours, to have no communication with strangers; a rule which, from having been adopted on that particular occasion, gradually became a religious institution. (16) After Moyses, his son Arruas, was made priest to supervise the Egyptian rites, and soon after created king; and ever afterwards it was a custom among the Jews to have the same persons both for kings and priests; and, by their justice combined with religion, it is almost incredible how powerful they became.

(3:1) The wealth of the nation was increased by the income from balsam, which is produced only in that country; (2) for there is a valley, encircled with an unbroken ridge of hills, as if it were a wall, in the form of a camp, the space enclosed being about two hundred iugera and called Aricus; (3) in which valley there is a wood remarkable both for its fertility and pleasantness, and chequered with groves of palm- and balsam-trees. (4) The balsam-trees resemble pitch-trees in shape, except that they are lower and are dressed after the manner of vines; and at a certain season of the year they exude the balsam. (5) But the place is no less admired for its [gentle] sunshine, than for its fertility; for though the sun in the whole region is the hottest in the world, there is, owing to the breath of tepid air, a constant and natural shadiness. (6) In that country is a huge lake, which, from its magnitude and the stillness of its waters, is called the Dead Sea; (7) for it is neither agitated by the winds, because the bitumen, which makes all the water stagnant, resists whirlwinds; nor does it admit of navigation, for all inanimate substances sink to the bottom; and it supports no material, except such as is incrusted with alum.

(8) The first who conquered the Jews was Xerxes, king of Persia. Thereafter they fell, with the Persians themselves, under the power of Alexander the Great; and they were then long subject to Macedonian domination under the kingdom of Syria. (9) On revolting from Demetrius and soliciting the favour of the Romans, they were the first of all the eastern peoples that regained their liberty, the Romans then readily bestowing what was not their own.

(a revised translation of J. S. Watson, London 1902)

1:10 *in Macedonico imperio*: The use of the term "Macedonian Empire" for the Seleucid kingdom is common in Justin; see C. Edson, *Classical Philology*, LIII (1958), pp. 153 ff.; see also D. Musti, *Studi classici e orientali*, XV (1966), pp. 111 ff.; cf. Tacitus, *Historiae*, V, 8 (No. 281).

Pompeius Trogus

sub Demetrio patre: Demetrius I is meant. Pompeius Trogus judged the reign of Demetrius to have been the crucial period in the progress of Judaea towards political liberty; see also below, XXXVI, 3 : 9.

2 : 1 *Namque Iudaeis origo* ...: Justin gives a relatively long account of the origin of the Jews, contrary to his custom of omitting similar digressions.

origo Damascena: This tradition differs from that recounted by Nicolaus of Damascus, apud: Josephus, *Ant.*, I, 159–160 (No. 83). Nicolaus recounts only that Abrahames was king of Damascus and that he came to this city from the country of the Chaldaeans. Still, it may be that the full narrative of Trogus conformed more with Nicolaus; cf. also Labhardt, *loc. cit.* (supra, p. 333).

unde et Assyriis regibus genus ex regina Samirami fuit: Among the traditions concerning the famous sanctuary of the Syrian Goddess Atargatis at Hierapolis-Bambyce, there was one that connected Semiramis with that temple, presumably identifying her with Atargatis; see Lucianus, *De Dea Syria*, 33. Since Atargatis, in the Damascene tradition, was thought to have been born at Damascus, this city also could be regarded as the birth-place of Semiramis (Diodorus, II, 4, from Ctesias, connects Semiramis with Ascalon and declares her to be the daughter of Derceto-Atargatis.) On the rise of the cult of Atargatis, see G. Goossens, *Hiérapolis de Syrie*, Louvain 1943, pp. 57 ff.

2 : 2 *nomen urbi a Damasco rege inditum*: For an eponym derived from the name of a nation, e.g., Armenius from Armenia, see Iustinus, XLII, 3 : 8. It may be that, under the name of Damascus, Iupiter Damascenus is implied; cf. R. Dussaud, *Syria*, III (1922), pp. 219 ff.

sepulcrum Arathis: Cf. Strabo, *Geographica*, XVI, 4 : 27, p. 785; Hesychius, s.v. Ἀτταγάθη, where the form Ἀθάρη stands for Atargatis.

2 : 3 *Azelus* ... *Adores*: These names stand for Hadad and Hazael, both well known from the Bible as kings of Aram. Already Josephus (*Ant.*, IX, 93) relates that Ἄδερ and Ἀζάηλος were accorded divine honours by the people of Damascus. This form (Ἄδερ or Ἄδερος) of the name given to Hadad helps to explain the form Adores we meet in Pompeius Trogus; see *Ant.*, IX, 93; VIII, 199; cf. the Septuagint, I Kings xi : 14; cf. also W.W. Baudissin, *Studien zur semitischen Religionsgeschichte*, I, Leipzig 1876, p. 312.

Israhel: Pompeius Trogus does not seem to know the name Jacob, but only Israel (Israhel), the eponym of the kingdom of Israel.

2 : 4 *Sed Israhelem felix decem filiorum proventus*...: The tradition followed here centres on the Northern Kingdom of Israel, which was in close contact with Damascene Aram in the Biblical period. Pompeius Trogus is not familiar with the tradition of the twelve tribes of Israel or with the separate kingdoms of Judah and Israel. He knows, however, something about the peculiar position of Judah, or rather seeks to explain the present name of the people by the eponym Judah.

2 : 5 *cuius portio omnibus accesserat*: It seems likely that the full history of Pompeius Trogus referred to the emigration of the Jews' ancestors from Damascus to Palestine; cf. Nicolaus, *Historiae*, (No. 83). Having only Justin's Epitome, we cannot discern any difference in the respective spheres of activity between Azaelus and Adores, on the one hand, and Abrahames and Israhel, on the other.

2 : 6 *Minimus aetate*... *Ioseph fuit*: The story of Joseph in Pompeius Trogus is consistent with that of Genesis, though Trogus gives a rationalistic explanation of Joseph's advancement. Trogus ignores Benjamin by calling Joseph the youngest of the brothers.

2 : 7 *Magicas ibi artes ... percepisset*: Joseph's proficiency in the art of magic, which he learned from Egyptian teachers, replaces divine inspiration as an explanation of his rise to power.

2 : 8 *nihilque divini iuris humanique* ...: Pompeius Trogus is using the current Roman phraseology.

2 : 9 *ut etiam sterilitatem agrorum ... providerit*: Cf. Gen. xli.

2 : 10 *non ab homine, sed a deo responsa dari viderentur*: This remark should be related to the tradition, prevalent in literature from the second century C.E. onwards, which derives from a syncretistic Graeco-Egyptian environment; cf. Tertullianus, *Ad Nationes*, II, 8; Firmicus Maternus, *De Errore Profanarum Religionum* 13; Suda, s.v. *Sarapis* (ed. Adler), IV, p. 325. According to this tradition, Joseph was considered worthy of divine worship under the name of Serapis. The same tradition prevails in the talmudic sources; see Y. Gutman, *The Jewish-Hellenistic Literature*, II, Jerusalem 1963, pp. 109 f. (in Hebrew).

2 : 11 *Filius eius Moyses fuit*: Pompeius Trogus thinks Moyses was a son of Joseph. Later he made Aaron (Arruas) a son of Moyses. In Apollonius Molon, apud: Eusebius, *Praeparatio Evangelica*, IX, 19 : 3 (No. 46) Moses appears as the grandson of Joseph.

etiam formae pulchritudo commendabat: I. Heinemann (PW, XVI, p. 362) suggests that Pompeius Trogus' emphasis on Moses' beauty is to be connected with his descent from Joseph; cf. Gen. xxxix : 6. Josephus (*Ant.*, II, 231) also has much to say about the beauty of Moses. In addition, in the Septuagint Exodus ii : 2 and in Philo, *Vita Mosis*, I, 18, Moses is defined as ἀστεῖος.

2 : 12 *Sed Aegyptii, cum scabiem*...: Henceforth Pompeius Trogus mainly uses an Egyptian tradition, which is followed by many writers, starting with Hecataeus, apud: Diodorus, XL, 3 : 4 (No. 11). In Justin's narrative we miss any reference to the emigration of Joseph's brothers and their families to Egypt. Nor do we learn anything about the subsequent fate of the Jewish state. It seems that Pompeius Trogus is responsible for this, because he did not succeed in combining in his History the three versions that he used on the origin of the Jewish nation, namely, the Damascene, the Biblical and the Egyptian. He made, however, some effort in this direction; cf. Pompeius Trogus' remark: "Itaque Moyses Damascena, antiqua patria, repetita."

2 : 13 *sacra Aegyptiorum furto abstulit*: Exod. xii : 35–36 relates only that the Children of Israel borrowed jewellery from their neighbours. The Egyptian version about the stealing of the *sacra* probably arose under the influence of the Egyptians' later experience with their enemies, the Persians; cf. also *OGIS*, No. 54, ll. 20 f. (the inscription from Adulis); No. 56, ll. 10 f. (the inscription from Canopus). For the motif of stealing the *sacra*, see Gen. xxxi : 30 ff.

quae repetentes ...: This constitutes a rationalistic interpretation of the miracle of the Red Sea, which makes it possible to connect the Jewish version of Pharaoh's pursuit of the Children of Israel with the Egyptian one; cf. also Artapanus, apud: Eusebius, *Praeparatio Evangelica*, IX (*F. Gr. Hist.*, III, C 726, F 3, p. 686):

Μεμφίτας μὲν οὖν λέγειν ἔμπειρον ὄντα τὸν Μώυσον τῆς χώρας, τὴν ἄμπωτιν τηρήσαντα διὰ ξηρᾶς τῆς θαλάσσης τὸ πλῆθος περαιῶσαι· Ἡλιουπολίτας δὲ λέγειν ἐπικαταδραμεῖν τὸν βασιλέα μετὰ πολλῆς δυνάμεως,<ἅμα> καὶ τοῖς καθιερωμένοις ζῴοις, διὰ τὸ τὴν ὕπαρξιν τοὺς Ἰουδαίους τῶν Αἰγυπτίων χρησαμένους διακομίζειν.

Pompeius Trogus

2:14 *Damascena, antiqua patria, repetita*: This statement refers back to the Damascene version of Jewish origins.

montem Sinam: The name of the mountain is mentioned also by Apion, apud: Josephus, *Contra Apionem* II, 25 (No. 165).

Sabbata: The form *Sabbata* is the most common one in the Septuagint, and appears also in Horatius, *Sermones*, I, 9 : 69 (No. 129); Suetonius, *Divus Augustus*, 76 : 2 (No. 303); Iuvenalis, XIV, 96 (No. 301). See also A. Pelletier, *Vetus Testamentum*, XXII (1972), pp. 436 ff.

ieiunio sacravit: For the Jewish Sabbath as a day of fasting, see other writers of the Augustan age; see also the commentary to Strabo *Historica Hypomnemata*, apud: Josephus, *Ant.*, XIV, 66 (No. 104), and the letter of Augustus, apud: Suetonius, *Divus Augustus*, 76 : 2 (No. 303).

2:15 *quoniam metu contagionis ...*: For the expulsion of strangers by Jews, see Hecataeus, apud: Diodorus, XL, 3 : 4 (No. 11).

2:16 *ut eosdem reges et sacerdotes haberent*: Pompeius Trogus anachronistically depicts all Jewish history according to the conditions that prevailed during the Hasmonaean monarchy, when the king and the high priest were the same person; cf. Tacitus, *Historiae*, V, 8 (No. 281): "quia honor sacerdotii firmamentum potentiae adsumebatur." Morr's conclusion about the Posidonian origin of our passage is hardly justified; see Morr *op. cit.* (supra, p. 333), p. 278.

quorum iustitia ... coaluere: Here we have an instance of Pompeius Trogus' moralistic tendency; cf. M. Rambaud, *REL*, XXVI (1948), pp. 180 ff.

3:1 *ex vectigalibus opobalsami*: For the form *opobalsamum*, see Plinius, *Naturalis Historia* XII, 116 (No. 213); *BJ*, IV, 469.

in his tantum regionibus gignitur: This region's unique feature is also emphasized by both Diodorus (*Bibliotheca Historica*, II, 48 : 9 = No. 59) and Strabo (*Geographica*, XVI, 2 : 41, p. 763 = No. 115), who both mention its medical value. Diodorus, like Pompeius Trogus, stressed the income derived from the opobalsam.

3:2 *Est namque vallis*: Diodorus also speaks about a valley (αὐλών) where the balsam grows, while Strabo tells about a valley encompassed by a mountainous country.

spatium loci ducenta iugera: Strabo gives only the length of the palm-grove.

Aricus: Both in Pompeius Trogus and in Strabo this is the name of the valley, and not of the town, which is not mentioned.

3:4 *Et arbores opobalsami similem formam piceis arboribus habent*: Strabo's description of the shrub is compared to different trees than those in Trogus. Tacitus states only that the tree is a *modica arbor*.

balsamum sudant: Cf. Tacitus, *Historiae*, V, 6 (No. 281).

3:5 *Sed non minor loci eius ... admiratio est*: A similar contrast is noticed by Tacitus in connection with Mt. Libanus, which is covered by snow though situated in a hot region; see Tacitus, *loc. cit.* (No. 281).

3:6 *Mortuum Mare dicitur*: Diodorus and Pliny call the Dead Sea the "Lake of Asphalt", as does Josephus, *BJ*, IV, 455 f. Strabo calls it Sirbonis by mistake; see *Geographica*, XVI, 2 : 42, p. 763 (No. 115). Tacitus gives it no name at all. Among the Greek writers, Pausanias, *Graeciae Descriptio*, V, 7:5 (No. 356) calls it the Dead Sea: ἡ θάλασσα ἡ Νεκρά; cf. also Galenus, *De Symptomatum Causis*, III, 7 (No. 380); *De Simplicium Medicamentorum Temperamentis ac Facultatibus*, IV, 20 (No. 381); Dio Chrysostomus, apud: Synesius, *Vita Dionis* (No. 251).

From *Herodotus to Plutarch*

3:7 *...nec materiam ullam sustinet...*: Cf. the commentary to Diodorus, XIX, 99 : 2 (No. 62); Pausanias, *loc. cit.* (No. 356).

omnia vita carentia in profundum merguntur: We have no statement as to what happens to living things. For this omission the Epitome of Justin is to blame.

3:8 *Primus Xerxes... Iudaeos domuit*: Like almost all Greek and Roman writers, Pompeius Trogus betrays complete ignorance of Jewish history after Moses. Nor does he seem to have known of the Assyrian and Babylonian rule in Palestine. It is hard to account for the supreme importance given to Xerxes. Is it because this Persian king is connected with Greece, or is it because Trogus echoes a tradition that knew something about a collision between the Jews and the Persian government under Xerxes? The first explanation seems preferable. On Jewish servitude, see Tacitus, *Historiae*, V, 8 (No. 281): "Dum Assyrios penes Medosque et Persas Oriens fuit, despectissima pars servientium."

3:9 *A Demetrio cum descivissent*: It is clear that Demetrius I (162–150 B.C.E.) is meant, as emerges from a comparison with the earlier passage of Justin (XXXVI, 1 : 10), where he speaks about the revolt of the Jews against Demetrius I, the father of Antiochus VII; cf. Niese, III, p. 255, n. 1; Ed. Meyer, II, p. 246, n. 4; A. Momigliano, *Prime linee di storia della tradizione maccabaica*, Rome 1930, p. 161 (who refute the implausible view of H. Willrich, *Urkundenfälschung in der hellenistisch-jüdischen Literatur*, Göttingen 1924, pp. 48 ff.).

amicitia Romanorum petita: This alludes to Judas Maccabaeus' embassy to Rome in 161 B.C.E., which resulted in a treaty of alliance between Rome and Judaea; see I Macc. viii; *Ant.*, XII, 417 ff.; see also *BJ*, I, 38; *Ant.*, XIV, 233 (as commented upon by B. Niese, *Orientalische Studien Th. Nöldeke gewidmet*, II, Giessen 1906, pp. 817 ff.). On the nature of this treaty, see E. Täubler, *Imperium Romanum*, Leipzig–Berlin 1913, pp. 239 ff.; M. Sordi *Acme*, V (1952), pp. 509 ff.; H. Horn, "Foederati", Ph.D. Thesis, Frankfurt 1930, p. 81; T. Liebmann–Frankfort, *L'Antiquité Classique*, XXXVIII (1969), pp. 101 ff; A. Giovannini & H. Müller, *Museum Helveticum*, XXVIII (1971) pp. 167 ff.

libertatem acceperunt: The treaty with Rome was considered by Pompeius Trogus as tantamount to an acquisition of liberty for the Jews. It is true that Demetrius I defeated Judas in 160 B.C.E., but this was only a passing event, and the Hasmonaeans continued to wage war.

Trogus hardly knew the details of the political history of the Hasmonaean revolt. What mattered to him was that Judaea had obtained independence some time after she had become allied to Rome during the reign of Demetrius I.

facile tunc Romanis de alieno largientibus: This sentence has an ironic ring, aimed at Roman self-righteousness in politics. Some scholars discern the influence of Timagenes, the presumable source of Trogus, who is well known for his critical attitude to Rome; cf. Seneca, *Epistulae Morales*, XCI, 13; A. Klotz, PW, XXI, p. 2308. On the attitude of Pompeius Trogus to Rome, see also E. Schneider, "De Pompei Trogi Historiarum Philippicarum Consilio et Arte", Ph.D. Thesis, Leipzig 1913, pp. 50 ff.; H. Fuchs, *Der geistige Widerstand gegen Rom*, Berlin 1938, pp. 42 f. For a view against Pompeius Trogus' dependence on Timagenes, see Seel, *op. cit.* (supra, p. 333), pp. 18 ff.

138

Historiae Philippicae, Prologus, Libri XXXIX — Seel = F139R

Ut Syriam Iudaei et Arabes terrestribus latrociniis infestarint, mari Cilices piraticum bellum moverint, quod in Cilicia Romani per Marcum Antonium gesserunt.

How the Jews and the Arabs molested Syria by brigandage on land, and how the Cilicians started a piratical war on sea, which the Romans under the leadership of Marcus Antonius waged in Cilicia.

Ut Syriam Iudaei et Arabes terrestribus latrociniis infestarint : The Epitome of Justin in the XXXIXth book ignores the Jewish acts of robbery and mentions only the plundering of the Arabs under their king Erotimus. On Erotimus, see E. Täubler, *Klio*, X, (1910) pp. 251 ff. For an evaluation of the Jewish conquests as *latrocinia*, see Strabo, *Geographica*, XVI, 2 : 28, p. 759 (No. 114); 2 : 37, p. 761 (No. 115). However, an allusion to the sufferings of Syria from Jewish robbery is found in Pompeius Trogus, apud: Iustinus, Epitoma, XL, 2 : 4 (No. 139).

139

apud: Iustinus, *Historiae Philippicae*, Libri XL Epitoma, 2:4 — Seel = F140R

Igitur ut habenti ⟨scil. Antiocho⟩ regnum non ademerit, ita quo cesserit Tigrani, non daturum, quod tueri nesciat, ne rursus Syriam Iudaeorum et Arabum latrociniis infestam reddat.

Accordingly, as he had not taken the throne from Antiochus, so he would not give him what he himself had yielded to Tigranes and what he would not know how to defend, lest he should again expose Syria to the depredations of the Jews and Arabs.

On the last struggles of the Seleucid monarchy and the fate of its representatives, see A.R. Bellinger, "The End of the Seleucids", *Transactions of the Connecticut Academy of Arts and Sciences*, XXXVIII (1949), pp. 82 ff.; G. Downey, *TAPA*, LXXXII (1951), pp. 149 ff.

XLVIII. VITRUVIUS

First century B.C.E.[1]

In his treatment of different waters, Vitruvius, the greatest Roman writer on architecture, mentions Jaffa "in Syria". The asphalt lake of Babylon with liquid bitumen floating on it, the lakes of Jaffa "in Syria" and those of Arabia find their place among the various fountains and rivers distinguished by an oily surface. By the bitumen of Jaffa, that of the Dead Sea is undoubtedly implied. The connection of the Dead Sea with Jaffa was also made by the third-century writer Xenophilus (No. 22), as quoted through Callimachus by Antigonus of Carystus. It may be assumed that Vitruvius, too, as far as concerns this piece of information, draws upon some early Hellenistic source. It should be pointed out that in this fragment he does not locate Jaffa in Judaea, which would have been more natural for a contemporary of Caesar and Augustus.[2]

Vitruvius also depends on early sources when he uses the name Syria in the eighth book of his work. Thus, when he adduces examples for the fact that the most numerous and the largest rivers are found to issue from the north, he includes both the Tigris and the Euphrates, which rise "from Syria" (VIII, 2:6). In this respect, he employs the name in a way that is wholly consonant with its early use by Greek writers; cf. the commentary to Mela (No. 152). In any case, the view of Jacoby[3] that Vitruvius owes his knowledge of the Dead Sea to the Περὶ Ὠκεανοῦ of Posidonius carries no weight. Posidonius certainly had more accurate information about the location of the Dead Sea and its relation to Jaffa.[4]

It may also be presumed that when Vitruvius alludes to the perfumes in the reeds, rushes and all herbs, and to the incense-bearing trees found

---

1 For the problem of dating *De Architectura* in the last decades of the first century B. C. E., see Schanz & Hosius, II, p. 386; F. Granger, Introduction to the *LCL* edition, 1931, p. XIV; P. Thielscher, PW, Ser. 2, IX, pp. 431 f.

2 It is a quite different matter when Strabo maintains that Jerusalem is visible from Jaffa; cf. Strabo, *Geographica*, XVI, 2:28, p. 759 (No. 114).

3 *F. Gr. Hist.*, II C, p. 199.

4 Of course, Posidonius was one of the sources for *De Architectura*, as is stated by Vitruvius himself (VIII, 3:27), but so was, e.g., Theophrastus.

in Syria (*VIII, 3:13:* "*Quodsi terra generibus umorum non esset dissimilis et disparata, non tantum in Syria et Arabia in harundinibus et iuncis herbisque omnibus essent odores*"), *he has in mind the balsam of Judaea. In his* Historia Plantarum, *II, 6:2 (No. 6) Theophrastus also places the balsam in the* "*valley of Syria*".

140

De Architectura, VIII, 3:8–9 — Krohn

(8) Babylone lacus amplissima magnitudine, qui λίμνη ἀσφαλτῖτις appellatur, habet supra natans liquidum bitumen; quo bitumine et latere testaceo structum murum Samiramis circumdedit Babyloni. Item Iope in Syria Arabiaque Nomadum lacus sunt inmani magni-
5 tudine, qui emittunt bituminis maximas moles, quas diripiunt qui habitant circa. (9) Id autem non est mirandum; nam crebrae sunt ibi lapidicinae bituminis duri. Cum ergo per bituminosam terram vis erumpit aquae, secum extrahit et, cum sit egressa extra terram, secernitur et ita reicit ab se bitumen.

2 *quo*] *quod* HEG   3 *testatio* codd. / *Babyloni* Müller-Strübing   *baby-*
lonem codd.   4 *Iope* Jocundus   *tope* codd. / *Nomadum* Rode
                        numidarum codd.

(8) At Babylon there is a lake of wide extent which is called Asphalt Lake, with liquid bitumen floating on it. Samiramis built a wall round Babylon of this bitumen and burnt-brick. At Jope in Syria also and in Nomad Arabia are lakes of immense size producing much bitumen which is gathered by the neighbouring people. (9) This is not surprising, because, there are many quarries of hard bitumen there. When, therefore, a spring of water rushes through the bituminous land, it draws the bitumen within it, and passing outside, the water separates and deposits the bitumen.   (trans. F. Granger, *LCL*)

XLIX. OVID

43 B.C.E. to 17 or 18 C.E.

The two references of Ovid to the Jewish Sabbath, in Ars Amatoria
(c. 2 B.C.E.) and in the Remedia Amoris, *testify to the impression made
on the Roman society of the Augustan period by the presence of a vast
Jewish community in Rome. These references are paralleled by similar
references in Ovid's near predecessor Tibullus (No. 126), in Horace and
in a letter by Augustus himself that was preserved by Suetonius,* Augustus, *76:2 (No. 303).*[1]

---

1 In most of the manuscripts of Ovid's *Metamorphoses* there occurs, in the description of the Flood, the line "et ducit remos illic, ubi nuper ararat" (I, 294; "arabat" is read only by N¹, and "arabant" by ε; cf. the *apparatus criticus* of Ehwald in the Teubner edition). It may be that the poet was aware of the play on words and included "ararat" as an allusion to the biblical Ararat of the Flood (Gen. viii: 4). See the discussion of T.T.B. Ryder, *Greece and Rome*, XIV (1967), pp. 126 ff.

141

Ars Amatoria, I, 75–80 — Kenney = 134aR

75 Nec te praetereat Veneri ploratus Adonis
cultaque Iudaeo septima sacra Syro,
nec fuge linigerae Memphiti:a templa iuvencae
(multas illa facit, quod fuit ipsa Iovi);
et fora conveniunt (quis credere possit?) amori,
80 flammaque in arguto saepe reperta foro.

76 *sacra*] *festa* ç / *syro*] *viro* r S$_a$Aω   *deo* OP$_a$ 77 *linigerae*] *lanigerae*
    OAω   *niligenae* aç   79 *et*] *ad* ç

Nor let Adonis bewailed of Venus escape you, nor the seventh day
that the Syrian Jew holds sacred. Avoid not the Memphian shrine
of the linen-clothed heifer: many a maid does she make what she
was herself to Jove. Even the lawcourts (who could believe it?) are
suitable to love; often has its flame been found in the shrill-tongued
court.   (trans. J. H. Mozley, *LCL*)

75 *Adonis*: Before the time of the Severi the cult of Adonis was of secondary
importance in Rome; see F. Cumont, *Les religions orientales dans le paganisme
romain*[4], Paris 1929, p. 252, n. 23.
76 *septima sacra*: Knowledge of the Jewish seventh day was common, though
inaccurate, in the Augustan age.
Iudaeo . . . *Syro*: On the Jews as a part of the Syrians, according to the writers of
the early Hellenistic age, see Theophrastus, apud: Porphyrius, *De Abstinentia*, II,
26 (No. 4); Megasthenes, apud: Clemens, *Stromata*, I, 15 : 72 : 5 (No. 14); Clearchus, apud: Josephus, *Contra Apionem*, I, 176–183 (No. 15); cf. Juster, I, p. 172
n. 4. For the whole passage, cf. Iuvenalis, IX, 24: "nam quo non prostat femina
templo?"

142

Ars Amatoria, I, 413–416 — Kenney = 134bR

Tum licet incipias, qua flebilis Allia luce
vulneribus Latiis sanguinolenta fuit,
415 quaque die redeunt rebus minus apta gerendis
culta Palaestino septima festa Syro.

413 *tum*] *tu* RO   *tunc* Aω   414 *vulneribus Latiis*] *vulneribus nostris*
    AHO$_a$²   *nostris vulneribus* OP$_a$ 416 *festa*] *sacra* Oç

You may begin on the day on which woeful Allia flows stained with the blood of Latian wounds, or on that day, less fit for business, whereon returns the seventh-day feast that the Syrian of Palestine observes. (trans. J. H. Mozley, *LCL*)

416 *Palaestino ... Syro*: It is clear from the context, since Ovid mentions the *septima sacra*, that *Palaestinus Syrus* is the same as *Iudaeus Syrus* in the earlier passage. This contrasts with Tibullus (I, 7 : 18): "alba Palaestino sancta columba Syro", which refers to the gentile inhabitants of Palestine. It is not clear how much territory beyond the coastal area Herodotus included in the concept of Syria-Palaestine; cf. the commentary to No. 1. Aristotle had already included the Dead Sea in Palestine, and the name appears in Hellenistic literature; see the commentary to No. 3. Tibullus and Ovid are the first Latin writers to use the name Palaestinus; see also *Metamorphoses*, IV, 46; V, 145; *Fasti*, II, 464. In the first century C.E. the Jewish writers in Greek, Philo and Josephus, already use the name Palaestine or Syria-Palaestine to designate the whole Land of Israel; cf., e.g., Philo, *Quod Omnis Probus Liber sit*, 75; *De Abrahamo*, 133; *Vita Mosis*, I, 163; *De Virtutibus*, 221; Josephus, *Ant.*, I, 145; XX, 259. It seems that the official name of Judaea for the whole land in the Hasmonaean and early Roman period was somewhat misleading, as at that time Judaea also meant Judaea proper, that is, the area around Jerusalem. Therefore, even the Jewish writers found it quite convenient to use the name Palaestine with its broader connotations. For a somewhat different explanation, see M. Noth, *ZDPV*, LXII (1939), p. 143; see also E. Bikerman, *RB*, LIV (1947), p. 260, n. 4. The name Syria-Palaestine became official only in the time of Hadrian; cf. Noth, *op. cit.*, pp. 127 f.; R. Syme, *JRS*, LII (1962), p. 90. Palaestine, alone, became common in the Greek literature of the second century C.E.

143

Remedia Amoris, 217–220 — Kenney — 135R

Sed quanto minus ire voles, magis ire memento;
perfer, et invitos currere coge pedes.
Nec pluvias opta, nec te peregrina morentur
220 sabbata nec damnis Allia nota suis;

220 *Allia* ed. Ald. 1502   *alea* codd.

Yet the less you wish to go, the more be sure of going; persist, and compel your unwilling feet to run. Hope not for rain, nor let foreign sabbath stay you, nor Allia well-known for its ill-luck.

(trans. J. H. Mozley, *LCL*)

L. CONON

First century B.C.E.?

We find the name of Conon in the list of eight writers, beginning with Theophilus and ending with Zopyrion (most of whom are unidentifiable), who, according to Josephus, dealt with the Jews. This Conon may be the same as a writer of the same name who is mentioned by Servius: "Conon in eo libro, quem de Italia scripsit, quosdam Pelasgos aliosque ex Peloponneso convenas ad eum locum Italiae venisse dicit" (In Aeneidem, VII, 738). This, however, is no more than a conjecture. Still more open to doubt is the identification of the Conon referred to by Josephus — or, for that matter, by Servius — with Conon the Mythographer.[1]

---

1 Cf. F. Jacoby, PW, XI, p. 1335.

Conon

144

apud: Josephus, *Contra Apionem*, I, 215–216 — Niese = Reinach (Budé), p. 41

(215) 'Αρκοῦσι δὲ ὅμως εἰς τὴν ἀπόδειξιν τῆς ἀρχαιότητος αἵ τε Αἰγυπτίων καὶ Χαλδαίων καὶ Φοινίκων ἀναγραφαί, πρὸς ἐκείναις τε τοσοῦτοι τῶν Ἑλλήνων συγγραφεῖς· (216) ἔτι δὲ πρὸς τοῖς εἰρημένοις Θεόφιλος ⟨No. 38⟩ καὶ Θεόδοτος καὶ Μνασέας ⟨No. 27⟩ καὶ
5 *'Αριστοφάνης ⟨No. 24⟩ καὶ 'Ερμογένης ⟨No. 199⟩ Εὐήμερός ⟨No. 16⟩ τε καὶ Κόνων καὶ Ζωπυρίων ⟨No. 198⟩...*

3 ἔτι δὲ Eus.   ἔτι δὲ καὶ L

(215) However, our antiquity is sufficiently established by the Egyptian, Chaldaean, and Phoenician records, not to mention the numerous Greek historians. (216) In addition to those already cited, Theophilus, Theodotus, Mnaseas, Aristophanes, Hermogenes, Euhemerus, Conon, Zopyrion... (trans. H. St. J. Thackeray, *LCL*)

LI. CONON THE MYTHOGRAPHER

End of the first century B.C.E. to beginning of the first century C.E.

Conon, a contemporary of Archelaus of Cappadocia, wrote mythological tales that were preserved by Photius.[1] Among these tales is one that depicts the story of Andromeda, connecting it with Jaffa. This is in accord with a long tradition in Greek literature that goes back at least as far as pseudo-Scylax; cf. the commentaries to Pausanias, IV, 35 : 9 (No. 354) and to Tacitus, Historiae, V, 2 (No. 281). However, the story, as related by Conon, is characterized by a rationalistic approach that does away with the monster (τὸ κῆτος). Conon is aware of the connection of Cepheus' territory with what was later called Phoenicia, but, like some other writers, he fails to include Jaffa in Judaea.

---

1 Cf. U. Höfer, *Konon — Text und Quellenuntersuchung*, Greifswald 1890.

145

Narrationes, apud: Photius, Cod. 186, p. 138b–139a — Bekker = ed. Henry, Vol. III, pp. 29 f. = *F. Gr. Hist.*, I, 26, F1, pp. 204 f. = Höfer, *op. cit.*, p. 22

⟨p. 138b⟩ Ἡ μ' ἱστορία τὰ περὶ Ἀνδρομέδας ἱστορεῖ ἑτέρως ἢ ὡς ὁ Ἑλλήνων μῦθος· ἀδελφοὺς μὲν γὰρ δύο γενέσθαι Κηφέα καὶ Φινέα, καὶ εἶναι τὴν τοῦ Κηφέως βασιλείαν τότε ἐν τῇ μετονομασθείσῃ μὲν ὕστερον Φοινίκῃ, τηνικαῦτα δ' Ἰόππᾳ ἀπὸ Ἰόππης τῆς ἐπιθαλασσιδίου πόλεως
5 τοὔνομα λαβούσῃ. καὶ ἦν τὰ τῆς ἀρχῆς ὅρια ἀπὸ τῆς καθ' ἡμᾶς θαλάσσης μέχρι Ἀράβων τῶν πρὸς τὴν Ἐρυθρὰν θάλασσαν ᾠκημένων. εἶναι δὲ τῷ Κηφεῖ καὶ θυγατέρα πάνυ καλὴν Ἀνδρομέδαν, καὶ αὐτὴν μνᾶσθαι Φοινικά τε καὶ τὸν ἀδελφὸν Κηφέως Φινέα. Κηφεὺς δὲ μετὰ πολλοὺς τοὺς ἐφ' ἑκατέρῳ λογισμοὺς ἔγνω δοῦναι μὲν Φοίνικι, ἁρπαγῇ δὲ τοῦ
10 μνηστῆρος τὸ αὑτοῦ ἑκούσιον ἀποκρύπτειν· καὶ ἁρπάζεται ἀπό τινος νησῖδος ἐρήμου ἡ Ἀνδρομέδα ἐν ᾧ εἰώθει ἀπιοῦσα θυσίας τῇ Ἀφροδίτῃ θύειν· Φοίνικος δ' ἁρπάσαντος νηΐ (κῆτος δ' αὕτη ἐκαλεῖτο, ἢ μίμησιν ἔχουσα τοῦ ζῴου ἢ κατὰ τύχην), ἡ Ἀνδρομέδα, ὡς κατὰ ⟨p. 139a⟩ ἄγνοιαν τοῦ πατρὸς ἁρπαζομένη, ἀνωλοφύρατό τε καὶ μετ' οἰμωγῆς
15 τοὺς βοηθήσοντας ἀνεκαλεῖτο. Περσεὺς δ' ὁ Δανάης κατὰ δαίμονα παραπλέων κατίσχει καὶ πρὸς τὴν πρώτην ὄψιν τῆς κόρης, οἴκτῳ καὶ ἔρωτι συσχεθεὶς τό τε πλοῖον, τὸ κῆτος, διαφθείρει καὶ τοὺς ἐμπλέοντας ὑπὸ ἐκπλήξεως μόνον οὐχὶ λιθωθέντας ἀναιρεῖ. καὶ τοῦτο Ἕλλησι τὸ τοῦ μύθου κῆτος καὶ οἱ παγέντες εἰς λίθους ἄνθρωποι τῆς Γοργόνος τῇ
20 κεφαλῇ. ἄγεται δ' οὖν γυναῖκα τὴν Ἀνδρομέδαν, καὶ οἴχεται αὐτὴ συμπλέουσα εἰς τὴν Ἑλλάδα τῷ Περσεῖ, καὶ βασιλεύοντος τὸ Ἄργος οἰκεῖται.

1 καὶ ὡς A	2 γενέσθαι φασὶ M	4 δ ἀπὸ A	5 λαβούσῃ edd.
λαβούσης codd.	10 αὑτοῦ edd.	αὐτοῦ codd.	12 αὕτη Bekker
αὐτὴ codd.	13 ἢ] ἢ καὶ M	17 ἐμπεσόντας M	19 τῆς om. M

(p. 138b) The fortieth story tells the history of Andromeda in a way different from that found in Greek mythology. There were two brothers, Cepheus and Phineus, and the kingdom of Cepheus was situated in the country called later Phoenicia, but at that time called Joppe, having received its name from the coastal city of Joppe. The boundaries of this realm extended from our sea till the land of the Arabs living near the Red Sea. Cepheus had a very pretty daughter, Andromeda, who was wooed by both Phoenix and Phineus, the brother of Cepheus. After he had given much thought to each of them, he decided to choose Phoenix, but to conceal his intention under the guise of a violent seizure by the suitor. And Andromeda was seized from a desolate islet where she used to retire in order to sacrifice to Aphrodite. Having been carried off by Phoenix in a ship (it was named "Sea-monster" either because it resembled one or by chance), Andromeda, like one violently carried away (p. 139a) and not with the knowledge of her father, started lamenting and piteously invoking help. Perseus the son of Danae, having by chance sailed by the islet, put in there and at the first sight of the girl became overpowered by a feeling of pity and love for her; he destroyed the vessel, the "Sea-monster", and killed its crew who became almost petrified by consternation. And this is the basis of the Greek myth that the Sea-monster and the people were turned into stone by the head of Gorgo. Perseus indeed married Andromeda, and she left sailing away with Perseus to Greece, and it was during his reign that Argos became inhabited.

LII. PTOLEMY THE HISTORIAN

End of the first century B.C.E.?

The following passage of Ptolemy derives from a work known as De Adfinium Vocabulorum Differentia, which is usually attributed to Ammonius. This work seems to have been composed not later than the end of the first century or the beginning of the second century C.E.[1] As for Ptolemy, it is not easy to identify him, as his name is one of the most common in the Greek onomasticon. Some scholars, e.g. Schürer, Otto and Hölscher, think that he is the well-known grammaticus Ptolemy of Ascalon, who lived presumably at the end of the first century B.C.E.[2] and who is assumed to have written, apart from his grammatical works, a History (or Life) of Herod.[3] If we accept this identification, the History of Herod by Ptolemy becomes the work of a contemporary writer. Yet, some doubt attaches to this identification, and Jacoby emphasizes the fact that the list of the works of Ptolemy of Ascalon in Suda does not include any composition that is not grammatical.

Josephus does not mention Ptolemy as the author of a work about Herod. Nevertheless, Ptolemy is thought by Hölscher to have been one of Josephus' main sources for the narrative in his Antiquitates. No proof, however, can be furnished for this view.

Bibliography

Schürer, I, pp. 48 ff.; G. Hölscher, *Die Quellen des Josephus*, Leipzig 1904, pp. 57, 80; idem, PW, IX, p. 1981; Otto, pp. 5 f.; *F. Gr. Hist.*, II D, pp. 625 f.; A. Dihle, PW, XXIII, p. 1861.

---

1 See Cohn, PW, I, p. 1866 (following Valckenaer); *Ammonii Qui Dicitur Liber De Adfinium Vocabulorum Differentia*, edited by K. Nickau, Leipzig 1966, pp. LXVI f.; see also *ibid.* concerning the name of the author. Nickau thinks that it was Herennius Philo rather than Ammonius.

2 Cf. M. Baege, "De Ptolemaeo Ascalonita", Ph. D. Thesis, Halle 1882, p. 6. Baege, however, does not identify Ptolemy of Ascalon with the historian of Herod.

3 Ptolemy of Ascalon is expressly quoted in *De Adfinium Vocabulorum Differentia* (436, 477), but not in connection with the life of Herod.

146

Historia Herodis, apud: Ammonius, *De Adfinium Vocabulorum Differentia*, No. 243 — Nickau = F47R = *F. Gr. Hist.*, II, B199, F1

᾿Ιουδαῖοι καὶ ᾿Ιδουμαῖοι διαφέρουσιν, ὥς φησι Πτολεμαῖος ἐν πρώτῳ Περὶ Ἡρώδου τοῦ βασιλέως. ᾿Ιουδαῖοι μὲν γάρ εἰσιν οἱ ἐξ ἀρχῆς φυσικοί· ᾿Ιδουμαῖοι δὲ τὸ μὲν ἀρχῆθεν οὐκ ᾿Ιουδαῖοι, ἀλλὰ Φοίνικες καὶ Σύροι, κρατηθέντες δὲ ὑπ᾿ αὐτῶν καὶ ἀναγκασθέντες περιτέμνεσθαι
5 καὶ συντελεῖν εἰς τὸ ἔθνος καὶ τὰ αὐτὰ νόμιμα ἡγεῖσθαι ἐκλήθησαν ᾿Ιουδαῖοι.

1 ἰδουμαῖοι καὶ ἰουδαῖοι θG / διαφέρει Eπ   1–2 ὥς φησι... βασιλέως om. Pt., Egud.   3 φυσικοί om. Pt. / ᾿Ιουδαῖοι] ᾿Ιδουμαῖοι Pt., Eren.
5 ἔθος θ   6 ᾿Ιουδαῖοι] ᾿Ιδουμαῖοι ηπ Eren., Egud.

Jews and Idumaeans differ, as Ptolemy states in the first book of the History of King Herod. Jews are those who are so by origin and nature. The Idumaeans, on the other hand, were not originally Jews, but Phoenicians and Syrians; having been subjugated by the Jews and having been forced to undergo circumcision, so as to be counted among the Jewish nation and keep the same customs, they were called Jews.

᾿Ιουδαῖοι καὶ ᾿Ιδουμαῖοι διαφέρουσιν: For the confusion between Judaea and Idumaea by Latin authors, see, e.g., Vergilius, *Georgica*, III, 12 (No. 125) and the commentary *ad loc.*

ὥς φησι Πτολεμαῖος: It seems that Ptolemy discussed the difference between Idumaeans and Jews in connection with the origin of Herod.

ἀλλὰ Φοίνικες: We are fairly well informed about the considerable Phoenician elements in Hellenistic Idumaea as a result of the excavations at Marissa. The Greek inscriptions found there indicate the existence of a community of Hellenized Phoenicians; see *OGIS*, No. 593; J.P. Peters & H. Thiersch, *Painted Tombs in the Necropolis of Marissa*, London 1905.

καὶ ἀναγκασθέντες περιτέμνεσθαι: The Judaization of the Idumaeans was accomplished in the time of John Hyrcan; see *Ant.*, XIII, 257; XV, 254; Strabo, *Geographica*, XVI, 2 : 34, p. 760 (No. 115).

καὶ συντελεῖν εἰς τὸ ἔθνος: The reference to Lucianus, *Timon*, 4 : 106 — εἰς ἔθος τι ἀρχαῖον συντελῶν — has relevance only on the basis of the reading ἔθος (the reading of the group θ).

καὶ τὰ αὐτὰ νόμιμα ἡγεῖσθαι: Hölscher emphasizes the similarity of language in this passage and in *Ant.*, XV, 254: Ὑρκανοῦ δὲ τὴν πολιτείαν αὐτῶν εἰς τὰ ᾿Ιουδαίων ἔθη καὶ νόμιμα μεταστήσαντος.

ἐκλήθησαν ᾿Ιουδαῖοι: At the end of the period of the Second Temple the Idumaeans felt themselves to be Jews in every respect; see, e.g., *BJ*, IV, 270 ff.

LIII. VALERIUS MAXIMUS

Beginning of the first century C.E.

The following passages are based on that part of Valerius Maximus which is found under the heading De Superstitionibus. *They contain a reference to the expulsion of Jewish missionaries from Rome in 139 B. C. E. — the first event in the history of the Jews of Italy that is known to us. In the expulsion ordered by the* praetor peregrinus *the Jews were coupled with the astrologers. Their expulsion was an expression of the concern felt by the ruling classes of Rome towards the diffusion of Eastern cults and ideas.*

The full text of Valerius Maximus relating to the expulsion of the Jews has not been preserved, and we get its contents only through the two epitomists, Paris (fourth century C.E.?) and Nepotianus (fourth–fifth century C. E.?). The Epitome of Paris is the more detailed of the two and seems also to be the more accurate.[1]

It may be that Valerius Maximus derived his information about the above-mentioned events from Livy.[2]

---

1 Wessner, PW, IX, pp. 697 ff.; Kappelmacher, PW, X, pp. 686 ff.; Schanz & Hosius, II, pp. 591 f.; M. Galdi, *L'epitome nella letteratura latina*, Naples 1922, pp. 128 ff.

2 See F. Cumont, *Le musée belge*, XIV (1910), pp. 57 f.; Ed. Meyer, III, p. 460, n. 1; E. J. Bickerman, *RIDA*, V, (1958), p. 144, n. 19. On the sources of Valerius Maximus, see also A. Ramelli, *Athenaeum*, NS XIV (1936), pp. 117 ff.; A. Klotz, *Studien zu Valerius Maximus und den Exempla*, Munich 1942, pp. 63 ff.; G. Comes, *Valerio Massimo*, Rome 1950, pp. 21 ff.

147 a

Facta et Dicta Memorabilia, I, 3:3, Ex Epitoma Ianuarii Nepotiani — Kempf

Chaldaeos igitur Cornelius Hispalus urbe expulit et intra decem dies
Italia abire iussit, ne peregrinam scientiam venditarent. Iudaeos quoque, qui Romanis tradere sacra sua conati erant, idem Hispalus urbe
exterminavit arasque privatas e publicis locis abiecit.

1 hippalus N   3 hippalus N

Cornelius Hispalus expelled from Rome the astrologers and ordered
them to leave Italy within ten days and thus not offer for sale their
foreign science. The same Hispalus banished the Jews from Rome,
because they attempted to transmit their sacred rites to the Romans,
and he cast down their private altars from public places.

arasque privatas e publicis locis abiecit: This may allude to a synagogue service.
Yet, Bickerman suggests that it implies real altars used by pagans to honour the
Jewish God; see Bickerman, *op. cit.* (supra, p. 357, n. 2), p. 150.

147 b

Facta et Dicta Memorabilia, I, 3:3, Ex Epitoma Iulii Paridis — Kempf = F 141 R

Cn. Cornelius Hispalus praetor peregrinus M. Popilio Laenate L.
Calpurnio coss. edicto Chaldaeos citra decimum diem abire ex urbe
atque Italia iussit, levibus et ineptis ingeniis fallaci siderum interpre-
tatione quaestuosam mendaciis suis caliginem inicientes. Idem Iudaeos,
5 qui Sabazi Iovis cultu Romanos inficere mores conati erant, repetere
domos suas coegit.

5 sabzi P¹   zabazi P²

Cn. Cornelius Hispalus, *praetor peregrinus* in the year of the consulate
of P. Popilius Laenas and L. Calpurnius, ordered the astrologers
by an edict to leave Rome and Italy within ten days, since by a fallacious interpretation of the stars they perturbed fickle and silly minds,
thereby making profit out of their lies. The same praetor compelled
the Jews, who attempted to infect the Roman customs with the cult
of Jupiter Sabazius, to return to their homes.

Cn. Cornelius Hispalus: The true name of the praetor was Cn. Cornelius Scipio
Hispanus; see *ILS*, No. 6; Appianus, *Libyca*, 80 : 375; see also F. Münzer, PW,
IV, p. 1493; T. R. S. Broughton, *The Magistrates of the Roman Republic*, I, New
York 1951, p. 482.

Valerius Maximus

M. Popilio Laenate L. Calpurnio coss.: They were consuls in 139 B. C. E. Paris gives the praenomen of the second consul as Lucius, but the correct praenomen Gnaeus is confirmed by the fragments of the Livian epitome found in Oxyrhynchus; see *P. Oxy.*, No. 668, l. 191 = R. Cavenaile, *Corpus Papyrorum Latinarum*, Wiesbaden 1958, p. 111. It is also confirmed by the Fasti Antiates; see A. Degrassi, *Inscriptiones Latinae Liberae Rei Publicae*, Florence 1957, p. 17.

Chaldaeos ... abire ... iussit: On the background of the astrologers' expulsion, see F. H. Cramer, *Astrology in Roman Law and Politics*, Philadelphia 1954, p. 58; idem, *Classica et Mediaevalia*, XII (1951), pp. 14 ff.

Sabazi Iovis cultu: Sabazius was a Phrygian deity identified with Dionysus. It seems that the similarity of the name Sabazius to that of the Jewish Sabaoth also induced an identification with the Jewish God; see Schürer, III, pp. 58 f.; Friedländer, *Sittengeschichte*, III, p. 209; F. Cumont, *Les religions orientales dans le paganisme romain* [4], Paris 1929, p. 60; W. Fink, *Der Einfluss der jüdischen Religion auf die griechisch-römische*, Bonn 1932, pp. 40 ff. For the diffusion of Sabaoth, see, e.g., *Oracula Sibyllina*, I, 304, 316; II, 239; K. Preisendanz, *Papyri Graecae Magicae*, Leipzig 1928, IV, ll. 981, 1485, 3052 f.; V, 352. Yet Nilsson explains the connection between the Jewish God and Sabazius by the conception of Sabazius as the God of the Sabbath; see M.P. Nilsson, *Geschichte der griechischen Religion*, II [2], Munich 1961, p. 662. He was anticipated in this explanation by Radin, p. 179; see also K. Latte, *Römische Religionsgeschichte*, Munich 1960, p. 275.

Whatever the derivation, it seems clear that in Valerius Maximus, and probably in his presumable source, Livy, Iupiter Sabazius is meant to be the Jewish God. For a view that Livy, the ultimate source, confused two *senatus consulta*, one dealing with Jews and the other with the votaries of Sabazius, see J. Lewy, *Zion*, VIII (1942–1943), p. 64, n. 215 = *Studies in Jewish Hellenism*, Jerusalem 1960, p. 166.

Cumont has suggested that the people who spread the worship of Iupiter Sabazius were votaries of a syncretistic Jewish-pagan cult; see F. Cumont, *Le Musée Belge*, XIV (1910), pp. 55 ff.; see also R. Reitzenstein, *Die hellenistischen Mysterienreligionen* [3], Leipzig–Berlin 1927, pp. 104 f. This interpretation is, however, somewhat contradicted by the express statement of the two epitomists that they were Jews. Only the appearance of Jupiter and the reference to the *arae* by Nepotianus lend some support to Cumont. The identification of the Jewish God (not a syncretistic deity) with Dionysus is well attested in pagan literature; see Tacitus, *Historiae*, V, 5 (No. 281); Plutarchus, *Quaestiones Convivales*, IV, 6 (No. 258). It is not surprising that the Jewish God was identified with Sabazius, though it may be that the identification with Sabazius was made prior to that with Dionysus. The latter identification was mainly derived from the connection between Dionysus and Sabazius.

repetere domos suas coegit: Many scholars thought that the expulsion was caused by the missionary zeal shown by people in Simon the Hasmonaean's delegation to Rome (I Macc. xiv : 24; xv : 15 ff.); see Schürer, III, p. 59; Friedländer, *loc. cit.*; and see also Leon, pp. 2 ff. Since the Roman consul Lucius is mentioned in I Macc. xv : 16 (his *gentilicium* has not been preserved), it was supposed by Ritschl and scholars who followed him that the consul Lucius Calpurnius Piso is meant, and that the year 139 B.C.E. is the probable date of Simon's embassy; see F. Ritschl, *Opuscula Philologica*, V, Leipzig 1879, pp. 99 ff. However, as we have already mentioned, the praenomen Lucius in Paris is mistaken, and, consequently, the

359

main argument for dating the embassy to 139 B. C. E. is invalidated. It looks as though the consul Lucius in I Macc. xv is Lucius Caecilius Metellus, one of the two consuls of 142 B. C. E. Therefore, the embassy should be dated to that year; cf. O. Roth, *Rom und die Hasmonäer*, Leipzig 1914, p. 37; E. Bickermann, *Gnomon*, VI (1930), p. 359; F. Münzer, *Klio*, XXIV (1931), pp. 333 ff. It also follows that there is no reason to connect the embassy of Simon with the expulsion of 139 B. C. E. Many other Jews found their way to Rome, the centre of the Mediterranean world. For the opinion that the missionary activity was due to Jews from Phrygia, see H. Gressmann, *Jewish Studies in Memory of Israel Abrahams*, New York 1927, pp. 170 ff.; see also H. Janne, *Latomus*, I (1937), pp. 40 ff.; A. D. Nock, apud: V. M. Scramuzza, *The Emperor Claudius*, Cambridge (Mass.) 1940, p. 283, n. 6; J. B. Mc Minn, *JNES*, XV (1956), pp. 211 f.; W.H.C. Frend, *Martyrdom and Persecution in the Early Church*, Oxford 1965, p. 141; Bickerman, *op. cit.* (supra, p. 357, n. 2), pp. 144 ff.; Hengel, pp. 478 f. Alessandrí's arguments against the historicity of the Jews' expulsion from Rome in 139 B.C.E. are not very convincing; see S. Alessandrí, *Studi classici e orientali*, XVII (1968), pp. 187 ff.

LIV. THE ANONYMOUS AUTHOR OF *DE SUBLIMITATE* (PSEUDO-LONGINUS)

First half of the first century C. E.

The author of De Sublimitate *is conspicuous in that he is, it seems, one of the very few Greek writers to quote the Bible before the spread of Christianity in the realm of the Roman Empire.[1] The exact date of the work is still a matter of sharp dispute, though we now find very few scholars who identify the author with the neoplatonic Longinus.[2] Current opinion dates him to the first century C. E., either in the age of Augustus or in the later Julio-Claudian period.[3] This opinion is mainly based on the impression conveyed by the spirit, style and general atmosphere that pervades his work. The fact that it criticizes a book on the same subject by Caecilius of Caleacte, the contemporary of Augustus, also slightly favours the dating of pseudo-Longinus either in the time of the first princeps or in the early years of Tiberius. None of the attempts to identify the author with one of the known literary critics is based on sufficient evidence.[4]*

Pseudo-Longinus quotes the opening section of Genesis as an example of literature that represents the divine nature as it really is — pure and great and undefiled — and he cites it immediately after the Homeric description of Poseidon. Moses the author is designated not by name,

1 The others are, perhaps, Hecataeus, apud: Diodorus, XL, 3:6 (No. 11) and Ocellus Lucanus *De Universi Natura*, 45–46 (No. 40).
2 This was still the view of F. Marx, *Wiener Studien*, XX (1898), pp. 169 ff. Marenghi has recently argued for a later date (late second or early third century C. E.), but whithout committing himself to the third-century Longinus; see G. Marenghi, *Rendiconti dell' Istituto Lombardo*, LXXXIX (1956), pp. 485 ff. For a recent identification with Longinus, see G. Luck, *Arctos*, V (1967), pp. 97 ff.
3 Among recent attempts to date the work in the Principate of Augustus are those of Marin and Goold; see D. Marin, *Studi in Onore di Aristide Calderini e Roberto Paribeni*, I, Milan 1956, pp. 157 ff. Most scholars tend to date it somewhat later in the first century, e. g., Rhys Roberts, Rostagni and Norden; see especially M. J. Boyd, *CQ*, LI (1957), pp. 39 ff. Cf. the discussion on the date by Russell in his commentary, pp. XXII ff.
4 See, e. g., Richards, who saw the literary critic Gnaeus Pompeius as the author of *De Sublimitate*; G. C. Richards, *CQ*, XXXII (1938), pp. 133 f. This view has recently been endorsed by Goold.

but only as the Legislator of the Jews,[5] and he is, incidentally, the only non-Greek writer other than the Latin Cicero (12 : 4) who is even mentioned in De Sublimitate.

The way in which pseudo-Longinus speaks of Moses and, above all, the context of the quotation, imply an even higher regard for the Jewish legislator and for the Bible than that shown by the more sympathetic pagan writers who write about Moses, e.g., Hecataeus, apud: Diodorus, XL, 3 (No. 11) and Strabo, Geographica, *XVI, 2 : 35 f. (No. 115). Some scholars are, therefore, inclined to think that pseudo-Longinus was a Jew,[6] while others have even made a rather unsuccessful attempt to athetize the passage.[7] The Jewishness of the writer is an unnecessary assumption, especially if it amounts to saying that he was a Jew by origin or that he became a proselyte. Moreover, there is some positive though slight proof that he was not a Jew; cf. 12 : 4, where the writer definitely declares himself to be a Greek: ἡμῖν ὡς ″Ελλησιν.[8] This is contrary to the habit of Jews writing Greek, even those who, like Philo, were deeply imbued with Greek culture. What we do know is that we have before us a gentile writer who displays more sympathy for Moses and the Bible than any other pagan writer. This should not surprise us if we bear in mind that the first century C. E. was not only the age of Apion, Chaeremon and Seneca, but was also a century marked by the unprecedented diffusion of Jewish ideas and customs among various classes of society — even if this did not result in proselytism; cf. the commentary to Tacitus,* Annales, *XIII, 32 (No. 293) and Cassius Dio, LXVII, 14 : 1–2 (No. 435). Indeed, it would be the lack of any literary expression of such a phenomenon that would call for an explanation.*

Some scholars — e.g. Reinach — suppose that pseudo-Longinus is indebted for his quotation to Caecilius of Caleacte, who, according to Suda, was a Jew; cf. the commentary to Plutarchus, Vita Ciceronis, *7 : 6*

5 Moses is designated by Quintilian as "Iudaicae superstitionis auctor", without his name having been mentioned; see *Institutio Oratoria*, III, 7:21 (No. 230).

6 E. g., Mommsen, basing himself only on a general feeling, but without advancing any specific arguments; and Sedgwick, who infers this from the style of the writer. Goold expresses himself as follows: "In Longinus we have one who has been brought up under its influence (i. e., of the Graeco-Judaic movement), for Longinus is in some sense a Jew. So was Caecilius of Calacte, and so possibly Theodorus of Gadara"; Goold, *TAPA*, XCII, p. 177. Cf. also Gager, p. 63.

7 Thus it was still argued by Ziegler; see also Mutschmann's reply. Hermann also thinks that it is a Jewish or a Christian interpolation.

8 Less conclusive perhaps is the argument from the use of νὴ Δία (11:2; 33:1; 35:4; 43:1; 44:2), which is even used by Josephus, *Contra Apionem*, I, 255.

The Anonymous Author of De Sublimitate

(*No. 263*). *Others* [9] *suggest Theodorus of Gadara, a view that has not much to commend itself. A citizen of a city that had suffered much from the Hasmonaean conquest and the rule of Herod (cf. Ant., XIII, 356; BJ, I, 86; Ant., XV, 351) would not be especially likely to transmit knowledge of the Bible to Greek readers.* [10]

After all, there is nothing to preclude the assumption that our author acquired his knowledge of the opening section of Genesis directly from Jews and not through the channels of Greek literature. Moreover, it is clear from the way he expresses himself that his acquaintance with Moses was by no means confined to this quotation.

It has been powerfully argued by Norden, and also by Rostagni, that the anonymous philosopher of the forty-fourth chapter should be identified with Philo, but this suggestion still cannot be proved.

Bibliography
Freudenthal, p. 179, note; L. Martens, *De Libello Περὶ "Υψους*, Bonn 1877, pp. 18 f.; Bernays, I, pp. 351 ff.; T. Reinach, *REJ*, XXVI (1893), pp. 43 f.; W. Rhys Roberts, *Classical Review*, XI (1897), pp. 431 ff.; idem, *JHS*, XVII (1897), p. 194; I. C. Vollgraf, *Mnemosyne*, NS XXVI (1898), pp. 123 f.; G. Kaibel, *Hermes*, XXXIV (1899), pp. 129 f.; W. Rhys Roberts, *Longinus on the Sublime*[2], Cambridge 1907, pp. 231 ff.; T. Mommsen, *Römische Geschichte*, Berlin 1909, V, p. 494; Schürer, III, pp. 631 f.; H. Mutschmann, *Tendenz, Aufbau und Quellen der Schrift vom Erhabenen*, Berlin 1913, pp. 109 ff.; K. Ziegler, *Hermes*, L (1915), pp. 572 ff.; H. Mutschmann, *Hermes*, LII (1917), pp. 161 ff.; Friedländer, III, p. 217; O. Immisch, "Bemerkungen zur Schrift vom Erhabnen", *Sitzungsberichte der Heidelberger Akademie der Wissenschaften*, 1924–1925, No. 2, pp. 9 ff.; Aulitzky, PW, XIII, p. 1416; W. Rhys Roberts, *Philological Quarterly* (Iowa), VII (1928), pp. 209 ff.; R. Munz, *Poseidonios und Strabon*, I, Göttingen 1929, pp. 218 ff.; Q. Cataudella, *REG*, XLIII (1930), pp. 165 ff.; H. C. Puech, *Mélanges Bidez*, Brussels 1934, p. 752; J. P. Hoogland, *Longinus "Over het verhevene"*, Groningen 1936, pp. 91 ff.; A. Rostagni, *Anonimo, Del Sublime*, Milan 1947, pp. VII ff.; XXIX ff.; W. B. Sedgwick, *AJP*, LXIX (1948), pp. 197 ff.; E. Norden, "Das Genesiszitat in der Schrift vom Erhabenen", *Abhandlungen der Deutschen Akademie der Wissenschaften zu Berlin*, 1954, Klasse für Sprachen, Literatur und Kunst, No. 1 (1955) = *Kleine Schriften*, pp. 286 ff.; D. Marin, *Studi in onore di Aristide Calderini e Roberto Paribeni*, I, Milan 1956, p. 185; M. J. Boyd, *CQ*, LI (1957) p. 43; G. P. Goold, *TAPA*, XCII (1961), pp. 168 ff.; Longinus, *On the Sublime*, edited with introduction and commentary by D. A. Russell, Oxford 1964, pp. 92 ff.; W. Bühler, *Beiträge zur Erklärung der Schrift vom Erhabenen*, Göttingen 1964, pp. 34 ff.; L. Herrmann, *L'antiquité classique*, XXXIII (1964), p. 84; G. J. de Vries, *Mnemosyne*, Ser. 4, XVIII (1965), pp. 234 f.; G. Kennedy, *AJP*, LXXXVII (1966), p. 358; P. L. Donini, *Rivista di filologia*, XCV (1967), p. 51; Hengel, p. 473; Gager, pp. 56 ff.

9 E.g., Rhys Roberts in his article in the *Philological Quarterly*, and also Rostagni.
10 It should also be added that the great influence Theodorus is presumed to have exerted on Longinus is rather questionable; cf. G. M. A. Grube, *AJP*, LXXX (1959), pp. 337 ff., especially pp. 356 ff.

148

De Sublimitate, IX, 9 — Russell = F57R

Ταύτῃ καὶ ὁ τῶν Ἰουδαίων θεσμοθέτης, οὐχ ὁ τυχὼν ἀνήρ, ἐπειδὴ
τὴν τοῦ θείου δύναμιν κατὰ τὴν ἀξίαν ἐχώρησε κἀξέφηνεν, εὐθὺς ἐν
τῇ εἰσβολῇ γράψας τῶν νόμων «εἶπεν ὁ Θεός», φησί, – τί; «γενέσθω
φῶς, καὶ ἐγένετο· γενέσθω γῆ, καὶ ἐγένετο.»

2 ἐχώρησε] ἐγνώρισε Manutius

A similar effect was achieved by the lawgiver of the Jews—no mean
genius, for he both understood and gave expression to the power
of the divinity as it deserved—when he wrote at the very beginning
of his laws, I quote his words: "God said"—what? "Let there be
light. And there was. Let there be earth. And there was."

(trans. D. A. Russell on p. 93 of his commentary)

Opinions have always differed concerning the correct syntactical understanding
of this sentence and no definite solution has yet been offered. Which is the main
verb of the sentence? How much is to be included in the main clause and in the
subordinate one, respectively? I have included the text as it stands in the edition
of Russell, who implies that φησί is parenthetical and that the main verb is to be
understood from the context; see Russell's commentary, pp. 92 f. Russell also
adopts the view that the ἐπειδή clause is dependent on οὐκ ὁ τυχὼν ἀνήρ. For
other recent solutions, cf. especially Bühler, *op. cit.*; De Vries, *op. cit.*

The whole sentence shows close affinity with *Ant.*, I, 15: ἤδη τοίνυν τοὺς ἐντευξο-
μένους τοῖς βιβλίοις παρακαλῶ τὴν γνώμην θεῷ προσανέχειν καὶ δοκιμάζειν τὸν
ἡμέτερον νομοθέτην, εἰ τήν τε φύσιν ἀξίως αὐτοῦ κατενόησε καὶ τῇ δυνάμει πρε-
πούσας ἀεὶ τὰς πράξεις ἀνατέθεικε πάσης καθαρὸν τὸν περὶ αὐτοῦ φυλάξας λόγον
τῆς παρ' ἄλλοις ἀσχήμονος μυθολογίας.

ταύτῃ καί: Cf. III, 2; IX, 3; XXXI, 1; cf. also Mutschmann, *Hermes*, LII (1917),
pp. 171 f.

θεσμοθέτης: Moses is more commonly described as the Jewish νομοθέτης; see,
e.g., Philo, *Quod Omnis Probus Liber*, 43; *De Aeternitate Mundi*, 19; Josephus,
Ant., I, 15, 18, 23. It is doubtful, however, if it was the author of περὶ Ὕψους who
coined θεσμοθέτης; cf. Philo, *De Migratione Abrahami*, 23: παρέπεται θεσμοθέτῃ
λόγῳ Μωυσῇ ποδηγετοῦντι. (In *Quis Rerum Divinarum Heres*, 167, it is God
who is the θεσμοθέτης.) The emendations of Robortello (θεσμοδότης) and others
are unnecessary.

οὐχ ὁ τυχὼν ἀνήρ: For the same adjective applied to the type of government instituted by Moses (συνεστήσατο [scil. Moses] ἀρχὴν οὐ τὴν τυχοῦσαν), see Strabo,
Geographica, XVI, 2 : 36, p. 761 (No. 115).

ἐχώρησε: χωρεῖν as meaning *animo concipere* is well attested in various writers;
see, e.g., Philo, *De Specialibus Legibus*, I, 44; *Quod Deus Sit Immutabilis*, 77; see
also, e.g., *Sylloge*, No. 814, l.11 f. There is no such usage, however, in the Septuagint. Hence, it should not be connected with a Jewish environment. In any case,

the various emendations suggested for it by Manutius, Rohde, Vollgraff and others are entirely unjustified.

κἀξέφηνεν: Rhys Roberts rightly opposes Ziegler's interpretation of ἐκφαίνειν, in the sense of "to reveal" as an expected explanation from a Jew or Christian; see Rhys Roberts, *Philological Quarterly*, pp. 211 f.; Ziegler, *op. cit.*, p. 584.

εἶπεν ὁ θεός...: This is not an exact quotation of a single verse, but a combination of three verses from Gen. i : 3, 9, 10, which was done to produce a stronger, cumulative effect.

The Septuagint Gen. i : 3 reads as follows: καὶ εἶπεν ὁ θεός Γενηθήτω φῶς. καὶ ἐγένετο φῶς. Gen. i : 9–10 reads: καὶ εἶπεν ὁ θεός Συναχθήτω τὸ ὕδωρ τὸ ὑποκάτω τοῦ οὐρανοῦ εἰς συναγωγὴν μίαν, καὶ ὀφθήτω ἡ ξηρά. καὶ ἐγένετο οὕτως... καὶ ἐκάλεσεν ὁ θεὸς τὴν ξηρὰν γῆν. This procedure is consonant with that applied by the author to the Ilias; cf. the combination of lines from different books of the Ilias in IX, 6.

LV. SENECA THE RHETOR

c. 55 B.C.E. to 40 C.E.

*Seneca the Elder mentions the Jews only incidentally, in order to clarify
the personality of Sosius before whom the rhetor Corvus declaimed at
Rome.*[1]

1 Cf. H. Volkmann, *Zur Rechtsprechung im Principat des Augustus*, Munich
1935, p. 62.

149

Hic est Corvus qui cum temptaret scolam Romae Sosio illi qui Iudaeos subegerat declamavit controversiam de ea quae apud matronas disserebat liberos non esse tollendos et ob hoc accusatur reipublicae laesae.

1 *Sosio* Gronovius   *sunio* codd.   2–3 *dissirebat* C

This Corvus when he conducted a school at Rome declaimed, in the presence of that Sosius who subdued the Jews, a controversia about her who argued in the presence of married women that they should rear no children, and on this account was accused of injuring the commonwealth.   (trans. W. A. Edward, Cambridge 1928)

Sosio illi qui Iudaeos subegerat: Gaius Sosius was one of the chief partisans of Antony; see Fluss, PW, Ser. 2, III, pp. 1176 ff.; R. Syme, *The Roman Revolution*, Oxford 1939, p. 200 He was appointed to the governorship of Syria by Antony, and, after capturing Jerusalem in 37 C.E., he delivered it to Herod, ordering his enemy Antigonus to be beheaded; see *Ant.*, XIV, 176, 447, 468 f.; XX, 246; *BJ*, I, 19, 327, 345 f., 355 ff.; V, 398, 408 f.; VI, 436; Tacitus, *Historiae*, V, 9 (No. 281); see also Otto, pp. 33 f. As a result of his victory, Gaius Sosius earned a triumph; see *CIL*, I, 1², p. 76; see also *CIL*, IX, No. 4855. For a coin from Zacynthus commemorating Sosius' victory over Judaea, see E. A. Sydenham, *The Coinage of the Roman Republic* ², London 1952, p. 199, No. 1272. This coin shows a military trophy, at the base of which two captives are seated: Judaea and Antigonus.

Though a partisan of Antony, Sosius kept his position in Roman society after the victory of Octavian; see Syme, *op. cit.*, p. 349.

LVI. CORNELIUS CELSUS

First half of the first century C.E.

Cornelius Celsus compiled an encyclopaedic work, of which only the medical part has remained. It is noteworthy that among the authorities quoted by this Latin author, who apparently lived in the time of Tiberius,[1] we find a Jewish medical writer, Iudaeus; cf. the commentary. First Celsus states that among the plasters useful for broken heads, there is one that is ascribed to Iudaeus (No. 150). Later in his work he describes a compound suggested by the same Iudaeus.[2]

1 For his time, see Cichorius, pp. 411 ff.; Schanz & Hosius, II, pp. 724 f.
2 For Jewish medicine in ancient times, see S. Krauss, *Talmudische Archäologie*, I, Leipzig 1910, pp. 252 ff.; J. Preuss, *Biblisch-talmudische Medizin*, Berlin 1911; Juster, II, pp. 254 f.; M. Neuburger, *Die Medizin in Flavius Josephus*, Reichenhall 1919, pp. 46 ff. On doctors in Jerusalem society, see Jeremias, p. 19. Josephus stresses the interest that the Essenes took in medicine; see *BJ*, II, 136. From his casual remarks one may also infer that doctors were to be found in different parts of the country, even in distant Galilaea (see *Vita* 404).

150

De Medicina, V, 19:11 — Marx = F142R

At inter ea, quae fracto capiti accommodantur, habent quidam id, quod ad auctorem Iudaeum refertur. Constat ex his: salis P. Ӿ IIII; squamae aeris rubri, aeris combusti, singulorum P. Ӿ XII; Hammon-iaci thymiamatis, turis fuliginis, resinae aridae, singulorum P. Ӿ XVI; 5 resinae Colophoniacae, cerae, sebi vitulini curati, singulorum P. Ӿ XX; aceti sesquicyatho, olei minus cyatho.

Ӿ = Uncia denarii

But among those suitable for broken heads, some include the one which is ascribed to Iudaeus. It is composed of salt 16 grms, red copper scales and calcined copper, 48 grms each, ammoniacum for fumigation, frankincense soot and dried resin, 64 grms each, Colophon resin, wax, and prepared calf's suet, 80 grms each, vinegar 65 c. cm, less than 40 c. cm of oil. (trans. W. G. Spencer, *LCL*)

ad auctorem Iudaeum: Here it is auctor Iudaeus, but in the next passage it is only Iudaeus. There are two ways of interpreting the name: (a) to regard it as a reference to a "Jewish writer", whose name Celsus does not know (this writer might have first been known as "so-and-so the Jew", and later Celsus knew him only as "the Jew"); (b) to assume that Iudaeus is really a proper name for Judas. On Iudaeus as a Jewish proper name, see *CII*, Nos. 710–711. These Delphian inscriptions date from the second century B. C. E. Cf. also the 'Ιουδαῖος of Plutarchus, *De Iside et Osiride*, 31 (No. 259).

We have no means of dating Iudaeus the medical writer. Most of the sources quoted by Celsus are from the early Hellenistic period, though many of them, e.g. Meges of Sidon, also belong to the first century B. C. E. Euelpides, the great oculist, had just died when Celsus wrote his work.

151

De Medicina, V, 22:4 — Marx = F143R

Est Iudaei, in qua sunt calcis partes duae; nitri quam ruberrumi pars tertia, quae urina inpuberis pueri coguntur, donec strigmenti crassitudo sit. Sed subinde is locus, cui id inlinitur, madefaciendus est.

The compound of Iudaeus contains lime two parts; the reddest soda one part, mixed with the urine of a young boy to the consistency of strigil scrapings. But the place on which it is smeared should from time to time be moistened. (trans. W. G. Spencer, *LCL*)

LVII. POMPONIUS MELA

First century (wrote *c.* 40 C.E.)

The following passage well reflects the general character of Mela's De Chorographia, *which partakes of the nature of a* periplus[1] *and pays only scant attention to the inland parts. Thus, Judaea is barely mentioned by Mela, who dwells only on the three coastal towns: Gaza, Ascalon and Jaffa. Moreover, the chorographer's dependence on old Greek sources is seen quite clearly.[2] There is nothing here to show that Mela's description expresses the conditions in the Julio-Claudian age, and it could have been written by a Greek in the time of the Persian Empire.*

1 See Schanz & Hosius, II, p. 654.
2 See F. Gisinger, PW, Suppl. IV, p. 674.

370

(62) Syria late litora tenet, terrasque etiam latius introrsus, aliis aliisque nuncupata nominibus: nam et Coele dicitur et Mesopotamia et Damascene et Adiabene et Babylonia et Iudaea et Commagene et Sophene. (63) Hic Palaestine est qua tangit Arabas, tum Phoenice; et ubi se
5 Ciliciae committit Antiochia, olim ac diu potens, sed cum eam regno Semiramis tenuit longe potentissima. Operibus certe eius insignia multa sunt; duo maxime excellunt; constituta urbs mirae magnitudinis Babylon, ac siccis olim regionibus Euphrates et Tigris immissi. (64) Ceterum in Palaestina est ingens et munita admodum Gaza: sic
10 Persae aerarium vocant, et inde nomen est, quod cum Cambyses armis Aegyptum peteret, huc belli et opes et pecuniam intulerat. Est non minor Ascalon; est Iope ante diluvium ut ferunt condita, ubi Cephea regnasse eo signo accolae adfirmant, quod titulum eius fratrisque Phinei veteres quaedam arae cum religione plurima retinent:
15 quin etiam rei celebratae carminibus ac fabulis, servataeque a Perseo Andromedae clarum vestigium marinae beluae ossa immania ostentant.

3 *Commagene et Sophene* Ranstrand.   *colophone* A   4 *tum*] *cum* A
7 *excellent* A   12 ⟨*as*⟩ *calo⟨n⟩*A (litteras in ras. add. A³) / ⟨*est i*⟩*ope* A
  (litteras in ras. add. A³)   16 *marinae* A²   *matrinae* A¹

(62) Syria extends widely along the coasts, and even more widely over the lands of the interior, and she is called by many different names. Thus she is named Coele-Syria and Mesopotamia and Damascene and Adiabene and Babylonia and Judaea and Commagene and Sophene. (63) There is situated Palestine, where Syria touches the Arabs, then Phoenicia, and Antiochia, where Syria borders on Cilicia. Syria had once been and for a long time powerful, but above all she was a great power in the reign of Semiramis. Among the achievements of that queen there are many that are distinguished. Two of them excel conspicuously, namely, the founding of Babylon, a city of admirable size, and the irrigation of the once-dry regions by the Euphrates and the Tigris. (64) In Palestine there is Gaza, an immense and very fortified city; that is the Persian name for treasury. The name derives from the fact that when Cambyses made preparations for the invasion of Egypt he concentrated there the treasure and money. Ascalon is not smaller. There is also Jope, founded, as is said, before the Flood. Its inhabitants base their view that Cepheus was king there on the fact that some ancient altars retain, with utmost reverence, his and his brother's

titles. Moreover, the enormous bones of the sea-monster constitute a manifest indication of the deliverance of Andromeda by Perseus, a subject celebrated in poetry and myth.

62 *Syria . . . nam et Coele dicitur*: On the history of Coele-Syria, see the commentary to Theophrastus, *Historia Plantarum*, II, 6 : 2, 5, 8 (No. 6).

et Mesopotamia: Mela, depending on his old sources, includes Mesopotamia in Syria, thus using the name's original meaning from the classical period (Syria = Assyria); see, e.g., Herodotus, VII, 63; T. Nöldeke, *Hermes*, V (1871), p. 443 ff.; E. Schwartz, *Philologus*, LXXXVI, pp. 373 ff. = *Gesammelte Schriften*, II, Berlin 1956, pp. 240 ff. We also find this use in other Latin writers; see Nöldeke, *op. cit.*, p. 452.

Iudaea: It is uncertain whether Judaea is used here in the broad sense of the Roman province Judaea, or if it covers only Judaea proper. Since Mela lists Palaestine separately, the second possibility is more probable.

63 *Palaestine*: It seems that Palaestine refers to the coastal strip from Mt. Carmel to Egypt.

64 *Gaza . . . Ascalon*: Both were important cities in Mela's time; see Schürer, II, pp. 115, 123. However, in view of the general character of the passage, it is doubtful whether even here Mela refers to contemporary conditions. The etymology that he gives for Gaza has no basis whatsoever.

Iope ante diluvium . . . condita: Cf. the commentary to Plinius, *Naturalis Historia*, V, 69 (No. 204).

ubi Cephea regnasse . . . servataeque a Perseo Andromedae clarum vestigium marinae beluae ossa immania ostentant: Cf. Plinius, *Naturalis Historia*, V, 69.

LVIII. SEXTIUS NIGER

First half of the first century C.E.

Although Dioscorides criticizes him strongly in the introduction to his De Materia Medica, *Niger seems to have been one of his main sources. Pliny also used Niger's work.*[1]

---

1 See M. Wellmann, *Hermes*, XXIV (1889), pp. 530 ff.

373

apud: Dioscorides, *De Materia Medica*, I, Praefatio, 3 — Wellmann

Ὁ γοῦν διαπρεπὴς δοκῶν εἶναι ἐν αὐτοῖς Νίγερ τὸ Εὐφόρβιόν φησιν ὀπὸν εἶναι χαμελαίας γεννωμένης ἐν Ἰταλίᾳ καὶ τὸ ἀνδρόσαιμον ταὐτὸ ὑπάρχειν ὑπερικῷ, ἀλόην δὲ ὀρυκτὴν ἐν Ἰουδαίᾳ γεννᾶσθαι, καὶ ἄλλα τούτοις ὅμοια πλεῖστα παρὰ τὴν ἐνάργειαν ἐκτίθεται ψευδῶς, ἅπερ
5 ἐστὶ τεκμήρια οὐκ αὐτοψίας ἀλλὰ τῆς ἐκ παρακουσμάτων ἱστορίας.

1 ἐν αὐτοῖς δοκῶν HDa / ἐφόρβιον F   2 χαμαιλέας FDa / γενομένης Da / Ἰταλίᾳ] Γαλατίᾳ? Wellmann   3 ὑπερικῷ ὑπάρχειν HDa / δὲ] τε HDa   3–4 ἄλλα πλεῖστα ὅμοια τούτοις HDa / ἐνάργειαν] ἀλήθειαν HDa

Indeed Niger, who seems to be the most conspicuous among them, says that the spurge is a juice of spurge-olive growing in Italy, and that St. John's wort is identical with hypericum, and that dug-out aloes is produced in Judaea, and he sets forth falsely many things like those contrary to manifest facts, which is evidence not of autopsy but of information based on false stories.

ἀλόην δὲ ὀρυκτὴν ἐν Ἰουδαίᾳ: On the aloe of Judaea, see Plinius, *Naturalis Historia*, XXVII, 15 (No. 219).

LIX. PHILIP OF THESSALONICA

First half of the first century C.E.

The following epigram becomes linked to Jewish history only through the brilliant emendation and interpretation of Cichorius (pp. 351 ff.). The general meaning of the epigram is fairly clear. Some piece of artistic tapestry depicting the lands of the Roman Empire and the sea has been presented to a reigning Roman Emperor. The embroidery was the gift of a queen (ἦν γὰρ ἀνάσσης δῶρα), and it seems that the name of the queen lurks somehow in the word καρπος of the manuscript (l. 3), which Cichorius emended into Κύπρος. Now, Queen Cyprus, a grand-daughter of Herod and the wife of Agrippa I, played a prominent role in the life of her husband. Cichorius has even made an attempt, on the basis of the narrative of Josephus, to connect the gift with a known event, namely, the mission of Agrippa's freedman Fortunatus in 39 C.E.[1]

1 Cf. Ant., XVIII, 247. This interpretation of the epigram has also been accepted by Beckby and by Page; see H. Beckby, Anthologia Graeca, III, Munich 1958, p. 810; A. S. F. Gow & D. L. Page, The Greek Anthology — The Garland of Philip, II, Cambridge 1968, p. 334. The date of The Garland of Philip is debatable. Cichorius thinks that it should be dated to the reign of Gaius, as do Wifstrand and Page; see A. Wifstrand, Gnomon, XIII (1937), p. 452; Gow & Page, loc. cit. Müller, on the other hand, thinks that c. 53 C.E. should be taken as terminus post quem for its publication; see K. Müller, Die Epigramme des Antiphilos von Byzanz, Berlin 1935, pp. 14 ff. Small and Cameron agree with Müller; see S. G. P. Small, YCS, XII (1951), p. 71; A. Cameron, Greek, Roman and Byzantine Studies, IX (1968), p. 323, n. 2.

From Herodotus to Plutarch

154

Anthologia Graeca, IX, 778 = Page, in: A.S.F. Gow & D.L. Page, *The Greek Anthology — The Garland of Philip*, I, Cambridge 1968, p. 300 No. VI

Γαῖαν τὴν φερέκαρπον ὅσην ἔζωκε περίχθων
ὠκεανὸς μεγάλῳ Καίσαρι πειθομένην
καὶ γλαυκήν με θάλασσαν ἀπηκριβώσατο Κύπρος
κερκίσιν ἱστοπόνοις πάντ᾽ ἀπομαξαμένη·
5 Καίσαρι δ᾽ εὐξείνῳ χάρις ἤλθομεν, ἣν γὰρ ἀνάσσης
δῶρα φέρειν τὰ θεοῖς καὶ πρὶν ὀφειλόμενα.

3 Κύπρος Cichorius   καρπος P   5 δ᾽ εὐξείνῳ Page   δ᾽ ακεινου P

Modelling all with shuttle labouring on the loom, Kypros made me, a perfect copy of the harvest-bearing earth, all that the land-encircling ocean girdles, obedient to great Caesar, and the gray sea too. We have come as a grateful return for Caesar's hospitality; it was a queen's duty to bring gifts so long due to the gods.

(trans. D. L. Page, Cambridge 1968)

LX. SCRIBONIUS LARGUS

First century C.E.

The pharmacological work of Scribonius Largus contains two allusions to the use of Judaean bitumen (i. e. the asphalt of the Dead Sea): for healing recent wounds and for mending broken bones. The medical qualities of the Dead Sea asphalt are also mentioned in BJ, IV, 481: καὶ χρήσιμος...πρὸς ἄκεσιν σωμάτων· εἰς πολλὰ γοῦν τῶν φαρμάκων παραμίσγεται; and in Galenus, De Simplicium Medicamentorum Temperamentis ac Facultatibus, XI, 2 : 10 (No. 386). For the excellence of the Judaean asphalt, see also Galenus, De Antidotis, I, 12 (No. 392). For the use of asphalt for general medical purposes, see, e.g., Aretaeus (ed. Hude²), Berlin 1958, VI, 2 : 6, p. 122; VII, 5 : 12, p. 158.

155

Conpositiones, 207 — Helmreich

Emplastrum nigrum eius ⟨scil. Glyconis chirurgi⟩, barbara dicitur, facit ad omne recens vulnus et contusum; hoc plerique in gladiatoribus utuntur: picis Bruttiae p. ℥ C, resinae frictae p. ℥ C, bituminis Iudaici p. ℥ C, cerae p. ℥ C.

His [scil. Glyco's] black plaster, which is called "barbara", is useful for every fresh wound and bruise. Most use it in the healing of gladiators. It is composed of Bruttian pitch, 400 gm; of rubbed resin, 400 gm, of Jewish bitumen, 400 gm; of wax, 400 gm.

156

Conpositiones, 209 — Helmreich

Emplastrum nigrum Aristi chirurgi facit ad omne recens vulnus mirifice... Habet autem haec: spumae argenteae p. ℥ CC, alnminis fissi p. ℥ XXX, picis Hispanae p. ℥ C, bituminis Iudaici p. ℥ C, propolis p. ℥ XXX, aeruginis p. ℥ X, cerae p. ℥ C, ammoniaci gut-
5 tae p. ℥ XXIIII, terebinthinae p. ℥ L, olei veteris sextarios quattuor.

The black plaster of Aristus the surgeon is wonderfully useful for every fresh wound... It is composed of the following materials: silver spume, 800 gm; cleft alum, 120 gm; Spanish pitch, 400 gm; Jewish bitumen, 400 gm; propolis, 120 gm; verdigris, 40 gm; wax, 400 gm; Ammoniac gum, 96 gm; turpentine gum, 200 gm; old oil, 4 sextarii.

LXI. PTOLEMY OF MENDES

Date unknown

Ptolemy was an Egyptian priest from Mendes, who composed an Egyptian Chronology in Greek. His date is unknown, but he must have lived before Apion, since that writer refers to him.

157a

apud: Tatianus, *Oratio ad Graecos*, XXXVIII — Schwartz = F46R = *F. Gr. Hist.*,
III, C611, T1a+F1a

Αἰγυπτίων δέ εἰσιν ἀκριβεῖς χρόνων ἀναγραφαί, καὶ τῶν κατ' αὐτοὺς
γραμμάτων ἑρμηνεύς ἐστι Πτολεμαῖος, οὐχ ὁ βασιλεύς, ἱερεὺς δὲ
Μένδητος. οὗτος τὰς τῶν βασιλέων πράξεις ἐκτιθέμενος κατ' Ἄμωσιν
Αἰγύπτου βασιλέα γεγονέναι Ἰουδαίοις φησὶ τὴν ἐξ Αἰγύπτου πορείαν
5 εἰς ἅπερ ἤθελον χωρία, Μωσέως ἡγουμένου. λέγει δὲ οὕτως· «ὁ δὲ
Ἄμωσις ἐγένετο κατ' Ἴναχον βασιλέα.»

1 ἀκριβεῖς Eus.   αἱ ἐπ' ἀκριβεῖς MP   αἱ ἐπακριβεῖς V   2 γραμμάτων
Eus.   πραγμάτων MPV / ἐστι om. Eus. / Πτολεμαῖος om. V   2–3 ἐκ
μένδητος Eus., ND   4 Αἰγύπτου βασιλέα Eus.   βασιλέα αἰγύπτου MPV /
γεγονέναι φησὶν Ἰουδαίοις Schwartz   ἰουδαίους P   5 ἤθελον Eus.   ἠλ-
θον MPV / Μωσέως Eus.   μωϋσέως MP   μωϋσεως V   6 κατατίναχον V
τὸν ἴναχον Eus., J / τὸν βασιλέα Eus.

Of the Egyptians also there are accurate chronicles. Ptolemy, not
the king, but a priest of Mendes, is the interpreter of their affairs. The
writer, narrating the acts of the kings, says that the departure of the
Jews from Egypt to the places whither they went occurred in the time
of king Amosis, under the leadership of Moses. He thus speaks:
"Amosis lived in the time of king Inachus."

(trans. B. P. Pratten, Edinburgh 1867)

Ἄμωσιν: This Amosis should be identified with Ahmose I, who was celebrated as
Egypt's redeemer from the Hyksos and who founded the eighteenth dynasty; see
Pietschmann, PW, I, pp. 1744 f.; A. Gardiner, *Egypt of the Pharaohs*, Oxford 1961,
pp. 168 f.
κατ' Ἴναχον βασιλέα: Inachus, the father of Phoroneus, is considered the first
king of Argos; see Acusilaus, in: *F. Gr. Hist.*, I, 2, F23c; Castor, *ibid.*, II, B
250, F 3. On Inachus as Moses' contemporary, apart from the account of Apion,
who is dependent on Ptolemy, see Tertullianus, *Apologeticus*, 19 : 3. For the
implication that the Exodus took place at the time of Apis, the grandson of Inachus,
see Polemon, apud: Eusebius, *Praeparatio Evangelica*, X, 10 : 15 (No. 29). From
Porphyry (No. 460) it emerges that Moses preceded Inachus.

157b

apud: Clemens Alexandrinus, *Stromata*, I, 21:101:5 — Stählin & Früchtel = *F. Gr. Hist.*,
III, C611, T1b+F1b

Ὁ δὲ Πτολεμαῖος οὗτος ἱερεὺς μὲν ἦν, τὰς δὲ τῶν Αἰγυπτίων βασιλέων
πράξεις ἐν τρισὶν ὅλαις ἐκθέμενος βίβλοις κατὰ Ἄμωσίν φησιν Αἰγύπτου

2 ἐκτιθέμενος Tatianus

Ptolemy of Mendes

βασιλέα Μωυσέως ἡγουμένου γεγονέναι Ἰουδαίοις τὴν ἐξ Αἰγύπτου
πορείαν, ἐξ ὧν συνῶπται κατὰ Ἴναχον ἠκμακέναι τὸν Μωσέα.

This Ptolemy was a priest, and narrating the acts of the Egyptian kings
in three books he says that the departure of the Jews from Egypt
occurred in the time of Amosis under the leadership of Moyses.
From which it has been seen that Moses flourished in the time of
Inachus.

LXII. LYSIMACHUS

Date unknown

Next to Apion, Lysimachus was the Graeco-Egyptian writer who displayed the most marked anti-Semitic tendencies. It seems that he lived before Apion, perhaps in the second or the first century B.C.E. Lysimachus did not compose a special book about the Jews, but deals with them only in his Aegyptiaca. *According to him, the ancestors of the Jews were not only disease-ridden beggars, distinguished by deeds of both murder and sacrilege, but they were also so shameless that the very name of their city openly declared their sacrilegious nature.*

The different name of the King, Bocchoris, and the absence of all mention of the Hyksos and of the Egyptian origins of Moses prove that the historical construction of Lysimachus is founded on a different version of the rise of the Jewish nation than that of Manetho, or, for that matter, of Chaeremon. As far as we can judge from the fragments preserved in Josephus, Lysimachus does not refer to the rule of the Jewish ancestors in Egypt itself or to the alleged crimes committed by them there, but concentrates on the age of violence supposedly instituted by them in Judaea. We have no sure basis for assessing to what extent Apion is indebted to Lysimachus or whether he merely draws upon the same stream of Graeco-Egyptian tradition. For the dependence of Tacitus on the same tradition, cf. the commentary to No. 281.

It cannot be determined whether Lysimachus the anti-Semitic writer is the same as Lysimachus the Greek mythographer of Alexandria.[1]

---

1 See G. [W.] Radtke, "De Lysimacho Alexandrino", Ph. D. Thesis, Strasbourg 1893, p. 101; Gudeman, PW, XIV, pp. 32f.; Fraser, II, p. 1092, n. 475.

Aegyptiaca, apud: Josephus, *Contra Apionem*, I, 304–311 — Niese = F59R = *F. Gr. Hist.*, III,
C621, T1a + F1 = Reinach (Budé), pp. 56 f.

(304) Ἐπεισάξω δὲ τούτοις Λυσίμαχον εἰληφότα μὲν τὴν αὐτὴν
τοῖς προειρημένοις ὑπόθεσιν τοῦ ψεύσματος περὶ τῶν λεπρῶν καὶ
λελωβημένων, ὑπερπεπαικότα δὲ τὴν ἐκείνων ἀπιθανότητα τοῖς
πλάσμασι, δῆλος συντεθεικὼς κατὰ πολλὴν ἀπέχθειαν· *(305)* λέγει
5 γὰρ ἐπὶ Βοκχόρεως τοῦ Αἰγυπτίων βασιλέως τὸν λαὸν τῶν Ἰουδαίων λεπροὺς ὄντας καὶ ψωροὺς καὶ ἄλλα νοσήματά τινα ἔχοντας
εἰς τὰ ἱερὰ καταφεύγοντας μεταιτεῖν τροφήν. παμπόλλων δὲ ἀνθρώπων νοσηλείᾳ περιπεσόντων ἀκαρπίαν ἐν τῇ Αἰγύπτῳ γενέσθαι.
(306) Βόκχοριν δὲ τὸν τῶν Αἰγυπτίων βασιλέα εἰς Ἄμμωνος πέμψαι
10 περὶ τῆς ἀκαρπίας τοὺς μαντευσομένους, τὸν θεὸν δὲ ἐρεῖν τὰ ἱερὰ
καθᾶραι ἀπ᾽ ἀνθρώπων ἀνάγνων καὶ δυσσεβῶν, ἐκβάλλοντα αὐτοὺς
ἐκ τῶν ἱερῶν εἰς τόπους ἐρήμους, τοὺς δὲ ψωροὺς καὶ λεπροὺς βυθίσαι,
ὡς τοῦ ἡλίου ἀγανακτοῦντος ἐπὶ τῇ τούτων ζωῇ, καὶ τὰ ἱερὰ ἁγνίσαι
καὶ οὕτω τὴν γῆν καρποφορήσειν. *(307)* τὸν δὲ Βόκχοριν τοὺς χρησμοὺς
15 λαβόντα τούς τε ἱερεῖς καὶ ἐπιβωμίτας προσκαλεσάμενον κελεῦσαι
ἐπιλογὴν ποιησαμένους τῶν ἀκαθάρτων τοῖς στρατιώταις τούτους
παραδοῦναι κατάξειν αὐτοὺς εἰς τὴν ἔρημον, τοὺς δὲ λεπροὺς εἰς
μολιβδίνους χάρτας ἐνδῆσαι, ἵνα καθῶσιν εἰς τὸ πέλαγος. *(308)* βυ-
θισθέντων δὲ τῶν λεπρῶν καὶ ψωρῶν τοὺς ἄλλους συναθροισθέντας
20 εἰς τόπους ἐρήμους ἐκτεθῆναι ἐπ᾽ ἀπωλείᾳ, συναχθέντας δὲ βουλεύσασθαι
περὶ αὐτῶν, νυκτὸς δὲ ἐπιγενομένης πῦρ καὶ λύχνους καύσαντας φυλάττειν ἑαυτοὺς τήν τ᾽ ἐπιοῦσαν νύκτα νηστεύσαντας ἱλάσκεσθαι τοὺς θεοὺς
περὶ τοῦ σῶσαι αὐτούς. *(309)* τῇ δ᾽ ἐπιούσῃ ἡμέρᾳ Μωσῆν τινα
συμβουλεῦσαι αὐτοῖς παραβαλλομένους μίαν ὁδὸν τέμνειν ἄχρι ἂν
25 ὅτου ἔλθωσιν εἰς τόπους οἰκουμένους, παρακελεύσασθαί τε αὐτοῖς
μήτε ἀνθρώπων τινὶ εὐνοήσειν μήτε ἄριστα συμβουλεύσειν ἀλλὰ τὰ
χείρονα θεῶν τε ναοὺς καὶ βωμούς, οἷς ἂν περιτύχωσιν, ἀνατρέπειν.
(310) συναινεσάντων δὲ τῶν ἄλλων τὰ δοχθέντα ποιοῦντας διὰ τῆς
ἐρήμου πορεύεσθαι, ἱκανῶς δὲ ὀχληθέντας ἐλθεῖν εἰς τὴν οἰκουμένην

5 Βοκχόρεως ed. pr.   βοχχόρεως L   bochore Lat.   6 ἔχοντας ed. pr.
ἐχόντων L   7 καταφυγόντας Herwerden   9 Βόκχοριν ed. pr.   βόχ-
χοριν L /   Ἄμμωνος Bekker   ἄμμωνα L   10 ἐρεῖν] εἰπεῖν ed. pr.
ἀνελεῖν Niese   11 ἐκβαλόντα ed. pr.   17 κατάξειν ... ἔρημον om. Lat.
κατάγειν? Reinach   κατάξουσιν G. Giangrande, *CQ*, LVI 1962, p. 115
18 χάρτας] λάρνακας Naber / ἐνδῆσαι Thackeray   ἐνδήσαντας L / καθ-
εθῶσιν Niese   mergerentur Lat.   24 παραβαλλομένους ed. pr.   παραβαλ-
λομένοις L   25 ὅτου om. ed. pr.   26 εὐνοῆσαι et συμβουλεῦσαι
Niese / μηδὲ Bekker / τἄριστα Herwerden

383

30 χώραν καὶ τούς τε ἀνθρώπους ὑβρίζοντας καὶ τὰ ἱερὰ συλῶντας καὶ
ἐμπρήσαντας ἐλθεῖν εἰς τὴν νῦν Ἰουδαίαν προσαγορευομένην, κτίσαντας
δὲ πόλιν ἐνταῦθα κατοικεῖν. *(311)* τὸ δὲ ἄστυ τοῦτο Ἱερόσυλα ἀπὸ τῆς
ἐκείνων διαθέσεως ὠνομάσθαι. ὕστερον δ᾽ αὐτοὺς ἐπικρατήσαντας χρόνῳ
διαλλάξαι τὴν ὀνομασίαν πρὸς τὸ ⟨μὴ⟩ ὀνειδίζεσθαι καὶ τήν τε πόλιν
35 Ἱεροσόλυμα καὶ αὐτοὺς Ἱεροσολυμίτας προσαγορεύεσθαι.

32 Ἱερόσυλα ed. pr.   ἱεροσόλυμα L   34 ⟨μὴ⟩ ὀνειδίζεσθαι Hudson
    35 Ἱεροσολυμίτας Niese   ἱεροσολύμους L   hierosolymitae Lat.

(304) I will next introduce Lysimachus. He brings up the same theme
as the writers just mentioned, the mendacious story of the lepers and
cripples, but surpasses both in the incredibility of his fictions, obviously composed with bitter animus. (305) His account is this: In
the reign of Bocchoris, king of Egypt, the Jewish people, who were
afflicted with leprosy, scurvy, and other maladies, took refuge in
the temples and lived a mendicant existence. The victims of disease
being very numerous, a dearth ensued throughout Egypt. (306) King
Bocchoris thereupon sent to consult the oracle of Ammon about the
failure of the crops. The god told him to purge the temples of impure
and impious persons, to drive them out of these sanctuaries into the
wilderness, to drown those afflicted with leprosy and scurvy, as the
sun was indignant that such persons should live, and to purify the
temples; then the land would yield her increase. (307) On receiving
these oracular instructions, Bocchoris summoned the priests and
servitors at the altars, and ordered them to draw up a list of the
unclean persons and to deliver them into military charge to be conducted into the wilderness, and to pack the lepers into sheets of lead
and sink them in the ocean. (308) The lepers and victims of scurvy
having been drowned, the others were collected and exposed in the
desert to perish. There they assembled and deliberated on their
situation. At nightfall they lit up a bonfire and torches, and mounted
guard, and on the following night kept a fast and implored the gods
to save them. (309) On the next day a certain Moses advised them to
take their courage in their hands and make a straight track until they
reached inhabited country, instructing them to show goodwill to
no man, to offer not the best but the worst advice, and to overthrow
any temples and altars of the gods which they found. (310) The rest
assenting, they proceeded to put these decisions into practice. They
traversed the desert, and after great hardships reached inhabited
country: there they maltreated the population, and plundered and set
fire to the temples, until they came to the country now called Judaea,

where they built a city in which they settled. (311) This town was
called Hierosyla because of their sacrilegious propensities. At a later
date, when they had risen to power, they altered the name, to avoid
the disgraceful imputation, and called the city Hierosolyma and
themselves Hierosolymites.   (trans. H. St. J. Thackeray, *LCL*)

304 ἐπεισάξω... Λυσίμαχον: Although Josephus deals with Chaeremon before
Lysimachus, we should not necessarily infer that Chaeremon's work preceded that
of Lysimachus. This order may merely be due to the great similarity between the
versions of Chaeremon and Manetho.

ὑπερπεπαικότα δὲ τὴν ἐκείνων ἀπιθανότητα...: Lysimachus' version of Jewish
origins as reflected by Josephus is more anti-Semitic in detail than that of the two
previously-mentioned authors, and it justifies the criticism of the Jewish apologist,
δῆλος συντεθεικὼς κατὰ πολλὴν ἀπέχθειαν. We must disagree with Gudeman's
too-favourable view of Lysimachus' Jewish chapters; see Gudeman, *op. cit.*
(supra, p. 382), p. 35.

305 ἐπὶ Βοκχόρεως: By ascribing the story of the Jews' expulsion to a Pharaoh
of the twenty-fourth dynasty, Lysimachus dates it much later than Manetho
or Chaeremon. Tacitus directly connects Bocchoris with the story of the Exodus;
see Tacitus, *Historiae*, V, 3 (No. 281). Bocchoris ranks very high among the
Pharaohs in the Greek tradition; see, e.g., Diodorus, I, 94 : 5; Plutarchus,
Demetrius, 27. For other Greek sources, see Sethe, PW, III, pp. 666 f. On
Bocchoris' reign, see J. H. Breasted, *A History of Egypt*[2], London 1945, pp.
546 f., p. 550; Ed. Meyer, *Geschichte des Altertums*, Vol. II, Part 2 [2], Stuttgart–
Berlin 1931, pp. 56 f.; Vol. III [2], 1937, pp. 41 f. Bocchoris is the only Pharaoh of
the twenty-fourth dynasty who is known from the fragments of Manetho. Bocchoris' connection with the Jews may be accounted for by the Egyptian tradition that
dated the Prophecy of the Lamb — i.e. the prophecy about the rule of foreigners
over Egypt — to his reign; see H. Gressmann, *Altorientalische Texte zum alten
Testament* [2], Berlin–Leipzig 1926, pp. 48 f.; see also U. Wilcken, *Hermes*, XL
(1905), pp. 558 f.

τὸν λαὸν τῶν Ἰουδαίων: Like Chaeremon, Lysimachus already uses the name
Jews when he refers to the sojourn in Egypt.

μεταιτεῖν τροφήν: Perhaps this emphasis on the needy condition of the Jews
should be connected with the recurring theme of the Jew as a beggar; cf. *De Motu
Circulari*, II, 1 : 91 (No. 333); Martialis, *Epigrammata*, XII, 57 : 13 (No. 246);
Iuvenalis, *Saturae*, VI, 542 ff. (No. 299); and, perhaps, Artemidorus, *Onirocritica*,
III, 53 (No. 395).

παμπόλλων... νοσηλείᾳ περιπεσόντων ἀκαρπίαν... γενέσθαι: It seems that here
Lysimachus adduces a natural explanation for the dearth, namely, a shortage of
workers resulting from the disease. However, we see from what follows that the
source underlying his account contained another explanation, which attributed
the dearth to the pollution of the temples by impure and impious persons. The
removal of these persons and the purification of the temples would cause the
earth to yield fruit.

306 ἀπ᾽ ἀνθρώπων ἀνάγνων καὶ δυσσεβῶν... τοὺς δὲ ψωροὺς καὶ λεπροὺς βυθίσαι:
Lysimachus distinguishes here between those who are impure and impious and
those afflicted with leprosy and scurvy. The god ordered that the former should be

banished to the wilderness, and that the latter should be drowned. Since the king executed the order, the Jews must be identified with the first category, which clearly emerges from the following narrative. On the other hand, this not only contradicts Apion (No. 165) and Tacitus, *Historiae*, V, 3, (No. 281), both of whom identified the Jews with the lepers, but even Lysimachus himself, who explicitly asserted that the Jews were afflicted with leprosy. Perhaps we should blame the way in which the account has been transmitted for this apparent confusion. We may only suggest that Lysimachus grouped immoral persons and physically polluted persons with lepers from the outset of his work. He may even have stressed the immorality of the Jews at the same time. It is worthwhile citing a passage from Manetho, apud: Josephus, *Contra Apionem*, I, 233 (No. 21): καθαρὰν ἀπό τε λεπρῶν καὶ τῶν ἄλλων μιαρῶν ἀνθρώπων τὴν χώραν ἅπασαν ποιήσειεν. μιαρός, as is well known, has a connotation of moral baseness.

ὡς τοῦ ἡλίου ἀγανακτοῦντος: Cf. Clemens Alexandrinus, *Stromata*, V, 7 : 43 : 2: τὰς λοιμικὰς νόσους ἡλίῳ ἀνατιθέασιν; cf. also Herodotus (I, 138), who gives the Persian view of the connection between leprosy and the Sun's wrath.

308 πῦρ καὶ λύχνους καύσαντας ... νηστεύσαντας: Presumably Lysimachus is concerned with the origin of the Sabbath. For the kindling of the lights as a striking feature of the Jewish Sabbath in the eyes of pagan writers, see Persius, *Saturae*, V, 180 f. (No. 190); see also Seneca, *Epistulae Morales*, XCV, 47 (No. 188).

309 Μωσῆν τινα: According to Lysimachus, Moses is one of the exiles. While this agrees with Tacitus, *Historiae*, V, 3 (No. 281), the view that Moses was an Egyptian priest, which is found in Manetho and Chaeremon, is missing in both Lysimachus and Tacitus.

310 καὶ τὰ ἱερὰ συλῶντας καὶ ἐμπρήσαντας: The tale of atrocities committed by Jews, especially in regard to pagan temples, echoes the indignation that arose as a consequence of the religious policy adopted by the Hasmonaean conquerors of Palestine.

311 Ἱερόσυλα ἀπὸ τῆς ἐκείνων διαθέσεως ὠνομάσθαι: An example of the etymology of a name of a nation, ἀπὸ διαθέσεως.

159

apud: Josephus, *Contra Apionem*, II, 16 — Niese = *F. Gr. Hist.*, III, C621, F2 = Reinach
(Budé), p. 61

Μανεθὼς μὲν γὰρ κατὰ τὴν Τεθμώσιος βασιλείαν ἀπαλλαγῆναί φησιν ἐξ Αἰγύπτου τοὺς Ἰουδαίους πρὸ ἐτῶν τριακοσίων ἐνενηκοντατριῶν τῆς εἰς Ἄργος Δαναοῦ φυγῆς, Λυσίμαχος δὲ κατὰ Βόκχοριν τὸν βασιλέα, τουτέστι πρὸ ἐτῶν χιλίων ἑπτακοσίων, Μόλων ⟨No. 47⟩
5 δὲ καὶ ἄλλοι τινὲς ὡς αὐτοῖς ἔδοξεν.

3 *bochore* Lat.

Well, Manetho states that the departure of the Jews from Egypt occurred in the reign of Tethmosis, 393 years before the flight of

Lysimachus

Danaus to Argos; Lysimachus says, under King Bocchoris, that is to say, 1700 years ago; Molon and others fix a date to suit themselves.

(trans. H. St. J. Thackeray, *LCL*)

Λυσίμαχος...: That Lysimachus precedes Molon does not prove that he published his work before Molon, since the order is reversed in *Contra Apionem*, II, 145 (No. 161). Molon again follows Lysimachus in *Contra Apionem*, II, 236 (No. 162).

160

apud: Josephus, *Contra Apionem*, II, 20 — Niese = F 59b R = *F. Gr. Hist.*, III, C 621, F 3 = Reinach, (Budé), p. 62

Τὸν δὲ ἀριθμὸν τῶν ἐλαθέντων τὸν αὐτὸν Λυσιμάχῳ σχεδιάσας ⟨scil. ᾿Απίων⟩ ⟨No. 165⟩, ἕνδεκα γὰρ αὐτοὺς εἶναί φησι μυριάδας...

After stating that the fugitives numbered 110,000, in which imaginary figure he agrees with Lysimachus... (trans. H. St. J. Thackeray, *LCL*)

161

apud: Josephus, *Contra Apionem*, II, 145 — Niese = *F. Gr. Hist.*, III, C 621, F 4 = Reinach (Budé), p. 82 f.

᾿Επεὶ δὲ καὶ ᾿Απολλώνιος ὁ Μόλων ⟨No. 49⟩ καὶ Λυσίμαχος καί τινες ἄλλοι τὰ μὲν ὑπ᾿ ἀγνοίας, τὸ πλεῖστον δὲ κατὰ δυσμένειαν περί τε τοῦ νομοθετήσαντος ἡμῖν Μωσέως καὶ περὶ τῶν νόμων πεποίηνται λόγους οὔτε δικαίους οὔτε ἀληθεῖς, τὸν μὲν ὡς γόητα καὶ ἀπατεῶνα διαβάλλοντες, τοὺς νόμους δὲ κακίας ἡμῖν καὶ οὐδεμιᾶς ἀρετῆς φάσκοντες εἶναι διδασκάλους, βούλομαι συντόμως καὶ περὶ τῆς ὅλης ἡμῶν καταστάσεως τοῦ πολιτεύματος... εἰπεῖν.

1 ἐπεὶ δὲ Dindorf   ἐπειδὴ L   quoniam vero Lat.
3 moyse Lat. Μωϋσέως Reinach

Seeing, however, that Apollonius Molon, Lysimachus, and others, partly from ignorance, mainly from ill will, have made reflections, which are neither just nor true, upon our lawgiver Moses and his code, maligning the one as a charlatan and impostor, and asserting that from the other we receive lessons in vice and none in virtue, I desire to give, to the best of my ability, a brief account of our constitution.

(trans. H. St. J. Thackeray, *LCL*)

387

From *Herodotus* to *Plutarch*

162

apud: Josephus, *Contra Apionem*, II, 236 — Niese = *F. Gr. Hist.*, III, C 621, T 1b = Reinach (Budé), pp. 100 f.

Εἶτα Λυσίμαχοι καὶ Μόλωνες ⟨No. 50⟩ καὶ τοιοῦτοί τινες ἄλλοι συγγραφεῖς, ἀδόκιμοι σοφισταί, μειρακίων ἀπατεῶνες, ὡς πάνυ ἡμᾶς φαυλοτάτους ἀνθρώπων λοιδοροῦσιν.

1 Μόλωνες ed. pr.   σόλωνες L

For all that, the Lysimachuses and Molons and other writers of that class, reprobate sophists and deceivers of youth, rail at us as the very vilest of mankind.   (trans. H. St. J. Thackeray, *LCL*)

LXIII. APION

First half of the first century C.E.

Apion was a Greek writer and scholar of Egyptian origin, who played a prominent part in the cultural and political life of his time. He gained fame in many branches of literature and scholarship, above all as a Homeric scholar and as the author of a work on the history of Egypt. During the reigns of Tiberius and Claudius he was active as a teacher in Rome. His journey through Greece in the time of Gaius Caligula (Seneca, Epistulae Morales, LXXXVIII, 40) brought him to the attention of many circles.

Although Apion was born outside Alexandria,[1] he won Alexandrian citizenship and represented the Greeks of Alexandria in the charges they levelled against the Alexandrian Jews before the Emperor Gaius, while Philo the philosopher represented the Jews (Ant., XVIII, 257 ff.). Apion, like his younger contemporary Chaeremon, lived at the meeting-place of both the Greek and the Egyptian worlds and was instrumental in drawing a picture of Egypt and its past for educated Greeks and Romans.

His references to the Jews, their past and their religious customs derive from the third and fourth books of his Αἰγυπτιακά. Since Clemens of Alexandria (Stromata, I, XXI : 101 : 3) and writers dependent on him state that Apion composed a work against the Jews (ὡς καὶ κατὰ 'Ιουδαίων συντάξασθαι βιβλίον), it has been suggested — e.g. by Gutschmid and Sperling — that, apart from the remarks concerning Jews found in his general Egyptian history, he also wrote an entire book about the Jews. It seems more probable, however, that he allotted a portion of his History of Egypt (either the third or fourth book) to the story of the Jewish Exodus and its consequences.

Josephus divides Apion's treatment of the Jews into the following three sections: (a) the Exodus; (b) an attack on the rights of the Alexandrian Jews; (c) a disparagement of the sanctity of the Temple and of Jewish religious customs.

---

1 Willrich's arguments against Josephus' statement concerning the origin of Apion do not carry much conviction; see his *Juden und Griechen*, pp. 172 ff.; *Klio*, III, (1903), p. 413, n. 2. See also I. Lévy *REJ*, XLI, (1900) pp. 188 ff.

His account of the Exodus reflects the views prevalent in Graeco-Alexandrian circles, e. g., the story of the lepers and the Egyptian origin of Moses. Chronologically he stands nearest to Lysimachus, and it is noteworthy that Apion, too, finds a place in his narrative for the biblical tradition about Moses' forty-day sojourn at Mount Sinai. In his polemic against Alexandrian Jews Apion's views were also the views of his fellow-citizens in Alexandria.

Because he had considerable influence on the educated classes of his times (although not all of them treated him with the same respect), Apion constituted a danger to the Jews. His Aegyptiaca became one of the authoritative works on ancient Egypt; cf. Aulus Gellius, Noctes Atticae, V, 14 : 2 : "eius libri non incelebres feruntur." Pliny the Elder is dependent on him, and his work presumably coloured the Egyptian tradition found in Plutarch. It is doubtful that Tacitus drew on Apion directly.

His flowing style, which may be inferred from the narrative fragments transmitted by Aulus Gellius in the story of Androclus and the Lion, (Noctes Atticae, V, 14 : 5 ff.) leads us to surmise that Apion was a rather popular writer. It is, therefore, small wonder that it was Apion, among all the anti-Semitic Graeco-Egyptian writers, whom Josephus chose as his main target.

Bibliography

Müller, pp. 14 ff.; A. Sperling, *Apion der Grammatiker und sein Verhältnis zum Judentum—Ein Beitrag zu einer Einleitung in die Schriften des Josephos*, Dresden 1886; Gutschmid, IV, pp. 356 ff.; Cohn, PW, I, pp. 2803 ff.; H. Willrich, *Juden und Griechen vor der makkabäischen Erhebung*, Göttingen 1895, pp. 172 ff.; Stähelin, pp. 29 ff.; I. Lévy, *REJ*, XLI (1900), pp. 188 ff.; Schürer, III, pp. 538 ff.; B. Motzo, "Il κατὰ 'Ιουδαίων di Apione", *Atti dell' Accademia delle Scienze di Torino*, XLVIII (1912–1913), pp. 459 ff.; Juster, I, p. 33; Radin, pp. 199 ff.; Schmid & Stählin, II, 1, 1920, pp. 437 f.; I. Heinemann, PW, Suppl. V, pp. 30 f.; Böhl, pp. 118 f.; Gager, pp. 122 ff.

On Apion's influence on Greek and Latin literature, see M. Wellmann, *Hermes*, XXXI (1896), pp. 249 ff.; I. Lévy, *Latomus*, V (1946), pp. 339 f.; X (1951), p. 161.

Apion

163 a

Aegyptiaca, apud: Tatianus, *Oratio ad Graecos*, 38 — Schwartz = F62R = *F.Gr.Hist.*,
III, C616, T 11a + F2a

Μετὰ δὲ τοῦτον ⟨scil. Πτολεμαῖον Μενδήσιον⟩ 'Απίων ὁ γραμματικὸς
ἀνὴρ δοκιμώτατος, ἐν τῇ τετάρτῃ τῶν Αἰγυπτιακῶν (πέντε δέ εἰσιν
αὐτῷ γραφαί) πολλὰ μὲν καὶ ἄλλα, φησὶ δὲ ⟨καὶ⟩ ὅτι κατέσκαψε τὴν
Ἀϑαρίαν "Αμωσις κατὰ τὸν 'Αργεῖον γενόμενος "Ιναχον ὡς ἐν τοῖς
5 Χρόνοις ἀνέγραψεν ὁ Μενδήσιος Πτολεμαῖος ⟨Νο. 157a⟩.

1 τοῦτον Eus.   τούτων MPV   3 ⟨καὶ⟩ Wilamowitz   4 Ἀϑαρίαν
Clemens   λναρίαν MV   λναριαν P   Αὔαριν Eus.

After him [scil. Ptolemy of Mendes], Apion the grammarian, a man
most highly esteemed, in the fourth book of his Aegyptiaca (there are
five books of his), says, besides many other things, that Amosis
destroyed Avaris in the time of the Argive Inachos, as the Mendesian
Ptolemy wrote in his Chronicle.   (trans. B. P. Pratten, Edinburgh 1867)

163 b

Aegyptiaca, apud: Clemens Alexandrinus, *Stromata*, I, 21:101:3-4 — Stählin & Früchtel = *F. Gr. Hist.*, III, C616, T11b + F2b

(3) 'Απίων τοίνυν ὁ γραμματικός, ὁ Πλειστονίκης ἐπικληθείς, ἐν τῇ
τετάρτῃ τῶν Αἰγυπτιακῶν ἱστοριῶν, καίτοι φιλαπεχθημόνως πρὸς
῾Εβραίους διακείμενος, ἅτε Αἰγύπτιος τὸ γένος, ὡς καὶ κατὰ 'Ιουδαίων
συντάξασθαι βιβλίον, 'Αμώσιος τοῦ Αἰγυπτίων βασιλέως μεμνημένος
5 καὶ τῶν κατ' αὐτὸν πράξεων, μάρτυρα παρατίθεται Πτολεμαῖον τὸν
Μενδήσιον. *(4)* καὶ τὰ τῆς λέξεως αὐτοῦ ὧδε ἔχει· «κατέσκαψε δὲ
τὴν 'Αουαρίαν "Αμωσις κατὰ τὸν 'Αργεῖον γενόμενος "Ιναχον, ὡς ἐν τοῖς
Χρόνοις ἀνέγραψεν ὁ Μενδήσιος Πτολεμαῖος» ⟨Νο. 157b⟩.

5 παρατίθεσθαι L   7 αϑυρίαν L   'Αούαριν Eus.   Λναρίαν Tat.

Thus, in the fourth book of his *Egyptian History*, Apion the grammarian, nicknamed Pleistonikes [victor in many contests], being an
Egyptian, displayed hatred toward the Hebrews so as to compose
a book *Against the Jews*; nevertheless he refers to Amosis the king
of the Egyptians and the events of his reign, adducing Ptolemy the
Mendesian as a witness. And he says as follows: "He destroyed
Avaris in the time of the Argive Inachus, as the Mendesian Ptolemy
wrote in his Chronicle."

391

163 c

Aegyptiaca, apud: Africanus, apud: Eusebius, *Praeparatio Evangelica*, X, 10:16 — Mras (cf. Ps.
Iustinus, *Cohortatio ad Graecos*, 9) = *F. Gr. Hist.*, III, C616, T11c + F2c

Ἀπίων δὲ ὁ Ποσειδωνίου, περιεργότατος γραμματικῶν, ἐν τῇ κατὰ
Ἰουδαίων βίβλῳ καὶ ἐν τῇ τετάρτῃ τῶν ἱστοριῶν φησὶ κατὰ Ἴναχον
Ἄργους βασιλέα, Ἀμώσιος Αἰγυπτίων βασιλεύοντος, ἀποστῆναι Ἰου-
δαίους, ὧν ἡγεῖσθαι Μωσέα.

4 ἡγεῖσθαι] γίνεσθαι Sync.

Apion, the son of Poseidonius, the most inquisitive of grammarians,
in his book *Against the Jews*, which constitutes the fourth book of
his *History*, writes that the Jews under the leadership of Moses
left in the time of Inachus, the king of Argos, who was a contemporary
of Amosis king of Egypt.

Ἀπίων... ἐν τῇ κατὰ Ἰουδαίων βίβλῳ: On the question of the existence of a
special book dealing with Jews, see the introduction.
κατὰ Ἴναχον... Ἀμώσιος Αἰγυπτίων βασιλεύοντος: See the commentary to
Ptolemy of Mendes (No. 157).

164

Aegyptiaca, apud: Josephus, *Contra Apionem*, II, 1-11 — Niese = F63Ra + b = *F. Gr. Hist.*,
III, C616, T15 + F1 = Reinach (Budé), pp. 59 f.

*(1) Διὰ μὲν οὖν τοῦ προτέρου βιβλίου, τιμιώτατέ μοι Ἐπαφρόδιτε,
περί τε τῆς ἀρχαιότητος ἡμῶν ἐπέδειξα τοῖς Φοινίκων καὶ Χαλδαίων
καὶ Αἰγυπτίων γράμμασι πιστωσάμενος τὴν ἀλήθειαν καὶ πολλοὺς
τῶν Ἑλλήνων συγγραφεῖς παρασχόμενος μάρτυρας, τήν τε ἀντίρρη-*
5 *σιν ἐποιησάμην πρὸς Μανεθὼν καὶ Χαιρήμονα καί τινας ἑτέρους.
(2) ἄρξομαι δὲ νῦν τοὺς ὑπολειπομένους τῶν γεγραφότων τι καθ᾽ ἡμῶν
ἐλέγχειν ★ καὶ τοῖς τῆς πρὸς Ἀπίωνα τὸν γραμματικὸν ἀντιρρήσεως
τετολμημένοις ★ ἐπῆλθέ μοι διαπορεῖν, εἰ χρὴ σπουδάσαι· (3) τὰ
μὲν γάρ ἐστι τῶν ὑπ᾽ αὐτοῦ γεγραμμένων τοῖς ὑπ᾽ ἄλλων εἰρημένοις*
10 *ὅμοια, τὰ δὲ λίαν ψυχρῶς προστέθεικεν, τὰ πλεῖστα δὲ βωμολοχίαν ἔχει
καὶ πολλήν, εἰ δεῖ τἀληθὲς εἰπεῖν, ἀπαιδευσίαν ὡς ἂν ὑπ᾽ ἀνθρώπου
συγκείμενα καὶ φαύλου τὸν τρόπον καὶ παρὰ πάντα τὸν βίον ὀχλαγωγοῦ
γεγονότος. (4) ἐπεὶ δ᾽ οἱ πολλοὶ τῶν ἀνθρώπων διὰ τὴν αὐτῶν ἄνοιαν
ὑπὸ τῶν τοιούτων ἁλίσκονται λόγων μᾶλλον ἢ τῶν μετά τινος σπου-*

5 Μανεθὼν Niese   μανεθῶνα L   7 καὶ τοῖς] καίτοι περὶ ed. pr.
8 τετολμημένοις om. ed. pr.   13 αὐτῶν om. ed. pr.

15 δῆς γεγραμμένων, καὶ χαίρουσι μὲν ταῖς λοιδορίαις, ἄχθονται δὲ τοῖς
ἐπαίνοις, ἀναγκαῖον ἡγησάμην εἶναι μηδὲ τοῦτον ἀνεξέταστον καταλιπεῖν
κατηγορίαν ἡμῶν ἄντικρυς ὡς ἐν δίκῃ γεγραφότα. (5) καὶ γὰρ αὖ κἀκεῖνο τοῖς πολλοῖς ἀνθρώποις ὁρῶ παρακολουθοῦν, τὸ λίαν ἐφήδεσθαι
ὅταν τις ἀρξάμενος βλασφημεῖν ἕτερον αὐτὸς ἐλέγχηται περὶ τῶν αὐτῷ
20 προσόντων κακῶν. (6) ἔστι μὲν οὖν οὐ ῥάδιον αὐτοῦ διελθεῖν τὸν λόγον
οὐδὲ σαφῶς γνῶναι, τί λέγειν βούλεται, σχεδὸν δ' ὡς ἐν πολλῇ ταραχῇ
καὶ ψευσμάτων συγχύσει τὰ μὲν εἰς τὴν ὁμοίαν ἰδέαν πίπτει τοῖς προεξητασμένοις περὶ τῆς ἐξ Αἰγύπτου τῶν ἡμετέρων προγόνων μεταναστάσεως, (7) τὰ δ' ἐστὶ κατηγορία τῶν ἐν Ἀλεξανδρείᾳ κατοικούντων
25 Ἰουδαίων. τρίτον δ' ἐπὶ τούτοις μέμικται περὶ τῆς ἁγιστείας τῆς κατὰ
τὸ ἱερὸν ἡμῶν καὶ τῶν ἄλλων νομίμων κατηγορία.

(8) Ὅτι μὲν οὔτε Αἰγύπτιοι τὸ γένος ἦσαν ἡμῶν οἱ πατέρες οὔτε
διὰ λύμην σωμάτων ἢ τοιαύτας ἄλλας συμφοράς τινας ἐκεῖθεν
ἐξηλάθησαν, οὐ μετρίως μόνον, ἀλλὰ καὶ πέρα τοῦ συμμέτρου
30 προαποδεδεῖχθαι νομίζω. (9) περὶ ὧν δὲ προστίθησιν ὁ Ἀπίων ἐπι-
μνησθήσομαι συντόμως. (10) φησὶ γὰρ ἐν τῇ τρίτῃ τῶν Αἰγυπτιακῶν
τάδε·«Μωσῆς, ὡς ἤκουσα παρὰ τῶν πρεσβυτέρων τῶν Αἰγυπτίων,
ἦν Ἡλιοπολίτης, ὃς πατρίοις ἔθεσι κατηγγυημένος αἰθρίους προσευχὰς
ἀνῆγεν εἰς οἵους εἶχεν ἡ πόλις περιβόλους, πρὸς ἀφηλιώτην δὲ πάσας
35 ἀπέστρεφεν· ὧδε γὰρ καὶ Ἡλίου κεῖται πόλις. (11) ἀντὶ δὲ ὀβελῶν
ἔστησε κίονας, ὑφ' οἷς ἦν ἐκτύπωμα σκάφη, σκιὰ ⋆ δ' ἀνδρὸς ἐπ' αὐτὴν
διακειμένη, ὡς ὂν ἐν αἰθέρι τοῦτον ἀεὶ τὸν δρόμον ἡλίῳ συμπεριπολεῖ.»

22–23 προεξητασμένοις ed. pr.   προεξετασμένοις L   25 ἁγιστείας Dindorf
ἁγιστίας L   26 κατηγορία Bekker   κατηγορίας L   29 ἐξηλάσθησαν
L¹ / μόνον μετρίως Naber   32 moyses Lat.   33 Ἡλιοπολίτης
Niese   ἡλιουπολίτης L   heliopolitanus Lat.   34 ἡ πόλις ed. pr.   ἥλιος L
35 ἀπέστρεψεν Reinach   36 σκάφης Huet / ἀνδρὸς] ἀνδριάντος Thackeray
ἀπ' ἄκρων Huet   37 διικνουμένη Holwerda / ὂν Huet ὅτι L

(1) In the first volume of this work, my most esteemed Epaphroditus,
I demonstrated the antiquity of our race, corroborating my statements by the writings of Phoenicians, Chaldaeans, and Egyptians,
besides citing as witnesses numerous Greek historians; I also challenged the statements of Manetho, Chaeremon, and some others.
(2) I shall now proceed to refute the rest of the authors who have attacked us. I am doubtful, indeed, whether the shameless remarks of
Apion the grammarian deserve serious refutation. (3) Some of these
resemble the allegations made by others, some are very indifferent
additions of his own; most of them are pure buffoonery, and, to tell the
truth, display the gross ignorance of their author, a man of low character and a charlatan to the end of his days. (4) Yet, since most people

are so foolish as to find greater attraction in such compositions than in works of a serious nature, to be charmed by abuse and impatient of praise, I think it incumbent upon me not to pass over without examination even this author, who has written an indictment of us formal enough for a court of law. (5) For I observe, on the other hand, that people in general also have a habit of being intensely delighted when one who has been the first to malign another has his own vices brought home to him. (6) His argument is difficult to summarize and his meaning to grasp. But, so far as the extreme disorder and confusion of his lying statements admit of analysis, one may say that some fall into the same category as those already investigated, relating to the departure of our ancestors from Egypt; (7) others form an indictment of the Jewish residents in Alexandria; while a third class, mixed up with the rest, consists of accusations against our temple rites and our ordinances in general.

(8) That our ancestors neither were Egyptians by race nor were expelled from that country in consequence of contagious diseases or any similar affliction, I think I have already given not merely sufficient, but even super-abundant, proof. (9) I propose, however, briefly to mention the details added by Apion. (10) In the third book of his *History of Egypt* he makes the following statement: "Moses, as I have heard from old people in Egypt, was a native of Heliopolis, who, being pledged to the customs of his country, erected prayer-houses, open to the air, in the various precincts of the city, all facing eastwards; such being the orientation also of Heliopolis. (11) In place of obelisks he set up pillars, beneath which was a model of a boat; and the shadow cast on this basin by the statue described a circle corresponding to the course of the sun in the heavens."

(trans. H. St. J. Thackeray, LCL)

3 ἔχει καὶ πολλήν ... ἀπαιδευσίαν: Josephus impugns the scholarly reputation of Apion, who gloried in his vast learning, by imputing ignorance to him.
ὀχλαγωγοῦ γεγονότος: Josephus does not stand alone in his negative characterization of Apion; cf. Aulus Gellius,V, 14 : 3: "Studioque ostentationis sit loquacior ... in praedicandis doctrinis sui venditator"; see also Plinius, *Praefatio*, 25.

6 περὶ τῆς ἐξ Αἰγύπτου ... μεταναστάσεως: Josephus refutes Apion's narration of the Exodus in *Contra Apionem*, II, 8 ff. It seems that Apion's version is related to that of Lysimachus; see Josephus, *Contra Apionem*, I, 304–311 (No. 158). However, we should not assume that Apion derived his account directly from Lysimachus. In any event, he embellished Lysimachus' version. Josephus dwells only on those arguments or details that Apion added to the works of his predecessors; see *Contra Apionem*, II, 3: προστέθεικεν; *ibid.*, 9: περὶ ὧν δὲ προστίθησιν; *ibid.*, 28: ὁ Αἰγύπτιος 'Απίων ἐκαινοποίησεν παρὰ τοὺς ἄλλους.

394

Apion

7 τὰ δ' ἐστὶ κατηγορία τῶν ἐν Ἀλεξανδρείᾳ κατοικούντων Ἰουδαίων: Josephus answers Apion's arguments concerning the status of the Jews of Alexandria in *Contra Apionem*, II, 32–78.

10 φησὶ γὰρ ἐν τῇ τρίτῃ τῶν Αἰγυπτιακῶν τάδε: This statement indicates that Apion discussed the Exodus in the third book of his *Egyptian History*. On the other hand, we learn from a passage deriving from Africanus and quoted by Eusebius that Apion treated the subject in the fourth book of his *History*; see Eusebius, *Historia Ecclesiastica*, X, 10 : 16 (No. 163). Either Apion referred to the Exodus in two consecutive books, or there must be a mistake in one of the passages. The second possibility is more probable.

ἦν Ἡλιοπολίτης: Manetho had already described Moses as a priest from Heliopolis; see Manetho, apud: Josephus, *Contra Apionem*, I, 250 (No. 21). The connection between Heliopolis and the Jews in Graeco-Egyptian literature seemed more probable to the generation after Manetho, since a Jewish temple had been founded in the Heliopolite nomos; see *Ant.*, XII, 388; XIII, 70, 285; XX, 236; *BJ*, I, 33; VII, 426.

προσευχὰς ἀνῆγεν: προσευχή was the common word to describe Jewish prayer-houses in the lands of the Hellenistic Diaspora; see Schürer, II, 517; M.A. Beek, *Oudtestamentische Studiën*, II (1943), pp. 132 ff.; *CPJ*, I, 1957, p. 8; cf. the list of Jewish synagogues in Graeco-Roman Egypt. For προσευχή, see also Iuvenalis, *Saturae*, III, 296 (No. 297); Artemidorus, *Onirocritica*, III, 53 (No. 395) and the commentary *ad loc.*

11 ἀντὶ δὲ ὀβελῶν ἔστησε κίονας: These famous obelisks seem to be referred to already in the Bible; see Jer. xliii : 13: מצבות בית שמש; Herodotus, II, 111 : 4. σκάφη: Cf. Vitruvius, *De Architectura*, IX, 8; see also H. Diels, *Antike Technik* 2, Leipzig and Berlin 1920, pp. 163 ff.

165

Aegyptiaca, apud: Josephus, *Contra Apionem*, II, 15–17, 20–21, 25, 28 — Niese = F63bR = *F. Gr. Hist.*, III, C616, F4a–d = Reinach (Budé), pp. 61 ff.

(15) Τὰ δὲ δὴ τῶν χρόνων, ἐν οἷς φησι τὸν Μωσῆν ἐξαγαγεῖν τοὺς λεπρῶντας καὶ τυφλοὺς καὶ τὰς βάσεις πεπηρωμένους, σφόδρα δὴ τοῖς πρὸ αὐτοῦ συμπεφώνηκεν, ὡς οἶμαι, ὁ γραμματικὸς ὁ ἀκριβής. *(16)* Μανεθὼς μὲν γὰρ κατὰ τὴν Τεθμώσιος βασιλείαν ἀπαλλαγῆναί
5 φησιν ἐξ Αἰγύπτου τοὺς Ἰουδαίους πρὸ ἐτῶν τριακοσίων ἐνενηκοντατριῶν τῆς εἰς Ἄργος Δαναοῦ φυγῆς, Λυσίμαχος ⟨No. 159⟩ δὲ κατὰ Βόκχοριν τὸν βασιλέα, τουτέστι πρὸ ἐτῶν χιλίων ἑπτακοσίων, Μόλων ⟨No. 47⟩ δὲ καὶ ἄλλοι τινὲς ὡς αὐτοῖς ἔδοξεν. *(17)* ὁ δέ γε πάντων πιστότατος Ἀπίων ὡρίσατο τὴν ἔξοδον ἀκριβῶς κατὰ τὴν ἑβδόμην
10 ὀλυμπιάδα καὶ ταύτης ἔτος εἶναι πρῶτον, ἐν ᾧ, φησί, Καρχηδόνα Φοίνικες ἔκτισαν... *(20)* τὸν δὲ ἀριθμὸν τῶν ἐλαθέντων τὸν αὐτὸν Λυσιμάχῳ ⟨No. 160⟩

1 moysen Lat.   7 bochore Lat.   10 καὶ ταύτης ... πρῶτον om. Lat.
12 ἐλασθέντων L¹

395

σχεδιάσας, ἕνδεκα γὰρ αὐτοὺς εἶναί φησι μυριάδας, θαυμαστήν τινα
καὶ πιθανὴν ἀποδίδωσιν αἰτίαν, ἀφ' ἧς φησι τὸ σάββατον ὠνομάσθαι.

15 *(21)* «ὁδεύσαντες γάρ, φησίν, ἐξ ἡμερῶν ὁδὸν βουβῶνας ἔσχον καὶ
διὰ ταύτην τὴν αἰτίαν τῇ ἑβδόμῃ ἡμέρᾳ ἀνεπαύσαντο σωθέντες εἰς
τὴν χώραν τὴν νῦν Ἰουδαίαν λεγομένην καὶ ἐκάλεσαν τὴν ἡμέραν
σάββατον σώζοντες τὴν Αἰγυπτίων γλῶτταν· τὸ γὰρ βουβῶνος ἄλγος
καλοῦσιν Αἰγύπτιοι σαββάτωσιν»...

20 *(25)* ὁ δὲ θαυμαστὸς Ἀπίων διὰ μὲν ἐξ ἡμερῶν αὐτοὺς ἐλθεῖν εἰς τὴν
Ἰουδαίαν προείρηκε, πάλιν δὲ τὸν Μωσῆν εἰς τὸ μεταξὺ τῆς Αἰγύπτου
καὶ τῆς Ἀραβίας ὄρος, ὃ καλεῖται Σίναιον, ἀναβάντα φησὶν ἡμέρας
τεσσαράκοντα κρυβῆναι κἀκεῖθεν καταβάντα δοῦναι τοῖς Ἰουδαίοις τοὺς
νόμους ...

25 *(28)* τοιαῦτα μέν τινα περὶ Μωσέως καὶ τῆς ἐξ Αἰγύπτου γενομένης
τοῖς Ἰουδαίοις ἀπαλλαγῆς ὁ Αἰγύπτιος Ἀπίων ἐκαινοποίησεν παρὰ
τοὺς ἄλλους ἐπινοήσας.

14 τὸ] τὸν L¹   19 σαββάτωσιν ed. pr.   σαββάτωσις L   sabbato Lat.
σαββώ Reinach   21 moysen Lat.

(15) On the question of the date which he assigns to the exodus of the
lepers, the blind and the lame under Moses' leadership, we shall
find, I imagine, this accurate grammarian in perfect agreement with
previous writers. (16) Well, Manetho states that the departure of
the Jews from Egypt occurred in the reign of Tethmosis, 393 years
before the flight of Danaus to Argos; Lysimachus says, under King
Bocchoris, that is to say, 1700 years ago; Molon and others fix a date
to suit themselves. (17) Apion, however, the surest authority of all,
precisely dates the exodus in the seventh Olympiad, and in the first
year of that Olympiad, the year in which, according to him, the
Phoenicians founded Carthage...
(20) After stating that the fugitives numbered 110,000, in which imaginary figure he agrees with Lysimachus, he gives an astonishing
and plausible explanation of the etymology of the word "sabbat"!
(21) "After a six days' march", he says, "they developed tumours in
the groin, and that was why, after safely reaching the country now
called Judaea, they rested on the seventh day, and called that day
sabbaton, preserving the Egyptian terminology; for disease of the
groin in Egypt is called sabbatosis."[1]
(25) This astonishing Apion, after stating that they reached Judaea
in six days tells us elsewhere that Moses went up into the mountain
called Sinai, which lies between Egypt and Arabia, remained in con-

1 This translation differs from that of Thackeray, who adopts Reinach's σαββώ.

cealment there for forty days, and then descended and gave the Jews their laws. . .
(28) Such are some of the novel features which the Egyptian Apion, improving upon other authors, has introduced into the story of Moses and the departure of the Jews from Egypt.

(trans. H. St. J. Thackeray, *LCL*)

15 τὸν Μωσῆν ἐξαγαγεῖν τοὺς λεπρῶντας. . .: We learn here that Apion accepted Manetho's version of the lepers' expulsion, but that he differs with respect to the chronology, where he almost agrees with Lysimachus.

17 Ἀπίων ὡρίσατο τὴν ἔξοδον ἀκριβῶς κατὰ τὴν ἑβδόμην ὀλυμπιάδα. . . ἐν ᾧ . . . Καρχηδόνα Φοίνικες ἔκτισαν: The first year of the seventh Olympiad was 752 B. C. E., which, according to Apion, was also the year that Carthage was founded. According to Timaeus, the founding of Carthage should be dated to the 38th year before the first Olympiad, i.e. to 814 B. C. E.; see Timaeus, apud: Dionysius of Halicarnassus, *Antiquitates Romanae*, I, 74 : 1 = *F. Gr. Hist.*, III, B 566 F 60. Also in Timaeus we find synchronization between the founding of Carthage and that of Rome, which caused the founding of Rome to be transferred to an earlier date than the one canonized later. However, Apion's date for the founding of Carthage reflects a synchronism that had started with the founding of Rome, *c.* 751 B.C.E., according to the Catonian system; see the commentary to Menander of Ephesus (No. 35). The choice of the year 752 B.C.E. as the date of the Exodus is in accord with Lysimachus' account, which connects the Exodus with King Bocchoris; see the commentary to Lysimachus (No. 158); cf. Gutschmid, IV, p. 367.

21 σαββάτωσιν: Cf. M. Scheller, *Glotta*, XXXIV 1955, pp. 298 ff. Scheller thinks that Σαββάτωσις "ist. . . die Bezeichnung einer Krankheit, welche die Betroffenen nötigt, in rebus Venereis Sabbatruhe zu beobachten". For the emendation σαββώ, see T. Reinach, *Gedenkbuch zur Erinnerung an David Kaufmann*, Berlin 1900, p. 14 f.

25 ὁ δὲ θαυμαστὸς Ἀπίων. . .: Josephus, of course, was happy to exploit the contradiction found in Apion's account. The contradiction may be explained by the fact that Apion added some details from the Biblical narrative to the common Graeco-Egyptian tradition without making a serious attempt to harmonize his two different sources. For a similar unsuccessful attempt, see Pompeius Trogus (No. 137). He may have used biblical material to help show that Moses' sojourn on the mountain constituted a ruse to deceive the people and to convince them that the laws that he invented were really of divine origin. Apion's polemic against the divine origin of the Law of Moses had precedents in the rationalistic criticism of the revelations by the old legislators such as Minos, Lycurgus and Numa; see Strabo, *Geographica*, XVI, 2 : 38 f., pp. 761 f. (No. 115).

166

Aegyptiaca, apud: Josephus, *Contra Apionem*, II, 32–33, 38, 42 — Niese = F63cR = *F. Gr. Hist.*, III, C616, F4d = Reinach (Budé), pp. 64 f.

(32) Ὁ δὲ γενναῖος Ἀπίων δοκεῖ μὲν τὴν βλασφημίαν τὴν καθ᾽ ἡμῶν ὥσπερ τινὰ μισθὸν ἐθελῆσαι παρασχεῖν Ἀλεξανδρεῦσι τῆς δοθείσης

αὐτῷ πολιτείας, καὶ τὴν ἀπέχθειαν αὐτῶν ἐπιστάμενος τὴν πρὸς τοὺς
συνοικοῦντας αὐτοῖς ἐπὶ τῆς Ἀλεξανδρείας Ἰουδαίους προτέθειται μὲν
5 ἐκείνοις λοιδορεῖσθαι, συμπεριλαμβάνειν δὲ καὶ τοὺς ἄλλους ἅπαντας, ἐν
ἀμφοτέροις ἀναισχύντως ψευδόμενος.

(33) Τίνα τοίνυν ἐστὶ τὰ δεινὰ καὶ σχέτλια τῶν ἐν Ἀλεξανδρείᾳ κατοικούντων Ἰουδαίων, ἃ κατηγόρηκεν αὐτῶν, ἴδωμεν. «ἐλθόντες, φησίν,
ἀπὸ Συρίας ᾤκησαν πρὸς ἀλίμενον θάλασσαν γειτνιάσαντες ταῖς τῶν
10 κυμάτων ἐκβολαῖς»...

(38) Τὸ δὲ δὴ θαυμάζειν, πῶς Ἰουδαῖοι ὄντες Ἀλεξανδρεῖς ἐκλήθησαν,
τῆς ὁμοίας ἀπαιδευσίας...

(42) ὁ δ᾽ οὕτως ἐστὶ γενναῖος, ὡς μετέχειν ἀξιῶν αὐτὸς ὢν τυχεῖν
ἐκωλύετο συκοφαντεῖν ἐπεχείρησε τοὺς δικαίως λαβόντας.

3 τὴν¹ ed. pr.　τὸν L　/　τὴν² ed. pr.　τοὺς L　　4 προτέθειται Niese
προυτέθειται L　προυτέθειτο ed. pr.　　5 συμπεριλαμβάνει ed. pr.

(32) The noble Apion's calumny upon us is apparently designed as
a sort of return to the Alexandrians for the rights of citizenship
which they bestowed upon him. Knowing their hatred of their Jewish
neighbours in Alexandria, he has made it his aim to vilify the latter,
and has included all the rest of the Jews in his condemnation. In both
these attacks he shows himself an impudent liar.

(33) Let us investigate the grave and shocking charges which he has
brought against the Jewish residents in Alexandria. "They came",
he says, "from Syria and settled by a sea without a harbour, close
beside the spot where the waves break on the beach." ...

(38) His astonishment at the idea of Jews being called Alexandrians
betrays similar stupidity...

(42) Yet Apion displays such noble generosity as to claim for himself privileges from which he was debarred, while he undertakes to
calumniate those who have fairly obtained them.

(trans. H. St. J. Thackeray, *LCL*)

33 ἐλθόντες ἀπὸ Συρίας: Syria here includes, of course, Judaea. On the Roman
emperor's warning to the Jews of Alexandria not to bring in or to invite Jews from
Syria, see the *Letter of Claudius*, *CPJ*, No. 153, ll. 96 f. This also agrees with the
traditional administrative usage of the Ptolemaic age, when Judaea was considered
one of the many parts of Ptolemaic Syria or Ptolemaic Syria and Phoenicia. On
this terminology, see, e.g., H. Liebesny (ed.), *Aegyptus*, XVI (1936), p. 258, Col. 1,
ll. 33 f.; Col. 2, ll. 14, 19 = M. T. Lenger, *Corpus des Ordonnances des Ptolémées*,
Brussels 1964, No. 22, ll. 1 f., 19, 24; *OGIS*, I, No. 54, l.6; J. Bingen (ed.), *Papyrus
Revenue Laws*, Göttingen 1952, Col. 54, l. 17; *PCZ*, I, No. 59012, l. 125; No. 59093,
l. 5; *PSI*, IV, Nos. 324, 325, 327; VI, No. 648.

ᾤκησαν πρὸς ἀλίμενον θάλασσαν...: Josephus' reply to Apion asserts that no fault is to be found with the locality inhabited by the Jews, as the seaboard forms part of the city and is, by universal consent, its finest residential quarter. Josephus adds that Alexander presented the quarter to the Jews. From *BJ*, II, 495, we learn that this quarter is identified with the area known as the Delta. The Jews were concentrated there, according to Josephus; see also Strabo, *Histories*, apud: Josephus, *Ant.*, XIV, 117 (No. 105): καὶ τῆς ᾿Αλεξανδρέων πόλεως ἀφώρισται μέγα μέρος τῷ ἔθνει τούτῳ, though Strabo does not tell us where the Jewish quarter was situated; see also the commentary *ad loc.* For the Delta, we should look in the north-eastern part of Alexandria; see Puchstein, PW, I, p. 1388. By no means should the allotment of a special quarter to the Jews be considered the creation of a compulsory ghetto, though this is the mistaken notion of some modern scholars, e.g. A. Bludau, *Juden und Judenverfolgungen im alten Alexandria*, Münster 1906, p. 12; U. Wilcken, "Zum alexandrinischen Antisemitismus", *Abhandlungen der philologisch-historischen Klasse der Königlichen Sächsischen Gesellschaft der Wissenschaften*, XXVII, Leipzig 1909, No. XXIII, 788 (8); P. Jouguet, *La vie municipale dans l'Égypte romaine*, Paris 1911, p. 19. For the correct view, see Juster, II, pp. 177 f.; L. Fuchs, *Die Juden Aegyptens in ptolemäischer und römischer Zeit*, Vienna 1924, pp. 104 f.; H. I. Bell, *JRS*, XXXI (1941), p. 1. The Jews had a natural inclination to live together, and the allotment of a special quarter to them was considered a favour. Jewish quarters and streets in the townships of the χώρα are known from the papyri; see *CPJ*, Nos. 423, 454, 468. The strategi of Sardis set aside a place in that city for the Jews to build and to inhabit (εἰς οἰκοδομίαν καὶ οἴκησιν αὐτῶν); see *Ant.*, XIV, 261. Only Flaccus, in the time of Caligula, compelled the Jews of Alexandria to be confined to their quarter; cf. Fraser, I, p. 56.

38 πῶς ᾿Ιουδαῖοι ὄντες ᾿Αλεξανδρεῖς ἐκλήθησαν...: Apion undoubtedly referred to the Jewish claim to be considered Alexandrians, that is, citizens of Alexandria according to the common Greek terminology. This raises the very complicated question of the Jews' right to Alexandrian citizenship. Josephus, in his criticism of Apion (*Contra Apionem*, II, 35), maintains that the Jews were granted their right of residence by Alexander, who must have also given them the same status that he assigned the Macedonians: καὶ ἴσης παρὰ τοῖς Μακεδόσι τιμῆς ἐπέτυχον. As proof Josephus adduces the fact that the Jews have been called Macedonians down to his time. Josephus also refers to the letters of Alexander, of Ptolemy the son of Lagos and of their successors the Egyptian kings, as well as to a bronze tablet in Alexandria that records the rights bestowed on the Jews by Caesar the Great. In the following passages Josephus is even more explicit as to the rights of the Jews. Referring to the status of the Jewish inhabitants of Antiochia, he asserts that they are called Antiochenes, because Seleucus, the founder of the city, conferred the right of citizenship (πολιτεία) upon them. The same applies, according to Josephus, to the Jews of Ephesus and the other cities of Ionia; *ibid.*, 39 f. In his other works Josephus maintains the same view of the Jews' right to citizenship. Thus, referring to Ptolemy Soter (*Ant.*, XII, 8), he tells us that the king granted the Jews in Alexandria equal civic rights with the Macedonians: καὶ τοῖς Μακεδόσιν ἐν ᾿Αλεξανδρείᾳ ποιήσας ἰσοπολίτας. He also states that Seleucus Nicator conferred citizenship on the Jews in the cities that he had founded in Syria and Asia, and that he declared them to have equal rights with the Macedonian and Greek settlers: ἰσοτίμους ἀπέφηνεν Μακεδόσιν καὶ ῞Ελλησιν (*Ant.*, XII, 119). Josephus adds that this citizenship remains "to this time", and, as evidence of this right, he adduces the fact that the king ordered that the Jews, who were unwilling to

use non-Jewish oil, should receive a fixed sum of money from the gymnasiarchs. According to Josephus, the Greeks of the Ionian cities petitioned Agrippa that only they should be allowed to enjoy the citizenship granted them by Antiochus II Theos, adding that if the Jews were to participate in it, they should worship the city gods; see *Ant.*, XII, 125 f. However, instead of subsequently reverting to the question of citizenship, Josephus surprisingly states only that the Jews won the right to follow their own customs.

Josephus again refers to the bronze tablet erected by Julius Caesar declaring the Jews to be citizens of Alexandria: ἐδήλωσεν ὅτι ᾿Αλεξανδρέων πολῖταί εἰσιν (*Ant.*, XIV, 188). Also, when speaking of the Jews of Asia and Libya in the time of Augustus, Josephus says that the Hellenistic kings had formerly granted the Jews equality of civic status: τῶν μὲν πρότερον βασιλέων ἰσονομίαν αὐτοῖς παρεσχημένων; see *Ant.*, XVI, 160. A reference to the fact that the kings granted the Jews civil rights equal to those of the Alexandrians is found in the edict of Claudius; see *Ant.*, XIX, 281: καὶ ἴσης πολιτείας παρὰ τῶν βασιλέων τετευχότας.

The two main passages in *Bellum Judaicum* that have a bearing on the question of Jewish citizenship in the Hellenistic cities are in full accord with those of *Antiquitates*. In *BJ*, II, 487 f., we read that, having received active support from the Jews against the Egyptians [*sic*], Alexander granted them permission to reside in Alexandria on terms of equality with the Greeks (ἔδωκεν τὸ μετοικεῖν κατὰ τὴν πόλιν ἐξ ἰσομοιρίας πρὸς τοὺς ῞Ελληνας), and that this permission was confirmed by his successors. The Jews, according to Josephus, were also allowed to style themselves "Macedonians": καὶ χρηματίζειν ἐπέτρεψαν Μακεδόνας. Concerning the Jews of Antiochia, Josephus states that the kings succeeding Antiochus Epiphanes granted the Jews ἐξ ἴσου τῆς πόλεως τοῖς ῞Ελλησι μετέχειν (*BJ*, VII, 44).

The evidence of Josephus with respect to the Jewish right of citizenship in Alexandria, and, for that matter, in Antiochia and other Hellenistic cities as well, may be summarized under three headings: (a) The Jews were πολῖται of Alexandria and other Greek cities. (b) The Jews had equal civic rights (ἴση πολιτεία, ἰσονομία, ἰσομοιρία). This formulation is much more frequent than the one that plainly asserts the Jews' right to citizenship. However, Josephus apparently means the same thing in both instances; cf. E. Szanto, *Das griechische Bürgerrecht*, Freiburg 1892, p. 72. (c) The Jews obtained a status on a par with that of the Macedonians or were allowed to style themselves Macedonians.

Philo, our other main literary authority on the question of Jewish civic rights, did not leave us an explicit statement concerning this question. However, chance references in his two historical works have a direct bearing on the problem. Thus, we read in *Legatio ad Gaium*, 194, about the Jews' struggle to prove that they were Alexandrians: ἀγωνίζεσθαι δεικνύντας ὡς ἐσμὲν ᾿Αλεξανδρεῖς, which is the exact opposite of Apion's statement discussed here. See also *ibid.*, 349: μεταπεμφθέντες ἀγωνίσασθαι τὸν περὶ τῆς πολιτείας ἀγῶνα. In this passage the exact meaning of πολιτεία cannot be assessed, as it may mean the general rights of the Jews of Alexandria, and not necessarily the right to Alexandrian citizenship. In another passage of the same work Philo speaks of "our" Alexandria: κατὰ τὴν ἡμετέραν ᾿Αλεξάνδρειαν (*ibid.*, 150). Also, some importance attaches to two passages of *In Flaccum*, 47 and 78 ff. In the first passage the Jewish inhabitants of different places are referred to as πολῖται of their respective cities, though perhaps no juridical meaning should be attached to this word. From the second passage we learn that the Alexandrian Jews had the right to be punished like Alexandrians, which was not the case for native Egyptians. In general, the impression we get from Philo is that the Jews strove to be considered Alexandrians, that Philo voiced their demands and that they were violently opposed by the leaders of the Greeks of Alexandria. On the other hand, Philo (*In Flaccum*, 172) alludes to the Alexandrian Jews as κατοῖκοι, though it is not certain whether we should understand κατοῖκοι here in a technical sense.

The question of Jewish civic rights also plays a conspicuous part in the narrative of the third book of the Maccabees, a book that seems to reflect the conditions of Alexandria in the early Roman period; see V.A. Tcherikover, *Scripta Hierosolymitana*, VII (1961), pp. 1 ff. According to this narrative, Ptolemy Philopator gave the Jews civic rights, stipulating that they should be initiated into the mysteries of Dionysos; see III Macc. ii : 30: ἐὰν δέ τινες ἐξ αὐτῶν προαιρῶνται ἐν τοῖς κατὰ τὰς τελετὰς μεμνημένοις ἀναστρέφεσθαι τούτους ἰσοπολίτας ᾿Αλεξανδρεῦσιν εἶναι. See also III Macc. iii : 21: ἐβουλήθημεν καὶ πολιτείας αὐτοὺς ᾿Αλεξανδρέων καταξιῶσαι... A comparison of both passages seems to leave no doubt that, for the writer, there was no difference between civic rights and ἰσοπολιτεία with the Alexandrians.

Strabo does not allude to the civic rights of the Alexandrian Jews and refers only to their autonomous organization; see Strabo, *Historica Hypomnemata*, apud: Josephus, *Ant.*, XIV, 117 (No. 105). More direct information on the question of the Jews' right to citizenship in the Hellenistic cities may be gleaned from his description of the different sections of the population of Cyrene, which is found at the beginning of the same fragment. Strabo divides the population of Cyrene into four classes: citizens (πολῖται), farmers (γεωργοί), resident aliens (μετοῖκοι) and Jews. It is clear that he does not include the Jews of Cyrene among the citizens of that city.

Among the papyrological evidence bearing on the civic rights of the Alexandrian Jews, the chief document is the famous letter of Claudius, dated 41 C.E. (*CPJ*, No. 153). The crucial passage is found in ll. 82 ff., where the emperor warns the Alexandrians in strong terms to behave gently and kindly towards the Jews, who have inhabited the city for many years (᾿Ιουδαίο‹ι›ς τοῖς τὴν αὐτὴν πόλειν ἐκ πολλῶν χρόνων οἰκοῦσει), and to allow them to follow their own customs. However, he orders the Jews to seek no further favours, since they enjoy what is their own, and, in a city that is not their own (ἐν ἀλλοτρίᾳ πόλει), they possess an abundance of all good things. Thus, Claudius sees in Alexandria a city foreign to the Jews living there, which is hardly compatible with the view that the Jews were full citizens of Alexandria.

The question of the status of the Alexandrian Jews is also implied in a petition to the Prefect of Egypt by a certain Helenus, son of Tryphon, dated 5–4 B. C. E. (*BGU*, No. 1140 = *CPJ*, No. 151). It is interesting to note that Helenus had first been designated in this papyrus "an Alexandrian", and that this designation was changed to "Jew from Alexandria" (᾿Ιουδαίου τῶν ἀπὸ ᾿Αλεξανδρείας), i.e. in Augustus' time there was a juridical difference between an Alexandrian and a Jew from Alexandria. Cf. Fraser, II, p. 139, n. 144.

On the other hand, some papyrological evidence exists corroborating Josephus' statement about the connection between the Alexandrian Jews and the status of the Macedonians. Among the few examples of Macedonians in Alexandria known from the papyri found at Abusir el-Meleq there is one Jew, Alexander the son of Nicodemus (*BGU*, No. 1132 = *CPJ*, No. 142, dated 14 B. C. E.), whose Jewishness is established by the fact that his brother deposited his will in the Jewish archive

(*BGU*, No. 1151 = *CPJ*, No. 143). To this may be added the recently discovered inscriptional evidence from Cyrene, which testifies that a Jew filled the post of a νομοφύλαξ in that city during the time of Nero (60–61 C. E.); see *Quaderni di archaeologia della Libia*, IV (1961), p. 16. In addition, Jewish names appear in a list of ephebi from 3–28 C. E.; see the commentary to Strabo, No. 105.

Some scholars, e.g. Schürer (III, pp. 121 ff.) and Juster (II, pp. 1 ff.), have accepted Josephus' statement at face value and hold the view that Jews had the full rights of active citizenship in all the cities founded by the Hellenistic kings, including Alexandria. Some continued to hold this view even after publication of the letter of Claudius, in which the emperor states, as mentioned above, that the Alexandrian Jews live in a city that is not their own; see, e.g., G. De Sanctis, *Rivista di Filologia Classica*, LII (1924), pp. 473 ff. A similar view is held by A. Momigliano, *The Emperor Claudius and His Achievement*, Oxford 1934, p. 96, n. 25. In Momigliano's opinion the edict of Claudius in *Ant.*, XIX, 281, and the reference to the equality of the punishment meted out to the Jews and to the Alexandrians in Philo's *In Flaccum* (80) are decisive. A similar view is expressed by Dessau, although he thinks that the Jewish citizens generally renounced enlistment into the phylae and demi for religious reasons; see H. Dessau, *Geschichte der römischen Kaiserzeit*, II, 2, Berlin 1930, pp. 668 f.

An intermediate view is taken by Tarn, who admits that it was impossible for the Jews as a group to be full citizens of Alexandria. He maintains that the kings bestowed isopolity upon the Jewish settlers, by which he means that they were given potential citizenship, on condition that they apostatized by worshipping the city gods; see W.W. Tarn, *Hellenistic Civilisation* [3], London 1952, pp. 220 ff. For doubts as to the real difference between citizenship and potential citizenship at this time, see M. Hammond, *Harvard Studies in Classical Philology*, LX (1951), p. 169, n. 40. Jones also thinks that it cannot be assumed that members of the Jewish πολίτευμα, as such, possessed full Alexandrian citizenship, i.e. the status of ἀστοί; see H.S. Jones, *JRS*, XVI (1926), p. 29. He suggests that the Jews belonged to an intermediate class, somewhere between the ἀστοί and the native Egyptians. The members of this intermediate class, known as πολῖται, were entitled to πολιτικοὶ νόμοι. Most scholars, however, wholly reject the view that the Jews *en bloc* obtained citizenship in Alexandria; see, e.g., T. Mommsen, *Römische Geschichte*, V, Berlin 1894, p. 491, n. 1; Stähelin, p. 35. Stähelin, who wrote before the letter of Claudius was published, thought that Claudius, as a friend of the Jews, granted them the citizenship that they had not originally possessed; *ibid.*, p. 45. See also A. Bludau, *op. cit.* (supra, p. 399), pp. 17 ff.; P. Jouguet, *op. cit.* (supra, p. 399), pp. 19 ff.; Wilcken, in: L. Mitteis & U. Wilcken, *Grundzüge und Chrestomathie der Papyruskunde*, Volume I, Part 2, Leipzig–Berlin 1912, p. 82; M. Engers, *Klio*, XVIII (1923), pp. 79 ff.; Fuchs, *op. cit.* (supra, pp. 399), pp. 94 f.; H. I. Bell, *Juden und Griechen im römischen Alexandreia*, Leipzig 1926, p. 11; W. Otto, *Berliner Philologische Wochenschrift*, XLVI (1926), p. 11; T. Hopfner, *Die Judenfrage bei Griechen und Römern*, Prague 1943, pp. 36 f.; V. M. Scramuzza, *The Emperor Claudius*, Cambridge (Mass.) 1940, pp. 74 ff. Scramuzza suggests that the term πολιτεία used in reference to the Alexandrian Jews expresses the sum of the rights enjoyed by the Jewish πολίτευμα. For similar views, see E.M. Smallwood, *Philonis Alexandrini Legatio ad Gaium*, Leiden 1961, p. 10.

The most complete investigation of Jewish civic rights in Alexandria was made by Tcherikover, (pp. 309 ff.), who also arrives at a negative conclusion in regard to the validity of Josephus' information. Indeed, we may conclude that the main papyrological evidence is contrary to Josephus' view. The evidence of Philo is not clear enough, and the information supplied by Strabo on the parallel example of Cyrene also contradicts Josephus. Even in Josephus himself we may detect some points that negate his main arguments. General considerations seem to preclude the assumption that the Jews, who had a well-organized πολίτευμα in Alexandria, were full citizens of the Greek πόλις. On the other hand, it does seem that there was much confusion concerning Jewish civic rights at the beginning of the Roman rule. This was in part due to the extensive rights and privileges bestowed on the members of the Jewish πολίτευμα, which put them, in many respects, on a par with the Greek citizen body and much above the Egyptian population of the city. Moreover, a number of Jews may have been descendants of the early settlers and have had the right to style themselves Macedonians, and to enjoy whatever privileges were attached to that group. We must also remember that under the early Roman Empire the Greek πόλις of Alexandria lacked some of the most important features of Greek political life and, above all, lacked the city council, the βουλή. Thus, the difference between the members of the Greek πόλις and those of the Jewish πολίτευμα has become somewhat blurred.

Still we see that in the Roman period the Jews thought it of the utmost importance for them to be considered citizens of Alexandria, and it seems that this question became more acute during this period than it had been under the Ptolemies. This may be connected (as Tcherikover has done) with the payment of the poll tax (λαογραφία), from which the Greek citizens of Alexandria were exempted. There may have been other practical reasons — such as privileges in respect to the Roman government — that now made Alexandrian citizenship more valuable to the Jews than citizenship *per se*. Although many seem to have found their way into the body of Greek citizens as individuals, the official Jewish claim to the Roman government was that the various privileges bestowed on them showed that they were, in fact, Alexandrians. Their opponents, such as Apion, not only objected to this interpretation, but also attempted to annul the various rights that put the Jews in a privileged position in the city, and tried to degrade them to the class of the native Egyptians. On Jewish rights in ancient cities, see the illuminating remarks of A. D. Nock, *Greek, Roman and Byzantine Studies*, IV (1963), pp 50 f. (= *Essays on Religion and the Ancient World*, II, Oxford 1972, pp. 960 ff.).

167

Aegyptiaca, apud: Josephus, *Contra Apionem*, II, 48–52, 56 — Niese = F63cR = *F. Gr. Hist.* III, C616, F4e = Reinach (Budé), pp. 66 ff.

(48) Ἀπίωνα δὲ σχεδὸν ἐφεξῆς πάντες ἔλαθον οἱ τῶν προγόνων αὐτοῦ Μακεδόνων βασιλεῖς οἰκειότατα πρὸς ἡμᾶς διατεθέντες... *(49)* ὁ δὲ Φιλομήτωρ Πτολεμαῖος καὶ ἡ γυνὴ αὐτοῦ Κλεοπάτρα τὴν βασιλείαν ὅλην τὴν ἑαυτῶν Ἰουδαίοις ἐπίστευσαν, καὶ στρατηγοὶ 5 πάσης τῆς δυνάμεως ἦσαν Ὀνίας καὶ Δοσίθεος Ἰουδαῖοι, ὧν Ἀπίων

1 Ἀπίωνα] quae Lat. 2 Μακεδόνων secl. Naber
5 Δοσίθεος ed. pr. δωσίθεος L

403

From Herodotus to Plutarch

σκώπτει τὰ ὀνόματα, δέον τὰ ἔργα θαυμάζειν καὶ μὴ λοιδορεῖν, ἀλλὰ
χάριν αὐτοῖς ἔχειν, ὅτι διέσωσαν τὴν Ἀλεξάνδρειαν, ἧς ὡς πολίτης
ἀντιποιεῖται. (50) πολεμούντων γὰρ αὐτῶν τῇ βασιλίσσῃ Κλεοπάτρᾳ
καὶ κινδυνευόντων ἀπολέσθαι κακῶς οὗτοι συμβάσεις ἐποίησαν καὶ
10 τῶν ἐμφυλίων κακῶν ἀπήλλαξαν. ἀλλὰ «μετὰ ταῦτα, φησίν, Ὀνίας
ἐπὶ τὴν πόλιν ἤγαγε στρατὸν ὀλίγον ὄντος ἐκεῖ Θέρμου τοῦ παρὰ
Ῥωμαίων πρεσβευτοῦ καὶ παρόντος.» (51) ὀρθῶς δὲ ποιῶν, φαίην
ἄν... ὁ γὰρ Φύσκων ἐπικληθεὶς Πτολεμαῖος ἀποθανόντος αὐτῷ τοῦ
ἀδελφοῦ Πτολεμαίου τοῦ Φιλομήτορος ἀπὸ Κυρήνης ἐξῆλθε Κλεοπάτραν
15 ἐκβαλεῖν βουλόμενος τῆς βασιλείας... (52) propter haec ergo Onias
adversus eum bellum pro Cleopatra suscepit...
(56) Apion autem omnium calumniator etiam propter bellum adversus Physconem gestum Iudaeos accusare praesumpsit.

11 ⟨οὐκ⟩ ὀλίγον Holwerda   11-12 ὄντος... παρόντος] cum esset illic thermus
(hermus codd.) praesens romanorum legatus Lat.

(48) Apion has further ignored the extreme kindness shown to us
successively by nearly all the kings of his Macedonian ancestors...
(49) Again, Ptolemy Philometor and his consort Cleopatra entrusted
the whole of their realm to Jews, and placed their entire army under
the command of Jewish generals, Onias and Dositheus. Apion ridi-
cules their names, when he ought rather to admire their achievements,
and, instead of abusing them, to thank them for saving Alexandria,
of which he claims to be a citizen. (50) For, when the Alexandrians
were at war with Queen Cleopatra and in imminent danger of annihi-
lation, it was they who negotiated terms and rid them of the horrors
of civil war. "But", says Apion, "Onias subsequently advanced at
the head of a large army against the city, when Thermus, the Roman
ambassador, was actually on the spot." (51) He was right... I venture
to say... For, on the death of his brother Ptolemy Philometor,
Ptolemy, surnamed Physcon, left Cyrene with the intention of de-
throning Cleopatra... (52) That was why, on Cleopatra's behalf,
Onias took up arms against him...
(56) Apion, however, whose calumny nothing escapes, ventures to
find another charge against the Jews in their war on Physcon.

(trans. H. St. J. Thackeray, LCL)

49 Ὁ δὲ Φιλομήτωρ Πτολεμαῖος καὶ ἡ γυνὴ αὐτοῦ Κλεοπάτρα τὴν βασιλείαν
ὅλην τὴν ἑαυτῶν Ἰουδαίοις ἐπίστευσαν: That the Jews were much favoured by
Ptolemy Philometor (180–145 B.C.E.) is attested by other sources as well. Thus, the
Jewish philosopher Aristobulus is designated as the teacher of the king in II Macc.

Apion

i : 10.The fact that they had a common enemy, Antiochus Epiphanes, seems to have strengthened the ties between Philometor and the Jews,and many Jews persecuted by the Seleucid government in Judaea found refuge in Egypt. Later, Jonathan the Hasmonaean, the Jewish high priest, supported Ptolemy Philometor when Philometor invaded the coast of Palestine on behalf of Alexander Balas; see I Macc. x : 57 ff.; cf. H.Volkmann, *Klio*, XIX (1925), pp. 405 f. For papyrological evidence on Jews in Egypt in the reign of Ptolemy Philometor, see *CPJ*, Nos. 24–28, 131–132. The most conspicuous event in the history of Egyptian Jewry at that time was the building of a temple in the Heliopolite nomos, which was known as the Temple of Onias after the name of its builder.

'Ονίας: This Onias should be identified with Onias IV, the son of Onias III. I do not see any basis for Neppi Modona's doubts concerning the connection of Onias in our passage with Onias the high priest of Leontopolis, i.e. Onias IV; see A. Neppi Modona, *Aegyptus*, III (1922), p. 23, n. 9. As related in II Macc. iv : 30–38, Onias III, the last legitimate high priest of the Temple of Jerusalem, was killed at Antioch *c*. 170 B. C. E. by Andronicus, the minister of Antiochus Epiphanes, at the instigation of Menelaus, who had been appointed high priest by Antiochus. Thus, Onias III himself cannot be identical with the Onias who emigrated to Egypt, participated in Egyptian politics and founded the temple named after him. Indeed, it emerges from Josephus that it was Onias, the son of Onias the high priest, who went to Egypt; see *Ant.*, XII, 387 f. Onias the son of Onias the high priest, seeing that Menelaus had been killed and that the high priesthood had been transferred to Alcimus, fled to Ptolemy. He was treated favourably by the king and his wife Cleopatra, and, having acquired a place in the Heliopolite nomos, built a temple there similar to the one in Jerusalem; see *Ant.*, XIII, 62 ff.; XX, 235 f.

Nevertheless, there are many scholars who doubt the truth of the version in II Maccabees concerning the murder of Onias III and also that of *Antiquitates* relating to the migration of Onias' son to Egypt; see G.Wernsdorff, *Commentatio Historico-Critica de Fide Historica Librorum Maccabaicorum*, Breslau 1747, pp. 90 f.; F. Baethgen, *ZAW*, VI (1886), pp. 276 ff.; J. Wellhausen, *Israelitische und jüdische Geschichte* [8], Berlin–Leipzig 1921, pp. 236 f.; H.Willrich, *Urkundenfälschung in der hellenistisch-jüdischen Literatur*, Göttingen 1924, pp. 27 ff.; A. Momigliano, *Prime linee di storia della tradizione maccabaica*, Rome 1930, pp. 38 f.; S. Zeitlin, *PAAJR*, IV (1932–1933), pp. 194 ff.; I. L. Seeligmann, *The Septuagint Version of Isaiah*, Leiden 1948, pp. 91 ff.; R. Hanhart, *Zur Zeitrechnung des I. und II. Makkabäerbuches* (*Beihefte zur Zeitschrift für die alttestamentliche Wissenschaft*, No. 88), 1964, pp. 87 ff. Their chief arguments may be summarized as follows:

a. The version of II Maccabees is somewhat improbable and is legendary in nature. While it ascribes the death of Andronicus to the king's anger at the murder of Onias, another story emerges from Greek sources; see Diodorus, XXX, 7 : 2; *Johannes of Antioch* = Müller, *FHG*, IV, 558, F 58. According to these sources, the death of Andronicus was connected with the murder of the royal nephew; cf. M.Zambelli, *Rivista di filologia classica*, LXXXVIII (1960), pp.363 ff.; O. Mørkholm, *Antiochus IV of Syria*, Copenhagen 1966, p. 141, n. 21.

b. II Maccabees purposely invented the murder of Onias III in order to deprive the Temple of Onias of the glory of having been founded by the famous high priest. Seeligmann even attributes this to the epitomist, whose ideology was contrary to that of Jason. It was the epitomist who attributed the foundation of the temple to Onias IV. This explanation is also implicitly accepted by Hanhart, *op. cit.*

c. In *Bellum Judaicum* (I, 33; VII, 423 ff.) it is implied that Onias III was the founder of the temple, and this version should be given preference over that of *Antiquitates*.

d. The version of *Bellum Judaicum* is confirmed by Theodorus of Mopsuestia (died 428 C. E.) in his commentary to the Psalms; see R. Devreesse, "Le commentaire de Théodore de Mopsueste sur les Psaumes", *Studi e Testi*, XCIII (1939), p. 353; see also some talmudic sources, *TP Yoma*, vi : 43d; *TB Menaḥot* 109b; cf. O. Murray, *JTS*, XVIII (1967), p. 365, n. 2.

To these arguments we may reply:

a. Although the murder of the royal nephew may have been the official reason for the execution of Andronicus, there is still nothing to be said against the possibility that Onias, too, was killed at the instigation of Andronicus. In order to shed lustre on Onias, II Maccabees explains the subsequent death of Andronicus as a punishment for his murder; cf. B. Niese, *Kritik der beiden Makkabäerbücher*, Berlin 1900, p. 97.

b. There is no trace whatever in II Maccabees of an ideological difference between Jason of Cyrene and the epitomist. Onias III is, after Judas the Maccabaean, the main hero of II Maccabees. If the epitome had implicitly aimed at diminishing the sanctity of the Temple of Onias in Egypt, it would hardly have glorified Onias III in such glowing terms. Even though it did imply that Onias could not have founded the temple himself, he was still the ancestor of the family that fostered the building of the Jewish temple in Egypt.

c. *BJ*, I, 33, is rather a confused passage. The expression τῶν ἀρχιερέων relating to Onias may here have the loose meaning it had during the period of the Second Temple; cf. *Contra Apionem*, I, 187 (No. 12). Thus, it may even refer to Onias IV. The situation is different in *BJ*, VII, 423, where Onias is called the son of Simon. In any event, Josephus corrected himself in his later and more circumstantial version in *Antiquitates*, which is, incidentally, not dependent on II Maccabees.

d. Theodorus of Mopsuestia is not an independent source, since he drew here from *Bellum Judaicum*, as is undoubtedly proved by the common factual mistakes made by him and Josephus, but not by any of the other relevant sources; see M. Stern, *Zion*, XXV (1960), pp. 13 ff. The above-mentioned talmudic sources are hardly accurate in the matter of names, though they well reflect the atmosphere of Hellenistic Jerusalem.

To conclude, the somewhat confused information of *Bellum Judaicum* cannot invalidate the version of II Maccabees, which is supported by *Antiquitates*. For a more detailed study of the whole question, see Stern, *op. cit.*, pp. 1 ff.

In addition, we now have some papyrological evidence testifying to the activities of one Onias in Egypt in 164 B. C. E.; see U. Wilcken, *Urkunden der Ptolemäerzeit*, Berlin 1927, No. 110, l.1 = *CPJ*, No. 132. Wilcken has suggested that this Onias functioned as a strategos of the Heliopolite nomos; see also Bengtson, III, p. 58. Tcherikover, in his commentary in *CPJ*, has suggested the identification of this Onias with Onias IV; see also M. Delcor, *RB*, LXXV (1968), p. 192. If so, this document supports Josephus' statement about Onias' high position in the Ptolemaic administration. The sons of Onias IV became commanders in the Ptolemaic army.

Δοσίθεος: We know next to nothing about the personality of this Dositheus. The name itself is fairly common in the Jewish-Hellenistic onomasticon. I see no reason to regard Dositheus as a Samaritan, as suggested by A. Büchler, *Die Tobiaden und die Oniaden*, Vienna 1899, p. 247.

Apion

ὧν Ἀπίων σκώπτει τὰ ὀνόματα: For a somewhat far-fetched interpretation, see D.L. Drew, *Bulletin of the Faculty of Arts of the Cairo University*, XIII, Part 2 (1951), pp. 53 f.

50 πολεμούντων γὰρ αὐτῶν τῇ βασιλίσσῃ Κλεοπάτρᾳ: It is obvious that the events described here are dated after Ptolemy Philometor's death in 145 B.C.E., since Josephus refers only to the struggle of the Alexandrians against Cleopatra II. Intending to reign conjointly with her son, Cleopatra II, the widow and sister of Ptolemy Philometor, continued the war against their brother and enemy Ptolemy Euergetes II, nicknamed Physcon. The city of Alexandria supported the candidature of Ptolemy Physcon, who had been staying at Cyrene, while the Jewish commanders remained loyal to Cleopatra. After some time an agreement was reached and cemented by the marriage of Cleopatra to Ptolemy Physcon. On the situation in Egypt after the death of Philometor, see Iustinus, XXXVIII, 8 : 2 ff. For a discussion of the events, see W. Otto, *Zur Geschichte der Zeit des 6. Ptolemäers*, Munich 1934, pp. 131 ff.; W. Otto & H. Bengtson, *Zur Geschichte des Niederganges des Ptolemäerreiches*, Munich 1938, pp. 25 f.; A. Bouché-Leclercq, *Histoire des Lagides*, II, Paris 1904, pp. 55 ff.; E. R. Bevan, *A History of Egypt under the Ptolemaic Dynasty*, London 1927, pp. 306 f.

μετὰ ταῦτα Ὀνίας ἐπὶ τὴν πόλιν ἤγαγε στρατὸν ὀλίγον: Against the insertion of οὐκ before ὀλίγον, see J. Cohen, *Judaica et Aegyptiaca*, Groningen 1941, p. 33. The force under the command of Onias consisted, at least in part, of Jewish military settlers from the land of Onias; see Strabo, *Histories*, apud: Josephus, *Ant.*, XIII, 287 (No. 99).

Θέρμου τοῦ παρὰ Ῥωμαίων πρεσβευτοῦ: The reference here is to Lucius Minucius Thermus, who already in 154 B. C. E. had been a member of a Roman delegation on behalf of Ptolemy Physcon; see Polybius, XXXIII, 11 (8) : 6; see also W. Otto, *op. cit.*, p. 118 f.; T. R. S. Broughton, *The Magistrates of the Roman Republic*, I, New York 1951, p. 451. On Thermus' activity in Alexandria, see E. Manni, *Rivista di filologia classica*, LXXVIII (1950), p. 249, n. 2; J. Briscoe, *Historia*, XVIII (1969), p. 61.

The discussion of the events by Willrich is quite unsatisfactory; see H. Willrich, *Juden und Griechen vor der makkabäischen Erhebung*, Göttingen 1895, pp. 146 ff. The same applies to Büchler, *op. cit.* (supra, p. 406), p. 248, n. 67.

168

Aegyptiaca, apud: Josephus, *Contra Apionem*, II, 56, 60, 63 — Niese = F63cR = *F. Gr. Hist.* III C616, F4f = Reinach (Budé), pp. 68 f.

(56) Is autem etiam ultimae Cleopatrae Alexandrinorum reginae meminit veluti nobis improperans, quoniam circa nos fuit ingrata, et non potius illam redarguere studuit...

(60) Putasne gloriandum nobis non esse, si quemadmodum dicit Apion famis tempore Iudaeis triticum non est mensa?...

(63) Si vero Germanicus frumenta cunctis in Alexandria commorantibus metiri non potuit, hoc indicium est sterilitatis ac necessitatis frumentorum, non accusatio Iudaeorum...

(56) He further alludes to Cleopatra, the last queen of Alexandria, apparently reproaching us for her ungracious treatment of us. He ought, instead, to have set himself to rebuke that woman. . .

(60) If, as Apion asserts, this woman in time of famine refused to give the Jews any rations of corn, is not that, pray, a fact of which we should be proud? . . .

(63) If Germanicus was unable to distribute corn to all the inhabitants of Alexandria, that merely proves a barren year and a dearth of corn, and cannot be made an accusation against the Jews.

(trans. H. St. J. Thackeray, *LCL*)

60 *putasne gloriandum nobis non esse*, . . .: Here Josephus evades a direct reply and implicitly admits that Cleopatra did not distribute corn to the Jews. We may add that by this discrimination she showed that she did not consider the Jews citizens of Alexandria.

63 *si vero Germanicus frumenta*, . . .: Germanicus, the nephew of the Emperor Tiberius, visited Egypt in 19 C. E. On the hunger prevailing there and Germanicus' attempt to alleviate it, see Tacitus, *Annales*, II, 59: "levavitque apertis horreis pretia frugum"; Suetonius, *Tiberius*, 52. On Germanicus' sojourn in Egypt, see Cichorius, pp. 375 ff.; E. Koestermann, *Historia*, VII (1958), pp. 348 ff.; J. van Ooteghem, *Les études classiques*, XXVII (1959), pp. 241 ff.

Josephus' explanation for the exclusion of the Jews from those helped by Germanicus is unacceptable. Germanicus excluded the Jews because he, too, believed that they were not citizens of Alexandria; cf. U. Wilcken, *Hermes*, LXIII (1928), pp. 51 f.; D. G. Weingärtner, *Die Ägyptenreise des Germanicus*, Bonn (1969), pp. 91 ff.

169

Aegyptiaca, apud: Josephus, *Contra Apionem*, II, 65, 68, 73, 78 — Niese = F63cR = *F. Gr. Hist.* III, C616, F4g = Reinach (Budé), pp. 69 ff.

(65) Sed super haec, quomodo ergo, inquit, si sunt cives, eosdem deos quos Alexandrini non colunt?...

(68) Is autem etiam seditionis causas nobis apponit, qui si cum veritate ob hoc accusat Iudaeos in Alexandria constitutos, cur omnes nos
5 culpat ubique positos eo quod noscamur habere concordiam...?

(73) Itaque derogare nobis Apion conatus est, quia imperatorum non statuamus imagines tamquam illis hoc ignorantibus aut defensione Apionis indigentibus, cum potius debuerit ammirari magnanimitatem mediocritatemque Romanorum...

10 (78) Haec itaque communiter satisfactio posita sit adversus Apionem pro his, quae de Alexandria dicta sunt.

408

(65) "But", Apion persists, "why, then, if they are citizens, do they not worship the same gods as the Alexandrians?" ...

(68) He further accuses us of fomenting sedition. But, if it be granted that he is justified in bringing this accusation against the Jews of Alexandria, why then does he make a grievance against the Jews at large of the notorious concord of our race?...

(73) Apion has consequently attempted to denounce us on the ground that we do not erect statues of the emperors. As if they were ignorant of the fact or needed Apion to defend them! He should rather have admired the magnanimity and moderation of the Romans...

(78) I have now given, I think, a comprehensive and sufficient reply to Apion's remarks on the subject of Alexandria.

(trans. H. St. J. Thackeray, LCL)

65 *quomodo... si sunt cives eosdem deos... non colunt?*: The same argument was advanced by the Jews' opponents in the cities of Asia Minor in the time of Augustus; see *Ant.*, XII, 126: ἀξιούντων δ', εἰ συγγενεῖς εἰσιν αὐτοῖς Ἰουδαῖοι, σέβεσθαι τοὺς αὐτῶν θεούς.

68 *seditionis... concordiam*: The Jewish *concordia* is stressed by both Cicero, *Pro Flacco*, 28 : 66 (No. 68), and Tacitus, *Historiae*, V, 5 (No. 281).

73 *quia imperatorum non statuamus imagines* ...: On the Jews and the imperial cult, see Juster, I, pp. 339 ff.

170

Aegyptiaca, apud: Josephus, Contra Apionem, II, 79–80 — Niese = F 63d R = F. Gr. Hist., III, C616, F4h = Reinach (Budé), p. 72

(79) Ammiror autem etiam eos, qui ei huiusmodi fomitem praebuerunt id est Posidonium ⟨No.44⟩ et Apollonium Molonem ⟨No.48⟩, quoniam accusant quidem nos, quare nos eosdem deos cum aliis non colimus, mentientes autem pariter et de nostro templo blasphemias componentes
5 incongruas non se putant impie agere, dum sit valde turpissimum liberis qualibet ratione mentiri multo magis de templo apud cunctos homines nominato ⟨et⟩ tanta sanctitate pollente. (80) In hoc enim sacrario Apion praesumpsit edicere asini caput collocasse Iudaeos et eum colere ac dignum facere tanta religione, et hoc affirmat fuisse depala-
10 tum, dum Antiochus Epiphanes expoliasset templum et illud caput inventum ex auro compositum multis pecuniis dignum.

2 Molonem Reinach   molonis Lat.   8 eum] id Naber

(79) I am no less amazed of the proceedings of the authors who

supplied him with his materials, I mean Posidonius and Apollonius Molon. On the one hand they charge us with not worshipping the same gods as other people; on the other, they tell lies and invent absurd calumnies about our temple, without showing any consciousness of impiety. Yet to high-minded men nothing is more disgraceful than a lie, of any description, but above all on the subject of a temple of world-wide fame and commanding sanctity. (80) Within this sanctuary Apion has the effrontery to assert that the Jews kept an ass's head, worshipping that animal and deeming it worthy of the deepest reverence; the fact was disclosed, he maintains, on the occasion of the spoliation of the temple by Antiochus Epiphanes, when the head, made of gold and worth a high price, was discovered.

(trans. H. St. J. Thackeray, LCL)

79 *Ammiror etiam eos, qui ei huiusmodi fomitem praebuerunt, id est Posidonium et Apollonium Molonem...*: From Josephus we learn that these writers supplied Apion with his material and that this referred to the Temple. Josephus' general statement is followed by the story of the worship of the asinine head in the Temple of Jerusalem. It seems that this is the story for which the two writers furnished the material. The next story, which is also connected with the Temple, tells of the annual murder of a Greek. It is possible, though much less certain, that this story, as well, ultimately derives from one or both of these writers. In any case, the extent of Apion's debt to them is still not known. Bickermann maintains that Apollonius Molon alone is responsible for Apion's account; see E. Bickermann, *MGWJ*, LXXI (1927), p. 260. This assumption is based on Diodorus, XXXIV–XXXV, 1, (No. 63). Diodorus, whose source presumably was Posidonius, contradicts Apion and is more favourable to the Jews. He states that all Antiochus found in the Temple was the statue of a man, who was identified with Moses, sitting on an ass. But, after all, Diodorus' dependence on Posidonius is only a matter of conjecture; see the introduction to Posidonius. On the other hand, there is a possibility that Josephus' statement about Posidonius and Apollonius Molon furnishing Apion with his material does not necessarily mean that Apion's circumstantial narrative was entirely dependent on it. Apion may have embellished his story so that neither Posidonius nor Apollonius Molon could be considered responsible for all the details.

80 *asini caput collocasse Iudaeos*: On Jewish ass-worship and its various versions, see the introduction to Mnaseas of Patara.

171

Aegyptiaca, apud: Josephus, Contra Apionem, II, 89, 91–96 — Niese = F63dR = F. Gr. Hist.,
III, C616, F4i = Reinach (Budé), pp. 73 ff.

(89) Alteram vero fabulam derogatione nostra plenam de Graecis apposuit...

(91) Propheta vero aliorum factus est Apion et dixit Antiochum in templo invenisse lectum et hominem in eo iacentem et propositam
5 ei mensam maritimis terrenisque et volatilium dapibus plenam, et obstipuisset his homo. (92) Illum vero mox adorasse regis ingressum tamquam maximum ei solacium praebiturum ac procidentem ad eius genua extensa dextra poposcisse libertatem; et iubente rege, ut confideret et diceret, quis esset vel cur ibidem habitaret vel quae
10 esset causa ciborum eius, tunc hominem cum gemitu et lacrimis lamentabiliter suam narrasse necessitatem. (93) Ait, inquit, esse quidem se Graecum, et dum peragraret provinciam propter vitae causam direptum se subito ab alienigenis hominibus atque deductum ad templum et inclusum illic, et a nullo conspici sed cuncta dapium
15 praeparatione saginari. (94) Et primum quidem haec sibi inopinabilia beneficia prodidisse et detulisse laetitiam deinde suspicionem postea stuporem, ac postremum consulentem a ministris ad se accedentibus audisse legem ineffabilem Iudaeorum, pro qua nutriebatur, et hoc illos facere singulis annis quodam tempore constituto. (95) Et com-
20 praehendere quidem Graecum peregrinum eumque annali tempore saginare et deductum ad quandam silvam occidere quidem eum hominem eiusque corpus sacrificare secundum suas sollemnitates et gustare ex eius visceribus et iusiurandum facere in immolatione Graeci, ut inimicitias contra Graecos haberent, et tunc in quandam
25 foveam reliqua hominis pereuntis abicere. (96) Deinde refert eum dixisse paucos iam dies de vita sibimet superesse atque rogasse, ut erubescens Graecorum deos et superantes in suo sanguine insidias Iudaeorum, de malis eum circumastantibus liberaret.

13 *direptum* ed. Basil.　　*directum* Lat.　　　　26 *de vita* Boysen　　*debita* Lat.

(89) He adds a second story, about Greeks, which is a malicious slander upon us from beginning to end...
(91) Apion, who is here the spokesman of others, asserts that: Antiochus found in the temple a couch, on which a man was reclining, with a table before him laden with a banquet of fish of the sea, beasts of the earth, and birds of the air, at which the poor fellow was gazing in stupefaction. (92) The king's entry was instantly hailed by him with adoration, as about to procure him profound relief; falling at the king's knees, he stretched out his right hand and implored him to set him free. The king reassured him and bade him tell him who he was, why he was living there, what was the meaning of his abundant fare. Thereupon, with sighs and tears, the man, in a pitiful tone, told the tale of his distress. (93) He said, Apion continues, that he was

411

a Greek and that, while travelling about the province for his livelihood, he was suddenly kidnapped by men of a foreign race and conveyed to the temple; there he was shut up and seen by nobody, but
was fattened on feasts of the most lavish description. (94) At first
these unlooked for attentions deceived him and caused him pleasure;
suspicion followed, then consternation. Finally, on consulting the
attendants who waited upon him, he heard of the unutterable law
of the Jews for the sake of which he was being fed. The practice was
repeated annually at a fixed season. (95) They would kidnap a Greek
foreigner, fatten him up for a year, and then convey him to a wood,
where they slew him, sacrificed his body with their customary ritual,
partook of his flesh, and, while immolating the Greek, swore an oath
of hostility to the Greeks. The remains of their victim were then
thrown into a pit. (96) The man (Apion continues) stated that he
had now but a few days left to live, and implored the king, out of
respect for the gods of Greece, to defeat this Jewish plot upon his
life-blood and to deliver him from his miserable predicament.

(trans. H. St. J. Thackeray, LCL)

89 *Alteram vero fabulam* . . .: On a brilliant analysis of this passage, see E. Bickermann, *MGWJ*, LXXI (1927), pp.171 ff. Bickermann concludes that Apion's narrative
of the incident consists of two main components. The first part is one of the many
references to the King of Saturnalia, who is known from many countries and ages;
the second constitutes a description of a cannibalic *coniuratio*, in which the partners
are joined by the strong bonds of a common crime; see Sallustius, *Catilina*, 22;
Diodorus, XXII, 5. Bickermann finds a trace of the combination of these two
different motifs in the words "et deductum ad quandam silvam occidere quidem
eum hominem eiusque corpus sacrificare . . ."; see Bickermann, *op. cit.*, p. 181:
"Einen schon Toten zu opfern, ist etwas zu spät." See also the introduction to
Damocritus, who, like Apion, gives his version of human sacrifice perpetuated, as
it were, by the Jews immediately after he describes their worship of the asinine head.
Bickermann holds the view that Apion's story about the murder of the Greek
ultimately derives from official Seleucid propaganda, which attempted to justify the
proceedings of the king against the Temple of Jerusalem. However, we may suggest
with no less reason that the writers whom Josephus describes as *volentes Antiocho
praestare* are anti-Semitic Alexandrians, who regarded Antiochus as the prototype
of a champion of Hellenic anti-Semitism against the enemies of mankind; cf.
Tacitus, *Historiae*, V, 8 (No. 281).

172

Aegyptiaca, apud: Josephus, *Contra Apionem*, II, 112–114 — Niese = F63dR = *F. Gr. Hist.*, III,
C 616, F4k = Reinach (Budé), p.77 (cf. Mnaseas, No. 28)

(112) Rursumque tamquam piissimus deridet adiciens fabulae suae

412

Mnaseam ⟨No.28⟩. Ait enim illum retulisse, dum bellum Iudaei contra Idumaeos haberent longo quodam tempore in aliqua civitate Idumaeorum, qui Dorii nominantur, quendam eorum qui in ea Apollinem cole-
5 bat venisse ad Iudaeos, cuius hominis nomen dicit Zabidon deinde qui eis promisisset traditurum se eis Apollinem deum Doriensium venturumque illum ad nostrum templum, si omnes abscederent. (113) Et credidisse omnem multitudinem Iudaeorum; Zabidon vero fecisse quoddam machinamentum ligneum et circumposuisse sibi et in eo
10 tres ordines infixisse lucernarum et ita ambulasse, ut procul stantibus appareret, quasi stellae per terram *(114)* τὴν πορείαν ποιουμένων, τοὺς μὲν Ἰουδαίους ὑπὸ τοῦ παραδόξου τῆς θέας καταπεπληγμένους πόρρω μένοντας ἡσυχίαν ἄγειν, τὸν δὲ Ζάβιδον ἐπὶ πολλῆς ἡσυχίας εἰς τὸν ναὸν παρελθεῖν καὶ τὴν χρυσῆν ἀποσῦραι τοῦ κάνθωνος κεφαλήν, οὕτω
15 γὰρ ἀστεϊζόμενος γέγραφεν, καὶ πάλιν εἰς Δῶρα τὸ τάχος ἀπελθεῖν.

2 *Mnaseam* Niese   *mnafeam* Lat.   2–3 *Idumaeos* Gelenius
iudaeos Lat.   3 *Idumaeorum* Gelenius   *iudaeorum* Lat.   5 *quia* Boysen
13 μένοντας Bekker   μὲν ὄντας L   *constitutos* Lat.   14 κάνθωνος Hudson
ἀκανθῶνος L   *asini* Lat.   15 εἰς Δῶρα Niese   *ad dora* Lat.   εἰς δῶριν
L   εἰς δῶραν ed. pr. / τὸ τάχος] κατὰ τάχος ed. pr.

(112) This model of piety derides us again in a story which he attributes to Mnaseas. The latter, according to Apion, relates that in the course of a long war between the Jews and the Idumaeans, an inhabitant of an Idumaean city, called Dorii, who worshipped Apollo and bore (so we are told) the name of Zabidus, came out to the Jews and promised to deliver into their hands Apollo, the god of his city, who would visit our temple if they all took their departure. (113) The Jews all believed him; where-upon Zabidus constructed an apparatus of wood, inserted in it three rows of lamps, and put it over his person. Thus arrayed he walked about, presenting the appearance to distant onlookers of stars perambulating the earth. (114) Astounded at this amazing spectacle, the Jews kept their distance, in perfect silence. Meanwhile, Zabidus stealthily passed into the sanctuary, snatched up the golden head of the pack-ass (as he facetiously calls it), and made off post-haste to Dora.   (trans. H. St. J. Thackeray, *LCL*)

173

Aegyptiaca, apud: Josephus, *Contra Apionem*, II, 121 — Niese = F63dR = *F. Gr. Hist.*, III, C616, F41 = Reinach (Budé), pp. 78 f.

Καταψεύσασθαί τινα καὶ ὅρκον ἡμῶν ὡς ὀμνυόντων τὸν θεὸν τὸν
1 καταψεύσασθαί] καταψεύδεται δὲ ed. pr.

ποιήσαντα τὸν οὐρανὸν καὶ τὴν γῆν καὶ τὴν θάλασσαν μηδενὶ εὐνοήσειν ἀλλοφύλῳ, μάλιστα δὲ ῞Ελλησιν.

Then he attributes to us an imaginary oath, and would have it appear that we swear by the God who made heaven and earth and sea to show no good-will to a single alien, above all to Greeks.

(trans. H. St. J. Thackeray, *LCL*)

μηδενὶ εὐνοήσειν ἀλλοφύλῳ, μάλιστα δὲ ῞Ελλησιν: Bickermann aptly refers to *Sylloge*[3], No. 527: μὴ μὰν ἐγὼ ποκα τοῖς Λυττίοις καλῶς φρονήσειν μήτε τέχνᾳ μήτε μαχανᾷ μήτε ἐν νυκτὶ μήτε πεδ᾽ἀμέραν...; see E. Bickermann, *loc. cit.* (supra, p. 412). Damocritus' version does not contain the emphasis on Greeks.

174

Aegyptiaca, apud: Josephus, *Contra Apionem*, II, 125 — Niese = F63dR = *F. Gr. Hist.*, III, C616, F4m = Reinach (Budé), p. 79

Σφόδρα τοίνυν τῆς πολλῆς συνέσεως καὶ ἐπὶ τῷ μέλλοντι ῥηθήσεσθαι θαυμάζειν ἄξιόν ἐστιν ᾿Απίωνα· τεκμήριον γὰρ εἶναί φησιν τοῦ μήτε νόμοις ἡμᾶς χρῆσθαι δικαίοις μήτε τὸν θεὸν εὐσεβεῖν ὡς προσῆκεν, ⟨τὸ μὴ ἄρχειν⟩, δουλεύειν δὲ μᾶλλον ἔθνεσιν [καὶ] ἄλλοτε ἄλλοις καὶ
5 τὸ κεχρῆσθαι συμφοραῖς τισι περὶ τὴν πόλιν.

4 ⟨τὸ μὴ ἄρχειν⟩ ed. pr. / καὶ secl. Niese

In the argument to which I now proceed Apion's extraordinary sagacity is most astonishing. A clear proof, according to him, that our laws are unjust and our religious ceremonies erroneous is that we are not masters of an empire, but rather the slaves, first of one nation, then of another, and that calamity has more than once befallen our city.

(trans. H. St. J. Thackeray, *LCL*)

τεκμήριον γὰρ... : For the same argument, see Cicero, *Pro Flacco*, 28 : 69 (No. 68).

175

Aegyptiaca, apud: Josephus, *Contra Apionem*, II, 135 — Niese = F63dR = *F. Gr. Hist.*, III, C616, F4n = Reinach (Budé), p. 81

᾿Αλλὰ θαυμαστοὺς ἄνδρας οὐ παρεσχήκαμεν οἷον τεχνῶν τινων εὑρετὰς ἢ σοφίᾳ διαφέροντας. καὶ καταριθμεῖ Σωκράτην καὶ Ζήνωνα καὶ

414

Κλεάνθην καὶ τοιούτους τινάς. εἶτα τὸ θαυμασιώτατον τοῖς εἰρημένοις
αὐτὸς ἑαυτὸν προστίθησι καὶ μακαρίζει τὴν 'Αλεξάνδρειαν, ὅτι τοιοῦτον
ἔχει πολίτην.

3 τοῖς εἰρημένοις Niese   τῶν εἰρημένων L   *his* Lat.

"But" (urges Apion) we "have not produced any geniuses, for example, inventors in arts and crafts or eminent sages." He enumerates
Socrates, Zeno, Cleanthes, and others of that calibre; and then — most
astounding master-stroke — adds his own name to the list, and felic-
itates Alexandria on possessing such a citizen!

(trans. H. St. J. Thackeray, *LCL*)

'Αλλὰ θαυμαστοὺς ἄνδρας οὐ παρεσχήκαμεν: Cf. Apollonius Molon, apud:
Josephus, *Contra Apionem*, II, 148 (No. 49): ἀφυεστάτους εἶναι τῶν βαρβάρων
καὶ διὰ τοῦτο μηδὲν εἰς τὸν βίον εὕρημα συμβεβλῆσθαι μόνους. Apion is probably
dependent here on Apollonius Molon. On the pride that the Hellenistic world
took in the great εὑρεταί and on the catalogues of the εὑρεταί, see the commentary
to Apollonius Molon (No. 49).

176

Aegyptiaca apud: Josephus, *Contra Apionem*, II, 137 — Niese = F63dR = *F. Gr. Hist.*, III, C616,
F4o = Reinach (Budé), p. 81

Τὰ δὲ λοιπὰ τῶν ἐν τῇ κατηγορίᾳ γεγραμμένων ἄξιον ἦν ἴσως ἀναπολό-
γητα παραλιπεῖν, ἵν' αὐτὸς αὐτοῦ καὶ τῶν ἄλλων Αἰγυπτίων ᾖ ὁ κατηγο-
ρῶν· ἐγκαλεῖ γάρ, ὅτι ζῷα <ἥμερα> θύομεν καὶ χοῖρον οὐκ ἐσθίομεν καὶ
τὴν τῶν αἰδοίων χλενάζει περιτομήν.

1 τὰ δὲ λοιπὰ ed. pr.   τὰ λοιπὰ L   3 ἥμερα add. Niese
animalia consueta Lat.

The remaining counts in his indictment had better perhaps have remained unanswered, so that Apion might be left to act as his own and
his countrymen's accuser. He denounces us for sacrificing domestic
animals and for not eating pork, and he derides the practice of circumcision.   (trans. H. St. J. Thackeray, *LCL*)

καὶ χοῖρον οὐκ ἐσθίομεν: Cf. the commentaries to Petronius (No. 195) and
Plutarch (No. 258).

415

177

Aegyptiaca, apud: Josephus, *Contra Apionem*, II, 148, 295 — Niese = *F. Gr. Hist.*, III, C616,
T15b = Reinach (Budé), pp. 83, 110

(148) Ἄλλως τε καὶ τὴν κατηγορίαν ὁ Ἀπολλώνιος ⟨No. 49⟩ οὐκ
ἀθρόαν ὥσπερ ὁ Ἀπίων ἔταξεν...
(295) Ἀπίωνες μὲν καὶ Μόλωνες ⟨No. 50⟩ καὶ πάντες ὅσοι τῷ ψεύδεσθαι καὶ λοιδορεῖν χαίρουσιν ἐξεληλέγχθωσαν.

(148) Especially because Apollonius, unlike Apion, has not grouped
his accusations together...
(295) The Apions and Molons and all who delight in lies and abuse
may be left to their own confusion.

(trans. H. St. J. Thackeray, *LCL*)

148 τὴν κατηγορίαν... οὐκ ἀθρόαν ὥσπερ ὁ Ἀπίων ἔταξεν: Apion apparently
concentrated his attack on the Jews in that part of his *Egyptian History* that
included the story of the Exodus.

LXIV. CHAEREMON

First century C.E.

The Graeco-Egyptian writer Chaeremon may be considered an Egyptian intellectual in the tradition of Manetho — one who took great pride in his country's past and immemorial institutions, describing them in Greek. He was also deeply imbued with much of Greek culture, and he became one of its most conspicuous representatives in the first century C.E. These two traits of Chaeremon are well illustrated by the fact that he is sometimes labelled an Egyptian priest (ἱερογραμματεύς), while elsewhere he appears as Chaeremon the Stoic. Insofar as he partakes of two cultural traditions, he resembles Apion, who preceded him a little, and some of his Jewish contemporaries, among whom Philo was most notable.

According to Suda, s. v. Ἀλέξανδρος Αἰγαῖος, he was a teacher of Nero. It has also been assumed by many scholars that Chaeremon the son of Leonidas,[1] who was one of the Alexandrian Greeks to appear before the emperor Claudius, is the same as Chaeremon the Graeco-Egyptian historian.[2] If this is so, would Chaeremon again resemble Apion, who fulfilled a similar task for the Alexandrian Greeks in the time of Gaius Caligula?

The fragment of Chaeremon on the Jews has been preserved in Contra Apionem. *Josephus states that the passage was culled from Chaeremon's History of Egypt, which included an Egyptian version of the Exodus.*

In general outline, Chaeremon's narrative is not unlike that of Manetho; however, he also uses traditions independent of Manetho. These are reflected, above all, in the appearance of Isis in a dream and in the mention of Phritibautes. Manetho's version ignores the part played by Isis, and Amenophis, the son of Paapis, takes the place of Phritibautes. Additionally, Chaeremon does not seem to identify the allies of the "defiled" with the Hyksos, and he gives Moses an Egyptian name

---

1 See P. London, No. 1912, l. 17, in: H. I. Bell, *Jews and Christians in Egypt,* London 1924, p. 23 (= *CPJ*, No. 153).

2 See H. Stuart-Jones, *JRS*, XVI (1926), p. 18; J. Vergote, *Le Muséon*, LII (1939), p. 220.

417

From Herodotus to Plutarch

different from the one found in Manetho, mentioning him alongside Joseph. The reference to these two leaders echoes the biblical tradition that found its way to non-Jewish circles.

Bibliography

J. Bernays, *Theophrastos' Schrift über Frömmigkeit*, Berlin 1866, pp. 21 f.; E. Zeller, *Hermes*, XI (1876), pp. 430 ff.; E. Schwartz, PW, III, pp. 2025 ff.; Stähelin, p. 48; Schürer, III, pp. 536 ff.; R. Weill, *La fin du moyen empire égyptien*, Paris 1918, pp. 105 f. (517 f).; I. Heinemann, PW, Suppl. V, p. 27; H. R. Schwyzer, *Chairemon*, Leipzig 1932, (see comment on our passage on pp. 57–59); Böhl, p. 111; Gager, pp. 120 ff.; Fraser, II, p. 1107, n. 46.

418

Aegyptiaca Historia, apud: Josephus, *Contra Apionem*, I, 288–292 — Niese = F58R = H. R. Schwyzer, *Chairemon*, Leipzig 1932, F1 = *F. Gr. Hist.*, III, C618, F1 = Reinach (Budé), pp. 53 f.

(288) Μετὰ τοῦτον ἐξετάσαι βούλομαι Χαιρήμονα· καὶ γὰρ οὗτος Αἰγυπτιακὴν φάσκων ἱστορίαν συγγράφειν καὶ προσθεὶς ταὐτὸ ὄνομα τοῦ βασιλέως ὅπερ ὁ Μανεθὼς Ἀμένωφιν καὶ τὸν υἱὸν αὐτοῦ Ῥαμεσσήν, *(289)* φησὶν ὅτι κατὰ τοὺς ὕπνους ἡ Ἶσις ἐφάνη τῷ Ἀμενώφει μεμ-
5 φομένη αὐτόν, ὅτι τὸ ἱερὸν αὐτῆς ἐν τῷ πολέμῳ κατέσκαπται. Φριτι-
βαύτην δὲ ἱερογραμματέα φάναι, ἐὰν τῶν τοὺς μολυσμοὺς ἐχόντων ἀνδρῶν καθάρῃ τὴν Αἴγυπτον, παύσεσθαι τῆς πτοίας αὐτόν. *(290)* ἐπι-
λέξαντα δὲ τῶν ἐπισινῶν μυριάδας εἰκοσιπέντε ἐκβαλεῖν. ἡγεῖσθαι δ᾽
αὐτῶν γραμματέας Μωσῆν τε καὶ Ἰώσηπον, καὶ τοῦτον ἱερογραμματέα,
10 Αἰγύπτια δ᾽ αὐτοῖς ὀνόματα εἶναι τῷ μὲν Μωσῇ Τισιθέν, τῷ δὲ Ἰωσή-
πῳ Πετεσήφ. *(291)* τούτους δ᾽ εἰς Πηλούσιον ἐλθεῖν καὶ ἐπιτυχεῖν
μυριάσι τριακονταοκτὼ καταλελειμμέναις ὑπὸ τοῦ Ἀμενώφιος, ἃς οὐ
θέλειν εἰς τὴν Αἴγυπτον διακομίζειν· οἷς φιλίαν συνθεμένους ἐπὶ τὴν
Αἴγυπτον στρατεῦσαι. *(292)* τὸν δὲ Ἀμένωφιν οὐχ ὑπομείναντα τὴν
15 ἔφοδον αὐτῶν εἰς Αἰθιοπίαν φυγεῖν καταλιπόντα τὴν γυναῖκα ἔγκυον,
ἣν κρυβομένην ἔν τισι σπηλαίοις τεκεῖν παῖδα ὄνομα Ῥαμέσσην, ὃν
ἀνδρωθέντα ἐκδιῶξαι τοὺς Ἰουδαίους εἰς τὴν Συρίαν ὄντας περὶ εἴκοσι
μυριάδας καὶ τὸν πατέρα Ἀμένωφιν ἐκ τῆς Αἰθιοπίας καταδέξασθαι.

2 προθεὶς Cobet   5–6 *fritobautis* Lat.   φριτιφάντην ed. pr.
Φριτοβαύτην Reinach   7 παύσεσθαι Niese   παύσασθαι L / πτοίας
ed. pr. πτόας L   *timor* Lat.   8 μυριάδας εἰκοσιπέντε] $\overline{CCCL}$ Lat.
9 *moysen* Lat.   13 οἷς ed. pr.   εἰς L   16 κρυπτομένην ed. pr. /
Ῥαμέσσην Lat., cod. Eliensis   μεσσήν L   18 ἀναδέξασθαι L in marg.

(288) The next witness I shall cross-examine is Chaeremon. This writer likewise professes to write the history of Egypt, and agrees with Manetho in giving the names of Amenophis and Ramesses to the king and his son. (289) He then proceeds to state that Isis appeared to Amenophis in his sleep, and reproached him for the destruction of her temple in war-time. The sacred scribe Phritibautes told him that, if he purged Egypt of its contaminated population, he might cease to be alarmed. (290) The king, thereupon, collected 250,000 afflicted persons and banished them from the country. Their leaders were scribes, Moses and another sacred scribe—Joseph! Their Egyptian names were Tisithen (for Moses) and Peteseph (Joseph). (291) The exiles on reaching Pelusium fell in with a body of 380,000 persons, left there by Amenophis, who had refused them permission to cross the Egyptian frontier. With these the exiles concluded an alliance

419

From Herodotus to Plutarch

and marched upon Egypt. (292) Amenophis, without waiting for their attack, fled to Ethiopia, leaving his wife pregnant. Concealing herself in some caverns she gave birth to a son named Ramesses, who, on reaching manhood, drove the Jews, to the number of about 200,000, into Syria, and brought home his father Amenophis from Ethiopia.

(trans. H. St. J. Thackeray, *LCL*)

288 Αἰγυπτιακὴν φάσκων ἱστορίαν συγγράφειν: This is the only place in the fragments of Chaeremon where he expressly refers to his Egyptian History.

289 κατὰ τοὺς ὕπνους ἡ Ἶσις ἐφάνη τῷ Ἀμενώφει μεμφομένη: There is no allusion to this in the fragments of Manetho or in those of other Graeco-Egyptian writers, but a papyrus dating from the third century C. E. affords an excellent parallel to the wrath of Isis in Chaeremon; see *PSI*, No. 982 = *CPJ*, No. 520. This papyrological text, which contains a prophecy concerning Egypt, has been related to the so-called Oracle of the Potter. However, while the texts of this work do not show any anti-Semitic traits, this papyrus refers to the Jews with hostility. In l. 4. of the papyrus the reading Ἰου(δαίοις), proposed by the first editor (Vitelli), has been endorsed by the scholars who subsequently dealt with the text. In l. 8 there is a reference to the Jews as ἐξ Ἐγύπτου ἐγβεβλημένοι,who are also labelled παράνομοι. Manteuffel, who has analysed the text, relates the papyrus to the Jewish revolt under Trajanus; see G. Manteuffel, *Mélanges Maspero*, II, Cairo 1934–1937, pp. 119 ff.; see also L. Koenen, *Gnomon*, XL (1968), p. 258. However, there is nothing to support Manteuffel's view, and the prophecy may originally date from the Hellenistic age. In l. 9 of the papyrus we read, after mention has been made of the people expelled from Egypt (i.e. the Jews), about the wrath of Isis, which, it seems, was connected with the expulsion. Because of the deteriorated state of the papyrus, we do not know whether there were more parallels between the fragment of the Graeco-Egyptian prophecy and the version of Chaeremon, nor can we tell whether there is any interdependence between the two. It seems more likely that both represent a common Graeco-Egyptian tradition, although Chaeremon might well have been known in the χώρα; cf., e.g., the much later Manetho papyrus referred to by C. H. Roberts, *Museum Helveticum*, X (1953), p. 265. See also R. A. Pack, *The Greek and Latin Literary Texts from Graeco-Roman Egypt* ², Ann Arbor 1965, p. 74.

ὅτι τὸ ἱερὸν αὐτῆς ἐν τῷ πολέμῳ κατέσκαπται: Cf. Varro, apud: Augustinus, *De Civitate Dei*, XVIII, 12: "ut placaretur ira eius [scil. Apollinis], qua putabant adflictas esse sterilitate Graeciae regiones, quia non defenderint templum eius quod rex Danaus cum easdem terras bello invasisset, incendit."

Φριτιβαύτην: Here Phritibautes replaces Manetho's Amenophis, son of Paapis.

ἐὰν ... παύσεσθαι τῆς πτοίας αὐτόν: The solution of Phritibautes, as it stands, seems to be missing a link. Its meaning surely was that by his pious act Amenophis would gain the favour of the goddess. However, Chaeremon, or more likely his abridger, did not succeed in connecting the story of Isis' dream to that about the defiled people.

290 καὶ Ἰώσηπον: Two other non-Jewish sources refer to Joseph: Pompeius Trogus (apud: Iustinus, Epitoma, XXXVI, 2 : 6 = No. 137), according to whom Joseph is the father of Moses, and Apollonius Molon (apud: Eusebius, *Praeparatio Evangelica*, IX, 19:3 = No. 46).

420

Chaeremon

καὶ τοῦτον ἱερογραμματέα: Chaeremon himself belonged to ἱερογραμματεῖς; see the introduction.

Τισιθέν... Πετεσήφ: There may be some justification for discerning here an Egyptian tradition that knew the leaders of the defiled people as the priests Tisithen and Peteseph, who were supposedly identified with Moses and Joseph at a later stage; cf. Schwyzer, op. cit. (supra, p. 418), p. 57. The name Peteseph, slightly emended, could easily be identified with the name of Joseph; cf. Böhl, op. cit. (supra, p. 418), p. 485, n. 8. Hopfner thinks that the name is Peteseth ("the gift of Seth"); see T. Hopfner, Plutarch über Isis und Osiris, II, Prague 1941, p. 145.

291 εἰς Πηλούσιον ἐλθεῖν: According to Chaeremon's version, the defiled people escaped directly to the border separating Egypt from Asia. Here Chaeremon's version is much clearer than that of Manetho. On the localization of these events, both in Chaeremon and in Manetho's second version, see J. Schwartz, BIFAO, XLIX (1950), pp. 75 ff. Schwartz points out that the Palestinian Targum locates Pithom and Rameses at Tanis and Pelusium.

ἃς οὐ θέλειν εἰς τὴν Αἴγυπτον διακομίζειν: Instead of the Hyksos inhabiting Jerusalem as they seem to do in Manetho, here we have nomad tribes at the border of the Egyptian kingdom, who were prevented from entering Egypt. In the passage from Chaeremon the identity of the people on the border is rather obscure. Although Josephus (Contra Apionem, I, 298) blames Chaeremon for being vague, it stands to reason that he did not have Chaeremon's original work before him, but only some fragments from a collection that may have been made by a Hellenistic Jew.

292 τὸν δὲ Ἀμένωφιν... Ῥαμέσσην: The narrative in this section is consonant with that of Manetho. The story about the wife of Amenophis who secretly gave birth to the saviour of Egypt is typical of the myth of the saviour-child and its persecution; cf. S. Luria, ZAW, XLIV (1926), pp. 120 f.

Ἰουδαίους: The people expelled from Egypt are labelled Jews without any explanation. Were the Jews, according to Chaeremon, identical with both the defiled people and with those from the border?

ὄντας περὶ εἴκοσι μυριάδας: How did Chaeremon arrive at this figure? He had previously mentioned 250,000 defiled people and 380,000 people from Pelusium, altogether 630,000. Did he identify the Jews only with the defiled? Even if he did so, some 50,000 people are unaccounted for. Again, we get the impression that Josephus only used fragments from Chaeremon.

LXV. DIOSCORIDES

First century C.E.

As one might expect in a work like De Materia Medica, *compiled under the Julio-Claudian dynasty by a writer from Cilician Anazarba, it contains allusions to products of Judaea. Thus, we find mentioned here the balsam that grows only in a certain valley in Judaea (No. 179); the Judaean asphalt, which differs from other types of asphalt (No. 181); and the resin (No. 180). Dioscorides also describes the medical uses of "the Jewish stone", which is helpful to sufferers from difficult micturition and stones in the bladder (No. 184). It is noteworthy that Petra is described once as* κατὰ 'Ιουδαίαν *(No. 182).[1]*

---

1 See also the reference to Sextius Niger, *Praefatio*, 3 (No. 153).

179

De Materia Medica, I, 19:1 — Wellmann = F64R

Βάλσαμον· τὸ μὲν δένδρον κατὰ μέγεθος λυκίου ἢ πυρακάνθης βλέπεται,
φύλλα ἔχον ὅμοια πηγάνῳ, λευκότερα δὲ πολλῷ καὶ ἀειθαλέστερα,
γεννώμενον ἐν μόνῃ Ἰουδαίᾳ κατά τινα αὐλῶνα, διαφέρον αὐτὸ ἑαυτοῦ
τραχύτητι καὶ μήκει καὶ ἰσχνότητι. λέγεται γοῦν τὸ λεπτὸν καὶ τριχῶδες
5 τοῦ θάμνου εὐθέριστον, ἴσως διὰ τὸ εὐχερῶς θερίζεσθαι ἰσχνὸν ὄν.

1 πυρακάνθης] πυξακάνθης Saracenus   3 post αὐλῶνα add. καὶ ἐν αἰγύπτῳ
HDiDA   5 εὐθέριστον Wellmann   θερίσερον F   θεριστόν cett.

Balsam. The tree seems to be as big as lycium or fiery thorn, and
it has leaves which resemble rue, yet they are whiter and ever-green.
It grows only in Judaea in a certain valley, and its parts differ from
each other according to their roughness, length and thinness. Indeed,
the fine and the hair-like part of the shrub is called Eutheriston,
perhaps because being thin it is easily harvested.

φύλλα ἔχον ὅμοια πηγάνῳ... καὶ ἀειθαλέστερα: Cf. Theophrastus, *Historia Plantarum*, IX, 6:1.
γεννώμενον ἐν μόνῃ Ἰουδαίᾳ: Cf. Diodorus, *Bibliotheca Historica*, II, 48:9 (No.
59); ibid., XIX, 98 (No. 62): γίνεται δὲ περὶ τοὺς τόπους τούτους ἐν αὐλῶνί τινι
καὶ τὸ καλούμενον βάλσαμον... οὐδαμοῦ μὲν τῆς ἄλλης οἰκουμένης εὑρισκομένου τοῦ φυτοῦ; Plinius, *Naturalis Historia*, XII, 111 (No. 213).
εὐθέριστον: Cf. Plinius, *Naturalis Historia*, XII, 114 (No. 213): "tenue et capillacea coma quod vocatur eutheriston."

180

De Materia Medica, I, 71:1 — Wellmann

Ἡ δὲ ἐξ αὐτῆς ⟨scil. τερμίνθου⟩ ῥητίνη κομίζεται μὲν ἐξ Ἀραβίας τῆς
ἐν Πέτρᾳ, γεννᾶται δὲ καὶ ἐν Ἰουδαίᾳ καὶ Συρίᾳ καὶ ἐν Κύπρῳ καὶ
ἐν Λιβύῃ καὶ ἐν ταῖς Κυκλάσι νήσοις, ἣ δὴ καὶ διαφέρει διαυγεστέρα
οὖσα, λευκή, ὑελίζουσα τῷ χρώματι [καὶ κυανίζουσα], εὐώδης, τερμίνθου
5 πνέουσα.

4 ὑαλίζουσα Oribasius, Di / καὶ κυανίζουσα om. Oribasius, Dl, secl. Wellmann

The resin of the terebinth is brought from Arabian Petra, and it
is produced also in Judaea and Syria and Cyprus and Libya and in the
Cyclades; it excels in that it is more translucent, white, like glass in
colour, fragrant, redolent of terebinth.

423

'Η δὲ ἐξ αὐτῆς ῥητίνη: Cf. Theophrastus, *Historia Plantarum*, IX, 1 : 6; Plinius, *Naturalis Historia*, XIV, 122 (No. 215); XXIV, 32.

181

De Materia Medica, 1, 73:1 — Wellmann

Ἄσφαλτος διαφέρει ἡ Ἰουδαικὴ τῆς λοιπῆς. ἔστι δὲ καλὴ ἡ πορφυροειδῶς
στίλβουσα, εὔτονος τῇ ὀσμῇ καὶ βαρεῖα, ἡ δὲ μέλαινα καὶ ῥυπώδης
φαύλη· δολοῦται γὰρ πίσσης μειγνυμένης.

1 ἡ² om. Oribasius

The Jewish asphalt differs from the other. That which has a purple
sheen and a strong odour and is heavy, is beautiful; while the black
and dirty kind is bad, since it is adulterated by an admixture of pitch.

182

De Materia Medica, IV, 157: 1 — Wellmann

Βάλανος μυρεψική. καρπός ἐστι δένδρου μυρίκῃ ἐοικότος, ὅμοιος τῷ
λεγομένῳ Ποντικῷ καρύῳ, οὗ τὸ ἐντὸς θλιβόμενον ὥσπερ τὰ πικρὰ
ἀμύγδαλα ἐξίησιν ὑγρόν, ᾧ εἰς τὰ πολυτελῆ μύρα ἀντὶ ἐλαίου χρῶνται.
γεννᾶται δὲ ἐν Αἰθιοπίᾳ καὶ Αἰγύπτῳ καὶ Ἀραβίᾳ καὶ ἐν τῇ κατὰ
5 Ἰουδαίαν Πέτρᾳ.

1 μυρίκῃ] μυρρίνῃ Sprengel   3 ἐξίεις F   4 δὲ] γὰρ H   δ' ἐν E
5 τὴν Ἰουδαίαν Oribasius, E

Bān (*Balanites aegyptiaca*). It is a fruit of a tree similar to tamarisk,
like the so-called pontic nut, of which the inner part, when crushed
like bitter almonds, discharges a fluid that is used for very expensive
unguents instead of olive oil. It grows in Aethiopia and in Egypt and
in Arabia and in Petra, which is near Judaea.

183

De Materia Medica, IV, 170:3 — Wellmann

Ὁ δὲ Συριακὸς καὶ ὁ ἐν Ἰουδαίᾳ γεννώμενος ⟨scil. ὀπὸς σκαμμωνίας⟩

1 γενόμενος FH

χείριστοι, βαρεῖς, πυκνοί, δολούμενοι τιθυμάλλῳ καὶ ἀλεύρῳ μεμειγμένοις αὐτοῖς.

2 καὶ ὀροβίνῳ ἀλεύρῳ REDi   ἀλεύροις H
2-3 μεμειγμένοις αὐτοῖς om. R   μεμιγμένος P

The Syriac juice of scammony and that produced in Judaea are
the worst, being heavy, compact and adulterated by an admixture of
sea-spurge and wheat-meal.

184
De Materia Medica, V, 137 — Wellmann = F65R

Ὁ δὲ Ἰουδαικὸς λίθος γεννᾶται μὲν ἐν τῇ Ἰουδαίᾳ, τῷ σχήματι
βαλανοειδής, λευκός, εὔρυθμος ἱκανῶς, ἔχων γραμμὰς παραλλήλους
ὡς ἀπὸ τόρνου, ἀνιέμενος δέ ἐστιν ἄποιος ἐν τῇ γεύσει. δύναται δὲ
ἐρεβινθιαῖον μέγεθος διεθὲν ὡς κολλούριον ἐπ' ἀκόνης σὺν ὕδατος
5 θερμοῦ κυάθοις τρισὶ καὶ ποθὲν δυσουρίαις βοηθεῖν καὶ τοὺς ἐν κύστει
λίθους θρύπτειν.

1 ἰουδία F / post Ἰουδαίᾳ c. 16 litt. del. E²   3 ὡς ἀπὸ τόρνου γεγονυίας
Galenus ed. Kühn, XII, p. 199   4 κολλύριον QDi   5 θερμοῦ om. Q

The Jewish stone is produced in Judaea, has an acorn-like form, is
white and fairly well-proportioned, has parallel lines as though made
by a turning-lathe, and when dissolved is tasteless. It is strong enough,
being of the size of a chick-pea and diluted like collyrium on a whet-
stone with three cyathi of hot water, when drunk to alleviate difficult
micturition and to crush stones of the bladder.

On the "Jewish stone", see also Galenus, *De Simplicium Medicamentorum Temperamentis ac Facultatibus*, IX, 2 : 5 (ed. Kühn, Vol. XII, p. 199). Galen learned by
experience that this medicine is not useful for stones in the bladder, but that it
helps with kidney stones.

LXVI. COLUMELLA

First century C.E.

Columella, in his work on agriculture, touches twice on Jews or Judaea: once when he tells of a Jewish giant and a second time when he couples Judaea, because of its odorous plants, with Arabia.

Columella may have visited Judaea. In any event, according to his own statement (II, 10:18) he visited Syria. This sojourn is well illustrated by a Latin inscription in which Columella appears as a Tribunus Militum in the Legio VI Ferrata (ILS, No. 2923),[1] a legion whose stay in Syria in the Julio-Claudian period is well attested.[2]

1 See also R. Saxer, *Untersuchungen zu den Vexillationen des römischen Kaiserheeres von Augustus bis Diokletian*, Cologne–Graz 1967, p. 9.
2 See T. R. S. Broughton, apud: F. J. Foakes-Jackson & Kirsopp Lake, *The Beginnings of Christianity*, Part I, Vol. 5, London 1933, p. 435; Ritterling, PW, XII, pp. 1589 f.

(1) Igitur si rerum naturam, Publi Silvine, velut acrioribus mentis oculis intueri velimus, reperiamus parem legem fecunditatis eam dixisse virentibus atque hominibus ceterisque animalibus nec sic aliis nationibus regionibusve proprias tribuisse dotes, ut aliis in totum
5 similia numera denegaret: quibusdam gentibus numerosam generandi subolem dedit, ut Aegyptiis et Afris, quibus gemini partus familiares ac paene sollemnes sunt, sed et Italici generis esse voluit eximiae fecunditatis Albanas Siciniae familiae trigeminorum matres; (2) Germaniam decoravit altissimorum hominum exercitibus, sed et alias gentes
10 non in totum fraudavit praecipuae staturae viris: nam et Cicero testis est Romanum olim fuisse civem Naevium Pollionem pede longiorem quam quemquam longissimum, et nuper ipsi videre potuimus in adparatu pompae circensium ludorum Iudaeae gentis hominem proceriorem celsissimo Germano...
15 (4) Sed ad genera frugum redeo. Mysiam Libyamque largis aiunt abundare frumentis, nec tamen Apulos Campanosque agros optimis defici segetibus, Tmolon et Corycon flore croceo, Iudaeam et Arabiam pretiosis odoribus inlustrem haberi.

2 *repperiamus* A   *reperiemus* R | *eam*] *eadem* A   3 *ceterisque*] *cele-riterque* SA   5 *progenerandi* R   6 *sobolem* S²AR | *dedit, ut*] *dedita* S *dedit* A | *partus*] *artus* SA   8 *Siciniae* Hedberg   *aequitiae* codd. 11 *olim* om. R | *pede* h²lp   *pedem* SAR   13 *iudae* S   15 *sed* om. AR

(1) Therefore, Publius Silvinus, if we will look at nature through the keener eyes of the mind, so to speak, we shall find that she has established an equable law of fertility for all green things even as for human beings and other living creatures; and that she has not so bestowed special endowments upon some nations or regions as to deny like gifts altogether to others. To some peoples she has granted the gift of producing numerous progeny, as to the Egyptians and Africans, with whom the birth of twins is common and almost an annual occurrence; but of Italian stock, too, she has willed that there be women of extraordinary fertility — Alban women of the Sicinian family, mothers of three children at one birth. (2) She has adorned Germany with armies of exceedingly tall men; but she has not wholly deprived other nations of men of exceptional stature. For Cicero bears witness that there was once a Roman citizen, Naevius Pollio, who was a foot taller than the tallest of other men; and recently we

ourselves might have seen, among the exhibits of the procession at the games at the Circus, a man of the Jewish race who was of greater stature, than the tallest German.

(4) But I return to various kinds of crops. They say that Mysia and Libya produce enormous quantities of grain, but that the fields of Apulia and Campania, are not wanting in rich crops; that Tmolus and Corycus are considered famous for the saffron-flower, and Judaea and Arabia for their precious scents.   (trans. H. Boyd, *LCL*)

2 *et nuper ipsi videre potuimus*: We know that Columella's third book was written before 65 C. E., since he refers to Seneca as still alive (III, 3:3). The expression *nuper* does not necessarily preclude a period of thirty years; cf. Cichorius, p. 421, n. 2.

Iudaeae gentis hominem proceriorem celsissimo Germano: Josephus also speaks of a Jewish giant called Eleazar (ἄνδρα ἑπτάπηχυν τὸ μέγεθος Ἰουδαῖον τὸ γένος Ἐλεάζαρον ὄνομα); see *Ant.*, XVIII, 103. He was sent by Artabanus, King of Parthia, as a gift to Tiberius. His nickname, because of his height, was Gigas. Cichorius (p. 421) suggests that the tall Jew of Columella is identical to the giant Eleazar. Less convincing is the identification of both of them with Gabbara, the Arab giant from the time of Claudius referred to in Plinius, *Naturalis Historia*, VII, 74.

LXVII. SENECA THE PHILOSOPHER

The end of the first century B.C.E. to 65 C.E.

Seneca was the first Latin writer to give vent to deliberate animadversions on the Jewish religion and its impact on Roman society. Cicero's outbursts against the Jews in Pro Flacco, *28:66–69 (No. 68) and in* De Provinciis Consularibus, *5:10–12 (No. 70), are well explained by the special necessities of the case, though the personal antipathy of the speaker may have had something to do with it, while Horace's references to Jewish credulity and proselytizing zeal lack acrimony and have a touch of humour.*

We know that in his youth Seneca stayed for some time with his aunt in Egypt,[1] and that his prolific writings include a work "de situ et de sacris Aegyptiorum" (Servius, In Aeneidem, VI, 154). As may be inferred from his existing works, Seneca shows a marked antipathy towards Oriental religions in general.[2] However, it should be noted that his viewpoint, at least as it emerges from the fragments of De Superstitione, is that of a philosophical critic rather than of a defender of mos maiorum.

Seneca's references to Jews derive from works that he composed in the sixties of the first century C.E.,[3] that is, at the height of the Jewish proselytizing movement and the diffusion of Jewish customs throughout the Mediterranean world. What mattered to Seneca was the spread of the religion of the gens sceleratissima—the fact that the "victi victoribus leges dederunt". Not only does he include the Jewish rites among the super-

---

1 See L. Cantarelli, *Aegyptus*, VIII (1927), pp. 89 ff.; P. Faider, *BIFAO*, XXX (1930–1931) = *Mélanges Victor Loret*, p. 83 ff.

2 Worshippers of Isis and Cybele are implied in his *De Vita Beata*, 26 : 8. The Galli of the cult of Cybele are censured in strong terms in *De Superstitione*, apud: Augustinus, *De Civitate Dei*, VI, 10. See in general R. Turcan, *Sénèque et les religions orientales*, Bruxelles 1967; M. Lausberg, *Untersuchungen zu Senecas Fragmenten*, Berlin 1970, pp. 211 ff.

3 Münscher dates *De Superstitione* to the very last years of Seneca; see K. Münscher, *Senecas Werke*, Leipzig 1922, pp. 80 ff. Turcan argues for an earlier date (40–41 C. E.); see Turcan, *op. cit.*, pp. 12 ff For the date of *Naturales Quaestiones* and *Epistulae Morales*, see K. Abel, *Bauformen in Senecas Dialogen*, Heidelberg 1967, pp. 165 ff.

stitions of civilis theologia *in* De Superstitione, *but, in his criticism of ceremonial worship in the* Epistulae Morales (*No. 188*), *he takes the Jewish custom of lighting lamps on Sabbath as his first example. The emphasis on Jewish customs in such contexts might be explained as an attempt to counter the claims of the Jews, who dwelt much on the excellence of Jewish abstract monotheism (see, e.g.,* Contra Apionem, *II, 190 ff.), and as a reply to those circles of Roman society that were impressed by this aspect of the Jewish religion.*[4]

We have no proof that Seneca preferred Christianity to Judaism. We cannot accept as valid Augustine's explanation for his ignoring the Christians in De Civitate Dei, *VI, 11: "Christianos iam tunc Iudaeis inimicissimos, in neutram partem commemorare ausus est, ne vel laudaret contra suae patriae veterem consuetudinem vel reprehenderet contra propriam forsitan voluntatem."*

It should be remembered that the Roman government distinguished Christians from Jews only at the very end of Seneca's life; it is even reasonable to suppose that the spread of the new and dangerous sect could only serve in the eyes of Seneca as an additional argument to incriminate Judaism.[5]

---

4 Not a few times Philo calls Judaism a philosophy; cf., e. g., *Legatio ad Gaium*, 245; *Vita Mosis*, II, 216; *De Somniis*, II, 127. For Seneca and Judaism, see J. A. Hild, *REJ*, XI (1885), pp. 55 ff.; L. Hermann, *Revue belge*, XXXI (1927), pp. 43 ff.; Turcan, *op. cit.*, pp. 21 ff.

5 For the question of the relationship between Seneca and Paul, and their apocryphal correspondence, see Schanz & Hosius, II, pp. 715 ff.; J. N. Sevenster, "Paul and Seneca", *Novum Testamentum*, Suppl. IV, Leiden 1961. The identification of Seneca with Theophilus mentioned in Luke, as suggested by Lee, is rather fantastic; see G. M. Lee, *Hommages à Marcel Renard*, I Brussels 1969, pp. 515 ff.

186

De Superstitione, apud: Augustinus, De Civitate Dei, VI, 11 — Dombart & Kalb = F145R =
F593, H. Hagendahl, Augustine and the Latin Classics, I, Göteborg 1967

Hic ⟨scil. Seneca⟩ inter alias civilis theologiae superstitiones reprehen-
dit etiam sacramenta Iudaeorum et maxime sabbata, inutiliter eos
facere adfirmans, quod per illos singulos septenis interpositos dies
septimam fere partem aetatis suae perdant vacando et multa in tem-
5 pore urgentia non agendo laedantur... De illis sane Iudaeis cum
loqueretur, ait: "Cum interim usque eo sceleratissimae gentis consuetudo convaluit, ut per omnes iam terras recepta sit; victi victoribus
leges dederunt." Mirabatur haec dicens et quid divinitus ageretur
ignorans subiecit plane sententiam, qua significaret quid de illorum
10 sacramentorum ratione sentiret. Ait enim: "Illi tamen causas ritus sui
noverunt; maior pars populi facit, quod cur faciat ignorat."

1 hinc a

Along with other superstitions of the civil theology Seneca also
censures the sacred institutions of the Jews, especially the sabbath.
He declares that their practice is inexpedient, because by introducing
one day of rest in every seven they lose in idleness almost a seventh
of their life, and by failing to act in times of urgency they often suffer
loss... But when speaking of the Jews he says: "Meanwhile the customs
of this accursed race have gained such influence that they are now received throughout all the world. The vanquished have given laws to their
victors." He shows his surprise as he says this, not knowing what was
being wrought by the providence of God. But he adds a statement that
shows what he thought of their system of sacred institutions: "The
Jews, however, are aware of the origin and meaning of their rites. The
greater part of the people go through a ritual not knowing why they
do so."   (trans. W. M. Green, LCL)

septimam fere partem aetatis suae perdant vacando: On the same censure, see
Tacitus, Historiae, V, 4 (No. 281). In another context, however, Seneca knows
well the value of relaxation; see De Tranquillitate Animi, 17 : 7: "Legum conditores
festos instituerunt dies, ut ad hilaritatem homines publice cogerentur, tamquam
necessarium laboribus interponentes temperamentum; et magni, ut dixi, viri
quidam sibi menstruas certis diebus ferias dabant, quidam nullum non diem inter
otium et curas dividebant." It is perhaps worthwhile referring to Philo's Hypothetica,
apud: Eusebius, Praeparatio Evangelica, VIII, 7 : 12 ff., where, after describing the
Essenes assembling on Sabbath to listen to the laws read to them, he says: ἆρά σοι
δοκεῖ ταῦτα ἀργούντων εἶναι καὶ οὐ παντὸς σπουδάσματος μᾶλλον ἀναγκαῖα
αὐτοῖς (7 : 14).

431

From Herodotus to Plutarch

ut per omnes iam terras recepta sit: Cf. Strabo, *Historiae*, apud: Josephus, *Ant.*, XIV, 115 (No. 105).

victi victoribus leges dederunt: Cf. Horatius, *Epistulae*, II, 1 : 156: "Graecia capta ferum victorem cepit"; see also Florus, Epitoma, I, 47 : 7: "Syria prima nos victa corrupit"; Plinius, *Naturalis Historia*, XXIV, 5: "vincendoque victi sumus"; cf. in Seneca himself, *De Vita Beata*, 14 : 2: "captaeque cepere"; see also Rutilius Namatianus, *De Reditu Suo*, I, 398 (No. 542).

Illi tamen causas ritus sui noverunt; *maior pars populi facit, quod cur faciat ignorat*: Cf. Posidonius, apud: Athenaeus, *Deipnosophistae*, VI, 106, p. 273d: συνετῶν γάρ ἐστιν ἀνδρῶν ἐμμένειν τοῖς παλαιοῖς ζηλώμασιν. The *illi* are the Jews, while *maior pars populi* implies the non-Jews who adopt Jewish customs. This interpretation, accepted also by Reinach, seems to be preferable to the one, recently revived by Turcan, namely, that the implied contrast is between the Jewish priests and the rest of the Jewish people; see Turcan, *op. cit.* (supra, p. 429, n. 2), p. 23.

187

Naturales Quaestiones, III, 25:5 — Oltramare

Quosdam lacus esse qui nandi imperitos ferant notum est; erat in Sicilia, est adhuc in Syria stagnum in quo natant lateres et mergi proiecta non possunt, licet gravia sint.

2 ⟨et⟩ est adhuc B   est ⟨et⟩ adhuc EV

It is known that there are some lakes in which even those who do not know how to swim remain on the surface. There was such a lake in Sicily, and there is still a place of standing water in Syria, where bricks float and things thrown in, however heavy they may be, do not sink.

est adhuc in Syria stagnum in quo natant lateres et mergi proiecta non possunt: This refers, of course, to the Dead Sea, since we know of no other Syrian lake with such features; see H. Öhler, "Paradoxographi Florentini Anonymi Opusculum de Aquis Mirabilibus", Ph. D. Thesis, Tübingen 1913, p. 104. The specific emphasis on *lateres* is confined to Seneca. The inclusion of Judaea within the territory of Syria is used by pagan writers like Theophrastus and in documents like the letter of Claudius to the Alexandrians (*CPJ*, No. 153, l. 96), as well as by the Jewish writers Philo and Josephus.

188

Epistulae Morales, XCV, 47 — Reynolds = F146R

Quomodo sint dii colendi solet praecipi. Accendere aliquem lucernas

432

sabbatis prohibeamus, quoniam nec lumine dii egent et ne homines
quidem delectantur fuligine. Vetemus salutationibus matutinis fungi et
foribus adsidere templorum: humana ambitio istis officiis capitur,
5 deum colit qui novit. Vetemus lintea et strigiles Iovi ferre et speculum
tenere Iunoni: non quaerit ministros deus. Quidni? ipse humano
generi ministrat, ubique et omnibus praesto est.

2 *prohibebamus* Bφ   5 *ferre* ς   *ferri* codd.

Precepts are commonly given as to how the gods should be worshipped. But let us forbid lamps to be lighted on the Sabbath, since
the gods do not need light, neither do men take pleasure in soot. Let
us forbid men to offer morning salutation and to throng the doors of
temples; mortal ambitions are attracted by such ceremonies, but God
is worshipped by those who truly know him. Let us forbid bringing
towels and flesh-scrapers to Jupiter, and proffering mirrors to Juno;
for God seeks no servants. Of course not; he himself does service to
mankind everywhere, and to all he is at hand to help.

(trans. R. M. Gummere, *LCL*)

Accendere aliquem lucernas sabbatis prohibeamus: On the lighting of the Sabbath
lamps and the diffusion of this custom in the Roman world, see Seneca's contemporary, Persius, V, 180 f. (No. 190) and the commentary *ad loc.*
nec lumine dii egent ... deum colit qui novit: On the views of Seneca, cf. Lactantius,
Divinae Institutiones, VI, 25: "Quanto melius, et verius Seneca? Vultisne vos,
inquit, Deum cogitare magnum et placidum, et maiestate leni verendum, amicum
et semper in proximo? Non immolationibus nec sanguine multo colendum (quae
enim ex trucidatione immerentium voluptas est?), sed mente pura, bono hones-
toque proposito? Non templa illi congestis in altitudinem saxis extruenda sunt:
in suo cuique consecrandus est pectore."

189

Epistulae Morales, CVIII, 22 — Reynolds

His ego instinctus abstinere animalibus coepi, et anno peracto non tantum facilis erat mihi consuetudo sed dulcis. Agitatiorem mihi animum
esse credebam nec tibi hodie adfirmaverim an fuerit. Quaeris quomodo
desierim? In primum Tiberii Caesaris principatum iuventae tempus
5 inciderat: alienigena tum sacra movebantur et inter argumenta
superstitionis ponebatur quorundam animalium abstinentia. Patre
itaque meo rogante, qui non calumniam timebat sed philosophiam

2 *sed*] *sed et* ψ   4 *primum* om. φψ | *iubente* φ   5 *amovebantur*
vel *removebantur* Summers   *vovebantur* ψ | *et* Schweighaeuser   *sed* codd.

433

oderat, ad pristinam consuetudinem redii; nec difficulter mihi ut inciperem melius cenare persuasit.

I was imbued with this teaching, and began to abstain from animal food; at the end of a year the habit was as pleasant as it was easy. I was beginning to feel that my mind was more active; though I would not today positively state whether it really was or not. Do you ask how I came to abandon the practice? It was this way: The days of my youth coincided with the early part of the reign of Tiberius Caesar. Some foreign rites were at that time being inaugurated, and abstinence from certain kinds of animal food was set down as a proof of interest in the strange cult. So at the request of my father, who did not fear prosecution, but who detested philosophy, I returned to my previous habits; and it was no very hard matter to induce me to dine more comfortably.   (trans. R. M. Gummere, *LCL*)

his ego instinctus abstinere animalibus coepi: In his early years Seneca came under Pythagorean influence. For the whole passage, see I. Lana, *Lucio Anneo Seneca*, Turin 1955, pp. 72 ff.

alienigena tum sacra movebantur: It is commonly, and rightly, assumed that the events of 19 C. E. bearing upon the persecution of Jewish and Egyptian rites under Tiberius are meant here; see the commentary to Tacitus, *Annales*, II, 85 (No. 284). *Movebantur* may probably stand without the proposed emendations. On the emendation *amovebantur*, see B. Axelson, *Neue Senecastudien*, Lund–Leipzig 1939, p. 21, n. 31; cf. Turcan, *op. cit.* (supra, p. 429, n. 2), p. 7, n. 6.

LXVIII. PERSIUS
34–62 C.E.

Persius, the son of a man of equestrian standing, was born in Etrurian Volaterrae. In his twelfth year he came to Rome, where he studied under the famous grammarian Remmius Palaemon. Later he became a pupil of the Stoic philosopher Cornutus. He also became intimate with some of the outstanding writers of his day — among them Lucanus and Servilius Nonianus — and he knew Seneca personally, though he was not much impressed by him.[1] He was also connected, with Paetus Thrasea, the illustrious leader of the senatorial and Stoic opposition in the time of Nero.[2]

As a pupil of Cornutus and an exponent of first-century C. E. Stoicism, Persius had a lofty conception of the moral foundations of religious worship.[3] These did not, however, draw his attention to the moral aspects of the Jewish religion, whose customs served him only as an example of one of the many types of superstitions that emanated from the East. In his fifth satire the Jewish customs head a list in which Phrygian and Egyptian superstitious beliefs are the other components. In this way Persius seems to be typical of the majority of the educated classes of Roman society in his time.

Among the Jewish customs chosen by Persius as targets for his satire, first place is accorded to observance of the Sabbath with the attendant lighting of lamps, which is also criticized by the contemporary Seneca (No. 188); red-ware dishes full of tunnyfish; and white jars brimming over with wine. It is interesting that the picture of the Jewish Sabbath drawn by Persius, who is commonly labelled a literary recluse much dependent on his poetical predecessors, is much more vivid and true to the reality of the Sabbath celebrated by the Jews than most allusions to Jewish customs in ancient literature. In addition to the Sabbath, Persius also refers to circumcision.

---

1 See *Vita* of Persius, Clausen's Oxford edition of Persius and Juvenalis, p. 32: "Sero cognovit et Senecam, sed non ut caperetur eius ingenio."
2 E. V. Marmorale, *Persio* [2], Florence 1956, pp. 117 ff.
3 *Saturae*, II, 71 ff.; "Quin damus id superis, de magna quod dare lance non possit magni Messalae lippa propago? Conpositum ius fasque animo sanctosque recessus mentis et incoctum generoso pectus honesto. Haec cedo ut admoveam templis et farre litabo."

435

190

Saturae, V, 176–184 — Clausen = F 147 R

Ius habet ille sui, palpo quem ducit hiantem
cretata Ambitio? vigila et cicer ingere large
rixanti populo, nostra ut Floralia possint
aprici meminisse senes. Quid pulchrius? at cum
180 Herodis venere dies unctaque fenestra
dispositae pinguem nebulam vomuere lucernae
portantes violas rubrumque amplexa catinum
cauda natat thynni, tumet alba fidelia vino,
labra moves tacitus recutitaque sabbata palles.

176 *ducit*] *tollit* P

And that white-robed wheedler there, dragged open-mouthed by
his thirst for office — is he his own master? Up with you before dawn,
and deal out showers of chick-peas for the people to scramble for,
that old men sunning themselves in their old age may tell of the splendour of our Floralia! How grand! But when the day of Herod[1] comes
round, when the lamps wreathed with violets and ranged round the
greasy window-sills have spat forth their thick clouds of smoke, when
the floppy tunnies' tails are curled round the dishes of red ware, and
the white jars are swollen out with wine, you silently twitch your lips,
turning pale at the sabbath of the circumcised.

(trans. G. G. Ramsay, *LCL*)

[1] Ramsay has translated "Herod's birthday".

179f. *at cum Herodis venere dies*: From a satire on the subject of the real freedom
of man as contrasted to formal freedom. Persius defends the thesis that all men
are slaves to their desires, fears, etc. He adduces the Jewish Sabbath as his first
proof that superstition enslaves man, and then alludes to the cults of Isis and
Cybele.
Herodis dies: This should not necessarily mean the day of Herod's accession or of
his *dies natalis* celebrated by the Herodiani; see, e.g., J. Conington, *The Satires of
A. Persius Flaccus* (ed. H. Nettleship), Oxford 1893, p. 119; B. L. Gildersleeve,
The Satires of A. Persius Flaccus, New York, 1875, p. 184. It should be interpreted
from the following to mean the Day of the Sabbath celebrated by Herod; see
F. Villeneuve, *Essai sur Perse*, Paris 1918, p. 486; W. Fink, *Der Einfluss der jüdischen Religion auf die griechisch-römische*, Bonn 1932, p. 16. Persius' labelling of the
Sabbath as the Day of Herod should be explained by the fame not only of Herod I
(37–4 B. C. E.), but also by that of his descendants. Derenbourg's suggestion
that the festival of Hanukkah is implied here seems less likely; see Derenbourg,
p. 165, n. 1. cf. T. F. Brunner, *California Studies in Classical Antiquity*, I, pp. 63 ff.

436

181 *pinquem nebulam vomuere lucernae*: The lighting of lamps is one of the most conspicuous features of the celebration of the Sabbath; see, e.g., *M. Shabbat*, ii : 6–7. *Contra Apionem* (II, 282) testifies to the diffusion of the custom among those gentiles who were influenced by the Jewish religion: οὐδ᾽ ἔστιν οὐ πόλις ʿΕλλήνων, οὐδ᾽ ἡτισοῦν οὐδὲ βάρβαρον οὐδὲ ἓν ἔθνος ἔνθα μὴ τὸ τῆς ἑβδομάδος, ἣν ἀργοῦμεν ἡμεῖς τὸ ἔθος διαπεφοίτηκεν καὶ αἱ νηστεῖαι καὶ λύχνων ἀνακαύσεις; see also Tertullianus, *Ad Nationes*, I, 13. It is noteworthy that Seneca finds it necessary to attack this custom; see *Epistulae Morales*, XCV, 47 (No. 188); see also Marmorale, *op. cit.* (supra, p. 435, n. 2), p. 313.

183 *cauda natat thynni*: On the Jewish custom of having fish at the Friday evening meal, see S. Krauss, *Talmudische Archäologie*, I, Leipzig 1910, pp. 110 f.; p. 483, n. 514; I. Scheftelowitz, *Archiv für Religionswissenschaft*, XIV (1911), pp. 18 f.; Goodenough, V, pp. 42 f. Interesting passages are found in *TB Shabbat* 119a; *Genesis Rabba*, 11 (ed. Theodor), Jerusalem 1965, pp. 91 f. = *Pesiqta Rabbati*, 23. These last two passages refer to a Jewish tailor, who, on the eve of the Day of Atonement, bought a fish for twelve dinars, thereby overbidding the servant of an important Roman personage.

184 *recutitaque sabbata* = *sabbata recutitorum*.

palles: Cf. Iuvenalis, XIV, 96 (No. 301): "metuentem sabbata."

LXIX. LUCANUS
39–65 C.E.

Three facts relating to Jews are found in Lucanus' Pharsalia: their subjugation by Pompey, their worship of the incertus deus and the military help sent by the rulers of Judaea (= Idumaea) to Pompey. The last two probably derive from Livy, as does most of Lucan's historical material.[1]

1 Schanz & Hosius, II, p. 499.

Lucanus

191

Pharsalia, II, 590–594 — Housman = 148R

590 Me domitus cognovit Arabs, me Marte feroces
Heniochi notique erepto vellere Colchi,
Cappadoces mea signa timent et dedita sacris
incerti Iudaea dei mollisque Sophene,
Armenios Cilicasque feros Taurumque subegi.

The Arab owns me conqueror; so do the warlike Heniochi, and
the Colchians famous for the fleece they were robbed of. My standards overawe Cappadocia, and Judaea given over to the worship of
an unknown god, and effeminate Sophene; I subdued the Armenians,
the fierce Cilicians, and the range of Taurus.   (trans. J.D. Duff, *LCL*)

590   *Me domitus cognovit Arabs* . . .: In Pompey's speech the Jews figure among
the nations he subjugated.
593   *incerti Iudaea dei*: Lucan called the Jewish God *incertus deus* mainly because
there was no specific name for him in post-biblical times. Varro called him Jao;
see Lydus, *De Mensibus*, IV, 53 (No. 75). See also Livy, as quoted by the scholia
to Lucan (No. 133): "Hierosolyma fanum cuius deorum sit non nominant";
cf. the commentary *ad loc.*; see also Cassius Dio, XXXVII, 17 : 2 (No. 406). The
concept of *di incerti* is found already in Varro's terminology, where he used it for
those gods of whom he had no clear knowledge; see G. Wissowa, *Hermes*, LVI
(1921), pp. 113 ff. Varro did not, however, include the Jewish God among the
incerti; see E. Norden, *Agnostos Theos*, Leipzig–Berlin 1913, p. 61. It is doubtful
whether Lucan was influenced by Varro. In any case, the expression seems to have
been quite common; see Vergilius, *Aeneis*, VIII, 352: "quis deus incertum est,
habitat deus."

192

Pharsalia, III, 214–217 — Housman

Accedunt Syriae populi; desertus Orontes
215 et felix, sic fama, Ninos, ventosa Damascos
Gazaque et arbusto palmarum dives Idume
et Tyros instabilis pretiosaque murice Sidon.

The nations of Syria came also, leaving behind the Orontes, and
Ninos of whose prosperity legend tells; they left wind-swept Damascus,
Gaza, Idume, rich in palm-plantations, tottering Tyre, and Sidon pre-
cious for its purple.   (trans. J. D. Duff, *LCL*)

439

216 *et arbusto palmarum dives Idume*: Idume stands for Judaea, as is common in Latin poets; see Vergilius, *Georgica*, III, 12 (No. 125). Gaza and Idumaea, both rich in palm plantations, are listed among the countries that sent help to Pompey. The military help that Hyrcan II and Antipater sent to Pompey from Judaea is referred to by Appianus, *Bella Civilia*, II, 71 : 294 (No. 349).

LXX. PETRONIUS

First century C.E.[1]

The references to the Jews in the Satyricon *(Nos. 193–195) have mainly to do with circumcision, which was, in the eyes of Petronius, their specific trait. In one of his poetic fragments he also adds the Jews' alleged worship of the pig and the sky. There are no convincing arguments to support the view that Habinnas, the master of the circumcised slave Massa and a member of the collegium of the Seviri, was a Jew. Nor can it be stated that the name is a Jewish one.[2]*

1 It has been commonly assumed that the writer of the *Satyricon* should be identified with the famous Petronius Arbiter of the age of Nero; see, e. g., Schanz & Hosius, II, p. 514; W. Kroll, PW, XIX, p. 1202. Not only has this identification been disputed, but even his date in the first century C. E. has been called into question by Marmorale, who argues for a *c.* 200 C. E. date; see E. V. Marmorale, *La Questione Petroniana*, Bari 1948. However, his view cannot be accepted. For arguments in favour of the earlier date, see, e. g., A. Momigliano, *CQ*, XXXVIII (1944), p. 100; R. Browning, *Classical Review*, LXIII (1949), pp. 12 ff.; J. Whatmough, *Classical Philology*, XLIV (1949), pp. 273 f.; G. Bagnani, *Arbiter of Elegance*, Toronto 1954; H. T. Rowell, *TAPA*, LXXXIX (1958), pp. 14 ff.; H. C. Schnur, *Latomus*, XVIII (1959), pp. 790 ff.; K. F. C. Rose, *CQ*, LVI (1962), pp. 166 ff.; H. D. Rankin, *Classica et Mediaevalia*, XXVI (1965), pp. 233 f.; J. P. Sullivan, *The Satyricon of Petronius*, London 1968, pp. 21 ff.; K. F. C. Rose, *The Date and Author of the Satyricon*, Leiden 1971.

2 Flores takes Habinnas for a Jew, but even if Habinnas were a Semitic name, it does not necessarily follow that it is a Hebrew one; see E. Flores, "Un Ebreo cappadoce nella 'Cena Trimalchionis'", *Rendiconti del' Accademia di Archaeologia, Lettere e Belle Arte di Napoli*, XXXVIII (1963), pp. 1 ff. The Hebraic influences in the *Satyricon* have been somewhat exaggerated in M. Hadas, *AJP*, L (1929), pp. 378 ff. Against him, cf. L. Pepe, *Studi petroniani*, Naples 1957, pp. 75 ff.

Satyricon, 68:4–8 — Müller

(4) Ecce alius ludus. Servus qui ad pedes Habinnae sedebat, iussus, credo, a domino suo proclamavit subito canora voce:

interea medium Aeneas iam classe tenebat.

(5) Nullus sonus umquam acidior percussit aures meas; nam praeter er-
5 rantis barbariae aut adiectum aut deminutum clamorem ⟨im⟩miscebat Atellanicos versus, ut tunc primum me etiam Vergilius offenderit. (6) Lassus tamen cum aliquando desisset, [adiecit] Habinnas "et num-⟨quam" in⟩quit "didicit, sed ego ad circulatores eum mittendo eru-dibam. (7) Itaque parem non habet, sive muliones volet sive circula-
10 tores imitari. Desperatum valde ingeniosus est: idem sutor est, idem cocus, idem pistor, omnis musae mancipium. (8) Duo tamen vitia habet, quae si non haberet, esset omnium numerum: recutitus est et stertit. Nam quod strabonus est, non curo: sicut Venus spectat. Ideo nihil tacet, vix oculo mortuo umquam. Illum emi trecentis denariis."

5 *adiectum* Scheffer *abiectum* H / *deminutum* Scheffer *diminutum* H /
⟨*im*⟩*miscebat* Scheffer *miscebat* H 7 *desisset* Scheffer *dedisset* H /
adiecit del. Fraenkel ⟨*plausum*⟩ *adiecit* Bücheler 7–8 *numquam inquit*
Bücheler *numquid* H 8–9 *erudibam* Jahn *audibant* H 10 *despe-*
ratum Bücheler *desperatus* H 11 *vitia* ed. pr. *vina* H 12 *num-*
erum Scheffer *nummorum* H 14 *emi trecentis* Scheffer *emit retentis* H

(4) Then there was another joke. A slave, who was sitting at the feet of Habinnas, began, by his master's orders I suppose, suddenly to cry in a loud voice:

Now with his fleet Aeneas held the main.

(5) No sharper sound ever pierced my ears; for besides his making barbarous mistakes in raising or lowering his voice, he mixed up Atellane verses with it, so that Virgil jarred on me for the first time in my life. (6) When he at last tired left off, Habinnas said: "He never went to school, but I educated him by sending him round the hawkers in the market. (7) So he has no equal, when he wants to imitate mule-drivers or hawkers. He is terribly clever; he is a cobbler too, a cook, a confectioner, a slave of all talents. (8) He has only two faults, and if he were rid of them he would be simply perfect. He is circumcised and he snores. For I do not mind his being cross-eyed; he has a look like Venus. So that is why he cannot keep silent,

442

and scarcely ever shuts his eyes. I bought him for three hundred
denarii." (trans. M. Heseltine, *LCL*)

8 *recutitus est et stertit*: From the description of the festival of Trimalchio. One
of the slaves began to recite, or rather cry in a loud voice, the fifth book of the
Aeneis. This greatly annoyed Encolpius, the hero of the *Satyricon*, who was told
that the slave possessed great natural talents. Although he had not received any
systematic education, the slave was very clever, was unequalled in imitating mule-
drivers and hawkers, and was also a cobbler, a cook, a confectioner, and, in fact,
omnis musae mancipium. However, he had two faults: he was circumcised and
he habitually snored.
As we learn from the following passage (No. 194), Petronius thought that circumcision was the msot characteristic feature of the Jews. Thus, we may assume
that here, too, circumcision implies Judaism. On *recutitus*, see Martialis, VII,
30 : 5 (No. 240): "nec recutitorum fugis inguina Iudaeorum"; Persius, *Saturae*,
V, 184 (No. 190).
trecentis denariis: On the price of slaves at that time, cf. A. H. M. Jones, *The
Economic History Review*, IX (1956), pp. 193 f.

194
Satyricon, 102:13–14 — Müller

(13) Eumolpus tamquam litterarum studiosus utique atramentum habet. Hoc ergo remedio mutemus colores a capillis usque ad ungues. Ita
tamquam servi Aethiopes et praesto tibi erimus sine tormentorum iniuria hilares et permutato colore imponemus inimicis. (14) "Quidni?"
inquit Giton "etiam circumcide nos, ut Iudaei videamur, et pertunde
aures, ut imitemur Arabes, et increta facies, ut suos Gallia cives
putet: tamquam hic solus color figuram possit pervertere."

5 etiam] et rtp

(13) Eumolpus, as a man of learning, is sure to have some ink. We
will use this medicine to dye ourselves, hair, nails, everything. Then
we will stand by you with pleasure like Aethiopian slaves, without
undergoing any tortures, and our change of colour will take in our
enemies. (14) "Oh, yes", said Giton, "and please circumcise us too,
so that we look like Jews, and bore our ears to imitate Arabians, and
chalk our faces till Gaul takes us for her own sons; as if this colour
alone could alter our shapes." (trans. M. Heseltine, *LCL*)

14 *etiam circumcide nos, ut Iudaei videamur*: Encolpius and his companions
attempt to escape from their enemy. After it was suggested that they paint themselves to deceive their enemies, Giton proposed circumcision, so they would look

like Jews, although members of other nations also practiced circumcision; see the commentary to Herodotus, *Historiae*, II, 104 : 3 (No. 1). Nevertheless, for Greek and Latin writers the Jews were the circumcised *par excellence*; see Sallustius, *De Deis et Mundo*, IX, 5 (No. 488).

195

Fragmenta, No. 37 — Ernout = F149R = Baehrens, *PLM*, IV, 97, p. 98

Iudaeus licet et porcinum numen adoret
et caeli summas advocet auriculas,
ni tamen et ferro succiderit inguinis oram
et nisi nodatum solverit arte caput,
5 exemptus populo Graias migrabit ad urbes
et non ieiuna sabbata lege tremet.

1 *numen* Binet in marg.   *nomen* in textu   3 *oram* Binet in marg.
aram in textu   5 *Graias migrabit ad urbes* Binet in marg.   *Graia migrabit ab*
urbe in textu   *sacra migrabit ab urbe* Baehrens   6 *tremet* Bücheler premet cod.

The Jew may worship his pig-god and clamour in the ears of high heaven, but unless he also cuts back his foreskin with the knife, he shall go forth from the people and emigrate to Greek cities, and shall not tremble at the fasts of Sabbath imposed by the law.

(trans. M. Heseltine, *LCL*)

1 *Iudaeus licet et porcinum numen adoret*: The view that the Jews worshipped the pig came about because they abstained from eating pork. Another writer whose works reflect this view is Plutarch; see *Quaestiones Convivales*, IV, 5 (No. 258) and the commentary *ad loc*. It is worthwhile quoting here Epiphanius, *Panarion*, 26 : 10 : 6: φασὶ δὲ τὸν Σαβαὼθ οἱ μὲν ὄνου μορφὴν ἔχειν, οἱ δὲ χοίρου. On the impression made by the Jews' abstention from pork, see Iuvenalis, XIV, 98 f. (No. 301): "nec distare putant humana carne suillam, qua pater abstinuit"; cf. Macrobius, *Saturnalia*, II, 4 : 11 (No. 543).
2 *et caeli summas advocet auriculas*: For the view that the Jews were sky-worshippers, see Hecataeus, apud: Diodorus, *Bibliotheca Historica*, XL, 3 : 4 (No. 11); Strabo, *Geographica*, XVI, 2 : 35, p. 761 (No. 115); Iuvenalis, *Saturae*, XIV, 97 (No. 301).
5 *exemptus populo*: Excommunication is probably implied here; see Juster, II, p. 159, n. 5; A Cabaniss, *Classical Philology*, XLIX (1954), p. 99.
Graias migrabit ad urbes: The reading of the codex Bellovacensis, as attested by Binet, "Graia migrabit ab urbe", makes no sense here.
non ieiuna sabbata lege tremet: On the Sabbath as a fast day, see, e.g., Pompeius Trogus, apud: Iustinus, Epitoma, XXXVI, 2 : 14 (No. 137); Suetonius, *Divus Augustus*, 76 (No. 303).

444

LXXI. EROTIANUS

Second half of the first century C.E.

The fact that the glossator of Hippocrates finds the abhorrence of pork typical of the Jews shows that this abhorrence had become a matter of common knowledge, as indeed it had from the time of the persecution of Antiochus Epiphanes. Cf. Diodorus, XXXIV–XXXV, 1 : 4 (No. 63); Petronius (No. 195); Tacitus, Historiae, V, 4 (No. 281); Plutarchus, Quaestiones Convivales, IV, 5 (No. 258); Juvenalis, Saturae, XIV, 98 (No. 301); Sextus Empiricus, III, 223 (No. 334). A good example for the first century C.E. is afforded by Philo, Legatio, 361, where the emperor Gaius asks the Jewish representatives: "διὰ τί χοιρείων κρεῶν ἀπέχεσθε."

196

Vocum Hippocraticarum Collectio cum Fragmentis. F33: *De Morbo Sacro,* p. 108 —
Nachmanson, 1918

θειοτέρη· θεῖον] θεῖόν τινές φασι τὴν ἱερὰν νόσον. ταύτην γὰρ εἶναι
θεόπεμπτον ἱεράν τε λέγεσθαι ὡς θείαν οὖσαν. ἕτεροι δὲ ὑπέλαβον τὴν
δεισιδαιμονίαν. «ἐξεταστέον γάρ,» φασί, «ποταπῷ χρῆται τύπῳ ὁ νοσῶν,
ἵνα, εἰ μὲν Ἰουδαῖός τις ᾖ, τὰ χοίρεια ἐπ᾽ αὐτῷ παρατηρώμεθα, εἰ δ᾽
5 Αἰγύπτιος, τὰ προβάτεια ἢ αἴγεια.»

3 φασί Ermerins   φησί codd.

More divine... divine] Some say that the "Sacred Disease" is of
divine origin, because this disease is god-sent, and being of divine
origin it is said to be sacred. Others suppose that superstition is
implied. They say that one should inquire to which type the sick
man belongs, in order that if he is a Jew we should refrain from giving
him pig's flesh, and if he is an Egyptian we should refrain from giving
him the flesh of sheep or goats.

LXXII. CURTIUS RUFUS

First century C.E. ?

*The Greek sources concerning Alexander the Great's conquest of
Palestine in 332 B.C.E. centre on the siege and capture of Gaza:
Arrianus, Anabasis, II, 25 ff.; Diodorus, XVII, 48:7; Plutarchus,
Vita Alexandri, 25; and Hegesias, apud: F. Gr. Hist., II, B 142, F 5.
The Latin sources add little. Plinius, Naturalis Historia, XII, 117
(No. 213) refers to the activities of Alexander's army in the vicinity
of Jericho. Only Curtius Rufus, in addition to his description of the
capture of Gaza (IV, 6:25:7 ff.), supplies us with some valuable,
though very brief, information. He relates the burning of the Macedonian governor by the Samaritans during Alexander's sojourn in Egypt
and their punishment after the King's return from Egypt (331 B.C.E.).*
*His information on the Samaritan revolt and its repression by Alex-
ander is somewhat paralleled by the Jewish tradition as reflected in
Josephus' Antiquitates and in talmudic literature. It is implicitly
corroborated by the results of recent excavations (cf. the commentary).
We know almost nothing about Curtius Rufus, and even his date is still
a matter of dispute.*[1]

---

1 Some date him to the time of Augustus; others, to the reigns of Claudius or
Vespasian, and even much later. See D. Korzeniewski, "Die Zeit des Quintus
Curtius Rufus", Ph. D. Thesis, Köln 1959; R. D. Milns, *Latomus*, XXV (1966),
pp. 490 ff.; G. Scheda, *Historia*, XVIII (1969), pp. 380 ff.
For his evaluation as a historical source, see G. Radet, *Comptes rendus de
l'académie des inscriptions et belles lettres*, Paris 1924, pp. 356 ff.; Schanz &
Hosius, II, pp. 599 ff.; W.W. Tarn, *Alexander the Great*, II, Cambridge 1950,
pp. 91 ff.

447

(9) Oneravit hunc dolorem nuntius mortis Andromachi, quem praefecerat Syriae: vivum Samaritae cremaverant. (10) Ad cuius interitum vindicandum, quanta maxima celeritate potuit, contendit, advenientique sunt traditi tanti sceleris auctores. (11) Andromacho
5 deinde Menona substituit adfectisque supplicio, qui praetorem interemerant.

1 *quem*] *quam* L   3 *maxima* Acidalius   *maxime* codd.   5 *Menona*
                           Blancardus   *memnona* codd.

(9) The sorrow was made greater by news of the death of Andromachus, to whom he had given the charge of Syria; the Samaritans had burned him alive. (10) To avenge his murder, he hastened to the spot with all possible speed, and on his arrival those who had been guilty of so great a crime were delivered to him. (11) Then he put Menon in place of Andromachus and executed those who had slain his general.

(trans. J. C. Rolfe, *LCL*)

9 *Oneravit hunc dolorem*: What is meant by this sorrow is the death of Hector, the son of Parmenio.

nuntius mortis Andromachi, quem praefecerat Syriae: In a former passage (IV, 5: 22 : 9) Curtius Rufus mentions that Coele-Syria had been allotted to Andromachus: "Syriam quae Coele appellatur Andromacho Parmenio tradidit." The only other writers to mention Andromachus are Christian writers (Eusebius, Syncellus). There is no reason to deny his existence and regard him as a duplicate of the Andromachus who was one of the chief Ptolemaic commanders in the Fourth Syrian War, as suggested by L. Haefeli, *Geschichte der Landschaft Samaria*, Münster 1922, pp. 66 f. On Andromachus, see also H. Berve, *Das Alexanderreich auf prosopographischer Grundlage*, II, Munich 1926, pp. 38 f.

vivum Samaritae cremaverant: We learn of the friendly relations that prevailed between the Samaritans, under the leadership of Sanbalat, and Alexander from *Ant.*, XI, 321 ff.; however, we do not know what caused the deterioration of these relations; see I. Spak, "Der Bericht des Josephus über Alexander den Grossen", Ph. D. Thesis, Königsberg 1911, pp. 30 ff.

11 *Menona substituit*: That Menon was formerly appointed governor of Coele-Syria we learn from Arrian, who draws on good sources, but who does not refer to Andromachus; see *Anabasis*, II, 13 : 7. His version is preferable to that of Curtius Rufus, who is not meticulous in administrative details; see Tarn, *op. cit.* (supra, p. 447, n. 1), p. 102. For another view, see Kahrstedt, p. 9. It seems that Andromachus was only a subordinate governor and a commander under Menon. After the murder of Andromachus, Menon took over the direct command of the Macedonian troops in Samaria in order to quell the rebellion. On the discrepancy between Arrian and Curtius, see also O. Leuze, *Die Satrapieneinteilung in Syrien und im*

Zweistromlande, Halle 1935, pp. 413 (257) ff.; Y. Gutman, *Tarbiz*, XI (1939–1940), pp. 275 ff.

adfectisque supplicio ...: Those events are also implied in Eusebius, *Chronicon* (ed. Schoene), II, p. 114; Hieronymus, *Chronicon* (ed. Helm), p. 123; Syncellus, I (ed. Dindorf), p. 496. These writers relate the punishment of the Samaritans and the founding of a Macedonian military colony in Samaria; see H. Willrich, *Juden und Griechen vor der makkabäischen Erhebung*, Göttingen 1895, pp. 16 f. Curtius' narrative accords well with the literary tradition that emphasizes Alexander's preference for the Jews; see Hecataeus, apud: Josephus, *Contra Apionem*, II, 43 (No. 13); *Ant.*, XI, 340 ff.; *TB Joma* 69a; see also Tcherikover, pp. 42 ff.; R. Marcus, *Josephus* (*LCL*), VI, App. C, pp. 512 ff.

As stated in the introduction, new discoveries support the information supplied by Curtius Rufus concerning a clash between the Samaritans and the Macedonian conquerors in the second half of the fourth century B. C. E. On the Samaria Aramaic papyri found north of Jericho (Wadi Daliyeh), see F.M. Cross, *Biblical Archaeologist*, XXVI (1963), pp. 110 ff. These documents, which are of a legal and administrative character, range, according to Cross (p. 115), from *c.* 375 to *c.* 335 B. C. E. It seems that when large numbers of Samaritans fled from the Macedonian forces that came to punish the rebellious population of Samaria, they took many legal documents with them. Subsequently, they were slaughtered at their refuge north of Jericho.

The results of the archaeological excavations at Samaria and Shechem also reveal that Samaria became a Hellenistic city in the late fourth century. At the same time there was a revival of Shechem, which supplanted Samaria as the religious and social centre of the Samaritans. For a summary of the results of the excavations at Shechem, see G.E. Wright, *HTR*, LV (1962), pp. 357 ff.

LXXIII. ZOPYRION

Date unknown

Zopyrion is mentioned by Josephus in Contra Apionem *as the last of eight writers who gave more than passing attention to Jews. We cannot identify this Zopyrion with any certainty, and we cannot even be sure that Josephus presents the eight names in chronological order. We may only point to Suda, s.v. Πάμφιλος (the Alexandrian), where a Zopyrion appears as the author of the first parts of the work Περὶ γλωσσῶν ἤτοι λέξεων, most of which was compiled by the grammaticus Pamphilus in the middle of the first century C. E.*[1]

---

1 Schmid & Stählin, p. 436.

450

Zopyrion

198

apud: Josephus, *Contra Apionem*, I, 215–216 = Reinach (Budé), p. 41

(215) Ἀρκοῦσι δὲ ὅμως εἰς τὴν ἀπόδειξιν τῆς ἀρχαιότητος αἵ τε
Αἰγυπτίων καὶ Χαλδαίων καὶ Φοινίκων ἀναγραφαὶ πρὸς ἐκείναις τε
τοσοῦτοι τῶν Ἑλλήνων συγγραφεῖς· (216) ἔτι δὲ πρὸς τοῖς εἰρημένοις
Θεόφιλος ⟨No. 38⟩ καὶ Θεόδοτος καὶ Μνασέας ⟨No. 27⟩ καὶ Ἀρισ-
τοφάνης ⟨No. 24⟩ καὶ Ἑρμογένης ⟨No. 199⟩ Εὐήμερός ⟨No. 16⟩ τε
καὶ Κόνων ⟨No. 144⟩ καὶ Ζωπυρίων καὶ πολλοί τινες ἄλλοι τάχα, οὐ
γὰρ ἔγωγε πᾶσιν ἐντετύχηκα τοῖς βιβλίοις, οὐ παρέργως ἡμῶν ἐμνη-
μονεύκασιν.

3 ἔτι δὲ Eus.   ἔτι δὲ καὶ L

(215) However, our antiquity is sufficiently established by the Egyptian,
Chaldaean, and Phoenician records, not to mention the numerous
Greek historians. (216) In addition to those already cited, Theophilus,
Theodotus, Mnaseas, Aristophanes, Hermogenes, Euhemerus, Conon,
Zopyrion, and, may be, many more — for my reading has not been
exhaustive — have made more than a passing allusion to us.

(trans. H. St. J. Thackeray, *LCL*)

451

LXXIV. HERMOGENES
Date unknown

Hermogenes is the fifth in the list of eight writers adduced by Josephus (Contra Apionem, I, 216) as authors who gave more than passing attention to the Jews; see also the introduction to Zopyrion.

It is hardly possible to identify this Hermogenes. Some scholars[1] suggest that he is the same as the Hermogenes, also of unknown date,[2] who is known as the writer of a history of Phrygia; see Scholia to Apollonius Rhodius, II, 722; Zenobius, Proverbia, 6:10 = E. L. Leutsch & F. G. Schneidewin, Paroemiographi Graeci, I, Göttingen 1839, p. 164.

The identification rests on the following: In the fragment preserved by Zenobius we read about a certain Nannacus (Νάνναχος), a Phrygian king who foretold the coming of the Deluge and who consequently gave rise to the proverb κῆν τὰ Ναννάχου κλαύσῃ. *The same proverb also occurs in Suda, s.v.* Νάνναχος *(ed. Adler, III, p. 435; cf. IV, p. 494), but without any reference to Hermogenes, and in Stephanus Byzantius, s.v.* Ἰχόνιον *(= F. Gr. Hist., III, C 800, F 3), who likewise does not mention Hermogenes. Stephanus Byzantius has the reading* Ἀνναχός. *It has been surmised that this is the original reading, and that in view of the later diffusion of the Jewish tale of the Flood in Phrygia (Apamea), the* Ἀνναχός *should be identified with the biblical Enoch.[3]*

However, the reading Νάνναχος *is vouched for by the third-century B.C.E. Herondas, who (III, 10) has* κῆν τὰ Ναννάχου κλαύσω. *At most, one can agree with Schürer that the original proverb* κλαύσειν ἐπὶ Ναννάχου *was transformed under Jewish influence and became connec-*

---

1 E. g. Müller, p. 181; Schürer, III, p. 20.
2 Jacoby dates him, with a question mark, to the Hellenistic age; see *F. Gr. Hist.*, III C, p. 833. Other scholars think of the historian Hermogenes of Tarsus, known from Suetonius, *Domitianus*, 10; cf. on him J. Janssen, *C. Suetonii Tranquilli Vita Domitiani*, Groningen 1919, p. 47. Yet, this is a conjecture that cannot be substantiated, as we do not know that this Hermogenes dealt with the history of Phrygia.
3 Cf. E. Babelon, *RHR*, XXIII (1891), p. 180.

ted with Enoch;[4] *however, even this seems rather doubtful.*[5] *In any case, the Jewish colouring of the legend should not be supposed to have already occurred in Hermogenes.*

4 Cf. Schürer, III, p. 20.
5 Cf. Scherling, PW, XVI, p. 1681.

apud: Josephus, *Contra Apionem*. I, 215–216 = Reinach (Budé), p. 41

'Αρκοῦσι δὲ ὅμως εἰς τὴν ἀπόδειξιν τῆς ἀρχαιότητος αἵ τε Αἰγυπτίων
καὶ Χαλδαίων καὶ Φοινίκων ἀναγραφαὶ πρὸς ἐκείναις τε τοσοῦτοι τῶν
Ἑλλήνων συγγραφεῖς· (216) ἔτι δὲ πρὸς τοῖς εἰρημένοις Θεόφιλος
⟨No. 38⟩ καὶ Θεόδοτος καὶ Μνασέας ⟨No. 27⟩ καὶ 'Αριστοφάνης
5 ⟨No. 24⟩ καὶ Ἑρμογένης Εὐήμερός ⟨No. 16⟩ τε καὶ Κόνων ⟨No. 144⟩
καὶ Ζωπυρίων ⟨No. 198⟩ καὶ πολλοί τινες ἄλλοι τάχα, οὐ γὰρ ἔγωγε
πᾶσιν ἐντετύχηκα τοῖς βιβλίοις, οὐ παρέργως ἡμῶν ἐμνημονεύκασιν.

3 ἔτι δὲ Eus.   ἔτι δὲ καὶ L

(215) However, our antiquity is sufficiently established by the Egyptian,
Chaldaean, and Phoenician records, not to mention the numerous
Greek historians. (216) In addition to those already cited, Theophilus,
Theodotus, Mnaseas, Aristophanes, Hermogenes, Euhemerus, Conon,
Zopyrion, and, may be, many more — for my reading has not been
exhaustive — have made more than a passing allusion to us.

(trans. H. St. J. Thackeray, *LCL*)

454

LXXV. THE ANONYMOUS AUTHORS ON
THE WAR BETWEEN THE ROMANS AND THE JEWS

The seventies of the first century C. E.

In the introductory sentences of his Bellum Judaicum *Josephus distinguishes between two types of historians who wrote about the history of the Great War of the Jews with the Romans: those who were not eye-witnesses and only wrote down stories casually collected from others, and those who did write on the basis of personal experience, but whose representation of the facts was either burdened by excessive flattery of the Romans or by hatred towards the Jews, with the result that their works assumed the character of encomium or invective.*

Since Josephus published his work between 75 and 79 C.E.,[1] it follows that the historians he alludes to composed their writings in the years immediately following the capture of Jerusalem in 70 C.E. Such a crop of contemporary historiography dealing with a great war waged by Rome recalls Lucianus' passage concerning the Parthian War under Marcus Aurelius in his "Quo modo historia sit conscribenda." Josephus' criticism is couched in a language that is conventional in ancient historiography.[2]

We cannot state with any certainty whom Josephus has in mind here. Antonius Iulianus may be one of the writers. His emphasis on the motif of flattering the Romans suggests that Josephus may allude to some Greek writers.[3]

1 H. Vincent, *RB*, 1911, pp. 370 f.; H. St. J. Thackeray, *Josephus, the Man and the Historian*, New York 1929, pp. 34 f.

2 See, in general, G. Avenarius, *Lukians Schrift zur Geschichtsschreibung*, Meisenheim 1956.

3 On this passage, see also W. Weber, *Josephus und Vespasian*, Berlin–Stuttgart–Leipzig 1921, pp. 3 ff.

455

(1) Ἐπειδὴ τὸν Ἰουδαίων πρὸς Ῥωμαίους πόλεμον συστάντα μέγιστον
οὐ μόνον τῶν καθ' ἡμᾶς, σχεδὸν δὲ καὶ ὧν ἀκοῇ παρειλήφαμεν ἢ πόλεων
πρὸς πόλεις ἢ ἐθνῶν ἔθνεσι συρραγέντων, οἱ μὲν οὐ παρατυχόντες τοῖς
πράγμασιν, ἀλλ' ἀκοῇ συλλέγοντες εἰκαῖα καὶ ἀσύμφωνα διηγήματα
5 σοφιστικῶς ἀναγράφουσιν, *(2)* οἱ παραγενόμενοι δὲ ἢ κολακείᾳ τῇ πρὸς
Ῥωμαίους ἢ μίσει τῷ πρὸς Ἰουδαίους καταψεύδονται τῶν πραγμάτων,
περιέχει δὲ αὐτοῖς ὅπου μὲν κατηγορίαν ὅπου δὲ ἐγκώμιον τὰ συγγράμματα, τὸ δ' ἀκριβὲς τῆς ἱστορίας οὐδαμοῦ, *(3)* προυθέμην ἐγὼ τοῖς
κατὰ τὴν Ῥωμαίων ἡγεμονίαν Ἑλλάδι γλώσσῃ μεταβαλὼν ἃ τοῖς ἄνω
10 βαρβάροις τῇ πατρίῳ συντάξας ἀνέπεμψα πρότερον ἀφηγήσασθαι...
(7) Καίτοι γε ἱστορίας αὐτὰς ἐπιγράφειν τολμῶσιν, ἐν αἷς πρὸς τῷ
μηδὲν ὑγιὲς δηλοῦν καὶ τοῦ σκοποῦ δοκοῦσιν ἔμοιγε διαμαρτάνειν. βούλονται μὲν γὰρ μεγάλους τοὺς Ῥωμαίους ἀποδεικνύειν, καταβάλλουσιν
δὲ ἀεὶ τὰ Ἰουδαίων καὶ ταπεινοῦσιν· *(8)* οὐχ ὁρῶ δέ, πῶς ἂν εἶναι
15 μεγάλοι δοκοῖεν οἱ μικροὺς νενικηκότες· καὶ οὔτε τὸ μῆκος αἰδοῦνται
τοῦ πολέμου οὔτε τὸ πλῆθος τῆς Ῥωμαίων καμούσης στρατιᾶς οὔτε τὸ
μέγεθος τῶν στρατηγῶν, οἳ πολλὰ περὶ τοῖς Ἱεροσολύμοις ἱδρώσαντες
οἶμαι ταπεινουμένου τοῦ κατορθώματος αὐτοῖς ἀδοξοῦσιν.

1 τῶν C / συστησάντων C   3 οἱ] τινὲς M   8 προεθέμην V
9 ἄνω om. PM   13 γὰρ μεγάλους μὲν tr. LVNC   14 τά] τὸ V /
          ὁρῶ] ὁρῶσι MLVNC   15 οἱ] καὶ C

(1) The war of the Jews against the Romans—the greatest not only
of the wars of our own time, but, so far as accounts have reached us,
well nigh of all that ever broke out between cities or nations—has
not lacked its historians. Of these, however, some, having taken no
part in the action, have collected from hearsay casual and contra-
dictory stories which they have then edited in a rhetorical style;
(2) while others, who witnessed the events, have, either from flattery
of the Romans or from hatred of the Jews, misrepresented the facts,
their writings exhibiting alternatively invective and encomium, but
nowhere historical accuracy. (3) In these circumstances, I propose to
provide the subjects of the Roman Empire with a narrative of the facts,
by translating into Greek the account which I previously composed
in my vernacular tongue and sent to the barbarians in the interior...
(7) Though the writers in question presume to give their works the
title of histories, yet throughout them, apart from the utter lack of
sound information, they seem, in my opinion, to miss their own

mark. They desire to represent the Romans as a great nation, and yet they continually depreciate and disparage the actions of the Jews. (8) But I fail to see how the conquerors of a puny people deserve to be accounted great. Again, these writers have respect neither for the long duration of the war, nor for the vast numbers of the Roman army that it engaged, nor for the prestige of the generals, who, after such herculean labours under the walls of Jerusalem, are, I suppose, of no repute in these writers' eyes, if their achievement is to be underestimated. (trans. H. St. J. Thackeray, *LCL*)

1 πόλεμον συστάντα μέγιστον: This, of course, has a Thucydidean ring. For the influence of Thucydides on the works of Josephus, see H. Drüner, "Untersuchungen über Josephus", Ph.D. Thesis, Marburg 1896, pp. 1 ff.
οἱ μὲν οὐ παρατυχόντες τοῖς πράγμασιν... ἀναγράφουσιν: The same criticism is applied, e.g., in Lucianus, *op. cit.* (supra, p. 455), 29 : 38: "Ἄλλος... οὐδὲ τὸν ἕτερον πόδα ἐκ Κορίνθου πώποτε προβεβηκὼς οὐδ᾽ ἄχρι Κεγχρεῶν ἀποδημήσας; cf. 24 : 32–33. The requirement of autopsy, or, at any rate, of first-hand information, was a recurrent theme in ancient historiography; see, e.g., Polybius, III, 4 : 13; cf. F. W. Walbank, *A Historical Commentary on Polybius*, I, Oxford 1957, p. 302; see also Avenarius, *op. cit.* (supra, p. 455, n. 2), pp. 71 ff.; G. Nenci, *Studi classici e orientali*, III (1953), pp. 14 ff.
2 ἢ κολακείᾳ τῇ πρὸς ῾Ρωμαίους ἢ μίσει πρὸς ᾽Ιουδαίους: On the motive of flattery, see Tacitus, *Historiae*, I, 1: "simul veritas pluribus modis infracta . . . mox libidine adsentandi aut rursus adversus dominantes." On the attitude of historians towards Nero see *Ant.*, XX, 154.
ὅπου δὲ ἐγκώμιον τὰ συγγράμματα: Cf. Lucianus, *op. cit.*, 7 : 9: ἀμελήσαντες γὰρ οἱ πολλοὶ αὐτῶν τοῦ ἱστορεῖν τὰ γεγενημένα τοῖς ἐπαίνοις ἀρχόντων καὶ στρατηγῶν ἐνδιατρίβουσι, τοὺς μὲν οἰκείους εἰς ὕψος ἐπαίροντες, τοὺς πολεμίους δὲ πέρα τοῦ μετρίου καταρρίπτοντες, ἀγνοοῦντες ὡς οὐ στενῷ τῷ ἰσθμῷ διώρισται καὶ διατετείχισται ἡ ἱστορία πρὸς τὸ ἐγκώμιον.

LXXVI. ANTONIUS JULIANUS

Second half of the first century C.E.?

Antonius Julianus is mentioned as a writer on the Jews only in the Octavius of Minucius Felix. In this dialogue the pagan disputant Caecilius Natalis adduces the argument that the Jews' reverent worship of one God, with altars and temples, was of no avail to them. To this argument the Christian replies that so long as the Jews worshipped God and obeyed his precepts they attained great success; misfortune was brought on them by their own wickedness. This, he continues, may be read in the Jewish writings, and if one prefers Roman writers, he may consult what Antonius Julianus wrote on Jews (for the text, see the commentary).

More than one Antonius Julianus is known to have lived in the Roman Empire.[1] One of them was the Antonius Julianus who acted as procurator of Judaea in 70 C.E. and who took part in the consilium of Titus that discussed the policy to be adopted towards the Jewish Temple (BJ, VI, 238).[2] Since there were many writers who dealt with the Jewish War (see No. 200) it has been quite plausibly suggested that one of them should be identified with the procurator of Judaea and that he is the writer on the Jews referred to by Minucius Felix. This view, propounded by Tillemont, has been endorsed by many scholars, e.g. Bernays, Norden, Weber, Paratore.[3] See also the introduction to Tacitus for the question of Tacitus' dependence on Antonius Julianus.

It has been maintained by Hertlein, and approved by Quispel, that Antonius Julianus was a Jew, like Josephus, and was also mentioned as such by Minucius Felix. Minucius, however, emphasizes that Antonius Julianus was a Roman, while the name of Josephus should probably be transposed to another part of the sentence. Of course, the reference to him by Minucius Felix does not imply Antonius Julianus' acceptance of

---

1 *PIR*[2], I, pp. 163 f., Nos. 843–846.
2 Cf. H. G. Pflaum, *Les procurateurs équestres sous le Haut-Empire romain*, Paris 1950, p. 145.
3 See also R. Syme, *Tacitus*, I, Oxford 1958, p. 178. Münter prefers to identify him with the rhetor Antonius Julianus, a contemporary of Hadrian; see *PIR*[2], I, No. 844. This Antonius, however, is no more than a name to us, and there is nothing to suggest his preoccupation with the Jews.

Antonius Julianus

the biblical philosophy of history concerning transgression and punishment, but refers only to his description of the misdeeds of the Jewish rebels in Jerusalem before and during the siege. In the eyes of Minucius these were tantamount to a desertion of God.

Bibliography:

F. Münter, *Der jüdische Krieg unter den Kaisern Trajan und Hadrian*, Altona–Leipzig 1821, p. 12; K. Peter, *Flavius Josephus und der jüdische Krieg*, Programm, Perleberg 1871, p. 4, n. 2; Bernays, II, p. 173; A. Schlatter, *Zur Topographie und Geschichte Palästinas*, Stuttgart 1893, pp. 97 ff., 344 ff.; E. Schürer, *Theologische Literaturzeitung*, XVIII (1893), p. 326; Schürer, I, p. 58; E. Norden, *Neue Jahrbücher für das klassische Altertum*, XXXI (1913), pp. 664 ff. = *Kleine Schriften*, pp. 272 ff.; W. Weber, *Josephus und Vespasian*, Berlin–Stuttgart–Leipzig 1921, p. 4; E. Hertlein, *Philologus*, LXXVII, pp. 174 ff.; A. Rosenberg, *Einleitung und Quellenkunde zur römischen Geschichte*, Berlin 1921, p. 256; H. J. Baylis, *Minucius Felix and his Place Among the Early Fathers of the Latin Church*, London 1928, p. 86, n. 2; Schanz & Hosius, II, p. 649; A. M. A. Hospers-Jansen, *Tacitus over de Joden*, Groningen 1949, pp. 1 f., 113, 172 ff.; G. Quispel, *Vigiliae Christianae*, III (1949), p. 115; E. Paratore, *Tacito* [2], Rome 1962, pp. 664 ff; A. Schlatter, *Kleinere Schriften zu Flavius Josephus*, Darmstadt 1970, pp. 1 ff.

apud: Minucius Felix, *Octavius*, 33: 2–4 — Beaujeu = F173R = H. Peter, *Veterum Historicorum Romanorum Reliquiae*, II, Leipzig 1906, pp. 108 f.

(2) Sed Iudaeis nihil profuit, quod unum et ipsi deum aris atque templis maxima superstitione coluerunt. Ignorantia laberis, si, priorum aut oblitus aut inscius posteriorum recordaris; nam et ipsi deum nostrum — idem enim omnium deus est — ⋆ (3) Quamdiu enim eum
5 caste, innoxie religioseque coluerunt, quamdiu praeceptis salubribus obtemperaverunt, de paucis innumeri facti, de egentibus divites, de servientibus reges, modici multos, inermi armatos, dum fugiunt insequentes, dei iussu et elementis adnitentibus obruerunt. (4) Scripta eorum relege ⋆ vel, ut transeamus veteres, Flavi Iosephi ⋆ vel, si
10 Romanis magis gaudes, Antoni Iuliani de Iudaeis require: iam scies nequitia sua hanc eos meruisse fortunam nec quidquam accidisse, quod non sit his, si in contumacia perseverarent, ante praedictum.

4 *est, dereliquerunt* Waltzing   *dereliquerant* Synnerberg   *experti sunt* Halm
9–10 *vel, ut transeamus . . . magis gaudes,* ordinem restituit Lindner   verba *si romanis magis gaudes* ante *ut transeamus* P   9 *Iosephi*] *iosepi* P

(2)"But what did it profit the Jews that they too, with reverence the most scrupulous, worshipped one God with altars and with temples?" There you are betrayed into ignorance, if you forget or ignore their earlier history, and remember only the later; (3) the Jews, so long as they worshipped our God — one God, the same for all — in purity and innocence and holiness — so long as they obeyed his precepts of salvation, grew from a small people to a numberless, from being poor to rich, from being slaves to kings; few in numbers and unarmed they overwhelmed armed hosts, and at the command of God with the assistance of the elements pursued them in their flight. (4) Read their own writings; or omitting the ancients, turn to Flavius Josephus; or, if you prefer Romans, consult Antonius Julianus on the Jews, and you will see that it was their own wickedness which brought them to misfortune, and that nothing happened to them which was not predicted in advance, if they persisted in rebelliousness.

(trans. G. H. Rendall, *LCL*)

4 *Scripta eorum relege*: This is an allusion to the Bible.
Flavi Iosephi: The inclusion of Flavius Josephus among the Roman writers justly causes some surprise, even if we take into account the fact that the Jewish historian obtained Roman citizenship and that his political views were affected by his loyalty to the Flavian dynasty. Therefore, Davis (in his Cambridge edition of 1707),

followed by Halm and Norden, treated the inclusion of Josephus as an interpolation. What seems a better solution was adopted, however, by other editors (e.g. Lindner, Waltzing and Beaujeu), who transpose "si Romanis magis gaudes" after "Flavi Iosepi"; see also Hospers-Jansen, *op. cit.* (supra, p. 459), p. 175.

de Iudaeis: This, by itself, does not necessitate the assumption that the title of the work was *De Iudaeis*. It could just as well have been a History of the Jewish War.

LXXVII. MEMNON OF HERACLEIA

First century C.E.?

Memnon, the author of a voluminous chronicle of his native city, mentions Judaea in connection with the war between the Roman Republic and Antiochus III. First, he states that Judaea was among the countries ruled by Antiochus. Second, he emphasizes the fact that Judaea was not detached from the territories of Antiochus after his defeat by the Romans. That a Greek writer from Asia Minor should pay special attention to the Jews need not cause much surprise; see the introduction to Teucer. What does invite comment is that in both references Judaea is coupled with Commagene, and that both are singled out from the many parts of the Seleucid Empire. This may be because Memnon wrote his chronicle when both countries were simultaneously much "in the news", which happened three times during the first century C.E.: (a) when Gaius Caligula made Antiochus of Commagene and Agrippa I kings; (b) when Claudius restored the same Antiochus to the throne and enlarged the kingdom of Agrippa so that it included the entire former province of Judaea; (c) c. 70 C.E., when the Flavians destroyed Jerusalem and incorporated Commagene into the Empire (72 C.E.)

These last events were, of course, the most impressive. The existing portion of Memnon's chronicle, which consists of a summary of books nine to sixteen by Photius, end at the time of Julius Caesar. Photius himself, however, expressly states that he saw neither the first eight books nor those coming after the sixteenth: τὰς δὲ πρώτας ἡ ἱστορίας καὶ τὰς μετὰ τὴν ἕκτην καὶ δεκάτην οὔπω εἰπεῖν εἰς θέαν ἡμῶν ἀφιγμένας ἔχω. Memnon presumably wrote eight more books covering the period subsequent to Caesar. This accords well with a date in the second half of the first century C.E.[1]

---

1 R. Laqueur would make Memnon a contemporary of Julius Caesar; see PW, XIII, pp. 1098 f. This dating involves him in an unjustified denial of the validity of Photius' statement concerning the existence of books after the sixteenth. About the question of the number of the books in Memnon's chronicle, see also Jacoby, who does not exclude the possibility that Memnon should be dated to the second century C. E.; *F. Gr. Hist.*, III b, 1955, pp. 267 f. Wachsmuth regards Memnon as a contemporary of Plutarch; see C. Wachsmuth, *Einlei-*

Memnon of Heracleia

tung in das Studium der alten Geschichte, Leipzig 1895, p. 209. His view is based on the fact that Memnon describes the activities, character, life and end of the Heracleian tyrants in a way that resembles Plutarch's attitude towards such persons.

202

apud: Photius, cod. 224, p. 229 a–b — Henry, IV, pp. 68 f. = F. Gr. Hist., III, B434, F18

Καὶ ὡς πέραν τοῦ ᾿Ιονίου ῾Ρωμαῖοι διέβησαν· καὶ ὡς Περσεὺς ὁ
Φιλίππου τὴν Μακεδόνων ἀρχὴν ἐκδεξάμενος, καὶ τὰς συνθήκας τὰς πρὸς
τὸν αὐτοῦ πατέρα ῾Ρωμαίοις γεγενημένας νεότητι κινῶν, κατεπολεμήθη,
Παύλου τὸ κατ᾿ αὐτὸν ἀναστήσαντος τρόπαιον· ὅπως τε πρὸς ᾿Αντίοχον
5 τὸν Συρίας καὶ Κομαγήνης καὶ ᾿Ιουδαίας βασιλέα δυσὶ μάχαις νική-
σαντες τῆς Εὐρώπης ἐξέβαλον...
Μετ᾿ οὐ πολὺ δὲ πάλιν εἰς μάχην ᾿Αντίοχος ῾Ρωμαίοις κατέστη, καὶ
ἀνὰ κράτος ἡττηθεὶς ἐπὶ συνθήκαις διελύσατο τὴν ἔχθραν, αἳ καὶ τῆς
᾿Ασίας αὐτὸν ἁπάσης ἀπεῖργον καὶ τοὺς ἐλέφαντας καὶ τῶν νηῶν
10 συναφῃροῦντο τὸν στόλον, τῆς Κομαγήνης αὐτῷ καὶ τῆς ᾿Ιουδαίας
εἰς ἀρχὴν ὑπολειπομένων.

5 τῆς ἰουδαίας M   10 αὐτῷ Stephanus   αὐτῶν codd.

And that the Romans crossed the Jonian Sea, and that Perseus the
son of Philip, having succeeded to the throne of Macedonia and,
because of his youth, having cancelled the agreements made with
his father by the Romans, was subdued after Paulus had defeated
him; how they won two battles against Antiochus king of Syria, Commagene and Judaea and expelled him from Europe. . .
Not long afterwards Antiochus was again in conflict with the Romans,
and having yielded to their might, put an end to the hostilities by a
treaty, which excluded him from the whole of Asia [i.e. Asia Minor].
He was at the same time deprived of his elephants and fleet; but
Commagene and Judaea were left under his rule.

464

LXXVIII. PLINY THE ELDER

23 / 24–79 C.E.

The Naturalis Historia *of Pliny includes not a few references to Judaea and the Jews. Most of the references relate to the natural features of the country and to its products — above all to the remarkable properties of the Asphaltitis and its bitumen (Nos. 203, 204 and 207). Pliny dwells on the superiority of the balsam over all other aromatic shrubs and stresses that it has been vouchsafed only to the country of Judaea; he also gives us a description of the balsam shrub (No. 213). Nor does he fail to mention the fame of Judaea as a palm-growing country, excelling in* caryotae, *which grow especially in Jericho and in the valleys of Archelais, Phasaelis and Livias (No. 214). In addition, he lists, among various aquatic marvels, a stream in Judaea that dries up every Sabbath (No. 222). Among the schools of magic, the branch originating with Moses and the Jews has its place (No. 221).*

Most important, however, are the chapters Pliny devotes to Judaea in the geographical books of his Naturalis Historia *(No. 204). Judaea is described, after Egypt, among the first areas in Syria. Pliny distinguishes Judaea from the Palestinian coast and Idumaea, though not very clearly. He also implies the well-known division of the Jewish population into Judaea proper, Galilaea and Peraea. His is the only description of the administrative districts of Judaea proper that is as detailed as the one furnished by Josephus. Of course, he does not fail to include a short account of the nature of the Dead Sea, which was considered an indispensable feature of all the ancient descriptions of Judaea; it is connected with the famous passage relating to the Essenes. Like some other ancient authorities, Pliny also refers to the Jordan and the Lake Gennesareth. The celebrated fortresses of Gamala, Machaerus and Massada, all three of which played a prominent part in the Great War between the Jews and the Romans, are mentioned by him. A list of the cities of the Decapolis and a reference to the tetrarchies in the vicinity link the account of Judaea with that of the other parts of Syria.*

The Judaean chapters of Pliny are by no means free from error. Cases in point are the faulty location of Tarichea(e) and the implied connection of Gamala with Samaria. There is nothing in the whole range of the Naturalis Historia *to indicate that Pliny was personally acquainted with*

Judaea. The assertion that he actually saw the country is mainly based on the very dubious connection of Pliny with an inscription from Aradus (OGIS, No. 586) that relates the equestrian career of a deputy to Tiberius Julius Alexander in the Roman army encamped before the walls of Jerusalem in 70 C.E.[1]
Pliny does not state his sources for the geography of Judaea. It seems (cf. the commentary) that for describing the administrative division of Judaea proper he used a source reflecting the conditions of the age of Herod. Sometimes he adapts this source to the contemporary situation of the Flavian age. Thus he refers to the destruction of Jerusalem and to Vespasian's founding the colonies of Prima Flavia (at Caesarea) and Neapolis. On the other hand, we also find traces of older sources prior to the main Herodian source. An example of this is afforded by

---

1 Mommsen restored the inscription so it would imply Pliny; T. Mommsen, *Hermes*, XIX (1884), pp. 644 ff. His restoration was accepted by Dittenberger and by many other scholars, among them D. Detlefsen, *Untersuchungen über die Zusammensetzung der Naturgeschichte des Plinius*, Berlin 1899, pp. 8 ff.; P. Fabia, *Revue de philologie*, NS XVI (1892), pp. 149 ff.; E. Groag, *Jahrbücher für Classische Philologie*, Suppl. XXIII, 1897, p. 783; Schürer, I, p. 625, n. 87. Mommsen's restoration has recently been approved by K. Ziegler, PW, XXI, pp. 275 ff. J. Beaujeu also accepts the restoration in his introduction to the Budé edition of Pliny, I, p. 9. The relevant part of the inscription reads as follows: .....ἡ βουλὴ [καὶ ὁ δῆμος] / ......ίνιον Σεκουν [δ.....] / [ἔπαρ]χον σπείρης (Θ)ρα [κῶν] / [πρ]ώτης, ἔπαρχον ΝΘ.... / ...ων, ἀντεπίτρο[πον Τιβε] / [ριο]υ 'Ιουλίου 'Αλ (ε) ξ [άνδρου] / [ἐπ]άρχου τοῦ 'Ιουδαΐ[κοῦ στρατοῦ]. Other scholars have challenged the restoration and the connection of Pliny with the inscription of Aradus. Foremost among them is F. Münzer, *Bonner Jahrbücher*, CIV (1899), pp. 103 ff. According to Münzer the *contubernium* of Titus and Pliny, alluded to in the *Praefatio* to *Naturalis Historia*, (written in 77 C.E.), implies a common sojourn to Germany in the fifties, and not to Judaea in 70 C.E. Münzer contends, moreover, that in 70 C.E., the presumable date of his presence in Judaea, Pliny acted as procurator in Gallia Narbonensis. Syme and Pflaum concur with Münzer; see R. Syme, *Tacitus*, I, Oxford 1958, p. 60, n. 5; idem, *Harvard Studies in Classical Philology*, LXXIII (1969), pp. 205 f.; H. G. Pflaum, *Les carrières procuratoriennes équestres sous le Haut-Empire romain* I, Paris 1960, pp. 106 ff., especially p. 108. See also G. Lopuszański, *Mélanges d'archéologie et d'histoire*, LV (1938), p. 156, n. 2; B. Dobson, in his edition of A. v. Domaszewski, *Rangordnung des römischen Heeres*, Köln–Graz 1967, p. XL. A. M. A. Hospers-Jansen (*Tacitus over de Joden*, Groningen 1949, pp. 89 ff.) somewhat complicates the problem. Nor does Pliny seem to have known Egypt by autopsy; cf. M. Malaise, *Latomus*, XXVII (1968), pp. 852 ff. The inscription is to be found now in *Inscriptions grecques et latines de la Syrie*, VII, Paris 1970, No. 4011 (ed. J. P. Rey-Coquais, who also rejects Mommsen's reading).

the designation of Jaffa as a Phoenician city, which negates its inclusion among the toparchies of Judaea in the administrative list that follows. Once, at least, it seems that either Pliny, or some intermediate source used by him, misunderstood the meaning of the first source (cf. the statement about the bulls and camels floating in the Dead Sea).[2]

Additional Note;

I do not think that it is necessary to include here Plinius, Naturalis Historia, *XXXVII, 169, which mentions Zachalias of Babylon, a writer who attributed man's destiny to the influence of precious stones: "Zachalias Babylonius in iis libris quos scripsit ad regem Mithridatem gemmis humana fata adtribuens."* Cf. Naturalis Historia, *I,* ad fin.
Some scholars have suggested that he was a Jew, Zachalias standing for Zacharias.[3] *Yet, it seems that this view has not much to recommend it.*[4]

2 For the use of his sources by Pliny, see the general remarks of F. Münzer, *Beiträge zur Quellenkritik der Naturgeschichte des Plinius,* Berlin 1897, pp. 8 ff.; cf. A. H. M. Jones, *The Cities of the Eastern Roman Provinces,* Oxford 1971, p. 503. For a rather far-fetched attempt to use Pliny's geographical description for a reconstruction of the administrative division of Palestine by the Seleucids, see G. Hölscher, *Palästina in der persischen und hellenistischen Zeit,* Berlin 1903, pp. 52 ff. See in general M. Stern, *Tarbiz,* XXXVII (1968), pp. 215 ff. (in Hebrew).
3 E. g. J. Neusner, *A History of the Jews in Babylonia,* I, Leiden 1965, p. 10, n. 2.
4 See K. Ziegler, PW, Ser. 2, IX, p. 2210.

203
Naturalis Historia, II, 226 — Beaujeu = F151R

Nihil in Asphaltite Iudaeae lacu, qui bitumen gignit, mergi potest nec in Armeniae maioris Aretissa; is quidem nitrosus pisces alit.

2 *Aretissa* Barbarus   *aretisa* R   *aritissa* AE²F²e   *aretisso* o   *artisa* (-*issa* D¹) D¹E¹F¹a   *aretesa* d   *arecussa* D³

In Lake Asphaltis in Judaea, which produces bitumen, nothing can sink, and also in Aretissa in Greater Armenia; the latter indeed is a nitrous lake that supports fish.   (trans. H. Rackham, *LCL*)

Nihil in Asphaltite Iudaeae lacu . . . *mergi potest*: Pliny qualifies this statement in V, 72 (No. 204); cf. the commentary *ad loc.*

204
Naturalis Historia, V, 66–73 — Mayhoff = F150R = D. Detlefsen, *Die geographischen Bücher der Naturalis Historia*, Berlin 1904, pp. 102 ff.

(66) Iuxta Syria litus occupat, quondam terrarum maxuma et plurimis distincta nominibus. Namque Palaestine vocabatur qua contingit Arabas, et Iudaea et Coele, dein Phoenice et qua recedit intus Damascena, ac magis etiamnum meridiana Babylonia, eadem Mesopotamia
5 inter Euphraten et Tigrin quaque transit Taurum Sophene, citra vero eam Commagene et ultra Armeniam Adiabene, Assyria ante dicta, et ubi Ciliciam attingit Antiochia. (67) Longitudo eius inter Ciliciam et Arabiam C̄C̄C̄C̄L̄X̄X̄ p. est, latitudo a Seleucia Pieria ad oppidum in Euphrate Zeugma C̄L̄X̄X̄V̄. Qui subtilius dividunt,
10 circumfundi Syria Phoenicen volunt et esse oram maritimam Syriae, cuius pars sit Idumaea et Iudaea, dein Phoenicen, dein Syriam. Id quod praeiacet mare totum Phoenicium appellatur. Ipsa gens Phoenicum in magna gloria litterarum inventionis et siderum navaliumque ac bellicarum artium.
15 (68) A Pelusio Chabriae castra, Casius mons, delubrum Iovis Casii, tumulus Magni Pompei. Ostracine Arabia finitur, a Pelusio L̄X̄V̄ p. Mox Idumaea incipit et Palaestina ab emersu Sirbonis lacus, quem quidam C̄L̄ circuitu tradidere. Herodotus Casio monti adplicuit, nunc est palus modica. Oppida Rhinocolura et intus Rhaphea, Gaza et intus
20 Anthedon, mons Argaris. Regio per oram Samaria; oppidum Ascalo

4 *mediterranea* Littré | *eadem* Mayhoff   *et eadem* D(?), v   *ex eadem* cett.
5 *quoque* Eao   6 *antea* Fao   10 *et* del. R² Basileensis   19 *rinocorura* o | *Gaza*] *gaia* F²E²   del. R²   *zaza* cett.   20 *ascalon* R²

Pliny the Elder

liberum, Azotos, Iamneae duae, altera intus. (69) Iope Phoenicum, antiquior terrarum inundatione, ut ferunt, insidet collem, praeiacente saxo, in quo vinculorum Andromedae vestigia ostendit. Colitur illic fabulosa Ceto. Inde Apollonia, Stratonis Turris, eadem Caesarea ab
25 Herode rege condita, nunc colonia Prima Flavia a Vespasiano Imperatore deducta, finis Palaestines, $\overline{\text{CLXXXVIIII}}$ p. a confinio Arabiae. Dein Phoenice; intus autem Samariae oppida Neapolis, quod antea Mamortha dicebatur, Sebaste in monte, et altiore Gamala.

(70) Supra Idumaeam et Samariam Iudaea longe lateque funditur.
30 Pars eius Syriae iuncta Galilaea vocatur, Arabiae vero et Aegypto proxima Peraea, asperis dispersa montibus et a ceteris Iudaeis Iordane amne discreta. Reliqua Iudaea dividitur in toparchias decem quo dicemus ordine: Hiericuntem palmetis consitam, fontibus riguam, Emmaum, Lyddam, Iopicam, Acrabatenam, Gophaniticam, Thamniti-
35 cam, Betholeptephenen, Orinen, in qua fuere Hierosolyma, longe clarissima urbium Orientis non Iudaeae modo, Herodium cum oppido inlustri eiusdem nominis.

(71) Iordanes amnis oritur e fonte Paneade, qui cognomen dedit Caesareae, de qua dicemus. Amnis amoenus et, quatenus locorum
40 situs patitur, ambitiosus accolisque se praebens velut invitus Asphaltiten lacum dirum natura petit, a quo postremo ebibitur aquasque laudatas perdit, pestilentibus mixtas. Ergo ubi prima convallium fuit occasio, in lacum se fundit, quem plures Genesaram vocant, $\overline{\text{XVI}}$ p. longitudinis, $\overline{\text{VI}}$ latitudinis, amoenis circumsaeptum oppidis, ab
45 oriente Iuliade et Hippo, a meridie Tarichea, quo nomine aliqui et lacum appellant, ab occidente Tiberiade, aquis calidis salubri. (72) Asphaltites nihil praeter bitumen gignit, unde et nomen. Nullum corpus animalium recipit, tauri camelique fluitant; inde fama nihil in eo mergi. Longitudine excedit $\overline{\text{C}}$. p. latitudine maxima $\overline{\text{LXXV}}$ implet,
50 minima $\overline{\text{VI}}$. Prospicit eum ab oriente Arabia Nomadum, a meridie Machaerus, secunda quondam arx Iudaeae ab Hierosolymis. Eodem

---

21 *Iamneae* Salmasius   *Iamniae* Sillig cum B² *iamnes* F³B¹ *hiomnes* R¹ *hamnes* D   *amnes* F cett.   23 *ostendunt* E(?) pv   24 *Derceto* Gelenius   28 *mamortha* E (?) v   *mamorta* F²   *amamorta* cett. 29 *Samariam* v   *samaritim* R²   *samaridim* (*de* a) cett.   33 *hiericontem* d   *iericontem* ao   34 *liddam* R²o   *hyddam* D   *yddam* F¹   *chiddam* R¹ / *iopeticam* R²   34–35 *thamniticam* (*tamni-* o) F²E²o Gelenius   *thamnicam* E¹ *thanicam* (*ta-* a) cett.   38 *Paneade* Solinus E³v   *paniade* DRo   *paniada* F¹ *paniadae* cett.   43 *genesaram* F²v   *gennesarum* R²   *gentes aram* (*arum* R¹) cett.   45 *culiade* DF¹Ea /   *tarichea* ed. Coloniensis   *tarlacea* R *tharicea* E²   *taracea* cett.   51 *macherus* Fa   *macharon* v

469

latere est calidus fons medicae salubritatis Callirhoe, aquarum glo-
riam ipso nomine praeferens.

(73) Ab occidente litora Esseni fugiunt usque qua nocent, gens sola
55 et in toto orbe praeter ceteras mira, sine ulla femina, omni venere abdicata, sine pecunia, socia palmarum. In diem ex aequo convenarum
turba renascitur, large frequentantibus quos vita fessos ad mores eorum
fortuna fluctibus agit. Ita per saeculorum milia — incredibile dictu —
gens aeterna est, in qua nemo nascitur. Tam fecunda illis aliorum vi-
60 tae paenitentia est! Infra hos Engada oppidum fuit, secundum ab Hierosolymis fertilitate palmetorumque nemoribus, nunc alterum bustum.
Inde Masada castellum in rupe, et ipsum haut procul Asphaltite. Et
hactenus Iudaea est.

54 *hesseni* FRa   60 *Engadda* Gelenius   62 *Massada* Solinus

(66) The next country on the coast is Syria, formerly the greatest of
lands. It had a great many divisions with different names, the part
adjacent to Arabia being formerly called Palestine, and Judaea, and
Coele Syria, then Phoenicia and the more inland part Damascena,
and that still further south, Babylonia, as well as Mesopotamia between the Euphrates and the Tigris, the district beyond Mount Taurus
Sophene, that on this side of Sophene Commagene, that beyond
Armenia Adiabene, which was previously called Assyria, and the
part touching Cilicia Antiochia. (67) Its length between Cilicia and
Arabia is 470 miles and its breadth from Seleucia Pieria to Zeugma
on the Euphrates 175 miles. Those who divide the country into smaller parts hold the view that Phoenicia is surrounded by Syria, and
that the order is — the seacoast of Syria of which Idumaea and Judaea
are a part, then Phoenicia, then Syria. The whole of the sea lying off
the coast is called the Phoenician Sea. The Phoenician race itself
has the great distinction of having invented the alphabet and the
sciences of astronomy, navigation and strategy.

(68) After Pelusium come the Camp of Chabrias, Mount Casius, the
Temple of Jupiter Casius, and the tomb of Pompey the Great. At
Ostracine, 65 miles from Pelusium, is the frontier of Arabia. Then
begins Idumaea, and Palestine at the point where the Serbonian Lake
comes into view. This lake is recorded by some writers as having
measured 150 miles round — Herodotus gave it as reaching the foot
of Mount Casius; but is now an inconsiderable fen. There are the town
of Rhinocolura and inland Raphia, Gaza and inland Anthedon,
and Mount Argaris. Further along the coast is the region of Samaria,
the free town Ascalon, Azotos, the two towns named Iamnea, one

of the inland, (69) and the Phoenician city of Jope. This is said
to have existed before the flood; it is situated on a hill, and in front
of it is a rock on which they point out marks made by the chains
with which Andromeda was fettered; here there is a cult of the legendary Ceto. Next Apollonia, and the Tower of Strato; otherwise
Caesarea, founded by King Herod, but now the colony called Prima
Flavia established by the Emperor Vespasian; this is the frontier
of Palestine, 189 miles from the confines of Arabia. After this comes
Phoenicia, and inland the towns of Samaria; Neapolis, formerly
called Mamortha; Sebaste on a mountain; and on a loftier mountain
Gamala.

(70) Beyond Idumaea and Samaria stretches the wide expanse of
Judaea. The part of Judaea adjoining Syria is called Galilee, and that
next to Arabia and Egypt, Peraea. Peraea is covered with rugged
mountains, and is separated from the other parts of Judaea by the
river Jordan. The rest of Judaea is divided into ten toparchies in the
following order: the district of Jericho, which has numerous palm-
groves and springs of water, and those of Emmaus, Lydda, Jope,
Acraba, Gophna, Timna, Betholeptephe, Orine, where Jerusalem
was formerly situated, by far the most famous city of the East and
not of Judaea only, and Herodium with the celebrated town of the
same name.

(71) The source of the river Jordan is the spring of Panias from which
Caesarea described later takes its second name. It is a delightful
stream, winding about so far as the conformation of the locality
allows, and showing itself to the people who dwell on its banks, as
though moving with reluctance towards that gloomy lake, the Dead
Sea, which ultimately swallows it up, its much-praised waters mingling
with the pestilential waters of the lake and being lost. For this reason
at the first opportunity afforded by the formation of the valleys
it widens out into a lake usually called Genesara. This is 16 miles
long and 6 broad, and is skirted by the pleasant towns of Iulias and
Hippo on the east, Tarichea on the south (the name of which place
some people also give to the lake), and Tiberias with its salubrious
hot springs on the west. (72) The only product of the Dead Sea is
bitumen, from which it derives its name [scil. Asphaltites]. The bodies
of animals do not sink in its waters, even bulls and camels floating;
this has given rise to the report that nothing at all can sink in it. It
is more than 100 miles long, and fully 75 miles broad at the broadest
part but only 6 miles at the narrowest. On the east it is faced by
Arabia of the Nomads, and on the south by Machaerus, at one

471

time next to Jerusalem the most important fortress in Judaea. On the same side there is a hot spring possessing medicinal value, the name of which, Callirhoe, itself proclaims the celebrity of its waters.

(73) On the west side of the Dead Sea, but out of range of the noxious exhalations of the coast, is the solitary tribe of the Essenes, which is remarkable beyond all the other tribes in the whole world, as it has no women and has renounced all sexual desire, has no money, and has only palm-trees for company. Day by day the throng of refugees is recruited to an equal number by numerous accessions of persons tired of life and driven thither by the waves of fortune to adopt their manners. Thus through thousands of ages (incredible to relate) a race in which no one is born lives on forever: so prolific for their advantage is other men's weariness of life! Lying below the Essenes was formerly the town of Engeda, second only to Jerusalem in the fertility of its land and in its groves of palm-trees, but now, like Jerusalem, a heap of ashes. Next comes Massada, a fortress on a rock, itself also not far from the Dead Sea. This is the limit of Judaea.

(trans. H. Rackham, *LCL*)

66 *Syria . . . quondam terrarum maxuma et pluribus distincta nominibus*: For this broad meaning of Syria, see the commentary to Mela (No. 152). Mela also includes Adiabene and Babylonia in Syria. Pliny presumably follows him (see T. Nöldeke, *Hermes*, V, 1871, p. 452), or a common source. On Mela and Pliny, see also F. Münzer, *Beiträge zur Quellenkritik der Naturgeschichte des Plinius*, Berlin 1897, pp. 122 f.

68 *mox Idumaea incipit et Palaestina ab emersu Sirbonis lacus*: One may agree with Burchard's translation: "qu'au débouché du Lac Sirbonis commence l'Idumée, subdivision de la Palestine"; see C. Burchard, *RB*, LXIX (1962), p. 544, n. 44.

Rhinocolura (Rhinokorura): Modern el-'Arish, on the border of Palestine and Egypt (*BJ*, IV, 662). It was the southern-most point of Alexander Jannaeus' kingdom (*Ant.*, XIII, 395) and also, presumably, of the Herodian monarchy and the Roman province.

et intus Rhaphea: In fact, Rhaphea was situated only a short distance from the sea, but it had no anchorage and was surrounded by shoals (Diodorus, XX, 74). It is listed among the towns captured by Alexander Jannaeus (*BJ*, I, 87; *Ant.*, XIII, 357) and restored by Gabinius (*BJ*, I, 166), but it is not referred to in connection with either the Herodian monarchy or procuratorial Judaea.

Gaza: After Herod's death Gaza was not incorporated into the ethnarchy of Archelaus, nor was it brought under the rule of Judaea's praefect or procurator. From the confirmation (*intus Anthedon*) it seems that Pliny implicitly considers Gaza to have been situated on the seacoast. Strictly speaking, this is only true of the port of Gaza, Maiumas (el-Mineh); see Abel, II, pp. 374 f.; M. Avi-Yonah, *Historical Geography of Eretz-Israel* 2, Jerusalem 1962, p. 117 (in Hebrew); cf. the commentary to Strabo, *Geographica*, XVI, 2 : 30, p. 759 (No. 114).

intus Anthedon: This contradicts our other sources, which expressly refer to Anthedon's location on the coast; see Stephanus Byzantius: ἔστι καὶ ἑτέρα πόλις πλησίον Γάζης πρὸς τῷ παραλίῳ μέρει; Josephus, *Ant.*, XVIII, 158: Ἀγρίππας εἰς Ἀνθηδόνα παραγενόμενος καὶ λαβὼν ναῦν ἐν ἀναγωγαῖς ἦν. Pliny does not refer to the town by the new name Agrippias or Agrippeion (in honour of Marcus Agrippa), which it received during Herod's reign; see *BJ*, I, 87, 118, 416; *Ant.*, XIII, 357; see also Abel, II, pp. 244 f.

mons Argaris: Mount Gerizim is meant here. As the Samaritans' religious centre it still played a part in the turmoils of the procuratorial period and in the Great Revolt; see *Ant.*, XVIII, 85. Since it was situated in Samaria, Pliny obviously made a mistake in referring to the mountain after Anthedon and before the southern cities of Ascalon, Azotus, Jamnia and Jaffa. Moreover, the mention of Samaria is also out of place here, since none of these southern cities had ever been included in Samaria.

regio per oram Samaria: Samaria seems to have included the coast from somewhere north of Jaffa up to and including Caesarea; see *Ant.*, XIX, 351.

oppidum Ascalo liberum: Ascalon was freed from the Seleucid rule in 104–103 B. C. E.; see *Chronicon Paschale* (ed. Dindorf), Bonn 1832, I, p. 346. For numismatic evidence, see A. B. Brett, *AJA*, XLI (1937), pp. 452 ff. It had never been incorporated in the Hasmonaean state; see M. Stern, *Zion*, XXVI, 1961, pp. 20 f. Nor was it ever a part of Herod's kingdom. Its military importance and power are attested by its pertinacious struggle against the Jews in the time of the Great Revolt.

Azotos: Azotus is the old Philistine Ashdod, which was still important in the first century C. E.; see the commentary to Strabo, *Geographica*, XVI, 2 : 2, p. 749 (No. 111). Pompey detached it from Judaea; see *BJ*, I, 156; *Ant.*, XIV, 75. However, the Jews continued to be a significant factor among Azotus' population, as is implied by Vespasian's need to capture the town and to garrison it; see *BJ*, IV, 130.

Iamneae duae, altera intus: The two Iamneae are the town of this name and the port of Jamnia (Ἰαμνειτῶν λιμήν). On the Hellenistic Jamnia, i.e. Jabneh, see the commentary to Strabo, XVI, 2 : 28, p. 759 (No. 114). This town, together with Azotus, was allotted in Herod's testament to his sister Salome; see *BJ*, II, 98; *Ant.*, XVII, 321. Salome left it to the Empress Livia, thus making Jamnia an estate of the imperial house, administered by a special procurator; see *BJ.*, II, 167; *Ant.*, XVIII, 31. It was a city with a mixed population, but with a Jewish majority; see Philo, *Legatio*, 200. In the years after the destruction of the Second Temple Jabneh became the main centre of Judaism and the seat of the Sanhedrin. Pliny makes no connection between Jamnia and the Jews and does not include it among the toparchies of Judaea. For the Ἰαμνειτῶν λιμήν, cf. Ptolemy *Geographia*, V, 16 : 2 (No. 337).

69 *Iope Phoenicum*: The designation of Jaffa as a Phoenician city does not accord with the actual situation in the first century C. E. It also contradicts the statement that follows,where Pliny includes the toparchy of Jaffa as an integral part of Judaea. Jaffa had been attached to Phoenicia in the Persian period; see the commentary to Diodorus, I, 31 : 2 (No. 56). However, it became a Jewish city in the Hasmonaean period, and in the first century C. E. it constituted one of Judaea's chief bulwarks. Thus, Pliny and the other writers who connect Jaffa with Phoenicia, e.g. Strabo, *Geographica*, I, 2 : 35 (No. 109), are archaizing.

473

antiquior terrarum inundatione: This refers to the flood that is related in Greek mythology with Deucalion. Mela (No. 152) also refers to Jaffa as having been founded before the flood. Indeed, Jaffa was a very ancient town, which already appeared in Egyptian documents dating from the eighteenth dynasty; see J.B. Pritchard, *Ancient Near Eastern Texts Relating to the Old Testament*[2], Princeton 1955, pp. 22 f., 242; H. Goedicke, *Chronique d'Egypte*, XLIII (1968), pp. 219 ff.

praeiacente saxo, in quo vinculorum Andromedae vestigia ostendit. Colitur illic fabulosa Ceto: Jaffa is often mentioned in ancient literature, from Pseudo-Scylax on, as the site of the *Andromeda* myth; see the commentary to Pausanias, *Graeciae Descriptio*, IV, 35 : 9 (No. 354). The monster (κῆτος) appears already in Pseudo-Scylax; see *ZDPV*, LXI (1938), p. 90. For a rationalistic explanation, see Conon, *Narrationes* (No. 145).

inde Apollonia: Apollonia should be identified with modern Arsuf. Apart from the mention in Pliny, it appears in Josephus among the cities belonging to the kingdom of Alexander Jannaeus (*Ant.*, XIII, 395) and among those restored by Gabinius (*BJ*, I, 166); cf. Abel, II, p. 247.

Stratonis turris eadem Caesarea: Stratonis turris (Στράτωνος πύργος) was the old name. The connection of Caesarea with the Tower of Strato is also stressed by other sources from the Roman period; see Ptolemy, *Geographia*, V, 16 : 2 (No. 337).

Nunc colonia Prima Flavia a Vespasiano imperatore deducta: On the coinage of the new colony, see L. Kadman, "The Coins of Caesarea Maritima", *Corpus Nummorum Palaestinensium* II, Tel Aviv 1957, p. 46.

Neapolis, quod antea Mamortha dicebatur: Cf. *BJ*, IV, 449: παρὰ τὴν Νέαν πόλιν καλουμένην, Μαβαρθὰ δ'ὑπὸ τῶν ἐπιχωρίων. Pliny again refers to the conditions prevailing after the fall of Jerusalem. Neapolis was founded in 72 C. E.

Sebaste in monte, et altiore Gamala: Sebaste, indeed, replaced ancient Samaria. Pliny is strangely mistaken concerning Gamala, since the town belonged not to Samaria but to the Lower Gaulanitis. For a description of Gamala, see *BJ*, IV, 4 ff.

70 *Supra Idumaeam et Samariam Iudaea longe lateque funditur* ...: Judaea should be construed here not as Judaea proper or as the Roman province of Judaea, but in the less common sense, as the whole territory inhabited by a Jewish majority, i.e. Judaea proper (implied here by "reliqua Iudaea"), as well as the Galilee and Peraea. This three-fold division of the Jewish territory is well attested elsewhere; cf., e.g., *Mishnah Shevi'it* 9 : 2; *Ketubot* 13 : 10; *Bava Batra* 3 : 2. Although Idumaea had been inhabited by Jews from the last quarter of the second century B. C. E., Pliny did not include it in the Jewish territory. From Pliny's phrasing one may get the false impression that Idumaea and Samaria formed a continuous territory, beyond which there was a continuous Jewish territory. *Supra* is to be understood in the sense of *in mediterraneo*, in contrast to *in ora*.

pars eius Syriae iuncta Galilaea vocatur: Cf. *BJ*, III, 35: Δύο δ'οὔσας τὰς Γαλιλαίας... περιίσχει μὲν ἡ Φοινίκη τε καὶ Συρία. Pliny is the first Latin writer known to us to refer expressly to the Galilee; the second is Tacitus, *Annales*, XII, 54 (No. 288); cf. also Strabo, *Geographica*, XVI, 2 : 34, p. 760 (No. 115).

Peraea: I.e. the territory east of the Jordan, which is considered Jewish by both Josephus and the *Mishnah*; cf. Schürer, II, p. 15.

asperis dispersa montibus: Cf. *BJ*, III, 44: ἡ Περαία... ἔρημος δὲ καὶ τραχεῖα τὸ πλέον.

reliqua Iudaea dividitur in toparchias decem quo dicemus ordine: The administrative

Pliny the Elder

division of the country into toparchies goes back to the Hellenistic age. We first meet it in connection with Palestine in I Macc. xi : 28. However, in the Hellenistic age, we encounter the term νομοί for the same administrative units in I Macc. x : 38; I Macc. xi : 34. Toparchy was the standard term for Roman Judaea.

For the list of toparchies in Pliny and the parallel one in *BJ*, III, 54 ff., see Schürer, II, p. 229 ff.; E. Nestle, "Judaea bei Josephus", Ph.D. Thesis, Tübingen 1911, pp. 51 f.; Kahrstedt, pp. 114 f.; Momigliano, pp. 366 ff.; A. H. M. Jones, *JRS*, XXI (1931), p. 78; XXV (1935), pp. 230 f.; idem, *The Cities of the Eastern Roman Provinces*, Oxford 1971, pp. 273; 462, n. 63; 508; S. Klein, *The Land of Judaea*, Jerusalem 1939, pp. 213 ff. (in Hebrew); M. Avi-Yonah, *op. cit.* (supra, p. 472), p. 62; M. Stern *Tarbiz*, XXXVII (1968), pp. 215 ff.; A. Schalit, *König Herodes*, Berlin 1969, pp. 208 ff.

As against the ten of Pliny, Josephus divides the country into eleven toparchies. The main differences between the two lists are that Pliny omits the toparchies of Idumaea and 'En Gedi (cf. *BJ*, III, 55) and includes that of Jaffa, while Josephus (*loc. cit.*, 56) refers to the toparchies of Jaffa and Jamnia only in an appendix, thereby, strictly speaking, not including Jaffa in Judaea. It is of little import that Pliny called the toparchy of Jerusalem, Orine and that he used Bethleptephene instead of Josephus' Πέλλη.

The discrepancies between Pliny and Josephus may be accounted for either by conjecturing that Josephus and Pliny represent different stages in Judaea's administrative history, or by assuming that one of them was grossly inaccurate. Beyer, thinks that Josephus confused the issue by attributing Idumaea and 'En Gedi to Judaea; see G. Beyer, *ZDPV*, LIV (1931), pp. 249 f; see also Kahrstedt, p. 115, n. 1. It seems worthwhile to me to pursue the first interpretation, since we may assume that Josephus, a native of Judaea and a member of the ruling priestly class, did not find it necessary to draw on written sources in order to compile a list of Judaea's contemporary administrative divisions. Thus, his list may truly represent the conditions prevailing there in the last decades before the Temple's destruction. On the other hand, Pliny, as a foreigner, must have used a written source. Jones suggests that Pliny's list derives from the *formula provinciae* drawn up after Archelaus' banishment in 6 C. E.; see A. H. M. Jones, *JRS*, XXV (1935), p. 231. Momigliano holds the view that the list is dependent on the *commentarii* of Agrippa. It seems to me that whatever the case, there is reason to adduce a source dating from Herod's time, since only such a source would explain Pliny's omission of Idumaea and 'En Gedi. In Herod's time Idumaea, with the attached coastal area of Gaza, constituted an administrative unit separate from Judaea; see *Ant.*, XV, 254; cf. Otto, p. 47, n. 2. Upon Herod's death in 4 B. C. E. Gaza and its territory were not incorporated into the newly created province, but were joined directly to the province of Syria; see *BJ*, II, 97; *Ant.*, XVII, 320. It may be suggested that the toparchies of the now diminished Idumaea were not considered a big enough territory to form an independent division, the more so as their populations were almost purely Jewish. Consequently, they were attached to the toparchies of Judaea proper and constituted its southern part. There were two Idumaean toparchies of southern Judaea, one in the west and one in the east. At an unknown time 'En Gedi became the capital of the eastern Idumaean toparchy. Since 'En Gedi suffered one of its periods of decline under Herod and experienced a revival in the last decades before the destruction of the Temple, it is quite likely that it was the centre of a toparchy in the time of Josephus, but not during Herod's reign. Of course, Pliny somewhat

475

modified his list in consideration of contemporary events. Thus, he alludes to the destruction of Jerusalem and of 'En Gedi.

One may also be inclined to explain the differences between the two lists by the natural supposition that, contrary to Josephus, Pliny reflects the conditions after the Great Revolt and after the destruction of Jerusalem and 'En Gedi. In that case, however, we should also suppose a new separation between Judaea and Idumaea in the period following 70 C. E., which seems unlikely to me. It should be noted that the second-century geographer Ptolemy also includes 'En Gedi in Judaea; see Ptolemy, *Geographia*, V, 16 : 8 (No. 337). His separate Idumaea implies a much more southern territory than that commonly known as Idumaea in the period of the Second Temple. We should also observe that, in his description of the Essenes that follows, Pliny presumably includes the area of 'En Gedi in a Judaea whose extremity is marked by Massada, which is much further to the south.

Although Josephus only mentions the toparchy of Jaffa in an appendix, while Pliny includes it in Judaea, it is noteworthy that Josephus (*BJ*, II, 567) equates Jaffa with the centres of the toparchies of Lydda and Emmaus.

Hiericuntem palmetis consitam, fontibus riguam: Jericho was still important during the Hellenistic and Roman ages. On the Persian period, see the commentary to Solinus, *Collectanea*, 35 : 4 (No. 449). On the pre-Roman period, see *PCZ*, No. 59004, Col. I, l. 4 (dated probably 259 B.C.E.), which is taken from the itinerary of Zeno and his companions. On Jericho as one of the strongholds that Bacchides raised to encircle Judaea, see I Macc. ix : 50.

At the time of Gabinius' partition of Judaea, Jericho became one of the five seats of the newly-created Synhedria; see *Ant.*, XIV, 91; *BJ*, I, 170. It achieved a new period of greatness under Herod's rule (37–4 B. C. E.), when it served as a royal winter residence and was embellished by splendid buildings and establishments, such as a palace, a hippodrome and an amphitheatre; see *BJ*, I, 659, 666; *Ant.*, XVII, 175, 194. Josephus gives a vivid description of its vicinity in *BJ*, IV, 452 ff. It seems to have been a populous Jewish town at the end of the period of the Second Temple; see A. Büchler, *Die Priester und der Cultus im letzten Jahrzehnt des jerusalemischen Tempels*, Vienna 1895, pp. 161 f. The Jericho of this period is now commonly identified with a group of mounds at Talul Abu el-'Alayiq. On the excavations there, see J. L. Kelso, D.C. Baramki et al., "Excavations at New Testament Jericho and Khirbet En-Nitla", *AASOR*, XXIX–XXX for 1949–1951 (1955); J. B. Pritchard, "The Excavation at Herodian Jericho", *AASOR*, XXXII–XXXIII for 1952–1954, (1958).

The famous palm-groves in the vicinity of Jericho are emphasized by Strabo, *Geographica*, XVI, 2 : 41, p. 763 (No. 115), although he only mentions Jericho as the name of a valley. The same holds true for Pompeius Trogus, apud: Iustinus, *Epitoma*, XXXVI, 3 : 2 (No. 137); cf. *BJ*, IV, 468.

Emmaum: Pliny skips the adjacent toparchies. Emmaus was situated in western Judaea, and its toparchy bordered on Orine ("hill country", i.e. Jerusalem) in the east, on the toparchy of Lydda in the north and north-west and on Bethleptephene in the south. Emmaus is first known from the Maccabaean wars; see I Macc. iii : 40; ix : 50. Later it gained much as it eclipsed and annexed Gezer (Gazara). Emmaus figures among the Jewish cities whose inhabitants were reduced to servitude by Cassius after Caesar's death; see *BJ*, I, 222; *Ant.*, XIV, 275 (the other cities were Gophna, Lydda and Thamna). Undoubtedly, by then Emmaus was already the centre of its toparchy. Later, this toparchy became the territory of Nicopolis; see G. Beyer, *ZDPV*, LVI (1933), p. 242.

Lyddam: Lydda had already been the centre of its district — either toparchy or nomos — under the Seleucid rule (I Macc. xi : 34) and remained so during the entire period of the Second Temple. It was a place of much importance, and Josephus defines it as a κώμη πόλεως τὸ μέγεθος οὐκ ἀποδέουσα; see *Ant.*, XX, 130.

Iopicam: Jaffa was included in Judaea since the time of Simon the Hasmonaean; see I Macc. xiii : 11. After a short period of separation Julius Caesar restored it to Judaea; see *Ant.*, XIV, 205. Also, Josephus, in his list of toparchies mentioned above, refers to Jaffa as the centre of a toparchy.

Acrabatenam: This is the northern-most toparchy of Judaea proper, cutting deeply into Samaria. It was named after the township of Akrabe; see *BJ*, II, 652: 'Ακρα-βετηνὴν τοπαρχίαν. It did not belong to Judaea in the Hellenistic age and was not annexed to the three south-Samaritan toparchies in the time of Jonathan the Hasmonaean, but seems to have been incorporated into Judaea only in the days of John Hyrcan; cf. Alt, II, pp. 349 f.

Gophaniticam: This toparchy, named after its capital Gophna, lay to the north of Orine and to the south of Acrabatena. Gophna superseded Aphairema (I Macc. xi : 34) as the capital of the toparchy; see A. H. M. Jones, *JRS*, XXI (1931), p. 78; G. Beyer, *ZDPV*, LIV (1931), p. 260.

Thamniticam: This place, named after Thamna, superseded Ramathaim; see I Macc. xi : 34.

Betholeptephenen: The same toparchy is referred to in *BJ*, IV, 445: ἐπὶ τὴν Βεθλε-πτηνφῶν τοπαρχίαν. The Πέλλη of *BJ*, III, 55, is either a mistake of Josephus' copyists, or, as some scholars suppose, the name of the toparchy's chief city, which was assimilated into Pella; see Abel, II, p. 277, based on an inscription found near Lydda. This inscription, which was published by Savignac, reads Μαρχίων Κρονίδου Πελλεύς; see R. Savignac, *RB*, XIII (1904), p. 83. In any case, it is not very likely that Josephus himself confused it with Pella across the Jordan. Against this supposition, see also A. H. M. Jones, *JRS*, XXV (1935), p. 231. For the centre of the Bethleptephene toparchy we must look at Bet-Nettif, south of Emmaus. The whole toparchy was bordered in the north by that of Emmaus. On this toparchy, see G. Beyer, *ZDPV*, LIV (1931), pp. 259 ff.

Orinen, in qua fuere Hierosolyma: For Orine ('Ορεινή), see Luke: i : 39 (ἐπορεύθη εἰς τὴν ὀρεινὴν... εἰς πόλιν 'Ιούδα); i : 65 here we find Pliny's allusion to contemporary conditions. It may be assumed that the name Orine became official only after the destruction of Jerusalem.

longe clarissima urbium orientis: Cf. the *famosa urbs* of Tacitus, *Historiae*, V, 2 (No. 281). Nothing expresses the growth of Jerusalem's fame from the Hellenistic age to the Julio-Claudian period more clearly than a comparison of the ways in which Polybius and Pliny referred to it. Polybius mentions Jerusalem only in relation to the temple; see Polybius, apud: Josephus, *Ant.*, XII, 136 (No. 32). However, Pliny's characterization seems to surpass in some respects that of the Jew Philo (*Legatio*, 281), to whom Jerusalem constituted the metropolis not only of Judaea, but also of most other countries, as it had at various times established colonies in neighbouring lands. On the kingdom of Jerusalem that was promised to Nero before his death and on the well-known Flavian inscription from 80 C. E. (*ILS*, No. 264), where Jerusalem is described as having been an

477

impregnable city, see Suetonius, *Nero*, 40 : 2 (No. 309); and the commentary to Livius, *Periochae*, 102 (No. 131).

Herodium cum oppido inlustri eiusdem nominis: The toparchy of Herodium included the south-eastern territory of Judaea proper, excluding the Idumaean toparchies. The town was built by Herod about 15 km south-east of Jerusalem and should be identified with Gebel el-Fureidis; see Abel, II, p. 348; P. Benoit, J. T. Milik & R. de Vaux, *Discoveries in the Judaean Desert*, II, Oxford 1961, pp. 124 ff. Pliny's list begins with the north-eastern part of Judaea (Jericho), passes abruptly to the west (Emmaus), lists the northern toparchies without regard to any logical order, proceeds to the south-west and to Jerusalem, and then concludes with the south-east. Josephus' list is much more systematic: It begins with Gophna in the north, lists all the northern toparchies, continues to the west, south-west and south-east, and ends with Jericho in the north-east; see *BJ*, III, 55 f.

71 *Iordanes amnis oritur a fonte Paneade*: Cf. Pausanias, *Graeciae Descriptio*, V, 7 : 4 (No. 356), where its name is given as Ἰόρδανος; see also Strabo, *Geographica* XVI, 2 : 16 (No. 112); Tacitus, *Historiae*, V, 6 (No. 281). On the sources of the Jordan, see *BJ*, III, 509: καὶ δοκεῖ μὲν Ἰορδάνου πηγὴ τὸ Πάνειον.

amnis amoenus et . . . ambitiosus: On the Jordan, see Abel, I, pp. 474 ff.; N. Glueck, *The River Jordan*, Philadelphia 1946.

velut invitus Asphaltiten lacum dirum natura petit: Mention of the mouth of the Jordan precedes the reference to the Lake of Gennesareth, thus obscuring the account.

in lacum se fundit, quem plures Genesaram vocant: Lake Tiberias often appears under this name in the works of Josephus; see, e.g., *Ant.*, XVIII, 28, 36; *Vita*, 349; *BJ*, II, 573; cf. the description in *BJ*, III, 506 ff.; see also I Macc. xi : 67 (τὸ ὕδωρ τοῦ Γεννήσαρ); Abel, I, p. 495. For the mention of this lake in Strabo, see *Geographica*, *loc. cit.*; see also the commentary *ad loc*. Pausanias (*loc. cit.*) refers to it as Tiberias. Tacitus, *Historiae*, V, 6 (No. 281), presents a clearer picture of the Jordan's course through the lakes ("unum atque alterum lacum integer perfluit, tertio retinetur"), than Pliny. Tacitus, however, does not name any of the lakes.

XVI passum longitudinis, VI latitudinis: The present length of lake Tiberias is given as 21 km; its maximum width at the northern end is 12 km.

ab oriente Iuliade: This city was founded by Herod's son Philippus on the site of Bethsaida (*Ant.*, XVIII, 28; *BJ*, II, 168) and was named Iulias after Iulia, the daughter of Augustus. It was situated east of the Jordan, near the head of Lake Tiberias; see Abel, II, pp. 279 f.; Avi-Yonah, *op. cit.* (supra, p. 472), p. 152.

Hippo: Ἵππος is one of the cities of the Decapolis, east of Lake Tiberias; see Schürer, II, pp. 155 ff.

a meridie Tarichea: On Tarichea (Taricheae) and the details of its location, see the commentary to Strabo, *Geographica*, XVI, 2 : 45 (No. 115). Tarichea should be located to the west of Lake Tiberias, which is north of the city of Tiberias, and not to the south of it, as Pliny states.

quo nomine aliqui et lacum appellant: It seems that here Pliny confuses Tiberias with Taricheae, since Tiberias sometimes gave its name to the lake; cf. Pausanias, *loc. cit.*

ab occidente Tiberiade aquis calidis salubri: Tiberias, the foremost among the cities of the Galilee, was founded by Herod Antipas *c.* 23 C. E.; see H. W. Hoehner, *Herod Antipas*, Cambridge 1972, pp. 93 ff.

72 *Asphaltites*: Pliny uses the name Asphaltites for the Dead Sea, as do Diodorus (No. 62), Josephus and Galen (No. 381).

nullum corpus animalium recipit, tauri camelique fluitant: The first part of the statement is found in Pliny as well as in other writers, from Aristotle, *Meteorologica*, II, p. 359a (No. 3) onwards. The second part, concerning the bulls and the camels, may be cited by Pliny as a concrete example of the first part. In fact, the reference to the bulls and camels arose from Pliny's negligent use of his sources, which, as we may see from a comparison with Diodorus, XIX, 98 (No. 62) and Josephus, referred to the asphalt lumps that took the form of certain animals; see the commentary to Diodorus *ad loc.*

inde fama nihil in eo mergi: Pliny uses only "fama", and, indeed, we miss an absolute statement such as this in most of our other ancient authorities. Cf., however, Xenophilus, apud: Antigonus Carystius, 151 (No. 22): ἐν μὲν τῇ πλησίον Ἰόππης [scil. λίμνῃ]...ἐπινήχεσθαι πᾶν βάρος; see also Pliny himself in No. 203, where "nihil in Asphaltite lacu . . . mergi potest" is just presented as a fact.

Longitudine excedit C passuum . . .: On the size of the Dead Sea, see the commentary to Diodorus *ad loc.* The measurements given here differ considerably from the true ones, especially in respect to the maximum width. There is a variant "XXV M passuum" (for LXXV), which may be correct; see C. Burchard, *RB*, LXIX (1962), pp. 545 f.

a meridie Machaerus: Pliny locates both Machairus and Callirhoe south of the Dead Sea. This is clearly a mistake, since both were situated to the east of it.

secunda quondam arx Iudaeae ab Hierosolymis: Machairus was fortified by Alexander Jannaeus and again by Herod. It fulfilled its function as one of Judaea's chief fortresses and served as a bulwark against the Nabataeans. It was the last stronghold but one to withstand the Roman army at the time of the Great Revolt. For a description of the place, see *BJ*, VII, 164 ff.; cf. O. Plöger, *ZDPV*, LXXI (1955), pp. 151 ff.

Callirhoe: On the warm baths of Callirhoe used, e.g., by King Herod, see *BJ*, I, 657; *Ant.*, XVII, 171; see also H. Donner, *ZDPV*, LXXIX (1963), pp. 59 ff.; A. Strobel, *ibid.*, LXXXII (1966), pp. 149 ff.

73 *Ab occidente litora Esseni fugiunt*: Pliny and Dio Chrysostom (No. 251) are the only two independent sources to connect the Essenes with the Dead Sea. Solinus, *Collectanea Rerum Memorabilium* XXXIV, (No. 449) and Capella, *De Nuptiis Philologiae et Mercurii*, VI, 679 (No. 536) derive from Pliny. The Graeco-Jewish writers never refer to the Dead Sea in connection with this sect, and the impression one gains from both Philo and Josephus is that the sect was dispersed over many parts of Judaea. In one place Philo says that the Essenes live in villages, eschewing town life: διὰ τὰς τῶν πολιτευομένων χειροήθεις ἀνομίας; see *Quod Omnis Probus Liber*, 76. However, in a fragment of Philo's *Apologia* we read that the Essenes inhabited many towns and villages of Judaea; see Eusebius, *Praeparatio Evangelica*, VIII, 11 : 1. This last reference agrees with Josephus, *BJ*, II, 124: Μία δ'οὐκ ἔστιν αὐτῶν πόλις, ἀλλ' ἐν ἑκάστῃ μετοικοῦσιν πολλοί.

On the order's functionaries, who were appointed in every city to attend to strangers belonging to the order and to provide them with clothes and other necessities, see *BJ*, II, 125. From *BJ*, V, 145, which is a description of Jerusalem before its destruction by Titus, we learn about the Gate of the Essenes, which implies the existence of an Essene community in Jerusalem. Presumably, Pliny knows only of the Essenes living in the vicinity of the Dead Sea, although he does not mention a specific town where the Essenes lived, as Dio Chrysostom does. If he had, he would have contradicted Josephus, *BJ*, II, 124. In fact, the only information that may be derived from Pliny, and, for that matter, from Dio Chrysostom, is that there was at one time a considerable concentration of Essenes somewhere in the neighbourhood of the Dead Sea. For a convenient collection of the ancient sources relating to the Essenes, see A. Adam, *Antike Berichte über die Essener (Kleine Texte für Vorlesungen und Übungen*, Berlin 1961, No. 182).

The various views on the origins and nature of Essenism have been discussed in a huge number of books and articles; see, e.g., S. Wagner, *Die Essener in der wissenschaftlichen Diskussion vom Ausgang des 18. bis zum Beginn des 20. Jahrhunderts*, Berlin 1960; Schürer, II, pp. 651 ff.; C. Bugge, *ZNTW*, XIV (1913), pp. 145 ff.; Bauer, PW, Suppl. IV (1924), pp. 386 ff.; F. Cumont, *Comptes rendus de l'Académie des Inscriptions et Belles-Lettres*, 1930, pp. 99 ff. For a discussion of the connection of the Essenes with the Dead Sea sect, see C. Burchard, *Bibliographie zu den Handschriften vom Toten Meer*, Berlin 1957; II, Berlin 1965; A. Dupont-Sommer, *Les écrits esséniens découverts près de la Mer Morte*[2], Paris 1960; H. Kosmala, *Hebräer–Essener–Christen*, Leiden 1959. For an interpretation of the present passage, as related to the problem, see R. de Vaux, *L'archéologie et les manuscrits de la Mer Morte*, London 1961, pp. 100 ff.; J. P. Audet, *RB*, LXVIII (1961), pp. 346 ff.; C. Burchard, *RB*, LXIX (1962), pp. 533 ff.; L. Herrmann, *Revue Belge de Philologie et d'Histoire*, XLI (1963), pp. 80 ff.; P. Sacchi, *Parola del Passato*, XVIII (1963), pp. 451 ff.

gens sola: Did Pliny or his source think of the Essenes as a special *gens*, separate from the Jewish nation though geographically included in Judaea (note the words that follow: "et hactenus Judaea est")? This view is perhaps echoed by Josephus, who finds it necessary to emphasize that the Essenes are Ἰουδαῖοι μὲν γένος (*BJ*, II, 119).

sine ulla femina, omni venere abdicata: Cf. Philo, apud: Eusebius, *Praeparatio Evangelica*, VIII, 11 : 14: Ἐσσαίων γὰρ οὐδεὶς ἄγεται γυναῖκα, διότι φίλαυτον γυνὴ καὶ ζηλότυπον...; cf. Josephus, *BJ*, II, 120: καὶ γάμου μὲν παρ' αὐτοῖς ὑπεροψία, τοὺς δ' ἀλλοτρίους παῖδας ἐκλαμβάνοντες ἁπαλοὺς ἔτι πρὸς τὰ μαθήματα, συγγενεῖς ἡγοῦνται. Josephus does, however, mention another branch of the Essenes who may marry under special conditions, but then only to propagate the race; see *BJ*, II, 160 f. Philo, on the other hand, never refers to these Essenes.

sine pecunia: Cf. Philo, *Quod Omnis Probus Liber Sit*, 76:...οὐκ ἄργυρον καὶ χρυσὸν θησαυροφυλακοῦντες...[77] μόνοι γὰρ ἐξ ἁπάντων σχεδὸν ἀνθρώπων ἀχρήματοι καὶ ἀκτήμονες γεγονότες... On the communal sharing of goods practised by the Essenes, cf. Philo, *Apologia*, apud: Eusebius, *Praeparatio Evangelica*, VIII, 11 : 4 f.; *BJ*, II, 122: καταφρονηταὶ δὲ πλούτου, καὶ θαυμάσιον παρ' αὐτοῖς τὸ κοινωνικόν. Pliny's *sine pecunia* expresses the fact that the Essenes used no money in their internal dealings, since their sharing of goods and earnings made this unnecessary. Perhaps this also shows their general contempt for money.

Infra hos Engada oppidum fuit: The exact meaning of this passage has given rise to more discussion than that of any other in Pliny, because many scholars think it provides decisive proof in favour of identifying the Essenes with the Qumran Sect. Khirbet Qumran is situated near the north-western shore of the Dead Sea, i.e. north of 'En Gedi. If we interpret *infra* in accordance with this situation, it would, it seems, clinch the arguments for identifying the Essenes with that sect. Unfortunately, this question cannot be answered solely by Pliny's use of *infra* or on any other purely linguistic grounds. Audet has argued strongly for an interpretation of *infra* that would give it the meaning of *in ora*, in contrast to *in medi-*

terraneo, a usage that occurs many times in Pliny, though it never relates to a lake instead of to a sea; see Audet, *loc. cit.* (supra, p. 480). If that is the case, we must assume that the Essenes' habitations were situated on the heights west of 'En Gedi, and not at Qumran. However, this interpretation of *infra* is not the only one to be considered in Pliny. Some other uses are attested both in Latin literature generally and in Pliny himself, e.g. "down-stream" (of the river Jordan), or even "south". Moreover, the impression one gets from reading Pliny is that he describes the Dead Sea by starting from the north, and that 'En Gedi, which is mentioned after the Essenes, should therefore be located south of the Essene habitations. Similarly, Massada, which is therefore mentioned after 'En Gedi, indeed lies south of it. Also, archaeological evidence does not favour the location of a large Essene settlement west of 'En Gedi; see R. de Vaux, *op. cit.* (supra, p. 480); F.M. Cross, *The Ancient Library of Qumran and Modern Biblical Studies*, New York 1958, p. 75. For a forceful answer to the various arguments of Audet, see Burchard, *op. cit.* (supra, p. 480).

I would add that even if Pliny had used *infra* in the sense Audet supposes, it would not have precluded our placing the Essenes' habitat more to the north. Pliny is so inaccurate in his description of Palestine that he could easily confuse the exact location of the Essene habitations in their relation to the Dead Sea. He did, however, preserve the bare fact that there was an Essene concentration in the vicinity of that sea, which is independently attested by Dio Chrysostom.

We know much more about the history of 'En Gedi since the excavations there by Mazar. It prospered under the Persian rule, suffered a great disaster sometime in the middle of the fourth century B. C. E., enjoyed a revival in the Ptolemaic period and experienced a second decline in the Herodian age; see B. Mazar & I. Dunayevsky, *IEJ*, XIV (1964), pp. 121 ff. Under the procurators it regained some importance as the centre of one of Judaea's toparchies (*BJ*, III, 55). Josephus calls it a πολίχνη (*BJ*, IV, 402).

secundum ab Hierosolymis fertilitate palmetorumque nemoribus, nunc alterum bustum: Josephus does not furnish direct information about the Romans' destruction of 'En Gedi, but only refers to the sack of this township by the Sicarii of Massada (*BJ*, IV, 402 ff.).

As to Jerusalem, it could hardly be famous for the fertility of its land and its palm-groves, a description that would apply rather to Jericho. On the other hand, the reference to a heap of ruins does fit Jerusalem. It seems, therefore, that Pliny carelessly refers to the two cities in one sentence.

inde Masada castellum in rupe: On Massada, see the commentary to Strabo, *Geographica* (No. 115). It is noteworthy that Pliny does not mention Massada's capture by the Romans in 73 C. E. or rather in 74 C. E.

205

Naturalis Historia, V, 128 — Mayhoff = D. Detlefsen, *Die geographischen Bücher der Naturalis Historia*, Berlin 1904, p. 118.

In Phoenicio deinde mari est ante Iopen Paria, tota oppidum, in qua obiectam beluae Andromedam ferunt.

1 *Iopen* Sillig   *iope* AF   *ioppen* DdE³   *ioppe* cett.

Then in the Phoenician Sea off Jope lies Paria, the whole of which
is a town—it is said to have been the place where Andromeda was
exposed to the monster. (trans. R. Rackham, *LCL*)

ante Iopen Paria: We know next to nothing about this place. Perhaps there was
once a settlement on the rocks in front of Jaffa; see M. Avi-Yonah, *op. cit.* (supra,
p. 472), p. 108; see also Conon, *Narrationes* (No. 145): καὶ ἁρπάζεται ἀπό τινος
νησῖδος ἐρήμου ἡ ᾿Ανδρομέδα.
in qua obiectam beluae Andromedam: Cf. the commentary to Pausanias, IV, 35 : 9
(No. 354).

206

Naturalis Historia, VI, 213 — Mayhoff = Detlefsen, *op. cit.*, pp. 174 f.

Sequens circulus incipit ab India vergente ad occasum, vadit per
medios Parthos, Persepolim, citima Persidis, Arabiam citeriorem, Iudaeam, Libani montis accolas, amplectitur Babylonem, Idumaeam,
Samariam, Hierosolyma, Ascalonem, Iopen, Caesaream, Phoenicen,
5 Ptolemaidem, Sidonem, Tyrum, Berytum, Botryn, Tripolim, Byblum,
Antiochiam, Laodiceam, Seleuciam, Ciliciae maritima, Cypri austrina,
Cretam, Lilybaeum in Sicilia, septentrionalia Africae et Numidiae.

2 *medos* FTo   4 *hierosolima* F² *ierosolima* ao | *iopem* p *ioppen* o

The next parallel begins with the western part of India, and runs
through the middle of the Parthians, Persepolis, the nearest parts
of Persis, Hither Arabia, Judaea and the people living near Mount
Lebanon, and embraces Babylon, Idumaea, Samaria, Jerusalem,
Ascalon, Jope, Caesarea, Phoenicia, Ptolemais, Sidon, Tyre, Bery-
tus, Botrys, Tripolis, Byblus, Antioch, Laodicea, Seleucia, seaboard
Cilicia, Southern Cyprus, Crete, Lilybaeum in Sicily, Northern
Africa and Northern Numidia. (trans. H. Rackham, *LCL*)

207

Naturalis Historia, VII, 65 — Mayhoff

Quin et bituminum sequax alioqui ac lenta natura in lacu Iudaeae,
qui vocatur Asphaltites, certo tempore anni supernatans non quit si-

1 *iudaae* F¹ *iude* R *iuda* a   2 *vocatur* om. o | *asphaltites* (*aspa-* o) ov
asphaltides F² *asphaltites et* E² *asphaltite et* cett. | *nequit* a

bi avelli, ad omnem contactum adhaerens praeterquam filo..., quem
tale virus infecerit.

Moreover bitumen, a substance generally sticky and viscous that
at a certain season of the year floats on the surface of the lake of
Judaea called Asphaltites, adheres to everything touching it, and
cannot be drawn asunder except by a thread soaked in the poisonous
fluid in question. (trans. H. Rackham *LCL*)

certo tempore anni: Cf. Tacitus, *Historiae*, V, 6 (No. 281): "Certo anni tempore
bitumen egerit."
non quit sibi avelli...: Cf. below, No. 220; see also *BJ*, IV, 480; Tacitus, *Historiae*,
V, 6 (No. 281).

208

Naturalis Historia, VII, 98 — Mayhoff = F160R

Hoc est breviarium eius ab oriente. Triumphi vero, quem duxit
a.d. III kal. Oct. M. Pisone M. Messala cos., praefatio haec fuit:
Cum oram maritimam praedonibus liberasset et imperium maris populo Romano restituisset ex Asia, Ponto, Armenia, Paphlagonia,
5 Cappadocia, Cilicia, Syria, Scythis, Iudaeis, Albanis, Hiberia, insula
Creta, Basternis et super haec de rege Mithridate atque Tigrane
triumphavit.

2 *hoc* F¹a   3 *et* om. a   6 *Basternis* v   *bastenis* R   *bastrenis* cett.

This is his summary of his exploits in the east. But the announcement
of the triumphal procession that he led on September 28 in the
consulship of Marcus Piso and Marcus Messala was as follows:
After having rescued the sea coast from pirates and restored to the
Roman People the command of the sea, he celebrated a triumph
over Asia, Pontus, Armenia, Paphlagonia, Cappadocia, Cilicia, Syria,
the Scythians, Jews and Albanians, Iberia, the Island of Crete, the
Basternae, and, in addition to these, over King Mithridates and
Tigranes. (trans. H. Rackham, *LCL*)

triumphi vero, quem duxit...: This is a passage from the description of Pompey's
achievements; cf. the commentary to Appianus, *Mithridatica*, 117 : 571 ff. (No.
346).

209

Naturalis Historia, IX, 11 — Saint-Denis

Beluae, cui dicebatur exposita fuisse Andromeda, ossa Romae apportata ex oppido Iudaeae Iope ostendit inter reliqua miracula in aedilitate sua M. Scaurus longitudine pedum XL, altitudine costarum Indicos elephantos excedente, spinae crassitudine sesquipedali.

2 *ioppe* xlaV

The skeleton of the monster to which Andromeda in the story was exposed was brought by Marcus Scaurus from the town of Joppe in Judaea and shown at Rome among the rest of the marvels during his aedileship; it was 40 ft. long, the height of the ribs exceeding the elephants of India, and the spine being 1 ft. 6 inches thick.

(trans. H. Rackham, *LCL*)

ostendit inter reliqua miracula in aedilitate sua M. Scaurus: This passage is part of Pliny's survey of Tritons, Nereids and aquatic monsters. Cf. Ammianus Marcellinus, XXII, 15 : 24: "monstruosas antehac raritates in beluis, in aedilitate Scauri vidit Romanus populus primitus."

210

Naturalis Historia, XII, 64 — Ernout

Caput eorum Thomna abest a Gaza, nostri litoris in Iudaea oppido, ⌐XXIIII⌐ · XXXVII. D p., quod dividitur in mansiones camelorum LXV.

1 *Gaza*] zaza D¹F   2 $\overline{XXIIII}$ Mayhoff $\overline{LXXIIII}$ L M   xxxxiiii cett. / $\overline{XXXVII}$ M   xxxvi cett.

Their capital is Thomna, which is 1487½ miles distant from the town of Gaza in Judaea on the Mediterranean coast; the journey is divided into 65 stages with halts for camels. (trans. H. Rackham, *LCL*)

This passage is from a description of the transport of frankincense to the Mediterranean.
Thomna: On Thomna, the capital of the Gebbanitae, see VI, 153.

211

Naturalis Historia, XII, 100 — Ernout

Myrobalanum Trogodytis et Thebaidi et Arabiae, quae Iudaeam ab Aegypto disterminat, commune est.

484

Pliny the Elder

The Trogodytes and the Thebaid and Arabia, where it separates
Judaea from Egypt, all alike have the myrobalanum...

(trans. H. Rackham, *LCL*)

et Arabiae, quae Iudaeam ab Aegypto disterminat: This is a passage from the description of myrobalanum; cf. Dioscorides, *De Materia Medica*, IV, 157.

212

Naturalis Historia, XII, 109 — Ernout

Cypros in Aegypto est arbor, ziziphi foliis, semine coriandri, candido,
odorato. Coquitur hoc in oleo premiturque postea quod cypros vocatur. Pretium ei in libras ＊ V. Optimum e Canopica in ripis Nili nata,
secundum Ascalone Iudaeae, tertium ⟨in⟩ Cypro insula.

A tree found in Egypt is the cypros which has the leaves of the jujube-
tree and the white, scented seed of the coriander. Cypros-seed is
boiled in olive oil and afterwards crushed, producing the cypros of
commerce, which sells at 5 denarii a pound. The best is made from the
tree grown at Canopus on the banks of the Nile, the second best at
Ascalon in Judaea, and the third quality on the island of Cyprus.

(trans. H. Rackham, *LCL*)

213

Naturalis Historia, XII, 111–124 — Ernout = F153R

(111) ... Sed omnibus odoribus praefertur balsamum, uni terrarum Iudaeae concessum, quondam in duobus tantum hortis, utroque regio,
altero iugerum viginti non amplius, altero pauciorum. Ostendere ＊
arbutum ＊ hanc urbi Imperatores Vespasiani, clarumque dictu, a
5 Pompeio Magno in triumpho arbores quoque duximus. (112) Servit
nunc haec ac tributa pendit cum sua gente, in totum alia natura quam
nostri externique prodiderant. Quippe viti similior est quam myrto.
Malleolis seri didicit nuper, vincta ut vitis, et inplet colles vinearum
modo. Quae sine adminiculis se ipsa sustinet, tondetur similiter fruticans,
10 ac rastris nitescit properatque nasci, intra tertium annum fructifera.

2 *ortis* DEFa   *hores* R   3 *paucorum* M   *pauciorem* Ea   4 *arbutum*] *arborum* Mayhoff   *arbustum hoc*? Ernout   8 *dicit* D¹EFa   *dicitur*
R(?) D² / *vincta*] *dicta* D¹EFa   9 *fructificans* DEFa

Folium proximum tuburi, perpetua coma. (113) Saeviere in eam Iudaei sicut in vitam quoque suam; contra defendere Romani, et dimicatum pro frutice est; seritque nunc eum fiscus, nec umquam fuit numerosior. Proceritas intra bina cubita subsistit. (114) Arbori tria
15 genera: tenue et capillacea coma quod vocatur eutheriston: alterum scabro aspectu, incurvum, fruticosum, odoratius: hoc trachy appellant, tertium eumeces, quia est reliquis procerius, levi cortice. Huic secunda bonitas, novissima eutheristo. (115) Semen eius vino proximum gustu, colore rufum, nec sine pingui. Peius in grano quod levius
20 atque viridius. Ramus crassior quam myrto. Inciditur vitro, lapide osseisve cultellis; ferro laedi vitalia odit, emoritur protinus, eodem amputari supervacua patiens. Incidentis manus libratur artifici temperamento, ne quid ultra corticem violet. (116) Sucus e plaga manat quem opobalsamum vocant, suavitatis eximiae, sed tenui gutta plo-
25 ratu: lanis parva colligitur in cornua, ex his novo fictili conditur, crassiori similis oleo et in musto candida; rufescit deinde simulque durescit e tralucido. (117) Alexandro Magno res ibi gerente, toto die aestivo unam concham impleri iustum erat, omni vero fecunditate e maiore horto congios senos, e minore singulos, cum et duplo rependebatur
30 argento, nunc etiam singularum arborum largior vena. Ter omnibus percutitur aestatibus, postea deputatur. (118) Et sarmenta quoque in merce sunt. $\overline{DCCC}$ HS amputatio ipsa surculusque veniere intra quintum devictae ⟨Iudaeae⟩ annum; xylobalsamum vocatur et coquitur in unguentis. Pro suco ipso substituere officinae. Corticis etiam ad
35 medicamenta pretium est. Praecipua autem gratia lacrimae, secunda semini, tertia cortici, minima ligno. (119) Ex hoc buxosum optimum, quod et odoratissimum, e semine autem maximum et ponderosissimum, mordens gustu fervensque in ore. Adulteratur Petraeo hyperico, quod coarguitur magnitudine, inanitate, longitudine, odoris ig-
40 navia, sapore piperis. (120) Lacrimae probatio ut sit e pingui tenuis ac modice rufa et in fricando odorata. Secundus candidi coloris, peior viridis crassusque, pessimus niger, quippe ut oleum senescit. Ex omni incisura maxime probatur quod ante semen fluxit. Et alias adulteratur seminis suco, vixque maleficium deprehenditur gustu amar-

---

11 *tuberi* DEFa   15 *tenue*] *tribui* DEFa   *eutheriston* Barbarus e Diosc.
entheristrum D¹EFa   *epentheristion* M   *henthesiscum* R   *antheristum* D²
16 *thracy* R   *tracy* DF   *traci* Ea   18 *eius*] *est* D¹EFa   21 *odit*]
laedit R   23 *ne quid*] *nequit* DF   *neque* R   25 *novo*] *nova* F   *non*
M   30 *argento* vett.   *argentum* codd.   33 ⟨*Iudaeae*⟩ C. F. W.
Müller   37 *et*] *est* DEFa   41 *odora* M | *candidi coloris* Mayhoff
candidi colos M   *candido, colos* RD¹EF   *candidus colos* D²   43 *incisura*] *inclusura* D¹EFa

45 iore; esse enim debet lenis, non subacidus, odore tantum austerus. (121) Vitiatur et oleo rosae, cypri, lentisci, balani, terebinthi, myrti, resina, galbano, cera Cypria, prout quaeque res fuit; nequissime autem cummi, quoniam arescit in manu inversa et in aqua sidit; quae probatio eius gemina est. (122) Debet sincerum et inarescere, sed hoc cummi
50 addita fragili crusta evenit. Et gustu deprehenditur, carbone vero quod cera resinaque adulteratum est, nigriore flamma. Nam melle mutatum statim in manu contrahit muscas. (123) Praeterea sinceri densatur in tepida aqua gutta sidens ad ima vasa, adulterata olei modo innatat et, si metopio vitiata est, circulo candido cingitur. Summa est probatio
55 ut lac coagulet, in veste maculas non faciat. Nec manifestior alibi fraus, quippe milibus denarium sextarii, empti vendente fisco trecenis denariis, veneunt: in tantum expedit augere liquorem. Xylobalsamo pretium in libras ⋆ VI.
(124) Proxima Iudaeae Syria supra Phoenicem styracem gignit circa
60 Gabala et Marathunta et Casium Seleuciae montem...

56–57 *trecentis* E   *tricenis* R

(111) But every other scent ranks below balsam. The only country to which this plant has been vouchsafed is Judaea, where formerly it grew in only two gardens, both belonging to the king; one of them was not more than twenty iugera in extent and the other less. This variety of shrub was exhibited in the capital by the emperors Vespasian and Titus; and it is a remarkable fact that ever since the time of Pompey the Great even trees have figured in our triumphal processions. (112) The balsam-tree is now a subject of Rome, and pays tribute together with the race to which it belongs; it differs entirely in character from the accounts that had been given of it by Roman and foreign writers, being more like a vine than a myrtle: it has quite recently been taught to grow from mallet-shoots tied up on trelisses like a vine, and it covers whole hillsides as vineyards do. A balsam unsupported by a trellis and carrying its own weight is pruned in a similar manner when it puts out shoots; the use of the rake makes it thrive and sprout rapidly, bearing in its third year. Its leaf is very near that of the tuber-apple, and it is evergreen. (113) The Jews vented their wrath upon this plant as they also did upon their own lives, but the Romans protected it against them, and there have been pitched battles in defence of a shrub. It is now cultivated by the fiscus, and was never before more plentiful; but its height has not advanced beyond three feet. (114) There are three varieties of balsam-tree: one with thin foliage like hair, called easy-to-gather; another with

a rugged appearance, curving over, of a bushy growth and with a stronger scent — they call this rough balsam, and the third tall balsam because it grows higher than the rest; this has a smooth bark. This last is the second best in quality, and the easy-to-gather kind is the lowest grade. (115) Balsam-seed tastes very much like wine, and has a red colour and a rather greasy consistency; that contained in a husk, which is lighter in weight and greener in colour, is inferior. The branch is thicker than that of a myrtle; an incision is made in it with a piece of glass or a stone, or with knives made of bone — it strongly dislikes having its vital part wounded with steel and dies off at once, though it can stand having superfluous branches pruned with it. The hand of the operator making the incision has to be poised under skilful control, to avoid inflicting a wound going below the bark. (116) The juice that oozes out of the incision is called opobalsamum; it is extremely sweet in taste, but exudes in tiny drops, the trickle being collected by means of tufts of wool in small horns and poured out of them into a new earthenware vessel to store; it is like rather thick olive-oil and in the unfermented state is white in colour; later on it turns red and at the same time hardens, having previously been transparent. (117) When Alexander the Great was campaigning in that country, it was considered a fair whole day's work in summer to fill a single shell, and for the entire produce of a rather large garden to be six congii and of a smaller one congius, at a time moreover when its price was twice its weight in silver; whereas at the present day even a single tree produces a larger flow. The incision is made three times in every summer, and afterwards the tree is lopped. (118) There is a market even for the twigs too; within five years of the conquest of Judaea the actual loppings and the shoots fetched 800.000 sesterces. The trimmings are called wood of balsam; they are boiled down in perfumes, and in manufacture they have taken the place of the actual juice of the shrub. Even the bark fetches a price for drugs; but the tears are valued most, the seed coming second, the bark third and the wood lowest. (119) Of the wood the sort resembling boxwood is the best, and also has the strongest scent; the best seed is that which is largest in size and heaviest in weight, which has a biting taste and is hot in the mouth. Balsam is adulterated with the ground-pine of Petra, which can be detected by its size, hollowness and long shape and by its weak scent and its taste like pepper. (120) The test of tear of balsam is that it should be thinning out in consistency, and slightly reddish, and give a strong scent when rubbed. The second quality is white in colour; the next inferior is green and thick and the worst kind black, inasmuch as like olive oil it deteriorates with age. Out of all the incisions the oil that has flowed out before the formation of the seed is considered the best. Also another mode of adulteration is by using the juice of the seed, and the fraud can be with difficulty detected by the greater bitterness of the taste; for the proper taste is smooth, without a trace of acidity, the only pungency being in the smell. (121) It is also adulterated with oil of roses, of cyprus, of mastich, of behen-nut, of the turpentine-tree and of myrtle, and with resin, galbanum and wax of Cyprus, just as the occasion serves; but the worst adulteration is with gum, since this dries up on the back of the hand and sinks in water, which is a double test of the genuine article — (122) pure tear of balsam ought to dry up likewise, but the sort with gum added to it turns brittle and forms a skin. It can also be detected by the taste; or when adulterated with wax or resin, by means of a hot coal, as it burns with a blacker flame. When mixed with honey, its quality alters immediately, as it attracts flies even, when held in the hand. (123) Moreover a drop of pure balsam thickens in warm water, settling to the bottom of the vessel, whereas when adulterated it floats on the top like oil, and if it has been tampered with by using metopium, a white ring forms round it. The best test of all is that it will cause milk to curdle and will not leave stains on cloth. In no other case is more obvious fraud practised, in as much as every pint bought at a sale of confiscated property for 300 denarii when it is sold again makes 1000 denarii; so much does it pay to increase the quantity of adulteration. The price of wood-balsam is six denarii a pound.

(124) The region of Syria beyond Phoenicia nearest to Judaea produces styrax in the part round Gabala and Marathus and Mount Casius in Seleucia. (trans. H. Rackham, *LCL*)

111 *Sed omnibus odoribus praefertur balsamum*: On the *balsamum*, see Wagler, PW, II, pp. 2836 ff.; I. Löw, *Die Flora der Juden*, I, Vienna–Leipzig 1928, pp. 299 ff. The other major descriptions of balsam in ancient literature are found in Theophrastus, *Historia Plantarum*, IX, 6 (No. 9); Dioscorides, *De Materia Medica*, I, 19 : 1 (No. 179); see also Strabo, *Geographica*, XVI, 2 : 41, p. 763 (No. 115); Pompeius Trogus, apud: Iustinus, XXXVI, 3 : 4 (No. 137); Tacitus, *Historiae*, V, 6 (No. 281).
uni terrarum Iudaeae concessum: For similar statements, see Diodorus, II, 48 : 9 = XIX, 98 (Nos. 59, 62); Pompeius Trogus, apud: Iustinus, XXXVI, 3 : 1; Strabo, *Geographica*, XVI, 2 : 41, p. 763 (No. 115); Dioscorides, *loc. cit*. From Diodorus, III, 46 : 2, we learn about the growth of balsam in Arabia. According to *Ant.*, VIII, 174, it was the queen of Sheba who first imported the *opobalsamum* into

Judaea: λέγουσι δ' ὅτι καὶ τὴν τοῦ ὀποβαλσάμου ῥίζαν, ἣν ἔτι νῦν ἡμῶν ἡ χώρα φέρει, δούσης ταύτης τῆς γυναικὸς ἔχομεν. Pliny does not state where in Judaea the balsam grew. We know from other sources that the two main centres for the growth of balsam in Judaea were Jericho and 'En Gedi. On Jericho, see Strabo, *Geographica*, XVI, 2 : 41, p. 763 (No. 115); Pompeius Trogus, apud: Iustinus, XXXVI, 3 : 2 (No. 137); *BJ*, IV, 469. On 'En Gedi, see *Ant.*, IX, 7; Galenus, *De Antidotis*, I, 4 (No. 391); cf. *TB Shabbat* 26a. Theophrastus refers to the Valley of Syria as the place where balsam grew; see Theophrastus, *Historia Plantarum*, IX, 6 : 1 (No. 9).

quondam in duobus tantum hortis: Cf. Theophrastus, *loc. cit.*: παραδείσους δ'εἶναί φασι δύο μόνους.

altero iugerum viginti non amplius, altero pauciorum. Cf. Theophrastus, *loc. cit.*: τὸν μὲν ὅσον εἴκοσι πλέθρων τὸν δ'ἕτερον πολλῷ ἐλάττονα.

ostendere: I.e. *in triumpho.*

112 *ac tributa pendit*: Cf. A. Büchler, *The Economic Conditions of Judaea after the Destruction of the Second Temple*, London 1912, pp. 62 f.

113 *seritque nunc eum fiscus*: Cf. F. Millar, *JRS*, LIII (1963), p. 30.

115 *inciditur vitro . . . ferro laedi vitalia odit*: Contrary to this, Theophrastus says: ἐντέμνειν δὲ ὄνυξι σιδηροῖς. Tacitus' description is closer to Pliny; see *Historiae*, V, 6 (No. 281): "si vim ferri adhibeas, pavent venae; fragmine lapidis aut testa aperiuntur." Josephus' description is also similar to Pliny; see *Ant.*, XIV, 54: ὀποβάλσαμον μύρων ἀκρότατον, ὃ τῶν θάμνων τεμνομένων ὀξεῖ λίθῳ ἀναπιδύει ὥσπερ ὀπός. On the other hand, Dioscorides agrees with Theophrastus; see Ernout's note to the Budé edition of the twelfth book of Pliny, p. 101.

117 *Alexandro Magno res ibi gerente*: I.e. the time when Alexander the Great conquered all of Palestine. It does not imply Alexander's presence at either Jericho or 'En Gedi; see Y. Gutman, *Tarbiẓ*, XI (1939–1940), pp. 278 f.

toto die aestivo unam concham impleri: Cf. Theophrastus, *Historia Plantarum*, IX, 6 : 2 (No. 9): τὴν δὲ συλλογὴν ὅλον τὸ θέρος ποιεῖσθαι· οὐκ εἶναι δὲ πολὺ τὸ ῥέον ἀλλ' ἐν ἡμέρᾳ τὸν ἄνδρα συλλέγειν ὅσον κόγχην.

cum et duplo rependebatur argento: Cf. Theophrastus, *op. cit.*, 4: πωλεῖσθαι δὲ τὸ μὲν ἄκρατον δὶς πρὸς ἀργύριον.

214

Naturalis Historia, XIII, 26–49 — Ernout = F154R

5 (26) Iudaea vero incluta est vel magis palmis, quarum natura nunc dicetur. Sunt quidem et in Europa volgoque Italia, sed steriles. Ferunt in maritimis Hispaniae fructum, verum inmitem; dulcem in Africa, sed statim evanescentem. (27) Contra in Oriente ex iis vina gentiumque aliquis panis, plurimis vero etiam quadrupedum cibus; quam ob 10 rem iure dicentur externae; nulla est in Italia sponte genita nec in alia parte terrarum, nisi in calida, frugifera vero nusquam nisi in fervida. (28) Gignitur levi sabulosaque terra, maiore in parte et nitrosa; gaudet riguis totoque anno bibere, cum amet sitientia. Fimo quidam

10–11 *sponte... alia* om. D¹EF¹   *sponte et ratio* R   13 *gaudet et* DEF

490

etiam laedi putant, Assyriorum pars aliqua, si non rivis misceat. Ge-
15 nera earum plura, et prima fruticem non excedentia, sterilem hunc,
aliubi et ipsum fertilem, brevisque rami, orbe foliosum. Tectorii vicem hic parietibus plerisque in locis praestat contra aspergines. (29) Est
et procerioribus silva, arbore ex ipsa foliorum aculeo fruticante
circa totas pectinatim. Quas silvestres intellegi necesse est; incerta
20 tamen libidine etiam mitioribus se miscent. Reliquae, teretes atque
procerae, densis gradatisque corticum pollicibus aut orbibus faciles ad
scandendum Orientis se populis praebent, vitilem sibi arborique indutis
circulum mira pernicitate cum homine subeuntem...

(43) ... Quarta auctoritas sandalidum a similitudine appellatarum.
25 Iam in Aethiopiae fine quinque harum, qui plurimas, arbores
tradunt, non raritate magis quam suavitate mirabiles. (44) Ab his
caryotae maxime celebrantur, et cibo quidem, sed et suco uberrimae,
ex quibus praecipua vina orienti, iniqua capiti, unde pomo nomen.
Sed ut copia ibi atque fertilitas, ita nobilitas in Iudaea, nec in tota, sed
30 Hiericunte maxime, quamquam laudatae et Archelaide et Phaselide
atque Liviade, gentis eiusdem convallibus. Dos iis praecipua suco
pingui lactantibus quodamque vini sapore in melle praedulci. (45) Sicciores ex hoc genere Nicolai, sed amplitudinis praecipuae: quater-
ni cubitorum longitudinem efficiunt. Minus speciosae, sed sapore
35 caryotarum sorores et ob hoc adelphides dictae proximam suavita-
tem habent, non tamen eandem. Tertium ex his genus patetae: nimio
liquore abundant, rumpitque se pomi ipsius, etiam in sua matre, ebri-
etas, calcatis similis. (46) Suum genus e sicciore turba dactylis, prae-
longa gracilitate curvatis interim. Nam quos ex his honori deorum
40 damus, chydaeos appellavit Iudaea gens contumelia numinum insignis.
(47) In totum arentes Thebaidi atque Arabiae macroque corpore exiles, et adsiduo vapore torrente crustam verius quam cutem obducunt.
In ipsa quidem Aethiopia friatur haec — tanta est siccitas — et farinae
modo spissatur in panem. Gignitur autem in frutice ramis cubitalibus,
45 folio latiore, pomo rotundo, sed maiore quam mali amplitudine; coïcas vocant. Triennio maturescunt, semperque frutici pomum est subnas-
cente alio. (48) Thebaidis fructus extemplo in cados conditur cum
sui ardoris anima. Ni ita fiat, celeriter expirat marcescitque non re-
tostus furnis. E reliquo genere plebeiae videntur Syriae et quas tra-
50 gemata appellant. Nam in alia parte Phoenices Ciliciaeque populari

---

15 *fruticem* vett.   *frutice* codd.   17 *asparagine* D¹EF¹   *asparagines* D²F²
23 *cum*] *tum* vett.   28 *iniqua*] *inimica* C. F. W. Müller   30 *laudatae*
et vett.   *laudata et* (*ad* M) codd.   45–46 *coïcas* Harduin   *coecas* codd.
    49 *Syriae et* Jan   *syriae...* M   *syri et* DEF   *et* (om. *Syriae*) R

etiam nomine a nobis appellantur balani. (49) Eorum quoque plura genera. Differunt figura rotunditatis aut proceritatis, differunt et colore, nigriores ac rubentes. Nec pauciores fico traduntur colores; maxime tamen placent candidi. Distant et magnitudine prout multi cu-
55 bitum effecere, quidam sunt non ampliores faba. Servantur ii demum qui nascuntur in salsis atque sabulosis, ut in Iudaea atque Cyrenaica Africa, non item in Aegypto, Cypro, Syria, Seleucia, Assyria; quam ob rem sues et reliqua animalia ex iis saginantur.

52–53 *colore*] *odore* R

(26) But Judaea is even more famous for its palm-trees, the nature of which will now be described. It is true that there are also palms in Europe, and they are common in Italy, but these are barren. In the coastal regions of Spain they do bear fruit, but it does not ripen, and in Africa the fruit is sweet but will not keep for any time. (27) On the other hand, in the east the palm supplies the native races with wine, and some of them with bread, while a very large number rely on it also for cattle fodder. For this reason, therefore, we shall be justified in describing the palms of foreign countries; there are none in Italy not grown under cultivation, nor are there in any other part of the earth except where there is a warm climate, while only in really hot countries does the palm bear fruit. (28) It grows in a light sandy soil and for the most part in one containing nitrates. It likes running water, and to drink all the year round, though it loves dry places. Some people think that dung actually does it harm, while a section of the Assyrians think that this happens if they do not mix the dung with water from a stream. There are several kinds of palm, beginning with kinds not larger than a shrub—a shrub that in some cases is barren, though in other districts it too bears fruit—and having a short branch. In a number of places this shrub-palm with its dome of leaves serves instead of plaster for the walls of a house to prevent their sweating. (29) Also the taller palms make a regular forest, their pointed foliage shooting out from the actual tree all round them like a comb — these it must be understood are wild palms, though they also have a wayward fancy for mingling among the cultivated varieties. The other kinds are rounded and tall, and have compact rows of knobs or circles in their bark which render them easy for the eastern races to climb; they put a plaited noose round themselves and round the tree, and the noose goes up with the man at an astonishingly rapid speed. . .

(43). . . The sandalis date, so called from its semblance to a sandal,

492

ranks fourth; of this kind again there are said to be at the most five trees in existence, on the border of Ethiopia, and they are as remarkable for the sweetness of their fruit as they are for their rarity. (44) Next to these the most famous are the caryotae, which supply a great deal of food but also of juice, and from which the principal wines of the East are made; these strongly affect the head, to which the date owes its name. But not only are these trees abundant and bear largely in Judaea, but also the most famous are found there, and not in the whole of that country but especially in Jericho, although those growing in the valleys of Archelais and Phaselis and Livias in the same country are also highly spoken of. Their outstanding property is the unctuous juice which they exude and an extremely sweet sort of wine-flavour like that of honey. (45) The Nicholas date, belonging to this class is not so juicy but exceptionally large in size, four put end to end making a length of eighteen inches. The date that comes next in sweetness is less attractive to look at, but in flavour is the sister of the caryotae and consequently is called in Greek the sister-date. The third class among these, the pateta, has too copious a supply of juice, and the excess of liquor of the fruit itself bursts open even while on the parent tree, looking like dates that have been trodden on. (46) Of the many drier dates the finger-date forms a class of its own: it is a very long slender date, sometimes of a curved shape. The variety of this class, which we offer to the honour of the gods is called chydaeus by the Jews, a race remarkable for their contempt for the divine powers. (47) All over the Thebaid and Arabia, the dates are dry and small, with a shrivelled body, and as they are scorched by the continual heat, their covering is more truly a rind than a skin. Indeed in Ethiopia itself the climate is so dry that the skin of these dates is rubbed into powder and kneaded to make loaves of bread like flour. This date grows on a shrub, with branches eighteen inches long, a rather broad leaf, and fruit of a round shape, but larger than the size of an apple. The Greek name for this date is koix; it comes to maturity in three years, and the shrub always has fruit on it, another date sprouting in place of one picked. (48) The date of the Thebaid is packed into casks at once, before it has lost the aroma of its natural heat; if this is not done, it quickly loses its freshness and dries up unless it is warmed up again in an oven. Of the rest of the date kinds, the Syrian variety, called sweetmeats, seem to be a low-class fruit; for those in the other part of Phoenicia and Cilicia have the level name of acorn-dates, also used by us. (49) These too are of several kinds, differing in shape, some rounder and others longer, and also in colour, some being blacker and others reddish; indeed, they are reported to have as many varieties of colour as the fig, though the white ones are the most in favour. They also differ in size, many having reached half a yard in length while some are no longer than a bean. The best kinds for keeping are those that grow in salt and sandy soils, for instance in Judaea and the Cyrenaic district of Africa; the dates in Egypt, Cyprus, Syria and Seleucia in Assyria do not keep, and consequently are used for fattening swine and other stock. (trans. H. Rackham, *LCL*)

26 *Iudaea vero incluta est vel magis palmis*: This passage is from a survey of countries in which palm trees grow. On the palm tree in antiquity in general, see Steier, PW, XX, pp. 386 ff.; cf. especially Theophrastus, *Historia Plantarum*, II, 6. The excellence of Judaea's palms is repeatedly emphasized in ancient literature; see, above all, Strabo, *Geographica*, XVI, 2 : 41, p. 763 (No. 115); XVII, 1 : 15, p. 800 (No. 121); 1 : 51, p. 818 (No. 123); see also Varro, *Res Rusticae*, II, 1 : 27 (No.73); Diodorus, II, 48 : 9 (No. 59); Horatius, *Epistulae*, II, 2 : 184 (No. 130); Vergilius, *Georgica*, III, 12 (No. 125); Pausanias, *Graeciae Descriptio*, IX, 19 : 8 (No. 359); Galenus, *De Alimentorum Facultatibus*, II, 26 (No. 379); Josephus, *Ant.*, IV, 100; IX, 7; XVIII, 31 (Phasaelis and Archelais).

44 *ab his caryotae maxime celebrantur*: Cf. the commentary to Varro, *Res Rusticae*, II, 1 : 27 (No. 73).

sed Hiericunte maxime: The connection between the palms and Jericho is also emphasized by Pompeius Trogus, apud: Iustinus, XXXVI, 3 : 3 (No. 137); *BJ*, *IV*, 468; *Ant.*, IV, 100. The connection is well known from the Bible (Deut. xxxiv : 3; II Chron. xxviii : 15) and from talmudic literature; cf. Löw, *op. cit.* (supra, p. 489), II, p. 308, n. 1.

et Archelaide: On Archelais, north of Jericho, see Abel, II, p. 249; Avi-Yonah, *op. cit.* (supra, p. 472), p. 120. It is located at Khirbet Auja et-Tahta. Archelais was named after its founder; see *Ant.*, XVII, 340. Josephus refers to the palms of both Archelais and Phasaelis in *Ant.*, XVIII, 31: τήν τ' ἐν τῷ πεδίῳ Φασαηλίδα καὶ 'Αρχελαΐδα, ἔνθα φοινίκων πλείστη φύτευσις καὶ καρπὸς αὐτῶν ἄριστος.

et Phaselide: On Phasaelis, see Schürer, II, p. 204; Abel, II, pp. 408 f. It is located at Khirbet Fasay'ijl, to the north of Archelais; see L. Mowry, *Biblical Archaeologist*, XV (1952), pp. 31 f.; G. Harder *ZDPV*, LXXVIII (1962), pp. 54 ff. It was founded by Herod and named after his brother Phasael; see *Ant.*, XVI, 145; *BJ*, I, 418. On its palm-groves, see *Ant.*, XVIII, 31; *BJ*, II, 167: καὶ τοὺς ἐν Φασαηλίδι φοινικῶνας κατέλιπεν.

atque Liviade: Livias, which was named after the Empress Livia, was founded by Herod Antipas in the Peraea, in the same place as the old Betharamptha. Josephus (*Ant.*, XVIII, 27; *BJ*, II, 168, 252) calls it Iulias, after the adopted name of the Empress. Eusebius, *Onomasticon* (ed. Klostermann), p. 48, and Ptolemaeus, *Geographia*, V, 16 : 9 (No. 337) call it Livias. On its location, see Avi-Yonah, *op. cit.* (supra, p. 472), p. 166; Harder, *op. cit.* pp. 60 ff. The sixth-century pilgrim Theodosius still refers to its palms: "Civitas Leviada trans Jordanen habens de Hiericho milia XII... ibi habet dactalum Nicolaum majorem"; see Theodosius, apud: Geyer, p. 145.

494

Pliny the Elder

45 *sicciores ex hoc genere Nicolai*: For this type of date, named after the historian Nicolaus of Damascus, who according to Athenaeus sent it to Augustus, see *Deipnosophistae*, XIV, 66, p. 652 A = Jacoby, *F. Gr. Hist.*, II, A 90, T 10a: περὶ δὲ τῶν Νικολάων καλουμένων φοινίκων ... τῶν ἀπὸ τῆς Συρίας καταγομένων ὅτι ταύτης τῆς προσηγορίας ἠξιώθησαν ὑπὸ τοῦ Σεβαστοῦ αὐτοκράτορος... Νικολάου τοῦ Δαμασκηνοῦ ἑταίρου ὄντος αὐτῷ καὶ πέμποντος φοίνικας συνεχῶς. See also Plutarchus, *Quaestiones Convivales*, VIII, 4 : 1, p. 723 D; Theodosius, *loc. cit.*; Isidorus, *Origines*, XVII, 7 : 1; *Descriptio Orbis Terrae* (fourth century C. E.), apud: T. Sinko, in: *Archiv für lateinische Lexikographie und Grammatik*, XIII (1904), p. 552: "Nicolaam itaque palmulam ⟨invenies⟩ in Palaestines regio ⟨nis⟩ loco, qui sic vocatur Hiericho" (= ed. Rougé, XXXI, p. 164). Cf. also S. Lieberman, *JQR*, NS XXXVII (1946–1947), pp. 51 f.

46 *contumelia numinum insignis*: This is Pliny's one reference to Jews or Judaea that has an undisputably anti-Semitic ring. For the expression *contumelia numinum*, see also Pliny the Younger, Panegyricus, 11 : 2.

215

Naturalis Historia, XIV, 122 — Mayhoff = F156R

Arabica resina alba est, acri odore, difficilis coquenti, Iudaea callosior et terebinthina quoque odoratior, Syriaca Attici mellis similitudinem habet.

Arabian resin is white and has a sharp scent, stifling to a person engaged in boiling it; the resin of Judaea dries harder and has a stronger scent than even that from the turpentine-tree; and Syrian resin has a resemblance to Attic honey.   (trans. H. Rackham, *LCL*)

Iudaea callosior et terebinthina quoque odoratior: This is a passage from Pliny's discussion of the resin.

216

Naturalis Historia, XIX, 101 — Mayhoff

Cepae genera apud Graecos Sarda, Samothracia, Alsidena, setania, schista, Ascalonia, ab oppido Iudaeae nominata.

2 *schista* Barbarus   *scista* DGFd   *scirta* E

Among the Greeks the varieties of onion are the Sardinian, Samothracian, Alsidenian, setanian, the split onion, and the Ascalon onion, named from a town in Judaea.   (trans. H. Rackham, *LCL*)

495

cepae genera: This passage is from the description of the various types of onions. *Ascalonia*: Cf. Strabo, *Geographica*, XVI, 2 : 29, p. 759: κρομμύῳ τ᾽ ἀγαθός ἐστιν ἡ χώρα τῶν Ἀσκαλωνιτῶν; see also Theophrastus, *Historia Plantarum*, VII, 4 : 9.

217

Naturalis Historia, XXIV, 85 — Mayhoff

Harundinis genera XXVIII demonstravimus, non aliter evidentiore illa naturae vi, quam continuis his voluminibus tractamus, siquidem harundinis radix contrita inposita felicis stirpem corpore extrahit, item harundinem felicis radix. Et, quo plura genera faciamus, illa, quae
5 in Iudaea Syriaque nascitur odorum unguentorumque causa, urinam movet cum gramine aut apii semine decocta; ciet et menstrua admota.

I have pointed out twenty-eight kinds of reed, and nowhere is more obvious that force of Nature which I describe in these books one after another, if indeed the root of the reed crushed and applied, draws a fern stem out of the flesh, while the root of the fern does the same to a splinter of reed. To increase the number of the various reeds, that which grows in Judaea and Syria and is used for scents and unguents; boiled down with grass or celery seed this is diuretic, and when made into a pessary acts as an emmenagogue.

(trans. W. H. S. Jones, *LCL*)

218

Naturalis Historia, XXVI, 60 — Ernout & Pepin = F157R

Radix ⟨scil. scamonii⟩ circa Canis ortum excavatur, ut in ipsam confluat sucus, qui sole siccatus digeritur in pastillos. Siccatur et ipsa, vel cortex. Laudatur natione Colophonium, Mysium, Prienense, specie autem nitidum et quam simillimum taurino glutini, fungosum
5 tenuissimis fistulis, cito liquescens, virus redolens, cumminosum, linguae tactu lactescens, quam levissimum, cum diluatur, albescens. Hoc evenit et adulterino, quod fit ervi farina et tithymalli marini suco fere in Iudaea.

7 *erbi* V   *herbi* E   *herbae* vett.

Near the rising of the Dogstar a hollow is made in this root [i.e. scamonium], so that the juice may collect in it automatically; this is dried

in the sun and worked into lozenges. The root of the skin is also
dried. The kind most approved grows in the regions of Colophon,
Mysia and Priene. This is shiny, as like as possible to bull glue;
spongy with very fine cracks; quickly melting, with a poisonous smell;
gummy, becoming like milk at a touch of the tongue, extremely
light, and turning white when dissolved. This happens too with bastard
scamonium, which is made, generally in Judaea, with flour of bitter
vetch and juice of sea spurge.

(trans. W. H. S. Jones, *LCL*)

hoc evenit et adulterino . . .: This is a passage from the description of *scamonium*,
the juice of which was used as a purgative.

219

Naturalis Historia, XXVII, 15 — Ernout = F155R

Quidam et caulem ⟨scil. aloes⟩ ante maturitatem seminis incidunt
suci gratia, aliqui et folia. Invenitur et per se lacrima adhaerens; ergo
pavimentandum ubi sata sit censent, ut lacrima non absorbeatur.
Fuere qui traderent in Iudaea super Hierosolyma metallicam eius
5 naturam, sed nulla magis improba est, neque alia nigrior est aut
umidior.

4 *Hierosolyma* Gronovius   *hierosolymam* codd.   6 *tumidior* E

Some, before the seed [of the aloe] ripens, make an incision in the
stem to get the juice; some so in the leaves as well. Drops too form
spontaneously on it, and adhere. Some therefore recommend that the
ground where the aloe has been planted should be beaten down hard,
so as to prevent absorption. Some have reported that in Judaea beyond
Jerusalem can be found mineral aloes. This, however, is the most
inferior kind of all, and no other is darker or more moist.

(trans. W. H. S. Jones, *LCL*)

fuere qui traderent . . .: This is from the description of the aloe; cf. Wagler, PW,
I, pp. 1593 f.; I. Löw, *Die Flora der Juden*, II, Vienna–Leipzig 1924, pp. 149 ff.
On its medical qualities, see Celsus, *De Medicina*, V, 1; Dioscorides, *De Materia
Medica*, III, 22; Galenus, *De Simplicium Medicamentorum Temperamentis ac
Facultatibus*, VI, 1 : 23. On aloes in Judaea, see also John, xix : 39. Pliny lists the
chief medical uses of the aloe: to relax the bowel, to prevent hair from falling out,
to relieve headaches when applied in vinegar, to cure eye troubles and to stop
haemorrhages.
super Hierosolyma metallicam eius naturam: Pliny seems to refer to the asphalt of

the Dead Sea; cf. the notes of Ernout in the Budé edition of the twenty-seventh book of Pliny and those of Jones in the Loeb edition.

220

Naturalis Historia, XXVIII, 80 — Ernout

Nam bitumen in Iudaea nascens sola hac vi superari filo vestis contactae docuimus. Ne igni quidem vincitur, quo cuncta, cinisque etiam ille, si quis aspargat lavandis vestibus, purpuras mutat, florem coloribus adimit, ne ipsis quidem feminis malo suo inter se inmunibus: abortus facit inlitu aut si omnino praegnans supergradiatur.

5

    1 *nam ut* V¹   *nam* <*et*> Detlefsen / *in Iudaea* vett.
    Iudaea in d   om. VR.

But the bitumen also that is found in Judaea can be mastered only by the power of this fluid, as I have already stated, a thread from an infected dress is sufficient. Not even fire, the all-conquering, overcomes it; even when reduced to ash, if sprinkled on clothes in the wash, it changes purples and robs colours of their brightness. Nor are women themselves immune to the effect of this plague of their sex; a miscarriage is caused by a smear, or even if a woman with child steps over it.   (trans. W. H. S. Jones, *LCL*)

bitumen in Iudaea nascens sola hac vi superari: Cf. above, No. 207.

221

Naturalis Historia, XXX, 11 — Mayhoff = F158R

Est et alia magices factio a Mose et Ianne et Lotape ac Iudaeis pendens, sed multis milibus annorum post Zoroastren.

    1 *ianno* E / *Iotape* Gelenius   *Iochabela* Barbarus

There is yet another branch of magic, derived from Moses, Jannes, Lotapes and the Jews, but living many thousand years after Zoroaster.   (trans. W. H. S. Jones, *LCL*)

Est et alia magices factio: This is a passage from the history of magic.
a Mose: On Moses as a magician, see the commentary to Apuleius, *Apologia*, 90 (No. 361). On the part played by Moses in magic, see also I. Heinemann, PW, XVI, p. 363.

Pliny the Elder

et Ianne et Lotape: Since Pliny puts Iannes and Lotapes between Moses and the Jews in general, one gets the impression that he considers Iannes and Lotapes to have been Jews. Other sources that refer to Iannes know him to have been an Egyptian magician and an opponent of Moses; see the commentary to Numenius, apud: Eusebius, *Praeparatio Evangelica*, IX, 8 : 1–2 (No. 365). He is usually coupled with another Egyptian magician, Iambres, although Apuleius does not mention him. The name Lotapes remains an enigma and the attempt made by Torrey to solve it is not successful; see C. C. Torrey, *JBL*, LXVIII (1949), pp. 325 ff. Ernout, in his search for an Aramaic origin, prefers Iotape to Lotape in his notes to the Budé edition of 1963, p. 82. For the large part that the Jewish names of God and angels played in ancient magic, see Goodenough, II, pp. 153 ff.; M. Simon, *Verus Israel*[2], Paris 1964, pp. 394 ff. See also the commentaries to Lucianus, *Tragodopodagra*, 171–173 (No. 374) and Damascius, *Vita Isidori*, 55–56 (No. 547). For magic in Pliny, see A. Ernout, *Hommages à J. Bayet*, Brussels 1964, pp. 190 ff.

222

Naturalis Historia, XXXI, 24 — Mayhoff = F152R

Singuli siccantur duodenis diebus, aliquando vicenis, citra suspicionem ullam aquae, cum sit vicinus illis fons sine intermissione largus. Dirum est non profluere eos aspicere volentibus, sicut proxime Larcio Licinio legato pro praetore post septem dies accidit. In Iudaea rivus sabbatis omnibus siccatur.

5

4 *pro praetore* Detlefsen   *post praeturam* codd.

Each one dries up for periods of twelve, occasionally of twenty days, without the slightest trace of water, although there is a copious spring near them that never dries up. It is an evil portent of those wishing to look at them find them not flowing, as recently Larcius Licinius a legate pro-praetore discovered after seven days. In Judaea is a stream that dries up every Sabbath.   (trans. W. H. S. Jones, *LCL*)

in Iudaea rivus sabbatis omnibus siccatur: Perhaps this should be connected with the later Jewish tradition about the river Sambation; cf. already *TB Sanhedrin* 65b; *Bereshit Rabba* (ed. Theodor), 11, p. 93. There is a description of a Sabbatical river that Josephus locates not in Judaea, but in Syria, between Arcea and Raphanea (*BJ*, VII, 96 ff.). However, one of the features ascribed to this river by Josephus — the phenomenon of a dry bed during six days and a copious stream only every seventh day — renders it completely different from the river described by Pliny.

223

Naturalis Historia, XXXI, 95 — Mayhoff = F159R

Aliud vero est castimoniarum superstitioni etiam sacrisque Iudaeis dicatum, quod fit e piscibus squama carentibus.

1 *catimoniarum* V   2 *squama maceretnentibus* V

But another kind of garum is devoted to superstitious sex-abstinence and Jewish rites, and is made from fish without scales.

(trans. W. H. S. Jones, *LCL*)

aliud vero est castimoniarum superstitioni . . . dicatum: This passage is from the description of *allex*, a sediment of *garum*; cf. Friedländer, III, p. 211. On the *garum castum* on an inscription from Pompeii, see J.B. Frey, *RB*, XLII (1933), pp. 372 ff.; C. Giordano & I. Kahn, *Gli Ebrei in Pompei, in Ercolano et nelle città della Campania Felix*, Pompei [1966], pp. 58 f.
quod fit e piscibus squama carentibus: As Reinach (*ad loc.*) notes, this statement seems strange in view of the fact that eating fish without scales is expressly prohibited in Lev. xi : 10.

224

Naturalis Historia, XXXIII, 136 — Mayhoff (cf. Varro, No. 74)

Congerant excedentes numerum opes, quota tamen portio erunt Ptolemaei quem Varro ⟨No. 74⟩ tradit Pompeio res gerente circa Iudaeam octona milia equitum sua pecunia toleravisse, mille convivas totidem aureis potoriis, mutantem ea vasa cum ferculis, saginasse!

But let them amass uncountable riches, yet what fraction will they be of the riches of the Ptolemy who is recorded by Varro, at the time when Pompey was campaigning in the regions adjoining Judaea, to have maintained 8000 horse at his own expense, to have given a lavish feast to a thousand guests, with 1.000 gold goblets, which were changed at every course. (trans. H. Rackham, *LCL*)

225

Naturalis Historia, XXXV, 178 — Mayhoff

Et bituminis vicina natura est. Aliubi limus, aliubi terra est, limus e

1 *aliubi* Sillig   *aliube* B¹   *alibi* cett.

Iudaeae lacu, ut diximus, emergens, terra in Syria circa Sidonem oppidum maritimum.

Near to the nature of sulphur is also that of bitumen. In some places it is a slime and in others an earth, the slime being emitted, as we have said, from the lake of Judaea and the earth being found in the neighbourhood of the seaside town of Sidon in Syria.

(trans. H. Rackham, *LCL*)

LXXIX. VALERIUS FLACCUS

Second half of the first century C. E.

The prooemium of the Argonautica, *which glorifies the Flavian dynasty, puts due emphasis on its great military achievement: the overthrow of Judaea (= Idume), which was accompanied by the burning of Jerusalem.[1]*
Concerning the exact date of the prooemium's composition, the opinions of scholars have always varied. Some adhere to the view that it was composed while Vespasian, who, with Phoebus, is the object of the poet's invocation, was still alive.[2] Others date it as late as the reign of Domitian,[3] pointing out that the "delubra genti" (l. 15) implies the "templum gentis Flaviae" on the Quirinal, erected by the last-mentioned emperor. However, it appears strange that, whereas the military glory of Titus is painted in glowing colours by Valerius Flaccus, Domitian is relegated to the rather subordinate position of a poet who sings of his elder brother's greatness. Taking into consideration the jealous character of Domitian, it is perhaps better to suppose a date in the reign of Titus rather than in that of his younger brother.[4] Furthermore, a date in the lifetime of

---

1 For the part that the victory over the Jews played in the propaganda of the Flavians, see, in general, G. C. Picard, *Les trophées romains*, Paris 1957, pp. 343 ff.: "Jérusalem a été l'Actium des Flaviens."

2 See, e. g., Langen's Commentary; Bernays, II, pp. 163 ff.; Schanz & Hosius, II, p. 520; R. Preiswerk, *Philologus*, LXXXIX, p. 442; A. Kurfess, PW, Ser. 2, VIII, p. 10. Cf. E. Wistrand, *Die Chronologie der Punica des Silius Italicus*, Göteborg 1956, p. 27. Wistrand dates the prooemium either to the lifetime of Vespasian or to a time shortly after his death, though he seems to prefer the first possibility. For the history of the problem of dating the prooemium, see V. Ussani Jr, *Studio su Valerio Flacco*, Rome 1955, pp. 9 ff.

3 The case for Domitian was put brilliantly by R. Syme, *CQ*, XXIII (1929), pp. 129 ff. Syme suggests that the poet may well have preferred an indirect method of flattery, namely, to pretend that the prooemium was written under Vespasian and, by subtly foreshadowing future things, to gain credit for having seen even then that it was Domitian who would be the true successor. For a date in the reign of Domitian, see also K. Scott, *Rivista di Filologia*, NS XII (1934), pp. 474 ff.; idem, *The Imperial Cult under the Flavians*, Stuttgart 1936, p. 70.

4 Among the scholars who date the prooemium to the reign of Titus are R. J. Getty, *Classical Philology*, XXXI (1936), pp. 53 ff.; Ussani, *op. cit.* (supra,

Vespasian should by no means be excluded, as such a date is, after all, naturally accounted for by the prooemium itself, in which the divinity of Vespasian is mainly referred to as a thing of the future.[5]

n. 2), pp. 37 ff.; E. M. Smallwood, *Mnemosyne*, Ser. 4, XV (1962), pp. 170 ff. The last-mentioned scholar argues that the reference to the Caledonian Ocean had relevance only at a time when Caledonia was "in the news", and that Caledonia proper — the area north of the Forth-Clyde line — is known to have first been penetrated by Agricola in the course of his third campaign, probably in 80 C. E.

5 Wistrand rightly reminds us that Flaccus' invocation to Vespasian resembles the homage paid to the living rulers Octavianus (*Georgica*, I, 24 ff.) and Nero (*Pharsalia*, I, 45 ff.); see Wistrand, *op. cit.* (supra, n. 2), p. 27, n. 2. A date in the reign of Vespasian is also defended by G. Cambier, *Hommages à Marcel Renard*, I, Brussels 1969, p. 191 ff. The same date is endorsed by Courtney in the *apparatus criticus* of his edition of Valerius Flaccus. See also Lefèvre *Das Prooemium der Argonautica des Valerius Flaccus*, Mainz 1971. On the other hand, see P. Venini, *Athenaeum*, LX (1972). pp. 176 ff. She disapproves of the metaphorical interpretation of *delubrum* by Lefèvre.

226

Prima deum magnis canimus freta pervia natis
fatidicamque ratem, Scythici quae Phasidis oras
ausa sequi mediosque inter iuga concita cursus
rumpere flammifero tandem consedit Olympo.
5 Phoebe, mone, si Cymaeae mihi conscia vatis
stat casta cortina domo, si laurea digna
fronte viret; tuque o, pelagi cui maior aperti
fama, Caledonius postquam tua carbasa vexit
Oceanus Phrygios prius indignatus Iulos,
10 eripe me populis et habenti nubila terrae,
sancte pater, veterumque fave veneranda canenti
facta virum. Versam proles tua pandet Idumen
(namque potest): Solymo nigrantem pulvere fratrem
spargentemque faces et in omni turre furentem.
15 Ille tibi cultusque deum delubraque gentis
instituet, cum tu, genitor, lucebis ab omni
parte poli, neque iam Tyriis Cynosura carinis
certior aut Grais Helice servanda magistris,
sed tu signa dabis, sed te duce Graecia mittet
20 et Sidon Nilusque rates.

1 *natis*] *nautis* V   11 *sancte pater*] *namque potes* Courtney / *venerande*
Baehrens *veneranda* V   12 *pandet* Gryphius   *pandit* V   13 *namque
potest* Pius   *namque potes* VC   *sancte pater* Courtney / *<et> pulvere*
Getty, *Classical Philology*, XXXV (1940), p. 269   15 *gentis* cod. Bon.
genti V   *centum* Haupt   17 *iam* Sudhaus   *in* V   *enim* Itali /
Tyriis... carinis Friesemann   *tyrias... carinas* V   *Tyriae... carinae* Heinsius
19 *sed tu* Caussin vel Lemaire   *seu tu* V   *tu <si>* Bury

My song is of the straits first navigated by the mighty sons of gods,
of the prophetic ship that dared to seek the shores of Scythian Phasis,
that burst unswerving through the clashing rocks, to sink at length
to rest in starry firmament.
Phoebus, be thou my guide, if there stands in a pure home the tripod
that shares the secrets of the Cymaean prophetess, if the green laurel
lies on a worthy brow. And thou too, that didst win still greater glory
for opening up the sea, after the Caledonian ocean had borne thy
sails, the ocean that of yore would not brook the Phrygian Juli, do
thou, holy sire, raise me above the nations and the cloud-wrapped
earth, and be favourable unto me as I hymn the wondrous deeds of

Valerius Flaccus

old time heroes. Thy son shall tell of the overthrow of Idume — for well he can — of his brother foul with dust of Solyma, as he hurls the brands and spreads havoc in every tower. In thy honour shall he ordain sacred rites and shall raise temples to his house, what time thou, Sire, shinest all over the sky; for if thy star guides then Cynosura shall not be a surer beacon to Tyrian ships, nor Helice, whom Grecian helmsmen must watch, but beneath thy guidance Greece and Sidon and Nile shall send forth their fleets. (trans. J. H. Mozley, *LCL*)

8f *Caledonius postquam tua carbasa vexit Oceanus*: Vespasian had already taken part in Claudius' conquest of Britain, and the court flatterers could easily magnify him into the chief conqueror of that country; see *BJ*, III, 4: προσκτησάμενον δὲ τοῖς ὅπλοις Βρεττανίαν τέως λανθάνουσαν. Cf. Silius Italicus, III, 597 f. (No. 227); Tacitus, *Agricola*, 13 : 5. For magnification of the Vespasianic achievement in Britain cf. A. Momigliano, *JRS*, XL (1950), pp. 41 ff. It seems, as Momigliano points out, that the adjective Caledonius was used rather loosely by the writers of that time and, consequently, by no means implies a reference to the territory north of the Forth-Clyde line.

12 *Idumen*: Here Idume designates Judaea. *Versam Idumen* seems to be equivalent to *eversorem Idumes*, i.e. Titus; cf. J. H. Waszink, *Mnemosyne*, XXIV (1971), pp. 298 f.

13 *Solymo nigrantem pulvere fratrem*: On Solymus, see Martialis, *Epigrammata*, VII, 55 : 7 (No. 242); Iuvenalis, *Saturae*, VI, 544 (No. 299); Tacitus, *Historiae*, V, 2 (No 281). Against Courtney's insertion of *et* after *nigrantem*, cf. Waszink, *loc. cit.*

14 *spargentemque faces*: Valerius Flaccus does not expressly allude to the burning of the Temple, though "spargentemque faces" may imply that. It is well known that Josephus intended to absolve Titus from the blame of burning the Temple. Flaccus, however, had no reason to slur over this fact; cf. the commentary to Sulpicius Severus, *Chronica*, II, 30 : 3, 6–7 (No. 282).

15 *ille*: This word can refer to Domitian only on the assumption that the prooemium was really composed under that emperor. For both of the other suppositions, we should equate *ille* with Titus.

delubraque gentis instituet: Again, an identification with the "templum Flaviae gentis" would require a date in Domitian's reign. Other possibilities, however, are at least as probable (Getty, Ussani, Wistrand).

LXXX. SILIUS ITALICUS

26–101 C.E.

Like other Flavian poets, Silius Italicus (Consul, 69 C.E.), who composed the Punica under the Flavian dynasty, found it fitting to make mention of the greatest military triumph of the Flavians, namely, the subjugation of Judaea (No. 227). The mention of the Idumaean palms won from Pallas by Venus sounds like a reminiscence of Vergilius, Georgica, III, 12–15 (No. 125).

227

Punica, III, 597–606 — Bauer = F165R

Hinc pater ignotam donabit vincere Thylen
inque Caledonios primus trahet agmina lucos;
compescet ripis Rhenum, reget impiger Afros
600 palmiferamque senex bello domitabit Idymen.
Nec Stygis ille lacus viduataque lumine regna,
sed superum sedem nostrosque tenebit honores.
Tum iuvenis, magno praecellens robore mentis,
excipiet patriam molem celsusque feretur,
605 aequatum imperio tollens caput. Hic fera gentis
bella Palaestinae primo delebit in aevo.

597 *thilen* LO   599 *ripis*] *remis* Schrader
600 *idimen* FOV   602 *superam* Heinsius

The father of that family shall give Rome victory over Thule, unknown till then, and shall be the first to lead an army against the Caledonian forests; he shall set banks to restrain the Rhine, he shall rule Africa with vigour, and, in his old age, he shall subdue in war the palm-groves of Idume. Nor shall he descend to the pools of the Styx and the realm deprived of light; but he shall attain to the habitation of the gods and the honours we enjoy. Then his son, unrivalled in mighty strength of mind, shall take up his father's task and move on in majesty, raising his head as high as his power. While yet a youth, he shall put an end to war with the fierce people of Palestine.

(trans. J. D. Duff, *LCL*)

597 *Hinc pater ignotam donabit* . . .: In the third book of his *Punica*, recounting Hannibal's crossing the Pyrenees and the Alps, Silius Italicus took the opportunity to praise the Flavian emperors. He describes how Venus, perturbed by Hannibal's victories, became anxious about Rome's future. Jupiter, in response to her anxiety, foretells Rome's future splendour. In ll. 586 ff. some of the great personalities of Roman history — the heroes of the Second Punic War, Marcellus and Scipio — pass before us, and the Julio-Claudian emperors are only briefly referred to. From l. 594 on the god speaks of the three Flavian emperors. Cf. R. Rebischke, "De Silii Italici Orationibus", Ph.D. Thesis, Königsberg 1913, pp. 20 f.

598 *Inque Caledonios primus trahet* . . .: The poet reviews the main stages of Vespasian's military career: the battles in Britain, the service on the Rhine, the proconsulate of Africa and the victories in Judaea: see *BJ*, III, 4 f; Suetonius, *Vespasianus*, 2 : 3–4 : 3. From Suetonius we learn that Vespasian served on the German frontier before going on active service in Britain. On Silius Italicus's possible dependence on Valerius Flaccus, see E. M. Smallwood, *Mnemosyne*, Ser. 4, XV (1962), p. 172.

600 *Palmiferamque ... domitabit Idymen*: Cf. the commentary to Statius, *Silvae*, I, 6 : 13 (No. 232). Vespasian, in fact, led the military operations that culminated in the conquest of most of Palestine, including the groves of Jericho; see *BJ*, IV, 443 ff.
603 *tum iuvenis*: I.e. Titus.
606 *Bella Palaestinae*: Silius Italicus uses the as yet unofficial name Palaestina, as does Statius, *Silvae*, III, 2 : 105 (No. 234).

228

Punica, VII, 449–457 — Bauer

Alloquitur natos: "Testis certissima vestrae
450 ecce dies pietatis adest. Quis credere salvis
hoc ausit vobis? de forma atque ore — quid ultra
iam superest rerum? — certat Venus. Omnia parvis
si mea tela dedi blando medicata veneno,
si vester, caelo ac terris qui foedera sancit,
455 stat supplex, cum vultis, avus: victoria nostra
Cypron Idumaeas referat de Pallade palmas,
de Iunone — Paphos centum mihi fumet in aris."

455 *nostram* Heinsius   456 *Cypros* Scaliger   457 *et iunone* LFO

She [scil. Venus] addressed her children: "See, the day has come that will prove beyond all doubt your love for your mother. Who would dare to believe, that while you still live, the claim of Venus to the prize for beauty is contested? What worse remains behind? If I gave to my children all my arrows steeped in delicious poison — if your grandsire, the Lawgiver of heaven and earth, stands a suppliant before you when so you please, then let my triumph bear back to Cyprus, the palm of Edom won from Pallas, and let the hundred altars of Paphos smoke for my conquest of Juno." (trans. J. D. Duff, *LCL*)

The seventh book of the *Punica* deals with the strategy of Fabius Maximus, the Roman dictator. The Italian nymphs are worried by the Punic navy's arrival at the Italian coast and they want Proteus to tell them the future. Thus, in ll. 437 ff. we are given Proteus' prophecy.

456 *Idumaeas referat de Pallade palmas*: Idumaeas here designates Iudaeas.

LXXXI. FRONTINUS

c. 40–104 C.E.

Frontinus, a contemporary of the Flavians, composed his Strategemata
*in the reign of Domitian. He refers to the Jews only in the second book,
where he adduces, as an example of how to choose the proper time for
battle, the way in which Vespasian took advantage of the Sabbath to
attack the Jews on that day.*

229

Divus Augustus Vespasianus Iudaeos Saturni die, quo eis nefas est quicquam seriae rei agere, adortus superavit.

1 *uespasionus* H

The deified Augustus Vespasian attacked the Jews on the day of Saturn, a day on which it is sinful for them to do any business, and defeated them.

Saturni die: Like Tibullus, Frontinus identifies the Sabbath with the Day of Saturn; see the commentary to Tibullus, I, 3 : 15–18 (No. 126).

Divus Augustus Vespasianus . . . superavit: Apart from his minor inaccuracy of making Vespasian the conqueror of Jerusalem instead of Titus, which may be explained by the fact that the hostilities against Jerusalem were conducted in Vespasian's name, Frontinus' statement cannot be accepted at face value.

He clearly contradicts our other sources, which relate that the Jews did not refrain from fighting on the Sabbath during the Great Revolt. Our sources make no allusion to the Sabbath observances constituting a major obstacle to Jewish military operations of that period. It is indeed true that the famous regulation of Mattathias the Hasmonaean (I Macc. ii : 41) allowed only purely defensive operations on the Sabbath. Even these, it seems, were to take place only in the case of a direct attack that threatened disaster. After this proclamation the enemies of the Jews still found it convenient to engage them on the Sabbath whenever possible; see II Macc. xv : 1; I Macc. ix : 43; *Ant.*, XIII, 337. However, this was because the attackers expected the Jews to be less ready for action on the sacred day; cf. M.D. Herr, *Tarbiz*, XXX 1961, p. 248 f. For events connected with Babylonian Jews in the first century C. E., see also *Ant.*, XVIII, 319, 354. It should be emphasized that during Pompey's siege of Jerusalem (63 B. C. E.) the Jews reacted only to a direct attack on the Sabbath and did nothing to prevent hostile operations such as the building of mounds, which subsequently proved fatal to them. Their reluctance to act greatly assisted the Romans; see *Ant.*, XIV, 63; *BJ*, I, 146.

It seems that the new view, that military operations on the Sabbath should not be confined to cases of direct and dangerous aggression, won many adherents at a somewhat later period. It became prevalent at the time of the Great Revolt. Graetz thinks that the School of Shammai played an important part in this development and that the Jewish fighters presumably acted according to this view; see H. Graetz, *Geschichte der Juden*, III 2⁵, Leipzig 1905, p. 799; cf. *BJ*, II, 456, 517. At any rate, Iohannes of Gischala fled from Titus on the Sabbath; see *BJ*, IV, 100 ff. See also *Tosephta 'Eruvin*, 3 : 5 according to the Vienna manuscript (4 : 5 according to the Erfurt manuscript), which refers to the general permission to fight on the Sabbath whenever the gentiles march against the cities of Israel; cf. *Tosefta Mo'ed*, edited by S. Lieberman, New York 1962, p. 99; 3 : 7, p. 100; idem, *Tosefta Kifshutah*, III, New York 1962, pp. 342 ff.; cf. also *TB Shabbat* 19a.

On the other hand, Agrippa II, in the speech attributed to him by Josephus (*BJ*, II, 392 f.), still alludes to the older usage as valid. However, his assertion should not be taken at face value and may be explained by the exigencies of the moment, or rather by what Josephus thought proper to put into his mouth in that situation. On the Zealots and the Sabbath, see M. Hengel, *Die Zeloten*, Leiden–Cologne 1961, pp. 293 ff. An extremist view against waging war on the Sabbath finds expression in the Book of Jubilees L : 12–13; cf. C. Albeck, *Das Buch der Jubiläen und die Halacha*, Berlin 1930, p. 11.

Frontinus' inaccurate statement on the Sabbath as the chief cause of Jerusalem's capture seems to derive from the opinion about the Sabbath that was prevalent since the time of Agatharchides; cf. also Plutarchus, *De Superstitione*, 8, p. 169c (No. 256). It may also be that Frontinus knew something about the Jews' exemption from military service in the Roman army on religious grounds, especially on account of their strict observance of the Sabbath; see *Ant.*, XIV, 226. It is even possible that Frontinus confused the siege of Jerusalem in 63 B.C.E. with that of 70 C.E., although he was a contemporary of the Flavians; cf. Herr, *op. cit.* (supra, p. 510), p. 256. In any case, Frontinus was not always meticulous about the dates of events. For example, he connects an episode concerning Darius' capture of Babylon with Babylon's capture by Cyrus, in *Strategemata*, III, 3 : 4. However, such a mistake is hardly comparable to one that confuses dates relating to recent Roman history.

LXXXII. QUINTILIAN

Second half of the first century C.E.

Quintilian, no less than the other great Spaniards in Latin literature of the first century C.E.— e.g. Seneca and Martial— had pronounced anti-Semitic views. This is evidenced by his reference to Moses as the father of Jewish superstition and as the man who was responsible for founding a nation pernicious to other people. In his hostility to Jews, Quintilian may have drawn inspiration from Domitian,[1] in whose reign the Institutio Oratoria was published, even though he owed his advancement to the influence of Flavius Clemens,[2] who was executed for his Jewish tendencies; cf. Cassius Dio LXVII, 14 : 1-2 (No. 435).

---

1 See J. A. Hild, REJ, XI (1885), pp. 166 ff.
2 See Ausonius, Gratiarum Actio ad Gratianum, 7 : 31, edited by R. Peiper, Leipzig 1886, p. 361 : "Quintilianus consularia per Clementem ornamenta sortitus." Clarke thinks it possible that Quintilian inserted the anti-Semitic passage after Clemens' fall; see M. L. Clarke, Greece and Rome, XIV (1967), p. 35; cf. also Gager, pp. 80 ff.

512

230

Institutio Oratoria, III, 7:21 — Winterbottom — No. 162R

Et parentes malorum odimus: et est conditoribus urbium infame contraxisse aliquam perniciosam ceteris gentem, qualis est primus Iudaicae superstitionis auctor: et Gracchorum leges invisae: et si quod est exemplum deforme posteris traditum, quale libidinis vir Perses in
5 muliere Samia instituere ausus dicitur primus.

4 *libidinosus* A

The vices of the children bring hatred on their parents; founders of cities are detested for concentrating a race which is a curse to others, as for example the founder of the Jewish superstition; the laws of the Gracchi are hated, and we abhor any loathsome example of vice that has been handed down to posterity, such as the criminal form of lust which a Persian is said to have been the first to practise on a woman of Samos. (trans. H. E. Butler, *LCL*)

et parentes malorum odimus: This is a passage from the chapter "De Laude et Vituperatione". After dwelling on points that may be useful in a laudatory speech, Quintilian discusses the possibilities open to the vituperative speaker. Moses is placed here among the instigators of malice.
conditoribus urbium: I.e. κτίσται.
contraxisse = συνοικίσαι.
Iudaicae superstitionis auctor: Quintilian supposes that the name Moses is known to his readers. The author of *De Sublimitate* (No. 148) makes a similar supposition, though he differs diametrically in his judgment: ταύτῃ καὶ ὁ τῶν ᾽Ιουδαίων θεσμο-οθέτης, οὐκ ὁ τυχὼν ἀνήρ; cf. I. Heinemann, PW, XVI, p. 361. On the Jewish religion as *superstitio*, see Tacitus, *Historiae*, V, 8, 13 (No. 281); *Annales*, II, 85 (No. 284).

231

Institutio Oratoria, IV, 1:19 — Winterbottom

Nam et in libris observationum a Septimio editis adfuisse Ciceronem tali causae invenio, et ego pro regina Berenice apud ipsam eam dixi.

I note, for instance, in the body of observations published by Septimius that Cicero appeared in such a case, while I myself, when I appeared on behalf of Queen Berenice, actually pleaded before her. (trans. H. E. Butler, *LCL*)

From Herodotus to Plutarch

Quintilian discusses the exordium of a speech and analyses the ways of influencing a judge. He reminds the reader that judges sometimes pass judgment on cases in which they have an interest. This once happened to Cicero, and also to Quintilian, acting as attorney to Queen Berenice "when she herself was the judge".

pro regina Berenice: Queen Berenice was the eldest daughter of Agrippa I and the sister of Agrippa II (Ant., XVIII, 132; BJ, II, 220). She was first married to Marcus, the son of Alexander the Alabarch. After his death she married her uncle Herod, the King of Chalcis (Ant., XIX, 276 f.; cf. Ant., XIX, 354; BJ, II, 217). Herod died in 48 C. E., leaving Berenice with two sons (BJ, II, 221; Ant., XX, 104). Some years later she married her third husband, Polemon, King of Cilicia, who submitted to the rite of circumcision; however, this marriage did not last long (Ant., XX, 145 f.). Later we hear of her intervention on behalf of the Jews at the time of the riots in Jerusalem under Florus' procuratorship (BJ, II, 310 ff.). Queen Berenice was among those who appealed to Cestius Gallus, the governor of Syria, against Florus (op. cit., 333). Together with her brother she tried to calm down public feeling in Jerusalem (op. cit., 402, 405). She shared property with her brother (op. cit., 595; Ant., XVIII, 194; Vita, 48; cf. Alt, II, p. 389) and used to accompany him (Acts, xxv : 13 ff.). Their relationship gave rise to scandalous rumours (Ant., XX, 145; cf. Iuvenalis, VI, 158 = No. 298). Josephus, like Quintilian, calls her a queen (BJ, II, 598; Vita, 49: καταστησάντων αὐτὸν τῶν βασιλέων, i.e. Agrippa and Berenice; cf. Tacitus, Historiae, II, 2 = No. 275). She is likewise designated as a queen in inscriptions, such as the one from Athens (OGIS, No. 428), which reads: 'Ιουλίαν Βερενείκην βασίλισσαν μεγάλην. In a Latin inscription from Beyrouth, she is called "regina Berenice"; see Comptes rendus de l'Académie des Inscriptions, (1927, p. 243 f.) = Gabba, No. XXX. During the Civil War she aided the Flavian cause, and she acquired wide renown at Rome because of Titus' love for her. This, of course, is not mentioned at all in the works of Josephus, but we know about it from Tacitus (loc. cit.); Suetonius (Titus, 7 : 2 = No. 318); Cassius Dio (LXVI, 15 : 3–4 = No. 433) and the Epitome de Caesaribus (10 : 4 : 7 = No. 532). Berenice did not reside in Rome right after the Jewish revolt was crushed. She arrived there only in 75 C.E. and remained there for some years. She came to Rome a second time in 79, after Titus had become sole ruler, but was compelled by circumstances to leave again. See the commentaries to Cassius Dio, loc. cit., and to Suetonius, loc. cit.; cf. G.H. Macurdy, AJP, LVI (1935), pp. 246 ff.; E. Mireaux, La Reine Bérénice, Paris 1951; J.A. Crook, AJP, LXXII (1951), pp. 162 ff.

apud ipsam eam dixi: We are somewhat at a loss to interpret Quintilian's statement regarding Berenice's acting as a judge. Of course, it is impossible to take it literally, and it probably means only that her influence over the court was so great that she actually was the judge. Presumably she was present at the trial. Crook suggests that she appeared on some occasion when the imperial consilium was dealing with a matter concerning her; see Crook, op. cit., pp. 169 f.

LXXXIII. STATIUS

Second half of the first century C.E.

Statius does not mention the Jews expressly in any of his works. His Silvae includes only references to the celebrated products of Judaea — the dates and the balsam — and to the Flavian triumph over Judaea. It is noteworthy, however, that usually Idyme (= Idumaea), and sometimes Palestine, stands for Judaea, though Statius does use the adjective "Hebraei" once.

Statius awards the Idumaean dates first place among the delicacies distributed by Domitian (No. 232), and he refers to Idyme's luxuriant groves. The "juices of Palestine" (Nos. 233 and 236) or the "Hebrew juices" (No. 236) refer to balsam. That the Flavian victory over Judaea is not neglected by Statius is only to be expected from a Flavian poet. This victory is alluded to in the "Idumaean triumph" (No. 235), in "the ashes of Solyma" and in "the captive palm-groves of Idyme" (No. 237).

232

Silvae, I, 6:9–16 — Marastoni

Vix aurora novos movebat ortus,
10 iam bellaria linea pluebant:
hunc rorem veniens profudit Eurus.
Quicquid nobile Ponticis nucetis,
fecundis cadit aut iugis Idymes;
quod ramis pia germinat Damascos,
15 et quod percoquit ⋆ aebosia ⋆ Caunos,
largis gratuitum cadit rapinis;

10 *bellaria*] *vellaria* M   *velaria* ε*A*   15 *Et quo percoquit aebosia caunos*
             M   *quod* G¹K¹Q / *aestuosa* Imhof

Scarce was the new dawn stirring, when already sweetmeats were raining from the line, such was the dew the rising East wind was scattering; the famous fruit of Pontic nut-groves, or of Idume's fertile slopes, all that devout Damascus grows upon its boughs or hot[1] Caunus ripens, falls in generous profusion.

(trans. J. H. Mozley, *LCL*)

1 The translation according to the emendation of Imhof.

The exact date of this poem's composition is unknown; see F. Vollmer, *P. Papinii Statii Silvarum Libri*, Leipzig 1898, p. 6. Its subject is the celebration of the December Kalendae in one of the years of Domitian's reign. Among the presents distributed in the early morning were Pontic nuts, Damascene fruit and Judaean dates.

12 *Ponticis nucetis*: On Pontic nuts, see Plinius, *Naturalis Historia*, XV, 88.
13 *Idymes*: Idyme here designates Judaea, as it often did in Latin literature; cf. Vergilius, *Georgica*, III, 12 (No. 125). On the palms of Idumaea, see below, *Silvae*, III, 2 : 138 (No. 234); V, 2 : 139 (No. 237); cf. "palmarum dives" in Lucanus, *Pharsalia*, III, 216 (No. 192); Silius Italicus, *Punica*, III, 600 (No. 227); VII, 456 (No. 228).

233

Silvae, II, 1:157–162 — Marastoni

Quid ego exsequias et prodiga flammis
dona loquor maestoque ardentia funera luxu?
quod tibi purpureo tristis rogus aggere crevit,
160 quod Cilicum flores, quod munera graminis Indi,

158 *loquor*] *loquar* c   159 *quod*] *quo* KQ
160 *quod ... quod*] *quot ... quot* G¹IK

Statius

quodque Arabes Phariique Palaestinique liquores
arsuram lavere comam?

161 *Palaestinique* Selden   *palam est vidique* M

Why should I tell of the funeral rites, the gifts flung prodigally to
the flames, the melancholy pomp of the blazing pyre? How thou
didst heap the purples high on the sad pile, how Cilician blooms and
gifts of Indian herbs and juices of Arabia and Palestine and Egypt
steeped the hair that was to burn?   (trans. J. H. Mozley, *LCL*)

This passage is from a poem about the death of a boy in the house of Melior.
161 *Palaestinique liquores*: The *opobalsamum* of Jericho was probably among the
various materials used in cremating the boy's body; cf. below, "Palaestini simul
Hebraeique liquores". Statius, who never uses Iudaicus or Judaea in his works,
implies the widespread, though as yet unofficial, use of Palaestina by using the
adjective *Palaestini* for the *liquores*.

234

Silvae, III, 2:101–107, 131–141 — Marastoni

Isi, Phoroneis olim stabulata sub antris,
nunc regina Phari numenque Orientis anheli,
excipe multisono puppem Mareotida sistro;
ac iuvenem egregium, Latius cui ductor Eoa
105 signa Palaestinasque dedit frenare cohortes,
ipsa manu placida per limina festa sacrosque
duc portus urbesque tuas...
131 O tum quantus ego aut quanta votiva movebo
plectra lyra, cum me magna cervice ligatum
attolles umeris atque in mea pectora primum
incumbes e puppe novus, servataque reddes
135 colloquia inque vicem medios narrabimus annos;
tu rapidum Euphraten et regia Bactra sacrasque
antiquae Babylonis opes et Zeuma, Latinae
pacis iter, qua dulce nemus florentis Idymes,
qua pretiosa Tyros rubeat, qua purpura suco
140 Sidoniis iterata cadis, ubi germine primum
candida felices sudent opobalsama virgae;

140 *cadis* Gronovius   *vadis* M   *bafis* Frère

517

Isis, once stalled in Phoreneus' caves, now queen of Pharos and a deity of the breathless East, welcome with sound of many a sistrum the Mareotic bark, and gently with thine own hand lead the peerless youth, on whom the Latian prince hath bestowed the standards of the East and the bridling of the cohorts of Palestine, through festal gate and sacred haven and the cities of thy land...
How proud then shall I be! How bravely shall I sound my votive lyre! When you lift me to your shoulders and I cling about your stalwart neck, and you, fresh from the ship, fall first upon my breast, and give me all your stored-up converse, and in turn we tell the story of the years between, you of Euphrates and royal Bactra and the sacred wealth of ancient Babylon, and of Zeugma, the way of the Peace of Rome; how sweet is Idume's luxuriant grove, with what dye costly Tyre glows scarlet, and the purple, twice plunged in Sidonian vats, is stained, where the fruitful sprays first exude the shining spikenard from the bud. (trans. J. H. Mozley, *LCL*)

101 *Isi, Phoroneis olim stabulata sub antris* ...: This poem was written on the occasion of Maecius Celer's departure for the East. Statius asks the gods to grant Maecius a successful voyage.
105 *Palaestinasque dedit frenare cohortes*: Already in the introduction to the third book of the *Silvae* Statius refers to the Emperor's sending Maecius Celer to a Syrian legion: "Maecium Celerem a sacratissimo imperatore missum ad legionem Syriacam." The expression *Palaestinae cohortes* implies that Maecius Celer served in Judaea, which was then garrisoned by the tenth Legion. Although in Statius' time Judaea constituted a separate province, the poet speaks of Celer having been ordered to a Syrian legion, thus including Judaea in Syria.
140f. *ubi germine ... sudent opobalsama virgae*: This is another allusion to the *opobalsamum* of Jericho.

235
Silvae, III, 3:138–142 — Marastoni = F163R

Illum et qui nutu superas nunc temperat arces,
progeniem claram terris partitus et astris,
140 laetus Idymaei donavit honore triumphi
dignatusque loco victricis et ordine pompae
non vetuit, tenuesque nihil minuere parentes.

138 *temperat*] *temperet* M

He who with his nod now sways the heights of heaven, and has given of his glorious offspring to earth and sky alike, gladly granted

Statius

to him the honour of an Idumaean triumph, and deeming him worthy of
the distinction and rank that the procession of victory brings, forbade
it not, nor did obscurity of birth diminish his renown.

(trans. J. H. Mozley, *LCL*)

This is a poem of consolation, which was addressed to Claudius Etruscus upon
the death of his father, a freedman who advanced to the highest positions of the
imperial service; cf. P. R. C. Weaver *Familia Caesaris*, Cambridge 1972, pp. 282 ff.
138 *qui nutu superas nunc temperat arces*: I.e. Vespasian, who became a god.
139 *progeniem claram terris partitus*: I.e. Domitian.
et astris: I.e. Titus, who died in 81 C. E.

236

Silvae, V, 1:208–214 — Marastoni

... Quis carmine digno
exsequias et dona malae feralia pompae
210 perlegat? omne illic stipatum examine longo
ver Arabum Cilicumque fluit floresque Sabaei
Indorumque arsura seges praereptaque templis
tura, Palaestini simul Hebraeique liquores
Coryciaeque comae Cinyreaque germina; ...

211 *cilicumque*] *ciliciumque* M   213 *palestini* Q   *palestinis* M
214 *coritiaeque* IQ   *corsciaeque* M

Who could recount in worthy song the obsequies and funeral gifts
of that unhappy train? There heaped together in long array is all
the liquid wealth of Arabian and Cilician springs, Sabaean blooms
and Indian produce destined for the flames, and incense, spoil of
shrines, Palestinian and Hebrew essences withal and Corycian petals
and Cinyrean buds... (trans. J. H. Mozley, *LCL*)

This is a passage from a dirge on the death of Priscilla.
213 *Palaestini simul Hebraeique liquores*: This is the first time that *Hebraei* occurs
in Latin literature and one of the first times that it is used in the whole of Graeco-
Roman pagan literature.

237

Silvae, V, 2:132–139 — Marastoni = F164R

Quasnam igitur terras, quem Caesaris ibis in orbem?
Arctoosne amnes et Rheni fracta natabis

519

flumina, an aestiferis Libyae sudabis in arvis?
135 an iuga Pannoniae mutatoresque domorum
Sauromatas quaties? an te septenus habebit
Hister et umbroso circumflua coniuge Peuce?
an Solymum cinerem palmetaque capta subibis
non sibi felices silvas ponentis Idymes?

134 *librae* M / *arvis*] *armis* M   137 *peuce*] *pauce* M
138 *Solymum*]*solidum* M

To what lands then, to which of Caesar's worlds wilt thou go? Wilt
thou swim Northern rivers and the broken waters of Rhine, or sweat
in the hot fields of Libya? Wilt thou make Pannonian mountains
tremble, and the Sauromatae that shift their dwelling? Shall seven-
fold Danube hold thee, and Peuce that lies amid her lover's shady
streams? Or wilt thou tread the dust of Solyma, and the captive palm-
groves of Idume, who not for herself did plant her fruitful orchards?

(trans. J. H. Mozley, *LCL*)

This is a poem in honour of young Crispinus, who is beginning his career as an
officer in the Roman army, thereby following in the footsteps of his late father.
Statius lists the various distant countries to which Crispinus will go during his
service. Judaea is included among them, but this, in itself, does not prove that the
country was in a state of revolt at the time of Domitian. Such a possibility was
suggested on the basis of *CIL*, III, p. 857, No. XIV = *CIL*, XVI, No. 33 (86 C. E.);
see A. Darmesteter, *REJ*, I (1880), pp. 37 ff.; Juster, II, p. 185; Schürer, I, p. 644,
n. 4 (who expresses his doubts); K. Friedmann, *Atene e Roma*, NS XII (1931),
pp. 69 ff.

138 *an Solymum cinerem*: Cf. Valerius Flaccus, *Argonautica*, I, 13 (No. 226).

LXXXIV. MARTIAL

Second half of the first century C.E.

Martial, like the Senecas, Lucan and Quintilian, is one of the great Spaniards who rose to fame in Latin letters. At least two of them — Seneca the Younger and Quintilian — were conspicuous for their anti-Semitic feelings.[1] In view of the nature of Martial's epigrams, we should not expect to find in them general statements of his opinion concerning the Jews.[2] He does not even refer to what constituted, in the eyes of the Roman society, the chief danger of Judaism, namely the proselytizing zeal of the Jews and their success among the different classes of Roman society — a problem that bulked so large in the mind of Seneca, Tacitus and Juvenal.

Martial's views on the relative importance of the Jews among the foreign elements of Rome are illustrated by the several references to them in his Epigrammata. *The number of such references are second only to those concerning the Phrygian cults of Cybele and Attis, which were connected with the institution of the castrated Galli.[3] It is the Jewish rite of circumcision that serves as the main target for the epigrammatist's wit (Nos. 240, 241, 243, and 245). The only other Jewish rite mentioned by Martial is the observance of the Sabbath, which he mistakenly views as a fast — a mistake long-established in pagan literary tradition.*

Among the variety of types that enliven the epigrams we find a circumcised poet, born in the very midst of Solyma (No. 245) and Menophilus (the name may be fictitious),[4] a circumcised actor or singer (No. 243). A Jewish beggar, taught by his mother to ask for alms, is listed, after

---

1 For Martial's connections with the other Spanish literary celebrities, see L. Friedländer, *M. Valerii Martialis Epigrammaton Libri*, Leipzig 1886, pp. 4 f., 8.

2 For a well-balanced evaluation of Martial's attitude to the Jews, see J.A. Hild, *REJ*, XI (1885), pp. 169 ff. With regard to Egypt, Martial expresses himself in stronger terms: "Niliacis primum puer hic nascatur in oris: nequitias tellus scit dare nulla magis"; see *Epigrammata*, IV, 42 : 3 f.

3 II, 45; III, 24 : 13; 47 : 2; 81 : 5 f.; 92; V, 41; VIII, 46; IX, 20 : 8; XI, 72; 74; 84 : 4; XIII, 25; XIV, 204. See also the references to the Egyptian cults; VIII, 81; IX, 29 : 6; X, 48 : 1; XII, 28 : 19 f.

4 For the question of fictitious names in Martial, see II, 23; IX, 95 b.

521

the raving throng of Bellona and a ship-wrecked seaman with his swathed
body, and before the bleary-eyed huckster of sulphur wares, among the
nuisances found in the city of Rome (No. 246).

The allusion to Titus' triumph over the Jews (No. 238) is only to be
expected from a Flavian poet.[5]

5 I fail to see that the reference to the box-bearer in V, 17 refers to a Jew.

238

Epigrammata, II, 2 — Lindsay

Creta dedit magnum, maius dedit Africa nomen,
Scipio quod victor quodque Metellus habet;
nobilius domito tribuit Germania Rheno,
et puer hoc dignus nomine, Caesar, eras.
5 Frater Idumaeos meruit cum patre triumphos,
quae datur ex Chattis laurea, tota tua est

3 *domino* CA   4 *nomine*] *munere* prius scripserat BA

Crete gave a great name, Africa gave a greater, the one victorious
Scipio, the other Metellus bears; a nobler yet Germany bestowed
when the Rhine was subdued; and of this name, thou, Caesar, wert
worthy while still a boy! Along with his sire thy brother won his
Idumaean triumph; the bay given for the Chatti is wholly thine.

(trans. W. C. A. Ker, *LCL*)

1 *Creta dedit magnum*: This is a passage from an epigram honouring Domitian.
3 *nobilius domito tribuit Germania Rheno*: Domitian became Germanicus after
his triumphant operations against the Chatti near the end of 83 C. E.; see R. Syme,
CAH, XI, p. 164, n. 2.
4 *et puer hoc dignus nomine eras*: In 70 C.E., when Domitian was little more
than a boy, he took part in restoring Gaul to the Roman Empire and in saving it
from German domination.
5 *Idumaeos... triumphos*: Idumaeos here designates Iudaeos; cf. *Epigrammata*,
X, 50 (No. 244), and the commentary to Vergilius, *Georgica*, III, 12 (No. 125).
Vespasian and Titus celebrated the triumph without assuming the name of Iudaicus;
see Cassius Dio, LXVI, 7 : 2 (No. 430).

239

Epigrammata, IV, 4 — Lindsay = F166R

Quod siccae redolet palus lacunae,
crudarum nebulae quod Albularum,
piscinae vetus aura quod marinae,
quod pressa piger hircus in capella,
5 lassi vardaicus quod evocati,
quod bis murice vellus inquinatum,
quod ieiunia sabbatariarum,

1 *sica* T | *paulus* T   *thalus* CA

maestorum quod anhelitus reorum,
quod spurcae moriens lucerna Ledae,
10 quod ceromata faece de Sabina,
quod volpis fuga, viperae cubile,
mallem quam quod oles olere, Bassa

12 *mallem*] *malles* BACA

The stench of the bed of a drained marsh; of the raw vapours of
sulphur springs; the putrid reek of a sea-water fishpond; of a stale
he-goat in the midst of his amours; of the military boot of a fagged
out veteran; of a fleece twice dyed with purple; of the breath of fasting
Sabbatarian women; of the sighs of depressed defendants; of filthy
Leda's lamp as it expires; of ointment made of dregs of Sabine oil; of
a wolf in flight; of a viper's lair—all these stenches would I prefer
to your stench, Bassa! (trans. W. C. A. Ker, *LCL*)

1 *Quod siccae redolet palus lacunae*: This epigram from 88 C. E. is one of the
many places in which Martial attacks Bassa. Among the bad smells that he prefers
to that of Bassa is the smell coming from women who fast on the Sabbath. For the
same motif, see VI, 93: "Tam male Thais olet quam non fullonis avari testa . . ."
7 *sabbatariarum*: The nearest form to this may be the Sabbatistae (Σαββατισταί)
in a Greek inscription from Cilicia, *OGIS*, No. 573; cf. V. A. Tcherikover, *CPJ*,
the introduction to Section XIII, p. 46; Gressmann, PW, Ser. 2, I, pp. 1560 ff.
For the notion of the Sabbath as a fast day, see Strabo, *Histories*, apud: Josephus,
Ant., XIV, 66 (No. 104); Pompeius Trogus, apud: Iustinus, XXXVI, 2 : 14 (No.
137); Suetonius, *Divus Augustus*, 76:2 (No. 303). The reading *sabbatariarum*,
implying women fasting on the Sabbath, seems justified in view of the special
attraction that the Jewish religion had for women; see, e.g., *BJ*, II, 560; Acts
xiii : 50. Thus, we see no reason for preferring *sabbatariorum*, as suggested by
S. Sabbadini, *Annali Triestini*, XIX (Ser. IV, Vol. III) 1949, pp. 5 ff.
12 *Bassa*: Cf. I, 90; IV, 61 : 8; IV, 87; V, 45; VI, 69.

240

Epigrammata, VII, 30 — Lindsay = F167aR

Das Parthis, das Germanis, das, Caelia, Dacis,
nec Cilicum spernis Cappadocumque toros;
et tibi de Pharia Menphiticus urbe fututor
navigat, a rubris et niger Indus aquis;
5 nec recutitorum fugis inguina Iudaeorum,
nec te Sarmatico transit Alanus equo.

3 *fututor*] *salitor* AA

524

Martial

Qua ratione facis, cum sis Romana puella,
quod Romana tibi mentula nulla placet?

You grant your favours to Parthians, you grant them to Germans,
you grant them, Caelia, to Dacians, and you do not spurn the couch
of Cilicians and Cappadocians; and for you from his Egyptian city
comes sailing the gallant of Memphis, and the black Indian from the
Red Sea; nor do you shun the lecheries of circumcised Jews, and the
Alan on his Sarmatian steed does not pass you by. What is your
reason that, although you are a Roman girl, no Roman lewdness
has attraction for you? (trans. W. C. A. Ker, *LCL*)

The subject of this epigram is Caelia, who readily bestows her affections on the
men of every nation except those of Rome; see L. Pepe, *Marziale*, Naples 1950,
p. 40.
5 *recutitorum* . . . *Iudaeorum*: On *recutiti*, see Petronius, *Satyricon*, 68 : 8 (No.
193).

241

Epigrammata, VII, 35 — Lindsay = F 167b R

Inguina succinctus nigra tibi servos aluta
stat, quotiens calidis tota foveris aquis.
Sed meus, ut de me taceam, Laecania, servos
Iudaeum nuda sub cute pondus habet,
5 sed nudi tecum iuvenesque senesque lavantur.
An sola est servi mentula vera tui?
Ecquid femineos sequeris, matrona, recessus,
secretusque tua, cunne, lavaris aqua?

4 *nuda*] *nulla* BACA | *habet* om. BA   5 *sed*] *et* BA | *lauamur* P
7 *et quid* BA   *et qui* CA

Un servo, cinto le pudende con un nero cuojo, attende a te ogni
volta che tutta t'immergi nelle calde acque. Ma il mio servo, senza
parlare di me, ha il giudaico peso sott'un nudo cuojo; ma ed i giovani,
ed i vecchi si lavano nudi teco. La mentola del tuo servo è solamente
la vera? O matrona, siegui tu i feminei recessi, e ti lavi tu di nascosto
Oc — o, nella tua acqua? (trans. W. C. A. Ker, *LCL*)

3-4 *sed meus . . . servos Iudaeum nuda sub cute pondus habet*: Martial alludes to
his Jewish slave as being circumcised.

525

242

Epigrammata, VII, 55 — Lindsay

Nulli munera, Chreste, si remittis,
nec nobis dederis remiserisque:
credam te satis esse liberalem.
Sed si reddis Apicio Lupoque
5 et Gallo Titioque Caesioque,
linges non mihi — nam proba et pusilla est —
sed quae de Solymis venit perustis
damnatam modo mentulam tributis.

5 *utioque* BA   6 *lingis* BA   /   *puella* BA

If you give presents in return to no man, Chrestus, give and return none to me either: I will believe you to be generous enough. But if you give them to Apicius, and Lupus and Gallus and Titius and Caesius, you shall assault, not my person (for that is chaste and petty), but the one that comes from Solyma now consumed by fire, and is lately condemned to tribute. (trans. W. C. A. Ker, *LCL*)

8 *damnatam modo mentulam tributis*: The allusion is to the Jewish tax, imposed by Vespasian and cruelly levied by Domitian after the destruction of Jerusalem; cf. the commentary to Suetonius, *Domitianus*, 12 : 2 (No. 320).

243

Epigrammata, VII, 82 — Lindsay

Menophili penem tam grandis fibula vestit
ut sit comoedis omnibus una satis.
Hunc ego credideram — nam saepe lavamur in unum —
sollicitum voci parcere, Flacce, suae:
5 dum ludit media populo spectante palaestra,
delapsa est misero fibula: verpus erat.

3 *unum*] *uno* CA

Menophilus' person a sheath covers so enormous that it alone would be sufficient for the whole tribe of comic actors. This fellow I had imagined—for we often bathe together—was solicitous to spare his voice, Flaccus; but while he was exercising himself in the view of the people in the middle of the exercise ground, the sheath unluckily fell off: lo, he was circumcised! (trans. W. C. A. Ker, *LCL*)

Martial

This epigram mocks a Jewish singer or actor who tried, and failed, to conceal the fact that he had been circumcised. We also know of Alityrus, another Jewish actor in Rome, who lived in the time of Nero (*Vita*, 16); cf. Juster, II, p. 309; Leon, p. 234; see also S. Krauss, *Talmudische Archäologie*, III, Leipzig 1912, pp. 118 ff.

3–4 *hunc ego credideram ... solicitum voci parcere*: On the actors' practice of abstaining from sex in order to preserve the quality of their voices, see XI, 75 : 3; XIV, 215; Iuvenalis, VI, 73 f.

6 *verpus erat*: Cf. XI, 94 (No. 245). For a similar effect, see V, 35 : 6 ff.; "equiti superbo, nobili, locupleti cecidit repente magna de sinu clavis. Numquam, Fabulle, nequior fuit clavis."

244

Epigrammata, X, 50 — Lindsay

Frangat Idumaeas tristis Victoria palmas,
plange, Favor, saeva pectora nuda manu;
mutet Honor cultus, et iniquis munera flammis
mitte coronatas, Gloria maesta, comas.
5 Heu facinus! prima fraudatus, Scorpe, iuventa
occidis et nigros tam cito iungis equos.
Curribus illa tuis semper properata brevisque
cur fuit et vitae tam prope meta tuae?

8 *cur*] *cui* CA

Let Victory sadly break her Idumaean palms; beat, Favour, with cruel hand thy naked breast; let Honour change her garb; and do thou, sorrowful Glory, cast on the cruel flames the offering of thy crowned locks. Ah, crime of fate! Robbed, Scorpus, of thy first youth, art thou fallen, and so soon dost yoke Death's dusky steeds! That goal, whereto thy car sped ever in brief course, and swiftly won, why to thy life also was it so nigh? (trans. W. C. A. Ker, *LCL*)

1 *Frangat Idumaeas tristis Victoria palmas...*: This is an epigram on the death of Scorpus, the charioteer. On palms as a victory symbol, see Iuvenalis, VIII, 57 ff., and especially Vergilius, *Georgica*, III, 12 (No. 125): "primus Idumaeas referam tibi, Mantua, palmas."

245

Epigrammata, XI, 94 — Lindsay = F168R

Quod nimium lives nostris et ubique libellis
detrahis, ignosco; verpe poeta, sapis.

527

Hoc quoque non curo, quod cum mea carmina carpas,
conpilas: et sic, verpe poeta, sapis.
5 Illud me cruciat, Solymis quod natus in ipsis
pedicas puerum, verpe poeta, meum.
Ecce negas iurasque mihi per templa Tonantis.
Non credo: iura, verpe, per Anchialum.

3 *tum* C A (*tu* V) / *carpas*] *carpis* C A   8 *anchalium* T

Your overflowing malice, and your detraction everywhere of my
books, I pardon: circumcised poet, you are wise! This, too, I dis-
regard, that when you carp at my poems you plunder them: so, too,
circumcised poet, you are wise! What tortures me is this, that you,
circumcised poet, although born in the very midst of Solyma, outrage
my boy. There! you deny it, and swear to me by the Thunderer's
Temple. I don't believe you: swear, circumcised one, by Anchialus.

(trans. W. C. A. Ker, *LCL*)

The subject of this epigram is a Jewish poet, who speaks disparagingly of the works
of Martial while stealing from them and who also has sexual relations with the
poet's beloved boy. On other rival poets that Martial accuses of being plagiarists,
see Friedländer, the introduction to his commentary, pp. 9 f.

2 *verpe*: Martial repeats "verpe" four times (three times with "poeta"); cf.
R. Helm, PW, Ser. 2, VIII, p. 75.

6 *pedicas puerum, verpe poeta, meum*: Cf. Meleager, *Anthologia Graeca*, V,
160 (No. 43).

8 *per Anchialum*: Many suggestions have purported to explain Anchialus; see
Friedländer, *loc. cit.* (including the older explanations); H. Lewy, *Rhein. Mus.*,
XLVIII (1893), pp. 472 ff.; Juster, II, p. 125, n. 1; J. H. Mordtmann, *Festschrift
Max Oppenheim*, Berlin 1933, pp. 80 f.; H. Seyrig, *Annuaire de l'institut de philologie
et d'histoire orientales et slaves*, VII (1939–1944), pp. 283 ff. (Anchialus = היכל‎);
J. Gagé, *REA*, LIV (1952), p. 299, n. 4 (Anchialus is the name of the *procurator
fisci Iudaici*); J. Schwartz, *Syria*, XXX (1953), pp. 362 ff.

Since Anchialus was a common name, especially among slaves and libertini, it
seems that Martial means an unidentified man of that name, who lived in Rome at
the time. The name, because of its phonetic similarity to the names of foreign
deities — and perhaps to the Hebrew אל‎ as well — was easy for Martial to use
as the counterpart to Jupiter Tonans.

246

Epigrammata, XII, 57:1–14 — Lindsay = F169R

Cur saepe sicci parva rura Nomenti
laremque villae sordidum petam, quaeris?

1 *momenti* C A

Martial

Nec cogitandi, Sparse, nec quiescendi
in urbe locus est pauperi. Negant vitam
5 ludi magistri mane, nocte pistores,
aerariorum marculi die toto;
hinc otiosus sordidam quatit mensam
Neroniana nummularius massa,
illinc palucis malleator Hispanae
10 tritum nitenti fuste verberat saxum;
nec turba cessat entheata Bellonae,
nec fasciato naufragus loquax trunco,
a matre doctus nec rogare Iudaeus,
nec sulphuratae lippus institor mercis.

3 cogitandis pare T   cogitandis pars CA   5 magistri] magister BA
7 hic AA   9 palucis Friedlaender   pollicent AA   paludis BACA
            10 fuste] veste BA   13 mare BA

Do you ask why I often resort to my small fields in arid Nomentum, and the unkempt household of my villa? Neither for thought, Sparsus, nor for quiet is there any place in the city for a poor man. Schoolmasters in the morning do not let you live; before daybreak, bakers, the hammers of the coppersmiths all day. On this side the money-changer idly rattles on his dirty table Nero's coins, on that the hammerer of Spanish gold-dust beats his well-worn stone with burnished mallet; and Bellona's raving throng does not rest, nor the canting ship-wrecked seaman with his swathed body, nor the Jew taught by his mother to beg, nor the blear-eyed huckster of sulphur-wares. (trans. W. C. A. Ker, *LCL*)

1 *Cur saepe sicci parva rura* . . .: Martial explains why he leaves Rome so often for rustic Nomentum; cf. the third satire of Juvenal. Among Rome's characteristic nuisances, he lists, the Jewish beggar, who is taught to beg by his mother. On Jewish beggars in Rome, see H. J. Lewy, *Studies in Jewish Hellenism*, Jerusalem 1960, pp. 197 ff. (in Hebrew).

LXXXV. DAMOCRITUS

First century C.E.?

Damocritus was a historian and the writer of a book on tactics. He is known to us only from Suda, according to which he was the author of a book about the Jews. We have no knowledge of Damocritus' time; we do not even know whether to date him before or after Apion. Like the latter, he knows the fable about the worship of the golden asinine head (cf. the introduction to Mnaseas), and, apart from Apion, he is the only Greek writer, as far as we know, to have maintained that the Jews practised ritual slaughter of foreigners.

Damocritus undoubtedly differs from Apion in matters of detail. While Apion emphasizes that the man sacrificed in the ritual slaughter was a Greek, Damocritus refers only in general terms to a ξένος. Moreover, Apion maintains that the sacrifice was annual, while, according to Damocritus, it occurs once in seven years. This implies that there was no close interdependence between the two writers; cf. also the commentary to Apion, apud: Contra Apionem, *II, 89 ff. (No. 171).*

It is well known that human sacrifice was practised widely in the ancient world.[1] The enlightened opinion of Greece and Rome saw it as a crude expression of barbarian superstition; cf., Cicero, Pro Fonteio, *31. The Roman government prohibited human sacrifice in Rome and found it incumbent upon itself to abolish it among other people who fell under the sway of Rome, above all among the Gauls.[2] By labelling the Jewish religion as one that fosters the custom of human sacrifice, Damocritus implies that Judaism condoned both superstition and misanthropy.*

---

1 See F. Schwenn, *Die Menschenopfer bei den Griechen und Römern*, Giessen 1915; Cichorius, pp. 7 ff. The accusation lodged against Apollonius of Tyana, namely, that he sacrificed a boy in order to learn the future from an inspection of his entrails, belongs to another category of libel. See Philostratus, *Vita Apollonii*, VII, 11; see also Iuvenalis, VI, 552.

2 See H. Last, *JRS*, XXXIX (1949), pp. 1 ff.

Damocritus

247

De Iudaeis, apud: Suda, s.v. Δαμόκριτος — Adler = F60R = F. Gr. Hist.,III, C730, F1

Δαμόκριτος, ἱστορικός. Τακτικὰ ἐν βιβλίοις β', Περὶ Ἰουδαίων· ἐν ᾧ φησιν, ὅτι χρυσῆν ὄνου κεφαλὴν προσεκύνουν καὶ κατὰ ἑπταετίαν ξένον ἀγρεύοντες προσέφερον καὶ κατὰ λεπτὰ τὰς σάρκας διέξαινον, καὶ οὕτως ἀνῇρουν.

1 Περὶ] περὶ τῶν V

Damocritus, an historian.—He wrote a work about tactics in two volumes, and a work *On Jews*. In the latter he states that they used to worship an asinine golden head and that every seventh year they caught a foreigner and sacrificed him. They used to kill him by carding his flesh into small pieces.

ἑπταετίαν: Seven years, instead of one year in Apion. The number seven may have some connection with the Jewish sabbatical year known to some pagan writers; cf. Tacitus, *Historiae*, V, 4 (No. 281), and, perhaps, Suetonius, *Tiberius*, 32 (No. 305).

προσεκύνουν . . . προσέφερον . . . διέξαινον . . . ἀνῇρουν: If we were certain that this is the *ipsissima verba* of Damocritus, this series of imperfects would have implicitly proven that Damocritus wrote his work about the Jews after the destruction of the Temple in 70 C. E. Schwartz categorically states that Damocritus composed his work in the first century B.C.E. at the earliest, and not later than 70 C.E.; see Schwartz, PW, IV, p. 2070. However, he adduces no proof for this view.

κατὰ λεπτὰ τὰς σάρκας διέξαινον: Flusser points out the similarity between this description and the description of human sacrifice known from the Dionysiac cult, in Porphyry, *De Abstinentia*, II, 55; see D. Flusser, in: *Commentationes Iudaico-Hellenisticae in Memoriam Iohannis Lewy*, Jerusalem 1949, pp. 104 f. (in Hebrew). In Porphyry we read, on the authority of Euelpis of Carystus and in connection with the cult of Dionysus Omadios: ἔθυον δὲ καὶ ἐν Χίῳ τῷ Ὠμαδίῳ Διονύσῳ ἄνθρωπον διασπῶντες καὶ ἐν Τενέδῳ; cf. Schwenn, *op. cit.* (supra, p. 530, n. 1), pp. 71 ff.; L. R. Farnell, *The Cults of the Greek States*, V, Oxford 1909, pp. 156, 304.

LXXXVI. NICARCHUS

First century C.E. ?

From the fragment preserved in Photius' lexicon we learn that Nicarchus, in a special monograph on the Jews, stated that Moses was called "Αλφα because of his leprosy: διὰ τὸ πολλοὺς ἔχειν ἀλφοὺς ἐν τῷ σώματι. *Nicarchus seems to be an Egyptian Greek, and his statement is in line with the Graeco-Egyptian tradition that the Jews were lepers. The name "Αλφα for Moses also appears in the writings of Ptolemy Chennos (No. 331) and Helladius (No. 473); cf. the commentary ad loc.*

Nicarchus

248

De Iudaeis, apud: Photius, *Lexicon*, s.v. ἄλφα—R.Reitzenstein *Der Anfang des Lexikons des Photios,*
Leipzig–Berlin 1907, p. 83 = F61R = *F. Gr. Hist.*, III, C731, F1

῎Αλφα· τοῦτο ὑπὸ Φοινίκων βοὸς κεφαλὴ ἐκαλεῖτο, καὶ Μωυσῆς δὲ
ὁ νομοθέτης ὑπὸ Ἰουδαίων διὰ τὸ πολλοὺς ἔχειν ἀλφοὺς ἐν τῷ σώματι
οὕτως ἐκαλεῖτο· ἀλλὰ καὶ τοῦτο Νίκαρχος ὁ τοῦ Ἀμμωνίου ἐν τῷ
Περὶ Ἰουδαίων φλυαρεῖ.

Alpha.—A cow-head was thus called by the Phoenicians, and also
Moyses the legislator by the Jews was so called because he had much
dull-white leprosy on his body. That sort of nonsense is told by
Nicarchus, the son of Ammonius, in his work on Jews.

LXXXVII. CLAUDIUS IOLAUS

First century C.E.?

Claudius Iolaus wrote a work on Phoenician history, of which some fragments have been preserved by Stephanus Byzantius, and one has been brought down to us in Etymologicum Magnum. *The two fragments relating to Acre and Dora are expressly stated to come from the Phoenician History.*[1] *The fragment in the* Etymologicum Magnum *is also said to derive from the Φοινιϰιϰαὶ ἱστοϱίαι.*[2]

We may, therefore, suppose that the fragment about Udaeus and Judaea was also included in the same work.

Both the personality and the date of Claudius Iolaus remain unknown. Since he refers to Caesarea (apud: Stephanus Byzantius, s.v. Δῶϱος = F. Gr. Hist., III, C788, F2) we may take the date that Herod founded the city as terminus post quem.

1 *F. Gr. Hist.*, III, C 788, F 1–2.
2 *Ibid.*, F 3.

Claudius Iolaus

249

apud: Stephanus Byzantius s.v. ᾿Ιουδαία — Meineke = F124R = F. Gr. Hist., III, C 788, F4

᾿Ιουδαία· ᾿Αλέξανδρος ὁ Πολυΐστωρ ⟨No. 53⟩ ἀπὸ τῶν παίδων Σεμιράμιδος ᾿Ιούδα καὶ ᾿Ιδουμαίας ⟨?⟩· ὡς δὲ Κλαύδιος ᾿Ιόλαος, ἀπὸ Οὐδαίου
Σπάρτων ἑνὸς ἐκ Θήβης μετὰ Διονύσου ἐστρατευκότος.

1 ὡς μὲν ante ᾿Αλέξανδρος add. Holstenius   2 ᾿Ιδουμαίας? Meineke
ἰδουμαία codd. λαύδιος R   καιαύδιος P / ἰόαλος V   ᾿Ιούλιος Holstenius
2-3 Οὐδαίου Σπάρτων ἑνὸς Schubart, Meineke   ἰουδαίου σπάρτωνος codd.

Judaea.—Alexander Polyhistor says that the name derives from that
of the children of Semiramis Judas and Idumaea [?]. According,
however, to Claudius Iolaus, it comes from that of Udaeus, one of
the 'Sown-men' at Thebes, who was among the military companions
of Dionysus.

Οὐδαίου: Udaeus was counted among the σπάρτοι sown by Cadmus at Thebes.
While most of the others killed each other, Udaeus was among the few who
survived; see F. Gr. Hist., I 4 (Hellanicus), F 1b; I 3 (Pherecydes), F 22; Pausanias,
Graeciae Descriptio, IX, 5 : 3; Apollodorus, Bibliotheca, III, 4 : 1; Hyginus,
Fabulae, 178; Scholia in Euripidem, Berlin 1887 (ed. E. Schwartz), I, p. 350. On the
various traditions, see F. Vian, Les origines de Thèbes, Paris 1963, pp. 158 ff.
The reading ᾿Ιουδαῖος of the MSS of Stephanus Byzantius is an obvious corrup-
tion. The connection between the mythological name Udaeus and Judaea may be
explained by their similarity in sound. This connection may have originated from
the tradition of friendship between the Jews and Sparta, which arose in the
Hellenistic age, as well as from the story of the emigration of the σπάρτοι from
Thebes to Sparta. On the relations between the Jews and Sparta, see I Macc. xii : 20
ff.; cf. Ant., XII, 226 ff.; II Macc. v : 9. For modern literature on the subject, see
A. Büchler, Die Tobiaden und die Oniaden, Vienna 1899, pp. 127 ff.; A. Momigliano,
Prime linee di storia della tradizione maccabaica, Rome 1930, pp. 141 ff.; M.S. Gins-
burg, Classical Philology, XXIX (1934), pp. 117 ff.; F. Dornseiff, Würzburger
Jahrbücher für die Altertumswissenschaft, I (1946), pp. 128 ff.; S. Schüller,
Journal of Semitic Studies, I (1956), pp. 257 ff.; Y. Gutman, The Beginnings of
Jewish-Hellenistic Literature, Jerusalem 1958, pp. 108 ff. (in Hebrew); M. Stern,
The Documents on the History of the Hasmonaean Revolt, Tel Aviv 1965, pp. 91 ff.
(in Hebrew); B. Cardauns, Hermes, XCV (1967), pp. 317 ff.
The connection between Sparta and the Spartoi is well illustrated by another tradi-
tion, which is related, on Timagoras' authority, in Stephanus Byzantius, s.v.
Σπάρτη. On the cult of Cadmus at Sparta, see Pausanias, Graeciae Descriptio,
III, 15 : 8: ἐν Σπάρτῃ δὲ λέσχη τέ ἐστι καλουμένη Ποικίλη καὶ ἡρῷα πρὸς αὐτῇ
Κάδμου τοῦ ᾿Αγήνορος τῶν τε ἀπογόνων...
μετὰ Διονύσου: On Dionysus and the Jews, see Tacitus, Historiae, V, 5 (No. 281);
Plutarchus, Quaestiones Convivales, IV, 6 : 1 ff. (No. 258); see also T. Labhardt,
Quae de Iudaeorum Origine Iudicaverint Veteres, Augsburg 1881, pp. 26 ff.

LXXXVIII. ANTONIUS DIOGENES

End of the first century C.E.

Antonius Diogenes is the author of an adventurous romance about Thule that was quoted in Porphyry's work on the life of Pythagoras. He repeats the well-known tradition that Pythagoras was a student of Eastern nations, and he lists the Hebrews among them (cf. the introduction to Hermippus).

250

apud: Porphyrius, *Vita Pythagorae*, 11 — Nauck = F83R

Ἀφίκετο δὲ καὶ πρὸς Αἰγυπτίους, φησίν ‹scil. ὁ Διογένης›, ὁ Πυθαγόρας καὶ πρὸς Ἄραβας καὶ Χαλδαίους καὶ Ἑβραίους, παρ᾽ ὧν καὶ τὴν περὶ ὀνείρων γνῶσιν ἠκριβώσατο.

2 ἄρραβας V

He says [scil. Diogenes] that Pythagoras came also to the Egyptians, the Arabs, the Chaldaeans and the Hebrews, from whom he learnt the exact knowledge of dreams.

ἀφίκετο δὲ καὶ πρός... Ἑβραίους: Antonius Diogenes is said to have lived at the end of the first century C. E.; see, e.g., W. Schmid, PW, p. 2616; B. Lavagnini, *Studi sul romanzo greco*, Messina–Florence 1950, p. 181. If he did live at that time, we have here one of the first instances of the term "Hebrews" used for Jews in pagan literature.

καὶ τὴν περὶ ὀνείρων γνῶσιν ἠκριβώσατο: Cf. Pompeius Trogus, apud: Iustinus, Epitoma, XXXVI, 2 : 8 (No. 137), concerning Joseph: "nam et prodigiorum sagacissimus erat et somniorum primus intellegentiam condidit." See also J.H. Waszink, "Porphyre", *Entretiens sur l'antiquité classique* (*Fondation Hardt*), XII (1965), pp. 52 f.

LXXXIX. DIO CHRYSOSTOM

c. 40 to after 112 C.E.

Nowhere in his existing works does Dio Chrysostom refer to either Jews or Judaism. We learn that he was among the writers who described the Essenes only from his biography, which was compiled by Synesius, the Bishop of Cyrene.[1] It seems that Dio's writings on the Essenes did not appear in a special work on them, but that he mentioned them in one of his lost speeches.[2]

---

1 See J. R. Asmus, *Byzantinische Zeitschrift*, IX (1900), pp. 85 ff.; Campenhausen, PW, Ser. 2, IV, p. 1364; K. Treu, *Synesios von Kyrene*, Berlin 1958.
2 Asmus, *op. cit.*, p. 86; Treu, *op. cit.*, p. 42.

Dio Chrysostom

251

apud: Synesius, *Vita Dionis* — Arnim II, p. 317 = A. Adam, *Antike Berichte über die Essener*, Berlin 1961, No. 8

Ἔτι καὶ τοὺς Ἐσσηνοὺς ἐπαινεῖ που, πόλιν ὅλην εὐδαίμονα τὴν παρὰ τὸ νεκρὸν ὕδωρ ἐν τῇ μεσογείᾳ τῆς Παλαιστίνης κειμένην παρ᾽ αὐτά που τὰ Σόδομα.

1 Ἔτι] ὅτι L

Moreover, he praises the Essenes, a very blessed city situated near the Dead Water in the interior of Palestine, in the very vicinity of Sodoma.

καὶ τοὺς Ἐσσηνοὺς ἐπαινεῖ: Dio Chrysostom is the only pagan writer to refer to the Essenes apart from Plinius, *Naturalis Historia*, V, 73 (No. 204), and writers dependent on him, like Solinus, *Collectanea Rerum Memorabilium*, XXXV, 9–11 (No. 449). Unlike the Graeco-Jewish writers Philo and Josephus, who do not mention any connection between the Dead Sea and the Essenes, both Pliny and Dio dwell on it. But it is doubtful whether we should assume a common source for Pliny and Dio, as do Lucius and Schürer; see P.E. Lucius, *Der Essenismus in seinem Verhältniss zum Judentum*, Strasbourg 1881, p. 32; Schürer, II, p. 658, n. 6.

πόλιν ὅλην εὐδαίμονα: Dio differs from Pliny in that he allots a separate town to the Essenes. Pliny refers to Engada ('En Gedi), denoting it by the words "infra hos fuit", but he does not imply that it was an Essene town.

τὸ νεκρὸν ὕδωρ: Cf. Pompeius Trogus, apud: Iustinus, Epitoma, XXXVI, 3 : 6 (No. 137); Pausanias, *Graeciae Descriptio*, V, 7 : 4 (No. 356); Galenus, *De Simplicium Medicamentorum Temperamentis ac Facultatibus*, IV, 20 (No. 381); XI, 2 : 10 (No. 386); *De Symptomatum Causis*, III, 7 (No. 380).

ἐν τῇ μεσογείᾳ τῆς Παλαιστίνης: While Pliny speaks of Judaea, Dio uses the then unofficial name of Παλαιστίνη. But it may be that Παλαιστίνη owes its appearance to Synesius.

παρ᾽ αὐτά που τὰ Σόδομα: For other references to Sodoma in Greek literature, see Strabo, *Geographica*, XVI, 2 : 44, p. 764 (No. 115); Galenus, (No. 381): οἱ Σοδομηνοὶ χόνδροι; (Σόδομα designates here the mountains that surround the Dead Sea). We cannot say with any degree of certainty where Dio or his source located Sodoma. Strabo undoubtedly thought that it was situated at the southern end of the Dead Sea. Josephus' references to it are not consistent; see E. Power, *Biblica*, XI (1930), p. 160. Philo, however, seems to have located Sodoma north of the Dead Sea, namely in the vicinity of Jericho, as is probably implied by his description of the catastrophe of Sodoma in *De Abrahamo*, 141: τῆς δὲ περὶ τὴν χώραν παλαιᾶς εὐδαιμονίας ἐναργέστατον ὑπολείπεται δεῖγμα πόλις μία τῶν ὁμόρων καὶ ἡ ἐν κύκλῳ γῆ, πολυάνθρωπος μὲν ἡ πόλις... It has been surmised that the πολυάνθρωπος πόλις, which Philo referred to, is the same as Jericho. If this is so, Philo would be an early witness for the opinion that Sodoma is situated north of the Dead Sea. However, in view of Strabo's opinion to the contrary and Josephus' somewhat vague view, it would be inaccurate to state that the unanimous opinion at the time

539

of Dio, or in the period preceding him, located Sodoma in the north. Thus, in Dio the connection of the Essenes with Sodoma cannot, by itself, be cited as clear evidence that the Essenes lived to the north of the Dead Sea. For later views locating Sodoma at the north, see, e.g., *Antonini Placentini Itinerarium*, 15, apud: Geyer, p. 169; 24, p. 176.

XC. EPICTETUS

c. 50–130 C. E.

While the other great Stoic, Seneca, was markedly hostile in his references to Jews, Epictetus' references to them are of a neutral character. The first mention appears in his discussion on the need for a criterion of good and evil. Here Epictetus points out the differences in the opinions of the Jews, the Syrians, the Egyptians and the Romans on the subject of food, all of which were diametrically opposed (No. 252). These four nations are again listed as professing conflicting views not over the principle of whether holiness should be pursued, but on whether the particular act of eating the flesh of the swine is a holy one or not (No. 253). Both these examples are, thus, connected with Jewish dietary laws. The third reference (No. 254) implies that Epictetus knew of the significance of the rite of baptism in the conversion to Judaism — a rite which was no less essential for converts to the Jewish religion than for converts to Christianity. There is, therefore, no basis for the supposition that Epictetus confused Jews with Christians.[1]

---

1 On the other hand, it seems that the Galilaeans of IV, 7:6, are to be considered Christians: Εἶτα ὑπὸ μανίας μὲν δύναταί τις οὕτως διατεθῆναι πρὸς ταῦτα καὶ ὑπὸ ἔθους οἱ Γαλιλαῖοι. See Ed. Meyer, III, p. 530, n. 1; A. Harnack, *Mission und Ausbreitung des Christentums*, Leipzig 1924, p. 412, n. 1. Hengel interprets the passage as referring to the Zealots, since the founder of that sect hailed from Galilee; see M. Hengel, *Die Zeloten*, Leiden–Cologne 1961, pp. 60 f., followed by S. Applebaum, *JRS* LXI (1971), p. 169. It remains doubtful, however, to what extent, if any, the name Galilaeans was used for the Zealots.

252

apud: Arrianus, *Dissertationes* I, 11 : 12–13 — Souilhé = F78bR, pp. 361 f.

(12) Φέρε, εἰπέ μοι, πάντα ἃ δοκεῖ τισιν εἶναι καλὰ καὶ προσήκοντα, ὀρθῶς δοκεῖ; καὶ νῦν Ἰουδαίοις καὶ Σύροις καὶ Αἰγυπτίοις καὶ Ῥωμαίοις οἷόν τε πάντα τὰ δοκοῦντα περὶ τροφῆς ὀρθῶς δοκεῖν; — καὶ πῶς οἷόν τε; (13) — ἀλλ' οἶμαι πᾶσα ἀνάγκη, εἰ ὀρθά ἐστι <τὰ> Αἰγυπτίων, μὴ
5 *ὀρθὰ εἶναι τὰ τῶν ἄλλων· εἰ καλῶς ἔχει τὰ Ἰουδαίων, μὴ καλῶς ἔχειν τὰ τῶν ἄλλων.*

2 νῦν] μὴν J   4 <τὰ> Schweighaeuser

(12) Come, tell me, are all things that certain persons regard as good and fitting, rightly so regarded? And is it possible at this present time that all the opinions which Jews, and Syrians, and Egyptians and Romans hold on the subject of food are rightly held? — (13) And how can it be possible? — But, I fancy, it is absolutely necessary, if the views of the Egyptians are right, that those of the others are not right; if those of the Jews are well founded, that those of the others are not.   (trans. W. A. Oldfather, *LCL*)

253

apud: Arrianus, *Dissertationes*, I, 22 :4 — Souilhé

Αὕτη ἐστὶν ἡ Ἰουδαίων καὶ Σύρων καὶ Αἰγυπτίων καὶ Ῥωμαίων μάχη, οὐ περὶ τοῦ ὅτι τὸ ὅσιον πάντων προτιμητέον καὶ ἐν παντὶ μεταδιωκτέον, ἀλλὰ πότερόν ἐστιν ὅσιον τοῦτο, τὸ χοιρείον φαγεῖν, ἢ ἀνόσιον.

3 ὅσιόν ἐστι J / χοιρίου Salmasius

This is the conflict between Jews and Syrians and Egyptians and Romans, not over the question whether holiness should be put before everything else and should be pursued in all circumstances, but whether the particular act of eating swine's flesh is holy or unholy.
                (trans. W. A. Oldfather, *LCL*)

254

apud: Arrianus, *Dissertationes*, II, 9:19–21 — Souilhé = F78R

(19) Τί γὰρ διαφέρει ταῦτα ἐξηγεῖσθαι ἢ τὰ τῶν ἑτεροδόξων; τεχνολόγει

Epictetus

νῦν καθίσας τὰ Ἐπικούρου καὶ τάχα ἐκείνου χρηστικώτερον τεχνολογήσεις. τί οὖν Στωικὸν λέγεις σεαυτόν, τί ἐξαπατᾷς τοὺς πολλούς, τί ὑποκρίνῃ Ἰουδαῖον ὢν Ἕλλην; (20) οὐχ ὁρᾷς, πῶς ἕκαστος λέγεται 5 Ἰουδαῖος, πῶς Σύρος, πῶς Αἰγύπτιος; καὶ ὅταν τινὰ ἐπαμφοτερίζοντα ἴδωμεν, εἰώθαμεν λέγειν «οὐκ ἔστιν Ἰουδαῖος, ἀλλ' ὑποκρίνεται.» ὅταν δ' ἀναλάβῃ τὸ πάθος τὸ τοῦ βεβαμμένου καὶ ᾑρημένου, τότε καὶ ἔστι τῷ ὄντι καὶ καλεῖται Ἰουδαῖος. (21) οὕτως καὶ ἡμεῖς παραβαπτισταί, λόγῳ μὲν Ἰουδαῖοι, ἔργῳ δ' ἄλλο τι, ἀσυμπαθεῖς πρὸς τὸν λόγον, 10 μακρὰν ἀπὸ τοῦ χρῆσθαι τούτοις ἃ λέγομεν, ἐφ' οἷς ὡς εἰδότες αὐτὰ ἐπαιρόμεθα.

4 Ἰουδαῖον ex corr. F   ἰουδαῖος SPVBF²J   ἰουδαίους U / ἕλληνας SPVBFJ
7 βεβαμμένου] βεβαιουμένου Bernays / περιῃρημένου Petavius, Upton

(19) For how much better is it to set forth these principles than those of other schools of thought? Sit down now and give a philosophical discourse upon the principles of Epicurus, and perhaps you will discourse more effectively than Epicurus himself. Why, then do you call yourself a Stoic, why do you deceive the multitude, why do you act the part of a Jew, when you are a Greek? (20) Do you not see in what sense men are severally called Jew, Syrian, or Egyptian? For example, whenever we see a man halting between two faiths, we are in the habit of saying, "He is not a Jew, he is only acting the part". But when he adopts the attitude of mind of the man who has been baptized and has made his choice, then he both is a Jew in fact and is also called one. (21) So we also are counterfeit "Baptists", ostensibly Jews, but in reality something else, not in sympathy with our own reason, far from applying the principles which we profess, yet priding ourselves upon them as being men who know them.

(trans. W. A. Oldfather, *LCL*)

20 ὅταν δ' ἀναλάβῃ τὸ πάθος τὸ τοῦ βεβαμμένου καὶ ᾑρημένου, τότε καὶ ἔστι τῷ ὄντι καὶ καλεῖται Ἰουδαῖος: Since some of the older scholars held the erroneous view that baptism did not constitute an indispensable element in the rite of conversion to Judaism in Epictetus' time, they inferred that Epictetus confused Christianity with Judaism. Even Oldfather shares this view in his introduction to the Loeb edition, p. XXVI. This opinion, however, no longer seems tenable. The setting of the discourses of Epictetus at Nicopolis is dated *c.* 108 C.E.; see F. Millar, *JRS*, LV (1965), p. 142. The philosopher should have known the difference between Jews and Christians by that time. The specific name "Galilaeans" which he applies to Christians makes it almost certain that he did know the difference. Moreover, it should be stressed that baptism was considered obligatory for any conversion in the Tannaitic age; see *M. Pesaḥim*, viii : 8; *M. 'Eduyot*, v : 2; see also the Tannaitic text in the *Mekhilta de-Rabbi Shim'on b. Yoḥai* on Exod. xii : 48, edited by

J. N. Epstein and E. Z. Melamed, p. 37 (= *TB Keritot* 9a): "... the proselyte enters into the covenant in three ways: by circumcision, immersion and sacrifice"; see also *TB Yevamot* 46a–b. On Jewish proselyte baptism at that period, see W. Brandt, *Die Jüdischen Baptismen*, Giessen 1910, pp. 57 ff.; Strack & Biller-beck, I, pp. 102 ff. (on Matt. iii : 6); G. F. Moore, *Judaism in the First Centuries of the Christian Era*, I, Cambridge (Mass.) 1927, pp. 331 ff.; H. H. Rowley, *HUCA*, XV (1940), pp. 313 ff.; W. G. Braude, *Jewish Proselyting*, Providence 1940, pp. 74 ff.; T. F. Torrance, *New Testament Studies*, I (1954–1955), pp. 150 ff.; T. M. Taylor, *New Testament Studies*, II (1955–1956), pp. 193 ff. Taylor emphasizes, perhaps too strongly, the difference between proselyte baptism and the old immersion bath that followed a proselyte's atonement offering.

τοῦ βεβαμμένου καὶ ἠρημένου: After βεβαμμένου one would naturally expect a word implying circumcision; see D. S. Sharp, *Epictetus and the New Testament*, London 1914, pp. 134 f. But ἠρημένου cannot mean this, and the emendation περιηρημένου, proposed by Petavius is also far from satisfactory. If we leave ἠρημένου, we get the sense it has in Oldfather's translation ("and has made his choice"), or in that of Souilhé ("sectateur").

XCI. PLUTARCH

The forties of the first century to the twenties of the
second century C.E.

*Plutarch, scion of an old Boeotian family, was a priest of Delphi. He
is the only resident of Greece proper among the Greek and Latin authors
of the Roman imperial period who expressed views on the Jews and their
religion. It is difficult to determine exactly where he obtained his impres-
sions of Judaism because he was widely read and well travelled, having
visited such Jewish centres as Alexandria and sojourned for a rather
long time at Rome, where he could have met many Jews. He might
also have come in contact with Jews in his native Boeotia, where a
Jewish population undoubtedly existed.[1]*

*Plutarch's most elaborate treatment of the Jewish religion is found in
his* Quaestiones Convivales, *which was written during his years of
maturity.[2] The occasion for a discussion of Judaism arises at a sympo-
sium held at Aidepsos in Euboea. Symmachus pleads for the superiority of marine food when Lamprias, Plutarch's brother, mentions
that his grandfather used to remark on the Jews' abstention from the
most legitimate food (τὸ δικαιότατον κρέας οὐκ ἐσθίουσιν). This
raises the problem of whether the Jews abstain from pork because
they honour the pig or because they abhor it.[3] One of the disputants,
Callistratus, maintains that the Jewish attitude derives from a feeling
of respect and gratitude for the part that the pig played in the history
of agriculture, as exemplified by the experience of Egypt. For, he
continues, if the Jews really abhor pork, they should treat it the same*

---

1 It is noteworthy that the first reference we find to Jews in Greece proper derives
   from Oropus, on the border of Boeotia and Attica (third century B. C. E.).
   See *SEG*, XV, No. 293; D. M. Lewis, *Journal of Semitic Studies*, II (1957),
   pp. 264 ff. For Jews in Boeotia under the Roman Empire, see Philo, *Legatio*, 281.
2 Probably at the end of the first decade of the second century C. E.; see
   K. Ziegler, *Plutarchos von Chaironeia*, Stuttgart 1949, p. 77 = PW, XXI, p. 713.
   See also C. P. Jones, *JRS*, LVI (1966), pp. 72 f. He dates the book after 99 and
   before 116 C. E.
3 This problem is paralleled in other parts of the *Quaestiones Convivales*, where
   reference is made to the Pythagoraean abstention from fish (VIII, 8) and to
   the eschewing of salt by the Egyptian priests (V, 10 : 1).

way that the magi treat mice. According to Callistratus, therefore, we must assume that the Jews honour the swine with the same feeling of gratitude that they show towards the ass, which helped them find water, i.e. during their wanderings in the desert.

Callistratus' view is in accordance with the trend in ancient literature that is represented by Petronius (No. 195), who even goes to the length of suggesting that the Jews worship the swine.

Lamprias objects to this view of the question. He maintains that the Jewish abstention from pork originated in the common fear of leprosy, a disease that may be incurred from this food. He adds that the swine is remarkably dirty, and its living quarters are disgusting. Moreover, if one also adduces mythical evidence, it might be pointed out that Adonis, who should be identified with Dionysus, was killed by a boar.

This leads back to the discussion of the identity of the Jewish God, since Lamprias' last statement implies a connection between Dionysus and Hebrew religious mysteries. The implication surprises Symmachus, but Moiragenes, the Athenian, responds in full; he proves his case by finding a link between the Dionysiac and the Jewish cults. Moiragenes' argument has been only partially preserved, because the latter part of the sixth problem in the fourth book of the Quaestiones — *and also the last four problems of this book — have not reached us. In what remains of the problem, Moiragenes concentrates on the Dionysiac character of the Jewish feasts, mainly on the Feast of the Tabernacles. He also finds a close relationship between the Sabbath and Dionysus, because: "even now many people call the Bacchi 'Sabboi' and call out that word when they perform the orgies of Bacchus." He adduces at least as powerful an argument from the nature of the dress worn by the High Priest and from the sounding of trumpets during nocturnal celebrations.[4] An argument, based on what seems to imply the institution of nazariteship, breaks off in the middle.*

Plutarch's description obviously derives at least partially from a source prior to the destruction of the Second Temple. Whether he was also influenced by the practice of contemporary synagogues is less certain.[5]

The Jews are also quite conspicuous in one of Plutarch's early essays,

---

4 Cf. also the identification of Dionysus with Osiris in *De Iside et Osiride*, 35, p. 364 E. See also G. Soury, *La démonologie de Plutarque*, Paris 1942, pp. 91 f.
5 This is hinted at by Goodenough, VI, p. 134. For a discussion of the whole passage, see A. Büchler, *REJ*, XXXVII (1898), pp. 181 ff.; see also B. Latzarus, *Les idées religieuses de Plutarque*, Paris 1920, pp. 161 ff.

Plutarch

namely, De Superstitione,[6] *where the Jewish religion is singled out two times. In* §*3, p. 166 A (No. 255), the keeping of the Sabbath (σαββατισ-μοί) is listed among the many barbarian customs adopted by the Greeks. In* §*8, p. 169 C (No. 256), it is Jewish inaction on the day of Sabbath that brought disaster upon Jerusalem. Yet, the Jews are not the only nation blamed for their superstitions. While it is their superstitious observance of the Sabbath that draws Plutarch's attention to the Jews, he blames the Gauls, the Scythians and above all the Carthaginians for human sacrifice* (De Superstitione, *13). He also quotes with approval Xenophanes' censure of the Egyptians* (loc. cit.).

The labelling of the Jews as a superstitious nation is quite in accord with the Graeco-Roman tradition, represented by, e.g., Agatharchides, apud: Contra Apionem, *I, 205–211 (No. 30); Horatius, Sermones, I, 5; 100 f. (No. 128) and Apuleius, Florida, 6 (No. 362). However, while the Jews are the "superstitiosi" par excellence to Apuleius, Plutarch does not consider superstition an exclusive Jewish attribute.[7]*

We find allusions to Jews in Plutarchus, De Stoicorum Repugnantiis, *38, p. 1051 E (No. 257) and in* De Iside et Osiride, *31, p. 363 C–D (No. 259). In the first-mentioned work the Jews are coupled with the Syrians as people who do not have the right concept of the divinity and who worship it from fear. In the latter work the ancestors of the Jewish nation (Hierosolymus and Iudaeus) emerge in connection with the myth of Typhon and his escape on the back of an ass.*

We are hardly warranted to include in this collection a passage found in the Amatorius, *25, p. 771 C. There we learn that one of the sons of the Gallic rebel Sabinus fell in Egypt, presumably in some skirmish: Τῶν δὲ υἱῶν ὁ μὲν ἐν Αἰγύπτῳ πεσὼν ἐτελεύτησεν, ὁ δ' ἕτερος ἄρτι καὶ πρῴην γέγονεν ἐν Δελφοῖς παρ' ἡμῖν, ὄνομα Σαβῖνος. It has been suggested,[8] on insufficient grounds, that his death occurred during the Jewish revolt under Trajan; cf. Cassius Dio, LXVIII, 32 (No. 438).[9]*

---

6 Volkmann's view that the essay was composed in 70 C. E., immediately after the capture of Jerusalem, is apparently based on a fallacious dating of the reference to the Jews in the essay; see R. Volkmann, *Leben, Schriften und Philosophie des Plutarch von Chaeronea,* I, Berlin 1869, p. 78. An early dating is, however, possible; see Ziegler, *op. cit.* (supra, n. 2), p. 72 = PW, XXI, p. 708.

7 The Christians are not mentioned at all in the works of Plutarch; see R. Hirzel, *Plutarch,* Leipzig 1912, pp. 87 f.

8 By Cichorius, pp. 406 ff. Cichorius also attributes the authorship of the essay to Plutarch's son Autobulus.

9 Against Cichorius, see Ziegler, *op. cit.* (supra, n. 2), pp. 78 f. = PW, XXI, pp. 715 f.; Jones, *op. cit.* (supra, n. 2), p. 66.

The Regum et Imperatorum Apophthegmata, *which ranges from Semiramis and the Persian kings to Augustus, should not be attributed to Plutarch.*[10] *The story about events connected with the relationship between Antiochus Sidetes and the Jews (No. 260) may be compared with other sources that narrate the relations between that king and the Jews; cf. Diodorus, XXXIV–XXXV, 1.*

The Vitae *do not include general remarks about Jews or Judaism, but merely furnish us with details of Jewish history, some of which we know from other sources.*

10 Volkmann, *op. cit.* (supra n. 6), pp. 210 ff.; Ziegler, *op. cit.* (supra, n. 2), pp. 226 f. = PW, XXI, pp. 863 f.

Plutarch

255

De Superstitione, 3, p. 166A — Paton

«ὦ βάρβαρ᾽ ἐξευρόντες Ἕλληνες κακά» ⟨Euripides, *Troiades*, 764⟩ τῇ δεισιδαιμονίᾳ, πηλώσεις, καταβορβορώσεις, σαββατισμούς, ῥίψεις ἐπὶ πρόσωπον, αἰσχρὰς προκαθίσεις, ἀλλοκότους προσκυνήσεις.

2 σαββατισμούς] βαπτισμούς Bentley   3 προσκαθίσεις Θ

"Greeks from barbarians finding evil ways!" [Euripides, *The Trojan Women*, 764], because of superstition, such as smearing with
mud, wallowing in filth, keeping of the Sabbath,[1] casting oneself
down with face to the ground, disgraceful besieging of the gods, and
uncouth prostrations.   (trans. F. C. Babbitt, *LCL*)

1 The translation differs here from that of Babbitt.

σαββατισμούς: The word does not occur in the Septuagint, but we find it in
the New Testament (Epistle to the Hebrews iv : 9) and in patristic literature.
Cf. A. Pelletier, *Comptes rendus de l'académie des inscriptions et belles lettres*,
1971, pp. 75 ff.

256

De Superstitione, 8, p. 169C — Paton = F66R

Ἀλλ᾽ Ἰουδαῖοι σαββάτων ὄντων ἐν ἀγνάπτοις καθεζόμενοι, τῶν πολεμίων
κλίμακας προστιθέντων καὶ τὰ τείχη καταλαμβανόντων, οὐκ ἀνέστησαν
ἀλλ᾽ ἔμειναν ὥσπερ ἐν σαγήνῃ μιᾷ τῇ δεισιδαιμονίᾳ συνδεδεμένοι.

1 ἰουδαίοις ΓWYN

But the Jews, because it was the Sabbath day, sat in their places
immovable, while the enemy were planting ladders against the walls
and capturing the defences, and they did not get up, but remained
there, fast bound in the toils of superstition as in one great net.

(trans. F. C. Babbitt, *LCL*)

ἀλλ᾽ Ἰουδαῖοι σαββάτων ὄντων...: The example that best illustrates the story
told by Plutarch is the one related by Agatharchides, apud: Josephus, *Contra
Apionem*, I, 205–211 (No. 30); cf. G. Abernetty, "De Plutarchi Qui Fertur de
Superstitione Libello", Ph.D. Thesis, Königsberg 1911, pp. 45 ff. However, in
view of the fallacious notion about the Sabbath and the nature of the prohibition
to fight on the Sabbath that was generally held by ancient writers, one cannot be
certain that Plutarch actually derived his information from a source referring to
the capture of Jerusalem by Ptolemy Soter. For ancient views on the Sabbath, see
Frontinus, *Strategemata*, II, 1 : 17 (No. 229).

ὥσπερ... μιᾷ τῇ δεισιδαιμονίᾳ συνδεδεμένοι: On Plutarch's attitude to *deisidaim-*

onia, see, e.g., *De Superstitione,* 1, p. 164 E; *De Iside et Osiride,* 11, p. 355 D; 67, p. 378 A. On the use of the word by Plutarch, see P. J. Koets, "Δεισιδαιμονία — A Contribution to the Knowledge of the Religious Terminology in Greek", Ph.D. Thesis, Utrecht 1929, pp. 68 ff. Plutarch seems to have consistently used δεισιδαιμονία to describe a mentality he condemns. See, in general, H. A. Moellering, *Plutarch on Superstition,* Boston 1963.

257

De Stoicorum Repugnantiis, 38, p. 1051 E — Pohlenz & Westman

"Ὅρα γὰρ οἷα Ἰουδαῖοι καὶ Σύροι περὶ θεῶν φρονοῦσιν, ὅρα τὰ τῶν ποιητῶν πόσης ἐμπέπλησται δεισιδαιμονίας· φθαρτὸν δὲ καὶ γενητὸν οὐδεὶς ὡς ἔπος εἰπεῖν διανοεῖται θεόν.

2 γεννητὸν g Bn   ὠνητὸν O

See the opinions held on gods by Jews and Syrians; see with how much superstition are filled the works of the poets. Still, hardly anybody conceived divinity as perishable and begotten.

258

Quaestiones Convivales, IV, 4:4–6:2, pp. 669 C – 672 B — Hubert = F 69 R

«Ὀρθῶς» ἔφη «λέγεις» ὁ Λαμπρίας, «ἀλλ' ἔτι τῷ λόγῳ προσφιλοσοφή-σωμεν. ὁ γὰρ ἐμὸς πάππος εἰώθει λέγειν ἑκάστοτε τοὺς Ἰουδαίους ἐπισκώπτων, ὅτι τὸ δικαιότατον κρέας οὐκ ἐσθίουσιν· ἡμεῖς δὲ φήσομεν δικαιότατον ὄψον εἶναι τὸ ἐκ θαλάττης...»
5 ⟨669 E⟩ Πότερον οἱ Ἰουδαῖοι σεβόμενοι τὴν ὗν ἢ δυσχεραίνοντες ἀπέχονται τῶν κρεῶν.
(5:1) Ἐπεὶ δὲ ταῦτ' ἐρρήθη, βουλομένων τινῶν ἀντικατατείνειν τὸν ἕτερον λόγον ἐκκρούων ὁ Καλλίστρατος ἔφη «πῶς ὑμῖν δοκεῖ λελέχθαι τὸ πρὸς τοὺς Ἰουδαίους, ⟨669 F⟩ ὅτι τὸ δικαιότατον κρέας οὐκ ἐσθίουσιν;»
10 «ὑπερφυῶς» ἔφη ὁ Πολυκράτης, «ἐγὼ δὲ καὶ προσδιαπορῶ, πότερον οἱ ἄνδρες τιμῇ τινι τῶν ὑῶν ἢ μυσαττόμενοι τὸ ζῷον ἀπέχονται τῆς βρώσεως αὐτοῦ· τὰ γὰρ παρ' ἐκείνοις λεγόμενα μύθοις ἔοικεν, εἰ μή τινας ἄρα λόγους σπουδαίους ἔχοντες οὐκ ἐκφέρουσιν.»
(5:2) «Ἐγὼ μὲν τοίνυν» εἶπεν ὁ Καλλίστρατος «οἶμαί τινα τιμὴν
15 τὸ ζῷον ἔχειν παρὰ τοῖς ἀνδράσιν· ⟨670 A⟩ εἰ δὲ δύσμορφον ἢ ὗς καὶ θολερόν, ⟨ἀλλ' οὐ⟩, κανθάρου καὶ γρυ... καὶ κροκοδείλου καὶ ⟨αἰλο⟩ύρου

16 ⟨ἀλλ' οὐ⟩ Turnebus / καὶ κροκοδείλου Aldina   ἐκ κροκοδείλου T
⟨αἰλο⟩ ύρου Basileensis

τὴν ὄψιν ἀτοπώτερον ἢ τὴν φύσιν ἀμουσότερον· οἷς ὡς ἁγιωτάτοις
ἱερεῖς Αἰγυπτίων ⟨ἄλλοις⟩ ἄλλοι προσφέρονται, τὴν δ᾽ ὗν ἀπὸ χρησ-
τῆς αἰτίας τιμᾶσθαι λέγουσι· πρώτη γὰρ σχίσασα τῷ προὔχοντι τοῦ
20 ῥύγχους, ὥς φασι, τὴν γῆν ἴχνος ἀρόσεως ἔθηκεν καὶ τὸ τῆς ὕνεως
ὑφηγήσατ᾽ ἔργον· ὅθεν καὶ τοὔνομα γενέσθαι τῷ ἐργαλείῳ λέγουσιν
ἀπὸ τῆς ὑός. οἱ δὲ τὰ μαλθακὰ καὶ κοῖλα τῆς χώρας Αἰγύπτιοι
γεωργοῦντες οὐδ᾽ ἀρότου δέονται τὸ παράπαν· ⟨670 B⟩ ἀλλ᾽ ὅταν ὁ
Νεῖλος ἀπορρέῃ καταβρέξας τὰς ἀρούρας, ἐπακολουθοῦντες τὰς ὗς
25 κατέβαλον, αἱ δὲ χρησάμεναι πάτῳ καὶ ὀρυχῇ ταχὺ τὴν γῆν ἔτρεψαν
ἐκ βάθους καὶ τὸν σπόρον ἀπέκρυψαν. οὐ δεῖ δὲ θαυμάζειν, εἰ διὰ
τοῦτό τινες ὗς οὐκ ἐσθίουσιν, ἑτέρων ζῴων μείζονας ἐπ᾽ αἰτίαις γλίσχραις,
ἐνίων δὲ καὶ πάνυ γελοίαις, τιμὰς ἐχόντων παρὰ τοῖς βαρβάροις.
τὴν μὲν γὰρ μυγαλῆν ἐκτεθειάσθαι λέγουσιν ὑπ᾽ Αἰγυπτίων τυφλὴν
30 οὖσαν, ὅτι τὸ σκότος τοῦ φωτὸς ἡγοῦντο πρεσβύτερον· τίκτεσθαι
δ᾽ αὐτὴν ἐκ μυῶν πέμπτῃ γενεᾷ νουμηνίας οὔσης· ἔτι δὲ μειοῦσθαι
τὸ ἧπαρ ἐν τοῖς ἀφανισμοῖς τῆς σελήνης. τὸν ⟨δὲ⟩ λέοντα τῷ ἡλίῳ
συνοικειοῦσιν ⟨670 C⟩ ὅτι τῶν γαμψωνύχων τετραπόδων βλέποντα
τίκτει μόνος, κοιμᾶται δ᾽ ἀκαρὲς χρόνου καὶ ὑπολάμπει τὰ ὄμματα
35 καθεύδοντος· κρῆναι δὲ [καὶ] κατὰ χασμάτων λεοντείων ἐξιᾶσι
κρουνούς, ὅτι Νεῖλος ἐπάγει νέον ὕδωρ ταῖς Αἰγυπτίων ἀρούραις
ἡλίου τὸν λέοντα παροδεύοντος. τὴν δ᾽ ἶβίν φασιν ἐκκολαφθεῖσαν
εὐθὺς ἕλκειν δύο δραχμάς, ὅσον ἄρτι παιδίου γεγονότος καρδίαν·
ποιεῖν δὲ τῇ τῶν ποδῶν ἀποστάσει πρὸς ἀλλήλους καὶ πρὸς
40 τὸ ῥύγχος ἰσόπλευρον τρίγωνον. καὶ τί ἄν τις Αἰγυπτίους αἰτιῷτο
τῆς τοσαύτης ἀλογίας, ὅπου καὶ τοὺς Πυθαγορικοὺς ἱστοροῦσιν καὶ
ἀλεκτρυόνα λευκὸν ⟨670 D⟩ σέβεσθαι καὶ τῶν θαλαττίων μάλιστα
τρίγλης καὶ ἀκαλήφης ἀπέχεσθαι, τοὺς δ᾽ ἀπὸ Ζωροάστρου μάγους
τιμᾶν μὲν ἐν τοῖς μάλιστα τὸν χερσαῖον ἐχῖνον, ἐχθαίρειν δὲ τοὺς
45 ἐνύδρους μῦς καὶ τὸν ἀποκτείνοντα πλείστους θεοφιλῆ καὶ μακάριον
νομίζειν; οἶμαι δὲ καὶ τοὺς Ἰουδαίους, εἴπερ ἐβδελύττοντο τὴν ὗν,
ἀποκτείνειν ἄν, ὥσπερ οἱ μάγοι τοὺς μῦς ἀποκτείνουσι· νῦν δ᾽ ὁμοίως
τῷ φαγεῖν τὸ ἀνελεῖν ἀπόρρητόν ἐστιν αὐτοῖς. καὶ ἴσως ἔχει λόγον,

---

17 ἀτοπώτερον Basileensis ἀτοπωτάτην T / ἀμουσότερον] μυσαρώτερον Hirschig
18 ἱερεῖς] ⟨καὶ⟩ ἱεροῖς Pohlenz / ⟨ἄλλοις⟩ Basileensis   18–19 ἀπὸ χρη-
στῆς αἰτίας Madvig ἀποχρηστῆσαι καὶ καὶ T   19–20 τοῦ ῥύγχους Reiske
τῆς ὀρυχῆς T   22 ἀπὸ τῆς ὑός del. Hubert   23 ἀρότρου Aldina
24 ἀπορρέῃ Stephanus ἀπορέῃι T / ἐπακολουθοῦντες ⟨καὶ σπείροντες⟩ Doehner
25 εἰσέβαλλον Reiske / ἔστρεψαν Aldina   32 ⟨δὲ⟩ Reiske   35 δὲ κατὰ
χασμάτων Turnebus δὲ καὶ κατασχάμματα τῶν T   38 δραχμάς Aldina
δαχμὰς T / καρδίαν Aldina καρδία T   39 ποδῶν Basileensis
πόνων T / ἀποστάσει Hubert ἀποτάσει T / ἀλλήλους Basileensis ἄλλους T

551

ὡς τὸν ὄνον [δὲ] ἀναφήναντα πηγὴν αὐτοῖς ὕδατος τιμῶσιν, οὕτως
50 καὶ τὴν ὗν σέβεσθαι σπόρου καὶ ἀρότου διδάσκαλον γενομένην· ⟨εἰ μή,⟩
νὴ Δία, καὶ τοῦ λαγωοῦ φήσει τις ⟨670E⟩ ἀπέχεσθαι τοὺς ἄνδρας
ὡς μυσερὸν καὶ ἀκάθαρτον δυσχεραίνοντας τὸ ζῷον.»
(5:3) «Οὐ δ⟨ῆτ'⟩» εἶπεν⟩ ὁ Λαμπρίας ὑπολ⟨αβών⟩ «ἀλλὰ τοῦ μὲν
λαγωοῦ ⟨φείδον⟩ται διὰ τὴν πρὸς τὸν * μένον ὑπ' αὐτῶν μυ...στα
55 θηρίον ἐμφερέστατον * ὁ γὰρ λαγὼς μεγέθους ἔοικε καὶ πάχους
ἐνδεὴς ὄνος εἶναι· καὶ γὰρ ἡ χρόα καὶ τὰ ὦτα καὶ τῶν ὀμμάτων ἡ
λιπαρότης καὶ τὸ λαμυρὸν ἔοικε θαυμασίως· ὥστε μηδὲν οὕτω *
μηδὲ μικρὸν μεγάλῳ τὴν μορφὴν ὅμοιον γεγονέναι. εἰ μὴ νὴ Δία καὶ
πρὸς τὰς ποιότητας αἰγυπτιάζοντες τὴν ὠκύτητα τοῦ ζῴου θεῖον ἡγοῦνται
60 καὶ τὴν ἀκρίβειαν τῶν αἰσθητηρίων· ⟨670 F⟩ ὅ τε γὰρ ὀφθαλμὸς ἄτ-
ρυτός ἐστιν αὐτῶν, ὥστε καὶ καθεύδειν ἀναπεπταμένοις τοῖς ὄμμασιν,
ὀξυηκοΐᾳ τε δοκεῖ διαφέρειν, ἣν Αἰγύπτιοι θαυμάσαντες ἐν τοῖς ἱεροῖς
γράμμασιν ἀκοὴν σημαίνουσιν οὓς λαγωοῦ γράφοντες. τὸ δ' ὕειον
κρέας οἱ ἄνδρες ἀφοσιοῦσθαι ⟨δο⟩κοῦσιν, ὅτι μάλιστα... οἱ βάρβαροι
65 τὰς ἐπὶ ⟨χρωτὸς⟩ λεύκας καὶ λέπρας δυσχεραίνουσι καὶ τῇ προσβολῇ
τὰ τοιαῦτα καταβόσκεσθαι πάθη τοὺς ἀνθρώπους οἴονται, ⟨671A⟩ πᾶσαν
δ' ὗν ὑπὸ τὴν γαστέρα λέπρας ἀνάπλεων καὶ ψωρικῶν ἐξανθημάτων
ὁρῶμεν, ἃ δή, καχεξίας τινὸς ἐγγενομένης τῷ σώματι καὶ φθορᾶς,
ἐπιτρέχειν δοκεῖ τοῖς * σώμασιν. οὐ μὴν ἀλλὰ καὶ τὸ θολερὸν περὶ
70 τὴν δίαιταν τοῦ θρέμματος ἔχει τινὰ πονηρίαν· οὐδὲν γὰρ ἄλλο βορβόρῳ
χαῖρον οὕτω καὶ τόποις ῥυπαροῖς καὶ ἀκαθάρτοις ὁρῶμεν, ἔξω λόγου
τιθέμενοι τὰ τὴν γένεσιν καὶ τὴν φύσιν ἐν αὐτοῖς ἔχοντα τούτοις. λέγουσι
δὲ καὶ τὰ ὄμματα τῶν ὑῶν οὕτως ἐγκεκλάσθαι καὶ κατεσπάσθαι ταῖς
ὄψεσιν, ὥστε μηδενὸς ἀντιλαμβάνεσθαι μηδέποτε ⟨671B⟩ τῶν ἄνω μηδὲ
75 προσορᾶν τὸν οὐρανόν, ἂν μὴ φερομένων ὑπτίων ἀναστροφήν τινα παρὰ
φύσιν αἱ κόραι λάβωσιν· διὸ καὶ μάλιστα κραυγῇ χρώμενον τὸ ζῷον
ἡσυχάζειν, ὅταν οὕτω φέρηται, καὶ σιωπᾶν κατατεθαμβημένον ἀηθείᾳ
τὰ οὐράνια καὶ κρείττονι φόβῳ τοῦ βοᾶν συνεχόμενον. εἰ δὲ δεῖ καὶ

49 δὲ del. Basileensis   50 ⟨εἰ μή⟩ Xylander   51 φήσει Reiske   φησί Τ
53 ⟨ῆτ' εἶπεν⟩ Hubert / ὑπολ⟨αβών⟩ Aldina   54 ⟨φείδον⟩ται Doehner
54–55 διὰ τὴν πρὸς τὸν ⟨ὄνον τιμώ⟩μενον ὑπ' αὐτῶν μά⟨λι⟩στα θηρίων ἐμφέρειαν
Franke   διὰ τὸ εἶναι πρὸς τὸ ⟨τιμώ⟩μενον ὑπ' αὐτῶν μά⟨λι⟩στα θηρίον
ἐμφερέστατον Hubert   55–56 πάχους ἐνδεὴς ὄνος Doehner   τάχους ἐν
δεινοῖς Τ   57 λαμυρὸν Reiske   ἁλμυρὸν Τ   58 μηδὲ del. Doehner
59 ποιότητας Reiske   ὁμοιότητας Τ   61 αὐτῶν] αὐτῷ Reiske
62 τε Hubert   δὲ Τ   63 σημαίνουσιν οὓς λαγωοῦ Reiske   σημαίνουσι
τοὺς λαγωοὺς Τ   64 ⟨δο⟩κοῦσιν Stephanus / μάλιστα ⟨πάντων⟩ Bernardakis   65 ἐπὶ ⟨χρωτὸς⟩ λεύκας Hubert   ἐπι... λευκίας Τ   66 πᾶσαν
Stephanus   ἐς ἂν Τ   67 ἐξανθημάτων Stephanus   ἐξανθησάντων Τ
68 ἐγγενομένης Reiske   ἐκγενομένης Τ   72 τὰ Reiske   μετὰ Τ
73 ἐγκεκλίσθαι Ziegler   77 ἀηθείᾳ Ziegler   ἀηθίαι Τ

552

τὰ μυθικὰ προσλαβεῖν, λέγεται μὲν ὁ Ἄδωνις ὑπὸ τοῦ συὸς διαφθα-
80 ρῆναι, τὸν δ᾽ Ἄδωνιν οὐχ ἕτερον ἀλλὰ Διόνυσον εἶναι νομίζουσιν, καὶ
πολλὰ τῶν τελουμένων ἑκατέρῳ περὶ τὰς ἑορτὰς βεβαιοῖ τὸν λόγον· οἱ δὲ
παιδικὰ τοῦ Διονύσου γεγονέναι· καὶ Φανοκλῆς, ἐρωτικὸς ἀνήρ, οὐ...
δήπου πεποίηκεν.
⟨671C⟩ «ἠδ᾽ ὡς θεῖον Ἄδωνιν ὀρειφοίτης Διόνυσος ⟨cf. J.U. Powell,
85 Collectanea Alexandrina, Oxford 1925, p. 108⟩ ἥρπασεν, ἠγαθέην
Κύπρον ἐποιχόμενος.»

Τίς ὁ παρ᾽ Ἰουδαίοις θεός

(6:1) Θαυμάσας οὖν τὸ ἐπὶ πᾶσι ῥηθὲν ὁ Σύμμαχος «ἆρ᾽» ἔφη «σὺ τὸν
πατριώτην θεόν, ὦ Λαμπρία, «εὔιον ὀρσιγύναικα μαινομέναις ἀνθέοντα
90 τιμαῖσι Διόνυσον ἐγγράφεις καὶ ὑποποιεῖς τοῖς Ἑβραίων ἀπορρήτοις;
ἢ τῷ ὄντι λόγος ἔστι τις ὁ τοῦτον ἐκείνῳ τὸν αὐτὸν ἀποφαίνων;» ὁ
δὲ Μοιραγένης ὑπολαβὼν «ἔα τοῦτον» εἶπεν· «ἐγὼ γὰρ Ἀθηναῖος ὢν
ἀποκρίνομαί σοι καὶ λέγω μηδέν᾽ ἄλλον εἶναι· καὶ τὰ μὲν πολλὰ τῶν
εἰς τοῦτο τεκμηρίων μόνοις ἐστὶ ῥητὰ καὶ διδακτὰ τοῖς μυουμένοις
95 παρ᾽ ἡμῖν εἰς τὴν τριετηρικὴν παντέλειαν. ⟨671D⟩ ἃ δὲ λόγῳ διελθεῖν
οὐ κεκώλυται πρὸς φίλους ἄνδρας, ἄλλως τε καὶ παρ᾽ οἶνον ἐπὶ τοῖς
τοῦ θεοῦ δώροις, ἂν οὗτοι κελεύωσι, λέγειν ἕτοιμος.»
(6:2) Πάντων οὖν κελευόντων καὶ δεομένων «πρῶτον μέν» ἔφη,
«τῆς μεγίστης καὶ τελειοτάτης ἑορτῆς παρ᾽ αὐτοῖς ὁ καιρός ἐστιν
100 καὶ ὁ τρόπος Διονύσῳ προσήκων. τὴν γὰρ λεγομένην νηστείαν
⟨ἄγοντες⟩ ἀκμάζοντι τρυγητῷ τραπέζας τε προτίθενται παντοδαπῆς
ὀπώρας ὑπὸ σκηναῖς καὶ καλιάσιν ἐκ κλημάτων μάλιστα καὶ κιττοῦ
διαπεπλεγμέναις· καὶ τὴν προτέραν τῆς ἑορτῆς σκηνὴν ὀνομάζουσιν.
⟨671E⟩ ὀλίγαις δ᾽ ὕστερον ἡμέραις ἄλλην ἑορτήν, οὐκ * ἂν δι᾽ αἰνιγ-
105 μάτων ἀλλ᾽ ἄντικρυς Βάκχου καλουμένην, τελοῦσιν. ἔστι δὲ καὶ
κραδηφορία τις ἑορτὴ καὶ θυρσοφορία παρ᾽ αὐτοῖς, ἐν ᾗ θύρσους ἔχοντες
εἰς τὸ ἱερὸν εἰσίασιν· εἰσελθόντες δ᾽ ὅ τι δρῶσιν, οὐκ ἴσμεν, εἰκὸς δὲ
βακχείαν εἶναι τὰ ποιούμενα· καὶ γὰρ σάλπιγξι μικραῖς, ὥσπερ
Ἀργεῖοι τοῖς Διονυσίοις, ἀνακαλούμενοι τὸν θεὸν χρῶνται, καὶ κι-
110 θαρίζοντες ἕτεροι προΐασιν, οὓς αὐτοὶ Λευίτας προσονομάζουσιν, εἴτε παρὰ τὸν Λύσιον εἴτε μᾶλλον παρὰ τὸν Εὔιον τῆς ἐπικλήσεως
γεγενημένης. οἶμαι δὲ καὶ τὴν τῶν σαββάτων ἑορτὴν μὴ παντάπασιν

82 οὖ ⟨τω⟩ Pohlenz   οὐ ⟨κ εἰκῇ⟩ Hubert   84 ἠδ᾽ ὡς Paton   ἠδὼς T   εἰδὼς
Aldina   86 Κύπρον Xylander   κύπριν T   88 πᾶσι Reiske   πᾶν T
95 εἰς del. Ziegler   101 ⟨ἄγοντες⟩ Madvig   ⟨ἀγαγόντες⟩ Heinrich Lewy
102 καλιάσιν Scaliger   καθιᾶσιν T   /   κλημάτων Aldina   κλημμάτων T
104 οὐκ αὖ Reiske   105 καλουμένην Reiske   καλουμένου T
106 κραδηφορία Turnebus   κρατηφορία T   110 προΐασιν Reiske   προσιᾶσιν T
111 Εὔιον Aldina   εὔειον T   112 σαββάτων Aldina   σαμβάτων T

ἀπροσδιόννσον εἶναι· ⟨671F⟩ Σάβους γὰρ καὶ νῦν ἔτι πολλοὶ τοὺς
Βάκχους καλοῦσιν καὶ ταύτην ἀφιᾶσι τὴν φωνὴν ὅταν ὀργιάζωσι
115 τῷ θεῷ, ⟨οὗ πίστω⟩σιν ἔστι δήπου καὶ παρὰ Δημοσθένους λαβεῖν
καὶ παρὰ Μενάνδρου, καὶ οὐκ ἀπὸ ⟨τρό⟩που τις ἂν φαίη τοὔνομα πε-
ποιῆσθαι πρός τινα σόβησιν ἢ κατέχει τοὺς βακχεύοντας· ⟨672A⟩ αὐτοὶ δὲ τῷ λόγῳ μαρτυροῦσιν, ὅταν σάββατα τελῶσι, μάλιστα μὲν
πίνειν καὶ οἰνοῦσθαι παρακαλοῦντες ἀλλήλους, ὅταν δὲ κωλύῃ τι μεῖζον,
120 ἀπογεύεσθαί γε πάντως ἀκράτου νομίζοντες. καὶ ταῦτα μὲν εἰκότα φαίη
τις ἂν εἶναι· κατὰ κράτος ⟨δὲ τοὺς⟩ ἐναντίους πρῶτον μὲν ὁ ἀρχιερεὺς
ἐλέγχει, μιτρηφόρος τε προϊὼν ἐν ταῖς ἑορταῖς καὶ νεβρίδα χρυσόπαστον
ἐνημμένος, χιτῶνα δὲ ποδήρη φορῶν καὶ κοθόρνους, κώδωνες δὲ πολλοὶ
κατακρέμανται τῆς ἐσθῆτος, ὑποκομποῦντες ἐν τῷ βαδίζειν, ὡς καὶ παρ'
125 ἡμῖν· ψόφοις δὲ χρῶνται περὶ τὰ νυκτέλια, καὶ χαλκοκρότους τὰς τοῦ
θεοῦ τιθήνας προσαγορεύουσιν ⟨672B⟩ καὶ ὁ δεικνύμενος ἐν τοῖς *
ἐναντίοις τοῦ νεὼ θύρσος ἐντετυπωμένος καὶ τύμπανα· ταῦτα γὰρ οὐδενὶ
δήπουθεν ἄλλῳ θεῶν ἢ Διονύσῳ προσῆκεν. ἔτι τοίνυν μέλι μὲν οὐ προσφέρουσι ταῖς ἱερουργίαις, ὅτι δοκεῖ φθείρειν τὸν οἶνον κεραννύμενον καὶ
130 τοῦτ' ἦν σπονδὴ καὶ μέθυ, πρὶν ἄμπελον φανῆναι· καὶ μέχρι νῦν τῶν τε
βαρβάρων οἱ μὴ ποιοῦντες οἶνον μελίτειον πίνουσιν, ὑποφαρμάσσοντες
τὴν γλυκύτητα οἰνώδεσι ῥίζαις καὶ αὐστηραῖς, Ἕλληνές τε νηφάλια
ταὐτὰ καὶ μελίσπονδα θύουσιν, ὡς ἀντίθετον φύσιν μάλιστα τοῦ μέλιτος
πρὸς τὸν οἶνον ἔχοντος. ὅτι δὲ τοῦτο νομίζουσι, κἀκεῖνο σημεῖον οὐ
135 μικρόν ἐστι, τὸ πολλῶν τιμωριῶν οὐσῶν παρ' αὐτοῖς, μίαν εἶναι μάλιστα
διαβεβλημένην, τὴν οἶνον τοὺς κολαζομένους ἀπείργουσαν, ὅσον ἂν τάξῃ
χρόνον ὁ κύριος τῆς κολάσεως· τοὺς δ' οὕτω κολα...

113 ἔτι Stephanus   ὅτι Τ   115 ⟨οὗ πίστω⟩ σιν Hubert   116 ⟨τρό⟩ που
Stephanus / τοὔνομα Turnebus   τοῦ ἅμα Τ   117 πρός τινα Stephanus
πρὸς τὴν Τ / σόβησιν Reiske   ἀσέβησιν Τ   118 σάββατα τελῶσι Hubert
σάμβα τιμῶσι Τ   121 ⟨δὲ τοὺς⟩ ἐναντίους Madvig   ἐν αὐτοῖς Τ
125 νυκτέλια Turnebus   νῦν τέλεια Τ / χαλκοκρότους τὰς Coraes   χαλκο-
κροδύστας Τ   127 ἐναντίοις] ἐνωπίοις Wyttenbach / θύρσος Aldina
θύρσους Τ   128 θεῶν Bernardakis   θεῷ Τ / προσήκει Meziriac
132 οἰνώδεσι] ὀπώδεσι Hirschig

"You are right", said Lamprias, "but let us add a little to our speculations. My grandfather used to say on every occasion, in derision
of the Jews, that what they abstained from was precisely the most
legitimate meat. But we shall say that of all delicacies the most
legitimate kind is that from the sea."...

Question 5

Whether the Jews abstain from pork because of reverence or aversion
for the pig

(5:1) When he had finished, and some of those present would have made an extended reply to his arguments, Callistratus headed them off by saying, "What do you think of the assertion that it is precisely the most proper type of meat that the Jews avoid eating?" "I heartily agree with it", replied Polycrates, "but I have another question: do they abstain from eating pork by reason of some special respect for hogs or from abhorrence of the creature? Their own accounts sound like pure myth, but perhaps they have some serious reasons which they do not publish."

(5:2) "My impression", said Callistratus, "is that the beast enjoys a certain respect among that folk; granted that he is ugly and dirty, still he is no more absurd in appearance or crude in disposition than dung-beetle, crocodile, or cat, each of which is treated as sacred by a different group of Egyptian priests. They say, however, that the pig is honoured for a good reason: according to the story, it was the first to cut the soil with its projecting snout, thus producing a furrow and teaching man the function of a ploughshare. Incidentally, this is the origin, they say, of the word *hynis* (from *hys*, 'swine') for that implement. The Egyptians who cultivate the soft soil of their low-lying areas have no use for ploughing at all. After the Nile over-flows and soaks their acres, they follow the receding water and unload the pigs, which by trampling and rooting quickly turn over the deep soil and cover the seed. We need not be surprised if some people do not eat pork for this reason. Other animals receive even greater honours among the barbarians for slight and in some cases utterly ridiculous reasons. The field-mouse is said to have been deified among the Egyptians because of its blindness, since they regarded darkness as superior to light; and they thought that the field-mouse was born of ordinary mice every fifth generation at the new moon, and also that its liver was reduced in size at the dark of the moon. "They associate the lion with the sun because it, alone of quadrupeds that have claws, bears young that can see at birth, sleeps only for a moment, and has eyes that gleam in sleep. Egyptian fountains pour forth their water through lion mouths, because the Nile brings new water to the fields of Egypt when the sun passes through Leo. They say that the ibis when hatched weighs two drachms, as much as the heart of a new-born infant, and forms an equilateral triangle by the position of its outspread feet and bill. How could anyone blame the Egyptians for such irrationality when it is recorded that the Pytha-goreans respect even a white cock, and that they abstain particularly from the red mullet and the sea anemone among marine animals?

Or when we remember that the Magi, followers of Zoroaster, especially esteem the hedgehog and abominate water mice, regarding the person who kills the greatest number of the latter as blest and dear to the gods? So I think the Jews would kill pigs if they hated them, as the Magi kill water mice; but in fact it is just as unlawful for Jews to destroy pigs as to eat them. Perhaps it is consistent that they should revere the pig who taught them sowing and plowing, inasmuch as they honour the ass who first led them to a spring of water. Otherwise, so help me, someone will say that the Jews abstain from the hare because they can't stomach anything so filthy and unclean."

(5:3) "No indeed", countered Lamprias, "they abstain from the hare because of its very close resemblance to the ass which they prize so highly. The hare appears to be simply an ass inferior in bulk and size; for its coat, ears, bright eyes, and salacity are amazingly similar, so much so that nothing small ever so closely resembled something large. Perhaps, to be sure, following the Egyptians even in their conception of traits of animals, they regard the swiftness of the creature and the keenness of its senses as something divine. For its eye is untiring: the hare even sleeps with its eyes wide open. In acuteness of hearing it is found to be unrivalled; the Egyptians admire this so much that in their hieroglyphics they draw a hare's ear to represent the idea of hearing.

"The Jews apparently abominate pork because barbarians especially abhor skin diseases like lepra and white scale, and believe that human beings are ravaged by such maladies through contagion. Now we observe that every pig is covered on the under side by lepra and scaly eruptions, which, if there is general weakness and emaciation, are thought to spread rapidly over the body. What is more, the very filthiness of their habits produces an inferior quality of meat. We observe no other creature so fond of mud and of dirty, unclean places, if we leave out of account those animals that have their origin and natural habitat there. People say also that the eyes of swine are so twisted and drawn down that they can never catch sight of anything above them or see the sky unless they are carried upside down so that their eyes are given an unnatural tilt upward. Wherefore the animal, which usually squeals immoderately, holds still when it is carried in this position, and remains silent because it is astonished at the unfamiliar sight of the heavenly expanse and restrained from squealing by an overpowering fear. If it is legitimate to bring in mythology too, Adonis is said to have been slain by the boar. People hold Adonis to be none other than Dionysus, a belief supported by many of the rites at the festivals of both; though others have it that he was the favourite of Dionysus. Phanocles, an erotic poet, surely knew whereof he spoke when he wrote the following lines: 'And how mountain-coursing Dionysus seized the divine Adonis, as the god did visit holy Cyprus.' "

Question 6

Who the god of the Jews is

(6:1) Symmachus, surprised at this last statement, asked, "Lamprias, are you enrolling your national god in the calendar of the Hebrews and insinuating into their secret rites 'him of the orgiastic cry, exciter of women, Dionysus, glorified with mad honours'? Is there actually some tradition that demonstrates identity between him and Adonis?" Moeragenes interposed, "Never mind him. I as an Athenian can answer you and say that the god is no other. Most of the relevant proofs can lawfully be pronounced or divulged only to those of us who have been initiated into the Perfect Mysteries celebrated every other year, but what I am going to speak of is not forbidden in conversation with friends, especially over after-dinner wine, while we are enjoying the god's own bounty. I am ready to speak if these gentlemen urge me."

(6:2) At this, all did urge him and beg him to go on. "First", he said, "the time and character of the greatest, most sacred holiday of the Jews clearly befit Dionysus. When they celebrate their so-called Fast, at the height of the vintage, they set out tables of all sorts of fruit under tents and huts plaited for the most part of vines and ivy. They call the first of the days of the feast Tabernacles. A few days later they celebrate another festival, this time identified with Bacchus not through obscure hints but plainly called by his name, a festival that is a sort of 'Procession of Branches' or 'Thyrsus Procession,' in which they enter the temple each carrying a thyrsus. What they do after entering we do not know, but it is probable that the rite is a Bacchic revelry, for in fact they use little trumpets to invoke their god as do the Argives at their Dionysia. Others of them advance playing harps; these players are called in their language *Levites*, either from *Lysios* (Releaser) or, better, from *Evius* (God of the Cry). "I believe that even the feast of the Sabbath is not completely unrelated to Dionysus. Many even now call the Bacchants *Sabi* and utter that cry when celebrating the god. Testimony to this can be found in Demosthenes and Menander. You would not be far off the track if you attributed the use of this name *Sabi* to the strange excitement (*sobesis*) that possesses the celebrants. The Jews themselves testify to a connection with Dionysus when they keep the Sabbath by inviting each other to drink and to enjoy wine; when more important business interferes with this custom, they regularly take at least a sip of neat wine. Now thus far one might call the argument only probable; but the opposition is quite demolished, in the first place by the High Priest, who leads the procession at their festival wearing a mitre and clad in a gold-embroidered fawnskin, a robe reaching to the ankles, and buskins, with many bells attached to his clothes and ringing below him as he walks. All this corresponds to our custom. In the second place, they also have noise as an element in their nocturnal festivals, and call the nurses of the god 'bronze rattlers.' The carved thyrsus in the relief on the pediment of the Temple and the drums (provide other parallels). All this surely befits (they might say) no divinity but Dionysus. Further, the Jews use no honey in their religious services because they believe that honey spoils the wine with which it is mixed; and they used honey as libation and in place of wine before the vine was discovered. Even up to the present time those of the barbarians who do not make wine drink mead, counteracting the sweetness somewhat by the use of winelike bitter roots. The Greeks, on the other hand, offer the same libations as 'sober libations' and *meli-sponda* on the principle that there is a particular opposition between honey and wine. To show that what I have said is the practice of the Jews we may find no slight confirmation in the fact that among many penalties employed among them the one most disliked is the exclusion of a convicted offender from the use of wine for such a period as the sentencing judge may prescribe. Those thus punished..." (trans. H. B. Hoffleit LCL,)

---

4 *Λαμπρίας*: A brother of Plutarch.
ὁ γὰρ ἐμὸς πάππος: Also named Lamprias. He appears often as an interlocutor in *Quaestiones Convivales*; see Ziegler, *op. cit.*, pp. 6 f. = PW, XXI, pp. 642 f.; R. H. Barrow, *Plutarch and His Times*, London 1967, p. 16.
5:1 *Καλλίστρατος*: A sophist who excelled as a host at Aidepsos.
Πολυκράτης: From an old family of Sicyon and a descendant of the Achaian strategos Aratus; see C. P. Jones, *Plutarch and Rome*, Oxford 1971, p. 40.
Callistratus maintains that the Jews' veneration of the pig does not differ in principle from the attitude of Egyptian priests towards animals that are not superior to swine in form and nature. The veneration of swine derives from feelings of gratitude for the part they played in agriculture; cf. *De Iside et Osiride*, 74, p. 380 F. This explanation certainly accords with that suggested by the Egyptian priests in Diodorus, I, 87. The population's gratitude to animals that have served and benefited

Plutarch

mankind ranks among the three reasons for animal worship, though Diodorus does not refer to the pig as one of these beneficial animals. However, Aelianus tells us, on the authority of Eudoxus, that the Egyptians do not sacrifice sows, which are useful to agriculture, since sows press the seed into the moist soil, thereby retaining their fertility and preventing their consumption by birds; see Aelianus, *Historia Animalium*, X, 16. On the Egyptian abstention from pork, see Sextus Empiricus, III, 223 (No. 334).

In this connection it is worthwhile referring to a fragment of the story told by Agathocles (third century B. C. E.?) in his History of Cyzicus, which is paralleled by Neanthes in his περὶ τελετῶν; cf. Athenaeus, *Deipnosophistae*, IX, 18, p. 376 A = F. Gr. Hist., III, B 472, F 1a = II, A 84, F 15. Here we read about the service that a sow rendered to Zeus. It was for this reason that the Cretans abstain from eating pork, and the people of Praisos offer sacrifices to the pig.

ὡς τὸν ὄνον ἀναφήναντα πηγὴν αὐτοῖς ὕδατος τιμῶσιν: Cf. Tacitus, *Historiae*, V, 3–4 (No. 281) and the commentary ad loc.; see also A.H. Krappe, *Classical Philology*, XLII (1947), p. 231.

καὶ τοῦ λαγωοῦ φήσει τις ἀπέχεσθαι τοὺς ἄνδρας: On the Jewish abstention from eating hare, see Lev. xi : 6, where the hare precedes the pig among the forbidden animals.

5:3 Lamprias represents the opposite view, namely, that the Jews refrain from eating pork because they abhor it. For the explanation that the Jewish abhorrence of pork derives from the fear of leprosy, to which the pig is prone, see Manetho, apud: Aelianus, *loc. cit.*: ἀκούω δὲ καὶ Μανέθωνα τὸν Αἰγύπτιον σοφίας ἐς ἄκρον ἐληλακότα ἄνδρα εἰπεῖν ὅτι γάλακτος ὑείου ὁ γευσάμενος ἀλφῶν ὑποπίμπλαται καὶ λέπρας· μισοῦσι δὲ ἄρα οἱ Ἀσιανοὶ πάντες τάδε τὰ πάθη. πεπιστεύκασι δὲ Αἰγύπτιοι τὴν ὗν καὶ ἡλίῳ καὶ σελήνῃ ἐχθίστην εἶναι.

Φανοκλῆς: An elegiac poet; see J. U. Powell, *Collectanea Alexandrina*, Oxford 1925, pp. 106 ff.; Blumenthal, PW, XIX, pp. 1781 ff.

τίς ὁ παρ' Ἰουδαίοις θεός: Cf. Lydus, *De Mensibus*, IV 53, p. 109 (Wünsch): Ὅτι πολλὴ τοῖς θεολόγοις διαφωνὴ περὶ τοῦ παρ' Ἑβραίων τιμωμένου θεοῦ καὶ γέγονε καὶ ἔστιν.

6:1 Σύμμαχος: A man from Nicopolis; see *Quaestiones Convivales*, IV, 4:2, p. 667 E.

πατριώτην θεόν: An allusion to Dionysus' Boeotian descent.

τοῖς Ἑβραίων ἀπορρήτοις: Plutarch belongs to the generation of writers who started to use "Hebrews" instead of or together with "Jews"; see the commentary to Charax of Pergamon, apud: Stephanus Byzantius (No. 335). In the earlier chapters, in the speeches of Callistratus and Lamprias, the term "Jews" is employed; the same is true in *Vita Pompei*, 45 (No. 262); *Vita Ciceronis*, 7 : 6 (No. 263); *Vita Antonii*, 3 (No. 264); 61 (No. 267); 71 (No. 268); *Vita Othonis*, 15 : 6 (No. 272); *De Superstitione*, 8 (No. 256); *De Stoicorum Repugnantiis*, 38 (No. 257). Ἑβραῖοι, on the other hand, is found, apart from the present passage, in *Vita Antonii*, 27 : 4 (No. 265).

Μοιραγένης: This Athenian argues in favour of identifying the Jewish form of worship with that of the god Dionysus in a way that displays a rather sympathetic attitude towards the Jewish religion. On Jews in Athens in the Hellenistic and early Roman ages, see *IG* 2, No. 12609; see also L. Robert, *Hellenica*, III, Paris 1946, p. 101; Acts xvii : 17; *IG* 2, Nos. 8934, 10219–10220 (Samaritan women); L. B. Urdahl, *Symbolae Osloenses*, XLIII (1968), pp. 39 ff.; J. & L. Robert, *REG*,

559

LXXXII (1969), pp. 453 f. It emerges clearly from Moiragenes' argument that he thinks of himself as the interpreter of the idea, and not as its originator.

6:2 The supposed Dionysiac nature of the Jewish worship is well known to Tacitus, who disposes of it in the strongest terms; see Tacitus, *Historiae*, V, 5 (No. 281). For the view that the Temple of Jerusalem belongs to Dionysus, see Lydus, *De Mensibus*, IV, 53, p. 109, ll. 18 ff. (Wünsch): "Ελληνες δὲ τὸν 'Ορφέως Διόνυσον, ὅτι, ὡς αὐτοί φασι, πρὸς τῷ ἀδύτῳ τοῦ ἐν 'Ιεροσολύμοις ναοῦ ἐξ ἑκατέρων σταθμῶν τὸ πρὶν ἄμπελοι ἀπὸ χρυσοῦ πεποιημένοι ἀνέστελλον τὰ παραπετάσματα ἐκ πορφύρας καὶ κόκκου πεποικιλμένα, ἐξ ὧν καὶ ὑπέλαβον Διονύσου εἶναι τὸ ἱερόν. What underlies this passage is the common trend of Greek thought that tended to disguise the Greek gods under the names of foreign deities. This is well illustrated by Plutarch's statement in *De Iside et Osiride*, 67. In our specific case, we may surmise that the equation of the God of the Jews with Dionysus was due primarily to Dionysus' identification with Sabazius. On Sabazius and the Jews, see Valerius Maximus, *Facta et Dicta Memorabilia*, I, 3 : 3 (No. 147).

The cult of Dionysus was introduced to Jerusalem in 167 B.C.E., the time of the religious persecution by Antiochus Epiphanes; see II Macc. vi : 7: γενομένης δὲ Διονυσίων ἑορτῆς ἠναγκάζοντο κισσοὺς ἔχοντες πομπεύειν τῷ Διονύσῳ; see also the discussions on the nature of this cult by O. Kern, *Archiv für Religionswissenschaft*, XXII (1923–1924), pp. 198 f.; H. Willrich, *ibid.*, XXIV (1926), pp. 170 ff.; E. Bickermann, *Der Gott der Makkabäer*, Berlin 1937, pp. 113 f. The restoration of the traditional Jewish way of life in Jerusalem put an end to the Dionysiac cult in Judaea, and there is little reason to assume that the cult left any imprint on the subsequent development of Jewish worship. Also, the attempt of Ptolemy IV Philopator to force the cult of Dionysus on the Egyptian Jews was in no way connected with an inherent affinity between Jewish worship and that of Dionysus, but was derived from royal policy; see III Macc. ii : 29; cf. L. Cerfaux & J. Tondriau, *Le culte des souverains*, Paris 1957, pp. 218 ff.

τῆς μεγίστης καὶ τελειοτάτης ἑορτῆς παρ' αὐτοῖς: The following makes it clear that the Feast of Tabernacles is meant here. It is also signified as μεγίστη ἑορτή in the pseudo-Plutarchian Apophthegmata (No. 260) and in *Ant.*, VIII, 100: ἑορτῆς σφόδρα παρὰ τοῖς 'Εβραίοις ἁγιωτάτης καὶ μεγίστης. The main biblical passage prescribing the feast is found in Lev. xxiii : 33 ff.; cf. Exod. xxiii : 16; xxxiv : 22; Num. xxix : 12 ff.; Deut. xvi : 13 ff.; Neh. viii : 14 ff.; Zech. xiv : 16 ff.; Ezra iii : 4; The Book of Jubilees xvi : 20 ff. The joyful celebration connected with the feast is described in *M. Sukka* and the parallel sources, the Talmuds and the Tosefta; cf. D. Feuchtwang, *MGWJ*, LV (1911), pp. 47 ff.; Goodenough, IV, pp. 147 ff.; S. Zeitlin, *The Rise and Fall of the Judaean State*, I, Philadelphia 1964, pp. 247 ff. The feast also left its mark on the life of the Jewish Diaspora; see, e.g., the well-known inscription of Berenice, *REG*, LXII (1949), p. 283: ἐπὶ συλλόγου τῆς σκηνοπηγίας. Cf. Gabba, no. XIX; and a papyrus from the second century C.E. (*CPJ*, 452a, ll. 15 f.), which may be from Edfu, where a παννυχὶς τῆς σκηνοπηγίας is mentioned.

ὁ καιρός ἐστιν καὶ ὁ τρόπος Διονύσῳ προσήκων: The suitability of the time indicates that it was the time of the vintage, and not that it coincided with the common Dionysiac feasts, though some of these were connected with the vintage; cf. M. P. Nilsson, *Griechische Feste von religiöser Bedeutung*, Leipzig 1906, p. 266; L. R. Farnell, *The Cults of the Greek States*, V, Oxford 1909, pp. 201 f. Yet, as Farnell points out, the evidence for Dionysiac autumn celebrations is less than we might expect. Thus, it seems that there is no vintage festival in the Dionysiac cycle of Athenian feasts; cf. H. Jeanmaire, *Dionysos*, Paris 1951, p. 486.

νηστείαν: This can only mean the Day of Atonement, the most impressive day of the Jewish Temple worship. This day precedes the first day of the Feast of Tabernacles by four days. Although it is a fast-day, in ancient times it had some characteristics of a feast; see *M. Ta'anit* iv : 8. It may have been this feature, as well as the date of its celebration, that caused Plutarch to confuse it with the Feast of Tabernacles. For an attempt to insert μετὰ before τὴν γὰρ and to strike out τε after τραπέζας, see Büchler, *op. cit.* (supra, p. 546, n. 5), p. 193.

σκηναῖς καὶ καλιάσιν: On the injunction to spend the feast in σκηναί, see Lev. xxiii : 42 f.; Neh. viii : 14. καλιάσιν is an emendation of Scaliger. The word does not occur in the Septuagint.

ἐκ κλημάτων μάλιστα καὶ κιττοῦ διαπεπλεγμέναις: Cf. Neh. viii : 14–15; see also W. Rudolph, *Esra und Nehemia* (*Handbuch zum Alten Testament*), ed. O. Eissfeldt, Tübingen 1949, pp. 150 f. On the κισσός in Dionysiac worship, see E.R. Dodds (ed.), *Bacchae*, Oxford 1960, p. 77.

τὴν προτέραν τῆς ἑορτῆς σκηνὴν ὀνομάζουσιν: In Lev. xxiii : 34 ἑορτὴ σκηνῶν covers the seven days of the feast, but in Lev. xxiii : 35 the first day is expressly distinguished from those that followed, a distinction that prevailed in Jewish practice throughout the ages.

ὀλίγαις δὲ ὕστερον ἡμέραις ἄλλην ἑορτὴν... τελοῦσιν: Perhaps this is an allusion to *Shemini Azeret*, the feast that follows the seven days of the Tabernacles; see Lev. xxiii : 36; Num. xxix : 35; Neh. viii : 18. If this is the case, we cannot understand what was the specific Dionysiac character of the feast.

Also, in *De Iside et Osiride*, 37, p. 365 F, the similarities between the feasts serve to corroborate the identification between Dionysus and Osiris: αἱ γὰρ εἰρημέναι περὶ τὰς ἑορτὰς καὶ τὰς θυσίας οἰκειότητες ἐναργεστέραν τῶν μαρτύρων τὴν πίστιν ἔχουσι.

ἔστι δὲ καὶ κραδηφορία τις ἑορτή: Thus, Plutarch mentions a third Dionysiac feast celebrated by the Jews. In its description he does not state outright that it is dedicated to Dionysus, as he did concerning the former feast, but he deduces the Dionysiac character from its features: εἰκὸς δὲ βακχείαν εἶναι τὰ ποιούμενα. It should also be noted that Plutarch does not connect the date of the third with that of the two former feasts; yet, a connection with the Feast of Tabernacles is implied by the bearing of the thyrsus, which is characteristic of the last-mentioned feast. It has been plausibly surmised, e.g. by Büchler, that the κραδηφορία may be identified with the Day of Willow, i.e. the seventh day of the Feast of Tabernacles; see Büchler, *op. cit.* (supra, p. 546, n. 5), p. 186. A special place was alloted for this celebration in the calendar of feasts of the Second Temple; see *M. Sukka* iv : 3, 5. Yet, there is nothing in the name κραδηφορία itself that infers a connection with willows.

θυρσοφορία: The carrying of θύρσοι (*lulavim* = palm-branches) was characteristic of all seven days of the feast. The only distinction was that on the seventh day the procession went round the altar seven times.

ἐν ᾗ θύρσους ἔχοντες: Jewish writers in Greek used θύρσος for the *lulav*; cf. II Macc. x : 7; *Ant.*, XIII, 372: νόμου ὄντος παρὰ τοῖς 'Ιουδαίοις ἐν τῇ σκηνοπηγίᾳ ἔχειν ἕκαστον θύρσους ἐκ φοινίκων καὶ κιτρίων. See also Judith xv : 12. On the thyrsus in the Dionysiac cult, see A. Reinach, *RHR*, LXVI (1912), pp. 1 ff.; F. v. Lorentz, PW, Ser. 2, VI, pp. 747 ff.

εἰσελθόντες δ᾽ ὅ τι δρῶσιν, οὐκ ἴσμεν: This gives Jewish worship the air of a mystery religion and also suits the character that Moiragenes attributed to it at the beginning of his speech.

σάλπιγξι μικραῖς ... χρῶνται: In the Septuagint σάλπιγξ is translated as both trumpet (חצוצרה) and shofar. The trumpet is typical of the Feast of Tabernacles, as well as of other celebrations in the Temple; see M. Sukka, v : 4–5; Eccles. L : 15 f.; see also L. Ginzberg, *MGWJ*, LVI (1912), pp. 546 ff. Thus, I see no necessity to follow Reinach in discerning any specific allusion here to the feast of the first of the seventh month (Rosh Hashana), which was accompanied by the sound of the *shofar*; see Lev. xxiii : 24; Num. xxix : 1. On the *shofar* as illustrated by the monuments, see Goodenough, IV, pp. 168 ff. On the *shofar* in Jewish worship, see S.B. Finesinger, *HUCA*, VIII–IX (1931–1932), pp. 193 ff.

ὥσπερ ᾽Αργεῖοι τοῖς Διονυσίοις: This is more circumstantially described in *De Iside et Osiride*, 35. The place of the celebrations is identified with Lake Alcyonia in the vicinity of Lerna; see Farnell, *op. cit.* (supra, p. 560), pp. 183 f.; M. P. Nilsson, *op. cit.* (supra p. 560), p. 288.

οὓς αὐτοὶ Λευίτας προσονομάζουσιν: This is the first and only mention of the Levites in pagan literature. The singers (משוררים) were Levites; see Jeremias, pp. 234 ff.; cf. R. Meyer, apud: Kittel, *Theologisches Wörterbuch*, IV, p. 245 ff.

Σάβους... τοὺς Βάκχους καλοῦσιν: Cf. Stephanus Byzantius, s.v. Σάβοι, ἔθνος Φρυγίας. λέγονται καὶ ἀντὶ τοῦ Βάκχοι παρὰ Φρυξίν; see also A. B. Cook, *Zeus*, I, Cambridge 1914, p. 395.

οὗ πίστωσιν... παρὰ Δημοσθένους λαβεῖν καὶ παρὰ Μενάνδρου: Cf. *De Corona*, 260; Menander, F 905 (Körte).

πίνειν... παρακαλοῦντες ἀλλήλους: Here, again, Plutarch is the only pagan writer to emphasize the association of wine with the Sabbath celebration. We may refer to the custom of ushering in the Sabbath with benedictions over a cup of wine; see M. *Berakhot* viii : 1.

ὁ ἀρχιερεὺς ἐλέγχει, μιτρηφόρος τε προϊὼν ἐν ταῖς ἑορταῖς: For a description of the high priest dressed in his solemn raiment, see *Ant.*, III, 159 ff.; *BJ*, V, 230 ff.; see also the remark of Latzarus, *op. cit.* (supra, p. 546, n. 5), p. 163, n. 8. Dionysus himself was spoken of as χρυσομίτρης; see Sophocles, *Oedipus Tyrannus*, 209; see also C. Picard, *Mélanges Glotz*, II, Paris 1932, pp. 707 ff. The μίτρα became characteristic of the high priest's votaries.

νεβρίδα χρυσόπαστον ἐνημμένος: On the fawnskin as the traditional dress of the Mainads, see Dodds, *op. cit.* (supra, p. 561), p. 81.

περὶ τὰ νυκτέλια: On νυκτέλιος as a cultic designation for Dionysus, see Pausanias, *Graeciae Descriptio*, I, 40:6; Plutarch, *De E apud Delphos*, 9, p. 389 A; Ovidius, *Metamorphoses*, IV, 15; see also Soury, *op. cit.* (supra, p. 546, n. 4), p. 92, n. 3.

μέλι μὲν οὐ προσφέρουσι: This is in accordance with the prescription of Lev. ii : 11. For the mistaken notion of Theophrastus that Jewish sacrifices abounded in honey, see Porphyrius, *De Abstinentia*, II, 26 (No. 4).

τὴν οἴνου τοὺς κολαζομένους ἀπείργουσαν: This is probably a vague allusion to the institution of Nazariteship.

259

De Iside et Osiride, 31, p. 363C–D — Sieveking = F68R

Οἱ δὲ λέγοντες ἐκ τῆς μάχης ἐπ' ὄνου τῷ Τυφῶνι τὴν φυγὴν ἑπτὰ ἡμέρας γενέσθαι καὶ σωθέντα γεννῆσαι παῖδας Ἱεροσόλυμον καὶ Ἰουδαῖον, αὐτόθεν εἰσὶ κατάδηλοι τὰ Ἰουδαϊκὰ παρέλκοντες εἰς τὸν μῦθον.

2 ἡμέρας Markland   ἡμέραις codd.

But those who relate that Typhon's flight from the battle was made on the back of an ass and lasted for seven days, and that after he had made his escape, he became the father of sons, Hierosolymus and Judaeus, are manifestly, as the very names show, attempting to drag Jewish traditions into legend.   (trans. F. C. Babbitt, *LCL*)

ἐπ' ὄνου τῷ Τυφῶνι τὴν φυγὴν ... γενέσθαι ... : Plutarch dwells on the sacrifices that were offered to the god Typhon and on the connection between this god and the ass. After referring to the Persian king who had been nicknamed "the Ass" by the Egyptians, he tells the story of the relations between Typhon, Hierosolymus and Iudaeus, the eponymous ancestors of the city of Jerusalem and the Jewish nation. It is clear that this story arose among circles hostile to Jews, who attributed ass-worship to them; see T. Hopfner, *Plutarch über Isis und Osiris*, II, Prague 1941, pp. 143 ff.; J. G. Griffiths, *Plutarch, De Iside et Osiride*, [Cardiff] 1970, pp. 418 f. With regard to Apion as Plutarch's possible source on this subject, see M. Wellmann, *Hermes*, XXXI (1896), pp. 221 ff.; for a different view, see K. Ziegler, *Plutarchos von Chaironeia*, Stuttgart 1949, p. 208 = PW, XXI, p. 845.

260

Regum et Imperatorum Apophthegmata, p. 184E–F — Nachstädt = F67R

Τῶν δ' Ἰουδαίων, πολιορκοῦντος αὐτοῦ ⟨scil. Ἀντιόχου⟩ τὰ Ἱεροσόλυμα, πρὸς τὴν μεγίστην ἑορτὴν αἰτησαμένων ἑπτὰ ἡμερῶν ἀνοχὰς οὐ μόνον ἔδωκε ταύτας, ἀλλὰ καὶ ταύρους χρυσοκέρως παρασκευασάμενος καὶ θυμιαμάτων καὶ ἀρωμάτων πλῆθος ἄχρι τῶν πυλῶν ἐπόμπευσε· καὶ
5 παραδοὺς τοῖς ἐκείνων ἱερεῦσι τὴν θυσίαν αὐτὸς ἐπανῆλθεν εἰς τὸ στρατόπεδον, οἱ δ' Ἰουδαῖοι θαυμάσαντες εὐθὺς ἑαυτοὺς μετὰ τὴν ἑορτὴν ἐνεχείρισαν.

The Jews, when he [i.e. Antiochus] was besieging Jerusalem, asked for an armistice of seven days for their most important festival, and he not only granted this, but he also made ready bulls with gilded horns, and a great quantity of incense and spices, and brought all

these in solemn procession as far as the gates. Then having transferred
the offerings to the hands of their priests, he returned to his camp.
The Jews were amazed, and immediately after the festival placed
themselves in his hands. (trans. F. C. Babbitt, *LCL*)

πολιορκοῦντος αὐτοῦ τὰ Ἱεροσόλυμα: Cf. *Ant.*, XIII, 236 ff.; Schürer, I, pp.
259 f.; the commentary to Diodorus, XXXIV–XXXV, 1 : 1–5 (No. 63).
πρὸς τὴν μεγίστην ἑορτήν: The Feast of Tabernacles is meant here; cf. *Ant.*,
XIII, 241. The Feast of Tabernacles is also so designated in *Ant.*, VIII, 100;
cf. Plutarchus, *Quaestiones Convivales*, IV, 6 : 2 (No. 258) and the commentary
ad loc.
αἰτησαμένων ἑπτὰ ἡμερῶν ἀνοχάς...: Cf. *Ant.*, XIII, 242: πέμψαντος δ᾽ Ὑρκανοῦ
πρὸς Ἀντίοχον καὶ σπονδὰς ἡμερῶν ἑπτὰ διὰ τὴν ἑορτὴν ἀξιώσαντος γενέσθαι,
τῇ πρὸς τὸ θεῖον εὐσεβείᾳ εἴκων σπένδεται καὶ προσέτι θυσίαν εἰσέπεμψε μεγ-
αλοπρεπῆ, ταύρους χρυσοκέρωτας καὶ μεστὰ παντοίων ἀρωμάτων ἐκπώματα
χρύσεά τε καὶ ἀργύρεα. (243) καὶ τὴν μὲν θυσίαν δεξάμενοι παρὰ τῶν κομιζόντων
οἱ πρὸς ταῖς πύλαις ὄντες ἄγουσιν εἰς τὸ ἱερόν. Undoubtedly, Josephus and pseudo-
Plutarch ultimately derive from a common source, but Büchler's view that
pseudo-Plutarch draws directly upon *Antiquitates* does not seem probable; see
A. Büchler, *REJ*, XXXVII (1898), p. 197, n. 2.

261
Vita Pompei, 39:3, p. 639 E — Lindskog & Ziegler = F70R

Χειρωσάμενος δὲ ⟨scil. ὁ Πομπήϊος⟩ δι᾽ Ἀφρανίου τοὺς περὶ Ἀμανὸν
Ἄραβας, καὶ καταβὰς αὐτὸς εἰς Συρίαν, ταύτην μὲν ὡς οὐκ ἔχουσαν
γνησίους βασιλεῖς ἐπαρχίαν ἀπέφηνε καὶ κτῆμα τοῦ δήμου Ῥωμαίων, τὴν
δ᾽ Ἰουδαίαν κατεστρέψατο, καὶ συνέλαβεν Ἀριστόβουλον τὸν βασιλέα.

After his legate Afranius had subdued for him the Arabians about
Amanus, he himself went down into Syria, and since this country
had no legitimate kings, he declared it to be a province and possession of the Roman people; he also subdued Judaea, and made a prisoner of Aristobulus the king. (trans. B. Perrin, *LCL*)

καὶ συνέλαβεν Ἀριστόβουλον τὸν βασιλέα: Cf. *Ant.*, XIV, 57: καὶ τὸν Ἀριστόβουλον ἐν φυλακῇ καταστήσας αὐτὸς ἐπὶ τὴν πόλιν ἔρχεται...; *BJ*, I, 141.

262
Vita Pompei, 45:1–2, 5, p. 642D–643A — Lindskog & Ziegler

(1) Τοῦ δὲ θριάμβου τῷ μεγέθει, καίπερ εἰς ἡμέρας δύο μερισθέντος,

ὁ χρόνος οὐκ ἐξήρκεσεν, ἀλλὰ τῶν παρεσκευασμένων πολλὰ τῆς θέας
ἐξέπεσεν, ἑτέρας ἀποχρῶντα πομπῆς ἀξίωμα καὶ κόσμος εἶναι. (2) γράμμασι δὲ προηγουμένοις ἐδηλοῦτο τὰ γένη καθ' ὧν ἐθριάμβευεν. ἦν δὲ
5 τάδε· Πόντος, Ἀρμενία, Παφλαγονία, Καππαδοκία, Μηδία, Κολχίς,
Ἴβηρες, Ἀλβανοί, Συρία, Κιλικία, Μεσοποταμία, τὰ περὶ Φοινίκην καὶ
Παλαιστίνην, Ἰουδαία, Ἀραβία, τὸ πειρατικὸν ἅπαν ἐν γῇ καὶ θαλάσσῃ
καταπεπολεμημένον...
(5) αἰχμάλωτοι δ' ἐπομπεύθησαν ἄνευ τῶν ἀρχιπειρατῶν υἱὸς Τιγράνου
10 τοῦ Ἀρμενίου μετὰ γυναικὸς καὶ θυγατρός, αὐτοῦ τε Τιγράνου τοῦ
βασιλέως γυνὴ Ζωσίμη, καὶ βασιλεὺς Ἰουδαίων Ἀριστόβουλος, Μιθριδάτου δ' ἀδελφὴ καὶ πέντε τέκνα καὶ Σκυθίδες γυναῖκες, Ἀλβανῶν δὲ καὶ
Ἰβήρων ὅμηροι καὶ τοῦ Κομμαγηνῶν βασιλέως, καὶ τρόπαια πάμπολλα
καὶ ταῖς μάχαις ἰσάριθμα πάσαις, ἃς ἢ αὐτὸς ἢ διὰ τῶν στρατηγῶν
15 ἐνίκησε.

5 μηδεία GL   14 καὶ om. NZ

(1) His triumph had such a magnitude that, although it was distributed
over two days, still the time would not suffice, but much of what had
been prepared could not find a place in the spectacle, enough to
dignify and adorn another triumphal procession. (2) Inscriptions
borne in advance of the procession indicated the nations over which
he triumphed. These were: Pontus, Armenia, Paphlagonia, Cappadocia, Media, Colchis, the Iberians, the Albanians, Syria, Cilicia,
Mesopotamia, Phoenicia and Palestine, Judaea, Arabia, and all the
power of the pirates by sea and land which had been overthrown. . .
(5) The captives led in triumph, besides the chief pirates, were the
son of Tigranes the Armenian with his wife and daughter, Zosime,
a wife of king Tigranes himself, Aristobulus, king of the Jews, a
sister and five children of Mithridates, Scythian women, and hostages
given by the Albanians, by the Iberians and by the King of Commagene; there were also very many trophies, equal in number to all
the battles in which Pompey had been victorious either in person
or in the persons of his lieutenants.   (trans. B. Perrin, *LCL*)

5 βασιλεὺς Ἰουδαίων Ἀριστόβουλος: On the triumph of Pompey, see the commentaries to Plinius, *Naturalis Historia*, VII, 98 (No. 208); Appianus, *Mithridatica*,
117 : 571 ff. (No. 346).

From Herodotus to Plutarch

263

Vita Ciceronis, 7:6, p. 864 C — Ziegler = F74R

"Ὅμως δὲ πολλὰ χαρίεντα διαμνημονεύεται καὶ περὶ ἐκείνην αὐτοῦ
τὴν δίκην. βέρρην γὰρ οἱ Ῥωμαῖοι τὸν ἐκτετμημένον χοῖρον καλοῦσιν.
ὡς οὖν ἀπελευθερικὸς ἄνθρωπος ἔνοχος τῷ ἰουδαΐζειν ὄνομα Κεκίλιος
ἐβούλετο παρωσάμενος τοὺς Σικελιώτας κατηγορεῖν τοῦ Βέρρου, «τί
5 Ἰουδαίῳ πρὸς χοῖρον;» ἔφη ὁ Κικέρων.

2 τὸν μὴ ἐκτετμημένον Amyot

(4) Nevertheless, many witty sayings of his in connection with this
trial are on record. (5) For instance "verres" is the Roman word
for a castrated porker; when, accordingly, a freedman named Caecilius, who was suspected of Jewish practices, wanted to thrust aside
the Sicilian accusers and denounce Verres himself, Cicero said:
"What has a Jew to do with a Verres?"   (trans. B. Perrin, LCL)

ἔνοχος τῷ ἰουδαΐζειν: For this expression, see, e.g., the Septuagint Esther
viii : 17; Ep. Gal. ii : 14; Eusebius, *Praeparatio Evangelica*, IX, 22 : 5.

Κεκίλιος ἐβούλετο ... κατηγορεῖν τοῦ Βέρρου: Verres, the propraetor of
Sicily, was accused of extortion by the inhabitants of the island. Cicero acted for
the Sicilians, while Quintus Caecilius Niger, the former quaestor of Verres, endeavoured to have himself placed in charge of the prosecution in order to thwart the
judicial proceedings against Verres; see Münzer, PW, III, p. 1231.

τί Ἰουδαίῳ πρὸς χοῖρον: Only Plutarch alludes to the Jewishness of the quaestor
Caecilius. Since Cicero, in his *Divinatio in Caecilium*, does not mention this detail,
and, considering the improbability that a freedman (ἀπελευθερικός) would be
appointed a quaestor at that time, there is sufficient reason to doubt the truth of
Plutarch's statement. It has been suggested that the pun is apocryphal and that it
derives from the fact that the namesake of the quaestor Caecilius — Caecilius of
Caleacte in Sicily who was a Greek writer, historian and rhetor in the time of
Augustus — was a Jew; see T. Reinach, REJ, XXVI (1893), pp. 36 ff.; Schürer,
III, p. 632. On the Jewish religion of Caecilius, see Suda, s.v. Καικίλιος (ed.
Adler), III, p. 83 = F. Gr. Hist., II, B 183, T 1, where Caecilius is designated τὴν δὲ
δόξαν Ἰουδαῖος. The same article of Suda states that Caecilius was a slave by
origin. Caecilius seems to have been the first to attain fame as a writer in Greek on
non-Jewish subjects, in marked contrast to most Jewish-Hellenistic writers, who
dealt almost exclusively with Jewish problems. The truth of Plutarch's statement
concerning the Jewishness of the quaestor is maintained, e.g., by Friedländer,
III, p. 212; see also Leon, pp. 15 f.

264

Vita Antonii, 3:1–3, p. 916E — Ziegler = F71R

(1) Ἐπεὶ δὲ Γαβίνιος ἀνὴρ ὑπατικὸς εἰς Συρίαν πλέων ἀνέπειθεν αὐτὸν ⟨scil. τὸν Ἀντώνιον⟩ ὁρμῆσαι πρὸς τὴν στρατείαν, ἰδιώτης μὲν οὐκ ἂν ἔφη συνεξελθεῖν, ἀποδειχθεὶς δὲ τῶν ἱππέων ἄρχων συνεστράτευε. (2) καὶ πρῶτον μὲν ἐπ' Ἀριστόβουλον Ἰουδαίους ἀφιστάντα πεμφθείς, αὐτὸς
5 *μὲν ἐπέβη τοῦ μεγίστου τῶν ἐρυμάτων πρῶτος, ἐκεῖνον δὲ πάντων ἐξήλασεν· (3) εἶτα μάχην συνάψας καὶ τρεψάμενος ὀλίγοις τοῖς σὺν αὐτῷ τοὺς ἐκείνου πολλαπλασίους ὄντας, ἀπέκτεινε πλὴν ὀλίγων ἅπαντας· αὐτὸς δὲ μετὰ τοῦ παιδὸς Ἀριστόβουλος ἥλω.*

3 τῶν ἱππέων ἄρχων] ἵππαρχος Π

(1) Gabinius, a man of consular dignity, was sailing for Syria, he tried to persuade Antony to join the expedition. Antony refused to go out with him in a private capacity, but being appointed commander of the horse, accompanied him on the campaign. (2) And first, having been sent against Aristobulus, who was bringing the Jews to a revolt, he was himself the first man to mount the highest of the fortifications, and drove Aristobulus from all of them, (3) then he joined battle with him, routed his many times more numerous forces with his own small band, and slew all but a few of them. Aristobulus himself was captured, together with his son.

(trans. B. Perrin, *LCL*)

3 αὐτὸς δὲ μετὰ τοῦ παιδὸς Ἀριστόβουλος ἥλω: Cf. *Ant.*, XIV, 92 ff.; *BJ*, I, 171 ff. The sequence of events in Josephus is as follows: the mission of Antony, who was accompanied by two officers; the defeat of Aristobulus in battle; his occupation of the fortress of Machaerus and his being taken prisoner. The sequence of events in Plutarch is: first the capture of the big fortress and then the battle. The big fortress that is implied in Plutarch's narrative seems to be Alexandrion and not Machaerus, which, according to Josephus, was captured only after the battle. Josephus only dwells on Aristobulus' attempt to rebuild Alexandrion and his being prevented from doing so by the Roman commanders.
The son of Aristobulus referred to by Plutarch is Antigonus. Plutarch's narrative reveals the use of a source very sympathetic to Antony (Dellius?). While Josephus relates the exploits of Antony and the other two Roman officers, Sisenna and Servilius, Plutarch stresses Antony's part in the battle, putting further emphasis on his courage in the capture of the fortress and on his victory in a battle of few against many. On the revolt of Aristobulus (56 B. C. E.), see Schürer, I, p. 341; see also the commentary to Cassius Dio, XXXIX, 56 : 6 (No. 408).

265

Vita Antonii, 27:4, p. 927E — Ziegler

Καὶ τὴν γλῶτταν ὥσπερ ὄργανόν τι πολύχορδον εὐπετῶς τρέπουσα
⟨scil. ἡ Κλεοπάτρα⟩ καθ' ἣν βούλοιτο διάλεκτον, ὀλίγοις παντάπασι
δι' ἑρμηνέως ἐνετύγχανε βαρβάροις, τοῖς δὲ πλείστοις αὐτὴ δι' αὐτῆς
ἀπεδίδου τὰς ἀποκρίσεις, οἷον Αἰθίοψι Τρωγλοδύταις Ἑβραίοις Ἄραψι
5 Σύροις Μήδοις Παρθυαίοις.

3 τοῖς βαρβάροις L¹ / ἑαυτῆς P

And her tongue, like an instrument of many strings, she [scil. Cleo-
patra] could readily turn to whatever language she pleased, so that
in her interviews with barbarians she very seldom had need of an
interpreter, but made her replies to most of them herself and un-
assisted, whether they were Ethiopians, Troglodytes, Hebrews,
Arabians, Syrians, Medes or Parthians.   (trans. B. Perrin, *LCL*)

Ἑβραίοις: On the use of the name "Hebrews" instead of "Jews", see the commentary to Charax of Pergamon (No. 335). On the attitude of Cleopatra VII to the
Jews, see Apion, apud: Josephus, *Contra Apionem*, II, 56 (No. 168). Although,
according to Apion, Cleopatra VII did not distribute corn to the Jews, there is no
reason to assume that she was consistently anti-Semitic. We know of her support
of Alexandra the Hasmonaean and her children; see *Ant.*, XV, 23 ff., 42 ff. See also
OGIS, No. 742, which some attribute to the reign of this queen; cf. M.L. Strack,
Archiv für Papyrusforschung, II (1903), p. 559; W. W. Tarn, *CAH*, X, pp. 35 f.

266

Vita Antonii, 36:3–4, p. 932B–C — Ziegler = F72R

(3) Ἐλθούσῃ δὲ ⟨scil. τῇ Κλεοπάτρᾳ⟩ χαρίζεται καὶ προστίθησι
μικρὸν οὐδὲν οὐδ' ὀλίγον, ἀλλὰ Φοινίκην, Κοίλην Συρίαν, Κύπρον,
Κιλικίας πολλήν· ἔτι δὲ τῆς τ' Ἰουδαίων τὴν τὸ βάλσαμον φέρουσαν
καὶ τῆς Ναβαταίων Ἀραβίας ὅση πρὸς τὴν ἐκτὸς ἀποκλίνει θάλασσαν.
5 *(4)* αὗται μάλιστα Ῥωμαίους ἠνίασαν αἱ δωρεαί. καίτοι πολλοῖς ἐχαρί-
ζετο τετραρχίας καὶ βασιλείας ἐθνῶν μεγάλων ἰδιώταις οὖσι, πολλοὺς
δ' ἀφῄρειτο βασιλείας ὡς Ἀντίγονον τὸν Ἰουδαῖον, ὃν καὶ προαγαγὼν
ἐπελέκισεν, οὐδενὸς πρότερον ἑτέρου βασιλέως οὕτω κολασθέντος.

(3) And when she [scil. Cleopatra] was come, he made her a present
of no slight or insignificant addition to her dominions, namely,
Phoenicia, Coele Syria, Cyprus, and a large part of Cilicia; and

still further, the balsam-producing part of Judaea, and all that part of Arabia Nabataea which slopes toward the outer sea. (4) These gifts particularly annoyed the Romans. And yet he made presents to many private persons of tetrarchies and realms of great peoples, and he deprived many monarchs of their kingdoms, as, for, instance Antigonus the Jew, whom he brought forth and beheaded, though no other king before him had been so punished. (trans. B. Perrin, *LCL*)

ἐλθούσῃ δὲ χαρίζεται καὶ προστίθησι μικρὸν οὐδὲν οὐδ᾽ ὀλίγον, ἀλλὰ Φοινίκην... ἔτι δὲ τῆς τ᾽ Ἰουδαίων τὴν τὸ βάλσαμον φέρουσαν: On this passage, the question of Antony's gifts to Cleopatra and their chronology, see J. Kromayer, *Hermes*, XXIX (1894), pp. 571 ff.; Schürer, I, p. 362, n. 5; Otto, p. 45, n. 1; V. Gardthausen, *Neue Jahrbücher für das klassische Altertum*, XXXIX (1917), pp. 164 ff.; L. Craven, *Antony's Oriental Policy until the Defeat of the Parthian Expedition*, Columbia, Missouri 1920, p. 70, n. 27; T. Rice Holmes, *The Architect of the Roman Empire*, I, Oxford 1928, p. 228, n. 11; J. Dobiáš, *Annuaire de l'institut de philologie et d'-histoire orientales et slaves*, II, 1934 (= *Mélanges Bidez*), pp. 287 ff.; K.W. Meiklejohn, *JRS*, XXIV (1934), p. 191, n. 3; R. Syme, *The Roman Revolution*, Oxford 1939, pp. 260 f.; A. Zwaenepoel, *Les études classiques*, XVIII (1950), p. 13; H. U. Instinsky, *Studies Presented to David M. Robinson*, II, St. Louis 1953, pp. 975 ff.; H. Volkmann, *Kleopatra*, Munich 1953, p. 121; H. Buchheim, *Die Orientpolitik des Triumvirn M. Antonius*, Heidelberg 1960, pp. 68 ff.; A. Schalit, *König Herodes*, Berlin 1969, pp. 772 ff.

In a prior passage, Plutarch refers to the treaty of Tarentum and states that, after signing it, Antony arrived in Syria, invited Cleopatra to come there and gave her the various territories listed in the passage. Then Plutarch continues with a description of Antony's Parthian campaign. Since the treaty of Tarentum was concluded during the autumn of 37 B. C. E. and because of its relative position in Plutarch's narrative, we must date the bestowal of Antony's gifts to the winter of 37–36 B.C.E. Plutarch mentions that Antony gave Cleopatra a second gift of territory after the Armenian campaign in 34 B.C.E.; see *Vita Antonii*, 54:6–7, p. 941 B: πρῶτον μὲν ἀπέφηνε Κλεοπάτραν βασίλισσαν Αἰγύπτου καὶ Κύπρου καὶ Λιβύης καὶ Κοίλης Συρίας, συμβασιλεύοντος αὐτῇ Καισαρίωνος... Πτολεμαίῳ δὲ Φοινίκην καὶ Συρίαν καὶ Κιλικίαν. The only part of Judaea that was included in the gift of 37–36 B. C. E., as related by Plutarch, is the part where the balsam grows, i.e. the vicinity of Jericho. This chronology, based on Plutarch, seems to conflict with that of Josephus, who deals with this question summarily in *Bellum Judaicum* by stating that the palm grove of Jericho (ἐν ᾧ γεννᾶται τὸ βάλσαμον) was among the many territories that Antony took from his friends; see *BJ*, I, 361. He presented the grove to Cleopatra, together with all the towns south of the river Eleutherus, except Tyre and Sidon. This gift is mentioned only after we read of Cleopatra's charges against Herod, made before Antony. The *terminus post quem* for the presentation is the death of Antigonus in 37 B.C.E.; *ibid.*, 357. The *terminus ante quem* is afforded by Antony's campaign against the Parthians, which, from the sequel of the narrative, should be equated with the campaign against the Armenian king in 34 B.C.E.; *ibid.*, 363: καὶ μετ᾽ οὐ πολὺ παρῆν ἐκ Πάρθων Ἀντώνιος ἄγων αἰχμάλωτον Ἀρταβάζην τὸν Τιγράνου παῖδα δῶρον Κλεοπάτρᾳ.

On the Armenian campaign, see Buchheim, *op. cit.* (supra, p. 569), p. 90 f. Josephus gives us a more circumstantial account in *Ant.*, XV. First he explains Cleopatra's policy towards Herod and her support of Alexandra and her son Aristobulus, Herod's brother-in-law (*Ant.*, XV, 23 ff.). Then he relates how, following the murder of Aristobulus, Cleopatra, on Alexandra's plea, persuaded Antony to question Herod about the facts. Antony ordered Herod to appear before him at Laodicea to clear himself of the accusation. After his meeting with Antony, Herod wrote a letter home (*ibid.*, 74 ff.), in which he states that Cleopatra's arguments were of little avail. At the end of the letter he adds that she could no longer cherish any hope of satisfying her greed: δόντος Ἀντωνίου ἀνθ᾽ ὧν ἠξίου τὴν Κοίλην Συρίαν καὶ διὰ τούτου παρηγορήσαντος ὁμοῦ καὶ ἀποσκευασαμένου τὰς ἐντεύξεις ἃς ὑπὲρ τῆς Ἰουδαίας ἐποιεῖτο (*ibid.*, 79). The letter of Herod refers only to Antony's gift of Coele-Syria and the area included therein. Somewhat later Josephus tells us that during the turmoil in Syria Cleopatra persuaded Antony to annex the dominions of the rulers, and that she contrived to get them into her possession when she passed through Syria; cf. *Ant.*, XV, 88 ff. She brought about the death of Ptolemy's son, Lysanias, the ruler of Chalcis, and asked Antony to grant her Judaea and Arabia. He did not comply with all her wishes, but nevertheless cut off portions of both territories and gave them to her (*ibid.*, 94). He also presented her with the cities between the Eleutherus River and Egypt, with the exception of Tyre and Sidon (*ibid.*, 95). However, Josephus does not specify the Judaean territory that was granted to Cleopatra. After obtaining the territories and escorting Antony to the Euphrates on his expedition against Armenia, Cleopatra, on her return, passed through Judaea. There she met Herod, who leased the parts of Arabia that had been presented to her, as well as the region around Jericho (*ibid.*, 96). Josephus, in *Antiquities*, had not previously referred to the fact that Jericho was taken away from Herod but this is implied by the lease of the region around Jericho by Herod.

In *Antiquitates* the immediate *ante quem* for the gift is the same as in *Bellum Judaicum*, namely, the Armenian expedition of Antony in 34 B. C. E. The *terminus post quem* is provided by the murder of Aristobulus and the meeting between Herod and Antony, the first event taking place sometime at the end of 35 B. C. E., and the second at the beginning of 34 B. C. E.; see Schürer, I, p. 362, notes 3–4. Otto's doubts regarding this chronology do not seem convincing; see Otto, p. 40, n. 2. Some information about the cession of Judaean territory to Cleopatra may be inferred from the description of the territorial aggrandizement of Herod's kingdom after the victory of Octavian. In *BJ*, I, 396, we read that Octavian τῇ βασιλείᾳ προσέθηκεν τήν τε ὑπὸ Κλεοπάτρας ἀποτμηθεῖσαν χώραν καὶ ἔξωθεν Γάδαρα καὶ Ἵππον καὶ Σαμάρειαν, πρὸς δὲ τούτοις τῶν παραλίων Γάζαν καὶ Ἀνθηδόνα καὶ Ἰόππην καὶ Στράτωνος πύργον. Exactly the same list is found in *Ant.*, XV, 217. We do not know the status of most of these towns at the beginning of the reign of Herod, but in view of the fact that Jaffa was restored to the Jews by Julius Caesar in the time of Hyrcan II, we are almost certain that it was originally included in the Herodian kingdom. Also, we learn from Appianus, that *c.* 39 B. C. E. Samaria constituted a part of the Herodian kingdom; see *Bella Civilia*, V, 75 : 319 (No. 352). Thus, we must conclude that if Jaffa and Samaria had to be restored to Herod by Octavian, they had undoubtedly been taken from him at some time before Actium. I would suggest that they formed a part of Antony's gifts to Cleopatra. However, since Josephus was mainly concerned with the territory of Jericho, he included Jaffa and Samaria among the towns that Octavian annexed to the Jewish kingdom, in addition (ἔξωθεν) to the territory that had been ceded to Cleopatra earlier. It may also be argued that Jaffa and Samaria are implied by the incorporation of the towns between the Eleutherus River and Egypt into the kingdom of Cleopatra; see *Ant.*, XV, 95. In any case, this does hold true for Jaffa. We may also add that in *Antiquitates* Josephus does not expressly mention Jericho in the territorial cession of 34 B. C. E., where he speaks only of certain parts of Jewish territories. That, of course, could also cover Samaria.

For another source referring to Antony's gift, see Cassius Dio, XLIX, 32 : 5 (No. 415). This historian speaks of areas bestowed on Cleopatra and her children, which include parts of the kingdom of the Arabian Malchus; the country of the Ituraeans, which had been ruled by Lysanias, who was sentenced to death because of his treacherous dealings with the Parthians; many parts of Phoenicia and Palestine; and sections of Crete, together with Cyrene and Cyprus. These gifts were made in 36 B. C. E., the same year that Plutarch gives for Antony's gifts to Cleopatra. There is a small chronological discrepancy between Plutarch and Cassius Dio: While the former states that the gifts were made before the Parthian campaign of that year, the latter places them after the campaign. But this discrepancy may prove illusory, since Cassius Dio arranges his narrative within the year according to subject matter and not to fit a strict chronological system; see Kromayer, *op. cit.* (supra, p. 569), p. 576; W. W. Tarn, *JRS*, XXII (1932), p. 145. Craven prefers Cassius Dio to Plutarch in this case; see Craven, *loc. cit.* (supra, p. 569). Some new distributions of the provinces are alluded to in Cassius Dio, XLIX, 41.

Porphyry, in his Chronicle, also tells us about Antony's gifts to Cleopatra; see *F. Gr. Hist.* II, B 260, F 2 (17), p. 1202 f. He expressly refers to Chalcis and its vicinity, and dates its transfer to 36 B. C. E.

There is undoubtedly a discrepancy between Plutarch and Josephus in the *Antiquities*, as to the year in which Jewish territory was ceded to Cleopatra by Antony. The former dates it to 36 B. C. E., and the latter to 34 B. C. E. Plutarch is supported in his dates by Cassius Dio. Porphyry does not refer at all to Jewish territory, but his date for the cession of Chalcis (36 B. C. E.) indirectly lends plausibility to Plutarch's version.

Some scholars wholly discredit Josephus' chronology in this case. The main arguments against Josephus have been made by Kromayer, *op. cit.* (supra, p. 569). They are as follows: (a) Josephus refers to Cleopatra's presence in Syria in connection with the gifts. This does not fit with 34 B. C. E. but rather with 36 B. C. E. (b) According to Josephus, Cleopatra followed Antony to the Euphrates. This accords with 36 B. C. E., when Antony launched his campaign against the Parthians, but not with 34 B. C. E., when his army did not proceed to the Euphrates. (c) Josephus cites a letter of Herod referring to the granting of Coele-Syria to Cleopatra. This gift should be equated with that of the territory of Lysanias, the date of which (winter 37-36 B. C. E.) is vouched for by Porphyry. (d) Josephus tells of the execution of Lysanias, which he links with the story of the gifts; see *Ant.*, XV, 92. If the execution took place in 36 B. C. E., the territorial grants referred to must also pertain to that date. (e) Also according to Josephus (*Ant.*, XV, 96), after the cession of Jewish and Arab territories to Cleopatra, Herod met the Queen and leased the Arab territory from her (standing, as it seems, surety for the Arab king himself) and accrued the revenues from the region of

Jericho. The Arab king, for whose payments Herod had become responsible, continued for some time (χρόνον μέν τινα) to pay him the two hundred yearly talents, but when he became refractory and was slow in making the payments, there was an outbreak of hostility between the two kingdoms. Since, according to Kromayer, the question had already become acute in 33 B. C. E., there was not enough time between 34 B. C. E. and 33 B. C. E. to justify Josephus' statement that χρόνον μέν τινα the Arab king was regular in his payment. Otto goes even further than Kromayer and thinks that even Josephus did not date the gifts to 34 B. C. E.; cf. Otto, p. 45, n. 1.

On the other hand, Schürer, Dobiáš and Buchheim cling to Josephus' chronology and to 34 B. C. E. as the date of the cession of Judaean territory to Cleopatra. Dobiáš, in particular, answered Kromayer's arguments in detail and apparently refuted most of them. Still, certain doubts prevent us from accepting the chronological implications of Josephus *en bloc* and dating the whole presentation of Jewish and Arab territory to 34 B. C. E.: (a) It is difficult to account for the fact that both Plutarch and Cassius Dio give the date as 36 B. C. E. (b) We know from Porphyry that Chalcis was granted to Cleopatra in 36 B. C. E. Josephus (*Ant.*, XV, 92) relates that the death of Lysanias of Chalcis, at the hands of Antony and at the instigation of Cleopatra, took place just before the grant of Jewish and Arab territories. It is quite reasonable to assume that Lysanias had already been killed when his territory was annexed in 36 B. C. E., even if we agree with Dobiáš and assume that the Arab king became refractory in his payments two years after 34 B.C.E.; see also Meiklejohn, *loc. cit.* (supra, p. 569).

The most satisfactory solution to the problem seems to be to assume that, in addition to the cession of Jewish territory in 36 B. C. E., which is referred to by Plutarch and Cassius Dio, there was a second grant in 34 B.C.E. The first one presumably included the territory of Jericho, expressly mentioned by Plutarch; the second one included some parts of the coastal area, e.g. Jaffa. It should be added that in *Antiquitates* Josephus does not even expressly assert that Jericho was taken from Herod and given to Cleopatra as part of the gift of 34 B. C. E. We may add that Plutarch himself alludes to a second cession of territories by Antony to Cleopatra (cf. supra, p. 569).

Κοίλην Συρίαν: Josephus refers to the cession of Coele-Syria to Cleopatra in *Ant.*, XV, 79 (a letter of Herod). The exact geographical definition of Coele-Syria is not specified in this passage of Josephus; however, a comparison with his other passages relating to the same period may suggest that the area refers to a part of Trans-Jordan and should not be equated with Chalcis; see Dobiáš, *op. cit.* (supra, p. 569), pp. 301 ff.; Kahrstedt, p. 105. Plutarch may have had the same region in mind.

'Αντίγονον τὸν 'Ιουδαῖον... οὐδενὸς πρότερον ἑτέρου βασιλέως οὕτω κολασθέντος: Cf. Strabo, *Historica Hypomnemata*, apud: Josephus *Ant.*, XV, 9 (No. 108): 'Αντώνιος δὲ 'Αντίγονον τὸν 'Ιουδαῖον ἀχθέντα εἰς 'Αντιόχειαν πελεκίζει. καὶ ἔδοξε μὲν οὗτος πρῶτος 'Ρωμαίων βασιλέα πελεκίσαι. Cf. Cassius Dio, XLIX, 22 : 6 (No. 414).

267

Vita Antonii, 61:1–3, p. 944 B–C — Ziegler = F 73 R

(1) Συνιόντων δὲ πρὸς τὸν πόλεμον, 'Αντωνίῳ μὲν ἦσαν αἱ μάχιμοι νῆες

Plutarch

οὐκ ἐλάττους πεντακοσίων, ἐν αἷς ὀκτήρεις πολλαὶ καὶ δεκήρεις κεκοσμημέναι σοβαρῶς καὶ πανηγυρικῶς, στρατοῦ δὲ μυριάδες δέκα, δισχίλιοι δ᾽ ἱππεῖς ἐπὶ μυρίοις· (2) βασιλεῖς δ᾽ ὑπήκοοι συνεμάχουν Βόκχος
5 ὁ Λιβύων καὶ Ταρκόνδημος ὁ τῆς ἄνω Κιλικίας, καὶ Καππαδοκίας μὲν Ἀρχέλαος, Παφλαγονίας δὲ Φιλάδελφος, Κομμαγηνῆς δὲ Μιθριδάτης, Σαδάλας δὲ Θρᾴκης. (3) οὗτοι μὲν αὐτῷ παρῆσαν, ἐκ δὲ Πόντου Πολέμων στρατὸν ἔπεμπε, καὶ Μάλχος ἐξ Ἀραβίας καὶ Ἡρώδης ὁ Ἰουδαῖος, ἔτι δ᾽ Ἀμύντας ὁ Λυκαόνων καὶ Γαλατῶν βασιλεύς· ἦν δὲ καὶ παρὰ τοῦ
10 Μήδων βασιλέως ἀπεσταλμένη βοήθεια.

7 Σαδάλας Oudendorp   ἀδάλλας codd. / αὐτῷ] αὐτοὶ Reiske
8 Μάλχος Xylander   μάγχος ΠL   μάγχος μὲν K

(1) When the forces came together for the war, Antony had no fewer than five hundred fighting ships, among which were many vessels of eight and ten banks of oars, arrayed in pompous and festal fashion; he also had one hundred thousand infantry soldiers and twelve thousand horsemen. (2) Of subject kings who fought with him, there were Bocchus the king of Libya, Tarcondemus the king of Upper Cilicia, Archelaus of Cappadocia, Philadelphus of Paphlagonia, Mithridates of Commagene, and Sadalas of Thrace. (3) These were with him, while from Pontus Polemo sent an army, and Malchus from Arabia, and Herod the Jew, besides Amyntas the king of Lycaonia and Galatia; the king of the Medes also sent an auxiliary force.   (trans. B. Perrin, LCL)

3 οὗτοι μὲν αὐτῷ παρῆσαν, ἐκ δὲ Πόντου Πολέμων στρατὸν ἔπεμπε, καὶ Μάλχος ἐξ Ἀραβίας καὶ Ἡρώδης ὁ Ἰουδαῖος...: Herod did not take part in the campaign of Actium personally, as he was engaged in the war against Malchus, King of the Nabataeans; see Ant., XV, 109 ff. (= BJ, I, 364 ff.): τῆς γὰρ ἐπ᾽ Ἀκτίῳ μάχης προσδοκωμένης... Ἡρώδης δὲ καὶ τῆς χώρας εὐβοτουμένης αὐτῷ πολὺν ἤδη χρόνον καὶ προσόδων καὶ δυνάμεως εὑρημένων, Ἀντωνίῳ συμμαχίαν κατέλεξεν ἐπιμελέστατα ταῖς παρασκευαῖς χρησάμενος. Ἀντώνιος δὲ τῆς μὲν ἐκείνου συμμαχίας οὐδὲν ἔφη δεῖσθαι...
Josephus explains that Antony's policy was prompted by Cleopatra's desire to weaken both vassal kings. From these passages of Josephus it emerges, contrary to Plutarch, that Herod did not send military help to Antony but only made preparations to do so. However, from Herod's statement when he met Octavian at Rhodes after Antony's defeat we learn that he sent at least money and wheat to Antony; see Ant., XV, 189: στρατείας μὲν οὐ κοινωνήσας κατὰ περιολκὰς τῶν Ἀράβων, πέμψας δὲ καὶ χρήματα καὶ σῖτον ἐκείνῳ; cf. BJ, I, 388.

From Herodotus to Plutarch

268

Vita Antonii, 71:1, p. 949B — Ziegler = F73R

Τῷ δ' Ἀντωνίῳ Κανίδιός τε τῆς ἀποβολῆς τῶν ἐν Ἀκτίῳ δυνάμεων
αὐτάγγελος ἦλθε, καὶ τὸν Ἰουδαῖον Ἡρώδην ἔχοντά τινα τάγματα καὶ
σπείρας ἤκουσε Καίσαρι προσκεχωρηκέναι, καὶ τοὺς ἄλλους ὁμοίως
δυνάστας ἀφίστασθαι καὶ μηδὲν ἔτι συμμένειν τῶν ἐκτός.

1 τε om. L

As for Antony, Canidius in person brought him word of the loss of
his forces at Actium, and he heard that Herod the Jew, with some
legions and cohorts, had gone over to Caesar, and that the other
dynasts in like manner were deserting him and nothing longer remained of his power outside Egypt. (trans. B. Perrin, LCL)

Ἡρώδην ἔχοντά τινα τάγματα καὶ σπείρας ἤκουσε Καίσαρι προσκεχωρηκέναι:
There was a Roman force stationed in Judaea to protect Herod from his rebellious
subjects; see Ant., XV, 72. On the help given by Herod to Octavian, even before
their meeting at Rhodes, see Ant., XV, 195. On an action against the gladiators
trained for Antony at Cyzicus, who attempted to join their master, see BJ, I, 392;
see also Otto, p. 50.

269

Vita Antonii, 72:3, p. 949F = 950A — Ziegler = F73R

Καὶ γὰρ Ἀλεξᾶς ὁ Λαοδικεύς, γνωρισθεὶς μὲν ἐν Ῥώμῃ διὰ Τιμαγένους
καὶ πλεῖστον Ἑλλήνων δυνηθείς, γενόμενος δὲ τῶν Κλεοπάτρας ἐπ'
Ἀντώνιον ὀργάνων τὸ βιαιότατον καὶ τῶν ὑπὲρ Ὀκταουίας ἱσταμένων ἐν
αὐτῷ λογισμῶν ἀνατροπεύς, ἐπέμφθη μὲν Ἡρώδην τὸν βασιλέα τῆς
5 μεταβολῆς ἐφέξων, αὐτοῦ δὲ καταμείνας καὶ προδοὺς Ἀντώνιον, ἐτόλ-
μησεν εἰς ὄψιν ἐλθεῖν Καίσαρος, Ἡρώδῃ πεποιθώς. ὤνησε δ' αὐτὸν
οὐδὲν Ἡρώδης, ἀλλ' εὐθὺς εἰρχθεὶς καὶ κομισθεὶς εἰς τὴν ἑαυτοῦ πατρίδα
δέσμιος, ἐκεῖ Καίσαρος κελεύσαντος ἀνῃρέθη. τοιαύτην μὲν Ἀλεξᾶς ἔτι
ζῶντι δίκην Ἀντωνίῳ τῆς ἀπιστίας ἐξέτεισε.

1 ἀλέξας ΠΚ   7 ἡρώδης οὐδὲν L

For Alexas the Laodicean, who had been known to Antony in Rome
through Timagenes and had more influence with him than any
other Greek, who had also been Cleopatra's most effective instrument against Antony and had overthrown the considerations arising
in his mind in favour of Octavia, had been sent to keep Herod the

Plutarch

king from apostasy; but after remaining there and betraying Antony he had the audacity to come into Caesar's presence relying on Herod. Herod, however, could not help him, but the traitor was at once confined and carried in fetters to his own country, where he was put to death by Caesar's orders. Such was the penalty for his treachery which Alexas paid to Antony while Antony was yet alive.

(trans. B. Perrin, *LCL*)

Ἀλεξᾶς ὁ Λαοδικεύς: Cf. *Ant.*, XV, 197: ᾔτεῖτο δὲ καὶ τῶν Ἀντωνίῳ συνήθων Ἀλέξανδρον ὡς μηδὲν ἀνήκεστον παθεῖν, ἀλλὰ τούτου μὲν οὐκ ἔτυχεν ὅρκῳ προκατειλημμένου Καίσαρος; cf. *BJ*, I, 393; Buchheim, *op. cit.* (supra, p. 569), p. 121, n. 210; see also H. Volkmann, *Zur Rechtsprechung im Principat des Augustus*, Munich 1935, p. 41.

270
Vita Galbae, 13:4, p. 1058 C — Ziegler

Ἐπεὶ δὲ ταῦτα λέγων ⟨scil. Νυμφίδιος⟩ οὐκ ἔπειθεν, ἀλλ' ἄτοπον ἐδόκει καὶ ἀλλόκοτον ἡγεμόνα πρεσβύτην, ὥσπερ ἄρτι γενόμενον ἐξουσίας μειράκιον, οἷς χρήσεται φίλοις ἢ μή, ῥυθμίζειν, ἑτέραν ὁδὸν τραπόμενος, ἔγραψε τῷ Γάλβᾳ δεδιττόμενος, νῦν μὲν ὡς ὕπουλα καὶ μετέωρα πολλὰ
5 τῆς πόλεως ἐχούσης, νῦν δὲ Κλώδιον Μᾶκρον ἐν Λιβύῃ τὰ σιτηγὰ κατέχειν, αὖθις δὲ παρακινεῖν τὰ Γερμανικὰ τάγματα, καὶ περὶ τῶν ἐν Συρίᾳ καὶ Ἰουδαίᾳ δυνάμεων ὅμοια πυνθάνεσθαι.

5 Μᾶκρον Ziegler   μάρκον codd.

But this speech of Nymphidius did not convince his hearers; nay, they thought it a strange and unnatural thing to dictate to an aged emperor, as if he had been a youth just tasting power — what friends he was to have or not to have. Nymphidius therefore took another course, and wrote to Galba messages intended to alarm him — now, that here was much hidden distemper and unrest in the city, now that Clodius Macer was holding back the grain supplies in Africa; again, that the legions in Germany were mutinous, and that like news came concerning the forces in Syria and Judaea.

(trans. B. Perrin, *LCL*)

271
271 *Vita Othonis*, 4:3, p. 1068 B — Ziegler

Ταχὺ δ' ἀφίκετο καὶ παρὰ Μουκιανοῦ γράμματα καὶ παρὰ Οὐεσπασιανοῦ

575

φίλια, τοῦ μὲν ἐν Συρίᾳ τοῦ δ' ἐν Ἰουδαίᾳ μεγάλας δυνάμεις ἐχόντων.

And quickly there came also friendly letters from Mucianus and Vespasian, who were at the head of large forces, the one in Syria, the other in Judaea. (trans. B. Perrin, *LCL*)

ταχὺ δ' ἀφίκετο καὶ παρὰ Μουκιανοῦ γράμματα καὶ παρὰ Οὐεσπασιανοῦ φίλια...:
Cf. Tacitus, *Historiae*, II, 6: "antequam Titus adventaret sacramentum Othonis acceperat uterque exercitus."

272

Vita Othonis, 15:6, p. 1073E — Ziegler

Οἶδα τὴν νίκην τοῖς ἐναντίοις οὐ[δὲ] βεβαίαν οὐδ' ἰσχυρὰν οὖσαν·
ἀπαγγέλλουσι τὴν ἐκ Μυσίας ἡμῶν δύναμιν οὐ πολλῶν ἡμερῶν ὁδὸν
ἀπέχειν, ἤδη καταβαίνουσαν ἐπὶ τὸν Ἀδρίαν· Ἀσία καὶ Συρία καὶ
Αἴγυπτος καὶ τὰ πολεμοῦντα Ἰουδαίοις στρατεύματα μεθ' ἡμῶν, ἥ τε
5 σύγκλητος παρ' ἡμῖν, καὶ τέκνα τῶν ἐναντίων καὶ γυναῖκες.

1 οὐ Ziegler   οὐδὲ codd.   οὔτε βεβαίαν οὔτε ἰσχυρὰν Corais
3 καταβαίνουσαν Solanus   καταβαίνουσιν codd.

I know that the victory of our adversaries is neither decisive nor assured. I have word that our forces from Mysia are already approaching the Adriatic and are only a few days distant from us. Asia, Syria, Egypt and the armies fighting against the Jews, are on our side; the senate, too, is with us, as well as the wives and children of our adversaries. (trans. B. Perrin, *LCL*)

כתבי האקדמיה הלאומית הישראלית למדעים

החטיבה למדעי־הרוח

מקורות לתולדות עם ישראל

היהודים והיהדות בספרות היוונית והרומית

ההדיר וצירף מבואות וביאורים

מנחם שטרן

כרך ראשון

מהרודוטוס עד פלוטארכוס

ירושלים תשל״ד